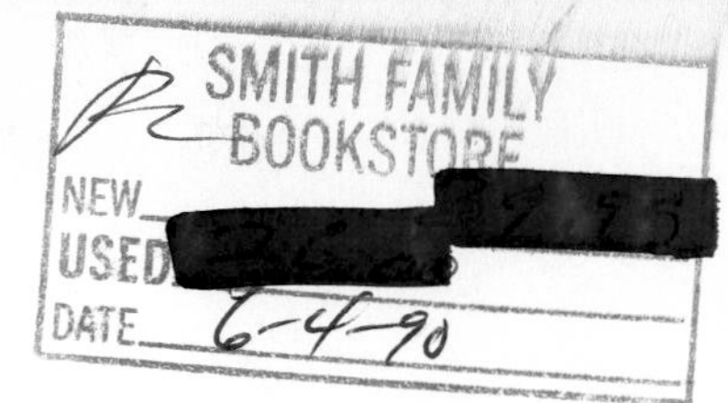

BUSINESS COMMUNICATION TODAY

Second Edition

Courtland L. Bovée

Professor of Business Communication
C. Allen Paul Distinguished Chair
Grossmont College

John V. Thill

Chief Executive Officer
Communication Specialists of America

Random House
New York

NOTE TO STUDENTS

A study guide for this textbook can be obtained from college bookstores under the title *Study Guide, Business Communication Today,* Second Edition, by Courtland L. Bovée and John V. Thill.

You can use the *Study Guide* throughout the course for reviewing the content of this textbook, for developing communication skills, and for increasing your knowledge of business communication. It is also an ideal aid when preparing for tests.

If the *Study Guide* is not in stock, ask the bookstore manager to order a copy from the publisher.

Second Edition

98765432

Copyright © 1986, 1989 by Random House, Inc.

All rights reserved under International and Pan-American Copyright Conventions. No part of this book may be reproduced in any form or by any means, electronic or mechanical, including photocopying, without permission in writing from the publisher. All inquiries should be addressed to Random House, Inc., 201 East 50th Street, New York, N.Y. 10022. Published in the United States by Random House, Inc., and simultaneously in Canada by Random House of Canada Limited, Toronto.

Library of Congress Cataloging-in-Publication Data

Bovée, Courtland L.
Business communication today.

Bibliography: p.
Includes index.
1. Business communication—United States—Case studies.
2. Communication in organizations—United States—Case studies. 3. Business writing—United States—Case studies.
I. Thill, John V. II. Title.
HF5718.B66 1989 658.4'5 88-4498

ISBN 0-394-37417-7

Manufactured in the United States of America
Cover: Inset art based on the design by Betty Binns Graphics
Color graphics section Figures C, D, and E courtesy of Genigraphics® Corporation
Composed by Monotype Composition Co., Inc.
Separations and printing by Lehigh Press Lithographers
Printed and bound by Rand McNally

Because this page cannot legibly accommodate all the copyright notices, pages iv–v in the back constitute an extension of the copyright page.

PREFACE

Teaching people the concepts and skills they need to communicate effectively in business is not easy. Business communication requires judgment and flexibility; because of the human element, it is more an art than a science. Yet most textbooks have taken a dry, academic approach to the subject.

Three years ago, when the first edition of *Business Communication Today* was published, we hoped to avoid that mistake by emphasizing real-life business situations and employing a lively, conversational writing style. Apparently we had the right idea: *Business Communication Today* is the most successful business communication textbook published in the past 35 years.

Business Communication Today, Second Edition, is another step forward in the evolution of business communication textbooks. Of course, this new edition covers all the basic principles and presents them in a traditional sequence. But it also provides expanded coverage of important issues and up-to-date discussions of the latest developments. Even more than before, an involving writing style and eye-opening graphics bring the subject to life. And this second edition contains an increased number of examples and applications revolving around actual companies. All told, we believe *Business Communication Today*, Second Edition, captures the dynamics of business communication like no other textbook.

The textbook itself is the centerpiece of a comprehensive teaching and learning package that targets a single goal: to successfully demonstrate how business communication works in the real world, thus helping students to understand the concepts behind effective communication and to develop and refine their own skills.

Features that link concepts to the real world

Business Communication Today, Second Edition, paints a vivid picture of the world of business communication. It offers an overview of the wide range of communication skills used by businesspeople to present ideas clearly and persuasively. It gives a close-up look at communication techniques that have led to sound decision making and effective teamwork. Its insights into the way organizations operate help clarify students' career interests and identify the skills they need for a lifetime of career success.

Because it encourages students to view themselves as part of an actual organization when completing assignments, *Business Communication Today* is the next best thing to on-the-job training. It shows how standard approaches to routine assignments can help them complete work quickly and efficiently. But it also stresses that every situation is different and advises students to think for themselves.

Examples from Actual Companies The opportunity to learn from other people's successes and failures is what sets this textbook apart from others. To understand our commitment to that concept, glance at the table of contents. You'll see that this textbook was written with the cooperation of many small and large businesses, among them such well-respected giants as Xerox, General Mills, Apple Computer, and AT&T.

Each chapter begins with an instructive Communication Close-Up featuring a communication expert who, in his or her own words, applies the chapter's concepts to common business situations. That expert reappears from time to time throughout the chapter to dramatize the connection between the chapter's contents and life on the job. This on-the-scene, internal company information was gathered through personal interviews with our business associates, friends, and contacts and is exclusive to *Business Communication Today*.

A significant new feature in this edition is chapter-ending projects called Communication Challenges, which are related to the situations described in the Communication Close-Ups. Each chapter has one *individual challenge* (to give students "on-the-job" practice in applying principles they've just learned) and one *team challenge* (to give students an opportunity to experience collaborative writing, the team approach prevalent in business). This feature provides a dimension of reality unmatched by any other textbook in the field.

37 Special Features Boxed and strategically placed within each chapter, Special Features are extensions of the chapter material. Ever since the first edition of *Business Communication Today* was published, we have been searching business publications and interviewing respected authorities to provide you with insights into the business world that are not found in other textbooks.

The Special Features center on five well-integrated themes:

- SHARPEN YOUR SKILLS. Practical pointers and confidence-building guidelines for improving writing and speaking skills.
- BUSINESS COMMUNICATION TODAY. Contemporary issues of vital importance and practical solutions to common communication problems.
- LEGAL ALERT. Instructions on how to identify areas of legal vulnerability, how to steer clear of legal perils, and when to seek legal advice.
- INTERNATIONAL OUTLOOK. Tested techniques for communicating successfully in the critical global arena.
- TEST YOURSELF. Self-scoring tests to help students identify their strengths and weaknesses in skills integral to successful communication in business.

The Special Features in the first four categories each include a discussion question and an application exercise—all new in this edition.

Example After Example of Letters, Memos, and Reports Throughout *Business Communication Today*, Second Edition, you'll find numerous up-to-date sample documents, many collected in our consulting work. These superb business examples provide students with benchmarks for achievement.

The chapters on letters and memos contain outstanding examples from many different types of organizations and from people working in a variety of functional areas. Many of these documents are fully formatted, and some are presented on the letterhead of such well-known companies as TWA, JC Penney, Kentucky Fried Chicken, and Mattel Toys. Accompanying sentence-by-sentence analyses help students see precisely how to apply the principles discussed in the text. Poor and improved examples illustrate common errors and effective techniques for correcting them.

The report-writing chapters give examples too. For instance, one chapter presents six case histories of reports (one a proposal), from inception through completion. And the last chapter of the unit illustrates the step-by-step development of a long report, which appears in its entirety to show how all the parts fit together.

Excellent Coverage of Today's Most Important Topics According to several surveys, recent graduates are not prepared to handle the full range of communication assignments that come across their desks. *Business Communication Today*, Second Edition, addresses that problem in two ways: (1) by emphasizing basic principles that can be applied to many different situations and (2) by including coverage of such important topics as organizational communication, the writing process, ethics, listening, nonverbal communication, and intercultural business communication.

The boundaries of business communication are always expanding. So in addition to covering all the traditional subjects, *Business Communication Today*, Second Edition, examines many new topics. For example, because technology is so advanced and so important in today's business world, we have carefully updated the chapter on office technology. The book also contains an unparalleled discussion of employment-related topics, including indispensable techniques for getting a job in our service-oriented economy.

Tools that help develop skills and enhance comprehension

Having an accurate picture of how businesspeople communicate is important, but students need more if they are to develop usable skills. That's why, in *Business Communication Today*, Second Edition, we've included a number of helpful learning tools.

Checklists To help students organize their thinking when they begin a communication project, make decisions as they write, and check their own work, we've included numerous checklists throughout the book. The checklists appear as close as possible to the related discussions. The checklists are reminders, however—not "recipes." They provide useful guidelines for writing, without limiting creativity. Students will find them handy when they're on the job and need to refresh their memory about effective communication techniques.

Documents for Analysis In this edition we have expanded the selection of documents that students can critique and revise to 30 documents in 11 different chapters. Documents include letters and memos, a letter of application and a resume, and visual aids. This hands-on experience in analyzing and improving documents will help students revise their own.

Exercises and Cases A wealth of new exercises and cases, many of them memo-writing tasks, provide assignments like those that students will most often face at work. The exercises and cases deal with all types and sizes of organizations, domestic and international. And we have written them for a variety of majors: management, marketing, accounting, finance, information systems, office administration, and many others. With such variety to choose from, students will have ample opportunities to test their problem-solving skills.

Business Communication Today, Second Edition, is the first business communication textbook to include numerous cases featuring real companies: Kodak, Nike, Merrill Lynch, Ford Motor Company, United Airlines, and dozens of others. These cases are yet another tool for demonstrating the role of communication in the real business world.

Component Chapters For maximum flexibility in designing a course tailored to students' needs, this textbook contains five Component Chapters. Placed near the end of the book, they are (A) Intercultural Business Communication, (B) Business Communication Technology, (C) Fundamentals of Grammar and Usage, (D) Format and Layout of Business Documents, and (E) Documentation of Report Sources. Students will find them informative and useful, even those not assigned.

Lively, Conversational Writing Style Read a few pages of this textbook, then read a few pages of another textbook. We think you'll immediately notice the difference.

The lucid writing style in *Business Communication Today*, Second Edition, makes the material pleasing to read and easy to comprehend. It stimulates interest and promotes learning. The writing style also exemplifies the principles presented in this book.

We have also carefully monitored the reading level of *Business Communication Today* to make sure it's neither too simple nor too difficult.

Learning Objectives Each chapter begins with a concise list of goals that students are expected to achieve by reading the chapter and completing the exercises and cases. These objectives are meant to guide the learning process, motivate students to master the material, and aid them in measuring their success.

Margin Notes Short summary statements that highlight key points and reinforce learning appear in the margins of *Business Communication Today*, Second Edition. They are no substitute for reading the chapters but are useful for quickly getting the gist of a section, rapidly reviewing a chapter, and locating areas of greatest concern.

Chapter Summaries Each chapter ends with a concise overview. We have included the summaries to help students understand and remember the relationships among key concepts.

End-of-Chapter Discussion Questions The Questions for Discussion are designed to get students thinking about the concepts introduced in each chapter. They may also prompt students to stretch their learning beyond the chapter content. Not only will students find them useful in studying for examinations, but the instructor may also draw on them to promote classroom discussion of issues that have no easy answers.

Appendixes *Business Communication Today*, Second Edition, contains two appendixes:

- BUSINESS COMMUNICATOR'S RESOURCE DIRECTORY. New in this edition, this appendix provides a quick reference guide to the best books on language and writing, the most frequently used handbooks and manuals, key periodicals and newsletters, the professional associations most important to business communicators, and useful computer data bases and software. It also lists the current five best-selling books on the subject of careers and job-hunting, the five best-selling word-processing programs, and the most frequently used software for feedback on spelling, grammar, and punctuation. Students will find themselves referring to this appendix again and again as they begin their careers.
- CORRECTION SYMBOLS. This appendix shows some common codes to use in proofreading and revising. The instructor can use them to grade assignments, and students can use the appendix to interpret the instructor's corrections.

Color Art and Strong Visual Program Full-color illustrations enliven the beginning of the book and the first-of-its-kind insert in Chapter 14, Report Writer's Portfolio: Creating Colorful Visual Aids with Computers. We hope you'll agree that the book has been attractively printed and that the dramatic use of a second color throughout gives it exceptional visual appeal. In addition, students will learn from carefully crafted illustrations of important concepts in each chapter: graphs, charts, tables, and photographs.

Book Design The state-of-the-art design, based on extensive research, invites students to delve into the content. It also makes reading easier, reinforces learning, and increases comprehension. The Special Features do not interfere with the flow of text material, a vital factor in maintaining attention and concentration. The design of this book, like much communication, has the simple objective of gaining interest and making a point.

Revision with a purpose

In preparing the second edition of *Business Communication Today*, we dedicated ourselves to a thorough revision. Virtually every sentence has been critically evaluated. We have made literally hundreds of refinements. Members of the academic and business communities have carefully reviewed it, and we have tested it in the classroom. Instructors, businesspeople, and students have all praised its competent coverage of subject matter, its up-to-date examples, its flexible organization, and its authentic portrayal of business.

Here is an overview of the major content changes in the second edition:

- CHAPTER 1: COMMUNICATING SUCCESSFULLY IN AN ORGANIZATION. Now covers communication climate, communication management, and ethics, in addition to organizational communication.
- CHAPTER 2: UNDERSTANDING BUSINESS COMMUNICATION. Integrates a more detailed and academic discussion of nonverbal communication into the original discussion of communication theory.
- CHAPTER 3: PLANNING BUSINESS MESSAGES. Introduces the writing process by showing how to analyze a message's purpose and audience and how to decide on a main idea.
- CHAPTER 4: ORGANIZING AND COMPOSING BUSINESS MESSAGES. Shows more clearly than before how choosing an organizational plan and a writing style fits into the writing process.
- CHAPTER 5: REVISING BUSINESS MESSAGES. By discussing revision and word skills at the end of the unit instead of the beginning, reinforces the book's new emphasis on the writing process.
- CHAPTER 6: WRITING DIRECT REQUESTS. Now presents the different types of direct requests in a more logical order and puts more emphasis on memos.
- CHAPTER 7: WRITING ROUTINE, GOOD-NEWS, AND GOODWILL MESSAGES. Condenses material that was covered in two chapters in the first edition, with a greater emphasis on internal communication, and adds material on writing directives, instructions, and press releases.
- CHAPTER 8: WRITING BAD-NEWS MESSAGES. Discusses more thoroughly how to decide between the direct plan and the indirect plan, and provides more examples of buffers.
- CHAPTER 9: WRITING PERSUASIVE MESSAGES. Reduces the first edition's emphasis on sales letters and collection letters by first discussing the uses of persuasion in messages to both co-workers and outsiders.
- CHAPTER 10: WRITING RESUMES AND APPLICATION LETTERS. Introduces three distinct varieties of resume, acknowledging the diverse job histories and goals of today's students.
- CHAPTER 11: INTERVIEWING FOR EMPLOYMENT AND FOLLOWING UP. Adds a discussion about the stages of an interview, and provides pointers on negotiation during the interview process.
- CHAPTER 12: USING REPORTS AND PROPOSALS AS BUSINESS TOOLS. More clearly defines what reports and proposals are and how they may be classified.
- CHAPTER 13: GATHERING AND INTERPRETING INFORMATION. Takes more of a process approach by focusing on the planning and research phase, and provides a clearer, more detailed discussion of data analysis.
- CHAPTER 14: DEVELOPING VISUAL AIDS. Strengthens the original chapter's "how-to" emphasis, and provides more examples of well-designed visual aids.
- CHAPTER 15: WRITING REPORTS AND PROPOSALS. Explains more carefully the complex or-

ganization of long messages and the factors that affect the choice of organizational plan.

- CHAPTER 16: COMPLETING FORMAL REPORTS AND PROPOSALS. Elaborates on the teamwork necessary to produce a formal report, and incorporates a new section describing the elements of a formal proposal.

- CHAPTER 17: LISTENING, INTERVIEWING, AND CONDUCTING MEETINGS. Amplifies the discussion of oral communication (both speaking and listening), adds information on negotiating, and provides a better overview of group dynamics.

- CHAPTER 18: GIVING SPEECHES AND ORAL PRESENTATIONS. Now shows how analysis of purpose and audience, development of a main idea, and development of an outline apply to speech making as well as writing, and provides more practical information on designing and presenting visual aids.

- COMPONENT CHAPTER A: INTERCULTURAL BUSINESS COMMUNICATION. Discusses subcultures as well as foreign cultures, and provides more practical tips.

- COMPONENT CHAPTER B: BUSINESS COMMUNICATION TECHNOLOGY. Now appears as a component chapter instead of a regular chapter, with updates reflecting current developments.

- COMPONENT CHAPTER C: FUNDAMENTALS OF GRAMMAR AND USAGE. Refines the discussion from the first edition, on the basis of feedback from instructors, and adds some exercises.

- COMPONENT CHAPTER D: FORMAT AND LAYOUT OF BUSINESS DOCUMENTS. Combines information about report formatting (which was previously in the report unit) with information about formatting other types of documents.

- COMPONENT CHAPTER E: DOCUMENTATION OF REPORT SOURCES. Adds information about doing secondary research (taken from the report unit), and expands discussion of reference citations.

- APPENDIX I: BUSINESS COMMUNICATOR'S RESOURCE DIRECTORY. Provides a new classified listing of print materials, computer resources, and organizations useful to business communicators.

- APPENDIX II: CORRECTION SYMBOLS. Divides the first edition's list into two parts (content and style; grammar, usage, and mechanics), and adds examples of how proofreading marks are applied.

A teaching/learning package that meets real needs

The instructional package for this textbook is specially designed to simplify the task of teaching and learning. The instructor may choose to use the following supplements.

Study Guide This paperback book contains a wealth of material reinforcing the information presented in the textbook. Students who are interested in maximizing their learning will appreciate its fill-in-the-blank chapter outlines, self-scoring quizzes on chapter contents, skill-building exercises, supplementary readings, and vocabulary and spelling exercises. In addition, to help students brush up on their English skills, the study guide includes an extensive review of grammar, punctuation, and mechanics interspersed with reinforcement exercises.

Computer Software for Students The instructor may also choose to use our interactive software, *Activities in Business Communication*, which has been revised for this edition. Three modules—dealing with job-search strategies, vocabulary development, and writing style—contain innovative learning activities specifically designed to accompany the textbook. All the modules are interactive learning tools, so students are continually reinforced by word and sound.

Instructor's Resource Manual This comprehensive paperback book is an instructor's toolkit. Among the many things it provides are a wealth of supplementary tidbits of information for enriching lectures (new to this edition), a section about collaborative writing (also new), suggested solutions to exercises, suggested solutions and fully formatted letters for *every* case in the letter-writing chapters, and a grammar pretest and posttest.

An audiovisual guide is also included in the manual. It lists over 200 videotapes, films, and audio cassettes that can be used to supplement the course. Each entry is fully described and keyed to the textbook.

The *Instructor's Resource Manual* includes an extensive bank of test questions for each chapter (ready for duplication), carefully written to provide a fair, structured program of evaluation.

An answer key to selected exercises in the *Study Guide* is also in the *Instructor's Resource Manual.*

Acetate Transparency Program A set of 100 large-type transparency acetates, available to instructors on request, helps bring concepts alive in the classroom and provides a starting point for discussion of communication techniques. All are keyed to the *Instructor's Resource Manual*. Many contrast poor and improved solutions to featured cases from the textbook.

Testing Services Two major programs are available:

- COMPUTERIZED TEST BANK FOR BUSINESS COMMUNICATION TODAY. *RHTest* is a powerful microcomputer program that allows the instructor to create customized tests using the questions from the test bank in the *Instructor's Resource Manual*, self-prepared items, or a combination. This versatile program incorporates a broad range of test-making capabilities, including editing and scrambling of questions to create different versions of a test. This program is available for both Apple and IBM computers.

- CUSTOMIZED TEST SERVICE. Through its Customized Test Service, Random House will supply adopters of *Business Communication Today* with custom-made tests consisting of items selected from the test bank in the *Instructor's Resource Manual*. The test questions can be renumbered in any order. Instructors will receive an original test, ready for reproduction, and a separate answer key. Tests can be ordered by mail or by phone, using a toll-free number.

Additional Ancillary Items For information concerning free videos, the Random House/Penn State University Media Resource Library, the Random House Business Library, the Random House Audio Library, and Report Card (classroom management program), please contact your local Random House sales representative.

Personal acknowledgments

Business Communication Today, Second Edition, is the product of the concerted efforts of a number of people. A heartfelt thanks to our many friends, acquaintances, and business associates who agreed to be interviewed so a business communication textbook could, at last, feature real people at actual companies: Joseph Varilla, Xerox; Lee Dunham, Harlem McDonald's; Irma Cameron, General Mills; David Petree, Mercy Hospital; Marcus Smith, Bear Creek; Julie Regan, Toucan-Du; Jacqueline Millan, PepsiCo Foundation; Wanda Williams, Southland; Stephen Bernard, *Newsweek*; Donald Greiner, Price Waterhouse; Ann Bowers, Apple Computer; Bert Browse, Calvin Klein; Jim Lowry, Lowry & Associates; Chuck Wettergreen, Firestone; Bill Beer, Maytag; Jane Trimble, Tupperware; David Anderson, Kelly Services; and Martha Tapias, AT&T Information Systems.

We are also indebted to Virginia Johnson, Minnesota Mining & Manufacturing Company; Donald Morrison, Trans World Airlines; Candace Irving, Mattel Toys; G. M. Reynolds, Kentucky Fried Chicken; and Ann Roberts, JC Penney.

A special acknowledgment to Jane D. Pogeler, whose exceptional background, experience, and professionalism gives this book an added dimension of reality.

Our thanks also to Rebecca Smith, whose outstanding communication skills, breadth of knowledge, and organizational ability assured this project of clarity and completeness. She has aided us admirably throughout the long and complicated process of preparing a major textbook package.

We extend our deep gratitude to Marie Painter for her diligence and expertise in word processing and her work beyond the call of duty.

For their friendship we thank Susan Badger; Doris Hill; Jane White; Robert P. Irwin; Mark Stephen Martinez; John S. Jackson; Kevin, Lynelle, and Ryan Coates; and Gary and Marilyn Bovée.

We are grateful to Angela Fox Dunn, whose wisdom and persistence helped immensely; to Michael Moynihan, for his tenacity and expertise; to Brian Williams, for his unique insights and perspectives; to Terry Sherf, for her specialized knowledge and sound advice; and to Jackie Estrada, for her expert assistance and remarkable talents.

Recognition and thanks to Ivan L. Jones, Eve Lill, Michele Nelson, Gerald Ashley, Donald Anderson, Margie Culbertson, Phyllis Miller, Mary Leslie, Lawrence Barry, and Carolyn Barry.

We also feel it is important to acknowledge and thank the Association for Business Communication, an organization whose meetings and publications provide a valuable forum for the exchange of ideas and for professional growth.

Thanks to the many individuals whose valuable suggestions and constructive comments contributed to the success of the first edition. The authors are deeply grateful for the efforts of Maxine Hart, Baylor University; Evelyn P. Morris, Mesa Community College; Susan Currier, California Polytechnic State University; Paul J. Killorin, Portland Community College; Ethel A. Martin, Glendale Community College; Kenneth R. Mayer, Cleveland State University; Devern Perry, Brigham Young University; Thomas L. Means, Louisiana Technological University; Gene Rupe, San Diego Mesa College; Mimi Will, Foothill College; Lois J. Bachman, Community College of Philadelphia; Earl A. Dvorak, Indiana University—Bloomington; W. J. Salem, Central Michigan University; Grant T. Savage, Texas Tech University; and Kathryn Jensen White, University of Oklahoma.

A special debt is owed to the individuals who reviewed the first edition in preparation for the second edition: Dona Vasa, University of Nebraska; Reva Leeman, Portland Community College; Mary Bresnahan, Michigan State University; Roberta M. Supnick, Western Michigan University; John L. Waltman, Eastern Michigan University; Carol David, Iowa State University; Thomas P. Proietti, Monroe Community College; Linda N. Ulman, University of Miami; and Norma J. Gross, Houston Community College.

The insightful comments and helpful ideas of the individuals who reviewed the manuscript of the second edition were invaluable. Thanks to David P. Dauwalder, California State University, Los Angeles; Gertrude M. McGuire, University of Montevallo; Willie Minor, Phoenix College; Richard David Ramsey, Southeastern Louisiana University; Linda S. Munilla, Georgia Southern College; Paul Preston, University of Texas, San Antonio; Rod Davis, Ball State University; Sumner B. Tapper, Northeastern University; and J. Kenneth Horn, Southwestern Missouri State University.

Appreciation is also extended to Ruth A. Walsh, University of South Florida, who reviewed the second edition and made important contributions to Chapters 17 and 18. Randolph H. Hudson, Northeastern Illinois University, is to be congratulated for his inventiveness and creativity in writing selected exercises and cases.

We gratefully acknowledge the contributions of the business communication professionals who serve on the Editorial Advisory Board for *Business Communication Today*: Robert Allen, Northwest Connecticut Community College; Gerald Alred, University of Wisconsin—Milwaukee; Jane Bennett, Dekalb College; Julian Caplan, Borough of Manhattan Community College; Donald Crawford, West Georgia College; David P. Dauwalder, California State University, Los Angeles; Carol David, Iowa State University; Norma Gross, Houston Community College System; Florence Grunkemeyer, Ball State University; Susan Hilligoss, Clemson University; Louise C. Holcomb, Gainesville Junior College; Edna Jellesed, Lane Community College; Betty Johnson, Stephen F. Austin State University; Gary Kohut, University of North Carolina; Lorraine Krajewski, Louisiana State University; Patricia Kuriscak, Niagara County Community College; Reva Leeman, Portland Community College; Gertrude M. McGuire, University of Montevallo; Linda Munilla, Georgia Southern College; Tom Musial, Saint Mary's University; Alexa North, Georgia State University; Thomas P. Proietti, Monroe Community College; Nelda Pugh, Jefferson State College; Lillian E. Rollins, Dekalb Junior College; Dorothy Sibley, Brevard Community College; Roberta M. Supnick, Western Michigan University; Vincent Trofi, Providence College; Linda N. Ulman, University of Miami; Dona Vasa, University of Nebraska; and John L. Waltman, Eastern Michigan University.

We also want to extend our warmest appreciation to the very devoted professionals at Random House. They include Executive Editor June Smith, Seib Adams, Anita Kann, Dan Alpert, Safra Nimrod, Liz Israel, Marie Schappert, and the outstanding Random House sales representatives. Finally, we salute project editor Bob Greiner, whose expertise and dedication is unmatched, and copyeditor Evelyn Katrak and designer David Lindroth for their superb work.

To my parents,
Courtney and Shirlee Bovée
Courtland L. Bovée

To D. John Thill and Regina Werner
John V. Thill

CONTENTS

Chapter 8 Writing Bad-News Messages 225

Chapter 9 Writing Persuasive Messages 260

CHECKLISTS

PART ONE

FOUNDATIONS OF BUSINESS COMMUNICATION

CHAPTER ONE

COMMUNICATING SUCCESSFULLY IN AN ORGANIZATION

After studying this chapter, you will be able to

- Understand how organizations use communication
- Recognize the distinctions between formal and informal communication channels
- Understand how management style influences an organization's communication climate
- Appreciate the considerations involved in making ethical communication decisions
- Understand how companies manage the creation and distribution of messages
- Explain how companies prepare for handling communication in times of crisis
- Identify the communication skills you will need in your career

COMMUNICATION CLOSE-UP AT XEROX

Joseph Varilla

Like many big U.S. companies, Xerox Corporation cruised complacently through the 1970s, feeling that business was going along about as well as could be expected. But as the 1980s dawned, the Stamford, Connecticut, company suddenly woke up to the fact that foreign competitors were nibbling away at its market share, offering surprisingly good products at surprisingly low prices. That's when the company's top executives started to take a hard look at how they were running the business. After some serious soul-searching, they formulated a new plan focusing on quality.

Having established this objective, top executives faced the problem of altering the company's habits and attitudes. How could they make 130,000 employees understand that quality was now the main goal? For help, they turned to Joseph A. Varilla, Xerox's director of corporate communications, who oversees the development and production of all formal messages to employees in the United States and abroad, as well as the preparation of messages to shareholders. "I become involved whenever we need to communicate to large groups," Joe says. This was certainly one of those occasions.

In producing high-quality photocopiers, computer work stations, and other office equipment, Xerox Corporation shows its commitment to effective communication.

Xerox developed a multifaceted approach to creating a new corporate value system. Joe's staff publicized all phases of the campaign, which was dubbed Leadership Through Quality, in internal publications and reports to shareholders. To kick off the campaign, all Xerox employees, from senior executives to entry-level clerks and production workers, went through a training course. Quality-control officers assigned to each of the company's major units reinforced the message. Staff members were also told to study what other companies were doing, then compare themselves against the "best in the business." Employees were encouraged to offer their own suggestions for improving quality. People at all levels began talking about how to close the gap between the ideal and the actual.

Through their own actions, Xerox executives hammered home the message that quality is the ultimate objective. Instead of rushing new products into the market, management insisted that everything be perfect. Executives delayed the launch of a new copier for three months to iron out a minor engineering flaw. "The decision was important because it proved to employees that top management was not willing to compromise on quality," Joe notes.

The message now permeates Xerox. Although top executives took the lead, others in the ranks played a crucial role. "We are a decentralized company," Joe says, "and so we are convinced that the best way to communicate with our people is through our middle managers, those who stand between top management and lower-level employees. We expend a great deal of effort to ensure that the middle managers understand the corporate philosophy and our total business thrust. We rely on them to put this information into a context that is useful to their people. They have to communicate, not just because it's good for morale, but because people need information to do their jobs effectively. And the information they need is not limited to the nitty-gritty details of a particular job. People contribute most if they understand how their job relates to the larger mission."[1]

THE COMMUNICATION CONNECTION

As Joe Varilla points out, understanding the organization's "mission" is important, because the better you become at deciphering what your employer wants from you, the more effective you will be in your job. Some organizations, like Xerox, bend over backward to see that employees understand their mission.

Communication occurs when an exchange of messages results in shared meaning.

When you join an organization—be it a club, a college, or a company—you join a little society. Communication is the glue that holds the society together and enables it to function. Through the process of communication, the members of the organization exchange messages using a common system of symbols that result, at least to some degree, in shared meanings. Thus communication has two important functions in an organization: It enables people to exchange necessary information, and it helps set members of the organization apart from nonmembers.

Two functions of organizational communication:

- Helps group members fulfill organizational goals
- Helps bind group members into a cohesive unit

The nature of the organization and the personalities of its members affect the way communication occurs. Nevertheless, most organizations depend heavily on communication to accomplish their objectives. In fact, one study has shown that people in organizations spend 69 percent of their working day in one form of verbal communication or another—whether speaking or listening, writing or reading.[2]

Impressive as this statistic may be, it understates the importance of communication because it fails to take into account nonverbal communication. Research suggests that people derive only 7 percent of the meaning of a spoken message from the sender's words. Tone of voice, facial expressions, and body language convey 93 percent of the meaning.[3] Taking these nonverbal messages into account, it would be fair to say that people communicate almost constantly during business hours. The simple fact is that organizations cannot function without effective communication.

THE USES OF ORGANIZATIONAL COMMUNICATION

When you stop to think about it, just about everything an organization does requires communication. Here are the organizational activities that rely on an exchange of views and facts:

Organizations rely on communication among employees at all levels to decide on and implement their goals.

- *Setting goals and objectives.* Most organizations have a variety of formal and informal objectives to accomplish. These goals are established by thinking and talking about them, then committing them to paper. The objective might be defined in terms of financial results, product quality (as at Xerox), market dominance, employee satisfaction, or service to customers. But regardless of what the particular goal may be, the fact that someone has thought about it and communicated it enables everyone to work toward a common purpose. Given the overall mission, the division and department heads can develop specific plans, usually in writing, for carrying out their activities. Supervisors can then get together with lower-level employees to work out assignments that will further the aims of the organization.

Managers make decisions by collecting facts and analyzing them, often with the help of lower-level employees; implementing these decisions requires communication between managers and others.

- *Making and implementing decisions.* In an effort to achieve their goals, people in business must make and implement many decisions. To

BUSINESS COMMUNICATION TODAY

Eight Ways Communication Skills Can Help Advance Your Career

What's the main career handicap of young people today? Poor communication skills, according to a recent survey of company personnel directors and business school deans. Does this weakness stand in *your* way? Let's look at the reasons you should sharpen your communication skills.

- *Getting the job you want.* Employers form lasting impressions on the basis of what they see and know about a job candidate. The first items that a prospective employer is likely to see are your resume and application letter. If they are well written, they'll make a good first impression and help you get the job. If not, you may fail to get an interview, even though you may be well qualified for the job.
- *Boosting your chances for promotion.* Many new employees soon have a chance to write a memo or report that will be read by management. These documents often stay in company files for a long time as a permanent record of employees' abilities. Good writing skills can draw attention to you and increase your chances for promotion. So can other well-honed communication skills. They make you a more effective member of the team; if your boss knows you can communicate well and deliver under pressure, you are likely to get more chances to prove your worth.
- *Helping others get ahead.* Once you are established in your career, communication skills can help you conduct impressive performance appraisals or compose letters of recommendation for employees. The ability to do a good job may show you to be a developer of people, a quality prized in any company.
- *Helping you get things done.* Good communication is important even in your daily routine. The right choice of words, even of a single word, may make the difference between settling an important issue at hand or igniting a company-wide dispute.
- *Benefiting your own business.* Perhaps your goal is to start your own business. Today, nearly half of the approximately 500,000 new businesses launched each year fail within 36 months. The reasons? Lack of management skills, inadequate financing, and poor communication ability—often reflected in a fear of writing. Nobody likes to do what he or she does poorly, and in a small business there's often no secretary to handle what the owner doesn't do well. One aspiring entrepreneur lost credibility with his stockholders and his banker because he couldn't

make these decisions, they collect facts and evaluate alternatives. They do so by reading, asking questions, talking things over with one another, and just plain thinking. Often their deliberations depend on reports, prepared by others, analyzing the pros and cons of various actions. Once a decision has been made, it has to be implemented, and this requires more communication. They have to explain what needs to be done and gain the support of people affected by the decision, as top management did at Xerox.

Keeping track of results requires the transmission of information from lower-level employees to management.

- *Measuring results.* As the decisions are translated into action, management needs to determine whether the desired outcome is being reached. Statistics on such factors as costs, sales, market share, productivity, employee turnover, inventory levels, and others are compiled. In larger companies, the data may be put together using a computerized management information system that prepares reports

write a report that would sell them on giving him further support. He soon went bankrupt. A decade later, another group, better managed, has made a nationwide success out of his idea: a television network devoted to covering amateur and professional sporting events.

- *Advancing you socially.* The ability to communicate well can help you get along with others. It can inspire others to like and follow you. In addition, if you adopt the habit of making cordial comments to those you work with and of sending short notes to people you know, you will soon have an extensive network of contacts who wish you well.
- *Ensuring your future.* Whatever may happen with new communication technologies, the basic communication skills will always be essential. For example, letters and memos will continue to be the main carriers of business communication for years to come, whether transmitted by computer printout, electronic display, or other devices. In fact, the volume of written communication will increase with the growing use of word/information-processing systems, so the ability to write clearly and concisely will become ever more important.
- *Enhancing your other skills.* As you apply your improved communication skills to more and more business functions, you'll learn how to use them to motivate prospects to buy, speed collections, improve customer relations and claims adjustments, and recruit and hire personnel. You'll also learn how to save time and effort. For example, you'll find you can write one letter to seal a business transaction that otherwise would have required two or three. With improved communication skills will come new self-confidence. You'll be able to plan and send messages faster, more freely, and with greater ease. You'll also discover that every act of communication is a potential public relations tool, and you'll try to make each one work for you.

Start your study of business communication by adopting a positive attitude. If you *can't* perform a task, you have a skill problem. But if you *won't* perform a task, you have a motivation problem. With real motivation, you can learn to communicate well and advance your career.

1. You receive a brief application letter from a man who states that he really needs a job because he has been out of work for six months. He writes, "I have completed only one year of college, and my grades are just average, but I am willing to work hard." What is your reaction to this letter?

2. For the next five days, write one letter a day to someone: a friend or relative, business associate, newspaper, government official, or customer-relations department. Make your letters as conversational as possible. Pretend you are talking to the other person. As the week progresses, do you notice any changes in your attitude toward writing or the ease with which you think of things to say? What responses do you receive to your letters?

automatically. In smaller companies, management may obtain the required information through face-to-face contact with lower-level employees or in the form of hand-prepared memos or reports.

Organizations attract, train, motivate, and evaluate their employees by communicating with them.

- *Hiring and developing staff.* If a company wants to hire someone, it must first advertise the opening, screen resumes, interview applicants, and eventually make a job offer. Then the new person must be introduced to the organization, instructed in the responsibilities of the position, and motivated to perform. As time goes on, the new employee must be given feedback on her or his performance, which involves more communication. The supervisor often fills out a standard form covering attitude, initiative, competence in handling assignments, suitability for promotion, and the like. The review is discussed with the employee, then forwarded to higher management for approval.

Both written and oral communication are essential to a company's interactions with customers.

- *Dealing with customers.* All of an organization's interactions with customers involve communication in one form or another. Even the price tags on products are a form of communication. Sales letters and brochures, advertisements, personal sales calls, telephone solicitations, and formal proposals are all used to stimulate the customer's interest. Communication also plays a part in such customer-related functions as credit checking, billing, and handling complaints and questions.

Organizations rely on communication to obtain needed supplies at favorable prices and to attract investment capital.

- *Negotiating with suppliers and financiers.* To obtain necessary supplies and services, companies develop written specifications that outline their requirements. They place orders for materials, bargaining to get the best price. To arrange financing, they negotiate with lenders and fill out loan applications, or they sell stock to the public, which involves still more paperwork. Once they have obtained the necessary capital, they must keep their investors informed about the status of the business.

The production process is, in part, a communication process.

- *Producing the product.* Getting an idea for a new product out of someone's head, pushing it through the production process, and finally getting the product out the door also require communication. Designers draw plans, marketing people conduct studies, product managers develop sales campaigns. When the time comes for full-scale production, the company prepares a manufacturing plan. Supervisors get instructions and pass them on to production workers. As production gets under way, workers report any problems that arise. Records are kept regarding raw materials, inventory levels, and product quality. Finally, arrangements are made by phone or in writing for shipping the product. Similar steps are required when a company's product is a service, such as accounting or air transportation.

Government regulation and services depend on a two-way flow of information.

- *Interacting with regulatory agencies.* Communication also occurs between businesses and the government. With input from companies and the public, government agencies establish rules and regulations that both protect companies and ensure that they operate in the general interest. Often, companies must then demonstrate their compliance with regulations by preparing reports that describe their efforts to meet such goals as cleaning up the environment or hiring women and minorities. Should a company fail to respond to the government's requirements, it may get an opportunity for further communication—in a court of law.

As you can see, speaking, listening, writing, and reading are involved in everything that an organization does.

PATTERNS OF COMMUNICATION IN ORGANIZATIONS

Each organization has its own approach to transmitting information throughout the organization.

Although all companies have to communicate in order to function, their approaches to communication vary. These variations are not surprising when you consider the vastly different requirements that organizations face. In a small business with only five or six employees, much information can be exchanged casually and directly. But in a giant organization like

FIGURE 1.1
Formal Communication Network

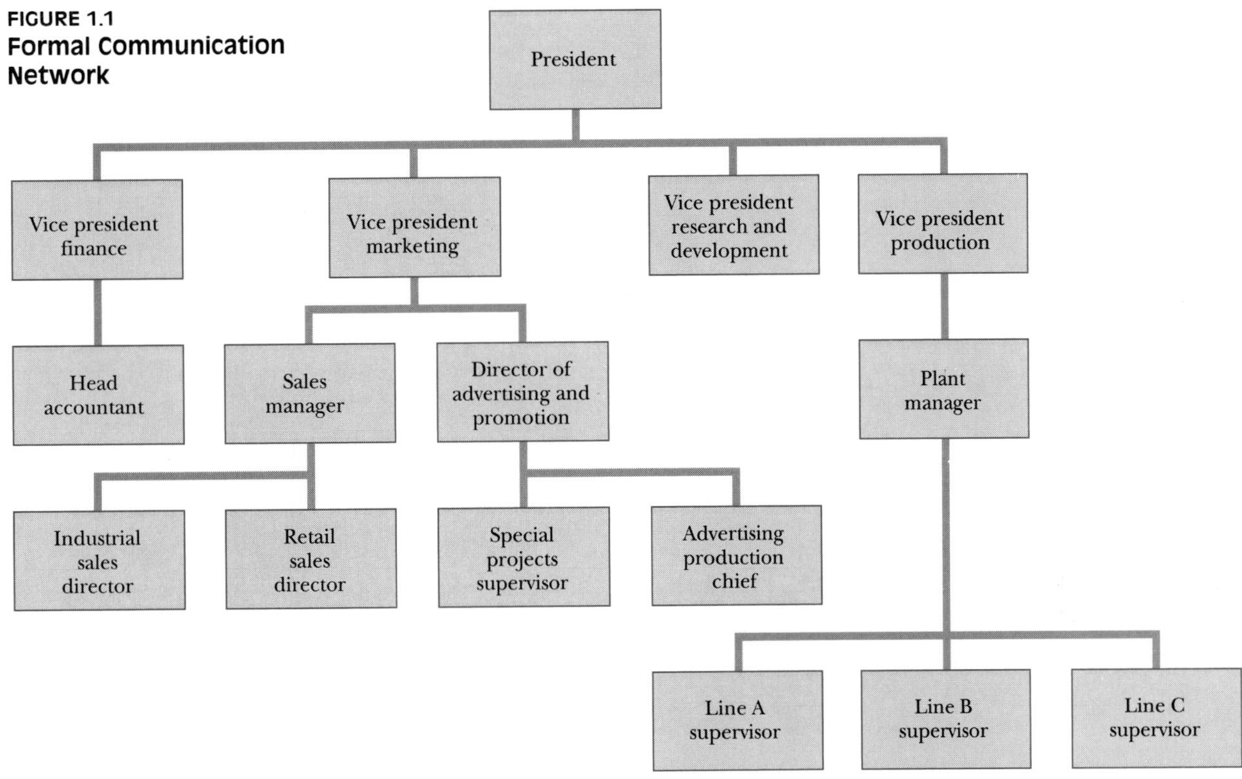

Xerox, with hundreds of thousands of employees scattered around the world, transmitting the right information to the right people at the right time is a real challenge.

Some companies are better at communicating than others. At top-performing companies like Procter & Gamble, Disney, and IBM, communication is a way of life. At IBM, for example, stands with big rolls of paper are placed throughout the building so that people can jot down their thoughts during informal discussions. Because managers communicate freely with employees, everyone in these companies develops a very clear sense of mission, derived from a constant repetition of the organization's values. In these firms, management *is* communication.[4]

How do these companies achieve superior communication? What sets them apart from other organizations? To answer that question, take a closer look at how communication occurs in organizations.

FORMAL COMMUNICATION CHANNELS

The formal flow of information follows the official chain of command.

The official structure of an organization is typically depicted in an organization chart like the one in Figure 1.1. The chart summarizes the lines of authority within the company and depicts the formal hierarchy. Each box represents a link in the chain of command; each line represents a formal channel for the transmission of official information. (Employees also communicate informally, of course.) Information may travel up, down, and across the formal hierarchy.

TABLE 1.1 Employee Satisfaction with Official Communication Network

STATEMENT	PERCENTAGE AGREEING
Company tries to keep employees well informed	68.5
Official communication doesn't tell the full story	68.2
Communication is two-way street within company	52.3
Communication is candid and accurate within company	48.9

Downward information flow

Managers direct and control the activities of lower-level employees by sending messages down through formal channels.

When a manager transmits information to an underling, communication is flowing downward. The message might take the form of a casual conversation or formal interview between a supervisor and an individual employee, or it might be disseminated orally to a group through a meeting, workshop, or videotape. On other occasions, the message might be a written memo, training manual, newsletter, bulletin board announcement, or policy directive.

Although companies like Xerox make a point of letting management decisions be known, many employees are dissatisfied with both the quality and quantity of information they receive through official channels. This is the conclusion reached in one survey, the results of which are summarized in Table 1.1. In another survey of 2 million employees, almost half expressed a desire to be better informed. Employees at lower levels in the organization are particularly likely to feel out of touch with what's happening.[5]

The real problem may lie in the differing communication priorities of managers and employees. As Table 1.2 illustrates, employees are particularly curious about things that affect them personally. They want to know how secure their jobs are, how their salary is determined, and when they'll get a raise. Often, this is the type of information that management prefers to keep confidential.

Upward information flow

From the organization's standpoint, upward communication is just as vital as downward communication. To solve problems and make intelligent

TABLE 1.2 Information Priorities of Employers and Employees

EMPLOYER RATING	TYPE OF INFORMATION	EMPLOYEE RATING
1	News about the company and its prospects for the future	2
2	Employee compensation, benefits, and service	3
3	Personal news	5
4	Company rules, policies, and programs	6
5	Promotions and opportunities for training and advancement	4
6	Social activities	7
7	Information that affects employees personally	1

Messages directed upward provide managers with the information they need to make intelligent decisions.

decisions, management must learn what's going on in the organization. Because they can't be everywhere at once, executives depend on lower-level employees to furnish them with accurate, timely reports.

The danger, of course, is that employees will report only the good news. People are often afraid to admit their own mistakes or to report data that suggest their boss was wrong. Companies try to guard against the "rose-colored glasses" syndrome by creating reporting systems that require employees to furnish vital information on a routine basis. Many of these reports have a "red flag" feature that calls attention to deviations from planned results.

Other formal methods for channeling information upward include group meetings, interviews with employees who are leaving the company, and formal procedures for resolving grievances. In recent years, many companies have also set up systems that give employees a confidential way to get a message to top management outside the normal chain of command. If an employee has a problem or an idea that might be difficult to discuss with the person's immediate supervisor, he or she can talk to a neutral third party (sometimes called an ombudsman) who will consider the issue and see that appropriate action is taken without putting the employee in an awkward position.[6]

Horizontal information flow

Official channels also permit messages to flow from department to department.

In addition to transmitting messages up and down the organization, the formal communication network also carries messages horizontally from one department to another. For example, the marketing director might write a memo to the production director, outlining sales forecasts for the coming period. Or the head of electronic data processing might call a meeting of department heads from throughout the company to inform them of changes in the computer system.

The amount of horizontal communication that occurs through formal channels depends on the degree of interdependence among departments. If the business requires coordinated action by its organizational units, horizontal communication may be frequent and intense. But if each department operates independently, official communication between departments is minimal.

Limitations of formal communication channels

The formal communication network may limit lower-level employees' access to decision makers.

Although formal communication channels are essential in large organizations, they have drawbacks for both the company and the individual. From the standpoint of the individual, formal communication is often frustrating because it limits access to decision makers. In a big, formally structured organization, the only official way to communicate with people at higher levels is to go through one's immediate supervisor. Someone who has a sensational idea but whose boss doesn't agree is effectively stymied. Some people then try to go over the boss's head, but they risk endangering their future at that company and possibly their careers.

Each link in the communication chain is a potential source of blockage or distortion.

From the company's standpoint, the biggest problem with formal communication channels is the opportunity for distortion. Every link in the communication chain opens up a chance for misunderstanding. By the time a message makes its way all the way up or down the chain, it may bear little resemblance to the original idea. As a consequence, people at

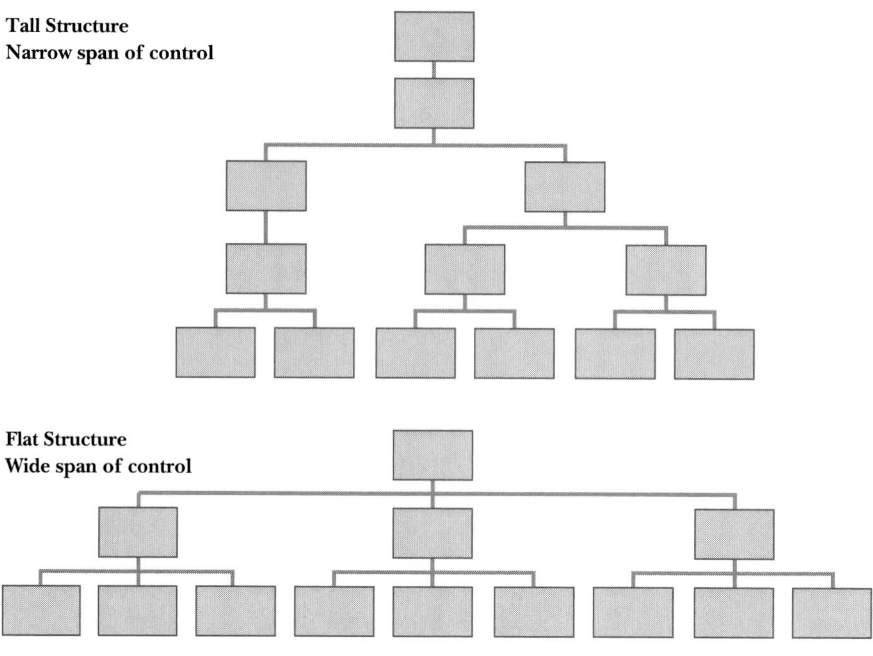

FIGURE 1.2
Organizational Structure and Span of Control

lower levels may have only a vague idea of what top management expects of them, and executives may get an imperfect picture of what's happening lower down.

One way to facilitate accurate communication is to reduce the number of links in the communication chain.

One way to reduce distortion is to reduce the number of levels in the organizational structure. The fewer the links in the communication chain, the less likely it is that misunderstandings will occur.[7] Generally speaking, bigger companies have more levels. But as Figure 1.2 illustrates, size does not necessarily force a company to have a hierarchy with many levels. By increasing the number of people who report to each supervisor, the company can reduce the number of levels in the organization and simplify the communication chain. In other words, a "flat" structure (with fewer levels) and a wider span of control (with more people reporting to each supervisor) are less likely to introduce distortion than are a "tall" structure and a narrow span of control.

Apart from being vulnerable to distortion, the formal communication chain has another potential disadvantage: Information may become fragmented. Unless management encourages horizontal communication and diligently practices downward communication, only the person at the very top can see the "big picture." People lower down in the organization obtain only enough information to perform their own isolated tasks. They don't learn much about other areas, and as a consequence, they cannot suggest ideas that cut across organizational boundaries. Their flexibility is limited by their lack of information. The solution is to make sure communication flows freely up, down, and across the organization chart.

INFORMAL COMMUNICATION CHANNELS

Formal organization charts illustrate how information is supposed to flow. In actual practice, however, lines and boxes on a piece of paper cannot prevent people from talking with one another. Every organization has an

FIGURE 1.3
Where Employees Get Their Information

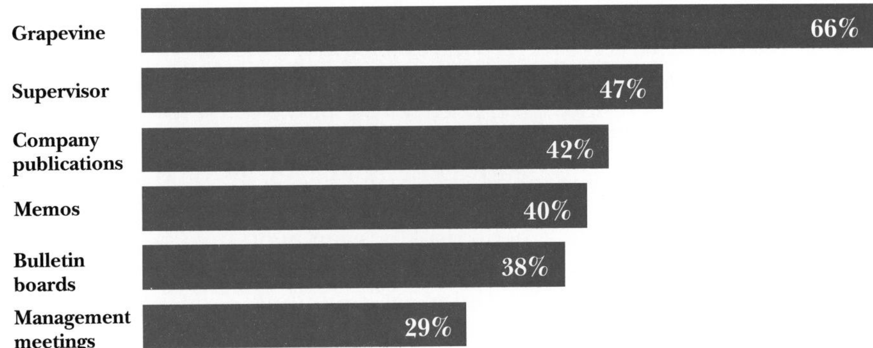

The grapevine is an important source of information in most organizations.

informal communication network—a "grapevine"—that supplements official channels. As people go about their work, they have casual conversations with their friends in the office. They joke and kid around and discuss many things: their apartments, their families, restaurants, movies, sports, other people in the company.

Although many of these conversations deal with personal matters, business is often discussed as well. In fact, about 80 percent of the information that travels along the grapevine pertains to business.[8] Furthermore, many employees rely on the informal network as their main source of information about the organization, as Figure 1.3 illustrates.

Although the grapevine is a potential source of distortion, organizations can limit its negative effects by supplementing it with a free flow of official information.

Unfortunately, information gained through informal channels may be inaccurate. Most grapevines mix facts and assumptions. Party A knows a little bit and supposes a little bit more. Party B adds to that, and so it goes. By the time the information makes the rounds, between 10 and 30 percent of the facts will be distorted.[9] Nevertheless, sophisticated companies rarely try to eliminate the grapevine. Instead, they minimize its less desirable effects by making certain that the official word gets out. The best way to stop false rumors is to spread the truth as quickly as possible.

Figure 1.4 illustrates a typical informal communication network, which is, as usual, somewhat different from the structure outlined in the orga-

FIGURE 1.4
Informal Communication Network

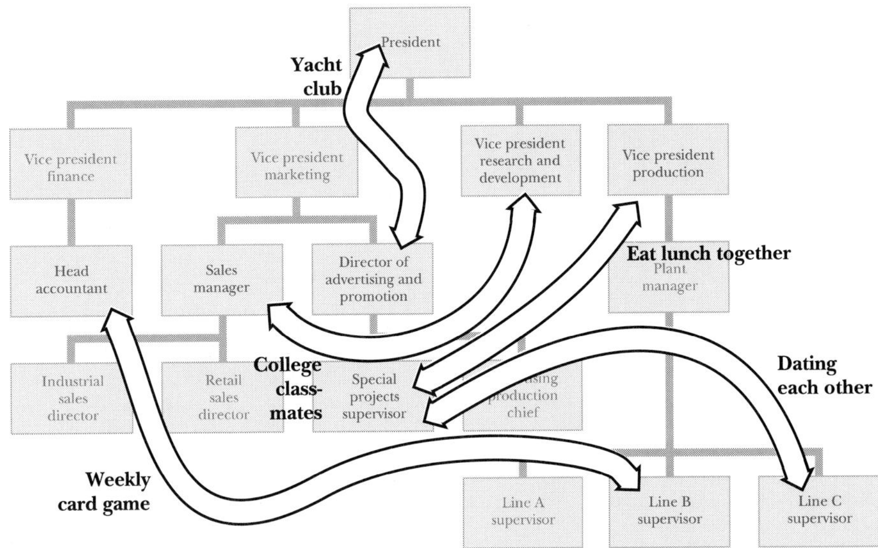

The informal communication network carries information along the organization's unofficial lines of activity and power.

nization chart. This informal network is often the company's real power structure. In every company, certain people seem to know everything, regardless of the position they officially fill. As a consequence, they play a very active role in the grapevine.

Unlike official channels, the informal network is in a constant state of flux. For example, for six or eight months someone might spend a good deal of time communicating with people from another department about a particular assignment; then, when the job is completed, their interaction might cease. And during periods of change in an organization, the amount of informal communication might increase, only to subside when the situation calms.

The informal network has its pluses. Peer-to-peer contact and interdepartmental interaction save the company a great deal of time. If two people from different departments need to work together to accomplish a task, it is often more efficient for them to talk directly to each other instead of passing messages through their bosses. And in an era when mergers, acquisitions, and reorganization are the norm, the informal communication network often plays a particularly vital role. As organizations become more complex structurally, the formal lines of communication become increasingly cumbersome. Informal communication helps people continue to do their jobs effectively until the formal structure catches up with the changes.

ALTERNATIVE COMMUNICATION NETWORKS

The actual pattern of communication flow in an organization is not necessarily the best. The optimum pattern depends on the nature of the task to be performed. This fact emerged from research designed to determine the impact of communication patterns on a group's ability to perform a task. The researchers varied the ways in which five people were allowed to interact, then measured how efficiently they did their work.

Figure 1.5 illustrates four of the alternative communication networks that were tested. The lines indicate who was allowed to talk to whom during the course of the experiment. No "unofficial" communication was permitted.

- *Wheel network.* One person acts as the focal point for all communication. The other members of the group transmit and receive all messages through the leader, who makes decisions and tells people what to do. This is the most structured and centralized of the communication patterns tested.
- *Chain network.* A chain network is also centralized, but in this pattern others serve as relay points between the central figure and individuals at the end of the communication line.
- *Circle network.* All members of the group have equal communication opportunities. Each person can talk with two other people. Information circulates from person to person. Individuals make their own decisions based on shared information.
- *Star network.* All members talk to one another directly. There are no restrictions on who communicates with whom, and all group members make their own decisions.

FIGURE 1.5
Communication Patterns

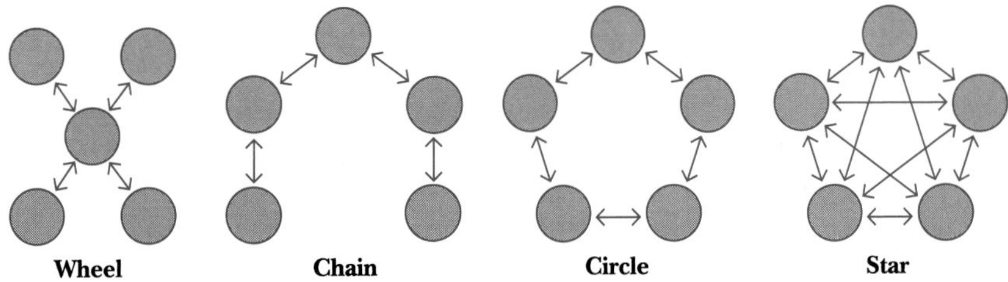

Each of the four alternative communication networks has advantages and disadvantages that make it more appropriate for some types of tasks than for others.

As Table 1.3 illustrates, each of these patterns has advantages and disadvantages. The wheel network is effective when a rather mundane task needs to be accomplished quickly and accurately. A chain network is also accurate but is slightly slower than a wheel network; the members of the chain tend to be somewhat more satisfied and adaptable. The circle ranks high when adaptability and individual satisfaction are important. The star network is not always very efficient, but it ranks very high in terms of job satisfaction and adaptability.[10]

Bear in mind that the networks tested in the experiment involved only five people; different results might have been obtained if more people were involved. Nevertheless, the experiment illustrates an important principle: Different communication networks are suitable for different tasks. If a group is engaged in complex or creative activities, an open communication network like the circle or star is probably most effective. But if success depends on rapid decision making and quick reactions, a more centralized communication pattern is faster, more accurate, and more efficient.[11]

THE INFLUENCE OF COMMUNICATION CLIMATE

The organization's communication climate affects the quantity and quality of information that passes through the pipeline.

Setting up an effective network for transmitting information is obviously important; but the best transmission links in the world won't do an organization much good if the information that flows through them is insufficient, unreliable, or ignored. When people are reluctant to report or acknowledge the truth, the nature of the communication network is irrelevant.

TABLE 1.3 Comparison of Four Communication Patterns

	COMMUNICATION PATTERN			
MEASURE	WHEEL	CHAIN	CIRCLE	STAR
Speed	very fast	fast	slow	slow/fast
Accuracy	good	good	poor	poor/excellent
Morale	very low	low	high	very high
Role clarity	very high	high	none	none
Stability	very stable	stable	unstable	unstable
Creativity	very low	low	high	very high
Adaptability	low	low	high	high

An organization's communication climate is a reflection of its corporate culture, the mixture of values, traditions, and habits that give a place its atmosphere or personality. Some companies foster candor and honesty. Their employees feel free to confess their mistakes, to disagree with the boss, to express opinions. Other companies tend to choke off the upward flow of communication, believing that debate is time consuming and unproductive.

For an example of how communication climate affects performance, consider the *Challenger* disaster. Months before the space shuttle went up in flames, engineers at Morton Thiokol wrote memos to executives warning of problems with the rubber O-ring seals, which ultimately failed. Morton Thiokol management apparently dismissed the warnings as being excessively cautious. Then, on the night before the fateful launch, Morton Thiokol engineers tried again to point out that the seals might fail in cold weather. They expressed their concerns directly to officials of the National Aeronautics and Space Administration at the launch site and also to Morton Thiokol's top management. Again, their worries were dismissed as negative thinking. The next day, immediately before the launch, the NASA officials who had received the engineers' warnings didn't even mention them to their bosses, despite the fact that NASA was debating postponement of the launch in light of the cold weather. Seven people died in a stunning disaster because bad news was unacceptable in NASA's "can-do," success-oriented culture.[12]

The communication climate suffers when management distorts or ignores information from below or when management limits the flow of information to employees.

NASA's communication climate was unhealthy because it established unspoken limits on the kind of information that could be transmitted. In a culture of this type, the discouraging word is never heard; it is never even expressed. Morton Thiokol's problem was somewhat different. There, the engineers were willing to pass along the bad news. But unfortunately, their bosses refused to acknowledge the truth. In both of these cases, top management limited its view of reality by impeding or ignoring the flow of information from below.

Another type of problem arises when top management limits the amount or type of information that is transmitted downward. In many organizations, knowledge is viewed as a form of currency in a power game. People attempt to build their power by hoarding information, like misers embracing a pot of gold. They are afraid to let employees in on the organization's "secrets," fearing that by sharing information they might diminish their control. In extreme cases, people in power even release disinformation, intentionally misleading reports designed in this case to placate lower-level employees.

Many factors influence an organization's communication climate, including the nature of the industry, the company's physical setup, the history of the company, and passing events. However, two of the most important variables are the style of the top management group and the organization's code of ethics.

MANAGEMENT STYLE

The management style of the top executives influences the organization's communication climate.

Experts on management describe four basic management styles, each associated with a different communication climate:[13]

- *Directive style.* Top managers make most of the decisions. This type of firm operates on the assumption that the workers cannot be trusted, that their overriding motive is to avoid work, that they lack initiative and responsibility, and that they must be told precisely what to do. In firms with this philosophy, communication is tightly controlled from the top, and people are discouraged from expressing their opinions. Top management limits the flow of information to employees and restricts communication between departments.

- *Coaching style.* Top executives still provide direction and tell lower-level employees what to do. However, management assumes that employees are members of the team, willing to do their share to accomplish the organization's goals. Management explains the rationale for decisions and listens to ideas and suggestions from below.
- *Supportive style.* Executives assume that employees are competent and motivated. Management establishes goals and plans, but it delegates much of the day-to-day decision making and problem solving to people at lower levels. Communication is a two-way street, flowing both up and down the hierarchy. Employees are free to establish their own informal communication channels.
- *Delegating style.* Top management allows employees to "run their own show." The chief executive provides broad direction but delegates responsibility for determining how tasks and goals are to be accomplished. Because employees are encouraged to solve their own problems, top management may become isolated and lose control of the operations of the organization.

There are other ways to categorize management styles, among them Douglas McGregor's Theory X and Theory Y.[14] Theory X considers workers lazy and irresponsible, motivated to work only by fear of losing their jobs; Theory X managers therefore adopt a directive style. Theory Y, on the other hand, assumes that people like to work and take responsibility when they believe in what they're doing; it's therefore a more supportive management style. Theory Z, developed by William Ouchi, describes yet another management approach.[15] Like the coaching management style, Theory Z encourages employees to work together as a family or a team. Although the company still looks after employees, it also gives them the opportunity to take responsibility and to participate in decision making.

Today, more and more companies are recognizing the value of an open communication climate.

The trend in management today is toward the styles that encourage an open communication climate. In this environment, managers spend more time listening than issuing orders. Workers offer suggestions, help set goals, and collaborate on solving problems.[16] However, some managers have trouble making the switch from a directive management style to a more participatory style. They accept the concept of participation but continue to restrict the flow of information.

COMMUNICATION ETHICS

Conflicting priorities pose ethical problems for an organization's communicators.

Although most organizations pay lip service to such virtues as honesty, courtesy, and moral integrity, doing the "right thing" is not as easy as it sounds. Corporations and their employees are often caught in moral dilemmas, trapped between conflicting loyalties. On the one hand, executives are supposed to protect the interests of the company's shareholders, which means doing everything within reason to maximize profits. At the same time, however, these executives have responsibilities to their employees, their customers, and the public. Sometimes it is impossible to serve all these constituencies at once.

Let's say, for example, that you are the president of a company that is losing money. You have a duty to your shareholders to try to cut your losses. After looking at various options, you conclude that you will have to lay off 500 people immediately. You suspect that you may have to lay off another 100 people later on, but right now you need these 100 workers to finish a project. What do you tell them? If you confess that their jobs are shaky, many of them may quit just when you need them most. But if you tell them that the future is rosy, you will be stretching the truth.

Consider another example. Suppose that you are a salesperson for a new company. You are about to book a big order, a very important piece of business for both you and your firm. You know that the customer is concerned about delivery, and you also know that your company has had some production delays lately. Do you confess that there may be a problem with meeting the delivery schedule, or do you smile, cross your fingers behind your back, and say, "Don't worry about a thing"?

There are no easy answers to these questions. Between the clearly right and the clearly wrong lies a vast gray area, full of difficult ethical trade-offs. How do you negotiate this minefield?

Legal considerations

Laws provide ethical guidelines for certain types of messages.

One place to look for guidance is the law. If saying or writing something is clearly illegal, there is no dilemma: You obey the law.

Human resource management is one problem area where the law provides a lot of answers. For example, people in organizations must be very careful to avoid doing or saying anything that might be interpreted as illegal discrimination. If you are interviewing an applicant for a job, the law says that you cannot ask any questions that relate to the individual's race, religion, age, marital status, political affiliation, or gender. It is also illegal to make unsubstantiated negative comments about someone (slander if the comment is oral, libel if it is written). So if you are asked to give an employment reference for a former employee, stick to the facts and state them in a positive way. Avoid offering any opinion that might hurt that individual's chances of getting the job, even if to do so you must turn down the request for a reference.

Advertising is another area regulated by laws, some of which prohibit unfair and deceptive trade practices. For example, companies should not make false or misleading promises about their products. If you claim that your herbal tea cures baldness, you'd better be able to prove your claim. If you list the contents on the package, the list must be complete; and if you compare your product to another, the comparison should be fair and verifiable. Similarly, in advertising you cannot use visual distortion to make your product look better than it is. Nor can you advertise an item at a low price, then try to convince prospective customers to buy something more expensive by telling them that the original item is defective or out of stock. You're also in legal trouble if you present false testimonials or if you make a statement in large print, then qualify it into meaninglessness in smaller type somewhere else in an ad.[17]

Regardless of whether a specific situation is covered by law, you should be aware of the legal implications of anything you say or write on the job. For better or for worse, we live in litigious times. That innocent memo for the files may well end up as evidence in court. Before you commit words to paper, ask yourself whether you would want to defend your remarks before a judge and jury.

Moral judgment

Although legal considerations will resolve some ethical questions, you and your organization will often have to fall back on your own judgment and principles in making communication decisions. Your organization may have a written code of ethics that outlines standards of conduct, or it may have well-established traditions that provide some guidance. If not, you might apply the Golden Rule: Do unto others as you would have them do unto you.

Ethical messages are well intentioned, honest, moral, professional, and kind.

You might also want to ask yourself these questions when faced with a murky decision:

- *What effect will your message have?* Are you advocating something that will benefit others, or is your purpose potentially harmful? If your message will help people in some way, you can make a strong ethical case for delivering it. But if it helps only you and hurts others, the communication is morally wrong.
- *Is the message true?* In attempting to accomplish your objectives, have you stretched the facts or covered up important information? Have you distorted the evidence to improve your case? If so, the message is dishonest and should be revised. Bear in mind, however, that business involves persuasion. You are trying to sell a product, attract resources, and advance your own career. As long as everything you say is true, there is nothing wrong with accentuating the positive and minimizing the negative. You are not morally obliged to call attention to the disadvantages associated with your products or activities.
- *Does your message appeal to good or bad values?* Are you using rational arguments and humanistic appeals? Or are you trying to persuade people by exploiting their baser motives? Let's say, for example, that you're advocating that your boss reorganize the department. You might argue that reorganization will increase efficiency, or you could point out that reorganization will increase your boss's power and diminish that of a rival. Both arguments might be true, but the first is more ethical because it appeals to your boss's better motives.[18]
- *Does your message reflect the wishes of your organization?* Occasionally, your own views or communication style may conflict with the organization's. If that happens, remember that during the working day, you represent your employer. You are paid to express the organization's position, not your own. In exchange for your paycheck, you owe your employer a certain amount of loyalty. Of course, you should not lie, cheat, or steal, even if you are instructed to do so. But within reason, you should adhere to the "party line."
- *Is the message expressed in a tactful manner?* Although bluntness is occasionally appropriate, nine times out of ten it's better to be kind

than inconsiderate. Why hurt someone's feelings if you can avoid it? Being polite makes life more pleasant for everyone. If you are diplomatic, you'll feel good about yourself, and other people will remember your courtesy.

HOW COMPANIES MANAGE COMMUNICATION

Routine communication is essential to business, but it represents a major expense.

Now that you've gained some insight into the nature of organizational communication, think for a minute about the logistics of moving all those messages, both within the organization and to and from the outside world. A few statistics may help you put the problem in perspective:

- For every white-collar employee on the payroll, the typical organization maintains 18,000 pages of paper, enough to fill a four-drawer filing cabinet. The size of the file increases by 4,000 pages a year.
- Various studies indicate that white-collar workers spend between 21 and 70 percent of their time handling paperwork: preparing, reading, recording, interpreting, filing, and maintaining information.
- Americans create 30 billion documents a year at a cost of over $100 billion. Many of these documents are filed away, but 75 to 85 percent of the time we don't look at the information again.'[19]
- U.S. companies waste $2.6 billion each year on unnecessary photocopies. Roughly one-third of the copies made are tossed into the trash.[20]
- Every year, a single division headquarters of a typical large corporation mails 9 million documents to the outside world. These documents include letters, memos, reports, brochures, news announcements, policy statements, product catalogs, and the like.[21]

And those are just the routine written messages. How many meetings are a waste of time? And how much effort is involved in handling messages in times of crisis? One begins to wonder whether companies are in business to produce products or words.

HANDLING ROUTINE MESSAGES

Obviously, most routine messages are produced for a reason. People in organizations need to communicate their ideas, and they need to document their activities. By establishing paper trails that provide background on operations and personnel, managers are able to keep track of what has occurred. They can review past decisions and evaluate what was done when, why, and by whom. And if they need to prove that they took some action, a written message retrieved from the files may keep them out of trouble.

Although organizations need to document their activities, they also need to manage the flow of messages as efficiently as possible.

The volume of messages is greater in large organizations than in small ones, but all companies are concerned about holding down costs while maximizing the benefits of their communication activities. To a great extent, they expect managers to control communication efforts. Some of the measures that managers may take are to reduce the number of messages being produced, to make assignments and procedures clearer, to distribute communication responsibility more evenly, and to make writers and speakers better at their jobs.

Reduce the number of messages

Modern society is adrift in a sea of paper, fighting a tide of "urgent" messages. Currently, the U.S. Postal Service handles about 100 billion pieces of business mail a year.[22] Think of all the mail you got in the past week. How much of it was business mail? And how much of it did you really pay attention to? You're not alone: The sheer number of messages that people receive dulls their ability to focus on any of them.

The overproduction of messages hurts businesses, too. It takes time and resources to produce even a one-page letter, so the organization must be concerned with how many letters it sends out. The average cost of dictating, transcribing, and mailing a business letter is over $9;[23] the typical business letter, which contains only 190 words, takes eight minutes to dictate.[24] If a message must genuinely be put in writing, a letter is a good investment. But if a letter merely adds to the information overload, the message is probably better left unsent or handled in some other way—say, by a quick telephone call or a face-to-face chat.

Organizations save time and money by sending only necessary messages.

This caution applies to communication within the organization as well. Many memos are superfluous, many meetings are a waste of everyone's time. Thus even these types of communication should be evaluated. How long does the message need to be? Can it be conveyed over the telephone? Can the answer to a question posed in a memo simply be penciled onto the original memo? How many copies of a letter really need to be made? How many copies need to be filed? Can the information be conveyed more concisely with a standardized form, such as a sales report? A thrifty approach to questions like these will save the organization both time and money.

Make instructions clearer

Ironically, even the communication experts in an organization sometimes communicate poorly with one another. Writers may be assigned a project but not given a clear understanding of what they are expected to write. On the other hand, people often neglect to ask the questions that would help them understand their assignment better. Communication breakdowns can be blamed on almost anyone, but managers have a special responsibility to make sure everyone knows what to do.

The manager is responsible for making sure that employees understand their role in preparing messages.

The person who is passing out communication assignments must have a clear understanding of the organization's overall needs and goals, together with a grasp of the purpose of a particular message. Only then can she or he fully explain the communicator's role.

Another aspect of this problem is a lack of follow-through. To keep everyone on course and to provide feedback about the developing message, managers should keep in touch with staff members throughout a project. Communicators, too, have a responsibility to seek clarification as the need arises.

Delegate responsibility

Follow-through and feedback are helpful; breathing down people's necks is not. A manager should be able to trust others to do their assigned jobs.

Managers should delegate some communication jobs to others.

Imagine how much of the organization's time is wasted when a manager feels the need to redo every message in his or her own style.

One thing managers have to realize is that everyone approaches a task differently. Given an assignment to write a report on a bank's branch operations, for example, one writer may organize the report around the bank's services, another around chronological events. Of course, if the company requires a certain approach, the manager must make those requirements clear. If, however, the structure of the report is a matter of personal perspective, the manager should allow the report to be organized in the way that makes the most sense to the writer.

Train writers and speakers

A person who can hold a pencil is not necessarily a good writer; someone with an attractive voice is not always able to explain something clearly to an audience. In fact, even writers and speakers with unusual natural talent need some sort of guided practice to become really good.

In-house training benefits even experienced communicators.

An organization would be well advised, therefore, to provide some sort of in-house training in communication skills for those who communicate on its behalf. Obviously, such training should cover at least the organization's style preferences and communication philosophies, so all can speak with one voice or as close to one voice as possible. Communicators may also need to brush up on their language and presentation skills.

One of the nice things about such training is the sense of pride and professionalism that it creates in those who go through the program. They can do their jobs with confidence, and so the organization operates more smoothly.

HANDLING CRISIS COMMUNICATION

Managing the day-to-day flow of messages is one thing, but the real test of an organization's communication skills comes in times of crisis. Consider the following situations, which you may remember from news stories. If you had been in charge of communications, how would you have handled the flow of information?

- Your firm manufactures pain relievers. A woman dies after taking some of your capsules, and the police investigation reveals that the medicine is laced with cyanide. After several more deaths occur, it becomes clear that someone is tampering with your products.
- In separate incidents, consumers from 30 states report finding fragments of glass in your firm's jars of baby food. You investigate but can find no evidence to substantiate any of these claims. A thorough review of your manufacturing and distribution operations suggests that the problem simply does not exist.

The organizations that faced these events in real life, Johnson & Johnson and Gerber, each handled the crisis in its own way. Johnson & Johnson recalled its Tylenol pain-reliever capsules immediately and cooperated fully with the press and the police. Within months, the company reintroduced Tylenol in a tamper-proof form and recovered its position in the market. But Gerber handled the negative publicity about the glass fragments in baby food by maintaining silence. When the state of Maryland ordered retailers to remove the company's strained peaches from their shelves, Gerber fought back by suing the state for $150 million. Although the suit is still pending, the publicity has subsided, and Gerber has resumed its position of leadership in the baby food market.[25]

The way a company handles a crisis says a lot about its communication skills.

The way an organization handles these one-time situations can have a profound impact on its future. If it copes well, it will not suffer and may even come out ahead. But if it fails to deal effectively with a crisis, its reputation and profitability will suffer.

Recognizing the importance of crisis management, many companies are adopting special plans. A survey of *Fortune* magazine's top 1,000 industrial companies and top 500 service companies reveals that almost half these firms now have crisis management plans in place. The first step is to identify the organization's most likely sources of trouble, such as industrial or environmental accidents, product recalls, regulatory problems, labor disputes, and other high-visibility events. Many companies then set up crisis management teams and specify the actions those teams should take to deal with problems that arise.[26]

Most crisis management plans adhere to one of two communication philosophies: (1) say nothing or (2) tell all and tell it fast. Both approaches can succeed, as the Gerber and Johnson & Johnson cases demonstrate. However, many public relations professionals favor Johnson & Johnson's approach of presenting the facts candidly and openly.[27] They advise companies to counteract rumors and panic by explaining problems to both the public and the employees. At the same time, companies should attack the source of the problem and bring it under control. This is easier said than done, of course. The important thing is to remain calm. A deliberate, rational response inspires more confidence than a hasty statement that has to be corrected a few hours later.

Although keeping a low profile in a crisis is occasionally wise, most experts recommend handling problems with candor and honesty.

HOW YOU CAN IMPROVE YOUR COMMUNICATION SKILLS

So far, this chapter has emphasized communication from the organization's viewpoint. But remember that communication is the link between the individual and the organization. Your ability to understand what is going on depends on your sensitivity as a communicator. Once you know the dynamics of communication within an organization, you can read between the lines to get an accurate picture of what is happening. At the same time, you can adjust your own messages, using the communication network to best advantage and tailoring your style to the organization's communication climate.

In addition, communication skills—the ability to read, write, listen, and speak—are highly prized by most employers. One survey asked, "In assessing an individual's chance of success in your company, how important do you think communication skills are, relative to other kinds of abilities?" About 85 percent of those surveyed replied that communication skills are extremely important.[28] Thus your communication skill, or lack of it, will have a profound impact on your success in the business world.

All jobs require communication skills of one sort or another.

Whether you're a secretary, a management trainee, an accountant, a salesperson, a financial analyst, a human resource specialist, chairman of

TEST YOURSELF

Check Your Communication Skills

To become more aware of your communication skills, complete the following self-evaluation. It will give you an idea of which habits you can congratulate yourself on and which ones you might want to reshape. Carefully think about each question, then answer "most times," "many times," "sometimes," or "few times." Place a check mark in the appropriate column, and then refer to the scales at the end of this chapter to analyze your skills.

WHEN WRITING, DO YOU	MOST TIMES	MANY TIMES	SOME-TIMES	FEW TIMES
1. Think about the kind of person who will be reading your message?	____	____	____	____
2. Make an outline before starting to write?	____	____	____	____
3. Try to use big words that will make the message sound important?	____	____	____	____
4. Revise and polish what you write?	____	____	____	____
5. Use long, complex sentences?	____	____	____	____
6. Proofread your document for errors in grammar, punctuation, and spelling?	____	____	____	____
7. Check your facts and figures for accuracy?	____	____	____	____

WHEN SPEAKING, DO YOU	MOST TIMES	MANY TIMES	SOME-TIMES	FEW TIMES
1. Plan the best time to say what you want to say?	____	____	____	____
2. Think about how the listener might react to what you have to say?	____	____	____	____
3. Avoid eye contact with listeners?	____	____	____	____
4. Assume that listeners share your background and attitudes?	____	____	____	____

the board, or something else entirely, you will need the ability to communicate effectively. Some jobs require greater communication skill than others, however. A salesperson needs to be an excellent communicator, and so does an advertising copywriter or public relations specialist. But even if your job involves staring through a microscope in a remote laboratory, you will sometimes need to work with other people. And that means you will need to communicate. If you can do it well, you will have an advantage. You will be able to get what you need more quickly, your contributions to the organization will be more useful, and you will be rewarded accordingly.

Seven communication skills are typically required in business.

Among the specific skills required in business communication are

- Reading
- Listening
- Engaging in casual conversation
- Interviewing
- Dealing with small groups
- Delivering speeches and presentations
- Writing letters, memos, and reports

The extent to which you use each of these skills depends on where you work and what you do, but you should try to be competent in all of them "just in case."

5. Formulate what you want to say before you begin speaking? ____ ____ ____ ____
6. Monopolize the conversation? ____ ____ ____ ____
7. Pronounce words clearly and correctly? ____ ____ ____ ____

WHEN READING, DO YOU

1. Look up the meanings of unfamiliar words? ____ ____ ____ ____
2. Become easily distracted by other things going on around you? ____ ____ ____ ____
3. Know what words and phrases you respond to emotionally? ____ ____ ____ ____
4. Stop reading when you think you know what the writer is going to say? ____ ____ ____ ____
5. Mentally summarize the key points being made? ____ ____ ____ ____
6. Go beyond reading for information and try to read for understanding? ____ ____ ____ ____
7. Become angry and critical when the author's viewpoint differs from your own? ____ ____ ____ ____

WHEN LISTENING, DO YOU

1. Tune out if the person says something you don't want to hear? ____ ____ ____ ____
2. Repeat in your own words what the speaker has just said? ____ ____ ____ ____
3. Give the appearance of listening when you aren't? ____ ____ ____ ____
4. Look at the person who is speaking? ____ ____ ____ ____
5. Form a rebuttal in your head while the speaker is talking? ____ ____ ____ ____
6. Take notes when necessary to help you remember? ____ ____ ____ ____
7. Concentrate on what is being said even if you're not really interested? ____ ____ ____ ____

Focus on building skills in the areas where you've been weak.

Perhaps the best place to begin any improvement program is with an honest assessment of where you stand. All of us have developed some communication skills to a higher degree than others. Maybe you're a good listener, or maybe writing is your strong suit. In the next few days, watch how you handle the communication situations that arise. Try to figure out what you're doing right and what you're doing wrong. Then, in the months ahead, try to focus on building your competence in areas where you need the most work.

Set goals for improvement that are related to your career plans.

Establish some realistic goals for yourself. What do you hope to accomplish? What part do you think communication will play in your own career plans, and how can you best prepare yourself?

Practice using all communication skills so you can learn from your mistakes.

Perhaps the best way to improve your ability is to practice. People are not "born" writers or speakers. They become good at these things by doing them. Someone who has written ten reports is better at it than someone who has written only two reports. You learn from experience. And some of the most important lessons are learned through failure. Learning what *not* to do is just as important as learning what *to* do.

One of the great advantages of taking a course in business communication is that you get to practice in an environment that provides honest and constructive criticism. A course of this kind also gives you an understanding of acceptable techniques, so you can avoid making costly mistakes on the job.

This book has been designed to provide the kind of communication practice that will prepare you for whatever comes along later in your career. The next chapter introduces the general concepts of communication, so that you will be better able to analyze and predict the outcome of various situations. Chapters 3, 4, and 5 explain how to plan and organize business messages and perfect their style and tone. These chapters are followed by ones that deal with specific forms of communication: letters and memos, resumes and application letters, reports, interviews and meetings, speeches and presentations. As you progress through this book, you will also meet many business communicators, like Joe Varilla of Xerox. Their experiences will give you insight into what it takes to communicate effectively on the job.

SUMMARY

Communication, the link between an organization and its members, is essential to the organization's major functions. When you understand how an organization communicates, you are equipped to become a productive member of the group. Communication also facilitates interactions among management, employees, customers, suppliers, financiers, and government officials.

Communication occurs through both formal and informal channels and flows up and down the hierarchy, as well as across the lines of authority. Open communication patterns encourage links among all members of the organization and facilitate complex activities that require creativity. Tightly controlled communication patterns that depend on an official hierarchy are well suited to situations that call for a rapid response. An organization's communication climate is affected by the corporation's management style and ethics.

Given the volume of messages flowing into, around, and out of modern organizations, communication management has become an issue. In many organizations, managers are encouraged to limit the number of messages, clarify communication assignments, delegate responsibility for writing and speaking, and build employees' communication skills. Many organizations have also developed plans for communicating during times of crisis.

Regardless of where you work or what you do, communication will play a part in your career. By analyzing your strengths and weaknesses, setting realistic goals, and practicing different types of communication, you can improve your oral and written communication skills.

COMMUNICATION CHALLENGES AT XEROX

Xerox is concerned about hiring and promoting women and minorities, as are many responsible companies. The human resource department has asked Joseph Varilla to develop an internal communication campaign that will boost Xerox's success rate in attracting qualified women and minorities.

Individual Challenge: Joe has asked you, as a member of his department, to create a plan for increasing employee awareness of the importance of recruiting minorities and women. List five things that Xerox can do to communicate this message internally, and provide a rationale for each measure.

Team Challenge: Xerox wants to be certain that women and minorities who join the organization receive fair opportunities on assignments and in promotions. Joe has formed a task force (made up of you and a few classmates) to find out if there are any significant problems and to ensure that Xerox provides a positive environment for all employees. Working with the task force, develop a plan for providing a safe communication channel for all employees who might have comments and suggestions about Xerox's equal employment opportunity program.

QUESTIONS FOR DISCUSSION

1. Think about the different groups you belong to. What role does communication play in establishing your membership in each group?
2. What would (or would not) happen if all written communication at your college came to a stop for one day?
3. Do you think that downward or upward communication is more important to an organization? Why?
4. As president of a company, what would you do if you discovered that employees were spending too much time talking to one another about outside activities and too little time doing their jobs?
5. Suppose that you were the commander of an army fighting an unpopular war. What management style would you employ? What kind of communication patterns would you establish?
6. Let's say you are a stockbroker. The amount of money that you and your company make depends on the amount of stock you buy and sell for your clients. The more they trade, the richer you become. From an ethical standpoint, you are justified in recommending that they buy or sell stocks when it's clearly to their advantage to do so. But what are the ethics involved in encouraging them to buy or sell stocks when it is not so clearly in their best interests? Where would you draw the line?
7. Some companies have a policy of limiting all memos to one page. Do you think this is a good idea? Why or why not?
8. Why are some companies reluctant to issue public statements during times of crisis? What are the advantages of maintaining a low profile?
9. What types of communication have you engaged in today? Are you satisfied with the results?
10. Pick three jobs that you might like to have after you graduate. What communication skills do you think would be most important to you in these positions?

EXERCISES

1. Think of someone in business who communicates successfully. Why did you choose this person? Write a one-page explanation of your choice.
2. Interview a businessperson on the following subjects:
   - What types of communication occur in his or her job?
   - How important are written communications to the person's company?
   - How important are oral communications to the person's company?

   Your instructor will tell you whether to report your results orally or in writing.
3. Think of two organizations you are familiar with. (If you have not worked for a company, think of large clubs you've belonged to.) For each organization, make a list of the means used for downward communication. This list should include methods used by top executives to inform individuals about the organization itself, organization policies, employee or member responsibilities, and so forth. Why, do you suppose, do the two organizations have different systems? Which system is better? What are the effects of each organization's communication style on individuals? How could the organization improve its downward communication?
4. Choose two organizations that you are familiar with (the same organizations you used in exercise 3, if you like), and list the methods that each uses for upward communication. Your list should include all means by which people in the ranks convey information to those at higher levels, such as regular reports, meetings, and so on. Which of

the two organizations seems to encourage more input from individuals? What methods might each of these organizations use to improve upward communication? Do you see any correlations between the quality of an organization's downward communication and the quality of its upward communication?

5. Which alternative communication pattern (wheel, chain, circle, star) would work best for handling each of the following situations? Explain your choices.
   a. Coordinating your small company's move to new offices
   b. Gathering information for the company newsletter
   c. Informing employees of a new company policy
   d. Having people sign up to bring food for the company picnic
   e. Soliciting suggestions for ways to handle parking problems in the employee lot
   f. Putting together a budget under a severe deadline
6. Which management style (directive, coaching, supportive, delegating) would be best for handling each of the following situations? Explain your choices.
   a. Training the staff to use all the features of a new phone system
   b. Planning the Christmas parties that will be held in each department of the local branch of a national insurance company
   c. Coordinating an annual inventory, using mainly temporary workers
   d. Conducting a twice-yearly sale in a large department store, which requires marking down nearly every item
   e. Putting together a $5 million promotional campaign for a new product, including advertising and publicity
7. Moral dilemmas are bound to arise in any job. But imagine that one of your salespeople, who also happens to be a good friend, says that the only way to land the big account she's been wooing is to go against company policy on entertainment expenses. She wants you to "bend" company policy and authorize her expenses. What would you tell her, and by what means would you tell her?
8. Imagine that you are the manager of a clothing store. During the day, the following communication tasks arise. For which would you phone and for which would you write? Briefly explain your answers.
   a. You want to inform the placement office of the nearby college of your need for a part-time salesclerk.
   b. You have to turn down an applicant for an assistant manager position because she does not have sufficient experience in retail clothing.
   c. You want to announce a new line of pants to your steady customers.
   d. You need to check on an order for two dozen shirts that should have arrived last week.
   e. You want to congratulate one of your regular customers, whose job promotion was just announced.
   f. You need to confirm details of an upcoming trade show.
   g. You need to respond to an inquiry from another merchant about a customer whose account with you is six months delinquent.
   h. You want to order several items from a supplier's catalog.
   i. You want to decline a request for a $50 contribution to the Neighborhood Improvement Council.
9. What are your strengths and weaknesses as a writer and speaker? Consider your personality, training, and preferences. Present your analysis in a way that will help your instructor plan this course to meet your needs.
10. In the career you have selected or are considering, what kind of communicating do you expect to be doing? How does it differ from the communicating you do in college?

SCORING FOR "CHECK YOUR COMMUNICATION SKILLS" (pp. 24–25)

For each item, circle the number in the column that represents your response.

	MOST TIMES	MANY TIMES	SOME-TIMES	FEW TIMES
WRITING				
1.	4	3	2	1
2.	4	3	2	1
3.	1	2	3	4
4.	4	3	2	1
5.	1	2	3	4
6.	4	3	2	1
7.	4	3	2	1
SPEAKING				
1.	4	3	2	1
2.	4	3	2	1
3.	1	2	3	4
4.	1	2	3	4
5.	4	3	2	1
6.	1	2	3	4
7.	4	3	2	1
READING				
1.	4	3	2	1
2.	1	2	3	4
3.	4	3	2	1
4.	1	2	3	4
5.	4	3	2	1
6.	4	3	2	1
7.	1	2	3	4
LISTENING				
1.	1	2	3	4
2.	4	3	2	1

	MOST TIMES	MANY TIMES	SOME-TIMES	FEW TIMES
LISTENING				
3.	1	2	3	4
4.	4	3	2	1
5.	1	2	3	4
6.	4	3	2	1
7.	4	3	2	1

Total the circled numbers:

Writing score = _____

Speaking score = _____

Reading score = _____

Listening score = _____

Total = _____

Find your score:

100–112	Superior
84–99	Above average
70–83	Average
56–69	Fair

In which of the four categories did you score highest? In which did you score lowest? In the years ahead, recheck your skills from time to time to make sure you're improving.

After studying this chapter, you will be able to

- Understand how nonverbal and verbal communication convey meaning
- Explain the process of communication
- Describe how misunderstandings arise during the communication process
- Recognize the special difficulties of business communication
- Understand how common barriers to communication may be overcome

CHAPTER TWO

UNDERSTANDING BUSINESS COMMUNICATION

Lee Dunham

COMMUNICATION CLOSE-UP AT McDONALD'S

Lee Dunham, chief executive officer of Harlem McDonald's and self-made millionaire, is a very busy person. With seven McDonald's restaurants, some 400 employees, and obligations to a variety of industry and community groups, it is no wonder that he works seven days a week. About two of those days he's in his New York City office, making phone calls and dealing with correspondence; another two days he's visiting his stores; one day a week he's meeting with his staff, another day helping to train his young and inexperienced employees in good work habits. The rest of the time he's sitting on various committees and speaking to groups who want to hear what he knows about motivating the underprivileged and disadvantaged to participate in the world of work.

Lee is a practiced communicator, but he still makes mistakes from time to time. For instance, a supervisor once approached him with the unpleasant news that $10,000 was missing from one of the stores. "Our policy is to fire the person who's responsible when that much is missing," Lee explains. "But in this case, the young woman had been with me for eight years, had a lot of responsibility, and was making a very good salary. I thought I said to her supervisor, 'I'm busy right now, so let me think about it and get back to you.' But the supervisor thought we had agreed to fire the employee." The young woman called Lee crying and explained that she had mistakenly

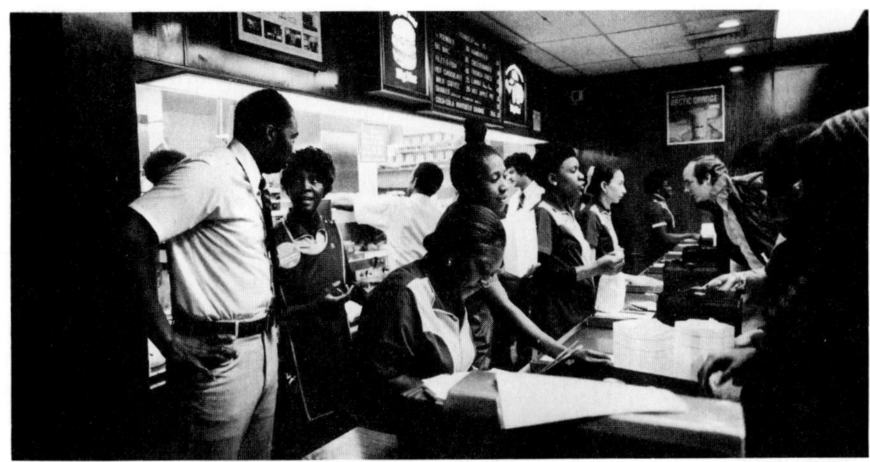

Breaking down communication barriers is a key element of McDonald's business philosophy.

gone to a meeting with the $10,000 instead of waiting for the armored truck to pick it up. "After I heard her explanation, I asked the supervisor to rethink the decision. Fortunately, it was reversed."

This sort of problem can be avoided. According to Lee, "The art of communication is very simple. You first have to get the other person's attention. Then make sure that you look the person in the eye while you're talking. It's a good idea, too, to make no more than three points at a time. Something gets lost when you try to bring up too much at once.

"Another problem is that we tend to make a lot of assumptions when we communicate," Lee notes. He has a suggestion for overcoming that one too: "I've seen a lot of mistakes made because somebody hasn't taken the time to understand what's being said. Make sure you do. And ask the other person to explain what you said."

Lee's specialty is oral communication, but he also has some observations about written messages. "It's a good idea to be very specific and get right to the point," he says, "because if you don't, the person you're writing to may never get the message. Cut through the garbage, get to the meat. Many times, you need only three or four paragraphs to do the job."

Lee's suggestions make good sense for any kind of message, but he notes that business communication is even more difficult than the everyday variety: "Business communication is very precise. And it's more important because more is riding on it."

Many of the young people Lee deals with don't have much opportunity for an education. But even college graduates are at a disadvantage in the business world, he feels, if they haven't used their time in school to learn how to communicate effectively. "Each time you get an opportunity, practice writing and speaking," he advises. "If you begin to polish your skills today, by the time you're out of school, you'll be in a good position to get the plum assignments."

THE BASIC FORMS OF COMMUNICATION

Effective communicators like Lee Dunham have many tools at their disposal when they want to get across a message. Whether writing or speaking, they know how to put together the words that will convey their meaning. They reinforce their words with gestures and actions. They look you in the eye, listen to what you have to say, and think about your feelings and needs. At the same time, they study your reactions, picking up the nuances of your response by watching your face and body, listening to your tone of voice, and evaluating your words. They absorb information just as efficiently as they transmit it, relying on both nonverbal and verbal cues.

NONVERBAL COMMUNICATION

The most basic form of communication is nonverbal. Anthropologists theorize that long before human beings used words to talk things over, our ancestors communicated with one another by using their bodies. They gritted their teeth to show anger; they smiled and touched one another to indicate affection. Although we have come a long way since those primitive times, we still use nonverbal cues to express superiority, dependence, dislike, respect, love, and other feelings.[1]

Nonverbal communication has few rules and often occurs unconsciously.

Nonverbal communication differs from verbal communication in fundamental ways. For one thing, it is less structured, which makes it more difficult to study. A person cannot pick up a book on nonverbal language and master the vocabulary of gestures, expressions, and inflections that are common in our culture. We don't really know how people learn nonverbal behavior. No one teaches a baby to cry or smile, yet these forms of self-expression are almost universal. Other types of nonverbal communication, such as the meaning of colors and certain gestures, vary from culture to culture.

Nonverbal communication also differs from verbal communication in terms of intent and spontaneity. We generally plan our words. When we say, "Please open the door," we have a conscious purpose. We think about the message, if only for a moment. But when we communicate nonverbally, we sometimes do so unconsciously. We don't mean to raise an eyebrow or blush. Those actions come naturally. Without our consent, our emotions are written all over our faces.

Why nonverbal communication is important

Although nonverbal communication is often unplanned, it has more impact than verbal communication. Nonverbal cues are especially important in conveying feelings, accounting for 93 percent of the emotional meaning that is exchanged in any interaction.[2]

Nonverbal communication is more reliable and more efficient than verbal communication.

One advantage of nonverbal communication is its reliability. Most people can deceive us much more easily with words than they can with their bodies. Words are relatively easy to control; body language, facial expressions, and vocal characteristics are not. By paying attention to these nonverbal cues, we can detect deception or affirm a speaker's honesty. Not surprisingly, we have more faith in nonverbal cues than we do in verbal messages. If a person says one thing but transmits a conflicting message nonverbally, we almost invariably believe the nonverbal signal.[3] To a great degree, then, an individual's credibility as a communicator depends on nonverbal messages.

Nonverbal communication is important for another reason as well: It can be efficient from both the sender's and the receiver's standpoint. You

TEST YOURSELF

How Does Your Nonverbal Credibility Measure Up?

If you want to establish credibility with listeners, you need to manage four aspects of your nonverbal behavior: eye behavior, gestures, posture, and voice. How do you currently measure up in each of these areas? For each question, answer "most times," "sometimes," or "few times." You can analyze your skills by referring to the scales at the end of this chapter.

EYES	MOST TIMES	SOME-TIMES	FEW TIMES
1. Do you maintain eye contact while talking to others?	____	____	____
2. Do you maintain eye contact while others talk to you?	____	____	____
3. Do you try to sustain eye contact throughout a conversation?	____	____	____
4. Do you look down before responding to questions?	____	____	____
5. Do you glance around the room while others are talking?	____	____	____
6. Do you blink a lot, or do your eyelids flutter?	____	____	____
GESTURES			
1. Are your gestures unrehearsed and relaxed?	____	____	____
2. Do you keep your elbows and hands away from your body while you talk?	____	____	____
3. Do you use gestures to signal when you want to continue talking or when you want another person to begin talking?	____	____	____
4. Are your gestures weak and tentative?	____	____	____
5. During a conversation, do you fidget or tug at your clothing?	____	____	____
6. Do you touch your hands to your face or lick your lips?	____	____	____
POSTURE			
1. Do you assume an open and relaxed posture?	____	____	____
2. Do you walk confidently?	____	____	____
3. Do you establish rapport by leaning forward and smiling (if appropriate) when beginning to answer a question?	____	____	____
4. Do you hold your body rigid?	____	____	____
5. When sitting, do you cross your arms and legs?	____	____	____
6. Do you keep your hands and arms close to your body?	____	____	____
VOICE			
1. Do you strive for a conversational speaking style?	____	____	____
2. Do you speak loudly enough for people to hear you?	____	____	____
3. Do you vary your pitch, rate, and volume when speaking?	____	____	____
4. Do you have a flat or nasal tone when you speak?	____	____	____
5. Do you talk too fast?	____	____	____
6. Do you pause frequently in the middle of sentences?	____	____	____

can transmit a nonverbal message without even thinking about it, and your audience can register the meaning unconsciously. By the same token, when you have a conscious purpose, you can often achieve it more economically with a gesture than you can with words. A wave of the hand, a pat on the back, a wink—all are streamlined expressions of thought.

The functions of nonverbal communication

People use nonverbal signals to support and clarify verbal communication.

Although nonverbal communication can stand alone, it frequently works hand in hand with speech. Our words carry part of the message, and nonverbal signals carry the rest. Together, the two modes of expression make a powerful team, augmenting, reinforcing, and clarifying each other.

For example, imagine that you are running a meeting. You might clear your throat and straighten up in your chair as you say, "I'd like to call the meeting to order now." Later you might hold up three fingers and say, "There are three things we need to decide today." As the meeting progresses, you might substitute gestures for comments—nodding your head and smiling to show approval, frowning to express reservations. You might also use nonverbal communication to regulate the flow of conversation; by tilting your head, for example, you could invite a colleague to continue with a comment. Finally, you might hedge your bets by saying one thing but implying another nonverbally.

Experts in nonverbal communication suggest that it has six specific functions:

- To provide information, either consciously or unconsciously
- To regulate the flow of conversation
- To express emotion
- To qualify, complement, contradict, or expand verbal messages
- To control or influence others
- To facilitate specific tasks, such as teaching a person to swing a golf club[4]

By controlling the nonverbal messages you send, you can project the image you desire.

Nonverbal communication plays a role in business, too. For one thing, it helps establish credibility and leadership potential. If you can learn to manage the impression you create with your body language, facial characteristics, voice, and appearance, you can do a great deal to communicate that you are competent, trustworthy, and dynamic.

By watching for nonverbal cues, you can get a more accurate picture of others.

At the same time, if you can learn to read other people's nonverbal messages, you will be able to interpret their underlying attitudes and intentions more accurately. In dealing with co-workers, customers, and clients, watch carefully for small signs that reveal how the conversation is going. If you aren't having the effect you want, check your words; then, if your words are all right, try to be aware of the nonverbal meanings you are transmitting. At the same time, stay tuned to the nonverbal signals that the other person is sending.

The varieties of nonverbal communication

According to one estimate, there are over 700,000 different forms of nonverbal communication.[5] For discussion purposes, however, these forms can be grouped into general categories, which include facial expressions and eye behavior, gestures and postures, vocal characteristics, personal appearance, touching behavior, and use of time and space.

Researchers have drawn some interesting conclusions about the meaning of certain nonverbal signals. But remember that the meaning of nonverbal communication is in the observer, who both reads the meaning of specific signals and interprets in the context of the particular situation.

The face and eyes command particular attention as a source of nonverbal messages.

- *Facial expressions and eye behavior.* The face is a powerful source of nonverbal messages; it is the primary site for the expression of emotion, revealing both the type and the intensity of a person's feelings.[6] A person's eyes are especially effective as a tool of communication. They can be used to indicate attention and interest, to influence others, to regulate interaction, and to establish dominance. Although the eyes and the face are usually a reliable source of meaning, people sometimes manipulate their expressions to simulate an emotion they do not feel or to mask their true feelings.

Body language, whether intentional or unconscious, reveals a lot about a person's emotions and attitudes.

- *Gestures and postures.* By moving their bodies, people can express both specific and general messages, some of which are voluntary and some of which are involuntary. Many gestures—a wave of the hand, for example—have a specific and intentional meaning, such as "hello" or "goodbye." These movements clarify and supplement verbal communication. Other types of body movement are unintentional and express a more general message. Slouching, leaning forward, fidgeting, and walking briskly all fall into this category. These unconscious signals reveal whether a person feels confident or nervous, friendly or hostile, assertive or passive, powerful or powerless.

Your tone of voice and other vocal characteristics augment verbal communication.

- *Vocal characteristics.* Like body language, a person's voice carries both intentional and unintentional messages. On a conscious level, we can use our voices to create different impressions. For example, consider the phrase "What have you been up to?" If you repeat that question four or five times, using a different tone of voice and stressing different words, you can convey quite different messages. However, your vocal characteristics also reveal many things that you are unaware of. The tone and volume of your voice, your accent and speaking pace, and all the little *um*'s and *ah*'s that creep into your speech say a lot about who you are, your relationship with the audience, and the emotions underlying your words.

Physical appearance and personal style contribute to our identity.

- *Personal appearance.* An individual's appearance helps to establish his or her social identity. To a great degree, we are what we appear to be. People respond to us on the basis of our physical attractiveness. Some teachers, for example, expect nice-looking students to excel.[7] Because we see ourselves as others see us, these expectations are often a self-fulfilling prophecy. When people think we're capable and attractive, we feel good about ourselves. We develop a positive outlook on life, and this affects our behavior, which in turn affects other people's perception of us. Although an individual's body type and facial features impose limitations, most of us are able to control our attractiveness to some degree. Our grooming, our clothing, our accessories, our "style"—all modify our appearance. Even without the gift of beauty, we can create a favorable impression, tailoring our physical appearance to send the message we want to convey.

Touch suggests both affection and dominance.

- *Touching behavior.* Touch is an important vehicle for conveying warmth, comfort, and reassurance. Even the most casual contact can create positive feelings. This fact was revealed by an experiment in which librarians alternately touched and avoided the hands of students while returning their library cards. Although the contact lasted only half a second, the students who had been touched reported far more positive feelings about themselves and the library, even though many of them did not consciously remember being touched.[8] Perhaps because it implies intimacy, touching behavior is governed by relatively strict customs that establish who can touch whom, and how, in various circumstances. The accepted norms vary, depending on the gender, age, relative status, and cultural background of the individuals involved. In business situations, touching suggests dominance, and so a higher-status person is more likely to touch a lower-status one than the other way around. Touching has become controversial, however, because it can sometimes be interpreted as sexual harassment.

The use of time and space, which is affected by culture, helps establish social relationships.

- *Use of time and space.* Like touch, time and space can be used to assert authority. In many cultures, people demonstrate their importance by making other people wait; they show respect by being on time. However, attitudes toward punctuality are cultural. In North America, being on time is a mark of good manners; in other places it is more polite to be somewhat late. People can also assert their status by occupying the best space. In an organization, the person who wields power usually has the corner office and the prettiest view. Apart from serving as a symbol of status, space determines how comfortable people feel in talking with each other. When people stand too close or too far away, we feel ill at ease. In intimate conversation, North Americans typically stand 1½ to 4 feet apart; in business or social groups, 4 to 12 feet; and in public, 12 to 25 feet. But in Latin America, people communicate more comfortably at closer range.

VERBAL COMMUNICATION

Language is composed of words and grammar.

Although you can express many things nonverbally, there are limits to what you can communicate without the help of language. If you want to discuss past events, ideas, or abstractions, you need words—symbols that stand for thoughts—arranged in meaningful patterns. In the English language, we have a growing pool of words, currently about 750,000, although most of us recognize only about 20,000 of them.[9] To create a thought with these words, we arrange them according to the rules of grammar, putting the various parts of speech in the proper sequence.

We then transmit the message in spoken or written form, hoping that someone will hear or read what we have to say. Figure 2.1 shows how much time business people devote to the different types of verbal communication. They use speaking and writing to send messages and use listening and reading to receive them.

Speaking and writing

When it comes to sending business messages, speaking is more common than writing. Giving instructions, conducting interviews, working in small groups, attending meetings, making speeches, and the like are all important activities. You'll learn more about them in Chapters 17 and 18.

Writing takes up less time, but it too is important. If you're dealing with a complex message of lasting significance, you will probably want to put it in writing. Chapters 6 through 16 deal with writing letters, memos, and reports.

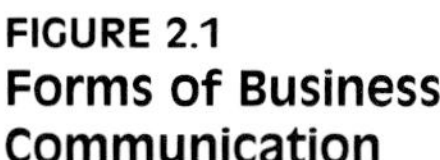
FIGURE 2.1
Forms of Business Communication

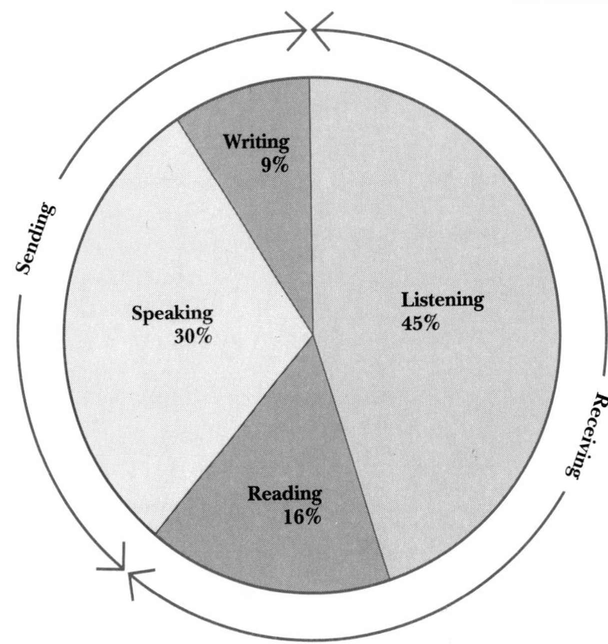

Listening and reading

Although this book focuses on writing and speaking, it's important to bear in mind that effective communication is a two-way street. People in business spend more time obtaining information than transmitting it. To do their jobs effectively, therefore, they need good listening and reading skills. Unfortunately, most of us are not very good listeners. Immediately after hearing a ten-minute speech, we typically remember only half of what was said. A few days later, we've forgotten three-quarters of the message.[10] To some extent, our listening problems stem from our education, or lack of it. We spend years learning to express our ideas, but few of us ever take a course in listening.

Effective business communication depends on skill in receiving messages as well as on skill in sending them.

By the same token, our reading skills often leave a good deal to be desired. Recent studies indicate that approximately 20 percent of the adults in the United States are functionally illiterate; 14 percent cannot fill out a check properly; 38 percent have trouble reading the help wanted ads in the newspaper; and 26 percent can't figure out the deductions listed on their paychecks.[11] Even those who read adequately often do not know how to read effectively. They have trouble extracting the important points from a document, and so they cannot make the most of the information in the document.

As a college student, you are probably better at listening and reading than many people, partly because you get so much practice. You spend your days going to classes and your nights studying. If you attend school full-time, you read between eight and ten textbooks per year, or roughly 5,000 pages.[12] On the basis of your own experience as a student, you no doubt realize that your listening and reading efficiency varies tremendously, depending on how you approach the task. Obtaining and remembering information takes a special effort.

Although listening and reading obviously differ, both require a similar approach. The first step is to register the information, which means that you must tune out distractions and focus your attention. You must then

To absorb information, you must concentrate, evaluate, and retain what you read or hear.

interpret and evaluate the information, respond in some fashion, and file away the data for future reference.

The most important part of this process is interpretation and evaluation, which is no easy matter. While absorbing the material, you must decide what is important and what isn't. One approach is to look for the main ideas and the most important supporting details, rather than trying to remember everything you read or hear. If you can discern the structure of the material, you can also understand the relationships among the ideas.

If you're listening as opposed to reading, you have the advantage of being able to ask questions and interact with the speaker. Instead of just gathering information, you can cooperate in solving problems. This interactive process requires additional listening skills, which Chapter 17 discusses.

THE PROCESS OF COMMUNICATION

Whether you are speaking or writing, listening or reading, communication is more than a single act. Instead, it is a chain of events that can be broken into five phases, as Figure 2.2 illustrates:

The communication process consists of five phases linking sender and receiver.

1. The sender has an idea.
2. The idea becomes a message.
3. The message is transmitted.
4. The receiver gets the message.
5. The receiver reacts and sends feedback to the sender.

Then the process is repeated, until both parties have finished expressing themselves. Communication is effective only when each step is successful.

THE SENDER HAS AN IDEA

All ideas are simplifications and abstractions of reality, filtered through the individual mind.

The world constantly bombards us with information: sights, sounds, scents, and so on. Our minds filter this stream of sensation and organize it into a mental map that represents our perception of reality. In no case is the map in a person's mind the same as the world itself, and no two maps are

FIGURE 2.2
The Communication Process

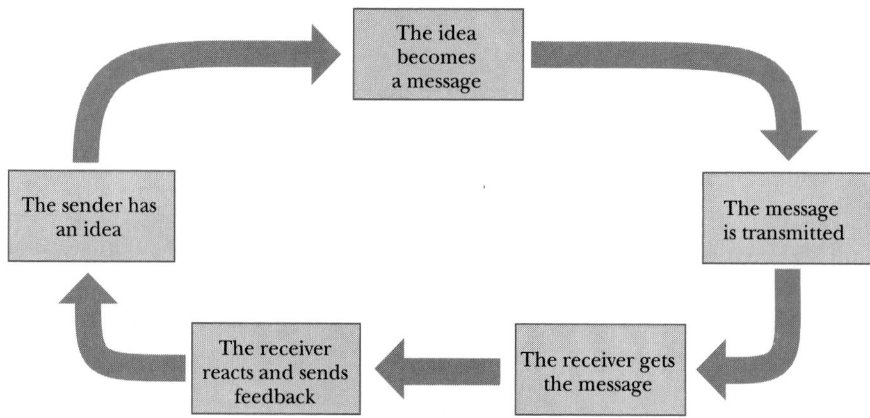

exactly alike. As you view the world, your mind absorbs your experiences in a unique and personal way. For example, if you and a friend go out for a pizza, you will mentally grasp different things. One of you may notice the coolness of the air conditioning as you enter the restaurant; the other may notice the aroma of pizza or the sound of the jukebox.

Because your perceptions are unique, the ideas that you want to express are different from other people's. Even when two people have experienced the same event, their mental images of that event will not be identical. As a communicator, you filter out the details that seem unimportant and focus your attention on the most relevant and general, a process known as abstracting.

Abstracting: considering the most general characteristics and ignoring the specific details

You also make assumptions and draw conclusions, even though you cannot directly verify those assumptions. You assume, for example, that the sound of music in the pizza parlor comes from the jukebox, although you cannot see it as you enter the door. Often your inferences are correct, but sometimes they are not.

When you send a message, you inevitably distort reality. The idea in your mind is a simplification of the real world. In the process of conceiving an idea, you leave out many things and assume many others.

THE IDEA BECOMES A MESSAGE

In a process not completely understood, the idea in your mind is transformed into words; you decide such issues as the message's length, organization, tone, and style. You can express an idea in an almost infinite number of ways, but something makes you choose one approach over another. For example, you may decide to say, "The man was driving a car," rather than, "The old geezer was poking along in a beat-up green 1982 Ford." Your choice of words depends on your subject, your purpose, your audience, and your personal style or mood.

Any given idea may be expressed in many ways, depending on your

- Subject
- Purpose
- Audience
- Personal style or mood
- Cultural background

To some extent, your choice of words also depends on your cultural background. If you are a government bureaucrat, you might say, "Expedited adjustment assistance may be ineffective in helping the industry cope with current problems of severe inventory overhang, low prices, and financial losses." That sort of language is considered appropriate in some bureaucracies. On the other hand, if you're a straightforward manager, you might say, "Even a swift government bailout won't save us from going broke." When you choose your words, you signal that you are a member of a particular club and that you know the code.

The nature of your code—your language and vocabulary—imposes its own limits on your message. For example, Eskimos are unable to express the difference between a car and a motorcycle. They use the same word for both. But their language has at least 30 separate terms for snow. Similarly, the language of a lawyer differs from that of an accountant or a doctor, and the difference in their vocabularies affects their ability to recognize and express ideas.

THE MESSAGE IS TRANSMITTED

The third step in the communication process is physical transmission of the message from sender to receiver. The channel may be nonverbal or verbal, written or spoken. Beyond that, you can convey a message by phone, computer, letter, memo, report, face-to-face exchange, or other medium.

The choice of a transmission channel depends on the

- Message
- Audience
- Need for speed
- Situation

The transmission channel and the medium you choose depend on the message you want to convey and on other factors, such as the location of your audience, the need for speed, and the formality of the situation. Let's say, for example, that you are trying to sell books. You might advertise in newspapers and magazines, put a sign in your store window, hire a door-to-door sales force, launch a direct-mail campaign, or solicit sales over the phone. Whichever approach you choose, the nature of the channel and the medium will influence the message. The wording of a newspaper ad should be, and usually is, different from the wording used in a face-to-face sales call.

The transmission channel and the medium used within that channel affect the content and reception of a message.

The transmission channel and medium also affect what the receiver gets from the message. Watching a movie on television is different from watching it in a theater, even though the movie is exactly the same. A theater offers no outside distractions, no commercials, no lights. Reading a handwritten report is different from reading a perfectly typed copy of the same material. The paper, the binding, and the graphics of a document all influence its reception.

THE RECEIVER GETS THE MESSAGE

For communication to occur, the receiver has to get the message. If you send a letter, the recipient has to read it before she or he can understand it. If you're giving a speech, the people in the audience have to be able to hear you, and they have to be paying attention.

A receiver is most likely to receive the message accurately if

- Nothing physical interrupts or distorts the message
- The receiver's mind processes the message as the sender intended

Physical reception is only the first step. The receiver also has to absorb the message mentally. In other words, the message has to be understood and stored in the receiver's mind. If all goes well, the message is interpreted correctly: The receiver assigns the same basic meaning to the words as the sender intended and responds in the desired way.

THE RECEIVER GIVES FEEDBACK TO THE SENDER

Feedback is the final link in the communication chain. After getting the message, the receiver responds in some way and signals that response to the sender. The signal may take the form of a smile, a long pause, a spoken comment, a written message, or an action of some sort. Even a lack of response is, in a sense, a form of response.

Feedback is the receiver's response; it permits the sender to evaluate the message's effectiveness.

Feedback is a key element in the communication process, because it enables the sender to evaluate the effectiveness of the message. If your audience doesn't understand what you mean, you can tell by the response and refine the message. In business, many written messages are also designed to elicit a response of some sort. If that response indicates you have not made your point, you may repeat the communication cycle as often as necessary. You may find, however, that you need to make some changes in the way you encode and transmit the message.

HOW MISUNDERSTANDINGS ARISE

Although most acts of communication are at least partially successful, very few are perfect. Generally speaking, some meaning is lost as the message encounters various barriers to communication along the pathway between sender and receiver. Communication barriers can arise while the message is being developed, transmitted, received, or processed.

PROBLEMS IN DEVELOPING THE MESSAGE

Problems in formulating your message get communication off to a bad start.

The first potential source of trouble is formulation of the message. Problems involve indecision about message content, lack of familiarity with the situation or the receiver, emotional conflicts, or difficulty in expressing ideas. If you aren't successful at this point, the communication process starts out wrong and rapidly goes downhill.

Indecision about content

Deciding what to say is the first hurdle in the communication process. If you know too little about a subject, you cannot develop an effective or convincing message. In business, however, you will generally have an adequate background for formulating your messages. Most of the time, you will be asked to provide information about your area of responsibility or expertise. Your major problem will be to sort through your knowledge and select the points that are useful for your audience.

Include only the information that is useful to the receiver, and organize it in a way that encourages its acceptance.

Communication often fails because the sender tries to convey everything that she or he knows about a subject. When a message contains too much information, it is difficult to absorb. If you want to get your point across, therefore, you have to decide what to include and what to leave out, how much detail to provide, and what order to follow. If you try to explain something without first giving the receiver adequate background, you will create confusion. And if you recommend actions without first explaining why they are justified, your message may provoke an emotional response that inhibits understanding.

Lack of familiarity with the situation or the receiver

Creating an effective message is difficult if you don't know how it will be used. Let's say that you're writing a report on the market for sports equipment. If you don't know the purpose of the report, it's hard to know what to say. What sort of sports equipment should you cover? Should you include team sports as well as individual sports? Should you subdivide the market geographically or according to price ranges? How long should the report be? Should it provide conclusions and recommendations or simply facts and figures? Unless you know why the report is needed, you really can't answer these questions intelligently. You are forced to create a very general document, one that covers a little bit of everything. In the process, you are likely to leave out some important information and to include some irrelevant material.

Ask why you are preparing the message and for whom you are preparing it.

Lack of familiarity with your audience is an equally serious handicap. You need to know something about the biases, education, age, status, and style of the receiver in order to create an effective message. If you're writing for a specialist in your field, for example, you can use technical

terms that might be unfamiliar to a layperson. If you're addressing a lower-level employee, you might approach a subject differently than if you were talking to your boss. Decisions about the content, organization, style, and tone of your message all depend, at least to some extent, on the relationship between you and the audience. If you don't know the audience, you will be forced to make these decisions in the dark. As a consequence, at least part of your message may miss the mark.

Emotional conflicts

Another potential problem in developing the message arises when the sender has conflicting emotions about the subject or the audience. Let's say that you've been asked to prepare a report recommending ways to improve the organization of your department. After analyzing the situation, you come to believe that the best approach is to combine two positions. But this solution will mean eliminating the job of one of your close associates. When the time comes to write your report, you find yourself apologizing for your recommendation. Even though you know your position is justified, you cannot make a convincing case.

In business communication, try to maintain your objectivity.

Or let's say that you have asked your boss for a raise and your request has been turned down. You are angry and feel that you're being treated unfairly. When you try to explain your feelings to your boss, you lose your temper. You know that you sound childish, and your embarrassment makes you even more angry. A conversation that takes place under such circumstances only makes matters worse; your emotions have prevented you from expressing yourself in an effective way.

Difficulty in expressing ideas

Lack of experience in writing or speaking can also prevent a person from developing effective messages. Some people have limited education or a lack of aptitude when it comes to expressing ideas. Perhaps they have a limited vocabulary or are uncertain about questions of grammar, punctuation, and style. Or perhaps they are simply frightened by the idea of writing something or appearing before a group. In any case, they are unable to develop an effective message because they lack expertise in using language.

An inability to put thoughts into words can be overcome through study and practice.

Problems of this sort can be overcome but only with some effort. The important thing is to recognize the problem and take action. Taking courses in communication at a college is a good first step. Some companies offer their own in-house training programs in communication; others have tuition reimbursement programs to help cover the cost of outside courses. Self-help books are another good, inexpensive alternative. Or you might prefer to join a club—Toastmasters or the League of Women Voters, for example—that provides opportunities for practicing communication skills in an informal setting.

PROBLEMS IN TRANSMITTING THE MESSAGE

Communication may also break down because of problems in getting the message from sender to receiver. The most obvious transmission problems are physical: bad connections, poor acoustics, illegible copy. Although defects of this sort (called "noise") seem trivial, they can completely block an otherwise effective message. For this reason, you should exercise as much control as possible over the physical transmission link. If you're preparing a written document, make sure that its appearance doesn't detract from your message. If you're delivering an oral presentation, choose a setting that permits the audience to see and hear you without straining.

A more subtle transmission problem arises when two messages compete for the receiver's attention or when two messages have conflicting meanings. When two messages are transmitted at once, there is interference in the communication line, just as there is interference when two radio signals overlap. Both messages are garbled, and the receiver has trouble deciphering either one. A similar problem arises when two messages are contradictory. For example, when Lee Dunham of Harlem McDonald's told the store supervisor that he needed time to think about whether to fire an employee, the supervisor misunderstood, possibly because Lee's remark conflicted with company policy. The supervisor might have been uncertain about which message had higher priority. The result was a failure of communication. You should be aware that a conflicting message may also be conveyed nonverbally—by a tone of voice, a wink, a casual shrug—instead of in words.

Transmission of a message may be blocked by

- Physical factors
- Conflicting signals
- Too many transmission links

Aside from conflicting signals, perhaps the most troublesome transmission problem arises when the communication chain has too many links. Because everyone's mental map is different, some distortion is likely when messages are transferred from person to person. The original message is interpreted and retold differently by each person in the chain. By the time the message reaches the end of the line, it may have only a vague resemblance to the original version. The longer the chain, the bigger the problem.

PROBLEMS IN RECEIVING THE MESSAGE

Like transmission problems, reception problems often have a physical cause. The receiver may be distracted by competing sights and sounds, an uncomfortable chair, poor lighting, or some other irritating condition. In some cases, the barrier may be related to the receiver's health. Hearing or visual impairment, for example, or even a headache, can interfere with reception of a message. These annoyances don't generally block communication entirely, but they may reduce the receiver's concentration.

Reception problems arise from

- Physical distractions
- Mental distractions

Perhaps the most common barrier to reception is simply lack of attention on the receiver's part. We all let our minds wander now and then, regardless of how hard we try to concentrate. People are especially likely to drift off when they are forced to listen to information that is difficult to understand or that has little direct bearing on their own lives. If they are tired or concerned about other matters, they are even more likely to lose interest.

PROBLEMS IN UNDERSTANDING THE MESSAGE

Although messages may get lost anywhere along the communication chain, the biggest potential trouble spot is the final link, where the message is interpreted by the receiver. Differences in background, vocabulary, and emotional state can all lead to misunderstanding.

SHARPEN YOUR SKILLS

Communication Barriers to Watch For and Avoid

Communication barriers may block any phase of the communication process. To help messages at work flow more smoothly, try to avoid the following:

- *Allness.* Avoid *always, never,* and similar words conveying a know-it-all attitude.
- *Bad appearance.* Send only messages that are neat and clean (including nonverbal messages), and try to overlook others' appearance so you can focus on the message.
- *Bad effects of group size.* The larger the group, the harder it is to communicate clearly with everyone. Try to involve as many members of your audience as possible, and put complicated messages in writing.
- *"Blindering."* Avoid putting blinders on by trying to apply the same solution to every problem. Look for solutions to fit specific problems.
- *Defensiveness.* Be sensitive to your audience's beliefs and feelings, and be open and flexible when you are the audience.
- *Emotional reactions.* Be aware of the emotions that arise in yourself and in others as you communicate, and attempt to control them.
- *Fact-inference confusion.* Don't jump to conclusions based on inferences. Things are not always as they seem.
- *Hostile, competitive, or aggressive attitudes.* Be understanding and willing to listen; your openness will help those who feel threatened accept you and your ideas.
- *Ignorance of personal differences.* Clarify your own and understand others' background, sphere of knowledge, personality, and perceptions.
- *Information overload.* Avoid inundating the receiver with facts. Too much information is as bad as too little, because it reduces the audience's ability to concentrate effectively on the most important messages.
- *Inability to understand nonverbal cues.* When you communicate with someone else, watch and listen for clues to his or her reactions. Try to keep your nonverbal cues consistent with your words.
- *Lack of concern for reference groups.* Recognize the fact that individuals are more open to messages that go along with the values of the groups they identify with.
- *Lack of credibility.* Show that you are competent, enthusiastic, and trustworthy. Evaluate someone else's message in light of what you know about his or her credibility.
- *Lack of feedback.* Ask questions, listen carefully, and make your own reactions known.

Different backgrounds

When the receiver's life experience differs substantially from the sender's, communication becomes more difficult. If you've ever tried to explain something to someone distinctly different from yourself, you know the problem. Age, education, gender, social status, economic position, cultural background, temperament, health, beauty, popularity, religion, political belief, even a passing mood can all separate one person from another and make understanding difficult. Figure 2.3 shows how shared experience contributes to shared meaning and understanding; the portion of each diagram where the circles overlap represents the level of understanding between sender and receiver.

Communicating with someone from another country is probably the most extreme example of how background may impede communication. (Component Chapter A details the problems and opportunities of intercultural communication.) But you don't have to seek out a person from an exotic locale to run into cultural gaps. You can misunderstand even your

Different emotional reactions

Interestingly enough, one person may react differently to the same words on different occasions. A message that might be perfectly clear and acceptable in one situation can lead to confusion and hostility in another, depending on the emotional relationship between receiver and sender.

A receiver may react either to the content of a message or to the relationship between sender and receiver that it implies.

Every message contains both a content meaning, which deals with the subject of the message, and a relationship meaning, which suggests the nature of the interaction between sender and receiver. Communication can break down when the receiver reacts negatively to either of these meanings. When the boss says, "Get that monthly report on my desk by 5:00 tonight," the employee may become angry on two counts:

- The content of the message means work for the employee, perhaps under difficult circumstances.
- The wording of the message implies that the employee is a pawn lacking freedom and power.

Although in this case the receiver may understand the message perfectly, communication suffers because the receiver is reacting emotionally.

As you know from your own experience, discussing something with another person is difficult when either of you is upset. An upset person tends to ignore or distort what the other person is saying and is often unable to present his or her own feelings and ideas effectively. This is not to say that you should avoid all communication when you are emotionally involved, but you should be alert to the greater potential for misunderstanding that accompanies aroused emotions.

SPECIAL PROBLEMS OF BUSINESS COMMUNICATION

Although all communication is subject to misunderstandings, business communication is particularly difficult. The material is often complex and controversial, yet both the sender and the receiver may face distractions that divert their attention. Furthermore, the opportunities for feedback are often limited, making it difficult to correct misunderstandings. Unfortunately, when business communication goes awry, the consequences can be grave. As Lee Dunham points out, there is often a lot riding on the outcome of a business message.

Complexity of the message

Business messages are often hard to formulate. For one thing, you must communicate both as an individual and as a representative of an organization. Thus you must adjust your own ideas and style so that they are acceptable to your employer. In fact, you may be asked occasionally to write or say something that you disagree with personally. Let's suppose, for example, that you work in the personnel department as a recruiter for your firm. You have interviewed a person that you believe would make an excellent employee, but others in the firm have rejected this person's application. Now you are in the position of having to write a letter telling the candidate, in effect, "Sorry, we don't want you." That's a tough assignment.

Even when you agree with the message, you may have emotional reservations about expressing it. You may know that you are doing the right thing, that you have no choice but to fire this or that person or to cancel this or that program, but you also would rather avoid causing hardship or disappointment. Business is full of difficult decisions like these, decisions that affect people's lives.

Even in purely unemotional situations, you may be dealing with subject matter that is difficult to express. Imagine trying to write an interesting insurance policy, for example. Or a set of instructions on how to operate a scraped-surface heat exchanger. Or the guidelines for checking credit references. Or an explanation of why profits have dropped by 12 percent in the last six months. Or a description of your solid-waste management program. These topics are dry, and making them clear and interesting is a real challenge.

The complexity of messages relates to

- Your conflicts about the content
- The dry or difficult nature of the subject
- The difficult conditions you are working under

On top of everything else, you may not know as much as you need to know about the purpose or audience of your message. Furthermore, you may be asked to prepare it under difficult conditions. You may be under time pressure, with two days to do a job that should take ten. You may be interrupted in the middle of your work. You may have to collaborate with other people and incorporate their ideas, regardless of whether they fit or not. You may be told to produce a document that looks professional but, at the same time, not to waste a lot of time and money. And you may have to revise your message over and over to please everybody in the chain of command.

Difficult conditions for transmission and reception

Assuming that you survive the ordeal of preparing the message, you still have to get through to your audience. In business, the filters between you and the receiver are many; secretaries, assistants, receptionists, and answering machines line the path between you and your audience. Just getting through by telephone can take a week if you're calling someone who's protected by layers of gatekeepers. Worse yet, your message may be digested and distilled, and probably distorted, before it is passed on to the intended receiver. Those same gatekeepers may also translate, embellish, and augment the receiver's ideas before passing them on to you.

Transmission and reception of messages may be hindered by

- Numerous layers of message processors
- Interruptions from other message senders

When the message finally does reach the receiver, he or she may be unable to digest it in peace. You may have to compete with a variety of interruptions: The phone rings every five minutes, people intrude, meetings are called, crises arise. In short, you rarely have the benefit of the receiver's undivided attention. Your message may be picked up and put down several times.

Differences between sender and receiver

Your biggest problem is the gulf between you and your receiver. In business, you often communicate with an unknown and unseen audience. And even when you know the other party, you may be separated by differences in function, status, age, or allegiance. These differences make communication very difficult indeed.

The problem of communicating with someone who has a different frame of reference is twofold. You have to establish credibility with the other person and, at the same time, try to understand that person's needs and reactions.

Whether you're writing a letter, making a phone call, or meeting face-to-face, the first step is convincing the receiver to trust you. In some circumstances, you may have to overcome hostility. For example, if you're a customer service representative, you often have to pacify disgruntled customers. Or if you're a problem solver from headquarters, you may have to convince people in other areas that you won't take away their power or put them in a bad light. What do you say or write in such situations to convince the audience of your reliability and intelligence?

Differences between sender and receiver are bridged by

- Getting the other person to trust you
- Sharing the other person's perspective

Building trust is a difficult problem, and the solution depends on your ability to "read" the other person. The approach you take with one individual might not work at all with another. And how do you read someone you've never met, someone who may be in another city? If you're communicating by phone or face-to-face, you can glean something from the person's tone of voice, appearance, and replies. But if all you have between you is the printed page, drawing meaningful conclusions about the other person is very difficult. Yet, as you know, unless you can develop a shared perspective with your audience, your message is likely to be misunderstood.

HOW TO IMPROVE COMMUNICATION

Effective communication requires perception, precision, credibility, control, and congeniality.

Think about the people you know. Which of them would you call successful communicators? What do these people have in common? Chances are, the individuals on your list share five qualities:

- *Perception.* They are able to predict how their message will be received. They anticipate your reaction and shape the message accordingly. They read your response correctly and constantly adjust to correct any misunderstanding.
- *Precision.* They create a "meeting of the minds." When they finish expressing themselves, you share the same mental picture.
- *Credibility.* They are believable. You have faith in the substance of their message. You trust their information and their intentions.
- *Control.* They shape your response. Depending on their purpose, they can make you laugh or cry, calm down, change your mind, or take action.
- *Congeniality.* They maintain friendly, pleasant relations with the audience. Regardless of whether you agree with them, good communicators command your respect and goodwill. You are willing to work with them again, despite your differences.

Look at your list of good communicators once more. Chances are, it's fairly short. When you think about it, effective communication is relatively rare.

What sets the effective communicators apart is their ability to overcome the main barriers to communication. They do this by creating their messages very carefully, minimizing noise in the transmission process, and facilitating feedback.

CREATE THE MESSAGE CAREFULLY

The sender has responsibility for creating a communicative message.

If you want the people in your audience to understand and accept your message, you have to help. You cannot depend on others to carry the communication ball; the burden is yours, not theirs.

Think about your purpose and your audience

The first step is to define your goal in communicating. Why are you sending your message? What do you want your audience to do or know as a consequence?

In general terms, your purpose is to bring the audience closer to your views.

When you have answered this question, you can begin to build a message to achieve your purpose. You must create a bridge of words that leads the audience from their current position to your point. Before you can do this, of course, you have to know something about the audience's current position. What do they know now, and what do they need to know? If you're addressing strangers, try to find out more about them; if that's impossible, try to project yourself into their position by using your common sense and imagination.

Tell the audience what to expect

Once you have defined your readers' or listeners' information needs, you can launch them on their journey toward the intended destination. As they travel, you must be their guide, providing them with a map of the territory they will cover. Tell them at the outset what they can expect to gain from the trip. Let them know the purpose of the message; tell them what main points they will encounter on the way. Even if you do not want to reveal controversial ideas at the beginning of the message, you can still give receivers a preview of the topics you plan to cover.

Give your audience a framework for understanding the ideas you communicate.

By telling your audience what to expect, you help them recognize the relationship among the ideas you hope to convey. When they encounter individual facts and thoughts, they can then fit them into a rational framework. By telling the audience how to categorize the information in your message, you eliminate one of the main barriers to communication: the discrepancy between your mental filing system and theirs. In addition, you make it easier for the audience to cope with the distractions that occur in most environments. If people know the basic framework of the message, they can pick it up and put it down without getting lost.

Use concrete, specific language

Because business communication often involves difficult, abstract, and even boring material, you must do something to help your audience understand and remember the message. The best way to do this is to balance the general concepts with specific illustrations. At the beginning, state the overall idea; then develop that idea by using vivid, concrete examples to help the audience visualize the concept.

To make your message memorable

- Use words that evoke a physical, sensory impression
- Use telling statistics

The most memorable words are the ones that create a picture in the receiver's mind by describing colors, objects, scents, sounds, tastes. Specific details can also be very vivid. For example, did you know that by the year 2000, the average car will be driven 22 years before it wears out?

Stick to the point

You can also help your audience by eliminating any information that doesn't directly contribute to your purpose. Many business messages contain too much material. The sender, in hopes of being thorough, tries to explain everything there is to know about a subject. But most receivers don't need everything. All they need are a few pertinent facts, enough information to answer their questions or facilitate their decisions.

The key to brevity is to limit the number of ideas, not to short-change their development.

By keeping your messages as lean as possible, you make them easier to absorb. With few exceptions, one page is better than two, especially in a business environment where the receiver is bombarded by competing claims for attention. By eliminating unnecessary ideas, you focus the other person's thoughts on those few points that really matter.

You have to be careful, however, to develop each main idea adequately. You're better off covering three points thoroughly than eight points superficially. Don't rush the audience through a laundry list of vague generalities in the mistaken belief that you are being brief. If an idea is worth including, it's worth explaining.

Connect new information to existing ideas

The mind absorbs information by categorizing it into mental files. If you want the receiver to understand and remember new ideas, you have to indicate how those ideas are related to the files that already exist in her or his mind. When the connection with familiar concepts is lacking, the new material tends to get lost, to become mentally misplaced, because it doesn't fit into the receiver's filing cabinet.

By showing the audience how new ideas relate to familiar ones, you increase the likelihood that your message will be understood correctly. The audience can say, "Oh yes, I see. We can market the new cosmetics line the way we did nylon stockings. We're trying to reach the same consumer." The meaning of the new concept is clarified by its relationship to the old. The receiver already has a wealth of information on the subject; all she or he has to do is apply it to the new idea.

Tie the message to the receiver's frame of reference.

Connecting new ideas to existing ones also helps make the new concepts acceptable. Most of us approach anything unfamiliar with caution. When we discover that it's similar to something familiar, we become more confident. We pick it up and look it over more carefully, then take it home with us. It becomes part of our collection, one of many related things.

Emphasize and review key points

Another way to help the audience is to call their attention to the most important points of the message. You can do this with your words, your format, and your body language. When you come to an important idea, say so. By explicitly stating that an idea is especially significant, you wake people up; you also make it easier for them to file the thought in the proper place. Underscore key points by calling attention to them visually. Use headlines, bold type, and indented lists to emphasize major ideas. Reinforce the text of your message by using charts, graphs, maps, diagrams, and illustrations that will help your audience "see" the point. If you are delivering the message orally, use your body and voice to highlight important concepts.

By highlighting and summarizing key points, you help the audience understand and remember the message.

Before you conclude your message, take a moment or two to review the essential points. Restate the purpose, and show how the main ideas relate to it. This simple step will help your audience remember the message.

Because business audiences are frequently interrupted, it's a good idea to provide summaries at the ends of major sections of a long message as well as at the end of a document or presentation. Such summaries not only refresh people's memories but also help simplify the overall meaning of complex material.

MINIMIZE NOISE

Even the most carefully constructed message will fail to achieve results if it does not reach the receiver. To the extent possible, you should try to eliminate potential sources of interference that stand between you and your audience. The key to getting through to the receiver often lies in the choice of communication channels and media. You should choose the method that will be most likely to attract the receiver's attention and enable him or her to concentrate on the message.

The careful choice of channel and medium helps focus the receiver's attention on your message.

If a written document seems the best choice, try to make it physically appealing and easy to comprehend. Use an attractive, convenient format, and pay attention to such details as the choice of paper and quality of type. If possible, deliver the document when you know the reader will have time to study it.

If the message calls for an oral delivery channel, try to eliminate environmental competition. The location should be comfortable and quiet, with adequate lighting, good acoustics, and few visual distractions. In addition, you should think about how your own appearance will affect the audience. An outfit that screams for attention creates as much noise as a squeaky air conditioning system.

Another way to reduce interference, particularly in oral communication, is to deliver your message directly to the intended audience. The more people who filter your message, the greater the potential for distortion.

PROVIDE FOR FEEDBACK

In addition to minimizing noise, you frequently need to give the receiver a chance to provide feedback. But one of the things making business communication difficult is the complexity of the feedback loop. If you're talking face-to-face with one other person, feedback is immediate and clear. But if you're writing a letter, memo, or report that will be read by several people, feedback will be delayed and mixed. Some of the readers will be enthusiastic or respond promptly, others will be critical or reluctant to respond. As a consequence, revising your message to take account of their feedback will be difficult.

When you plan a message, think about the amount of feedback that you want to encourage. Although feedback is generally useful, it reduces your control over the communication situation. You need to know whether your message is being understood and accepted, but you may not want to respond to comments until you have completed your argument. If you are communicating with a group, you may not have the time to react to every impression or question.

Make feedback more useful by
- Planning how and when to accept it
- Being receptive to others' responses
- Encouraging frankness
- Using it to improve communication

For this reason, think about how you want to obtain feedback and choose a form of communication that suits your needs. Some channels and media are more compatible with feedback than others. For example, if you want to adjust your message quickly, you must talk to the receiver face-to-face or by phone. If feedback is less important to you, you can use a written document or give a prepared speech.

Feedback is not always easy to get, even when you have chosen a transmission method that encourages feedback. In some cases, you may have to draw out the other person by asking questions. If you want to know specific things, ask specific questions. But also encourage the other person to express general reactions; you can often learn something very interesting that way.

Remember, too, that in order to get feedback you have to listen, which is more difficult than you might think. We tend to let our minds wander and miss important points, or we jump in too quickly with comments of our own, so the other person doesn't have a chance to complete a thought. We make the mistake of prejudging other people because we don't like the way they look or because they represent an opposing group. Often we lack patience, objectivity, and understanding. We send signals, subconsciously perhaps, that we don't value the other person's comments.

Regardless of whether the response to your message is written or oral, you have to encourage people to be open if you want them to tell you what they really think and feel. You can't say, "Please tell me what you think," and then get mad at the first critical comment. So try not to react defensively. Your goal is to find out whether the people in your audience have understood and accepted your message. If you find that they haven't, don't lose your temper. After all, the fault is at least partially yours. Instead of saying the same thing all over again, only louder this time, try to find the source of the misunderstanding. Then revise your message. Sooner or later, if you keep trying, you'll achieve success. You may not win the audience to your point of view, but at least you'll make your meaning clear. And you'll part with a feeling of mutual respect.

SUMMARY

Effective communicators use both nonverbal and verbal signals to get their messages across. And they pay as much attention to receiving information as they do to transmitting it.

Communication is a five-step process: The sender has an idea, the idea becomes a message, the message is transmitted, the receiver gets the message, and the receiver reacts and sends feedback. Misunderstandings arise when any part of this process breaks down.

Business communication is especially prone to misunderstandings, because the message is complex, conditions are difficult, and psychological and social differences often separate the sender and receiver.

To overcome communication barriers, think about your audience, let them know what to expect, use vivid language, stick to the point, connect new ideas to familiar ones, emphasize and review key points, minimize noise, and provide opportunities for feedback.

COMMUNICATION CHALLENGES AT McDONALD'S

One of the things that has made McDonald's the top name in fast food is its employees. They have the reputation for doing their jobs efficiently and for treating customers well. Although many McDonald's employees start out with few job skills, the company is committed to training them thoroughly.

The current training program at Harlem McDonald's covers specific job duties, work habits, and customer relations. Those who go through the program seem highly motivated to do a good job, yet there is a wide discrepancy in their level of performance. Lee Dunham understands that individual differences account for at least part of the discrepancy, but he worries that his basic training program might also be partly to blame. He wonders if his company is doing an effective job of communicating with all the trainees.

Individual Challenge: Lee wants to study the effectiveness of Harlem McDonald's current training methods and to develop improvements in the basic training course. As a first step, he asks those on his training staff (including you) to outline how their own attitudes and assumptions might differ from those of the trainees. As you write your analysis, bear in mind what you have learned about the communication process and barriers to understanding.

Team Challenge: Because customer service is so important in the restaurant business, Lee wants to put extra effort into teaching his employees the fine art of dealing with the public. He has assigned you and several others to a task force charged with developing a new program. The goal is to teach new employees how to use nonverbal communication to build good relations with customers. Your program should be geared for a class of 15 people and should last for three hours. Develop an outline and activities for the course.

QUESTIONS FOR DISCUSSION

1. Why does talking to someone with your feet on the desk transmit different messages in different situations?
2. Which party bears more responsibility for the outcome of communication, the sender or the receiver?
3. Some communication experts contend that good communication does not necessarily produce agreement between the parties. Do you agree or disagree?
4. Is written communication or spoken communication more susceptible to noise?
5. Do you believe it is easier to communicate with members of your own sex? Why or why not?
6. "One of the things making business communication difficult is the complexity of the feedback loop." Show what this sentence means by giving some examples.
7. "Be brief!" "Don't short-circuit your development of ideas!" Do these two pieces of advice contradict each other? Explain your answer.
8. "A good business writer can make any piece of writing interesting." Do you agree? Why or why not?
9. What are some of the techniques that advertisers use to capture the audience's attention and make people ignore competing stimuli?
10. Under what circumstances might you want to limit the feedback you receive from an audience of readers or listeners?

DOCUMENT FOR ANALYSIS

Read the following memo, and then (1) analyze the strengths and/or weaknesses of each numbered sentence and (2) revise the memo so it follows this chapter's guidelines.

(1) It has come to my attention that many of you are lying on your time cards. **(2)** If you come in late, you should not put 8:00 on your card. **(3)** If you take a long lunch, you should not put 1:00 on your time card. **(4)** I will not stand for this type of cheating. **(5)** I simply have no choice but to institute a time clock system. **(6)** Beginning next Monday, all employees will have to punch in and punch out whenever they come and go from the work area. **(7)** The time clock will be right by the entrance to each work area, so you have no excuse for not punching in. **(8)** Anyone who is late for work or late coming back from lunch more than three times will have to answer to me. **(9)** I don't care if you had to take a nap or if you girls had to shop. **(10)** This is a place of business, and we do not want to be taken advantage of by slackers who are cheaters to boot.

(11) It is too bad that a few bad apples always have to spoil things for everyone.

EXERCISES

1. Observe a small group of people in the college cafeteria or lounge area. Closely examine the dress of each person to see what he or she is communicating. Start with such easily visible matters as color combinations and general styles. Then notice matters that are often ignored but contribute to a person's total appearance: shoes, jewelry, the presence or absence of a belt. Finally, include personal grooming (hair style and cleanliness). Select two members of the group and write a one- or two-paragraph description of what they are communicating about themselves, without naming them. Remember that for this exercise your job is not to judge their dress; rather it is to try to understand the image that, consciously or unconsciously, they present through their dress and grooming.
2. Choose a popular television drama or soap opera and turn it on to watch it, but don't turn on the sound. Watch for ten minutes and see whether you can guess from nonverbal cues what is going on. Then turn up the sound to see whether you were right. Make a list of the kinds of cues you noticed and what they indicated. Were any of the cues misleading?
3. A friend of yours is a talented artist who would like to get a job in advertising, but he's discouraged because ad agencies want people who are good at expressing themselves verbally, a skill that he lacks. He says he never really had to do much writing or speaking in school because he took mostly art classes. What advice would you give your friend for improving his verbal communication skills?
4. Find a detailed picture in a magazine and show it to three or four people individually for, say, 10 to 15 seconds each. Then ask each of them to describe the picture without looking at it again. What differences do you note in their descriptions? What is the lesson to be learned and applied to business?
5. The channel and medium chosen for transmitting a message influence the way the message is received. For each of the following, indicate whether it would be best to use a form letter, a memo, a personal letter, a phone call, face-to-face contact, or some other medium:
   - **a.** Inviting the mayors of ten cities in your county to attend a luncheon honoring your company president
   - **b.** Informing three employees that they have won this month's sales awards
   - **c.** Announcing the ground breaking for a multimillion-dollar plant to the major daily newspapers in the area
   - **d.** Informing a middle manager that her job has just been eliminated
   - **e.** Finding out the cost of having a banquet for 20 at each of four local restaurants
   - **f.** Informing your boss that you want to take your vacation next month
   - **g.** Informing your boss that you want maternity leave

6. In conversations with three different people, pay attention to the type of feedback each gives you. What are the main methods of feedback used by each person: gestures, nods, questioning about what you said? How does the amount of feedback differ? Do you adjust your communication in any way as a result of this feedback? How can this exercise help you become more responsive to others?
7. Think of a communication experience you have had recently. Describe in a paragraph or two how your experience fits the model of the communication process presented in the chapter. In other words, identify the sender, message, transmission channel and medium, receiver, and feedback. Also identify any barriers that affected the communication.
8. Cultural background determines, in part, the mental images that words produce. Imagine three people: a 19-year-old man who grew up on a ranch in Idaho, a 19-year-old woman who grew up in an elegant Baltimore home, and a retired mechanic who has lived all his life in a working-class neighborhood of Chicago. Describe the differences in the images or feelings that the following nouns might call to mind for each of them:
   a. rose
   b. shotgun
   c. snake
   d. wealth
   e. education
   f. horse
   g. danger

   What have you learned in this exercise that will help you communicate more effectively in business?
9. In business, people communicate both as individuals and as representatives of their organizations. Naturally, situations arise that create a conflict between what one would like to say as an individual and what one must say as a company representative. It is unprofessional to resolve this conflict by saying such things as, "If I had my way you would get the job, but 'they' turned you down," or, "You're right, but I don't make the rules around here." How might you resolve a conflict between the personal and professional sides of yourself in the following situations? Instead of writing what you would say, write a few sentences for each example telling what you would try to accomplish.
   a. You must try to collect on a past-due account from someone who is obviously very short of money.
   b. On behalf of a publisher, you must write to a would-be author to reject a manuscript that he has worked on for two years.
   c. You must refuse a loan to a friend because you don't think she will be able to repay it.
   d. You must respond to a rude and drunken passenger on the bus you're driving.
   e. You must respond to a former co-worker who was fired for incompetence and who has asked you for a letter of recommendation.
10. Some business communicators supply too much information, making it difficult for the recipient to sort out the key points. Here is the first draft of a memo written by a busy office manager to her immediate supervisor. Rephrase it so that it gets to the point quickly and fits easily onto a half-sheet memo form.

    I can't ever remember being so frustrated in my life! Here is what happened. I ordered six regional U.S. maps last week at $17 each against our office equipment budget, but Mr. Olson in Purchasing said that I had to place the order against the office supplies budget because the maps cost less than $25 each. The problem is, of course, that we are going to be overspent this year in the office supplies budget, but we still have equipment money because we got such a good price on the terminals I ordered last month. Anyway, Olson and I went round and round about this. He wouldn't budge, and I couldn't budge, but I do see a possible way out of the dilemma. Do you think that I could put the order through again, this time for a single set of U.S. maps costing $102? You'll probably be hearing from Mr. Olson, so I wanted to alert you to the problem and get your advice. We do need the maps!

SCORING FOR "HOW DOES YOUR NONVERBAL CREDIBILITY MEASURE UP?" (p. 33)

In each category (Eyes, Gestures, Posture, and Voice), give yourself points according to the following key:

QUESTION	MOST TIMES	SOME-TIMES	FEW TIMES
1.	3	2	1
2.	3	2	1
3.	3	2	1
4.	1	2	3
5.	1	2	3
6.	1	2	3

A score of 15 or higher in any category indicates high credibility; a score of 10–15 indicates average credibility; a score below 10 indicates low credibility. You might use this test to give yourself an annual credibility checkup.

INTERPRETATION

- *Eyes.* Eye contact is a highly important nonverbal cue to credibility. Maintaining eye contact while both speaking and listening is a sign of confidence and interest. Behaviors such as looking down, looking away, and excessive blinking are damaging to credibility.
- *Gestures.* A credible communicator uses spontaneous, relaxed gestures to emphasize the points he or she is making and to communicate the intensity of his or her emotions. Behaviors such as fidgeting, tugging at clothing, touching the face, lip licking, and so on suggest lack of confidence, defensiveness, and nervousness.
- *Posture.* Posture is particularly important in communicating an individual's status or power, as well as his or her responsiveness and desire to establish a warm rapport. Credible communicators assume an open, relaxed posture and walk confidently. They avoid constricted postures that might suggest they are timid or lack assertiveness.
- *Voice.* Vocal cues often play a key role in shaping a person's credibility, status, and power. A conversational speaking style with appropriate variations in pitch, rate, and volume is particularly important in projecting the image of a confident, competent, dynamic person. Communicators should avoid speaking in a voice that sounds flat, tense, or nasal. Stuttering and frequent pauses, punctuated by *ah*'s, *um*'s, or *you know*'s, suggest a lack of confidence.

PART TWO

THE WRITING PROCESS

CHAPTER THREE

After studying this chapter, you will be able to

- Describe the basic steps in the process of planning business messages
- Establish both the general and the specific purposes of your business messages
- Develop a profile of your audience
- Establish the main idea of your messages
- Select an appropriate channel and medium for transmitting a particular message to a particular audience

PLANNING BUSINESS MESSAGES

Irma Cameron

COMMUNICATION CLOSE-UP AT GENERAL MILLS

"Dear Betty Crocker," the letter began. "I've just moved to Leadville, Colorado. How will the altitude affect my recipes?"

"There was a whole box of recipes, but we helped with all of them," recalls Irma Cameron, manager of consumer relations for General Mills in Minneapolis. "We searched our files, and when they weren't enough, we went to our test kitchens to check on things like whether to add more liquid."

Every year, Irma's department receives 200,000 consumer inquiries—by letter, by phone, and even, on occasion, in person. Few require as much research as the one from Leadville, but all receive the same careful attention. Nine people (out of a staff of 21) handle inquiries about product and recipe performance—and incidentally field most of the telephone calls that come in. A small group handles requests for refunds from consumers who are dissatisfied with a product. And one person specializes in handling inquiries about TV programs sponsored by General Mills.

General Mills gets a large number of letters on the same subjects. Nevertheless, Irma makes sure her staff pays attention to the individual variations in each. They have found that the most important thing in answering any inquiry is truly to answer it. So Irma and her staff make a point of thinking about each inquirer as an individual. As she says, "We try to address every person's particular needs."

In recognition of its customers' changing interests and needs, over the years General Mills has changed the appearance of Betty Crocker, its fictitious spokesperson.

And yet, respondents must answer similar inquiries in a consistent fashion. To achieve precisely this mix of individuality and consistency, General Mills has developed a computerized system of 1,200 sample paragraphs. Working with word processors, Irma explains, "respondents can pull paragraphs and then customize them for each individual consumer." Approximately 80 percent of all correspondence can be answered this way. "But we leave in enough variables so that any letter you receive from us will not sound like a form letter." And letters are all hand-signed by the respondent.

The average turnaround time for a letter is three to five days. If a response is going to take longer, "we often just call up the consumer in the meantime," says Irma.

The 20 percent of the letters that are composed from scratch obviously require more time and effort. At weekly meetings, the respondents confer about unusual letters, evaluating the inquirers' needs and deciding on the basic thrust of the replies. To be certain the responses are acceptable to General Mills's management, the correspondents check out company policy with other parts of the corporation and consult the company's published guidelines.

Armed with the necessary information and policy guidelines, the respondents answer the nonroutine letters in a style suited to their subject matter. For example, a man who lamented, tongue in cheek, that his Nature Valley Granola didn't sing and dance, even when he shined a flashlight on it, received a similarly whimsical response. A complaint about a TV special, on the other hand, received a thoughtful, positively phrased explanation of the sponsorship decision, together with an assurance that the writer's concern had been conveyed to those responsible for advertising.

The respondents have worked for General Mills an average of 10 to 11 years, and most have a homemaking background. A knowledge of recipes, although helpful, is not critical. What is most important is the ability to write a letter that responds to the recipient's needs.

UNDERSTANDING THE COMPOSITION PROCESS

Like Irma Cameron and her staff, you will face a variety of business communication assignments in your career. Some of them will be routine; others will require reflection and research. But regardless of the complexity of the task, you will employ the same basic process for preparing both written and oral messages: You will plan what you want to say, compose the message, then revise and refine it before sending it.

Three steps are involved in preparing business messages: planning, composing, and revising.

Here's what each step in the process involves:

1. *Planning.* During the planning phase, you think about the fundamentals of the message: your purpose in communicating, the audience who will receive your message, the main idea of your message, and the channel and medium you will use to convey your thoughts. You also decide on the organization of ideas and the tone you will adopt.
2. *Composing.* As you compose the message, you commit your thoughts to words, creating sentences and paragraphs and selecting illustrations and details to support your main idea.
3. *Revising.* Having formulated your thoughts, you step back to see if you have expressed them adequately. You review the purpose and content of the message, its overall structure and tone, the choice of words, and details like grammar, punctuation, and format.

This basic process varies somewhat with the situation, the communicator, and the organization. Routine messages obviously require less planning and revision than more complex messages; if time for completing the project is limited, one or two of the steps may also be slighted. In addition, different people approach the process in different ways. Some compose quickly, then revise slowly; others revise as they go along. And finally, the steps do not necessarily occur in 1-2-3 order. Writers often jump back and forth from one step to another.

In many organizations the process of preparing a message is a collaborative effort. For example, you might sit down with your boss to plan a memo, then work independently during the writing phase. After completing a rough draft, you might ask your boss to review the message and suggest revisions, which you would then incorporate. If you were working on a particularly long and important document, the preparation process might involve more people: an editor, a team of writers, typists, graphic artists. For efforts of this type, the review and revision process might be repeated several times to respond to input from different departments. Of course, deadline pressures must also be considered. If the message was due yesterday, the process must be compressed.

In the remainder of this chapter, you'll learn more about planning a message, which is the first phase of the process: defining the purpose, analyzing the audience, establishing the main idea, and selecting the channel and medium. Chapter 4 discusses how to organize and compose the message; Chapter 5 deals with revision. Although all three chapters focus on the task of writing a message, remember as you read that many of the same issues are important in composing an oral message.

DEFINING YOUR PURPOSE

The first step in planning a business message is to think about your purpose. Obviously, you want to maintain the goodwill of the audience and create a favorable impression for your organization. But in every situation, you also have a particular goal you want to achieve. That purpose may be straightforward and obvious—like placing an order, for example—or it may be more difficult to define. When the purpose is unclear, it pays to spend a few minutes thinking about what you hope to accomplish.

SHARPEN YOUR SKILLS

Fear of the Blank Page and How to Overcome It

For some people, writing is a breeze. But many of us struggle to put words on paper. We may even get stuck so often that we develop a mental block. Here are some ways to overcome this block:

- *Use positive self-talk.* Reasons for writer's block include worry about not being able to write well or easily and belief that writing is too difficult, too time consuming, or too complicated. You need to replace such negative ideas about writing by telling yourself that you are a resourceful, capable person who knows how to do the job. Try to think of past examples of your writing that were successful as proof that you really can write when you want to.
- *Visualize your audience.* Picture their backgrounds, interests, knowledge of the subject, and vocabulary, including the technical jargon they're familiar with. This exercise will help you choose an appropriate slant for your writing.
- *Know your purpose.* What do you want to accomplish with this particular piece of writing? Without a clear purpose, writing can indeed be impossible.
- *Create a productive environment.* When you are blocked, you're easily distracted by sights, sounds, and other elements in your environment. Make sure the place where you do your writing is for writing only, and make that environment pleasant. Then set "appointments" with yourself in which you will write and only write. Be sure to build in break times as well. A writing appointment for, say, 9:30 to 12:00 seems less imposing than an indefinite writing session.
- *Make an outline.* Even if formal outlines make you restless, you should at least jot down a few notes about how your ideas fit together. As you go along, you will probably revise these notes. No matter, as long as you end up with a plan

WHY YOU NEED A CLEAR PURPOSE

The purpose of the message determines content, organization, style, tone, and format.

Suppose that your boss has asked you to prepare a memo describing the company's policy on vacation time. This is a fairly broad topic. What should you say about it? Until you know what the memo is supposed to accomplish, you can't really do a very effective job of writing it. You need a purpose to help you make decisions about the message.

To decide whether to proceed

Thinking about your purpose is important because it helps you decide whether to put time and effort into communicating. Frankly, many business documents shouldn't be created at all. They serve no practical purpose, apart from giving the creator a chance to show off. It's tempting, when you've done a great deal of work, to say, "Look at me; haven't I done this well?"

But unnecessary messages can backfire, even if the material is dazzling. Like the little boy who cried "Wolf!" once too often, you can rapidly use up your credibility by writing memos that merely fill up filing cabinets. So when you're tempted to fire off a message, pause to ask yourself, "Is this really necessary? Will it make a difference?" If you suspect that your ideas will have very little impact, hold off. Wait until you have a more practical purpose.

that gives direction and coherence to your writing.

- *Just start.* Put aside all worries, fears, and distractions—everything that gives you an excuse to postpone writing. Then start putting down on paper any thoughts you have about the topic. Don't worry about whether these ideas can actually be used; just let your mind range freely.
- *Write the middle first.* You don't necessarily have to start at the beginning. Instead, start where your enthusiasm is greatest and your ideas most developed. If your thoughts head in a different direction, feel free to follow them. Make notes about ideas that you want to come back to later. When you've finished with this first section, pick out another; but don't worry about sequence. The idea is to get all your thoughts in writing.
- *Push obstacles aside.* You may very well get stuck at some point. If so, you can get unstuck quite easily. First, don't worry too much. These things happen, and they're not the end of the world. Second, rid yourself of any distractions. Third, if you are stuck on one thought or sentence or paragraph, go on to another that is easier for you. You can always come back later. Fourth, prime the pump simply by writing about why you are stuck: "I am stuck because . . ." Before you know it, you will be writing about your topic. You can also try talking about your problem aloud. Finally, you can try brainstorming. Make notes about things you have not yet covered. Soon enough you will feel the urge to write.

When deadlines loom, you may become paralyzed with panic. But if you keep things in perspective, you will survive. Concentrate on the major ideas first, and save the details for later, after you have something on the page.

1. Procrastination is a skill that many writers have developed into a fine art. List as many ways to procrastinate as you can think of. Then discuss what a procrastinator might do to break these habits.

2. One reason for writer's block is negative self-talk. Try to analyze your own writing experiences. When you know that your material is really good, do you still have trouble getting started? What negative self-talk do you use? What might you do to overcome this tendency?

To respond to the audience

In addition to preventing pointless messages, thinking about your purpose will help you respond to the needs of your audience. You want to be certain that your purpose in creating a message is compatible with the audience's purpose in considering it. Otherwise you're likely, in effect, to serve fruit punch and peanut butter when they're expecting champagne and caviar.

Vague assignments often give rise to this kind of mismatch. So when someone asks you to prepare a message, try to pin down the issues. What is the person's objective in requesting the information? Exactly what is expected of you? What does the audience need to know?

Even when you initiate the message yourself, you still need to consider the audience's motives. Why will they pay attention to the material? What do they hope to gain? Are their expectations compatible with your own? If not, both you and the audience will fail to get what you want.

To focus the content

Establishing a clear purpose will also help you focus the message. It's all too easy to accumulate more information than you need, much of it interesting tidbits that really don't prove anything. If you include them in your message, your audience will suffer an overload. But what should you discard?

When you know your purpose, the answer becomes clear. You include only the information that is necessary to accomplish your objective. Everything else is irrelevant and should be eliminated. Even though the extraneous information may be interesting, it diverts the audience from the real point and reduces the impact of your message.

To establish the channel and medium

Depending on your purpose, you will choose a channel for your message (oral or written) and then a medium within that channel. For example, if your purpose is to put together a company softball team, you may decide to use the written channel so that you can send the same message simultaneously to everyone in the office. Then you may decide that the appropriate medium is a casual memo. Other purposes call for using the oral channel and for using other media, as you will discover later in the chapter. The thing to remember at this point is that your purpose is the foundation for many decisions you will have to make about the message. If you don't know your purpose, or have only a vague definition of it, you will make these decisions haphazardly.

COMMON PURPOSES OF BUSINESS MESSAGES

Every business message has both a general and a specific purpose, and both influence the way the message develops.

Your general purpose may be to inform, persuade, or collaborate.

There are three general purposes common to business communication: informing, persuading, and collaborating with the audience. Figure 3.1 shows how these general purposes affect communication. For example, messages at the informative end of the continuum require relatively less interaction with the audience. Readers or listeners absorb the information and accept it or reject it, but they don't contribute to the content of the message. The writer or speaker controls the message. Collaborative messages, at the other end of the spectrum, reduce the writer's or speaker's control of the material and require maximum audience participation. When collaboration is your goal, you cannot adhere to a rigid plan. You must be

FIGURE 3.1
General Purposes of Business Messages

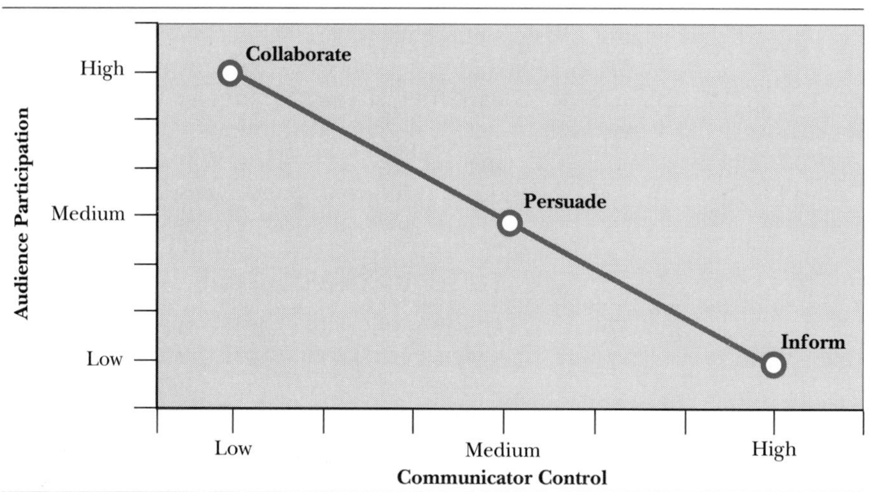

prepared to adjust to new input and unexpected reactions. Persuasive messages fall in the middle: They require a moderate amount of audience participation and allow a moderate amount of control.

To determine the specific purpose, think of how the audience's ideas or behavior should be affected by the message.

In addition to satisfying a general purpose, every presentation must accomplish a specific objective. To formulate this objective, ask yourself, "What should my audience do or think after reviewing this message?" Be as precise as possible in stating your purpose; identify the individuals in the audience who should respond. Here are some examples:

GENERAL PURPOSE	SPECIFIC PURPOSE
To inform	To present last month's sales figures to the vice president of marketing
To persuade	To convince the vice president of marketing to hire more sales representatives
To collaborate	To help the personnel department develop a training program for new members of the sales staff

Sometimes you will want to accomplish several related things with the same message. For example, you might want to advance your own career while providing objective information about a business matter, or you might want to convince the audience to approve two decisions. When you find yourself facing twin goals, ask yourself whether they are compatible. Can both be accomplished with the same message? Even if one message can accommodate multiple goals, you must analyze how those goals are related and try to establish a priority. Focus on the more important one, especially if time or space is limited. And if one of the goals is personal, stress the business goal.

HOW TO TEST YOUR PURPOSE

Once you have established your purpose, pause for a moment to consider whether it is worth pursuing at this time. There's no point in creating a message that is unlikely to accomplish its purpose. You quickly use up your credibility in an organization when you become the sponsor of lost causes. So, before you decide to pursue the message, ask yourself these questions:

Defer a message, or do not send it at all

- If the purpose is not realistic
- If the timing is not right
- If you are not the right person to deliver the message
- If the purpose is not acceptable to the organization

- *Is the purpose realistic?* Human nature being what it is, you can't expect to work miracles overnight. Most people resist change. In addition to fearing the unknown, they may be responsible for the status quo. If your purpose involves a radical shift in action or attitude, you may have better luck going slowly. Instead of suggesting your whole program at once, consider proposing the first step. View your message as the beginning of a learning process.
- *Is this the right time?* Timing is vital in transmitting any message. An idea that is unacceptable when profits are down, for example, may easily win approval when results improve. If an organization is undergoing changes of some sort, you may want to defer your

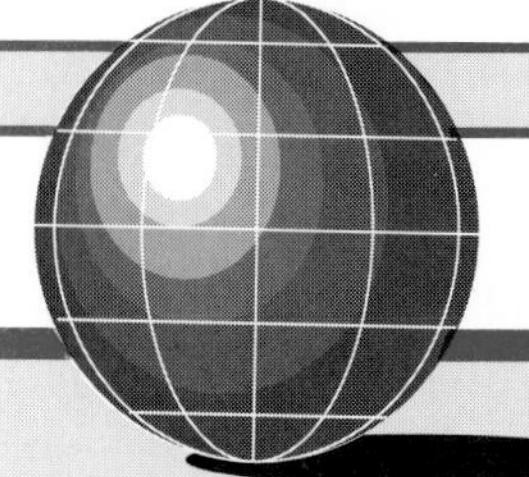

INTERNATIONAL OUTLOOK

Ten Tips for Communicating Successfully with a Global Audience

In your job, you may have occasion to communicate with people in other countries or from other cultures. Whether you are buying, selling, consulting, or simply trying to obtain information, you will need to get across ideas to an audience you are not used to dealing with. Just as you need to understand the characteristics of your audience when you communicate with others from your own country, you need to understand something about the culture, business customs, and communication styles of foreign audiences.

Here, then, are some tips to assist you in your intercultural communications:

- *Be clear and simple.* Whether communicating orally or in writing, you should avoid long, complex sentences, highly technical language, jargon, and colloquialisms. Don't be condescending, but do use simpler words when they are available (*pay* rather than *compensate*, *soon* rather than *momentarily*).
- *Don't assume that someone you hear speaking English will understand you.* If you talk too fast, slur your words, have an accent, or use slang, even a foreigner who seems to speak impeccable English will have a hard time following you. An added problem is that many English-speaking foreigners are too polite to let you know they haven't understood.
- *Learn the business customs and terminology of those you'll be communicating with.* Most countries, for example, use the metric system, unlike the system of measurement used in the United States. And many countries use the day/month/year system for dating as opposed to the U.S. system of month/day/year. A meeting arranged in one of these countries on 7.5.89 is scheduled for May, not July.
- *Use written messages whenever possible.* Foreigners read English more easily than they understand spoken English. If you communicate by phone, follow up with a confirmation in writing to guard against miscommunication.
- *Don't be in a hurry to get to the point.* Europeans, Africans, and Arabs in particular are put off by the straight-to-the-point style of North American business communication. They prefer a more roundabout approach. The French, for

message until things stabilize and people can concentrate on your ideas.

- *Is the right person delivering the message?* Some people have more leverage in an organization than others. Even though you may have done all the work yourself, your boss may have a better chance of accomplishing results because of her or his higher status. If this is the case, let your boss deliver the message. Achieving your objective is more important than taking the credit. In the long run, people will recognize the quality of your work. Also bear in mind that some people are simply better writers or speakers than others. If the stakes are high and you lack experience or confidence, you might want to play a supporting role rather than take the lead.
- *Is the purpose acceptable to the organization?* As the representative of your company, you are obligated to work toward the organization's goals. Let's say, for example, that you are a customer service representative who answers letters from customers, much as the correspondents do at General Mills. And let's say that you have received a truly abusive letter that attacks your company unfairly. What would you do? Your initial reaction might be to fire back an angry reply that defends the organization. But would the management want you

example, like to have time to digest information and ideas and tend to look on a letter as only one in a series.

- *Don't ask questions that require a yes or no answer.* Whereas North Americans tend to say yes when they mean yes and no when they mean no, that's simply not the case in most other cultures. In Asian countries, for example, it is considered impolite to say no, so Asians may answer affirmatively if only to mean "Yes, I heard you." (The Japanese have more than a dozen ways to avoid saying no.) Europeans, on the other hand, may initially react negatively to any question, but they actually mean "maybe" or "it depends." In many countries, the answer you get is what the person thinks you want to hear.
- *Learn about the country's body language.* Gestures have different meanings in different places. In Yugoslavia, turning the head from side to side means yes; in Japan, looking someone in the eye is considered judgmental or hostile; and in Ghana, thumbs up is a rude gesture. To avoid giving offense, keep your hands quiet.
- *Control your style of expression.* The North American style of expressing emotions is considered impulsive and wild by Asians but restrained and cold by Latin Americans. You need to be aware of how your habits of emotional expression will affect people in a particular culture.
- *Don't interrupt periods of silence.* Many foreigners are offended by the North American penchant for jumping in to fill any gaps in a conversation. Speakers in many cultures enjoy periods of silence and use them to gather their thoughts. Be patient. Allow the person to formulate what he or she wants to say, and try not to be "helpful" by putting words into the other person's mouth.
- *Use an interpreter or a translator.* Whenever possible, have your messages translated into the other person's language. A translated letter is more likely to be read sooner—and by the right person—than one in English, and your message is more likely to be understood as intended. When choosing an interpreter or translator, be sure to find someone who is familiar with both cultures and with the terminology of your business.

1. Have you ever had to communicate with someone who spoke little or no English? How successful were you in communicating? What problems did you encounter? How might you have handled the situation differently?

2. Interview a foreign student attending your school. Find out what kinds of communication difficulties he or she has encountered. In the course of your interview, what communication problems or misunderstandings do you note?

to counterattack, or would it want you to regain the customer's goodwill? Your response should reflect the organization's priorities.

ANALYZING YOUR AUDIENCE

Once you are satisfied that you have a legitimate purpose in communicating, take a good look at your intended audience. Who are the members, what are their attitudes, and what do they need to know? The answers to these questions will indicate something about the material you need to cover and the way you should cover it.

Ask yourself some key questions about your audience:

- Who are they?
- What is their probable reaction to your message?
- How much do they already know about the subject?
- What is their relationship to you?

DEVELOPING AN AUDIENCE PROFILE

If you are communicating with someone you know well, perhaps your boss or a co-worker, audience analysis is relatively easy. When you know people well, you can predict their reactions fairly accurately. On the other hand, if your audience is a group of strangers, you have to do some investigating and use common sense to anticipate their reactions.

What is the size and composition of the audience?

Large audiences behave differently from small ones and require different communication techniques. For example, if you were giving a speech to 500 people, you would have to limit the amount of audience participation, because fielding comments from such a large audience could be chaotic. And if you were writing a report for wide distribution, you might choose a more formal style, organization, and format than you would if the report was directed to only three or four people in your department.

Size and diversity often go hand in hand. The larger the audience, the more diverse their backgrounds and interests are likely to be. People with different education, status, and attitudes are likely to react differently to the same message, so you must look for the common denominators that tie the group together.

Focus on the common interests of the audience, but be alert to their individual concerns.

At the same time, you often have to respond to the particular concerns of individuals. The head of marketing needs different facts about a subject than the head of production or finance needs, for example. As you compose the message, keep these differences in mind. Include a variety of evidence that touches on everyone's area of interest.

Who is the primary audience?

When several people will be receiving your message, try to identify those who are most important to your purpose. If you can reach these decision makers or opinion molders, the other members of the audience will fall into place. Ordinarily, those with the most organizational status are the key people, but occasionally someone will surprise you. A person in a relatively low position may have power in one or two particular areas.

What is the audience's probable reaction?

Your approach to organizing your message should depend on your audience's probable reaction. If you expect a favorable response with very little criticism or debate, you can be straightforward about stating your conclusions and recommendations. You can also use a bit less evidence to support your points. On the other hand, when you face a skeptical audience, you may have to introduce your conclusions and recommendations more gradually and provide more proof.

A gradual approach and plenty of evidence are required to win over a skeptical audience.

In addition to considering the audience's general reaction, try to anticipate how key decision makers will respond to specific points. From past experience, you may know that the boss is especially concerned about certain issues: profits, market share, sales growth, or whatever. By anticipating this bias, you can incorporate evidence in your presentation that will address these issues.

What is the audience's level of understanding?

If you and your audience share the same general background, you can assume they will understand your material without any difficulty. If not, you will have to decide how much you need to educate them. The trick is to provide the information they need without being pedantic or obvious. In general, you're better off explaining too much rather than too little, particularly if you're subtle about it. The audience may get a bit impatient, but at least they will understand your message.

With luck, most of the audience will have roughly the same general level of understanding. If not, gear your coverage to the key decision makers.

What is your relationship with the audience?

Are you communicating with people from within the organization or with outsiders? What is your relative status? How much credibility do you have? The answers to these questions should influence the way you organize and style your message.

If you're an unknown, you will have to build the audience's confidence in you before you can win them to your point of view. The initial portion of your message will be devoted to gaining credibility. As you proceed, you will have to prove your points carefully, because the audience will be judging your abilities as well as your information.

Vary the tone and structure of the message to reflect your relationship with the audience.

If you are communicating with a familiar group, your credibility will already be a given. You can get down to business immediately. However, you may have to overcome people's preconceptions about you. Some members of the audience may have trouble separating your arguments from your personality. If they think of you as being a certain type, say, a "numbers person," they may question your competence in other areas. As you develop your message, you can overcome these prejudices by providing ample evidence on points outside your usual area of expertise.

Your status relative to the audience also affects the style and tone of your presentation. You address your peers differently than you do your boss, and you use still another tone when you're communicating with those who are lower in the hierarchy. And you handle a customer or supplier differently from a co-worker.

SATISFYING THE AUDIENCE'S INFORMATION NEEDS

As Irma Cameron points out, the key to effective communication is to determine your reader's needs and then respond to them. "Fine," you say to yourself, "but how should I do that?" The answer is quite simple: Try to tell people what they need to know in terms that are meaningful to them.

A good message answers all of the audience's questions. For example, if you're ordering office supplies, you have to tell the other person everything she or he needs to know to fill your order: the number and type of items you want, when and where you want delivery, the price you are prepared to pay. If you leave out any of the necessary information, your order will not be filled correctly. Whether you're placing a simple order or preparing a complicated report with hundreds of pages, you have a responsibility to take the following five steps:

Five questions to ask yourself that will help you satisfy the audience's information needs:

- What does the audience want to know?
- What does the audience need to know?
- Have I provided all desired and necessary information?
- Is the information accurate?
- Have I emphasized the information of greatest interest to the audience?

1. Find out what the audience wants to know.
2. Anticipate unstated questions.
3. Provide all the required information.
4. Be sure the information is accurate.
5. Emphasize ideas of greatest interest to the audience.

Find out what the audience wants to know

In many cases, the audience's information needs are readily apparent. For example, when Irma Cameron and her staff at General Mills answer letters requesting information about recipes, all they normally have to do is respond to the consumers' questions.

You will probably find during your career, however, that some people are not particularly good at telling you what they want. For example, your boss might tell you, "Find out everything you can about the Polaroid Corporation, and write a memo on it." That's a pretty big assignment. Ten days later, you could submit a 25-page report. But it's entirely possible that the boss, instead of heaping you with praise, will say, "I don't need all this. All I wanted is their five-year financial record."

If you have questions about what your reader wants to know, don't guess—ask.

When you get a vague request, pin it down. One good approach is to restate the request in more specific terms. For example, if your boss says, "Find out everything you can about Polaroid," you might respond, "You want me to track down their market position by product line and get sales and profit figures by division for the past five years, right?"

Another way to handle a vague request is to get a fix on its priority. Faced with an ambiguous assignment, you might ask, "Should I drop everything else and devote myself to this for the next week?"

Asking a question or two forces the person to think through the request and define more precisely what is required. You can then provide that information more efficiently.

Anticipate unstated questions

It's also a good idea to try to think of information needs that your audience may not even be aware of. For example, suppose that your company has just hired a new employee from out of town, and you've been assigned to coordinate the person's relocation. At a minimum, you would write a welcoming letter describing your company's procedures for relocating employees. But with a little extra thought, you might decide to include some information about the city: perhaps a guide to residential areas, a map or two, brochures about cultural activities, information on schools and transportation facilities.

Include any additional information that might be helpful, even though the reader didn't specifically ask for it.

Providing the little extras can be a big help to your audience. In some cases, you may be a better judge of their information needs than they are. You may be able to tell them something new that will be important to them, something they wouldn't have thought to ask. Although adding information of this sort lengthens your document, it creates goodwill.

Provide all the required information

Test the completeness of your document by making sure it answers all the important questions: who, what, when, where, why, and how.

Once you've defined your audience's needs, you have to be certain to satisfy those needs completely. One good way to test the thoroughness of your message is to check it for what reporters call the five *w*'s and one *h*: *who*, *what*, *when*, *where*, *why*, and *how*.

Here's an example that fails to pass the test. It's a request for free promotional materials that was sent by a director of corporate travel arrangements to a major hotel chain.

Dear Ms. Hill:

The Martin-Norton sales division is holding its annual meeting soon. Would you be interested in supplying us with some promotional materials that we can use as gifts for our sales representatives? Last year you were kind enough to provide key chains engraved with your logo, which were a big hit with our people. I'm sure they were a constant reminder that your hotels are good places for Martin-Norton sales representatives to stay while traveling on business. Our records show that 342 Martin-Norton people spent a total of 2,346 nights with you last year, an increase of 37 percent over the year before.

Although the style of the letter is fine, it won't get the desired results. The trouble is that the author fails to tell Ms. Hill everything she needs to know. The *what* and *why* are covered fairly well, but Ms. Hill won't know how many gifts are needed or when they will be required or where to send them or to whom. Because the document doesn't answer the five *w*'s and one *h*, Ms. Hill will have to either write or call the sender to get the missing details. The inconvenience of doing so may be just enough to prevent her from agreeing to the request.

When you want to induce action
- Be specific
- Cover all the essential points

You must take particular care to explain any action that you want to induce. Until readers get a clear picture of what they're supposed to do, they can't possibly do it. If you want them to send you a check for $5, tell them; if you want them to turn in their time cards on Friday by 3 p.m., spell it out. Don't be tactlessly blunt, but don't beat around the bush hoping to be subtle. If you want somebody to do something, be specific in stating your request. Cover all the essential points.

Be sure the information is accurate

In addition to being thorough, you must be accurate. There's no point in answering all your audience's questions if the answers are wrong.

Be certain that the information you provide is accurate and that the commitments you make can be kept.

In business, you have a special duty to check things before making a written commitment, especially if you are writing to someone who is outside the company. Your organization is legally bound by any promises you make, so make sure your company is able to follow through. People from production, inventory control, or shipping and delivery might be involved in supplying an item by a given date. Upper-level management might need to approve any purchases that you agree to make. If you have any doubt about the organization's ability or willingness to back up your promises, check with the appropriate people *before* you make the commitment. If you write the letter first and check for approval later, you may get some nasty surprises. Unreliability is embarrassing and harmful to the reputation of any company.

Of course, honest mistakes are possible. You may sincerely believe that you have answered someone's questions correctly, then later realize that your information was wrong. If that happens, contact the person immediately and correct the error. Most people will respect you for your honesty.

You can minimize mistakes, however, by trying to be accurate and double-checking everything you write or say. Check first to be certain that the organization can meet any commitments you make involving other people. Then check again to be certain you have not made any errors of fact or logic. If you are using outside sources of information, ask yourself whether they are up-to-date and reliable. Review any mathematical or financial calculations. Check all dates and schedules. Examine your own assumptions and conclusions to be certain they are valid, and be alert to the sources of misunderstanding discussed in Chapter 2.

Emphasize ideas of greatest interest to the audience

In deciding how to respond to your audience's information needs, remember that some points will be of greater interest and importance than others. Say, for example, that you're summarizing a recent conversation you had with one of your company's oldest and best customers. The emphasis you give to each point of the conversation should depend on the audience's concerns. The head of engineering might be interested in the customer's reaction to the design features of your product. Someone in the shipping department might be concerned about comments on delivery schedules. In other words, pick out the points that will have the most impact on the reader, and emphasize those points.

Try to figure out what points will especially interest your audience, and then give these points the most attention.

If you don't know the audience, or if you are communicating with a group of people, you'll have to use your common sense to identify points of particular interest. Possibly such factors as age, job, location, income, or education will give you a clue to the person's interests. For example, let's say that you're trying to sell memberships in the Book of the Month Club. How would you adjust your sales message for college students? Suburban homemakers? Retired residents of Sun City, Arizona? Traveling sales representatives? Auto mechanics? All these people would need to know the same facts about membership. But each group would be more interested in one point than another. Economy might be important to college students or retired people. Convenience might attract sales representatives or homemakers. Remember that your main goal as a business communicator is to tell your audience what they need to know.

SATISFYING THE AUDIENCE'S MOTIVATIONAL NEEDS

Some types of messages, particularly persuasive messages and bad news, have the purpose of motivating the audience to change their beliefs or behavior. The problem for the communicator is that resistance occurs when people hear ideas that conflict with their existing ideas. For example, if you try to sell financial planning services to someone who has always managed her own finances, she has to rethink her way of doing things. She is being asked to give up a system that she's familiar with for one that's entirely new. Faced with mutually exclusive concepts like these, people sometimes reject the new information without even really listening.[1] They may selectively screen out threatening ideas or distort your message to fit their preconceived map of reality.

To prevent resistance, you must arrange your message so the information will be as acceptable as possible. One approach is to use rational arguments, presented in an objective tone. For example, if you're arguing that a loan applicant should reduce his existing debts before he borrows more, you might use cause-and-effect reasoning to prove your point: "Adding this amount to your current debt might endanger your credit standing." Or you could use an analogy to support your position: "A study of debt as a percentage of income suggests that this loan would put you over the safe limit." Presenting both sides of an argument is another rational approach that is often quite effective. For example, you could point out how both the bank and the individual might benefit if the loan were approved but then conclude your argument by stating the risks. Two-sided approaches like this increase the communicator's credibility and defuse the receiver's counterarguments.[2]

Rely mainly on reason to win your audience to your point of view, but don't overlook their underlying emotions.

Although appealing to reason is often the best approach, you might also try to convince the audience by appealing to their emotions. For example, in attempting to sell a product, you might suggest that the item will enhance the customer's status or confer social acceptability. You can also build a convincing case by making the audience respect your honesty and fairness. This technique is frequently used in advertisements, where an "expert" delivers the message. Readers accept the product because they trust the spokesperson. Your credibility with an audience depends on their perception of your competence and integrity. People are more likely to believe you if they feel comfortable with you: if you have similar backgrounds or friends in common, if you wear the same style of clothes, enjoy the same sports, and aspire to the same goals. To establish rapport, you need to emphasize these common denominators.

If an audience trusts you, they are more likely to agree with you.

Remember that your success in getting your points across depends as much on the other person's receptivity as it does on your arguments. When you are writing or speaking to a resistant audience, presenting information isn't enough. You must address the other person's motivational needs before you introduce controversial material.

SATISFYING THE AUDIENCE'S PRACTICAL NEEDS

Many business messages are directed toward people who are themselves in business—as customers, suppliers, or co-workers. Regardless of where these people work or precisely what they do, they will receive your communication under distracting circumstances. Recent research on managerial work habits shows how fragmented a manager's day is:

Remember that your audience

- May have little time
- May be distracted
- May give your message low priority

- First-level supervisors are involved in at least 200 separate activities or incidents in an 8-hour day.
- Most activities are very brief. A study of supervisors shows one activity every 48 seconds.
- Another study of chief executives reports that periods of desk work average 10 to 15 minutes each.
- Responding to mail is a minor, routine part of a manager's day, taking less than 5 percent of her or his time. Most executives react to only about 30 percent of the mail they receive.[3]

In other words, many in your audience have very little time to devote to your message. They will review it under difficult circumstances with many interruptions, and they are likely to give it a low priority.

These facts suggest that you should make your message as convenient as possible to grasp. Try to be brief. Generally speaking, a 5-minute talk is easier to follow than a 30-minute presentation; a two-paragraph letter is more manageable than one that's two pages long, and a two-page memo is more likely to be read than a ten-page report. In recognition of this fact, Procter & Gamble, one of the most successful companies in the United States, has a tradition of limiting all memos to one typewritten page. Richard Deupree, who started the tradition when he was president of Procter & Gamble, explained the practice this way: "Part of my job is to train people to break down an involved question into a series of simple matters. Then we can all act intelligently."[4]

Devices that make your messages easier to comprehend include summaries and overviews, headings, lists, enclosures and appendixes, handouts, charts and graphs.

If your written message has to be long, make it easy for the reader to follow, so that she or he can pick it up and put it down several times without losing the thread of what you're saying. For example, begin with a summary of key points; use plenty of headings; put important points in list format so they will stand out. Put less important information in separate enclosures or appendixes. Use charts and graphs to dramatize important ideas.

If you're delivering your message orally, be sure to give listeners an overview of the message's structure and then express your thoughts clearly and logically. You might also use flip charts, slides, or handouts to help listeners understand and remember key points.

By using these simple devices to make the information easy to grasp, you will be responding to one of your audience's key needs: the need for convenience.

DEFINING THE MAIN IDEA

Once you've analyzed both your purpose and your audience, you're ready to deal with the basic question of how to achieve that purpose. What message will work best with this particular audience?

The main idea is the "hook" that sums up why a particular audience should do or think as you suggest.

Every business message can be boiled down to one main idea. Regardless of the issue's complexity, one central point sums up everything. This is your theme, your main idea. Everything else in the message either supports this point or demonstrates its implications.

A topic and a main idea are different, as Table 3.1 illustrates. The topic is the broad subject of the message. The main idea makes a statement about the topic—one of many possible statements—providing a rationale, explaining your purpose in terms that the audience can accept. For example, you might give a presentation on the topic of company health clubs, with the aim of convincing management to build an on-site exercise facility. Your main idea might be that the costs of providing a company health club would be more than offset by gains in productivity and reductions in insurance costs.

Developing the main idea is something like creating an advertising campaign. Let's say that you're trying to sell a new perfume called Finesse. And let's say that your target customer is the young professional woman. What message will persuade this woman to buy your product as opposed to the hundreds of other perfumes on the market? You toy with various concepts: romance, elegance, economy. Finally, you decide to promote Finesse as the fragrance that works at the office. Once you have the main idea, the campaign begins to take shape. You create a commercial that

TABLE 3.1 Topic, Purpose, and Main Idea

GENERAL PURPOSE	TOPIC	SPECIFIC PURPOSE	MAIN IDEA
To inform	Filing insurance claims	To teach customer service representatives how to file an insurance claim	Proper filing by employees saves the company time and money.
To persuade	Funding for research and development	To get top management's approval for increased spending on research and development	Competitors spend more than we do on research and development.
To collaborate	Incentive pay	To get the human resources and accounting departments to jointly devise an incentive system that ties wages directly to profits	Tying wages to profits will automatically reduce compensation costs in tough years while motivating employees to be more productive.

shows a well-dressed, attractive young woman in various office scenes—scoring points at meetings, laughing with colleagues, assigning work to her staff. As she negotiates a successful deal, two of her male co-workers say, "Leave it to Ellen to handle everything with Finesse." You could achieve your purpose in many other ways, but the main idea has to strike a response in the intended audience. It has to motivate people to do what you want by linking your purpose with their own.

When you're preparing a brief letter, memo, or meeting, the main idea may be pretty obvious, especially if you're dealing with simple facts that have little or no emotional content for the audience. In such cases the main idea may be nothing more than "Here is what you wanted." For example, if you're responding to a request for information about the price and availability of one of your company's products, your main idea would be something like this: "We have the item you want at a competitive price."

Finding the "angle" or "hook" becomes a bit more complicated when you are trying to persuade someone or have disappointing information to convey. In these situations, you have to look for a main idea that will establish a good relationship between you and your audience. What you're after is some point of agreement or common interest.

In longer documents and in presentations, in which a large mass of material needs to be unified, the problem of establishing a main idea becomes still more challenging. You need to identify a generalization that encompasses all the individual points you want to make. For tougher assignments like these, you may need to take special measures to come up with a main idea.

USE BRAINSTORMING TECHNIQUES

Identifying the main idea often requires creativity and experimentation. The best approach is to "brainstorm," letting your mind wander over the possibilities, testing various alternatives against your purpose, your audience, and the facts at your disposal. But how do you generate those possibilities? Different people use different approaches. You have to experiment until you find a brainstorming method that fits your mental style. Here are a few approaches that might work for you:

Some techniques for establishing the main idea:

- Storyteller's tour
- Random list
- FCR worksheet
- Journalistic approach
- Question-and-answer chain

- *Storyteller's tour.* Turn on your tape recorder and pretend that you've just run into an old friend on the street. She says, "So, what are you working on these days?" Give her an overview of your message, focusing on your reasons for communicating, your major points, your rationale, and implications for the message's recipient. Listen critically to the tape, then repeat the exercise until you are able to give a smooth, two-minute summary that conveys the gist of your message. This exercise should reveal your main idea.
- *Random list.* On a clean sheet of paper, list everything that pops into your head pertaining to your message. When you've exhausted the possibilities, study the list for relationships. Sort the items into groups as you would sort a deck of cards into suits. Look for common denominators; the connection might be geographic, sequential, spatial, chronological, or topical. Part of the list might break down into problems, causes, and solutions, another part into pros and cons. Regardless of what categories finally emerge, the sorting process will help you sift through your thoughts and decide what's important and what isn't.
- *FCR worksheet.* If your subject involves the solution to a problem, you might try using an FCR worksheet to help you visualize the relationships among your findings (F), your conclusions (C), and your recommendations (R). For example, you might find that you are losing sales to a competitor who offers lower prices than you do (F). From this, you might conclude that your loss of sales is due to your pricing policy (C). This conclusion would lead you to recommend a price cut (R). To make an FCR worksheet, divide a sheet of paper into three columns. List the major findings in the first column, then extrapolate conclusions and write them in the second column. These conclusions form the basis for the recommendations, which are listed in the third column. An analysis of the three columns should help you focus on the main idea.
- *Journalistic approach.* For informational messages, the journalistic approach may provide a good point of departure. The answers to six questions—who, what, when, where, why, how—should clarify the main idea.
- *Question-and-answer chain.* Perhaps the best approach is to look at the subject from your audience's perspective. Ask yourself, "What is the audience's main question? What do they need to know?" Examine your answer to that question. What additional questions emerge? Follow the chain of questions and answers until you have replied to every conceivable question that might occur to the audience. By thinking about your material from their point of view, you should be able to pinpoint the main idea.

LIMIT THE SCOPE

The main idea should be geared to the length of the message.

Whether the audience expects a one-page memo or a one-hour speech, you will have to select a main idea that can be developed within that framework. So once you have a tentative statement of your main idea, test it against the length limitations that have been imposed for your message.

There's a limit to how much you can communicate in a given number of words. What can be accomplished depends on several variables: the nature of the subject, the audience's familiarity with the topic, its receptivity to your conclusions, your existing credibility. In general, presenting routine information to a knowledgeable audience that already knows and respects you takes fewer words. Building consensus about a complex and controversial subject takes longer, especially if the audience is composed of skeptical or hostile strangers.

Although the main idea of your message should be adjusted to fit the time or space available, the number of major points should not. Regardless of how long the message will be, you should stick with three or four major points—five at the very most. According to communication researchers, that's all your audience will remember.[5]

If you're delivering a long message, say, a 60-minute presentation or a 20-page report, the major points can be developed in considerable detail. You can spend about 10 minutes or 10 paragraphs (or over 3 pages of double-spaced, typewritten text) on each of your key points and still have room for the introduction and conclusion. Instead of introducing additional points, you can deal more fully with complex issues, offer a variety of evidence, and overcome resistance.

Say your message is brief: 4 minutes or 1 page. You will have only a minute or a paragraph each for the introduction, conclusion, and major points. The amount of evidence you can present is limited, which means that your main idea must be both easy to understand and easy to accept.

SELECTING THE CHANNEL AND MEDIUM

Have you ever worn the wrong thing to a party? There you are in shorts and sandals mingling with folks wearing fancy outfits. The shorts are nice, and the sandals are new; but this is clearly the wrong time and place for them, and you feel self-conscious.

Different types of messages require different communication channels.

Business messages have "clothes" too, and the clothing has to suit the occasion, or the message is ineffective. You can dress your ideas in one of two basic outfits: oral or written. Within those basic channels, you can vary the length, format, style, and tone in an almost infinite variety of ways to create the ideal vehicle for your message. The basic choice between speaking and writing depends on the purpose, the audience, and the characteristics of the two communication channels (see Table 3.2).

ORAL COMMUNICATION

In general, use oral communication if your purpose is to collaborate with the audience.

The chief advantage of oral communication is the opportunity it provides for immediate feedback. This is the channel to use when you want the audience to ask questions and make comments or when you are trying to reach a group decision. The oral approach is also useful when you are presenting controversial information, because you can read the audience's reaction in their body language and adjust your message accordingly.

Oral communication takes many forms, including unplanned conversations between two people, telephone calls, interviews, small group meetings, seminars, workshops, training programs, formal speeches, and

TABLE 3.2 **When to Talk It Through, When to Write It Out**

AN ORAL MESSAGE IS APPROPRIATE WHEN	A WRITTEN MESSAGE IS APPROPRIATE WHEN
You want immediate feedback from the audience	You do not need immediate feedback
Your message is relatively simple and easy to accept	You have a detailed and complex message that requires careful planning
You do not need a permanent record	You need a permanent, verifiable record
You can assemble the audience conveniently and economically	You are trying to reach an audience that is large and geographically dispersed
You want to encourage interaction to solve a problem or reach a decision	You want to minimize the chances for distortion that occurs when a message is passed orally from person to person

major presentations. Chapters 17 and 18 explore these "media" in more detail.

In general, the smaller the audience, the more interaction among the members. If your purpose involves reaching a decision or solving a problem, you should select an oral medium geared toward a small audience. The program should be relatively informal and unstructured so ideas can flow freely. Although a certain amount of planning should precede the meeting, the participants need not prepare a script or rehearse their remarks. Gatherings of this sort can be arranged quickly and economically.

At the opposite extreme are formal presentations to large audiences, which are common at events like sales conventions, shareholder meetings, presentations to security analysts, and ceremonial functions. Often, these major presentations take place in a big facility, where the audience can be seated auditorium style. The audiovisual aids are frequently elaborate as well: films, audio recordings, multi-image slide shows. Because of the difficulty of coordinating all the audiovisual effects, the presentation must follow a carefully rehearsed plan. Long lead times, fancy equipment, a professional crew, and a big budget are required to stage one of these events. Their formality makes them unsuitable for collaborative purposes requiring audience interaction.

WRITTEN COMMUNICATION

Written communication increases the sender's control but eliminates the possibility of immediate feedback.

Written messages also vary in formality. At one extreme are the scribbled notes that people use to jog their own memories; at the other are elaborate, formal reports that rival magazines in graphic quality. But regardless of the degree of formality, written messages have one big advantage: They give the writer an opportunity to plan and control the message. A written format is called for when the information is complex, when a permanent record is needed for future reference, when the audience is large and geographically dispersed, and when immediate interaction with the audience is either unimportant or undesirable.

Although there are many specialized types of written communication, the most common media are letters, memos, and reports. Letters and memos are covered extensively in Chapters 6 through 9, reports in Chapters 12 through 16. In addition, Component Chapter D is a detailed discussion of formats for business documents.

FIGURE 3.2
A Typical Letter

Irma Cameron uses letterhead enhanced with her name to give a personal touch.

The formal salutation indicates Irma's respect for a customer she doesn't know.

The body of the letter is brief but still includes a number of friendly remarks designed to maintain goodwill.

The signature also demonstrates a personal touch.

GENERAL MILLS, INC. · GENERAL OFFICES · 9200 Wayzata Boulevard · Minneapolis, Minnesota

IRMA K. CAMERON
Manager, Consumer Relations

May 6, 1988

Mr. Ron Philip
280 Lake Drive
Kalispell, MT 59901

Dear Mr. Philip:

Your letter was a day brightener for the Cheerio brand group and for us in the Consumer Relations Department. We were all delighted to learn how much you enjoy Cheerios.

You are right! Cheerios was first introduced in the same year you were born, 1941. Perhaps that explains your affection for those little Cheerioats, as the product was initially called.

Congratulations to you and your wife as you await the arrival of your baby. I am sending something separately to help welcome the newest member of your "Cheerios family."

Best wishes,

Irma K. Cameron

Irma K. Cameron
Manager, Consumer Relations

ss

Enclosure

Letters and memos

With a few exceptions, most letters and memos are relatively brief documents, generally one or two pages. Memos, the "workhorses" of business communication, are used for the routine, day-to-day exchange of information within an organization. Letters, which go to outsiders, perform an important public relations function in addition to conveying a particular message.

Letters and memos are organized according to their purpose; the relationship between writer and reader dictates their style and tone.

Letters and memos can be classified by purpose into four categories: direct requests; routine, good-news, and goodwill messages; bad-news messages; and persuasive messages. The purpose determines the organization of main points. Style and tone, however, are governed by the relationship between the writer and the reader. The options range from forceful to passive, from personal to impersonal, and from colorful to bland.

FIGURE 3.3
A Typical Memo

Every memo is headed with four pieces of information—date, to, from, and subject—even when a plain sheet of paper is used.

The writer, Irma Cameron, states her business right away.

Direct phrasing may be used more frequently in memos than in letters, especially when a boss is telling an employee what to do.

Common courtesy never hurts.

General Mills, Inc.

INTRA-COMPANY CORRESPONDENCE

Copy to Carol Thomas At 4N

To Mike Gamache At 4N

From Irma Cameron At 4N Date 6/25/88

Subject 1988/1989 Human Resource Needs

We need to evaluate our human resource needs against anticipated growth in the volume of calls coming over our toll-free consumer service telephone lines.

Please compile a list of all General Mills products that currently carry the right toll-free phone number and another list of products expected to carry the number within this fiscal year.

The next step is to project call volume by month. I suggest that you use past history on call volume as well as our established volume-projection formulas for estimating the monthly totals.

Work with Carol to define our staffing needs. Use current individual productivity statistics as a guide, and take into account the impact of increased use of the toll-free phone number.

Please have this data ready for review on July 25. Let me know if you have any conflict in meeting this due date.

IC:ss
IC91J

The format for a letter depends on the traditions of the organization. Figure 3.2 is a typical example of a letter from Irma Cameron's department at General Mills. Memo format is somewhat different, as Figure 3.3 demonstrates. The body of a memo, especially a longer one, often includes headings and lists to call attention to important points and make the information more convenient to readers. Introductions and transitions may be given less attention in a memo than in a letter, because the writer and reader share a common frame of reference.

Many organizations rely on form letters (and sometimes memos) to save time and money in handling routine correspondence. Form letters are particularly handy for such one-time mass mailings as sales messages about products, explanations of policies and procedures, information about organizational activities, goodwill messages such as seasonal greetings, and acknowledgments of job applications. A variation of the form letter is used for slightly more individualized messages, such as General Mills's replies to inquiries about its products and activities. Letters of this type are made up of optional paragraphs that can be selected to suit the occasion.

Reports and proposals

Reports are generally longer and more formal than letters and memos and have more components.

These factual, objective documents may be distributed to either insiders or outsiders, depending on their purpose and subject. They come in many formats, including preprinted forms, letters, memos, and manuscripts. In length, they range from a few pages to several hundred. Generally, however, reports and proposals are longer than letters and memos, with a larger number of distinct pieces.

Reports and proposals also tend to be more formal than letters and memos. But in reports and proposals, as in all forms of business communication, organization, style, and tone depend on the message's purpose, on the relationship between writer and reader, on the traditions of the organization. Thus the basic composition process is much the same for all.

■ Checklist for Message Planning

A. Purpose

- ☐ 1. Determine whether the purpose of your message is to inform, persuade, or collaborate.
- ☐ 2. Identify the specific behavior you hope to induce in the audience.
- ☐ 3. Make sure that your purpose is worthwhile and realistic.

B. Audience

- ☐ 1. Identify the primary audience.
- ☐ 2. Determine the size and composition of the group.
- ☐ 3. Analyze the audience's probable reaction to your message.
- ☐ 4. Determine the audience's level of understanding.
- ☐ 5. Evaluate your relationship with the audience.
- ☐ 6. Analyze the audience's informational, motivational, and practical needs.

C. Main Idea

- ☐ 1. Stimulate your creativity with brainstorming techniques.
- ☐ 2. Identify a "hook" that will motivate the audience to respond to your message in the way you intend.
- ☐ 3. Evaluate whether the main idea is realistic given the length limitations imposed on the message.

D. Channel and Medium

- ☐ 1. If your purpose is to collaborate, give an informal, relatively unstructured oral presentation to a small group.
- ☐ 2. If you are celebrating an important public occasion, give a prepared speech to a large audience.
- ☐ 3. If you need a permanent record, if the message is complex, or if immediate feedback is unimportant, prepare a written message.
  - ☐ a. Send a letter if your message is relatively simple and the audience is outside the company.
  - ☐ b. Send a memo if your message is relatively simple and the audience is inside the company.
  - ☐ c. Write a report if your message is objective and complex.

SUMMARY

The process of preparing business messages consists of three basic steps: planning, composing, and revising. During the planning phase, you need to establish both the general and the specific purposes for your message and to decide whether that purpose is worth pursuing.

Also during the planning phase, you need to analyze the audience. Their information needs will help you decide on the content of the message; their motivational needs will help you organize your points in a convincing way. The audience's practical needs will guide your decisions regarding format.

Another step in the planning process is to establish the main idea of the message. The main idea summarizes what the audience should do or think as a result of your message and provides them with a rationale. By defining this idea, you provide direction for composing the message.

You also need to plan the channel of communication for your message. Oral communication gives you the opportunity to interact with the audience;

written communication gives you a greater opportunity to plan and control your message. Within these two basic channels, you must select from alternative media, such as speech versus presentation or letter versus report.

COMMUNICATION CHALLENGES AT GENERAL MILLS

Teaching new correspondents how to reply to letters from customers is an important part of Irma Cameron's job. Even with the company's computerized inventory of 1,200 sample paragraphs to rely on, the correspondents must make many communication decisions. Irma wants to be certain those decisions are responsive to the customers' needs.

Individual Challenge: As a veteran member of the General Mills letter-writing staff, you have been asked to help teach new recruits the ropes. Prepare some guidelines for the new correspondents to use in planning their replies to customers. Indicate how letters should be organized to respond to different types of inquiries, and provide suggestions on techniques for personalizing the replies.

Team Challenge: Although producing letters of high quality is the consumer relations department's main goal, efficiency is also important. Irma has asked a team from her department to analyze the letter preparation process. She is specifically interested in knowing what steps could be taken to enable the existing staff to produce more letters in a given period of time. As part of your effort, develop a list of questions that you will use to guide your analysis. For example, you might want to find out how long it takes to compose a letter using the sample paragraphs versus starting from scratch.

QUESTIONS FOR DISCUSSION

1. Some writers argue that planning a message is a waste of time, because they inevitably change their plans as they go along. How would you respond to this argument?
2. What proportion of your time would you expect to spend on the three steps in the preparation process (planning, composing, and revising) for these writing projects: (a) memo to a colleague, (b) report for the president's office, (c) letter to a client.
3. "An effective memo always has a single purpose." Do you agree? Why or why not?
4. What would you do if your supervisor asked you to prepare a message that, in your opinion, would serve no worthwhile purpose?
5. How would the size of an audience affect your ability to communicate if you were (a) preparing a written message, (b) delivering a speech, (c) conveying information nonverbally?
6. What are some of the things a communicator might do to respond to the audience's practical needs?
7. What are some alternative main ideas that you might consider using if you were trying to convince an audience to add three more people to the office typing pool?
8. What main idea might you try to develop in a one-page memo on cigarette smoking in the office? In a three-page memo?
9. Which channel and medium would you use to convince your boss, the director of planning, to reconsider the company's policy of requiring MBA degrees for all members of the planning staff?
10. As a student, you receive many messages in the form of lectures, seminars, laboratories, and textbooks. What purposes does each of these media serve?

EXERCISES

1. For each of the following communication tasks, write a statement of purpose (if you have trouble, try beginning with "I want to . . ."):
   a. A report to your boss, the store manager, about the outdated items in the warehouse
   b. A memo to clients about your plans to have a booth at an upcoming trade show
   c. A letter to a customer who has not made a payment for three months
   d. A memo to employees about the office's high water bills
   e. A phone call to a supplier to check on an overdue shipment of parts
   f. A report to future users on the computer program you have chosen for the company's mailing list
2. Make a list of communication tasks you will need to accomplish in the next week or so (a job application, a letter of complaint, a speech to a class, an order for some merchandise, and so on). For each, determine a general purpose and a specific purpose.
3. List five messages that you have received lately, such as direct-mail promotions, letters, phone solicitations, and lectures. For each, determine the general purpose of the message and the specific purpose, and then answer the following questions: Was the message well timed? Did the sender choose an appropriate channel and medium for the message? Was an appropriate person used for delivery of the message? Was the sender's purpose realistic?
4. Barbara Marquardt is in charge of public relations for a cruise line that operates out of Miami. She is shocked to read a letter in a local newspaper from a disgruntled passenger, complaining about the service and entertainment on a recent cruise. Barbara will have to respond to these publicized criticisms in some way. What audiences will she need to consider in her response? What channels and media should she choose? If the letter had been published in a travel publication widely read by travel agents and cruise travelers, how might her course of action differ?
5. For each communication task below, write brief answers to three questions: Who is the audience? What are the audience's general attitudes toward my subject? What does the audience need to know?
   a. A "final notice" collection letter from an appliance dealer, sent ten days before initiating legal collection procedures
   b. An unsolicited sales letter asking readers to purchase computer disks at near-wholesale prices
   c. An advertisement for peanut butter
   d. Fliers to be attached to doorknobs in the neighborhood, announcing reduced rates for chimney lining or repairs
   e. A cover letter sent by a job applicant along with her resume
   f. A request (to the seller) for a price adjustment on a piano that incurred $150 in damage during delivery
   g. A letter to the editor of the local newspaper, protesting a scheduled rise in utility rates
6. Rewrite the following message so that it includes all the information that the reader needs. (Make up any necessary details.)

   I am pleased to offer you the position of assistant buyer at Marcus Industries at an annual salary of $15,500. I hope to receive notice of your acceptance soon.

7. Frank Kroll has been studying a new method for testing the durability of the electric hand tools his company manufactures. Now he needs to prepare three separate reports on his findings: one for the administrator who will decide whether to purchase the new equipment needed for using this method, one for the company's engineers who design and develop the hand tools, and one for the workers who will be using the new equipment. To determine the audience's needs for each of these reports, Frank has made a list of the following questions: (1) Who are the readers? (2) Why will they read my report? (3) Do they need introductory or background material? (4) Do they need definitions of terms? (5) What level and type of language is needed? (6) What level of detail is needed? (7) What result does my report aim for? Put yourself in Frank's shoes and answer these questions for each of the three audiences:
   a. The administrator
   b. The engineers
   c. The workers
8. Choose a type of electronic device that you know how to operate well, such as a videocassette recorder, a home computer, or a telephone answering machine. Write two sets of instructions for operating the device: one geared toward a reader who has never used that type of machine and one geared toward a person who is familiar with that

type of machine in general but who has never operated the specific model you have in mind.

9. As the new manager of a music store, you are dismayed to find a storeroom full of discontinued guitars. This model of guitar is an inexpensive one, designed for beginners wanting to learn to play. It is also smaller than full-size guitars, which makes it good for children to learn on. One reason it may not have sold is the paint job: red, white, and blue stripes, with stars. You want to move these guitars out—fast. Write the copy for two different newspaper ads: one with a rational appeal, one with an emotional appeal.

10. You are looking for a job as a salesperson. If you are going to be able to sell something, you'd better be able to sell yourself first. What special qualities do you have that will make you a desirable sales employee? Use the techniques described in the chapter to come up with a main idea you can use in your efforts to market yourself. Draft a statement of your main idea—from a sentence to a paragraph long—that tells your audience (potential employers) what to do or think about you and why.

After studying this chapter, you will be able to

- Identify the characteristics of a well-organized message
- Explain why organization is important to both the audience and the communicator
- Break a main idea into subdivisions of thought, grouped into logical categories
- Arrange ideas in direct or indirect order, depending on the audience's probable reaction
- Compose a message using a style and tone that are appropriate to your subject, purpose, audience, and format
- Use the "you" attitude to interest the audience in your message

CHAPTER FOUR

ORGANIZING AND COMPOSING BUSINESS MESSAGES

David Petree

COMMUNICATION CLOSE-UP AT MERCY HOSPITAL

Communication is important in any organization, but it's especially vital in a place like Mercy Hospital in San Diego, where the product is healthy people. David Petree, associate administrator of the 523-bed facility, says: "When you have 2,200 employees, 1,200 affiliated physicians, and a constantly changing flow of patients, you know that you have to communicate effectively. The consequences of a simple misunderstanding can be horrifying."

In the course of an average day, David has plenty of opportunities to perfect his communication skills: "Most days begin with an early-morning medical meeting with physicians, followed by an hour or two of general office time. That's when I go through the mail, catch up on my reading, and plan my day. I usually attend a few more meetings before lunch, which is often a business affair too. Afternoons are generally reserved for meetings dealing with special projects. The afternoon is also when I do my writing, which generally includes a couple of letters and brief memos. I prepare longer reports and presentations less frequently; they usually require a day or two of concentrated effort.

A complex concern like Mercy Hospital demands good organization—in terms of both management and communication.

"Because communication is such an important part of my job, I've tried hard to improve my writing and speaking skills. I'm not what you'd call a 'natural' communicator," David confesses. "I have a cluttered mind. When I try to explain my thoughts, I'm stymied by the fact that I can only say one thing at a time. Language is linear, but my mind is multidimensional. I can't stick to one point, because in my head I know that doing so is an oversimplification."

Although David has written hundreds of letters, memos, and reports in the past ten years, each one has been a struggle. "I'm better than I used to be," he says, "but I still have a rough time sorting my ideas into neat little piles and talking about one pile at a time. But I know I have to do that to be effective. I know I can't just dump a bunch of ideas on my audience and expect them to understand how all the pieces fit together."

To David, developing a business message is somewhat like making a movie: "You have to create a series of scenes. At the start of each scene, you use a wide angle: the big, broad shot of the cowboy riding across the plains. Then you focus on the horse, the man, the eyes. Then you switch back to the wide angle. You show the Indians on the rim of the canyon, and then you home in again on the details: the war paint, the bows and arrows, the glistening flesh of the chief." As David so colorfully explains, each new scene in the movie—and each new section in a business message—moves from the general to the specific. And each scene, each thought, connects with the next to create a story.

THE CASE FOR BEING WELL ORGANIZED

Like David Petree, all business communicators face the problem of developing a story, of finding a way to compress a multidimensional web of ideas into a linear message that proceeds point by point. Meeting the challenge is important: Research clearly demonstrates that people simply do not remember disassociated facts and figures.[1]

WHY SOME MESSAGES SEEM DISORGANIZED

If you've ever been on the receiving end of a disorganized message, you're familiar with the frustration of trying to sort through a muddle of ideas. For example, consider this letter, which was sent to the customer service department of a department store in Mason City, Iowa:

My dad was in an accident last year, and he hasn't been able to work full-time, so we don't have as much money to spend as we used to. But my mom works as a clerk at the city hall, so we aren't destitute by any means. And soon my dad will be going back full-time.

My family has shopped at your store since I was a kid. It was smaller then, and it was located on the corner of Federal Avenue and 2nd N.W. My dad bought me my first bike there when I was six. I still remember the day. He paid cash for it. We always pay cash.

I have five brothers and sisters, and they need plenty of things. The cassette player that I bought for my sister Suzanne for Christmas has been a problem. We've taken it in for repairs three times in three months to the authorized service center, and my sister is very careful with the machine and hasn't abused it. She likes piano music. It still doesn't work right, and I'm tired of hauling it back and forth, because I work at McDonald's after school and don't have a lot of spare time. I paid cash for the tape player.

This is the first time I've returned anything to your store, and I hope you'll agree that I deserve a better deal.

Most disorganized communication suffers from problems with content, grouping, or sequence.

This letter displays the sort of disorganization that readers find frustrating. Here's a closer look at what's wrong:

- *Taking too long to get to the point.* The most obvious problem with the letter is that the writer wrote three paragraphs before introducing the topic, which is the faulty cassette player. She then waited until the final paragraph to state her purpose: She wants an adjustment.
- *Including irrelevant material.* Another big problem is that the writer introduced extraneous information that has no bearing on her purpose or topic. Does it matter, for example, that the department store used to be smaller or that it was at a different location? And what difference does it make, at least as far as solving the problem is concerned, whether the writer works at McDonald's? Or whether Suzanne likes piano music?
- *Getting ideas mixed up.* In addition, some of the ideas seem to be in the wrong place. Their grouping and sequence are illogical. The writer seems to be making six points: (1) her family has money to

spend; (2) they are old customers; (3) they pay cash; (4) they buy many things at the store; (5) the cassette player doesn't work; and (6) the buyer wants an adjustment. Wouldn't it be more logical to begin with the fact that the machine doesn't work? And shouldn't some of these ideas be combined under the general idea that the writer is a valuable customer?

- *Leaving out necessary information.* A final problem with the letter is that the writer left out some necessary information. The customer service representative may want to know the make, model, and price of the cassette player; the date on which it was purchased; the specific problems the machine has had; whether the repairs were covered by the warranty. The writer also failed to specify what she wants the store to do. Does she want a new cassette player of the same type? A different model? Or simply her money back?

These four common faults are responsible for most of the organization problems you'll find in business communication.

WHAT GOOD ORGANIZATION IS

Achieving good organization is a challenge sometimes. It's easier, however, if you know what good organization is. These four guidelines will help you recognize a well-organized message:

A message is well organized when all the pieces fit together in a coherent pattern.

- The subject and purpose must be clear.
- All of the information must be related to the subject and purpose.
- The ideas must be grouped and presented in a logical way.
- All necessary information must be included.

Watch how observing these four rules would change the previous letter:

I bought an Olympia Model 124 cassette player from your store on November 25, during your pre-Christmas sale, when it was marked down to $19.95. I didn't use the unit until Christmas, because it was bought as a gift for my sister. You can imagine how I felt when she opened it on Christmas morning and it didn't work.

I took the machine to the authorized service center and was assured that the problem was merely a loose connection. The service representative fixed the machine, but three weeks later it broke again--another loose connection. For the next three weeks, the machine worked reasonably well, although the volume tended to vary at random. Two weeks ago, the machine stopped working again. Once more, the service representative blamed a loose connection and made the repair. Although the machine is working now, it isn't working very well. The volume is still subject to change without notice, and the speed seems to drag sometimes.

What is your policy on exchanging unsatisfactory merchandise? Although all the repairs have been relatively minor and have been covered by our six-month warranty, I am not satisfied with the machine. I would like to exchange it for a similar model from another manufacturer. If the new set costs more than the old one, I will pay the difference, even though I generally look for sale merchandise.

My family and I have shopped at your store for 15 years and until now have always been satisfied with your merchandise. We are counting on you to live up to your reputation for standing behind your products. Please let us hear from you soon.

This version meets the definition of a well-organized message. The main point is clear and is introduced early. All the information is directly related to the subject and purpose of the letter. The ideas are arranged in logical groups and presented in a logical sequence. And all necessary information is included. The result is a unified, coherent, and businesslike document.

WHY GOOD ORGANIZATION IS IMPORTANT

You might now be asking yourself, "Does it really matter? Who cares whether the message is well organized, as long as the point is eventually made? Why not just let the ideas flow naturally and trust that the audience will grasp my meaning?"

In general, the answer is simple: By arranging your ideas logically and diplomatically, you are able to satisfy the audience's informational, motivational, and practical needs. A well-organized message presents all the required information in a convincing pattern, with maximum efficiency.

Helps the audience understand the message

To see how important organization is to the communication process, read the following passage. It's from a linen supply company's report on the pros and cons of buying a new type of washing machine known as a CLM, or a continuous laundry machine.

The CLM washing-drying cycle does not involve much tumbling of the sheets. Sheets are held in one position while a water spray dislodges particles and removes stains. Several sheets have been processed through the CLM over 200 times. A conventional washer uses a tumbling action that pounds the sheet to remove foreign matter. This action is followed by squeezing to extract excess water and additional tumbling during drying. A typical sheet's life expectancy in conventional laundering may be on the order of 100 washings.

From what you've read, which of the two machines—the CLM or the conventional machine—would seem like the better choice if you were running the linen supply house? Are you even sure what a CLM does?

Now look at the revised version:

A key advantage of the CLM is that it increases the average life of a sheet--that is, the number of washings the sheet will withstand before it has to be replaced. In a CLM, the sheet is held in one position while a spray of water dislodges particles and removes stains; the washing-drying cycle is also very fast. A conventional washer, on the other hand, tumbles and pounds the sheet to remove foreign matter. This action is followed by squeezing to remove excess water and additional tumbling during the drying cycle. With this type of process, a typical sheet's life expectancy is only about 100 washings. The CLM process, by contrast, extends a sheet's useful life to at least 200 washings.

This version contains essentially the same facts, but it is organized so that the main point of those facts is clear at the outset.

The main reason for being well organized is to improve the chances that people will understand exactly what you mean.

One disorganized paragraph may not be too much of a problem, but imagine trying to make sense out of an entire disorganized document or presentation. If you're interested in getting your message across, good organization is one of your handiest tools. It pays off because it makes your message easier to understand and remember. A well-organized message satisfies the audience's need for information.

Helps the audience accept the message

Good organization also helps you get your ideas across without upsetting the audience.

Good organization pays off in another way too: It helps make your message more acceptable to your audience from a motivational standpoint. Let's say, for example, that you are the customer with the broken cassette player referred to earlier. And let's say that you get the following reply from Laura Hampton, a customer service representative at the department store:

> Your letter has been referred to me for a reply. I'm sorry, but we are unable to grant your request for a cassette player. Our store does not accept returns on sale merchandise or on merchandise that was purchased over 30 days ago. Because you bought the machine on sale 3 months ago, we cannot help you. I suggest that you have it repaired before the warranty runs out.
>
> We do hope that you will understand our position and that you will continue to shop at our store. As you said yourself, this is the first problem you've ever had with our merchandise.

How do you feel now?

Although Laura's letter appears at first glance to be logical enough, she has made no effort to select and organize her points in a diplomatic way. With greater care in choosing and presenting her ideas, Laura could have come up with something more acceptable, like the letter in Figure 4.1. Although this letter is still not likely to leave the customer totally satisfied, isn't the bad news a little easier to take?

As Laura knows, writers can soften refusals and leave a better impression by organizing messages diplomatically. They can also use good organization to enhance their credibility and add authority to their messages. In a recent survey of chief executives, 89 percent said that they interpret clear, well-organized writing as an indication of clear thinking.[2]

Saves the audience's time

Well-organized messages are efficient because they contain only relevant information.

In addition to being convincing, well-organized messages are efficient. They satisfy the audience's need for convenience. When a message is well organized, it contains only relevant ideas. Those in the audience do not waste time on information that is superfluous. Effective organization is the foundation of brevity.

In addition, all the information in a well-organized message is in a logical place. The audience can follow the thought pattern without a struggle. And because the organization is clear and logical, they can save even more time, if they want to, by looking for just the information they need instead of reading everything.

FIGURE 4.1
Sample Letter Demonstrating the Importance of Good Organization

WAINWRIGHT'S DEPARTMENT STORE
660 Sixth Avenue, N.W.
Mason City, Iowa 50401
(515) 988-9900

March 15, 1989

Miss Evelyn Kittrell
Route 3, Hancock Highway
Clear Lake, IA 50401

Dear Miss Kittrell:

The letter begins with a neutral statement that the reader should not find objectionable.

Thank you for letting us know about your experience with the Olympia cassette player that you bought in November. It's important that we learn of unusual problems with merchandise we stock.

The refusal is stated indirectly and is linked with a solution to the reader's problem.

As you know, regularly priced merchandise returned to Wainwright's within 30 days is covered by the unconditional refund policy that has been our tradition for 22 years. But your machine is still covered by the manufacturer's warranty. Your needs will receive immediate attention if you write to

Ms. Bonnie Bendek
Olympia Manufacturing
P.O. Box 6671, Terminal Annex
Los Angeles, CA 90010

From experience, I know that the people at Olympia truly care about having satisfied customers.

The letter closes on an appreciative note and confidently assumes normal dealings in the future.

We too value your business, Miss Kittrell. Please don't miss our Tax Days sale in April, which will feature more of the low prices and high-quality merchandise that you've come to rely on.

Sincerely,

Laura Hampton

Laura Hampton
Customer Service

sb

Simplifies the communicator's job

Organizing what you're going to say before you start to write makes tne job much easier.

There's one final reason why being well organized is a good idea: It helps you get your message down on paper more quickly and efficiently. This is an important factor in business, where the objective is to get a job done, not to produce paper. In fact, when the chief executives in the survey mentioned earlier were asked what they would most like to improve about their own business writing, they mentioned speed of composition more often than any other factor.[3]

By thinking about what you're going to say and how you're going to say it before you begin to write, you can proceed more confidently. The draft will go more quickly, because you won't waste time putting ideas in the wrong places or composing material you don't need. In addition, you can use your organizational plan to get some advance input from your boss so you'll be sure you're on the right track *before* you spend hours working on a draft. And if you're working on a large and complex project, you can use the plan to divide the writing job among co-workers so you can finish the assignment as quickly as possible.

GOOD ORGANIZATION THROUGH OUTLINING

To organize a message, first group the ideas and then put them in sequence.

"Alright," you say, "I'm willing to admit that good organization makes sense. But just how do I achieve it?" Basically, achieving good organization is a two-step process. First you define and group the ideas; then you establish their sequence with a carefully selected organizational plan.

DEFINE AND GROUP IDEAS

In business, deciding what to say is more important than deciding how to say it.

Deciding what to say is the most basic problem that any business communicator has to solve. If the content is weak, no amount of style will camouflage that fact. Sooner or later, your audience will conclude that you really don't have anything worthwhile to say. Whether you're making a phone call, composing a 3-paragraph letter, or writing a 250-page report, you should begin by defining the content. The longer and more complicated the message, the more important this step is.

The brainstorming techniques described in Chapter 3 will help generate your main idea, but they won't necessarily tell you how to develop it or how to group the supporting details in the most logical and effective way. To decide on the final structure of your message, you need to visualize how all the points fit together. One way to do this is to construct an outline. Even if all you do is jot down three or four points on the back of an envelope, making a plan and sticking to it will help you cover the important details.

When you're preparing a long and complex message, an outline is indispensable, because it helps you visualize the relationship among the various parts. Without an outline, you may be inclined to ramble. As you're describing one point, another point may occur to you—so you describe it. One detour leads to another, and before you know it, you've forgotten the original point. With an outline to guide you, however, you can communicate in a more systematic way, covering all the ideas you must include in an effective order, with proper emphasis. Following a plan also helps you express the transitions between ideas, so that the audience will understand the relationships among your thoughts.

An outline or schematic diagram will help you visualize the relationship among parts of a message.

You're no doubt familiar with the basic alphanumeric outline, which uses numbers and letters to identify each point and indents them to show which ideas are of equal status. (Chapter 13 tells more about the different formats that can be used in this type of outlining.) But you may never have tried a more schematic approach, which illustrates the structure of your message in an "organization chart" like one that depicts a company's management structure. The main idea is shown in the highest-level box (see Figure 4.2). Like a top executive, the main idea establishes the big picture. The lower-level ideas, like lower-level employees, provide the details. All of the ideas are arranged into logical divisions of thought, just as a company is organized into divisions and departments.[4]

FIGURE 4.2
"Organization Chart" for Organizing a Message

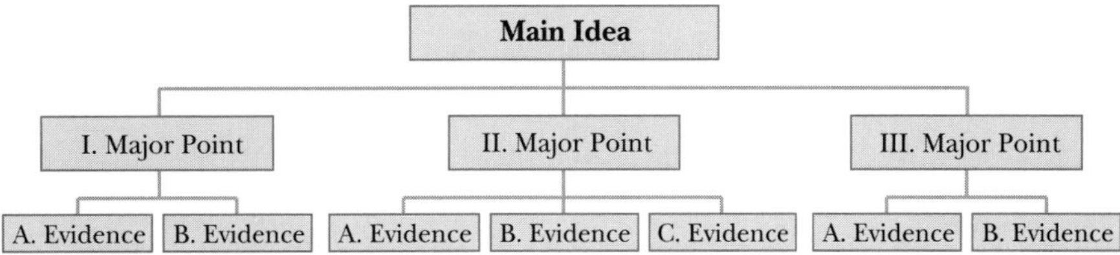

Start with the main idea

The main idea is the starting point for constructing an outline.

The main idea, placed at the top of an organization chart, helps you establish the goals and general strategy of the message. This main idea summarizes two things: (1) what you want the audience to do or think and (2) the basic reason why they should do it or think it. Everything in the message should either support this idea or explain its implications.

State the major points

In an organization chart, the boxes directly below the top box represent the major supporting points, corresponding to the main headings in a conventional outline. These are the "vice presidential" ideas that clarify the message by expressing it in more concrete terms.

The main idea should be supported by three to five major points, regardless of the message's length.

To fill in these boxes, you break the main idea into smaller units. Generally, you should try to identify three to five major points. If you come up with more than seven main divisions of thought, go back and look for opportunities to combine some of the ideas. The big question then is deciding what to put in each box. Sometimes the choices are fairly obvious. But sometimes you may have hundreds of ideas to sort through and group together. In such situations, you should consider both your purpose and the nature of the material.

If your purpose is to inform and the material is factual, the groupings are generally suggested by the subject itself. They are usually based on something physical that you can visualize or measure: activities to be performed, functional units, spatial or chronological relationships, parts of a whole. For example, when you're describing a process, the major support points are almost inevitably steps in the process. When you're describing a physical object, the "vice presidential" boxes correspond to the components of the object. When you're giving a historical account, each box represents an event in the chronological chain.

When your purpose is to persuade or collaborate, the major support points may be more difficult to identify. Instead of relying on a natural order imposed by the subject, you need to develop a line of reasoning that proves your central message and motivates your audience to act. The boxes on the organization chart then correspond to the major elements in a logical argument. Basically, the supporting points are the main reasons why your audience should accept your message.

Illustrate with evidence

The third level on the organization chart shows the specific evidence you will use to illustrate your major points. This evidence is the flesh and blood that helps your audience understand and remember the more abstract concepts. For example, let's say you're advocating that the company increase

TABLE 4.1 Six Types of Details

TYPE OF DETAIL	EXAMPLE	COMMENT
Facts and figures	Sales are strong this month. We have received two new contracts worth over $5 million and have a good chance of winning another with an annual value of $2.5 million.	Most common form of detail in business messages. Adds more credibility than any other form of development. May become boring if used in excess.
Example or illustration	We've spent the past four months trying to hire recent accounting graduates for our internal audit staff, and so far, only one person has agreed to join our firm. One woman told me that she would love to work for us but can't afford to. She can get $5,000 more a year from another employer.	Adds life to a message, but one example does not prove a point. Idea must be supported by other evidence as well.
Description	Upscale hamburger restaurants are designed for McDonald's graduates who still love the taste of a Big Mac but who want more from a restaurant than convenience and low prices. The adult hamburger establishments feature attractive waitresses, wine and beer, half-pound hamburgers, and substantial side dishes such as nachos or potato skins. "Atmosphere" is a key ingredient in the formula for success.	Useful when you need to explain how something looks or functions. Helps audience visualize the subject by creating a sensory impression. Does not prove a point but clarifies points and makes them memorable. Begins with overview of object's function; defines its purpose, lists major parts, and explains how it operates; relies on words that appeal to senses.

its advertising budget. To support this point, you could provide statistical evidence that your most successful competitors spend more on advertising than you do. You could also describe a specific case in which a particular competitor increased its ad budget and achieved an impressive sales gain. As a final bit of evidence, you could show that over the past five years, your firm's sales have gone up and down in unison with the amount spent on advertising.

If you're developing a long, complex message, you may need to carry the organization chart (or outline) down several levels. Remember that every level is a step along the chain from the abstract to the concrete, from the general to the specific. The lowest level contains the individual facts and figures that tie the generalizations to the observable, measurable world. The higher levels are the concepts that reveal why those facts are significant.

Each major point should be supported with enough specific evidence to be convincing but not enough to be boring.

The more evidence you provide, the more conclusive your case will be. If your subject is complex and unfamiliar or if your audience is skeptical, you will need a lot of facts and figures to demonstrate your points. On the other hand, if the subject is routine and the audience is positively inclined, you can be more sparing with the evidence. You want to provide enough support to be convincing but not so much that your message becomes boring or inefficient.

Another way to keep the audience interested is to vary the type of detail. As you plan your message, try to incorporate the methods described

TABLE 4.1 (Continued)

TYPE OF DETAIL	EXAMPLE	COMMENT
Narration	Under former management, the company operated in a casual style. Executives came to work in blue jeans, meetings rarely started on time, and lunch rarely ended on time. But when Mr. Wilson took over as CEO, the company got religion—financial religion. A Harvard MBA who favors Brooks Brothers suits, Mr. Wilson has embarked on a complete overhaul of the operation. He has cut the product line from 6,000 items to 1,200 and chopped $12 million off expenses.	Good for attracting attention and explaining ideas but lacks statistical validity.
Reference to authority	I talked with Jackie Lohman in the Cleveland plant about this idea, and she was very supportive. As you know, Jackie has been in charge of that plant for the past six years. She is confident that we can speed up the number 2 line by 150 units per hour if we add another worker.	Bolsters a case and adds variety and credibility. Works only if "authority" is recognized and respected by audience, although he or she may be ordinary person.
Visual aid	Graphs, charts, tables	Essential in presenting specific information. Provides visual impression of information. Used more often in memos and reports than in letters.

in Table 4.1. Switch from facts and figures to narration; add a dash of description; throw in some examples or a reference to authority. Reinforce it all with visual aids. Think of your message as a stew, a mix of ingredients, seasoned with a blend of spices. Each separate flavor adds to the richness of the whole.

ESTABLISH SEQUENCE WITH ORGANIZATIONAL PLANS

Once you have defined and grouped your ideas, you are ready to decide on their sequence. You have two basic options:

- *Direct approach (deductive).* Puts the main idea first, followed by the evidence
- *Indirect approach (inductive).* Puts the evidence first and the main idea later

These two basic approaches may be applied to either short messages (memos and letters) or long ones (reports, proposals, presentations). To choose between the two alternatives, you must first analyze your audience's likely reaction to your purpose and message.

FIGURE 4.3
Audience Reaction and Organizational Approach

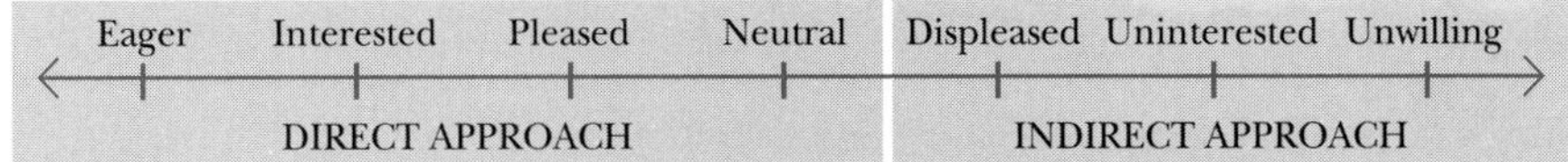

Use direct order if the audience's reaction is likely to be positive and indirect order if it is likely to be negative.

Your audience's reaction will fall somewhere on the continuum shown in Figure 4.3. In general, the direct approach is fine when your audience will be receptive: eager, interested, pleased, or even neutral. If they will be resistant to your message—displeased, uninterested, or unwilling—you will generally have better results with the indirect approach.

Bear in mind, however, that each message is unique. You can't solve all your communication problems with a simple formula. If you're sending bad news to outsiders, for example, an indirect approach is probably best. On the other hand, you might want to get directly to the point in a memo to an associate, even if your message is unpleasant. The direct approach might also be the best choice for long messages, regardless of the audience's attitude, because delaying the main point could cause confusion and frustration. Just remember when planning your approach that the first priority in business communication is to make the message clear.

Short messages follow one of four organizational plans, depending on the audience's probable reaction.

Once you have analyzed your audience's probable reaction and chosen a general approach, you can choose the most appropriate organizational plan. The four basic plans for short messages are

- *Direct requests.* When the audience will be interested in complying or eager to respond. Let's say you're inquiring about products or placing an order. Usually the recipient will want to comply and will welcome your request.
- *Routine, good-news, and goodwill messages.* When the audience will feel neutral about your message or will be pleased to hear from you. If you are providing routine information as part of your regular business, the audience will probably be neutral, meaning neither very pleased nor displeased. And if you are announcing a price cut, granting an adjustment, accepting an invitation, or congratulating a colleague, the audience will be pleased to hear from you.
- *Bad-news messages.* When the audience will be displeased about what you have to say. If, for example, you are turning down a job applicant, refusing credit, or denying a request for an adjustment, the audience will be disappointed.
- *Persuasive messages.* When the audience really isn't very interested in your request or will be unwilling to comply without extra coaxing. If you write to ask for a favor, request an adjustment, collect a debt, or make a sale, the audience will initially resist.

Table 4.2 summarizes how each type of message is structured. In each organizational plan, the opening, the body, and the close all play an important part in getting your message across.

TABLE 4.2 **Four Organizational Plans for Short Messages**

AUDIENCE REACTION	ORGANIZATIONAL PLAN	OPENING	BODY	CLOSE
Eager or interested	**Direct requests**	Begin with the request or main idea.	Provide necessary details.	Close cordially and state the specific action desired.
Pleased or neutral	**Routine, good-news, and goodwill messages**	Begin with the main idea or the good news.	Provide necessary details.	Close with a cordial comment, a reference to the good news, or a look toward the future.
Displeased	**Bad-news messages**	Begin with a neutral statement that acts as a transition to the reasons for the bad news.	Give reasons to justify a negative answer. State or imply the bad news, and make a positive suggestion.	Close cordially.
Uninterested or unwilling	**Persuasive messages**	Begin with a statement or question that captures attention.	Arouse the audience's interest in the subject. Build the audience's desire to comply.	Request action.

Direct requests

Direct requests get straight to the point, because the audience usually wants to respond.

One of the most common types of business messages, and the most straightforward, is the direct request. In making a direct request, says David Petree of Mercy Hospital, "I always get to the point in the first paragraph. Or if I'm talking with the person face-to-face or on the phone, I get right down to business."

Here's a letter that David wrote concerning the purchase of oak paneling for the main lobby of the hospital's new addition. He expected the reader to be interested in the request and willing to comply with it.

Of the two grades of paneling that you wrote about in your October 4 letter, we are more interested in the less expensive of the two. Could you please show us a sample of that paneling at one of our upcoming Thursday morning meetings.

The letter begins with the main idea.

If the paneling is acceptable to the rest of the committee, we'll probably use it, because the price is closer to the original cost estimate for the paneling. In fact, if you have other paneling materials that are even less expensive, we'd like to look at those as well.

The midsection makes a request and provides essential details.

We appreciate your supplying the bids for our paneling and look forward to working with you. Please let me know the date you prefer to meet with us.

In closing, the letter refers to the main point and states the action desired.

David's direct approach is appropriate in this case because it focuses attention on the main point. The reader finds out right away that he wants to see a sample of the paneling. A quick scan of the remaining paragraphs yields additional details.

Aside from being easy to understand, direct requests have the added advantage of being easy to formulate. You can state your point directly without searching for some creative introduction. As David explains, "The direct approach is the most natural approach, and I think it's the most useful and businesslike." This type of message is discussed in greater detail in Chapter 6.

Routine, good-news, and goodwill messages

The direct approach is effective for messages that will please the reader or will cause no particular reaction.

Other messages that call for the direct approach are also easy to organize. Here's a good-news letter that David Petree wrote to inform a medical clinic that Mercy Hospital would be happy to join in a contract to provide health services to the local Bureau of Prisons. David knew that the director of the clinic would be pleased with this response, so he came right to the point:

We'd be delighted to participate with Smith Hanna Medical Group in delivering health-care services to the Bureau of Prisons. The contract attached to your letter of September 29 is basically acceptable, although we would like to make one or two minor changes. I have noted these on the enclosed copy.

The letter begins with the good news.

I should add that our participation is based on the assumption that there will not be an excessive number of Bureau prisoners. You mentioned on the phone that typically only a few low-security patients need hospitalization each year and that each is accompanied by a security guard from the Bureau of Prisons.

All necessary details are provided in the middle part.

As soon as the revised contract is ready for signature, please send it to me. Sister M. Joanne, our executive director, will be signing the contract. She has asked that her signature noting acceptance of the contract be included at the end of the agreement to reflect Mercy Hospital's acceptance of all terms contained in the document.

This paragraph gives additional specifics.

Thank you for giving us the opportunity to join with you in this contract. We hope it will be the first of many joint ventures to deliver health services to the people of our community.

The letter closes with a reference to the main idea and a gracious look toward the future.

Using the direct approach for routine, good-news, and goodwill messages has many advantages. By starting off with the positive point, you put your audience in a good frame of mind and help make them receptive to whatever else you have to say. Also, this approach emphasizes the pleasing aspect of your message by putting it right up front, where it is the first thing recipients see. This type of message is discussed in more detail in Chapter 7.

Bad-news messages

If you have bad news, try to put it somewhere in the middle, cushioned by other, more positive ideas.

You may be tempted to blurt out an unpleasant message in the most direct and unvarnished terms, with the excuse that you're just being businesslike or that the audience is too far away or unimportant to matter. But bluntness is in many cases more expedient than practical. Astute businesspeople know that everyone has the potential to be a customer or supplier sometime or to influence someone else who may be. They are willing to take a little extra care with their bad-news messages, because they know it often pays off in the end.

The challenge lies in being honest but kind. You don't want to mislead the audience, but at the same time you don't want to be too blunt in expressing the bad news. To achieve a good mix of candor and kindness, imagine that you are talking face-to-face with someone you want to remain on good terms with. Wouldn't you focus on some aspect of the situation that makes the bad news a little easier to take?

David Petree avoids writing bad news whenever possible: "If I have something negative to say, I make a point of communicating orally first. I prefer to talk things through in person, because I've found that written documents are more likely to leave a lasting negative impression. When you talk to people face-to-face, you can usually work things out in a constructive way."

At times, however, personal interaction is simply not possible. You may have to officially refuse a request, cancel an agreement, turn down an order, or refuse to make an adjustment. Often, the person you're writing to is a complete stranger at a distant location. Then the best way to make your point without alienating the audience is to use the indirect approach.

Here's how David responded when he was asked to act as industry chairman for a dinner sponsored by the National Conference of Christians and Jews. Notice how he cushioned the bad news:

Your invitation to act as industry chairman for NCCJ's upcoming Anniversary Citation Dinner is a great honor. I thoroughly enjoyed serving in the role last year. Your members are a fine group with high ideals, and working with them was a privilege.

The letter begins with a neutral statement that provides a transition to the refusal.

This year I'm involved with a construction project here at the hospital that is consuming all my time--and then some. Therefore, although I would enjoy repeating the experience of working with NCCJ, I believe someone else would be better able to give the assignment the attention it deserves.

The midsection explains the reason for the refusal and then states the bad news.

Perhaps one of my colleagues would have the time to do the job the way it ought to be done. If you'll give me a call, I'll be happy to suggest some names for you. We want the health-care industry to be well represented.	The writer takes care to introduce a positive thought.
I wish you and the rest of your committee the greatest success in achieving the goals set this year by NCCJ.	The letter closes on a cordial note.

The first and last sections of a message make the biggest impression. If David had stated his refusal in the first sentence of the letter, his reader might never have bothered to go on to the reasons or might have been in the wrong frame of mind to consider them. By putting the explanation before the refusal, David focused attention on the reasons. But at the same time, David advises, "you have to be sincere about your reasons. A reader can spot a phony excuse in a minute."

As long as you can be honest and reasonably brief, you're better off to open a bad-news message with a neutral point and put the negative information after the explanation. Then if you can close with something fairly positive, you're likely to leave the audience feeling okay—not great, but not hostile either. When you're the bearer of bad tidings, that's often about all you can hope for. This type of message is discussed further in Chapter 8.

Persuasive messages

Using the indirect approach gives you an opportunity to get your message across to a skeptical or hostile audience.

The indirect approach is also useful when you know that the audience will resist your message. This might be the likely reaction to a sales or collection letter, an unsolicited job application, or a request for a favor of some kind. In such cases, you have a better chance of getting through to the person if you lead off with something catchy. This doesn't mean that you should go in for gimmicks, but do try to think of something that will make your audience receptive to what you have to say. Mention a possible benefit or refer to a problem that the recipient might have. Pose a question or mention an interesting statistic.

The following letter is one that David Petree wrote to raise funds for Mercy Hospital:

How good is "good enough" when it comes to health care? Do you want the best treatment available, no matter what it costs, or are you willing to settle for less--for old equipment, cheaper programs, something a little less reliable?	These questions are likely to catch the reader's attention.
These are tough questions for anyone, but they're especially tough for a hospital like Mercy, which is under pressure to contain health-care costs. We want to give our patients the best care available, yet we have to face economic realities. We need your help.	The letter leads up to the main point by arousing the reader's interest.
As you know from your visit to our hospital last week, we are working hard to raise funds for our	This section gives the reader a motive for com-

building program. We've received generous pledges from A. O. Reed and Bergelectric as well as from the M. H. Golden Company. But we still have a long way to go before we can start construction. Needless to say, we're eager to have the E. F. Brady Company join in our campaign to build the hospital's new addition.

plying with the request.

Thanks again for taking the time to visit the hospital and discuss our needs. We appreciate your consideration of our request for support and look forward to a favorable decision from you soon.

The letter closes with an appeal for action.

Although you might argue that people are likely to feel manipulated by the indirect approach, the fact remains that you have to capture people's attention before you can persuade them to do something. If you don't, there's really no way to get the message across. You also have to get your audience to consider with an open mind what you have to say; to do this, you have to make an interesting point and provide supporting facts that encourage the audience to continue paying attention. Once you have them thinking, you can introduce your real purpose. This type of message is discussed at greater length in Chapter 9.

Longer messages

Most short messages can use one of the four basic organizational plans. But longer messages (namely, reports and presentations) require a more complex pattern to handle the greater mass of information. These patterns can be broken into two general categories: informational and analytical. Figure 4.4 shows how the choice of plan for a longer message relates to the purpose.

In general, the easiest reports and presentations to organize are the informational ones that provide nothing more than facts. Operating instructions, status reports, technical descriptions, and descriptions of company procedures all fall into this category.

When your purpose is to inform, the major points are based on a natural order implied by the subject's characteristics.

Long informational messages have an obvious main idea, often with a descriptive or "how to" overtone. The development of subordinate ideas follows the natural breakdowns of the material to be explained. These subtopics can be arranged in order of importance, sequentially, chronologically, spatially, geographically, or categorically. Suppose, for example, that your boss asks you to give a presentation on how to fill out time sheets. The procedure involves a certain number of obvious steps, so organizing the message should be almost automatic. You simply list the steps in sequence and describe each one.

FIGURE 4.4
Organizational Plans for Longer Messages

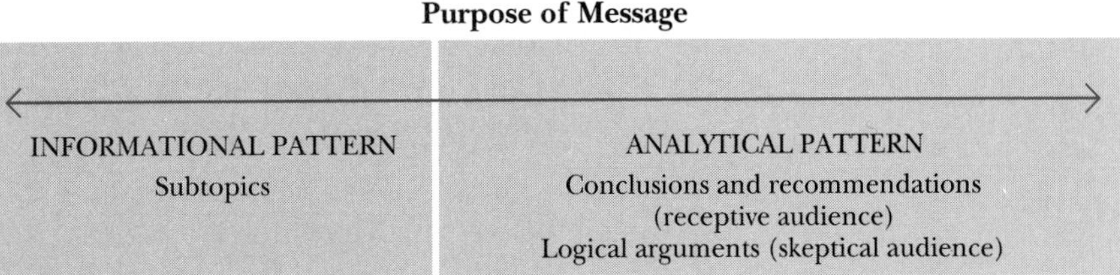

SHARPEN YOUR SKILLS

How Personal Computers Aid the Composition Process

For many business writers, the computer keyboard has replaced the pen, pencil, and typewriter as the basic technology for capturing their ideas. Whatever the hardware and word-processing software used, a personal computer can be an indispensable aid to writing, eliminating much of the drudgery.

In particular, a personal computer can help you

- *Generate ideas.* Many writers are intimidated by a blank piece of paper but somehow find a keyboard and screen much more inviting. As one business writer put it, "I used to dread writing reports. But now I just sit down at the computer and start typing whatever comes to mind, knowing that I can always erase it from the screen at any time. What's surprising is that when I go back and read what I've written, I'm usually pretty happy with it."
- *Organize ideas.* You can create outlines on screen and then fill them in, and you can freely rearrange your material as you produce it. You can also use outliner software to create agendas for meetings, to set priorities for tasks to accomplish, or for other such purposes.
- *Make corrections.* Many word-processing programs have spelling checkers that search for spelling errors. Other types of writing software check for errors in grammar and usage, flag use of the passive voice, and analyze your document for readability. Most errors found by these programs can easily be corrected. (Appendix I, "Business Communicator's Resource Directory," lists some of this software.)
- *Perform cosmetic typing tasks.* Tasks such as setting up tables, centering material, and indenting chunks of type can be done more easily on a computer than on a typewriter.
- *Find and change items within the document.* If you wanted to change the word *accountant* to *comptroller* throughout a document, you could simply instruct the computer to search for all instances of *accountant* and to replace them with *comptroller*. It would complete the task within a few seconds.
- *Revise documents.* Moving a paragraph from the middle of page 4 to the end of page 2 no

When your purpose is to persuade or collaborate, the approach is analytical, with major points corresponding to logical arguments or to conclusions and recommendations.

It is more difficult to organize analytical reports and presentations, which are designed to lead the audience to a specific conclusion. When your purpose is to collaborate with the audience in solving a problem or to persuade them to take a definite action, you have to choose an organizational plan that highlights logical arguments or focuses the audience's attention on what needs to be done. Your audience may respond in one of two ways to your material, and your choice of organizational plan should depend on the reaction you anticipate:

> If you expect your audience to agree with you, use a structure that focuses attention on conclusions and recommendations.
>
> If you expect your audience to be skeptical about your conclusions and recommendations or hostile toward them, use a structure that focuses attention on the rationale that supports your point of view.

You'll learn more about organizing longer messages in Chapter 15. For now, the important thing is to master the basic steps in structuring a message.

longer requires scissors and glue. A few keystrokes make that change—and others, such as inserting words and sentences, deleting material, and revising paragraph breaks—without your having to retype the entire document.

- *Produce final drafts.* When you are satisfied with your revised document, you need only press a key or two to have the final draft printed out for you. The computer will even number the pages and give you multiple copies if you like.
- *Personalize form letters.* In the past, sending a similar letter to a dozen different people required separately typing each letter, which took a considerable amount of time. Now you can take the same basic letter, customize it for each recipient, and print out letter-quality copies in a fraction of the time.
- *Conduct research.* If you can't find what you're looking for in your own files, you can turn to data bases, which are computer stockpiles of information. If your computer has a modem, you can use the phone lines to get immediate access to news services, stock market reports, research abstracts, and other resources. Information is displayed on the screen of your computer.

Computers do have their drawbacks, of course. Some writers find themselves compulsively revising because it is so easy to make changes. Others are frustrated by limitations of their software or problems with their hardware. Everyone who has ever done writing on a computer has tales of woe about crashed programs, power outages, damaged disks, and other technical problems that mean the loss of hours or even days of work.

Despite the capability of personal computers, using one does not automatically make you a better writer. If you write poorly with a pencil or typewriter, you may write no better with a word processor. But you may write faster.

Furthermore, using a software program that checks your spelling can lull you into a false cents of security because the program checks only spelling, not context. (For example, "cents" in the last sentence is spelled correctly; it just happens to be the wrong word.) No matter how many spelling and punctuation programs are available, you still need to proofread everything you write. A computer does not use common sense. You must provide that.

1. Although personal computers can cut your writing time, learning to use one can be a time-consuming and frustrating experience. Given your own situation, do you feel that a personal computer would be worth the time you would have to invest to learn how to use it?

2. Assume that you are going to be buying a word processor or personal computer. First, analyze the type of writing that you now do or expect to be doing. Then visit a computer store to find out what make and model would best suit your needs. Write a memo about your findings, specifying the reasons for your final choice.

FROM OUTLINE TO FIRST DRAFT

Once you have completed the planning process, you are ready to begin composing the message. If your schedule permits, put your outline or organization chart aside for a day or two, then review it with a fresh eye, looking for opportunities to improve the flow of ideas. When you feel confident that you finally have the structure that will achieve your purpose with the intended audience, you can begin to write.

THE COMPOSITION PROCESS

As you compose the first draft, don't worry too much about getting everything perfect. Just put down your ideas as quickly as you can. You'll have time to revise and refine the material later.

Composition is relatively easy if you've already figured out what to say and in what order, although you may need to pause now and then to find the right word. You may also discover as you go along that you can improve

CHECKLIST FOR DICTATION

A. Preparation for Dictation

- ☐ 1. Review the operating instructions for the dictation equipment, and see that it is working properly.
- ☐ 2. Gather notes, files, and reference materials that you may need to use during the dictation session.
- ☐ 3. Plan the message.
  - ☐ a. Determine your purpose.
  - ☐ b. Think about the audience's needs and interests.
  - ☐ c. Organize your thoughts into logical groups, and decide on the sequence of points.

B. Dictation Procedures

- ☐ 1. Start with messages that have the greatest priority.
- ☐ 2. Speak clearly and distinctly, in a natural tone of voice.
- ☐ 3. Avoid eating, gum chewing, smoking, and other audible distractions while you are dictating.
- ☐ 4. Provide full instructions for the transcriber.
  - ☐ a. Identify yourself and your department, indicating where you can be reached if the transcriber has any questions.
  - ☐ b. Identify the form of the message—letter, memo, report, slide presentation, or whatever—and specify whether you want a draft or a final copy.
  - ☐ c. Request any special stationery you want used, and specify any special format instructions, such as margin widths, single or double spacing, and blocked or indented paragraphs.
  - ☐ d. Indicate how many copies are required, who should receive them, and how copies should be filed.
  - ☐ e. Identify enclosures, and if necessary, tell the transcriber where they can be found.

on your outline. Feel free to rearrange ideas, to delete, and to add as long as you don't lose sight of your purpose.

If you're writing the draft in longhand, leave space between lines so you'll have plenty of room to make revisions. If you're using a typewriter, leave wide margins and double-space the text. Probably the best equipment for drafting the message is a word processor, which allows you to make changes very easily. Alternatively, you might try dictating the message, particularly if you're practicing for an oral delivery or if you're trying to create a conversational tone. For details on the equipment available for the composition process and other communication tasks, see Component Chapter B.

STYLE AND TONE

In composing the message, vary the style to create a tone that suits the occasion.

Style is the way you use words to achieve a certain tone, or overall impression. You can vary your style—your sentence structure and vocabulary—to sound forceful or passive, personal or impersonal, colorful or colorless. The right choice depends on the nature of your message and your relationship with the reader.

Your use of language is one of your credentials, a badge that identifies you as being a member of a particular group. Although your style should be clear, concise, and grammatically correct, it should also conform to the norms of your group. Every organization has its own stylistic conventions, and many occupational groups share a particular vocabulary.

Style can be refined during the revision phase (see Chapter 5). But you will save yourself time and a lot of rewriting if you compose in an appropriate style. Before you even begin writing, focus on the role you're playing, your

- ☐ f. Describe special mailing and transmission requirements.
- ☐ g. Specify the necessary turnaround time for each message.
- ☐ h. Spell out clearly the name and address of each person who is to receive the message.

☐ 5. Use the pause or stop button on the dictation machine if you need to think through a statement or locate additional material.

☐ 6. Clarify ambiguous grammar, spelling, and punctuation.

- ☐ a. Clearly enunciate plurals, past-tense endings, and sounds that might be confused (such as *b* and *p*).
- ☐ b. Spell out names, homonyms (words that sound alike), and trade or technical terms.
- ☐ c. Specify punctuation where a question may arise: periods, commas, colons and semicolons, question marks, exclamation points, hyphens, dashes, parentheses, and quotation marks.
- ☐ d. Specify capitalization: "all caps" for entire words, "initial cap" for the first letter of a word.
- ☐ e. Identify the use of underlining, indention, and columns.
- ☐ f. Dictate long or unusual numbers digit by digit.
- ☐ g. Indicate paragraph endings by saying "paragraph."

☐ 7. Make corrections as soon as you notice that you have made a mistake or that revision is needed.

☐ 8. Conclude the dictation by saying "end of dictation" and thanking the transcriber.

C. Dictation Follow-up

☐ 1. Proofread the typed document carefully, then double-check to be certain that required changes were made.

☐ 2. Sign or initial the final version.

☐ 3. Ask the transcriber for feedback on how to improve your dictation technique.

purpose, the probable reaction of your audience. All these elements of a message almost subconsciously influence tone.

Think about the relationship you want to establish

The first step toward getting the right tone is to think about your relationship with the audience. Who are you and who are they? Are you friends of long standing with common interests, or are you total strangers? Are you equal in status, experience, and education, or are you clearly unequal? Your answers to these questions will help you define your relationship with the audience so you can use the right "voice" in your message.

If you're addressing an old friend, you can often take an informal tack. But if you're near the bottom of the hierarchy in a large organization, you generally have to adopt a respectful tone in communicating with the people above you. Some people in high positions are extremely proud of their status and resent any gesture from a lower-level employee that is even remotely presumptuous. For example, they may not like you to offer your own opinions, and they may resent any implied criticism of their actions or decisions. If you are writing to someone of this type, you have to show a keen appreciation of rank, or your message will be ineffective.

To achieve a warm but business-like tone

- Don't be too familiar
- Use humor only with great care
- Don't flatter the other person
- Don't preach
- Don't brag
- Be yourself

Although different situations require different tones, most business communication should sound businesslike without being stuffy. The tone should suggest that you and your audience are sensible, logical, unemotional people—objective, interested in the facts, rational, competent, and efficient. You are civilized people who share a mutual respect.

To achieve this tone, you must avoid being too familiar. For example, don't mention things about anyone's personal life unless you know the

SHARPEN YOUR SKILLS

Tailor Your Writing Style to Get the Results You Want

Business writers are less concerned with style than novelists are, but they do have some leeway. Sometimes you want impact and adopt a forceful style; other times a passive style is preferable. Sometimes, friend, you want to get personal; other times, it behooves one to be impersonal. Some messages cry out for a razzle-dazzle, colorful style; in others, colorless prose fits the requirements. With practice, you can tailor your writing to fit these six basic styles.

FOR A FORCEFUL STYLE

- Use the active voice.
- Give orders; use the imperative.
- Step up front and be counted.
- Don't beat around the bush; say things directly.
- Use a subject-verb-object order in sentences.
- Adopt a tone of confidence about what you say.

A forceful style conveys courage and a sense of personal responsibility for what is being said.

FOR A PASSIVE STYLE

- Avoid the imperative; never give an order.
- Use the passive voice heavily.
- Avoid taking responsibility for negative statements; attribute them to faceless, impersonal "others."
- Use "weasel words" such as *possibly*, *maybe*, and *perhaps*.
- Use long sentences and heavy paragraphs to slow down reader comprehension of sensitive or negative information.

A passive style conveys softness and a lack of blunt abrasiveness. It can be particularly useful in communicating negative information.

FOR A PERSONAL STYLE

- Use the active voice, which puts you in front of the sentences.
- Use people's names instead of referring to them by titles.
- Use personal pronouns, especially *I* and *you*, when saying positive things.
- Use short sentences that capture the rhythm of ordinary conversation.

individual very well. Such references are indiscreet and presumptuous. You should also avoid phrases that imply intimacy, such as "just between you and me," "as you and I are well aware," and "I'm sure we both agree." And you should be careful about sounding too folksy or chatty, because the audience may interpret this tone as an attempt on your part to seem like an old friend when in fact you're not.

Humor is another type of intimacy that may backfire. It's fine to be witty in person with old friends but very difficult to hit just the right note of humor in a written document, particularly if you don't know the reader very well.

You should also avoid obvious flattery. Although most of us respond well to honest praise and proper respect, we are suspicious of anyone who seems too impressed. When someone says, "Only a person of your outstanding intellect and refined tastes can fully appreciate this point," little warning lights flash in our minds. We suspect that we are about to be conned.

We are also quick to take offense when someone starts preaching to us. Few things are more irritating than a person who assumes that she or he knows it all while we know nothing. People who feel compelled to give lessons in business are particularly offensive. If for some reason you have to tell your audience something obvious, try to make the information unobtrusive. Place it in the middle of a paragraph, where it will sound like

- Use contractions to sound informal and conversational.
- Direct questions at the reader.
- Interject positive personal references that will let the reader know the letter is really to him or her and is not a form letter.

A personal style exudes charm and warmth. It sounds just like one human being talking to another.

FOR AN IMPERSONAL STYLE

- Avoid using people's names, especially first names.
- Avoid using personal pronouns, especially *I* and *you*. (The corporate *we* is acceptable.)
- Use the passive voice to make yourself conveniently disappear.
- Make some of your sentences complex and some paragraphs long.

An impersonal style is withdrawn and often cerebral. It sounds like a policy manual or legal document.

FOR A COLORFUL STYLE

- Insert some adjectives and adverbs.
- Use concrete rather than abstract words.
- Choose interesting active verbs (*grab* rather than *take*, for example).
- If appropriate, use metaphors, similes, or other figures of speech to make a point.

A colorful style usually conveys a literary quality. When used well, it increases the impact of your prose.

FOR A COLORLESS STYLE

- Avoid using adjectives and adverbs.
- Use abstract rather than concrete words.
- Avoid using metaphors, similes, and other figures of speech.
- Blend an impersonal style with a passive style.
- Use only formal words and expressions that freeze wit, liveliness, and vigor out of the writing.

A colorless style is dull and lacks emotional impact.

1. What would be the most appropriate situations for using each of the six styles? What would be the least appropriate situations?

2. Choose a writing task, such as a letter to a boss asking for a week off. Write six letters, each in a different style. Which letter turns out to be the most appropriate to the task? Which is the least appropriate?

a casual comment as opposed to a major revelation. Alternatively, you might preface an obvious remark with "as you know" or some similar phrase.

Bragging is closely related to preaching, and it is equally offensive. When you praise your own accomplishments or those of your organization, you imply that you are better than your audience. References to the size, profitability, or eminence of your organization may be especially annoying (unless, of course, those in your audience work for the same organization). For example, you are likely to evoke a negative reaction with comments like "We at McMann's, which is the oldest and most respected firm in the city, have a reputation for integrity that is beyond question."

Perhaps the most important thing you can do to establish a good relationship with your audience is to be yourself. People can spot falseness very quickly, and they generally don't like it. If you don't try to be someone you're not, you will sound sincere.

Use the "you" attitude

The "you" attitude is best implemented by expressing your message in terms of the audience's interests and needs.

Once you've thought about the kind of relationship you want to establish, try to project yourself into your audience's shoes. What do they want from you? What are their expectations? How will they feel about what you have to say? By asking yourself these questions, you can begin to establish empathy with your audience. You can see the subject through their eyes.

Too many business messages have an "I" or "we" attitude, which causes the sender to sound selfish and not interested in the receiver. The message tells what the sender wants; the recipient is expected to go along with it. If you want to get your message across, you have to adopt the "you" attitude instead and talk in terms of your receiver's wishes, interests, hopes, and preferences. Talk about the other person, and you are talking about the thing that most interests him or her.

On the simplest level, you can adopt the "you" attitude by substituting terms that refer to your audience for terms that refer to yourself. In other words, use *you* and *yours* instead of *I, me,* and *mine* or *we, us,* and *ours*:

INSTEAD OF THIS	USE THIS
To help us process this order, we must ask for another copy of the requisition.	So that your order can be filled promptly, please send another copy of the requisition.
We are pleased to announce our new flight schedule from Atlanta to New York, which is any hour on the hour.	Now you can take a plane from Atlanta to New York any hour on the hour.
We offer the typewriter ribbons in three colors: black, blue, and green.	Take your pick of typewriter ribbons in three colors: black, blue, and green.

Using *you* and *yours* requires finesse. If you overdo it, you are likely to create some rather awkward sentences. You also run the risk of sounding like a high-pressure carnival barker at the county fair. The most effective approach is to balance references to yourself with references to your audience.

Avoid using *you* and *yours*
- To excess
- When assigning blame
- If your organization prefers a more formal style

On some occasions, too, you are justified in avoiding the use of "you." For instance, when you need to establish blame but want to do so impersonally to minimize the possibility of ill will, you might say "there is a problem" instead of "you caused a problem." Using "you" in a way that might sound dictatorial is also impolite:

INSTEAD OF THIS	USE THIS
You should never use that kind of paper in the copy machine.	That type of paper doesn't work very well in the copy machine.
You must correct all five copies before noon.	All five copies must be corrected by noon.
You need to make sure the staff follows instructions.	The staff may need guidance in following instructions.

Keep in mind the attitudes and policies of your organization as well. Some companies have a tradition of avoiding references to *you* and *I* in their memos and formal reports. If you work for a company that expects a formal, impersonal style, confine your use of personal pronouns to informal letters and memos.

In any case, the best way to implement the "you" attitude is to be sincere in thinking about the audience. The "you" attitude is not just a matter of using one pronoun as opposed to another; it is a matter of genuine

The word *you* does not always indicate a "you" attitude, and the "you" attitude can be displayed without using the word *you*.

empathy. You can use *you* 25 times in a single page and still ignore your audience's true concerns. In the final analysis, it's the thought that counts, not the pronoun. If you're talking to a retailer, try to think like a retailer; if you're dealing with a production supervisor, put yourself in his or her position; if you're writing to a dissatisfied customer, imagine how you would feel at the other end of the transaction. The important thing is your attitude toward the audience and your appreciation of that person's position.

One way of touching the right spots in your audience is to find a parallel situation in your own experience. Build your message around this experience, or use what you have learned as a basis for your thoughts.

Emphasize the positive

Explain what you can do and what you will do—not what you haven't done, can't do, or won't do.

Another way of showing sensitivity to your audience is to emphasize the positive side of your message. Focus on the silver lining, not the cloud. Stress what is or will be instead of what isn't or won't be. Most information, even bad news, has at least some redeeming feature. If you can make your audience aware of that feature, you will make your message more acceptable. For example:

INSTEAD OF THIS	USE THIS
It is impossible to repair this vacuum cleaner today.	We can repair your vacuum cleaner by Tuesday.
We apologize for inconveniencing you during our remodeling.	The renovations now under way will enable us to serve you better.
We never exchange damaged goods.	We are happy to exchange merchandise that is returned to us in good condition.

When you are offering criticism or advice, focus on what the person can do to improve.

In the same vein, when you are criticizing or correcting, don't hammer on the other person's mistakes. Avoid referring to failures, problems, or shortcomings. Focus instead on what the person can do to improve:

INSTEAD OF THIS	USE THIS
The problem with this department is a failure to control costs.	The performance of this department can be improved by tightening up cost controls.
You filled out the order form wrong. We can't send you the paint until you tell us what color you want.	Please check your color preferences on the enclosed card so we can process your order properly.
You broke the dish by running cold water on it right after you took it from the oven.	These dishes are sensitive to temperature shock and should be allowed to cool gradually after they are removed from the oven.

Show your audience how they will benefit from complying with your message.

If you're trying to persuade the audience to buy a product, pay a bill, or perform a service for you, emphasize what's in it for them. Don't focus on why *you* want them to do something. Instead of saying, "Please buy this book so I can make my sales quota," say, "The plot of this novel will keep you in suspense to the last page." Instead of saying, "We need your contribution to the Boys and Girls Club," say, "You can help a child make friends and build self-confidence through your donation to the Boys and Girls Club." An individual who sees the possibility for personal benefit is more likely to respond positively to your appeal.

Avoid words with negative connotations; use meaningful euphemisms instead.

In general, try to state your message without using words that might hurt or offend your audience. Substitute mild terms (euphemisms) for those that have unpleasant connotations. Instead of advertising "cheap" merchandise, announce your bargain prices. Don't talk about "pimples and zits"; refer more delicately to complexion problems. You can be honest without being harsh. Gentle terms won't change the facts, but they will make those facts more acceptable:

POSSIBLY OFFENSIVE	INOFFENSIVE
toilet paper	bathroom tissue
used cars	resale cars
sweaty armpits	underarm wetness
constipation	irregularity
high-calorie food	high-energy food

On the other hand, don't carry euphemisms to extremes. If you're too subtle, people won't know what you're talking about. "Derecruiting" someone to the "mobility pool" instead of telling them they have six weeks to find another job isn't really very helpful. There's a fine line between softening the blow and hiding the facts. In the final analysis, people respond better to an honest message, delivered with integrity, than they do to sugar-coated double-talk.

Establish credibility

It's to your advantage to communicate your credibility to the audience. Experiments show that an audience's faith in a communicator has a profound impact on their acceptance of the message. In one experiment, three groups of college students heard the same prerecorded talk recommending leniency toward juvenile delinquents. One group was told that the speaker was a judge, another that he was an anonymous member of the audience, and the third that he was a former juvenile offender out on bail on a drug charge. As you might guess, 73 percent of the audience agreed with the "judge," but only 29 percent of the audience agreed with the "offender."[5]

Don't make false promises.

Because the success of your message may depend on the audience's perception of you, their belief in your competence and integrity is important. You want people to believe that you know what you're doing and that your word is dependable. The first step in building credibility is to promise only what you can do and then to do what you promise. After that, you can enhance credibility through your writing style.

People are more likely to react positively to your message when they have confidence in you.

If you're communicating with someone you know well, your previous interactions influence your credibility. The other person knows from past experience whether you are trustworthy and capable. And if the person is familiar with your company, the firm's reputation may be ample proof of your credibility.

But what if you are complete strangers? Or worse, what if the other person starts off with doubts about you? First and foremost, show an understanding of the other person's situation by calling attention to the things you have in common. For example, if you're communicating with someone who shares your professional background, you might say, "As a fellow engineer (lawyer, doctor, teacher, or whatever), I'm sure you can appreciate this situation." Or you might use technical or professional terms that identify you as a peer.

You can also gain the audience's confidence by explaining your credentials, but you need to be careful that you don't sound pompous. Generally, one or two aspects of your background are all that you need to mention. Possibly your title or the name of your organization will be enough to impress the audience with your abilities. If not, perhaps you can mention the name of someone who carries some weight with your audience. For example, you might begin a letter with "Professor Goldberg suggested that I contact you." Or you could quote a recognized authority on a subject, even if you don't know the authority personally. The fact that your ideas are shared by a credible source adds prestige to your message.

To enhance your credibility

- Show that you understand the other person's situation
- Establish your own credentials or ally yourself with a credible source
- Back up your claims with evidence, not exaggerations
- Use words that express confidence
- Believe in yourself and your message

Your credibility is also enhanced by the quality of the information you provide. If you support your points with evidence that can be confirmed through observation, research, experimentation, or measurement, your audience will recognize that you have the facts, and they will respect you. But exaggerated claims do more harm than good. Here's an example from a mail-order catalog advertising rose bushes: "You'll be absolutely amazed at the remarkable blooms on this healthy plant. Gorgeous flowers with brilliant color and an intoxicating aroma will delight you week after week." Terms like *amazing*, *incredible*, *extraordinary*, *sensational*, and *revolutionary* exceed the limits of believability, unless they're backed up with some sort of factual proof.

You also risk losing credibility if you seem to be currying favor with insincere compliments. So support compliments with specific points:

INSTEAD OF THIS	USE THIS
My deepest heartfelt thanks for the excellent job you did. It's hard these days to find workers like you. You are just fantastic! I can't stress enough how happy you have made us with your outstanding performance.	Thanks for the fantastic job you did of filling in for Gladys at the convention with just an hour's notice. Despite the difficult circumstances, you managed to attract several new orders with your demonstration of the new line of coffeemakers. Your dedication and sales ability are truly appreciated.

Doesn't the more restrained praise seem more credible?

The other side of the credibility coin is too much modesty and not enough confidence. Many writing authorities suggest that you avoid such words as *if*, *hope*, and *trust*, which express a lack of confidence on your part:

INSTEAD OF THIS	USE THIS
We hope this recommendation will be helpful.	We're glad to make this recommendation.
If you'd like to order, mail us the reply card.	To order, mail the reply card.
We trust that you'll extend your service contract.	By extending your service contract, you can continue to enjoy topnotch performance from your equipment.

The ultimate key to being believable is to believe in yourself. If you are convinced that your message is sound, you can state your case with authority so that the audience has no doubts. When you have confidence in your own success, you automatically suggest that your audience will respond in the desired way. But if you lack faith in yourself, you're likely to communicate a "maybe this, maybe that" attitude that undermines your credibility.

Be polite

The best tone for business messages is almost always a polite one. When you are courteous to your audience, you show consideration for their needs and feelings. You express yourself with kindness and tact.

Although you may be tempted now and then to be brutally frank, try to express the facts in a kind and thoughtful manner.

Undoubtedly, you will be frustrated and exasperated by other people many times in your career. When those times occur, you will be tempted to say what you think, in blunt terms. To be sure, it's your job to convey the facts, precisely and accurately. But venting your emotions will rarely improve the situation and may jeopardize the goodwill of your audience. Instead, be gentle in expressing yourself:

INSTEAD OF THIS	USE THIS
I've seen a lot of dumb ideas in my time, but this takes the cake.	This is an interesting suggestion, but I'm not sure it's practical. Have you considered the following possible problems?
You really fouled things up with that last computer run.	Let me tell you what went wrong with that last computer run so we can make sure things run smoothly next time.
You've been sitting on my order for two weeks now. When can I expect delivery?	As I mentioned in my letter of October 12, we are eager to receive our order as soon as possible. Could you please let us know when to expect delivery.
I told you before you hired the guy that he wouldn't work out. You made your bed, now lie in it.	We all make mistakes about people from time to time, and maybe this was one of them. Why don't you give the new person a few more weeks to get adjusted?

Of course, some situations require more diplomacy than others. If you know your audience well, you can get away with being informal. However, correspondence with people who outrank you or with those outside your organization generally calls for an added measure of courtesy. And in general, written communication requires more tact than oral communication. When you're speaking, your words are softened by your tone of voice and facial expression. You can adjust your approach depending on the feedback you get. Written communication, on the other hand, is stark and self-contained. If you hurt a person's feelings in writing, you can't soothe them right away. In fact, you may not even know that you have hurt the other person, because the lack of feedback prevents you from seeing his or her reaction.

Use extra tact when writing and when communicating with higher-ups and outsiders.

In addition to avoiding things that give offense, try to find things that might bring pleasure. Remember a co-worker's birthday, send a special note of thanks to a supplier who has done a good job, acknowledge someone's help, send a clipping to a customer who has expressed interest in a subject. People remember the extra little things that indicate you care about them as individuals. In this impersonal age, the human touch is particularly effective.

Being courteous means taking the time to do a little extra for someone.

Another simple but effective courtesy is to be prompt in your correspondence. If possible, answer your mail within two or three days. Or if you need more time to prepare a reply, write a brief note or call to say that you're working on an answer. Most people are willing to wait if they know how long the wait will be. What annoys them is the suspense.

Promptness is a form of courtesy.

Project the company's image

Although establishing the right tone for your audience should be your main goal, you must also give some thought to projecting the right image for your company. When you communicate with outsiders, on even the most routine matter, you serve as the spokesperson for your organization. The impression that you make can enhance or damage the reputation of the entire company. Thus your own views and personality must be subordinated, at least to some extent, to the interests and style of the company.

Subordinate your own style to that of the company.

Let's say, for example, that you have just taken a job with a very conservative company based in Boston, a firm that manages trust funds for the wealthy offspring of old, established families. One of your first assignments is to answer a letter addressed to your supervisor (a partner in the firm). In your first draft, you try to write the way you would talk:

Dear Ms. Hopkins:

Thanks for the invitation to address the American Society of Securities Analysts. It's a great group, and I'm honored that you want me to talk to you.

The thing is, I really don't know much about the subject you have in mind. I handle convertible debentures, not municipal bonds. Given time, I could come up with something, but it would take a lot of effort--and frankly, I'm awfully busy right now.

How about calling me again when you need a convertible debentures specialist?

When your supervisor reads your draft, he is less than delighted. He complains that it just doesn't sound like something from The Firm. The style is too casual. So you try again:

Dear Ms. Hopkins:

The American Society of Securities Analysts is an organization of the highest caliber, and I am honored that you have asked me to address the group.

The topic you suggest--tax-free municipal bonds--is a complex and rapidly changing subject. I can see why your membership is concerned about being up-to-date on trends in this area.

However, my particular field is convertible debentures. Preparing a speech on municipal bonds that would give your group the depth of information they deserve would be a time-consuming endeavor for me.

Might I suggest that you contact Ms. Shirley Whitfield of Whitfield, Collingsworth & Hamilton. She recently wrote an article on municipal bonds for the Wall Street Observer that was far and away the most authoritative thing I have seen on the subject.

I will miss the opportunity to appear before your group. Please keep me in mind for another occasion.

This time your boss is pleased. He signs the letter and tells you that you have the makings of a valuable member of The Firm.

You can save yourself a great deal of time and frustration if you master the company style early in your career. In a typical corporation, 85 percent of the letters, memos, and reports are written by someone other than the higher-level managers who sign them. Most of the time, managers reject first drafts of these documents for stylistic reasons. In fact, the average draft goes through five revisions before it is finally approved.[6]

You might wonder whether all this effort to fine-tune the style of a message is worthwhile. But the fact is, people in business care very much about saying precisely the right thing in precisely the right way. Their willingness to go over the same document five times demonstrates just how important style really is.

SUMMARY

In a well-organized message, all the information is related to a clear subject and purpose, the ideas are presented in a logical order, and all necessary information is included. Good organization is important because it makes the message more effective and simplifies the communicator's job.

Organizing a message requires grouping ideas and deciding on the order of their presentation. Direct and indirect order are the two basic organizational approaches. With the direct approach, the main idea comes first; with the indirect approach, the main idea comes later. The indirect approach is best for people who are likely to react with skepticism or hostility to the message, but the direct approach is best in most other cases.

When you communicate, you establish a relationship with the audience. The success of the relationship depends on the tone, or overall impression, that you create. Try to be both businesslike and likable; try to look at the subject through the audience's eyes. Emphasize positive ideas. Convey your credibility, and be courteous. Also remember that you represent your organization and must adjust your style to reflect its standards.

COMMUNICATION CHALLENGES AT MERCY HOSPITAL

David Petree is currently working on a letter that will be sent to several major employers in his community. He hopes to persuade the companies to participate in an innovative plan that would allow their employees to use physicians associated with Mercy Hospital for all of their medical care. Instead of insuring their employees through such plans as Blue Cross, the companies would enroll their employees in Mercy's program and pay a fee directly to the hospital. The advantage of the idea from Mercy's standpoint is that it would encourage use of their hospital, which would help the administration manage its finances. As David points out, "The more patients we have, the easier it is to distribute our fixed costs and keep our charges in line."

Team Challenge: David needs help in deciding on a strategy for convincing companies to enroll in Mercy's plan. He has asked a group of you for ideas. Try to put yourself in the audience's position. What arguments could David use to persuade you to drop your regular insurance plan and sign up with Mercy instead? Using your common sense and imagination to flesh out the details, develop an outline for the letter. Decide on the main idea, the major supporting points, and the sequence of development.

Individual Challenge: David was pleased with the outline you and your colleagues prepared. Now he has asked you to draft the letter asking companies to enroll in Mercy's health-care plan. Sister M. Joanne, the hospital's executive director, will sign it. Working independently, put the letter into final form. Make up any facts you need to create a convincing message.

QUESTIONS FOR DISCUSSION

1. "There is a perfect way to organize every message." Do you agree or disagree? Why?
2. Some people feel that cushioning bad news is manipulative. What do you think?
3. Is it ever appropriate to write a message without outlining it first? If so, why? What might the circumstances be? If not, why not?
4. Do you agree that every message, regardless of its length, can be boiled down to a single main idea? Why or why not?
5. Why is it important to support major points with specific details?
6. What is the difference between the style and the tone of a business message?
7. "You are a good communicator when you know how to change your style to suit every audience." Do you agree or disagree?
8. What considerations determine the degree of familiarity to use in a business message?
9. How can one reconcile these conflicting instructions: "In all your correspondence, be yourself" and "In all your correspondence, keep the image of the company in mind"?
10. Where does a company's style originate?

DOCUMENTS FOR ANALYSIS

DOCUMENT 1

Revise the following outline for an insurance information brochure, putting the information in a more logical sequence with appropriate subordination of ideas and parallel phrasing.

ACCIDENT PROTECTION INSURANCE PLAN

I. Coverage is only pennies a day
II. Benefit is $100,000 for accidental death on common carrier
III. Benefit is $100 a day for hospitalization as result of motor vehicle or common carrier accident
IV. Benefit is $20,000 for accidental death in motor vehicle accident
V. Individual coverage is only $17.85 per quarter; family coverage is just $26.85 per quarter
VI. No physical exam or health questions
VII. Convenient payment--billed quarterly
VIII. Guaranteed acceptance for all applicants
IX. No individual rate increases
X. Free, no-obligation examination period
XI. Cash paid in addition to any other insurance carried
XII. Covers accidental death when riding as fare-paying passenger on public transportation, including buses, trains, jets, ships, trolleys, subways, or any other common carrier
XIII. Covers accidental death in motor vehicle accidents occurring while driving or riding in or on automobile, truck, camper, motorhome, or nonmotorized bicycle

DOCUMENT 2

Read the following letter, and then (1) analyze the strengths and/or weaknesses of each numbered sentence and (2) revise the letter so it follows this chapter's guidelines.

(1) I am a new publisher with some really great books to sell. (2) I saw your announcement in Publishers Weekly about the bookseller's show you're having this summer, and I think it's a great idea. (3) Count me in, folks! (4) I would like to get some space to show my books. (5) I thought it would be a neat thing if I could do some airbrushing on tee shirts live to help promote my hot new title, Tee Shirt Art. (6) Before I got into publishing, I was an airbrush artist and I could demonstrate my techniques. (7) I have done hundreds of advertising illustrations and been a sign painter all my life, too, so I will also be promoting my other book, hot off the presses, How to Make Money in the Sign Painting Business.

(8) I will be starting my PR campaign about May 1989 with ads in PW and some art trade papers, so my books should be well known by the time the show comes around in August. (9) In case you would like to use my appearance there as part of your publicity, I have enclosed a biography and photo of myself.

(10) P.S. Please let me know what it costs for booth space as soon as possible, so I can figure out if I can afford to attend. (11) Being a new publisher is mighty expensive!

EXERCISES

1. Suppose that, as he was preparing to recommend to the board of directors of Mercy Hospital the installation of a new heating system (called cogeneration), David Petree had the following information in his files:
   - History of the development of the cogeneration heating process
   - Scientific credentials of the developers of the process
   - Risks assumed in using this process
   - His plan for installing the equipment at Mercy Hospital
   - Stories about its successful use in comparable facilities
   - Specifications of the equipment that would be installed
   - Plans for disposing of the old heating equipment
   - Costs of installing and running the new equipment
   - Advantages and disadvantages of using the new process
   - Detailed ten-year cost projections
   - Estimates of the time needed to phase in the new heating system
   - Alternate systems that the board might wish to consider

   Help David by eliminating from the list topics that aren't essential; then arrange the other topics so his report will give the board a clear understanding of the heating system and a balanced, concise justification for using it.
2. Indicate whether the direct or indirect approach would be best in each of the following situations, and briefly explain your reasoning:
   a. A letter asking when next year's automobiles will be put on sale locally
   b. A letter from a recent college graduate requesting a letter of recommendation from a former instructor

c. A letter turning down a job applicant
d. An announcement that, because of high air-conditioning costs, the plant temperature will be held at 78 degrees during the summer months
e. An invitation to the annual company picnic
f. A request for a price adjustment to cover shipping damage to a desk
g. A final request to settle a delinquent debt
h. A letter to a restaurant owner from a regular customer, informing the owner of unusually bad service

3. If you were trying to persuade someone to take the following actions, how would you structure your argument?
   a. You want your boss to approve your plan for hiring two new people.
   b. You want professional photographers to purchase your cameras.
   c. You want amateur photographers to purchase your cameras.
   d. You want to be hired for a job.
   e. You want to be granted a business loan.
   f. You want to collect a small amount from a regular customer whose account is slightly past due.
   g. You want to collect a large amount from a customer whose account is seriously past due.
   h. You want a manufacturer to switch to your brand of chrome products.
4. Suppose that end-of-term frustrations have produced this letter to Professor Anne Brewer from a student who feels he should have received a B in his accounting class:

   I think that I was unfairly awarded a C in your accounting class this term, and I am asking you to change the grade to a B. It was a difficult term. I don't get any money from home, and I have to work mornings at the Pancake House (as a cook), so I had to rush to make your class, and those two times that I missed class were because they wouldn't let me off work because of special events at the Pancake House (unlike some other students who just take off when they choose). On the midterm examination I originally got a 75 percent, but you said in class that there were two different ways to answer the third question and that you would change the grades of students who used the "optimal cost" method and had been counted off 6 points for doing this. I don't think that you took this into account, because I got 80 percent on the final, which is clearly a B. Anyway, whatever you decide, I just want to tell you that I really enjoyed this class, and I thank you for making accounting so interesting.

   If this letter were recast into three or four clear sentences, the teacher might be more receptive to the student's argument. Rewrite the letter to show how you would improve it.
5. Substitute inoffensive phrases for the following:
   a. you claim that
   b. it is not our policy to
   c. you neglected to
   d. it is our definite policy
   e. in which you assert
   f. we are sorry you are dissatisfied
   g. you failed to enclose
   h. we request that you send us
   i. if we are at fault
   j. apparently you overlooked our terms
   k. we hereby deny your claim
   l. we have been very patient
   m. we are at a loss to understand
   n. you forgot
   o. we will be forced to
6. Rewrite the following letter to Mrs. Bruce Crandall (1597 Church Street, Grants Pass, Oregon 97526) so that it conveys a helpful, personal, and interested tone:

   We have your letter of recent date to our Ms. Dobson. Owing to the fact that you neglected to include the size of the dress you ordered, please be advised that no shipment of your order was made, but the aforementioned shipment will occur at such time as we are in receipt of the aforementioned information.
7. Rewrite these sentences to reflect the reader's viewpoint:
   a. We request that you use the order form supplied in the back of our catalog.
   b. We insist that you always bring your credit card to the store.
   c. We want to get rid of all our typewriters, last year's models, in order to make room in our warehouse for new models. Thus we are offering a 25 percent discount on all sales this week.
   d. I am applying for the position of bookkeeper in your office. I feel that my grades prove that I am bright and capable, and I think I can do a good job for you.
   e. As requested, we are sending the refund for $25.
   f. *Personal Money Management* is read weekly by millions of people who get useful information from it. We include tips on how to make money in real estate, banking, and other fields.
8. Revise these sentences so they're positive rather than negative:

a. Unfortunately, your order cannot be sent until next week.
b. To avoid the loss of your credit rating, please remit payment within ten days.
c. We don't make refunds on returned merchandise that is soiled.
d. Because we are temporarily out of Baby Cry dolls, we won't be able to ship your order for ten days.
e. You failed to specify the color of the blouse that you ordered.
f. You should have realized that waterbeds will freeze in unheated houses during winter months. Therefore, our guarantee does not cover the valve damage and you must pay the $9.50 valve-replacement fee (plus postage).

9. Provide euphemisms for the following words and phrases:
   a. stubborn
   b. wrong
   c. stupid
   d. strike (labor)
   e. incompetent
   f. small gift
   g. loudmouth
   h. unchanging
   i. retail store losses (due to theft)
10. Rewrite the following sentences to show confidence and conviction:
    a. It is our sincere hope that we will hear from you again.
    b. We feel that you will enjoy owning the Odd-Ark toy chest.
    c. Perhaps you'll like it well enough to recommend it to your friends.

CHAPTER FIVE

REVISING BUSINESS MESSAGES

After studying this chapter, you will be able to

- Edit a message for content and organization, style and readability, and mechanics and format
- Identify functional words and content words, and explain their qualities
- Choose the most correct and most effective words to make your point
- Use the three different types of sentences to clarify the relationships among ideas and to make your writing interesting
- Use techniques of style for writing more effective sentences
- Describe the elements of a paragraph
- Develop paragraphs in a variety of ways

Marcus Smith

COMMUNICATION CLOSE-UP AT BEAR CREEK

"Dear Fruit-of-the-Month Club Member: The recent heavy rains in Southern California have delayed the harvest of the Royal Oranges that were listed as your February selection. . . ." Two things stand out about this passage from a note once sent to Harry & David customers. First, the language is simple and direct. Second, the note is signed by David, who's been dead for almost twenty years.

The guardian of both the writing style and David's signature is Marcus Smith, copy administrator in promotional services at Bear Creek Corporation of Medford, Oregon. Bear Creek is the parent organization for several mail-order companies, including Harry & David and rose growers Jackson & Perkins. Marcus's job is to write original copy in David's voice for Harry & David catalogs, sales letters, order blanks, enclosures that tell gift recipients what they're getting, and explanatory notes like the one about the Royal Oranges. Besides carefully revising everything that he writes himself, he edits the writing of other copywriters and proofreads copy.

Fifty years ago, the real Harry and David Rosenburg ran an ad in *Fortune* with an approach unusual for the times and for a publication directed to the affluent. "Out here on the ranch we don't pretend to know much about advertising," it began. Today, Marcus still aims to create a special tone in the copy he writes for Harry & David—a conversational,

Careful selection and artful arrangement are the secrets of Harry & David fruit sales and of Bear Creek Corporation's messages to customers.

down-to-earth, "just folks" tone, although admittedly less cornball than once was the case. "There's a built-in style here," he notes. "Most of the catalogs and other customer messages I write are ostensibly written by David. I try to keep in mind what David would say and what he wouldn't."

Marcus doesn't have a formula in his head to guide him in his work. "My style varies to fit the need," he says, "although all my sentences are fairly direct. In a business like ours, the written message is often the only kind of contact we have with a customer. If our mailing doesn't draw in the reader immediately, it just becomes junk mail. We need to be as clear as we can, to say exactly what we mean. People need to be able to read the copy and understand it."

Not all business messages are advertising copy, but all business communicators need to understand the impact of words. "My vocabulary includes more positive words than negative words," Marcus says. "And I have to be sensitive to connotations, to the nuances of words."

Bear Creek is equally careful about the spoken messages that customers receive. "Our customer service department is one of the best in the business," according to Marcus. "When customers call, they want to hear a personal, personable concern. Before our customer service representatives can talk to a single customer, they go through at least 40 hours of training."

As part of a sizable organization, Marcus sees a lot of written messages from co-workers. "None of the memos I get are completely incomprehensible, although some are the butt of jokes. The main abuse I see is the use of overblown language." Awkward phrasing may also leave a message less than crystal clear: "One time, somebody in another department fiddled with some copy so it ended up reading, 'We have over 50 years' experience in shipping behind us.' That sentence makes it seem like the shipping's been going on behind our backs all these years."

Marcus is a professional communicator, but he believes language skill is important no matter what your job. "If I come to a misspelled word in a letter of application," he says, "I stop. An audience that has any appreciation at all for good language skills will think better of you if you know how to use language correctly."

FIGURE 5.1
Sample Revised Letter

November 12, 1989

Miss Louise Wilson

Corporate Travel Department

Brother's Electric Corp.

2300 Wacker Drive

Chicago, IL 60670

Dear Miss Wilson:

Thank you for your interest in ~~I enjoyed our recent conversation regarding~~ the *frequent-guest* ~~FG~~ program *at the Commerce Hotel. We are* ~~and am~~ delighted to hear that the people at Brother's Electric are thinking about joining. ~~Incidentally, we are planning a special Thanksgiving weekend rate, so keep that in mind in case you happen to be in Chicago for the Holiday.~~

The ~~I have~~ enclosed ~~a~~ brochure ~~that~~ explains the details of the *frequent-guest* ~~FG~~ program. *As a corporate member, Brother's Electric will be entitled to a 20 percent discount on all rooms and services.* ~~Your FG ID card is enclosed.~~ Use *the enclosed ID card* ~~it~~ whenever you make reservations with us to obtain your corporate discount. ~~We will see to it that~~ your executives *will receive* ~~are treated with~~ special courtesy, *including free* ~~and that they get to~~ use *of* the health club ~~free~~.

Organizations enrolled in the frequent-guest program also qualify for discounts on ~~We also have excellent~~ convention facilities and banquet rooms ~~should you want to book a convention or meeting here~~. We hope you and your company will take advantage of these *facilities the next time you book a convention.* ~~outstanding, world-class amenities~~. If you have any questions, please feel free to call me personally. I will be happy to answer them.

Sincerely,

Mary Cortez

Account Representative

Content and organization: Stick to the point, the main idea, in the first paragraph. In the middle, highlight the key advantage of the frequent-guest program and discuss details in subsequent paragraphs. Eliminate redundancies.

Style and readability: Reword to stress the "you" viewpoint. Clarify the relationships among ideas through placement and combination of phrases. Moderate the excessive enthusiasm, and eliminate words (like "amenities") that may be unfamiliar.

Mechanics and format: To prevent confusion, spell out the abbreviated phrase, "FG." Fix typos, as in "advantage."

PRACTICING THE CRAFT OF REVISION

Once you have completed the first draft of your message, you may be tempted to breathe a sigh of relief and get on with the next project. Resist the temptation. As professional communicators like Marcus Smith are aware, the first draft is rarely good enough. You owe it to yourself and to your audience to review and refine your messages.

In fact, many writing authorities suggest that you plan to go over a document at least three times: once for content and organization, once for style and readability, and once for mechanics and format. The letter in Figure 5.1 has indeed been thoroughly revised, using the proofreading marks shown in Appendix II.

SHARPEN YOUR SKILLS

Fifteen Secrets of Successful Business Writers

One of life's little-noted joys is the production of an effective piece of writing. But such a joy is not easily attained; your audience, your employer, and your own standards all make demands. The best way to be sure you've met everyone's needs is to write more than one draft. Revision is a skill that the most successful business writers learn early, and here's how it's done:

- *Type your first draft in a double-spaced format.* (Skip every other line if you're writing in longhand.) You want plenty of room to insert corrections.
- *If possible, compose and revise on a word processor* so you can easily make corrections and can take advantage of software that checks style and spelling.
- *Set aside the draft for a while* before you tackle the final revision. You'll be able to evaluate it more objectively.
- *Make a photocopy or printout of the original,* and mark your changes on the copy. That way, if you decide you don't like the changes you've made, you won't have to redo the original.
- *Pretend you are reading someone else's work.* It is easier to detect faults in other people's work than in our own.
- *Mark corrections with the standard proofreading symbols,* which are shown in Appendix II. Standardized markings make it easier for a typist to understand the changes you want.
- *For lengthy inserts, use a separate page* labeled with the number of the page the insert is supposed to merge with and a letter identifying it as a separate page (for example, Insert 13A, 13B, and so on). On the original page, use the circled word *Insert* to show where it goes. Put the insert page directly behind the original page.
- *Check the document for completeness.* Omitting a key point may defeat your case. Insert any miss-

Although most people separate revision from composition, editing is an ongoing activity that occurs throughout the creative process. You edit and revise as you go along, then edit and revise again after you have completed the first draft. Your mind constantly searches for the best way to say something, probing for the right words, testing alternative sentences, and arranging paragraphs in various patterns.

The basic editing principles discussed here apply to both written and oral communication. However, the steps involved in revising a speech or oral presentation are slightly different, as Chapter 18 explains.

EDIT FOR CONTENT AND ORGANIZATION

After a day or two, review your message for content and organization.

Ideally, you should let your draft age a day or two before you begin the editing process, so you can approach the material with a fresh eye. As you get under way, read through the document quickly to evaluate its overall effectiveness. At this point, you are mainly concerned with content, organization, and flow. Compare the draft to your original plan. Have you covered all points in the most logical order? Is there a good balance between the general and the specific? Do the most important ideas receive the most space, and are they placed in the most prominent positions? Have you provided enough support and double-checked the facts? Would the message be more convincing if it were arranged in another sequence? Do you need to add anything?

On the other hand, what can you eliminate? In business, it's particularly important to weed out unnecessary material. Three-fourths of the executives

ing facts or details, rewriting your draft as needed to accommodate them. You may also think of new information you want to add. If it will help to satisfy both your audience's needs and the purpose of the message, add it. If not, omit it.

- *Check your facts and figures for accuracy.* Building a whole case on an incorrect fact or figure is embarrassing, if not fatal. Be careful not to treat an assumption as a fact.
- *Check your organization.* The work should have a beginning, a middle, and an end.
- *Check the document for unity and continuity.* Unity means that only one idea is developed in each paragraph. Continuity means that each sentence, and paragraph, grows logically out of the preceding one and flows smoothly into the following one.
- *Check your style.* Be on the lookout for lengthy, obscure sentences, wordiness, and pretentiousness. Eliminate needless words or phrases. Read your work aloud: If any parts of it sound dull or boring, revitalize them by substituting active verbs and concrete nouns. Put the ideas you want to emphasize at the beginning or end of a sentence, where they'll stand out.
- *Check the length.* A work is too long if it tells readers more than they want to know and too short if it fails to draw key conclusions. Be sure you have given your audience the information they'll need to see your point and accept it. But don't overdo it.
- *Check the format.* Make sure it is the correct one for the type of document you've written.
- *Check for errors in word usage, grammar, spelling, and punctuation.* Look up the spelling of any words you habitually misspell. Because spotting your own errors is difficult, you may want another person to read your draft.

By heeding these simple points, you can achieve a final draft you'll be proud of.

1. How important is revision? Many busy businesspeople feel that revising and rewriting are a waste of time, that the first draft is good enough. They believe that the audience will overlook small errors and certainly understand what was meant. The important thing is getting the message out. Discuss the pros and cons of this argument.

2. Find a paper you wrote for a class sometime in the past. Check it over. What sorts of errors did you miss when you originally produced the paper? What might you have done at the time to avoid submitting a paper with these sorts of mistakes?

who participated in one survey complained that most written messages are too long.[1] They are most likely to read documents that efficiently say what needs to be said.

In the first phase of editing, spend a few extra moments on the beginning and ending of the message. These are the sections that have the greatest impact on the audience. Be sure that the opening of a letter or memo is relevant, interesting, and geared to the reader's probable reaction. In longer messages, check to see that the first few paragraphs establish the subject, purpose, and organization of the material. Review the conclusion to be sure that it summarizes the main idea and leaves the audience with a positive impression.

EDIT FOR STYLE AND READABILITY

Once you are satisfied with the content and structure of the message, turn your attention to its style and readability. Ask yourself whether you have achieved the right tone for your audience. Look for opportunities to make the material more interesting through the use of lively words and phrases.

At the same time, be particularly conscious of whether your message is clear and readable. You want the audience to understand you with a minimum of effort. Check your vocabulary and sentence structure to be sure you are relying mainly on familiar terms and simple, direct statements. You might even want to apply a readability formula to gauge the difficulty of your writing.

The most common readability formulas measure the length of words and sentences to give you a rough idea of how well educated your audience

FIGURE 5.2
The Fog Index

I called Global Corporation to ask when we will receive copies of their insurance policies and engineering reports. Cindy Turner of Global said that they are putting the documents together and will send them by Express Mail next week. She told me that they are late because most of the information is in the hands of Global's attorneys in Boston. I asked why it was in Boston; we had understood that the account is serviced by their carrier's Dallas branch. Turner explained that the account originally was sold to Global's Boston division, so all paperwork stays there. She promised to telephone us when the package is ready to ship.

1. Select writing sample that is 100 to 125 words long. Count number of words in each sentence. Treat independent clauses (stand-alone word groups containing subject and predicate) as separate sentences. For example, "In school we studied; we learned; we improved" counts as three sentences. Count dates and other number combinations as single words. Then add all word counts for each sentence to get total word count, and divide by number of sentences to get average sentence length.	1. *Average sentence length*: 18 + 21 + 21 + 7 + 13 + 17 + 12 = 109 words ÷ 7 sentences = 16
2. Count number of long words—that is, all words that have three or more syllables (underlined in sample). Omit proper nouns; combinations of short words, such as *butterfly* and *anyway*; and verbs that gain third syllable by adding *es* or *ed*, as in *trespasses* and *created*. Divide number of long words by total number of words in sample to get percentage of long words in sample.	2. *Percentage of long words*: 11 long words ÷ 109 words total = 10
3. Add numbers for average sentence length and percentage of long words. Multiply sum by 0.4; drop number following decimal point. Result is number of years' schooling required to read sample passage easily.	3. *Fog Index*: 16 words per average sentence + 10 percent long words = 26 × 0.4 = 10.4 = 10

must be to understand your message. Figure 5.2 shows how one readability formula, the Fog Index, has been applied to a passage from a memo. (The "long words" in the passage have been underlined.) As the calculation shows, anyone who reads at a 10th-grade level should be able to read the passage with ease. For technical documents, you can aim for an audience that reads at a 12th- to 14th-grade level; for general business messages, your writing should be geared to those who read at the 8th- to 11th-grade level. The Fog Index of such popular business publications as the *Wall Street Journal* and *Forbes* magazine, for example, is about 10 to 11.

Readability depends on word choice, sentence length, sentence structure, organization, and the message's physical appearance.

Readability formulas are easy to apply, but they ignore some important variables that contribute to reading ease, such as sentence structure, the organization of ideas, and the appearance of the message on the page.[2] To fully evaluate the readability of your message, ask yourself whether you have effectively highlighted the important information. Are your sentences easy to decipher? Do your paragraphs have clear topic sentences? Are the transitions between ideas obvious?

In addition, give some thought to the visual presentation of the message. People have trouble comprehending long, uninterrupted pages of text. By

SHARPEN YOUR SKILLS

How to Proofread Effectively

You've carefully revised and polished your document, and it's been sent off to the typist or word-processing department to be put into final form. You can breathe a sigh of relief, but only for the moment: You'll still need to proofread what comes out of the typewriter or printer. You should always proofread the final version of any document that goes out with your name on it to ensure that it is error-free.

Here are some hints to help make your proofreading more effective:

- Go through the document several times, each time focusing on a different aspect. The first pass might be to look for omissions and errors in content; the second scan could be for layout, spacing, and other aesthetic features; a final pass might be to check for typographical, grammatical, and spelling errors.
- In normal reading, our perceptual processes have been trained to ignore transposed letters, improper capitalization, misplaced punctuation, and the like. To short-circuit these normally helpful processes, you need to try some tricky techniques. Professional proofreaders recommend reading each page from the bottom to the top, starting at the last word in each line; placing your finger under each word and reading it silently; making a slit in a sheet of paper that will reveal only one line of type at a time; and reading the document aloud, pronouncing each word carefully.
- Have a friend or colleague proofread the document for you. Others are likely to catch mistakes that you continually fail to notice. (All of us have blind spots when it comes to reviewing our own work.)
- Look for the most common typographical errors ("typos"): transposed letters (such as *teh*), substitution errors (such as *ecomonic*), and errors of omission (such as *productvity*).
- Look for errors in spelling, grammar, punctuation, and capitalization. If you aren't sure about something, look it up in a dictionary, usage book, or other reference work.
- Double-check the spelling of names and the accuracy of dates, addresses, and all figures (quantities ordered, prices, and so on). It would not do to order 500 staplers when you really want only 50.
- If you have time, set the document aside and proofread it the next day.
- Avoid reading large amounts of material in one sitting, and try not to proofread when you are tired.
- Concentrate on what you're doing. Try to block out distractions, and focus as completely as possible on your proofreading task.
- Take your time. Quick proofreading is not careful proofreading.

Proofreading may require patience, but it adds a measure of credibility to your document.

1. What qualities does a person need to be a good proofreader? Are such qualities inborn, or can they be learned?

2. Proofread the following sentence:

aplication of thse methods in stores in San Deigo nd Cinncinati have resultted in a 30% drop in roberies an a 50 precent decling in violnce there, acording ot thedevelpers if the securty sytem, Hanover brothrs, Inc..

using headlines, indented lists, boldface type, and white space, you can provide visual clues to the importance of various ideas and their relationships. These clues will help the reader grasp the message more easily, particularly if it exceeds a page or two.

EDIT FOR MECHANICS AND FORMAT

Credibility is affected by your attention to the details of mechanics and format.

The final step is to edit the document so it is letter perfect. Although things like grammar, spelling, punctuation, and typographical errors may seem trivial to you, your readers will view your attention to detail as a sign of your professionalism. If you let mechanical errors slip through, people automatically wonder whether you're unreliable in more important ways. Marcus Smith of Bear Creek, for example, rejects application letters containing misspelled words. You might want to refresh your memory of the details of grammar and usage by reviewing Component Chapter C.

Give some attention, too, to the finer points of format. Have you followed accepted conventions and company guidelines for laying out the document on the page? Have you included all the traditional elements that belong in documents of the type you are creating? Have you been consistent in handling margins, page numbers, headings, exhibits, source notes, and other details? To resolve questions about format and layout, see Component Chapter D.

SELECTING THE RIGHT WORDS[3]

The two key aspects of word choice are

- Correctness
- Effectiveness

As a business communicator, you have two things to worry about in choosing and revising your words: correctness and effectiveness. Correctness is generally the easier of the two qualities to achieve, particularly if you have heard "good" English all your life. Without even thinking about grammar and usage, you will generally know what's correct; the words will sound "right" to you. But sometimes you may stumble over an unusual situation. Editors and grammarians themselves occasionally have questions—and even disputes—about correct usage. The "rules" of grammar are constantly changing to reflect changes in the way people speak. For example, many experts now prefer to treat *data* as a singular noun when it refers to a body of information, even though technically speaking it is the plural form of *datum*. You be the judge: Which of the following sentences sounds better to you?

The data on our market share is very consistent from region to region.

The data on our market share are very consistent from region to region.

Although debating the finer points of usage may seem like nitpicking, using words correctly is important. A writer or speaker who makes grammatical errors loses credibility with the audience. Poor grammar is a mark of ignorance, and—rightly or wrongly—nobody puts much faith in an ignorant source. Even if an audience is broad-minded enough to withhold judgment of the speaker, a grammatical error is distracting, like a mosquito buzzing around one's ears.

If in doubt, check it out.

So if you have doubts about what is correct, don't be lazy. Look up the answer and use the proper form of expression. And if you suspect that your ear for correct usage is not particularly good, check the grammar and usage guide in this book or any number of special reference books available in libraries and bookstores. Most authorities agree on the basic conventions.

Effectiveness depends on writing style.

Just as important as using the correct words is choosing the best words for the job at hand. Word effectiveness is generally more difficult to achieve than correctness, particularly in written communication. Professional writers like Marcus Smith have to work at their craft, using what you might call tricks of the trade to improve their writing style. In the rest of this chapter, you will learn some of these techniques.

FUNCTIONAL WORDS AND CONTENT WORDS

Words can be divided into two categories: functional words and content words. Functional words express relationships and have only one unchanging meaning in any given context. They include conjunctions, prepositions, articles, and pronouns. Your main concern with functional words is to use them correctly.

Functional words (conjunctions, prepositions, articles, and pronouns) express relationships among content words (nouns, verbs, adjectives, and adverbs).

Content words, on the other hand, are multidimensional and therefore subject to various interpretations. Nouns, verbs, adjectives, and adverbs are in this category. These are the words that carry the meaning of the sentence. They are the building blocks; the functional words are the mortar. In the following sentence, all the content words are in italics:

Some objective observers of the *cookie market give Nabisco* the *edge* in *quality*, but *Frito-Lay is lauded* for *superior distribution*.

Both functional words and content words are necessary, but your effectiveness as a communicator depends largely on your ability to choose the right content words for your message. So let's take a closer look at two important dimensions for classifying content words.

Connotation and denotation

Content words have both a denotative (dictionary) meaning and a connotative (associative) meaning.

As you know from reading Chapter 2, content words have both a denotative and a connotative meaning. The denotative meaning is the literal, or dictionary, meaning; the connotative meaning includes all the associations and feelings evoked by the word. Take *dirt,* for example, a word that has many different connotations. A disapproving mother remarks, "Just look at you; you're covered in dirt." An investigative reporter tells the editor, "I've uncovered some interesting dirt on that politician." But an Iowa farmer says, "My land is good; you've never seen darker dirt." The word is the same, but the connotations are different.

Some words have more connotations than others. If you say that a person has failed to pass the test, you're making a strong statement; you suggest that she or he is inferior, incompetent, second-rate. But if you say that the person has achieved a score of 65 percent, you suggest something else. By replacing the word *failed,* you avoid a heavy load of negative connotations.

In business communication you should generally use terms that are low in connotative meaning. Words that have relatively few possible interpretations are less likely to be misunderstood. Furthermore, because you are generally trying to deal with things in an objective, rational manner, you should avoid emotion-laden comments.

Abstraction and concreteness

The more abstract a word, the more it is removed from the tangible, objective world of things that can be perceived with the senses.

In addition to varying in connotative impact, content words also vary in their level of abstraction. An abstract word expresses a concept, quality, or characteristic instead of standing for a thing you can touch or see. Abstractions are usually broad, encompassing a category of ideas. They are often intellectual, academic, or philosophical. For example, *love*, *honor*, *progress*, *tradition*, and *beauty* are abstractions.

Concrete terms, on the other hand, are anchored in the tangible, material world. They stand for something particular: *chair*, *table*, *horse*, *rose*, *kick, kiss, red, green, two*. These words are direct and vivid, clear and exact.

You might suppose that concrete words are better than abstract words, because they are more precise. But try to rewrite this sentence without using the italicized abstract words:

> We hold these *truths* to be *self-evident*, that all men are *created equal*, that they are *endowed* by their *Creator* with certain *unalienable Rights*, that among these are *Life*, *Liberty*, and the *Pursuit* of *Happiness*. . . .

As you can see from this extract, the opening words of the Declaration of Independence, we need abstractions. They permit us to rise above the common and tangible. Can you imagine trying to talk about business without referring to such concepts as *morale*, *productivity*, *profits*, *motivation*, and *guarantees*?

In business communication, use concrete, specific terms whenever possible; use abstractions only when necessary.

Although they are indispensable, abstractions are also troublesome. They tend to be fuzzy, subject to many interpretations. And they also tend to be boring. It isn't always easy to become excited about ideas, especially if they are unrelated to concrete experience. The best way to minimize the problem is to blend abstract terms with concrete ones, the general with the specific. State the concept, then pin it down with details expressed in more concrete terms. Save the abstractions for ideas that cannot be expressed any other way.

As an experiment, you might take a sample of your writing and circle all the nouns. How many of them point to a specific person, place, or object? The ones that do are concrete and specific. Look at the vague nouns; can you replace them with more vivid terms? Now underline all the adjectives. How many of them describe the exact color, size, texture, quantity, or quality of something? Bear in mind that such words as *small*, *numerous*, *sizable*, *near*, *soon*, *good*, and *fine* are imprecise. You should usually try to replace them with more accurate terms. For example, instead of referring to "a sizable loss," talk about "a loss of $32 million."

WORD CHOICE

With an understanding of the two main types of words, you are ready to learn about wordsmithing. Wordsmiths are journalists, public relations specialists, editors, letter and report writers—anyone who earns a living by crafting words. Unlike poets, novelists, or dramatists, wordsmiths do not try for creative effects. They are mainly concerned with being clear, concise, and accurate in their use of language. To reach this goal, they emphasize words that are strong, familiar, and short, and they avoid hiding them under unnecessary extra syllables. When you edit your message, try to think like a wordsmith.

Strong words

Verbs and nouns are more concrete than adverbs and adjectives.

Nouns and verbs are the most concrete words in any message, so use them as much as you can. Although adjectives and adverbs obviously have parts to play, use them sparingly. They often call for subjective judgments, and business communication should be objective.

Verbs are especially powerful, because they carry the action; they tell what's happening in the sentence. The more dynamic and specific the verb, the better. Instead of settling for *is* or *are*, look for something more meaningful and descriptive, like *remains* or *exemplifies*.

Given a choice of words, choose the one that most clearly and specifically expresses your thought:

AVOID WEAK PHRASES	USE STRONG TERMS
wealthy businessperson	tycoon
business prosperity	boom
fall	plummet

Familiar words

You will communicate best with words that are familiar to your readers. But bear in mind that words familiar to one reader could be unfamiliar to another:

AVOID UNFAMILIAR WORDS	USE FAMILIAR WORDS
ascertain	find out, learn
consummate	close, bring about
peruse	read, study
circumvent	avoid
increment	growth, increase
unequivocal	certain

Although familiar words are generally the best choice, beware of terms so common that they have become virtually meaningless. Readers tend to slide right by such clichés as these to whatever is coming next:

Familiar words are preferable to unfamiliar ones, but try to avoid overworked terms (clichés).

interface	time frame	strategic decisions
track record	frame of reference	dialogue
viable	prioritize	scenario

Technical or professional terms should also be handled with care. Used in moderation, they add precision and authority to a message. But many people simply do not understand them, and even a technically sophisticated audience will be lulled to sleep by too many. Let your audience's vocabulary be your guide. If they share a particular jargon, you may enhance your credibility by speaking their language. For example, in addressing a group of engineers, you might want to use wording like this:

> The passive solar illumination assembly (PSIA) is a vertically installed, moisture-resistant photon-transmission aperture for sub-exospheric microclimate monitoring, with polished planar transparent amorphous-fused silicate surfaces and manually adjustable gaseous infiltration/exfiltration capability.[4]

On the other hand, if you're addressing an ordinary audience, you might have better luck referring to a *window*.

Short words

Make an effort to use short words. Because they're more vivid and easier to read, they tend to communicate better than long words.

Short words are generally more vivid than long ones and improve the readability of a document.

AVOID LONG WORDS	USE SHORT WORDS
During the preceding year, the company was able to accelerate productive operations.	Last year the company was able to speed up operations.
The action was predicated on the assumption that the company was operating at a financial deficit.	The action was based on the belief that the company was losing money.

Camouflaged verbs

Turning verbs into nouns or adjectives weakens your writing style.

Watch for these endings in the words you use: *ion, tion, ing, ment, ant, ent, ence, ance,* and *ency.* Most of them change verbs into nouns and adjectives. In effect, the words that result are camouflaged verbs. Get rid of them and strengthen your writing:

AVOID CAMOUFLAGED VERBS	USE VERBS
The manager undertook implementation of the rules.	The manager implemented the rules.
Verification of the shipments occurs weekly.	Shipments are verified weekly.

BIAS-FREE WRITING

Avoid biased language that might offend the audience.

Most of us like to think of ourselves as being sensitive, unbiased, and fair. But being fair and objective isn't enough; you must also *appear* to be fair.[5] The following suggestions will help you avoid embarrassing blunders with language related to gender, race, ethnic group, age, and disability.

Sexist language

For many years, the word *man* was used to denote humanity, describing a human being of either gender and any age. Today, however, *man* is associated more with an adult, male human being. The fact that some of the most commonly used words contain the word *man* creates a problem, but some simple solutions exist:

UNACCEPTABLE	PREFERABLE
mankind	humanity, human beings, human race, people
if a man drove 50 miles at 60 miles per hour	if a person (or someone or a driver) drove 50 miles at 60 miles per hour
man-made	artificial, synthetic, manufactured, constructed, of human origin
manpower	human power, human energy, workers, work force

Here are some simple ways to replace occupational terms that contain the word *man* with words that can represent people of either gender:

UNACCEPTABLE	PREFERABLE
businessman	business executive, business manager, businessperson
salesman	sales representative, salesperson, salesclerk

insurance man	insurance agent
foreman	supervisor

Replace words that inaccurately exclude women or men.

Avoid using female-gender words like *authoress* and *actress; author* and *actor* denote both women and men. Similarly, avoid special designations, such as *woman doctor* or *male nurse*. Use the same label for everyone in a particular group. For example, don't refer to a woman as a *chairperson*, then call the man a *chairman*.

The pronoun *he* has also traditionally been used to refer to both males and females. Here are some simple ways to avoid this outdated usage:

UNACCEPTABLE	PREFERABLE
The average worker . . . he	The average worker . . . he or she
The typical professional athlete spends four hours a day practicing his sport.	Most professional athletes spend four hours a day practicing their sports.

Certain roles should not always be identified with a specific gender:

UNACCEPTABLE	PREFERABLE
the consumer . . . she	consumers . . . they
the nurse/teacher . . . she	nurses/teachers . . . they

If you are discussing categories of people, such as bosses and office workers, avoid referring to the boss as *he* and the office worker as *she*. Instead, reword sentences so you can use *they*, or reword them so you don't have to use any pronoun. In today's business world, it's also appropriate sometimes to use *she* when referring to a boss and *he* when referring to an office worker.

Another way to avoid bias is to make sure you don't always mention men first. Vary the traditional pattern with *women and men, gentlemen and ladies, she and he, her and his.*

Finally, identify women by their own names, not by their role or marital status—unless it is appropriate to the context:

UNACCEPTABLE	PREFERABLE
Phil Donahue and Marlo	Phil Donahue and Marlo Thomas
Phil Donahue and Ms. Thomas	Mr. Donahue and Ms. Thomas

The preferred title for women in business is Ms., unless the individual asks to be addressed as Miss or Mrs. or has some other title, such as Dr.

Racial and ethnic bias

Eliminate references that reinforce racial or ethnic stereotypes.

The guidelines for avoiding racial and ethnic bias are much the same as those for avoiding gender bias. The main rule is to avoid language suggesting that members of a racial or ethnic group have the same stereotypical characteristics:

UNACCEPTABLE	PREFERABLE
disadvantaged black children	children from lower-income families
Jim Wong is an unusually tall Asian.	Jim Wong is tall.

The best solution is to avoid identifying people by race or ethnic origin unless such a label is relevant:

UNACCEPTABLE	PREFERABLE
Mario M. Cuomo, Italian-American governor of New York	Mario M. Cuomo, governor of New York

Age bias

As with gender, race, and ethnic background, mention the age of a person only when it is relevant:

UNACCEPTABLE	PREFERABLE
Mary Kirazy, 58, has just joined our trust department.	Mary Kirazy has just joined our trust department.

Avoid references to an individual's age or physical limitations.

In referring to older people, avoid such stereotyped adjectives as *spry* and *frail.*

Disability bias

There is really no painless label for people with a physical, mental, sensory, or emotional impairment. However, if you must refer to such individuals in terms of their limitations, call them *disabled* as opposed to *handicapped, crippled,* or *retarded.*

UNACCEPTABLE	PREFERABLE
Crippled workers face many barriers on the job.	Disabled workers face many barriers on the job.

Most of all, avoid mentioning disability unless it is pertinent. When it is pertinent, present the whole person, not just the disability, by showing the limitation in an unobtrusive manner:

UNACCEPTABLE	PREFERABLE
An epileptic, Tracy has no trouble doing her job.	Tracy's epilepsy has no effect on her job performance.

The goal is to abandon stereotyped assumptions about what a person can do or will do and to focus on an individual's unique characteristics.

CREATING EFFECTIVE SENTENCES

Every sentence contains a subject (noun or noun equivalent) and a predicate (verb and related word).

Although looking at individual words is important, you cannot revise your work effectively until you consider each word in relation to a particular sentence. What can you do to improve *Jill, receptionist, the, smiles,* and *at*? These words don't make much sense until they are combined in a sentence to express a complete thought: "Jill smiles at the receptionist." Then you can begin to explore the possibilities for improvement, looking at how well each word performs its particular function. The nouns and noun equivalents are the topics, or subjects, about which something is being said; the verbs and related words, or predicates, make a statement about the subjects. In a more complicated sentence, adjectives and adverbs modify the statement, and various connectors hold the words together.

THE THREE TYPES OF SENTENCES

Sentences come in three basic varieties: simple, compound, and complex. A simple sentence has a single subject and a single predicate, although it may be expanded by nouns and pronouns serving as objects of the action and by modifying phrases. Here's a typical example, with the subject underlined once and the predicate verb underlined twice:

Profits have increased in the past year.

To give your writing variety, use the three types of sentences:

- Simple
- Compound
- Complex

A compound sentence expresses two or more independent but related thoughts of equal importance, joined by *and, but,* or *or*. In effect, a compound sentence is a merger of two or more simple sentences (independent clauses) that deal with the same basic idea. For example:

Wage rates have declined by 5 percent, and employee turnover has been high.

The independent clauses in a compound sentence are always separated by a comma or by a semicolon (in which case the conjunction—*and, but, or*—is dropped).

A complex sentence expresses one main thought (the independent clause) and one or more subordinate thoughts (dependent clauses) related to it, often separated by a comma. The subordinate thought, which comes first in the following sentence, could not stand alone:

Although you may question the conclusions, you must admit that the research is thorough.

In constructing a sentence, use the form that best fits the thought you want to express. The structure of the sentence should match the relationship of the ideas. For example, if you have two ideas of equal importance, they should be expressed as two simple sentences or as one compound sentence. But if one of the ideas is less important than the other, it should be placed in a dependent clause to form a complex sentence. This compound sentence uses a conjunction to join two ideas that aren't truly equal:

The chemical products division is the strongest in the company, and its management techniques should be adopted by the other divisions.

In the complex sentence that follows, the first thought has been made subordinate to the second. Notice how much more effective the second idea is when the cause-and-effect relationship has been established:

Because the chemical products division is the strongest in the company, its management techniques should be adopted by the other divisions.

In complex sentences, the placement of the dependent clause should be geared to the relationship between the ideas expressed. If you want to emphasize the idea, put the dependent clause at the end of the sentence (the most emphatic position) or at the beginning (the second most emphatic position). If you want to downplay the idea, bury the dependent clause within the sentence:

Most Emphatic: The handbags are manufactured in Mexico, *which has lower wage rates than the United States.*

Emphatic: *Because wage rates are lower there,* the handbags are manufactured in Mexico.

Least Emphatic: Mexico, *which has lower wage rates,* was selected as the production point for the handbags.

The most effective writing balances all three sentence types. If you use too many simple sentences, you cannot properly express the relationship among ideas. On the other hand, if you use too many long, compound sentences, your writing will sound monotonous. And an uninterrupted series of complex sentences is hard to follow.

SENTENCE STYLE

Whether a sentence is simple, compound, or complex, it should be grammatically correct, efficient, readable, interesting, and appropriate for the audience. In general, you should strive for straightforward simplicity.

But some ideas, audiences, or occasions may call for a different tone. Take the following passage, for example:

> I am often accused of inordinate reliance on unusual words, and desire—as would you in my shoes, I think—to defend myself against the insinuation that I write as I do simply to prove that I have returned recently from the bowels of a dictionary with a fish in my mouth, establishing my etymological dauntlessness. Surely one must distinguish between those who plunder old tomes to find words which, in someone's phrase, should never be let out, belonging strictly to the zoo sections of the dictionary; and such others as Russell Kirk who use words because (a) the words signify just exactly what the user means, and because (b) the user deems it right and proper to preserve in currency words which in the course of history were coined as a result of a felt need.[6]

You could simplify this passage. But if William F. Buckley, Jr., its author, knows his readers and has responded to their tastes and needs, this passage will achieve its purpose far better than a simpler version would.

Bear in mind, however, that Buckley is not writing to a group of people who are chiefly interested in getting a job done. For most business audiences, clarity and efficiency take precedence over literary style. The following guidelines will help you achieve these qualities in your own writing.

Keep sentences short

Long sentences are usually harder to understand than short sentences, because they are packed with information that must all be absorbed at once. Most business writing should therefore have an average sentence length of 20 words or less. This figure is the average, not a ceiling. To be interesting, your writing should contain both longer and shorter sentences.

Break long sentences into shorter ones to improve readability.

Long sentences are especially well suited for grouping or combining ideas, listing points, and summarizing or previewing information. Medium-length sentences (those with about 20 words) are useful for showing the relationships among ideas. And short sentences are tailor-made for emphasizing important information.

Rely on the active voice

Active sentences are generally preferable to passive sentences because they are easier to understand.[7] The subject (the "actor") comes before the verb,

LEGAL ALERT

Plain-English Laws

Have you ever tried to make sense of an obtusely worded legal document or credit agreement? Then you can understand why there is a movement toward requiring contracts and other such documents to be written in plain English.

Plain English is language written and arranged so readers can understand its meaning. Because it's close to the way we speak, anyone with an eighth- or ninth-grade education should find plain English easy to understand.

In 1978, in an attempt to make government regulations understandable to those who must comply with them, President Jimmy Carter signed an Executive Order requiring that regulations issued by executive agencies be written in plain English. Since then, 28 states have passed legislation regarding the readability of insurance contracts, and more than a dozen states have approved laws aimed at making consumer contracts easier to understand.

Plain-English laws are designed to benefit consumers. When potential customers understand the terms of the contracts they are asked to sign, they have more power in the marketplace. Understandable contracts may also increase consumers' willingness to fulfill their obligations. Someone who signs a contract written in plain English can no longer get out of it by saying, "I couldn't understand what I was getting into."

Plain English is good for business in other ways. For example, it can help attract customers. Ads, labels, letters, instructions, and warranties written in everyday English show concern for customers, leading to customer loyalty and goodwill and thus to enhanced profits. For example, a buyer who understands what a product contains, how to use it, and what to do if it must be repaired or replaced is happier with the purchase and more likely to remember the company or product in the future.

The growing focus on plain-English laws has already led to plain-English loan and credit card application forms, insurance policies, real estate contracts, and other documents. One of the first large insurers to simplify its policies was the St. Paul Fire and Marine Insurance Company of St. Paul, Minnesota. For example:

BEFORE

a. Automobile and Watercraft Liability:

1. any Relative with respect to (i) an Automobile owned by the Named Insured or a Relative, or (ii) a Non-owned Automobile, provided his actual operation of (if he is not operating) the other actual use thereof is with the permission of the owner and is within the scope of such permission, or
2. any person while using an Automobile or Watercraft, owned by, loaned or hired for use in behalf of the Named Insured or any person or organization legally responsible for the use thereof is within the scope of such permission.

AFTER

We'll also cover any person or organization legally responsible for the use of a car, if it's used by you or with your permission. But again, the use has to be for the intended purpose. You loan your station wagon to a teacher to drive a group of children to the zoo. She and the school are covered by this policy if she actually drives to the zoo but not if she lets the children off at the zoo and drives to her parents' farm 30 miles away.

Which policy would you rather sign?

1. Why are so many legal documents written in language that is difficult to understand?

2. Find a document written in "legalese," such as an insurance policy, warranty, or savings account contract. Try drafting a new version in plain English.

and the object of the sentence (the "acted upon") follows it: "John rented the office." When the sentence is passive, the subject follows the verb and the object precedes it: "The office was rented by John." As you can see, the passive verb combines the helping verb *to be* with a form of the verb that is usually similar to the past tense.

Use of passive verbs makes sentences longer and de-emphasizes the subject. Active verbs produce shorter, stronger sentences:

Active sentences are stronger than passive ones.

AVOID PASSIVE SENTENCES	USE ACTIVE SENTENCES
Sales were increased by 32 percent last month.	Sales increased by 32 percent last month.
The new procedure is thought by the president to be superior.	The president thinks the new procedure is superior.

Use passive sentences to soften bad news, to put yourself in the background, or to create an impersonal tone.

Using the passive voice makes sense, however, in some situations. For example, when you want to be diplomatic in pointing out a problem or error of some kind, you might say, "The shipment was lost" as opposed to "You lost the shipment." In this case, the passive version seems less like an accusation; the emphasis is on the problem of the lost shipment rather than on the person responsible for the loss. Similarly, if you want to point out what's being done without taking or attributing either the credit or the blame, you might say something like "The production line is being analyzed to determine the source of problems." Passive verbs are also useful when you are trying to avoid personal pronouns and create an objective tone. For example, in a formal report, you might say, "Criteria have been established for evaluating capital expenditures."

Eliminate unnecessary words and phrases

Be on the lookout for

- Legalistic phrases
- Redundancies
- Unneeded relative pronouns and articles

Some words and combinations of words are either repetitious or have one-word equivalents. Legalistic language is a frequent offender: "This is to inform you that we have" (*We have* is enough); "for the sum of" (*for*); "in the event that" (*if*); "on the occasion of" (*on*); "prior to the start of" (*before*). Redundancy is a somewhat less serious flaw: "Visible to the eye" (*visible* is enough—nothing can be visible to the ear); "surrounded on all sides" (*surrounded* implies on all sides). Relative pronouns such as *who, that,* and *which* frequently cause clutter, and sometimes even articles are excessive (mostly too many *the*'s).

However, well-placed relative pronouns and articles serve an important function by preventing confusion. For example, without *that*, the following sentence is ambiguous:

Confusing:	The project manager told the engineers last week the specifications were changed.
Clear:	The project manager told the engineers last week *that* the specifications were changed.
Clear:	The project manager told the engineers *that* last week the specifications were changed.

Here are some more ways to prune your prose:

POOR	IMPROVED
consensus of opinion	consensus
at this point in time	at this time, now
irregardless	(no such word; use *regardless*)
each and every	(either word but not both)
due to the fact that	because
at an early date	soon (or a specific date)
at the present time	now

in view of the fact that	since, because
until such time as	when
we are of the opinion	we believe
with reference to	about
as a result of	because
for the month of December	for December

Avoid needless repetition.

In general, be on the lookout for the needless repetition of words or ideas. For example, try not to string together a series of sentences that all start with the same word or words, and avoid repeating the same word too often within a given sentence. Take a close look at double modifiers. Do you really need to say *modern, up-to-date equipment,* or would *modern equipment* do the job?

Use infinitives to replace some phrases.

Another way to save words is to use infinitives in place of some phrases. This technique not only shortens your sentences but makes them clearer as well:

POOR	IMPROVED
In order to be a successful writer, you must work hard.	To be a successful writer, you must work hard.
He went to the library for the purpose of studying.	He went to the library to study.
The employer increased salaries so that she could improve morale.	The employer increased salaries to improve morale.

Avoid obsolete and pompous language

Obsolete formal phrases can obscure meaning.

The language of business used to be much more formal than it is today, and a few out-of-date phrases remain from the old days. Perhaps the best way to eliminate them is to ask yourself: "Would I say this if I were talking face-to-face with someone?"

OBSOLETE	UP-TO-DATE
as per your letter	as in your letter (do not mix Latin and English)
hoping to hear from you soon, I remain	(omit)
yours of the 15th	your letter of June 15
awaiting your reply, we are	(omit)
in due course	today, tomorrow (or a specific time or date)
permit me to say that	(permission is not necessary; just say what you wish)
we are in receipt of	we have received
pursuant to	(omit)
in closing, I'd like to say	(omit)
attached herewith is	here is
the undersigned	I; me

kindly advise	please let us know
under separate cover	in another envelope; by parcel post
we wish to inform you	(just say it)
attached please find	enclosed is
it has come to my attention	I have just learned; Ms. Garza has just told me
our Mr. Lydell	Mr. Lydell, our credit manager
pleased be advised that	(omit)

The use of pompous language suggests that you are a pompous person.

Pompous language is similar to out-of-date phrases. It, too, sounds stiff, puffed up, and roundabout. People are likely to use pompous language when they are trying to impress somebody. In hopes of sounding imposing, they use big words, trite expressions, and overly complicated sentences:

POOR	IMPROVED
Upon procurement of additional supplies, I will initiate fulfillment of your order.	I will fill your order when I receive more supplies.
Perusal of the records indicates a substantial deficit for the preceding accounting period due to the utilization of antiquated mechanisms.	The records show a company loss last year due to the use of old equipment.

Moderate your enthusiasm

Business writing shouldn't be gushy.

An occasional adjective or adverb intensifies and emphasizes your meaning, but too many ruin your writing:

POOR	IMPROVED
We are extremely pleased to offer you a position on our staff of exceptionally skilled and highly educated employees. The work offers extraordinary challenges and a very large salary.	We are pleased to offer you a position on our staff of skilled and well-educated employees. The work offers challenges and an attractive salary.

Break up strung-out sentences

In many cases, the parts of a compound sentence should be separated into two sentences.

A strung-out sentence is a series of two or more sentences unwisely connected by *and*—in other words, a compound sentence taken too far. You can often improve your writing style by separating the string into individual sentences.

POOR	IMPROVED
The magazine will be published January 1, and I'd better meet the deadline if I want my article included.	The magazine will be published January 1. I'd better meet the deadline if I want my article included.

Avoid hedging sentences

Don't be afraid to present your opinions without qualification.

Sometimes you have to write *may* or *seems* to avoid stating a judgment as a fact. But when you have too many such hedges, particularly several in a sentence, you aren't really saying anything:

POOR	IMPROVED
I believe that Mr. Johnson's employment record seems to show that he may be capable of handling the position.	Mr. Johnson's employment record shows that he is capable of handling the position.

Watch for indefinite pronoun starters

Avoid starting sentences with *it* and *there*.

If you start a sentence with an indefinite pronoun (an expletive) like *it* or *there*, odds are that the sentence could be shorter:

POOR	IMPROVED
It would be appreciated if you would sign the lease today.	Please sign the lease today.
There are five employees in this division who were late to work today.	Five employees in this division were late to work today.

Express parallel ideas in parallel form

When you use the same grammatical pattern to express two or more ideas, you show that they are comparable thoughts.

When you have two or more similar (parallel) ideas to express, try to present them in the same grammatical pattern. The repetition of the pattern tells readers that the ideas are comparable and adds a nice rhythm to your message. In the following examples, parallel construction makes the sentences more readable:

POOR	IMPROVED
Miss Simms had been drenched with rain, bombarded with telephone calls, and her boss shouted at her.	Miss Simms had been drenched with rain, bombarded with telephone calls, and shouted at by her boss.
Ms. Reynolds dictated the letter, and next she signed it and left the office.	Ms. Reynolds dictated the letter, signed it, and left the office.

Parallelism can be achieved through a repetition of words, phrases, clauses, or entire sentences:

Parallel Words:	The letter was approved by Clausen, Whittaker, Merlin, and Carlucci.
Parallel Phrases:	We have beaten the competition in supermarkets, in department stores, and in specialty stores.
Parallel Clauses:	I'd like to discuss the issue after Vicki gives her presentation but before Marvin shows his slides.
Parallel Sentences:	In 1988 we exported 30 percent of our production. In 1989 we exported 50 percent.

Eliminate awkward pointers

Tell readers exactly where you want them to look.

To save words, business writers sometimes direct their readers' attention elsewhere with such expressions as *the above-mentioned, as mentioned above, the aforementioned, the former, the latter, respectively*. These words cause the reader to jump from one point in the message to another, a process that hinders effective communication. A better approach is to be specific in your references, even if you must add a few more words:

POOR	IMPROVED
Typewriter ribbons for legal secretaries and beginning clerks are distributed by the Law Office and Stenographic Office, respectively.	Typewriter ribbons for legal secretaries are distributed by the Law Office; those for beginning clerks are distributed by the Stenographic Office.

Correct dangling modifiers

Make sure that modifier phrases are really related to the subject of the sentence.

Sometimes a modifier is not just an adjective or adverb but rather an entire phrase defining a noun or verb. You must be careful to construct your sentences so this type of modifier refers to something in the main part of the sentence in a way that makes sense. For example:

Walking to the office, a red sports car passed her.

The way this sentence is constructed, it implies that the red sports car has the office and the legs to walk there. The modifier is said to be dangling because it has no real connection to the subject of the sentence—in this case, the sports car. This is what the writer is trying to say:

A red sports car passed her while she was walking to the office.

Flipping the clauses produces another correct sentence:

While she was walking to the office, a red sports car passed her.

Dangling modifiers make sentences confusing and ridiculous:

POOR	IMPROVED
Working as fast as possible, the budget soon was ready.	Working as fast as possible, the committee soon had the budget ready.
After a three-week slump, we increased sales.	After a three-week slump, sales increased.

Passive construction is often the cause of dangling modifiers.

The first example shows one frequent cause of dangling modifiers: passive construction in the independent clause. When the clause is made active instead of passive, the connection with the dangling modifier becomes more obvious.

Avoid long sequences of nouns

Stringing together a series of nouns may save a little space, but it causes confusion.

When nouns are strung together as modifiers, the resulting sentence is hard to read. You can clarify the sentence by putting some of the nouns in a modifying phrase. Although you are adding a few more words, your audience won't have to work as hard to understand the sentence.

POOR	IMPROVED
The window sash installation company will give us an estimate on Friday.	The company that installs window sashes will give us an estimate on Friday.

Keep words together that work together

To avoid confusing readers, keep the subject and predicate of a sentence as close together as possible. Otherwise, readers will have to read your sentence twice to figure out who did what:

Subject and predicate should be placed as close together as possible, as should modifiers and the words they modify.

POOR	IMPROVED
A 10 percent decline in market share, which resulted from quality problems and an aggressive sales campaign by Armitage, the market leader in the Northeast, was the major problem in 1989.	The major problem in 1989 was a 10 percent loss of market share, which resulted from both quality problems and an aggressive sales campaign by Armitage, the market leader in the Northeast.

The same rule applies to other parts of speech. Adjectives, adverbs, and prepositional phrases usually make the most sense when they are placed as close as possible to the words they modify:

POOR	IMPROVED
We will deliver the pipe soon that you ordered last Tuesday.	We will soon deliver the pipe that you ordered last Tuesday.

Emphasize key thoughts

In every message, some ideas are more important than others. You can emphasize these key ideas through your sentence style. One obvious technique is to give important points the most space. When you want to call attention to a thought, use extra words to describe it. Take this sentence, for example:

The chairman of the board called for a vote of the shareholders.

To emphasize the importance of the chairman, you might describe her more fully:

Emphasize parts of a sentence by

- Giving them more space
- Putting them at the beginning or the end of the sentence
- Making them the subject of the sentence

The chairman of the board, who has considerable experience in corporate takeover battles, called for a vote of the shareholders.

You can increase the emphasis even more by adding a separate, short sentence to augment the first:

The chairman of the board called for a vote of the shareholders. She has considerable experience in corporate takeover battles.

Another way to emphasize an idea is to place it at either the beginning or the end of a sentence:

LESS EMPHATIC	MORE EMPHATIC
We are cutting the *price* to stimulate demand.	To stimulate demand, we are cutting the *price*.

You can also call attention to a thought by making it the subject of the sentence. In the following example, the emphasis is on the person:

I can write letters much more quickly using a computer.

In this version, the computer takes center stage:

The *computer* enables me to write letters much more quickly.

Techniques like this one give you a great deal of control over the way your audience interprets what you have to say.

DEVELOPING COHERENT PARAGRAPHS

Paragraphs are functional units that revolve around a single thought.

A paragraph is a cluster of sentences all related to the same general topic. It is a unit of thought. A series of paragraphs makes up an entire composition. Each paragraph is an important part of the whole, a key link in the train of thought. As you edit a message, think about the paragraphs and their relationship to one another.

When you're talking to someone face-to-face, you develop your paragraphs informally, using tone of voice and gestures to signal the relationship among ideas. You pause to indicate that you have completed one topic and are ready to begin another, a new "paragraph." In a written document, on the other hand, paragraphs are developed more formally. Each paragraph is separated from other units of thought by the typographical device of skipping a line or indenting the first line.

ELEMENTS OF THE PARAGRAPH

Most paragraphs consist of a topic sentence, related sentences, and transitional elements.

Although paragraphs vary widely in length and form, the typical paragraph contains three basic elements: a topic sentence, related sentences that develop the topic, and transitional words and phrases.

Topic sentence

Every properly constructed paragraph is unified: It deals with a single topic. The sentence that introduces that topic is called the topic sentence. In informal and creative writing, the topic sentence may be implied rather than stated. But in business writing, the topic sentence is generally explicit and often the first sentence in the paragraph.

The topic sentence

- Reveals the subject of the paragraph
- Indicates how it will be developed

The topic sentence gives readers a summary of the general idea that will be covered in the rest of the paragraph. Notice in the following examples how the topic sentence introduces the subject and suggests the way it will be developed:

The medical products division has been troubled for many years by public relations problems. (In the rest of the paragraph, readers will learn the details of the problem.)

Relocating the plant in New York has two main disadvantages. (The disadvantages will be explained in subsequent sentences.)

To get a refund, you must supply us with some additional information. (The details will be described.)

Related sentences

The sentences that explain the topic sentence round out the paragraph. These related sentences must all have a bearing on the general subject, and they must provide enough specific details to make the topic clear. For instance:

The medical products division has been troubled for many years by public relations problems. Since 1980, the leading local newspaper has published 15 articles that portray the division in a negative light. We have been accused of everything from mistreating laboratory animals to polluting the local groundwater. Our facility has been described as a health hazard. Our scientists are referred to as "Frankensteins." And our profits are considered "obscene."

Paragraphs are developed through a series of related sentences that provide details about the topic sentence.

Notice that the developmental sentences are all more specific than the topic sentence. Each one provides another piece of evidence to demonstrate the general truth of the main thought. Notice also that each sentence is clearly related to the general idea being developed, which gives the paragraph its unity. A paragraph is well developed when it contains enough information to make the topic sentence convincing and interesting.

Transitional elements

Transitional words and phrases show readers how paragraphs and the ideas within them are related.

In addition to being unified and well developed, paragraphs need to be coherent. They need to be arranged in a logical order so the audience can understand the train of thought. Coherence is achieved through the use of transitions that show the relationship between paragraphs and among sentences within paragraphs. They show how one thought is related to another.

Some transitional devices:

- Connecting words (conjunctions)
- Repeated words or phrases
- Pronouns
- Words that are frequently paired

You can establish transitions in various ways:

- Use connecting words such as *and, but, or, nevertheless, however, in addition*, and *therefore*.
- Echo a word or phrase from a previous paragraph or sentence: "A system should be established for monitoring inventory levels. This system. . . ."
- Use a pronoun that refers to a noun used previously: "Ms. Arthur is the leading candidate for the president's position. She has excellent qualifications."
- Use words that are frequently paired: "The machine has a minimum output of. . . . Its maximum output is. . . ."

These techniques help readers understand the connections you are trying to make.

FIVE WAYS TO DEVELOP A PARAGRAPH

Five ways to develop paragraphs:

- Illustration
- Comparison or contrast
- Discussion of cause and effect
- Classification
- Discussion of problem and solution

Paragraphs can be developed in many ways, five of the more common being illustration, comparison or contrast, discussion of cause and effect, classification, and discussion of problem and solution. Your choice of approach should depend on your subject, the intended audience, and the purpose of the message. Remember also that in actual practice you will often combine two or more methods of development in a single paragraph. You might begin with illustration, shift to cause and effect, then shift again to problem and solution.

Before you settle for the first approach that comes to mind, think about the alternatives. Try different methods in your mind before committing yourself on paper. And don't fall into the easy habit of repeating the same old paragraph pattern time after time, or your writing will be boring.

By illustration

When you develop a paragraph by illustration, you give examples that demonstrate the general idea:

Some of our most popular products are available through local distributors. For example, Everett & Lemmings carries our frozen soups and entrees. The J. B. Green Company carries our complete line of seasonings, as well as the frozen soups. A third major distributor, Wilmont Foods, has just begun to carry our new line of frozen desserts.

By comparison or contrast

Similarities or differences among thoughts often provide a strong basis for paragraph development. Here's an example developed by contrast:

In previous years, when the company was small, the recruiting function could be handled informally. The need for new employees was limited, and each manager could comfortably screen and hire her or his own staff. Today, however, Gambit Products must undertake a major recruiting effort. Our successful bid on the Owens contract means that we will need to double our labor force over the next six months. To hire that many people without disrupting our ongoing activities, we need to create a separate recruiting group within the personnel department.

By discussion of cause and effect

When you develop a paragraph by cause and effect, you focus on the reasons for something:

The heavy-duty fabric of your Wanderer tent has probably broken down for one of two reasons: (1) A sharp object punctured the fabric, and the stress of erecting the tent daily for a week without reinforcing the hole has enlarged it; (2) the tent was folded and stored while still wet, which gradually rotted the fibers.

By classification

Paragraphs developed by classification show how a general idea is broken into specific categories:

Successful candidates for our supervisor trainee program generally come from one of several groups. The largest group, by far, consists of recent graduates of accredited data-processing programs. The next largest group comes from within our own company, as we try to promote promising clerical workers to positions of greater responsibility. Finally, we do occasionally accept candidates with outstanding supervisory experience in related industries.

By discussion of problem and solution

Another way to develop a paragraph is to present a problem and then discuss the solution:

Selling handmade toys by mail is a challenge, because consumers are accustomed to buying heavily advertised toys from major chains. However, if we develop an appealing catalog, we can compete on the basis of product novelty and quality. And we can provide craftsmanship at a competitive price: a rocking horse made from birchwood, with a hand-knit tail and mane; a music box with the child's name painted on the top; a real Indian tepee, made by a Native American.

PARAGRAPH POINTERS

Each paragraph should cover a single idea.

As you edit your paragraphs, check to be sure that they are unified, well developed, and coherent. Be particularly careful to limit each paragraph to one general idea. Your readers expect everything to be related; if you throw in unrelated thoughts, your readers will be puzzled by the unexpected shift. Similarly, when you complete a paragraph, your readers automatically assume that you have finished with a particular idea. If you then continue to discuss that idea in the next paragraph, you upset their expectations.

Short paragraphs are easier to read than long ones.

But some ideas are simply too big to be handled conveniently in one paragraph. Unless you break up the thoughts somehow, you'll end up with a three-page paragraph that's guaranteed to intimidate even the most dedicated reader. It's a fact that short paragraphs (of 100 words or less) are easier to read than long ones. Direct-mail letters almost always use very short paragraphs, because the writers know their letters will be read more carefully that way. Even in memos, letters, and reports, you may sometimes want to emphasize an idea by isolating it in a short, forceful paragraph.

What do you do when you want to package a big idea in a short paragraph? The solution is to break the idea into subtopics and treat each subtopic in a separate paragraph, being careful to provide plenty of transitional elements. Take a look at the following draft and the revised version:

DRAFT VERSION

Donner Corporation had to increase the size of its facilities and staff to keep up with rapid sales growth. It had to invest more in physical plant in 3 years ($18 million) than it had spent in the previous 17 years of its operation. It had to double its staff in 3 years. All this had to be accomplished in an increasingly competitive labor market, without the benefit of an experienced personnel department. The company had to transform itself from a small, single-product company into a broadly based corporation with several divisions. Much more was involved than simply adding on to the existing plant and hiring more people. The quality of the existing staff and products did not compare favorably to that of its main competitors. The corporation had to develop new operations while improving and expanding its traditional activities. And it needed to add to its professional staff by recruiting high-caliber people from many fields.

REVISED VERSION

Donner Corporation faced a major transformation, growing from a small, single-product company to a large, broadly based corporation in just 3 years. This changeover involved much more than simply adding on to the plant and hiring more people, because the quality of the existing staff and products was not good enough for a first-rate operation. The task therefore required both physical expansion and quality improvement.

The physical expansion alone represented a major undertaking. The investment in facilities required $18 million. Over a 3-year period, the organization spent more on new plant and equipment than it had spent in the past 17 years of its operation.

To raise its competitive capability, the company had to develop new programs and organizational units and, at the same time, expand and upgrade its existing operations. It also needed to double the size of its staff by recruiting high-caliber people from many fields. This staffing had to be accomplished in an increasingly competitive labor market and without benefit of an experienced personnel department.

By breaking the subject into three paragraphs rather than one, the writer of the revised version has increased the clarity and effectiveness of the message. Each paragraph is organized around a topic sentence, and the separate paragraphs are linked by transitional elements.

The writer has done a good job of revising this draft, but many other approaches might be as effective. There is no such thing as the "right" way to develop a paragraph. The first priority in business writing is to be clear and concise, but you should also try to be interesting. And the key to being interesting is variety. As you edit your message, look for opportunities to use different methods of paragraph development, varying your approach to suit the purpose and content of each thought. Also, try to vary the structure and length of sentences within paragraphs; this variation will make the message not only more interesting but more readable as well.

CHECKLIST FOR REVISION

A. Content and Organization

- ☐ 1. Review your draft against the message plan.
- ☐ 2. Cover all necessary points in logical order.
- ☐ 3. Organize the message to respond to the audience's probable reaction.
- ☐ 4. Provide enough support to make the main idea convincing and interesting.
- ☐ 5. Eliminate unnecessary material; add useful material.
- ☐ 6. Be sure the beginning and ending are effective.

B. Style and Readability

- ☐ 1. Pay attention to word choice.
  - ☐ a. Avoid words with negative connotations.
  - ☐ b. Use concrete words to clarify abstractions and prevent misunderstandings.
  - ☐ c. Rely on nouns, verbs, and specific adjectives and adverbs.
  - ☐ d. Use familiar words, but avoid clichés.
  - ☐ e. Avoid long words.
  - ☐ f. Replace camouflaged verbs.
  - ☐ g. Eliminate terms that suggest bias based on gender, race, religion, age, or disability.
- ☐ 2. Improve sentence style.
  - ☐ a. Use the sentence structure that best fits the thought.
  - ☐ b. Tailor the sentence style to the audience.
  - ☐ c. Aim for an average sentence length of 20 words.
  - ☐ d. Write mainly in the active voice, but use the passive voice to achieve specific effects.
  - ☐ e. Eliminate unnecessary words and phrases.
  - ☐ f. Avoid obsolete and pompous language.
  - ☐ g. Moderate your enthusiasm.
  - ☐ h. Break up strung-out sentences.
  - ☐ i. Avoid hedging sentences.
  - ☐ j. Watch for indefinite pronoun starters.
  - ☐ k. Express parallel ideas in parallel form.
  - ☐ l. Eliminate awkward pointers.
  - ☐ m. Correct dangling modifiers.
  - ☐ n. Avoid long sequences of nouns.
  - ☐ o. Keep subject and verb close together, and keep adverbs, adjectives, and prepositional phrases close to the words they modify.
  - ☐ p. Emphasize key points through sentence style.
- ☐ 3. Construct effective paragraphs.
  - ☐ a. Be sure each paragraph contains a topic sentence, related sentences, and transitional elements.
  - ☐ b. Edit for unity, effective development, and coherence.
  - ☐ c. Choose a method of development that suits the subject: illustration, comparison or contrast, cause and effect, classification, problem and solution.
  - ☐ d. Vary the length and structure of sentences within paragraphs.
  - ☐ e. Mix paragraphs of different lengths, but aim for an average of 100 words.

C. Mechanics and Format

- ☐ 1. Review sentences to be sure they are grammatically correct.
- ☐ 2. Correct punctuation and capitalization errors.
- ☐ 3. Look for spelling and typographical errors.
- ☐ 4. Review the format to be sure it follows accepted conventions.
- ☐ 5. Apply the format consistently throughout the message.

To write an interesting document

- Use different methods to develop the paragraphs
- Vary the length and structure of sentences
- Mix short and long paragraphs

Another way to add variety and improve readability is to mix short paragraphs with longer ones. You might even use a one-sentence paragraph occasionally for emphasis.

Above all, think about what you're doing and why. Consider your words, your sentences, and your paragraphs. You can almost always improve them if you try. The more you write, the easier revision becomes. When you've mastered the elements of style, you can create whatever impression you want. You can be forthright and sincere, crisp and businesslike, warm and sympathetic. Having control over your writing style gives you the flexibility to respond to many different communication situations.

SUMMARY

Revision is the final step in developing effective business messages. Each message should be edited for content and organization, style and readability, mechanics and format.

An effective writing style begins with word choice. A meaning may often be expressed in more than one way. In general, however, you should rely on strong words—nouns and verbs—to convey your meaning. Use short, familiar terms. Avoid verbs that have been turned into nouns or adjectives through the addition of suffixes.

The most effective writing also involves a balance of the three types of sentences: simple, compound, and complex. Sentences are more readable when you keep them short and use the active voice. Eliminate unnecessary words and phrases, and avoid obsolete, pompous, or overly enthusiastic language. Try to avoid strung-out sentences, hedging sentences, pronoun starters, awkward pointers, dangling modifiers, and long sequences of nouns. Express parallel ideas in parallel form, and keep words together that work together. Emphasize key thoughts by drawing them out and placing them in prominent positions.

Paragraphs consist of a topic sentence, related sentences, and transitional words and phrases. You can develop paragraphs in many ways: illustration, comparison or contrast, discussion of cause and effect, classification, and presentation of a problem and a solution. For best effect, focus each paragraph on a single idea, and keep each paragraph short.

COMMUNICATION CHALLENGES AT BEAR CREEK

Marcus Smith likes to experiment occasionally with new approaches for direct-mail letters seeking new members in the Fruit-of-the-Month Club. He has decided to test some alternatives and see which one gets the best response. These letters will be aimed specifically at young, affluent families with children. Marcus's main idea is that fruit makes a wonderful snack because of its nutritional value. He wants to emphasize that Harry & David is particularly careful to avoid using any chemicals that might have a harmful effect on consumers.

Individual Challenge: Draft a sample letter, using a style that you think reflects Harry & David's conversational, down-to-earth approach. Then revise it for content and organization, style and readability, mechanics and format.

Team Challenge: Get together with a small group of classmates. Make enough copies of your letter to give a copy to each person in your group; you will receive a copy of each person's letter in return. Edit the other letters. Then compare your revisions with the others. Did all editors make similar suggestions?

QUESTIONS FOR DISCUSSION

1. How would you feel about submitting your writing to a company editor whose job it was to review your letters and reports? What do you think you would like the editor to do to help you?
2. Which step in the revision process do you think is most important—editing for content and organization, editing for style and readability, or editing for mechanics and format? Explain your answer.
3. How does the revision phase affect oral communication?
4. Why do business writers tend to use words of low connotative meaning? In what types of business situations might one use words of high connotative value?
5. How would you answer someone who says, "In business letters I employ Latinate, unfamiliar words, because I desire to convey an image of traditional and consummate elegance"?
6. Some writers argue that trying to avoid stereotyping and bias makes a message sound unnatural and leads to awkward constructions. How would you respond to this criticism?
7. What specific techniques of style could you use to create a formal, objective tone? An informal, personal tone?
8. When, if ever, should a writer use poor grammar?
9. What technique might you use to develop a paragraph explaining the game of Frisbee? Explain your choice.
10. Why does a good writer develop the ability to express the same idea in several different styles?

DOCUMENTS FOR ANALYSIS

Read the following documents, and then (1) analyze the strengths and/or weaknesses of each numbered sentence and (2) revise each document so it follows this chapter's guidelines.

DOCUMENT 5.A

(1) The move to our new offices will take place over this coming weekend. (2) For everything to run smooth, everyone will have to clean out their own desk and pack up the contents in boxes that will be provided. (3) You will need to take everything off the walls too, and please pack it along with the boxes.

(4) If you have alot of personal belongings, you should bring them home with you. (5) Likewise with anything valuable. (6) I do not mean to infer that items will be stolen, irregardless it is better to be safe than sorry.

(7) On Monday, we will be unpacking, putting things away, and then get back to work. (8) The least amount of disruption is anticipated by us, if everyone does their part. (9) Hopefully, there will be no negative affects on production schedules, and current deadlines will be met.

DOCUMENT 5.B

Dear Ms. Giraud:

(1) Enclosed herewith please find the manuscript for your book, Three Bags Full. (2) After perusing the first two chapters of your 1,500-page manuscript, I was forced to conclude that the subject matter, handicrafts and artwork using wool fibers, is not coincident with the publishing program of Framingham Press, which to this date has issued only works on business endeavors, avoiding all other topics completely.

(3) Although our firm is unable to consider your impressive work at the present time, I have taken the liberty of recording some comments on some of the pages. (4) I am of the opinion that any feedback that a writer can obtain from those well versed in the publishing realm can only serve to improve the writer's authorial skills.

(5) In view of the fact that your residence is in the Boston area, might I suggest that you secure an appointment with someone of high editorial stature at the Cambridge Heritage Press, which I believe might have something of an interest in works of the nature you have produced.

(6) Wishing you the best of luck in your literary endeavors, I remain

Arthur J. Cogswell
Editor

DOCUMENT 5.C

(1) The popper is designed to pop 1/2 cup of popcorn kernels at one time. (2) Never add more than 1/2 cup. (3) A half cup of corn will produce three to four quarts of popcorn. (4) More batches may be made separately after completion of the first batch. (5) Popcorn is popped by hot air. (6) Oil or shortening is not needed for popping corn. (7) Add only popcorn kernels to the popping chamber. (8) Standard grades of popcorn are recommended for use. (9) Premium or gourmet type popping corns may be used. (10) Ingredients such as oil, shortening, butter, margarine, or salt should never be added to the popping chamber. (11) The popper, with popping chute in position, may be preheated for two minutes before adding the corn. (12) Turn the popper off before adding the corn. (13) Use electricity safely and wisely. (14) Observe safety precautions when using the popper. (15) Do not touch the popper when it is hot. (16) The popper should not be left unattended when it is plugged into an outlet. (17) Do not use the popper if it or its cord has been damaged. (18) Do not use the popper if it is not working properly. (19) Before using the first time, wash the chute and butter/measuring cup in hot soapy water. (20) Use a dishcloth or sponge. (21) Wipe the outside of the popper base. (22) Use a damp cloth. (23) Dry the base. (24) Do not immerse the popper base in water or other liquid. (25) Replace the chute and butter/measuring cup. (26) The popper is ready to use.

EXERCISES

1. Write a concrete phrase for each of these abstract phrases:
   - a. sometime this spring
   - b. a substantial saving
   - c. a large number attended
   - d. increased efficiency
   - e. expanded the work area
2. List words that are stronger than the following:
   - a. ran after
   - b. seasonal ups and downs
   - c. bright
   - d. suddenly rises
   - e. moves forward
3. As you rewrite these sentences, replace the clichés with fresh, personal expressions:
   - a. Being a jack-of-all-trades, Dave worked well in his new selling job.
   - b. But moving Leslie into the accounting department, where she was literally a fish out of water, was like putting a square peg into a round hole, if you get my drift.
   - c. I knew she was at death's door, but I thought the doctor would pull her through.
   - d. Movies aren't really my cup of tea; as far as I am concerned, they can't hold a candle to a good book.
   - e. It's a dog-eat-dog world out there in the rat race of the asphalt jungle.
   - f. There's been a lot of water under the proverbial bridge since you and I last rubbed elbows and chewed the fat together.
   - g. The meeting was a real barn burner. Jack was trying to get his fat out of the fire, but Suzy poured cold water on every idea that came down the pike, and he flipped out over her raining on his parade.
   - h. I was between a rock and a hard place because the decision was a real can of worms, and I couldn't win for losing, but I faced the music and bit the bullet and voted for Cynthia.
4. Suggest short, simple words to replace each of the following:
   - a. inaugurate
   - b. terminate

c. utilize
d. anticipate
e. assistance
f. endeavor
g. ascertain
h. procure
i. consummate
j. advise
k. alteration
l. forwarded
m. fabricate
n. nevertheless
o. substantial portion
p. fundamental
q. afford an opportunity
r. approximately
s. accomplished
t. accumulate
u. additionally
v. commence
w. compensate
x. demonstrate
y. encounter
z. expedite
aa. facilitate
bb. initiate
cc. indicate
dd. maintain
ee. objectives
ff. obligation
gg. participate
hh. remittance
ii. remuneration
jj. subsequent
kk. sufficient
ll. transmit
mm. unavailability
nn. voluminous

5. Revise the following sentences using shorter, simpler words:
   a. The antiquated calculator is ineffectual for solving sophisticated problems.
   b. It is imperative that the pay increments be terminated before an inordinate deficit is accumulated.
   c. There was unanimity among the executives that Ms. Jackson's idiosyncrasies were cause for a mandatory meeting with the company's personnel director.
   d. The impending liquidation of the company's assets was cause for jubilation among the company's competitors.
   e. The expectations of the president for a stock dividend were accentuated by the preponderance of evidence that the company was in good financial condition.
6. Rewrite each sentence so that the verbs are no longer camouflaged:
   a. Adaptation to the new rules was performed easily by the employees.
   b. The assessor will make a determination of the tax due.
   c. Verification of the identity of the employees must be made daily.
   d. The board of directors made a recommendation that Mr. Ronson be assigned to a new division.
   e. The auditing procedure on the books was performed by the vice president.
7. Rewrite each of the following to eliminate bias:
   a. For an Indian, Maggie certainly is outgoing.
   b. He needs a wheelchair, but he doesn't let his handicap affect his job performance.
   c. She's too sensitive; when I criticized her performance, she asked me to explain.
   d. A pilot must have the ability to stay calm under pressure, and then he must be trained to cope with any problem that arises.
   e. "And what would you ladies like us to do about absenteeism?"
   f. David is a teen-ager and has little experience to draw on when making career decisions.
   g. Kathryn Kentro, a female accountant, has been preparing our profit and loss statements for the past seven years.
   h. Henry Bates just bought a nice home with a swimming pool, and he's black.
   i. Candidate Renata Parsons, married and the mother of a teen-ager, will attend the debate.
   j. Senior citizen Sam Nugent is still an active salesman.
8. Shorten these sentences by adding more periods:
   a. The next time you write something, check your average sentence length in a 100-word passage; and if your sentences average more than 16 to 20 words, see if you can break up some sentences.
   b. Don't do what the village blacksmith did when he instructed his apprentice as follows: "When I take the shoe out of the fire, I'll lay it on the anvil; and when I nod my head, you hit it with the hammer." The apprentice did just as he was told and now he's the village blacksmith.
   c. Unfortunately, no gadget will produce excellent writing, but using a yardstick like the Fog Index gives us some guideposts to follow for making writing easier to read because its two factors remind us to use short sentences and simple words.
   d. Know the flexibility of the written word and its power to convey an idea, and know how to make your words behave so your readers will understand.
   e. Words mean different things to different people, and a word like *block* may mean city block, butcher block, engine block, auction block, or several other things.
   f. Mineral classifications will be made by areas, and these areas will show resources that are available now along with those that will probably become available at some time in the future.
9. Rewrite each sentence so it is active rather than passive:
   a. The raw data are submitted to the data-processing division by the sales representative each Friday.
   b. High profits are the responsibility of management.

c. The policies announced in the directive were implemented by the staff.
d. Our typewriters are serviced by the Santee Company.
e. The employees were represented by Janet Hogan.

10. Cross out unnecessary words in the following phrases:
  a. consensus of opinion
  b. exact replica
  c. new innovations
  d. most unique
  e. true facts
  f. surrounded on all sides
  g. the month of May
  h. visible to the eye
  i. maximum possible
  j. eight in number
  k. important essential
  l. red in color
  m. the state of California
  n. my personal opinion
  o. entirely complete
  p. just recently
  q. refer back
  r. whether or not
  s. continue on
  t. past experience
  u. long period of time
  v. at a distance of 100 feet
  w. at a price of $50
  x. remember the fact that
  y. until such time as
  z. I would like to recommend
  aa. during the course of reporting on
  bb. she is engaged in
  cc. circle around
  dd. the main problem is a matter of scheduling
  ee. throughout the entire week
  ff. came at a time when
  gg. still remains
  hh. repeat again
  ii. strict accuracy

11. Use infinitives as substitutes for the overly long phrases in these sentences:
  a. In order to live I require money.
  b. They did not find sufficient evidence for believing in the future.
  c. Bringing about the destruction of a dream is tragic.

12. Rephrase the following in fewer words:
  a. in the near future
  b. in the event that
  c. in order that
  d. for the purpose of
  e. with regard to
  f. I am of the opinion that
  g. please do not hesitate to let me know
  h. I wish to take this occasion to express my thanks
  i. the early part of next week
  j. your check in the amount of
  k. it is quite probable that
  l. it may be that
  m. at an early date
  n. in very few cases
  o. with reference to
  p. a large number
  q. at the present time
  r. there is no doubt that
  s. most of the time
  t. in the same way

13. Condense these sentences to as few words as possible:
  a. We are of the conviction that writing is important.
  b. In all probability, we're likely to have a price increase.
  c. The price increase exceeded the amount of 5 cents.
  d. We are engaged in the process of building this store.
  e. Our goals include making a determination about that in the near future.
  f. When all is said and done at the conclusion of this experiment, I would like to summarize the final windup.
  g. After a trial period of 3 weeks, during which time she worked for a total of 15 full working days, we found her work was sufficiently satisfactory so that we offered her full-time work.
  h. I find this to be an unexciting, nonstimulating situation.

14. Write up-to-date versions of the following phrases; write *none* if you believe there is no appropriate substitute:
  a. as per your instructions
  b. attached herewith
  c. hold in abeyance
  d. in lieu of
  e. in reply I wish to state
  f. in response to same
  g. kindly note same
  h. please be advised that
  i. pursuant to our agreement
  j. refer back to
  k. take the liberty of
  l. thanking you in advance
  m. this will acknowledge
  n. we wish to advise that
  o. yours of the 11th
  p. we deem it advisable
  q. allow me to express
  r. at all times
  s. according to our records

15. Remove all the unnecessary modifiers from these sentences:
  a. Tremendously high pay increases were given to the extraordinarily skilled and extremely conscientious employees.

b. The union's proposals were highly inflationary, extremely demanding, and exceptionally bold.

16. Rewrite these sentences so they no longer contain any hedging:
    a. It would appear that someone apparently entered illegally.
    b. It may be possible that sometime in the near future the situation is likely to improve.
17. Rewrite these sentences to eliminate the indefinite starters:
    a. There are several examples here to show that Elaine can't hold a position very long.
    b. It would be greatly appreciated if every employee would make a generous contribution to Mildred Cook's retirement party.
    c. It has been learned in Washington today from generally reliable sources that an important announcement will be made shortly by the White House.
18. Present the ideas in these sentences in parallel form:
    a. Mr. Hill is expected to lecture three days a week, to counsel two days a week, and must write for publication in his spare time.
    b. The office workers were hired to receive callers, to operate the duplicating equipment, and a variety of duties were handled by them.
    c. All the employees were given instruction in writing letters, using the photocopying machine, and how to keep all of our accounts in alphabetical order.
    d. She knows not only accounting, but she also reads Latin.
    e. My Uncle Bill is young, ambitious, and he is rich.
    f. Both applicants had families, college degrees, and were in their thirties, with considerable accounting experience but few social connections.
    g. This book was exciting, well written, and held my interest.
    h. Don is both a hard worker and he knows bookkeeping.
19. Revise these sentences to delete the awkward pointers:
    a. The vice president in charge of sales and the production manager are responsible for the keys to 34A and 35A, respectively.
    b. The keys to 34A and 35A are in executive hands with the former belonging to the vice president in charge of sales and the latter belonging to the production manager.
    c. The keys to 34A and 35A have been given to the production manager, with the aforementioned keys being gold-embossed.
20. Rewrite these sentences to clarify the dangling modifiers:
    a. Running down the railroad tracks in a cloud of smoke, we watched the countryside glide by.
    b. Lying on the shelf, Ruby saw the seashell.
    c. Based on the information, I think we should buy the property.
21. Rewrite the following sentences to eliminate the long strings of nouns:
    a. The focus of the meeting was a discussion of the bank interest rate deregulation issue.
    b. Following the government task force report recommendations, we are revising our job applicant evaluation procedures.
    c. The production department quality assurance program components include employee training, supplier cooperation, and computerized detection equipment.
    d. The supermarket warehouse inventory reduction plan will be implemented next month.
    e. The State University business school graduate placement program is one of the best in the country.
22. Rearrange the following sentences to bring the subjects closer to their verbs:
    a. Trudy, when she first saw the bull pawing the ground, ran.
    b. It was Terri who, according to Ted, who is probably the worst gossip in the office (Tom excepted), mailed the wrong order.
    c. William Oberstreet, in his book *Investment Capital Reconsidered*, writes of the mistakes that bankers through the decades have made.
    d. Judy Schimmel, after passing up several sensible investment opportunities, despite the warnings of her friends and family, invested her inheritance in a jojoba plantation.
23. In the following paragraph, identify the topic sentence and the related sentences (those that support the idea of the topic sentence):

    Each year McDonald's sponsors the All-American Band, made up of two high school students from each state. The band marches in Macy's Thanksgiving Day parade in New York City and the Rose Bowl Parade in Pasadena. Franchisees are urged to join their local Chamber of Commerce, United Way, American Legion, and other bastions of All-Americana. McDonald's tries hard to project an image of almost a charitable organization. Local outlets sponsor campaigns on fire prevention, bicycle safety, and litter cleanup, with advice from Hamburger Central on how to extract the most publicity from their efforts.[1]

Now add a topic sentence to this paragraph:

> Your company's image includes what a person sees, hears, and experiences in relation to your company. Every business letter you write is therefore important. The quality of the letterhead and typing, copy position on the page, format, the kind of typeface used, the color of the typewriter ribbon—all play a part in creating an impression of you and your company in the mind of the person you are writing to.[2]

24. Build a paragraph around each of the following topic sentences:

a. During its first decade of operations, Perkins Industries almost went bankrupt.

b. But as the advertising budget increased, so did the sales.

25. Write a paragraph on each of the following topics—one by illustration, one by comparison or contrast, one by discussion of cause and effect, one by classification, and one by discussion of problem and solution:

a. Types of cameras (or dogs or automobiles) available for sale

b. Advantages and disadvantages of eating at fast-food restaurants

c. Finding that first job

d. Good qualities of my car (or house, apartment, or neighborhood)

e. How to pop popcorn (or barbecue or cook a steak)

PART THREE

LETTERS, MEMOS, AND OTHER BRIEF MESSAGES

After studying this chapter, you will be able to

- Clearly state the main idea of each direct request you write
- Indicate your confidence that the request will be filled
- Provide sufficient detail for the reader to be able to comply with your request
- Clarify complicated requests with lists and tables
- Close with a courteous request for specific action

CHAPTER SIX

WRITING DIRECT REQUESTS

Julie Regan

COMMUNICATION CLOSE-UP AT TOUCAN-DU

"When my partner and I decided to go into business, we didn't know a lot of things," says Julie Regan, the founder of Toucan-Du (pronounced *two can do*). Their Honolulu company imports decorative accessories from Southeast Asia. Julie knew something about Southeast Asian arts, through her own travels and through friends abroad. Her partner, an interior decorator, knew something about the demand for exotic imports in the United States. But neither knew how to establish a business and line up sources of products.

"The first thing we did," Julie explains, "was to take a course from an international broker on how to run an import business. Our instructor gave us plenty of good ideas on whom we should correspond with (chambers of commerce in other countries and consulates), trade journals we should advertise in, trade representatives we should know or avoid, and companies that might be able to supply us with products."

Over the next three months, Julie and her partner wrote some 200 letters to potential suppliers. "Most of our letters were direct requests for information. We described what we were looking for and asked if the supplier might be able to meet our needs."

To save time, Julie used a form letter, which she refined as time went on. "We learned a lot from our first letters," she notes. "Many of the people who responded were selling things we really didn't want; the quality level was too low. So we became more specific in describing what we were looking for. We explained that we were selling to architects and interior designers and that we were interested in sculpture, paintings, crafts, and decorative objects. We were also very specific in stating what we didn't

A flurry of written requests to Southeast Asian merchants helped establish Toucan-Du's collection of exotic merchandise.

want. For example, we didn't want any brass, because there's so much of that already available. And we didn't want anything of museum quality, because the market for that is limited."

In response to their letters, Julie and her partner received catalogs, photographs, and samples from many potential suppliers. "The replies were interesting," Julie says. "Many of them were handwritten, and they were very personal. The English was simple and straightforward, and the tone was informal. So we made our replies to them much more personal as well."

In their replies, Julie and her partner arranged appointments to meet with the potential suppliers whose products, from carved masks to hand-painted chopsticks, appeared to be most interesting. Some of this correspondence was handled by Telex, because a letter to Southeast Asia may take three weeks to arrive.

During their initial buying trip, Julie and her partner obtained enough merchandise for their opening, including some rare imports available in this country for the first time. In addition, they established good relationships with several steady suppliers. "We constantly correspond with these suppliers," says Julie. "If we're looking for something special, we write to them, and every now and then we touch base to see what's new that might be interesting. They send us photographs or slides. I feel as though we have become 'pen pals' in a way. These people have become my friends. It's fun to write to them, and I look forward to their letters—not just because of the business, but because they are interesting people."

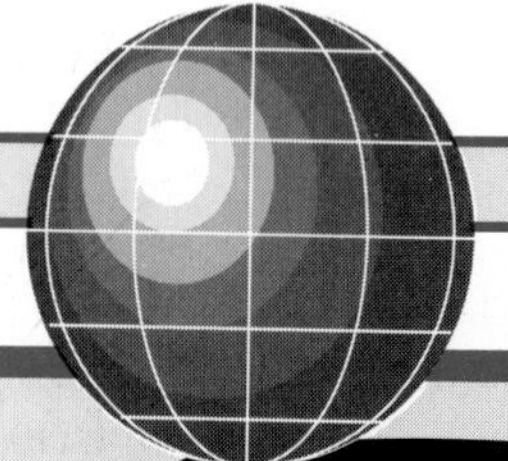

INTERNATIONAL OUTLOOK

Pitfalls of Writing International Business Letters

Written communication with people in other countries is often extremely frustrating, depending on the degree of red tape, the language barrier, availability of translators, familiarity with international trade practices, and mail systems. For example, business is very paper-oriented in European countries such as France, Germany, and England, where a steady stream of correspondence leads up to meetings and negotiations. In other countries, paperwork is anathema and correspondence is a poor second choice for conducting business. In India, for example, where street addresses are uncommon, mail is totally unreliable; letters often are lost or simply remain unanswered. And don't assume that a handwritten letter from a foreign company is an invitation to informality; in some locales, typewriters are not widely available.

Addressing foreign correspondence is a special challenge. Normally, the address you see on the letterhead or envelope is in the form you should use to address a return letter. For example:

Blaubach 13	Street address
Postfach 10 80 07	Post office box
D-5000 Koln I	District, city
Federal Republic of Germany	Country
10-I, Akasaka I-chome	Building/block address
Minato-ku 107	District, postal service
Tokyo	City
Japan	Country

But letterhead can be misleading; very often the return address is hard to distinguish from Telex information or promotional statements. Needless to say, the problem also exists in reverse, so the American firm doing business abroad should design stationery and business cards that will be intelligible to foreigners.

ORGANIZING DIRECT REQUESTS

For direct requests
- State the request or main idea
- Give necessary details
- Close with a cordial request for specific action

When you can assume that your audience will be interested in what you have to say or at least be willing to cooperate with you, your message should follow the direct, or deductive, plan. You should present the request or the main idea first, follow up with necessary details, and close with a cordial statement of the action you want. This approach works well when your request requires no special tact or persuasion.

Senders of direct requests may be tempted to begin with personal introductions ("I am the owner of an import company in Honolulu, and I am looking for decorative accessories that . . ."). But this type of beginning is usually a mistake. The essence of the message, the specific request, is buried and may get lost. A better way to organize a direct request is to state what you want in the first sentence or two and to let the the explanation follow this initial request.

Assume that your reader will comply once he or she understands your purpose.

Even though you expect a favorable response, the tone of your initial request is important. Instead of demanding immediate action ("Send me your catalog #33A"), soften your request with such words as *please* and *I would appreciate*. An impatient demand for rapid service is not necessary, because you can generally assume that the audience will comply with your request once he or she understands why the request is being made.

The middle part of a direct request usually explains the original request ("Our clients are architects and interior designers, so we are looking for unusual and dramatic pieces of exceptional quality"). Such amplifying details help your audience fill your request correctly.

It is important to get job titles right when addressing correspondence, but designations for a position may vary around the world. In England, for example, a "managing director" is often what Americans call the chief executive officer or president, and a British "deputy" is the equivalent of a vice president. In France, responsibilities are assigned to individuals without regard to titles or organizational structure. In China, *project manager* has meaning, but *sales manager* may not.

To make matters worse, individuals in some countries sign correspondence without their names typed below. Germans, for example, believe that employees represent the company, so it is inappropriate to emphasize their personal names. Indeed, German letters often have two signatures, either because some individuals may act only in concert with someone else or because two individuals have been assigned to a job. When signatures are illegible, the names of the signers can be found out by writing to the company and alluding to the reference numbers or initials that normally appear on a well-executed German letter.

Finally, remember that no answer does not necessarily mean no interest. David Chang, an executive at Nike, tells of a letter received in 1981 that began, "In response to your Telex of 1978. . . . " To a North American, failure to answer a letter is either an insult or sloppy business. But elsewhere, failure to answer a letter may be insignificant. Communication problems, a complex decision-making process, or other priorities may be at fault. Most foreigners, from Japan to South America to the Arab world, prefer face-to-face dealings with business associates and may "respond" to a letter by waiting for further contact.

1. With the exception of details like those discussed here, should letters to people in other countries be handled like those to people in North America? Discuss such factors as style, organization, and tone.

2. Imagine that you are the sales manager for a toy store that is contemplating adding a section of imported toys. Find out the names of major toy manufacturers in three other countries, and draft letters asking for information on each company's products.

In the last section, clearly state the action that you are requesting. You may wish to tell the audience where to send the sought-after information or product, indicate any time limits, or list details of the request that were too complex or numerous to cover in the introductory section. Then close with a brief, cordial note reminding the audience of the importance of the request ("Next month one of our clients will begin planning a major hotel redecoration project that seems well suited to the carved figures you are known for, so please send your catalog right away").

Now let's take a closer look at the three main sections of a direct request. Although this discussion focuses on letters and memos, remember that this organizational plan may be appropriate for brief oral messages as well.

DIRECT STATEMENT OF THE REQUEST OR MAIN IDEA

Word the request itself carefully so it says exactly what you want.

The general rule for the first part of a direct request is to write not only to be understood but also to avoid being misunderstood. If, for example, you request "1980 census figures" from a government agency, the person who handles your request won't know whether you want a page or two of summary figures or a detailed report running to several thousand pages. Therefore, you should be as specific as possible in the sentence or two that begins your message.

Use a period at the end of a request in question form that requires action; use a question mark at the end of a request that requires an answer in words.

Be aware of the difference between a polite request in question form, which requires no question mark, and a question that is part of a request.

POLITE REQUEST IN QUESTION FORM

Would you please help us determine whether Kate Kingsley is a suitable applicant for a position as landscape designer.

QUESTION THAT IS PART OF A REQUEST

Did Kate Kingsley demonstrate an ability to work smoothly with clients?

Many direct requests include both types of statements, but make sure you distinguish between the polite request that is your overall reason for writing and specific questions, which belong in the middle section of your letter or memo.

JUSTIFICATION, EXPLANATION, AND DETAILS

In the middle section

- Call attention to how the reader will benefit from granting your request
- Give details of your request

When Julie Regan and her partner were writing to potential suppliers across the Pacific Ocean, some of whom were barely familiar with the English language, the middle section of their letters was of great importance. True, they were looking for immediate product information, but they were also telling their unknown readers why they needed the information and explaining how long-term business and personal relationships might evolve.

To make the explanation a smooth and logical outgrowth of your opening remarks, you might make the first sentence of your letter's middle section you-oriented by stating a service-to-the-reader benefit. For instance, Julie might have written, "By keeping Toucan-Du informed about your products, you can help create a new distribution channel for your business.

For example, if an American market exists for one of your new specialty items, I can help you reach those customers."

Another possible approach for the middle section is to ask a series of questions, particularly if your inquiry concerns machinery or complex equipment. You might ask about technical specifications, exact dimensions, and the precise use of the product. The most important question should be asked first. For example, if cost is your main concern, you might begin with a question like "What is the price of your least expensive typewriter?" Then you may want to ask more specific but related questions about, say, the cost of ribbons and maintenance service.

Ask the most important question first, then related, more specific questions.

If you are requesting several items or answers, you should number the items and list them in logical order or in descending order of importance. Furthermore, so that your request can be handled quickly, remember (1) to ask only the questions that are central to your main request and (2) to avoid asking for information that you can find on your own, even if the effort takes considerable time.

Use numbered lists when you're requesting several items or answers.

If you are asking many people to reply to the same questions, you should probably word them so they can be answered yes or no or some other easily counted response. You may even want to provide respondents with a form or with boxes they can check to indicate their answers. But if you need more than a simple yes or no answer, you must pose an open-end question. For example, a question like "How fast can you repair typewriters?" is more likely to elicit the information you want than "Can you repair typewriters?" Keep in mind also that phrasing questions in a way that hints at the response you want is likely to get you less than accurate information. So try to phrase your questions objectively. Finally, deal with only one topic in each question. If the questions need amplification, keep each question in a separate paragraph.

When you prepare questions

- Ask only questions that relate to your main request
- Don't ask for information you can find yourself
- Make your questions open-ended and objective
- Deal with only one topic in each question

Other types of information that belong in this section include data about a product (model number, date and place of purchase, condition), your reason for being concerned about a particular matter, and other details about your request. When a reader finishes this section, he or she should understand why the request is important and be persuaded to satisfy it.

COURTEOUS CLOSE WITH REQUEST FOR SPECIFIC ACTION

Your letter should close with both a request for some specific response, complete with any time limits that apply, and an expression of appreciation or goodwill. Help your reader respond easily by including your phone number, office hours, and other helpful information.

Close with

- A request for some specific response
- An expression of appreciation
- Information about how you can be reached

But do not thank the reader "in advance" for cooperating. If the reader's reply warrants a word of thanks, send it after you have received the reply. If you are requesting information for a research project, you might offer to forward a copy of your report in gratitude for the reader's assistance. If you plan to reprint or publish materials that you ask for, indicate that you will get necessary permission. When asking for information about a person, indicate that you will keep responses confidential.

PLACING ORDERS

Because orders are usually processed without objection and refer to a product that the reader knows about, an order is considered one of the simplest types of direct request. In placing an order, you need not excite your reader's interest, just state your needs clearly and directly.

To see what to include in a good order letter, examine any mail-order form supplied by a large firm. It offers complete and concise directions for providing all the information that the company will need to fill an order.

After the date, the order form probably starts with "Please send the following" or "Please ship." If you complete the rest of the form and mail it, these statements constitute a legal and binding offer to purchase goods; the supplier's shipment of the goods constitutes an acceptance of the offer and thus completes a legal contract.

Order letters are like good mail-order forms, although they also provide more room for explaining special needs.

Order blanks are arranged to document the precise goods you want, describing them by catalog number, quantity, name or trade name, color, size, unit price, and total amount due. This complete identification helps prevent errors in filling the order. When drafting an order letter, you would do well to follow the same format, presenting information on the items you want in column form, double-spacing between the items, and totaling the price at the end.

Order blanks provide space for you to indicate the address where the goods should be sent. Your letter, too, should specify the delivery address, especially if it is not the address from which you send your letter. Sometimes the billing and delivery addresses are different.

Order blanks may also leave space for you to indicate how the merchandise is to be shipped: by truck, air freight, parcel post, air express, or delivery service. Unless you specify the mode of transportation, the seller chooses.

Like any letter sent with money, your order letter should mention the amount of payment as well as explain how the amount was calculated and, if necessary, to what account it should be charged. Again, the order form provides an excellent model. Most have spaces for showing unit prices, the total amount for each item, the cost of shipping and handling, the total amount of the payment, and the form of payment (check, money order, bank draft, or other means).

Here's an example that follows the order-form format and adds important information:

Please ship by air express to the above address the following four items, which are shown in your April sale catalog:

The general request is stated first.

1-#256 Men's nylon raincoat, in gray, size 42 long	$19.95
1-#5823 Women's plastic raincape, in yellow, size medium	17.50
2-#353898-C Children's rain parkas, in red, sizes 6 and 8, @ $8.95	17.90
Total sale	$55.35

All necessary details are provided, in a format similar to an order form.

FIGURE 6.1
Memo Requesting Routine Action from Company Insiders

MEMO

DATE: April 17, 1989

TO: All employees

FROM: Michael Nardi, Personnel MN

SUBJECT: Golden Time parties

We are very interested in learning your opinion about award dinners. Please take a few moments to respond to this questionnaire.

Traditionally, employees who have been with the company for 20 years are honored at annual departmental dinners, where their Golden Time pins are awarded.

Recently, however, management has proposed that a company-wide recognition dinner replace these departmental events. Because our firm has only 107 employees, such a dinner could still be a friendly affair. The interdepartmental ties and friendships that many of you share would be part of the celebration. However, our company is proud of the unity within each department, and you may feel that this closeness would be lost in a larger celebration.

Please consider these points and mark your choice below:

_____ VOTE FOR AN ALL-COMPANY PARTY

_____ VOTE FOR DEPARTMENTAL PARTIES

Please feel free to make additional signed or unsigned comments at the bottom of this memo. Return your completed questionnaire by Friday.

The basic request is stated at the beginning.

The next two paragraphs explain the problem that made the inquiry necessary.

The final paragraph requests action and, with a built-in questionnaire, makes a response easy.

In the following memo, notice how the writer refers to a previous memo on the same topic and then makes the request for a response from employees:

How do you feel about adopting flextime in your department?

The memo begins with the central question.

Last week you received an explanation of flextime schedules as they could apply to our organization. Now we need your opinion of the proposal.

A little background information orients the reader.

1. Would you want to go on a flextime schedule? Please summarize your reasons.

The numbered questions focus responses so they will be easier to tally.

2. The proposal listed four schedule patterns for employees to choose from. Which pattern now seems best for your department?

3. If your preferred schedule pattern is not available, what other pattern would suit you?

4. Should flextime be mandatory or optional?

5. If flextime is adopted, what problems might arise in your department?

Please write your answers directly on this sheet and return it to me by Friday. Complete responses will help us formulate the policy that works best for our company.

Specific instructions for replying close the memo. The courteous tone helps to ensure a prompt response.

Craft internal memos just as carefully as letters to outsiders, but adjust the writing style to take shared reference points into account.

Notice that this memo is matter-of-fact and assumes some shared background. This style is appropriate when you are writing about a routine matter to someone in the same company.

REQUESTS TO OTHER BUSINESSES

When writing a letter in response to an advertisement

- Say where you saw the ad
- Specify what you want
- Provide a clear and complete return address on the letter

Many letters to other businesses are requests for information about products, like Julie Regan's letters to exporters in Southeast Asia. They are among the easiest of all letters to write, because recipients welcome the opportunity to tell you about their goods and services. In fact, often you need only fill out a coupon or response card and mail it to the correct address. You might find, however, that you'd like to write a brief note requesting further information about something you've seen in an advertisement. One or two sentences will most likely do the job. Companies commonly check on the effectiveness of their advertisements, so they also like to know where you saw or heard them.

If the reader is not expecting your letter, you must supply more detail.

Inquiries that are not prompted by an advertisement demand a more detailed letter. If the letter will be welcome, or if the reader won't mind answering it, the direct approach is still appropriate. The following is such a letter:

Would you please supply information and recommendations on the type of refrigerator we might install in two-bedroom apartments.

The overall request is stated at the beginning; phrased politely in question form, it requires no question mark.

Ten refrigerators will be needed for our new apartment building, which is scheduled for completion within four months. Four other buildings now under construction in the same complex will need new appliances later.

The explanation for the request keeps the reader's attention by hinting at the possibility of future business.

Because we're considering your company as the supplier, please answer the following questions:

1. What size is appropriate for two-bedroom apartments? 14 cubic feet? 16? 18?

To avoid burdening the reader with an impossibly broad request, the writer asks a series of specific questions, itemized in a logical sequence.

2. Do you recommend putting self-defrosting refrigerators in rental units?

3. Do you provide service for the refrigerators you sell? If so, how quickly could you repair them in case of breakdown?

4. What models of apartment-size refrigerators do you carry, and what are their prices?

5. Which of your refrigerators has the best service record?

To avoid receiving useless yes or no answers, the writer asks some open-end questions.

The refrigerators must be ordered within a month, so we would appreciate receiving your reply by March 26.

The courteous close specifies a time limit.

This letter should bring a prompt and enthusiastic reply, because the situation is clearly described, the possibility of current and future business is suggested, and the questions are specific and easy to answer. Additionally, the letter implies confidence in the opinion and assistance of the reader. Because the letter will be sent to a business firm and pertains to a possible sale, the writer did not enclose a stamped, preaddressed envelope.

If you are writing as an individual and are therefore not using letterhead stationery, be sure to write your address on the letter clearly and completely. Many inquiries are not answered because the address was illegibly handwritten or was written only on the return envelope, which was tossed away by the recipient.

REQUESTS TO CUSTOMERS AND OTHER OUTSIDERS

Requests to customers must often spell out in detail

- What exactly is needed
- How filling the request will benefit them

Businesses often ask individuals outside the organization to provide information or to take some simple action: attend a meeting, return an information card, endorse a document, confirm an address, supplement information on an order. Often these messages can be short and simple, but other situations require a more detailed explanation. In such cases, readers may not be willing to respond unless they understand how the request benefits them. Thus more complex letters, with several paragraphs of explanation, are sometimes written. Because the same message must often be sent to many people at the same time, it may be prepared as a form letter and perhaps individualized with a word processor.

The following is an example of a well-planned, detailed form letter:

Under federal tax law, your annuity payments are considered "wages" for income tax withholding purposes. To simplify your record keeping, you may choose to have us withhold taxes from your annuity payments. Or you may choose to receive the full payments and pay estimated taxes yourself.

The opening states the purpose of the letter in simple, reader-oriented terms. Providing details of the law convinces the reader that the request is warranted.

Here's how to decide which option is best for you:

First, estimate your total taxable income this year from all sources: the taxable portion of all

An explanation of procedures is another reader-oriented feature of the letter. To make a complex procedure easier to

annuity payments you receive, dividends, interest, and salary from employment.

Second, estimate your total tax liability for this year by using the income figure you just calculated and your present tax rates. Then subtract your payments of estimated taxes and other amounts withheld for you.

understand, the writer breaks the directions into two clearly defined steps.

If your calculations show that you will have a tax liability, you may want us to withhold the taxable portion of your pension payments. Simply mark the appropriate box on the enclosed Tax Decision Form, fill in your Social Security number, sign and date the form, and mail it to us.

This paragraph begins to explain the particular action being requested. Again, clear directions are provided to help ensure a response.

If you do not want taxes withheld, mark the "no" box on the form, fill in your Social Security number, sign and date the form, and return it to us.

Providing boxes for the response helps readers comply with the request.

Please let us know your decision by November 1 so we can begin withholding in January. If you need further information about the new requirements, call Larry Bender, our customer service representative, at (919) 744-2063. He is in the office Monday through Friday from 9 a.m. to 5 p.m.

The courteous close motivates action by specifying a person to talk to and a deadline for a reply.

The clarity of the language in this letter—the nontechnical, easily understood words and the step-by-step directions—helps ease the reader's concerns about a complex procedure.

The purpose of routine requests to customers is often to reestablish communication.

Businesses sometimes need to reestablish a relationship with former customers. For example, customers who are unhappy about some purchase or the way they were treated often make no complaint: They simply stay away from the offending business. A letter of inquiry encouraging them to use idle credit accounts offers them an opportunity to register their displeasure and then move on to a good relationship. Additionally, a customer's response to an inquiry may provide the company with insights into ways to improve its products and customer service. Even if they have no complaint, customers still welcome the personal attention. Such an inquiry to the customer might begin in this way:

When a good charge customer like you has not bought anything from us in six months, we wonder why. Is there something we can do to serve you better?

Consider enclosing a stamped, preaddressed envelope in routine requests, especially those sent to individuals rather than other businesses.

Letters of inquiry sent to someone's home frequently include a stamped, preaddressed envelope to make a reply easier.

Similar inquiry letters are sent from one business to another. For example, the sales representatives of a housewares distributor might send a letter like this to their customers:

Because we haven't heard from you in a while, I thought it would be a good idea to touch base. In fact, I'd like to ask a favor.

The opening paragraph states the reason for the letter. The frank request arouses curiosity and encourages a frank response.

Will you take a minute today to give us your honest opinion about our merchandise and service. Just jot your ideas, pro and con, at the bottom of this letter and rush it back in this afternoon's mail. Your response will help us help you.

This request for action is a device for uncovering trouble without actually suggesting that there might be trouble.

So you'll have a good supply of order forms on hand, I'm enclosing some extra copies. And the enclosed spring bulletin and update on our cooperative advertising program may help you plan your spring promotions.

This paragraph recognizes the possibility that nothing particular is wrong, that the customer just needs a little push.

Remember, Ms. Skovie, that you can always count on us when you're in the market for high-style housewares. We have some new merchandise in today's most desirable colors that seems just right for your fashion-conscious customers. Do give us the opportunity to serve your needs soon. That's why we're here.

The actual request for action is left unstated until the end so it will leave an impression.

■ CHECKLIST FOR ROUTINE REQUESTS

A. Direct Statement of the Request

- ☐ 1. Phrase the opening to reflect the assumption that the reader will respond to your request favorably.
- ☐ 2. Phrase the opening so clearly and simply that the main idea cannot be misunderstood.
- ☐ 3. Write in a polite, undemanding, personal tone.
- ☐ 4. Preface complex requests with a sentence or two of explanation, possibly a statement of the problem that the response will solve.

B. Justification, Explanation, and Details

- ☐ 1. Justify the request or explain its importance.
- ☐ 2. Explain to the reader the benefit of responding.
- ☐ 3. State desired actions in a positive and supportive, not negative or dictatorial, manner.
- ☐ 4. Itemize parts of a complex request in a numbered series.
- ☐ 5. List specific questions.
  - ☐ a. Don't ask questions that you could answer through your own efforts.
  - ☐ b. Arrange questions logically.
  - ☐ c. Number questions.
  - ☐ d. Word questions carefully to get the type of answers you need: numbers or yes's and no's if you need to tally many replies; more lengthy, detailed answers if you want to elicit more information.
  - ☐ e. Word questions to avoid clues about the answer you prefer so as not to bias the reader's answers.
  - ☐ f. Limit each question to one topic.

C. Courteous Close with Request for Specific Action

- ☐ 1. Courteously request a specific action, and make it as easy as possible to implement, possibly by enclosing a return envelope or explaining how you can be reached.
- ☐ 2. Indicate gratitude, possibly by promising to follow up in a way that will benefit the reader.
- ☐ 3. Clearly state any deadline or time frame, and briefly justify it if it is genuinely important.

BUSINESS COMMUNICATION TODAY

Writing Claim Letters That Get Results

Sometime in the next couple of years, unless you are unusually lucky or very easily pleased, you are likely to buy merchandise or receive service that disappoints you: a toaster that shoots sparks two days after its warranty expires, a blouse or shirt that falls apart on its third trip through the wash, an airline ticket that gets you to your destination six hours too late.

If you get no satisfaction at the face-to-face level, from the retailer or the airline counter agent, your next step is to write a claim letter. Will your letter bring forth a satisfactory adjustment or a form letter that makes you angrier than you were before? The response depends to a large extent on how you go about making your claim. Here are some guidelines that have proved helpful in getting results:

- *Don't write "To Whom It May Concern."* Letters addressed to no one in particular are routinely sent to the customer service department, whereas letters addressed by name to the president or executive vice president stand some chance of coming to the attention of these individuals. You can find the name and address of almost any corporate officer in Standard & Poor's *Register of Corporations, Executives, and Directors,* available in most libraries. If your product carries a trade name but no clue as to its manufacturer, consult Ellen T. Crowley's *Trade Names Dictionary,* where you'll find, for example, that the toy named "Blinky" is produced by James Industries, Hollidaysburg, PA 16648. Writing to the president of a corporation often produces a satisfactory response because he or she has probably been shielded by underlings from the problem you've confronted and is glad to know about it and make amends.
- *Play politics.* A useful tactic is to send a copy of your letter to the president at the same time you send a copy to whichever vice president (manufacturing, advertising, retailing) you think is responsible for your problem. Be sure to include a copy notation at the bottom of the vice president's letter. When both executives get your letter, the junior one will want to settle your claim before her or his senior asks about it. A frequent result: prompt action.
- *Prevent detours.* To improve your letter's chances of getting to the eyes of an executive

WRITING DIRECT REQUESTS FOR CLAIMS AND ADJUSTMENTS

You are entitled to request an adjustment whenever you receive a product or experience service that doesn't live up to the supplier's standards.

For most of us, *claim* and *adjustment* are unpleasant words. But most progressive organizations want to know if you are dissatisfied with their services or merchandise, because satisfied customers bring additional business to the firm. Angry or dissatisfied customers do not. In addition, angry customers complain to anyone who will listen, creating poor public relations. If you do have a complaint, it is in your best interests, and the company's, to bring your claim or request for an adjustment to the organization's attention.

When you feel that you are justified in making a claim, communicate at once with someone in the company who can make the correction. A phone call or visit may solve the problem, but a written claim letter is better because it documents your dissatisfaction.

Tone is of primary importance; keep your claim businesslike and unemotional.

Your first reaction to a clumsy mistake or defective merchandise is likely to be anger or frustration, but the person reading your letter probably had nothing to do with the problem. Making a courteous, clear, concise

instead of being shunted elsewhere by an overprotective secretary, mark the envelope "Confidential." If you prefer, spend an additional sum to send your letter by certified mail, return receipt requested. These steps will convey the message that you mean business without your having to make threats in the letter itself.

- *Don't get mad, get specific.* A savage and sarcastic blast against the company and its products may make you feel better, but a calm, reasonable, specific letter gets better results. Indicate exactly what went wrong and, more important, whether you want a replacement, a prompt repair, a refund, or a reimbursement for whatever expenses the problem caused you. Instead of anger, try a wryly humorous approach. Some senior executives have a sense of humor and are secure enough to admit that their company sometimes makes mistakes.
- *If at first you don't succeed. . . .* If the first response to your claim is a form letter that doesn't really address your problem, write again more firmly. This time indicate that you intend to send copies to your state's consumer protection agencies and to any federal agencies that have jurisdiction, such as the Federal Trade Commission, the Interstate Commerce Commission, the National Highway Transportation Safety Agency, or the Environmental Protection Agency. Some companies brush off or ignore requests for adjustment but take seriously those who persist.
- *If at last you don't succeed. . . .* If several of your best efforts produce zero results, hold onto your carbons or photocopies as evidence, and file a complaint with your state or local consumer protection agency, your small-claims court, or a federal agency. At this point you may be tempted to give up and take your loss, but one consideration should motivate you to persist: Even if it's more trouble than it's worth, your formal claim, along with others, can strongly influence a company to mend its ways. The result will be better products and service not only for you but for thousands of other consumers. In this sense, your private claim letter or your appeal to a consumer protection agency becomes a public service.

1. When was the last time you were unhappy with a product or service? Did you do anything about it? Why or why not?

2. Pick a recent instance in which you were legitimately dissatisfied with a product or service. Write a claim letter that explains what happened, and ask for an adjustment. Keep a copy of your letter, and note the response you get. What conclusions can you draw about the willingness of most organizations to grant claims and make adjustments?

explanation of the difficulty will impress the reader much more favorably than an abusive, angry letter. Asking for a fair and reasonable solution will increase your chances of receiving a satisfactory adjustment.

In your claim letter

- Explain the problem and give details
- Provide backup information
- Request specific action

In most cases, and especially in the first letter, you can assume that a fair adjustment will be made. Thus your letter should follow the plan for direct requests. Begin with a straightforward statement of the problem, and follow with a complete, specific explanation of the details. In the middle part of your claim letter, provide any information the adjuster will need to verify your complaint about faulty merchandise or unsatisfactory service. Politely request specific action in your closing, and express the attitude that the business relationship will continue if the problem is solved satisfactorily.

Be prepared to document your claim. Send copies; keep the original documents.

Companies usually accept the customer's explanation of what is wrong, but you should be prepared to back up your claim with invoices, sales receipts, canceled checks, dated correspondence, catalog descriptions, and any other relevant documents. Send copies and keep the originals for your files.

If the remedy is obvious, tell your reader exactly what will return the company to your good graces—for example, an exchange of merchandise for the right item or a refund if the item is out of stock. If you are uncertain about the precise nature of the trouble, you could ask the company to make an assessment. When you are dissatisfied with a very costly item, you might request that an unbiased third person either estimate the cost of repair or suggest another solution. Be sure to supply your telephone number and the best time to call (as well as your address) so the company can discuss the situation with you if need be.

The following two letters have been written to a gas and electric company. As you read them, contrast the tone of the two versions. If you were the person who received the complaint, which version would you respond to more favorably?

I've lived here only three months, and I don't understand why my December utility bill is $115.00 and my January bill is $117.50. My neighbors on both sides of me, in apartments just like mine, are paying only $43.50 and $45.67 for the same months. We all have the same kind of appliances and equipment, so something must be wrong.

Consumers are helpless against big utility companies. How can I prove that you read the meter wrong or that the November bill before I even moved here got added to mine? I want someone to check this meter right away. I can't afford to pay these big bills.

Here's the second version:

The utility meters may not be accurate in my apartment. Please send someone to check them.

I have lived here since December 1, almost three months. My monthly bills are nearly triple those of my neighbors in this building, yet we all have similar apartments, furnished with the same appliances. In December I paid $115.00, and my January bill was $117.50; my neighbors' highest bills were $43.50 and $45.67.

If your representative could check the operation of the meters, he or she could also see how much energy our appliances are using. I understand that you regularly provide this helpful service to customers.

I would appreciate hearing from you this week. You can reach me by calling 878-2345 during business hours or 551-3971 in the evening.

A courteous approach gets the best results because it is non-threatening.

If you're like most people, you reacted much more favorably to the second letter than to the first. As the rational and clear second letter demonstrates, a courteous approach is best for any routine request. If you must write a letter that gives vent to your anger, go ahead; but then tear that one up and write a letter that will actually help solve the problem.

Generally, you should suggest specific and fair compensation when asking for an adjustment. However, the following complaint illustrates a case in which the customer does not request a specific adjustment but asks the reader to resolve the problem:

At our October 25 dinner meeting in your restaurant, your rum cake was a big success. You should know, however, that many who attended commented on three areas needing improvement:

1. Serving began half an hour late.
2. The roast beef was cold and tough.
3. The vegetables were cold and overcooked.

What can we do to guarantee that things go better at our next dinner meeting, which is scheduled for December 10?

In the past, we have been quite pleased with the quality of your food and service. Please call me at 372-9200, ext. 271, any time this week to discuss this situation further.

In a letter like this, you must define the problem and express your dissatisfaction in as much detail as possible while conveying a sincere desire to find a fair solution. A courteous tone will allow the reader to save face and still make up for the mistake.

■ CHECKLIST FOR CLAIMS AND REQUESTS FOR ADJUSTMENT

A. Direct Statement of the Request

- ☐ 1. Write a claim letter as soon as possible after the problem has been identified.
- ☐ 2. State the need for reimbursement or correction of the problem.
- ☐ 3. Maintain a confident, factual, fair, unemotional tone.

B. Justification, Explanation, and Details

- ☐ 1. To gain the reader's understanding, praise some aspect of the product or the service.
- ☐ 2. Present facts honestly, clearly, and politely.
- ☐ 3. Eliminate threats, sarcasm, exaggeration, and hostility.
- ☐ 4. Specify the problem: product failed to live up to advertised standards, product failed to live up to sales representative's claims, product fell short of company policy, product was defective, customer service was deficient.
- ☐ 5. Make no accusations against any person or company that you can't back up with facts.
- ☐ 6. Use a nonargumentative tone to show your confidence in the reader's fairness.
- ☐ 7. If necessary, refer to documentation (invoices, canceled checks, confirmation letters, and the like), but mail only photocopies.
- ☐ 8. Ask the reader to propose fair adjustment, if appropriate.
- ☐ 9. If appropriate, present your idea of fair settlement, such as credit against your next order, full or partial refund of the purchase price, replacement of the defective merchandise, performance of services as originally contracted, or repair of the defective merchandise.
- ☐ 10. Do not return the defective merchandise until you have been asked to do so.
- ☐ 11. Avoid uncertainty or vagueness that might permit the adjusters to prolong the issue by additional correspondence or to propose a less-than-fair settlement.

C. Courteous Close with Request for Specific Action

- ☐ 1. Summarize desired action briefly.
- ☐ 2. Simplify compliance with your request by including your name, address, phone number (including area code, if necessary), and hours of availability.
- ☐ 3. Note how complying with your request will benefit the reader.

MAKING ROUTINE CREDIT REQUESTS

The first step in requesting credit is to get an application form.

If your credit rating is sound, your application for business or personal credit may be as direct as any other type of simple request. Whether the application is directed to a local bank or retail store, a wholesaler or manufacturer, or a national credit card company, the information needed is the same. You might phone the company for a credit application or write a letter as simple as this:

We would like to open a credit account with your company. Please send an application blank and let us know what references you will need.

The second step is to supply the necessary information.

Before you get a credit account, you will have to supply such information as the name of your company or employer, the length of time you've been in business or on the job, the name of your bank, and the addresses of businesses where you have existing accounts. Businesses trying to establish credit are also expected to furnish a financial statement and possibly a balance sheet. In general, the lender wants proof that your income is stable and that you can repay the loan. You might put this information in your original letter, but it will probably be requested again on the standard credit application form.

Order letters are often combined with a request for credit.

A request for credit should

- Be supported by documentation
- Adopt a confident tone
- Hint at future business

A request to buy on credit is sometimes included with a company's first-time order for goods. In these cases, the customer often sends copies of the latest financial statement along with the order letter. If a company's credit standing is good, it may ask with confidence for the order to be accepted on a credit basis. Because the main idea in this situation is to get permission to buy on credit, the letter should open with that request. Figure 6.2 is an example of the way an order may be combined with a request for credit. Notice that the request for credit is supported by documentation of financial ability. In addition, the writer has encouraged a favorable response by adopting a confident tone and mentioning the probability of future business.

INQUIRING ABOUT PEOPLE

Some companies ask applicants to supply references before awarding credit, contracts, jobs, promotions, scholarships, memberships, and so on. For example, job seekers are often asked to provide the names and addresses of at least three people who can vouch for their ability, skills, integrity, character, and fitness for the job.

But recently some unsuccessful job and credit applicants have brought suit against those who wrote uncomplimentary letters about them. Not surprisingly, people have therefore become more wary about writing meaningful recommendation letters. Now they may simply confirm the facts of the relationship with the applicant, confine their remarks to the positive and bland, or refuse to recommend anyone, especially in writing.

Nevertheless, some applicants and companies still try to solicit recommendations. When they succeed, the recommendation letter is sent directly from the reference to the potential employer or creditor, and the information is considered confidential.

FIGURE 6.2
Letter Making a Routine Credit Request

ACTION
HARDWARE
1411 S. Gillette Avenue
Tulsa, Oklahoma 74104
(918) 754 - 3121

August 5, 1989

OK Distributors, Inc.
2143 16th Street S.W.
Oklahoma City, OK 73108

Ladies and Gentlemen:

Please fill the following order on a credit basis. We would like to have a supply of your small appliances to include in our October promotion:

The main idea is tied in with a statement implying a reader benefit.

12 - #210 WR Electric Toasters @ $18.00	$ 216.00
12 - #486 XL Electric Table-Top Broilers @ $27.00	324.00
12 - #489 XL Electric Table-Top Broilers @ $32.00	384.00
6 - #862 XL Food Blenders @ $28.00	168.00
Total	$1,092.00

Since opening in January 1985, Action Hardware has enjoyed a steady improvement in business. We are capable of paying our bills promptly, as you'll see from the enclosed financial statements. You are welcome to phone us if you need more information for granting credit or if you need names of references.

The background details of the business are necessary if credit is to be granted.

Your WR and XL appliances are of the quality and price range sought by our customers. Because of the steady demand for them, we expect to place orders comparable to this one about every four months. This order could mark the beginning of a profitable relationship between our companies.

The possibility of continuing orders is another reason for the reader to grant credit.

Sincerely,

Maggie Hastings

Maggie Hastings
Housewares Buyer

gh

Enclosures

LETTERS REQUESTING A RECOMMENDATION

Always ask for permission before you use someone's name as a reference.

Before volunteering someone's name as a reference, always ask that person's permission. Some people will not let you use their names, perhaps because they don't know enough about you to feel comfortable writing a letter or because they have a policy of avoiding recommendations. In any event, you are likely to receive the best recommendations from those who agree to write about you, so check first.

When asking a close personal or professional associate to serve as a reference, take the direct approach. Confidently assume that the reader will honor your request, and adopt a professional tone. Your opening paragraph should clearly state that you are applying for a position and that you want the person to write a letter of recommendation. If you have

Refresh the memory of any potential reference you haven't been in touch with for a while.

not had contact with the person for some time, use the opening to refresh the person's memory. Recall the nature of the relationship you had, the dates of association, and any special events that might bring a clear, favorable picture of you to mind.

If you are applying for a job or scholarship or the like, include a copy of your resume to give the reader an idea of the direction your life has taken. After reading the resume, your reader will know what favorable qualities to emphasize and will be able to write the recommendation that best supports your application. If you do not have a resume, you should include in your letter any information about yourself that the reader might use to support a recommendation, such as a description of related jobs you've held.

Close your letter with an expression of appreciation and the full name and address of the person to whom the letter should be sent. When you are asking for an immediate recommendation, you should also mention the deadline. You will make a response more likely if you enclose a stamped, preaddressed envelope.

The following letter covers all these points and adds important information about some special interests of the prospective employer:

May I have a letter of recommendation from you. I'm being considered for a position with Benson, Harley and Yates, Certified Public Accountants, and I have been asked for a recommendation from my major professor in accounting.

As you may recall, I was a student in your advanced accounting class the spring semester of 1986 (my grade was an A). You not only taught me a great deal about accounting but also guided my studies from 1983 until 1986. My grade-point average for all accounting courses was 3.8, as shown on the enclosed resume.

As the resume also shows, I have been working in the accounting department at Murphy's, Inc., since graduating in 1986. Although this job has given me good experience, the opportunity to join Benson, Harley and Yates means a great deal to me. It would be an important step forward in my career and would involve me in the kind of work I was educated to do.

During my interview with Carl Benson, senior member and head of the firm, he said he would like your honest opinion of my preparation and abilities in tax accounting. Your recommendation will surely enhance my chances of being hired.

Professor Gibson, I would greatly appreciate your sending a letter of recommendation to

> Mr. Carl Benson, CPA
> Benson, Harley and Yates
> 5342 Falstaff Street
> Milwaukee, WI 53211

Would you please send the letter so it arrives by May 2. The firm plans to make a decision on this position at a meeting on May 5.

If I'm selected, Professor Gibson, part of the credit will go to you. I'll let you know how things turn out.

LETTERS CHECKING ON A REFERENCE

Many companies prefer to write directly to the person named as a reference. Like letters requesting a recommendation, letters checking on a reference should be specific about the type of information needed and the use to which it will be put. If Carl Benson, the head of the accounting firm, had written the letter directly to Professor Gibson, his request might have read like this:

We are considering Joan M. Takahashi for a position in the tax division of our firm. Because you had close, continuing contact with Ms. Takahashi as her major professor in accounting, she has given your name as a reference.

Ms. Takahashi's overall academic record is excellent. But as you well know, work in taxation requires an ability to deal with complex situations as well as a thorough knowledge of accounting and tax laws. We are interested in your opinion of Ms. Takahashi's abilities in handling assignments in this specialized area.

Your evaluation will, of course, be kept confidential.

We would greatly appreciate having your comments by May 2, because our decision on this matter is an agenda item for our executive meeting of May 5.

Notice that this letter explains why Professor Gibson's opinions are valued, states that the applicant has authorized this request, and includes pertinent information about the requirements of the position and general qualities by which the applicant is being evaluated. Because it has been written to Professor Gibson at her business address (the university) and requests information about a third party (Joan Takahashi), no stamped, preaddressed envelope has been enclosed.

Guarantee confidentiality to help protect a reference from legal problems.

Promise confidentiality when you write a letter to check on a reference. The person supplying a frank recommendation could be subject to a libel suit if false, negative, written information were made available. Charges of discrimination are another potential problem, so avoid asking for information about an applicant's age, gender, race, color, religion, marital status, physical handicaps, or personal traits—unless it is directly related to the position and you are satisfied that you considered these factors under current laws.

ISSUING INVITATIONS

In issuing an invitation

- Present the main idea (the invitation)
- Provide full and accurate details about the event (where, when, and the like)

In the sense that they are simple messages requesting action from people who are interested or willing, invitations are direct requests. In writing invitations, therefore, you should present the main idea ("You are invited") as well as give accurate details of what the event is, who is giving it, the place, the date, and the time. Thoughtful additional details might include directions or a simple map, the location of parking, choice of menu, cost, and the simplest way to respond. If you don't check and recheck the accuracy of these details before mailing the invitations, you may find yourself without guests on the day of the event.

This invitation seeks to capture interest in the first line by mentioning the topic:

DISCOVER HOW TO BE A WINNER
UNDER PRESSURE!

The attention-catching opening presents the invitation.

Coping with competing demands is a problem we all face. But you can easily develop coping skills. Come and hear Julia Knight's incisive views on this important subject. She'll be the guest speaker at the

OMEGA PI CHAPTER MEETING

Tuesday, June 13, at 7:00 p.m.

Boyle Hall

The essential details are brief because the meeting is a regular one, but they are displayed prominently.

Ms. Knight, the national president of Omega Pi, is well known as an entertaining and stimulating speaker. You'll enjoy every minute. And after her talk, you're invited to stay for another of our lively after-the-speech discussions.

A note about the speaker creates interest.

To assure yourself of a seat, be sure to mail your reservation card today.

The close asks for action and makes it easy.

Even an informal invitation should

- State all the necessary details
- Convince the reader to attend

Informal invitations like this one may also take the form of a brief letter or memo, perhaps with a reservation blank at the bottom of the page. Although informal in style, they must still state all necessary details and convince the reader to attend.

Because invitations for an open house in honor of a special anniversary or for some other occasion are somewhat more formal, they should be printed. Notice how the listed details convey a tone of welcome in this invitation from a savings and loan association:

Formal invitations should be printed.

YOU are invited . . .

To an OPEN HOUSE in our spacious new building at a new location:

546 Lincoln Avenue
Sunday, February 5, 1989
10 a.m. to 3 p.m.

SEE OUR NEW FACILITIES

ENJOY REFRESHMENTS WITH US

RENEW YOUR ACQUAINTANCE WITH OUR SENIOR
STAFF AND MEET OUR NEW STAFF MEMBERS

We hope you'll come celebrate with us!

CHECKLIST FOR INVITATIONS

A. Direct Statement of the Request

- ☐ 1. Clearly indicate that the request is an invitation.
- ☐ 2. Indicate the central purpose of the event.

B. Justification, Explanation, and Details

- ☐ 1. Clarify the reason for inviting the reader.
- ☐ 2. Discuss the event in terms of the pleasures of attending, the significance of the event, the importance of attending, or the job to be done at the event.
- ☐ 3. Specify all necessary details, including the nature of the event, when the event takes place (date and time), where the event is being held and how to find the site, the program schedule, the expected formality of the attire, how many and what types of guests are permitted, what type of refreshments will be served, suggestions about parking, what guests are expected to bring.
- ☐ 4. Check the format of the invitation.
  - ☐ a. Lay out the invitations to be attractive and inviting.
  - ☐ b. Properly highlight essential information.
- ☐ 5. Specify the method for responding to the invitation.
- ☐ 6. Make a response as simple as possible by enclosing a form, phone number, or address in a prominent position.
- ☐ 7. Specify deadline for the response.

C. Courteous Close with Request for Specific Action

- ☐ 1. Close enthusiastically and graciously.
- ☐ 2. Emphasize how the reader may benefit by attending.

SUMMARY

The purpose of a direct request is to gain a specific response from the reader, whether the answer to a question, the delivery of goods or services, or some other sort of action. Although a favorable response is assumed, you can ensure cooperation by maintaining a cordial and you-oriented tone. Direct requests are used for placing orders, requesting routine information and action, requesting claims and adjustments, requesting credit, inquiring about people, and issuing invitations.

To ease the reader's task, you should begin with the request and then provide any justification and explanatory details that will help the reader execute the request correctly. If you request several items or pose several secondary questions, number them for clarity. The letter can then close courteously with a request for specific action and an indication of any deadline. By emphasizing a benefit to the reader, you also increase chances for a favorable and prompt response.

COMMUNICATION CHALLENGES AT TOUCAN-DU

One of the companies that Julie Regan and her partner encountered on their initial buying trip was a small exporter in Singapore called Tiger Balm Exports, Ltd. Although Julie and her partner had already bought products similar to those offered by Tiger Balm Exports, they especially liked the quality of the work and the imagination displayed by the artisans supplying the company. They asked the owner, Mr. Ang Kok Hin, to send them some information for future reference.

The brochure that Tiger Balm Exports sent lists three categories of products: Carved Mahogany Animal Figurines, approximately 12 to 15 inches in height ($21 U.S.) or 2 to 3 feet in height ($47 U.S.); Ornamental Brass Ceremonial Plaques, approximately 18 inches in diameter ($18 U.S.); and Indigo Batik Cotton Fabric Squares (Traditional Patterns or Pictorial Representations), approximately 1 yard square ($24 U.S.).

Individual Challenge: Julie has asked you to write out an order to Tiger Balm Exports. In the margins of the brochure, she's indicated that she wants a dozen of the smaller carved figurines (four each of elephants, monkeys, and tigers), a large carved elephant, and a large carved tiger. Although the brochure doesn't mention specific animals, you assume Julie saw figurines like the ones she wants when she was in Singapore. She has also penciled in "24—for pillows" next to the batik fabric entry and has circled the word "patterns." The brochure doesn't say anything about shipping fees, but you know Julie has an account with a cargo airline that lets her pay for air shipments from Southeast Asia in one monthly payment. She has already written out a check to Tiger Balm Exports to send with her initial order; all you have to do is fill in the total amount. Send the letter to Mr. Ang Kok Hin, Tiger Balm Exports, Ltd., 469 Bukit Timah Road, Singapore 1025.

Team Challenge: When ordered products arrive at Toucan-Du, a group of you usually work together to unpack and inspect them. You notice that the shipment from Tiger Balm Exports has a few problems, none of them too unusual for an import business like Toucan-Du. For one thing, instead of getting four carved monkeys, you get two monkeys and two exotic-looking birds (which are actually more attractive than the monkeys). For another, you get only 21 fabric squares instead of 24; yet there is no indication that Toucan-Du has been credited for the short shipment or that the other three fabric squares will ever be shipped. When Julie calls from the Philippines, where she's gone on another buying trip, you ask her what to do. "I trust your judgment on the birds," she says. "Talk it over, and if you think we should keep them, okay. Maybe we should even return the monkeys and get more birds. But be sure to write a letter to Mr. Ang about the batik squares." Discuss what you should do, have each member of the team draft a letter, and then evaluate one another's letters. Your end product should be a single letter.

QUESTIONS FOR DISCUSSION

1. What does a writer who plans to use the direct approach assume about the reader?
2. Why is it inappropriate to begin a request with a brief personal introduction?
3. What are some considerations that determine how friendly and personal the tone of a direct request should be?
4. What precautions should be taken in writing secondary questions in a direct request?
5. Why is it inappropriate to thank a reader "in advance" for a response?
6. What element of an order letter makes it a legally binding contract?
7. What types of request letters might businesses write to regular customers?
8. Why are you doing a business a favor when you speak up about defective products or careless service?
9. If you are writing to a firm to request an adjustment, to whom should you address your letter? Why?
10. If you want someone to write a letter of recommendation on your behalf, what information should you supply?

DOCUMENTS FOR ANALYSIS

Read the following letters, and then (1) analyze the strengths and/or weaknesses of each numbered sentence and (2) revise each letter so it follows this chapter's guidelines.

DOCUMENT 6.A

(1) Your ads in a recent local newspaper have caught my attention. (2) I'd appreciate it greatly if you could send me accurate answers to these questions:

(3) 1. What information can you provide about the stainless steel ElectroPerk coffee pot? Does it work O.K.?

(4) 2. Can it be repaired when it breaks, and are repairs covered by a warranty or store policy? Or will I have to pay for repairs on faulty merchandise?

(5) 3. What is the price range on the machine?

(6) 4. Does it come with attachments? Do attachments cost extra? Is the machine hard to use?

(7) Let me know the answers to these questions as soon as possible, please. (8) I am considering several other models.

DOCUMENT 6.B

(1) I'm writing to inquire about your recent order for a custom wedding suit. (2) You forgot to mention what color you want and also failed to include your measurements. (3) I'd like to clear up this confusion quickly so that we will be able to provide you with the suit before the wedding. (4) When, exactly, is the happy day?

(5) I know you must be busy getting ready for the wedding, but if you can spare the time, you might want to stop by in person to pick out your suit, because we do offer an incredibly wide selection of fine wedding attire. (6) At that time, you could also select an appropriate tie and shirt. (7) I would also suggest that you choose clothing for your best man and ushers, assuming that you are having a large wedding. (8) We are prepared to provide the best in both custom and rental formal attire for your entire wedding party, regardless of how large or small it may be. (9) Incidentally, you should also bring your fiancee along to coordinate the men's clothing with the bridesmaids' dresses. (10) You know how picky women are about clothes.

(11) If you can't come by in person, you should send me a letter stating your measurements and indicating your color and style preferences, or call me at 633-4296. (12) After we receive this information, we will need at least two weeks to complete the suit. (13) Thank you for your cooperation in this matter.

DOCUMENT 6.C

(1) About six months ago, I bought one of your watches at a store ten miles away from the town where I live and attend college. (2) Although the watch is attractive, it doesn't keep very good time. (3) Generally, it loses about 10 or 15 minutes every day or so. (4) This is inconvenient. (5) In fact, I have been late for class repeatedly, and my professors are annoyed with me.

(6) Finally, I decided to take the watch to the repair shop. (7) The repairman said the watch was cheap, then charged me $15 to fix it, which is almost as much as I paid for the silly thing. (8) It still doesn't work right, and I am out $15. (9) Would you be willing to cover the repair bill for me and replace the watch? (10) I am enclosing a copy of the repair bill, along with the watch. (11) Thank you for your help.

CASES

PLACING ORDERS

1. Team colors: Letter placing a complex order

Congratulations! You and five of your friends have just made the track team. Before competition begins, you, as team captain, have to order some matching warm-up suits.

The coach, Bud Schopp, passes along to you a slick four-color flier from All Sports Supply, Inc., P.O. Box 2107, Columbia, MD 21045. The outfit you decide to order is the Roadrunner style; it's available in just about any two-color combination you could imagine, including your school's colors. Each warm-up suit costs $59.95; postage and handling charges are $2.00 for each suit; the order is subject to a 5 percent sales tax.

Your task: Order the six warm-up suits you need from All Sports Supply. Remember to specify the main color and the accent color you want. The biggest problem is likely to arise in getting the right sizes. Find out from your friends the size they take for both jackets and pants, and provide All Sports Supply with a complete and accurate list. Use the coach's name and your school's address as the shipping and billing address, but sign the letter yourself as team captain.

2. Party time: Letter reserving party facilities As chairman of the Junior Civic Association's entertainment committee, you have the duty of reserving a site for the Spring Fling. You have called three facilities for information and prices and have decided to rent the Oak Room at the Lennox Hotel for the night of May 2. Renting the elegant old ballroom will cost $1,200, but the extra services that are available—complimentary valet parking, cloakroom, bar service, sound system, two large check-in tables with cloth covers, 120 deluxe folding chairs—justify the price.

Your task: Write to Samantha Wilde, the Lennox Hotel's facilities manager, to confirm the arrangements you discussed over the phone. Remind Ms. Wilde of the date and time you require and the services you expect to be provided. Don't forget that the band, The Ravers (led by Tommy Killeen), will need time to set up in advance; somebody from your organization will be there to greet them, but you want the hotel staff to be prepared for their arrival. You will also have a dozen large flower arrangements delivered by Yoshiko Flowers around the same time. The Lennox Hotel is located at 701 Brody Avenue, Missoula, MT 59806.

3. Real fatigues: Complex order for Banana Republic Ever since you saw *Indiana Jones and the Temple of Doom*, you've been intrigued with Banana Republic Travel & Safari Clothing Co. Becoming an assistant buyer has been a dream come true. Mel and Patricia Ziegler, the free-spirited husband-and-wife team who founded the firm, spend about half their time traveling to remote places looking for clothes that will appeal to weekend adventurers. You help handle the paperwork associated with their buying trips.

On a recent trip to West Germany, the Zieglers arranged to buy some authentic NATO (North Atlantic Treaty Organization) fatigues, first worn by Western armies in Korea and later by NATO troops on maneuvers in the North Atlantic. The fatigues are a brownish-green blend of wool flannel and nylon. They feature thigh pockets with an outside compartment for writing tools, flashlight, or knife; ribbon ties to secure keys, canteen, or ice axe; and suspender buttons. NATO is asking a price of $9 per pair.

The Zieglers originally ordered 9,000 pairs: 1,500 each in sizes 30, 32, 34, 36, 38, and 40. Within each size category, the Zieglers stipulated that the pants should be divided into three lengths: 500 short, 500 medium, and 500 long. After thinking over the order, however, the Zieglers have decided to request 500 additional medium-length pants in sizes 32, 34, and 36, a total of 1,500 pairs. At the same time, they have decided to decrease their order for size 30 pants in the long length from 500 to 250 and to decrease their order for size 40 short pants from 500 to 250.

Your task: Write to Lt. Colonel Karl Westheim at NATO headquarters, clarifying the change in the order. The address is 1110 Brussels, Belgium. Be sure to specify that the merchandise should be shipped to you within two weeks, care of Banana Republic Travel & Safari Clothing Co., P.O. Box 7737, San Francisco, CA 94120. The Zieglers have already paid a deposit of $1,800. The balance will be paid by check within 30 days of receiving the merchandise.[1]

REQUESTING ROUTINE INFORMATION AND ACTION

4. Who has the weakest knees? Memo requesting information from within the Hospital Corporation of America Your boss has been put in charge of planning new sports medicine facilities for the giant Hospital Corporation of America, which is based in Nashville, Tennessee. "Top management is really excited about this idea," he tells you. "They want us to come up with a plan for adding new sports medicine facilities throughout the country. The big question is, what should we add in which locations?"

"Well," you say, "I suppose that depends on population density to a great extent. But it also depends on how many people engage in which sports in different regions. And we need to know what injuries they sustain. Are there more sprained ankles per capita in Los Angeles than there are in New York City, for example?"

Your task: Seeing that you have a good grasp of the issues involved, your boss tells you to write a memo asking the marketing and industry research department for help in analyzing regional patterns in sports injuries. It should be addressed to David Young, who's the assistant vice president. Suggest the specific types of information you need, such as the numbers of various sports-related injuries currently being handled at existing HCA hospitals and the types of sports activities common to some well-defined regions. Your boss wants to receive this information within three weeks.[2]

5. Art attack: Memo requesting action from within Battery Park City Authority Battery Park City is a partially completed 92-acre complex of offices, residences, and stores on the banks of the Hudson River in lower Manhattan. Such notable firms as Merrill Lynch and American Express have already moved into the complex, helping to make it one of the most successful real estate developments in North America.

Meyer S. Frucher, president and chief executive officer of Battery Park City Authority, has purposely sought to achieve a luxurious ambience in the development. So far, he has spent $4.5 million on an art and architecture program, which includes a large glass-enclosed Winter Garden filled with exotic plants and many works of sculpture scattered among the buildings. His efforts to date have drawn rave reviews.

At the moment, Mr. Frucher is busy planning the next phase of Battery Park City, a 280,000 square foot retail complex designed to lure tourists and shoppers. He is trying to decide what sort of art to include in this part of the development, and he wants you to help.

Your task: Draft a memo to Evelyn Whitelaw, who has been conducting research for Battery Park City Authority, asking her to find some information on the impact of art in retail shopping developments. Before the end of next month, you need to know whether other shopping centers have benefited from the expense of high-quality art and architecture and what types of art they have found most practical. Give Evelyn as many specific guidelines for her research as you can.[3]

6. A possible turnaround investment: Inquiry about a troubled company You are examining the 1988 balance sheet of Mid-Continent Industries, Inc., a manufacturer and distributor of automobile replacement parts. Given the low price of Mid-Continent stock and the attractiveness of its products, you are interested in purchasing some of its stock for long-term investment. But you are concerned by the ratio of current assets to liabilities and by the general weakness of the balance sheet.

Your task: Write to Mid-Continent Industries to determine its prospects for improving its performance in the foreseeable future. The company's annual report indicates that queries should be addressed to Michael Washington, Public Relations Department, Mid-Continent Industries, Inc., 602 Rogers Avenue, Fort Smith, AR 72901. Explain the reason for your inquiry, and in your letter show that you understand something about accounting.

7. Please tell me: Request for information about a product You're a consumer, and you've probably seen hundreds of products that you'd like to buy. (If not, look at the advertisements in your favorite magazine for ideas.) Choose a big-ticket item that is rather complicated, such as a stereo system or vacation in the Caribbean.

Your task: You surely have some questions about the features of your chosen product or about its price, guarantees, local availability, and so on. Write to the company or organization offering it, and ask four questions that are important to you. Be sure to include

MID-CONTINENT INDUSTRIES, INC.
BALANCE SHEET
For period ending December 31, 1988

ASSETS		LIABILITIES AND SHAREHOLDERS' EQUITY	
Current Assets		Current Liabilities	
Cash	$ 240,132	Long-Term Debt (current)	$ 796,954
Notes Receivable	350,776	Notes Payable (to banks)	995,710
Inventory	2,576,401	Accounts Payable	2,539,099
Prepayments	442,958	Accrued Expenses	474,803
Total Current Assets	$3,610,267	Taxes Payable	78,883
		Total Current Liabilities	$4,885,449
Noncurrent Assets			
Notes Receivable	$ 432,958	Other Liabilities	
Land	286,357	Senior Notes Payable	$3,173,987
Buildings (net)	987,357	Total Other Liabilities	$3,173,987
Equipment (net)	1,847,341		
Total Noncurrent Assets	$3,554,013		
		Shareholders' Equity	
Goodwill (net)	$ 774,915	3,303,162 Shares @ 1¢	$ 33,032
		Retained Earnings	(153,273)
TOTAL ASSETS	$7,939,195	TOTAL LIABILITIES	$7,939,195

enough background information so the reader can answer your questions satisfactorily.

If requested to do so by your instructor, mail a copy of your letter (after your instructor has had an opportunity to review it) to the company or organization. After a few weeks, you and your classmates may wish to compare responses and to answer this question: How well do companies or organizations respond to unsolicited inquiries?

8. The bull is back: Inquiry about selecting a bull for a Merrill Lynch television commercial After several years of being "bullish on America," Merrill Lynch & Co. decided to change its advertising strategy. The veteran longhorn bull that starred in the brokerage firm's TV commercials was replaced by human actors who portrayed Merrill Lynch staff members solving their clients' investment problems.

Unfortunately, the new ads were not a success with either the viewing public or Merrill Lynch employees. Stampeded by loyal cattle fans, management has decided to revive the old campaign. But alas, they have discovered that their star bull has hung up his horns and is retired in California.

The problem now is to find a new bull. Your boss, Jim Walsh, corporate advertising manager, has specified one with a cooperative temperament, handsome horns, and a graceful lope. The bull will be required to film commercials this summer in California, Wyoming, Arizona, New Jersey, and Manhattan. Jim has been authorized to pay up to $100,000 to cover any fees and expenses associated with the bull during the filming of these commercials; Merrill Lynch prefers to rent the bull rather than buy it outright.

Your task: As an assistant to Jim Walsh, you have been asked to draft a letter to the Texas Longhorn Breeder's Association asking for their help in finding a bull for Merrill Lynch's commercials. Address your letter to William Clark, president of the association, whose office is at 2315 N. Main Street, Suite 402, Fort Worth, TX 76106.[4]

WRITING DIRECT REQUESTS FOR CLAIMS AND ADJUSTMENTS

9. The (slightly) mislaid carpet: Request for a small adjustment To make the old house look better, you started by contracting for three rooms of wall-to-wall carpeting. You chose the color burnt mauve and the "thistle" texture and requested the "three rooms for the price of two" special. Yesterday you turned the house over to Universal Carpeting.

Today you inspect the job. At first glance, the carpeting looks fine. But then you examine the job more closely. A small section of carpet laid in the living room in a corner near the fireplace has been carelessly fitted, and some of the flooring shows through. In the dining room, excess carpeting extends a quarter inch up the wall for several feet. You understood that one length would never be joined to another in the middle of a room, but in the dining room such a seam has obviously been made. (Universal presumably did this to save money; carpeting is wasted when rolls must be cut to reach from one wall to another.) As you inspect the perimeter of the job, you find that the tacking is too light in some sections. And finally, your rosewood coffee table sports a ring where a can of some sort of solvent must have been placed.

You feel that some follow-up work is in order, and you'd also like a modest price adjustment for the damage to your rosewood table and for the two roll-ends that join in your dining room.

Your task: Write a letter to Robert Wragg, the proprietor of Universal Carpeting, at 712 Fifth Avenue S.W., Calgary, Alberta T2P 0M9. Express precisely what you expect in both service and reduced charges. At this early stage of the negotiations, you have no reason to believe Mr. Wragg won't comply with your request. A positive close might suggest the mutual benefits that would follow successful adjustment of the difficulties.

10. The $30 lesson: Request for settlement of a dubious transaction The phone rang, and she spoke to you with a soft, confident voice: "I'm calling from Nationwide Renewals about your subscription to *National Photographer*. It expires in three months, but for $30 we can put through a three-year renewal. It's part of a promotion. That's a good price, isn't it?"

What could you say? "Yes, it is."

"That's fine," said the gentle voice. "You'll receive our statement in a day or so. Just send your check along with our statement to the California address. All right?"

After you paid the Nationwide Renewal bill, a statement from *National Photographer* appeared in the mail. Being patient and trusting, you waited for the matter to sort itself out. Another statement arrived, informing you that the magazine would stop appearing in your mailbox if you didn't renew.

You don't have the address of Nationwide Renewals, but you do have your check. The stamp on the back indicates that it cleared three months ago (to the day!) through "Bay Area Bank, Redwood City, CA," to the account of "Nationwide Renewal Service 0101379170." The check was endorsed by the firm's bank stamp.

Your task: Write to *National Photographer* to get the subscription problem solved. The magazine's business offices are at 3714 Dinsmore Street, Denver, CO 80225.

MAKING ROUTINE CREDIT REQUESTS

11. Footing the bill: Routine request for retail credit After 12 months in business, your shoe shop (named Rowdy's after the puppy who once chewed all your shoes) seems to be succeeding. You were clever enough to locate it near a campus, and you carry a limited but appropriate variety of footwear that appeals to the college crowd. At the moment, you have $5,000 worth of inventory, you just finished paying off the loan for the improvements the shop needed when you took over, and your remaining payments seem manageable given the way business has been growing.

Today Joe Randall, the representative for Bailey-Brown Shoes, stopped by to tell you about a new line of moderately priced, fashionable sandals that have been selling well near colleges. You're sure you could sell the sandals too, now that warm weather is approaching. Besides, Bailey-Brown's other shoes have always sold well in your shop.

The only problem is that you don't have a lot of ready cash. You mentioned the problem to Joe, but he shrugged it off. "We have credit arrangements with a lot of stores like Rowdy's," he said. "All you have to do is write to us on your letterhead, asking for credit. Enclose a financial statement, but summarize your financial position in the letter. We'll also need the name of your shop's bank and the account number."

Your task: Write the letter requesting credit. Address it to Amy Provol, Credit Department, Bailey-Brown Shoes, Ltd., 602 Warden Avenue, Scarborough, Ontario M1L 3Z7. Make up any financial details that you feel are necessary; you might also provide as references the names of three people who can vouch for your credit worthiness.

INQUIRING ABOUT PEOPLE

12. Remember me? Request for someone to write a letter on your behalf You are applying for a job similar to one you held before. Alonzo Montoya, your former employer, knows something of your abilities and would probably be willing to comment on your qualifications for the new job. However, it's been a while since you worked for Mr. Montoya, and he knows relatively little about your more recent accomplishments and aspirations.

Your task: Write to Mr. Montoya at 4124 Beaumont Boulevard, San Antonio, TX 78200, asking him whether he would be willing to write a letter of recommendation on your behalf to a potential employer. (As an alternative, write to an actual former employer.) Your letter should be both friendly and businesslike, and you should demonstrate that you are prepared for the job you are seeking. Bring Mr. Montoya up-to-date on your accomplishments since you worked for him.

13. Shopping for talent: Memo inquiring about an employee in another department As manager of women's apparel for Clovine's, a growing chain of moderate to upscale department stores in South Florida, you are always looking for smart, aggressive young buyers. Right now you're particularly in need of an assistant buyer for your women's sportswear division. Because Clovine's likes to promote from within, you've been scouting store personnel for likely candidates.

Angela Ramirez, a salesclerk in the designer sportswear boutique of your main store in Miami, has caught your attention. She's quick, friendly, and good at sizing up a customer's preferences. Moreover, at recent meetings she's made some intelligent remarks about new trends in South Florida.

Angela's supervisor is Rachel Cohen, who is on vacation this week. When Rachel returns, you'll be out of town for two weeks. Rachel could help you decide whether to interview this salesclerk, yet you need to have a list of candidates when you return.

Your task: Write a memo to Rachel Cohen, sales supervisor, inquiring about Angela Ramirez's performance at Clovine's. Ultimately, you want to know if Rachel thinks Angela has the energy and aptitude for the demanding job of assistant buyer. Mention to Rachel that you'll check with the personnel department about Angela's education and employment history; you're mainly interested in a character assessment. Ask any specific questions you consider appropriate, and indicate when you'd like to receive Rachel's comments.

ISSUING INVITATIONS

14. "Dear distinguished world figure": Letter inviting a special guest to be honored Every year, the Student-Faculty Commencement Committee of your college selects a distinguished person to receive an honorary degree in Humane Letters at the June graduation ceremony. The degree recipient usually gives a brief talk as part of the graduation ceremonies and attends a campus reception given in his or her honor. The honoree also has the opportunity to get to know your campus and the surrounding area.

It is campus policy not to reimburse travel costs for recipients of honorary degrees, but a member of the faculty provides housing for the two-day campus visit. It is also campus policy not to award the honorary degree unless the recipient is present.

Your task: As chairman of the Student-Faculty Commencement Committee, it is up to you to send an invitation to this year's honoree. (To whom should you write? You might look through a national or international Who's Who.) Tell why your college is highly regarded, and invite the honoree to your campus to accept the award.

15. Happy 80th! Form letter inviting Fuller Brush sales representatives to attend a party As a member of the public relations department at Fuller Brush, you have been busy preparing for the company's 80th birthday celebration. The president, Len Dunlap, wants the party to be a special event, something that will be remembered by both the public and the sales force, currently 15,000 to 20,000 strong.

To show his appreciation of the sales representatives' contribution to Fuller Brush's success, Mr. Dunlap has decided to invite all of them to an old-fashioned parade and chicken dinner on the lawn at company headquarters in Great Bend, Kansas. The party—which will also include entertaining speeches, displays of new products, music, dancing, games, and fireworks—will be held from 11:00 a.m. to 8:00 p.m. on September 4. Sales representatives are encouraged to bring their families.

Travel and accommodation expenses will be paid by the company. However, people coming from a long way must make their own flight reservations into nearby Wichita and book lodgings there at either the Holiday Inn or the Ramada Inn. Special express buses will transport the guests from the hotels to the party. Transportation from the airport to the hotels will also be provided.

Your task: Draft a form letter inviting the sales representatives to attend the birthday bash. Ask them to reply to the invitation by August 7, so you will have ample time to arrange the details of the party.[5]

CHAPTER SEVEN

After studying this chapter, you will be able to

- Understand when to write a routine, good-news, or goodwill letter or memo
- Adjust the basic pattern to fit the type of letter or memo you are writing
- Add resale and sales promotion material when appropriate
- Encourage your reader to take any desired action
- Avoid the pitfalls of writing credit approvals and recommendation letters
- Put such specialized messages as instructions and press releases in the correct form
- Adopt the proper tone in writing goodwill letters

WRITING ROUTINE, GOOD-NEWS, AND GOODWILL MESSAGES

Jacqueline Millan

COMMUNICATION CLOSE-UP AT PEPSICO

In her job as manager of corporate contributions for PepsiCo, Inc., and vice president–contributions of the PepsiCo Foundation, Jacqueline Millan has the opportunity to write many different kinds of letters and memos. Some are businesslike responses to requests for funding or information; some are "bread-and-butter" notes meant to enhance PepsiCo's relations with employees, potential customers, and the world at large. But the way Jackie writes them, they all have something in common. "It's important to put a lot of thought into how a letter or memo is going to be interpreted by the reader," Jackie says, "because that piece of paper can make a big difference in the reader's perception of you and your company."

As the parent company of Pepsi-Cola, Pizza Hut, Taco Bell, Frito-Lay, Kentucky Fried Chicken, and Seven-Up International, PepsiCo, Inc., is highly visible, and so people write constantly to the Purchase, New York, headquarters to request support for one worthy cause or another. After

Many messages sent out by PepsiCo Foundation bear good news to community-service organizations seeking support.

reviewing a proposal, Jackie constructs a memo (typically one page long) for the committee that makes the final decision. "I put the recommendation in the first paragraph," Jackie says, "so a committee member who already knows about the organization requesting the grant doesn't have to read the whole thing. I'm also a great believer in headings and bullets and attachments. One of the traps that many people fall into is writing long, comprehensive memos that look impressive but don't get read."

One of Jackie's other responsibilities is to oversee PepsiCo's scholarship program. Recently she received a letter from an employee requesting information. "In our reply, we tried to establish an understanding about the content up front," Jackie recalls. "We said thank you for your letter inquiring about the eligibility requirements for children of employees; here's the information. In the middle of the letter, we spelled out what the eligibility requirements are. After we answered the question, we mentioned that we were enclosing a brochure about the scholarship program. The closing statement was something like 'We're glad to provide you with this information. If you have any questions, please get in touch with us again. Best wishes to your son or daughter in applying for the scholarship.' "

When an employee succeeds in winning a scholarship, Jackie writes again. "PepsiCo is not a company to neglect the social graces," she says. "We send the student a personal note signed by the chairman of PepsiCo's board." The point in goodwill letters like these is to foster a sense that the sixth-largest employer in the United States is a warm, caring organization. Jackie feels that the important element is detail, "to try to personalize as much as you can. The more pieces of information you can glean about the person, the better your letter." Thus the congratulatory letter to one scholarship winner closed with this sentence: "We wish you much success in your studies in meteorology at the State University of New York at Oneonta."

Why does Jackie make this extra effort, even when time is in short supply? "In business we tend to concentrate so much on speedy responses that we may not think as much as we need to about the reader's perceptions. I'm always thinking, 'What will the reader think about PepsiCo after reading this letter?' " Even when the message is routine, it's a relevant question.

PLANNING POSITIVE MESSAGES

Organizational plan for routine, good-news, and goodwill messages:

- Main point
- Details
- Close

Most business communication consists of routine, good-news, and goodwill messages, so you will probably get a lot of practice composing them. But if you labor over these projects, you are budgeting your time inefficiently. A clear understanding of how such messages are organized will allow you to compose excellent examples quickly. Whether written or oral, they follow a simple formula: clear statement of the main idea, necessary details, courteous close. Because the main idea comes right at the beginning, this type of message is said to follow the direct plan.

CLEAR STATEMENT OF THE MAIN IDEA

Almost all business communication has two basic purposes: (1) to convey information and (2) to produce in the audience a favorable (or at least accepting) attitude or response. When you begin a message with a statement of your purpose, as Jackie Millan did in her memo to the PepsiCo employee who wanted scholarship information, you are preparing your audience for the explanation that follows.

The opening must be clear and concise. Notice that the following introductory statements make the same point. However, one is cluttered with unnecessary information that buries the purpose; the other is brief and to the point.

INSTEAD OF THIS	WRITE THIS
I am pleased to inform you that after deliberating the matter carefully, our personnel committee has recommended you for appointment as a staff accountant.	You've been selected to join our firm as a staff accountant, beginning March 20.

Before you begin, have a clear idea of what you want to say.

The best way to write a clear opening is to have a clear idea of what you want to say. Before you put one word on paper, ask yourself this: What is the single most important message I have for the audience?

NECESSARY DETAILS

The middle part is typically the longest section of a routine, good-news, or goodwill message. Your reason for communicating can usually be expressed in a sentence or two, but you'll need more space or time to explain your point completely so the audience will not be left with confusion or lingering doubt.

Answer questions in the order they were asked.

The task of providing necessary details is easiest when you are responding to a series of questions. You can simply answer them in order, possibly in a numbered sequence.

In addition to providing details in the middle section, you must maintain the supportive tone established at the beginning. This tone is easy to continue when your letter is purely good news. For example, consider this letter:

As we discussed, your major responsibilities as staff accountant in the internal accounting division will be to monitor our accounts receivable program. For this position, we're happy to offer you $2,750 monthly. You'll immediately be eligible for our health and pension plans and reduced membership fees at the Fitness and Racquet Club on Chestnut Avenue, near our office. Knowing how much you like to play squash, I'd also like to invite you to sign up right away for our Accountants' Squash Tournament, which begins next month.

Embed negative information in a positive context.

But when a routine message must convey mildly disappointing information, put the negative answer into as favorable a context as possible. Take a look at the following example:

INSTEAD OF THIS	WRITE THIS
No, we no longer carry the Sportsgirl line of sweaters.	The new Olympic line has replaced the Sportsgirl sweaters that you asked about. Olympic features a wider range of colors and sizes and more contemporary styling.

A bluntly negative explanation was replaced with a more complete description that emphasized how the audience could benefit from the change. Be careful, though: You can use negative information in this type of message only if you're reasonably sure the audience will respond positively to your message. Otherwise, use the indirect approach, which is described more thoroughly in Chapter 8.

COURTEOUS CLOSE

Make sure the audience understands what to do next and how that action will benefit her or him.

Your message is most likely to succeed if your audience is left with the feeling that you have their personal welfare in mind. In addition, if follow-up action is required, you should clearly state who will do what next. Highlighting a benefit to the audience, this closing statement clearly summarizes the desired procedure: "Mail us your order this week so you can be wearing your Shetland coat by the first of October."

WRITING POSITIVE REPLIES

Many memos and business letters are written in response to an order, inquiry, or request. If the answer is yes or straightforward information, the direct plan is appropriate.

ACKNOWLEDGING ORDERS

Acknowledgment letters play a role in building goodwill.

One of the simplest letters to write is one confirming that a customer's order has been received and is being filled. An order acknowledgment is unnecessary if the products are being shipped or the services provided immediately. But acknowledgments of large orders, first orders from a customer, and orders that cannot be filled right away are appropriate. To foster goodwill, the wise business communicator sends a letter personalized with the customer's name and specific product information, even though it may use stock paragraphs.

In accordance with the direct plan, the first paragraph of an acknowledgment letter is a statement of "good news." The customer has placed an order and looks forward to receiving the merchandise; all you have to say is that the order is being processed and that the merchandise is on its way.

The middle section should demonstrate the professionalism of the firm through a clear, accurate summary of the transaction: when the delivery may be expected; the cost of the merchandise, shipping, and taxes; an explanation of problems that might have arisen. If you have recently established a new credit account for this customer, you should summarize your credit terms.

Resale: information about the company or product that confirms the customer's good judgment in making the transaction

Sales promotion: information about goods or services that may supplement the customer's purchase

Letters of this type frequently do a bit of selling in the middle or closing section as well. Resale information bolsters the customer's confidence by pointing out the good points of the product or the company and the way those good points will benefit the customer. Sales promotion—talk about something you offer that the customer may not be aware of, may not have thought of buying, or hasn't yet purchased—takes advantage of the customer's obvious interest in your products. Sending along brochures or order blanks makes an additional purchase easier. To be effective, both resale and sales promotion material should demonstrate the "you" attitude. Emphasize benefits to the customer rather than benefits to the company.

Despite its business purpose, an order acknowledgment should end on a warm, personal note, with a look toward future dealings.

The following letter was designed to leave the customer satisfied with the handling of the order and prepared to do more business with the writer's firm:

In a little over two weeks, you'll receive your Span-a-Vision videocassette recorder. Be watching for the United Parcel Service delivery van.

The main message is stated clearly right at the start.

Because you live in Massachusetts, you're exempt from the Illinois sales tax. So I'm enclosing a check for $26.15, the amount of the sales tax that you included in your payment.

The middle section conveys specific details about the order.

Mr. Harmon, you're going to enjoy your new videocassette recorder, day after day. It's quite versatile. And to make it even more so, you might want to add a remote-control device. Wired and wireless models compatible with your new videocassette recorder are pictured in the enclosed brochure. Thanks to these state-of-the-art electronic controllers, you can run a videotape on fast forward, rewind the tape, and search quickly for specific portions of the tape--all without budging from your most comfortable chair! Many users have come to think of their remote-control devices as a "must have." Let me urge you to order yours now, during our limited-time 10%-Off Sale.

Resale and sales promotion build on the customer's goodwill toward the product and the company. The customer's name is mentioned, as in a personal conversation, to increase the feeling of friendliness.

When your new videocassette recorder arrives, spend a few minutes with the user's manual that accompanies it. It should answer all your

In closing, the writer offers friendly, accessible help.

questions about how to operate your recorder. If it doesn't, just pick up your phone and call toll-free 1-800-441-6446 from 9 a.m. to 6 p.m. weekdays (Central Standard Time). One of our expert staff members will be happy to help you.

REPLYING TO REQUESTS FOR INFORMATION AND ACTION

Any request is important to the person making it, whether inside or outside the organization. That person's opinion of your company and its products, your department, and you yourself will be influenced by how promptly, graciously, and thoroughly the request is handled. Readers' perceptions are the reason Jackie Millan of PepsiCo is so sensitive to the tone of her letters.

When written on letterhead stationery, a reply legally commits the company to any promised action.

Admittedly, complying with a request is not always easy. The information may not be immediately at hand, and decisions to take some action must often be made at a higher level. Furthermore, because a letter written on letterhead stationery is legally binding, you must often plan your response carefully.

Fortunately, however, many requests are similar. For example, a human resources department gets a lot of inquiries about job openings. Companies usually develop form responses to handle repetitive queries like these. Although form responses are often criticized as being cold and impersonal, much time and thought may go into wording them, and computers permit personalization and the mixing of paragraphs. Thus a computerized form letter prepared with care may actually be more personal and sincere than a quickly dictated, hastily typed "personal" reply.

When a potential sale is involved

Prospective customers often request an annual report, catalog, brochure, swatch of material, or other type of sample or information to help them make a decision about a product encountered through advertising. A polite and helpful response may prompt them to buy. When the customer has not requested the information and is not looking forward to a response, you must use persuasive techniques like those described in Chapter 9. But in a "solicited" sales letter, which the customer is anticipating, you may use the direct plan.

Three main goals when a potential sale is involved:

- Respond to the immediate request
- Encourage a sale
- Convey a good impression of you and your firm

When answering requests where a potential sale is involved, you have three main goals: (1) to respond to the inquiry or answer all the questions; (2) to encourage the future sale; and (3) to leave your reader with a good impression of you and your firm. The following letter succeeds in meeting these three objectives:

Here's the copy of "Brightening Your Bathroom" that you recently requested.

A clear, conversational statement of the main point is all that's required to start.

As beautiful as the full-color photographs are, you really need to inspect Brite-Tiles in person. Only then can you fully appreciate the sparkling

Key information—the address of the local store that carries the merchan-

beauty of their designer colors and patterns and the quality of their fabrication. Baywood Hardware, 313 Front Street in Clear Lake, is the nearest outlet carrying Brite-Tiles. While you're there, ask the salesperson to explain how easy it is to install Brite-Tiles with our chemically compatible cements and grouts.

dise—is presented immediately, along with resale and sales promotion.

From antique Victorian to sleek contemporary, Brite-Tiles will help you achieve just the look you want. Spend a few moments now with the handy chart, "The Right Pattern for Your Decor," on page 5 of the enclosed booklet. Then you'll know which patterns to look for when you visit Baywood Hardware.

A reference to a specific page further emphasizes the benefits of the product. This suggestion also encourages the reader to take one more step toward an actual purchase.

Mrs. Lyle, if you have any questions before or during installation, please phone our toll-free Service Hotline: 1-800-459-3678. You'll get easy-to-follow answers every time.

The personal close confidently points toward the possible sale.

Two goals when no sale is involved:

- Respond to the request
- Leave a favorable impression of your company or foster good working relationships

Some requests from outsiders and most requests from fellow employees are not opportunities to sell a product. In replies to those requests, you have two goals: (1) to answer all the questions honestly and completely and (2) to leave a favorable impression that prepares the way for future business or smooths working relationships. The following is a well-written response to a request from an outsider that does not involve an immediate sale:

Thanks for writing to ask us about the warranty on your Micro-9 computer. Here are the answers to your questions, in the order you asked them:

A brief statement introduces the purpose of the letter.

1. All needed repairs to your computer are covered by the warranty, with the exception of damage caused by abuse, such as dents on the external frame, sheared wiring, or shorting from water penetration. If the cause of damage is in dispute, you may appeal your claim to our independent consumer panel. We will accept their decision.
2. When repair is needed, we'll be happy to pick up your computer and return it repaired for a total delivery charge of only $40. Whenever possible, pickups are made on a next-day basis--and always within two working days of your call.
3. Yes, you can buy a one-year computer service policy any time before the expiration of your 12-month warranty. You can renew this policy indefinitely.

Specific questions are answered clearly and fully, in the order asked and with consideration for the reader's needs.

FIGURE 7.1
Memo Replying to a Routine Request

MEMO

DATE: May 9, 1989

TO: Mark Gundy

FROM: Bill Apodaca

SUBJECT: Temporary Measures to Alleviate Parking Problems

Today we have taken action that should relieve the situation you alerted me to in your memo:

1. We have asked the security department to post new signs at the entrances to the plant warning that our parking facilities are private. They have also been instructed to work with city police to ticket any nonemployee vehicles that block our driveways.

2. Until the problem is completely solved, plant workers have been given a "grace period" extending their clock-in time by five minutes so they can find a parking space.

Apparently, this problem arose because city streets in the surrounding neighborhood are being resurfaced. According to the city traffic department, this work should be completed by the end of next week. Until then, we'll do our best to be good neighbors despite the inconvenience.

Thanks for making me aware of the seriousness of the parking problem. If you have any other suggestions for improvements, please let me know. I plan to stay posted on this matter until parking is once more convenient for you and our other employees.

The good news is announced without any fanfare, and the specific actions are enumerated for easy reference.

The problem's cause and eventual solution are explained to demonstrate awareness and goodwill.

An appreciative, personal, cooperative close confirms the desire to foster good working relationships.

Making sure you're 100 percent satisfied is always our goal, Ms. Worthington. Whenever you have more questions, just let me know. And be sure to let me know how you like your new Micro-9 computer.

A warm, personalized, appreciative close encourages goodwill.

When writing to a fellow employee, you can assume a shared background and goals.

A similar approach is appropriate for responding to requests from fellow employees, although memo format should be used instead of letter format. The memo in Figure 7.1 is a reply written to an employee who had requested that something be done about nonemployee automobiles encroaching on plant parking facilities. Notice that the tone of the memo, while still respectful, is a bit less formal than the tone in the previous letter.

CHECKLIST FOR POSITIVE REPLIES

A. Initial Statement of the Good News or Main Idea

- ☐ 1. Respond promptly to the request.
- ☐ 2. Indicate in your first sentence that you are shipping the customer's order or fulfilling the reader's request.
- ☐ 3. Avoid such trite and obvious statements as "I am pleased to," "We have received," "This is in response to," or "Enclosed please find."
- ☐ 4. If you are acknowledging an order, summarize the transaction.
  - ☐ a. Describe the merchandise in general terms.
  - ☐ b. Express appreciation for the order and the payment, if it has arrived.
  - ☐ c. Welcome a new customer aboard.
- ☐ 5. Convey an upbeat, courteous, you-oriented tone.

B. Middle, Informational Section

- ☐ 1. Imply or express interest in the request.
- ☐ 2. If possible, answer all questions and requests, preferably in the order posed.
  - ☐ a. Adapt replies to the reader's needs.
  - ☐ b. Indicate what you have done and will do.
  - ☐ c. Include any necessary details or interpretations that the reader may need to understand your answers.
- ☐ 3. Provide all the important details about orders.
  - ☐ a. Provide any necessary educational information about the product.
  - ☐ b. Provide details of the shipment, including the approximate arrival time.
  - ☐ c. Clear up any questions of charges (shipping costs, insurance, credit charges, or discounts for quick payment).
- ☐ 4. Use sales opportunities when appropriate.
  - ☐ a. Enclose a brochure that provides routine information and specifications, if possible, pointing out its main value and the specific pages of potential interest to the reader.
  - ☐ b. Call the customer's attention to related products with sales promotion material.
  - ☐ c. Introduce price only after mentioning benefits, but make price and the method of payment clear.
  - ☐ d. Send a credit application to new customers and cash customers, if desirable.
- ☐ 5. If you cannot comply with part of the request, perhaps because the information is unavailable or confidential, tell the reader why this is so, and offer other assistance.
- ☐ 6. Embed negative statements in positive contexts, or balance them with positive alternatives.

C. Warm, Courteous Close

- ☐ 1. Avoid clichés ("Please feel free to").
- ☐ 2. Direct a request to the reader (such as "Please let us know if this procedure does not have the effect you're seeking") or specify the action you want the reader to take, if appropriate.
  - ☐ a. Make the reader's action easy.
  - ☐ b. Refer to the reader benefit of fulfilling your request.
  - ☐ c. Stimulate the reader to act promptly.
- ☐ 3. Use resale material in acknowledging orders to remind the reader of benefits to be derived from this order.
- ☐ 4. Offer additional service, but avoid suggestions of your answer being inadequate, such as "I trust that," "I hope," or other doubtful statements.
- ☐ 5. Express goodwill or take an optimistic look into the future, if appropriate.

RESPONDING FAVORABLY TO CLAIMS AND ADJUSTMENT REQUESTS

In general, it pays to give customers the benefit of the doubt.

As anyone in business knows, customers sometimes return merchandise to a company, complain about its services, ask to be compensated, and the like. The most sensible reaction is to assume that the customer's account of the transaction is an honest statement of what happened—unless the

BUSINESS COMMUNICATION TODAY

Turn Complaining Customers into Company Boosters

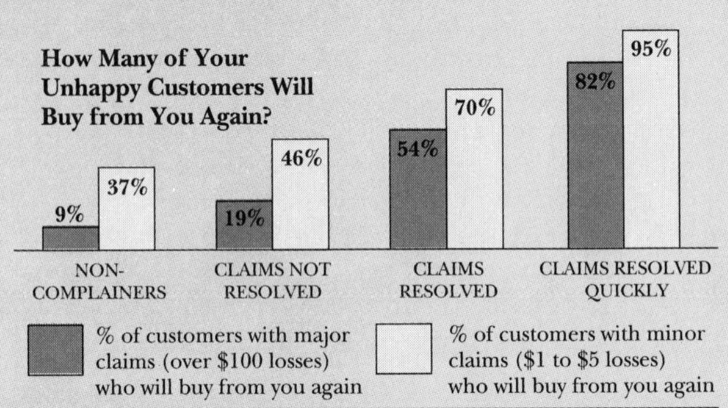

Most companies have many more dissatisfied customers than they realize, recent findings show. For every customer who complains about a problem, 26 do not.

A whopping 65 to 90 percent of these noncomplainers will not buy from the company again, as the chart indicates. What's worse, most noncomplainers will tell 9 or 10 others of their unpleasant experience with a company, and 13 percent will tell more than 20 others.

Is there a way to defuse this time bomb? Research shows that a firm can win back 54 to 70 percent of those who submit claims by resolving their problems. In fact, 95 percent of them will become loyal customers again if their claims are handled quickly and well. The solution, then, is to encourage customer complaints and to resolve them promptly and courteously.

But can business afford to do this? Statistics indicate that it normally costs five times as much to get a new customer as it does to keep an existing one. And customers whose claims are resolved quickly and well will tell an average of five others of their good treatment, thus spreading the news.

Here's how to turn customer claims into goodwill for your business:

- Develop a well-organized dialogue-by-mail with customers to solicit and encourage complaints.
- Except when a claim is clearly dishonest or when compensation will be too expensive, assume that the customer is right and that the claim is justified. If the claim doesn't seem justified, avoid making a point of your doubts.
- Reply to every customer claim within two days after receipt. Sound positive. Exhibit concern. If necessary, send the customer a holding letter until the claim can be investigated and positive action taken. A follow-up letter should also be sent to make certain that the customer is satisfied.
- Spell the customer's name correctly, and address the letter properly. Refer to the matter about which the customer has written.
- Take serious complaints, which can damage your company's public reputation, to the highest possible level. Although it would be physically impossible and a great waste of time for the chief executive to read every claim letter, he or she should see those that indicate real trouble.

Every complaining customer turned into a booster might bring the company five or more new customers, because a customer usually has that many friends who are influenced by his or her point of view.

1. What are some of the specific things a company might do to develop a dialogue-by-mail for soliciting and encouraging customer complaints?

2. Think of two places where you regularly do business and have a good relationship with the personnel. Try to pick a small business (such as your local market) and a large business (such as a department store). Ask the managers how customer claims are handled, and request samples of standard reply letters for claims. Analyze each business's letters, citing their strong and weak points.

same customer repeatedly submits dubious claims, a customer is patently dishonest (returning a dress that has obviously been worn, claiming it's the wrong size), or the dollar amount in dispute is very large. Very few people go to the trouble of requesting an adjustment unless they actually have a problem.

WHEN THE COMPANY IS AT FAULT

An ungracious adjustment may increase customer dissatisfaction.

The usual human response to a bad situation is to say, "It wasn't my fault!" But businesspeople who receive requests for claims or adjustments must take a different stance. Even when the company's terms of adjustment are generous, a grudging tone can actually increase the customer's dissatisfaction.

To protect your company's image and to regain the customer's goodwill, refer to your company's errors carefully. Don't blame an individual or a specific department, and avoid such lame excuses as "Nobody's perfect" or "Mistakes will happen." You shouldn't promise that problems will never happen again, because such guarantees are unrealistic and often beyond your control. But if you explain your company's efforts to do a good job, then you do imply that the error was an unusual incident.

Imagine that customers who complain to a food company receive the following form letter, which is customized through word processing and is individually signed:

> Your letter about the Golden Harvest canned fruit you recently purchased has been forwarded to our vice president of operations for review. We're pleased you took the time to write. Your satisfaction is important to us.
>
> Since 1906, Golden Harvest has been packaging fine food products. Our workers and inspectors monitor quality carefully, using the most up-to-date technology, but we want to do an even better job. Your letter will help us do just that.
>
> The next time you shop, use the enclosed half-price coupon to pick up a gift-boxed set of Golden Harvest Holiday Spices. This coupon, which will be honored wherever our fine specialty foods are sold, is our way of thanking you for your interest in our products.

You may send form letters in response to claims, but word them carefully so they are appropriate in a variety of circumstances.

Notice the following points about this letter:

- A form letter like this, which is sent to people with various types of requests or complaints, cannot start with a clear good-news statement, because different customers are seeking different types of good news.
- The letter starts instead with what might be called a "good attitude" statement; it is you-oriented to put the customer at ease.
- At no time does this letter suggest that the customer was mistaken in questioning the quality of the product; on the other hand, the writer does not admit to any defect in the product.
- The middle, explanatory section nicely combines the old and the new: Golden Harvest has been doing business for over 80 years, but its equipment is thoroughly modern. This explanation of the company's quality controls may restore the reader's confidence in the product.
- The letter closes with some resale and sales promotion made personal by the use of *you* and *your*.

A claim letter written as a personal answer to a unique situation would start with a clear statement of the good news: the settling of the claim according to the customer's request. Look, for example, at this letter:

In just a few days you'll receive a new factory-tested electronic metric scale to replace the one you returned. Thanks, Dr. Clark, for giving us the opportunity to back up our claim of total buyer satisfaction.

Our goal for the past 104 years has been to provide precise and reliable measuring devices that meet the most exacting standards. Throughout our manufacturing process, every scale must meet stringent factory tests for accuracy and durability. Technicians in our test laboratories have been alerted to your experience, however, so we can maintain the high ratings we have been given by all major professional journals.

We appreciate your interest in our products, Dr. Clark. Please continue telling us how we may supply your needs for dependable measuring devices.

WHEN THE BUYER IS AT FAULT

Say that a customer is technically wrong (he washed a shirt in water that's too hot) but feels in the right ("The washing instructions were impossible to find!"). You can refuse the claim and attempt to justify this refusal to the customer, or you can simply do what the customer asks. But as you try to decide which course to take, remember that refusing to make an adjustment may mean losing that customer as well as many of the customer's friends, who will hear only one side of the dispute. It makes sense, therefore, to weigh the cost of making the refund against the cost of losing future business from one or more customers.

If you choose not to contest the claim, you should start off with a statement of the good news: You are replacing the merchandise or refunding the purchase price. The explanatory section needs more attention, however. Your job is to make the customer realize that the merchandise was mistreated without falling into a tone that is condescending ("Perhaps you failed to read the instructions carefully") or preachy ("Next time, please allow the machine to warm up before using it at full power"). The dilemma is this: If the customer fails to realize what went wrong, you may commit your firm to an endless procession of returned merchandise; but if you insult the customer, your cash refund will have been wasted, because the customer will make his or her next purchase elsewhere. Keep in mind that a courteous tone is especially important to the success of your message, regardless of the solution you propose.

When complying with an unjustified claim, let the customer know that the merchandise was mistreated, but maintain a respectful and positive tone.

Without being offensive, the following letter educates a customer about how to treat a wristwatch:

With your approval, a brand-new Leico wristwatch will be shipped to you at once. We'll be happy to replace the one you returned yesterday.

A brief statement conveys the good news.

According to our service department, your watch cannot be repaired. Water has gotten into the mechanism, and the rust clogging the gears prevents the key parts from moving.

Here, the writer explains the defect using the passive voice to avoid blaming the customer for the damage.

Leico watches are guaranteed to resist water only when no pressure is exerted on the case. Thus they can confidently be worn in the rain but not while swimming or bathing. We

The account of what probably caused the damage is objective and impersonal.

■ CHECKLIST FOR FAVORABLE RESPONSES TO CLAIMS AND ADJUSTMENT REQUESTS

A. Initial Statement of the Good News or Main Idea

- ☐ 1. State immediately your willingness to honor the reader's claim.
- ☐ 2. Accept your reader's account as entirely accurate unless good business reasons demand a different interpretation of some points.
- ☐ 3. Adopt a tone of consideration and courtesy; avoid being defensive, recriminatory, or condescending.
- ☐ 4. Thank the reader for taking the time to write.

B. Middle, Informational Section

- ☐ 1. Minimize or, if possible, omit any disagreements with your reader's interpretation of events.
- ☐ 2. Maintain a supportive tone through such phrases as "Thank you for," "May we ask," "Please let us know," and "We are glad to work with you."
- ☐ 3. Apologize only under extreme circumstances; then do so crisply and without an overly apologetic tone.
- ☐ 4. Admit your firm's faults carefully.
  - ☐ a. Avoid blaming any particular person or office.
  - ☐ b. Avoid implying general company inefficiency.
  - ☐ c. Avoid blaming probability ("Mistakes will happen").
  - ☐ d. Avoid unrealistic promises about the future.
  - ☐ e. Remind the reader of your firm's quality controls.
- ☐ 5. Handle carefully the customer's role in producing the problem.
  - ☐ a. If appropriate, honor the claim in full but without negative comment.
  - ☐ b. If appropriate, provide an objective, nonvindictive, impersonal explanation.

C. Warm, Courteous Close

- ☐ 1. Clarify any necessary actions that your reader must take.
- ☐ 2. Remind the reader of how you have honored the claim.
- ☐ 3. Avoid negative information.
- ☐ 4. Encourage the customer to look favorably on your company and/or the product in question (resale).
- ☐ 5. Encourage the customer to continue buying other goods from you (sales promotion), but avoid seeming greedy.

encourage customers who want to wear their wristwatches under water to select models with plastic crystals, because they are mounted more snugly than glass crystals are. Some customers still prefer glass crystals, however, because even the best-quality plastic will scratch.

Mr. Jameson, which model would you prefer as a replacement, a sportswatch you can wear under water or the kind you returned? Just check your choice on the enclosed postage-paid card and rush it back today. Whichever one you choose, you can be confident that your new Leico will give you the years of precise timekeeping that you expect from a fine-quality watch.

A friendly alternative and a bit of resale give the reader a clear choice.

WHEN A THIRD PARTY IS AT FAULT

At times a customer will submit a legitimate claim for a defect or damage that was not caused by either of you. The merchandise may have been damaged while in transit, in which case the carrier is responsible; or the defect may have been caused by the manufacturer, in which case you have a claim for replacement from that firm.

Three options when a third party is at fault:

- Honor the claim
- Honor the claim with an explanation of what went wrong
- Refer the customer to the third party for satisfaction of the claim

When a third party is at fault, you have three options: (1) honor the customer's claim with the standard good-news letter and no additional explanation; (2) honor the claim but explain that you were not really at fault; or (3) take no action on the claim and suggest that your customer file against the firm that caused the defect or damage. Common business sense should tell you, however, that the third option is almost always a bad choice. (The exception is when you are trying to dissociate yourself from any legal responsibility for the damaged merchandise, especially if it has caused a personal injury, in which case you need to send a bad-news message.)

Of the other two options, the first is more attractive. By honoring the claim without explanation, you are maintaining your reputation for fair dealing at no cost to yourself; the carrier or manufacturer that caused the damage in the first place will reimburse you. But you may want to provide an explanation to the customer, possibly to correct an impression that the damage was caused by your negligence. In that case, you can still write the standard good-news letter, but stress the explanation more than usual.

HANDLING ROUTINE CREDIT REQUESTS

These days, much of our economy runs on credit. Consumers often carry a wallet full of plastic credit cards, and businesses of all sizes operate more smoothly because they can pay for their purchases over time. Because credit is so common, most credit requests are routine, as are credit approvals and credit references.

APPROVING CREDIT

Letters approving credit are, of course, good-news letters and the first step in what may be a decades-long business relationship. Thus the opening of a letter granting credit may start out with the main idea.

State credit terms factually and in terms of the benefits of having credit.

In the middle section of the letter, you must include a reasonably full statement of the credit arrangements: the upper limit of the account, dates that bills are sent, possible arrangements for partial monthly payments, discounts for prompt payments, interest charges for unpaid balances, and due dates. The terms should be stated positively and objectively, not negatively or in an authoritarian manner:

INSTEAD OF THIS	WRITE THIS
Your credit balance cannot exceed $5,000.	With our standard credit account, you can order up to $5,000 worth of fine merchandise.
We expect your payment within 30 days of receipt of our statement.	Payment is due 30 days after you receive our statement.

Because the letter approving credit is considered a legal document, the wording should be checked for accuracy, completeness, and clarity.

■ CHECKLIST FOR CREDIT APPROVALS

A. Initial Statement of the Good News or Main Idea

- ☐ 1. Cheerfully tell the reader that he or she now has approved credit with your firm.
- ☐ 2. Tell the reader, with brief resale, that he or she will soon be enjoying the use of any goods that were ordered with the request; specify the date and method of shipment and other purchase details.
- ☐ 3. Establish a tone of mutual warmth and trust.

B. Middle, Informational Section

- ☐ 1. Explain the conditions under which credit was granted.
- ☐ 2. Include or attach a full explanation of your firm's credit policies and expectations of payment.
- ☐ 3. Stress the advantages of prompt payment in a way that assumes your reader will take advantage of them ("When you pay your account in full within ten days . . .").
- ☐ 4. Include legally required disclosure statements.
- ☐ 5. Inform or remind the reader of the general benefits of doing business with your firm (resale).
  - ☐ a. Tell the consumer about free parking, mail and phone shopping, personalized shopping services, your home-decorating bureau, bridal consultants, restaurants, child care, gift wrapping, free deliveries, special discounts or purchase privileges, and other benefits, if your firm offers them.
  - ☐ b. If the customer is a retailer or wholesaler, tell about nearby warehouses, factory representatives, quantity discounts, free window or counter displays, national advertising support, ads for local newspapers and other media, repair services, manuals, factory guarantees, prompt and speedy deliveries, toll-free phone number, research department, and other benefits, if your firm offers them.
- ☐ 6. Inform or remind the reader of a special sale, discount, or promotion (sales promotion).
- ☐ 7. Avoid exaggerations or flamboyant language that might make this section of your letter read like an advertisement.

C. Warm, Courteous Close

- ☐ 1. Summarize the reasons why the reader will enjoy doing business with your firm.
- ☐ 2. Use the "you" attitude, and avoid clichés.
- ☐ 3. Invite the reader to a special sale or the like or provide resale information to motivate him or her to use the new account.

Include resale and sales promotion information in a credit letter.

The final section of the letter should provide resale information and sales promotion highlighting the benefits of buying from you.

The following letter was written both to approve credit and to bring in customers:

Welcome aboard! Here's your new Ship-to-Shore credit card, which will make shopping at Conrad's even easier than before. Now you can make credit purchases up to a total of $1,000.

The good-news opening gets right to the point.

With a Ship-to-Shore card in your wallet, you can enjoy storewide shopping. Or if you prefer, phone in orders to 834-2230, for delivery within two days. A statement mailed on the tenth of each month will list all credit purchases made within the period and the amount due. When you pay the entire balance by the due date, no interest is charged. Otherwise, you may pay as little as 10 percent of the balance or $20, whichever is greater. A monthly interest charge of 1-1/2 percent of the outstanding balance will be added to your next statement.

An objective statement of the terms constitutes a legal contract. Positive, you-oriented wording avoids an authoritarian tone.

LEGAL ALERT

Hazards of Writing Recommendation Letters

The most up-to-date advice for managers asked to write recommendation letters for employees: Don't. The reason? Our society's habit of addressing all slights in court has put the writer of recommendation letters in a no-win situation.

In the past five years some 8,000 suits have been filed by workers charging former employers with slander or libel. Those bringing suit, mainly people who have been fired, allege that false statements made by their former employers have damaged their reputation and hurt them in their attempts to gain new employment. Juries believe them. In a seven-year period in California, employees won 72 percent of libel and related cases they brought against employers, with an average award of $582,000.

To win damages, employees must prove that the employer made false and defamatory statements about them either in writing (libel) or orally (slander). In one such case, the employer had stated that an ex-employee, a lawyer, had "suddenly resigned." A federal district court ruled that this phrase suggested to prospective employers that "the party who resigned did so under a veil of suspicion or scandal" and thus constituted defamation. In another case, the court ruled that an employer's statement that an employee had been fired "for causes" constituted defamation.

If the worker can show that an employer showed malice in making defamatory statements, greater damages can sometimes be won. In Florida, a tugboat captain was fired for refusing to cross a picket line. When the company referred to the captain's action as "mutiny," he sued, and the court upheld his allegation that the term *mutiny* constituted malice.

Do visit Conrad's today. You'll find that every department is overflowing with up-to-the-minute merchandise for your whole family. From gourmet foods to casual clothing to appliances for land and sea, this is your one-stop shopping center. And remember our free delivery service. Even if you're berthed in the city docks, we'll deliver your purchases right to your door.

The courteous close provides resale for the store and sales promotion noting a range of customer benefits.

PROVIDING CREDIT REFERENCES

The great majority of credit applications are checked electronically: Computer terminals at many stores connect directly with data banks maintained by national credit-reporting agencies. Generally, the data are fed to the inquiring business without recommendation.

When responding to an inquiry about someone's credit worthiness

- Make sure the request is legitimate
- Limit yourself to factual statements

At times, however, one businessperson will request a credit rating directly from another. If you are supplying an answer to an inquiry about someone's credit worthiness, your first responsibility is to make sure the inquiry is legitimate. You are being asked to provide confidential information, which should not be made available unless it is requested by a stable business.

As you write a credit reference, remember that the decision is not yours but must be made by the company that has been asked to extend credit. Therefore, no matter how strong your opinion of the applicant may be, limit yourself to factual statements. If you don't, you may end up in court.

In the face of such litigation, most employers have established a policy of not providing recommendation letters. At most, they will supply basic employment information about a past worker, such as position held, dates of employment, and final rate of pay.

Those employers who do still write letters of recommendation tend to stick to positive statements about the employee. A problem with this approach is that the person who is hired on the basis of glowing recommendations may be unsuited to the new job, a situation that destroys the credibility of the former employer as well as hurting both the employee and the new employer. In addition, such recommendations may make the letter writer vulnerable to lawsuit on the basis of negligence—that is, failure to provide essential information about a person that could have significant bearing on job performance. One example: not mentioning that a person being considered for a job at a preschool was fired for being too rough with children in a previous job.

If you are asked to write a letter of recommendation, what should you do? You could politely refuse to do so. Or you could follow your company's policy (if there is one) to provide only essential employee information. But if you do choose to write a letter, be aware of the legal ramifications and keep in mind that your wording could one day be scrutinized in court. Make sure the information you provide is accurate. State what is known and pertinent. Stick to the facts. Avoid volunteering information that is not related to the person's work performance, and refrain from using abusive language. As long as you reply honestly and in good faith, you are within the law.

1. If you were an employer, would you continue to check the references of job applicants, or would you write off this step as a waste of time? What other measures could you take to verify a candidate's qualifications?

2. Step outside yourself for a moment and assume the role of a former employer. Write a letter of recommendation about yourself from this person's perspective. Try to be as honest as possible.

CONVEYING POSITIVE INFORMATION ABOUT PEOPLE

Professors, supervisors, and managers are often asked to write letters recommending students or employees for jobs, and nearly anyone may be asked to recommend acquaintances for awards, membership in organizations, and other honors. Such letters may take the direct approach when the recommendation is generally positive. Employers use the same type of organizational plan when telling job applicants the good news: They got the job.

RECOMMENDATION LETTERS

Letters of recommendation have an important goal: to convince readers that the person being recommended has the characteristics required for the job or other benefit. It is important, therefore, that they contain all the relevant details:

- The full name of the candidate
- The job or benefit that the candidate is seeking
- Whether the writer is answering a request or taking the initiative
- The nature of the relationship between the writer and the candidate
- Facts relevant to the position or benefit sought
- The writer's overall evaluation of the candidate's suitability for the job or benefit sought

A recommendation letter that will be held confidential may give a balanced view of the candidate.

Recommendation letters are usually confidential; that is, they are mailed directly to the person or committee who requested them and are not shown to the candidate. A writer who has been assured of confidentiality can be more candid and present the important negatives along with the positives.

Two devices for convincing the reader when the candidate is outstanding:

- Use examples
- Use comparisons to the "competition"

Oddly enough, the most difficult recommendation letters to write are those for truly outstanding candidates. A reader will have trouble believing uninterrupted praise for someone's talents and accomplishments. Thus good writers often illustrate the general points they are making with a specific example or two that point up the candidate's abilities, and they discuss the candidate's abilities in relation to the "competition."

Most candidates are not perfect, however. Omitting reference to a candidate's shortcomings may be justified, especially if the shortcomings are irrelevant to the demands of the job. But you have an obligation to the reader of your letter and to your own conscience—and possibly to a better-qualified candidate who is relying on honest references—to refer to any shortcoming that is serious and related to job performance.

A serious shortcoming should not be ignored, but beware of being libelous:

- Include only relevant, factual information
- Avoid value judgments
- Balance criticisms with favorable points

The danger in writing a critical letter is that you might engage in libel—that is, make a false and malicious written statement that injures the candidate's reputation. If you must refer to a possible shortcoming, you can best protect yourself by sticking to the facts and placing your criticism in the context of a generally favorable recommendation, as in the following example:

I am pleased to support Jim Esposito's application for membership in the West Bay Umpires' Association.

The candidate's full name and the main point are clearly stated.

For the past two years, Jim and I have officiated at both high school and college baseball games. Working closely with him, I have found that he is a good umpire. Not only is he alert on the field, but he makes his calls quickly and sticks by them. Even though Jim has changed his calls because of managers' complaints more often than most of our league's other umpires have, he is highly respected by both managers and players. I've really enjoyed working games with him.

The duration and nature of the relationship are specified to give weight to the evaluation. A possible weakness related to the position is embedded in the discussion of good qualities without resort to overly negative terms.

We need more umpires like Jim Esposito in the Association! I would be happy to elaborate on his skills if you call me at home any evening (231-0977).

A supportive, personal summary of the writer's evaluation provides a good close. The phone number and invitation to discuss the candidacy further constitute another helpful touch.

In this letter, the writer avoids the risk of libel by supporting his statements with facts and by steering clear of vague, critical judgments.

You can avoid trouble, too, if you ask yourself the following questions before mailing a recommendation letter:

- Does the person receiving this frank, personal information have a legitimate right to the information?
- Does all the information I have presented relate directly to the job or other benefit being sought?
- Have I put the candidate's case as strongly as I honestly can?
- Have I avoided overstating the candidate's abilities or otherwise misleading the reader?

If you can answer yes to all four questions, you may confidently mail off the letter and turn to your next project.

GOOD NEWS ABOUT EMPLOYMENT

Finding suitable job applicants and then selecting the right person is a task fraught with hard choices and considerable anxiety. In contrast, writing a letter to the successful applicant is a pleasure. Most of the time such a letter is eagerly awaited, and so the direct approach serves quite well:

> After interviewing a number of qualified applicants for the position of executive secretary to Cynthia Hargrove, our vice president of marketing, we have selected you. Welcome to Southwest Specialties, Inc.!
>
> We would like you to report for work on July 24 so the person who currently has the job can spend a week showing you around. You will be paid a monthly salary of $1,500 and will receive the standard benefits package described during the interview process.
>
> Please plan to arrive at 8:30 a.m. on the 24th; ask for me at the reception desk. We will spend an hour or so filling out the necessary forms and going over company employment policies. Then I will introduce you to the people in the marketing department--and your new career with Southwest Specialties will be under way!

Notice that this letter takes a friendly, welcoming tone and that it explains the necessary details: job title, starting date, salary, and benefits. The last paragraph, with its explanation of the first day's routine, helps allay the bewilderment and uncertainty that might afflict the new employee.

A letter telling someone that she or he got the job is a legal document, so make sure all statements are accurate.

Although letters like these are pleasant to write, you should be aware that, legally, a letter to a successful applicant constitutes a job offer. You and your company may be held to any promises you make. Thus attorneys sometimes recommend stating salary as a monthly amount and keeping the timing of performance evaluations and raises vague; you want to avoid implying that the employee will be kept on, no matter what, for a whole year or until the next evaluation.[1]

WRITING DIRECTIVES AND INSTRUCTIONS

Directives tell employees what to do; instructions tell readers how to do something.

Directives are memos that tell employees *what* to do. Instructions, which tell people inside and outside the company *how* to do something, may take the form of memos, letters, or even booklets. But directives and instructions are both considered routine messages, because readers are assumed to be willing to comply.

The goal in writing directives and instructions is to make the point so obvious and the steps so self-explanatory that readers will not have to ask for additional help. The following directive does a good job of explaining what employees are expected to do:

> Please send me employee vacation schedules for the third quarter, July through September, no later than June 16.
>
> Note that we have pushed back the deadline for submitting the schedules by two weeks. This change is made possible by the new computerized personnel system. The new deadline should give your line workers more time to firm up their vacation plans.
>
> Use the attached form, which has also been simplified, for reporting third-quarter vacation schedules.

Notice that this directive is brief and to the point. Drawn-out explanations are unnecessary, because readers are expected simply to follow through on a well-established procedure. Yet it also covers all the bases, answering these questions: Who? What? When? Where? Why? How?

Instructions need to answer the same questions, but they differ from directives in the amount of explanation they provide. For example, Jackie Millan of PepsiCo might write a simple three-sentence directive to employees to tell them of a change in the policies regarding employee scholarships; a detailed set of instructions, however, would be more appropriate for explaining the procedure for applying for a scholarship.

The key with instructions is to take nothing for granted. Assuming that readers know nothing about the process you're describing is better than risking confusion and possible damage or harm by overlooking some basic information. Figure 7.2 is a set of instructions for writing instructions.

CONVEYING GOOD NEWS ABOUT PRODUCTS AND OPERATIONS

It's good business to spread the word about such positive developments as the opening of new facilities, the appointment of a new executive, the introduction of new products or customer services, the sponsorship of community events. For example, imagine that So-Good Foods has successfully introduced a new line of vegetable chips (carrot, turnip, and yam chips, not the same old potato chips) to the stores it serves. To maintain its position on supermarket shelves, So-Good decides to offer a new discount program to stores that buy large quantities of its vegetable chips. It supplements the personal visits of its sales force with a good-news letter describing the new program to existing customers. The letter begins by trumpeting the news, fills in the details of the discount program in the middle, and closes with a bit of resale information and a confident prediction of a profitable business relationship.

Specially formatted press releases convey good news to the media, which in turn disseminate it to the public.

When the audience for a good-news message is large and scattered, however, it is usually easier to communicate through publications, television, or radio. Press releases are the specialized documents that convey news to the media. They are written to match the style of the medium they are intended for.

FIGURE 7.2
Instructions for Writing Instructions

HOW TO WRITE INSTRUCTIONS

When you need to explain in writing how to do something, a set of instructions is your best choice. By enumerating the steps, you make it easy for readers to perform the process in the correct sequence. Your goal is to provide a clear, self-sufficient explanation so readers can perform the task independently.

Equipment Needed: Writing materials

Preparing to Write Useful Instructions

1. Perform the task yourself, or ask experts to demonstrate it or describe it to you in detail.
2. Analyze prospective readers' familiarity with the process so you can write instructions at their level of understanding.

Making Your Instructions Clear

1. Include four elements as needed: an introduction, a list of equipment and materials, a description of the steps involved in the process, and a conclusion.
2. Explain in the opening why the process is important and how it relates to a larger purpose.
3. Divide the process into short, simple steps, presented in order of occurrence.
4. Present the steps in a numbered list, or present them in paragraph format, making plentiful use of words indicating time or sequence, such as first and then.
5. If the process involves more than ten steps, divide them into groups or stages identified with headings.
6. Phrase each step as a command ("Do this" instead of "You should do this"); use active verbs ("Look for these signs" instead of "Be alert for these signs"); use precise, specific terms ("three" instead of "several").
7. When appropriate, indicate how readers may tell whether a step has been performed correctly and how one step may influence another. Supply warnings when performing a step incorrectly could result in damage or injury, but limit the number of warnings so readers do not underestimate their importance.
8. Include diagrams of complicated devices, and refer to them in the appropriate steps.
9. Summarize the importance of the process and the expected results in the conclusion.

Testing Your Instructions

1. Review the instructions to be sure they are clear and complete. Also judge whether you have provided too much detail.
2. Ask someone else to read the instructions and tell you whether they make sense and are easy to follow.

Press releases should be typewritten on plain 8½- × 11-inch paper or on special letterhead—not on regular letterhead—and should be double-spaced for print media, triple-spaced for electronic media. Clean photocopies may be sent by first-class mail to radio and television news directors and to editors of magazines and weekly newspapers. But individually typed, hand-delivered copies are more impressive to city editors of the daily newspapers. These decision makers expect to see a format like the one shown in Figure 7.3.

FIGURE 7.3
Press Release Format

The name, affiliation, address, and phone number of the person who wrote the release and can provide more information is noted at the top.

Most news is released immediately.

Provide your own suggestion for a title, or leave two inches here so the editor can insert a headline.

This release for a newspaper starts with a dateline and a summary (who, what, when, where, why) of the rest of the story.

Put a release on one page if you can, but indicate carryover to a second page like this.

Head the second page like this, with a short title and the page number.

Do not split a paragraph; start the new page with a new paragraph. The "plug" is in the last paragraph.

Indicate the end of the release like this.

News Release

Time Inc.
Rockefeller Center
New York, NY 10020
212 586 1212

Time Inc.

For Immediate Release

Contact:
Louis J. Slovinsky
Director, Corporate Public Affairs
(212) 841-3911

A NEW LOGO FOR TIME INC.

NEW YORK, MARCH 13, 1985--Time Inc., the information and entertainment company, is introducing a new corporate logotype this week. It appears for the first time on the cover of Time Inc.'s 1984 Annual Report, now being distributed to the company's shareholders.

The new logotype, modeled on the classic Baskerville letterform, was designed by Walter Lefmann, who retired last year as *Time* magazine's promotion art director.

--more--

Time Inc. Logo 2-2-2-2

In announcing the new logo to the Time Inc. staff, J. Richard Munro, president and chief executive officer, said: "A key element in the way a company is perceived is its use of graphics. To establish a strong, consistent identity for Time Inc., we have designed this new logo. It will set a standard that is consistent with our goal of being a top-quality company in every respect."

# # #

Notice that the content of the press release in the figure follows the customary pattern for a good-news letter: good news first, followed by details and a positive close. However, it avoids explicit references to any reader. Instead, it displays the "you" attitude by presenting information presumed to be of interest to readers. Furthermore, because no honest editor will run a press release that sounds like an advertisement, the "plug" for the company's products has been relegated to the final section.

WRITING GOODWILL MESSAGES

Business is not all business. To a great extent, it's an opportunity to forge personal relationships. You can enhance your relationships with customers and other business people by sending friendly, unexpected notes with no

Goodwill: the positive feeling that encourages people to maintain a business relationship

direct business purpose. Goodwill messages like these have a positive effect on business, too, because people prefer to deal with those who are warm and human and not interested strictly in money.

One way to come across as sincere is to avoid exaggeration. What do you think a reader's reaction would be to these two sentences?

We were overjoyed to learn of your promotion.

Congratulations on your promotion.

Make sure your compliments are grounded in reality.

Most likely, the reader would not quite believe that anyone (except perhaps a relative or very close friend) would be "overjoyed." But the reader will accept the writer's simple congratulations, a human, understandable intention.

To demonstrate your sincerity, back up any compliments with specific points.

INSTEAD OF THIS	WRITE THIS
My deepest heartfelt thanks for the excellent job you did. It's hard these days to find workers like you. You are just fantastic! I can't stress enough how happy you have made us with your slam-bang performance.	Thanks for filling in for Gladys at the convention with just an hour's notice. You did a great job. Despite the difficult circumstances, you managed to bring in several orders for the new line of coffeemaker you demonstrated. Your dedication and sales ability have been noted and are truly appreciated.

Notice also the difference in the words used in these two examples. The reader would probably feel that the more restrained praise was the more sincere.

Offer help only when you are able and willing to provide it.

Offering help in a goodwill message is fine, but promise only what you can and will provide. Avoid giving even the impression of an offer of help where none is intended. What if Jackie Millan of PepsiCo had ended her letter to the scholarship winner like this?

Please let us know if we can help you in any way in the future.

It's possible that in a year or two PepsiCo might receive a request for a loan, prompted by inflation in college costs.

Only the slightest hint of a sales pitch should ever appear in a goodwill message.

Although goodwill messages have little to do with business transactions, they might include some sales information if you have the opportunity to be of particular service or want to remind the reader of your company's product. But any sales message should be subdued and secondary to the helpful, thoughtful message. In the following example, the dealer succeeds in seeming more interested in the relationship with the reader than in a possible sale:

Congratulations on reeling in the big one at the Grainger County fishing contest! The second we saw the newspaper picture of you holding that beauty in one hand and our Fish-Pro collapsible rod in the other, we felt button-popping proud.

Now that you're a local fishing expert, Lou, you might want to check out our other Fish-Pro equipment. At least come by sometime and let us shake your hand. Maybe we can talk you into telling us about your big catch.

The reader of this letter will not feel a great deal of pressure to buy but will feel that the dealer took special notice of his accomplishments. If you add a sales pitch, make sure that it takes a back seat to your goodwill message. Honesty and sincerity must come across above all else.

CONGRATULATIONS

One prime opportunity for sending congratulations is news of a significant business achievement—for example, being promoted or attaining an important civic position. Notice that the sample congratulatory note in Figure 7.4 moves swiftly into the subject of the letter, the good news. It gives reasons for expecting success and avoids such extravagances as "Only you can do the job!"

Highlights in people's personal lives—weddings and births, graduations, success in nonbusiness competitions—are another reason for sending congratulations. You may congratulate business acquaintances on their achievements or on their spouse's or children's achievements. You may also take note of personal events, even if you don't know the reader well. But if you are already friendly with the reader, you can get away with a very personal tone.

Taking note of significant events in someone's personal life helps cement the business relationship.

Some alert companies develop a mailing list of potential customers by assigning an employee to clip newspaper announcements of births, engagements, weddings, and graduations. They then introduce themselves by sending out a form letter that might read like this:

Congratulations!

We thought you might like this extra copy of your picture and wedding announcement from the Evening Herald.

It's a pleasure to send it to you. Please accept our good wishes for your happiness.

In this case, the company's letterhead and address is enough of a sales pitch. This simple letter has a natural, friendly tone, even though the sender has never met the recipient.

LETTERS OF APPRECIATION

A letter of appreciation documents a person's contributions.

An important managerial quality is the ability to see employees (and other business associates) as individuals and to recognize their contributions. People often value praise more highly than monetary rewards.

A letter of appreciation may also become an important part of an employee's personnel file:

Thanks a million for programming the computer for the fulfillment department. I suppose only those of us close to this task can really appreciate the size and complexity of the job you did in such a short time. Even during a time when your own work load is usually heavy, you managed to develop a

FIGURE 7.4
Letter Congratulating a Business Acquaintance

11495 NATURAL BRIDGE BRIDGETON (ST. LOUIS), MISSOURI, U.S.A. 63044

November 8, 1988

Mr. Lawrence Andrews, General Manager
St. Louis Landscape Design, Inc.
7600 Regents Road
St. Louis, MO 63155

Dear Mr. Andrews:

Congratulations! We noted in this morning's news that your firm has been chosen by the Lambert-St. Louis International Airport to redesign the landscaping at the airport.

We are delighted to learn that you have been awarded the contract. By beautifying the airport, you will help establish a pleasant atmosphere for our passengers and for our employees.

Judging by your award-winning work along the waterfront, we are indeed fortunate that your firm is handling the project. We are confident that you will make the entrance to the airport more beautiful and convenient.

Cordially,

Jessica Rogers

Jessica Rogers
Director, Airport Relations

nb

TRANS WORLD AIRLINES, INC.

The point of writing comes first.

The reason for congratulating the reader is expressed early and concisely.

Additional detail fleshes out the letter and clarifies the writer's purpose.

The letter ends with a personalized expression of confidence.

series of programs that will significantly improve our ability to handle the work of our department.

Always remember, Kathy, that your time and talents are truly appreciated. We view your accomplishment as outstanding!

cc: Personnel Department

With its references to specific qualities and deeds, this note may provide support for future pay increases and promotions.

Suppliers also like to know that you value some exceptional product or the service you received. Long-term support deserves recognition too. Your praise doesn't just make the supplier feel good; it also encourages further

Anyone who does you or your organization a special favor should receive written thanks.

excellence. Notice how the brief message that follows expresses gratitude and reveals the happy result:

Thank you for the quick service.

You got me that power pack in time for the 8 a.m. flight, and the customer was in service by noon!

Thanks again, especially to Brian McKee in your customer service department, for making us both look good.

When you write a letter of appreciation to a supplier, try to mention specifically the person or people you want to praise. Your expression of goodwill might net the employee some future benefit. In any case, your letter also honors the company that the individual represents.

Guest speakers at meetings should also be thanked, even if they have been paid an honorarium or their travel expenses—and surely if they have not. They may have spent hours gathering and organizing material for an informative and interesting presentation. Their hard work should be rewarded. An imaginative word picture makes this letter distinctive:

Please accept warmest thanks from me and all who were at yesterday's Technical Group meeting for spending some time with us.

And congratulations! You have that rare gift of making complex subjects crystal clear; you washed the muddy window, and we could all see right through.

Letters of appreciation are also appropriate for acknowledging money donations to campaigns or causes. They should usually include a few details about the success of the campaign or how the funds are being used, so that the donors will feel good about having contributed.

CONDOLENCES

In times of serious trouble and deep sadness, written condolences and expressions of sympathy leave their mark. Granted, this type of letter is difficult to write, but don't let the difficulty of the task keep you from responding promptly. Those who have experienced a health problem, death of a loved one, or business misfortune like to know that they are not alone.

Begin condolences with a brief statement of sympathy, such as "I was deeply sorry to hear of your loss." In the middle, mention the good qualities or the positive contributions made by the subject of the letter. State what the person or business meant to you. In closing, you can offer your condolences and your best wishes. One considerate way to end this type of message is to say something that will give the reader a little lift, such as a reference to a brighter future.

You are not obligated to offer help to the reader; a good condolence letter is often help enough. But if you want to and can offer assistance, don't hesitate to do so. Remember that the bereaved and grieving often suffer financially as well as emotionally and that reestablishing a business or a life often takes a great deal of time and effort. A simple gesture on your part may mean much to the reader.

In condolence messages, try to find a middle path between being superficial and causing additional distress.

Here are a few additional suggestions for writing condolence letters:

- *Don't reminisce at length.* And don't dwell on the details of the loss, lest you add to the reader's anguish.
- *Write in your own words,* as if you were speaking privately to the person. Don't quote "poetic" passages or use stilted or formal phrases. If the loss is a death, refer to it as such rather than as "passing away" or "departing."
- *Be tactful.* The bereaved and distressed take little comfort in such lines as, "Richard was too young to die" or "Starting all over again will be so difficult." Try to strike a balance between superficial expressions of sympathy and heart-rending references to a happier past and a possibly bleak future.
- *Take special care* to spell names correctly and to be accurate in your review of facts.

A supervisor sent the following condolence letter to the husband (whom she does not know) of a deceased employee:

The news of Georgia's accidental death was a great shock; please accept my sincere sympathy.

For many years I have enjoyed working with Georgia, as have her other friends and co-workers. She was a woman of integrity, ability, wit, and kindness. We will miss her greatly.

Here's a longer condolence letter sent by a friendly competitor on the occasion of a serious business disruption:

We just heard that your facilities were vandalized over the weekend to the point that you cannot operate on the air. Please accept our sympathy.

Promptness is especially important in condolence letters.

Your station has been a pioneer in efforts to present an informative alternative to all-news radio, and you have presented some points of view that other stations would shy away from. We would hate to see something like this happen to any of our fellow radio stations, but the fact that it happened to you is especially chilling.

These specifics reassure the reader that the station has friends as well as enemies.

Bill, we'd like to help you get back on the air somehow--and quickly. If there's anything we can do, such as lending engineers or equipment, don't hesitate to talk to me about it.

The offer of help is not too specific, so it doesn't intrude on the central message of sympathy.

I hope the unpleasant memory of this despicable act will soon be replaced by good feelings about the many people in this city who wish you well.

The closing ties together a reminder of friendship and a look toward the future.

GREETINGS

The basic message of greetings is simply "Hello—remember us."

Businesses often send seasonal greetings and messages of welcome to employees, suppliers, customers, and prospective customers. Readers of such messages are grateful for the evidence that you are aware of them and that you value a friendly, successful relationship.

For example, welcomes are often sent by retailers eager to serve new people in their trading areas. The ultimate purpose of sending such letters is to increase sales, of course, but writing an all-out sales letter for the occasion is a big mistake. Notice how the writer of this letter emphasizes the welcome and helpful information:

Welcome to the neighborhood from all of us at the Hanson Company. So we can get to know you, do stop by soon. Our nearest store to you is at 2248 Moore Street, just a few blocks from your home.

While you're visiting, Mr. and Mrs. Lee, why don't you apply for a Hanson charge account? Just ask anyone in the credit department (third floor) for a Newcomer Credit Application Form. Once credit is approved, you'll enjoy so many conveniences. For example, you can shop by phone or mail as well as in person. And you'll receive special advance notice of upcoming sales so you can save substantially.

Whatever your needs--men's, women's, and children's clothing, furniture, fine tableware, the newest time-saving kitchenware--you'll find us eager to make shopping a joy for you.

Mr. and Mrs. Lee, we look forward to your visit so we can say, "Welcome, neighbor."

Potential customers appreciate the friendliness and the helpful information supplied in such letters. The good feeling lingers.

Seasonal greetings need not always be end-of-year messages.

Additional opportunities to express good wishes, say thank you, or just keep in touch with clients and customers pop up in every season. The long winter holiday season is most popular for these types of messages. However, a business with a limited budget for seasonal greetings might want to avoid competing for the reader's attention at this busy time of year. In fact, some businesses relate much better to other seasons and holidays. For example, a candy store or florist might send greetings around Valentine's Day, and a canning factory might send end-of-harvest messages in October or November.

Some concentrated thought will help you plan messages that are different. For instance, you could include a calendar, a special recipe for the season, an attractive bookmark, or a minihistory of some landmark related to the holiday. The best of these little gifts relate to your business as well and can be used all year (thereby keeping your company on the recipient's mind all year).

In composing a greeting, try to avoid a pompous, wordy start. Instead, make a seasonal greeting warm, lively, and conversational:

Happy New Year--good health and good cheer to you this day!

'Tis the season to say how much your business is appreciated and to offer you a most sincere wish for success and happiness in the year ahead.

Smother the urge to add sales promotion in these special messages. Focus on good wishes and gratitude to your customers.

Here are some additional suggestions for writing seasonal greetings:

- Find a quiet moment when you can relax and write the message without interruption or pressure.
- Think of something you would like to read if you were getting the message, and then say it in the simplest way possible.
- Don't try to be too clever, cute, or spectacular.
- Try to keep your message brief, although there is no rule on length.

Now that you know about goodwill messages, you should be able to recognize many opportunities for writing them. Taking advantage of those opportunities will show that your business cares about people as individuals, not just as sales prospects. And your caring image could make all the difference when those people choose which firm to deal with.

CHECKLIST FOR GOODWILL MESSAGES

A. Planning Goodwill Messages

- ☐ 1. Choose the appropriate type of goodwill message for your purpose.
  - ☐ a. Offer congratulations to make the reader feel noticed.
  - ☐ b. Express praise or thanks to show your appreciation for good performance.
  - ☐ c. Offer condolences to show appreciation for the deceased or the person suffering a loss.
  - ☐ d. Send greetings to put a positive business image before the reader.
- ☐ 2. Be prompt in sending out goodwill messages so they lose none of their impact.
- ☐ 3. Send a written goodwill message rather than a telephone message, because a written message can be savored more than once; but keep in mind that a telephone message is better than none at all.

B. Format

- ☐ 1. Use the format most appropriate to the occasion.
  - ☐ a. Use letter format for condolences and for any other goodwill message sent to outsiders or mailed to an employee's home.
  - ☐ b. Use memo format for any goodwill messages sent through interoffice mail, except for condolences.
  - ☐ c. Use a preprinted greeting card for condolences (with a brief handwritten message added) or for seasonal greetings.
- ☐ 2. Handwrite condolences (and replies to handwritten invitations); otherwise type the goodwill message.
- ☐ 3. Use special stationery, if available.
- ☐ 4. For added impact, present congratulations in a folder with a clipping or photo commemorating the special event.

C. Opening

- ☐ 1. State the most important idea first to focus the reader's attention.
- ☐ 2. Incorporate a friendly statement that builds goodwill, right at the beginning.
- ☐ 3. Focus on the good qualities of the person or situation.

D. Middle

- ☐ 1. Provide sufficient details, even in a short message, to justify the opening statement.
- ☐ 2. Express personalized details in sincere, not gushy, language.
- ☐ 3. Be warm but concise.
- ☐ 4. Make the reader, not the writer, the focus of all comments.

E. Close

- ☐ 1. Use a positive or forward-looking statement.
- ☐ 2. Restate the important idea, when appropriate.

SUMMARY

Positive replies, favorable responses to claims and requests for adjustment, responses to routine credit requests, positive information about people, directives and instructions, good news about products and operations, and goodwill messages—these make up much of the daily correspondence in business. Their purpose is to convey a message that readers will either welcome or accept without question. Some of these messages also encourage readers to take a specific action.

Routine, good-news, and goodwill letters follow a straightforward pattern: first a clear statement of the news or main point, then the necessary explanatory details, and finally a warm and courteous close. Some include resale information or sales promotion, which are complimentary references to the writer's company and its products. Most are rather short and depend heavily on the "you" attitude. A sincere and courteous tone highlights the positive image that such messages seek to convey and helps maintain a warm business relationship.

COMMUNICATION CHALLENGES AT PEPSICO

With cutbacks in government support and changes in the tax laws, nonprofit organizations have become more likely than before to approach private funding sources like the PepsiCo Foundation. Jacqueline Millan has expanded her staff to cope with the greater volume of proposals and requests she has been receiving.

Individual Challenge: As a seasoned member of the corporate contributions staff, you have been drafted to write a new prototype for letters to successful grant applicants. Jackie gives you free rein, with only two guidelines: Be brief but explicit, and be businesslike but warm. She suggests that you craft your prototype letter around a specific nonprofit organization that you know about.

Team Challenge: With the influx of new staff members, some of the corporate contributions department's most hallowed policies and procedures risk being overlooked. Jackie assigns a group of her most trusted employees to prepare a set of instructions that the new writers can use in putting together one-page memos summarizing grant requests. PepsiCo Foundation board members will review the memos to decide which projects to fund. The traditional format is fine, but the new people in the department need clear, easy-to-follow instructions so they can quickly be put to work dealing with the flood of grant applications.

QUESTIONS FOR DISCUSSION

1. How should negative information be conveyed in a routine or good-news message? A goodwill message?
2. Why should anyone bother to write letters acknowledging orders?
3. Which is better for replying to requests for information and action—a form letter or a personal reply? Why?
4. How can selling information be incorporated in a routine or good-news message? A goodwill message?
5. Why must a business operate on the assumption (in the absence of contrary evidence) that its customers present their claims honestly?
6. If the customer is clearly at fault, should a claim be disallowed? Why or why not?
7. How can you write a letter of recommendation about someone who has limitations, without engaging in libel?
8. Why should directives and instructions be phrased as commands?
9. What is the value of sending goodwill messages?
10. What is a desirable balance between a sales message and a seasonal greeting to regular customers?

DOCUMENTS FOR ANALYSIS

Read the following letters, and then, (1) analyze the strengths and/or weaknesses of each numbered sentence and (2) revise each letter so it follows this chapter's guidelines.

DOCUMENT 7.A

(1) After receiving your shipment of returned books, we checked our records to see why we had sent them to you in the first place. (2) Our records show that you were late in returning your card indicating that you did not want the selections. (3) As you know, we will automatically send you the month's new books unless you specifically ask not to receive them by our clearly stated deadline. (4) This policy enables us to see that our subscribers have access to the newest books as soon as possible.

(5) However, you are in luck. (6) Because we value your membership in the Read-a-Lot Club, we are crediting your account for $29.18--the full price of the books that you returned!

(7) In the future, please try to return your reply card more promptly so you won't face the inconvenience of returning the books. (8) In any case, we want to express our thanks for your long-term patronage of the Read-a-Lot Club. (9) We think you will want next month's selection, which is a murder mystery by John D. MacDonald.

DOCUMENT 7.B

(1) Please accept our apologies for the delay in repairing your video game, which is being shipped under separate cover.

(2) Let me explain what happened: Four Star Games, the manufacturer of your video game system, had expanded their production facilities to capitalize on the boom in video game sales that occurred in the early 1980s. (3) When the market for such games declined, the firm was unable to meet the payments on their bank loans. (4) The firm went bankrupt early this year, and we bought their assets. (5) We also acquired their liabilities, which included all repairs under warranties.

(6) Your broken game was just one of many that fell in our lap, so to speak. (7) As you can imagine, it took us a while to sort out what was happening--hence the delay in repairing your video game.

(8) In the future, we will be handling any further repairs covered by warranties through a new dealer network, created through the combination of Four Star's best dealers and our own existing dealers. (9) If you have any further problems with the game, please contact one of these dealers for repairs.

(10) Thanks for your patience in this matter. (11) Again, we apologize for the delay. (12) Incidentally, I am enclosing a brochure showing some of our exciting new products.

DOCUMENT 7.C

(1) Your letter to Jason Nichols, president of Sunway Homes, has been given to me to answer because I am the director of personnel. (2) In that capacity, I keep the performance records on all of Sunway's personnel, which means that I am the person here who is best qualified to answer requests for references on former employees.

(3) In your letter of the 25th, you asked about the employment history of Karen Wilson, who has applied for a position with your organization. (4) Ms. Wilson was employed by Sunway from January 1985 until April of this year. (5) Her record shows that she consistently earned above-average merit raises because her supervisors felt that she was doing a good job. (6) From this, I would conclude that she is a good worker. (7) Although I did not work closely with Karen myself, I can assure you that we take great care in selecting all our employees. (8) I will say, however, that Karen's record shows that she took more than the usual number of days for personal business. (9) In my experience, this often indicates domestic difficulties and may be a sign of instability, although whether this is so in Karen's case, I don't know.

(10) In summary, Karen Wilson's record suggests that she was an above-average employee during her tenure with our firm. (11) If I can be of any further assistance in this matter, please feel free to contact me.

DOCUMENT 7.D

(1) I was really glad to hear that you were promoted to vice president of research and development at ChemCo. (2) I know that you have wanted that job for years, and I can imagine how happy you must be now that you have finally achieved your goal. (3) But before you break out the champagne, take a hard look at what you're getting into.

(4) As you know, I received an important promotion myself last year. (5) And let me tell you, it's not all a bed of roses up here in the executive suite.

(6) I've been working 12 and 15 hours a day since I became general manager of the Wingate plant; my wife and children hardly recognize me anymore, and my former friends in the company act like they're afraid of me. **(7)** As they say, it's lonely at the top. **(8)** If you find yourself wishing you could undo it all, give me a call. **(9)** Maybe we can run away and join the circus together.

CASES

WRITING POSITIVE REPLIES

1. Cooling it: Letter confirming details of a complex job The contract has been signed. For $2,300, you have agreed to install a central air-conditioning unit in the home at 3985 Magoo Terrace, Wichita, KA 67216.

The preliminary sheet-metal work has been done, and the main unit has arrived in your shop. The main unit is guaranteed for one year (materials and labor) and an additional two years for materials only. Working with a crew of three, you believe you can install the unit and the vents in two days, starting each day at 8:30 a.m. Your customer, Mrs. Valerie Franchasia, has suggested Thursdays and Fridays as the days most convenient for her.

You want to tell Mrs. Franchasia when your crew will be working in her house, to remind her that the job will be a noisy one, and to let her know you'll need access to the house through the driveway and garage. It is also possible that you won't be able to complete the job within two days.

Your task: You have been unable to reach Mrs. Franchasia by phone, so you must write to her. Confirm that Air-Whiz workers will install her air-conditioning system next Thursday and Friday and that they hope to have the job completed by 5:00 p.m. Friday. You usually sign letters of this type using your title, which is air-control specialist.

2. Mystery and romance: Memo updating Simon & Schuster management on the status of a marketing campaign A few years ago, New York publishing company Simon & Schuster acquired the rights to the Nancy Drew series, a collection of books about a spunky young sleuth who drives around in a little blue roadster solving such crimes as The Clue in the Jewel Box. For over 50 years, Nancy was a favorite among preteens. Although ostensibly written by Carolyn Keene, the stories were created by Edward Stratemeyer, whose stable of anonymous writers also churned out volumes on the Hardy Boys, Tom Swift, and the Bobbsey Twins.

Now Simon & Schuster is updating Nancy Drew for young adults (12- to 15-year-olds) who remember her from their younger days. The "new" Nancy books are also written by a "book factory" employing a corps of writers, but they are adult-looking paperbacks with glitzy covers. Romance plays a bigger role in the plots, and Nancy is portrayed in a more modern light: driving a Mustang, wearing designer jeans, and solving such trendy crimes as record piracy.

Ron Buehl, publisher of the juvenile division, hopes to build a loyal following of readers who will buy one Nancy paperback after another, month after month, at a price of $2.50 each. He is also working on a TV series and plans to license Nancy Drew clothes, cosmetics, and jewelry.

As a member of Simon & Schuster's marketing department, your role is to see that Nancy is doing well in the bookstores. So far, so good. The first four Nancy books have all made it to the young adult best-seller list and are moving well at major bookstore chains like Waldenbooks and B. Dalton. Sales are so strong that you have shipped an additional 500,000 copies to stores.

Because Nancy Drew already has a lot of name recognition, Simon & Schuster decided against a big advertising campaign, but it has given you a budget of $125,000 for other forms of promotion. You have used part of the money to buy special racks for bookstores and to print free Nancy Drew bookmarks. Your best idea, though, was to develop 400,000 "teaser" booklets with excerpts from the books. You distributed 100,000 of these to bookstores and gave 300,000 directly to junior high and high school students as part of a gift pack containing free samples of shampoo and other teen-oriented products. You are also planning to give away 3,200 books through a sweepstakes, which is being promoted in teen magazines.

These efforts have gotten the new Nancy books off to a strong start. You're hearing lots of encouraging comments from booksellers. Anne Hoppe, a senior buyer for Waldenbooks, confided, "I thought putting a Nancy Drew series in the young adult market was crazy. It was already so saturated, and I thought girls who read her when they were younger might not want her around anymore. I was shocked by the sales; they've been fantastic."

Your task: Mr. Buehl has asked you how the Nancy Drew books are doing in the marketplace. Write a memo updating him on your progress in promoting the new series.[1]

3. Fighting back: Letter replying to questions about Baskin Robbins's marketing strategy Like the rest of the employees at Baskin Robbins's corporate headquarters in Glendale, California, you've been worried about growing competition. Although Baskin Robbins still dishes out more ice cream than any other chain in America, it has been stung by such rivals as Haagen-Dazs and Frusen Gladje, which specialize in super-premium ice creams. While sales of such brands are increasing by 19 percent per year, Baskin Robbins's sales are inching up by only 4.3 percent annually. At the same time, frozen yogurt shops are gobbling up customers who are concerned about calories and fats.

Caught between a rock and a hard place, Baskin Robbins has responded by launching a multimillion-dollar revitalization plan. The basic thrust of the plan is to make Baskin Robbins more appealing to adults. A program is under way to spruce up at least 2,000 outlets so they will be more attractive and more comfortable. The school-desk chairs are being replaced by benches and tables, and the old pink and gray color scheme is giving way to a sleeker look.

At the same time, Baskin Robbins is introducing its own ultrarich International Creams line featuring adult-oriented flavors: Grand Marnier, chocolate raspberry truffle, cappuccino chip, almond amaretto, and brandied cherries. Designed to lure customers back from Haagen-Dazs, these flavors are priced at $1.25, 25 percent higher than Baskin Robbins's traditional roster of 31 flavors. To launch the line, management is spending $5 million on advertising, the first national campaign the company has undertaken.

Baskin Robbins is also experimenting with other options, such as adding yogurt, cookies, candy, and coffee in some stores. The downtown Pittsburgh franchise even features croissants and muffins at 6:30 a.m. Meanwhile, the research staff is hard at work concocting new flavors to add to Baskin Robbins's list of ice cream favorites.

Your boss, Carol Kirby, vice president of marketing, is confident that these measures will soon produce results. Nevertheless, company headquarters continues to receive letters from concerned franchisees, asking what is being done to meet the increasingly tough competition.

Your task: Prepare a form letter that can be used as a basis for replies to franchisees who inquire about headquarters' efforts to strengthen the chain.[2]

RESPONDING FAVORABLY TO CLAIMS AND ADJUSTMENT REQUESTS

4. Potholes and other problems: Letter granting a small adjustment During recent road repairs (in Regina, Saskatchewan S4P 0J2), members of the work crew inadvertently spilled several gallons of molten tar on an azalea bush belonging to Ernest Eberly, 312 Bishop Lane. Mr. Eberly is upset. He says that the crew members were noisy, that they blocked his driveway needlessly during a prolonged lunch break, and that they gouged up his lawn.

You are a claims adjuster for the Department of Streets & Sewers of Regina, and so you drove by to inspect the situation. The crew did its assigned job well; the formerly notorious Bishop Lane potholes are nicely smoothed over. You cannot see evidence of any recent lawn damage at 312 Bishop Lane. But the azalea is another matter. It definitely has been damaged.

Your task: Write to Mr. Eberly, offering him a settlement of $30.

5. Wining and dining: Adjustment offered in hopes of smoothing over a bad situation As manager of Schiller's Restaurant, you are responsible for making certain that the bartender serves only from polished glasses, that the tables are cleared after each course, that the servers don't hustle for larger tips by serving oversized portions ("Cut the pie in seven pieces, not six!" you remind them), and that everything is done to keep the restaurant popular and profitable. But you can't anticipate everything.

Three weeks ago, in the after-theater rush, one of your best servers spilled a glass of red wine into the lap of a patron. The wine was a lively Burgundy with a rich red color, which spread rapidly and deeply through the cotton fibers of the print dress. Your apologies were profound and profuse, and you asked the customer to send the cleaning bill directly to you. The customer (Ann Jefferson, Regency Towers 566A, 1857 Briar Oaks Lane, Houston, TX 77027) took the entire event in decent humor. Once again, your quick, confident, and decisive style appeared to have minimized the effects of a potentially bad situation.

You have just learned from Ann Jefferson, however, that the matter is not yet ended. She took the dress to SummerSweet Cleaners, where repeated trips through the dry cleaning tubs were necessary to remove the wine stain. In the process, the colors faded too, and the dress is no longer presentable. Ms. Jefferson tells you that it is a Kitsy Clark designer dress, for which she paid $135 last May.

Your task: Write a letter to Ms. Jefferson in which you offer a reasonable adjustment.

6. Satisfaction guaranteed: Letter from L. L. Bean granting a claim As a member of L. L. Bean's customer service department in Freeport, Maine, you've handled plenty of claims in your day. The famous mail-order sporting goods company processes thousands of orders every month, and inevitably, some items are returned. Your job is to respond to the customer by either exchanging the merchandise or refunding the person's money, regardless of why the item was returned. L. L. Bean guarantees satisfaction, no questions asked.

Today, you have received a package from Arvin Bummel (212 North Star, Traverse City, MI 49684). When you open it, you find (1) one Maine guide shirt, stiff as a board and two sizes smaller than it ought to be; (2) one pair of whipcord trousers, also stiff and shrunken; and (3) a nasty letter from Mr. Bummel saying that he expects better from L. L. Bean. According to him, the clothes were ruined the first time he washed them. He wants L. L. Bean to replace the shirt and pants with new ones.

You are not surprised that the clothes are ruined, because the label plainly says, "dry clean only." Regardless, $108.50 worth of clothes are now unwearable.

Your task: In the spirit of good customer relations, write to Mr. Bummel and grant his claim. You may want to suggest gently that he look for clothing that is washable.[3]

HANDLING ROUTINE CREDIT REQUESTS

7. Bing's: Form letter granting credit As manager of Bing's Bikes (799 Garnet Avenue, Pacific Beach, CA 92109), you've decided to open lines of credit to a score of your regular customers and to some newcomers whose jobs and credit standing the local credit bureau has confirmed. However, motorcyclists tend to come and go, so you want to get your customers in a frame of mind to pay their accounts when due and to keep you informed of their whereabouts.

Your credit terms: (1) Payment in full is due within 20 days of the date of your bill, (2) no credit is available to customers who have been 60 days delinquent, (3) 1½ percent interest a month is assessed for payments that are received after the 20th day.

Your task: Draft a model letter welcoming credit customers of Bing's Bikes.

CONVEYING POSITIVE INFORMATION ABOUT PEOPLE

8. The special courier: Reply to a request for a recommendation letter In today's mail you get a letter from Non-Stop Messenger Service, 899 Sparks Street, Ottawa, Ontario K1A 0G9. It concerns a friend of yours who has applied for a job. Here is the letter:

Your friend has applied for the position of special courier with our firm, and she has given us your name as a reference. Our special couriers convey materials of considerable value or confidentiality to their recipients. It is not an easy job. Special couriers must sometimes remain alert for periods of up to 20 hours, and they cannot expect to follow the usual "three square meals and eight hours' sleep" routine, because they often travel long distances on short notice. On occasion, a special courier must react quickly and decisively to threatening situations.

For this type of work we hire only people of unquestioned integrity, as demonstrated both by their public records and by references from people, like yourself, who have known them personally or professionally.

We would appreciate a letter from you detailing (1) how long and in what circumstances you have known the applicant, (2) qualities she possesses that would qualify her for the position of special courier, and (3) qualities that might be improved before she were put on permanent assignment in this job.

Your task: Write as supportive a letter as possible about your friend (choose someone you know) to Roscoe de la Penda, personnel specialist.

9. Welcome aboard, Ms. Scarpelli: Good news for a new employee Being a successful entrepreneur with a rapidly growing business has its rewards as well as its headaches. Fortunately, you've reached a point where you can afford to foist some of those headaches onto an executive assistant. All five of the people you interviewed for the position have excellent qualifications, and several seem compatible with your own personality and style. But the one who stands a little above the rest is Gina Scarpelli.

Maybe you're impressed by Gina's experience working as an assistant to someone you know to be rather difficult, maybe by her poise and resourcefulness, maybe by her hobby: stock-car racing. All three qualities will stand her in good stead in your office, where the only sure thing is that every new day will bring another crisis.

What will this paragon cost you? You think she'll accept an annual salary of $24,000 plus health benefits and one week of paid vacation. To sweeten the offer, however, you want to let her know that you're willing to accommodate her hobby by giving her an occasional long weekend—assuming, of course, that business does not absolutely demand her presence.

You'd like Gina to begin working yesterday, but she said she needs to give her present employer two weeks' notice. As soon as she joins you, she'll have to begin taking over some of the administrative detail that's bogged you down. You realize that your working relationship will evolve through trial and error, but you're excited about having someone to back you up.

You just hope you're right about Gina being able to cope with chaos for a while.

Your task: Write a letter to Ms. Scarpelli (731 Pickwick Drive, Wilmington, DE 19808) offering her the job.

WRITING DIRECTIVES AND INSTRUCTIONS

10. Wrinkle-free service: Memo directing Nordstrom employees to stress customer service Another great story has reached corporate headquarters in Seattle. It seems that a clerk in the menswear department of a Nordstrom store learned that a customer was buying a new dress shirt to wear to an important business meeting that afternoon. The clerk dashed into the back room and gave the shirt a good pressing to get the wrinkles out. The customer was so astonished by the good service that he wrote the store manager a note of appreciation. And the clerk received a $200 gift certificate in recognition of his efforts.

You're pleased to see additional proof that Nordstrom's emphasis on service is paying off. In the competitive world of retailing, your company is growing more rapidly than most department store chains, and your sales per square foot are twice the industry average. Furthermore, morale among your employees is high. Knowing that they are the company's chief competitive asset makes the clerks feel important. The company does everything it can to reinforce this feeling.

Your task: Draft a directive that your boss, the head of personnel, can send to store managers. The message isn't new, but it bears repeating: They are to encourage clerks to take initiative in serving customers, just as the menswear clerk did. And they are authorized to use Nordstrom gift certificates, within the constraints of their overall budget, as rewards to employees who best exemplify the company's philosophy.[4]

CONVEYING GOOD NEWS ABOUT PRODUCTS AND OPERATIONS

11. Solving the child-care dilemma: Memo announcing Steelcase's new child-care benefits Your boss, James C. Soule, vice president of human resources with the prosperous manufacturer of office furniture, has noticed that employee performance is increasingly affected by child-care problems. In the typical company, about half the work force (from production workers to top executives) are part of two-career couples or are single parents. Over 75 percent of the working mothers and almost that many fathers sometimes have to come in late, leave early, stretch their lunch hours, or spend time on the phone to deal with their children. And on top of that, they often take sick leave to stay at home when their children are ill. A company loses anywhere from $100 to $200 a day when someone does stay home, depending on the person's level in the organization.

In surveying employees from Steelcase headquarters in Grand Rapids, Michigan, you found diverging opinions about the options that might alleviate the problem. Some like the idea of an on-site day-care center, but many prefer to make their own arrangements. Mr. Soule has concluded that Steelcase should help employees with outside arrangements. Specifically, he approves your plan to provide a list of top-quality day-care centers, family-care homes, and babysitters and to offer the option of signing up for child-care assistance instead of another fringe benefit, such as dental insurance.

Your task: Draft a memo for Mr. Soule to send out announcing Steelcase's new child-care benefits.[5]

12. Time to grow: Press release from Wells Fargo San Francisco-based Wells Fargo Bank has actively implemented policies that help employees develop to their full potential. Now the company has instituted a program that enables employees to take time off to pursue worthwhile personal objectives. The employees who qualify continue to receive salaries and benefits during their sabbaticals; at the end, they can return to their old jobs or to positions at equivalent levels in the organization.

The program is designed to reward superior performers who have been with the bank for at least ten years. The applicants must spend their leave time on projects that will enrich both themselves and their communities. Nancy Thompson, the program's director, says, "These are not larks. We eliminate people who want to take a cruise or go to Hawaii."

Recently, the bank approved applications for two employees: Phyllis Jones, a bank operations officer who is studying Navajo rug weaving in New Mexico, and Patricia Lujan, a customer service representative who is preparing for a recital as a concert pianist.

Your task: Write a press release about the program that will interest newspapers and general-interest magazines.[6]

WRITING GOODWILL MESSAGES

13. That warm glow of success: Letter congratulating a friend Success feels good, but it feels especially good when someone else knows about it. Which of your friends has recently received an award or achieved a sought-after goal?

Your task: Let your successful friend know that you know. Give her or him a written confirmation of (1) success and (2) your support.

14. Back on track: Letter thanking Nike dealers for their support Rob Strasser, Nike's vice president in charge of new product development, is always eager to hear news from the company's sales representatives. During one of your brief visits to headquarters in Beaverton, Oregon, you oblige with a few observations on dealers' response to your company's shoes.

"Air Jordan basketball shoes are still selling like hotcakes," you tell Rob, "and some of our newer items are also catching on. I think we're going to have a winner with the EXW walking shoe." Rob agrees, with one caveat: Dealers must believe in the shoe and help sell it.

"I think we can count on them," you say. "You should have seen them at the mini walking races when we demonstrated the shoes. A couple of years ago, it was another story, but those days are over. The dealers I call on are all very enthusiastic about Nikes again, even though our shoes are expensive. Our name means a lot, and most of the athletic shoe stores are fighting to carry our brand."

That's welcome news to Rob. At one point, Nike had some serious problems with product designs, and the delivery system was fouled up too. But most of the dealers stuck with Nike. And as soon as the company started coming up with good designs again, the dealers really supported them. "I know that some people think the Air Jordan shoe rescued Nike," you observe, "but the shoes didn't sell themselves. The dealers were out there pushing for us." Rob agrees.

Your task: You know that the dealers will be pleased to know how much Nike appreciates their support through difficult times. With Rob's blessing, draft a form letter thanking them; it will go out over Rob's signature.[7]

15. Season's greetings: Letter combining seasonal greetings with a business message As your part-time, seasonal tax service evolved into a full-time, all-year tax and accounting business, you let it grow naturally through advertisements, satisfied clients, and word of mouth. But now, with your education and certification out of the way, you are taking your work more seriously. What had been a source of extra spending money while you were a college student is now your sole means of support.

In the past you have sent out stock Christmas cards imprinted with your name to your ongoing (and a few former) clients. The cards did not carry personal messages, nor were they of such quality that your clients would have them lead the parade of cards marching across the mantel. Maybe you should do better.

Your task: Using your home address, draft a message that would be appropriate for mailing to 45 tax and accounting clients. If you choose to, you might sketch the graphics.

After studying this chapter, you will be able to

- Choose correctly between the indirect and direct approach
- Establish the proper tone from the beginning of your message
- Present bad news in such a way that a reader will accept it as reasonable and understandable
- Motivate the reader to take constructive action
- Leave the reader willing to continue a business relationship with your firm

CHAPTER EIGHT

WRITING BAD-NEWS MESSAGES

Wanda Williams

COMMUNICATION CLOSE-UP AT SOUTHLAND

In the 1980s, as the American economy experienced major realignments, many workers felt the pain of layoffs. Some of them worked for Southland Corporation, which is best known as operator and franchiser of 7-Eleven convenience stores. The unpleasant task of letting people at the Dallas, Texas, headquarters know they'd lost their jobs fell to Wanda Williams, Southland's corporate personnel manager.

Wanda and her staff tried to make the layoffs as painless as possible. "We assembled a packet of materials for employees who were affected by the cutbacks," she says, "explaining what we were going to do for them and how the outplacement center operated and inviting them in to discuss the situation with someone in our department." Letters to those who had lost their jobs were personalized and tactful. "We tried to present the facts in as positive a tone as possible. For employees who'd been around for a long time, we made note of that fact. We said we'd try to work with employees to find another job. Anything positive is helpful when you're faced with the loss of your livelihood."

Wanda sometimes has to convey other types of bad news. Letters to unsuccessful job applicants, for example, are concise but still considerate. "They're organized along the lines of 'We appreciate your coming in for an interview; another candidate has been selected; we'll keep your resume on file for a certain time.'" The polite and positive opening helps the

Bad-news messages are a fact of business life, even for successful companies like Southland Corporation, operator and franchiser of 7-Eleven stores.

reader accept the bad news in the middle of the letter; the close leaves room for hope but doesn't make any false promises.

When employees aren't performing their jobs well, Wanda's department is called on again. "For a person with excessive absences or alcoholism or other personal problems, we need to motivate change. We write a letter that focuses on the performance issues, and we go into some detail to show that we're not just making idle criticisms. We say, 'This is serious, these are the facts, but you have a future with the company.' We try to give them something to hang on to."

Although her general approach is to wrap the bad news in positive statements, Wanda cautions against being too indirect and vague: "I tell my staff, first and foremost, that we want our bad-news messages to make a point. Sometimes we try so hard to soften the message that it doesn't come across. It's also important to be specific and stay away from personal accusations. Instead of making a general statement like 'You are careless in your work,' we say something like 'You had this assignment, and there were these specific problems with your performance.' And we always have a contact name on our letters, even letters to job applicants, so we can invite people to call us if they have any further questions."

These tactful touches are the norm in Southland's messages to both employees and aspiring employees, in form letters and more personalized letters. According to Wanda, "The person who's getting an unpleasant message doesn't want to hear it and could be hurt by it. So we do what we can to be both clear and considerate. We can't afford to squander our company's good name."

EASING THE PAIN OF BAD-NEWS MESSAGES

As Wanda Williams realizes, some people interpret as a personal failure being rejected for a job or for credit, and even rejections in less sensitive areas usually complicate people's lives. Admittedly, business decisions should not be made solely to avoid hurting someone's feelings, but mixing bad news with consideration for the other person's needs helps the audience understand that your unfavorable decision is based on a business judgment, not on personal judgment.

When the time comes to compose a bad-news message, you must address two basic questions. The first is, what tone will best contribute to the message's effectiveness? Try to adopt a tone that will support three specific goals:

In establishing tone, strive for:

- Firmness
- Fairness
- Goodwill

- You want your audience to understand that your bad-news message represents a firm decision.
- You want your audience to understand that, under the circumstances, your decision was fair and reasonable.
- You want your audience to remain well disposed toward your business and possibly toward you.

In a bad-news message, the "you" attitude translates into

- Emphasizing the audience's goals instead of your own
- Looking for the best in your audience
- Using positive rather than negative phrasing

With the right tone, you can make an unwelcome point while preserving the audience's ego. A key is to make liberal use of the "you" attitude. For example, point out how your decision might actually further the audience's goals, even though it first causes disappointment. You can also convey concern by looking for the best in your audience. Even if the person is at fault, assume that he or she is interested in being fair. You can also ease the pain by using positive instead of negative words.

Use the indirect plan or the direct plan, depending on the audience's needs.

The second question is, What arrangement of the main idea and supporting data will most completely ease the audience's disappointment? It can be answered by choosing between the two basic strategies described in Chapter 4: (1) the indirect plan, in which you present supporting data first and then the main idea, or (2) the direct plan, in which you present the main idea first and then the supporting data.

INDIRECT PLAN

The indirect plan is actually a familiar approach. You've probably used it many times to say something, in a roundabout way, that might upset another person. You can recognize, then, how beginning a business message with a blunt no may keep someone from reading or listening to your reasons. The point of using the indirect plan is to ease the audience into the part of your message that demonstrates you are fair-minded or eager to do business on some other terms.

The indirect plan consists of four parts: (1) a buffer; (2) reasons supporting the negative decision; (3) a clear, diplomatic statement of the negative decision; and (4) a helpful, friendly, positive close. By presenting the reasons for your decision before the bad news itself, you gradually prepare the audience for disappointment. In most cases, this approach is more appropriate than an abrupt statement of the bad news.

Buffer

Buffer: neutral lead-in to bad news.

The first step in using the indirect plan is to put the audience in an accepting mood by making a neutral, noncontroversial statement closely related to the point of the message. For example, in a memo telling another supervisor that you can't spare anyone from your customer service staff for a temporary assignment to the order fulfillment department, you might begin with a sentence like this: "Customer service, I'm sure you agree, is one of our major concerns at National Investments. And this department shares your goal of processing orders quickly and efficiently." If possible, base the buffer on statements made by the person you are responding to. The danger in using an unrelated buffer is that you will seem to be "beating around the bush" and therefore lose the audience's respect.

Also avoid giving the impression in the buffer that good news will follow. Building up the audience at the beginning only makes the subsequent letdown even more painful. Imagine your reaction to this opening: "Your resume indicates that you would be well suited for a management trainee position with our company." Now compare that opening with this: "Your resume shows very clearly why you are interested in becoming a management trainee with our company." The second opening, which emphasizes the applicant's favorable interpretation of her qualifications rather than the company's evaluation, is less misleading but still positive.

Here are some other things to avoid in writing a buffer:

Use a buffer that is

- Neutral
- Relevant
- Not misleading
- Assertive
- Succinct

- *Avoid saying no*, because an audience who encounters the unpleasant news right at the beginning will react negatively to the rest of the message, no matter how reasonable and well phrased it is.
- *Avoid using a know-it-all tone*, as in "you should be aware that," because the audience will expect your lecture to lead to a negative response and will therefore become resistant to the rest of your message.
- *Avoid wordy and irrelevant phrases*, such as "we have received your letter," "this letter is in reply to your request," and "we are writing in response to your request." You make better use of the space by referring directly to the subject of the letter.
- *Avoid apologizing*. An apology weakens your explanation of the unfavorable decision.
- *Avoid writing a buffer that is too long*. The point is to identify briefly something that both you and the audience are interested in and agree on and then to proceed in a businesslike way.

Table 8.1 shows some ways you could tactfully open a bad-news message.

After you have composed a buffer, evaluate it by asking yourself four questions: Is it pleasant? Is it relevant? Is it neutral, saying neither yes nor no? Does it provide for a smooth transition to the reasons that follow? If you can answer yes to all four, you may proceed confidently to the next section of your message.

Reasons

If you've done a good job of composing the buffer, the reasons will follow naturally. Cover the more positive points first; then move to the less positive ones. Provide enough detail so the audience will understand your reasons. But be concise, because a long, roundabout explanation may make the audience impatient.

Present reasons to show that your decision is reasonable and fair.

It is very important to explain *why* you have reached your decision before you explain *what* that decision is. If you present your reasons effectively, they will help convince the audience that your decision is justified, fair, and logical. However, someone who realizes you are saying

TABLE 8.1 Types of Buffers

BUFFER	EXAMPLE
Agreement: Find a point on which you and the reader share similar views.	We both know how hard it is to make a profit in this industry.
Appreciation: Express sincere thanks for receiving something.	Your check for $127.17 arrived yesterday. Thank you.
Cooperation: Convey your willingness to help in any way you realistically can.	Employee Services is here to smooth the way for those who work to achieve the company's goals.
Fairness: Assure the reader that you've closely examined and carefully considered the problem, or mention an appropriate action that has already been taken.	For the past week, we have carefully monitored those using the photocopying machine to see if we can detect any pattern of use that might explain its frequent breakdowns.
Good news: Start with the part of your message that is favorable.	A replacement knob for your range is on its way, shipped February 10 via UPS.
Praise: Find an attribute or an achievement to compliment.	Your resume shows an admirable breadth of experience, which should serve you well as you progress in your career.
Resale: Favorably discuss the product or company related to the subject of the letter.	With their heavy-duty, full-suspension hardware and fine veneers, the desks and file cabinets in our Montclair line have become a hit with many value-conscious professionals.
Understanding: Demonstrate that you understand the reader's goals and needs.	So you can more easily find the typewriter with the features you need, we are enclosing a brochure that describes all the Olsen typewriters currently available.

no before he or she understands why may either quit paying attention altogether or be set to rebut the reasons when they're finally given.

Focus on how the audience might benefit from your negative message.

The tactful business communicator highlights the benefits of the decision to the audience instead of focusing on the company. For example, when saying no to a credit request, show how your decision will keep the person from becoming overextended financially. Facts and figures are often helpful in convincing the audience that you are acting in her or his best interests.

Some business communicators try to cushion bad news by hiding behind company policy. A statement like "Company policy forbids our hiring anyone for this position who does not have two years' management experience" seems to imply that you have not considered the person on her or his own merits. A skilled and sympathetic communicator may sometimes quote company policy but will also briefly explain it so that the audience may try to meet the requirements at a later time.

The other common failing is to apologize. Apologies are appropriate only if someone in your company has made a severe mistake or done something terribly wrong. But if no one in the company is at fault, an apology gives the wrong impression.

The tone of your language does a great deal to make your audience receptive to the bad news that follows. Avoid negative, counterproductive words like these:

broken	dissatisfied	regret
cannot understand	error	shocked
damage	fault	unfortunately
delay	inconvenience	wrong

Sometimes the "you" attitude is best observed by avoiding the word *you.*

Also, protect the audience's pride by using language that conveys respect; do not adopt an accusing tone. Use third-person, impersonal, passive language to explain the audience's mistakes in an inoffensive way. For example, say "The appliance won't work after being immersed in water" instead of "You shouldn't have immersed the appliance in water." In this case, the "you" attitude is better observed by avoiding the word *you.*

In the case of the management trainee applicant, a tactfully worded letter might give these reasons for the decision not to hire:

> Because these management trainee positions are quite challenging, our human relations department has researched the qualifications needed to succeed in them. The findings show that the two most important qualifications are a bachelor's degree in business administration and two years' supervisory experience.

Well-written reasons are

- Detailed
- Tactful
- Individualized
- Unapologetic
- Positive

This paragraph does a good job of stating the reasons for the refusal, because

- It provides enough detail to make the reason for the refusal logically acceptable.
- It implies that the applicant is better off avoiding a program where she would probably fail, given the background of others who would be working alongside her.
- The case does not rest solely on company policy. Even though a relevant policy exists, it is presented as logical rather than rigid.
- It offers no apology for the decision.
- It avoids negative personal expressions ("You do not meet our requirements").

Sometimes detailed reasons should not be provided.

Although specific reasons help the audience accept bad news, reasons cannot always be given. When reasons involve confidential, excessively complicated, or purely negative information, or when the reasons benefit only you or your firm (for example, enhancing the company's profits), do not include them. Move directly to the next section.

The bad news

So that the audience is psychologically prepared, the bad news should be the logical outcome of the reasons that come before it. However, the audience may still react emotionally if the bad news is handled carelessly. Here are some methods for de-emphasizing the bad news:

- Minimize the space or time devoted to it.
- Subordinate it in a complex or compound sentence (for example, "My department is already short-handed, so I'll need all my staff for at least the next two months").
- Embed it in the middle of a paragraph.

Two other techniques are especially useful for saying no as clearly but painlessly as possible. First, using a conditional (*if* or *when*) statement implies that the audience could possibly have received or might someday

To make bad news less painful:

- De-emphasize the bad news visually and grammatically
- Use a conditional statement
- Tell what you did do, not what you didn't do

receive a favorable answer: "When you have more managerial experience, you are welcome to reapply." A statement like this could motivate the applicant to improve her qualifications.

The other technique is to tell the audience what you did do, can do, or will do rather than what you did not do, cannot do, or won't do. Say "We sell exclusively through retailers, and the one nearest you that carries our merchandise is . . ." rather than "We are unable to serve you, so please call your nearest dealer." Here's the same principle applied in the letter rejecting the job applicant: "The five positions currently open have been staffed with people whose qualifications match those uncovered in our research." A statement like this need not be followed by the explicit news that you will not be hiring the reader. By focusing on the positive and only implying the bad news, you soften the blow.

In writing a bad-news message, avoid negative wording and personal language.

If it seems that an implied message might leave any doubt, state your decision in direct terms. Just be sure to avoid blunt statements that are likely to cause pain and anger. The following phrases are particularly likely to offend:

I must refuse — we must deny — we cannot allow
I am unable to — we cannot afford to — much as I would like to
you must understand — we must reject — we must turn down

Use impersonal, positive language instead so you don't undermine the audience's feelings of self-worth. Your goal is for the audience not only to accept your unfavorable decision but also to pay attention to the end of your message.

Positive close

After giving the bad news, your job is to end the message on a more upbeat note. You might propose an attainable solution to the audience's problem: "The human resources department has offered to bring in temporary workers when I need them, and I'm sure they would consider doing the same for you." In a message to a customer or potential customer, an off-the-subject ending that includes resale information or sales promotion is also appropriate. If you've asked the audience to decide between alternatives or to take some action, make sure she or he knows what to do, when to do it, and how to do it with ease.

Whatever type of close you choose, observe these "don'ts":

- Don't refer to or repeat the bad news.
- Don't apologize for the decision or reveal any doubt that the reasons will be accepted ("I trust our decision is satisfactory").
- Don't urge additional communication ("If you have further questions, please write"), unless you're really willing to discuss your decision further.
- Don't anticipate problems ("Should you have further problems, please let us know").
- Don't include clichés that are insincere in view of the bad news ("If we can be of any help, please contact us").

- Don't reveal any doubt that you will keep the person as a customer ("We hope you will continue to do business with us").

In the case of the applicant for the management trainee position, you could observe these rules by writing a close like this:

An upbeat, positive close
- Builds goodwill
- Offers a suggestion for action
- Provides a look toward the future

Many companies seek other qualifications in management trainees, so I urge you to continue your job search. You'll certainly find an opening in which your skills and aspirations match the job requirements exactly.

Keep in mind that the close is the last thing the audience has to remember you by. Try to make the memory a positive one.

DIRECT PLAN

A bad-news message organized on the direct plan would start with a clear statement of the bad news, proceed to the reasons for the decision, and end with a courteous close. Stating the bad news at the beginning has two potential advantages: (1) It makes a shorter message possible, and (2) the audience needs less time to reach the main idea of the message, the bad news itself.

Use the direct plan when
- Your boss prefers that internal messages come right to the point
- The message has little personal impact
- You want to make your point emphatically

Although the indirect approach is preferable in bad-news messages, you may sometimes want to move right to the point. For example, memos are often organized so the bad news comes before the reasons. In fact, some managers expect all internal correspondence to be brief and direct, regardless of whether the message is positive or negative. But remember that a little bit of sugar—a tactful tone, a focus on reasons, a courteous close—helps any distasteful medicine go down.

Routine bad-news messages to other companies also commonly follow the direct plan, especially if they relay decisions that have little or no personal impact. Sometimes, too, you will know from prior experience that someone prefers the bad news first in any message. The direct plan is also appropriate when you want to present an image of firmness and strength; for example, the last message in a collection series, just before the matter is turned over to an attorney, usually gets right to the point.

CONVEYING BAD NEWS ABOUT ORDERS

The basic goal of a bad-news letter about orders is to protect or make a sale.

For several reasons, businesses must sometimes convey bad news concerning orders. In writing to a would-be customer, you have three basic goals:

- To work toward an eventual sale along the lines of the original order
- To keep instructions or additional information as clear as possible
- To maintain an optimistic, confident tone so your reader will not lose interest

UNCLEAR ORDERS

When you have received an incomplete or unclear order from a customer, your first job is to get the information needed to complete the order. You

Use the indirect plan to get additional information for unclear orders.

should make it as simple as possible for the customer to provide this information.

The first question to ask yourself is whether to phone or write for the data. If time is short, the information you need is uncomplicated, and the cost of the call is in proportion to the size of the order, you may want to use the phone. But write if you need a great deal of information, if the customer must spend time to assemble it, or if you need a written record of the transaction. Whether you phone or write, the indirect approach is usually best.

The first part of your message, the buffer, should confirm the original order; in doing so, it might bolster the sale by referring to desirable features of the product (resale). Then the source of the confusion could be stated or the problem defined. A friendly, helpful, and positive close should make it simple for the audience to place a corrected order. For instance:

Your order for two dozen Gregg McGhee tennis racquets is a wise decision. You'll find that they sell fast because of their reputation for durability. In fact, tests reveal that they outlast several other racquets costing over $10 more.

The buffer has a resale emphasis.

McGhee racquets have a standard face, but their patented "Handi-Grip" handles come in several sizes so players can enjoy the tightest, best-fitting grip possible. Handles range in 1/8-inch increments from 4-1/4 inch (for the average ten-year-old) to 4-3/4 inch (for a large adult male). Considering your customer mix, which sizes will sell best in your store?

The reason for not immediately filling the order precedes the actual bad news (which is implied) in order to show the positive side of the problem.

To let us know, simply fill in your preferences on the enclosed postage-paid card and mail it back today. All sizes are in stock, Mr. Wallace, so your order will be shipped promptly. You can be selling these handsome racquets within a week.

The close tells how the customer can solve the problem and describes the benefits of acting promptly.

BACK ORDERS

Use the indirect plan when telling a customer that you cannot immediately ship the entire order.

When you must "back order" for a customer, you have one of two types of bad news to convey: (1) You are able to send only part of the order, or (2) you are able to send none of the order.

When sending only part of the order, you actually have both good news and bad news. In such situations, the indirect plan works very well. The buffer should contain the good news that part of the order is en route, along with a resale reminder of the product's attractiveness. After the buffer come the reasons why the remainder of the shipment has been delayed. A strong close should encourage a favorable attitude toward the total transaction. For a customer whose order for a lawn mower and its companion grass catcher can be only partly filled, your letter might read like the one in Figure 8.1.

Had you been unable to send the customer any portion of this order, you would still have used the indirect approach. But because you would have had no good news to give, your buffer would only have confirmed

FIGURE 8.1
Letter Advising of a Back Order

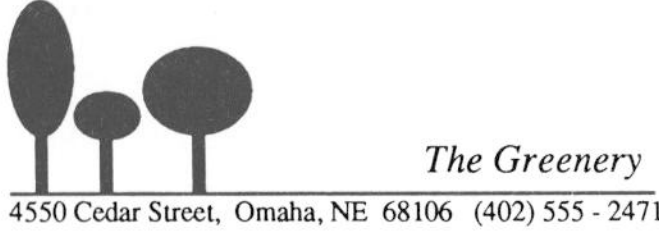

The Greenery
4550 Cedar Street, Omaha, NE 68106 (402) 555 - 2471

April 4, 1989

Mr. and Mrs. Eric Larsen
411 Fourth Street
Blue Springs, NE 68318

Dear Mr. and Mrs. Larsen:

Your lawn mower is being shipped to you today. The 22-inch Kleen-Kut mower with the vacuum grass catcher will not only give you a clean, beautifully manicured lawn but also give you one free of brown rot, the disease that afflicts lawns when cuttings are not removed.

So far this spring, almost every customer who has purchased a Kleen-Kut lawn mower has also taken advantage of the special savings on the vacuum grass catcher. Because such demand was not anticipated, our supply of grass catchers is temporarily depleted.

When we realized that we were running out of this popular product, we phoned the manufacturer to order additional vacuum grass catchers. This shipment is now on its way, and we should have it within one week. On the day the grass catchers reach us, we will send yours by parcel service. Within two weeks, you can be enjoying the convenience of your grass catcher.

Other Kleen-Kut products that will help you maintain your lawn and flower beds are shown in the enclosed catalog. Note that during our spring promotion, the prices of some products have been reduced by as much as 50 percent. At those savings, your yard could be the envy of the entire neighborhood.

Sincerely,

Art Brill

Arthur Brill
Manager

br

Enclosure

The buffer conveys the good news and confirms the wisdom of the customer's choice.

The reason for the bad news shows that the grass catcher is popular and therefore, again, a good choice.

The bad news itself is implied by telling the reader what is being done, not what cannot be done.

The positive close includes sales promotion material.

the sale, and the explanation section would have stated your reason for not filling the order promptly.

SUBSTITUTIONS

Use the indirect plan to notify a customer that you must send a substitute, especially when the replacement is more expensive than the original item.

Once in a while, a customer will request something that you no longer sell or that is no longer produced. If you are sure the customer will approve a substitute product, you may go ahead and send it. But when in doubt, first send a letter that "sells" the substitute product and gives the customer simple directions for ordering it. In either case, be careful to avoid calling the second product a *substitute,* because the term carries a negative connotation and detracts from your sales information. Instead, say that you now stock the second product exclusively.

As you can imagine, the challenge is greater when the substitute is more expensive than the original item. You must show that the more expensive item can do much more than the originally ordered item so additional charges seem justified to the customer. Say a customer has ordered a drill that is no longer manufactured. Because of problems with the original drill, the motor has been upgraded. As a result, the price of the drill has increased from $24.95 to $31.95. You must send a letter convincing the customer to buy the more expensive drill:

Alpha-Omega, manufacturer of the Mini-Max drill you ordered, is committed to your satisfaction with every product it makes.

The buffer includes resale information on the manufacturer.

For this reason, Alpha-Omega conducts extensive testing. Results for the 1/4-inch Mini-Max with the 1/8-horsepower motor show that although it can drill through two inches of wood or a quarter inch of metal, thicker materials put a severe strain on the motor. Alpha-Omega knows that household jobs come in all sizes and shapes, so it now makes a more powerful 1/4-inch drill with a 3/8-horsepower motor. The new Mini-Max can cut through materials twice as thick as those the former model could handle.

The reasons for the bad news are explained in terms of the customer's needs.

Even with its superior capabilities, the new Mini-Max costs only about 30 percent more. Using this beefed-up model, you'll know that even heavy-duty household drilling will cause no overheating.

The bad news is stated positively. The writer emphasizes the product the firm carries rather than the one it does not.

You can be using your new heavy-duty drill by this time next week if you just check the YES box on the enclosed form, tuck the form into the postage-paid envelope with $7.00, and mail it today. Your new, worry-free Mini-Max will be on its way to you at once.

The close, which asks the reader to authorize shipment of the substitute item, makes action easy and reinforces the benefits described earlier.

UNFILLABLE ORDERS

Use the indirect plan to say that you cannot fill an order at all.

Occasionally you will not be able to fill an order either in part or with a substitute. In this case, your job is to say no and yet be as helpful as possible. One good way to maintain the customer's confidence in you and your company is to mention another source where the requested product might be obtained, as in the following letter from an upholsterer:

Your couch and chair are truly exquisite antiques. And the upholstery fabric you've selected will enhance their beauty even more.

The buffer is simple appreciation for the customer's good taste, highlighting a point on which both writer and reader agree.

Antiques demand special care when being upholstered, because of their dry, delicate wood

The reasons for the bad news and the bad news it-

■ CHECKLIST FOR BAD NEWS ABOUT ORDERS

A. Overall Strategy

- ☐ 1. Use the indirect plan in most cases.
- ☐ 2. Use the direct plan when the situation is routine (between employees of the same company), when the reader is not emotionally involved in the message, or when you know that the reader would prefer the bad news first.

B. Buffer

- ☐ 1. Express appreciation for the specific order.
- ☐ 2. Extend a welcome to a new customer.
- ☐ 3. Avoid flashy, attention-getting devices or phrasing.
- ☐ 4. Avoid negative words (*won't, can't, unable to*).
- ☐ 5. Avoid expressions of pleasure in receiving the order.
- ☐ 6. Use resale information on the ordered merchandise to build the customer's confidence in her or his choice (except for unfillable orders).

C. Reasons

- ☐ 1. Emphasize what the firm is doing rather than what it isn't doing, what it does have rather than what it lacks.
- ☐ 2. Avoid apologies.
- ☐ 3. Avoid expressions of sorrow or regret.
- ☐ 4. Thoroughly explain the problem with unclear orders.
  - ☐ a. Stress your desire to send exactly what the customer wants.
  - ☐ b. Include details, such as styles and colors available, that will enable the customer to specify the merchandise desired.
  - ☐ c. Provide photographs, sketches, catalog numbers, and other aids for ordering properly.
  - ☐ d. Avoid negative personal expressions, such as "You forgot" and "You neglected to."
- ☐ 5. Handle back orders carefully.
  - ☐ a. Specify shipping dates.
  - ☐ b. Avoid negative phrases, such as "cannot send" or "out of stock."
  - ☐ c. Explain reasons why the item is out of stock, such as high popularity or exceptional demand, that may stimulate the customer's desire for the item.
  - ☐ d. Reinforce the customer's confidence with resale (for consumers: personal attention, credit, repair services, free delivery, special discounts, telephone shopping, and other

and intricate curves and pleats. I know how important it is to you that someone spend all the time needed to do a painstaking job. Because I have several unusually heavy commitments, May 15 is the soonest I could start work on your couch and chair and give them the special attention they need. If my shop were clear of this other work, I could easily promise you a two-week delivery date.

self are intertwined in one paragraph. By emphasizing the care that the writer believes this project deserves, she "resells" the reader on her services.

I know that you want the job done very soon. So let me recommend Peter Aarons of A & J Upholstery. I talked with him just this morning, and he assured me that he could complete work on your furniture within two weeks. You'll find his expertise and prices comparable to mine. To discuss the details, phone Peter at 257-2543.

The suggestion of an alternative, which is technically part of the bad-news section, rates a paragraph of its own.

Thank you, Mrs. Nasseri, for making me your first choice for this important job. The next time you call, you should receive my usual prompt, on-time service. Please let me know whenever I can help.

The main point of this close is to convince the customer to come back under other circumstances.

services; for dealers: free counter and window displays, advertising materials, sales manuals, factory guarantees, and nearby warehousing).

- ☐ e. Refer to sales promotion material, if desirable.

☐ 6. Explain substitutions in detail.
- ☐ a. Introduce the benefits of the substitute before the bad news that the ordered item is unavailable.
- ☐ b. Avoid the word *substitute*, because of its negative connotation.
- ☐ c. Describe enough reader benefits to justify any higher price.

☐ 7. Explain why orders can't be filled.
- ☐ a. Explain in positive terms the way you market your products (such as through authorized dealers, who may provide personal service, faster delivery, shipping at little or no cost, credit, adjustment and repair services, the opportunity to see goods before buying).
- ☐ b. Name alternate sources, with addresses, telephone numbers, and positive statements about them.
- ☐ c. Stress the benefits to the customer of dealing with other sources.

☐ 8. Thoroughly explain the problem with nonconforming orders.
- ☐ a. Stress your desire to send exactly what the customer wants.
- ☐ b. Explain the reasons for requiring a deposit or minimum order.

☐ 9. Avoid hiding behind company policy.

D. The Bad News

☐ 1. State the bad news as positively as possible.
☐ 2. State the bad news clearly but, when possible, by implication.
☐ 3. Stress the reader benefit of the decision.

E. Positive, Friendly, Helpful Close

☐ 1. Remind the reader of how his or her needs are being met, if appropriate.
☐ 2. Explain the desired reader action as clearly and simply as possible.
☐ 3. Use resale information to clinch the sale, especially for replies about unclear orders, back orders, and nonconforming orders.
☐ 4. Make reader action as easy as possible.
☐ 5. Adopt a tone that shows you remain in control of the situation and will continue to give customers' orders personal attention.

NONCONFORMING ORDERS

Use the indirect plan to get a customer to comply with your order policy.

Many companies require deposits before delivery or require orders of a certain minimum size. Customers do not always understand or conform with these conditions, so orders sometimes come in that do not meet the requirements. In these situations, you must explain to customers what they must do before the order can be filled.

Imagine that you have received an order for a dozen golf bags, which is fewer than your policy requires. You must write to tell the customer of the required minimum.

Your order for lightweight, all-nylon Ace golf bags arrived today. Golfers really go for these bags because of their durability and practicality. Your sales will soar when customers find the Ace bags on display.

The buffer contains resale information.

Because most of our time is spent manufacturing rather than distributing golf bags, our shipping department is very small. In fact, we chiefly supply wholesalers and a few large retailers from our plant, with a minimum order of four dozen bags.

The reasons for the bad news and the bad news itself easily fit into the same paragraph.

To increase your order of this fast-selling product to four dozen or more, you can phone me at our toll-free number: 1-800-319-GOLF. I will see that your bags are sent right out, Ms. Burns.

Phase 1 of the close offers an alternative action and resells the customer on the product by emphasizing its popularity.

But if an order of four dozen golf bags is more than you need, check with Garcia Sports Wholesalers, Inc. They carry the Ace bags and supply most of the retail stores in your area (at a slightly higher price, because they are wholesalers). Their toll-free number is 1-800-586-9437. I know you'll like their efficiency and speedy delivery service.

Phase 2 of the close offers yet another alternative, enabling easy action.

As you can see, your bad-news letter should follow a carefully thought out plan. Most important is the sequence of the elements: You should provide the buffer and reasons before the bad news, then offer helpful suggestions.

COMMUNICATING NEGATIVE ANSWERS AND INFORMATION

The businessperson who tries to say yes to everyone will probably not win many promotions or stay in business for long. Occasionally, your response to inquiries must simply be no. It is a mark of your skill as a communicator to be able to say no clearly yet not cut yourself off from future dealings with the other person.

Use the direct plan when your negative answer or information will have little personal impact, the indirect plan in more sensitive situations.

Depending on your relationship with the reader, you could use either the direct plan or the indirect plan in these situations. If the reader is unlikely to be deeply disappointed, use the direct plan. Otherwise, use a buffer that expresses appreciation for being thought of, assures the reader of your attention to the request, compliments the reader, or indicates your understanding of the reader's needs. Continue with the reasons for the bad news and the bad news itself, couched in terms that show how the reader's problem can be solved and what you can do to help. Then close with a statement of interest, encouragement, or goodwill. You can demonstrate your sincerity, and minimize the reader's hostility or disappointment, by promptly fulfilling any promises you make.

PROVIDING BAD NEWS ABOUT PRODUCTS

Consider the direct or indirect plan for telling the reader bad news about a product.

When you must provide bad news about a product, the situation and the reader will dictate whether to use the direct or indirect plan. For example, if you were writing to tell the bookkeeping department in your company about price hikes in your products, you would use the direct plan. The reader will have to make some arithmetical adjustments when the hikes are put into effect but presumably will not be emotionally involved in the matter. However, you should probably use the indirect plan to convey the same information to the sales department. A change that weakens your products' competitive edge threatens sales representatives' income and possibly even their jobs.

The memo in Figure 8.2 was written to tell one company's sales department of a 10 percent across-the-board price increase. Notice that

FIGURE 8.2
Memo Providing Bad News About Products

The memo begins on an appreciative note to buffer the bad news.

The reason for the bad news is carefully explained, and then the bad news is introduced. The "you" attitude is emphasized also.

The close indicates that some action will be taken to lessen the impact of the bad news.

MEMO

DATE: October 11, 1989

TO: Sales Representatives

FROM: Jerri Canfield, Marketing Liaison

SUBJECT: Price Changes

Congratulations on setting a new sales record last month! Your all-out efforts are apparent to all of us.

As you know, for the past three years we have held our product prices constant so we could increase our share of the market. Because of this price lid and because of your effectiveness, we have achieved an even greater market share than forecasted. But inflation over the past three years has driven up our product costs to the point where we are no longer operating as profitably as we must. To keep salaries in line with inflation and to maintain the industry-standard profit margin of 3 percent of gross sales, on the first of next month the prices of all our products will be raised 10 percent.

To generate ideas that will help motivate our customers to accept these price increases, the marketing department and sales department will hold a joint meeting at 10 a.m. next Tuesday in Room 247. Please plan to attend. We need to develop some good ways to minimize the impact of these price increases on total sales and to maximize your commissions on next year's sales.

Jerri

the middle section of this memo presents an honest statement of the bad news. But the effect of this bad news is diminished by the credible rationale that precedes it, by the avoidance of any overt statement that commissions may get smaller, and by the upbeat close.

DENYING COOPERATION WITH ROUTINE REQUESTS

Consider the direct or indirect plan to tell someone you cannot do what has been requested.

When people ask you for information or want you to do something and you cannot honor the request, you may answer with either the direct plan or the indirect plan. For example, let's assume that someone has asked your company to participate in a research project concerning sales promotion. But the company has a policy against disseminating any information about projected sales figures. If you were the researcher, how would you react to this letter?

This letter is to inform you that Blodgett Corporation has no interest in taking part in your Sales Management Techniques research project.

In fact, our company has a policy that prohibits dissemination of any projected sales figures.

Thank you for your interest in our organization. If we can help you in any other way, please let us know.

This letter would offend most readers, for several reasons:

- The direct plan is used, even though the reader is outside the company and may be emotionally involved in the response.
- The words "This letter is to inform you" are stodgy and condescending.
- The tone of the first paragraph is unnecessarily negative and abrupt.
- The phrase "has no interest in taking part" implies that the research is unimportant.
- The writer hides behind company policy, a policy that the reader may find questionable.
- Clichés in the final paragraph undercut any personal, friendly impact that the letter might have had.
- The offer to help is an unpleasant irony, given the writer's unwillingness to help in this instance.

Wording, tone, and format conspire to make a letter either offensive or acceptable. Notice how the letter that follows conveys the same negative message as the previous letter without sounding offensive:

Your upcoming research project sounds fascinating. Thanks for thinking of Blodgett Corporation as a possible contributor.

The buffer is supportive and appreciative.

Each year, we receive a number of requests for help in various studies. Although we would like to lend a hand to everyone who asks, we've had to set up guidelines for deciding which requests we can honor. Many competitors and shareholders would like to get an advance look at some of the figures that researchers request. That's why our sales and earnings projections must be kept within corporate headquarters until they are publicly announced through press releases.

Without falling back on references to "company policy," the reason for the policy is fully explained. The bad news is implied, not stated explicitly.

Ms. Dalle, we would like to help you in another way. If you can use sales and earnings data from a previous period, which are shown in the enclosed annual report, please do. Best of luck with your study.

The close is friendly, positive, and helpful.

Think about the different impact these two letters might have on the researcher, her associates, her family, and friends. Given this network, shouldn't a business writer take the time and trouble to give negative messages the attention they deserve?

DECLINING INVITATIONS AND REQUESTS FOR FAVORS

Consider the direct or indirect plan to turn down an invitation or a request for a favor.

The plan to use when saying no to an invitation or requested favor depends on your relationship with the reader. For example, suppose that the president of the local Chamber of Commerce asks you to speak at a luncheon five weeks away. You are, however, scheduled for a business trip at that time. If you do not know the president well, you would probably use the indirect plan.

The Chamber of Commerce has accomplished many worthwhile projects, and I've always admired the local organization. Thank you for asking me to speak at your luncheon meeting next month.

The buffer recaps the request and demonstrates respect.

As you know, I'm a sales representative for Midland Grain Cooperative, and I do quite a bit of traveling. In fact, I'm scheduled to be in Dubuque on the day you asked me to speak.

The reason for declining implies the bad news itself.

Can you suggest an alternate date? Any Thursday during April would be fine for me. The opportunity to speak to your members would be most rewarding.

The close suggests an alternate plan.

If you were writing a similar letter to a close friend instead of an acquaintance or stranger, you could use the direct plan:

Dave, I won't be able to speak at the Chamber of Commerce luncheon next month. As you know, I'm on the road about half the time, and the middle of next month puts me in Dubuque.

But I'm not always on the road! Keep me in mind; I'll be in town every Thursday during April. With you at the helm, the Chamber of Commerce is finally making a difference here. I'll be glad to contribute what I can to a good meeting.

This letter gets right to the point but still uses some blow-softening techniques, as Wanda Williams of Southland Corporation suggests: It compliments the person and organization making the request and looks toward future opportunities for cooperation.

REFUSING ADJUSTMENT OF CLAIMS AND COMPLAINTS

Use the indirect plan in most cases of refusing to make an adjustment.

In almost every instance, a customer who requests an adjustment is emotionally involved; therefore, the indirect plan is generally used for a reply. Your job as a writer is to avoid accepting responsibility for the unfortunate situation and yet avoid blaming or accusing the customer. To steer clear of these pitfalls, the tone of your letter is extremely important. Keep in mind that a tactful and courteous letter can build goodwill while denying the claim.

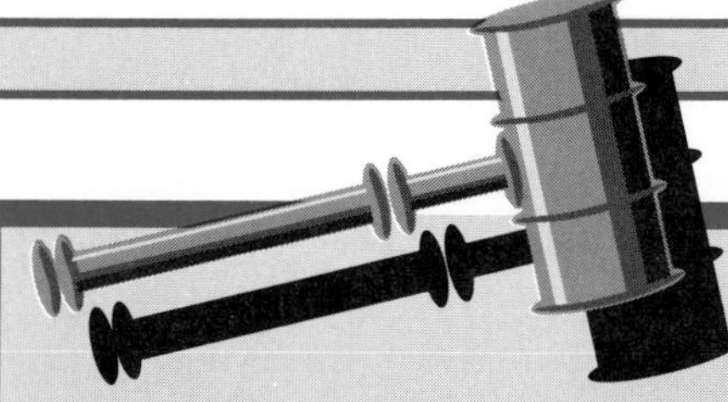

LEGAL ALERT

How to Avoid Libelous Letters

You may be tempted to respond to something particularly outrageous by calling the person responsible a crook, a swindler, or an incompetent. Resist! If you don't, you could be sued for defamation.

In technical terms, *defamation* is a false statement that tends to damage someone's character or reputation. (Written defamation is called *libel*; spoken defamation is called *slander*.) By this definition, someone suing for defamation would have to prove that (1) the statement is false, (2) the language is injurious to the person's reputation, and (3) the statement has been "published."

The issue of falsehood versus truth is the basis for defending against charges of defamation. If you can prove that your accusations are true, then you have not defamed the person. And the courts will give you the benefit of the doubt, because our society believes ordinary business communication should not be hampered by fear of lawsuits. Thus many messages within a company and with outsiders as well may carry uncomplimentary statements if the information is believed to be true and if it is communicated in good faith. Beware the irate letter intended to let off steam, however: If the message has no necessary business purpose and is expressed in abusive language that hints of malice, you will lose the case.

In attempting to define defamatory language, the courts have ruled a number of terms out of bounds. Among them are any words that could injure a person's trade, business, or profession (such as *quack*, *shyster*, *cheat*); any that impute a crime for which a person has not been convicted (*blackmailer*, *thief*, *racketeer*); and any that untruthfully attribute a loathsome disease (leprosy, syphilis). Among the many other terms that have been judged defamatory in the absence of fact are *bankrupt*, *liar*, *drug addict*, *Communist*, and *deadbeat*.

Legally, you could call someone names like these face-to-face in private and not be guilty of defamation. If no third party has witnessed the communication, you could not possibly have damaged the person's reputation. However, once you put something in writing, you are in potential trouble, because someone else could see the document. Marking a letter "Personal" or "Confidential" and sealing it in an opaque envelope might help. However, a recipient who can show, for example, that the letter was opened by a secretary and seen by others has proof of publication. And you could be proved guilty of defamation.

To avoid these legal traps,

- Avoid using any kind of abusive language or terms that could be considered defamatory.
- If you wish to express your own personal opinions about a sensitive matter, write a letter on your own stationery, not on company letterhead, and do not include your job title or position. Take responsibility for your own actions without involving your company.
- In all your messages, provide accurate information and stick to the facts.
- Never let anger or malice motivate your messages.
- Consult your company's legal department or an attorney whenever you think a message might have legal consequences.
- Always communicate honestly, and make sure what you are saying is what you believe to be true.

Keep these guidelines in mind whenever you're faced with the need to provide negative information about a person.

1. Many critics of the legal system have pointed out that there is a difference between what is legal and what is ethical. Do you think that it is ever ethical to say abusive things about another person, even if you can do so legally?

2. Research libel cases in your college library to find a good example of a business message that was judged libelous. How might the writer have avoided litigation?

■ CHECKLIST FOR REFUSALS TO MAKE ADJUSTMENTS

A. Buffer

- ☐ 1. Use a topic of mutual agreement or a neutral topic to start, but keep to the subject of the letter.
- ☐ 2. Indicate your full understanding of the nature of the complaint.
- ☐ 3. Avoid all areas of disagreement.
- ☐ 4. Avoid any hint of your final decision.
- ☐ 5. Keep the buffer brief and to the point.
- ☐ 6. Maintain a confident, positive, supportive tone.

B. Reasons

- ☐ 1. Provide an accurate, factual account of the transaction.
- ☐ 2. Offer enough detail to show the logic of your position.
- ☐ 3. Emphasize ways that the product should have been handled or the contract followed, rather than the reader's negligence.
- ☐ 4. Word the explanation so the reader can anticipate the refusal.
- ☐ 5. Avoid relying on unexplained company policy.
- ☐ 6. Avoid accusing or preaching ("You should have").
- ☐ 7. Do not blame or scold the reader.
- ☐ 8. Do not make the reader appear or feel stupid.
- ☐ 9. Inject a brief resale note after the explanation, if desirable.

C. The Bad News

- ☐ 1. Make the refusal clear by tactful wording, or possibly imply it.
- ☐ 2. Avoid any hint that your decision is less than final.
- ☐ 3. Avoid words like *reject* and *claim.*
- ☐ 4. Make a counterproposal for a compromise settlement or partial adjustment (if desirable), in a willing not begrudging tone, in a spirit of honest cooperation, and without making it sound like a penalty.
- ☐ 5. Include a resale note for the company or product.
- ☐ 6. Emphasize a desire for a good relationship in the future.
- ☐ 7. Extend an offer to replace the product or provide a replacement part at the regular price.

D. Positive, Friendly, Helpful Close

- ☐ 1. Eliminate any reference to your refusal.
- ☐ 2. Avoid any apology.
- ☐ 3. Eliminate words suggesting uncertainty (*hope, trust*).
- ☐ 4. Refer to enclosed sales material.
- ☐ 5. Make any suggested action easy to comply with.

Let's say that you work for a sportswear company. A customer who bought one of your swimsuits a month and a half ago has returned it to you because a seam has split. In a pleasant letter, she asks for a refund of the purchase price. Your negative response might read like this:

I agree. You have every right to expect high quality and a comfortable, lasting fit in the Fun 'n' Sun swimsuit you selected.	The buffer covers a point that reader and writer agree on.
Because sunshine and chlorine rapidly destroy the fabric of any swimsuit, few manufacturers are willing to take responsibility for wear-related problems. But we feel that the customer comes first. That's why a tag is attached to every Fun 'n' Sun swimsuit explaining our guarantee. We're always happy to refund every penny if the customer returns a suit within 30 days of purchase for reasons other than a change in taste or fit.	The reason puts the company's policy in a favorable light. The bad news, stated indirectly, tactfully puts some of the responsibility on the customer's shoulders.

But we do want to help. So you can continue enjoying your swimsuit, we've reinforced the inside seams with flexible cloth tape. The seam should now hold through many, many wearings. Inspect it carefully.

A positive alternate action should help soothe the customer.

And also inspect the new Hampton House catalog I'm enclosing. You'll find a full line of quality fashions, including a delightful variety of festive swim coverups. You'll also find an entry form for our big $2,000 Designer Wardrobe Giveaway. Fill it in and rush it back today, and you could be the lucky winner!

The close blends sales promotion with acknowledgment of the customer's interests.

When refusing to make an adjustment
- Demonstrate understanding of the complaint
- Explain your refusal
- Suggest alternative action

When refusing to adjust a claim, avoid language that might have a negative impact on the reader. Instead, demonstrate that you understand and have considered the complaint. Then, even if the claim is unreasonable, you must rationally explain why you are refusing the request. (But don't apologize or rely on company policy.) The letter should end on a respectful and action-oriented note.

REFUSING TO EXTEND CREDIT

Use the indirect plan when turning down a credit applicant.

Credit is refused for a variety of reasons, all involving sensitive personal or legal considerations.

In denying credit to the applicant with a proven record of delinquent payments and to the applicant with an unstable background, you would probably be justified in offering little hope for future credit approval. But you could be more encouraging to other types of applicants. You most certainly would like their current cash business, and you may want their future credit business. The following letter refuses credit for the present but points to the possibility of credit being extended in the future:

Your request for a charge account at Talton's Clothiers tells us something important: You enjoy the rewards of owning a smart, up-to-the-minute wardrobe.

The buffer expresses understanding and offers some subtle resale on the company.

Year after year, value-minded customers like you return to Talton's because of our low prices. How do we do it? We buy our entire inventory of fine men's clothing on a cash basis so we can get manufacturers' discounts and avoid interest charges. You benefit, because we can offer you superb quality at some of the lowest prices in the clothing industry.

The reasons for the refusal are explained in some detail.

So we can continue to deal with suppliers on a cash basis and to offer you low prices, customer credit applications are approved only when the applicant makes at least $20,000 yearly and has lived in the area for one year or more. As soon as you meet these criteria, we will be glad to reconsider your application.

The actual refusal is stated in positive terms, and the criteria are stated explicitly.

CHECKLIST FOR CREDIT REFUSALS

A. Buffer

- ☐ 1. Introduce a topic that is relevant and that both you and the reader can agree with.
- ☐ 2. Eliminate apologies and negative-sounding words.
- ☐ 3. Phrase the buffer to avoid misleading the reader.
- ☐ 4. Limit the length of the buffer.
- ☐ 5. Express appreciation for the credit request.
- ☐ 6. Introduce resale information.

B. Reasons

- ☐ 1. Check the lead-in from the buffer for smoothness.
- ☐ 2. Make a transition from the favorable to the unfavorable message.
- ☐ 3. Make a transition from the general to the specific.
- ☐ 4. Avoid a condescending lecture about how credit is earned.
- ☐ 5. Avoid relying on unexplained company policy.
- ☐ 6. Stress the benefits of not being overextended.
- ☐ 7. Encourage a later credit application, if future approval is realistic.
- ☐ 8. Phrase reasons in terms of experience with others.
- ☐ 9. Present reasons for the refusal carefully.
  - ☐ a. Clearly state the reasons if the reader will accept them.
  - ☐ b. Explain your general credit criteria.
  - ☐ c. Refer to a credit reporting agency you have used.
  - ☐ d. Use "insufficient information" as a reason only if this is the case.
  - ☐ e. To avoid the risk of legal action, omit reasons entirely for extraordinarily sensitive or combative readers or when evidence is unusually negative or involves behavioral flaws.
- ☐ 10. Remind the reader of the benefits of cash purchases.

C. The Bad News

- ☐ 1. Make the refusal clear to the reader.
- ☐ 2. Offer only honest encouragement about considering the credit application at a later date.
- ☐ 3. Avoid negative words, such as "must decline" or "not able."
- ☐ 4. Suggest positive alternatives, such as cash and layaway purchases.
- ☐ 5. Handle refusals of business credit somewhat differently.
  - ☐ a. Recommend cash purchases for small, frequent orders.
  - ☐ b. Describe cash discounts (include figures).
  - ☐ c. Suggest a reduction of inventory so the business can strengthen its credit rating.
  - ☐ d. Offer promotional and marketing aid.
  - ☐ e. Suggest a later review of the credit application, if future approval is realistic.

D. Positive, Friendly, Helpful Close

- ☐ 1. Avoid business clichés, apologies, and words of regret.
- ☐ 2. Suggest actions the reader might take.
- ☐ 3. Encourage the reader to look toward the future, when the application may be approved.
- ☐ 4. Include sales promotion material only if the customer would not be offended.

In the meantime, Mr. O'Neill, I want to show you how much we value your business. Enclosed is a certificate that entitles you to a 10 percent discount on any purchase from our Stagg Shoppe. Also, be sure to take advantage of our big storewide sale on August 25 and 26. You'll find some tremendous bargains!

The letter closes gracefully with some sales promotion.

Notice how the writer of this letter has taken pains to make the reader feel welcome and realize that his business is appreciated.

Denials of business credit, as opposed to denials of individual credit, are less personally sensitive but more financially significant. Businesses

SHARPEN YOUR SKILLS

How to Criticize yet Maintain Goodwill

People can't improve if they aren't evaluated, but criticism from others is often hard to take. The way you tell someone "You did it wrong" can destroy goodwill and cooperation, or it can build the relationship and improve the person's performance. Here's how to criticize people constructively:

- *Get all the facts first.* Don't accept hearsay or rumors. Be specific. Find out who did or said what, when, where, why, and how.
- *Don't act in haste.* And never act while you're angry, no matter how upset you or the other person may be. Take time to cool off and think things out before you start to write or speak. Remember that you are in control. Then explain your criticism calmly, rationally, and objectively.
- *Phrase your remarks impersonally.* Criticize the mistake, not the person. Focus your remarks on the action only. Analyze it thoughtfully. You'll help the person retain self-esteem and learn from the mistake.
- *Never criticize in an offhand manner.* Treat the situation seriously. Take the time to state what the problem is in detail. Explain what was wrong and why.
- *Don't ridicule, talk down, or use sarcasm.* An abusive tone will prevent the person from accepting what you have to say. Give her or him your respect and the benefit of the doubt, and you will make the criticism more acceptable.
- *Make the offense clear.* Don't talk in generalities. Be specific. Let the person know exactly what she or he did wrong.
- *Share responsibility.* Take the sting out of your criticism by sharing some of the blame for the person's mistake. One way to do this is by say-

In a letter denying credit to a business

- Be more factual and less personal than in a letter to an individual
- Suggest ways to continue doing business

have failed because major suppliers have suspended credit at inconvenient times. When refusing to grant business credit, explain your reasons as factually and impersonally as possible (perhaps the firm's latest financial statements don't meet your criteria or its credit rating has fallen below an acceptable minimum) and the steps that must be taken to restore credit. Emphasize the benefits of continued dealings on a cash basis until the firm's credit worthiness has been established or restored. You might also offer discounts for cash purchases or assistance in cooperative merchandising to reduce the firm's inventory and increase cash flow. Third-party loans are another possibility you might suggest.

Be aware that credit is a legally sensitive subject.

With any candidate, companies that deny credit must exercise good judgment in order to avoid legal action. A faulty decision may unfairly damage a person's reputation, which may in turn provoke a lawsuit and other bad publicity for the company. Handling credit denials over the phone instead of in writing is no guarantee of avoiding trouble; companies that orally refuse credit should still proceed with caution.

CONVEYING UNFAVORABLE NEWS ABOUT PEOPLE

Use the indirect plan when giving someone bad news about his or her own job, the direct plan when giving bad news about someone else's job.

From time to time, most managers must convey bad news about people. Letters to prospective employers may be written in direct order. But the indirect plan is used for letters to job applicants and employees, because the reader will most certainly be emotionally involved.

ing *we,* as in "What do you think we did wrong?"

- *Preface the criticism with a kind word or compliment.* It will make the other person more receptive and put her or him at ease. Start with a few words of praise or admiration. Say how much you value the person. Put good news first, then bad news.
- *Supply the answer.* When telling a person what she or he did wrong, also explain how to do it right. The emphasis shouldn't be on the mistake but on how to correct it and avoid repeating it.
- *Ask for cooperation; don't demand it.* Asking makes the person feel like a member of your team and provides an incentive to improve.
- *Limit yourself to one criticism for each offense.* Don't drag up past mistakes or rehash any that are over and done with. Focus on the present one.
- *End on a friendly note.* Until an issue has been resolved on a positive note, it hasn't been resolved. Don't leave things up in the air, to be discussed again later. Settle them now. A friendly close works wonders. Give the other person a pat on the back. Let the last memory of the matter be a good one. The person is much more likely to accept your criticism and to feel friendly toward you.
- *Forgive and forget.* Once the criticism has been made, let the person start with a clean slate. Don't look for more mistakes. Give the person a real chance to improve.
- *Take steps to prevent a recurrence.* After telling the person what to do to improve, follow up to make sure she or he is acting on your suggestions and doing things right.

If you follow these guidelines, constructive criticism can benefit you, your company, and—most important—the person you are criticizing.

1. Think back over the lessons you have learned in life. In what ways have you benefited when someone has told you the truth about something you were doing wrong?

2. With a partner, role-play a situation in which one of you is the boss and the other an employee. The boss is angry because the employee is repeatedly late for work, takes long lunches, and always leaves five to ten minutes early. However, the employee's work is always excellent. After the role-play, analyze what the boss did right and what areas could use improvement.

REFUSING TO WRITE RECOMMENDATION LETTERS

In letters informing prospective employers that you will not provide a recommendation, be direct, brief, and factual (to avoid legal pitfalls).

With all the legal hazards involved in writing recommendation letters, it is no wonder that some former employers are refusing to write them—especially for people whose job performance has been, on balance, unsatisfactory. Prospective employers do not usually have a personal stake in the response, so letters refusing to provide a recommendation may be brief and direct:

Anthony Wright did work at German Auto Repair as a mechanic from June 1988 through April 1989. In light of current legalities, however, we cannot comment on the job performance of people who no longer work here; I'm sure you understand the dilemma. Good luck in your hiring process.

In letters telling job applicants that you will not write a recommendation, use the utmost tact.

Letters to the applicants themselves are another matter. Any refusal to cooperate may seem a personal slight and a threat to the applicant's future. The only way to avoid ill feelings is to handle the applicant gently:

You have had an interesting year since you left Imperial Bottling. Thank you for bringing me up-to-date.

Your decision to pursue a new line of work seems well thought out, and the classes you have taken should help you get a job. Your instructors at the community college would have more relevant knowledge of your ability to perform the type of job you're applying for, so I suggest that you ask them for recommendations.

Good luck to you in your future endeavors.

By using positive comments about the reader's recent activities, an implied refusal, a suggested alternative, and a polite close, this letter deftly and tactfully avoids hurting the reader's feelings.

REJECTING JOB APPLICANTS

In a letter turning down a job applicant, treat the reader with respect; by applying for a job, he or she has complimented your company.

It's also hard to tell job applicants tactfully that you aren't going to offer them employment. A rejection letter need not be long, however. After all, the applicant wants to know only one thing: Did I land the job? This brief message conveys the information clearly and with some consideration for the applicant's feelings:

Congratulations on your fine undergraduate accounting education. Your record of academic achievement is impressive.

Because 35 well-qualified people applied for the position of staff accountant, the selection process was very difficult.

After much analysis, we settled on a person who has worked three years for a public accounting firm in Chicago.

Thank you for letting us review your resume. A person with your qualifications should have no trouble finding just the right position.

The letter implies that the applicant might have been selected if he or she had matched the qualifications of the successful candidate—in other words, the rejection was "nothing personal."

GIVING NEGATIVE PERFORMANCE REVIEWS

In performance reviews, say what's right as well as what's wrong and explain how the employee can improve performance.

A performance review is a manager's formal or informal evaluation of an employee. Almost always, even if the employee's performance has been disappointing, a performance review mentions some good points. But then the manager must clearly and tactfully state how the employee is failing to meet the responsibilities of the job. And if the performance review is to have a positive effect, it must also suggest ways that the employee can improve. For example, instead of telling an employee only that he damaged some expensive machinery, suggest that he take a refresher course in the correct operation of that machinery. The goal is to leave the impression that you want the employee to succeed.

TERMINATING EMPLOYEES

Carefully word a termination letter to avoid creating undue ill will and grounds for legal action.

Recognizing the ill will that might result if she treated laid-off employees callously or carelessly, Wanda Williams of Southland Corporation made every effort to protect their egos. In writing a termination letter, you too have three goals: (1) to present the reasons for this difficult action, (2) to avoid statements that might involve the company in legal action, (3) and to leave the relationship between the terminated employee and the firm as favorable as possible.

■ CHECKLIST FOR UNFAVORABLE NEWS ABOUT PEOPLE

A. Buffer

- ☐ 1. Identify the applicant or employee clearly when writing to a third party.
- ☐ 2. Express the reasons for writing—clearly, completely, and objectively.
- ☐ 3. Avoid insincere expressions of regret.
- ☐ 4. Avoid impersonal business clichés.

B. Reasons

- ☐ 1. Include only factual information.
- ☐ 2. Avoid negative personal judgments.
- ☐ 3. Word negative job-related messages carefully to avoid legal difficulties.
  - ☐ a. Avoid terms with legal definitions *(slanderous, criminal)*.
  - ☐ b. Avoid negative terms with imprecise definitions *(lazy, sloppy)*.
  - ☐ c. Embed negative comments in favorable or semifavorable passages, if possible.
  - ☐ d. Avoid generalities, and explain the limits of your observations about the applicant's or employee's shortcomings.
  - ☐ e. Eliminate secondhand information.
  - ☐ f. Stress the confidentiality of your letter.
- ☐ 4. For letters to job seekers refusing to supply a recommendation, suggest another avenue for getting a recommendation.
- ☐ 5. For rejection letters, emphasize the positive qualities of the person hired rather than the shortcomings of the rejected applicant.
- ☐ 6. For performance reviews, describe the employee's limitations and suggest methods for improving performance.

C. The Bad News

- ☐ 1. Understate negative decisions.
- ☐ 2. Imply negative decisions whenever possible.

D. Positive, Friendly, Helpful Close

- ☐ 1. For refusals to supply recommendations and for rejection letters, extend good wishes.
- ☐ 2. For performance reviews, express a willingness to help further.
- ☐ 3. For termination letters, make suggestions for finding another job, if appropriate.

For both legal and personal reasons, you must present specific reasons for asking the employee to leave. Make sure that all your reasons are accurate and verifiable. Avoid words that are open to interpretation, such as *untidy* and *difficult.* Make sure the employee leaves with feelings that are as positive as the circumstances allow.

HANDLING BAD NEWS ABOUT COMPANY OPERATIONS OR PERFORMANCE

At least three types of situations require bad-news letters about company operations or performance: (1) a change in company policy that has a negative effect on the reader, (2) performance problems in the company, and (3) controversial or unpopular company operations. In very trying situations, apologies may be in order. If so, good writers usually make the apology brief and bury it somewhere in the middle of the letter; they try to leave readers with a favorable impression by closing on a positive note.

When conveying bad news about the company, focus on the reasons and on possible benefits.

When a change in company policy will have a negative effect on the reader, the key is to state clearly and carefully the reasons for the change. The explanation section of the letter must convince readers that the change was necessary and, if possible, that this change will benefit them.

If your company is having serious performance problems, your customers and shareholders should ideally learn of the difficulty from you, not from newspaper accounts or from rumors. Even if the news leaks out, you should counter as soon as possible with your own explanation. Much business is based on mutual trust; if your customers and shareholders can't trust you to inform them of your problems, they may choose to work with someone they can trust. Common business sense, however, should tell you to minimize the bad news by presenting it in as favorable a light as possible.

Companies at times also find themselves caught in a political cross fire. In such cases the writer's general strategy should be to present the reasons why the company is manufacturing the controversial item or providing the unpopular service. The goal is to show that reason and need are behind the controversial decision, not villainy, carelessness, or greed.

SUMMARY

The purpose of a bad-news message is to convey unfavorable information without alienating the audience. To accomplish both ends, you must first consider the audience's point of view; if possible, explain how the bad news can work to the audience's advantage. You can convey tact and concern by assuming that the audience is basically honest and wants to be fair.

Bad-news messages can be based on either the indirect or direct plan, depending on the circumstances. The indirect plan begins with a buffer and moves to the reasons; it then states the bad news and closes on a courteous note that may suggest other options for the audience. The direct plan, which is used mainly for sending bad news that will have little emotional impact on the audience, begins with a clear statement of the bad news, moves to the reasons, and then provides a courteous close.

COMMUNICATION CHALLENGES AT SOUTHLAND

Since the layoffs at Southland's Dallas headquarters, everyone has been busier than ever trying to fill in the gaps. The corporate personnel department is no exception. For weeks, Wanda Williams has been putting in a lot of 10- and 11-hour days. But now that the immediate crisis is over, she's going to cut back.

Individual Challenge: As head of personnel for a large and visible company, Wanda gets her share of invitations to speak. Just today, this invitation arrived from Donna DeMarco (1277 Fox Hill Lane, Dallas, TX 75232), the president of Dallas Businesswomen's Association:

Dear Ms. Williams:

Your fine reputation as a businesswoman and speaker has spread throughout Dallas. In fact, Sammie Linton, our program chair, tells me that she heard you deliver a rousing speech about employee relations last fall at a Dallas Chamber of Commerce meeting.

Because of Ms. Linton's recommendation and the many other fine things I've heard about you, we'd be honored if you would address our group sometime in the next few months. Dallas Businesswomen's Association typically draws about 100 entrepreneurs and professionals to its monthly meetings. We mix and mingle from 5:30 p.m. to 6:30 p.m., then settle in for a 20- or 30-minute address by someone like you who can inspire women to attain their full potential in the business world.

Will you please let me know by the end of next week when you would be available to speak to us, Ms. Williams. We're all eager to learn the secrets of your success.

Wanda hands you this letter, mentioning that she's heard the group attracts many of the city's most powerful and successful women. Still, to preserve her health and sanity, Wanda must decline the invitation, at least for the next few months. She asks you to write to Ms. DeMarco to explain her decision.

Team Challenge: Wanda calls in several of her senior staff members to discuss another problem that has arisen since the layoffs. As former employees have gone out to seek new jobs, the volume of other employers' requests for recommendation letters has doubled. Wanda is inclined to institute a new policy of not supplying recommendation letters, in part because of the work entailed and in part because of the legal complications. She asks you to discuss the pros and cons and then to draft (1) a brief form letter to send to other employers who request recommendations and (2) a memo to be distributed to all employees at corporate headquarters explaining the new policy. As usual, Wanda wants you to use great tact, particularly in the memo to employees.

QUESTIONS FOR DISCUSSION

1. What is the single chief purpose behind all bad-news messages?
2. How do you decide whether to use the direct or the indirect approach in bad-news messages?
3. What are the qualities of a good buffer?
4. If a relevant company policy exists, why shouldn't a writer simply justify the bad news through reference to the policy?
5. If the purpose of your letter is to convey bad news, should you possibly suggest alternatives to the reader? Why or why not?
6. If you were writing a bad-news letter to someone you no longer wish to do business with, would you still close on a helpful, friendly, positive note? Explain.
7. What is the overriding goal in conveying bad news about an order?
8. How should you justify refusing credit to an applicant who is a credit risk?
9. What are the legal risks involved in writing a bad-news message about employment, and how can you avoid those risks?
10. When a company suffers a serious misfortune, should the impact be softened by letting out the bad news a little at a time? Why or why not?

DOCUMENTS FOR ANALYSIS

Read the following documents, and then (1) analyze the strengths and/or weaknesses of each numbered sentence and (2) revise each document so it follows this chapter's guidelines.

DOCUMENT 8.A

(1) We have included with this letter a list of videotapes, films, slides, and other material that you may wish to order on the subjects of business mathematics and economics. (2) Also included is a price list for these materials plus some other books you may wish to order.

(3) Per your request, we are sorry to tell you that we cannot ship to you free examination copies of the books you requested as a result of reading a review in the Business Education Journal. (4) The books, Business Mathematics Made Easy by Chester Sims and Economics Made Easy by Joanna Wesson, are well written in spite of being about a subject most people find difficult. (5) The cost of printing and publishing these supplementary textbooks is getting higher every year, so I'm sure you can understand the reason for our not complying with your request for free examination copies.

(6) We must request prompt payment for these books. (7) The cost is $5.95 each plus $1.00 per book for postage and handling. (8) These books would make good additions to your college's bookstore, even if you don't require them in your classes, because they are helpful supplements to the primary textbooks your students are probably using now. (9) Your students could use the extra help, we're sure. (10) Let us know whether you decide to buy these books or not; because the price is going up, let us know soon.

DOCUMENT 8.B

(1) Yes, in the past we always did provide free setup for parties using our Grand Ballroom. (2) We have found, however, that parties vary greatly in size. (3) Table settings also vary depending on the menu being served.

(4) Therefore, tell everyone in your department that the Banquet Department will no longer provide free setup.

(5) When working with customers to plan their events, please add a $1.00 setup charge for each person in the party. (6) That fee will cover arrangement of tables and chairs, table draping and place setting, bar setup, and setup of microphone and podium, if needed. (7) This policy takes effect immediately for any events for which contracts have not already been signed. (8) If any customers have a problem with the new policy, please have them call me.

DOCUMENT 8.C

(1) We'd like to express our thanks for your letter of about six weeks ago. (2) However, we regret to inform you that your claim for an adjustment on the Model XL dictation unit has been denied. (3) Careful inspection by our engineering staff confirmed our original supposition that the unit has been damaged by improper treatment, either by user or by carrier.

(4) Are you aware of the possibility that the Model XL dictation unit could have been dropped or abused by your employees? (5) If this has not happened, you may file a claim against the carrier. (6) It is more than likely that the unit was damaged in transit, because according to you the unit has never worked properly and because we are clearly not at fault.

(7) Our charges for repairing the unit will be $50 to cover labor costs; the parts will be replaced at no charge under the terms of our 90-day warranty. (8) Please remit payment to us promptly.

(9) We hope to see your representative at our sale, which will be held soon; pertinent facts appear in the promotional literature that is enclosed.

DOCUMENT 8.D

(1) I regret to inform you that we must reject your application for admission into our law school program. (2) This refusal is based on the fact that all applications must be received before July 1. (3) This policy is clearly stated in our catalog. (4) We even sent a letter to all law school candidates reminding them of this important deadline. (5) We have made every effort to prevent late applications; therefore, we cannot make any exceptions. (6) I trust you will understand the law school's position. (7) We deeply regret any inconvenience associated with our reply. (8) Some law schools consider applications after our deadline. (9) You should notify them of your interest.

CASES

CONVEYING BAD NEWS ABOUT ORDERS

1. Between a tomato and a carrot: Letter requesting clarification of an order When Mrs. Bernard Peyton selected a fabric for reupholstering her sofa, her order was taken by your newest salesperson, Alec Gallup. Alec Gallup is also the most recent of your salespeople to leave. Now you have Mrs. Peyton's couch and only the memory of Gallup's saying that she wanted it "real red, sort of halfway between a tomato and a carrot." Whatever Gallup put on paper left with him or has simply disappeared.

You do have several fabrics in stock that might be what Mrs. Peyton decided on, but you certainly don't want to begin a $900 job on such a shaky understanding. You decide against phoning her; letting her examine swatches of the material in her own home seems a better way to proceed.

Your task: Write to Mrs. Peyton on store letterhead, enclose samples of four fabrics, and ask which one she favors. Mrs. Peyton lives at 44 Grand Avenue, Vancouver, B.C. V6C 2X4. You assume that Alec Gallup quoted the standard price for a job of this size ($865 plus tax and a $35 delivery charge), but you should confirm this understanding.

2. Slow delivery ahead: Letter from Ford Motor Co. announcing delays in shipments Your fellow Ford employees in Dearborn, Michigan, are all excited about the phenomenal success of the Taurus and Sable models. People are snapping them up as fast as you can turn them out, and Ford dealers are clamoring for more.

However, like many new models, the Taurus and Sable have a few bugs. Since their introduction, they have been recalled several times, and now they are being recalled once again. Apparently, 600 sedans and station wagons have a potential problem with the steering equipment, and 630 sedans must be checked for problems involving rear suspension components. These are serious problems that affect the safety of the cars.

Although the recalls are obviously bad for the cars' image, they are not unusual. Many new models are recalled a dozen times or more. And the number of cars involved in this case is small; some recalls involve several hundred thousand cars.

Nevertheless, a recall of any type is inconvenient and expensive. In this case, the inconvenience is compounded by the fact that the recall will delay shipments of new cars to dealers, who are already anxiously awaiting delivery of their orders. Most of the cars being recalled were en route to showrooms when the problem was discovered. These cars will have to be returned and repaired, a process that will take at least a month. Furthermore, no additional Taurus and Sable cars will be shipped until all the problems are ironed out. Ford dealers will have to tell their customers, "I'm sorry, but we can't get that car to you for a couple of months."

Your task: Your boss, Howard Simpson, is in charge of relationships with dealers. He has asked you to draft a letter explaining the recall and alerting dealers to the delay in their orders. He has authorized you to say that Ford expects to begin shipping the cars again within two months.[1]

3. The card-carrying caterer: Letter declining a request to provide services Given the slow response to your catering advertisements, you felt safe adding this slogan to your business cards: "Maximum service on minimum notice."

But with two successive rings of your telephone, you have been offered two assignments on the same day. Of course, you agreed to take the first. The second request was from Janet Daley (611 Willow Avenue of your city and ZIP code) to cater a small wedding reception at her home a week from Sunday. Fortunately, you have an arrangement with Mike Listerman (1038 13th Street, of your city and ZIP code) to exchange overload assignments, but you want to keep in touch with Ms. Daley in case she has future business for you.

You told Ms. Daley over the phone that you would try to line up a replacement caterer, and Mike Listerman has agreed to handle the wedding. But given the confusion possible in such three-sided conversations, you decide to put the arrangements in writing.

Your task: Write to Janet Daley, telling her you will not be able to cater the reception. Briefly introduce Mike Listerman to her as a qualified replacement. Make it clear that Mr. Listerman, who will receive a copy of your letter, has already reserved the date and will phone Ms. Daley for specific instructions.

4. Package deals only: Letter from Lillian Vernon explaining a nonconforming order As a customer service representative for catalog merchandiser Lillian Vernon of Mount Vernon, New York, you have just received the following letter:

709 Green Hill Court
Mobile, AL 36609
February 12, 1989

Dear Customer Service Representative:

I just love all of the things in your new catalog, especially the pantyhose with valentines on them. Where does Lillian Vernon find such pretty things? Please send five pairs, one for each of my daughters. The hose are listed on page 4 of the catalog, item number 9279, at $4.98 each.

I'd also like to order the set of 12 woven-stripe cotton dish towels, which are listed on page 23 of your catalog. The order number is 6348, and the price is $12.98. But instead of sending me the red, white, and blue combination, would you please send me six white and six red. My kitchen is painted a funny shade of green, and I don't think the blue would be very attractive color-wise.

My check for $37.88 is enclosed. I'm so sorry, but I lost my order form. I think I filled it out, put it in an envelope, and then lost the envelope before I could write the check and stick it in the mail. Anyway, if you get two orders from me, disregard one, will you please?

Sincerely,

Mrs. Lucy Gloring

This order is a bit of a problem. For one thing, the dish towels come as a set, with four of each color; the sets cannot be broken down as Mrs. Gloring would like them to be. There are other towels in the catalog, however, some of which have a green stripe in them (on page 77).

Another problem is the money. If you could ship the towels and pantyhose together, the shipping charge would be $5.85. But the shipping charge for the pantyhose alone is $4.75. In any case, Mrs. Gloring's check is written for the wrong amount. She'll need a refund, because without knowing what she wants to do about the towels, you can only ship the pantyhose.

Your task: Write to Mrs. Gloring and tell her what you've discovered and what you plan to do. Inform her that the package will be delivered within three days via a delivery service. Mention the refund check that you're enclosing. You might also suggest that she call you at 1-800-633-6400 to clarify her order.[2]

5. Toys Aplenty: Letter attempting to straighten out a problem order This letter arrived in today's mail from Bill Breen, Manager, Toys Aplenty, 454 Cass Road, Brockton, MA 02401:

Please send as soon as possible the following:

1 doz	Puffees (Styrofoam filled), blue	#12231 A
1 doz	Clarence the Clown, 2-foot size	#12775
6	Smiley Face bedside lamps	
	2 lemon	#12998 C
	2 avocado	#12998 D
	2 plum	#12998 F
1 doz	Freddy Frogs, green	#12466 B
3 doz	I-See-Me mirrored dinner plates	#12423
6 doz	Baby Walkers (with attached Talkers)	#12969
4 gross	Polka Dot diaper sets	#12128
3 doz	Popeye bubble pipes	#12903

According to my calculations, this order qualifies for a 5 percent volume discount.

For several years Toys Aplenty has had an open account with your company, Happy Day Toys, and it generally pays promptly. Its orders are subject to your usual terms: 5 percent discount on orders over $500, with the smaller orders at 2/10, net 30 (which means a 2 percent discount for paying within 10 days and the total due within 30 days in any case). The customer is charged for shipping.

You have Smiley Face bedside lamps in lemon and plum, but no avocado lamps will be available for ten days. The order number given for the Freddy Frogs is for the yellow model, not green as specified in the order. You no longer carry Popeye bubble pipes. You do not stock the Baby Walkers; they are sent to customers directly from the Peoria, Illinois, factory. The other items present no problems. But if you pull the Popeye bubble pipes from this order, the reduced total no longer qualifies for the 5 percent quantity discount. When you try to reach Mr. Breen by phone to explain matters, you are told that he will be out of town for three days.

Your task: Make some professional decisions, and write to Mr. Breen, explaining as much as necessary and indicating the state of his order. Be prepared to explain why you chose to do what you did.

COMMUNICATING NEGATIVE ANSWERS AND INFORMATION

6. A friendly accounting: Letter breaking bad news gently The officers of Friends of Photography, a local photography club, have asked you, a student of accounting, to audit their books prior to distribution of the yearly financial report to members. After some arithmetical corrections, you find the following account balances:

ASSETS	
Cash in Bank Account	$ 645.17
Petty Cash	46.71
Library Collection	4,100.00
Furniture	2,750.00
Goodwill	55.00
TOTAL ASSETS	$7,596.88
LIABILITIES	
Accounts Payable (rent)	$1,200.00
Accounts Payable (janitorial)	480.00
Accounts Payable (furniture)	77.95
TOTAL LIABILITIES	$1,757.95
NET WORTH	$5,838.93

You are informed that the books in the library are carried at their cost (less any sales taxes paid), as is the furniture. You ask about the curious Goodwill item of $55 and are told that this account was opened to cover a similar amount found missing from the petty cash account several years ago, "to balance the books." The accounting practices of this club obviously do not conform with standard accounting practices. You decide that it hardly makes sense to carry the books and furniture as assets, because they are worth much less than their purchase price and will never be sold. And the Goodwill account should be written off.

Your task: Write a letter to Craig Williams, president of Friends of Photography, 224 Red Maple Road, Boston, MA 02127. The tone should be gentle; the message should convey the seriousness of the club's financial position.

7. It's a switch! Memo announcing that Wendy's is switching beverage suppliers For many years, Wendy's International has served Pepsi in its restaurants. In fact, Wendy's and PepsiCo signed a contract cementing their relationship through 1990.

Through a series of acquisitions, PepsiCo has gradually become a competitor to Wendy's as well as a supplier. As the owner of Pizza Hut, Taco Bell, and Kentucky Fried Chicken, PepsiCo is now a major force in the fast-food industry. As a result, Wendy's now finds itself in the uncomfortable position of buying its soda from one of its major competitors. Because PepsiCo uses its soft-drink profits to invest in its restaurant businesses, Wendy's is essentially helping to finance its competition. Furthermore, as a supplier PepsiCo has access to confidential information about Wendy's sales, information that can be used to Wendy's disadvantage by PepsiCo's restaurant subsidiaries.

In view of this conflict of interest, top management has decided to terminate Wendy's contract with PepsiCo. They want the company-owned restaurants to serve Coca-Cola beverages instead. The switch will not immediately affect Wendy's franchisees, but they will be urged to follow the example set by the company-owned outlets.

Some of the restaurant managers probably won't be too happy about this change, because they are very loyal to their suppliers, the changeover is bound to be inconvenient, and some customers may complain. Furthermore, some Wendy's managers will be annoyed that franchisees can still sell Pepsi even though company-owned outlets can't.

Your task: Your boss, Helene Sorenson, is in charge of relationships with Wendy's company-owned restaurants. She has asked you to draft a memo announcing that Pepsi is out and Coke is in. She wants you to emphasize that Wendy's headquarters staff in Dublin, Ohio, will try to make the transition as smooth as possible. There shouldn't be any interruption in soft drink supplies.[3]

8. Running a restaurant: Memo refusing an employee's request Amber Waves is a restaurant you opened six months ago in a suburb of St. Louis. You made this business decision after a rewarding but frenzied stint as chef at a popular restaurant in New York City. Although midwestern palates tend to be conservative, you think you can make your specialties, which were a hit in the Big Apple, popular back home in St. Louis. Still, business is slow.

Ever optimistic, you've recently added a chef's apprentice to your staff of ten. She is Janie Koontz, inexperienced but enthusiastic. Aware of the growing interest in cuisine of the American Southwest, she asks to take a company-paid trip to Santa Fe, where she would spend a week sampling the menus of various restaurants. Then she would report back to you with new recipes. Including food, accommodations, and air fare, the trip should cost no more than $1,500, Janie claims. Unfortunately, this expense could cripple your delicate budget.

Your task: Write a memo to Janie Koontz refusing her request. Your restaurant can't afford the expense, and you don't have time to do the work of two while she is having fun in Santa Fe. You still have a few of your own specialties to introduce, and the kitchen library of Amber Waves is well stocked with cookbooks and culinary magazines, including a complete collection of James Beard's books on American cooking. Because this is Janie's first professional position at a restaurant, you believe she is poorly equipped to judge other restaurants.

REFUSING ADJUSTMENT OF CLAIMS AND COMPLAINTS

9. The 108-year-old television set: Letter gently refusing an unreasonable request The last time Barbara Cottrell picked up her ten-year-old television set from your shop, Crestwood Television Repair, you warned her that the set was on its last cathodes. You tried to make a joke, which Ms. Cottrell apparently missed: "In human terms, this set is now 108 years old!"

At that time, you put in some components that you'd had to special order, and you tightened the horizontal hold so Ms. Cottrell would no longer have the impression of watching a passing freight train. Now she tells you that, in the process, you damaged the sound control, leaving her unable to turn off the sound and just "watch the pictures." She expects you to fix the set for nothing, given your 90-day guarantee on repairs.

Your 90-day guarantee applies only to the components that you worked with, so you must refuse her claim. But you appreciate Ms. Cottrell as a customer, however difficult she may be at times. If you could sell her one of the fine new television sets you have in stock, you wouldn't have to spend any more time hunting up long-outmoded parts for her ancient television set.

Your task: Write to Ms. Cottrell (Rural Route #3, Forest Hill, LA 71430) and explain in an acceptable way that you are unwilling to fix her television set for free. Explain why any repair of the old set would probably be a mistake, and encourage her to purchase a replacement set.

10. Covering the gap: Refusal to honor a claim You recently installed an Eazy-Air Model 77 air conditioner in the upstairs den of Mr. and Mrs. Norman E. Stocker's home (41 Citrus Place, Sumatra, FL 32691). Installation was unusually difficult, because the oak paneling in the room was old and brittle. With a lot of extra care, however, you managed to do the job with only one small problem: When you drilled a hole to bring in the 220 wiring, the paneling split a little.

Fortunately, the cover plate covered all but a fraction of an inch of the gap.

When you were finished, you made sure that Mrs. Stocker was aware of the problem. She said, "Don't worry about it" and wrote out a check for $100 as the first installment on the $650 bill. But now Mr. Stocker has written to express his disappointment with the work. He gives you two alternatives: Repair the damage, or refund $100. Mr. Stocker indicates that he will make no payments on his $550 one-year sales contract until this matter is settled.

Mr. Stocker's threat to withhold payment does not affect you directly, because you have sold his sales contract (at a discount) to the Goodwin Finance Company, which now has the legal right to collect on it. You also feel justified in refusing to make any adjustment because Mrs. Stocker approved the work. Nevertheless, as a goodwill gesture, you decide that a $25 refund will more than pay for the wood putty necessary to repair the damage. Although you dislike the thought of revisiting the Stocker home to make the repairs yourself, you could stop by if that's what will make Mr. Stocker happy.

Your task: Write to Mr. Stocker, denying his request but offering an alternative. Your business address is Hatcher Air Conditioning, 2379 Coconut Lane, Sumatra, FL 32691.

11. A taxing matter: Refusal to pay for another's mistake During the mid-April rush at tax time last year, Hilda Black phoned to ask if she could "roll over" funds from one retirement account into another without paying taxes on any gain. You answered that such a rollover was not considered a "tax event," as long as the transaction was completed in 60 days. You also informed her that when she eventually draws out the funds to support her retirement income, she will pay taxes on the portion that represents interest earned on the account.

Today Ms. Black phones to say that she is being billed by the Internal Revenue Service for $1,309.72 in penalties and back interest because she failed to declare interest income earned when she cashed in "those bonds that I told you about last April." You explain that bonds are not the same thing as a retirement account. One difference, unfortunately, is that cashing in bonds requires one to pay taxes the following April on any interest income or capital gains.

Your client is not satisfied. She demands "something in writing" to show to her lawyer. Her position is that you misled her; thus you should pay the penalties and interest charges—which, by the way, are getting larger every day. She is willing to pay the actual tax on the transaction.

Your task: Write to Hilda Black (622 N. Bank Lane, Park Forest, IL 60045), explaining why you are unwilling to pay the penalties and interest charges requested by the IRS. Your position should be that you have done nothing to make yourself vulnerable in this transaction.

12. Many happy returns: Letter refusing a claim in a complicated transaction Your policy at Prentiss Publishing is to give full credit to any bookstore that returns unsold copies of your books if you receive the books in salable condition within six months of their original shipment to the bookstore. The bookstore pays postage.

Today's mail includes a large return from the Silver Bridle Bookstore, Horse Creek, WY 82061, containing the following:

21 copies, *Wonder Horses of the Wild West,* list $21.95
6 copies, *Claypot Cooking,* list $15.95
12 copies, *The Letters of Herbert Hoover,* list $25.00
5 copies, *Butterflies of East Anglia,* list $12.95

The list price is the price typically charged to retail customers. You give the bookstores a 40 percent discount off the list price.

The cover note from Silver Bridle Bookstore indicates that 23 copies of the *Wonder Horses* book have been sent, but you count only 21. The carton has sustained some damage, but no books appear to have spilled out. Five of the books are worn to the extent that they cannot be resold. One copy of *Claypot Cooking* is water stained and cannot be resold. One copy of *The Letters of Herbert Hoover* was damaged in shipping, from a combination of careless packing and rough handling in transit. Because your firm did not publish the book about East Anglian butterflies, you owe the Silver Bridle Bookstore nothing for this title.

You decide to return the butterfly books to Silver Bridle (and charge them $2.20 for postage); to return the unsalable copies to them with an explanation; and to tell them that they shipped you only 21 copies, not 23 copies, of *Wonder Horses of the Wild West.*

Your task: Figure out where things stand and write a letter explaining your decision. Your job title is manager of customer service.

REFUSING TO EXTEND CREDIT

13. Jack's first job: Letter denying credit to a recent high school graduate On the strength of his recent high school graduation and subsequent employment as a bookkeeper, Jack Cornelius (23 River Road, Livonia, MO 63551) has applied for credit with your firm, the Livonia Computer Center. Jack has been in and out of your store for most of his young life, and he may be about to make the transition from electronic games to computers. He is also interested in automobiles and scuba diving, and you suspect that he unrealistically envisions his modest wages as being sufficient to support these varied interests. His credit record lists no open accounts, but yours is probably not the only firm that he is now approaching.

You know Jack to be sensible and probably a good long-term risk, but for now, given the absence of any credit experience on his part, you are unwilling to offer him an open account.

Your task: Write Jack Cornelius a tactful letter that declines his request for an account with your firm but leaves the way open for some future arrangement.

14. Pat the Painter: Letter refusing credit to a new business Patricia Whitman (doing business as Pat the Painter, 1427 Queen Street East, Sault Sainte Marie, Ontario P6A 5P2) is a young woman of boundless ambition. She proposes to blanket the area with fliers promoting her painting and carpentry business. She tells you that she has scaffold builders, scrapers, paint mixers, and commission salespeople in place and that paint and equipment will be delivered to work sites by college students before and after their classes. She also tells you that her start-up capital is small and her start-up expenses high. She wants to purchase paint, brushes, solvents, and ladders from your firm, Hobson's Builders Supply, with payments to begin in 60 days.

You admire Pat's energy and ambition, but you are less enthusiastic about the success of her venture. You certainly want to supply her business needs but prefer to deal on a cash basis, at least for now.

Your task: Write Pat a letter, turning down her request for credit. You are willing to help her in other ways, however—possibly by helping her submit an application for a government loan.

15. The late Mrs. Snyder: Letter holding the line against an irate customer Today's mail brings the following letter from Mrs. Katherine Snyder:

I have been shopping at Barrington's for ten years, but no more!

Yesterday, I tried to buy four sheets and an electric blanket. When I came to the counter to charge them, the clerk told me that there was a hold on my credit and that I would have to pay cash or not get the merchandise. I got her name, Idelle Lewis, in case you want to take action against her. I was with a friend, and you can imagine how I felt when I was publicly denied the right to take the sheets and blanket out of the store. Or maybe you can't imagine, but you should.

I was so mad I couldn't sleep last night. What are you going to do about it?

A look at Mrs. Snyder's file confirms the problem. Her account is 60 days past due, with two payments of $50 each needed to bring it current. Her unpaid balance is only $250, but when a computer check disclosed the delinquency in the account, Idelle Lewis correctly followed your policy. Mrs. Snyder has been a credit customer of Barrington's for five years and has been slow with her payments from time to time.

Your task: In your capacity as credit supervisor, answer Mrs. Snyder's letter on company letterhead. She resides at 3742 Devonshire Drive, Brookfield, WI 53005.

CONVEYING UNFAVORABLE NEWS ABOUT PEOPLE

16. Career moves: Refusal to write a letter of recommendation Tom Terwilliger worked in the office at Opal Pools and Patios for four months, under your supervision (you're office manager). On the basis of what he told you he could do, you started him off as a word processor. His keyboard skills were inadequate for the job, however, and you transferred him to logging in accounts receivable, where he performed almost adequately. Because he assured you that his "really long suit" was customer relations, you moved him to what you aggrandize as the complaint department. After he spent three weeks making angry customers even angrier, you were convinced that no place in your office was appropriate for the talents of Mr. Terwilliger. Five weeks ago, you encouraged him to resign before being formally fired.

Today's mail brings a request from Mr. Terwilliger for you to write a letter recommending him for a sales position with a florist shop. You have no knowledge one way or the other of Mr. Terwilliger's sales abilities, but you do know him to be an incompetent word processor, a careless bookkeeper, and an insensitive customer service representative. Someone is more likely to deserve the sales job than Mr. Terwilliger is. You decide that you have done enough favors for Mr. Terwilliger for one lifetime and plan to refuse his request.

Your task: Write to Mr. Terwilliger (now living with his parents at 2344 Bob-O-Link Road, Pineville, SC 29468), indicating that you have chosen not to write a letter recommending him for the sales job.

17. Bad news for 80: Form letter to unsuccessful candidates for a high-level job The Dean's Selection Committee screened 85 applications for the position of dean of arts and sciences at your campus. After two rounds of eliminations, the top five candidates were invited to "airport interviews," where the committee managed to meet with each for an hour. Then the top three candidates were invited to the campus to meet with students, faculty, and administrators.

The committee recommended to the university president that the job be given to Constance Pappas, who has a doctorate in American studies and has been chairman of the history department at Minneapolis Metropolitan College for the past three years. The president agreed, and Dr. Pappas accepted the offer.

One final task remains before the work of the Dean's Selection Committee is finished: Letters must be sent to the 84 unsuccessful candidates. The 4 who reached the "airport interview" stage will receive personal letters from the chairman of the committee. Your job, as secretary of the committee, is to draft the form letter that will be sent to the other 80 applicants.

Your task: Draft a letter of 100 to 200 words. All copies will be individually addressed to the recipients but will carry identical messages.

HANDLING BAD NEWS ABOUT COMPANY OPERATIONS OR PERFORMANCE

18. The high price of low fares: Memo announcing layoffs at United Airlines Fare wars can be murderous. When some companies offer big discounts, other airlines have to match their fares, whether they can afford to or not.

James J. Hartigan, president of United Airlines, watched his company lose $81 million in one year as it struggled to compete with more streamlined airlines. Finally, having decided that drastic measures are necessary, he has called a meeting with the company's top human resources staff. "We've got to cut our costs," Mr. Hartigan tells all of you gathered in his office. "And we've got to do it immediately."

He'd really like to convince the unions to make some wage and benefit concessions, but they're protected by contracts for another eight to ten months. In the short term, United can save $100 million by laying off about 1,000 nonunion people at headquarters in Chicago, freezing management salaries, and stopping unnecessary expenses. Safety and service are out of bounds.

"This is going to be awfully hard on morale," you point out. "You're talking about firing 25 percent of the executive office personnel." By the pained look on his face, you know that Mr. Hartigan has no more enthusiasm for the layoffs than you do. But there's no alternative.

As the meeting breaks up, Mr. Hartigan directs the human resources department to prepare a memo announcing United's cost-cutting moves. Affected individuals will be notified personally when the layoffs begin next week. Of course, the company will help all terminated employees find new jobs.

Your task: Draft the memo. It will go out under Mr. Hartigan's signature, so it should sound as though it comes from him.[4]

19. The losing bet: Memo from Northrup management announcing the loss of an important contract The suspense has been mounting for months at Northrup's headquarters in Los Angeles. Everybody has been wondering whether management's $1 billion bet will pay off. Over 2,000 jobs have been riding on the outcome.

In the defense industry, most new weapon systems are developed under contract at the government's expense. But without advance funding from the government, Northrup spent five years designing and developing the F-20, a new defensive fighter plane. Management hoped that the Air Force would like the final product well enough to replace the existing fleet of F-16s, which were built by a different defense contractor.

Unfortunately, the Air Force has decided to economize by modifying the F-16s for $2.3 million each instead of buying new defensive fighters at $10 million each. The money it saves will be used to buy new offensive fighters.

The good news is that the Air Force was so impressed with the company's work that it picked Northrup and only one other defense contractor to develop an advanced tactical fighter. The contract will keep Northrup engineers busy. However, unless Northrup is also chosen to build this other plane, production people in the F-20 division may have to be let go.

"That's what I wanted to talk to you about," your boss says. "We're supposed to write a memo that officially announces the government isn't buying any F-20s, but we're also supposed to reassure everybody that no layoffs are planned—at least not right away. But it's quite possible that next year we'll lay off as many as 2,000 workers. We just don't know for certain, one way or the other."

Your task: Your boss gives you responsibility for drafting the memo to Northrup's employees informing them of the F-20 decision and its implications.[5]

20. The linen suit fiasco: Memo explaining that a new line of Liz Claiborne suits is not selling well As you examine last week's sales figures for Liz Claiborne, Inc.'s various clothing lines, you fall to muttering: "This can't be right. We must have sold more linen suits than that." You are so puzzled by the low sales figures that you call the data-processing department to see if there has been some mistake. But no, the newly introduced linen suits are simply not selling well.

In your tenure as a sales analyst at Liz Claiborne's New York offices, you have never seen a line that fell so far short of the projected sales figures. In fact, since the company was founded in 1976, it has had one success after another, and already it has a spot on the

Fortune 500 list of America's biggest manufacturers. So your curiosity is aroused.

Talking on the phone with 25 retailers from around the country, trying to analyze what's gone wrong with the linen suits, you hear comments like these:

"It's November; nobody wants to buy linen in November."

"Maybe it's the wrinkle factor. Natural fabrics are fine up to a point, but let's face it, you have to iron a linen suit every time you wear it. That's a pain in the neck."

"The timing is wrong. People expect to see wool this time of year."

"The color and fabric are too springlike."

Judging from comments like these, you doubt that sales will pick up in the coming weeks. You know that this news will be a big disappointment to Robert Bernard, senior vice president in charge of the Collection and Sport Division, which brought out the suit line. But the sooner Mr. Bernard gets the facts, the sooner he can control the damage. Maybe the line would do better if it were withdrawn and reintroduced in the spring.

Your task: Write a memo to Mr. Bernard, explaining the disappointing sales statistics. You will include a copy of the computerized report as an attachment so he can analyze sales patterns in detail.[6]

CHAPTER NINE

WRITING PERSUASIVE MESSAGES

After studying this chapter, you will be able to

- Choose a persuasive appeal appropriate for the type of audience you are writing to
- Apply the organizational plan for persuasive messages—attention, interest, desire, action—to any task requiring persuasion
- Write a messsage persuading someone to take action or to make an adjustment on your behalf
- Design a sales letter around selling points and benefits
- Apply the techniques of persuasion to prompt someone to pay an overdue bill

COMMUNICATION CLOSE-UP AT *NEWSWEEK*

Stephen Bernard

Which premium will entice the most people to subscribe? The travel guide, the restaurant guide, or the calculator? As circulation promotion director for *Newsweek* magazine in New York, Stephen Bernard knows there's only one way to find out which one will work best: "Run a test. I take a cross section of my mailing list and then mail out a selection of direct-mail packages. All of them are identical except for the premium they offer. In this case, the calculator was what people wanted."

Stephen uses the same technique for deciding on copy. He'll come up with several "angles" to get potential subscribers' attention and then send out letters using these approaches to a cross section of people on his mailing list. The idea that generates the best response is the one he uses for subscription offers to the rest of the mailing list.

"In direct mail," says Stephen, "the copy is the most important element. Sure, you can increase results with premiums or eye-catching art or unusual layouts. But the copy—how you phrase it, the appeals you use, and the style of the copy—all affect the results.

"I entrust the creation of the copy itself to specialized copywriters, generally free-lancers or writers associated with an advertising agency. When the time comes to put together a package, I call in a few to develop potential concepts. Once I get their copy, we put the letters through an

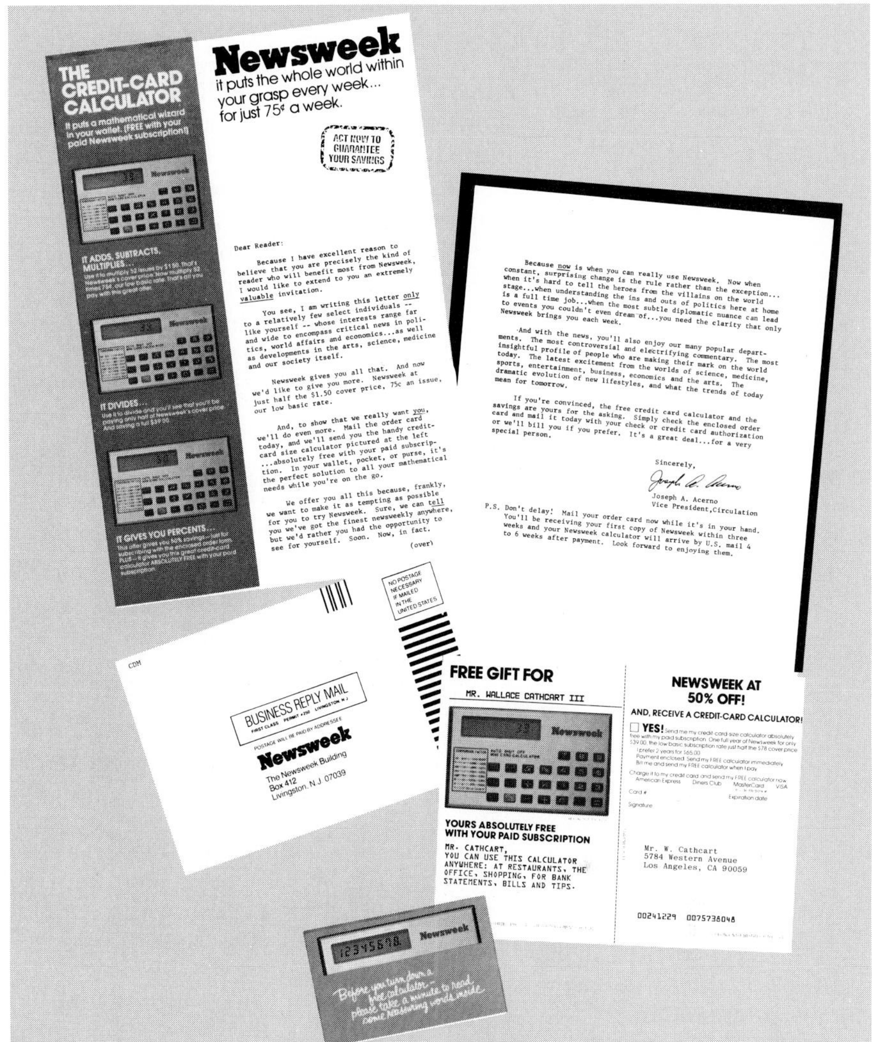

Persuasive messages, including *Newsweek*'s direct-mail packages, are effective only to the degree they take account of the audience's needs and interests.

editing process and then run a test. I'm always looking for a winner."

The writers that Stephen calls in do some careful analysis when they begin a new project. They don't write a word until they understand the objective of the letter, the offer to be made, and the market to whom the letter will be sent. Then they explain the features of the product in terms of the benefits they bring to the greatest number of people in the target audience.

This basic groundwork is only part of the task. As Stephen points out, "Top copywriters all have their own style. In fact, sometimes I can recognize who wrote a letter just by reading it. But what all good copy shares is the spark of imagination and a personal quality that can cut through the distance between writer and reader." This distance can be formidable, especially when the letter comes through the mail along with a handful of other letters that may be more important to the reader. But the skilled application of persuasive techniques can help overcome the reader's resistance and sell magazines.

PREPARING TO WRITE A PERSUASIVE MESSAGE

Because copywriting for direct mail is so specialized and requires such a knowledgeable touch, most business communicators never get this type of assignment. However, the persuasive techniques used by professionals are useful in many other types of business communication, which is why a chapter on the subject is included in this book.

Persuasion: a process of changing people's attitudes or influencing their actions, now or in the future

Persuasion is much more than simply asking somebody to do something. In formal terms, it's the process of changing people's attitudes or influencing their actions, either immediately or at some time in the future. Because persuasive messages aim to influence an audience that is inclined to resist, they depend heavily on strategic planning like that carried out by Stephen Bernard of *Newsweek*.

SETTING THE COURSE

It takes a good deal of skill to persuade someone to do what you want. Say you bought a pair of contact lenses and then realized that you had been overcharged. Your initial request for a partial refund prompted a rather rude response from the ophthalmologist's office assistant. How should you go about getting the ophthalmologist to adjust the charges?

First of all, you must be able to state the problem. Unless you stick to the facts, your emotions will only cloud the issue. In addition, you must clearly understand the sequence of events or the source of the dissatisfaction. In the case of the contact lenses, you might state the problem as follows:

> The problem is that I paid $50 more for contact lenses than I expected to pay. When I called for a quote on the charges for fitting and purchasing the lenses, Dr. Gibson's office assistant told me that the total charge would be $175. Later I paid a bill for $225.

Three questions to ask before you begin to write a persuasive message:

- What are you writing about?
- Who are you writing to?
- What do you want to happen as a result?

Notice that the core problem is stated in one sentence. The rest of the paragraph gives only the essential background, not such extra information as, for instance, the office assistant's uncooperative attitude.

The second item to focus on is the person you're writing to. Are you writing in this case to Dr. Gibson or to her assistant? If you are writing to Dr. Gibson, you might consider the possibility that the doctor has no direct hand in the billing process. Therefore, a little more explanation might be necessary. On the other hand, if you are writing to the assistant, you may want to consider the possibility that the setting of prices is out of her control. In addition, although both Dr. Gibson and the assistant deserve your respect and the benefit of the doubt, each has a different stake in the outcome of the dispute.

Finally, you must think about the outcome that you desire. How will you know if your persuasive efforts have succeeded? Do you want Dr. Gibson to take back the lenses and refund all your money? Do you want to keep the lenses and get $50 back? Do you want Dr. Gibson to fire her office assistant, or the state licensing agency or ophthalmologists' association to censure Dr. Gibson? Do you just want to vent your frustration? To achieve a solution to your problem, you must have a clear idea of what would solve it, so that you don't get sidetracked to a less important issue or overlook the signs indicating that you have succeeded.

FIGURE 9.1
Maslow's Hierarchy of Needs

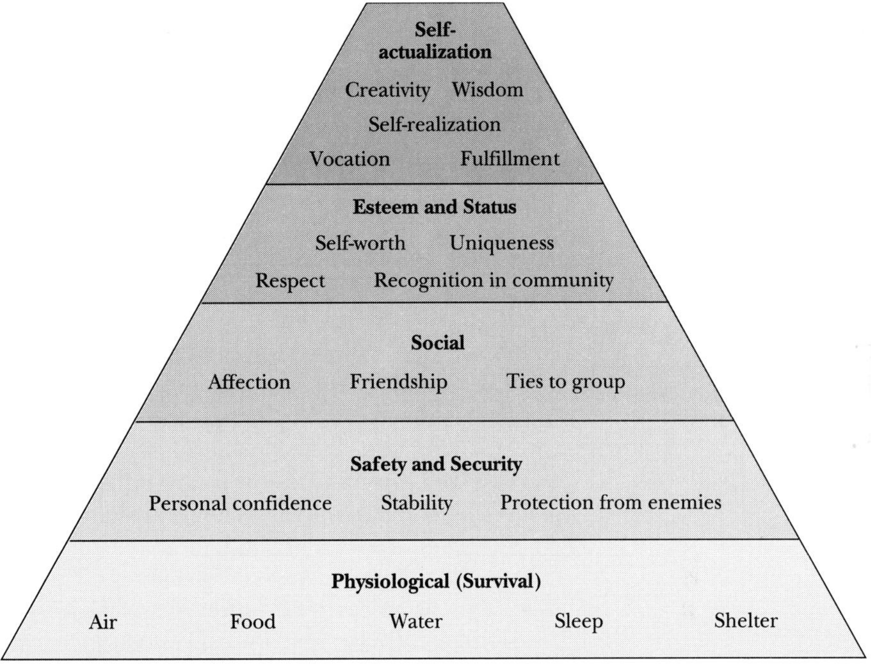

APPEALING TO THE AUDIENCE

Convincing an uninterested or wary audience is a very difficult job requiring much insight. Fortunately, a great deal of research has been conducted to determine how a communicator can overcome people's resistance to a message and motivate them to change their actions or beliefs.

Needs and appeals

People are motivated by needs.

What makes people think or act as they do? Needs. People have many different needs, of course, but some researchers believe that certain needs have priority. In Figure 9.1, a representation of Abraham Maslow's ideas, the most basic needs are those at the bottom of the pyramid. Only after they have been met will a person seek to fulfill higher-level needs.[1]

Imagine that you supervise someone who consistently arrives late for work. If he doesn't break this habit, you're going to have to fire him. But before you try to persuade him to change, you should find out why he's coming in late. For example, does he oversleep because he has a second job that he needs to support a family (a safety and security need)? Or might he be coming in late out of a misguided desire to have people notice his arrival (an esteem and status need)? Once you have analyzed the need motivating him to arrive late, you can craft an appeal, a "hook" that will make him interested in your message about changing his behavior. If the need for safety and security is behind his problem, you might begin with a statement like "Your job is very important to you, I know." If he craves esteem and status, you could say, "You have always seemed interested in being given more responsibility, perhaps even a promotion."

Advertising researchers have come up with long lists of appeals that make people take notice. But because their needs differ, people respond to any given message in different ways. Not everyone is interested in economy, for instance, or fair play; as a matter of fact, some people's innermost needs make appeals to status and greed much more effective. Because of these individual differences, you must analyze your audience and then construct a message that appeals to their needs. For example, a letter requesting an adjustment for defective merchandise could focus on issues of fairness or on legal issues, depending on the reader. A sales letter for sheepskin seat covers should perhaps emphasize their prestige to Porsche drivers and their comfort to Chevrolet drivers.

Choose appeals according to your audience's needs.

Emotion and logic

Emotional reactions may result when an audience's needs are overlooked.

When people's needs are not being met, they are likely to respond emotionally. For example, a person who lacks a feeling of self-worth is likely to be very sensitive to the tone of respect in a message. To yield the best results, a collection letter to such a person must therefore take care to avoid any hint that the person is considered dishonorable. The danger is that the person will become upset and not pay attention to the message. Not even the best-crafted, most reasonable message will persuade someone who is emotionally unable to accept it.

In some cases, emotional issues are a pitfall for persuasive messages; in many other cases, however, persuasive messages make use of the emotion surrounding certain words. *Freedom,* for instance, brings forth strong feelings, as do such words as *success, prestige, credit record, savings, free, value, comfort.* The use of words like these puts the audience in a certain frame of mind and helps them accept the message.

Although the need to think of oneself as rational is as strong as any of the other needs, logic and emotion work together in a rather strange way: People need to have reasons for an attitude they've already embraced in their hearts. To take advantage of this need, you should be sure to use both emotional appeals and logical proof when you write persuasive messages, as in the following excerpt:

Emotion and logic together are more powerful than either alone.

> The streets of Calcutta swarm with orphaned, homeless children. To you and me, a few cents for milk and bread seem so little. But to them, a supper like this would be a feast. Think how good you'd feel to know you're helping to feed the children of Calcutta and other burdened cities around the world. Your pledge of $5, $10, or more a month is all it takes to put food in the mouth of a starving child.

The scene described in this letter tugs at the heartstrings; the implication that $5 is relatively little to someone in this country and a fortune to a hungry, homeless orphan provides a logical reason for contributing.

Credibility

Without credibility, your skillful use of needs and appeals, emotion and logic may seem to be nothing more than manipulation. It is especially important that a skeptical or hostile audience believe you know what you are talking about and, furthermore, are not trying to mislead them.

Enhance your credibility by supplying evidence that is objective and specific.

One of the best ways to gain credibility is to support your message with facts. Testimonials, documents, guarantees, statistics, research results, and the like all provide seemingly objective evidence for what you have to say and thus make your message more credible. The more specific and relevant your proof, the better. It also helps to name your sources, especially if they are respected by your audience.

Express personal qualities that enhance credibility through your approach and writing style.

A number of personal qualities will enhance your own credibility. If you can demonstrate the following characteristics, your audience will more readily believe what you say.

- *Enthusiasm.* Infectious excitement about the subject of the message
- *Objectivity.* Understanding of and willingness to acknowledge all sides of an issue
- *Sincerity.* Honesty, genuineness, good faith, and truthfulness
- *Expertise.* Knowledgeability in the subject area of the message (or even some other area)
- *Good intentions.* Willingness to keep the audience's best interests at heart
- *Trustworthiness.* Honesty and dependability
- *Similarity.* Beliefs, attitudes, and background like those of the audience

If you want the audience to "buy" your message, let them know that you have or are associated with someone who has these qualities.

Semantics

How do you let an audience know that you are, for example, enthusiastic or trustworthy? An outright claim that you have these qualities is sure to raise suspicion. Word choice, however, can do much of the job for you.

Semantics: the meaning of words and other symbols

The words you choose to state your message say much more than their dictionary definition. For instance, *useful, beneficial,* and *advantageous* may be considered synonyms. Yet these three words cannot be used interchangeably and still convey the same meaning:

She suggested a *useful* compromise. (The compromise allowed the parties to get to work.)

She suggested a *beneficial* compromise. (The compromise not only resolved the conflict but also had a positive effect, perhaps for both parties.)

She suggested an *advantageous* compromise. (The compromise benefited her or her company more than it benefited the other party.)

Abstractions are most persuasive when combined with details.

Another way that semantics can affect persuasive messages is in the variety of meanings that people attribute to certain words. Because abstractions refer to things that people cannot experience with their senses, they are subject to interpretation. Thus they can be used to enhance the emotional content of a persuasive message. For example, you may be able to sell more flags by appealing to people's patriotism (which may be interpreted in many ways) than by describing the color and size of the flags. You may have better luck collecting an overdue bill by mentioning honesty and fair play than by repeating the sum owed and the date it was due. But you must include both the abstraction and the details for your message to have the effect you want, because the very fact that you are using abstract words creates room for misinterpretation.

ORGANIZING THE MESSAGE

The AIDA plan:
- Attention
- Interest
- Desire
- Action

Once you have laid a foundation, you may begin to build your message. Persuasion requires the indirect approach, often a specialized one called the AIDA plan (attention, desire, interest, action).

Your goal in the attention phase is to convince the audience right at the beginning that you have something useful or interesting to say. The audience wants to know "What's in this message for me?" Try to tell them without making extravagant claims or threats or bringing up irrelevant points. For example:

Begin every persuasive message with an attention-getting statement that is
- Personalized
- You-oriented
- Not extravagant
- Relevant

You've mentioned several times in the past two weeks that constructing an employee schedule has become increasingly difficult. Let me share an idea that could substantially reduce the time you spend making and revising schedules.

In the interest phase, you explain how your message relates to the audience. Continuing the theme that you started with, you paint a more detailed picture with words. Your goal is to get the audience thinking, "This is an interesting idea; maybe it is a possibility for solving my problems."

In the interest section
- Continue the opening theme in greater detail
- Relate benefits specifically to the attention getter

Inc. magazine ran an article in the July 2 issue about a scheduling concept called flextime. It gives employees leeway to schedule their own work, within certain guidelines. Two companies profiled in the article were having problems (as we have been) with late arrivals, long lunches, early departures, and too many "sick days." They found it nearly impossible to set up a schedule that everyone would adhere to. But once these companies instituted flextime, their problems practically disappeared.

Notice how this section ties together a factual description and the benefits of instituting the program. Notice also that the benefits relate specifically to the attention getter that precedes this paragraph. Even though the flextime system might help improve employee morale, that benefit is secondary to the main interest of the intended audience (to reduce the frustration of devising useless schedules) and is therefore not mentioned.

In the desire section
- Provide relevant evidence to prove your claim
- Draw attention to any enclosures

The desire section of a persuasive message is used to back up claims and thereby increase your audience's willingness to take the action that you will suggest in the next section. The point is to get the audience thinking, "I really need this." Whatever you use to prove your claim, make sure the evidence is directly relevant to your point. For example:

One of the people interviewed in the article, the head of manufacturing for a $10 million company, said: "I seemed to be spending all my time making schedules and then tearing them up. Now I let my employees figure out their own schedules. I have more time to oversee the work that's being done and to track the quality of the products we ship." This company had a flextime program in full operation within three months of deciding to start it. Attached is a copy of an article about the factors to consider before going to flextime and the three steps involved in instituting it.

Action ending: close of a persuasive message that suggests a specific step the audience may take

Notice how this example draws attention to the evidence and suggests the lessons that may be drawn from it.

All persuasive messages end with a section that urges specific action. But the so-called "action ending" should be more than a statement like

End by
- Describing precisely what you would like to happen
- Restating how the audience will benefit by acting as you wish
- Making action easy

"Institute this program as soon as possible" or "Send me a refund." In fact, it offers a good opportunity for one last reminder of the main benefit the audience will realize from taking the action you want. For example:

Let's meet early next week (Monday, 3 p.m.?) to see how we might implement a flextime schedule. With a little bit of extra effort now, you could soon be concentrating on something more important than scheduling.

The secret of the final section is to make action easy. In sales letters, for example, you might ask the audience to fill out an enclosed order form and use a preaddressed, postpaid envelope for reply.

WRITING PERSUASIVE REQUESTS FOR ACTION

Many persuasive messages are written to solicit funds, favors, information, or cooperation. In an organization, for example, persuasive techniques are often required to get someone to change policies or procedures, to spend money on new equipment and services, to promote a person or protect turf.[2] Persuasive letters to outsiders might solicit donations or ask for some other type of help.

Three problems with requests for action:
- They frequently offer nothing tangible in return
- They take time that could be used for something else
- There are so many competing requests

This type of message is one of the most difficult persuasive tasks you could undertake. For one thing, people are busy, and doing something new takes time without offering a guaranteed reward in return. Second, there are plenty of competing requests. In fact, the public relations departments of many large corporations receive so many requests for donations to worthy causes that they must sometimes resort to lotteries to decide which to support.

Why do people respond to requests for action on an issue that is more important to you than to them? They may, if you're lucky, believe in the project or cause that you're writing about. Even so, you must persuade them that your request will give them some benefit, perhaps an intangible benefit down the road or a chance to make a meaningful contribution. Also, especially in the case of requests for professional favors or information, people may believe that they are obliged to "pay their dues" by helping others.

Highlight the direct and indirect benefits of complying with your request.

When making a persuasive request, therefore, take special care to highlight direct and indirect benefits. Direct benefits might include a reduced work load for the supervisor who institutes flextime or a premium for someone who responds to a survey. Indirect benefits might include better employee morale or the prestige of giving free workshops to small businesses.

The attention-getting device at the beginning of a persuasive request for action usually serves to show the reader that you know something about his or her concerns and that you have some reason for making such a request. In this type of persuasive message, more than in most others, a flattering comment about the reader is acceptable, especially if it is sincere. The body of the letter or memo covers what you know about the problem you are trying to solve with the reader's help: the facts and figures, the benefits of helping, your experience in attacking the problem. The goal is to give you and your request credibility, to make the reader believe that

FIGURE 9.2
Memo Requesting Action

A provocative statement and remarkable statistics help get the reader's attention.

By detailing the nature and dimensions of the problem, the writer gives the request credibility.

The suggested solution is specific enough to appear workable.

The final paragraph tells the reader exactly what must be done and reinforces the main reason for doing it.

MEMO

TO: Elaine Tyson DATE: August 10, 1989

FROM: Bob Binks BB SUBJECT: Order Processing

We may not be getting our money's worth from the three new data-entry clerks we hired six months ago, although the clerks aren't really to blame. Take a look at these figures, which Sarah and I have compiled over the past month:

--About 18 percent of customer orders lack some piece of information, such as a ZIP code, needed to process and ship the merchandise efficiently.

--In six cases that we know about (because customers called to complain), orders never showed up in the computer records and were therefore never processed, although we did find the paperwork.

When the new order-processing system was installed two years ago, we selected computers with plenty of capacity. In fact, even at present growth rates they should be adequate for another two or three years.

The software is another matter. Although it was the best available at the time, new software on the market is much more "goof-proof." With audible prompts to remind operators when necessary information is missing and a simplified "save" function, OrderMaster II could solve our data-entry problems and upgrade customer service at the same time. OrderMaster II can easily be customized to suit our operations. And note this fact particularly: The total cost is less than we have spent in the past month to have someone resolve order-processing problems.

The requisition form we need to obtain OrderMaster II is attached, complete except for your signature. The software manufacturer assures me that we can have it within a week; a field representative will come out for a day or two to set it up and show the data-entry clerks how to use it.

Do you have any questions about this program? If so, call me at ext. 157. Otherwise, please sign the requisition form and send it back to me right away. The sooner we order the program, the sooner we can solve some serious problems with order processing.

helping you will indeed help solve a significant problem. Once you have demonstrated that your message is relevant to your reader, you can request some specific action. Take a look, for example, at the request in Figure 9.2. Be aware, however, that a persuasive memo is somewhat more subdued than a letter to an outsider might be.

Make only reasonable requests.

The most important thing to remember when you prepare a persuasive request for action is to keep your request within bounds. Nothing is so distressing as a request so general, all-encompassing, or inconsiderate that it seems impossible to grant, no matter how worthy the cause. And don't doom your request to failure by asking your reader to do all your work for you: to provide information that you were too lazy to seek, to spend time saving you from embarrassment or inconvenience, to provide total financial support for a cause that nobody else is supporting.

■ CHECKLIST FOR PERSUASIVE REQUESTS FOR ACTION

A. Attention

- ☐ 1. Demonstrate that you understand the audience's concerns.
- ☐ 2. Introduce a direct or indirect benefit that can be developed as a central selling point.
- ☐ 3. Craft statements so they don't sound like high-pressure sales tactics or bribes.
- ☐ 4. Use an effective opening: comment or assertion the audience will agree with, compliment (if sincere), frank admission that you need the audience's help, problem that is the basis of your request, one or two rhetorical questions, statement(s) of what is being done or has been done to solve a problem.

B. Interest and Desire

- ☐ 1. Early in the body of the message, introduce the reason you are writing.
  - ☐ a. Mention the main audience benefit before the actual request.
  - ☐ b. Thoroughly explain your reason for asking the favor.
- ☐ 2. Include all necessary description: physical characteristics and value of the project.
- ☐ 3. Include all facts and figures necessary to convince the audience that his or her contribution will be enjoyable, easy, important, and of personal benefit (as much as is true and possible).
  - ☐ a. In a request for cooperation, explain the problem, facts, suggestions, other participants' roles, and the audience's part.
  - ☐ b. In a request for a donation, explain the problem, past and current attempts to remedy it, future plans, your organization's involvement, and projected costs, along with suggestions about how the audience can help.
  - ☐ c. Describe the possible direct benefits.
  - ☐ d. Describe the possible indirect benefits.
- ☐ 4. Anticipate and answer possible objections.
  - ☐ a. Ignore objections if they are unimportant or might not occur to the audience or if you can focus on positive facts instead.
  - ☐ b. Discuss objections (usually) about half or two-thirds of the way through the body of the letter or memo.
  - ☐ c. Acknowledge objections calmly, then overcome them by focusing on more important and more positive factors.
  - ☐ d. Turn objections into an advantage by looking at them from another viewpoint or by explaining the facts of the situation more clearly.
  - ☐ e. Overcome objections to providing restricted material by giving assurance that you will handle it in whatever limited way is specified.
- ☐ 5. Introduce any enclosures after you have finished the key message, with an emphasis on what to do with them or what information they offer.

C. Action

- ☐ 1. Confidently ask for the audience's cooperation.
- ☐ 2. Make the desired action clear and easy.
- ☐ 3. Stress the positive results of action.
- ☐ 4. Include the due date for a response (if necessary), and tie it in with audience benefits (if possible): adequate time for ordering supplies, prominent billing on the program, and so forth.
- ☐ 5. Replace negative or tentative statements, such as "If you can donate anything," with positive, confident statements, such as "To make your contribution, just return. . . ."
- ☐ 6. Tie in the last sentence with an appeal or statement featured in the opening paragraph (if appropriate), as a last audience-benefit plug.

WRITING PERSUASIVE CLAIMS AND REQUESTS FOR ADJUSTMENT

Although persuasive claims and requests for adjustment are sometimes referred to as complaint letters, your goal should be to persuade someone to make an adjustment in your favor, not merely to get your complaint off

The goal of a persuasive claim or request for adjustment is to satisfy your expectations for a transaction.

your chest. You do that by demonstrating the difference between what you expected and what you actually got.

Persuasion is a necessity in pressing claims when you've already bought and paid for the product. You can't threaten to withhold payment. Instead, you must convey essentially negative information in a way that will get positive results. Fortunately, most people in business are open to fair settlement of your claim. It is to their advantage to maintain your goodwill and to resolve your problem quickly so that they may continue with other business.

Make your persuasive claims

- Complete and specific in reviewing the facts
- Confident and positive in tone

The key ingredients of a good persuasive claim are a complete and specific review of the facts and a confident and positive tone. Assume that the other person is not intentionally trying to cheat you but also that you have the right to be satisfied with the transaction. Talk only about the specific complaint at hand, not about other issues involving similar products or other complaints about the company. Your goal is to solve a particular problem; your audience is most likely to help when you focus on the benefits of solving the problem rather than on the horrors of neglecting your complaint.

As you read the following letter, take note of the improvements that could be made:

I am writing to you in regard to a cartridge I purchased on April 3, 1988. I have a Technic Automatic 300 that I equipped with the VDX-II. On September 12, 1988, the cartridge failed to perform as it should. I then drove to Dallas, Texas, the place of purchase (ABC Stereo, 5000 Independence Drive) to see about getting either a replacement or compensation for the defective cartridge.

This opening fails to attract attention or to clarify for the reader the benefits of solving the problem. The tone is rather pompous.

One of the salespeople briefly inspected the cartridge and said it was worn. Naturally, I asked for a free cartridge replacement, but the gentleman said that you, the manufacturer, do not guarantee the cartridge for wear; therefore ABC Stereo doesn't either. He said that I would have to buy a new cartridge at the retail price, but I chose not to because I feel justified in insisting on satisfaction.

These sentences tend to be hard to read, because they are long and cluttered with detail.

I'm requesting a replacement cartridge for the VDX-II from you, at no charge, for these reasons:

--The cartridge/stylus is less than one year old.

--Under the "implied warranty of merchantability," Section 2-314 of the Uniform Commercial Code, "any merchant who sells a product is guaranteeing to the purchaser that the product is merchantable--fit for the ordinary purposes for which such a product is used."

--Further, as a marketing student in business school, I don't believe that any manufacturer's warranty should exempt the product from

A hostile and haughty tone invites the reader to square off as an adversary. Instead, the writer should establish some common ground.

ordinary wear in a period of one year from the date of purchase, regardless of the exact provisions of the warranty.

It is difficult to believe that a product that retails for as much as the VDX-II could conceivably have a life cycle of only five months.

Criticism of the company's product and pricing invites disaster. A gracious close would work much better.

Here's a revised version of the same letter, one that should yield more favorable results:

After hearing so many good things about your VDX-II stereo cartridge, I bought one on April 3, 1988, and installed it on my Technic Automatic 300. The sound was terrific!

But on September 12, 1988, the cartridge suddenly stopped working. Because it was scratching my records and muffling the sound, I took it back to ABC Stereo in Dallas, Texas, where I'd bought it. The salesperson there told me the problem was not caused by a defect but by normal wear, for which you provide no warranty.

Please inspect the enclosed cartridge. I feel sure you'll agree that a product your company is so proud of should not wear out after only five months.

I like the design of the VDX-II, so I'd prefer that you replace the cartridge. Otherwise, a refund would be acceptable. Having treated my friends to the magnificent sound created by your VDX-II cartridge, I'd like to do it again.

As this example illustrates, resolving problems is more a matter of reasonable exchange than a struggle between adversaries.

■ CHECKLIST FOR PERSUASIVE CLAIMS AND REQUESTS FOR ADJUSTMENT

A. Attention

- ☐ 1. Use for the opening a sincere compliment, rhetorical question, agreeable comment or assertion, statement of the basic problem, or brief review of what has been done about the problem.
- ☐ 2. State at the beginning something that you and the audience can agree on or that you wish to persuade the audience about.

B. Interest and Desire

- ☐ 1. State all necessary facts and details, and interweave them with audience benefits.
- ☐ 2. Provide a description that shows the audience that his or her firm is responsible for the problem and that your request is factual, logical, and reasonable.
- ☐ 3. Appeal to the audience's sense of fair play, desire for customer goodwill, need for a good reputation, or sense of legal or moral responsibility.
- ☐ 4. Reflect your goal (business objective) of having the adjustment granted.
- ☐ 5. Present your case in a calm, logical manner.
- ☐ 6. Tell the audience how you feel (your disappointment with the products, policies, or services provided may well be the most important part of your argument).

C. Action

- ☐ 1. Make sure the action request is a logical conclusion based on the problem and the clearly stated facts.
- ☐ 2. State the request specifically and confidently.
- ☐ 3. Specify a due date for action (when desirable).
- ☐ 4. Provide a special inducement (when desirable).
- ☐ 5. State the main audience benefit as a reminder of benefits in earlier statements.

WRITING SALES LETTERS

In the United States, more than 55 billion pieces of direct mail promoting some product or organization were sent in 1987, and each piece included a persuasive sales letter.[3] By and large, sales letters are written by specialized and highly skilled professionals like the writers employed by Stephen Bernard of *Newsweek*. The letters come in letter-size or larger envelopes, with brochures or without. The common denominator is their attempt to motivate people to spend money or patronize an organization.

PREWRITING

The three steps involved in planning a sales letter are similar to those involved in planning any persuasive message: (1) determine the main idea (in sales letters, it revolves around a selling point and related benefits), (2) define the audience, and (3) plan the approach and format.

Determining selling points and benefits

Know the product's selling points, but talk about their benefits to consumers.

Selling points are the most attractive features of a product; consumer benefits are the particular advantages that buyers will realize from those features. For example, one selling point of a personal computer might be its numeric keypad; the consumer benefit of this selling point is that the user doesn't need a separate calculator or the skill to type numbers on the regular keyboard.

Start with a thorough knowledge of the product.

Obviously, you cannot write about either selling points or benefits without a thorough understanding of what you're going to write about. The first step in writing any sales letter is therefore to take a good look at the product. Ask yourself (or someone else, if necessary) everything that you think a potential buyer might want to know about it. For example, if you're supposed to write a sales letter for a wholesale bakery, you might want to get a full listing of the types of bread the bakery sells and find out whether the breads are prepared in any particular way, say, without preservatives or with only whole-grain wheat. You should also investigate prices and discounts, delivery schedules, packaging, and the availability of special display materials. At *Newsweek*, free-lance copywriters talk to Stephen Bernard to get information about the benefits of the specific offer and of subscribing to the magazine.

Think about how the product's features can help potential buyers, then concentrate on the most appealing benefits.

Once you have a complete file on the product, you must think of how its features can help potential buyers. In selling bread to a retailer, you might want to focus on the wholesale prices (and hence the markup that the retailer can impose) and the convenience of being able to call in orders for next-day delivery. But if you were selling the same bread to consumers, you might want to focus on the ingredients that are and are not included in the bread. Whatever the case, the product benefits that you focus on should be relatively few, and you should determine which are most appealing so you can direct your audience's attention to them. Ultimately you will want to single out one benefit, which will become the hallmark of your campaign.

LEGAL ALERT

Dangers in Writing Sales Letters

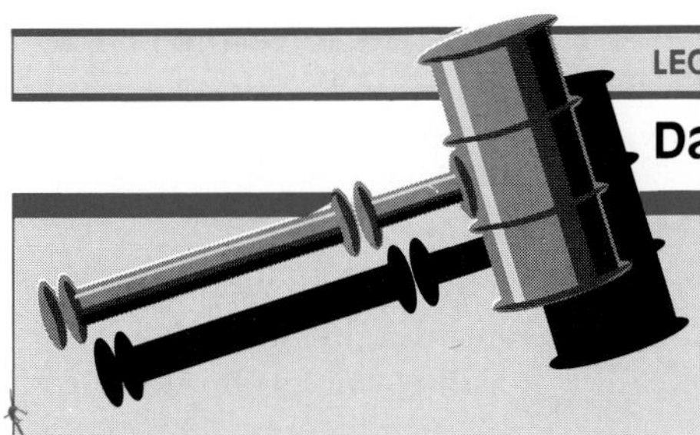

Knowing the laws that govern sales letters can help you avoid serious legal problems. Here are some points worth remembering.

CONTRACTS

Sales letters are considered contracts under the laws of many states. A "promise" made in a sales letter is held to be binding in these states, even if the person to whom the offer is made does not communicate in return. So avoid even implying offers or promises that you can't deliver.

FRAUD

Making a false statement in a sales letter is fraud if the recipient can prove that (1) the misstatement was made with the intent to deceive; (2) it was made regarding a fact rather than an opinion or a speculation; (3) the recipient relied on this false statement and was justified in doing so; and (4) he or she was damaged by it, in a legal sense.

Misrepresenting the price, quality, or performance capability of a product in a sales letter is an example of fraud. So is a testimonial by a person misrepresented to be an expert.

Fraudulent offers sent through the mail cost the nation's consumers an estimated $500 million a year, according to the U.S. Postmaster General. These bogus offers range from phony contests, fake charity appeals, and get-rich-quick schemes to product ripoffs, bogus business opportunities, and worthless self-improvement courses that promise to pay off in "exciting, high-paying careers."

INVASION OF PRIVACY

Using a person's name, photograph, or other identity in a sales letter without permission constitutes invasion of privacy, with some exceptions. For example, using a photo of the members of a local softball team in a Chamber of Commerce mailer may not be an invasion of the team members' privacy if they are public figures in the community and if the use of the photo does not falsely imply their endorsement. But the use of a photo of the President of the United States, without consent, on a letter about the profits to be made in worm farming could be deemed an invasion of privacy.

Legal problems can also result from publicizing a person's private life in a sales letter. For example, stating that the president of a local bank (mentioned by name) served six months in prison for income tax evasion is a potentially damaging fact and may therefore be considered an invasion of privacy. You can also risk a suit by publicizing another person's past-due debts or by publishing without consent another person's medical records, x-rays, or photograph.

Avoiding practices like these when writing sales letters can save you from the legal consequences—and costs—that may result.

1. A friend of yours is a food faddist who sincerely believes that seaweed has protective and curative health powers, although she has no scientific proof. She has started a seaweed food supplement company and has asked you to help by drafting a sales letter to potential customers. Would you be willing to help her? If so, what claims might you make in the letter?
2. Collect as many unsolicited sales letters as you can find, whether mailed to you or to friends. Go through them to see whether any make promises or claims that may be fraudulent. Summarize your findings.

Defining the audience

The most persuasive sales letters are written to appeal to a specific audience.

As you can see, you must start with a general idea of your audience in order to define benefits. However, you can and should learn a great deal more about them. For example, the bakery's pool of potential customers includes grocery stores, convenience markets, delicatessens, and so on, each with its own special needs. Bread retailers may also be divided on the basis of geographic location; rye bread, for instance, may sell much better in large cities and on the East Coast than in rural areas. Such considerations as the specific location of the retailer and the characteristics of the people who shop there would also be of interest.

Marketers seek to define consumers in terms of

- Demographics: age, gender, occupation, income, and education
- Psychographics: personality, attitudes, and life style

When analyzing an audience of individual consumers, marketers refer to *demographics* and *psychographics*. Demographic surveys determine the age, gender, occupation, income, education, and other quantifiable characteristics of people who buy products. Psychographics, the psychological characteristics of potential buyers (personality, attitudes, life style), are less easily determined but provide valuable insights into the preferences of potential customers.

After collecting data about your audience, you should try to form a mental image of the typical buyer for the product you wish to sell. The point of this exercise is to help you formulate an idea of the central concerns of potential buyers. Then you can check the selling points and benefits that you have already come up with against your audience's actual characteristics.

Planning the format and approach

Once you know what you need to say and who you want to say it to, you have to decide how you're going to say it. Will you send just a letter? Or will you include brochures, samples, response cards, and the like? Will the letter be printed with an additional color or special symbols or logos? How many pages will it run? You'll also need to decide whether to conduct a multistage campaign, with several mailings and some sort of telephone or in-person follow-up, or to rely on a single hard-hitting mailing.

The more difficult the selling job, the more elaborate the direct-mail package.

All these decisions depend on whom you are trying to reach—their characteristics, their likely acceptance of or resistance to your message—and what you are trying to get them to do. Generally speaking, expensive items and hard-to-accept propositions call for a more elaborate campaign than low-cost products and simple actions.

PREPARING THE COPY

Sales letters are prepared according to the AIDA plan used for any persuasive message—that is, they start with an attention-getting device, move to whet the reader's interest and desire, and end with a specific call to action. Special techniques give them added impact. Figure 9.3 is a typical example employing some of these techniques.

Getting attention

A number of tried-and-true attention-getting devices are used in sales letters for a wide variety of products.

Take a look at these attention-getting devices commonly used in sales letters:

- *A piece of genuine news.* "In the past 60 days, auto manufacturers' inventories have shrunk by 12 percent."
- *A personal appeal to the reader's emotions and values.* "The only thing worse than paying taxes is paying taxes when you don't have to."
- *The most attractive feature plus the associated benefit.* "New control device ends problems with employee pilferage!"
- *An intriguing number.* "Here are three great secrets of the world's most loved entertainers."

FIGURE 9.3
Letter Selling a Product

AUTO CARE CENTRE
MOWBRY'S
1401 Smith Street
Winnepeg, Manitoba
R3C 1J8

October 3, 1988

Dear Friend:

A single selling point, the service center's specialized cold-weather servicing, is emphasized.

Before you know it, the thermometer is going to be stuck on "Brrr." Yes, Old Man Winter is on his way, bringing some tough times for your automobile.

Don't wait for signs of trouble. Come in and give your auto the cold-weather servicing it needs, right now!

Benefits of the major feature have both a logical appeal (higher trade-in value) and an emotional appeal (family safety).

By having your automobile winterized now, you'll not only protect its trade-in value but also enjoy that great feeling of security every time you and your family back out of the driveway. You'll know your auto is going to get you where you have to go.

The emphasis on quality prepares the reader to pay more for these services.

To make sure your whole family is protected, our expert service facilities are ready and waiting. Factory-trained mechanics, up-to-the-minute equipment, the latest tools, genuine parts--all are ready to make sure your automobile performs at its best.

Do make a point to drive in during the next day or two. Let us give your auto a complete inspection, from fender to fender. Then you'll know what's needed to make sure it runs right, even on the coldest days.

The reader's intelligence and desire to save time and money are the basis of this appeal.

Remember, a check-up now can easily save you much time and hundreds of dollars later, when the really cold weather arrives.

The special time-limited offer should induce quick action.

Drive in today or tomorrow... Hand the enclosed card of introduction to one of our attendants for a 10 percent discount, which is good for the next ten days. The attendant will see that you get special, personal attention.

Don't put off your auto's winter checkup. It pays in every way to act now and beat the cold!

Sincerely,

Glen Mowbry

Glen Mowbry
Manager

- *A sample of the product.* "Here's your free sample of the new Romalite packing sheet."
- *A concrete illustration with story appeal.* "In 1979 Earl Colbert set out to find a better way to process credit applications. After ten years of trial and error, he finally developed a procedure so simple but thorough that he was cited for service to the industry by the American Creditors Association."
- *A specific trait shared by the audience.* "Busy executives need another complicated 'time-saving' device like they need a hole in the head!"
- *A provocative question.* "Are you tired of watching inflation eat away at your hard-earned profits?"
- *A challenge.* "Don't waste another day wondering how you're going to become the success you've always wanted to be!"

- *A solution to a problem.* "Tired of feeling that icy Arctic air rush through the cracks around your windows? Stay warm and save energy with StormSeal Weatherstripping."

A look at your own mail will show you how many different products these few techniques can be applied to.

Choose an attention getter that encourages the reader to read more.

But not all attention-getting devices are equally effective. The best is the one that makes the audience read the rest of the letter. Look closely at the three examples below. Which seems most interesting to you?

How would you like straight A's this semester?

Get straight A's this semester!

Now you can get straight A's this semester, with....

If you're like most people, you'll find the first option the most enticing. The question invites your response—and, by no mistake, a positive response designed to encourage you to read on. The second option is fairly interesting too, but its commanding tone may make you wary of the claim. The third option is acceptable, but it certainly conveys no sense of excitement, and its quick introduction of the product may lead you to a snap decision against reading further.

Sales letters prepared by professionals also use a variety of formats to get your attention, including personalized salutations, special sizes or styles of type, underlining, color, indentions, and so on. But whatever special techniques are used, the best attention getter for a sales letter is a "hook" that gets the reader thinking about the needs that your product might be able to help fill.

Emphasizing the central selling point

To determine your product's central selling point, ask

- What does the competition offer?
- What is special about my product?
- What are potential buyers really looking for?

Let's say that your company's alarm device is relatively inexpensive, durable, and tamperproof. Although these are all attractive features, you would be wise to focus on only one. To determine the central selling point, ask what the competition has to offer, what most distinguishes your product, and what most concerns potential buyers. The answers to these three questions will help you select the single point around which to build your sales message. Make this point a feature of your letter, in the heading or within the first paragraph, and make it stand out through typography, design, or high-impact writing.

Highlighting benefits

Selling points + "you" attitude = benefits.

The exercise you go through to determine the central selling point will help you define the benefits to potential buyers. For example, perhaps your company's alarm device has been built mainly to overcome the inadequacies of the competition in resisting tampering by would-be burglars. The benefits of this feature, your central selling point, are that burglars will not be able to break in so easily and that burglaries will therefore be reduced. You'll want to make this point repeatedly, in words and pictures (if possible), near the beginning and the end of your letter. You might get attention by using a news item to stress this benefit: "Burglaries of businesses in our county have increased 7.7 percent over the past year; police department officials cite burglars' increasing sophistication and familiarity with conventional alarm devices." Or: "Worried about the reliability of your current alarm system in repelling today's sophisticated burglars?"

In the rest of the letter, you should of course continue to stress this theme, but you should also weave in references to other benefits. For example: "You can get this worry-free protection for much less than you might think." And: "The same technology that makes it difficult for burglars to crack your alarm system makes the device durable, even where it must be exposed to the elements." Remember, sales letters reflect the "you" attitude through references to benefits, so always try to phrase the selling points in terms of what such features will do for potential customers.

Using action terms

Active words, which give force to any business message, are especially important in sales letters. Compare the following:

INSTEAD OF THIS	USE THIS
The NuForm desk chair is designed to support your lower back and relieve pressure on your legs.	The NuForm desk chair supports your lower back and relieves pressure on your legs.

To give force to a message

- Use action terms
- Use colorful verbs and adjectives

The second version says the same thing in fewer words and puts more emphasis on what the chair does for the user ("supports") than on the intentions of the design team ("is designed to support").

In general, you should use colorful verbs and adjectives that convey a dynamic image. Be careful, however, not to overdo it: "Your factory floors will sparkle like diamonds" is hard to believe and may prevent your audience from believing the rest of your message.

Talking about price

The price that customers will pay for a product depends on the prices of similar products, the general state of the economy, and the psychology of the buyer. Price is therefore a complicated issue and often a sensitive one.

You can prepare readers for your product's price by subtle choice and arrangement of words.

Whether the price of your product is highlighted or downplayed, your entire letter should prepare the reader for it. Such words as *luxurious* and *economical* provide unmistakable clues about how your price compares to that of competitors and helps the reader accept the price when you finally state it. If your price is relatively high, you should definitely stress features and benefits that justify it. If the price is low, you may wish to compare the features of your product to those of the competition, either directly or indirectly. In either case, if the price you eventually mention is a surprise to the reader, you've made a mistake that will be hard to overcome.

Here's an example of a sales letter offering a product at a bargain price:

All the Features of Name-Brand Pantyhose at Half the Price!

Why pay for fancy packaging or that little tag with a famous name on it when you can enjoy a cotton lining, reinforced toes, and matchless durability for only $1.99?

If the price is an attractive feature, emphasize it by displaying it prominently.

Notice in this example that the price falls right at the end of the paragraph, where it stands out. In addition, the price issue is featured in a bold headline. This technique may even be used as the opening of a letter if the price is the most important feature and the audience for the letter is value conscious.

If price is not a major selling point, you can handle it in several ways. For instance, you could leave out the price altogether or mention it only in an accompanying brochure. Or you could de-emphasize the price by putting the actual figures in the middle of a paragraph close to the end of your sales letter, well after you've presented the benefits and selling points. The same paragraph might include a discussion of related topics, such as credit terms, special offers, and volume discounts. Mentioning favorable money matters before the actual price also reduces its impact.

To de-emphasize price

- Bury actual figures in the middle of a paragraph near the end
- Mention benefits and favorable money matters before the actual price
- Break a quantity price into units
- Compare the price to the cost of some other product or activity

Only 100 prints of this exclusive, limited-edition lithograph will be created. Come June 1, they will be made available to the general public. But you can reserve one now for only $350, the special advance-reservation price. Simply rush the enclosed reservation card back today, so your order is in before the June 1 publication date.

Emphasis on the rarity of the edition signals value and thus prepares the reader for the big-ticket price that follows. The actual price, buried in the middle of a sentence, is tied in with another reminder of the exclusivity of the offer.

The pros use two other techniques for minimizing price. One is to break a quantity price into units. For example, instead of saying that a case of wine costs $60, you might say that each bottle costs $5. The other is to compare your product's price to the cost of some other product or activity: "The daily cost of owning your own spa is less than you'd pay for a health-club membership." Your aim should be to make the cost seem as small and affordable as possible, thereby eliminating price as a possible objection.

Supporting your claims

You can't assume that people will believe what you say about your product just because it's in writing. You will have to prove your claims, especially if your product is complicated, expensive, or representative of some unusual approach.

Types of support for product claims:

- Samples
- Brochures
- Examples
- Testimonials
- Statistics
- Guarantees

Support for your claims may take several forms. Samples and brochures, often with photographs, are enclosures in the sales package but should be referred to in the letter. The letter should also describe or highlight typographically examples of how the product has benefited others, include testimonials (actual quotations) from satisfied customers, or cite statistics from scientific studies of the product's performance. Guarantees of exchange or return privileges, which may also be woven into the letter or set off in a special way, indicate that you have faith in the product and are willing to back it up.

It's almost impossible to provide too much support. A highly regarded direct-mail writer recommends that you anticipate "each and every question that the recipient is likely to want answered. . . . You must put yourself in the role of the reader. You must ask, and answer, all of the 'what-ifs.' "[4]

Motivating action

The overriding purpose of a sales letter is to get the reader to do something. Many consumer products sold through the mail simply ask for a check—

in other words, an immediate decision to buy. On the other hand, big-ticket and more complex items frequently ask for just a small step toward the final buying decision, such as sending for more information or authorizing a call by a sales representative.

Aim to get the reader to act as soon as possible.

Try to persuade readers to take action, whatever it is, right away. You need to convince them that they must act now, perhaps to guarantee a specific delivery date. If there's no particular reason to act quickly, many sales letters offer discounts for orders placed by a certain date or prizes or special offers to, say, the first 500 people to respond. Others suggest that purchases be charged to a credit card or be paid off over time. Still others offer a free trial, an unconditional guarantee, or a no-strings request card for information, all in an effort to overcome readers' natural inertia.

CHOOSING THE FORMAT AND MAILING LIST

As mentioned earlier, sales letters do not stand alone. Instead, they are part of a package of materials and, much more, part of a campaign to market a product or idea.

Direct-mail packages

Direct-mail packages traditionally have five elements, all coordinated to reinforce the central selling point.

Traditionally a direct-mail package has five elements: (1) outer envelope telegraphing a sales message, (2) multipage sales letter, (3) brochure (usually in color), (4) order blank, and (5) postage-paid return envelope. A postage-paid order card sometimes takes the place of the order blank and return envelope. And sometimes other elements are included, such as samples or small gifts, catalogs, invitations, coupons, plastic "credit cards," and a short folded note "for those who have decided not to buy at this time." All these pieces should emphasize the same theme and be written in the same style and tone. Of course, the information in all elements should be consistent, although they should not merely repeat the same message.

An alternative to the traditional package is a self-mailer, a single piece of cleverly folded paper that both conveys a message to the reader and carries the order back to the original sender. Another format is the simulated telegram or invitation, which may entice recipients into reading the message.

Personalization of sales letters is not always cost-effective.

Very often, personalized letters are more effective than those addressed to, say, Occupant or Office Manager. However, people have become accustomed to personalization, and it is expensive. So before using it, determine whether the cost is justified by test-mailing letters with and without personalized messages.

In sales letters, use visual emphasis to keep the reader's attention.

Advertising professionals seem to agree that a longer letter is more effective than a short one, because it provides plenty of room for the specific information that will convince a reader to accept your message. Most sales letters are four pages long. However, because very few recipients have the patience to read all of a long letter, attention-getting devices such as underlining, indenting, and colored type are used to help them find the points of greatest interest. Enclosures give necessary details about the product too.

Mailing lists

Direct mail is an effective means of reaching a specialized audience.

Direct mail is especially useful for organizations trying to reach special groups of people. For example, perhaps you are trying to market expensive exercise equipment. Although exercise and fitness have become important to large segments of the public, television and magazine advertising is very expensive and scatters the message to many people who may not be interested in exercise or who may not be willing to spend much money for it. The secret is to find the people who would definitely be interested in hearing about your product.

A key to direct-mail success is to choose the right kind of mailing list.

Fortunately, you can rent, buy, or create a mailing list that focuses on people who buy certain products, subscribe to certain magazines, belong to certain organizations, and so on. Three types of direct-mail lists exist:

- *House lists* are compiled from the rolls of previous customers and even those who have inquired about the company's product. This is often the best type of list, because the people on it tend to be receptive to the company (assuming it has cultivated their goodwill).
- *Compiled lists* are taken from easily obtained sources of data, such as automobile registration lists or the telephone book. Compiled lists

CHECKLIST FOR SALES LETTERS

A. Planning the Direct-Mail Package

- ☐ 1. Determine the specific purpose of the mailing.
- ☐ 2. Define selling points and consumer benefits.
- ☐ 3. Analyze the audience, using demographic and psychographic information if available.
- ☐ 4. Plan the approach and format.
  - ☐ a. Determine the appeal, remembering that the most potent appeals relate to making money, saving money, saving time, or avoiding effort.
  - ☐ b. Write a sales letter that is long enough to present all necessary information.
  - ☐ c. Use short paragraphs, underlining, handwritten notes, bullets, color, and so on to make the letter visually appealing.
  - ☐ d. Include several enclosures to improve response.
  - ☐ e. Enclose or offer a free sample to demonstrate your product.
  - ☐ f. Telegraph your main appeal on the envelope.
- ☐ 5. Pretest every element of your package.

B. Attention

- ☐ 1. Design a positive opening that awakens in the reader a favorable association with the product.
- ☐ 2. Promise a benefit to the reader.
- ☐ 3. Write an opening that is appropriate, fresh, honest, interesting, specific, and relevant to the central selling point.
- ☐ 4. Keep the first paragraph short, preferably two to five lines, sometimes only one.
- ☐ 5. Design an attention-getting opening that uses any of the following techniques: significant fact about the product, solution to a problem, special offer or gift, testimonial, stimulation of the senses or emotions, reference to current events, action picture, startling fact, agreeable assertion, comparison, event or fact in the reader's life, problem the reader may face, quotation.

C. Interest

- ☐ 1. State information clearly, vividly, and persuasively, and relate it to the reader's concerns.
- ☐ 2. Develop the central selling point.
- ☐ 3. Feature the product in two ways: physical description and consumer benefits.
  - ☐ a. Interweave benefits with a physical description, or place benefits first.
  - ☐ b. Describe the objective details of the product: size, shape, color, scent, sound, texture, and so on.
  - ☐ c. Through psychological appeals, present the sensation, satisfaction, or pleasure your reader will gain, translating the product or

provide many names, but often they are too general to target interested parties. Selling exercise equipment by mailing promotional literature to every name in the telephone book, for example, would not be cost-effective; literature about tax-preparation services, however, might well be sent to every name in the phone book.

- *Mail-response lists* are like house lists, except that they come from other companies. Usually direct competitors do not trade mail-response lists; however, list brokers often accumulate competitors' lists and make them available temporarily or for a certain number of mailings. Mail-response lists are valuable because they contain the names of people who have responded to direct mail in the past.

Direct Mail List Rates & Data, published by Standard Rate and Data Service, tells who has lists for rent or sale. Columbia Record & Tape Club (Columbia House), for example, has 1,135,745 active members and rents their names for $60 per thousand. Its list can be subdivided by listening preference (country and western, jazz, and so forth), by ZIP code, by state, or by any one of a host of other factors.

service into the fulfillment of needs and desires.
- ☐ d. Blend cold facts with warm feelings.

D. Desire

- ☐ 1. Enlist one or more appeals to support the central selling point.
  - ☐ a. Provide one paragraph of desire-creating material in a one-page letter with descriptive brochure; provide several paragraphs if the letter itself is two or more pages long, with or without an enclosed brochure.
  - ☐ b. Emphasize reader use and benefits.
  - ☐ c. If the product is valued mainly because of its appearance, describe its physical details.
  - ☐ d. If the product is machinery or technical equipment, describe its sturdiness of construction, fine crafting, and other technical details in terms that help readers visualize themselves using it.
  - ☐ e. Include technical sketches and meaningful pictures, charts, and graphs, if necessary.
- ☐ 2. Anticipate and answer the reader's questions and objections.
- ☐ 3. Use an appropriate form of proof.
  - ☐ a. Include facts about users' experience with the product, including verifiable reports and statistics from users.
  - ☐ b. Provide names (with permission only) of other satisfied buyers and users.
  - ☐ c. Present unexaggerated testimonials from persons or firms that are users of the product and whose judgment the reader respects.
  - ☐ d. Provide the results of performance tests by recognized experts, testing laboratories, or authoritative agencies.
  - ☐ e. Offer a free trial.
  - ☐ f. Offer a guarantee.
  - ☐ g. Refer to samples if they are included.
- ☐ 4. Note enclosures in conjunction with a selling point.

E. Action

- ☐ 1. State clearly the action you desire.
- ☐ 2. Provide specific details on how to order or specific information on how to reach your place of business.
- ☐ 3. Make action easy through the use of a mail-back reply card, preaddressed envelope, phone number, or promise of a follow-up call or visit.
- ☐ 4. Offer a special inducement to act: time limit, special price for a limited time, premium for acting before a certain date, free gift for buying, free trial, no obligation to buy but more information or a suggested demonstration, easy payments with no money down, credit card.
- ☐ 5. Supply a final consumer-benefit plug.
- ☐ 6. Include a postscript conveying an important sales point (if desired for emphasis).

PREPARING COLLECTION MESSAGES

People have many reasons for not paying bills; give debtors the benefit of the doubt as long as reasonably possible.

The causes of overdue accounts are as varied as the individuals and companies they represent. Once in a while, the bill may truly be lost in the mail or misfiled. A few people mistakenly borrow more than they can possibly repay. Some have an unforeseen difficulty that makes timely repayment a problem. Still others are irresponsible about paying bills, dissatisfied with their purchase, or temporarily negligent. But luckily for the writers of collection letters, most individuals and businesses value their good name and credit rating and respond quickly to reminders and inquiries.

THE COLLECTION CONTEXT

Your dual goal in sending collection messages:

- Collect what is owed
- Maintain goodwill

The purpose of the collection process is to maintain goodwill while collecting what is owed. Three factors should influence decisions about how to achieve these twin goals:

- The amount of money owed, the time elapsed, the nature of the credit agreement, and the creditor's attitude
- The debtor's values, feelings of self-esteem, and attitudes toward financial responsibility
- The debtor's ability to solve the problem and withstand external and internal pressures

A debtor's response is likely to be emotional, especially when the debtor is conscientious, so use tact.

Credit is a sensitive issue. Ironically, the more the customer agrees with the justice of your claim, the more likely he or she is to react defensively. The true "deadbeat" expects to be dunned and has little reaction to requests for payment; but a conscientious customer is embarrassed about such a slip. In such an emotional state, the customer may resort, consciously or unconsciously, to blaming you for the problem, procrastinating, avoiding the situation altogether, or reacting aggressively. Your job is to neutralize those feelings by accentuating the positive: the benefits of complying with your request for payment.

Positive appeals are usually more effective than negative ones.

Here are a few examples of positive appeals:

- *Sense of pride.* "A good credit rating is something to be proud of. It isn't acquired overnight. Send in your payment today, and your credit standing with us will remain unblemished."
- *Need to belong.* "We want you back in the fold. Send us your payment today, and we will continue uninterrupted service."
- *Sense of fair play.* "We special-ordered your tools when you needed them. You know you can depend on us. We also depend on you to send in your payment today."
- *Need to follow rules.* "We supplied you with the products you required. You agreed to pay for them. Please send in your payment in the return envelope."
- *Recognition of mutual effort.* "If you're having budget problems, why not let us help? After all, our business is to help people solve their financial needs. Please let us know the reason for the delay so we can suggest a solution to the problem."

LEGAL ALERT

How to Write Collection Letters That Conform to the Law

Writing a collection letter is tricky not only because of the sensitivities of the recipient but also because of federal and state laws governing collections. The Fair Debt Collection Practices Act of 1978 outlines a number of restrictions on collection procedures. You may not, for example,

- Falsely imply that a lawsuit has been filed.
- Contact the debtor's employer or relatives about the debt.
- Communicate to other persons that the person is in debt.
- Harass the debtor (although definitions of harassment may vary).
- Use abusive or obscene language.
- Use defamatory language (such as calling the person a "deadbeat" or a "crook").
- Intentionally cause mental distress.
- Threaten violence.
- Communicate by postcard (not confidential enough).
- Send anonymous C.O.D. communications.
- Misrepresent the legal status of the debt.
- Communicate in such a way as to make the receiver physically ill.
- Give false impressions, as by labeling the envelope "Tax Information."
- Misrepresent the message as a government or court document.

The law also delineates when you may contact a debtor, how many times you may call, and what information you must provide to the debtor (timely responses, accurate records, and understandable documents).

The purpose of this law and of related state laws is to protect people from unreasonable persecution and harassment by debt collectors. Debtors who feel that this law has been violated may sue for damages.

That doesn't mean you can't be tough in collection letters, though. As long as what you state is true and lawful, it cannot be construed as harassment or misrepresentation. For instance, you're well within your rights to say, "If you don't pay this amount by June 20, we will take you to court."

1. Suppose that a client has owed your firm $6,000 for over a year. The client doesn't deny that the money is due, and evidence suggests that the firm is able to pay. Yet you have tried repeatedly, with no success, to collect your money. It appears that the client is simply unethical. You have decided to write one last letter before turning the matter over to your attorney. What are some of the things you might say in your letter? What things should you avoid saying?

2. Interview a representative from a local collection agency. Ask for copies of some of the standard collection letters. What, if anything, has the agency done to change its letter writing practices in light of the 1978 federal law?

- *Need for closure.* "You agreed to make your payments according to the schedule we worked out together. If you send us your check today, the matter will be settled and your credit protected."

If positive appeals fail, you may need to point out the actions legally available to you.

If positive appeals fail, you may have to consider a negative appeal, which stresses the unpleasant consequences of not acting rather than the benefits of acting. Still, it's not only ineffective but illegal to use abusive or threatening language or to harass the customer. Remembering that persuasion is the opposite of force, continue to use a polite and businesslike tone. But you may point out some of the actions legally available to you:

- Reporting the delinquent customer to a central credit agency
- Repossessing the purchased item
- Demanding the surrender of collateral put up to secure the loan
- Turning the account over to a collection agency
- Engaging the services of a lawyer and taking the matter to court

Indirect negative consequences, such as embarrassment and inconvenience, are also associated with these actions.

Don't forget that your real aim is to persuade the customer to make the payment. Thus your best approach is to try to maintain the customer's goodwill so the two of you can cooperate to solve the problem.

THE COLLECTION SERIES

In a well-managed company, past-due accounts are flagged early (often by computer), and simple reminders (often form letters) are sent out immediately. As the past-due period lengthens, a series of collection letters reflecting the increasing seriousness of the problem is sent to the customer at predetermined intervals.

Steps in the collection series:

- Notification
- Reminder
- Inquiry
- Urgent notice
- Ultimatum

The typical collection series includes a notification, reminder, inquiry, urgent notice, and ultimatum. Usually, only the first step or two is required for a simple oversight or temporary problem on the part of a debtor who normally pays bills; the latter steps are usually reserved for those who deliberately refuse to accept responsibility for a debt. At these later stages, the customer's past credit and buying history, the amount of money owed, and the customer's overall credit rating determine the content and style of collection messages.

Not all creditors follow exactly the same sequence for all debtors; some may, for instance, start with a notification, progress to a reminder, and then jump to an ultimatum. However, creditors with every reason to believe that the debtor will eventually pay usually go through every step (perhaps sending a few letters at each stage) and allow more time between the steps.

The timing of collection messages is important but varies widely. Often the reminder is sent a week or ten days after the due date, but the ultimatum may be sent anytime from weeks to months after the original due date.

Notification

The standardized notification is a sign of trust.

Most creditors send bills to customers on a regular schedule, depending on the terms of the credit agreement. Typically, this standard notification is a form letter or statement, often computerized, stating clearly the amount due, the date due, the penalties for late payment, and the total amount remaining to be paid. The standardized form, far from being an insult to the recipient, indicates the creditor's trust that all will go according to plan.

Reminder

The reminder notice, which still assumes only a minor problem, may be a standardized form or an informal message.

If the payment has not been received within a few days after the due date, most creditors send out a reminder. Again, a standardized letter is reassuring.

A reminder notice should be written under the assumption that some minor problem has delayed payment—in other words, that the customer has every intention of paying and needs only to be reminded. The tone should not be too serious:

As of October 1, we still hadn't received your September payment of $197.26. Has the payment been overlooked? Please check your records.

Using a different strategy, some companies send out a copy of the unpaid bill at this stage, with a handwritten note or preprinted stamp or sticker indicating that payment has not yet been received.

Inquiry

The inquiry
- Assumes that something unusual is preventing payment
- Is personalized
- Avoids any suggestion of customer dissatisfaction

As frustrating as it may be to send out a reminder and still get no response, the creditor cannot yet assume that the customer plans to ignore the debt, especially if the customer has paid bills promptly in the past. Thus the inquiry message must avoid accusations. However, the time has passed for assuming that the delay is merely an oversight; instead, you may now assume that some unusual circumstance is preventing payment:

> Because you're a valued customer who's been conscientious about paying bills on time, Ms. Jablonski, I'm wondering why we haven't received your September payment of $197.26. Is there a problem we should know about?
>
> Please send us your payment right away or phone me at 555-4495 to discuss your situation. We want to help you fulfill your obligations.

Notice that this letter uses a name. Personalization at this stage is appropriate, because you are asking the customer to work out an individualized solution. Notice also that the letter avoids any suggestion that the customer might be dissatisfied with the purchase. Instead, it emphasizes the reader's obligation to communicate about the problem and the creditor's willingness to discuss it. The inclusion of the writer's name and a phone number is very helpful in motivating a response at this stage.

Urgent notice

An urgent notice
- Might be signed by a top company official
- Might indicate the negative consequences of noncompliance
- Should leave an opening for payment without loss of face

This stage represents a significant escalation. The purpose here is to convey your desire to collect the overdue payment immediately and your willingness to get serious, although you want to avoid any overt threats. To communicate a sense of urgency, you may need to resort to a letter signed by a top official in the company or to a negative appeal. However, an urgent notice should still leave an opening for the debtor to make a payment without losing face:

> I was very surprised this morning when your file reached my desk with a big tag marked OVERDUE. Usually I receive customer files only when a serious problem has cropped up.

An attention getter focuses on the unusual circumstances leading to this letter.

> Opening your file, I found the following facts: Your order for five cases of Panza serving trays was shipped six months ago. Yet we still haven't received the $232.70 due. You're in business too, Mr. Rosen, so you must realize that this debt needs to be paid at once. If you had a customer this far behind, you'd be equally concerned.

The recipient is reminded of the order. Personalization and an attempt to emphasize common ground may motivate the reader to respond.

> Please see that a check for $232.70 is mailed to us at once. Or if you need to work out an alternate plan for payment, call me now at (712) 693-7300.

The preferred action is spelled out; an option is also suggested in case of serious trouble.

> Sincerely,
>
> Artis Knight
> Vice President

The signature of a ranking official lends weight to the message.

A well-written urgent notice has a good chance of persuading customers who still view themselves as responsible and trustworthy. At this stage, a telephone call backing up your written message may also get a promise to pay. However, the irresponsible debtor is unlikely to be swayed by anything less than an ultimatum.

Ultimatum

An ultimatum

- Should state the exact consequences of nonpayment
- Must avoid any hint of defamation or harassment
- Need not take a personal, helpful tone

Some people's finances are in such disorder that you won't get their attention until this stage. But do not send an ultimatum unless you intend to back it up and are well supported by company policy. Even then, maintain a polite, businesslike manner and avoid defaming or harassing the debtor.

By setting down on paper the precise consequences of not paying the bill, you can encourage debtors to reevaluate their priorities. You are no

CHECKLIST FOR COLLECTION MESSAGES

A. Effective Collections

- ☐ 1. Reflect in your message the fact that you are communicating with a person, not with an account number.
- ☐ 2. Employ a tactful, courteous "you" attitude, coupled with firmness and patience.
- ☐ 3. Assume that the customer honestly wants to pay as agreed.
- ☐ 4. Balance your two main goals—collecting the money and retaining the customer's goodwill—because too much emphasis on one reduces the chance of achieving the other.
- ☐ 5. Keep communication between collector and debtor open.
- ☐ 6. Focus on only one appeal in each letter.
  - ☐ a. Use positive appeals—cooperation, fair play, and pride—if possible.
  - ☐ b. Use negative appeals—self-interest and fear—after positive appeals have failed.
- ☐ 7. Avoid giving the debtor any reason for not paying you—for example, by writing "Your company has had a lot of problems this year, but. . . ."
- ☐ 8. Take the debtor's past behavior into account when deciding on the timing of collection messages.
  - ☐ a. Allow generous time intervals for a customer with a good credit record.
  - ☐ b. Shorten intervals for a customer who has earned the reputation of being slow.
- 9. Regardless of the stage in the collection procedure, clarify the amount due and the account number.
- ☐ 10. Include an easy-action envelope, postpaid, for every stage.

B. Collection Stages

- ☐ 1. At every stage, make it easy for the debtor to respond.
  - ☐ a. Clarify the account number and the amount due.
  - ☐ b. Include an easy-action envelope, postpaid.
- ☐ 2. Send out an initial notification.
  - ☐ a. Provide details on how much is owed, when it's due, where it should be sent, and what happens if it isn't paid on time.
  - ☐ b. Use a standard, impersonal format to avoid implying that anything is out of the ordinary.
- ☐ 3. In the reminder stage, provide a routine, direct request to jog the customer's memory.
  - ☐ a. Present the main question or subject first, then explain (when necessary), and follow up with a request for action.
  - ☐ b. Assume the payment is delinquent because of customer oversight.
  - ☐ c. Subordinate sales material or humorous gimmicks to the main goal: collecting the debt.
  - ☐ d. Include a duplicate copy of the original bill, perhaps stamped "Reminder" or "Past Due," with a short note (usually a form) specifying the amount, due date, late charge, and account number.

longer interested in hearing why it has taken them so long to respond; you are interested in putting your claim at the top of their list. The tone of the ultimatum need not be so personal or individualized as the inquiry or urgent notice. At this stage, you are in a position of justified authority and should no longer be willing to return to an earlier stage of communication and negotiation. For example:

On September 2, 1988, we shipped a standard assortment of consumer publications to City News (invoice number CN3-0014). Your application for credit was approved because of the credit references you supplied.

Under our usual terms, we sent a statement for $757.93, due October 3. Although we were concerned when we didn't receive payment by that date, we assumed there was some oversight. After all, you had a history of paying debts promptly.

- ☐ 4. In the inquiry stage, provide a personalized message with an inside address and a salutation with the customer's name.
  - ☐ a. Assume that something unusual has happened and that for some reason unknown to you the customer cannot or does not want to pay.
  - ☐ b. Employ a positive tone.
  - ☐ c. Avoid suggesting that reader dissatisfaction with your goods or services might be responsible for the late payment.
  - ☐ d. Demonstrate a genuine willingness to help.
  - ☐ e. Attract attention in the first paragraph with a reader-benefit theme: something beneficial, pleasant, interesting, and/or important to the reader.
  - ☐ f. Include in the body of the letter facts, figures, and/or reasons why the customer will benefit by doing as requested.
  - ☐ g. Leave the reader with alternatives that allow her or him to recover from the transaction with dignity intact.
  - ☐ h. Provide for easy action.
- ☐ 5. In an urgent notice, convey the seriousness of the situation.
  - ☐ a. Assume that the customer must pay.
  - ☐ b. Phrase the letter to retain the customer's goodwill and future business (although probably for cash), if possible.
  - ☐ c. Employ the strongest appeal—fear—by mentioning the unfortunate consequences of collection enforcement.
  - ☐ d. Tell the customer that you would prefer not to take this drastic action but (because of obligations to credit reporting agencies and company procedures) you must do so unless the debtor pays or explains.
  - ☐ e. Tell the customer that, by not paying, she or he is likely to lose credit privileges, goods or services not paid for, additional money or property, reputation, and self-respect.
  - ☐ f. Employ urgent language.
  - ☐ g. Insist on immediate payment, and set a date by which you must receive it.
  - ☐ h. To protect yourself from legal problems, state facts correctly, make no malicious or defamatory accusations, and send messages in sealed envelopes addressed to the debtor personally.
  - ☐ i. Offset the negativity of an appeal to fear with at least one positive appeal, to give the debtor a chance to avoid the drastic action and extra costs.
  - ☐ j. Arrange for the letter to be signed by a higher executive, such as a vice president or even the president (if desirable).
- ☐ 6. In an ultimatum, you may resort to a bad-news message.
  - ☐ a. Make the action request firm, and be definite about the amount to be sent and the place to which it should be sent.
  - ☐ b. Be polite, businesslike, and impersonal.
  - ☐ c. Put into effect any actions that you have stated you will take.

Over the past three months we've tried repeatedly to get you to send a check for $757.93. So far, we have had only your oral agreement to pay. Ms. Park in our credit department phoned you, as you'll recall. At that time you assured her a check would be mailed to us at once.

No longer can we accept such assurances. If we don't receive payment in full within the next five days, we will have to turn your account over to a collection agency.

To save embarrassment and a black mark on your permanent credit record, do mail your check today.

This letter outlines the steps that have already been taken, implying that the drastic action to come is the logical follow-up. Although earlier collection messages were based on persuasion, this one is essentially a bad-news letter.

If a letter like this doesn't yield results, the only remaining remedy is actually to begin legal collection procedures. As a final courtesy, you may wish to send the debtor a notice of the action you are about to take. By maintaining until the bitter end your respect for the customer, you may still salvage some goodwill.

SUMMARY

The purpose of a persuasive message is to influence attitudes and actions. Persuasive techniques are especially important for an audience that may not completely agree with you or gain any direct benefits from doing as you ask.

You can motivate an audience to do as you wish by using the AIDA plan for organizing persuasive messages: attention, interest, desire, action. The benefits of complying with your request should be stressed.

Persuasive messages are used in many business contexts, including requests for action and requests for adjustment of charges. In preparing a sales letter, highlight a major feature and related benefit of the product that's being promoted; in the close, make a response easy. Debt-collection letters also follow the AIDA plan.

COMMUNICATION CHALLENGES AT *NEWSWEEK*

Stephen Bernard, *Newsweek*'s circulation promotion director, has two diverging roles. On the one hand, he guides and evaluates the creative efforts of copywriters, most of whom are not *Newsweek* employees. On the other hand, he is part of the bureaucracy, working within channels to get the resources he needs.

Individual Challenge: Stephen needs your help with one bureaucratic battle. In the past couple of years, he has occasionally noticed some strange results in the test mailings conducted by the circulation promotion department: no clear-cut preference for one package or premium. He thinks these results might signify the emergence of a "new generation" that does not find any of the traditional devices particularly exciting. Just as baby boomers forged their own distinctive identity, Stephen feels, so are young people who grew up in the 1970s and 1980s. If *Newsweek* is to make inroads with this group, Stephen has to find out more about its needs, interests, and concerns.

He assigns you the task of writing a memo to Pat Wilson, director of market research, with the goal of persuading her to conduct a special study. Pat, of course, has plenty of her own work to do, but Stephen has already drafted a survey and has some ideas about the makeup of the sample. If Pat would just provide some guidance and some resources for conducting the study, it could be done quickly and inexpensively, and Stephen could make some breakthroughs in his own area of expertise.

Team Challenge: It's time again for the circulation promotion department to devise a new direct-mail package. Stephen wants to come up with some ideas that will appeal to the "new generation" of young people who have succeeded the baby boomers. You and the other copywriters that he calls in are asked to discuss the needs of this group and to settle on the strongest appeal that addresses those needs. Then you are to construct a sales letter based on that appeal. Don't forget that the objective of the letter is to get new subscribers for *Newsweek*. As an incentive, subscribers are being offered a 10 percent discount on the magazine and a one-time "credit card" for a 10 percent discount on the lowest fare available on any flight originating and ending in the United States or Canada.

QUESTIONS FOR DISCUSSION

1. "Persuasion is like rowing upstream against the current of an audience's attitudes." What does this sentence mean?
2. If you are genuinely angry about an unsatisfactory business situation, should you show this anger? Why or why not?
3. How can a business writer attain credibility?
4. Why is it sometimes necessary to use persuasive techniques in memos?
5. What is the difference between a complaint letter and a persuasive claim or request for adjustment?
6. What is the difference between a selling point and a benefit? Give an example.
7. What sorts of attention-getting devices used in sales letters might be appropriate in memos and other types of persuasive letters?
8. How should the issue of price be handled in a sales letter?
9. Why is it important to write collection letters that maintain goodwill while collecting what is owed?
10. What are some positive appeals that writers of collection letters employ?

DOCUMENTS FOR ANALYSIS

Read Documents 9.A through 9.D, and then (1) analyze the strengths and/or weaknesses of each numbered sentence and (2) revise each document so it follows this chapter's guidelines.

DOCUMENT 9.A

(1) We really appreciate your taking advantage of our two-day weekend seminar on "Accounting Fundamentals for the Small Businessperson." (2) I want to express my thanks to you for enrolling.

(3) We'd like to offer an even broader range of courses. (4) We want to grow and know that we can do so only if we satisfy the needs of our customers and offer them the benefits they truly desire.

(5) Please take just a few minutes of your time to fill out the enclosed card and place it in the mail. (6) It's crucial that we know whether you were happy with the seminar you took from us, and we'd appreciate your help, although it may seem like an unimportant thing.

(7) We are looking forward to conducting more seminars. (8) There will even be one next month--hope to see you there!

DOCUMENT 9.B

(1) It's United Way time again. (2) We need somebody to head up the drive. (3) Could you possibly take on the job?

(4) Serving as the chairman shouldn't take too much of your time. (5) You have to attend a couple of meetings with the United Way people downtown, but they generally buy you lunch. (6) You will be provided with pledge cards to pass out to our employees, and you will be briefed on techniques for motivating people to donate to the United Way.
(7) The biggest part of the job is taking the pledge cards around to all the employees and giving them a little sales pitch. (8) After a couple of days, you go around again and collect the cards. (9) Some companies have contests and skits to boost participation, but you don't have to go to all that trouble if you don't want to.

(10) Last year, Harry Huntley did a very fine job. (11) He had to twist a few arms, but he managed to achieve 100 percent participation. (12) Although he doesn't want to run the campaign again, he says that he will be willing to give you a hand with some of paperwork, which can get a little confusing if you've never done it before.

(13) As you know, the president is trying to build better relations between the company and the community. (14) He views the United Way Campaign as an important vehicle for projecting a positive image to civic and community leaders, who are deeply committed to surpassing last year's record-breaking campaign and who are counting on the active participation of the corporate community. (15) If you do a good job, he is sure to be impressed.

(16) It would be appreciated if you could get back to me about this immediately. (17) If you can't do the job, I'll need to find someone else as soon as possible.

DOCUMENT 9.C

(1) We have developed a revolutionary new fertilizer that can easily be applied to lawns to keep them green and weed-free during the summer months with a minimum of effort. (2) For just pennies, our trained experts will make weekly applications (in liquid form) of our fantastic fertilizer that kills weeds and strengthens the fibers of the roots. (3) It works in both shady and sunny areas and particularly well in your climate zone!

(4) Green-Gro works in any kind of climate and should not harm pets or birds, although it's poisonous to people (keep kids away). (5) All you have to do is water your lawn and keep the grass cut, and we will do all the rest to ensure that you have a green lawn for the entire season! (6) We look forward to having your business and trust that you'll want to purchase many of our other excellent lawn products.

(7) Please fill out the enclosed coupon and avail yourself of the "early-bird discount" of 25 percent off the prices we regularly charge.

DOCUMENT 9.D

(1) Even though you've been delinquent with your payment this past month, we have always been happy to serve you in any way. (2) Thanks for being one of our oldest customers.

(3) In the past, we have always received your payment right on time, so we are somewhat surprised by your recent carelessness and delay. (4) However, be assured that we keep excellent records of all late accounts.

(5) If you have a legitimate gripe, please write to us telling us about it on the enclosed business reply card. (6) Otherwise we'll expect payment right away for your outstanding bill of $762.32.

(7) Thanks for cooperating with us regarding this most distressing matter.

DOCUMENT 9.E

Find a direct-mail package that contains a letter. Bring the package to class, along with answers to the following questions:

1. Who is the intended audience?
2. What are the demographic and psychographic characteristics of the intended audience?
3. What is the purpose of the direct-mail package? Has it been designed to obtain a sales lead, make a mail-order sale, obtain a charitable contribution, or do something else?
4. What kind of letter is included? Is it fully printed, printed with computer fill-in, or fully computer typed? Is the letter personalized? If so, how many times?
5. Did the writer use the AIDA plan? If not, explain how the letter is organized.
6. What needs are being appealed to?
7. What emotional appeals and logical arguments are given in the letter?
8. How many and what kinds of enclosures (supporting pieces such as brochures and order cards) are used?
9. Is there anything distinctive about the outer envelope in which the literature arrived?
10. Is the message in the letter and on the supporting pieces believable? Would the letter sell the product to you?
11. What selling points and consumer benefits are offered?
12. Is an unusual format used? Are eye-catching graphics used?

CASES

WRITING PERSUASIVE REQUESTS FOR ACTION

1. Sending out for some software: Request to borrow some valuable merchandise The Student Advisory Committee to the business department at your college has asked the administration for a course called "Software Packages for the Personal Computer." Students want guidance in selecting programs from the hundreds advertised, and they want hands-on experience in using some of them.

Their request was relayed to the chairman of the computer science department, who rejected the idea on the grounds that neither department could afford to buy the many software packages that such a course would demand.

As a member of the Student Advisory Committee, you think that this problem may be solvable. You have agreed to write to a producer of packaged software (Micropoint Software, 1400 Eucalyptus Hills Road, Santa Barbara, CA 93103) to see whether it will lend you samples for use in the course. The software could be protected against copying, and surely many students educated to use Micropoint programs would be inclined to purchase such programs for themselves. You phone Micropoint corporate headquarters and learn that Melissa Weintraub is vice president of marketing.

Your task: Write to Ms. Weintraub, inquiring about the feasibility of Micropoint lending to your college for one term the 23 software packages they currently produce.

2. A new life: Letter requesting a personal review of someone's credit history Your cousin Tina Johnston, knowing of your growing skill in writing business letters, has called on you for help. Tina recently separated from her husband, Michael, and is facing heavy relocation expenses as she establishes a new home for herself and her three-year-old daughter. Thus she has applied for credit at Bates Company, a large department store at 4800 Dickerson Street, Detroit, MI 48215.

Tina has a job as bookkeeper for Enterprise Glass Company, a position she has held for six years. Her monthly salary is $1,245. Rent on her new apartment is $395 a month, and Tina knows that she can support herself and her daughter without help from her estranged husband. But during the past few years of their marriage, Tina and her husband incurred several thousand dollars' worth of indebtedness, which remains outstanding. Tina's attorney believes that Michael is responsible for the full amount, because the purchases were made in his name and were chiefly for his use.

Nevertheless, Tina was turned down by Bates Company, which checked only "no credit history" on the form she received. Tina asked to see her credit report and learned that the full history of Michael's purchases has been recorded under her name. Tina plans to straighten out this record, but meanwhile she needs credit from Bates Company.

Your task: Draft a letter from Tina to the credit manager at Bates Company, explaining her situation and presenting a case for obtaining a credit account. Tina's new address is 404 Coplin Avenue, Apartment 3E, Detroit, MI 48215.

3. Zoned for golf: Letter to a zoning board from Jack Nicklaus Development Corp. Ever since you first held a club, you have loved the game of golf. After graduating from college, you turned your passion for the game into a career by landing a job with Jack Nicklaus Development Corp., which builds residential communities focused around golf courses designed by Mr. Nicklaus himself.

You are currently working on a development known as Country Club of the South, located just north of Atlanta. Mr. Nicklaus and his partner, J. Robert Sierra, have purchased 800 acres that they are developing into a community for 600 families. The development, aimed at affluent buyers, features a 200-acre golf course that will cost an estimated $14.5 million to build. The clubhouse alone has a $1 million furniture budget. Mr. Sierra, who serves as president of the company, has budgeted $45 million for the entire residential community, a lavish walled enclave protected 24 hours a day by a manned security gate. Lots are priced from $70,000 up, about 35 to 45 percent higher than residential land elsewhere in the vicinity. The project is expected to take about eight years to complete.

Although you and your co-workers are very enthusiastic about Country Club of the South, you are aware that the local zoning board may have reservations about the project. But you can't get under way until they rezone your land from agricultural to residential uses. On the basis of your experience with other developments, you anticipate that some members of the zoning board may be concerned about population growth associated with the development. Board members will want reassurance that you have considered the impact of your community on the environment, economy, roads, schools, and public facilities in the area. Additionally, some board members may question your plan to build a playground for rich golfers, preferring to see a more balanced mix of income groups in the area.

Your task: You have been asked to draft a letter that will go out to the local zoning board from Mr. Sierra, requesting that the property be rezoned from agricultural to residential purposes. Address it to Michael Lomax, Chairman, Board of Commissioners, 165 Central Avenue, Room 208, Atlanta, GA 30335. This is a preliminary letter. You do not expect the commission to grant your request without a formal hearing; your immediate purpose is to pave the way for approval by obtaining the necessary rezoning application forms, setting up a date when Mr. Nicklaus and Mr. Sierra can appear before the commission, and establishing a friendly relationship with the commission members.[1]

4. Drugs in the office: Memo requesting a balanced approach at Kansas City *Star* and *Tribune* The newsroom staff at the Kansas City *Star* and *Tribune* is outraged. The publisher, James Hale, has issued a memo announcing that the paper's owner, Capital Cities/ABC of New York, is waging war on drugs in the workplace. The parent company is planning to send drug-sniffing dogs to ferret out any illegal substances.

"This is insane," says one of the paper's leading reporters. "It's an invasion of privacy. They have no right to do this. Nobody here defends drug abuse on the job, but we don't deserve to be treated like criminals. You have to have 'probable cause' to search somebody's property."

Reaction to the memo is so negative that Mr. Hale agrees to consider an alternative to using dogs. But he insists on doing something to satisfy the management of Capital Cities/ABC, who want to create a drug-free company one way or another.

Other companies have the same goal. Nearly half of all Fortune 500 companies have programs to identify drug abusers and rehabilitate employees. Some companies limit their testing to job applicants, but many test their existing employees as well. The most common approach is to ask for urine samples on a random basis. A few companies resort to undercover operations. General Motors, for example, has used private undercover agents to identify employees who use or sell drugs on company premises. Those who are caught are fired and criminally prosecuted.

Such hard-nosed behavior is relatively rare, however. At most companies, the main concern is to help people with drug problems. Employees are encouraged to attend rehabilitation programs, which are often paid for by insurance benefits. Their paychecks continue while they are undergoing treatment, and when they are cured, they can return to their old jobs.

You are convinced that fighting drug abuse in the workplace is a good idea. But you think management should begin by deciding what they are trying to accomplish with the program: deterrence, punishment, or rehabilitation. As a first step toward creating a program that will satisfy everyone, you think the company should create a committee of employees and managers to develop guidelines for creating a drug-free workplace.

Your task: Draft a memo to Mr. Hale arguing on behalf of a drug-abuse program that will incorporate employee and management input.[2]

5. Please move your blimp: Letter requesting that Kodak stop flying its blimp in Fuji territory You are one of the few Americans working in the Tokyo office of Fuji Photo Film Co., having been recruited into a special training program aimed at building a corps of international managers. In the process of learning about Japanese language and culture, you have developed a deep respect for the Japanese, who seem adept at handling problems diplomatically.

Thus you are sympathetic when your boss, Hidenobu Miyata, the manager of Fuji's advertising department, walks into your office and points out your window. Hovering there is a large yellow blimp, adorned with the name of Fuji's archrival: KODAK. You are tempted to chuckle, but the look on Mr. Miyata's face tells you that this is no laughing matter. Kodak is making a big push into the Japanese film market, using the same advertising vehicle that Fuji employed when it began challenging Kodak in the United States a few years ago—namely, the blimp.

In hopes of soothing Mr. Miyata, you say, "You should be flattered that they are copying our approach. After all, Fuji was the official film company of the 1984 Olympics, and we flew our blimp over the games in Los Angeles. Kodak must have been quite upset."

Your task: Mr. Miyata doesn't feel so tolerant toward Kodak's incursions in Japan. He asks you to write a letter to a fellow American, the vice president and general manager of Kodak Japan, asking him to please move his blimp. The person's name is Albert L. Sieg, and his business address is Kodak Japan K.K.; Nishi-Shinbashi Mitsui Building; 1-24-14, Nishi-Shinbashi; Minato, Tokyo 105, Japan.[3]

6. A happier hospital: Memo asking a supervisor for additional funds Clarkson Memorial Hospital is the largest public hospital in your area, but it suffers from low employee morale and high turnover. As director of personnel, you know that the employees must take pride in Clarkson so they'll have a vested interest in the hospital's success. You would therefore like to establish an annual "Thanks to You" Day, which would feature employee picnics and awards. These festivities would encourage lower absenteeism and a greater commitment to job responsibilities, you believe. (A colleague of yours at Atlanta General Hospital found that such a program worked wonders, helping to decrease the turnover rate by 30 percent.)

Clarkson has been losing thousands of dollars each year through declining productivity, high absenteeism, and inefficient planning resulting from the hefty percentage of unfilled positions, nearly 25 percent at present. You believe the tab for "Thanks to You" Day would run around $17,000, a mere scratch on the hospital's multimillion-dollar budget. Alexandra Smith, director of Clarkson, has the authority to approve or refuse your request for these funds.

Your task: Write a persuasive memo to Alexandra Smith, explaining how your proposal can boost morale and productivity at Clarkson. Convince her that the money for "Thanks to You" Day will be well spent.

7. Store of the future: Memo lobbying for a new retailing concept at Murjani International Murjani International, a New York City fashion house, can claim a number of successes. The company introduced Gloria Vanderbilt jeans and turned an undiscovered fashion designer named Tommy Hilfiger into an overnight sensation. A more recent coup is an agreement with Coca-Cola to create and promote a line of clothing bearing the Coca-Cola logo.

Richard Hosp, Murjani's vice president of marketing, is your boss. He's given you the assignment of coming up with a captivating concept for retailing the Coca-Cola line through special boutiques within department stores as well as independent Coca-Cola clothing stores.

Initially, you pictured the stores with an ice-cream parlor motif, complete with formica counters and soda jerks in white hats. But your research showed that people identify Coke with the future, not the past. So with the "store of the future" in mind, you have now come up with some really revolutionary ideas. You picture the Coca-Cola clothing stores as being a cross between a video arcade and a cafeteria.

Twenty-four hours a day, pictures of the clothes will flash on a giant screen visible from the street through a wall of windows. Free-standing video terminals, similar to the automated teller machines used by banks, will stand outside. As people pass by, they can touch the screen and see the entire line of 125 styles in more detail. They can even insert a credit card to place an order.

As customers enter a store, they will see the giant screen on one wall and floor-to-ceiling bins of Coca-Cola clothes lining the other walls. By touching the screen on one of the video terminals placed inside the store, customers will be able to browse through the merchandise, checking out details like collar style, pocket design, price, fabric, sizes, and so on. The customer who wants to try something on will enter a "cafeteria" line and slide a stainless steel tray (with the Coke logo) around a high-tech counter, placing orders and receiving merchandise along the way.

You have tested this concept with your target market: teen-agers who grew up in the computer age. They are comfortable with video terminals, and they seem enthusiastic about the new store design.

Your task: Draft a memo explaining your ideas to Richard Hosp. Try to make a persuasive case for the "store of the future."[4]

8. Happy days may be here again: Letter persuading someone to sponsor a city event Times are tough. Roy Palmer ran for mayor of Everett, Washington, with the promise that, if elected, he would cut back on the "frills." He was elected, and one of his first official acts was to inform the public, through the press, that the city would no longer sponsor the annual Everett Feast. This event was initiated two mayors back by politicians of the other party and has grown to be a popular event. Rock, jazz, blues, and comedy groups perform, local restaurants set up tents and serve their specialties, and other shops sell wares from leased tables.

But no more. Although the past few Everett Feasts made a small profit, Roy Palmer points out that the city had to pay for the police protection and cleanup that were necessary. Taking these services into consideration, he argues that the Everett Feasts have been a drain on an already debt-ridden city government.

You are president of Fairs & Festivals, an independent consulting and organizing firm in Everett. For a substantial fee your organization has planned and managed the past few Everett Feasts. You booked the acts, negotiated with the restaurateurs and exhibitors, and then supervised the setup and operation of the ten-day event. It has been a mutually beneficial arrangement, and you would like to see it continue.

It occurs to you that the Everett Parks Department could sponsor this year's feast. The Parks Department maintains its own budget and is not subject to regulation from City Hall. The superintendent of parks, Carol Marine, is no great friend of the mayor, and she might appreciate the opportunity to sponsor this popular event through her department. The 37 acres of recreation fields that she controls provide adequate space for the 15,000 visitors per day needed to break even. They also provide enough space for parking and are convenient to existing bus services.

A feast thus modified would be smaller, with fewer acts, restaurants, and visitors needed to make a profit. But the spirit could remain, and the people of Everett would be keeping alive a happy traditional event.

Your task: Draft a letter to Carol Marine, whose office is at 2nd Avenue SE, Everett, WA 98204, asking her to sponsor this year's Everett Feast through the Parks Department. State your position in general terms, and encourage Ms. Marine to discuss the matter further with you.

9. A vote for short-time pay: Memo asking for approval from employees of Barrier Science & Technology As at many companies, business at the Port Jervis, New York, manufacturer ebbs and flows with orders. These cycles create considerable work for you, the company's personnel manager. During the upswings, you hire new people to handle the added business; during downswings, you lay people off to hold down your costs.

Currently Barrier is entering a downswing, and you face the unpleasant prospect of letting some workers go. However, you recently read about an alternative called short-time compensation. Instead of laying off workers during a temporary downturn, you could split the reduced workload among all your workers. Everybody would take a cut in hours and pay, but nobody would be out of a job. State unemployment compensation benefits would make up for some of the lost pay. In fact, with their state benefits and short-time pay, your workers could collect 90 percent of their current compensation for working a four-day week. And they would retain all their fringe benefits.

The biggest winners in a short-pay program are the newest workers, who would be the ones to be terminated under the traditional plan. The biggest losers are the senior employees, who would have to give up 10 percent of their pay to save the jobs of the others.

From the company's standpoint, short-time pay has one big advantage: You would save the expenses associated with hiring and training new workers when business turns up. On the negative side, the company has to bear the full cost of employee benefits during downswings in business. In addition, company payments to the state unemployment insurance system might increase. On balance, though, you believe that the company would be ahead financially if it adopted short-time compensation for the next three or four months, at which point you expect business to pick up again.

Your task: You have succeeded in convincing management to give the program a try. Now you face the job of convincing the workers. Write a memo explaining short-time pay and asking employees to vote on the issue by filling out a form and returning it to you within three days.[5]

10. Ruffled feathers: Letter lobbying the government to permit Hartz Mountain to import parakeets When you agreed to a transfer from headquarters in Harrison, New Jersey, to the Caribbean island of St. Lucia, you thought all you would have to contend with was tropical weather and parakeets. Little did you know that your employer, Hartz Mountain Corp., would get caught in a bird war between the U.S. parakeet industry and the government of St. Lucia.

It all started out innocently enough. The U.S. government, hoping to promote investment in the Caribbean basin, was highly enthusiastic when Hartz Mountain proposed to breed parakeets on St. Lucia, then import them duty free. Some exotic birds captured in the wild are quarantined for 30 days to make sure they won't spread avian diseases to the United States. But the government agreed that the St. Lucia parakeets would not need to be quarantined, because they would be raised in a special breeding facility and protected from disease.

Things were moving along beautifully until the U.S. parakeet industry got wind of the plan and fired off more than 800 angry letters to Congress. In their letters, the parakeet breeders contended that waiving the quarantine posed a serious danger to the domestic bird industry. According to the breeders, the St. Lucia parakeets could transmit diseases not only to other parakeets but also to turkeys and chickens.

The breeders were able to convince the U.S. Department of Agriculture to reimpose the 30-day waiting period on Hartz's birds. And you prepared to close down the Caribbean operation. But the Prime Minister of St. Lucia threatened to take the issue to a summit meeting of Caribbean leaders.

Hoping to avoid an international incident, the Agriculture Department decided to compromise. They agreed that the parakeets could escape the 30-day quarantine period if St. Lucia took certain measures to prevent bird diseases from spreading and infecting the parakeets—namely, quarantining all chickens imported to St. Lucia from Barbados.

When the Prime Minister of St. Lucia heard these terms, he was outraged, claiming that quarantining Barbados chickens was both ridiculous and impractical. He contended that the disease issue was a ruse and that the U.S. government was sacrificing St. Lucia's economic interests to satisfy a few parakeet breeders in Texas and Oklahoma who were afraid of a little competition.

Your task: As manager of the Hartz Mountain project in St. Lucia, you have been asked to write a letter to the U.S. Department of Agriculture protesting the quarantine of Barbados chickens. Try to convince the U.S. government that Hartz's parakeets should not be quarantined either. Address your comments to Mr. Franklin D. Lee, Caribbean Basin Area Officer, Foreign Agricultural Service, U.S. Department of Agriculture, Room 5084, South Agricultural Building, Washington, DC 20250.[6]

WRITING PERSUASIVE CLAIMS AND REQUESTS FOR ADJUSTMENT

11. Life's little hassles: Request for satisfaction It's hard to go through life in this world without becoming annoyed at the way things work. At some point, you have undoubtedly been dissatisfied with a product you've bought, the service you've received, or the action of some elected official or government body.

Your task: Write a three- to five-paragraph persuasive request expressing your dissatisfaction in a particular case. Specify the action you want the reader to take.

12. A temporary problem: Request for a sizable adjustment Your firm, Hernandez & Hernandez, Accountants, has had a good working relationship with Temps for Our Times, a firm that provides temporary office help. But problems have arisen. With quarterly tax reports coming due for a score of your clients, you requested three employees from Temps for Our Times: a CRT operator, someone who could operate a word processor, and a 65-wpm typist. Temps for Our Times reduces its charges slightly for full-week assignments; therefore, you requested each appointment for the entire week. You dealt with Bob Speller, the manager of the office, which is located at 35 White Heron Drive, Daytona, FL 32019.

If last week's service is any indication of the type of personnel that Temps for Our Times currently employs, you might be wise to switch firms. The CRT operator, Terri Hiller, was fine. She has been assigned to you before and each time has done all that was requested of her.

But Miller Sabat, the word processor, was unfamiliar with the coding and spent most of Monday learning to handle what he referred to as his "new toy." He started off Tuesday with a sharp bang, when he spilled coffee into the Lanier keyboard and shorted out the circuitry. (Damage from spilling coffee on the circuitry is not covered by your word-processor maintenance agreement. Repairs cost $125, and the smell of burnt insulation will be with you long after this bill is paid.) "Bet I know one fellow in this office who won't be asked back!" was Miller's running gag as he worked toward an early exit on Friday.

The typist could, in a manner of speaking, type 65 words a minute, but when asked to prepare errorless copy, her speed dropped to under half that. She worked through Thursday and then called in sick on Friday.

Temporary help is expensive. You were billed $1,050 ($375 for the CRT operator, $350 for the word processor, and $325 for the typist). Given the work of these three, you believe that an adjustment of a third from this contracted figure is in order. Bob Speller says only, "Send me the bill for the repairs to your word-processing unit, and I'll see what I can do." You decide to appeal this inadequate settlement to the president of the firm, Dorette Richards.

Your task: Request from Ms. Richards a one-third downward adjustment in the billing that you received from Bob Speller. Your job title is office manager.

WRITING SALES LETTERS

13. The $1,000 videotape ploy: Sales letter announcing the grand opening of a new Marshall Field's For the past three months, you have been planning "the grandest grand opening in the history of retailing." Your employer, Marshall Field & Company, based in Chicago, is expanding into San Antonio. You are responsible for seeing that the new store is promoted properly.

Your idea is to target people with money to spend on the new store's upscale merchandise. First you obtained a list of all the videocassette recorder owners in San Antonio and picked out 7,500 of them with the highest incomes. Then you made a videotape featuring scenes of San Antonio, interspersed with shots of Field's crystal department and diamond jewelry. You plan to send copies of the tape to the people on your list, along with a letter promoting the store and urging recipients to apply for a credit card.

Frankly, you consider your ploy a stroke of genius. But you have one major worry: What if nobody takes time to watch the videotape? To get around that problem, you decide to offer recipients a chance to win a $1,000 gift certificate. All they have to do is to correctly identify all the San Antonio landmarks on the tape.

Your task: Write a cover letter to go with the videotape. First, of course, you'll have to identify the features and benefits of your offer. In the letter, explain the videotape and the prize and announce the grand opening, scheduled for November 1. And don't forget to include a credit card application and a postage-paid return envelope.[7]

14. And a letter is born! Sales letter pulling together ideas generated by brainstorming The brainstorming session was called to develop ideas for a sales letter to be sent to retail stores in the greater Louisville, Kentucky, metropolitan area. Your firm is Jitney Deliveries; your service is local package delivery with price, speed, and personal attention that competitors cannot match. Drivers of your three jitneys keep in touch by mobile telephone so delivery routes can be adjusted during the day.

Here is an abridged transcript of the brainstorming session: "I don't see why everyone doesn't use our service. Who else actually gives you the delivery times you want? Other services just come when they want and dump the package on the porch if you're not home." . . . "The most important part of the letter is the first 12 words; that's where you have to hook them." . . . "Get the fixed price in there, exactly $2 for anything in the greater metropolitan area up to 10 pounds." . . . "The action part—probably we should give them a choice, either order our service right after reading the letter or send in a coupon for additional information. That way, we know who is interested in our service, and we can try again with them." . . . "Should we deliver this letter in our own jitneys, to show them how sharp we look?" . . . "Make it plain that we don't move stoves, refrigerators—maybe specify a 50-pound upper limit." . . . "And the prices for the heavy stuff should be set pretty high; we don't want to encourage the back breakers." . . . "I think the most important part of the letter is the close; we have to let them know exactly what kind of action they should take." . . . "We should anticipate their objections. Why deal with a new, unheard-of company when more established companies are around? It seems like the customer's attitude might be 'Why should we trust you with our jewels?' " . . . "This isn't going to be a letter; it's going to be a book! One page is enough. A full page, though." . . . "The mobile phones, so we can keep in touch with each other and plan routes during the day—isn't that our chief edge? Isn't that what we should stress?" . . . "O.K., right after the headline, let's pretend that we're answering the question 'What can your service do for me?' "

Your task: Draft the text of the sales letter.

15. Beginning with the bottlebag: Letter introducing products You met Ruby Kendall last month in Boston at the annual Kitchenware Convention and talked long enough to develop a first-name relationship. She owns Cook Smart, a retail outlet on Dorchester Road (no street number) in Niagara Falls, Ontario L2E 6V4. Her store generates annual sales of $220,000, carrying ordinary, high-quality kitchen items as well as unusual products. Anyone in Niagara Falls who is looking for an oyster shucker or a samovar looks first at Cook Smart. Ruby is creative, ambitious, and energetic; she likes golf and Mexican beer.

You carry a line of cloth and leather products, every piece handmade. You decide to approach Ruby first with the bottlebag, a cloth wine-bottle holder with a drawstring. It's handy for carrying wine to a picnic or a party; the drawstring secures the bottle and can hold an opener. The bottlebag comes in three colors: red with a designer logo, red with a three-colored stripe, or green with the same decorative stripe. It wholesales for $4.00 and retails for what the traffic will bear. It's unusual, attractive, well designed, made of washable suedecloth, and like all your products, can be monogrammed in old English style or script for $5.50. You decide to send Ruby a sample.

Once Ruby sees how well this product sells, you know that she will place orders for your distinctive children's and adults' quilted aprons, hot mitts, placemats, napkins, and more—but that's for later.

Your task: Write Ms. Kendall a sales letter that will encourage her to order a stock of your bottlebags.

16. "Why do I need an accountant?" Sales letter explaining accounting services to a nonbeliever Imagine that you have the following conversation with Lou Stanton, who owns Video to Go (a video rental store), 11523 N. Delaware, Indianapolis, IN 46280:

"What kind of accounting services do you use?" you ask.

"Someone comes in every March to do the taxes," Mr. Stanton says, "but that's all I need. I check the cash in the register each night against the register tape and make the deposits myself, and I order all the goods and pay the bills myself, so I don't need any outside help except at tax time."

"Have you ever thought of bringing someone in for an annual audit?"

"I don't think an audit would be worthwhile. What can an auditor tell me that I don't already know? I've got all the facts here."

"An auditor could prepare a statement of your financial position," you explain. "An audit done by an outsider gives you credibility if you need a loan on short notice. Also, an auditor might spot trends from year to year or sales patterns that you hadn't noticed. And by checking purchases against inventory and sales, an auditor could tell you if anyone's pilfering merchandise."

"Well, I don't know," Mr. Stanton says. "I might be interested, but I need to think about it."

Your task: Write a letter to send as a follow-up to Mr. Stanton, giving reasons for employing an outside accounting service for ongoing use, for a yearly audit, or for both.

PREPARING COLLECTION MESSAGES

17. A friendly reminder: Form collection letter from Sears, Roebuck & Co. You are sitting in your office in the Sears Tower in Chicago when your boss walks in and says, "I don't know what the world is coming to. Nobody seems to be paying their bills anymore. In all my years with Sears, we've never had such a high percentage of delinquent credit card accounts."

This is an unusual problem for Sears, which has always had one of the best collection rates in the country. Possible causes are many. In general, total consumer debt is higher than ever, and people in economically distressed areas (such as the farm belt) are having trouble repaying what they've borrowed. And then there's the crowded credit card market: In an attempt to increase their business, many credit card issuers are signing up people who don't really have the financial resources to handle the responsibility.

On the chance that Sears' collection methods might be partly at fault, your boss suggests revising the company's collection letters. The same form letters have been used for years.

Your task: Write a form letter reminding Sears' past-due accounts to pay their bills.[8]

18. The weeping willow follow-up: "Middle-stage" collection letter Many tree surgeons require cash payment immediately on completion of their work, but Cutter Tree Care has a different policy. Most of its work is done in the affluent communities of Austin, Texas, where people generally pay their bills. Furthermore, Cutter finds it most convenient to schedule work when the property owners may not be at home.

Bills are sent immediately after completion of the work, and three-fourths of the customers pay within 14 days. If payment has not been received by that time, a "friendly reminder" is sent, a brief note printed on letterhead with a picture of a sadly weeping willow tree on the bottom. If payment is not received within an additional 30 days, a "final notice" is sent, threatening legal action (which is taken) if the full amount due is not remitted within 14 days. Legal action has been taken in fewer than 4 percent of the cases, but given the expense in money and ill will, you have convinced Charlie Cutter that this figure is too high.

"Charlie," you say, "I think we'd get better results if we sent a middle-stage collection letter after the friendly reminder letter and before the final threat of legal action. We might not have to go to court so often if we could get people to agree to play fair."

The puzzled look on Charlie's face backs up his words: "Sorry. I'm not sure I know what you're talking about. Maybe you could write some kind of a model letter to show me what you mean."

Your task: Draft a form letter to be sent to nonpaying customers of Cutter Tree Care 30 days after the "friendly reminder" has been sent. The main thrust of the letter should be an appeal to fair play, but introduce other types of appeals if they seem helpful.

19. "Have no money": Last-ditch attempt to collect overdue bills When you signed on as part-time receptionist for David Cortez, D.D.S., you had no idea of the types of assignments you would get. Bill collecting has turned out to be one of them. Dr. Cortez usually refers all accounts more than 120 days past due to Medical Collectors, Inc. This agency keeps a commission of 50 percent of the first $100 it collects on an account and 35 percent of any amount over $100. Given the difficulty in collecting anything on accounts that old, the checks sent by Medical Collectors to Dr. Cortez are small and few.

You suggest to Dr. Cortez that a different approach might be more successful: seeking small monthly payments from those patients who are unable to settle their bills in full.

"O.K., you try it out," he answers, and he hands you the card for Billy Harris that he was about to send to Medical Collectors. Mr. Harris (1010 Shadrack Street, Houston, TX 77013) had a root canal job four months ago, for which Dr. Cortez billed him $450. Mr. Harris has simply returned the last bill with this scrawled note: "Have no money. Honest. Sorry. Sincerely, Billy."

Your task: Prepare for Dr. Cortez's signature a letter to Mr. Harris that will produce good results.

20. The stained couch: Final collection letter You stand politely at Dawn D'Arcy's front door, trying to reason with her through the screen. So far, you aren't having much luck. "You know why you won't repossess that couch?" she says. "The condition it's in, that's why. You should see what's been spilled on it—and all the cigarette burns. I owe $750 on the darn thing, but you couldn't get $100 for it."

You press on bravely: "You know, you still owe the full $750 whether we take back the couch or not."

"I can't pay what I don't have. You can't squeeze blood out of a whatchamacallit, you know what I mean?"

"O.K., so give me something to keep your account open. Let's say $50."

"Go home."

You try again: "How about $1? I don't want to turn your account over to a lawyer. Give me something, and we leave the lawyers off the case for a while."

"Go home. And take the couch with you if you want to. It's garbage. Just get off my property."

So much for the threat of repossession. You make a mental note to start repossession proceedings more promptly next time, but for the moment what Ms. D'Arcy says is true.

Back at the store, you decide that you have gone as far as you can with Ms. D'Arcy. Appeals to fair play, pride, and loss of credit standing haven't brought in a single payment, and Ms. D'Arcy has convinced you that repossession would be a waste of time.

Your task: Write one last letter to Dawn D'Arcy (1599 S. Kingston, Aurora, CO 80012), indicating that if she does not make a substantial payment on her account, you will turn it over to an attorney for full collection. Provide specific details. Sign as credit manager of Van Ness Furnishings.

PART FOUR

EMPLOYMENT MESSAGES

CHAPTER TEN

After studying this chapter, you will be able to

- Analyze your work skills and qualifications
- Find out what type of job and employer you want
- Identify your best prospects for employment
- Develop a strategy for "selling" yourself to these prospects
- Prepare an effective resume
- Write an application letter that gets you an interview

WRITING RESUMES AND APPLICATION LETTERS

Donald J. Greiner

COMMUNICATION CLOSE-UP AT PRICE WATERHOUSE

Donald J. Greiner has been with Price Waterhouse for 14 years and has been manager of human resources and administrative services in its Denver office since 1979. As the person in charge of recruiting for the accounting and consulting staff, Don uses a variety of avenues for finding good job candidates. "Like many major accounting firms, we have a very active campus recruiting program," he explains. "But we also run ads in newspapers and journals and occasionally use employment agencies or executive search firms. We also get referrals from our own staff, and we screen all the resumes that come in."

Don estimates that he receives 50 to 75 resumes with application letters every week. "Obviously, your chances of getting an interview from an unsolicited resume are pretty slim, but we're always looking for good people. If your qualifications match our needs, you'll be invited to come in, especially if we happen to be short-handed at the moment."

When an application arrives "over the transom," Don scans it quickly, looking for qualities that will separate the promising candidates from the clearly unqualified. "My initial impression is based on appearances," he confesses. "If your resume looks professional, you have a much better chance of selling yourself."

To find employees who can both do the job and fit in with the company, Price Waterhouse managers review application letters and resumes from vast numbers of job seekers.

Style is also important for making a good impression. "I tend to like crisp, concise language and a fairly simple sentence structure," Don says. "People who try to impress me with long, flowery sentences only make their applications more difficult to read. Another thing that helps is brevity. I'm more likely to read one or two pages than three or four.

"The best way to distinguish yourself from the pack is to display some knowledge of our firm," he says. "It's surprising how many people apply without knowing anything about us. If you want to make a good impression, address your letter and resume to a specific person. Make sure you have the right name and the right title, even if you have to phone first. I've been called everything from personnel manager to president of Price Waterhouse! Mistakes like those just show a lack of interest."

Next, check to see if there's a position available. "If there is, tailor your letter and resume to that position. And mention any contacts you have at the company. If a friend of yours works in one of our 81 offices, say so!" Don advises. "If you do, I get the idea that you know something about us. Better yet, do some research and say something specific about the reputation or performance or size of our firm."

Don recommends using the application letter to expand on your resume: "Resumes should be fact-oriented, but the cover letter can be used to convey your personality and style, the qualities that tell so much about you." Don also recommends that you use the letter to explain any points in your resume that could get a negative reaction. "For instance, tell me why you took 5½ years to earn a bachelor's degree. Explaining an item like this may help keep you in the running."

One more thing: If you're willing to relocate, state your reasons for wanting to make the change. "If you're writing from Boston," says Don, "I'd like to know why you want to relocate to Denver—specific reasons other than the job market. For example, maybe you have parents here or have visited the area. And if you're planning a trip to Denver, mention it, along with the specific dates. I'll be sure to respond in a timely manner."

Your application letter and resume won't get you a job, but they may get you through the initial screening process. "If you make them work for you," Don points out, "your resume and cover letter can get you an interview. They are more than a vehicle for presenting facts about your background. They are tangible evidence of your ability to communicate, and that's something we value very highly around here."

THINKING ABOUT YOUR CAREER

As Don Greiner points out, getting the job that's right for you takes more than sending out a few resumes. Planning and research are important if you want to make a good impression. The best way to begin is by analyzing what you have to offer: your skills, characteristics, values, and interests. Then you can identify employers that are likely to need someone with your qualifications.

ANALYZING WHAT YOU HAVE TO OFFER

To analyze what you have to offer:

1. List ten achievements in order of importance.
2. Look for a pattern in the skills that contributed to each achievement.
3. Ask a friend/relative what you're good at, and compare the answers with your own assessment.
4. List your employment qualifications, including education, work, and outside activities.
5. Ask a friend/relative to list four or five of your most obvious personal traits, and compare the answers with your own assessment.
6. List the things you liked best about work you've done before.
7. List your interests and hobbies.

What are your marketable skills? One way to find out is to jot down ten achievements over the years that gave you the most pride and satisfaction, whether they included learning to ski, taking a prize-winning photo, losing 12 excess pounds, tutoring a child in reading, or being editor of the school paper.

Which of these achievements is the most important to you? Rate them first, second, and so on in their order of importance. Then go back to the achievement that you rated first. Write down the specific skills that you feel went into this achievement. For example, leadership, speaking ability, and art/design talent may have been the skills that helped you coordinate a winning presentation to the college administration. Now do the same for each of the other nine achievements. Soon you will see a pattern of skills start to emerge. Which of these skills would you most enjoy using in your career? Which would be second, third, fourth, and so on?

Next, ask a friend or relative to make a list of your greatest abilities. Ask the person to be as honest and objective as possible. Have others evaluate your skills as well. Then compare their answers to your own assessment.

Now you are ready to analyze your employment qualifications: your educational preparation, work experience, activities, and achievements. What kinds of jobs have your education and work experience prepared you to do? Make a list of them. What have you learned from participating in volunteer work or class projects that could benefit you on the job? Other qualifications to consider are any offices you have held, awards or scholarships you have won, travel experiences, and fluency in languages other than English.

The next step is to take stock of your personal characteristics so you can determine the type of job you'll like best. Are you aggressive, a born leader? Or would you rather follow? Are you outgoing, articulate, great with people? Or do you prefer working in the background with ideas? Make a list of what you feel are your four or five most important qualities. Ask a relative or friend to rate your traits as well.

If you're having trouble figuring out your interests and capabilities, you might find out whether your college placement office or career guidance center offers any vocational testing services. Many campuses administer a variety of tests designed to help you identify your interests, aptitudes, and personality traits. Although these tests won't reveal the "perfect" job for you, they will help you focus on the types of work that best suit your personality.

Values are the things that are important to you.

Identifying your values will also help you discover the type of work that will satisfy you most. Values are those factors that give you satisfaction and happiness on the job—for example, helping others or being free to create your own ideas. Start by figuring out what you liked best about your last job or volunteer project. What seemed worthwhile about it? What did you get out of it? By learning which values are important to you, you can determine which types of work you'll find most rewarding in the future.

Finally, what are your interests and hobbies? Work can be fun, if it involves the things you enjoy. What courses in school did you like the most? If you enjoy travel, would you like a job that takes you to other countries? Or if you're interested in sports or fashion, how could you put your skills to use in that field? Analyzing your interests will tell you the types of work you'll enjoy doing.

DETERMINING WHAT YOU WANT

You are now ready to turn your self-evaluation into short-term career goals. You will need to determine your functional goals (those that will enable you to use your skills on the job), your performance goals (those that will help you to get ahead on the job), and the work environment that will be most comfortable for you.

Functional goals

In determining your functional goals, ask

- Do I want to work independently or as part of a team?
- With what materials do I want to work?
- In what setting do I want to work?

Your functional goals are related to the skills you want to use in your work. Because these are the same skills you identified earlier when analyzing your personal achievements, they are likely to increase your effectiveness and success on the job.

Start with a goal statement, such as "I would like a job in which I can use my ability to sell products" or "I would like a job that will put my writing skills to use." State only what you want to do; you'll determine where you want to do it later. And rewrite your goal statement as needed until you feel that it accurately reflects your goals.

One specific functional goal to consider is how much independence you want on the job. Do you prefer to work on your own or as part of a team? Would you like to be free to develop your own ideas, or are you the type who thrives on give and take with others? Would you be happier in an atmosphere of established procedures or in a relaxed, flexible atmosphere? Your answers will help define the right job situation for you.

Next, think about your work preferences. Would you like to work with products or machines? Or with people? Or with ideas and figures? Maybe your ideal is some combination of things, people, and ideas. Do you prefer physical work, brain work, or a combination? Would you like to work indoors? Outdoors? Or both? Do you need supervision to get things done? Or are you disciplined and on time? Do you thrive on variety and change, or do you prefer a predictable, stable environment?

Personal performance goals

In determining your personal performance goals, ask

- How much do I want to earn?
- How far do I want to go?
- How fast do I want to progress?

How much do you want to earn on your job after two years? After four? How high do you want to rise in the hierarchy? Setting these goals now can help you move faster up the ladder of success.

Start by jotting down on paper what you would like to earn at the outset. Then write what you would like to be earning at the start of the second year, the third year, and so on, in today's dollars. Finally, jot down your ultimate earnings goal. What types of occupations pay the kind of money you're looking for? Are these occupations realistic for a person with your qualifications? Are you willing to settle for less money in order to do something you really love to do?

Next, consider your place within the company or profession. Where would you like to start? Where do you want to go from there? What is the ultimate position you would like to attain? How soon after joining the company would you like to receive your first promotion? Your next one? Once you have established these goals, ask yourself what additional training or preparation you will need to be able to achieve them.

Establishing a timetable for each goal motivates you to achieve it. Review your timetables regularly to determine your rate of progress.

Work environment preferences

In determining your work environment preferences, ask

- What type of industry and organization do I want to work for?
- What kind of community do I want to work and live in?
- What type of facility do I want to work in?

Now you are ready to choose the environment you want to work in. Start by thinking in broad terms about the size and type of operation that appeals to you. Do you like the idea of working for a small, entrepreneurial operation, or would you prefer to be part of a large company? How do you feel about profit-making versus not-for-profit organizations? Are you attracted to service businesses or manufacturing operations? What types of products appeal to you? Do you want regular, predictable hours, or do you thrive on flexible, varied hours? Do you prefer to work from 9 to 5, or are you willing to work evenings and weekends, as in the entertainment and hospitality industries? Would you enjoy a seasonally varied job like education, which may give you summers off, or like retailing, with its selling cycles?

Location can also be important. Would you like to work in a big or medium-size city or in a small town? In an industrial area or an uptown setting? Do you favor a particular part of the country?

What about facilities? Is it important to you to work in an attractive place, or will simple, functional quarters suffice? Do you need a quiet office to work effectively, or can you concentrate in a noisy, open setting? Would you prefer to work in a high-rise building or in a low-profile one? In a large plant or in a small field office? Do such amenities as an in-house gym or handball court matter to you? Is access to public transportation or freeways important? Your answers can help identify the right work environment for you.

SEEKING EMPLOYMENT OPPORTUNITIES

When you're looking for work, you may occasionally feel rejected. But bear in mind that somebody out there is just as anxious to find employees as you are to find a job. In fact, American corporations spend roughly $11.5 billion annually trying to find the talent they need.[1] Somewhere, an employer is looking for someone with your skills, values, interests, and qualifications.

Sources of employment information

Find out where the job opportunities are.

Once you know what you have to offer and what you want, you can start finding an employer to match. If you haven't already committed yourself to any particular career field, you might first find out where the job opportunities are. Which industries are strong? Which parts of the country are booming, and which specific job categories offer the best prospects for the future?

Start your search for information by keeping abreast of business and financial news. If you don't already do so, subscribe to a major newspaper and scan the business pages every day. Watch some of the TV programs that focus on business, like "Wall Street Week," and read the financial articles in popular magazines like *Time* and *Newsweek*. You might even want to subscribe to a business magazine like *Fortune, Business Week,* or *Forbes.*

You can obtain information about the future for specific jobs in *The Dictionary of Occupational Titles* (U.S. Employment Service), *Occupational Outlook Handbook* (U.S. Bureau of Labor Statistics), and the employment publications of Science Research Associates. For an analysis of major industries, see the annual Market Data and Directory issue of *Industrial Marketing* and Standard & Poor's industry surveys.

You might also study professional and trade journals in the career fields that interest you. And talk to people in these fields; for names of the most prominent, consult *Standard & Poor's Register of Corporations, Directors and Executives.* Recent books about the career fields you are considering can be found by checking *Books in Print* at your library.

Find out which organizations that interest you need your skills.

Once you've identified a promising industry and a career field, you need to compile a list of specific organizations that appeal to you. You can do this by consulting directories of employers, such as *The College Placement Annual* and *Career: The Annual Guide to Business Opportunities.* (Other directories are listed in Chapter 11.) Write to the organizations on your list and ask for their most recent annual report and any descriptive brochures or newsletters that they've published. If possible, you might also visit some of the organizations on your list, contact their personnel departments, or talk with key employees.

Ads for specific job openings can be found in local and major-city newspapers. You might also check the trade and professional journals in career fields that interest you; *Ulrich's International Periodicals Directory,* available at the library, lists these journals. Job listings can also be obtained from your college placement office and from state placement bureaus.

Recruiter's sources

An understanding of how employers approach the recruiting process can save you considerable time and effort in searching for the job you want.

FIGURE 10.1
Avenues for Matching Jobs and Job Seekers

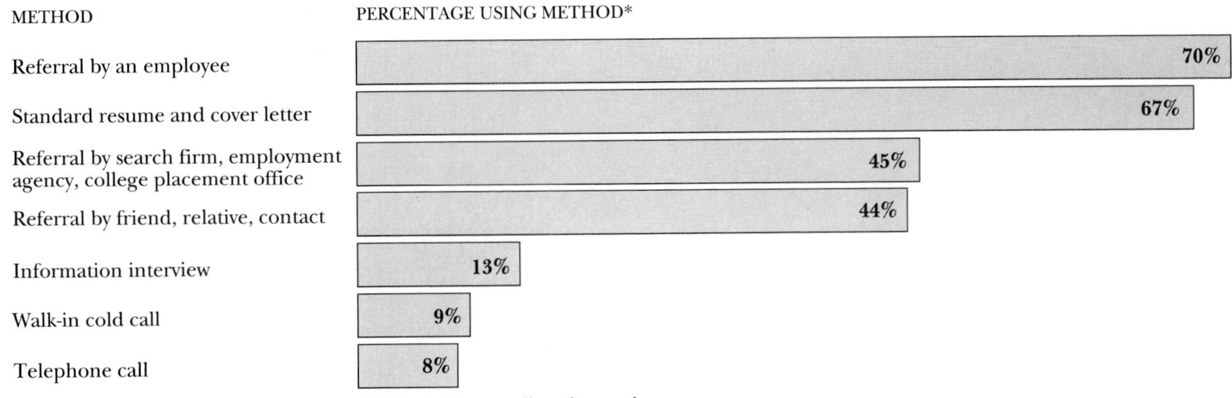

How Job Seekers Find Work

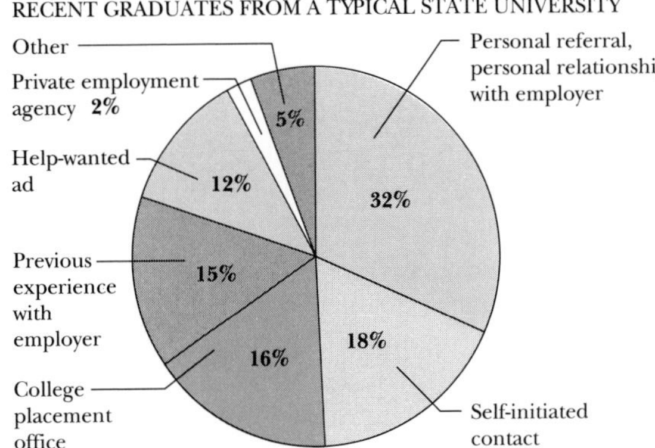

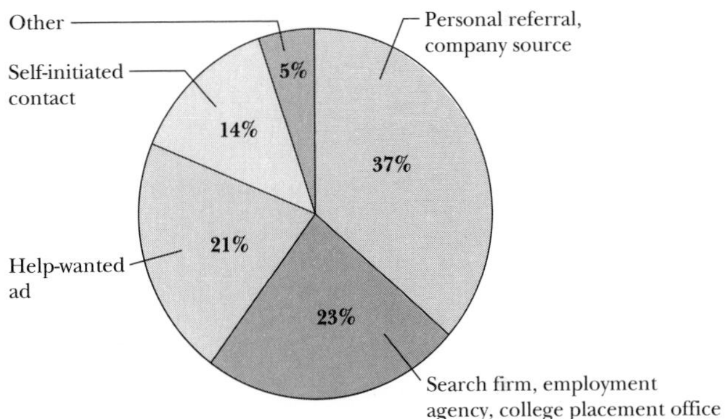

The quickest route is to get a referral from someone you know. In a recent survey by the American Management Society, 70 percent of the managers interviewed said that employee referrals are a useful source of job candidates. And personal contacts appear to be the prime source of jobs for job seekers, regardless of whether they are just graduating from college or have been out of school for several years.[2]

Employers find job candidates through

- Employee referrals
- On-campus interviews
- Advertisements
- Placement agencies
- Unsolicited resumes

Don't despair, however, if you lack contacts who can introduce you to potential employers. As Figure 10.1 shows, a variety of avenues are used by both job applicants and organizations seeking employees. Many organizations, like Price Waterhouse, send representatives to college campuses to interview students for job openings. These interviews are usually coordinated by the campus placement office, which keeps files containing college records, data sheets, and letters of recommendation for all students registered for the service.

Employers also recruit candidates through classified and display ads in newspapers, trade magazines, and campus publications, as well as through employment agencies, state employment services, and the employment bureaus operated by some trade associations.

Unsolicited resumes are also a vital source of candidates for many organizations. Some 67 percent of the employers who participated in the

American Management Society survey engage in this method of recruiting. And 18 percent of the job seekers graduating from a typical university found employment by sending unsolicited resumes to prospective employers. However, if you pursue this route, be prepared to buy a lot of postage stamps. For every 100 letters that you send out, you can expect to get only about 6 interviews.[3]

WRITING A RESUME

The purpose of the resume is to get you an interview.

Many people who are new to the job market have some misconceptions about resumes (see Figure 10.2). The fact is that a resume is a form of advertising, designed to help you get an interview. As in all forms of advertising, your objective is to call the reader's attention to your best features and to downplay your disadvantages, without distorting or misrepresenting the facts.

CONTROLLING THE FORMAT AND STYLE

The reader's initial reaction to your resume will be based on its appearance, not its content. For an impressive-looking resume, use clean, black type on letter-size white bond paper. Leave ample margins all around for easy reading. Corrections should be unnoticeable. To make duplicate copies, use offset printing or photocopying.

As a rule of thumb, try to write a one-page resume. But if you have a great deal of experience and are applying for a higher-level position, you may wish to prepare a somewhat longer resume. The important thing is to give yourself enough space to present a fair and persuasive portrait of your accomplishments and capabilities.

Skillful layout and graphic design make the resume visually appealing and easy to follow. Break up the text by using headings that call attention to different aspects of your background, such as your work experience and education. Underline or capitalize key points, or set them off in the left margin. Use indented lists to itemize your most important qualifications. Leave plenty of white space, even if doing so forces you to use two pages rather than one.

The key characteristics of a good resume are

- Neatness
- Simplicity
- Accuracy
- Honesty

Pay attention to mechanics. Check the headings and itemized lists to make sure they're grammatically parallel. Be sure that your grammar, spelling, and punctuation are correct.

Your resume has only seconds to make an impression, so keep the writing style simple and direct. Instead of whole sentences, use short, crisp phrases starting with action verbs. For example, you might say, "Coached a Little League team to the regional playoffs" or "Supervised a fast-food restaurant and four personnel."

TAILORING THE CONTENTS

Most potential employers have certain preconceived notions about what belongs in the resume. The bare essentials are your name and address, your academic credentials, and your employment history.

FIGURE 10.2
Fallacies and Facts About Resumes

Fallacy: The purpose of a resume is to list all your skills and abilities.
Fact: The purpose of a resume is to kindle employer interest and generate an interview.

Fallacy: A good resume will get you the job you want.
Fact: Hundreds of thousands of good resumes cross employers' desks every working day.

Fallacy: Your resume will be read carefully and thoroughly by an interested employer.
Fact: Your resume probably has less than ten seconds to make an impression.

Fallacy: The more good information you present about yourself in your resume, the better.
Fact: By including too much information, a resume may actually kill the appetite to know more.

Fallacy: If you want a really good resume, have it prepared by a resume service.
Fact: Many resume services use undistinguished standard formats, so you should prepare your own—unless the position you're after is very high-level and you choose the service very carefully.

Otherwise your resume should present your strongest, most impressive qualifications and skirt the areas that might raise questions. Don't exaggerate, and don't alter the past or claim to have skills you don't have. But don't dwell on negatives, either. For example, you may want to leave out any reference to the brief part-time job that just didn't seem to work out; potential employers for full-time jobs are likely to overlook such a small gap. Or if you've changed jobs rather frequently, you may want to "bury" the dates of employment instead of drawing attention to them with your format. By focusing on your strengths, you can tell the truth and still sound like a winner.

Name and address

The first thing an employer needs to know is who you are and where you can be reached: your name, address, and phone number. If you have an address and phone number at school and another at home, you may include both. By the same token, if you have a work phone and a home phone, list both and indicate which is which.

The opening section of your resume should show at a glance who you are, how to reach you, and what kind of job you're interested in.

Many resume headings are nothing more than the name and address centered at the top of the page. But you may also feature the title "Resume" or something more attention getting. For example:

Qualifications of Craig R. Crisp for Insurance Sales Representative

Data Sheet of Jean Gray, an Experienced Retail Fashion Buyer

Public Relations Background of Bradley R. (Brad) Howard

Susan Lee Selwyn's Qualifications
for the Position of Teaching Assistant
in the Dade County School District

Profile of Michael de Vito for Entertainment Management

Whatever heading you use, make sure the reader can tell in an instant who you are and how to communicate with you.

Career objective

There are two schools of thought on stating a career objective on your resume. Some experts argue that your objective will be obvious from your qualifications. They also point out that such a statement is counterproductive (especially if you would like to be considered for any suitable openings), because it labels you as being interested in only one thing. Other experts point out that employers will undoubtedly try to categorize you anyway, so you might as well be sure they attach the right label.

On balance, stating your objective is probably a good idea, because it provides the reader with a frame of reference for reviewing your qualifications. Be as specific as possible about what you want to do, but avoid making a narrow statement that will severely limit your prospects. The statement should indicate any special qualifications that pertain to your objective. Here's an example of this double-barrel type of career objective:

A junior accounting position in the aerospace industry in which my 1-1/2 years of computer programming experience would be valuable

Your objective should indicate what you want to do and why you are qualified to do it.

It is no simple matter to state in one short phrase both your objective and the reasons you are qualified for the job. But it can be done. Start by asking yourself these questions:

- *What specific position do I want?* Think in terms of the functions that the position might have. "Creating copy for a public relations firm" is much more meaningful than such vague wording as "A job in which I can use my creative talents."
- *What especially qualifies me for this job?* In a few brief words, focus on your key strengths and skills.

If you have two different types of qualifications (such as a certificate in secretarial science and two years' experience in retail sales), prepare two separate resumes, each with a different objective. If your immediate objective differs from your ultimate one, combine the two in a single statement:

A marketing position in a major communications company with an opportunity for eventual management status

To serve your organization as a proposal writer with the ultimate goal of becoming a contracts administrator

Summary of qualifications and date of availability

If your resume is long and your experience is varied, you might want to summarize your qualifications in a brief statement that highlights your

Summarize your strongest qualifications to focus and simplify the employer's evaluation.

strongest points. Use a short, simple heading, such as "Preparation for Financial Management" or "Significant Advertising Experience." Then summarize your strongest job-related qualifications.

As a convenience for the prospective employer, you may also list your date of availability. State the month and, if you know it, the day you will be available to start work.

Education

In the education section, list information about

- Postsecondary schools
- Off-campus workshops, seminars, and so on
- High school (only if pertinent)
- Military service (only if pertinent)
- Grades (only if pertinent and favorable)

If you're still in school, education is probably your strongest selling point. So present your educational background in depth. Give this section a heading, such as "Education," "Professional College Training," or "Academic Preparation." Then, starting with the postsecondary school you most recently attended, list for each school the name and location, the term of your enrollment (in months and years), your major and minor fields of study, significant skills and abilities you've developed in your course work, and the degree(s) or certificate(s) you earned. List courses that have directly equipped you for the job sought, and indicate any scholarships, awards, or academic honors you have received.

The education section should also include off-campus training sponsored by business, industry, or government. Indicate any relevant seminars or workshops you have attended, as well as the certificates or other documents you have received. Mention high school or military service here only if your achievements are pertinent to your career goals.

Whether you should list your grades depends on the nature of the work you want and whether they are favorable or unfavorable. If you choose to show grade-point averages for your total program or your major, be sure to say whether you're using a 4-point or a 5-point scale.

Education is usually given less emphasis in a resume after you've worked in your chosen field for a year or more. If work experience is your strongest qualification, save the section on education for later in the resume, where you can discuss it in less detail. But even those who have been out of school for several years should include the name and location of each postsecondary school attended, the dates of enrollment, and the degrees or certificates received.

Work experience

In the work experience section, give details of all the related jobs you've had.

In addition to describing your education, your resume should discuss your work experience off and on campus. Emphasize jobs that are relevant to your target field—including any part-time, summer, or volunteer work—to show that you like the type of position you are seeking. If your former jobs have no relation to your present career objective, list them anyway, without going into too much detail. Employers will see that you have the ability to get and hold a job, which is an important qualification in itself. And if you have worked your way through school, say so. Employers interpret this type of experience as a sign of character.

In describing your work experience, list your jobs in chronological order, with the current or last one first. Start each listing with the name and location of the employer. Then, if the reader is unlikely to recognize the organization or its name doesn't reveal what type of business it is, briefly describe what it does. When you want to keep the name of your present employer confidential, state "Name of organization (or company) on request," identify the firm by industry only (for example, "a large film-

For each work experience, state
- Name and location of employer
- What the organization does (if not clear from its name)
- Your functional title
- How long you worked there
- Your duties and responsibilities
- Your significant achievements or contributions

processing laboratory"), or use the name but request confidentiality in the application letter or in an underlined note ("Resume submitted in confidence") at the top or bottom of the resume. If an organization's name or location has since changed, state the present name or location and then "formerly. . . ."

Under each job listing, state your functional title, such as "clerk typist" or "salesperson." If you were a dishwasher, say so. Don't try to make your role seem more important by glamorizing your job title or functions.

You should also state how long you worked on each job, from month/year to month/year. Use the phrase "to present" to denote current employment. If a job was part-time, say so.

One of the most important features to emphasize is how your previous jobs relate to the position you are seeking. If you achieved something significant in a job, be sure to mention it—for example, "Devised a new collection system that accelerated payment of overdue receivables." Facts about your accomplishments are the most important information you can give a prospective employer. And quantify your accomplishments, where possible: "Designed a new ad that increased videotape sales by 9 percent." Figure 10.3 lists some other statements that may help you identify your own accomplishments. Remember to back them up with specific evidence.

Quantify your accomplishments whenever possible.

Activities and achievements

Nonpaid activities may provide valuable work-related skills.

Your resume should also describe any paid or unpaid activities that demonstrate your abilities. You should list projects that required leadership, organization, teamwork, and cooperation. Include speaking, writing, or tutoring experience, participation in athletics or creative projects, fundraising or community-service activities, and offices held in academic or professional organizations. (However, mention of political or religious organizations may be a red flag to someone with different views, so use your judgment.) Note any awards you have received.

Again, quantify your achievements with numbers wherever possible. Instead of saying that you addressed various student groups, state how many and the approximate audience sizes.

If your activities have been extensive, you may want to group them into divisions like these: "College Activities," "Community Service," "Professional Associations," "Seminars and Workshops," and "Speaking Activities." Or divide them into two categories: "Service Activities" and "Achievements, Awards, and Honors."

Other relevant facts

List anything else that might make you attractive to employers.

You may also want to include a section that describes other aspects of your background that pertain to your career objective. For example, if you were applying for a position with a multinational organization, you would mention your command of a foreign language or your travel experience. Other skills you might mention include the ability to operate a computer, word processor, photocopier, or other equipment.

Personal data

Sometimes included in a resume are references to hobbies, willingness to travel or relocate, and miscellaneous experiences that may help you get a job, such as military service and citizenship. However, civil rights laws

FIGURE 10.3
Accomplishment Statements for Resumes

Improved morale and teamwork
Introduced an improved filing system
Improved customer service
Stepped up work flow
Contributed new ideas
Reorganized procedures
Motivated co-workers
Increased typing speed and accuracy
Solved problems
Improved work efficiency
Increased sales
Reduced overdue accounts
Increased profits
Saved money
Reduced staff
Increased productivity
Improved existing products
Devised new products
Expanded markets
Arranged financing for company
Trained new employees
Reduced inventory
Increased financial reporting
Found companies to acquire
Reduced taxes
Improved management reporting
Used cost-saving purchasing techniques
Planned better meetings
Relieved boss of administrative details
Created a more effective advertising theme

prohibit employers from discriminating on the basis of gender, marital or family status, age (although only those 40 to 70 are protected), race, color, religion, or national origin. Thus you should exclude any items that could encourage discrimination and reduce your chances of being considered for the job.

Provide only the personal data that will help you get the job.

Good health warrants mention because it enhances work performance. You may say "Excellent health" or imply it by listing vigorous hobbies. If your health is less than excellent, say nothing. Of course, a physical disability is independent of health. If it has no bearing on your ability to do the job, you are justified in ignoring it in the resume.

If military service is relevant to the position you are seeking, you may list it in this section (or under "Education" or "Work Experience"). List the date of induction, the branch of service, where you served, the highest rank you achieved, any accomplishments related to your career goals, and the date you were discharged.

References

You may want to list the names of three to five people who can provide potential employers with insights into your abilities and personal characteristics. Your list might include the names of former and present employers, business associates, professors, and contacts who can attest to your character. The most convincing references are people who have a good reputation in their field and who are in a position to know a good deal about you. Because relatives are likely to be biased, they should not be used as references.

A list of three to five references may impress the prospective employer.

Experts argue about including the names of references in your resume. In general, you should try to list only names that will have credibility with the employer. But because you may be preparing a resume for distribution to a number of employers, you may not be able to come up with a list of names that will be appropriate in all cases. Or you may not want to bury the people who are your references under an avalanche of requests for information. In either case, simply state "References available on request" at the end of your resume. Another approach is to call on the services of your college placement office, which may have references on file for you. Then you can state in this section "References and supporting documents available from . . ."; be sure to include the exact address of the placement office.

Before naming someone as a reference, ask that person's permission.

Before you list anyone's name on your resume as a reference, ask for permission. Then get the person's name (correctly spelled), title, address, and telephone number. If you are currently employed and don't want your employer to know that you are seeking another job, omit his or her name from your list of references.

Supporting data

Instead of sending supporting documents with your resume, offer to supply them on request.

If your academic transcripts, samples of your work, and/or letters of recommendation might increase your chances of getting the job, insert a line at the end of your resume offering to supply these documents on request. But don't include them with your resume. The only thing that should accompany your resume is the letter of application.

CHOOSING THE BEST ORGANIZATIONAL PLAN

Select an organizational pattern that focuses attention on your strengths.

Although you may want to include a little information in all categories, you should emphasize the information that has a bearing on your career objective and minimize or exclude any that is irrelevant or counterproductive. You do this by adopting an organizational plan—chronological, functional, or targeted—that focuses attention on your strongest points. The "right" choice depends on your background and goals, as Table 10.1 illustrates.

The chronological resume

The most traditional way to organize a resume is chronologically. With this approach, the "Related Experience" section dominates the resume and is placed in the most prominent slot, immediately after the name/address and job objective. You develop this section by listing your jobs in reverse order, beginning with the most recent position and working backward toward earlier jobs. Under each listing, you describe your responsibilities and accomplishments, giving the most space to the most recent positions.

If you are just graduating from college, you can vary the chronological plan by putting your educational qualifications before your experience, thereby focusing attention on your academic credentials.

A chronological resume emphasizes your work history.

The chronological approach is the most common way to organize a resume, and many employers prefer it. It is especially appropriate if you have a strong employment history and are aiming for a job that builds on your current career path.

The chronological approach is a good choice for Roberto Cortez, who has had considerable experience. Notice in Figure 10.4 how Roberto calls attention to his most recent achievements by setting them off in list format with bullets. He includes a section titled "Personal Data" to emphasize his international background and fluency in Spanish, which are important qualifications for his target position.

TABLE 10.1 How to Choose an Organizational Plan for Your Resume

TYPE OF RESUME	WHEN TO USE	WHEN NOT TO USE
Chronological: Lists work experience and/or education in reverse chronological order; describes responsibilities and accomplishments associated with each job or educational experience	Your last employer is well known and highly respected You plan to continue along your established career path Your job history shows progressively more responsible positions You are applying to a traditional organization	You have changed jobs frequently You are changing your career goals You have not progressed in your career You have been away from the job market for some time You are applying for your first job
Functional: Lists functional experience separately from employment history	You want to emphasize capabilities not used in recent jobs You are changing careers You are entering the job market for the first time or are reentering after an absence Your past career progression has been disappointing You have held a variety of unrelated jobs Your work has been of a free-lance or temporary nature	You want to emphasize your career progress You have performed a limited number of functions Your most recent employers are well-known and prestigious You are applying to a traditional organization
Targeted: Lists capabilities and accomplishments pertaining to a specific job; briefly lists work experience in a separate section	You are very clear about your job target You have several career objectives and want a separate resume for each You want to emphasize capabilities that you may not have performed for a regular employer	You want to use one resume for several applications You are not clear about your capabilities or accomplishments You are just starting your career and have little experience

The functional resume

A functional resume focuses attention on your areas of competence.

In a functional resume, you emphasize your areas of competence by organizing around a list of accomplishments, then identifying your employers and academic experience in subordinate sections. This organizational pattern is useful for people who are just entering the job market or who are trying to redirect their career or minimize breaks in employment.

Figure 10.5 illustrates how a recent graduate used the functional approach to showcase her qualifications for a career in public relations. Although Glenda St. Johns has not held any paid, full-time positions in public relations, she knows a good deal about the profession from doing research and talking with people in the industry. As a result, she was able to organize her resume in a way that demonstrates her ability to handle such a position.

The targeted resume

A targeted resume shows how you qualify for a specific job.

A targeted resume is organized to focus attention on what you can do for a particular employer in a particular position. Immediately after stating your career objective, you list any capabilities that pertain to it. This list is followed by a list of your achievements, which provide evidence of your

FIGURE 10.4
Chronological Resume for an Accounting Position

The applicant emphasizes his achievements by using an indented list.

The chronological organization highlights the applicant's impressive career progress.

The applicant's special qualifications are presented as personal data.

RESUME

Roberto Cortez
5687 Crosswoods Drive
Falls Church, VA 22044
Home: (703) 987-0086
Office: (703) 549-6624

OBJECTIVE — To obtain a position in accounting management where my knowledge of international finance will be of value

EXPERIENCE

March 1986 to present — Staff Accountant/Financial Analyst
INTER-AMERICAN IMPORTS ALEXANDRIA, VA

Prepare general accounting reports for wholesale giftware importer with annual sales of $15 million. Audit all financial transactions between company headquarters and suppliers in 12 Latin American countries.
* Created a computerized model to adjust accounts for fluctuations in currency exchange rates
* Represented company in negotiating joint venture agreements with major suppliers in Mexico and Colombia

October 1982 to March 1986 — Staff Accountant
MONSANTO AGRICULTURAL CHEMICALS MEXICO CITY

Handled budgeting, billing, and credit processing functions for the Mexico City branch of Monsanto's Agricultural Chemicals division. Audited travel and entertainment expenditures for Monsanto's 30-member Latin American sales force. Assisted in launching an on-line computer system (IBM).

EDUCATION — GEORGE MASON UNIVERSITY FAIRFAX, VA
(1986-1989) M.B.A. with emphasis on international business

UNIVERSIDAD NACIONAL AUTÓNOMA DE MEXICO
MEXICO CITY, MEXICO
(1978-1982) B.B.A., Accounting

PERSONAL DATA — Born and raised in Mexico City; became U.S. citizen in 1987. Fluent in Spanish and German. Have traveled extensively in Latin America.

REFERENCES — Available on request.

Resume Submitted in Confidence

capabilities. Employers and schools are listed in subordinate sections.

Targeted resumes are a good choice for people who have a very clear idea of what they want to do and who can demonstrate their ability in the targeted area. This approach was very effective for Erica Vorkamp, whose resume appears in Figure 10.6. Instead of using a chronological pattern, which would have focused attention on her lack of recent work experience, Erica uses a targeted approach that emphasizes her ability to organize special events.

WRITING THE PERFECT RESUME

Regardless of what organizational plan you follow, the key to writing the "perfect" resume is to put yourself in the reader's position. Think about

FIGURE 10.5
Functional Resume for a Public Relations Position

Because she is a recent graduate, the applicant describes her education first.

The use of action verbs and specific facts enhances this resume's effectiveness.

The applicant's sketchy work history is described but not emphasized.

```
                              RESUME

Glenda St. Johns                        Objective: To obtain a
Box 6671, College Station               position in corporate
Iowa City, Iowa 52240                   public relations where
(515) 545-9856                          my experience is of use.

WRITING/EDITING:
     * Wrote arts and entertainment articles for college
       newspaper
     * Edited University of Iowa Handbook, guidebook
       mailed to all incoming freshmen
     * Published guest editorial on student attitudes in
       Des Moines Register
     * Wrote prize-winning script for sorority skit in
       Fall Follies talent show

PUBLIC SPEAKING:
     * Participated in over 100 debates as member of
       college debating team
     * Led seminars to teach job-search skills to under-
       privileged teen-agers as part of campus outreach
       program
     * Performed in summer theater productions in Clear
       Lake, Iowa

MANAGING:
     * Created and administered summer parks and recreation
       program for city of Osage, Iowa
     * Developed budget, schedule, and layouts for college
       handbook; assigned work to photographers and
       copywriters
     * Developed publicity campaign for Fall Follies,
       three-hour talent show that raised $7,000 for The
       University of Iowa's Panhellenic Council

EDUCATION:
The University of Iowa, Iowa City, September 1984-June 1989
B.A. Journalism (3.81 GPA on 4.0 scale)
Speech minor; two courses in public relations

EXPERIENCE:
June 1988-April 1989, Editor, University of Iowa Handbook
Summer 1987, Director, Summer Recreation Program, Osage, Iowa
Summer 1986, Actress, Cobblestone Players, Clear Lake, Iowa

PERSONAL DATA:
Excellent health; willing to relocate

REFERENCES AND SUPPORTING DOCUMENTS:  Available from Placement
Office, The University of Iowa, Iowa City, IA 52242
```

The "perfect" resume responds to the reader's needs and preferences and avoids some common faults.

what the prospective employer needs, then tailor your resume accordingly.

People like Don Greiner who read thousands of resumes every year complain about the following common resume problems:

- *Too long.* The resume is not concise, relevant, and to the point.
- *Too short or sketchy.* The resume does not give enough information for a proper evaluation of the applicant.
- *Hard to read.* A lack of "white space" and of such devices as indentions and underlining makes the reader's job more difficult.
- *Wordy.* Descriptions are verbose, with numerous words used for what could be said more simply.

FIGURE 10.6
Targeted Resume for a Position as Special Events Coordinator

The capabilities and achievements all relate to the specific job target, giving a very selective picture of the candidate's abilities.

This work history has little bearing on the candidate's job target, but she felt that recruiters would want to see evidence that she has held a paying position.

These high-powered references lend credibility to the candidate's claims.

ERICA VORKAMP'S QUALIFICATIONS
FOR THE POSITION OF SPECIAL EVENTS COORDINATOR
IN THE CITY OF BARRINGTON

993 Church Street
Barrington, IL 60010
(312) 884-2153

CAPABILITIES

* Plan and coordinate large-scale public events
* Develop community support for concerts, festivals, and entertainment
* Manage publicity for major events
* Coordinate activities of diverse community groups
* Establish and maintain financial controls for public events
* Negotiate contracts with performers, carpenters, electricians, and suppliers

ACHIEVEMENTS

* Arranged 1988's week-long Arts and Entertainment Festival for the Barrington Public Library, which involved performances by musicians, dancers, actors, magicians, and artists
* Served as chairperson for the 1988 Children's Home Society Fashion Show, a luncheon for 400 that raised $5,000 for orphans and abused children
* Supervised the 1987 PTA Halloween Carnival, an all-day festival with game booths, live bands, contests, and food service that raised $7,600 for the PTA
* Organized the 1987 Midwestern convention for 800 members of the League of Women Voters, which extended over a three-day period and required arrangements for hotels, meals, speakers, and special tours

EDUCATION

* Northwestern University (Evanston, Illinois), September 1965 to June 1970, B.A. Psychology; Phi Beta Kappa

WORK HISTORY

* Northwestern University, November 1967 to June 1970, Part-time Research Assistant

* First National Bank of Chicago, June 1970 to October 1972, Personnel Counselor/Campus Recruiter

REFERENCES

* John Detweiler, Mayor, Village of Barrington, Barrington, Illinois 60010; (312) 884-0100

* Jan Flapan, Co-President, Midwestern Division, League of Women Voters, 332 South Michigan Avenue, Chicago, Illinois 60004; (312) 236-0315

* Mark Nesbitt, President, Heartland Promotions, Inc., 433 W. Grand Avenue, Chicago, Ilinois 60651; (312) 864-9701

- *Too slick.* The resume appears to have been written by someone other than the applicant, which raises the question of whether the qualifications are exaggerated.
- *Amateurish.* The applicant appears to have little understanding of the business world or of the particular industry, a lack revealed by including the wrong information or presenting it awkwardly.
- *Poorly reproduced.* The print is faint and difficult to read.
- *Misspelled and ungrammatical throughout.* The applicant lacks verbal skills important on the job and shows poor judgment in failing to have another person proofread the resume.
- *Lacking a career objective.* The resume fails to identify the applicant's job preferences and career goals.

- *Boastful.* The overconfident tone makes the reader wonder if the applicant's self-evaluation is realistic.
- *Dishonest.* The applicant claims to have expertise that he or she does not possess.
- *Gimmicky.* The words, structure, decoration, or material used in the resume depart so far from the usual as to make it ineffective.[4]

Guard against making these mistakes in your own resume, and compare your final version with the suggestions in the accompanying checklist.

CHECKLIST FOR RESUMES

A. Contents and Style

- ☐ 1. Prepare the resume before the application letter to summarize the facts that the letter will be based on.
- ☐ 2. Present the strongest, most relevant qualifications first.
- ☐ 3. Use short noun phrases and action verbs, not whole sentences.
- ☐ 4. Use facts, not opinions.
- ☐ 5. Avoid personal pronouns.
- ☐ 6. Omit the date of preparation.
- ☐ 7. Omit mention of your desired salary, work schedule, or vacation schedule.

B. Contact Information

- ☐ 1. Use a title, such as "Resume," as a heading.
- ☐ 2. List your name, address, area code, and telephone number—for both school or work and home, if appropriate.

C. Career Objective and Skills Summary

- ☐ 1. State the type of work you want (not a job title) and your career objective.
  - ☐ a. State a broad and flexible goal to increase the scope of your job prospects.
  - ☐ b. Prepare two different resumes if you can do two unrelated types of work, such as bookkeeping and nursing.
- ☐ 2. Summarize your key qualifications.
- ☐ 3. State the month and, if you know it, the day on which you will be available to start work.

D. Education

- ☐ 1. List all relevant schooling and training since high school, with the most recent first.
  - ☐ a. List the name and location of every post-secondary school you have attended, with the dates you entered and left and the degrees or certificates you obtained.
  - ☐ b. Indicate your major (and minor) fields in college work.
  - ☐ c. State the numerical base for your grade-point average, overall or in your major, if your average is impressive enough to list.
- ☐ 2. List relevant required or elective courses in descending order of importance.
- ☐ 3. List any other relevant educational or training experiences, such as job-related seminars or workshops attended and certificates obtained.

E. Work Experience

- ☐ 1. List all relevant work experience, including paid employment and volunteer work.
- ☐ 2. List full-time and part-time jobs, with the most recent one first.
  - ☐ a. State the month/year when you started and left each job.
  - ☐ b. Provide the name and location of the firm that employed you.
  - ☐ c. List your job title and describe your functions briefly.
  - ☐ d. Note on-the-job accomplishments, such as an award or a suggestion that saved the organization time or money.

F. Activities, Honors, and Achievements

- ☐ 1. List all relevant unpaid activities, including offices and leadership positions you have held; significant awards or scholarships not listed elsewhere; projects you have undertaken that show an ability to work with others; and writing or speaking activities, publications, and roles in academic or professional organizations.
- ☐ 2. In most circumstances, exclude mention of religious or political affiliations.

(continued on p. 320)

Checklist continued from previous page

G. Other Relevant Facts

- ☐ 1. List other relevant information, such as your typing speed or your proficiency in languages other than English.
- ☐ 2. Mention your ability to operate any machines, equipment, or computer software used in the job.

H. Personal Data

- ☐ 1. Omit data that could be regarded negatively or be used to discriminate against you.
- ☐ 2. Omit or downplay references to age if it could suggest inexperience or approaching retirement.
- ☐ 3. Describe military service (branch of service, where you served, rank attained, and the dates of induction and discharge) here or, if relevant, under "Education" or "Work Experience."
- ☐ 4. List job-related interests and hobbies, especially those indicating stamina, strength, sociability, or other qualities that are desirable in the position you seek.

I. References

- ☐ 1. List three to five references, or offer to supply the names on request.
  - ☐ a. Supply names of academic, employment, and professional associates—but no relatives.
  - ☐ b. Provide a name, title, address, and telephone number for each reference.
  - ☐ c. List no name as a reference until you have that person's permission to do so.
- ☐ 2. Exclude your present employer if you do not want her or him to know you are seeking another position, or add "Resume submitted in confidence" at the top or bottom of the resume.

WRITING AN APPLICATION LETTER

If you're like most job seekers, you will send your resume to many employers, because the chances of getting an interview from each inquiry are relatively slight. To make the process more efficient, you will probably use the same resume repeatedly but tailor your application for each potential employer by including a cover letter that tells what you can do for that specific organization.

Follow the AIDA plan in writing your application letter: attention, interest, desire, action.

Like your resume, your application letter is a form of advertising, and it should be organized like a persuasive message. You need to stimulate the reader's interest, then show how you can satisfy the organization's needs. The style should project confidence, because you can't hope to sell a potential employer on your merits unless you truly believe in them yourself and sound as though you do.

Your letter should also reflect your personal style, so be yourself. But be businesslike too; avoid sounding cute. Don't use slang or a gimmicky layout. The only time to be unusually creative is when the job you're seeking requires imagination, such as a position in advertising.

Finally, showing that you know something about the organization can pay off, as Don Greiner points out. It gets attention. It conveys your desire to join the organization. The more you can learn about the organization, the better you'll be able to write about how your qualifications fit its needs.

WRITING THE OPENING PARAGRAPH

A solicited application letter is one sent in response to an announced job opening. An unsolicited, or "prospecting," letter is one sent to an organization that has not announced an opening. When you send a solicited letter, you usually know in advance what qualifications the organization is looking for. However, you also have more competition, because hundreds of other job seekers will have seen the listing and may be sending applications. In some respects, therefore, an unsolicited application letter stands a better chance of being read. Although it may initially be filed away, it will probably be considered eventually, and it may get more individualized attention.

Unsolicited application letters, which are not designed to respond to a particular opening, must do an especially good job of capturing attention and raising interest.

Whether your application letter is solicited or unsolicited, your qualifications are presented similarly. The main difference is in the opening paragraph. In a solicited letter no special attention-getting effort is needed, because you have been invited to apply. The unsolicited letter, however, must start by capturing the reader's attention and interest.

Getting attention

One way to spark attention in the opening paragraph is to show how your strongest work skills could benefit the organization. A 20-year-old secretary with 1½ years of college might begin like this:

When you need a secretary in your export division who can take shorthand at 125 words a minute and transcribe notes at 70--in English, Spanish, or Portuguese--call me.

Another attention getter consists of describing your understanding of the job's requirements and then showing how well your qualifications fit the job:

Begin an unsolicited application letter by focusing on one or more of the following:

- Your strongest work skills and how they would help the organization
- The match between job requirements and your qualifications
- The name of someone respected by the reader
- News about the organization that demonstrates your awareness
- A question that reflects your knowledge of the organization's needs
- An imaginative catch phrase
- The source of your knowledge about the job opening

From my research, I've learned that the IBM technician needs a diverse array of skills. These include mechanical aptitude, manual dexterity, and public relations skills. Please check the attached resume to see how well my background in telephone repair fits these specifications.

Mentioning the name of a person known to and highly regarded by the reader is also bound to capture some attention:

When Janice McHugh of your franchise sales division spoke to our Business Communication class last week, she said you often add promising new marketing graduates to your sales staff at this time of year.

References to publicized company activities, achievements, changes, or new procedures can also be used to gain attention:

Today's issue of the Detroit News reports that you may need the expertise of computer programmers versed in robotics when your Lansing tire plant automates this spring.

Another type of attention-getting opening uses a question to demonstrate an understanding of the organization's needs:

Can your fast-growing market research division use an interviewer with 1-1/2 years of field survey experience, a B.A. in public relations, and a real desire to succeed? If so, please consider me for the position.

A catch-phrase opening can also capture attention, especially if the job sought requires ingenuity and imagination:

Grande monde--whether said in French, Italian, or Arabic, it still means "high society." As an interior designer for your Beverly Hills showroom, I not only could serve, and sell to, your high-society clientele, but I could do it in all these languages. I speak, read, and write them fluently.

If you are writing a solicited application letter, in response to an advertisement or inquiry by the organization, begin by mentioning how you found out about the opening.

In contrast, a solicited letter written in response to a job advertisement usually opens by identifying the publication in which the ad ran and then describes what the applicant has to offer:

Your ad in the April issue of Travel & Leisure for a cruise-line social director caught my eye. My eight years of experience as a social director in the travel industry would allow me to serve your new Caribbean cruise division well.

Notice that all these openings demonstrate the "you" attitude and indicate how the applicant can serve the employer.

Clarifying your reason for writing

State in the opening that you are applying for a job.

The opening paragraph of your application letter should also state your reason for writing: You are applying for a job. It should therefore identify the desired job or job area:

I am seeking an entry-level position in technical writing.

Having had six months of new-car sales experience, I am applying for the fleet sales position advertised by your firm in the Baltimore Sun (March 23, 1989).

Another way to state your reason for writing is to use a title at the opening of your letter. For example:

Subject: Application for bookkeeper position

After this clear signal, your first paragraph can focus on getting attention and indicating how hiring you may benefit the organization.

SUMMARIZING YOUR KEY SELLING POINTS

The middle section of an application letter should

- Summarize those qualifications that are directly related to this job
- Show how you have put your qualifications to use
- Provide evidence of desirable personal qualities
- Tie salary requirements to the benefits of hiring you
- Refer to your resume

The middle paragraph(s) of the application letter should present your strongest selling points in terms of their potential benefit to the organization, thereby creating interest in you and a desire to interview you. If your selling points have already been mentioned in the opening, don't repeat them. Simply give supporting evidence. Otherwise, spell out your key qualifications, together with some convincing evidence of your ability to perform.

To avoid a cluttered application letter, mention only the qualifications that indicate you can do the job. For example, show how your studies and work experience have prepared you for it. Or tell the reader about how you grew up in the business. But be careful not to repeat the facts presented in your resume. Simply interpret them:

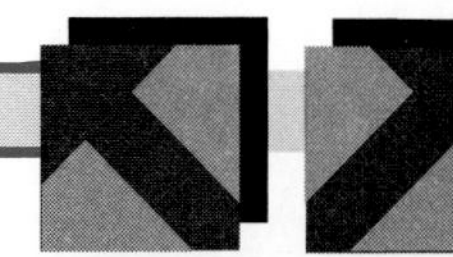

BUSINESS COMMUNICATION TODAY

Ten Skills That Can Help You Succeed in Any Career

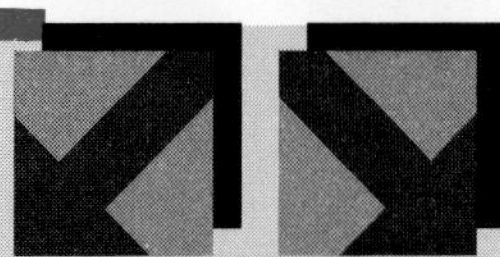

How good are you at supervising others? At coping with deadline pressures? At taking charge of a situation? At explaining things to others? These are a few of the many important skills you will need no matter what your career.

Instead of waiting to learn the following skills on the job, you should make every effort to cultivate them now. Perhaps you belong to a club or organization where you can take on responsibilities that require such skills. Or maybe you can do volunteer work that will give you needed experience. Or you might have a part-time job where you can practice them.

- *Budget management.* Get your hands on any budget you can find, and take responsibility for it. Manage how the funds are dispensed, and learn what fiscal control is all about.
- *Supervising.* Take responsibility for the work of others in a situation calling for accountability. Expose yourself to giving orders, delegating tasks, understanding the other person's viewpoint.
- *Public relations.* Accept a role in which you must meet the public. Greet visitors, answer complaints, talk to community groups, sell ads to businesspeople, or explain programs to prospective clients.
- *Coping with deadline pressure.* Search for opportunities to show that you can produce good work in time for deadlines. Prove that you can function on someone else's schedule, even when it is tight.
- *Negotiating/arbitrating.* Cultivate the fine art of dealing effectively with people in ambiguous situations. Taking a leadership role in almost any organization will help you learn how to bring warring factions together, resolve differences, and make demands on behalf of one constituency to those in positions of power.
- *Speaking.* Taking a leadership role in an organization will also force you to talk publicly, prepare remarks, get across ideas, and motivate people without feeling self-conscious.
- *Writing.* Write letters to the editors of every publication you read routinely. Write a newsletter, however informal, for a club or organization you belong to.
- *Organizing/managing/coordinating.* Take charge of an event. It doesn't matter what, as long as you have responsibility for bringing together people and resources. Organizing events or managing projects teaches you how to delegate tasks to others.
- *Interviewing.* Learn how to acquire information from people by questioning them directly, as a newspaper reporter would. Interview the neighbors, your friends, and others. Help them feel comfortable in your presence, even though you are asking difficult or touchy questions.
- *Teaching/instructing.* Refine your ability to explain things to other people. Become familiar and comfortable with passing on information and know-how. Any position of responsibility gives you many chances to teach ideas and methods to others.

If you cultivate any three or four of these skills, you are doing quite well. If you practice most of them and feel you are improving in each, expect to have a responsible decision-making position before long.

1. Think about the career you'd like to pursue. Which of the skills listed here might be especially valuable to you in your work? In what ways would these skills be useful?

2. Pick one of the skills listed here and develop a plan for building that skill during the next year. Be specific in identifying five or six activities that will help you build your skill.

Experience in customer relations and college courses in public relations have taught me how to handle the problem-solving tasks that arise in a leading retail clothing firm like yours. Such important tasks include identifying and resolving customer complaints, writing letters that build good customer relations, and above all, promoting the organization's positive image.

When writing a solicited letter responding to a help-wanted advertisement, fully cover each requirement specified in the ad. If you are deficient in any of these requirements, stress other solid selling points to help strengthen your overall presentation.

Stating that you have all the necessary requirements for the job is rarely enough to convince the reader, so back up assertions of your ability by presenting evidence of it. Cite one or two of your key qualifications, then show how you have effectively put them to use. For example:

INSTEAD OF THIS	WRITE THIS
I completed three college courses in business communication, earning an A in each course, and have worked for the past year at Imperial Construction.	Using the skills gained from three semesters of college training in business communication, I developed a collection system for Imperial Construction that reduced its 1989 bad-debt losses by 3.7 percent, or $9,902, over those of 1988. The new collection letters offered discount incentives for speedy payment rather than time-worn terminology.

This section of the letter should also present evidence of a few significant job-related qualities. For example, the following paragraph demonstrates that the applicant is diligent and hard working:

> While attending college full-time, I trained 3 hours a day with the varsity track team. Additionally, I worked part-time during the school year and up to 60 hours a week each summer in order to be totally self-supporting while in college. To your company I offer these same levels of energetic effort and perseverance.

Other relevant qualities worth noting include the ability to learn quickly, handle responsibility, and get along with people.

Another matter to bring up in this section is your salary requirements—but only if the organization has asked you to state them. Of course, you should have a reasonable figure in mind and should indicate some flexibility. It is also important to tie your desired salary to the benefits you would provide the organization, as you would handle price in a sales letter. For example:

> For the past two years, I have been helping a company similar to yours organize its data base. I would therefore like to receive a salary in the same range (the mid-20s) for helping your company set up a more efficient customer data base.

Toward the end of this section, refer the reader to your resume. You may do so by citing a specific fact on the resume or by mentioning the references or other information it contains.

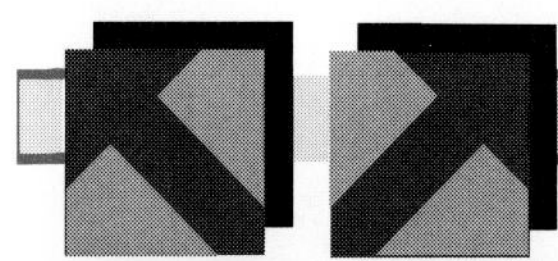

BUSINESS COMMUNICATION TODAY

Eight Ways to Sidestep Hidden Job-Hunting Hazards

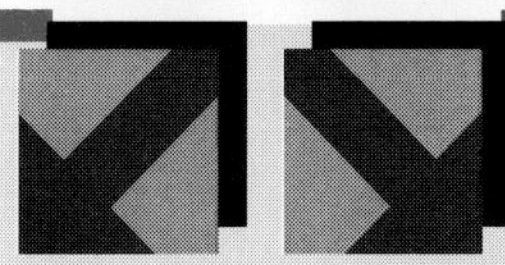

Errors in judgment can prevent even the finest candidate from landing the job she or he wants. These eight simple rules can help you avoid such mistakes.

- *Begin your job search before the pressure is really on.* Desperate candidates are much less attractive. And if you need a job fast, you may have to accept the first offer you get.
- *Conduct a complete search.* Touch all of the following bases to increase your chances of getting the job and the salary you want: (1) apply to companies; (2) ask your friends and relatives about jobs; (3) answer newspaper ads; (4) apply at private employment agencies, the state employment service, and the school placement office; (5) take civil service tests.
- *Set realistic goals.* (1) Make sure you aren't pursuing conflicting goals. For example, you may be unrealistic if you're unwilling to relocate, thereby narrowing your prospects, yet want a high salary. (2) Don't expect miracles. Expect to do about as well as others have. (3) Establish a priority for your goals. If getting a job quickly is essential, then realize that your needs probably rule out getting a high salary. (4) Review your goals periodically. If what seemed a realistic goal at the start appears unattainable 12 weeks later, change your goal.
- *Be willing to invest in yourself.* If your resume typed on a portable is less impressive than one typed on a full-size electronic typewriter, the few dollars saved may not be worth it. You'll have a better chance to succeed if you look successful.
- *Revise your strategies as needed.* Don't continue to send out a resume or an application letter that has gotten no results. And don't keep pursuing a position if it obviously isn't attainable. If you discover that you aren't as marketable as you assumed you would be, revise your resume and your goals.
- *Try to get every job offer you can.* (1) Even if you aren't sure you want a certain job, getting an offer may make you more attractive to a company you know you want to work for. (2) The job you're interviewing for may not appeal to you so much now but could prove to be your most appealing alternative later. (3) Interviews enable you to see how good you are at making people want you. If you get an offer, you'll know you've mastered the technique that can get you other offers. (4) Getting a job offer can build you up psychologically. This boost may be just what you need to succeed in your next interview, for a job you want more.
- *Follow up every lead you get.* The least likely contact may be the one that gets you a job or leads you to the contact that does.
- *Don't overdo it.* Trying to do too much at once may be a mistake. Be sure you schedule enough time to follow up every lead and every application. Getting a job is a matter of planning and persistence. It isn't a race.

1. Which of the hazards listed here are most likely to be a problem for recent college graduates?

2. Talk to several people who have recently been through the job-search process. What lessons can you learn from them?

WRITING THE CLOSING PARAGRAPH

The final paragraph of your application letter has two important functions: to ask the reader for a specific action and to make a reply easy.

The "action" section of an application letter should

- Almost always ask for an interview
- Make an interview easy to arrange

In almost all cases, the action you should ask for is an interview. But don't demand it. Try to sound natural and appreciative. Offer to come to the employer's office at a convenient time or, if the firm is some distance away, to meet with its nearest representative. Make the request easy to fulfill by stating your phone number and the best time to reach you. Refer again to your strongest selling point and, if desired, your date of availability.

FIGURE 10.7
Sample Unsolicited Application Letter

216 Westview Circle
Dallas, TX 75231
June 16, 1989

Mr. William DuPage, Managing Partner
Grant & Grant Financial Planning Associates
1775 Lakeland Drive
Dallas, TX 75218

Dear Mr. DuPage:

When Roberta Hawley of your personnel department spoke with me today, she indicated that you may be looking for a staff accountant. On the basis of our talk, I believe that my background would benefit Grant & Grant. Four years of college have trained me in accounting and full-charge bookkeeping through trial balance.

My 42 units of college accounting and courses in electronic data processing have equipped me to work with computer-based clients like yours. Training in business writing, human relations, and psychology should help me to achieve solid rapport with them. And advanced studies in tax accounting will enable me to analyze their financial needs from a planning perspective.

Because your company specializes in tax-shelter planning, my work experience could also be beneficial. After two years as a part-time bookkeeper for a securities brokerage firm, I was promoted to full-time financial analyst intern in the corporate investment division. In making recommendations to the firm's corporate clients, I analyzed and selected specific tax-shelter programs. After three months, my accomplishments were acknowledged by a substantial salary increase.

Harold Paul, vice president of CitiBank, and other references listed on the enclosed resume will confirm my potential for the staff accountant position.

At a time convenient for you, I would appreciate the opportunity to discuss my qualifications for beginning a career with your company. I will phone you early next Wednesday to see if we can arrange a meeting at your convenience.

Sincerely,

Diane Fahey

Diane Fahey

Enclosure

The applicant relates her educational qualifications to the requirements of the position as she understands them.

Knowledge of the company and a specialized capability are sure to interest the reader.

This paragraph emphasizes positive job-related qualities without emphasizing "I."

Mentioning a prominent name calls attention to the enclosed resume.

For example:

After you have reviewed my qualifications, could we discuss the possibility of putting my marketing skills to work for your company? Because I will be on spring break the week of March 8, I would like to arrange a time to talk then. You can reach me by calling (901) 235-6311 during the day or (901) 529-2873 any evening after 5.

An alternate approach is to ask for an interview and then offer to get in touch with the reader to arrange a time for it, rather than requesting a reply.

Whichever approach you use, mail your application letter and resume promptly, especially if they have been solicited. Do not enclose a pre-

FIGURE 10.8
Sample Solicited Application Letter

2893 Jack Pine Road
Chapel Hill, NC 27514
February 2, 1989

Ms. Angela Clair
Director of Administration
Cummings and Welbane, Inc.
770 Campus Point Drive
Chapel Hill, NC 27514

Dear Ms. Clair:

Your advertisement in the January 31 issue of the Chapel Hill Post attracted my attention because I believe that I have the "proven skills" you are looking for in an administrative assistant. In addition to having previous experience in a variety of office settings, I am familiar with the computer system that you use in your office.

The opening states the reason for writing and links the writer's experience to stated qualifications.

I recently completed a three-course sequence at Hamilton College on operation of the Beta computer system. I learned how to apply this technology to speed up letter-writing and report-writing tasks. A workshop on "Writing and Editing with the Beta Processor" gave me experience with other valuable applications.

By discussing how his specific skills apply to the job sought, the applicant shows that he understands the job's responsibilities.

As a result of this training, I am able to compose many different types of finished documents, including sales letters, financial reports, and presentation slides.

These specialized skills have proven valuable in my work for the past eight months as assistant to the chief nutritionist at the University of North Carolina campus cafeteria. As my resume indicates, my duties include drafting letters, typing finished correspondence, and handling phone calls. I'm particularly proud of the order-confirmation system I designed, which has sharply reduced the problem of late shipments and depleted inventories.

Because "proven skills" are best explained in person, I would appreciate an interview with you. Please phone me any afternoon between 3 and 5 p.m. at (919) 220-6139 to let me know the day and time most convenient for you.

In closing, the writer asks for an interview and facilitates action.

Sincerely,

Ken Sawyer

Kenneth Sawyer

Enclosure

addressed, stamped reply envelope unless you are applying for a job with a low-budget employer.

WRITING THE PERFECT APPLICATION LETTER

The "perfect" application letter, like the "perfect" resume, accomplishes one thing: It gets you an interview. But it conforms to no particular model because it's a reflection of your special strengths. Nevertheless, an application letter should contain the basic components. In Figure 10.7, an unsolicited letter for an accounting position, notice how the applicant seeks to gain attention by mentioning a person known to the reader. The letter in Figure 10.8, written in response to a help-wanted ad, highlights the applicant's chief qualifications.

■ CHECKLIST FOR APPLICATION LETTERS

A. Attention (Opening Paragraph)

- ☐ 1. Open the letter by capturing the reader's attention in a businesslike way.
  - ☐ a. *Summary opening.* Present your strongest, most relevant qualifications, with an explanation of how they can benefit the organization.
  - ☐ b. *Name opening.* Mention the name of a person who is well known to the reader and who has suggested that you apply for the job.
  - ☐ c. *Source opening.* When responding to a job ad, identify the publication in which the ad appeared and briefly describe how you meet each requirement stated in the ad.
  - ☐ d. *Question opening.* Pose an attention-getting question that shows you understand an organization's problem, need, or goal and have a genuine desire to help solve, meet, or attain it.
  - ☐ e. *News opening.* Cite a publicized organizational achievement, contemplated change, or new procedure or product, and then link it to your desire to work for the organization.
  - ☐ f. *Personalized opening.* Present one of your relevant interests or views, mention your previous experience with the organization, or cite your present position or status as a means of leading into a discussion of why you want to work for the organization.
  - ☐ g. *Creative opening.* Demonstrate your flair and imagination with colorful phrasing, especially if the job requires these qualities.
- ☐ 2. State that you are applying for a job, and identify the position or the type of work you seek.

B. Interest and Desire, or Evidence of Qualifications (Next Several Paragraphs)

- ☐ 1. Present your key qualifications for the job, highlighting what is on your resume: job-related education and training; relevant work experience; and related activities, interests, and qualities.
- ☐ 2. Adopt a mature and businesslike tone.
  - ☐ a. Eliminate boasting and exaggeration.
  - ☐ b. Back up your claims of ability by citing specific achievements in educational and work settings (or in outside activities).
  - ☐ c. Demonstrate a knowledge of the organization and a desire to join it by citing its operations or trends in the industry.
- ☐ 3. Link your education, experience, and personal qualities to the job requirements.
  - ☐ a. Relate aspects of your training or work experience to those of the target position.
  - ☐ b. Outline your educational preparation for the job.
  - ☐ c. Provide proof that you learn quickly, are a hard worker, can handle responsibility, and/or get along well with others.
  - ☐ d. Present evidence of personal qualities and work attitudes that are desirable for job performance.
  - ☐ e. If asked to state salary requirements, provide current salary or a desired salary range, and link it to the benefits of hiring you.
- ☐ 4. Refer the reader to the enclosed resume.

C. Action (Closing Paragraph)

- ☐ 1. Request an interview at the reader's convenience.
- ☐ 2. Request a screening interview with the nearest regional representative, if company headquarters is some distance away.
- ☐ 3. State your phone number (with area code) and the best time to reach you, to make the interview request easy to comply with, or mention a time when you will be calling to set up an interview.
- ☐ 4. Express appreciation for an opportunity to have an interview.
- ☐ 5. Repeat your strongest qualification, to help reinforce the claim that you have something to offer the organization.

WRITING OTHER TYPES OF EMPLOYMENT MESSAGES

In your search for a job, you may prepare three other types of written messages: job-inquiry letters, application forms, and application follow-up letters.

WRITING JOB-INQUIRY LETTERS

The purpose of a job-inquiry letter is to get you an application form.

Some organizations will not consider you for a position until you have filled out and submitted an application form. The inquiry letter is mailed to request such a form.

To increase your chances of getting the form, include enough information about yourself in the letter to show that you have at least some of the requirements for the position you are seeking. For example:

Please send me an application form for work as an interior designer in your home furnishings department. For my certificate in design, I took courses in retail merchandising and customer relations. I have also had part-time sales experience at Capwell's department store.

Instead of writing a letter of this kind, you may want to drop in at the office you're applying to. You probably won't get a chance to talk to anyone but the receptionist or a personnel assistant while you're there, but you can pick up the form, get an impression of the organization, and demonstrate your initiative and energy.

FILLING OUT APPLICATION FORMS

Some organizations require an application form instead of a resume, and many require both an application form and a resume, for all positions. The application form is a standardized data sheet that simplifies comparison of applicants' qualifications. In addition, it provides a convenient one-page source for the information most important to the employer.

The most important thing about filling out an application form is to be thorough and accurate.

When filling out an application form, make every effort to be thorough and accurate. Use your resume as a reference for such things as dates of employment. If you can't remember something and have no record of it, provide the closest estimate possible. If the form calls for information that you cannot provide because you have no background in it—for example, military experience—write "Not applicable."

Many application forms request that you provide information about the salary you want. The best strategy, unless you know what other people at the organization are earning for the job you are applying for, is to suggest a salary range or to write in "Negotiable" or "Open." You might also prepare for this question by consulting the latest government "Area Wage Survey" at the library; this document presents salary ranges for various job classifications and geographic areas.

Application forms rarely seem to provide the right amount of space or to ask the right kinds of questions to reflect one's skills and abilities accurately. Swallow your frustration, however, and show what a cooperative person you are by doing your best to fill out the form completely. If you get an interview, you'll have an opportunity to fill in the gaps. You might also ask the person who gives you the form if you may submit a resume and application letter as well.

WRITING APPLICATION FOLLOW-UPS

The purpose of an application follow-up is to keep your file active and up-to-date.

If your application letter and resume fail to bring a response within a month or so, follow them up with a second letter to keep your file active. This follow-up letter also gives you a chance to update your original application with any recent job-related information:

Since applying to you on May 3 for an executive secretary position, I have completed a course in office management. My typing speed has also increased to 75 words per minute.

Please keep my application in your active file and let me know when you need a skilled executive secretary.

Even if you have received a letter acknowledging your application and saying that it will be kept on file, don't hesitate to send a follow-up letter three months later to show that you are still interested:

Three months have elapsed since I applied to you for an underwriting position, but I want to let you know that I am still very interested in joining your company.

I recently completed a four-week temporary work assignment at a large local insurance agency. There I learned several new verification techniques and gained experience in using the on-line computer system. This experience could increase my value to your underwriting department.

Please keep my application in your active file, and let me know when an opening arises for a capable underwriter.

Unless you tell them otherwise, the personnel office is likely to assume that you've already found a job and are no longer interested in the organization. In addition, organizations' requirements change. Sending a letter like this demonstrates that you are sincerely interested in working for the organization, that you are persistent in pursuing your goals, and that you continue upgrading your skills to make yourself a better employee. And it might just get you an interview.

SUMMARY

Before writing a resume or application letter, analyze what you have to offer an employer and what you want from a job or career. Then look for employment opportunities.

After you have decided what kind of work you want to do and where you might want to do it, prepare a resume, a factual report on your qualifications, using action phrases and an abbreviated style. Organizing your resume to emphasize your strong points is entirely acceptable.

A resume should always be accompanied by an application letter, which is a selling piece. Therefore, follow the AIDA plan. The point of writing it is to win yourself an interview.

Other types of employment messages are job-inquiry letters, written to get you an application form; application forms, which should be filled out as completely as possible; and application follow-up letters, written to keep your name on the active list.

COMMUNICATION CHALLENGES AT PRICE WATERHOUSE

The senior managers at Price Waterhouse's Denver office are concerned about attracting high-caliber people to serve on the accounting and consulting staff. Every year, Don Greiner is expected to find 15 or 20 new people to fill vacancies and accommodate the growth of the office. However, attracting top-notch individuals is difficult, because competition for the "best and the brightest" is always intense.

Individual Challenge: To increase the efficiency of the campus recruiting effort, Don Greiner has asked you to develop a detailed form for evaluating the resumes of graduating students. Price Waterhouse is most interested in people with strong academic backgrounds who show evidence of communication skills and leadership potential. Previous work experience is a plus. After you have developed the evaluation form, evaluate the resumes of three or four fellow students.

Team Challenge: Don Greiner has been invited to conduct a workshop on writing resumes and application letters for a Career Day sponsored by local businesses. He asks a group of you to plan such a workshop for him. Prepare a detailed outline of the topics to be covered and prepare examples that can be distributed to workshop participants.

QUESTIONS FOR DISCUSSION

1. What advice would you give to a person who is interested in a career where opportunities are limited because of basic economic forces?

2. If you were running a company, which recruiting methods would you favor for identifying new employees? Why?

3. Do you think that employers are justified in reacting to a resume on the basis of its appearance?

4. "A good resume lists all your talents so potential employers know how versatile you are." Do you agree or disagree? Explain your answer.

5. Studies have found that many people inflate the credentials on their resumes, misrepresenting job qualifications, salaries, and academic credentials. If you were an employer, what would you do to detect resume inflation?

6. If you were a recruiter, would you prefer one organizational pattern for resumes over the others? If so, which one? Why?

7. Which do you think is more likely to convince an employer to interview you, your resume or the application letter that accompanies it?

8. How does one distinguish between an application letter that's unique (which is good) and one that's cute or gimmicky (which is bad)? Provide examples.

9. What role could phone calls play in your relationship with potential employers?

10. According to experts in the job placement field, "The average job seeker places too much importance on the resume and not enough on other elements of the job search." Which "other elements" do you think are more important?

DOCUMENTS FOR ANALYSIS

Read the following documents, and then (1) analyze the strengths and/or weaknesses of each numbered sentence and (2) revise each document so it follows this chapter's guidelines.

DOCUMENT 10.A

SYLVIA MANCHESTER
765 BELLE FLEUR BLVD.
NEW ORLEANS, LA 70113
(504) 312-9504

PERSONAL: Single, excellant health, 5'8", 116 lbs.; hobbies include cooking, dancing, and reading.

JOB OBJECTIVE: To obtain a responsible position in marketing or sales with a good company.

Education: B.A. degree in biology, University of Louisiana. Graduated with a 3.0 average. Member of the varsity cheerleading squad. President of Panhellenic League. Homecoming queen.

WORK EXPERIENCE

FISHER SCIENTIFIC INSTRUMENTS, 1985 TO PRESENT, FIELD SALES REPRESENTATVE. Responsible for calling on customers and explaining the features of Fisher's line of laboratory instruments. Also responsible for writing sales letters, attending trade shows, and preparing weekly sales reports.

FISHER SCIENTIFIC INSTRUMENTS, 1983-85, CUSTOMER SERVICE REPRESENTATIVE. Was responsible for handling incoming phone calls from customers who had questions about delivery, quality, or operation of Fisher's line of laboratory instruments. Also handled miscellaneous correspondence with customers.

MEDICAL ELECTRONICS, INC. 1981-83. ADMINISTRATIVE ASSISTANT TO THE VICE PRESIDENT OF MARKETING. In addition to handling typical secretarial chores for the vice president of marketing, I was in charge of compiling the monthly sales reports, using figures provided by members of the field sales force. I also was given responsibility for doing various market research activities.

NEW ORLEANS CONVENTION AND VISITORS BUREAU. 1977-81, SUMMERS. TOUR GUIDE. During the summers of my college years, I led tours of New Orleans for tourists visiting the city. My duties included greeting conventioneers and their spouses at hotels, explaining the history and features of the city during an all-day site-seeing tour, and answering questions about New Orleans and its attractions. During my fourth summer with the bureau, I was asked to help train the new tour guides. I prepared a handbook that provided interesting facts about the various tourist attractions, as well as answers to the most commonly asked tourist questions. The Bureau was so impressed with the handbook that they had it printed up so it could be given as a gift to visitors.

UNIVERSITY OF LOUISIANA. 1977-81. PART-TIME CLERK IN ADMISSIONS OFFICE. While I was a student in college, I worked 15 hours a week in the admissions office. My duties included filing, processing applications, and handling correspondence with high school students and administrators.

DOCUMENT 10.B

(1) I'm a motivated, experienced professional who can play a key managerial role in helping you become one of the aggressive and recognized leaders in the shopping center industry. **(2)** As the accountant for a prestigious real estate development company, I have extensive experience in such vital executive activities as:

--Administering and controlling accounting systems, reports, and project costs
--Preparing budgets and cash flow projections
--Managing and supervising a large accounting staff
--Interfacing with a variety of highly skilled development professionals

(3) In addition to offering you ten years of hands-on experience, I offer impressive academic and personal credentials, having both an MBA degree and a CPA certificate. **(4)** My knowledge of computers and my excellent interpersonal communications skills will be of value to you in your negotiations and transactions, in both the long run and the short run.

(5) Although I am extremely interested in your fine company, let me point out that this self-starter will not be available for long. **(6)** Five of your competitors in the real estate development industry have also received copies of my resume. (7) It will be advantageous for you to contact me in the immediate future.

DOCUMENT 10.C

(1) Two months ago, I sent you my resume. (2) As I'm sure you remember, you replied that you had no openings for which I was qualified. (3) But you said you would keep my resume in your files in case something turned up. (4) I was wondering if things had changed there, because I'm still looking for a job and would really like to work in Boston. (5) As you know, looking for a permanent job is not a pleasant task (especially if you've been looking as long as I have).

(6) However, I haven't been completely unemployed since I first wrote you. (7) I've taken a variety of odd jobs: waitress, baby-sitter, door-to-door salesperson. (8) Although none of these positions are in my chosen field of social work, they have increased my understanding of people. (9) I think I have matured considerably in the past two months and would make a better social worker now that I have seen how tough it is to make ends meet when you're making the minimum wage.(10) I'd like to come talk to you about the great things that I can do.

(11) And I have a real commitment to Boston.(12) Because it's one of my favorite cities, I am positive that I would be a real asset to the community.

DOCUMENT 10.D

(1) I saw your ad for a finance major in one of the papers last week, and I'd like to apply for the position. (2) I think I have all of the qualifications you're looking for, as you will see when you read my resume (attached).

(3) Let me tell you a little bit about myself.(4) Since I got my B.A. degree in finance (with honors) three years ago from State, I've been working for a little company in Sorrento Valley that makes magnetic tape heads for computers. (5) My title is financial analyst, and I do most of the things you mentioned in your ad: budgeting, cash forecasting, and computer modeling. (6) The work is interesting, but the company is having some problems, and I'd like to get into a more secure situation.(7) Although I don't know much about your outfit, the fact that you are owned by a large company is reassuring.

(8) I'd be grateful if you'd give me an interview. I know you must get a lot of resumes, and I guess mine is pretty much like all the rest, but I have a nice personality and would work hard. (9) You can reach me most of the time by calling 420-4665. (10) Thanks for taking the time to read this.

CASES

THINKING ABOUT YOUR CAREER

1. Taking stock and taking aim: Application package for the right job Think about yourself. What are some things that come easily to you? What do you enjoy doing? In what part of the country would you like to live? Do you like to work indoors? Outdoors? A combination of the two? How much do you like to travel? Would you like to spend considerable time on the road? Do you like to work closely with others or more independently? What conditions make a job unpleasant? Do you delegate responsibility easily, or do you like to take charge? Are you better with words or numbers? Better at speaking or writing? Do you like to be motivated by fixed deadlines? How important is job security to you? Do you want your supervisor to state clearly what is expected of you, or do you like the freedom to make many of your own decisions?

Your task: Mentally answer these questions. Next, with the help of some reference materials (from your college library or placement center), choose a location, a company, and a job that suit the profile you have just developed. With guidance from your instructor, you'll have to decide whether to apply for a job you're qualified for now or one you'll be qualified for with additional education. Then, as directed by your instructor, write one or more of the following: (a) a job-inquiry letter, (b) a resume, (c) a letter of application, and/or (d) a follow-up letter to your application letter.

WRITING A RESUME AND AN APPLICATION LETTER

2. "Help wanted": Application for a job listed in the classified section Among the jobs listed in today's *New Orleans Sentinel* (500 Canal Street, New Orleans, LA 70130) are the following:

ACCOUNTANT/MANAGER

Supervisor needed for 3-person bookkeeping department. Degree in accounting plus collection experience helpful. L. Cichy, Reynolds Clothiers, 1572 Abundance Dr., New Orleans 70119.

ACTIVIST—MAKE DEMOCRACY WORK

The state's largest consumer lobbying organization has permanent positions (full- or part-time) for energetic individuals with excellent communication skills who are interested in working for social change. Reply Sentinel Drawer 973.

ATTENDANT

For video game room, 4647 Almonaster Ave., New Orleans 70216.

CONVENIENCE FOOD STORE MANAGER

Vacancies for managers and trainees in New Orleans area. We are seeking energetic and knowledgeable individuals who will be responsible for profitable operation of convenience food stores and petroleum product sales. Applicants should possess retail sales and/or managerial training. Interested candidates mail resumes and salary requirements to Prestige Products, Inc., 444 Sherwood Forest Blvd., Baton Rouge, LA 70815. Equal opportunity employer M/F.

Your task: Send a resume and an application letter to one of these potential employers.

3. The goat and the tire: Application letter that shows the writer's creative abilities When Lillian Farmer opened her one-person advertising agency four years ago, it had two small accounts, no name, no office, no reputation. But all that has changed. Now it does more than $1 million in annual billings, and it has a name (Notorious, Inc.) and a statewide reputation for placing print and television advertisements that are visible, distinctive, memorable, varied, and compelling.

Her secrets for success are just that—secrets. But Lillian Farmer knows how to find the "heart" of the enterprise, the "drama" in the product, and to bring these intangibles to life through the color of her words and the bite of her graphics. She makes the ordinary memorable by showing it in unusual combinations or from odd angles, and she makes the extraordinary seem comfortably familiar.

Consider the Roadmaster tire draped around the body of a stuffed goat; almost nobody who saw the ad turned the page without reading the copy, and nobody will ever forget that tire.

Your task: Apply for a job as copywriter with Notorious, Inc. (674 Pellissippi Parkway, Atlanta, GA 30338). By its own example, your application letter must demonstrate your creative ability to write ad copy that gets results. Your resume lists the facts of your academic and professional life; your letter gives you the chance to show off your ability.

WRITING OTHER TYPES OF EMPLOYMENT MESSAGES

4. Crashing the last frontier: Letter of inquiry about jobs in Alaska Your friend can't understand why you would want to move to Alaska. So you explain: "What really decided it for me was that I'd never seen the Northern Lights."

"But what about the bears? The 60-below winters? The permafrost?"

"No problem. Anchorage doesn't get much colder than Buffalo. Just windier and wetter. But I want to live near Fairbanks, which is near the gold-mining area. And the university is there. Fairbanks has lots of small businesses, like a frontier town in the West about 50 years ago. I think they still have homesteading tracts for people who can do their own building and are willing to stay for a certain number of years."

"Your plans seem a little hasty. Maybe you should write for information before you just take off. How do you know you could get a job?"

Your task: Take your friend's advice and write to the Chamber of Commerce, Fairbanks, AK 99701. Ask what types of employment are available to someone with your education and experience and who specifically is hiring year-round employees.

5. Toward Florida employment: Letter to follow up a job application Three weeks ago, you applied for the position of sales trainee with Riverland Foods (323 Ted Hines Drive, Tallahassee, FL 32308), sending your resume and a strong cover letter to Christine Christopoulos, the director of personnel. Given your experience in the food industry and your good academic record, you believe that you have a chance to get the position.

Your application has not been acknowledged yet, so you decide to write a follow-up letter to show your genuine interest in the position. You begin to consider the points the letter might make:

- You are not certain that your original letter and resume arrived.
- Since you wrote, you have been named activities editor of the campus newspaper.
- You have been notified that you will have completed the requirements for graduation at the end of the term.
- You have submitted applications to several other firms but would prefer to work at Riverland Foods.

Your task: Write a follow-up letter to Ms. Christopoulos that will strengthen your application with Riverland Foods.

CHAPTER ELEVEN

After studying this chapter, you will be able to

- Prepare properly for a job interview
- Present your qualifications to an interviewer convincingly
- Find out whether an organization and a job are for you
- Pave the way for a second interview and a possible job offer
- Follow up effectively after the interview

INTERVIEWING FOR EMPLOYMENT AND FOLLOWING UP

Ann S. Bowers

COMMUNICATION CLOSE-UP AT APPLE COMPUTER

To score high marks with Ann S. Bowers, vice president of human resources for Apple Computer in Cupertino, California, applicants need to bone up on the organization in advance. "We find that most interviewees haven't done their homework," Ann confides. "They just don't know enough about our company." Thus one of Ann's aims during an interview is to make sure the applicant understands what the job entails and what her company is like.

"But most of all," she adds, "I try to get a clear picture of the applicant: his or her skills, preferences, and career goals." For this reason, Ann urges applicants to evaluate their skills in advance. "If they have specific professional abilities—like accounting, marketing, finance—they should be ready to let me know about them. They should also let me know about their interpersonal skills. Maybe they're good at getting people to talk to them. Maybe they've had experience in selling ideas or products. They need to spell out these capabilities and be ready to give evidence."

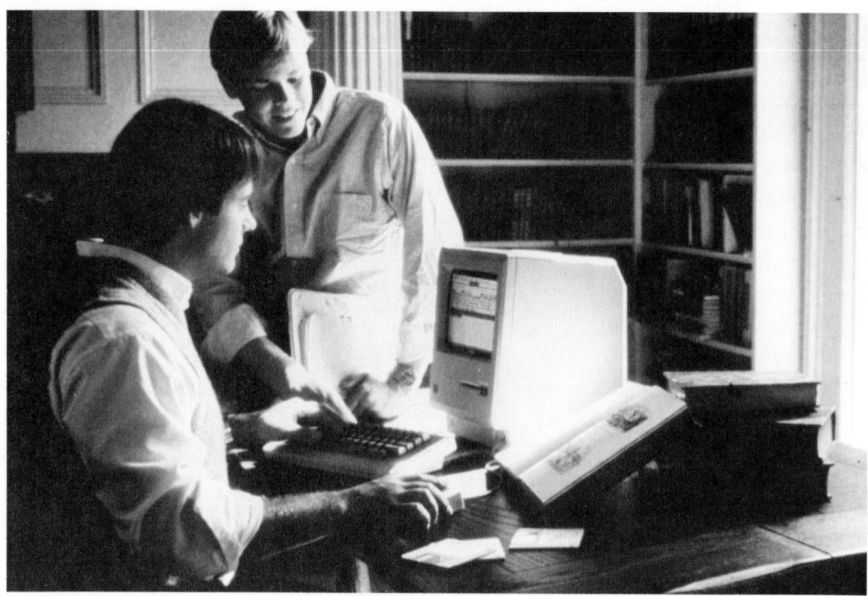

One reason Apple Computer is an industry leader is its ability to hire outstanding employees from among the hundreds of people interviewed each year.

They should also be ready to talk about their total experience, not merely classroom or work experience. "What impresses employers like Apple are people who are alive and alert, who have gotten involved in a variety of things, who have pursued opportunities to test themselves, learn a wide range of skills, and see how various situations fit them. We would be far more interested in this type of job applicant," she says candidly, "than in someone with just a super academic background."

In an interview, Ann likes to ask open-end questions: "For example, 'What do you think you would bring to Apple?' That's a tough one. I'm also likely to ask, 'What's really important to you?' 'Money' might be the answer, or 'recognition.' Whatever the response, it helps me know if we could meet that person's goals." Although the answers themselves are important, so is the way an interviewee handles the questions. "Some applicants are so busy figuring out what to say next that they fail to listen to the interviewer's questions. They also tend to say too much. A good interviewer notes how an applicant fills in the pauses."

Questions from applicants are usually not well thought out, Ann points out, mostly because many job seekers lack work experience. "But even from knowing their likes and dislikes, they should be able to define their job preferences. Then they could at least ask questions about the work environment and the nature of the job. Determining what they want ahead of time helps them come up with questions they can ask during the interview.

"One more thing," Ann says. "After the interview, whether they feel they did well or not, they should send a thank-you note. A short, polite note is a courtesy and helps them stand out from the applicants who didn't send one. If properly written, it also reinforces their strong points."

Unique, talented people are welcome at Apple. "We aren't a stuffy outfit," Ann laughs. "We're looking for pirates, not sailors. Not everyone wants to be an adventurer, of course. Many would rather be sailors. But by knowing which they are, applicants have a better chance of finding a job that fits, here or anywhere."

INTERVIEWING WITH POTENTIAL EMPLOYERS

An interview has benefits for both parties; the interviewer and the applicant both have legitimate goals.

As Ann Bowers points out, finding a job that fits is important. With the right job, you stand to be happy in your work. Thus it pays to approach job interviews with a sound appreciation of their dual purpose. The organization's main objective is to find the best person available for the job; the applicant's main objective is to find the job best suited to his or her goals and capabilities.

HOW INTERVIEWERS LEARN ABOUT APPLICANTS

Most organizations of any size have a well-developed system for finding and evaluating job applicants. Human resource specialists help supervisors and managers define the types of people they need and then recruit candidates. After the applications are evaluated and the most appropriate ones culled, the interviews may begin.

The interview process

Most organizations interview an applicant three times before extending a job offer.

Someone whose application makes an impression is normally invited to three interviews: preliminary screening on campus or elsewhere, initial evaluation at the organization's offices, and final evaluation at the organization. If you successfully negotiate all three phases of the interview process, chances are that you will be offered a job.

The preliminary screening is a means of eliminating unqualified applicants. The interviewer is typically a member of the organization's personnel department who may conduct hundreds of screening interviews each year. The interviews are generally quite structured, so that each interviewee is asked to respond to roughly the same questions. Many companies use standardized evaluation sheets to "grade" the interviewees, so that each candidate is measured against the same criteria. Screening interviews enable an organization to sort through a large number of candidates efficiently, which is a practical necessity when, say, 50 people respond to a help-wanted ad or 50 students sign up for interviews through their campus placement office.

Candidates who survive the screening are invited for a second interview, which is generally held at the organization's offices. This session is designed to let the personnel officer or department manager narrow the field a little further. If the initial evaluation goes well, the candidate is asked to come back for a final evaluation—and a possible job offer. (Sometimes the initial evaluation and the final evaluation are combined in a single visit.)

The goal of the final interview is to find the candidate best suited for the job. This interview is ordinarily conducted by the supervisor or department manager to whom the new employee will report, and this person usually has the authority to make the hiring decision. The final interview, then, is for the purpose of hiring.

In a typical job search, you can expect to have 20 or 30 interviews before you accept a job offer.

Because these three steps take time, it's a good idea to start seeking interviews well in advance of the date you want to start work. According to experts, it takes an average of 10 interviews to get one job offer. If you hope to have several offers to choose from, you can expect to go through 20 to 30 interviews during your job search.[1] No wonder some students start their job search as much as nine months before graduation.

Types of interviews

An interview for a specific job opening or for employment in the near future is a job interview. In contrast, a referral interview gives the employer a look at you for future reference. If you're uncertain about the purpose of an interview, ask a question like "Are you interviewing me for a specific position?" Sometimes a referral interview turns into a job interview, as when the interviewer finds that your qualifications are right for a specific opening. Thus a referral interview may open the door to a job opportunity before it is advertised.

Types of interviews:
- Job interview
- Referral interview
- Screening interview
- Selection interview

The aim of a screening interview is to narrow the field of applicants. The interviewer scrutinizes your qualifications to find reasons to reject you and checks your resume for inconsistencies. Your best approach to a screening interview is to follow the interviewer's lead. Keep your responses short and to the point. Volunteer no other information.

Those who successfully come through the screening interview usually go on to one or more selection interviews. The interviewer, generally a supervisor or department head, seeks to determine from your answers, actions, and attitudes whether you're right for the job. By noting how you listen, think, and express yourself, the interviewer can decide how likely you are to get along with others in the organization. The interview may end in a hiring decision. Your best approach in a selection interview is to show interest in the job, relate your training and experience to the organization's needs, listen attentively, and display enthusiasm.

Forms of interviews

Interviews may take three basic forms. The directed interview, generally used in screening, is planned from start to finish by the interviewer. Working from a checklist, she or he asks you a series of prepared questions within a specific time period. Your answers are noted. Although useful in gathering facts, the directed interview is generally regarded as too structured to measure an applicant's personal qualities.

Forms of interviews:
- Directed interview
- Unstructured interview
- Stress interview

In contrast, the less formal unstructured interview has an open, relaxed format. By posing broad, general questions, the interviewer encourages you to talk freely, perhaps even to divulge more than you should. Chiefly used in selection interviews, this form allows you to take control, with the interviewer acting as a moderator. The unstructured interview is therefore good for bringing out an applicant's personality.

The unstructured interview is often used in combination with the third form, the stress interview, which puts you under intentional stress so your reactions can be observed. For the unsuspecting applicant, the experience can be difficult. The stress interview may consist of pointed questions designed to irk or unsettle you, long periods of silence, criticisms of your appearance, highly personal or even insulting questions, deliberate interruptions, sudden challenges to your views, and abrupt or even hostile reactions by the interviewer. If you are alert, you cannot help but notice the use of stress techniques. The best way to deal with the situation is to remain calm.

Employment testing

To supplement the interview process, an increasing number of organizations administer tests to determine whether applicants have the necessary skills

FIGURE 11.1
What Employers Look For in an Applicant

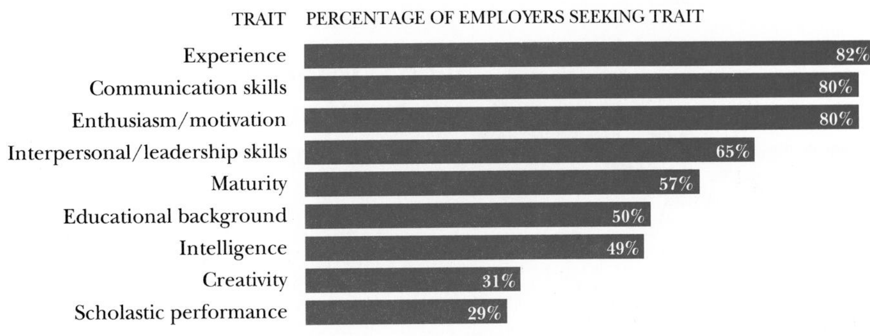

Interviews may be supplemented with employment tests, which are designed to provide objective, quantitative criteria for selecting new employees.

and psychological characteristics to handle a particular job. For example, some companies use "honesty" tests, which ask applicants a series of questions designed to bring out their attitudes toward stealing and doing a day's work for a day's pay. Other companies use handwriting analysis to evaluate candidates' personalities in areas considered necessary for good job performance.[2]

Tests have their critics, of course. Some employers prefer not to go to the extra expense of administering them or feel that educated judgment works just as well. And some job applicants consider employment tests an invasion of privacy. But the tests provide an objective, quantitative measure of applicants' qualifications, which may work to the advantage of both employer and job candidate. To protect candidates' interests, employment tests must meet strict criteria of fairness set forth by the Equal Employment Opportunity Commission.

WHAT EMPLOYERS LOOK FOR

Interviewers try to determine what you can do and what kind of person you are.

In general, employers are looking for two things: proof that a candidate can handle a specific job and evidence that the person will fit in with the organization. As Figure 11.1 illustrates, employers are most concerned with the candidate's experience, but communication skills, enthusiasm, and motivation are close behind.

Suitability for the job

Suitability for the specific job is judged on the basis of

- Academic preparation
- Work experience
- Job-related personality traits

Every position requires specific qualifications. To become an auditor, for example, you must know accounting; to become a sales manager, you must have several years of sales experience. When you are invited to interview for a position, the interviewer may already have a fairly good idea of whether you have the right qualifications, based on a review of your resume. But during the interview, you'll be asked to describe your education and previous jobs in more depth so the interviewer can determine how well your skills match the requirements.

Another consideration is whether a candidate has the right personality traits for the job. A personal interview is vital, because a resume is a poor vehicle for showing whether a person is lively and outgoing or subdued and low key, able to take direction or a take-charge type. Each job requires a different mix of personality traits. The task of the interviewer is to find out whether a candidate will be able to do the job comfortably.

LEGAL ALERT

Illegal Interview Questions: Your Rights When the Questions Are Wrong

Under federal law, employers may not discriminate against a job candidate on the basis of race, color, gender, age (from 40 to 70), marital status, religion, national origin, or handicap unrelated to job performance. If you are asked any of the following types of questions in an interview and then fail to get a job offer, you may have cause for legal complaint:

- Inquiries about your religious affiliation or about the organizations or lodges you belong to
- Questions about your marital status or former name
- Questions about the names or relationships of people you live with or questions about your spouse, spouse's employment or salary, dependents, children, or child-care arrangements
- Any questions about your height, weight, gender, or pregnancy that are not linked to actual job requirements
- Questions about health conditions or handicaps that are not reasonably related to your ability to perform the job
- Preinterview requests for a photograph or a question about the color of your skin, hair, or eyes
- Questions that would expose arrests or criminal convictions and that are not reasonably related to your fitness to perform the job, or questions about convictions that occurred more than seven years before the application date

If your reply to an unlawful question can't hurt you, answer the question. Then subtly let the interviewer know that you're aware of the law. But if the reply could hurt you, react lightheartedly, then decline to answer. If the interviewer presses you, explain, "I thought you were kidding, because that question is not job related."

Remember that an interviewer's job is to find out the sort of person you are. But if you feel that the interviewer is prying into prohibited areas in an attempt to discriminate, you may have cause for action. Complaints can be filed with the Equal Employment Opportunity Commission (EEOC) or with your state's agency that is responsible for fair employment practices. If discrimination relates specifically to age or a physical disability, contact the employer's equal opportunity officer or the U.S. Department of Labor. If none of these organizations provides you with satisfaction, you can file suit. But think before you take any of these actions. If you file a claim merely out of resentment that you didn't get a job offer, you risk losing time, money, and sympathy.

1. Although companies are reluctant to ask questions that might be considered discriminatory, candidates are free to mention their religion, ancestry, marital status, health, and so on. Do you believe that bringing up these issues is ethical for a candidate, or does it contribute to discrimination?

2. With another student acting as a probing interviewer, role-play a situation in which you are a 20-year-old unmarried woman, two months pregnant, applying for a job as a clerk in a convenience store.

A good fit with the organization

In addition to determining whether the applicant has the right professional qualifications and personality for a particular job, the interviewer must decide whether the person will be compatible with the other people in the organization.

Every interviewer approaches this issue of "fit" a little differently. Physical appearance is often a consideration, because clothing and grooming reveal something about a candidate's personality and awareness of industry standards. If you show up in casual clothes at Apple Computer, for example, you may be greeted as a kindred spirit, but the same outfit would work against you at a conservative law firm. Apart from noticing a candidate's clothes, interviewers also size up such physical factors as posture, eye contact, handshake, facial expressions, and tone of voice.

Compatibility with the organization is judged on the basis of

- Appearance
- Age
- Personal background
- Attitudes and style

An interviewer might also consider age in deciding whether an applicant will fit in with the organization (although job discrimination against the middle-aged is prohibited by law). If you feel your youth could count against you, counteract its influence by emphasizing your experience, dependability, and mature attitudes.

A candidate's personal background—interests, hobbies, awareness of world events, and the like—is also regarded as an indicator of how well the person will fit in with the organization. You can expand your potential along these lines by reading widely, making an effort to meet new people, and participating in discussion groups, seminars, and workshops.

Attitudes and style are other personal qualities that employers look at. Openness, enthusiasm, and interest are likely to impress an interviewer. So are courtesy, sincerity, willingness to learn, and a positive, self-confident style—all of which help a new employee adapt to a new workplace and new responsibilities.

WHAT APPLICANTS NEED TO FIND OUT

In an interview, you are entitled to find out whether the work and the organization are compatible with your goals and values.

What things should you find out about the prospective job and employer? By doing a little advance research and asking the right questions during the interview, you can probably find answers to all of the following questions and more:

- *Are these my kind of people?* Arrange to talk with an employee if you can, and when you go for an interview, observe the interviewer and other employees. Would you enjoy working with them?
- *Can I do this work?* Compare your qualifications with the requirements described in the notice for the job, in the job description on file at the placement office, or by the interviewer.
- *Will I enjoy the work?* To answer this one, you must know yourself and what is important to you. Is the work challenging? Will it give you feelings of accomplishment and satisfaction? Of making a real contribution?
- *Is the job what I want?* You may never find a job that fulfills all your wants, but the position you accept should satisfy at least your primary ones. Will the job make use of your best capabilities? Does it offer a career path to the long-term goals you've set for yourself?
- *Does the job pay what I'm worth?* Is the position comparable to those held by people with qualifications like your own? Is the pay in line with that for similar jobs in the field? By comparing jobs and salaries before you are interviewed, you will know what's reasonable for someone with your skills in your industry.
- *What kind of person would I be working for?* You can find out quite a bit by watching how others interact with your interviewer (if the interviewer is the supervisor for the position), by tactfully querying other employees, or by posing a careful question or two during the interview. If the interviewer is not your prospective boss, then ask who will be and what his or her job title and responsibilities are. Try to learn all you can, because that one person will have quite a bit to do

with whether you'll like the job and whether it will lead you somewhere or nowhere.

- *What sort of future can I expect with this organization?* This is a key question to ask during the interview and to research on your own. How healthy is the organization? And can you look forward to advancement?

HOW TO PREPARE FOR A JOB INTERVIEW

It's perfectly normal to feel a little anxious before an interview. So much depends on it, and you don't know quite what to expect. But don't worry too much, because preparation will help you perform well.

Do some basic research

As Ann Bowers points out, learning about the organization and the job is important. Figure 11.2 describes some good sources of information and the types of information to look for. You should also try to learn the interviewer's name and title. Knowing these facts shows that you have the interest and initiative to find out things on your own.

Be prepared to provide details about your qualifications that will interest the particular organization.

Once you have studied the organization, review your resume from the employer's point of view. What aspects of your background are likely to be of greatest interest to this particular organization? Practice relating what you have done and can do to the requirements of the job you want. Let each line of your resume serve as a cue for discussing relevant facts that may not be obvious from the resume.

Think ahead about questions

Most job interviews are essentially question-and-answer sessions: You answer the interviewer's questions about your background, and you ask questions of your own to determine whether the job and the organization are right for you. By planning ahead, you can handle these exchanges intelligently.

You can expect to be asked questions about what you have achieved, your interests and hobbies, how you feel about work and school, and your relationships with friends and family members. For a list of likely questions, see Figure 11.3. Jot down a brief answer to each one. Then read the answers over until you feel comfortable with each one. Or tape-record them, then listen to make sure they sound clear and convincing. This exercise will help you clarify your thinking and equip you with ready answers to even the toughest questions.

Practice answering interview questions.

The questions you ask in an interview are just as important as the answers you provide. By asking intelligent questions, you can demonstrate your understanding of the organization and steer the discussion into areas where you can present your qualifications to peak advantage. More important, you can get the information you need to evaluate the organization and the job.

Before the interview, prepare a list of about a dozen questions, using a mix of formats to elicit different types of information. Start with a warm-up question to help break the ice. For example, you might ask, "Have you already conducted many interviews for this job?" After that, ask only questions that can be answered without difficulty. Interviewers feel good

FIGURE 11.2
Finding Out About the Organization and the Job

WHERE TO LOOK	■ *Annual report:* Summarizes year's operations; mentions products, significant events, names of key personnel ■ *In-house magazine or newspaper:* Reveals information about company operations, events, personnel ■ *Product brochures and publicity releases:* Provide insight into organization's operations and values (obtain from public relations office) ■ *Stock research reports:* Help you assess stability and prospects for growth (obtain from local stockbroker) ■ *Business and financial pages of local newspapers:* Contain news items about organizations, current performance figures ■ *Periodicals indexes:* Contain descriptive listings of magazine and newspaper articles about organizations (obtain from library) ■ *Better Business Bureau and Chamber of Commerce:* Distribute information about some local organizations ■ *Former and current employees:* Have insight into job and work environment ■ *College placement office:* Collects information on organizations that recruit and on job qualifications and salaries
WHAT TO FIND OUT	About the Organization ■ *Full name:* What the organization is officially known as (for example, 3M is Minnesota Mining & Manufacturing Company) ■ *Location:* Where the organization's headquarters, branch offices, and plants are ■ *Age:* How long the organization has been in business ■ *Products:* What goods and services the organization produces and sells ■ *Industry position:* What the organization's current market share, financial position, and profit picture are ■ *Earnings:* What the trends in the organization's stock prices and dividends are (if the firm is publicly held) ■ *Growth:* What changes in earnings and holdings the organization has experienced in recent years and its prospects for expansion ■ *Organization:* What subsidiaries, divisions, and departments make up the whole About the Job ■ *Job title:* What you will be called ■ *Job functions:* What the main tasks of the job are ■ *Job qualifications:* What knowledge and skills the job requires ■ *Career path:* What chances for ready advancement exist ■ *Salary range:* What the organization typically offers and what pay is reasonable in this industry and geographic area ■ *Travel opportunities:* How often, how long, and how far you'll be allowed (or required) to travel ■ *Relocation opportunities:* Where you might be allowed (or required) to move to and how often you might be moved

Types of questions to ask during an interview:

- Warm-up
- Answerable
- Open-end
- Indirect

when they have an answer, especially when you acknowledge the answer with a smile. An open-end question—for example, "How do you see your organization improving on its product sales in the next few years?"—builds rapport by giving the interviewer a chance to express an opinion. Indirect questions are another approach. Comments like "I'd really like to know more about your space project" or "You must be busy with your new hotel acquisition" show your awareness and interest and may elicit useful

FIGURE 11.3
Twenty-five Common Interview Questions

1. What courses in school did you like most? Least? Why?
2. What jobs have you held? Why did you leave?
3. What percentage of your college expenses did you earn? How?
4. Why did you choose your particular field of work?
5. Do you prefer to work in any specific geographic location? If so, why?
6. How much money do you hope to earn at age 30? Age 35?
7. Do you think that your extracurricular activities while in college were worth the time you devoted to them? Why or why not?
8. What do you think determines a person's progress in a good organization?
9. What personal characteristics do you feel are necessary for success in your chosen field?
10. Why do you think you would like this particular type of job?
11. Do you prefer working with others or by yourself?
12. What type of boss do you prefer?
13. Tell me a story!
14. Have you served in the military? What rank did you achieve? What jobs did you perform?
15. When did you choose your college major? Did you ever change your major? If so, why?
16. Do you feel you did the best scholastic work you are capable of?
17. Have you ever had any difficulty getting along with other students? With instructors? With co-workers or supervisors?
18. Which of your college years was the toughest?
19. Would you prefer to work in a large or a small organization? Why?
20. What do you think about how this industry operates today?
21. Do you like to travel?
22. How do you feel about overtime work?
23. What are the disadvantages of your chosen field?
24. Do you think grades should be considered by employers? Why or why not?
25. What have you done that shows initiative and willingness to work?

information without putting any pressure on the interviewer. For a list of other good questions, see Figure 11.4.

Take your list of questions to the interview on a notepad or clipboard. Don't jot down the interviewer's answers during the meeting, but try to remember the answers and record them afterward. Having a list of questions should impress the interviewer with your organization and thoroughness. It will also show that you are there to evaluate the organization and the job as well as to sell yourself.

Bolster your confidence

By overcoming your tendencies to feel shy, self-conscious, nervous, or uncertain during an interview, you can build your confidence and make a

FIGURE 11.4
Fifteen Questions to Ask the Interviewer

1. What are this job's major responsibilities?
2. What qualities do you want in the person who fills this position?
3. Do you want to know more about my related training?
4. What is the first problem that needs the attention of the person you hire?
5. What are the organization's major strengths? Weaknesses?
6. Who are your organization's major competitors, and what are their strengths and weaknesses?
7. What makes your organization different from others in the industry?
8. What are your organization's major markets?
9. Does the organization have any plans for new products? Acquisitions?
10. What can you tell me about the person I would report to?
11. How would you define your organization's management philosophy?
12. What additional training does your organization provide?
13. Do employees have an opportunity to continue their education with help from the organization?
14. Would relocation be required, now or in the future?
15. Why is this job now vacant?

better impression. The best way to counteract these feelings is to identify and deal with their source.

For instance, being shy often results from having a real or an imagined deficiency that makes one shrink from contact with others. Here's how to overcome shyness:

- Realize that you are more aware of your seeming drawbacks than others are.
- If an aspect of your appearance makes you uneasy, correct it or exercise positive traits to offset it, such as warmth, wit, intelligence, or charm.
- If you feel inferior as a talker, emphasize modes of communication that you're good at, such as writing and researching.
- Make a list of your good points and compare them to your imagined shortcomings.
- Ask yourself this: With how many people whom you know well would you readily change places?

Learn to focus on your strengths so you can emphasize them to an interviewer.

You must also realize that it is natural to feel self-conscious in the presence of someone you regard as important, such as an interviewer. To conquer self-consciousness, keep this in mind: Everyone is just a person. You and the interviewer may not share all the same experiences and interests, but you are both human. To the extent that you can make the interviewer feel more comfortable, you will lose your own feelings of discomfort.

If you feel shy or self-conscious, remember that recruiters are human too.

BUSINESS COMMUNICATION TODAY

Winning Answers to 15 Challenging Interview Questions

Here are good answers to some of the tougher questions asked in job interviews. If you can smoothly supply answers like these during the interview, you're bound to make a good impression.

- *What is important to you in a job?* Mention specific rewards other than a paycheck—for example, challenge, the feeling of accomplishment, and knowing that you have made a contribution.
- *Why do you want to work for this organization?* Cite its reputation, the opportunities it offers, and the working conditions. Stress that you want to work for this organization, not just any organization.
- *Why should we employ you?* Point to your academic preparation, job skills, and enthusiasm about working for the firm. Mention your performance in school or previous employment as evidence of your ability to learn and to become productive quickly. If the job involves management responsibilities, refer to past activities as proof of your ability to get along with others and to work as part of a team.
- *If we hire you, how long will you stay with us?* Answer by saying something along these lines: "As long as my position here allows me to learn and to advance at a pace consistent with my abilities."
- *What are your greatest strengths?* Give a response like one of the following: "I can see what needs to be done and do it"; "I'm willing to make decisions"; "I work well with others"; "I can organize my time efficiently."
- *What are your greatest weaknesses?* Identify one or two, such as the following: "I tend to drive myself too hard"; "I expect others to perform beyond their capacities"; "I like to see a job done quickly, and I'm critical if it isn't." Notice that these weaknesses could also be regarded as desirable qualities. The trick with this question is to make a potential virtue sound like a problem.
- *What didn't you like about previous jobs you've held?* Discuss the things you didn't like, but avoid making slighting references to any of your former employers.

Many people also feel nervous when they think about being interviewed. Here are some simple ways to overcome nervousness:

- Identify the specific aspect of the interview that is making you feel nervous. Is it the large office building? The busy work atmosphere? The authoritative interviewer? The pressure of having to do well? Once you know what makes you feel uneasy, envision yourself facing it and dealing with it successfully. Repeat this process until you feel your nervousness subside.

Control your nervousness by thinking positively.

- Jot down the reasons you feel anxious about the interview. Then make a list of your positive points. Compare the two. You'll discover that you have more reasons to feel confident than to feel nervous.
- Review your capabilities until you can discuss them readily. Practice doing so aloud in front of a mirror, with a friend, with a tape recorder, or on videotape. Rehearse talking about yourself and selling yourself.
- Use small props during the interview to control nervousness: Keep your resume in front of you to prevent lapses of memory; carry a

- *How do you spend your leisure time?* Mention a cross section of interests—active and quiet, social and solitary—rather than just one.
- *Are there any weaknesses in your education or experience?* Take stock of your weaknesses before the interview. Practice discussing them in a positive light. You'll find that they are minor when discussed along with all the positive things you have to offer.
- *Where do you want to be five years from now?* Saying you'd like to be president is unrealistic, yet few employers want people who are content to sit still. You might say, "In five years, I'd like to have my boss's job." If you can't qualify for your boss's job by then, you may not be the right candidate.
- *What are your salary expectations?* If you are asked this at the outset, it's best to say, "Why don't we discuss salary after you decide if I'm right for the job?" But if the interviewer asks this after showing real interest in you, speak up. She or he will probably try to meet your price. If you need a clue about what to ask for, say "Can you discuss your salary range with me?"
- *What would you do if . . . ?* This question is designed to test your responses. For example: "What would you do if your computer broke down during an audit?" Your answer here isn't nearly so important as your approach to the problem. And a calm approach is best. Start by saying, "One thing I might do is . . . ." Then give several alternative choices.
- *What type of position are you interested in?* Job titles and responsibilities vary from firm to firm. So state your skills instead, such as "I'm good at figure work," and the positions that require these skills, such as "accounts payable."
- *Tell me something about yourself.* Say you'll be happy to talk about yourself, and ask what the interviewer wants to know. If this point is clarified, respond. If not, tell why you feel your skills will contribute to the job and the organization. This question gives you a great opportunity to sell yourself.
- *Do you have any questions about the organization or the job?* Employers like a candidate who is interested in the organization. So this is a perfect time to convey your interest and enthusiasm.

Many other answers might be appropriate, of course, so you need not memorize the ones suggested here. Just be sure that your answers are sincere, truthful, and positive. And take a moment to compose your thoughts before responding so your answers are to the point.

1. What makes an effective answer to an interviewer's question? Consider some of the ways in which answers can vary: specific versus general, assertive versus passive, informal versus formal.

2. Think of four or five additional questions that pertain specifically to your resume. Practice your answers.

piece of literature about the organization, such as an annual report, that you can refer to; or take along a sample of your work, if appropriate.

- Avoid looking nervous during the interview. Don't chew gum, smoke, tap your fingers on the desk or chair, or play with a key ring or other object. Instead, sit back in the chair, relax, and fold your hands in your lap. This posture will help you to look calm and feel calm.

Act confident, and you will feel confident.

And then there's uncertainty. If you are interviewing for an advertised position and don't feel fully qualified, realize that advertisements often overstate the job requirements. The interviewer may relax the requirements a bit after talking with you. And because such qualities as enthusiasm may overshadow all others, sound and act positive.

Polish your interview style

Confidence helps you walk into an interview, but you'll walk out without a job if you don't also give the interviewer an impression of poise, good manners, and good judgment. One way to develop an adept style is to

FIGURE 11.5
Black Marks Against Applicants (in General Order of Importance)

1. Has a poor personal appearance
2. Is overbearing, overaggressive, conceited; has a "superiority complex"; seems to "know it all"
3. Is unable to express self clearly; has poor voice, diction, grammar
4. Lacks knowledge or experience
5. Is not prepared for interview
6. Has no real interest in job
7. Lacks planning for career; has no purpose or goals
8. Lacks enthusiasm; is passive and indifferent
9. Lacks confidence and poise; is nervous and ill at ease
10. Shows insufficient evidence of achievement
11. Has failed to participate in extracurricular activities
12. Overemphasizes money; is interested only in the best dollar offer
13. Has poor scholastic record; just got by
14. Is unwilling to start at the bottom; expects too much too soon
15. Makes excuses
16. Is evasive; hedges on unfavorable factors in record
17. Lacks tact
18. Lacks maturity
19. Lacks courtesy; is ill-mannered
20. Condemns past employers
21. Lacks social skills
22. Shows marked dislike for schoolwork
23. Lacks vitality
24. Fails to look interviewer in the eye
25. Has limp, weak handshake

Staging mock interviews with a friend is a good way to hone your style.

stage mock interviews with a friend. After each practice session, have your friend critique your performance, using the list of interview faults shown in Figure 11.5 to identify opportunities for improvement.

Striking just the right tone in an interview is difficult. You want to avoid any hint of the following flaws:

- *Shrinking in the presence of authority*. Being in awe of the interviewer can reduce you to a quaking ninny, a condition that is unlikely to get you a job offer. To prevent it, project a warm, confident manner from the start. Ask questions and acknowledge answers. Be positive, outgoing, and professional.
- *Seeming "laid back" and flippant*. Perhaps you are so confident of your chances that you'll seem overly relaxed, perhaps even uncaring. To dispel this image, try to display real interest during the interview. Learn about the organization in advance, and ask relevant questions. Look alive and attentive. Show enthusiasm. Smile. Comment positively on what the interviewer is saying.

- *Talking too much or too little.* Either one can turn off an interviewer. Ask people close to you about your speaking habits. Do you tend to dominate the conversation? Or barely say a word? If you tend to have either problem, try to correct it.
- *Being overwhelming.* If you're a dynamic, exuberant type who talks rapidly, exudes enthusiasm, and sometimes overwhelms others, try to curb your energies during the interview. Sell yourself less assertively. Listen a little more. Promote your ideas a little less vigorously.

Nonverbal behavior has a great effect on the interviewer's opinion of you.

As you stage your mock interviews, pay particular attention to your nonverbal behavior. You are more likely to be invited back for a second interview or offered a job if you maintain eye contact, smile frequently, nod your head, sit in an attentive position, and use frequent hand gestures. These nonverbal signals convince the interviewer that you are alert, assertive, dependable, confident, responsible, and energetic.[3]

Like other forms of nonverbal behavior, the sound of your voice can have a major impact on your success in a job interview.[4] If you suspect that you are weak in this area, work with a tape recorder to overcome your faults. If you tend to speak too rapidly, practice speaking more slowly. If your voice sounds too loud or too soft, practice adjusting it. Work on eliminating annoying little speech mannerisms like *you know*, *like*, and *um*, which might make you sound inarticulate. Speak in your natural tone; trying to sound sophisticated may make you seem artificial or affected. But do try to vary the pitch, rate, and volume of your voice to express enthusiasm and energy. If you speak in a flat, emotionless tone, you convey the impression that you are passive or bored.

The way you speak is almost as important as what you say.

Plan to look good

You can impress an interviewer just by the way you look. The best policy is to dress conservatively. Wear the best-quality clothing you can. The traditional business colors are dark blue, brown, gray, and maroon, although lighter colors are acceptable if the clothing style is businesslike. At all costs avoid flamboyant styles, colors, and prints. Before you go to the interview, try to find out what type of clothing is worn by employees at your target job level. By dressing like them, or perhaps a little more conservatively for this special occasion, you'll seem to fit right in.

To look like a winner
- Dress conservatively
- Be well groomed
- Stand and sit up straight
- Smile

Good grooming makes any style of clothing look better. Make sure your clothes are clean and unwrinkled, your shoes unscuffed and well shined, your hair neatly styled and combed, your fingernails clean, your breath fresh. If possible, check your appearance in a mirror before entering the room for the interview. Don't spoil the effect by chewing gum or smoking cigarettes during the interview.

Good posture, another important aspect of appearance, conveys an air of pride and confidence. So avoid slouching during the interview. And avoid crossing your arms and your legs simultaneously.

Finally, remember that one of the best ways to look good is to smile.

Be ready when you arrive

For the interview, plan to take (perhaps in a neat, compact briefcase) a small notebook, a pen, a list of the questions you want to ask, two copies of your resume protected in a folder, an outline of what you have learned about the organization, and any past correspondence about the position. You may also want to take a small calendar, a transcript of your college grades, a list of references, and if appropriate, samples of your work. Recruiters are impressed by tangible evidence of your job-related accomplishments, such as reports, performance reviews, and certificates of achievement. In an era when many people exaggerate their qualifications, visible proof of your abilities carries a lot of weight.[5]

Be prepared for the interview:

- Take proof of your accomplishments
- Arrive on time
- Wait graciously

Finally, be sure that you know when and where the interview will be held. The worst way to start any interview is late. Check the route you will take, even if it means phoning the interviewer's secretary to ask. Find out how much time it takes to get there, then plan to arrive early. And allow a little extra time just in case you run into a problem on the way.

Once you arrive, relax. You may have to wait a little while, so bring along something to read or occupy your time (the less frivolous or controversial, the better). Or if company literature is available, read it while you wait. In either case, be polite to the interviewer's assistant. If he or she doesn't seem too busy, you might ask a few questions about the organization or express enthusiasm for the job. Just keep in mind that anything you do or say while you wait may well get back to the interviewer. So make sure your best side shows from the moment you enter the premises.

HOW TO BE INTERVIEWED

The way to handle the interview itself depends on where you stand in the interview process. If you are being interviewed for the first time, your main objective should be to differentiate yourself from the many other candidates who are also being screened. Let's say, for example, that you have signed up to talk with a recruiter on campus. A recruiter with a full interview schedule may talk with 10 or 15 applicants during the course of the day. Without resorting to gimmicks, you need to call attention to one key aspect of your background so the recruiter can say, "Oh yes, I remember Jones—the one who sold encyclopedias door to door in Detroit." Just be sure the trait you accentuate is relevant to the job in question.

Present a memorable "headline" during a screening interview.

If you have progressed to the initial selection interview, you should broaden your sales pitch. Instead of telegraphing the "headline," give the interviewer the whole story. Touch at least briefly on all your strengths, but explain three or four of your best qualifications in depth. At the same time, probe for information that will enable you to evaluate the position objectively. As important as it is to get an offer, it's also important to learn whether the offer is worth taking.

Cover all your strengths during a selection interview.

If you are asked back for a final visit, your chances of being offered a position are quite good. At this point, you will be talking to a person who has the authority to make the offer and negotiate terms. This individual may already have concluded that you have the right background for the job, so she or he will be concerned with sizing up your personality. In fact, both you and the employer need to find out whether there is a good psychological fit. Be honest about your motivations and values. If the interview goes well, your objective should be to clinch the deal on the best possible terms.

Emphasize your personality during a final interview.

Regardless of where you stand in the interview process, every interview will proceed through three stages: the warm-up, the question-and-answer-session, and the close.

The warm-up

The first minute of the interview is crucial.

Of the three stages, the warm-up is most important, although it may account for only a small fraction of the time you spend in the interview. Psychologists say that 50 percent of the interviewer's decision is made within the first 30 to 60 seconds, and another 25 percent is made within 15 minutes. If you've gotten off to a bad start, it's extremely difficult to turn the interview around.[6]

Body language is very important at this point. Because you won't have time to say much in the first minute or two, you must sell yourself nonverbally. Begin by using the interviewer's name if you're sure you can pronounce it correctly. If the interviewer extends a hand, respond with a firm but gentle handshake. Then wait until you are asked to be seated. Let the interviewer start the discussion. And listen for cues that tell you what he or she wants to hear.

The question-and-answer stage

Questions and answers will consume the greatest part of the interview. During this phase, the interviewer will ask you to restate your qualifications and expand on the points in your resume. You will also be asked if you have any questions of your own.

As questions are asked, tailor your answers to make a favorable impression. Remember that the interviewer will be observing you and noting every word you say. So don't limit yourself to yes or no answers, and pause to think before responding if you are asked a difficult question. Consider the direction of the discussion, and guide it where you wish with your responses.

Another way you can reach your goal is to ask the right questions. If you periodically ask a question or two from the list you've prepared, you will demonstrate interest. And form occasional questions by paraphrasing the interviewer's own words.

Paying attention when the interviewer speaks can be as important as giving good answers or asking good questions. Listening should make up about half of the time you spend in an interview. For tips on becoming a better listener, read Chapter 17.

Effective listening, with your eyes and ears, can help you turn the question-and-answer stage to your advantage.

Remember to listen with your eyes as well as your ears. The interviewer's facial expressions, eye movements, gestures, and posture may tell you the real meaning of what is being said. If the interviewer says one thing but sends a different message nonverbally, you may want to discount the verbal message. Be especially alert to how your comments are received. For example, does the interviewer nod in agreement or smile to show approval? If so, you're making progress. If not, you might want to introduce another topic or modify your approach.

The close

Like the opening, the end of the interview is more important than its duration would indicate. In the last few minutes, you need to evaluate how well you have done and correct any misconceptions the interviewer might have.

You can generally tell when the interviewer is trying to conclude the

SHARPEN YOUR SKILLS

Turning Tough Interview Situations to Your Advantage

Here are ten tough interview situations you may encounter in your job search. Before reading the suggested solutions, think about how you might handle each situation.

PROBLEM: You keep trying to promote a conversation, but your interviewer isn't saying much.

SOLUTION: The interviewer may want to see how you do on your own—or may even be uneasy talking with strangers. Your best bet is to keep on talking about how your skills can benefit the company.

PROBLEM: The interviewer won't stop talking and give you a chance to sell yourself or your talents.

SOLUTION: Interject good, solid questions as the interviewer talks, questions that show you know the subject. Then ask, "How do you see my abilities fitting in with your organization?"

PROBLEM: The interviewer seems to dislike you and shoots down every answer you give.

SOLUTION: The interviewer probably wants to see how you react to stress. Don't let negative responses upset your poise; maintain a positive attitude. For example, mention what you have done to help the companies you've worked for instead of dwelling on why you no longer work for them. The strategy is to keep the interviewer on your track, not to be dragged onto his or hers.

PROBLEM: The interviewer suddenly hits you with a series of tough, fast questions.

SOLUTION: The interviewer wants to see if you can think on your feet and under pressure. Take your time. Give specific answers. If you don't know an answer, say so. And keep cool; poise may be the most important quality you could demonstrate.

PROBLEM: Your interview starts 45 minutes late. You're due back at school or your office in 15 minutes and feel anxious about the time.

SOLUTION: If you can delay returning without feeling uneasy, go ahead with the interview. If not, level with the in-

Conclude the interview with courtesy and enthusiasm.

session by watching for verbal and nonverbal cues. The interviewer may ask if you have any more questions, sum up the discussion, change position, or indicate with a gesture that the interview is over. When you get the signal, respond promptly. Trying to prolong the interview will frustrate the recruiter and work to your disadvantage. But by the same token, don't rush. Be sure to thank the interviewer for the opportunity and express an interest in the organization. If you can do so comfortably, try to pin down what will happen next, but don't press for an immediate decision.

If this is your second or third visit to the organization, the interview may culminate with an offer of employment. You have two options: Accept it, or request time to think it over. The best course is usually to wait. If no job offer is made, the interviewer may not have reached a decision yet. But you may tactfully ask when you can expect to know the decision.

If you do receive an offer during the interview, you will naturally want to discuss salary. But let the interviewer raise the subject. If asked your salary requirements, say that you would expect to receive the standard

terviewer about the time bind and try to set up another date.

PROBLEM: The interviewer likes you and says so but adds that your background isn't exactly what the company is looking for.

SOLUTION: Agree that your experience may not be as deep as desired. Then persuade the interviewer that you are the best choice; after all, a year with the company would give you the desired level of experience.

PROBLEM: The interview is going well. Then the interviewer describes the specific job that is open. You know it isn't for you.

SOLUTION: If you're absolutely positive that you don't want the job, make clear that you are not interested in it. Then ask about other openings that may exist; or try to convince the interviewer that, in view of your ability and promise, he or she should try to create a new position for you.

PROBLEM: The interview goes well, and you're offered the job right there and then. But you recently interviewed at another firm and would prefer to work there. Should you take the job you've just been offered or hold out for the other one?

SOLUTION: Ask Company A (the company that just offered you the job) for time to think, without mentioning the job you want at Company B. Then tell Company B about the offer from Company A. Ask if Company B can move up its decision date or at least tell you where you stand. If you get no response, you have your answer.

PROBLEM: The interviewer tells you that although the company has no opening of the kind you seek, you can temporarily take an opening at a lower level.

SOLUTION: You have no assurance of when and how you will be promoted. Try to persuade the interviewer to offer you a job closer in level to the one you seek. If you have another job offer, mention it. If this tactic fails to get results, keep looking.

PROBLEM: The interviewer talks on and on about the company, its prospects, the wonderful working conditions, and the people—then asks when you can start. Without opening your mouth, you have a job offer.

SOLUTION: Be wary. Ask for time to think, then investigate. Don't jump into a job that may be a disaster.

1. **Try to think of some other tough interview situations. How would you handle them?**

2. **In class, role-play several of these situations with another student, taking turns as interviewer. Have the class critique the exchange.**

salary for the job in question. If you have added qualifications, point them out: "With my 18 months of experience in the field, I would expect to start in the middle of the normal salary range."

If you don't like the size of the offer, you might try to negotiate, provided that you are in a good bargaining position and the organization has the flexibility to accommodate you. You will be in a fairly strong position if your skills are in short supply and you have several other offers. It also helps if you are the favorite candidate and the organization is booming. But many organizations are relatively rigid in their compensation practices, particularly at the entry level. You might just ask, "Is there any room for negotiation?"

Don't be afraid to negotiate for a better salary and benefits package, but be realistic in your expectations and diplomatic in your approach.

Even if you can't bargain for more money, you might be able to win some concessions on benefits and perquisites. The value of negotiating can be significant, because benefits often cost the employer 25 to 45 percent of your salary. In other words, if you're offered an annual salary of $20,000, you'll ordinarily get an additional $5,000 to $9,000 in benefits: life, health, and disability insurance; pension and savings plans; vacation time; tuition reimbursement; club memberships; use of a car.[7] If you can trade one benefit for another, you may be able to enhance the value of the total package. For example, life insurance may be relatively unimportant to you if you are single, whereas extra vacation time might be very valuable indeed. Don't inquire about fringe benefits, however, until you know you have a job offer.

Interview notes

Careful record keeping will help you keep organized and will help you become more adept at interviewing.

If yours is a typical job search, you will have many interviews before you accept a final offer. To refresh your memory of each conversation, you should keep a record of your impressions. As soon as the interview ends, jot down the names and titles of the people you met. If you're unsure of any names or their spellings, phone the organization's receptionist for clarification.

Next write down in capsule form the interviewer's answers to your questions. Then briefly evaluate your performance during the interview, listing what you handled well and what you didn't. Going over these notes can help you improve your performance in the future.

■ CHECKLIST FOR INTERVIEWS

A. Preparation

- ☐ 1. Determine the requirements and general salary range of the job.
- ☐ 2. Research the organization's products, structure, financial standing, and prospects for growth.
- ☐ 3. Determine the interviewer's name, title, and status in the firm.
- ☐ 4. Prepare answers for the questions you are likely to be asked about your qualifications and achievements, your feelings about work and school, your interests and hobbies.
- ☐ 5. Develop relevant questions to ask, such as what training the organization might offer after employment, what type of management system the firm has, whether its executives are promoted from within, and why the position is vacant.
- ☐ 6. Plan your appearance.
  - ☐ a. Determine the mode of dress that prevails within the organization so you can copy it.
  - ☐ b. Select conservative, good-quality clothing to wear to the interview.
  - ☐ c. Check your clothing to make sure it's clean and wrinkle-free.
  - ☐ d. Choose traditional footwear, unscuffed and well shined.
  - ☐ e. Wear a minimum of jewelry, but wear a wristwatch to keep track of the time.
  - ☐ f. Use fragrances sparingly, and avoid excessive makeup.
  - ☐ g. Choose a neat, well-groomed, conventional hairstyle.
  - ☐ h. Clean and manicure your fingernails.
  - ☐ i. Check your appearance just before going into the interview, if possible.
- ☐ 7. Take a list of questions, two copies of your resume, and samples of your work (if appropriate) to the interview in a briefcase.
- ☐ 8. Double-check the location and time of the interview.
  - ☐ a. Map out the route beforehand, and estimate the time you'll need to get there.
  - ☐ b. Plan your arrival for 10 to 15 minutes before the interview.
  - ☐ c. Add 10 or 15 more minutes to cover problems that may arise en route.

B. Initial Stages of the Interview

- ☐ 1. Greet the interviewer by name, with a smile and direct eye contact.
- ☐ 2. Offer a firm but gentle handshake if the interviewer extends a hand.

FOLLOWING UP AFTER THE INTERVIEW

Touching base with the prospective employer after the interview, either by phone or in writing, shows that you really want the job and are determined to get it. It also brings your name to the interviewer's attention once again and reminds him or her that you are waiting to know the decision. Because few applicants send follow-up letters or call to say thank you, the prospective employer will probably be impressed if you do.

Six types of follow-up messages:
- Thank you
- Inquiry
- Request for a time extension
- Letter of acceptance
- Letter declining a job offer
- Letter of resignation

The two most common forms of follow-up are the thank you and the inquiry. These are generally handled by letter, but a phone call is often just as effective, particularly if the employer seems to favor a casual, personal style. The other four types of follow-up messages—request for a time extension, letter of acceptance, letter declining a job offer, and letter of resignation—are sent only in certain cases. These messages are better handled in writing, because it is important to document any official actions relating to your employment. However, regardless of whether you are communicating orally or in writing, you should follow the principles outlined in this chapter.

- ☐ 3. Take a seat only after the interviewer invites you to be seated or has taken his or her own seat.
- ☐ 4. Sit with an erect posture, facing the interviewer.
- ☐ 5. Listen for cues that tell you what the interviewer wants to hear.
- ☐ 6. Assume a calm and poised attitude.
- ☐ 7. Avoid gum chewing, smoking, and other displays of nervousness.

C. Body of the Interview

- ☐ 1. Display a genuine, not artificial, smile at appropriate times.
- ☐ 2. Convey interest and enthusiasm.
- ☐ 3. Listen attentively so you can give intelligent responses.
- ☐ 4. Take no notes, but remember key points and record them later.
- ☐ 5. Sell the interviewer on hiring you.
  - ☐ a. Relate your knowledge and skills to the position you are seeking.
  - ☐ b. Stress your positive qualities and characteristics.
- ☐ 6. Answer questions wisely.
  - ☐ a. Keep responses brief, clear, and to the point.
  - ☐ b. Avoid exaggeration, and convey honesty and sincerity.
  - ☐ c. Avoid slighting references to former employers.
- ☐ 7. Avoid cocktails if you are interviewed over lunch.

D. Salary Discussions

- ☐ 1. Put off a discussion of salary until late in the interview, if possible.
- ☐ 2. Let the interviewer initiate the discussion of salary.
- ☐ 3. If asked, state that you would like to receive the standard salary for the position in question.

E. Closing Stages of the Interview

- ☐ 1. Watch for signs that the interview is about to end.
- ☐ 2. Tactfully ask when you will be advised of the decision on your application.
- ☐ 3. If you're offered the job, either accept or ask for time to consider the offer.
- ☐ 4. Thank the interviewer for meeting with you, with a warm smile and a handshake.

THANK YOU

A note or phone call thanking the interviewer

- Should be organized like a routine message
- Should close with a request for a decision or future consideration

Express your thanks within two days after the interview, as Ann Bowers of Apple Computer suggests, even if you feel you have little chance for the job. Acknowledge the interviewer's time and courtesy. Convey the idea that you continue to be interested. Then ask politely for a decision.

Keep your thank you brief (less than five minutes or a page in length), and organize it like a routine message. Like all good business messages, it should demonstrate the "you" attitude. Although you don't want to sound doubtful about your chances of getting the job, you must also avoid sounding arrogant or too sure of yourself.

The following sample thank-you letter shows how to achieve all this in three brief paragraphs:

After talking with you yesterday, touring your sets, and watching the television commercials being filmed, I remain very enthusiastic about the possibility of joining your staff as a television/film production assistant. Thanks for taking so much time to show me around.	The opening reminds the interviewer of the reasons for meeting and graciously acknowledges the consideration shown to the applicant.
During our meeting, I said that I would prefer not to relocate. But I've reconsidered the matter. If my apartment can be sublet, I would be pleased to relocate wherever you need my skills in set decoration and prop design.	This paragraph indicates the writer's flexibility and commitment to the job if hired. It also reminds the recruiter of special qualifications.
Now that you've explained the details of your operation, I feel quite strongly that I can make a contribution in the sorts of productions you've begun to line up. You can also count on me to be an energetic worker and a positive addition to your crew. Please let me know your decision as soon as possible.	The letter closes on a confident and you-oriented note, ending with the request for a decision.

Even if the interviewer has said that you are unqualified for the job, a thank-you message like that shown in Figure 11.6 may keep the door open. A letter of this type will probably go into the file for future openings, because it demonstrates courtesy and interest.

INQUIRY

An inquiry about a hiring decision should follow the plan for a direct request.

If you are not advised of the interviewer's decision by the promised date or within two weeks, you might make an inquiry. An inquiry is particularly appropriate if you have received a job offer from a second firm and don't want to accept it before you have an answer from the first.

The following inquiry letter follows the general plan for a direct request; the writer assumes that a simple oversight, and not outright rejection, is the reason for the delay.

When we talked on April 7 about the fashion coordinator position in your Park Avenue showroom, you said you would let me know your	The opening paragraph identifies the position and introduces the main idea.

FIGURE 11.6
Sample Thank-You Note

585 Montoya Road
Las Cruces, NM 88005
January 16, 1989

Ms. Gloria Reynolds, Editor
Las Cruces News
317 N. Almendra Street
Las Cruces, NM 88001

Dear Ms. Reynolds:

The main idea is the expression of thanks for the interviewer's time and information.

Our conversation on Tuesday about your newspaper's opening for a food-feature writer was enlightening. Thank you for taking time to talk with me about it.

The writer specifically refers to points discussed in the interview. Enthusiasm and eagerness to improve skills are qualities that will impress the interviewer.

Your description of the profession makes me feel more certain than ever that I want to be a newspaper writer. Following your advice, I am going to enroll in an evening journalism course soon.

The letter closes with a specific and cordial request.

After I achieve the level of writing skills you suggested, I would deeply appreciate the chance to talk with you again.

Sincerely,

Michael Espinosa

Michael Espinosa

decision before May 1. I would still like the position very much, so I'm eager to know what conclusion you've reached.

To complicate matters, another firm has now offered me a position and has asked that I reply within the next two weeks.

The reason for the request comes second. The writer tactfully avoids naming the other firm.

Because your company seems to offer a greater challenge, I would appreciate knowing about your decision before Thursday, May 12. If you need more information before then, please let me know.

The courteous request for a specific action comes last, in the context of a clearly stated preference for this organization.

REQUEST FOR A TIME EXTENSION

A request for a time extension should follow the plan for a direct request but pay extra attention to easing the reader's disappointment.

If you receive a job offer while other interviews are still pending and you want more time to decide, write to the offering organization and ask for a time extension. Such a request can be risky, so be sure to preface it with a friendly opening like the one shown in the following sample letter. Then ask for more time, stressing your enthusiasm for the organization. Conclude by allowing for a quick decision if your request for additional time is denied. And ask for a prompt reply confirming the time extension if the organization grants it.

The customer relations position in your snack foods division seems like an exciting challenge and a great opportunity. I'm very pleased that you offered it to me.	The letter begins with a strong statement of interest in the job.
Because of another commitment, I would appreciate your giving me until August 29 to make a decision. Before our interview, I scheduled a follow-up interview with another company. Frankly, I'm more interested in your organization because of its impressive quality-control procedures and friendly, attractive work environment. I do feel obligated to keep my appointment, however.	The writer stresses professional obligations, not her desire to learn what the other company may offer. Specific reasons for preferring the first job offer help reassure the reader of her sincerity.
If you need my decision immediately, I'll gladly let you know. But if you can allow me the added time to fulfill the earlier commitment, I'd be grateful. Please let me know right away.	The expression of willingness to yield or compromise conveys continued interest in the position.

This type of letter is, in essence, a direct request. But because the recipient may be disappointed, you must temper your request for an extension with statements indicating your continued interest.

LETTER OF ACCEPTANCE

A letter of acceptance should follow the good-news plan.

When you receive a job offer that you want to accept, reply within five days. Begin by accepting the position and expressing thanks. Identify the job that you're accepting. In the next paragraph, cover any necessary details. Conclude by saying that you look forward to reporting for work.

I'm delighted to accept the graphic-design position in your advertising department at the salary of $1,575 a month.	The good-news statement at the beginning confirms the specific terms of the offer.
Enclosed are the health insurance forms you asked me to complete and sign. I've already given notice to my current employer and will be able to start work on Monday, January 18.	Miscellaneous details are covered in the middle.
The prospect of joining your firm is very exciting. Thank you for giving me this opportunity for what I'm sure will be a challenging future.	The letter closes with another reference to the good news and a look toward the future.

As always, a good-news letter should convey your enthusiasm and eagerness to cooperate.

Acceptance of a job offer is legally binding.

You should be aware that a job offer and a written acceptance of that job constitute a legally binding contract, for both you and the employer. So before you write an acceptance letter, be sure you want the job.

LETTER DECLINING A JOB OFFER

A letter declining a job offer should follow the bad-news plan.

After all your interviews, you may find that you need to write a letter declining a job offer. The best approach is to open warmly, state the reasons for refusing the offer, decline the offer explicitly, and close on a pleasant note, expressing gratitude. By taking the time to write a sincere, tactful letter like the one shown here, you leave the door open for future contact.

One of the most interesting interviews I have ever had was the one last month at your Durham textile plant. I'm flattered that you would offer me the computer-analyst position that we talked about.

The opening paragraph is a buffer.

During my job search, I applied to five highly rated firms like your own, each one a leader in its field. Both your company and another offered me a position. Because my desire to work abroad can more readily be satisfied by the other company, I have accepted that job offer.

Tactfully phrased reasons for the applicant's unfavorable decision precede the bad news and leave the door open.

I deeply appreciate the hour you spent talking with me. Thank you again for your consideration and kindness.

A sincere and cordial ending lets the reader down gently.

The bad-news plan is ideally suited to this type of letter.

LETTER OF RESIGNATION

A letter of resignation should also follow the bad-news plan.

If you get a job offer and are presently employed, you should write a letter of resignation to maintain good relations with your current employer. Make the letter sound positive, regardless of how you feel. Say something favorable about the organization, the people you work with, or what you have learned on the job. Then state your intention to leave and the termination date.

My sincere thanks to you and to all the other Emblem Corporation employees for helping me learn so much about serving the public these past 11 months. You have given me untold help and encouragement.

An appreciative opening serves as a buffer.

You may recall that, when you first interviewed me, my goal was to become a customer relations supervisor. Because that opportunity has been offered to me by another organization, I am

Reasons stated before the bad news itself and tactful phrasing help keep the relationship friendly,

■ CHECKLIST FOR FOLLOW-UP MESSAGES

A. Thank You's

- ☐ 1. Thank the interviewer by phone or in writing within two days after the interview.
- ☐ 2. Keep the message to less than five minutes or one page.
- ☐ 3. In the opening, express thanks and identify the job and the time and place of the interview.
- ☐ 4. Use the middle section for supporting details.
  - ☐ a. Express your enthusiasm about the organization and the job after the interview.
  - ☐ b. Add any new facts that may help your chances.
  - ☐ c. Try to undo any negative impressions you may have left during the interview.
- ☐ 5. Use an action ending.
  - ☐ a. Offer to submit more data.
  - ☐ b. Express confidence that your qualifications will meet the organization's requirements.
  - ☐ c. Look forward to a favorable decision.
  - ☐ d. Request an opportunity to prove that you can aid the organization's growth or success.

B. Inquiries

- ☐ 1. Phone or write an inquiry if you are not informed of the decision by the promised date, especially if another organization is awaiting your reply to a job offer.
- ☐ 2. Follow the plan for direct requests: main idea, necessary details, specific request.

C. Requests for a Time Extension

- ☐ 1. Send this type of letter if you receive a job offer while other interviews are pending and you want more time before making your decision.
- ☐ 2. Open with an expression of warmth.
- ☐ 3. In the middle section, explain why you need more time and express your continuing interest in the organization.
- ☐ 4. Conclude by allowing for a quick decision if your request for more time is denied and by asking the interviewer to confirm the time extension if it is granted.

D. Letters Accepting a Job Offer

- ☐ 1. Begin by stating clearly that you accept the offer with pleasure and by identifying the job you are accepting.
- ☐ 2. Fill out the letter with vital details.
- ☐ 3. Conclude with a statement that you look forward to reporting for work.

E. Letters Rejecting a Job Offer

- ☐ 1. Open a letter of rejection warmly.
- ☐ 2. Fill out the letter with an explanation of why you are refusing the offer and an expression of appreciation.
- ☐ 3. End on a sincere, positive note.

F. Letters of Resignation

- ☐ 1. Send a letter of resignation to your current employer as soon as possible.
- ☐ 2. Begin with an appreciative buffer.
- ☐ 3. Fill out the middle section with your reasons for looking for another job and the actual statement that you are leaving.
- ☐ 4. Close cordially.

submitting my resignation. I regret leaving all of you, but I can't pass up this opportunity.	should the writer later want letters of recommendation.
I would like to terminate my work here two weeks from today but can arrange to work an additional week if you want me to train a replacement.	An extra paragraph discusses necessary details.
My sincere thanks and best wishes to all of you.	A cordial close tempers any disappointment.

This letter follows the bad-news plan. By sending one like it, you show that you are considerate and mature, and you also help ensure the good feeling that may help you get another job in the future.

SUMMARY

An organization that invites you to an interview wants to find out if you are the best person to fill a job opening. Your goal is to find out about the job and the organization so you can make a decision should the job be offered.

You can relieve the anxious and nervous feelings that often accompany interviews by preparing ahead of time. First, analyze the organization, the job, and your own qualifications and needs. Then plan answers to the interviewer's likely questions and devise some questions of your own. The interview itself will go more smoothly if you adopt a relaxed style and an enthusiastic attitude.

Follow-up messages to the interviewer, such as thank you's and inquiries, may increase your chances of getting a job offer. Other courteous, well-planned employment letters—whether requesting a time extension, accepting an offer, declining an offer, or resigning—also demonstrate that you are a professional.

COMMUNICATION CHALLENGES AT APPLE COMPUTER

Apple Computer is gearing up for the campus recruiting season. The firm hopes to hire 6 or 7 trainees for the sales department as well as 10 to 15 engineers and computer scientists. Your boss, Ann Bowers, has asked you to take charge of the effort to recruit new graduates for the sales department.

Individual Challenge: A team of recruiters will visit college campuses to screen applicants. To ensure that the recruiters' evaluations of potential sales trainees are thorough and consistent, Ann has asked you to prepare a questionnaire they can use during screening sessions. Each interview will last about 20 minutes.

Team Challenge: After the screening interviews, a number of the most promising candidates for the position of sales trainee are invited back to Apple headquarters for selection interviews. Each candidate is evaluated by you and a group of sales department staffers; you decide whether the candidate should be invited back for a final interview with sales department management. To guide this phase of the interview process, your group needs to develop a checklist that covers all of the skills and interests that might indicate success in sales. Test the checklist by having one member of the group play the role of the candidate. Each of the other members of the team (yourself included) should interview the candidate separately, out of hearing of the rest. Afterward, meet to discuss the candidate, using the checklist to guide the discussion.

QUESTIONS FOR DISCUSSION

1. Why do companies use directed interviews for screening and less structured approaches for selection interviews?
2. Do you feel that stress interviews are a useful way to evaluate candidates? Why or why not?
3. What would you do if a potential employer asked you to submit to a handwriting analysis designed to reveal your personality traits?
4. Suppose that you have been invited to interview at a prestigious company. Prior to the interview, you happen to meet someone who used to work there. What would you ask this person about the company? If the person's comments were highly critical, how would you determine the truth during the interview?
5. How should a job applicant answer this question: "What are your greatest weaknesses?"
6. How might an applicant explain a desire to switch jobs because of an inability to work with the current supervisor?

7. What types of questions should an applicant not ask?
8. How can an applicant strike a balance between appearing to shrink before the interviewer's authority and appearing to be overconfident?
9. If you felt that you had gotten off to a bad beginning, what would you do to try to save the interview?
10. What are the advantages of thanking an interviewer over the phone instead of writing? What are the disadvantages?

DOCUMENTS FOR ANALYSIS

Read the following documents, and then (1) analyze the strengths and/or weaknesses of each numbered sentence and (2) revise each document so it follows this chapter's guidelines.

DOCUMENT 11.A

(1) Thank you for the really marvelous opportunity to meet you and your colleagues at Starret Engine Company. **(2)** I really enjoyed touring your facilities and talking with all the people there. **(3)** You have quite a crew! **(4)** Some of the other companies I have visited have been so rigid and uptight that I can't imagine how I would fit in. **(5)** It's a relief to run into a group of people who seem to enjoy their work as much as all of you do.

(6) I know that you must be looking at many other candidates for this job, and I know that some of them will probably be more experienced than I am. **(7)** But I do want to emphasize that my two-year hitch in the Navy involved a good deal of engineering work. **(8)** I don't think I mentioned all of my shipboard responsibilities during the interview.

(9) Please give me a call within the next week to let me know your decision. **(10)** You can usually find me at my dormitory in the evening after dinner (phone: 877-9080).

DOCUMENT 11.B

(1) I have recently received a very attractive job offer from the Warrington Company. **(2)** But before I let them know one way or another, I would like to consider any offer that your firm may extend. **(3)** I was quite impressed with your company during my recent interview, and I am still very interested in a career there.

(4) I don't mean to pressure you, but Warrington has asked for my decision within ten days.**(5)** Could you let me know by Tuesday whether you plan to offer me a position? **(6)** That would give me enough time to compare the two offers.

DOCUMENT 11.C

(1) I'm writing to say that I must decline your job offer. **(2)** Another company has made me a more generous offer, and I have decided to accept. **(3)** However, if things don't work out for me there, I will let you know. **(4)** I sincerely appreciate your interest in me.

CASES

INTERVIEWING WITH POTENTIAL EMPLOYERS

1. Interviewers and interviewees: Classroom exercise in interviewing Obviously, interviewing is an interactive process involving at least two people. The best way to practice for interviews is therefore to work with others.

Your task: You and all other members of the class should write letters of application for a management trainee position requiring a pleasant personality and intelligence but a minimum of specialized education or experience. Sign your letters with a fictitious name that conceals your identity. Next, polish (or prepare) a resume that accurately identifies you and your educational and professional accomplishments.

Three members of the class, who volunteer as interviewers, should divide equally among themselves all the anonymously written application letters. Then each interviewer should select for an interview the candidate who seems the most pleasant and convincing in his or her letter. At this time, the selected candidates should identify themselves and give the interviewers their resumes.

Each interviewer should then interview his or her chosen candidate in front of the class, seeking to understand how the items on the resume qualify the candidate for the job. At the end of the interviews, the class may decide who gets the job and discuss why this candidate was successful. Then retrieve your letter, sign it with the right name, and submit it to the instructor for credit.

FOLLOWING UP AFTER THE INTERVIEW

2. "Dear Mr. Chacon": Follow-up letter to straighten out a possible confusion You have been interviewed for the position of assistant manager of a retail outlet in the In-a-Minute, Inc., chain, consisting of company-owned stores that sell groceries, some medications, and petroleum products. The chain is successful, with new outlets opening regularly in Missouri, Kentucky, and Tennessee, and you would much appreciate the chance to join the firm.

During the interview, Roger Chacon asked you several questions about your academic record. Your answers, you feel, were somewhat scattered and left Mr. Chacon with no clear understanding of the courses you've taken, your proficiency in several key areas, and the date you expect to graduate—matters that he seemed most interested in.

Your task: Working with your own record, draft a follow-up letter to send to Mr. Chacon with a copy of your college transcript. Describe what you have accomplished in one or two academic areas. Mr. Chacon is with the personnel department at the corporation's headquarters, 99 Litzinger Lane, St. Louis, MO63124.

3. A slight error in timing: Letter asking for delay of an employment decision You botched up your timing and applied for your third-choice job before going after what you really wanted. What you want to do is work in marketing with Allied Stores in Dallas; what you have been offered is a similar job with Longhorn Leather and Lumber, 55 dry and dusty miles away in Commerce, just south of the Oklahoma Panhandle.

You review your notes. Your Longhorn interview was three weeks ago with the personnel manager, R. P. Bronson, a congenial person who has just written to offer you the position. The store's address is 27 Sam Rayburn Drive, Commerce, TX 75428. Mr. Bronson notes that he can hold the position open for ten days. You have an interview scheduled with Allied next week, but it is unlikely that you will know their decision within this ten-day period.

Your task: Write to R. P. Bronson, requesting a reasonable delay in your consideration of his job offer.

4. Journey to Long Island: Letter accepting a good job offer Today's mail brings you the following letter from Rhonda Frederick, Personnel Director, Chesterton Ceramics, 3 Chesterton Place, Long Island City, NY 11101:

We are pleased to offer you the position of Chemical Technician beginning 60 days from the date of this letter at a monthly salary of $1,650. Please let us know of your acceptance of this position within ten days.

Your work will be given six-month and twelve-month reviews; we offer 5 percent salary increases at these points if the employee's work progress is satisfactory. As was indicated to you in the interview, employee participation in the company pension plan is voluntary during the first full year of employment, after which time it is required. We will fund your moving expenses up to $850, with 50 percent of this amount sent to you in advance if you desire.

We hope that you will accept this position. Your academic record and experience indicate that you should do well in our laboratories, and you will find that Long Island provides easy access to Manhattan. We maintain a file of house and apartment listings; if you let me know your housing needs, I will send you whatever information you require.

If you plan to join our pension program during your first year, please let me know so I can start the paperwork prior to your arrival.

Enclosed is our check for $232.76, covering your interview expenses.

Your task: Write a letter accepting the job and answering the questions that Ms. Frederick asks.

5. Job hunt: Set of employment-related letters to a single company Where would you like to work? Pick a real or imagined company and assume that a month ago you sent your resume and application letter. Not long afterward, you were invited to come for an interview, which seemed to go very well.

Your task: Use your imagination to write the following: (a) a thank-you letter for the interview; (b) a note of inquiry; (c) a request for more time to decide; (d) a letter of acceptance; and (e) a letter declining the job offer.

PART FIVE

REPORTS AND PROPOSALS

After studying this chapter, you will be able to

- Identify the qualities of a good business report or proposal
- Base decisions about report format, style, and organization on factors relating to who, what, when, where, why, and how
- Identify six general purposes of reports
- Explain how the six types of reports are developed
- Understand how reports and proposals are used in a business setting

CHAPTER TWELVE

USING REPORTS AND PROPOSALS AS BUSINESS TOOLS

Bert Browse

COMMUNICATION CLOSE-UP AT CALVIN KLEIN

Bert Browse, senior vice president and director of manufacturing for Calvin Klein, Ltd., is responsible for seeing that 175 different styles of clothes in assorted colors and sizes are perfect, right down to the last stitch. On a typical day in his busy New York office, he receives roughly 300 orders, ranging in value from $10,000 to $100,000.

Reports are essential in filling these orders. "I couldn't do my job without them," says Bert. Each morning, he receives update reports on work in progress, cut-and-sew operations, and fabric inventory, so he always knows "what we've cut and what we still have left to cut."

These daily status reports are augmented by other reports. For example, every week Bert receives a report on the company's inventory of leftover raw materials. "On reading one of these reports," Bert recalls, "I noticed that we had 75,000 square feet of suede sitting in our factory in Hong Kong. The skins were just sitting there because they weren't in current 'fashion' colors."

Knowing the suede would dry out if it wasn't used soon, Bert took the report along with him on his next trip to Hong Kong. "When I arrived," he says, "I selected six styles from past seasons and worked up a small

Reports help maintain the status of one of the biggest names in the fashion world—Calvin Klein, Ltd.—which appears on everything from designer jeans to men's fragrances.

group of samples, tops and bottoms." When he returned to New York, he presented the samples to the sales manager. Within a few days, she had booked enough orders for these styles to use all the suede. "I was able to turn $150,000 of almost worthless skins into a profit," adds Bert, "because of the information in the inventory report.

"The person who prepared that report listed the kinds of fabric that we had the most of right up front, so I saw the most valuable inventory first," Bert observes. He likes this approach for business reports: "Put the main idea at the beginning and get the reader's interest. Spell out the highlights. Then get to the point quickly.

"One more thing," notes Bert. "Say it simply in clear, concise language." Many of his reports, he points out, are to associates abroad. Some don't understand English well. "So I write in a language that's easy to understand."

Bert relies on reports because "the more responsibility you have, the less time you have to run around and talk to everybody. Reports are the only intelligent way to monitor and control operations and to get the input you need to make the right decisions."

WHAT MAKES A GOOD BUSINESS REPORT

A business report is any factual, objective document that serves a business purpose.

You may be surprised at the variety of documents that qualify as reports. The term covers everything from preprinted forms to brief, informal letters and memos to formal three-volume manuscripts. Some reports are even delivered orally, as Chapter 18 explains. In general, however, when business people speak of reports, they are thinking of written, factual accounts that objectively communicate information about some aspect of the business.

In large part, reports are a management tool. Even the most capable managers must often rely on other people to observe events or collect information for them. They are often too far away to oversee everything themselves, and they don't have enough time. In addition, they often lack the specialized background required to research and evaluate certain subjects. Thus reports are usually for management or on its behalf.

Make business reports as concise as possible.

The goal in developing a report is to make the information as clear and convenient as possible. Because time is precious, you tell the readers what they need to know—no more, no less—and you present the information in a way that is geared to their needs.

SOLID CONTENT

Make sure that every report's content is accurate and that it reflects good judgment.

Reports vary widely in their purpose and, to a lesser but still significant degree, in the audience they're written for. They also vary in format, style, and organization. However, good reports all have at least two things in common: (1) The information is accurate, and (2) the content shows the writer's good judgment.

Accuracy

The first thing you have to learn as a business report writer is how to tell the truth. If your information is inaccurate or incomplete, the readers will make bad decisions. As a result the business will suffer, and so will your reputation.

To ensure accuracy
- Check the facts
- Reduce distortion

Unfortunately, telling the truth is not always a simple matter. Each of us sees reality a little bit differently, and each of us describes what we see in our own way. For instance, if you say, "That movie was great," your friend may respond, "Are you nuts? It was nothing but sex and violence."

What can you do to limit the distortions introduced by differences in perception? Here are some guidelines:

- *Describe facts or events in concrete terms.* It's better to say, "Sales have increased from $400,000 to $435,000 in the past two months" than to say, "Sales have skyrocketed." Indicate quantities whenever you can. Be specific.
- *Report all the relevant facts.* Regardless of whether these facts will support your theories or please your readers, they should be included. Omitting the details that undermine your position might be convenient, but it isn't accurate. You might also hesitate to be the bearer of bad news, but you will mislead readers if you leave out unpleasant information.
- *Put the facts in perspective.* If you tell readers, "The value of the stock has doubled in three weeks," you are giving only a partial picture. They will have a much clearer idea of reality if you say, "The value of the stock has doubled in three weeks, rising from $2 to $4 per share on the rumor of a potential merger." Taken out of context, even the most concrete facts can be misleading.
- *Give plenty of evidence for your conclusions.* You can't expect readers to fully understand your conclusions unless you offer substantial supporting evidence. Statements like "We've got to reorganize the sales force or we're bound to lose market share" may or may not be true. Readers have no way of knowing unless you provide enough data to support your claim.

- *Present only valid evidence and supportable conclusions.* You will, of course, check your facts and figures and obtain your information from reliable sources. In addition, try to avoid drawing hasty or ill-founded conclusions from your data. Just because one sales representative reports that customers are dissatisfied with your product doesn't mean that all customers are dissatisfied. You are likely to distort the truth when you generalize from too small a sample. In addition, you should not assume that a preceding event is the cause of what follows. The fact that sales declined right after you switched advertising agencies doesn't necessarily mean that the new agency is to blame. Other factors, such as the general state of the economy, may be responsible. When you offer a conclusion, be certain that you have ample evidence to support it, and avoid drawing conclusions in areas where you have limited experience or an inadequate professional background.
- *Keep your personal biases in check.* Even if you have strong feelings about the subject of your report, try to keep those feelings from influencing your choice of words. Here's an example of emotionally charged language taken from a relocation study: "Locating a plant in Kraymore is a terrible idea. The people there are mostly students, they'd rather play than work, and they don't have the ability to operate our machines." Language like this is not only offensive, but it obscures reality and provokes emotional responses.

Good judgment

Do not include anything in a report that might jeopardize you or your organization.

Some things simply don't belong in a report, whether or not they are true. You can do both yourself and your employer a great deal of harm by being indiscreet. Of course, you should not cover up wrongdoing, but you should be prepared to back up in a court of law whatever you write. Business documents are frequently used as evidence in legal proceedings.

Keep "politics" out of your reports; provide a clear, direct accounting of the facts.

You should also be aware that managers have distinct preferences when it comes to reports. They particularly dislike personal gripes, criticism, alibis, attempts to blame someone else, incomplete or sugar-coated data, unsolicited opinions, and attempts to by-pass the manager through the distribution of the document. On the other hand, they like five things:

- Getting the main idea at the beginning of the report
- Seeing the facts
- Receiving the whole story
- Reading language they can understand
- Learning something that will make their jobs easier[1]

It's fair to say that all readers, not just managers, will appreciate your attention to these five points.

Regardless of what type of report you are preparing, try to keep the likes and dislikes of your readers in mind. As you make decisions about the content of the report, their needs should be your main concern, and you should exercise your best judgment in trying to meet those needs.

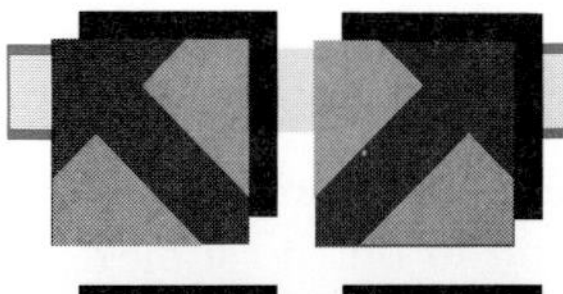

BUSINESS COMMUNICATION TODAY

Beyond the Typewriter: Using a Computer to Prepare Reports

A computer can speed and simplify the production of many types of reports, from routine informational ones to detailed analytical forecasts. For instance, with a microcomputer or computer terminal, you can obtain data from and send data to other computer users; search company, library, or other data bases; obtain data via computer screen and/or printout; organize data on the screen; store data and retrieve it when needed; test hypotheses by statistical analysis; and analyze trends in sales, revenues, costs, and profits.

In addition, some computers can store hundreds of reports and retrieve them on command. They can also reproduce them at a rate of over 600 words per minute. Thus you can have at your fingertips many already prepared documents that will ease your writing task.

With a computer you can also polish your report endlessly without ever having to retype it. The computer lets you recall your original draft, then add, delete, or replace words, phrases, or sentences. You can edit, revise, and proofread the report right on the screen. The computer can incorporate all these changes before you produce even one "hard copy" from a printer. If you like, you can print the report for proofreading and then go back to the computer to make further refinements.

All these advantages of using a computer to do reports assume that you have access to a computer with word-processing and text-editing capabilities. But you might also investigate desktop publishing systems if your reports must be fairly elaborate (including visual aids, for example) or if they need to look particularly professional.

Desktop publishing allows you to produce computer-created pages that look as though they've been typeset and professionally laid out. Special software helps you design the look of your pages, placing artwork on the same page as text and incorporating a wide variety of typefaces and sizes. You can then make a copy of the result on a laser printer, which gives the appearance of typesetting. Laser-printed pages can then be photocopied for distribution or, because they are of such high quality, can even be submitted to a print shop for reproduction in quantity.

To do desktop publishing, you will need access to a hardware system that can handle this type of application, such as an Apple Macintosh or IBM Personal System computer; to software such as PageMaker by Aldus; and to a laser printer. You will also need, of course, some knowledge of how to make this system work for your purposes. Just as using a word-processing program will not make you an expert writer, using a desktop publishing system will not automatically make you an expert at page design and layout. But if you have some flair for design and the need to do elaborate reports, a desktop system could save you a lot of time and effort and help you produce a visually pleasing product.

1. Do you feel that you are being adequately trained to take advantage of computer technology for report writing? If not, what can you do to gain the skills you need? Who do you think should be responsible for computer education? Employers, schools, or individuals?

2. Investigate the desktop publishing systems available for the Apple Macintosh and the IBM Personal System. What are the advantages and disadvantages of each? Which system would you choose?

RESPONSIVE FORMAT, STYLE, AND ORGANIZATION

Select a format, style, and organization that reflect the reader's needs.

The reader's needs should also be the the key factor in your decisions regarding the format, style, and organization of the report. Before you write, you have to decide whether to use letter, memo, or manuscript format (see Component Chapter D for details); whether to employ a formal or informal style; whether to group the ideas one way or another.

In thinking about these issues, you need to ask yourself the following questions and tailor the report accordingly:

In making decisions about the format, style, and organization of a report, consider its

- Origin
- Subject
- Timing
- Distribution
- Purpose
- Probable reception

- *Who initiated the report? Voluntary* reports, prepared on your own initiative, require more detail and support than *authorized* reports, which are prepared at the request of another person. In writing a voluntary report, you need to give more background on the subject and more carefully explain your purpose.
- *What subject does the report cover?* The subject of a business report affects its vocabulary and format. For example, an audit report (one that verifies an accountant's inspection of a firm's financial records) must contain a lot of numbers, often in the form of tables. A report from the corporate legal department about the company's patents would contain many legal terms. When both writer and reader are familiar with the subject and share the same background, the writer does not need to define terms or explain basic concepts.
- *When is the report prepared? Routine* reports submitted on a repeat basis (daily, weekly, monthly, quarterly, annually), like the reports that Bert Browse receives at Calvin Klein, require less introductory and transitional material than do *special,* nonrecurring reports that deal with unique situations. Often, routine reports are prepared on preprinted forms, which the writer simply fills in, or are organized in a standard way.
- *Where is the report being sent? Internal* reports, prepared for use within the organization, are generally less formal than *external* reports, which are sent to people in other organizations. Many internal reports, especially those under ten pages, are written in memo format. External reports, on the other hand, may be in letter format if they are no longer than five pages or in manuscript format if they exceed five pages.
- *Why is the report being prepared? Informational* reports focus on facts; *analytical* reports include analysis, interpretation, conclusions, and recommendations. Informational reports are usually organized around subtopics; analytical reports are generally organized around logical arguments. (Chapter 15 explains the difference in greater detail.)
- *How receptive is the reader?* When the reader is likely to agree with the content of the report, the material is presented in *direct order,* starting with the main idea (key findings, conclusions, recommendations). If the reader may have reservations about the report, the material is presented in *indirect order,* starting with the details and leading up to the main idea.

As you can see from this list and from Table 12.1, the origin, subject, timing, distribution, purpose, and probable reception of a report all have a substantial impact on its format, style, and organization.

HOW COMPANIES USE REPORTS AND PROPOSALS

Reports are like bridges, spanning time and space. Organizations use them to provide a formal, verifiable link among people, places, and times. Some reports are needed for internal communication; others are a vehicle for corresponding with outsiders. Some are required as a permanent record; others are needed to solve an immediate problem or answer a passing

TABLE 12.1 Factors Affecting Report Format, Style, and Organization

FACTOR	POSSIBILITIES	IMPLICATIONS FOR FORMAT, STYLE, AND ORGANIZATION
WHO originates it?	Voluntary reports prepared on the writer's own initiative	Require plenty of introductory information to explain purpose of report
	Authorized reports prepared at the request of another person	Require less introductory material than voluntary reports; should be organized to respond to the reader's request
WHAT subject does it cover?	Sales reports, compensation policies, affirmative action plans, engineering proposals, research studies, progress reports	Presentation dictated by characteristics of subject (for example, detailed statistical information summarized in tabular format)
WHEN is it prepared?	Routine, recurring reports prepared on daily, weekly, monthly, quarterly, or annual basis	Require standard format that facilitates comparisons from one period to next; need relatively little background and transitional information
	Special, nonrecurring reports prepared in response to unique situations	Do not need standardization; require plenty of background and transitional information
WHERE is it sent?	Internal reports prepared for use within the organization	Can be relatively informal; written in memo or manuscript format
	External reports sent to people outside the organization	Should be relatively formal in tone; written in letter or manuscript format
WHY is it prepared?	Informational reports providing facts	Organized around subtopics
	Analytical reports providing analysis, interpretation, conclusions, and often recommendations	Organized around conclusions/recommendations or logical arguments
HOW will it be received?	Receptive readers	Arranged in direct order
	Skeptical or hostile readers	Arranged in indirect order

question. Many move upward through the chain of command to help managers monitor the various units in the organization; some move downward to explain management decisions to lower-level employees responsible for day-to-day operations.

Before you start writing a report, ask yourself why it's being prepared.

Business reports may appear in many different guises, as Table 12.1 shows. However, *why* a report is prepared provides the best clues on how to organize it, write it, and set it up. Although business reports serve literally hundreds of purposes, most reports are used for one of the following six general purposes:

The most common uses of business reports fall into six categories.

- To monitor and control operations
- To help implement policies and procedures
- To comply with legal or regulatory requirements
- To obtain new business or funding
- To document work performed for a client
- To guide decisions on particular issues

Each of these purposes imposes different requirements on the report writer. If your readers need information to oversee an operation, for example, you would present your message differently than you would if you were contributing to a decision on a complex issue. In other words, the purpose of a report affects its form.

REPORTS FOR MONITORING AND CONTROLLING OPERATIONS

Monitor/control reports help managers find out what's happening.

One of the most common applications for business reports is to monitor and control the operations of the organization. Because managers cannot be everywhere at once, they rely on reports to find out what's happening to the operations under their control. Plans, operating reports, and personal activity reports are a few examples of this type.

Monitor/control reports are easy to write because they focus on data. The best way to approach them if you're new in an organization is to use previous reports of the same type as examples. Your objective should be to make your report very similar in appearance, style, and organization to the reports your boss is used to reviewing, so he or she can more easily absorb the information.

Be sure to cover the bad news along with the good news in preparing monitor/control reports.

With monitor/control reports, you must pay special attention to accuracy, thoroughness, and honesty. It is very tempting to cover up the bad news and emphasize only the accomplishments, but such distortions defeat the purpose of the report. In the final analysis, the problems will show up anyway, so you might as well get them out in the open early.

Plans

Plans help managers

- Coordinate the different activities of a business
- Guide the distribution of resources
- Motivate employees

One of the most widely used monitor/control reports is the plan. Plans come in all shapes and sizes: annual budgets, five-year plans, strategic plans, sales plans, recruiting plans, production plans, and so on. Just about every functional area of a company develops a plan to establish guidelines for future action. These plans are generally used to improve internal coordination, to guide the distribution of money and material, and to motivate employees.

Operating reports

A management information system comprises many operating reports that provide managers with statistics on company performance.

Bert Browse at Calvin Klein, like many other managers, gets information about operations from reports generated by a management information system (MIS), which captures statistics about everything happening in the organization. Like plans, these operating reports are a common tool for monitoring and controlling operations. In large companies the MIS is generally computerized, but operating reports can be created manually as well. In either case, someone must decide what facts to gather and in what form to report them. Either system then provides a constant stream of statistics on all operations of the company—sales, production, inventory, shipments, backlogs, costs, personnel—whatever management is interested in measuring. All this information can be given to management in its raw state through computer terminals, printouts, or pages of accounting numbers; or it can be analyzed in paragraph form by lower-level staff.

Personal activity reports

In addition to using statistical MIS reports, companies rely on a variety of personal activity reports to keep track of what individuals are doing. Sales-

Personal activity reports keep managers abreast of employees' work-related activities.

call reports are an example of this type. In a sales-call report, the salesperson summarizes the events that occurred during an appointment with a customer. The report outlines the topics that were discussed and gives the salesperson's evaluation of the prospects for a sale, together with plans for follow-up action. Other examples are conference reports, expense reports, performance reviews, recruiting reports, and any other document intended to keep management posted on the activities of individuals.

Case study: Arnold Miller's sales reports

To get an idea of how monitor/control reports are actually used, consider Arnold Miller's experience. Arnold, who works for a major corporation that produces packaging for foods and consumer goods, is one of five regional sales managers in the plastic packaging division.

As Arnold says, "The number-one objective of my sales region is to achieve or beat the annual sales plan. My region is supposed to achieve 1989 sales of $52 million, and I have assigned each of the five salespeople who work for me a share of that total.

"Obviously, it's important for me to know how well our sales are doing. I require two key reports from each salesperson on a monthly basis. The first is the sales forecast, which gives me a running update on anticipated sales (as opposed to actual shipments). The second report summarizes the most important events of the previous month for each salesperson. I collect both reports and then write my own report for senior management."

Figure 12.1 includes an excerpt from one of Arnold's reports (along with details about this type of report). Notice that he uses a "telegraphic" style so his boss can scan the report in seconds. Arnold wastes no time on introductions or transitions; he gets to the point immediately. This approach is appropriate because his boss already knows the background and purpose of the report. In this instance, the details are all that matter.

The forecasts and monthly sales summaries are the most important of the reports that Arnold uses to keep track of his salespeople and to keep his boss up to date on performance in his region. But, says Arnold, "I also require a weekly call or trip report, which allows me to track individual sales activity against planned activity. And of course, I receive expense reports.

"In cases involving major sales objectives, I also require my salespeople to prepare action plans. These plans begin with a statement of a sales objective and are followed by a description of the events that must occur for the objective to be accomplished."

Write reports only when they serve a meaningful purpose.

Although Arnold requires many reports, he warns that "reports are useful only if they serve a meaningful purpose. Some companies have a tendency to overburden people with reporting. Our objective is to create sales, not to write reports. I encourage my people to prepare their reports for me as efficiently as possible."

REPORTS FOR IMPLEMENTING POLICIES AND PROCEDURES

Policy/procedure reports help managers communicate the company's standards.

Another very common use for business reports is to help put company policies and procedures into effect. Like reports for monitoring and controlling operations, policy/procedure reports are necessary because managers cannot be everywhere at once. They often have to communicate

FIGURE 12.1
Excerpt from a Report for Monitoring and Controlling Operations

Arnold Miller's monthly sales report, excerpted on the opposite page, is typical of monitor/control reports. Important characteristics of these reports are summarized below.

PREPARATION AND DISTRIBUTION

Most monitor/control reports are routine, recurring documents prepared by many employees scattered throughout the organization for submission to upper-level management. A few higher-level readers receive many similar reports from a number of employees.

FORMAT

These reports are often submitted on preprinted forms or written to conform to a standard plan. The high degree of standardization allows readers to compare information from one report to another.

STYLE

The purpose of these reports is to provide a great deal of information as efficiently as possible. Their routine, recurring nature reduces the need for introductory and transitional material. Headings are used to establish topics. Major points are often made in a list.

ORGANIZATION

In these reports, ideas are presented in direct order and developed to emphasize the items being reviewed by management. For example, if readers want to monitor sales by region, the report is organized by region: Sales in Region 1, Sales in Region 2, and so on. If readers are interested in product costs by category, the headings might be Labor Costs, Overhead, and the like.

Factors affecting Arnold Miller's sales report:

WHO: Authorized
WHAT: Monthly sales report
WHEN: Routine, recurring
WHERE: Internal, upward
WHY: Informational
HOW: Receptive reader (direct order)

without talking firsthand to every person in the organization. Written policies and procedures can be read and reread by anyone who needs to know about a particular issue. Some of these documents are preserved as lasting guidelines; others are one-time explanations.

In general, make statements of policies and procedures as broad and simple as possible.

Reports for implementing policies and procedures are generally quite easy to organize, but they are more difficult to write than you might think. The goal should be to hit the right balance between the general and the specific. It is tempting to try to answer every question that every possible reader might have, but this approach often creates more confusion than illumination. Try to keep the policies broad and the procedures as simple as possible.

MEMO

TO: Wayne Pullman DATE: November 2, 1989
FROM: Arnold Miller

SUBJECT: October Sales Report--Northeast Region, Plastic Packaging Division

MONTHLY SUMMARY

We have exceeded our sales forecast for the month by $725,000. Most of the excess comes from three new developments:

1. Horton Foods. Barbara Gorble landed this new account for us with an order for $360,000 in flexible packaging for dry soup mix.

2. BioMed Laboratories. Because of an unexpected surge in BioMed's sales, we have been awarded an additional $250,000 order for blister-packs on sinus capsules.

3. AlmaLynn Cosmetics. Thanks to the efforts of Brenda Cano, we have been asked to provide plastic packaging for a new line of lipsticks that will be going into test marketing early next year. The initial order for $115,000 could increase to over $1.5 million if the product is successful.

MAJOR ACTIVITY BY PRODUCT LINE

Grocery Products

The order from Horton Foods was the bright spot for this product area this month. Other developments:

1. Sugar Sweet. We're running into tough competition for our packaging of individual sugar servings. In order to meet our sales forecast, we must retain this business. Lonny Haskins, who's in charge of the account, recommends offering a 10 per-

Lasting guidelines

Some policies and procedures provide lasting "recipes" for how things should be done.

Each organization typically has a collection of lasting policies and procedures. The head of personnel might write a memo announcing a new reimbursement program for employees who continue their education; the head of production might develop guidelines for standardizing quality-control procedures; the office manager might issue a memo explaining how to reserve the conference room for special meetings; the assistant to the president might draft a policy on business ethics for use in international operations. All these reports would then become part of the company's large body of lasting guidelines for doing things a certain way.

Position papers

Other policies and procedures explain management's position on passing events.

In contrast to lasting policy/procedure reports, position papers treat less permanent issues. They explain management's views on particular issues or problems as they arise. For example, an office manager might write a report on the need for extra security precautions following a rash of burglaries in the area. Countless other situations also call for written statements aimed at informing various groups about management's position on special, nonrecurring events.

Case study: Gary DeVille's compensation policy

Gary DeVille is vice president of human resources for a $500 million company that manufactures broadcasting equipment. Gary is responsible for overseeing corporate recruiting, management training, career-path planning, compensation and benefits, labor relations, and affirmative action programs. He monitors the human resources activities of the company's 26 operating divisions, which are scattered across the country, and also supervises a staff at corporate headquarters.

"At corporate headquarters," Gary says, "our role is to define the overall guidelines for human resources, then give the divisions responsibility for defining specific procedures. We try to prepare policies only when we clearly need to establish a position on an issue. But sometimes we need to update existing policies or issue new ones."

Figure 12.2 is an excerpt from a policy report that Gary prepared shortly after joining the company. "This is a refinement of an older, longer policy statement covering our compensation system," Gary explains. "We found that the old policy, which went into great detail, created confusion because it was so explicit. People were afraid they'd do something wrong if they didn't follow the directions precisely, especially in new situations that weren't covered very well in the policy. So we reduced the policy statement and made it more philosophical. We tried to emphasize why we have compensation, what we're trying to accomplish with our base salaries and merit increases. We focused on the compensation goals and asked the divisions to determine whether their specific programs conformed with the goals.

Make policy/procedure reports as concise as possible.

"Overall," says Gary, "policy statements have a way of ending up on a shelf or in a drawer somewhere once they've been read. They are necessary, and they can often have a strong short-term impact, but people tend to go on about their business and forget that policy statements even exist. That's why we try to keep our policies to a minimum and state them as succinctly as possible. They are more likely to be read that way."

REPORTS FOR COMPLYING WITH REGULATORY AGENCIES

Compliance reports explain what a company is doing to conform to government regulations.

The regulation of business by government agencies has spawned another type of report that is relatively easy to organize: the compliance report. All compliance reports are written in response to regulations of one sort or another, most of them imposed by government agencies. In a sense, then, compliance reports are monitor/control reports for the government.

These reports play a major role in relations between private industry and the government.

Compliance reports are generally easy to write because the regulatory agency issues instructions on how to write them. The important thing is to be honest, thorough, and accurate. Remember that these reports are required by law, that they generally serve the public interest, and that you and your company can get into trouble if you are caught being dishonest.

Many government agencies require businesses to submit reports on their activities.

Perhaps the most common example of a compliance report is the income tax return. Both the U.S. Internal Revenue Service and Revenue Canada also require a yearly report from every corporation with a pension plan.

Another common compliance report is the annual report to a company's shareholders, which is required in the United States by the Securities and Exchange Commission and in Canada by the provincial securities commissions. Annual reports also serve a public relations function. Many other documents are required as well, all of which contain financial information related to a company's stock and bond offerings.

Companies that do business with the U.S. government are required to submit a yearly report to the Equal Employment Opportunity Commission describing the composition of their work force and their plans for ensuring full use of qualified women, minorities, and other protected groups. The Canadian Human Rights Commission has similar reporting requirements.

Finally, depending on a company's size and industry, it may also encounter more specialized reporting requirements. For example, pharmaceutical companies operating in the United States are regulated by the Food and Drug Administration, and the Interstate Commerce Commission watches over transportation companies that do business across state lines.

Case study: Gary DeVille's affirmative action plan

Preparing his company's annual affirmative action plan is another of Gary DeVille's responsibilities. Actually, he oversees the preparation of 26 affirmative action plans, because his company's 26 operating divisions are required to submit separate reports. Each plan is roughly 100 pages long and consists of three distinct parts: one covering minorities and women, one for the handicapped, and one for veterans. Figure 12.3 includes an excerpt from one.

Gary estimates that writing an affirmative action plan takes one person a full month. He and his staff also prepare many other reports, including compliance reports for the Occupational Safety and Health Administration, the Environmental Protection Agency, and the National Labor Relations Board. In addition, the various states in which the company operates require reports.

Compliance reports require a format that conveniently displays statistical details.

As Gary says, "The key in preparing compliance reports is to design a format that captures the data in as simple and straightforward a fashion as possible."

PROPOSALS FOR OBTAINING NEW BUSINESS OR FUNDING

Proposals vary in length and complexity, but all are attempts to get products, plans, or projects accepted by outside business or government

FIGURE 12.2
Excerpt from a Report for Implementing Policies and Procedures

Gary DeVille's compensation policy, part of which appears on the opposite page, is a typical policy/procedure report. Important characteristics of these reports are summarized below.

PREPARATION AND DISTRIBUTION

Reports on policies and procedures move downward from management to a wide audience throughout the organization. They are prepared as needed to respond to specific situations and are usually retained (sometimes in a looseleaf binder) and updated periodically.

FORMAT

Most large companies have a policies and procedures manual that establishes a standard format for these reports. However, the variety of subjects covered limits the amount of standardization that is possible.

STYLE

Because they establish lasting guidelines or clarify management's position, these reports are comprehensive, detailed documents, written in paragraph form and containing ample introductory and background information.

ORGANIZATION

These reports are written in direct order, with the ideas arranged around subtopics that emphasize either the important elements of the policy or the steps in the procedure.

Factors affecting Gary DeVille's compensation policy:

WHO: Voluntary (originated by management)
WHAT: Compensation policy
WHEN: Special, with periodic updates
WHERE: Internal, downward
WHY: Informational
HOW: Receptive reader (direct order)

Proposals are reports written to obtain new business or funding from outsiders.

clients. Thus they are often called sales proposals. Such a proposal spells out precisely what the seller will provide under specific terms and conditions. If the proposal is accepted, it becomes the basis of a contract between the buyer and the seller.

SALARY PLANNING GUIDE

PURPOSE

Compensation is a major element of cost and has a significant influence on employee motivation and productivity. These costs, like other business expenses, must be carefully managed. Therefore, planning compensation levels is an important managerial function.

The overall objective of salary planning is to design a process for merit increases that will enable us to attract, retain, and reward employees equitably. At the same time, the concept of paying for performance means paying for results that contribute to the success of the business.

This salary planning guide is designed to give managers a common frame of reference for this undertaking.

Determining the Performance Rating

Merit increases should clearly motivate and reward better performance. Superior performance should be rewarded with superior merit increases, and performance falling below requirements should warrant lesser increases or no action at all.

Factors that managers may want to consider in determining an employee's contribution and corresponding performance rating are

--Level of individual performance against assigned objectives and position responsibilities

--Length of time since last increase and size of that increase

--Position in salary range

Proposals to outsiders are similar in many ways to reports soliciting approval of projects within the organization, which are called justification reports (discussed later in the chapter). However, there are some important differences:

FIGURE 12.3
Excerpt from a Report for Complying with Regulatory Agencies

One example of a compliance report is Gary DeVille's affirmative action plan, shown in part on the opposite page. Important characteristics of these reports are summarized below.

PREPARATION AND DISTRIBUTION

Compliance reports are prepared for external readers who review many reports of the same type. Many are recurring documents prepared on an annual basis.

FORMAT

These reports are highly standardized; many are essentially long forms filled out according to instructions issued by the regulatory agency.

STYLE

These reports are written in a style that emphasizes concise detail as opposed to broad concepts. Readers need plenty of detail to do their job of regulating the companies; they do not need lengthy introductions or transitions, because they have read hundreds of similar documents before. The language is often legalistic and impersonal.

ORGANIZATION

These reports follow a direct order dictated by the instructions of the regulatory agency.

Factors affecting Gary DeVille's affirmative action plan:

WHO:	Authorized
WHAT:	Affirmative action plan
WHEN:	Routine, recurring
WHERE:	External
WHY:	Informational
HOW:	Receptive reader (direct order)

- Sales proposals, unlike justification reports, are legally binding and must therefore be prepared with extreme care. If you propose to sell 500 units at a price of $250 each, you are bound to deliver at that price, come what may.

IDENTIFICATION OF PROBLEM AREAS

Any problems found in the following analyses will be discussed and solutions presented in the section titled Development and Execution of Programs.

1. The total selection process--including applicant flow, position descriptions, position titles, worker specifications, application forms, interview procedures, and similar factors--has been quantified.

   a. Applicant flow by minority group status, gender, and EEOC category

EEOC CATEGORY	NUMBER OF PERSONS			NUMBER IN MINORITY GROUP							
				MALE				FEMALE			
	TOTAL	MALE	FE-MALE	B	A/PI	AI/AN	H	B	A/PI	AI/AN	H
OFFICIALS/MGRS.	0										
PROFESSIONALS	0										
TECHNICIANS	5	4	1	1					1		
SALES WORKERS	0										
OFFICE & CLERICAL	23	13	10			1		3	3		
CRAFTS	12	10	2		1	2		2			
OPERATIVES	43	30	13	3		1	3	5			
LABORERS	0										
SERVICE WORKERS	5	4	1		2						1
TOTAL	88	61	27	4	3	4	3	10	4	0	1

Note: B = Black; A/PI = Asian/Pacific Islands; AI/AN = American Indian/Aleutian Islands; H = Hispanic.

   b. Selection and placement procedures

   We have carefully analyzed our selection process to ensure elimination of any possible bar to full equal employment

- Sales proposals involve competition with other organizations; justification reports do not. In the sales proposal, you must convince the buyer that your organization is the best source of the product. As a result, you must devote a considerable amount of space to explaining your experience, qualifications, facilities, and equipment.

The two basic types of sales proposals are those solicited by a prospective client and those sent without a specific invitation from a prospective client.

Solicited proposals

In a solicited proposal, you must demonstrate that your organization is better qualified than competitors are to handle a particular contract.

Solicited proposals are prepared at the request of clients, who need something done or want a certain product manufactured. The solicitation, or invitation to bid on the contract, is called a request for proposal (RFP). You respond to an RFP by preparing a proposal that shows how you would meet the potential customer's needs.

Let's say that the National Aeronautics and Space Administration decides to develop a new satellite. Nobody makes this particular satellite yet; it hasn't been invented. But NASA knows what the satellite ought to do and wants to get the best design at the lowest cost. Typically, NASA first prepares an RFP that specifies exactly what the satellite should accomplish. NASA then sends this RFP to several aerospace companies and invites them to bid on the job.

NASA is not the only branch of the government that awards contracts on the basis of written proposals. Every agency from the Library of Congress to the Department of Health and Human Services issues RFPs, as do many states, provinces, counties, and cities. In addition, private industry awards major contracts on the basis of proposals. The items procured in this fashion range from office equipment to power plants. Whenever a customer is spending a lot of money—especially for something that is unique, sophisticated, and difficult to produce—it makes sense to get several competing bids.

When a company gets an RFP, the managers have to decide whether they are interested in the job and have a reasonable chance of winning the contract. If they decide to submit a bid, the proposal effort begins in earnest. The company reviews the requirements, defines the scope of the work, determines the methods and procedures to be used, and estimates time requirements, personnel requirements, and costs. Then the proposal writers put it all down on paper, responding meticulously to every point raised by the RFP.

Most proposals are organized in the same way: They begin with an introductory section that states the purpose of the proposal, defines the scope of the work, presents background information, and explains any limitations that might apply to the contract. The body of the proposal gives details on the proposed effort and specifies what the anticipated results will be. The discussion covers the methods, schedule, facilities, equipment, personnel, and costs that will be involved in the contract. A final section generally summarizes the key points of the proposal and asks for a decision from the client.

Unsolicited proposals

In an unsolicited proposal, you must establish the need for your product.

The other major type of sales proposal, the unsolicited proposal, is initiated by a company that is attempting to obtain business or funding on its own, without a specific invitation from the client. Unsolicited proposals differ from solicited proposals in one important respect: The client has to be sold on the idea of buying something. As a consequence, unsolicited proposals generally spend more time explaining why the client should take action.

Unsolicited proposals vary widely in form and length, depending on the nature of the product being sold. One interesting type, known as a business plan, is used to raise funds through bank loans or private investments. In the business plan, the writer describes the business and its financial potential, with the objective of persuading the reader to provide capital. The plan is essentially a proposal to provide the lender or investor with a financial return in exchange for the use of the funds.

Case study: Jill Rivers's proposal for obtaining new business

Jill Rivers is vice president of engineering for a construction company that specializes in designing and building large-scale public facilities, such as sports stadiums, bridges, roads, parking structures, and government buildings. Jill supervises a staff of 250 engineers, plus assorted support personnel. At any given time, someone in her department is working on a proposal. She estimates that her group submits 50 to 100 proposals a year.

"About 90 percent of our work is the result of proposals," says Jill. "Some of them are for add-ons to existing contracts, and these are fairly easy to write. We have an established relationship with the customer. All we have to do is provide additional work—more of the same. The proposal just puts it in writing.

"But many of our most important jobs involve major proposals, some three volumes long, that take us several months to prepare. As many as 20 people might be involved in writing these proposals. We are usually bidding against several other companies, and we have a set of specifications to respond to.

"We usually split up the writing job, although sometimes one person handles the entire technical portion. But generally, proposals are a team effort, and the contributions have to mesh. Obviously you need a good outline for that, and you need people who can write clearly and quickly. You can't learn to write while you're working on a proposal. You've got to know how already. Time is essential, and quality is essential. We have a training program for our engineers that helps them develop their writing skills, and I think it's one of the reasons that we have established such a good record at winning proposals.

"Another important factor in our ability to write proposals is the way we use word processors to make the most of the time available. We can revise the final draft of a proposal until two hours before it has to be shipped. A lot of our competitors aren't able to do that. We're a young company, and we have developed our approach to proposal writing using all the latest equipment, so we're able to get a very professional report completed quickly. The word processor takes care of a lot of little things automatically: page numbers, table of contents, setups for charts and tables. We don't have to worry about all of that. It's amazing how having the right equipment changes the whole nature of the proposal process. We can spend our time worrying about the content instead of the form."

Figure 12.4 includes an excerpt from one of Jill's proposals. It will give you an idea of the flavor of these documents.

FIGURE 12.4
Excerpt from a Proposal for Obtaining New Business or Funding

An excerpt from a typical sales proposal, prepared by Jill Rivers, is shown on the opposite page. Important characteristics of proposals are discussed below.

PREPARATION AND DISTRIBUTION

A sales proposal is a nonrecurring document prepared for someone outside the organization. Solicited proposals submitted by separate companies respond to the same set of questions posed by the prospective client, who compares the various proposals and selects the best one. Unsolicited proposals are initiated by the seller. They are not compared against directly competing proposals, but they must motivate the client to buy the product.

FORMAT

Because a potential client can compare competing proposals more easily if all of them are presented in a similar way, solicited proposals follow a standard organization and format outlined in the client's request for proposal (RFP). Unsolicited proposals provide more room for creativity in format and organization, because they are not compared with competing proposals.

STYLE

All but the simplest proposals are written in fully developed paragraphs designed to convince the client that the bidder should be awarded the contract. The length of many proposals may make the reader lose track of the discussion. The writer should provide good introductory and transitional paragraphs as well as plenty of headings and lists.

ORGANIZATION

When issuing an RFP for a project, the client may outline the major topics that proposing companies must address. However, proposals tend to follow a predictable order: statement of the problem, scope of the problem, methods and procedures, work plan and schedule, qualifications, and projected costs.

Factors affecting Jill Rivers's proposal:

WHO: Authorized
WHAT: Engineering proposal
WHEN: Special, nonrecurring
WHERE: External
WHY: Analytical
HOW: Receptive reader (direct order)

REPORTS FOR DOCUMENTING CLIENT WORK

Reports documenting progress on a contract should provide all the information the client needs.

Once a company wins a contract, the engineers can't simply put their pens away and forget about writing. Indeed, their writing days have just begun. Now they have to document their work.

Reports that document client work vary in importance and complexity. Some are a mere formality; others are a vital element in the relationship

PROPOSAL TO DEVELOP A SERIES OF JETTIES
FOR THE CITY OF SANTA LUISA BEACH

INTRODUCTION

Seabold Engineering is pleased to submit this proposal in response to RFP SLB-8590, issued by the city of Santa Luisa Beach. The purpose of the proposal is to describe Seabold's approach to developing a series of jetties that will protect Santa Luisa Beach from sand erosion.

Background and Statement of the Problem

Santa Luisa Beach is a city of 189,000 located on the California coast. One of the chief natural resources of this city is its splendid beaches, which are a source of delight for the local population as well as a magnet for tourists.

Unfortunately, these beaches are beginning to erode. The problem began ten years ago with the construction of a breakwater 30 miles north of Santa Luisa Beach. The breakwater altered the natural flow of sand that would ordinarily replenish the beach. In addition, inland development has diminished the amount of sediment that washes down toward the beaches from two rivers, further reducing the natural sand replacement process.

Santa Luisa Beach's loss of sand has increased in the last two winters, which have been particularly stormy. The high tides, whipped by heavy winds and rains, have washed away a large portion of the sand that remained. In some areas the beach has essentially disappeared. All that remains are rocks and boulders, butting up against fragile cliffs.

Property along the beach has been heavily damaged in the past two years. Both private homes and commercial establishments have been flooded repeatedly. A luxury condominium development with 50 housing units has been condemned because of potential cliff

with the client. These reports may be difficult to write, particularly if the work is not going well or if the customer is unusually demanding. The important thing is to anticipate the reader's needs and to provide the required information clearly and tactfully.

Progress reports to clients are generally submitted on a regular basis: sometimes monthly, sometimes keyed to phases of the project. In many cases these periodic progress reports are followed by a final report at the conclusion of the contract.

Interim progress reports

A long or complex project is documented with periodic updates on the progress that has been made.

Interim progress reports naturally vary in length, depending on the period covered and the complexity of the contract. Their purpose is to give the customer an idea of the work that has been accomplished to date. These reports are often keyed to the work plan that was established at the beginning of the contract. The writer tells the customer what tasks have been accomplished, identifies problems, and outlines future steps. Important findings are summarized.

Final reports

At the end of the project, a final report provides a wrap-up of results.

Final reports are generally more elaborate than interim reports and serve as a permanent record of what was accomplished. They focus on results rather than progress. They deal with what was discovered as opposed to how the work got done.

Case study: Jill Rivers's progress report

As vice president of engineering, Jill Rivers has a great deal of experience in writing progress reports as well as proposals. She has these comments on documenting client work: "Most of our projects require at least two different kinds of documentation. The first kind, monthly letter reports, are fairly routine status reports that begin with a summary of events, followed by a discussion of any problems we're having. There's often an updated schedule as well. These reports range in length from 20 to 50 pages, but they aren't very difficult to write. Their contents are spelled out in the contract, and writing them is just a matter of pulling the information together.

"The second kind of documentation that we provide supports major client review meetings. We usually have three of these meetings for each project, spaced at the beginning, middle, and end of the contract. During these reviews, key members of our team give overviews on their portion of the work. We use transparencies as a communication tool at the meetings, but we generally provide a large written report as well, which the customer can study at leisure.

"We prepare a lot of documentation in our work, but we try to keep it in perspective. We provide tangible products, so the things we make speak for themselves. If they don't turn out right, nothing we can say in a report is really going to make much difference. And if they are successful, the customer is probably going to be pretty happy regardless of whether our reports are works of art or not, although the quality of the report is important in projecting our company image. But being a good writer is essential, because good writing skills enable you to get the writing done quickly and efficiently so you can go on to the next thing." Figure 12.5 is an excerpt from one of Jill's interim progress reports.

REPORTS FOR GUIDING DECISIONS

Reports that help managers make decisions about problems and opportunities are especially interesting to write.

In many respects, the most interesting business reports are those that help the managers in your organization make major decisions. Before responding to problems or opportunities, most managers study the pros and cons of alternatives. For this, they rely on reports from lower-level employees that provide information, analyses, and recommendations. Thus decision-oriented reports require a strong foundation of facts combined with good insight and excellent communication skills on the part of the writer. When you prepare one of these reports, you have the chance to present your skills to top management. You naturally want to give these assignments your best effort.

Although decision-oriented reports are extremely varied, all of them tend to have a "should we or shouldn't we" quality: Should we expand into this market? Should we reorganize the research department? Should we invest in new equipment? Should we close this plant? Should we make Mary Patchett a vice president? Because people performing the various functions of a company make different kinds of decisions, they require different types of decision-oriented reports. Some of the more common types are research reports, justification reports, and troubleshooting reports.

Research reports

Research reports provide management with background information and analysis of options.

People in management rely heavily on research reports, which analyze the pros and cons of various actions. The question may be whether to launch a new product, expand into a new territory, change the pricing strategy, withdraw from a business venture, redesign a product, or acquire another company.

In making these and similar decisions, managers need both basic information and analysis of the various options. The research report might cover supply and demand, growth projections, competitor profiles, and company strengths and weaknesses.

Justification reports

A justification report is a proposal to upper-level management from lower- or middle-level management.

Another common type of decision-oriented report is the justification report (or internal proposal), which is used to persuade top management to approve a proposed investment or project. For example, the writer might want to build a new plant, buy some new production equipment, or automate the warehouse system. Although many justification reports deal with the acquisition of tangible assets, others do not. The proposed project might be the reorganization of a department, the revision of recruiting procedures, a change in the company's training programs, the redesign of the information storage and retrieval system, or any one of hundreds of other ideas for improving the operations of a company that do not require the addition of physical assets. In preparing these sorts of documents, managers explain why the project is needed, what it will involve, how much it will cost, and what the benefits will be.

A capital appropriation request is a specific type of justification report that deals with a request for equipment or facilities. Most capital appropriation requests are aimed at justifying the investment from a financial standpoint. In many organizations, these requests are submitted on a standardized form so all projects can be evaluated according to the same financial criteria.

Justification reports vary widely in style and format. Some are brief informal memos, but others are lengthy, formal documents in manuscript format.

FIGURE 12.5
Excerpt from a Report for Documenting Client Work

The interim progress report excerpted on the opposite page is a typical report for documenting client work. Important characteristics of these reports are summarized below.

PREPARATION AND DISTRIBUTION

Interim reports are written for outsiders and are submitted over the life of a contract. As many as five or six progress reports are followed by a final report.

FORMAT

Interim progress reports are often in letter format and tend to be relatively brief. The final report is generally a longer manuscript.

STYLE

Because interim reports are written for outsiders, they are handled in a formal style. But they require less attention to introductions and transitions than final reports, which serve as a lasting record covering the contract. The writer of a final report cannot depend on future readers being familiar with the subject.

ORGANIZATION

Interim progress reports are organized to highlight what has been accomplished during the reporting period. The main headings correspond to the tasks that have been performed. A final section usually outlines plans for the coming period. Final reports, on the other hand, focus on results rather than progress.

Factors affecting Jill Rivers's interim progress report:

WHO:	Authorized
WHAT:	Interim progress report
WHEN:	Nonrecurring series
WHERE:	External
WHY:	Analytical
HOW:	Receptive reader (direct order)

Troubleshooting reports

Troubleshooting reports analyze problems and propose solutions.

Troubleshooting reports are another common decision-oriented document prepared for submission to top management. Whenever a problem exists, somebody has to investigate it and propose a solution. The vehicle for communicating this analysis is the troubleshooting report. Regardless of

SEABOLD ENGINEERING, INC.
5680 Ventura Boulevard
Los Angeles, CA 91601-2416

July 17, 1989

Mr. Jack Constable, City Manager
City of Santa Luisa Beach
2863 Calverra Street
Santa Luisa Beach, CA 92600

Dear Mr. Constable:

This report covers the work performed by Seabold Engineering on jetties for Santa Luisa Beach from May 1 to June 31 under the terms of contract SLB-659-X15.

BACKGROUND RESEARCH

Historical analysis of the beach erosion problem is under way. The Seabold project team has studied records dating back ten years to determine changes over time in the coastline of Santa Luisa Beach. In addition, city records and private property deeds for parcels along the coast have been analyzed. Lifeguards and local residents have been interviewed, as well as oceanographers from the Scripps Institution of Oceanography in La Jolla, California. The team has also reviewed newspaper accounts describing coastal storms, inland development, and efforts to halt sand erosion at Santa Luisa Beach.

Particular attention has been given to interviews with city officials responsible for previous efforts to deal with the erosion problem. Both Carlos Zamora and Richard Barta of the city manager's office have been extremely helpful in describing the effects of the Longard tube and the transportation of sand from inland river beds.

OCEANOGRAPHIC RESEARCH

The project team is conducting oceanographic experiments to test the direction and intensity of currents and tides and their effects on

the specific problem at hand, these reports deal with the same basic questions: How did we get into this predicament, what's the extent of the damage, and what can we do about it? These reports usually begin with some background information on the problem, then analyze alternative solutions and recommend the best approach.

FIGURE 12.6
Report for Guiding Decisions

Lia Chung's justification report, which begins on the opposite page, is typical of reports for guiding decisions. Important characteristics of these reports are summarized below.

PREPARATION AND DISTRIBUTION

Reports for guiding decisions are prepared for managers in response to unique, nonrecurring situations. They are directed upward within an organization; some decision-oriented reports are prepared by outside consultants.

FORMAT

Most decision-oriented reports are written in manuscript or memo format. In the case of capital appropriation requests, some companies provide guidelines on what should be included, because most capital investments are evaluated in a similar fashion.

STYLE

These documents must contain ample background information, facts, and analysis to guide both the decision and its implementation. They are written in complete paragraphs and include strong introductory and transitional elements. Headings, lists, and visual aids are used to help readers follow the material.

ORGANIZATION

The organization of these reports is based on the reader's probable reaction. When readers are considered receptive, as in this example, the reports are written in direct order, using conclusions or recommendations at the beginning. When readers are considered skeptical or potentially hostile, the material is presented in an indirect order that will highlight the reasons underlying the final conclusions or recommendations.

Factors affecting Lia Chung's justification report:

WHO: Authorized
WHAT: Justification report
WHEN: Special, nonrecurring
WHERE: Internal, upward
WHY: Analytical
HOW: Receptive reader (direct order)

Case study: Lia Chung's justification report

Lia Chung is director of training and development for a consulting firm that provides a wide variety of services to its clients, most of which are small to mid-sized companies in the Southeast. The firm, which is growing by leaps and bounds, currently employs about 40 professional consultants

MEMO

TO: J. P. Nordhoff
FROM: Lia Chung
DATE: March 8, 1989
SUBJECT: Proposed training program for consulting staff

As you requested at our meeting last week, I have prepared this written proposal outlining how the Dale Carnegie Institute of Atlanta can help us meet our training needs.

THE PROBLEM: UNEVEN SKILLS IN HANDLING CLIENT RELATIONSHIPS

In the past year we have hired 12 new consultants, boosting our total professional staff to 40 people. The new staff members all have excellent qualifications to advise our clients in general business matters. However, some of the new people have relatively little experience in handling client relationships, a skill that is important to their success.

THE SOLUTION: DALE CARNEGIE COURSE IN EFFECTIVE SPEAKING AND HUMAN RELATIONS

To help the 12 new members of our professional staff develop their human relations skills, I would like to offer a training program in communication and leadership. Rather than "re-invent the wheel" with an in-house training program, I would like to hire an organization with a proven track record in management education. After looking at a number of alternatives, I believe the best source of such training is the Dale Carnegie Institute.

Over the past 70 years, literally millions of people have improved their human relations skills by attending Dale Carnegie training programs. Their courses are offered throughout the United States and in 60 foreign countries.

The Dale Carnegie Method

Participants are encouraged to learn by doing. Instead of listening to dry lectures, students present reports and talks, engage in friendly competitions, and practice problem-solving and decision-making techniques. Applying the lessons in class reinforces the

(continued on p. 394)

and 40 administrators and clerical personnel. Lia's job is to see that the employees receive the training they need to do their jobs effectively.

"When we hire new people," Lia explains, "I'm responsible for teaching them the ropes. Because our firm is growing so rapidly, we have a constant stream of new employees who all have to be taught how to do things our way. If I notice that people are having a problem accomplishing some

Figure continued from previous page

-2-

learning process and gives students constructive feedback from instructors.

Anticipated Results of the Program

The Dale Carnegie course in effective speaking and human relations is ideally suited to the needs of our consulting staff. This course is designed to enhance communication skills and help people develop their leadership potential. Our consultants will be taught how to get better results from meetings and how to gain the cooperation of clients. During the course, the participants will study and practice various techniques to improve their business and personal relationships. They will learn how to handle responsibility, work under pressure, and motivate themselves and others. At the conclusion of the program, they will be more confident and effective in their work.

Instructor's Qualifications

Dale Carnegie instructors are carefully chosen and well trained. Each is a successful professional with experience directly related to the course. To ensure that the courses are uniform in quality, all instructors undergo a rigorous training program and use the same proven methods and course materials. Our course would be taught by Melissa Steinberg, who has been a Dale Carnegie instructor for five years. She has a master's degree in psychology from New York University.

Course Scheduling and Costs

The Dale Carnegie course in effective speaking and human relations consists of 14 sessions, which last approximately 3-1/2 hours each. Classes will be held here in our offices on Monday mornings from 9:00 to 11:30 for 14 consecutive weeks. The cost for 12 students will be $9,000.

CONCLUSION

If you have any questions about the course, I would be happy to answer them. I have had a number of conversations with Barry Furrow, who is in charge of the Dale Carnegie office in Atlanta, and I am confident that this is a worthwhile program.

aspect of their work, I create a training program to address the need. But first I need the approval of the firm's managing partner."

Figure 12.6 is an excerpt from Lia's proposal for a course to upgrade the communication and leadership skills of the firm's professional staff. "This particular justification report was pretty short because I knew that the firm's managing partner would be receptive. We had already discussed the need for such a program, and he was aware that I had looked at five or six different training courses before selecting one option as the best. However, some of the justification reports I write are considerably longer and contain more background on why a program is needed, what the alternatives are, and why a particular choice is best.

A successful justification report builds credibility for the next one.

"Regardless of their length, all of my justification reports have one thing in common: They offer to solve a problem for a specific price. Every time I write a proposal for a new training program, I follow the same basic formula: (1) Here's the problem; (2) here's the solution; and (3) here's what it will cost. And every time I sell a solution that works, I gain credibility, which makes the next idea that much easier to sell."

Because decision-oriented reports represent both a challenge and an opportunity for business report writers, they are the main focus of the remaining report-writing chapters. Table 12.2 is an overview of all the types of reports discussed in this chapter.

TABLE 12.2 Overview of the Six Most Common Uses of Reports

PURPOSE OF REPORT	COMMON EXAMPLES	PREPARATION AND DISTRIBUTION	FEATURES
To monitor and control operations	Plans, operating reports, personal activity reports	Internal, move upward on recurring basis	Standardized format (memo or preprinted form), telegraphic style, topical organization, direct order
To implement policies and procedures	Lasting guidelines, position papers	Internal, move downward on nonrecurring basis	Format that matches policy/procedure manual, fully developed text, topical organization, direct order
To comply with regulatory requirements	Reports for IRS, SEC, EEOC, and industry regulators	External, recurring	Standardized format (perhaps preprinted form), skeletal style, organized to follow reader's instructions, direct order
To obtain new business or funding	Sales proposals	External, nonrecurring	Letter or manuscript format, fully developed text, problem/solution organization, commonly direct order
To document client work	Interim progress reports, final reports	External, nonrecurring series	Letter or manuscript format, fully developed text, organized around sequential steps or key findings, usually direct order
To guide decisions	Research reports, justification reports, troubleshooting reports	Internal, move upward on nonrecurring basis	Memo or manuscript format, fully developed text, organized around conclusions or logical arguments, direct or indirect order

SUMMARY

A business report is a factual, objective document that serves a legitimate business purpose. It may be three pages long or three hundred pages. It may be a preprinted form, a memo, a letter, or a manuscript. The style may be abbreviated and specific or fully developed and generalized, the organization direct or indirect. The length, format, style, and organization of a business report all depend on who originates it, what subject it covers, when it is prepared, where it is sent, why it is prepared, and how receptive the reader is.

The way a report will be used suggests how it should be developed. Companies use reports for six basic functions: to monitor and control operations, to implement policies and procedures, to comply with regulatory agencies, to obtain new business or funding, to document client work, and to guide decisions.

COMMUNICATION CHALLENGES AT CALVIN KLEIN

Although Bert Browse finds the format of his current reports useful, he expects that at some point it will become outdated. Fortunately, Calvin Klein, Ltd., backs changes that increase the efficiency of its internal reporting system. Moreover, from time to time management undertakes its own review of the use, format, and frequency of its operating reports.

Individual Challenge: You have been asked to remedy a specific example of an inefficient reporting system. Sales managers for the blue jean product line are preparing sales reports in different formats. Because of the discrepancies, top management has a hard time comparing results from one region to another. Develop a standardized format that can be filled in each week by the blue jean sales managers from five different regions. Your report form should elicit data on total sales, actual versus planned sales, sales by major account, sales by style number, new business opportunities, and problems.

Group Challenge: A task force of which you are a member has been asked to help study other Calvin Klein operating reports. The first step is to establish a checklist for evaluating them. Give some thought to such issues as format, organization, content, and value of information relative to preparation time.

QUESTIONS FOR DISCUSSION

1. If a report is pushing strongly toward a specific recommendation, should the writer include information that might support a different recommendation? Why or why not?
2. Do you believe that employees have a moral obligation to express in writing their reservations about their company's decisions?
3. What would you do if your boss asked you to alter or destroy a report that might be used as evidence in legal proceedings?
4. Can you think of any reasons, other than length, for putting a report in memo or letter format as opposed to manuscript format?
5. How do you explain the fact that so many different kinds of documents qualify as reports? What makes them all reports?
6. What types of reports need fully developed text?
7. What dangers do you see in the practice of requiring people to "fill in the blanks" on a standardized reporting form?
8. In terms of the concepts in this chapter, how would you classify the reports you write for your college classes?
9. What are some of the ways in which reports you write for your college classes differ from business reports?
10. If you were a manager, how would you respond to the frequent employee lament that "all we do is write reports."

EXERCISES

1. Using the categories presented in Table 12.1, label each of the reports listed below. In addition, explain what type of data would be used and whether conclusions and recommendations would be appropriate.
   - **a.** A statistical study of the pattern of violent crime in a large city during the last five years
   - **b.** A report prepared by a seed company demonstrating the superiority of its seed corn for farmers
   - **c.** A report prepared by an independent testing agency evaluating various types of cold remedies
   - **d.** A trip report submitted at the end of a week by a traveling salesperson
   - **e.** A report indicating how 45 acres of undeveloped land could be converted to an industrial park
   - **f.** An annual report to be sent to the shareholders of a large corporation
   - **g.** A report from a wildlife officer to Washington headquarters reporting on the status of the California condor (a seriously endangered species of bird)
   - **h.** A written report by a police officer who has just completed an arrest
2. Identify a problem that exists in almost all businesses, such as out-of-control costs, poor quality of raw materials or finished products, employee dissatisfaction, unmotivated salespeople. Next, choose a particular business that you know something about and describe in detail the problem as it exists in that organization (for example, employees in a garage performing less-than-thorough lubrications or inside salespeople chatting while customers wait unattended). Finally, assume that you are to report to management about the nature and magnitude of the problem. How will your report be classified according to the categories listed in Table 12.1? What kinds of data would you need before you could draw logical conclusions and present convincing recommendations? Describe the type of report you would write, and justify your choices.
3. List three entry-level positions for which you will be qualified after graduation, and then list the types of reports that you would be responsible for preparing in each position.
4. Interview several people working in a career that you might like to enter, and ask them about the types of written reports they receive and prepare. How do these reports tie into the decision-making process? Who reads the reports they prepare? Summarize your findings in writing to your instructor, and be prepared to discuss them with the class.
5. Call for an appointment with a senior officer of a local business, possibly a bank, and arrive for the interview with most of your questions already written out. Learn what you can about how the business uses reports in its decision-making process and possibly for other purposes. Are most reports written or oral? Do the written reports follow a standardized format? (If so, see if you can obtain a copy of the style sheet or manual.) What types of reports must be made to local, state, and national government agencies? Does the company employ an in-house report writer, or are most reports drafted by the employees most closely involved with the work? Prepare a written account of your findings, and be prepared to discuss the project with your classmates.

CHAPTER THIRTEEN

GATHERING AND INTERPRETING INFORMATION

After studying this chapter, you will be able to

- Develop a statement defining the problem to be solved
- Identify and outline the issues that have to be analyzed during your study
- Prepare a work plan for conducting the investigation, laying out necessary steps, their timing, and sources of information required for each step
- Organize the research phase of the investigation, including the identification of secondary and primary sources of data
- Draw sound conclusions and develop practical recommendations

COMMUNICATION CLOSE-UP AT LOWRY & ASSOCIATES

Jim Lowry

"Heaven knows what possessed me to take a chance and start my own management consulting business," says Jim Lowry, president of Lowry & Associates. "I'd worked hard to get where I was, and I'd reached the point where I had a lot to lose: a good salary, status, security, work I liked. But I'm ambitious, and I wanted to have my own firm. If I'd had any sense, I'd probably still be working for someone else, playing racquetball three times a week. Now I'm running around like a crazy man between Washington, Oakland, and headquarters in Chicago, trying to keep track of what 150 people are doing. I can't believe it's been 13 years since I started the firm. I can't believe how much it has grown."

Although many things have contributed to Lowry & Associates' success, perhaps the single most important factor was their work for the Department of Commerce (DOC), which was aimed at developing a new government strategy for stimulating minority business development.

As Jim says of this study, "Our report for the DOC put us on the map. The business press picked up on our recommendations, and suddenly I started reading about myself in the newspapers. It was really exciting. I think the firm would have grown and succeeded in any case, but that study certainly helped."

To some extent, Jim owes the wide media coverage of his work for the DOC to the subject of his report. He was writing about a controversial

Information about minority-owned businesses was the basis of Lowry & Associates' massive report for the Department of Commerce.

issue, and his views on the subject were original and newsworthy. But to an even greater extent, his success depended on the quality of the work underlying the document. As Jim points out, "Our report for the DOC was a good one; we spent a lot of time on it. But the important things in that study happened a long time before we started writing. Solving the problem was the main thing. Writing the report was just the final step."

The other steps, the ones that occur before the writing begins, are the foundation of any report. Jim took these six steps in his work for the DOC:

1. Defined the problem
2. Outlined the issues for investigation
3. Prepared a work plan
4. Conducted research
5. Analyzed and interpreted data, drew conclusions, and developed recommendations
6. Prepared the final report

The relative importance of these steps depends on the type of assignment. Informational reports, which contain facts alone, may require very little in the way of conclusions and recommendations. Monitor/control reports, statements of policies and procedures, interim progress reports, and many compliance reports are examples. On the other hand, analytical documents that include conclusions and recommendations demand all six steps. Decision-oriented reports, proposals, final reports to clients, and some compliance reports are examples. Jim's report, a final report to an outside client, belongs in this second category.

DEFINING THE PROBLEM

Before you begin to write a report, you almost always have some work to do. Even if you're preparing a strictly informational report that does nothing more than transmit facts, you must still gather those facts and arrange them in a convenient format. But your first step is to write a statement of the problem. This exercise will help you decide what information you need to complete your report.

Let's say, for example, that you've been asked to study the extent of drug and alcohol abuse by assembly-line workers in your company's main plant. All you've been asked to do is to make a factual report on what is happening.

The first step in writing a report is to narrow the focus of your investigation.

Before conducting your investigation, you have to decide on a few boundaries for your report. For example, are you going to study the source and distribution of drugs and alcohol in the plant, or are you going to disregard the question of where these substances come from? What time period are you going to cover? This month? The past 12 months? The past 5 years? Your answers to these and similar questions establish the extent of your investigation and, ultimately, the content of your report.

If you're writing an analytical document that interprets facts and draws conclusions about them, you generally limit the investigation by the way you define the problem to be solved. For example, let's say that you've been asked to analyze the alcohol and drug abuse problem, not just report the facts. Do you try to determine why workers are using drugs and alcohol at the plant and recommend ways to keep them from turning to these substances? Or do you try to determine the impact of drug and alcohol abuse on productivity and product quality, then recommend measures that can be taken to make up for their effects? In other words, exactly what is the problem to be solved? The way you define the problem establishes the framework of your investigation.

ASKING THE RIGHT QUESTIONS

Your investigation takes its shape from the questions you ask and the purpose you delineate.

Often, the problem is defined for you by the person who authorizes the report. When this is the case, talk over the objectives of the report before you begin your investigation to ensure that you understand exactly what is required. Find out specifically

- What needs to be determined
- Why the issue is important
- Who is involved in the situation
- Where the trouble is located
- When it started
- How the situation originated

Not all these questions apply in every situation, but asking them helps you clarify the boundaries of your investigation.

DEVELOPING THE STATEMENT OF PURPOSE

Prepare a written statement of your purpose; then review it with the person who authorized the study.

Once you've asked some preliminary questions, you should develop a clear written statement of the purpose of your report. Then double-check this statement with the person who authorized the study. When the authorizer sees the purpose written down in black and white, she or he may decide to redirect the study toward other areas.

For example, let's say you've been asked to evaluate four candidates for the job of personnel director and recommend one to your boss. You might state your purpose in one of three ways:

A study's purpose may be stated in one of three ways.

- *Use an infinitive.* "The purpose of this report is to determine which of four job candidates is best qualified to be personnel director."
- *Use a question.* "This report answers the question, Which of four candidates is best qualified to be personnel director?"
- *Use a declarative statement.* "The best qualified of four job candidates will be selected to serve as personnel director."

Regardless of which form you choose for your statement of purpose, be sure to make the goal of the investigation clear so you will not be sidetracked into irrelevant issues.

Factors affecting Jim Lowry's report:

- WHO: Authorized
- WHAT: Final report to client
- WHEN: Special, nonrecurring
- WHERE: External
- WHY: Analytical
- HOW: Receptive reader (direct order)

In defining the purpose of his work for the Department of Commerce, Jim Lowry was dealing with a particularly complex situation. As he says, "Ever since the late 1960s, the government has been trying to help blacks and Hispanics get into business and stay in business. There's been some progress, but minorities still don't own very many companies, and those that they do own tend to be pretty small. Basically, our purpose was to find out why all these government programs weren't having more of an impact so we could advise the DOC on what the government ought to be doing differently.

"This problem may seem fairly straightforward, but there were some complicating factors. For one thing, the DOC is only one of several government agencies that offer programs to stimulate minority businesses. Should we limit our study to DOC programs, or should we review all the government's efforts? And what about the administration of programs, as opposed to program design? Some very fine programs might simply be poorly managed. Should we deal with that issue? Similarly, with respect to new programs, should we stop with program design, or should we extend our work to cover program implementation?"

After considering these and other questions, Lowry & Associates developed the following problem statement:

> The purpose of the proposed study is to help the Department of Commerce (DOC) develop and implement an improved plan for Minority Business Enterprise Development (MBED). During the study, new programs will be developed and existing programs of little value will be identified. Alternatives for creating and managing the new programs will be analyzed to determine which agencies of the government should be involved in putting the new MBED plan into action.

OUTLINING ISSUES FOR ANALYSIS

The second step is to outline the issues you plan to study.

Once you have defined the problem and established the purpose of the study, you are ready to begin your investigation. To organize the research effort, you need to break the problem into a series of specific questions. This process is sometimes called factoring. You probably subconsciously approach most problems this way. Let's say, for example, that your car's engine won't start. What do you do? You look at the various possibilities—

FIGURE 13.1
How Lowry & Associates Factored Their Problem

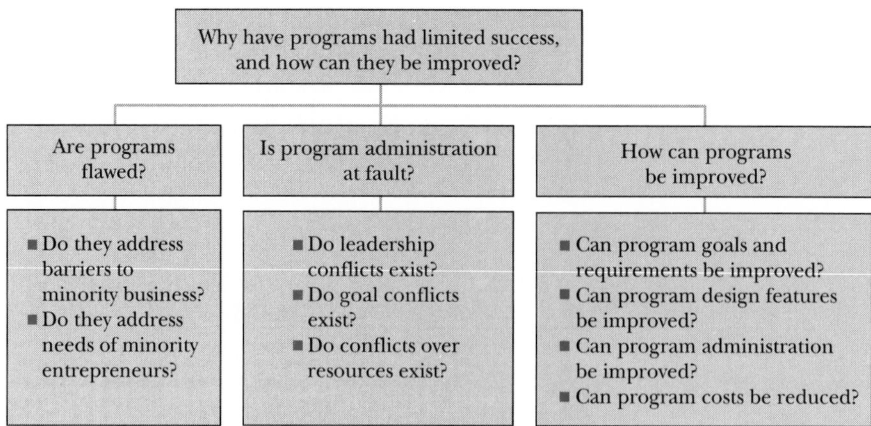

the battery, the gas, the ignition system—checking one thing at a time until you find the cause. Subdividing the problem like this helps you cover every important aspect.

Jim Lowry and his associates, because of the magnitude of their study for DOC, faced a complex factoring process (diagrammed in Figure 13.1). "We began with a general question," Jim says: "Why have government programs had such limited success in fostering minority-owned businesses, and how can they be improved? We then factored the question of why there had been so little success into two subquestions: Are the programs flawed? Is program administration at fault?

"Looking at the area of program design, we speculated that the government's programs have had limited success for a very basic reason: They have not provided the right kind of help to the right people. This hypothesis naturally led us to some more questions: What kind of help do minorities need in order to create and operate successful businesses? What specific barriers need to be removed for them to enter the economic mainstream? What are their general social and economic problems? And what are their specific business problems? We went through a similar thought process to come up with some specific questions in the area of program administration."

Once Jim had determined what was wrong with the DOC's program, he could address the second part of the main question: the problem of recommending improvements. He had to decide what the new programs ought to accomplish, how they should be designed, who should administer them, and what they would cost.

The outline of issues for analysis is often different from the outline of the final report.

The process of outlining the issues enabled Jim and his colleagues to solve a problem methodically, just as outlining a report enables you to write in a systematic way. It's worth noting, however, that the way you outline an investigation may be different from the way you outline the resulting report. Solving the problem is one thing; "selling" the solution is another.

DEVELOPING A LOGICAL STRUCTURE

Because any subject can be factored in many different ways, your job is to choose the most logical method, the one that makes the most sense. Start

Informational and analytical studies are factored differently.

by looking carefully at the purpose of your study. Informational assignments are structured differently from analytical assignments.

Be aware, however, that many assignments require both information and analysis. You must therefore be able to discern the overall purpose of the study. Is your general goal to provide background information that someone else will interpret? Then an informational outline is appropriate overall, even though subsections of the study may require some analysis to bring important facts to the fore. Or is the purpose of your study to scrutinize the data and generate your own conclusions and recommendations? Then you should use an analytical outline overall, even though your opinions must obviously be based on facts. In problem solving you may use a variety of structural schemes, as long as you avoid errors in logic.

Informational assignments

Studies that emphasize the discovery and reporting of facts may be factored by subtopic.

Studies that lead to factual reports with very little analysis or interpretation generally are factored on the basis of subtopics dealing with specific subjects. These subtopics can be arranged in various ways:

- *In order of importance.* Let's say you're reviewing five product lines. You might organize your study in order of sales for each product line, beginning with the line that produces the most revenue and proceeding to the one that produces the least revenue.
- *Sequentially.* If you're studying a process, proceed step by step—1, 2, 3, and so on.
- *Chronologically.* When investigating a chain of events, organize the study according to what happened in January, what happened in February, and so on.
- *Spatially.* If you're studying a physical object, study it left to right, top to bottom, outside to inside.
- *Geographically.* If location is important, factor your study geographically.
- *Categorically.* If you're asked to review several distinct aspects of a subject, look at one category at a time, such as sales, profit, cost, or investment.

These methods of subdivision are commonly used in the preparation of monitor/control reports, policies and procedures, compliance reports, and interim progress reports.

Analytical assignments

Studies that focus on problem solving may be factored on the basis of hypotheses; those that focus on the evaluation of alternatives, on relative merits.

Studies that result in reports containing analyses, conclusions, and recommendations are generally categorized by a problem-solving method. Hypotheses and relative merits are the two most common structural approaches of this type.

When the problem is to discover causes, predict results, or find a solution to a problem, one natural way to proceed is to formulate hypothetical explanations. Let's say your problem is to determine why your company is having trouble hiring secretaries. You would factor this problem by speculating on the reasons, then collect information that would confirm or disprove each reason. Your outline of the major issues might look something like this:

Why are we having trouble hiring secretaries?

I. Salaries are too low.
   A. What do we pay our secretaries?
   B. What do comparable companies pay their secretaries?
   C. How important is pay in influencing secretaries' job choices?

II. Our location is poor.
   A. Are we accessible by public transportation and major roads?
   B. Is the area physically attractive?
   C. Are housing costs affordable?
   D. Is crime a problem?

III. The supply of secretaries is diminishing.
   A. How many secretaries were available five years ago as opposed to now?
   B. What was the demand for secretaries five years ago as opposed to now?

When the problem is to evaluate how well different alternatives meet your criteria, the natural way to subdivide your analysis is to focus on the criteria. For example, if the problem is to decide where to build a new plant, you might factor the investigation along the following lines:

Where should we build a new plant?

I. Construction costs
   A. Location A
   B. Location B
   C. Location C

II. Labor availability
   A. Location A
   B. Location B
   C. Location C

III. Transportation facilities
   A. Location A
   B. Location B
   C. Location C

Another way of using relative merits is to identify the alternatives first and then to analyze how well each alternative meets your criteria.

Investigations that result in decision-oriented reports, final reports for clients, and some compliance reports are generally factored on the basis of either hypotheses or relative merits.

FOLLOWING THE RULES OF DIVISION

Dividing something physical, like a pie, is much easier than dividing something intangible, like an idea. How do you know that the pieces of an idea are cut in the right size and shape and number? Over the centuries,

Follow the rules of division to ensure that your study will be organized in a logical, systematic way.

scholars have developed a concise set of rules for dividing an idea into components:

- *Choose a significant, useful basis or guiding principle for the division.* For example, you could subdivide production problems into two groups: problems that arise when the machines are turned off and problems that occur when the machines are turned on. However, this basis for breaking down the subject would not be of much use to anyone. A better choice might be problems caused by human error versus problems caused by machine failure.
- *Limit yourself to one basis at a time in subdividing a whole into its parts.* If you switch from one basis to another, you get a mixed classification, which can confuse your analysis. Let's say you're subdividing your study of the market for toothpaste according to sales of fluoride versus nonfluoride brands. You would upset the investigation by adding another category to your analysis (say, sales of toothpaste in Alabama). If you are dealing with a long, complex subject, you will no doubt have to use several bases of division before you complete your work, but the shift from one basis to another must be made at a logical point, after you have completed your study of a particular issue. For example, after you have looked at sales of fluoride versus nonfluoride toothpaste, you might then want to look at toothpaste sales by geographic location or socioeconomic group.
- *Make certain that each group is separate and distinct.* The groups must be mutually exclusive, or you will end up talking about the same item twice under two different headings. Subdividing a population into males, females, and teen-agers wouldn't make any sense, because the categories overlap.
- *Be complete in listing all the components of a whole.* For example, it would be misleading to subdivide an engine into parts without mentioning the pistons. An important part of the whole would be missing, and the resulting picture of the engine would be wrong.

If you follow these rules, your investigation will be logical, systematic, and complete.

PREPARING A PRELIMINARY OUTLINE

Organize your study by preparing a detailed preliminary outline.

As you go through the factoring process, you may want to use an outline format to represent your ideas. But, you may ask, if a few notes on a piece of paper are enough to guide you, why should you bother with a more formal outline? Perhaps you shouldn't for a short, informal report in memo form. But a preliminary outline does give you a convenient frame of reference for your investigation. And a detailed outline is definitely worth the effort under these circumstances:

- When you are one of several people working on an assignment
- When your investigation will be extensive and will involve many different sources and types of data
- When you know from past experience that the person who requested the study will revise the assignment during the course of your investigation and you want to keep track of the changes

FIGURE 13.2
Two Common Outline Formats

ALPHANUMERIC	DECIMAL
I. _____	1.0 _____
A. _____	1.1 _____
B. _____	1.2 _____
1. _____	1.21 _____
2. _____	1.22 _____
a. _____	1.221 _____
b. _____	1.222 _____
3. _____	1.23 _____
C. _____	1.3 _____
II. _____	2.0 _____
A. _____	2.1 _____
1. _____	2.11 _____
a. _____	2.111 _____
b. _____	2.112 _____
2. _____	2.12 _____
3. _____	2.13 _____
B. _____	2.2 _____

Two widely used systems of outlining, the alphanumeric system and the decimal system, are illustrated in Figure 13.2. Both are perfectly acceptable, but some companies traditionally favor one method over the other.

Use the same grammatical form for each group of items in your outline.

You should usually write the captions at each level of your outline in the same grammatical form. In other words, if item I uses a verb, II, III, and IV should also use verbs. This so-called parallel construction enables readers to see that the ideas are related, of similar importance, and on the same level of generality. It makes the outline a more useful tool for establishing the table of contents and headings in your final report, and it is considered the correct format by most of the people who might review your outline.

In wording the outline, you must also choose between descriptive (topical) and informative (talking) captions. As Table 13.1 indicates, descriptive captions label the subject that will be discussed, whereas informative captions (in either question or summary form) suggest more about the meaning of the issues.

Informative outlines are generally more helpful than descriptive outlines.

Although outlines with informative captions take a little longer to write, they are generally more useful in guiding your work, especially if written in terms of the questions you plan to answer during the study. In addition, they have the advantage of being easier for others to review. If other people are going to comment on your outline, they may not have a very

TABLE 13.1 **Types of Outline Captions**

DESCRIPTIVE (TOPICAL) OUTLINE	INFORMATIVE (TALKING) OUTLINE	
	QUESTION FORM	SUMMARY FORM
I. Industry characteristics	I. What is the nature of the industry?	I. Flour milling is mature industry.
A. Annual sales	A. What are the annual sales?	A. Market is large.
B. Profitability	B. Is the industry profitable?	B. Profit margins are narrow.
C. Growth rate	C. What is the pattern of growth?	C. Growth is modest.
1. Sales	1. Sales growth?	1. Sales growth averages less than 3 percent a year.
2. Profit	2. Profit growth?	2. Growth in profits is flat.

clear idea of what you mean by the descriptive heading "Advertising." But they will get the main idea if you use the informative heading "Cuts in ad budget may explain sales decline."

Remember that at this point you are only developing a preliminary outline to guide your investigation. Later on, when you have completed your research and are preparing a final outline or a table of contents for the report, you may want to switch from an outline of your questions to an outline that summarizes your findings.

PREPARING THE WORK PLAN

The third step is to prepare a work plan that identifies the tasks you will perform.

Once you have defined the problem and outlined the issues for analysis, you are ready to establish a work plan based on your preliminary outline. If you are preparing this plan for yourself, it can be relatively informal: a simple list of the steps you plan to take, an estimate of their sequence and timing, and a list of the sources of information you plan to use.

If you're conducting a lengthy, formal study, however, the work plan should be quite detailed, because it will guide the performance of many tasks over a span of time. And most proposals require a detailed work plan, which becomes the basis for a contract if the proposal is accepted.

A formal work plan may specify a number of things.

A formal work plan might include these things (especially the first two):

- Statement of the problem
- Statement of the purpose and scope of your investigation
- Discussion of the sequence of tasks to be accomplished, indicating sources of information, required experiments or observations, and limitations (such as restrictions on time, money, or available data)
- Description of the end products that will result from the investigation, such as reports, plans, operating improvements, or tangible products
- Review of project assignments, schedules, and resource requirements, indicating who will be responsible for what, when tasks will be completed, and how much the investigation will cost

FIGURE 13.3
Sample Work Plan for a Formal Study

Statement of the Problem

The rapid growth of our company over the past five years has reduced the sense of community among our staff. People no longer feel like part of an intimate organization where they matter as individuals.

Purpose and Scope of Work

The purpose of this study is to determine whether a company newsletter would help rebuild employee identification with the organization. The study will evaluate the impact of newsletters in other companies and attempt to identify features that might be desirable in our own newsletter. Such variables as length, frequency of distribution, types of articles, and graphic design will be considered. Costs will be estimated for several approaches. In addition, the study will analyze the personnel and procedures required to produce a newsletter.

Sources and Methods of Data Collection

Sample newsletters will be collected from 50 companies similar to ours in size, growth rate, and types of employees. The editors will be asked to comment on the impact of their publications on employee morale. Our own employees will be surveyed to determine their interest in a newsletter and their preferences for specific features. Production procedures and costs will be analyzed through conversations with newsletter editors and possible printers.

Preliminary Outline

I. Do newsletters affect morale?
   A. Do people read them?
   B. How do employees benefit?
   C. How does the company benefit?

II. What are the features of good newsletters?
   A. How long are they?
   B. What do they contain?
   C. How often are they published?
   D. How are they designed?

III. How should a newsletter be produced?
   A. Should it be written, edited, and printed internally?
   B. Should it be written internally and printed outside?
   C. Should it be totally produced outside?

IV. What would a newsletter cost?
   A. What would the personnel costs be?
   B. What would the materials costs be?
   C. What would outside services cost?

V. Should we publish a company newsletter?

VI. If so, what approach should we take?

Work Plan

Collect and analyze newsletters	Sept. 1-14
Interview editors by phone	Sept. 16-20
Survey employees	Sept. 14-28
Develop sample newsletter	Sept. 28-Oct. 5
Develop cost estimates	Oct. 7-10
Prepare report	Oct. 10-24
Submit final report	Oct. 25

Some work plans also include a tentative outline of the report. Figure 13.3 is an example of a work plan for a study of whether to launch a company newsletter.

In his work plan for the DOC study, Jim Lowry wrote a 15-page explanation of the tasks and subtasks to be performed, indicating how they would be accomplished and which of nine associates would be responsible for each. He also provided a schedule and a breakdown of project costs.

DOING THE RESEARCH

The value of your report depends on the quality of the information it's based on. So when the time comes to gather information, your first concern is to get organized. If you're working alone on a project, getting organized may mean nothing more than setting up a file and checking out a few books and periodicals from the nearest library. But if you are part of a team, you have to work out your assignments and coordinate activities. Your work plan will be a big help during this research effort.

The fourth step is to do the research by consulting primary (firsthand) and secondary (secondhand) sources.

The work plan should contain a list of the primary and secondary sources you will consult. Primary sources provide, as the name implies, firsthand information; secondary sources are secondhand reports. Most business problems call for a mix of both secondary and primary sources. You are likely to find, however, that much of what you need to know has never been collected. This reliance on primary sources is one of the main differences between business reports and school reports.

REVIEWING SECONDARY SOURCES

Even though you may plan to rely heavily on primary sources, you are wise to begin your study with a thorough review of the information that has already been collected. By searching the literature, you are protected against the embarrassment of failing to report something that is common knowledge. You are also saved the trouble of conducting a study of something that has already been done. Once you gain a feel for the structure of the subject, you can decide what additional research will be required.

Do secondary research by locating information that has already been collected, usually in the form of books, periodicals, and reports.

Depending on your subject, you may find useful information in general reference works, popular publications, and government documents. In addition, however, each field of business has a handful of specialized references that are considered indispensable. You will quickly come to know these sources once you've joined a particular industry. And don't overlook internal sources. Often the most useful references are company reports and memos. Also check company brochures, newsletters, and annual reports to shareholders.

If you are working for a large organization with a company library, you may have direct access to the help of a professional librarian in identifying and obtaining other useful materials for your investigation. If not, look for the nearest public library or university library, and ask the librarians there for help. Reference librarians are trained to know where to find just about everything, and many of them are pleased to help people pursue obscure information.

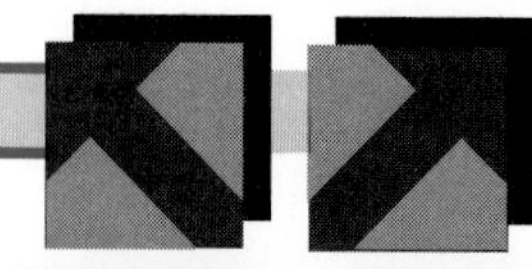

BUSINESS COMMUNICATION TODAY

Plugging into Electronic Data Bases

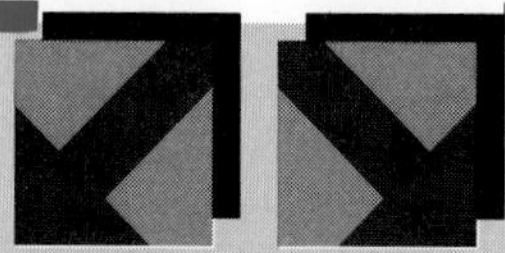

If you're looking for information, library shelves are a good place to start. But if you need up-to-the-minute data or have specialized needs, you may find a computerized data base more useful, less expensive, and less time consuming. A data base, a file of information on one subject or a family of subjects, can be stored and maintained in a computer's memory. The speed of the computer then enables you to recall any item in this file almost instantly.

The three main types of data bases are statistical, bibliographic, and full text. Statistical data bases store vast amounts of numerical data, such as wage and price indexes, census information, foreign exchange rates, and stock and bond prices. Bibliographic data bases store references to and summaries of articles in periodicals and newspapers. Full-text data bases offer the complete texts of such materials as newspaper, magazine, and journal articles.

Thousands of different data bases exist today, and their numbers are growing. Many companies have their own in-house data base, which is accessible to employees through computer terminals or microcomputers. In addition, several hundred commercial data bases are now available to the public, with literally millions of items of information readily retrievable. These data bases cover specific fields, such as law and financial forecasting, or general information, such as sports and weather data.

You can obtain access to commercial data bases in three ways. The first is to subscribe to a data base yourself. To do so, you need a computer, a modem (a device that allows your computer to tap into the phone system), and special communications software. If you are interested in reading an article, you can read it on screen or have it printed out on your own printer (if you are using a full-text data base) or request that a photocopy be sent to you through the mail (if you are using a bibliographic data base).

The second way is to go through an information retrieval service, which subscribes to many data bases. You ask a research question, and the service selects the appropriate data base, plans and conducts the search, and delivers the results to you.

The third way to gain access to a commercial

Choose reference works that are

- Up-to-date
- Objective

When it comes to choosing your references, be selective. Avoid dated or biased material. If possible, check on the author's qualifications and the reputation of the publisher.

The amount of library research you do depends on the subject you're studying and the purpose of your investigation. Jim Lowry's work for the DOC, for example, required an unusually thorough literature search. The subject of minority business development is well documented, and Jim knew that his report had to be especially authoritative to gain acceptance. His team read over 10,000 pages of evaluations and special reports prepared by the Office of Management and the Budget, the Office of Minority Business Enterprise, and the General Accounting Office. They also studied newspaper and magazine articles going back ten years to gain a feeling for changes in the status of minority businesses over time. They collected and reviewed a wide assortment of books on the subject as well. Was this effort excessive? No, it was necessary, because Lowry & Associates was dealing with an emotionally charged, politically sensitive issue. The size of the subject and the importance of the study justified extensive research.

In conducting library research, you will eventually reach the point where additional effort provides little new information.

Few projects would require so much research, however. In most cases, when you find yourself reading essentially the same things over and over again, move out of the library and on to the next phase of your work.

data base is to go to a library. Many offer computer bibliographies free or for a reasonable fee. The librarian can help you select the appropriate data bases.

Conducting a computerized search is not easy. Suppose, for example, that you want to know how successful 15-second television commercials have been. First you need to figure out which data base would be most likely to have information on this topic. You might go with a very specific data base, such as BAR (Broadcast Advertiser Reports), or you might choose a service, such as Dialog or Compuserve, that carries hundreds of data bases.

Then you need to determine exactly what to ask and translate your needs into "key words" that you can use in the search. The more specific the key words, the more likely you are to find exactly what you want. You might, for example, tell the data base that you want to see abstracts of all recent articles having to do with TELEVISION, ADVERTISING, and 15-SECOND SPOTS. That instruction may or may not yield the desired results, however. For instance, if there are no entries for 15-SECOND SPOTS, your search will yield nothing. Then you will have to come up with different key words, perhaps BROADCASTING and COMMERCIALS.

There are other drawbacks to using electronic data bases as well. One is the difficulty of use, especially if you're not really sure what you're looking for. Several data bases are so complicated that you must go through a training session or tutorial before you can use them. Once you've learned the basic principles of "logging on" to a particular data base system and of conducting a search, you still may not find what you want.

Another drawback is the cost. Data bases typically charge $15 to $200 per hour, depending on the time of day and the particular data base. Charges can add up very quickly.

Finally, the information you find may not be complete. Thus, if you are researching a particularly complex issue, you might conduct a library search for basic data and supplement it with current statistical data that you obtain through a data base search.

1. Given the skill required to use data bases effectively, do you foresee a day when doing computer research will be a specialized job? Does the idea of letting someone else find the answers to your questions bother you, or do you see this division of labor as a way to increase your personal productivity? What are the advantages and disadvantages of letting someone else do a data base search for you?

2. Investigate the data base services offered at your college. Devise a question you would like researched, and use the service to conduct the information search.

Remember that in business, time is money. Your objective is to be as accurate and thorough as possible within a reasonable length of time.

Regardless of the amount of research you do, retain complete and accurate notes on the sources of all the material you collect, using one of the systems explained in Component Chapter E, "Documentation of Report Sources." Documenting your sources through footnotes, endnotes, or some similar system lends credibility to your report.

COLLECTING PRIMARY DATA

Do primary research by collecting basic information yourself.

When the information you need is not available from secondary sources, you have to collect and interpret the data yourself by doing primary research. You must go out into the real world to gather information through your own efforts. The four main ways to collect primary data are to examine documents, observe things, survey people, and conduct experiments.

Documents

In business, a great deal of information is filed away for future reference. Your own company's files may therefore provide you with accurate, factual

Documentary evidence and historical records are sources of primary data.

historical records that you cannot obtain any other way. Business documents that qualify as primary data include sales reports prepared by field representatives, balance sheets and income statements, policy statements, correspondence with customers and suppliers, contracts, and log books. Many government and legal documents are primary sources as well, because they represent a decision made by those present at some official proceeding.

A single document may be both a secondary source and a primary source. For example, in citing summaries of financial and operations data from an annual report, you are using it as a secondary source. But that same report would be considered a primary source if you were analyzing its design features or comparing it with annual reports from other years or other companies.

Observations

Observation applies your five senses and your judgment to the investigation.

Informal observations are a rather common source of primary data in business. All you have to do is use your five senses, especially your eyes and ears, to gather information. Many reports, for instance, are based on the writer's visit to a facility to observe operations.

More objective information can be gathered through formal observations, which give observers a structure for noting what they see and minimize opportunities for interpretation. For example, when Jim Lowry and his associates wanted to test their recommendations for stimulating minority business development, they implemented their recommendations in three communities and watched what happened over three months. Observers had a specific list of developments to watch for. Later, when the team thoroughly analyzed the results, they came up with some relatively objective conclusions.

In general, observation is a useful technique when you are studying objects, physical activities, processes, the environment, or human behavior. It does have one major drawback, however: The value of the observation depends on the reliability of the observer. Many people have a tendency to see what they want to see or to interpret events in light of their own experience. But if the observer is trustworthy and has proper instructions, observation can provide valuable insights that would be difficult to obtain with other methods.

Surveys

Often the best way to obtain answers to your questions is to ask people with relevant experience and opinions. Such surveys include everything from a single interview to distribution of thousands of questionnaires.

A common way to conduct primary research is to interview well-qualified experts.

When you need specialized information that hasn't been recorded anywhere, you may want to conduct a personal interview with an expert, which is the simplest form of survey. Many experts come from the ranks of your own organization: people from other departments who have specialized knowledge, your predecessor in the job, "old-timers" who've seen it all. On occasion, you may also want to talk with outsiders who have some special expertise.

Always prepare for interviews with experts.

Doing an interview may seem an easy way to get information, but you should always prepare carefully. You don't want to waste anyone's time, and you want your efforts to be productive. Chapter 17 presents some pointers on conducting effective interviews.

A formal survey is a way of finding out what a cross section of people think about something.

Although they have the same purpose, interviews are quite different from formal, large-scale surveys in which a sample population answers a series of carefully tested questions. For example, in Jim Lowry's work for the DOC, he needed to know how government assistance programs for minority businesspeople were viewed. Jim and his team could have consulted thousands of people on that subject. But to keep the project within bounds, they questioned a sample of 50 representative minority business owners and over 100 government officials with knowledge of the field.

A formal survey requires a number of important decisions:

- Should you use face-to-face interviews, phone calls, or printed questionnaires?
- How many individuals should you contact to get results that are *reliable* (that is, reproducible if the same study were repeated)? And who should those people be (what sample is an accurate reflection of the population)?
- What specific questions should you ask to get a *valid* picture, a true reflection of the group's feelings on the subject?

Two important research criteria:

- Reliability—when the same results would be obtained if the research were repeated
- Validity—when research measures what it is intended to measure

Your answers to these questions have a profound effect on the results of your survey.

Having seen rival preelection polls that come up with conflicting projections of who's going to win, you may wonder if it makes sense to rely on survey results at all. The answer is yes, as long as you understand the nature of surveys. For one thing, surveys reveal only what people think about something at a specific point in time. For another, pollsters ask different people different questions in different ways and, not surprisingly, get different answers. Just because surveys produce different results does not mean that they are a poor form of research. But conducting a reliable, valid survey is not an easy matter. Generally speaking, it helps to have the advice of a specialist.

Developing an effective questionnaire requires care and skill.

One of the most critical elements of a survey is the questionnaire. To develop one, begin by making a list of the points you are trying to determine. Then break these points into specific questions, choosing an appropriate type of question for each point (Figure 13.4 shows some variations). The following guidelines will help you produce valid results:

- Provide clear instructions so respondents know exactly how to fill out the questionnaire.
- Keep the questionnaire short and easy to answer. People are more likely to respond if they can complete the questionnaire within 10 or 15 minutes. So ask only questions that are relevant to your research. And don't ask questions that require too much work on the respondent's part. People aren't willing to dig up the answers to questions like "What was your monthly rate of water consumption in 1988?"
- Formulate questions that provide easily tabulated or analyzed answers. Numbers and facts are easier to deal with than opinions are. Nevertheless, you may be able to elicit countable opinions with multiple-choice questions or to group open-ended opinions into a limited number of categories.

FIGURE 13.4
Types of Survey Questions

OPEN-END	How would you describe the flavor of this ice cream?
EITHER–OR	Do you think this ice cream is too rich? _______Yes _______No
MULTIPLE CHOICE	Which description best fits the taste of this ice cream? (Choose only one.) a. Delicious b. Good c. Creamy d. Too intensely flavored e. Too sweet f. Grainy
SCALE	Please make an X on the scale to indicate how you perceive the texture of this ice cream. ←――――――――――――――――→ Too light Light Creamy Too creamy
CHECKLIST	Which flavors of ice cream have you had in the past 12 months? (Check all that apply.) _______Vanilla _______Chocolate _______Strawberry _______Chocolate chip _______Coffee
RANKING	Rank these flavors in order of your preference, from 1 (most preferred) to 5 (least preferred): _______Vanilla _______Cherry _______Maple nut _______Chocolate ripple _______Coconut
FILL IN THE BLANK	In the past month, how many times did you buy ice cream in the supermarket? ________________________ In the past month, how many times did you buy ice cream in ice cream shops? ________________________

- Avoid questions that lead to a particular answer, because they bias your survey. For example, this question obviously calls for a yes answer: "Do you prefer that we stay open in the evenings for the convenience of our customers?" A less biased alternative would be: "What time of day do you normally do your shopping?"
- Ask only one thing at a time. When you pose a compound question like "Do you read books and magazines regularly?" you don't allow for the respondent who reads one but not the other.
- Avoid questions with vague or abstract words. Instead of asking "Are you frequently troubled by colds?" ask "How many colds did you have in the past 12 months?"
- Pretest the questionnaire on a sample group to identify questions that are subject to misinterpretation.
- Include a few questions that rephrase earlier questions, as a cross check on the validity of the responses.

If you are mailing your questionnaire, as opposed to administering it in person, include a persuasive cover letter that explains why you are conducting the research. Try to convince the person that her or his response is important to you. If possible, offer to share the results with the respondent. Include a self-addressed envelope with prepaid postage so the respondent won't have to find an envelope or postage to return the questionnaire to you. Remember, however, that even under the best of circumstances you may not get more than a 10 to 20 percent response.

Experiments

Although some general business questions justify their use, experiments are far more common in technical fields. That's because an experiment requires extensive manipulation of the factors involved, which is often very expensive and may be, when people are a factor, unethical. Nevertheless, experiments do have their place. For example, say that you want to find out whether a change in lighting levels increases the productivity of the pattern cutters in your dressmaking business. The most objective approach is to conduct an experiment using two groups of cutters: one working under existing conditions and the other working under the new lighting.

The aim in conducting an experiment is to keep all variables the same except for the one you are testing.

In conducting an experiment, you have to be very careful to control the factors (called variables) you are not testing. Thus in the lighting experiment, for the results to be valid, the only difference between the two groups and their environments should be the lighting. Otherwise, differences in productivity could be attributed to such factors as age differences between the two groups of pattern cutters or experience on the job. It's even possible that introducing any change in the pattern cutters' environment, whether it be lighting or something else entirely, is enough to increase their productivity.

ANALYZING DATA

Once you've completed your research, you have to analyze your findings. The analytical process is essentially a search for relationships among the

The fifth step is to analyze your results by calculating statistics, drawing reasonable conclusions, and if appropriate, developing a set of recommendations.

facts and bits of evidence you've compiled. Looking at the data from different angles, you attempt to detect patterns that will enable you to answer the questions outlined in your work plan. Your mind begins to fit pieces together and to form tentative conclusions. As your analysis proceeds, you either verify or reject these conclusions. Your mind constantly filters, sorts, and combines ideas.

CALCULATING STATISTICS

Much of the information you compile during the research phase will be in numerical form. Assuming that it's been collected carefully, this factual data is precise, measurable, and objective—and therefore credible. However, statistical information in its raw state is of little practical value. It must be manipulated so that you and your readers can interpret its significance.

Averages

The same set of data can be used to produce three kinds of averages: mean, median, and mode.

One useful way of looking at data is to find the average, which is the number representative of a group of numbers. Consider the data presented in Figure 13.5, for example, which shows the sales booked by a group of nine salespeople over one week. To analyze this information, you could calculate the average. But which average? Depending on how you planned to use the data, you would choose the mean, median, or mode.

The most commonly used average is the mean, or the sum of all the items in the group divided by the number of items in the group. The mean is useful when you want to compare one item or individual with the group. In the example, the mean is $7,000. If you were the sales manager, you might well be interested in knowing that Wimper's sales were average; that Wilson, Green, and Carrick had below-average sales; that Keeble, Kemble, O'Toole, Mannix, and Caruso were above average. One problem with using the mean, however, is that it can give you a false picture if one of the numbers is extreme. Let's say that Caruso's sales for the week were $27,000. The mean would then be $9,000, and eight of the nine salespeople would be "below average."

The median is the "middle of the road" average.[1] In a numerical ranking like the one shown in Figure 13.5, the median is the number right in the middle of the list: $7,500. The median is useful when one (or a few) of the numbers is extreme. For example, even if Caruso's sales were $27,000, the median would still be $7,500.

The mode is the "fashionable" average, the pattern followed most often, the case you're most likely to come across.[2] It's the best average for answering a question like "What is the usual amount?" For example, if you wanted to know what level of sales was most common, you would answer with the mode, which is $8,500. Like the median, the mode is not affected by extreme values. It's much easier to find than the median, however, when you have a large number of items or individuals.

While you're analyzing averages, you should also consider the range, or the spread of a series of numbers. The fact that, in the example, sales per person ranged from $3,000 to $9,000 may raise the question of why there is such a wide gap between Wilson's and Caruso's performance. A range tells you the context in which the averages were calculated and demonstrates what values are possible.

FIGURE 13.5
Three Types of Averages: Mean, Median, and Mode

SALESPERSON	SALES	
Wilson	$ 3,000	
Green	5,000	
Carrick	6,000	
Wimper	7,000	Mean
Keeble	7,500	Median
Kemble	8,500	Mode
O'Toole	8,500	Mode
Mannix	8,500	Mode
Caruso	9,000	
Total	$63,000	

Trends

Trend analysis involves an examination of data over time so that patterns and relationships can be detected.

If you were overseeing the work of Wilson, Caruso, and the rest, you might be tempted to make some important personnel decisions on the basis of the week's sales figures. But you would be a lot smarter to compare them with sales figures from other weeks, looking for a pattern in the performance of salespeople over time. You could begin to see which salespeople were consistently above average and which were consistently below. You could also see whether sales for the group as a whole were increasing, declining, or remaining steady and whether there were any seasonal fluctuations in the sales pattern.

This type of analysis, known as trend analysis, is very common in business. By looking at data over a period of time, you can detect patterns and relationships that will help you answer important questions.

Correlations

A correlation is a statistical relationship between two or more variables.

Once you have identified a trend, you should look for the cause. Let's say, for example, that Caruso consistently produces the most sales. You would undoubtedly be curious about the secret of her success. Does she call on her customers more often? Is she a more persuasive person? Does she have larger accounts or a bigger sales territory? Is she simply more experienced than the others?

To answer these questions, you could look for a consistent relationship between each person's sales and other variables, such as average account size or years of selling experience. For example, if salespeople with the largest accounts consistently produced higher sales, you might assume that these two factors were correlated, or related in a predictable way. And you might conclude that Caruso's success was due, at least in part, to the average size of her accounts.

However, your conclusion might be wrong. Correlations are useful evidence, but they do not necessarily prove a cause-and-effect relationship. Caruso's success might well be the result of several other factors. To know for sure, you would have to collect more evidence.

DRAWING CONCLUSIONS

Conclusions may be based on a combination of facts, value judgments, and assumptions.

Regardless of how much evidence you amass, at some point in every analysis you move beyond hard facts, which can be objectively measured and verified. When you reach that point, you begin to formulate conclusions, which are interpretations of what the facts mean. You then step into the realm of assumptions and value judgments, which have taken form out of your own experience. Nothing is inherently wrong with assumptions and value judgments; very few decisions are made on the basis of facts alone. But you must understand the extent to which conclusions may be based on subjective factors.

Imagine that, as sales manager, you have gathered these facts:

- Sales in New England are three times as high as sales in the Southeast.
- The two regions are roughly equal in the size and number of potential accounts.
- Both regions have the same number and type of salespeople, who have all been trained in the same selling techniques.

SHARPEN YOUR SKILLS

Seven Errors in Logic That Can Undermine Your Reports

For your report to be effective, it must be logical. If you learn how to think logically, you will also write more logically.

Here are some common errors to avoid:

- *Lack of objectivity.* Seeing only the facts that support your views and ignoring any contradictory information:

  Although half the survey population expressed dissatisfaction with our current product, a sizable portion finds it satisfactory. *(You may be tempted to ignore the dissatisfied half instead of investigating the reasons for their dissatisfaction.)*

- *Hasty generalizations.* Forming judgments on the basis of insufficient evidence or special cases:

  Marketing strategy Z increased sales 13 percent in Atlanta supermarkets. Let's try it in Fairbanks. *(Atlanta and Fairbanks are probably vastly different markets.)*

- *Hidden assumptions.* Hiding a questionable major premise:

  We are marketing product X in trade journals because we marketed product Y in trade journals. *(Who says product X and product Y should be marketed the same way?)*

- *Either/or.* Setting up two alternatives and not allowing for others:

  We must open a new plant by spring, or we will go bankrupt. *(Surely there are other ways to avoid bankruptcy.)*

- *False causal relationships.* Assuming that event A caused event B merely because A preceded B:

  Sales increased 42 percent as soon as we hired the new sales director. *(Something besides the new sales director may be responsible for increased sales.)*

- *Begged questions.* Assuming as proven what you are seeking to prove:

  We need a standard procedure so we will have standard results. *(But why is standardization important?)*

- *Personal attacks/appeals to popular prejudice.* Sinking people or ideas you don't like by chaining them to irrelevant but unpopular actions or ideas:

  Ellen mishandled the budget last year, so she can't be expected to motivate her staff. *(Ellen's accounting ability may have nothing to do with her ability to motivate a staff.)*

  It's un-American to impose government regulations. *(Regulations are unpopular, but they do exist in America.)*

1. Discuss some newsworthy business problem that arose from errors in logic. For example, Steven Jobs may have lost control of the company he co-founded, Apple Computer, because skill at starting new projects is quite different from skill at managing a going concern. Another example is the rapid demise of People Express after the innovative airline decided to compete more directly with traditional companies.

2. Go through the "Letters to the Editor" columns in recent newspapers or news magazines. Examine the arguments made by letter writers, and point out examples of errors in logic.

- In the past three years, six of the eight salespeople in the Southeast have requested a transfer.
- Sales in the Southeast have declined by 5 percent over the past three years.
- The current manager of the Southeast region has been there for three years.

With additional investigation, using scientific research and statistical analysis, you might come up with an objective, indisputable conclusion about the cause of these facts.

In the fast-paced world of business, however, you are far more likely to seek a quicker, more subjective conclusion. Again, there is nothing inherently wrong with this type of decision making; in fact, skill at making subjective decisions is often highly valued. You should be aware, however, of the possible pitfalls.

One inescapable factor in your thought process is your own personal values, which may tell you that the difference in sales between the two regions is unacceptable; another person, with different values, might be willing to accept the discrepancy. In analyzing the facts, you might also assume that something within your control is responsible for the disparity, although it's possible that some unknown characteristics of, say, buyers or competing products are responsible. To the extent your value judgments and assumptions correspond to the facts, however, you can draw a sound conclusion.

In this case, after applying a subjective thought process to objective evidence, you may well conclude that the current manager of the Southeast region is associated with the sales problem. You are probably right, although you might want more evidence to confirm your hunch before you recommend any action.

Check the logic that underlies your conclusions.

But what if you don't have enough hard facts to go on? Or what if the facts are inconclusive or inconsistent? In either case, subjectivity becomes more of a factor. For example, a decision to hire one candidate rather than another is largely a matter of personal judgment. In situations of this type, testing your logic is particularly important. Try to be as objective as possible; be aware of possible biases that aren't justified by the circumstances. Diminish subjectivity by establishing criteria and measuring each candidate against the same standards.

The best conclusion is often the one that gains the most support.

If you're working as part of a team, you have the benefit of being able to discuss your conclusions with co-workers, so values and assumptions come into focus. But don't expect everyone to agree all the time. Some business decisions are fuzzy; the "right" answers are not always clear. Often the best bet is to accept the consensus position rather than fight for a conclusion that others will not accept and therefore will not implement with enthusiasm. Then, once the decision has been made, stick with it unless conditions change significantly.

As Jim Lowry says, "Analysis is not something that involves simple steps, like baking a cake. It's a process involving a lot of intuition. In my organization, the best analysis usually arises from a lot of give and take among the members of the study team. But to me, the fun part of the business is the brainstorming, the interaction of good minds all working together on a problem."

DEVELOPING RECOMMENDATIONS

Conclusions are opinions or interpretations; recommendations are suggestions for action.

Concluding that the sales manager of the Southeast region is somehow associated with low sales is one thing. Deciding what to do about it and then recommending a solution is another. Be sure you know the difference between conclusions and recommendations, because recommendations are inappropriate in a report when you are not expected to supply them. A conclusion is an opinion or interpretation of what the facts mean; a recommendation suggests what ought to be done about the facts. Here's an example of the difference:

CONCLUSION

I conclude that, on the basis of its track record and current price, this company is an attractive buy.

RECOMMENDATION

I recommend that we write a letter to the president offering to buy the company at a 10 percent premium over the market value of its stock.

When you have been asked to take the final step and translate your conclusions into recommendations, be sure to make the relationship between them clear.

Jim Lowry has this to say about his final recommendations to the DOC: "Our conclusions were controversial, and our recommendations were even more so. Because we knew there would be some resistance to our ideas, we tested them carefully against the following criteria:

- The recommendations had to offer real advantages to the minority community and to the DOC administrators responsible for minority business development.
- The recommendations had to be financially and politically feasible.
- We had to have specific plans for dealing with roadblocks.
- The risks associated with the recommendations had to be acceptable.
- The picture of what should happen next, of who should do what, had to be clear."

Good recommendations are
- Practical
- Acceptable to readers
- Explained in enough detail so readers can take action

Although Jim developed these criteria for a specific situation, you might want to remember them when you develop recommendations of your own. Consider whether your recommendations are practical and acceptable to your readers, because they are the people who have to make the recommendations work. You must also be certain that you have adequately described the steps that come next. Don't leave your readers scratching their heads and saying, "This all sounds good, but what do I do on Monday morning?"

SUMMARY

Effective business reports begin with a clear definition of the problem to be investigated. Once the problem has been defined, you can determine what information will be required to solve it and develop a plan for obtaining that information.

During the research phase, you should review such secondary sources as books, periodicals, and reports. You may also conduct primary research to obtain information that is not available from existing sources. This research may involve interviews, surveys, experiments, and firsthand observation.

When you have completed your research and analyzed the data, you are ready to develop conclusions and recommendations. Be certain that your suggestions are both logical and practical.

COMMUNICATION CHALLENGES AT LOWRY & ASSOCIATES

After reading of Jim Lowry's work for the Department of Commerce, the administration of the city of Chicago has become interested in having Lowry & Associates conduct a study of the progress of minority businesses within the city. The mayor wants to know what the minority business community is like, what problems minority business people face, and what programs the local government should institute to deal with those problems.

Individual Challenge: Jim Lowry has asked you to work on the study for the city of Chicago. Your first assignment is to define the problem. Develop a statement of purpose.

Team Challenge: You have been assigned to a study team that will complete the investigation. To organize your efforts, you must develop a preliminary outline of the issues you plan to analyze. Work together to develop an informative outline phrased in question form.

QUESTIONS FOR DISCUSSION

1. Why is it to your advantage to develop a written statement of the problem before you begin your research?
2. How might you rephrase the statement of purpose for Jim Lowry's report to the DOC?
3. Why are informational assignments factored differently from analytical assignments?
4. Why is the outline for a study likely to differ from the outline used for the report on that study?
5. What are some uses of a work plan?
6. In terms of the mix of primary and secondary sources consulted, how do business reports differ from reports written for school?
7. If you were in charge of a study, would you instruct your assistants to limit their research, or would you prefer that they exhaust all possible sources of information? Explain your answer.
8. What are the advantages and disadvantages of primary research using documents, observations, surveys, and experiments?
9. What are the differences among an average, a trend, and a correlation?
10. After an exhaustive study of an important problem, what would you do if you came to a conclusion that you knew your company's management would reject?

EXERCISES

1. State the purpose of a report written to address each question below. Then factor the problem and indicate whether subtopics, hypotheses, or relative merits are the basis for the outline.
   a. Which of two careers would be best for you?
   b. What should be considered when renting an apartment?
   c. How should you go about starting a small business?
   d. How should convenience stores protect themselves against robberies?
   e. What computer printer would be the best for you to buy?
   f. What incentives should be implemented to reduce absenteeism at work?
   g. How could your bank improve its services?
2. The following statements of purpose indicate how problems have been factored. Critique each breakdown for violations of the rules of division.
   a. This report will analyze the pros and cons of advertising our hardware store in each of the major local media: radio, newspapers, and the yellow pages.
   b. This report will analyze the major market segments in the Pacific Northwest for our line of raincoats: teen-agers, yuppies, baby boomers, affluent over-50s, and senior citizens.
   c. This report focuses on the six main categories of products carried in our chain of music stores: keyboards, stringed instruments, beginning band instruments, professional band instruments, sheet music, and accessories.

d. This report analyzes inventory methods, distribution channels, point-of-purchase advertising, and product pricing for our line of suntan lotions, hand creams, and beauty soaps.

3. Assume that your college president has received many student complaints about campus parking problems. You are appointed to chair a student committee organized to investigate the problems and recommend solutions. The president turns over to you the file labeled "Parking: Complaints from Students," and you jot down the essence of the complaints as you inspect the contents. After this first pass at the file, your notes look like this:

```
--Inadequate student spaces at critical hours
--Poor night lighting near the science area
--Inadequate attempts to keep resident neigh-
  bors from occupying spaces
--Dim marking lines
--Motorcycles hogging full spaces
--Discourteous security officers
--Spaces (usually empty) reserved for college
  officials
--Unfairly high fees
--Full fees charged to night students even
  though they use the lots only during low-de-
  mand periods
--Vandalism to cars and a sense of personal
  danger
--Inadequate total space
--Resident harassment of students parking on
  the street in front of neighboring houses
```

Your first job is to organize for committee discussion four or five areas that include all (or almost all) of these specific complaints. Choose the main headings for your outline, and group these specific complaints under them.

4. Assume that your four-person accounting business specializes in going directly to clients' places of business. Your clients appreciate this personal attention, and often material is available on their premises that they would not have remembered to bring to your central office. Your policy has been for each accountant to log business mileage and then to be reimbursed 25 cents per mile. But accountants with large cars complain that they should be receiving more than the fixed rate. They argue that the large cars aid the company's image but that 25 cents per mile is inadequate reimbursement. "Do you want us all to show up in old Chevettes?" they ask.

   Thus you are considering leasing or purchasing four company cars. Before deciding, however, you want to "cost out" the three options: (a) maintaining the present system (possibly with some minor adjustments); (b) leasing four cars; or (c) purchasing four cars. If you provide the cars, accountants will use them only for company business and commuting to work.

   Your task now is to factor the problem in the form of an outline. To begin, list eight or ten factual questions that must be answered before you can seriously address the problem.

5. For one of the cases at the end of Chapter 16, draft a tentative work plan that includes the following:

   a. Statement of the problem
   b. Statement of the purpose
   c. Factors of the problem (in the form of an outline)
   d. Tasks to be accomplished, indicating general sources of information and any experiments or observations required
   e. Schedule that indicates when various tasks will be completed

6. The baking business is highly competitive, but say that you are succeeding with the small Philadelphia bakery turned over to you by your father. You produce an attractive line of sweet cookies, the type that children point to in the supermarket and that their mothers buy because of the low price. Your secret is to employ as bakers people who are certified "economically disadvantaged" and who have been unemployed for over two years. The federal government gives you tax credits for these workers, and you have found that they are very conscientious.

   You read in a trade journal of a fully operational small bakery outside Trenton, New Jersey, that is for immediate sale at a modest price, because of "failing health of owner." One of your workers has been with you for six years and understands your system; she could manage this bakery if you bought it. What you don't know is whether there is demand for your product in Trenton and, if so, the extent of the local competition. You are concerned, too, about the bakery itself: its size, the age and condition of its equipment, its location. Given your fairly modest budget for activities outside the normal sweep of your business, what types of primary research might you schedule to examine the feasibility of extending operations into the Trenton area? What specific questions would you like answered?

7. Imagine you have parlayed promises ("You'll get 3 percent of the gross"), a little luck, your contagious faith, and a lot of goodwill into an almost completed motion picture, the story of a group of unknown musicians finding work and making a

reputation in a difficult world. You have captured vibrant vignettes, both painful and happy, along with considerable footage of successful and less successful gigs. The work is almost done. Some of your friends leave the first complete screening saying that the 132-minute movie is simply too long; others (and you) can't imagine any more editing cuts. You decide to test the movie on a regular audience, members of which will be asked to complete a questionnaire that may or may not lead to additional editing. You obtain permission from a local theater manager to show your film at 4:30 and 8:15, straddling his scheduled presentation. Design a questionnaire that can solicit valid answers.

8. Select a business problem that interests you, and explain how you would conduct an experiment to solve it. Assume that you have sufficient time and money to conduct the experiment properly. Carefully define the problem, and describe the exact procedures you would use.
9. Prepare a list of ten questions about a current political issue or a class of consumer products. Then interview five randomly chosen people over the telephone. To obtain the five interviews, you will probably need to make more than twice that number of calls. Tabulate your results, and write a one- or two-page summary of your findings.
10. Visit a supermarket or fast-food outlet during a busy time in its operation, and observe customers passing through one cash register for half an hour. You are interested in the gender and approximate age of the customers, the size and composition of the groups they're in, and the size of their purchases. Before your investigation, you need to prepare a sheet that will help you collect data systematically; afterward, draft a brief narrative and statistical report of your findings for your instructor. You should be able to answer these three questions: Do men or women make larger purchases? Does the age of the customer help predict the size of the purchase? How many purchases can this check-out counter handle in 30 minutes?

CHAPTER FOURTEEN

DEVELOPING VISUAL AIDS

After studying this chapter, you will be able to

- Decide when using a visual aid would be appropriate
- Develop visual aids that conform to the principles of effective graphic design
- Select the right table, chart, or other illustration to simplify and dramatize your information
- Produce visual aids in an efficient manner
- Fit visual aids into the text of your report
- Analyze the effectiveness of a visual aid

COMMUNICATION CLOSE-UP AT FIRESTONE

Chuck Wettergreen

"Change" is the watchword at The Firestone Tire & Rubber Company these days. For nearly 100 years, the name Firestone has been synonymous with high-quality tires and with Akron, Ohio, where its headquarters were located. But today the company is consolidating its tire operations, adding automotive retail and service outlets, and moving its headquarters to Chicago.

"Change" is also an important word to Chuck Wettergreen, a senior financial analyst in Firestone's corporate accounting department. Increasingly, his job is to show graphically how Firestone is changing, for the benefit of shareholders, the board of directors, upper-level management, and such government bodies as the Securities and Exchange Commission. In addition to preparing financial statements, he uses bar charts, line graphs, pie charts, and tables to depict changes in Firestone's operations. He also uses visual aids to lay out statistics needed for strategic decision making, for instance data about a company that Firestone might consider purchasing.

"I make every attempt possible to take the intimidation out of financial data by using visual aids," Chuck says. "You can present numbers in the text and ask readers to make comparisons in their own minds, but you make their job easier if you simply show them two bars representing the numbers you want them to compare. The same principle applies when you're identifying a trend. If you give readers a line chart that shows the past ten years, they don't have to take the time to find meaning in the numbers themselves; they can see it. Charts and graphs are great for illustrating change."

The 1980s brought many changes to Firestone Tire & Rubber, including increased use of visual aids for charting the company's performance and trends in its major markets.

Some visual aids work better than others in particular situations. "If you're talking about something that's a percentage of a whole," Chuck advises, "use some sort of pie chart. Item-to-item comparisons are generally bar charts. Trends can best be portrayed by line charts, although bar charts can do that also. I use tables only when people need to know the details."

And when should color be used? Chuck believes that "color is best when you want to create excitement. It attracts people's attention. Specific colors are important too. Some people like to use red, because it tends to dominate; on the other hand, it's kind of an 'angry' color, so I use it sparingly. I also try to use lighter colors for things that are supposed to be in front and darker colors in back to show depth."

Chuck is something of a pioneer in his company, because he's the one who got Firestone to computerize the production of graphics. "Prior to putting in that system," he notes, "we didn't really use graphics. We had a lot of tabular financial statements, of course, and a bar chart here and there, but now we have a lot more."

Chuck sees few disadvantages to installing the computer. "Initially, the cost seemed high," he says, "but we've saved money in the long run. Buying a system like ours is a lot cheaper than hiring a graphic artist." Ironically, one disadvantage is that the computer is so easy to use: "Unfortunately, most people haven't learned yet how to make attractive visual aids. When they see what the computer can do, they often produce visual aids that are too 'busy,' putting things like little pictures of rocket ships all over their graphs. Plus we now have such a tremendously fast turnaround time that people think they can make a lot of changes and fiddle with the visual aids until the last minute."

But the advantages prevail. "The computer cuts the production time for a typical graph from 2 or 3 hours to 10 or 15 minutes," Chuck says, "so we are saving a lot of time. And we are also limiting the number of people who have access to confidential financial information, which is an important consideration in times when insider trading and hostile takeover attempts are a problem for many corporations. The speed and confidentiality and cost and superior quality we get far outweigh the disadvantages."

As Chuck has observed, visual aids are sometimes a problem as much as a solution: "Some people go overboard and put everything in graphic form. I've seen someone in charge of a presentation go so far as to put up a slide that announces the name of the next speaker. You've got to remember, though, that the visual aids are there to emphasize your points, not to do the whole job for you. Just show the things you want to highlight, and keep the graphics simple so people don't get lost in them. Remember that a visual aid is just that: an aid."

PLANNING VISUAL AIDS

Visual aid: illustration in tabular, graphic, schematic, or pictorial form

Let's say that you have just completed the research for an important report or oral presentation. You are about to begin the composition phase. Your first impulse might be to start with the introduction and proceed page by page until you have completed the text or script. Then, almost as an afterthought, you might throw in a few visual aids—tables, graphs, schematic drawings, photographs—to illustrate the words.

This approach makes some sense, but many experienced business people prefer to begin with the visual aids. Starting with the visual aids has three advantages. First, if much of the fact-finding and analytical work is already in tabular or graphic form, you already have a visual point of departure. Sorting through and refining your visuals will help you decide exactly what you're going to say. Second, many important business projects involve both a written report and an oral presentation of results. Similar visual aids, modified for different media, can be used for both communication situations. By starting with the visual aids, you develop a graphic story line that serves two purposes. Finally, the text or script has to explain and refer to the tables, charts, and graphs, so it makes sense to have them ready before you start to compose, particularly if you plan to use quite a few visuals.

WHY BUSINESS PROFESSIONALS USE VISUAL AIDS

"But wait a minute," you might be saying to yourself, "why should I use visual aids at all? I've written any number of successful papers in school without including a single table or chart."

School is one thing. Business is another. For instance, your audience in school is generally an individual (the instructor) with a built-in interest in your ideas. In business, however, your audience is generally much wider and may not have any interest in your ideas at all. In addition, in the numbers-oriented world of work, people rely heavily on visual images. They think in terms of trend lines, distribution curves, and percentages. An upward curve means good news in any language, be it English or Japanese.

Visual aids help communicators get through to an audience.

Visual aids also attract and hold people's attention and help them understand and remember the message. In one study, 36 audiences were exposed to presentations with and without graphic aids, with the following results:

TABLE 14.1 When to Use Visual Aids

PURPOSE	APPLICATION
To clarify	Support text descriptions of "graphic" topics: quantitative or numerical information; explanations of trends; descriptions of procedures, relationships, locations, or composition of an item
To simplify	Break complicated descriptions into components that can be depicted with conceptual models, flow charts, organization charts, or diagrams
To emphasize	Call attention to particularly important points by illustrating them with line, bar, and pie charts
To summarize	Review major points in the narrative by providing a chart or table that sums up the data
To reinforce	Present information in visual and written form to increase readers' retention
To attract	Make material seem more interesting by decorating the cover or title page and by breaking up the text with visual aids
To impress	Build credibility by putting ideas in visual form to convey the impression of authenticity and precision
To unify	Depict the relationship among points—for example, with a flow chart

- In presentations where visual aids were used, the speaker was able to convince the audience to accept the message two-thirds of the time. Speakers who did not use visuals won the audience to their point of view only half the time.
- The audience reached a consensus 79 percent of the time in presentations where graphics were used, but they agreed on a decision only 58 percent of the time when graphics were not used.
- Meetings involving graphic presentations were 28 percent shorter than meetings where no graphics were used.[1]

Although the study focused on oral presentations, to a considerable degree its results pertain to written reports as well.

Despite their value, visual aids must be used selectively, as Chuck Wettergreen of Firestone points out. The illustrative material in a report or presentation should supplement the written or spoken word, not replace it, so limit your use of visual aids to those situations in which they do the most good. Table 14.1 will help you identify those situations.

THE PROCESS OF "VISUALIZING" YOUR TEXT

When planning visual aids
- Decide what you want to say
- Pick out the points that can best be made visually
- Judge whether you have too many or too few graphics

Translating words and numbers into graphic format is generally an integral part of the process of preparing a report or presentation. As you sort through the information you have compiled during the research phase, you begin to see relationships and draw conclusions. An outline begins to take shape in your mind, and you select the facts you will use to support each point. Some of these facts lend themselves to a prose presentation; others may be expressed more easily in graphic form. As you think about how to convey your message, you begin to envision the balance between verbal and graphic elements.

Decide on the message

When you begin to compose a report or presentation, you usually have a lot of raw data that can be molded into a number of messages. Your first step, then, is to decide what you're trying to say. You do this by sorting through the facts you have compiled.

Suppose, for example, that you've been asked to compare your company's recent sales to those of a competitor. You have obtained the following data on market share for the past month:

SALES REGION	YOUR COMPANY'S SHARE	COMPETITOR'S SHARE
North	10%	25%
South	40	8
East	32	32
West	20	23

Analyze your raw data, which are often in tabular or graphic form, to identify the points supporting your main idea.

Now, what message can you derive from this set of data? Here are some of the possibilities:

- The two companies perform differently in different regions.
- Your company is strongest in the South, where your competitor is weakest.
- The two companies' performance is similar in the East and West.
- Both companies are uneven in their market share from region to region.

All of these messages are true, and all of them might be useful. You just have to decide which interpretation of the data is most useful for your purposes. As you sort through your facts, looking at different interpretations, an outline of a message will begin to emerge.

Identify points that require visual support

Once you have an outline in mind, you can begin to identify which points can be, and should be, illustrated graphically. Ask yourself whether there is some way to dramatize visually the key elements of your message. You might approach the problem as though you were writing a picture book or making a movie. Think of each main point on your outline as a separate scene. Your job is to think of a "picture," a chart or graph, that will communicate that point to the audience.

Use visual aids to simplify, clarify, and emphasize important information.

Then take your analysis a step further. Undoubtedly, some of the supporting items on your outline involve the presentation of detailed facts and figures. This sort of information may be confusing and tedious when presented in paragraph form. But tables are a convenient format for organizing and displaying detail. And if some points require a detailed description of physical relationships or procedures, you might want to use flow charts, drawings, or photographs to clarify the discussion.

Maintain a balance between illustrations and words

In planning the illustrations for your report or presentation, aim to achieve a reasonable balance between the verbal and the visual. The ideal blend depends on the nature of the subject. Some topics are more graphic than others and require more visual aids.

But remember that illustrating every point dilutes the effectiveness of all your visual aids. In a written report, particularly, too many visuals can be a problem. If readers are told every paragraph or two to consult a table or chart, they are likely to lose the thread of the argument you are trying to make. Furthermore, readers tend to assume that the amount of space allocated to a topic indicates its relative importance. If you use visual aids to illustrate a minor point, you may be sending a misleading message about its significance.

In general, use visual aids only to supplement the story you are telling in words.

In deciding on the mix of words and visuals, give some thought to your readers' needs and thought patterns. Some people ignore the visuals and focus on the words; others do the opposite. If you know that your audience prefers one form of communication over the other, you should obviously adjust the balance accordingly.

Another thing to consider is your production schedule. If you are producing the report or presentation without the aid of either an art department or a computer graphics system, you may want to limit the number of illustrations. Making charts and tables takes time, particularly if you are inexperienced.

DESIGNING VISUAL AIDS

Knowing what points you want to present visually and knowing exactly what format to use are two different things. The construction of visual aids requires a good deal of both imagination and attention to detail. Your main concern should always be your audience. What format is most meaningful and convenient for them?

UNDERSTANDING THE ART OF GRAPHIC DESIGN

You may not think of yourself as being the "artistic type," but chances are you have a better sense of design than you realize. Most people seem to subconsciously recognize good design when they see it, although they often don't know how to achieve the same effects on their own.[2]

The elements of design convey meaning in subtle ways.

Few of us have studied the "language" of line, mass, space, size, color, pattern, and texture. These elements of visual design, when arranged in certain ways, are pleasing to the eye. But more important for the business communicator, they have a meaning of their own. A thick line implies more power than a thin one; a bold color suggests strength; a solid mass seems substantial. To create effective visual aids, you must become conscious of both the aesthetic and the symbolic aspects of graphic art, lest you send the wrong message. Here are a few principles to be aware of:

When designing visual aids, observe the principles of continuity, contrast, and emphasis.

- *Continuity.* An audience views a series of visual aids as a whole and assumes that you will use the elements of design in a consistent way from one page to the next. You will confuse people if you make arbitrary changes in color, shape, size, texture, position, scale, or typeface. For example, if your first chart shows results for Division A in blue, the audience will expect Division A to be shown in blue throughout the report or presentation.
- *Contrast.* The audience also expects that visual distinctions will match verbal distinctions. If you are contrasting A and B, they should be depicted in a visually contrasting manner: red versus blue, black versus white. On the other hand, if you want to indicate similarities

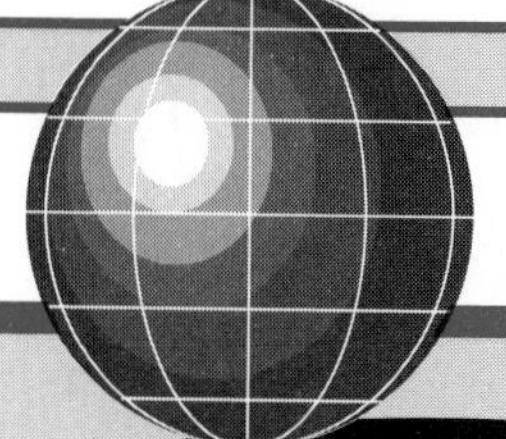

INTERNATIONAL OUTLOOK

Creating Visual Aids for an International Audience

When communicating to audiences made up of people from a different culture, visual aids can be a vital means of getting information across. Most of the guidelines for creating effective visuals for English-speaking audiences also apply to creating visuals for an international audience. But a few additional measures are required:

- Choose labels and wording that are simple and free of "Americanisms," and don't bog down visual aids with excess verbiage.
- Whenever possible, provide materials that are in the language of your audience and that are specifically geared to your audience. Take advantage of a reliable translator.
- Strive for a "modern" look to the visuals rather than a stodgy, dull approach. Many foreigners see Americans as behind the times when it comes to graphic appeal.
- In photographs and illustrations, do not call attention to the nationality of the people portrayed, unless that is an important point of the visual aid. Try to find "generic" models. Also, be aware of any cultural constraints on such portrayals. In some countries, for example, men and women should never be shown touching.
- Be aware that some people—Arabs, for example—are used to reading from right to left instead of left to right. In a sequence of three steps, then, step one will need to be on the right and step three on the left.
- Don't leave "blanks" to be filled in. Most foreign audiences prefer a presentation that is fully prepared beforehand. The common American practice of marking up transparencies and flip charts as part of a "dynamic" talk is considered unprofessional by such audiences as the Japanese. They see complete prior preparation as a sign of respect.
- Be aware of the cultural meanings of symbols. The "OK" symbol (thumb and first finger touching to form a circle) that we take for granted, for example, is a vulgar gesture in Greece and Turkey and means "You're a zero" in France and Belgium. The stork symbolizes maternal death in Singapore, owls are considered bad luck in India, and dogs are seen as filthy in Islamic countries. Be very careful in using national and religious symbols, such as flags and crosses. To avoid faux pas, you will need to consult someone knowledgeable about the particular culture your visuals will be geared to.
- Be careful about the colors you choose, because they also have different connotations in other parts of the world. We think of green as symbolizing freshness, but it is associated with disease in many countries. And a green hat in China is like a dunce cap. The color for mourning varies from culture to culture; it may be purple, yellow, dark red, or even white rather than black.
- Avoid humor. What is funny in one culture may be meaningless or insulting in another.

1. If you were writing a report for a foreign audience, would you be inclined to use the same type and number of visual aids that you would use for an American audience? Explain your answer.

2. Obtain a recent issue of *USA Today, Newsweek,* or *Time.* Examine the visual aids, especially charts and diagrams. Which would be most adaptable to foreign audiences? Which would be least adaptable?

between two items, the visual distinction between them should be more subtle. For example, you might have a pie chart in which two similar items are shown in two shades of blue and a dissimilar item is shown in yellow.

- *Emphasis.* An audience also assumes that the most important point will receive the most visual emphasis. The key item on the chart should therefore be presented in the most prominent way, through color, position, size, or whatever. Less important items should be

FIGURE 14.1
Parts of a Table

TABLE 1 Title

	Multicolumn Head		Single-Column Head*	Single-Column Head
Stub head	Subhead	Subhead		
Line head	XXX	XXX	XX	XX
Line head				
Subhead	XX	XXX	XX	XX
Subhead	XX	XXX	X	XX
Totals	XXX	XXX	XX	XX

Source: (in the same format as a text footnote; see Component Chapter E)

* Footnote (for explanation of elements in the table; a superscript number or small letter may be used instead of an asterisk or other symbol)

visually downplayed: Avoid using strong colors for unimportant data, and make sure that background features, like the grid marks on a chart, recede visually.

The best time to think about the principles of good design is before you prepare visual aids, because making changes after the fact increases the amount of time required to produce them.

SELECTING THE RIGHT VISUAL AID FOR THE JOB

Different types of messages call for different types of visual aids.

Once you've decided on the general design features for your report or presentation, you can begin to develop the individual visual aids, choosing the specific form that best suits your message.

Tables

Use tables to help your audience understand detailed information.

When you have to present detailed, specific information, choose a table. Tables are ideal when the audience needs the facts, all the facts, and when the information would be either difficult or tedious to handle in the main text.

Most tables contain the same standard parts, which are illustrated in Figure 14.1. What makes a table a table is the grid that allows you to find the point where two factors intersect. Every table must therefore include vertical columns and horizontal lines, with useful headings along the top and side. Tables that are projected on a screen for use in oral presentations should be limited to three column heads and six line heads; tables presented on paper may include from one or two heads to a dozen or more. If the table has too many columns to fit comfortably between the margins of the page, turn the paper horizontally and insert it in the report with the top toward the binding.

Tabular information can be introduced within the text without a formal title.

Although formal tables set apart from the text are necessary for complex information, some data can be presented more simply within the text. The table becomes, in essence, a part of the paragraph, typed in tabular format.

FIGURE 14.2 Word Table

Table 1

Transportation Resources of Six Cities Considered for the New Plant

Metro Area	Daily Commute	Public Transportation	Freeway Traffic	Interstate Highways	Air Service	Amtrak Service
Abilene, TX	34.8 min.	17 city buses Seat miles/capita: 1.14	Light	I - 20	Non-hub Abilene Municipal (ABI) 2 airlines, 18 flights/day	—
Akron, OH	43.8 min.	135 city buses Seat miles/capita: 1.74	Heavy	I - 76 I - 77	Part of Cleveland hub Akron - Canton Regional (CAK) 6 airlines, 24 flights/day	—
Albany, GA	38.9 min.	15 city buses Seat miles/capita: 1.13	Light	—	Non-hub Albany - Dougherty County (ABY) 2 airlines, 10 flights/day	—
Albany - Schenectady - Troy, NY	43.3 min.	236 city buses Seat miles/capita: 3.21	Light	I - 87 I - 88 I - 90	Medium hub Albany County (ALB) 13 airlines, 78 flights/day	11 trains/day
Albuquerque, NM	41.6 min.	82 city buses Seat miles/capita: 1.31	Heavy	I - 25 I - 40	Medium hub Albuquerque International (ABQ) 16 airlines, 118 flights/day	2 trains/day
Alexandria, LA	37.8 min.	16 city buses Seat miles/capita: 1.15	Light	—	Non-hub Esier Regional (ESF) 5 airlines, 10 flights/day	—

Source: Richard Boyer and David Savageau, Rand McNally Places Rated Almanac (Chicago: Rand McNally, 1985), 194.

These "text tables" are usually introduced with a sentence that leads directly into the tabulated information. Here's an example:

The farm population has declined steadily since 1960, but the average size of a farm has increased:

Year	Farm Population (in millions)	Average Farm Size (in acres)
1960	15.6	297
1970	9.7	374
1980	6.0	429
1990 (est.)	5.2	435

The flow of people away from farming seems likely to continue, but many experts believe that farm size will stabilize at around current acreages.

In setting up a numerical table, be sure to identify the units in which amounts are given: dollars, percentages, price per ton, or whatever. All items in a column should be expressed in the same units.

Use word tables

- To summarize survey results
- To compare items to some standard

Although many tables are numerical, word tables like Figure 14.2 can be just as useful. They are particularly appropriate for survey findings or comparisons of various items against a specific standard. In this example, notice how the author has shaded one column to call attention to the most important data.

Line and surface charts

Line charts, which illustrate trends over time or plot the interaction of two variables, are common in business reports. In charts showing trends, the

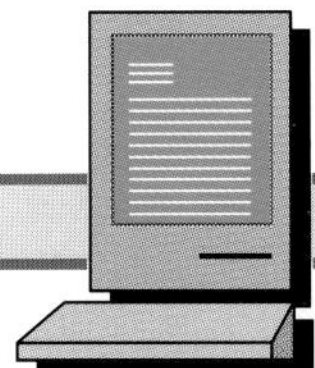

Creating Colorful Visual Aids with Computers

As computers become increasingly common in the workplace, more people are learning to use graphics software to create visual aids. But computer-generated visual aids may be ineffective if the computer's capabilities, especially color, aren't handled well.

Color helps make a point more effectively than black and white. But there's more to using color in visual aids than simply picking colors that appeal to you. To choose an effective color scheme, ask yourself these questions:

- *What colors will best convey the effect I want?* As a general rule, bright, solid colors are more pleasing to the eye and easier to distinguish than pastel, patterned colors. Yellow, blue, and green are usually good choices, but there are many other possibilities. Just keep in mind that too many colors may overwhelm the message. Use color as an accent, bright color for emphasis and darker or lighter colors for background information.
- *Are these colors appropriate for my message, purpose, and audience?* Liking red is not enough of a reason for using it in all your graphic designs. It's too "hot" for some people and conveys the wrong message in some instances. For example, using red to show profits in an annual report might confuse readers, because they are likely to associate it with "red ink," or losses. Be aware that people in other cultures also make associations with some colors.
- *Can I improve the effect by changing any of the colors?* When you have the opportunity to use more than one color, choose those that contrast. Colors without contrast blend together and obscure the message.

In this portfolio, you'll see some examples of color visual aids generated with various types of computer equipment. The captions accompanying the examples will help you duplicate their effect.

FIGURE A Computer with Graphic Capabilities

To create your own visual aids with a computer, you'll need hardware and software that are capable of producing them. Your hardware will limit your software choices and determine the form and quality of the visual aids you're able to produce. At a minimum, you'll need a microcomputer with ample memory and graphics capability, a monitor (preferably color), an input device (keyboard, joystick, or special stylus), and an output device (printer, plotter, or film recorder). The graphics software you choose must be compatible with the hardware. Some software is designed to create only a particular form of output: hard copy, 35-mm slides, or overhead transparencies. Other software is specialized according to the types of visual aids it produces: graphs, diagrams, word charts, maps.

FIGURE B Pie Chart with Color Overlay

Many of the most popular integrated software packages for microcomputers, including several spreadsheet and data base management programs, have built-in graphics capability that enables you to convert words and numbers into graphic output. Creating visual aids is a simple matter of selecting choices from a menu and responding to prompts that appear on the screen. Here's a typical sequence of events for constructing a chart:

1. *Give the chart a title, and indicate the categories of information that you wish to portray.*
2. *Enter the numerical values for each point or segment on the chart, either by using the keyboard or by instructing the computer to take the data from an existing file.*
3. *Select the kind of chart you want to create: pie, bar, or line chart.*
4. *Identify the range of data that will be portrayed (that is, the highest and lowest values you want on the chart).*
5. *Label the scales (the horizontal and vertical axes) or segments.*
6. *Choose colors, if you have a color output device.*
7. *Print the graph.*

The visual aid shown here was created with a very common combination of hardware and software: a microcomputer, integrated software, and a black-and-white dot matrix printer. Color was added by superimposing pieces of colored transfer film (available at most office supply stores). This type of visual aid is suitable for relatively informal communication.

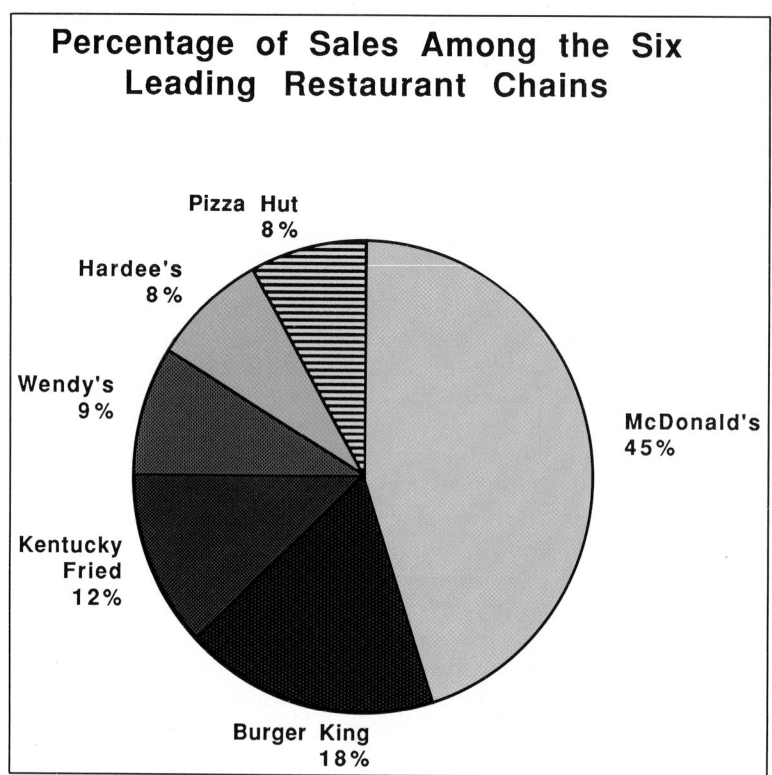

FIGURE C Bar Chart Produced on Color Printer

More professional looking visual aids require the use of specialized graphics software and output devices. This chart was created with a presentation-quality software program and printed out on a color printer that produces either paper copies or overhead transparencies. Because of its precise lines and dense colors, this type of visual aid is suitable for more formal communication.

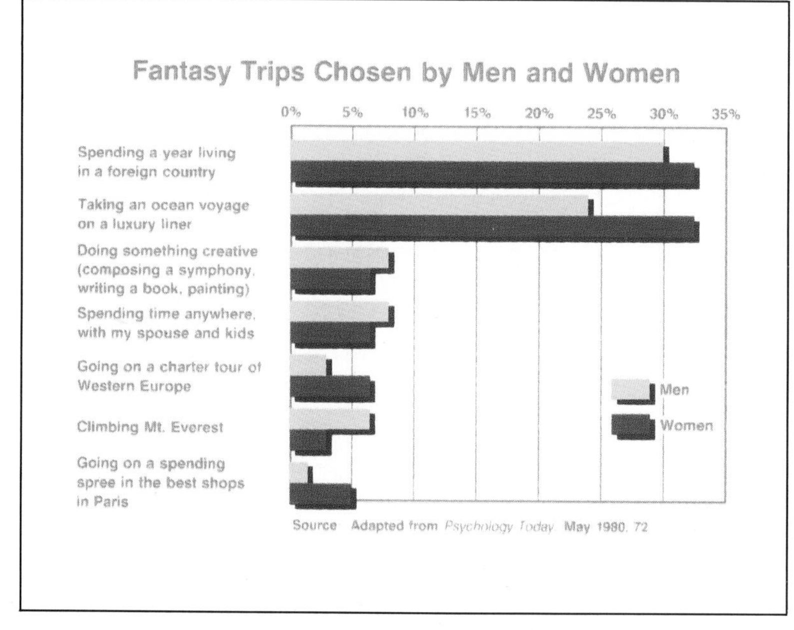

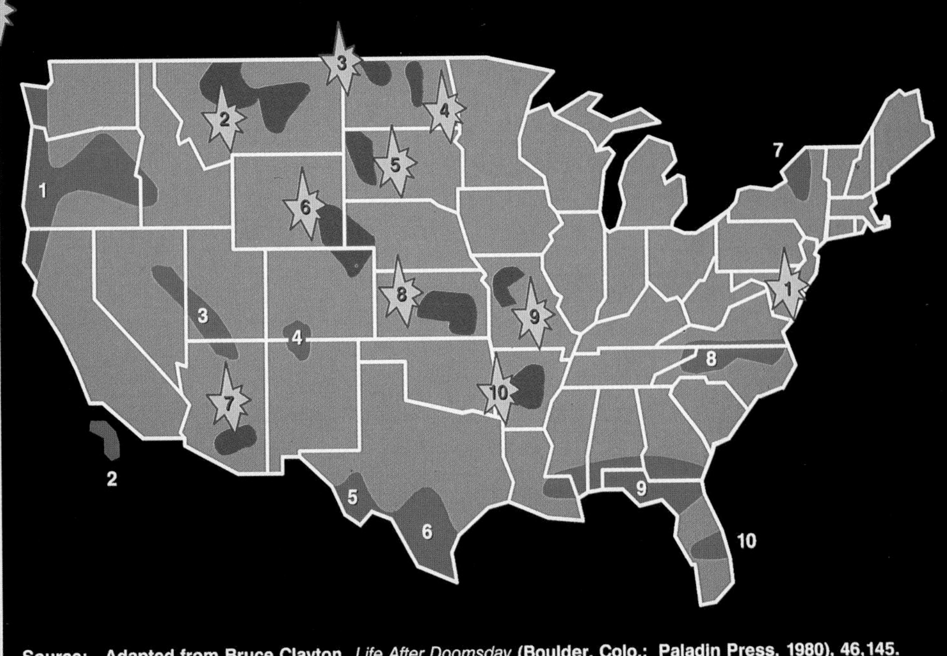

The Ten Safest and Most Dangerous Places in the United States in Case of Nuclear Attack
The Most Dangerous Places
1. Washington, DC
2. Central Montana
3. Minot, ND
4. Grand Forks, ND
5. Rapid City, SD
6. Cheyenne, WY
7. Tucson, AZ
8. Wichita, KA
9. Kansas City, MO
10. Little Rock, AR
The Safest Places
1. Pacific Northwest coast
2. Channel Islands
3. Southwestern Utah vicinity
4. Durango area
5. Big Bend region
6. San Antonio vicinity
7. Adirondacks
8. Northwest Carolina vicinity
9. Northern Florida vicinity
10. Okeechobee vicinity
Source: Adapted from Bruce Clayton, *Life After Doomsday* (Boulder, Colo.: Paladin Press, 1980), 46,145.

FIGURE D Map Produced with a Film Recorder

FIGURE E Line Chart Using Special Graphics

Mastery of top-of-the-line graphics packages requires dedication, because neither the hardware nor the software is simple. But the end result is superb. The examples in Figures D and E were originally produced in the form of 35-mm slides, using a film recorder (which can also produce overhead transparencies). Few companies find it worthwhile to buy equipment this specialized, but independent computer service bureaus are now available to serve those who need top-quality visual aids.

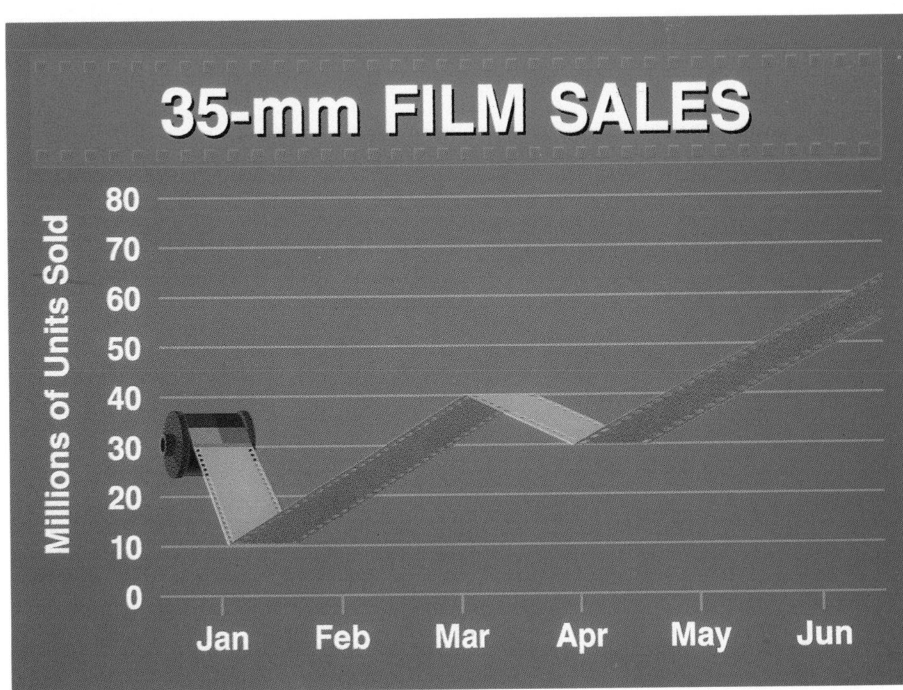

FIGURE F Memo with Embedded Bar Chart

One of the newer developments in computer graphics is the ability to combine text and graphics on the same page. Many simple hardware and software packages are capable of producing documents like this one. More sophisticated packages can produce complex layouts, with a column of text and a visual aid set side by side on the page.

CalPlus
9408 SEPULVEDA WAY, LOS ANGELES, CALIFORNIA 97402 (805) 555-4103

MEMO

DATE: April 14, 1989

TO: Alden Maxwell, V.P., Marketing

FROM: Louise Ellison, Manager, Promotions

SUBJECT: Using sports as a selling tool for promoting our newcalcium-plus soft drink

After doing a little research, I'm more convinced than ever that sponsoring a sporting event would be an excellent way to build awareness of our new calcium-plus soft drink.

The experiences of other companies show that **sports sponsorship is an extremely cost-effective approach to promotion.** For example, Volvo has found that it can reach as many people by spending $3 million on tennis tournaments as it can by spending $25 million on media advertising.

If we decide to go forward with a sponsorship, our first priority should be to identify a sport that is popular with our target customers. As the chart below indicates, auto racing is currently the number-one sport among corporate sponsors, possibly because it appeals to both men and women:

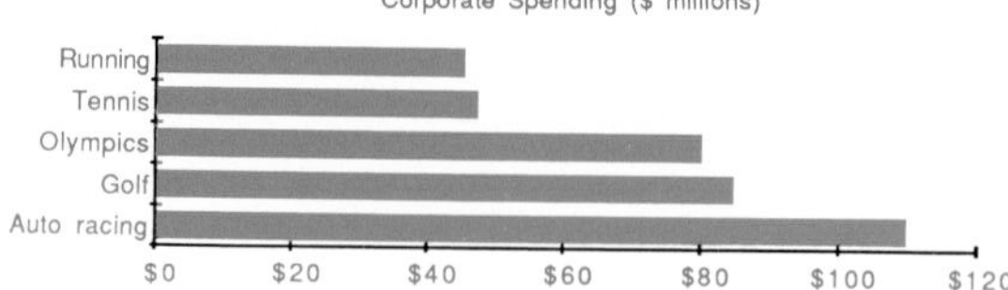

Although the "mainstream" sports currently receive the lion's share of coroporate dollars, we might achieve more impact with a lesser-known event. Timberline Company has really scored with its sponsorship of the Idatarod dog-sled race across Alaska, a contest that appeals to customers for rugged footwear.

Over the next few days, I plan to do some more research to identify sporting events that would give us the most exposure among the health-conscious women who represent our primary market. I hope to pinpoint three or four possibilities and prepare some preliminary cost estimates for discussion at the Tuesday staff meeting.

FIGURE 14.3 Line Chart with Broken Axis

Figure 1 Most Participants Are in the Moderate Income Bracket

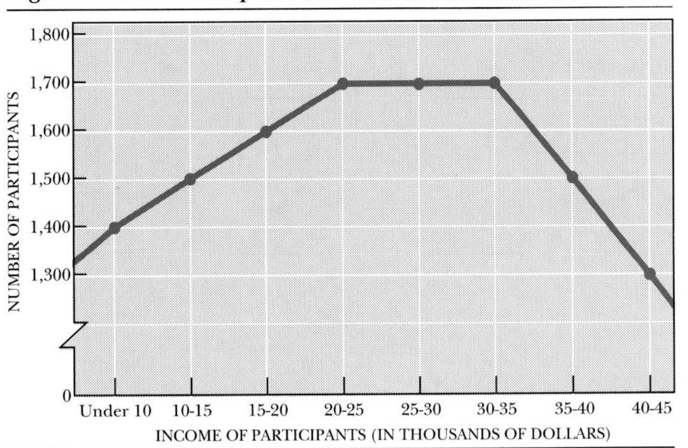

FIGURE 14.4 Line Chart Plotting Three Lines

Figure 1 Big Cars Lose Market Share, Little Cars Gain

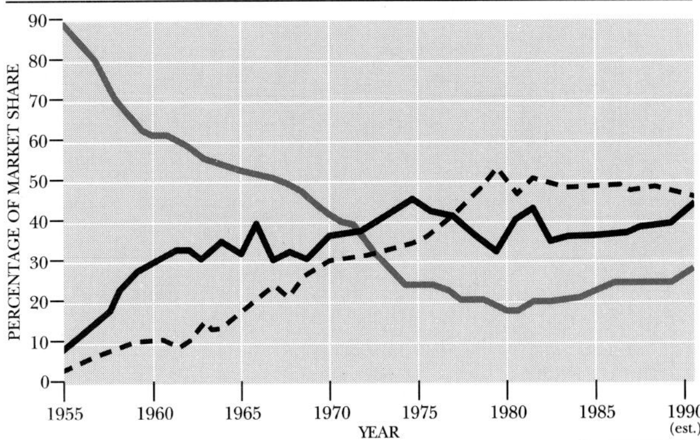

Source: Data from U.S. Department of Commerce.

Use line charts

- To indicate changes over time
- To plot the interaction of two variables

vertical axis is used to show amount and the horizontal axis to show time or quantity being measured. Ordinarily, both scales begin at zero and proceed in equal increments. In Figure 14.3, however, the vertical axis is broken to show that some of the increments have been left out. A broken axis is appropriate when the data are plotted far above zero, but the omission of data points should be clearly indicated.

A simple line chart may be arranged in many ways. One of the most common is to plot several different lines on the same chart for comparative purposes, as shown in Figure 14.4. If at all possible, use no more than three lines on any given chart, particularly if the lines cross.

Another variation of the simple line chart has a vertical axis with both positive and negative numbers (see Figure 14.5). This arrangement is handy when you have to illustrate losses.

A surface chart is a kind of line chart showing cumulative effect.

Surface charts are a form of line chart with a cumulative effect; all the lines add up to the top line, which represents the total (see Figure 14.6). This form of chart is useful when you want to illustrate changes in the composition of something over time. In preparing this type of chart, put the most important segment against the baseline, and limit the number of strata to four or five.

FIGURE 14.5 Line Chart with Positive and Negative Values on Vertical Axis

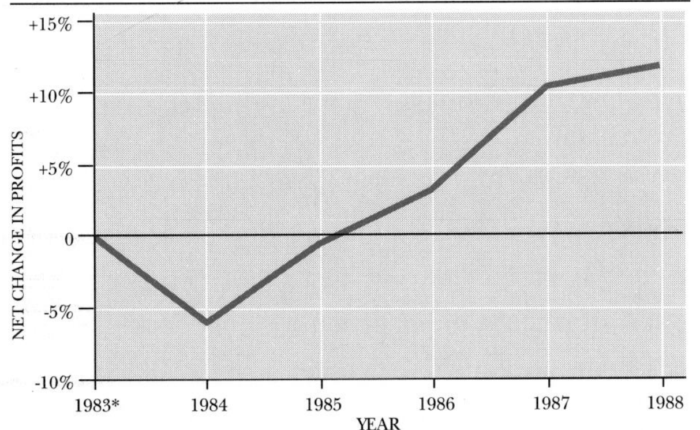

Figure 1 After Difficult Second Year, Division's Profits Are Rising
***First-year profit was approximately $97,000.**

FIGURE 14.6 Surface Chart

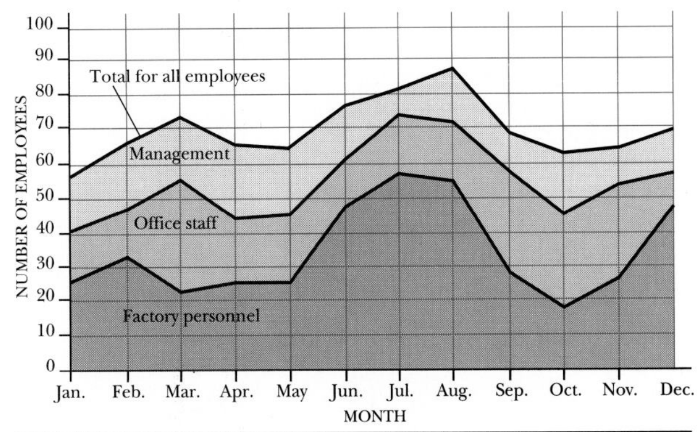

Figure 1 Average Daily Employee Absences

FIGURE 14.7
The Impact of Scale on the Slope of a Curve

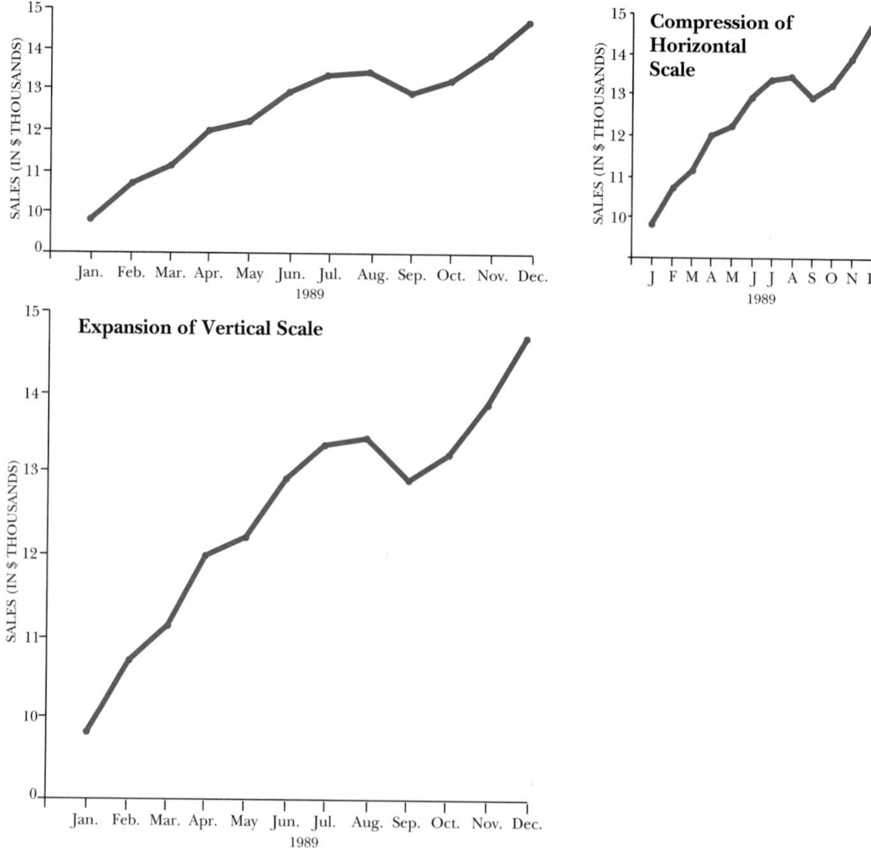

When using line and surface charts

- Choose a scale that presents a realistic picture
- Use the same scale in successive charts

The most important thing to be aware of in constructing a line chart of any kind is the impact of scale on the slope of the line. For example, if you double the size of the increments on the vertical axis while leaving the horizontal scale the same, the slope of the line becomes noticeably steeper, as Figure 14.7 shows. Compression of the horizontal scale has a similar effect. Thus modest results can be transformed into dramatic ones by a simple manipulation of the scale. You can avoid misleading your audience if you choose a scale that will give them a realistic view of what's happening. Likewise, you should maintain the same scale in successive charts comparing the same factors.

Bar charts

Bar charts are useful in many situations and take a variety of forms.

Bar charts are almost as common in business reports as line charts, and in some ways they are more versatile. As Figure 14.8 illustrates, they are particularly valuable when you want to

- Compare the size of several items at one time
- Show changes in one item over time
- Indicate the composition of several items over time
- Show the relative size of components of a whole

The opportunities for being creative with bar charts are almost infinite. You can align the bars either vertically or horizontally and double the bars

FIGURE 14.8
The Versatile Bar Chart

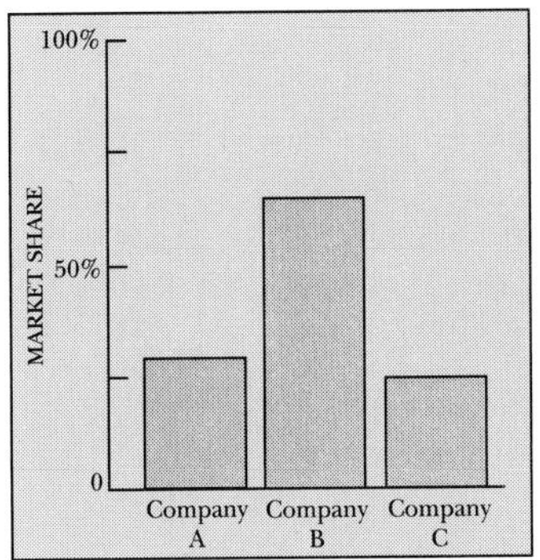

Figure 1
Company B Dominates the Market at This Time (August 1, 1989)

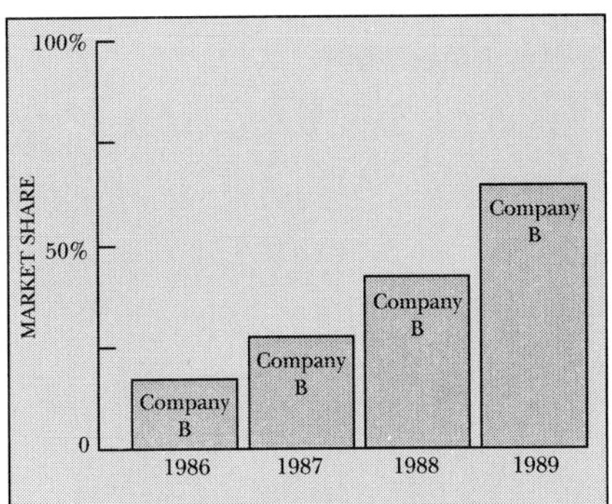

Figure 1
Company B Has Steadily Gained Market Share Over Time

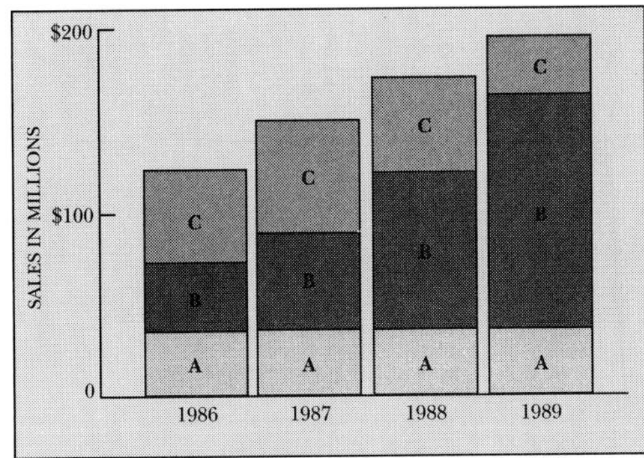

Figure 1
Company B Has Captured Most of the Growth in the Total Market Over the Past Four Years

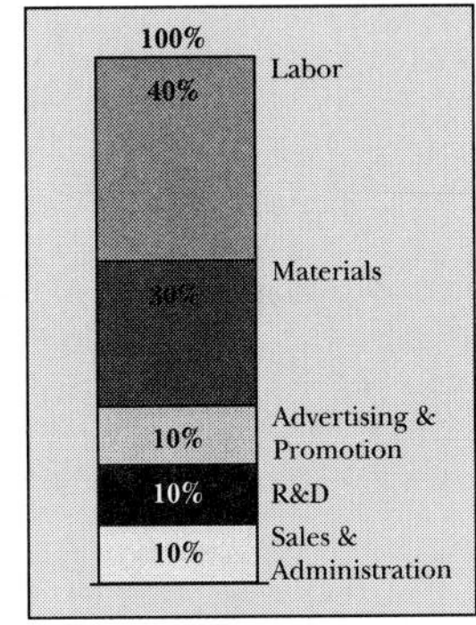

Figure 1
Advertising and Promotion Represent 10 Percent of Company B's Expenses

for comparisons. You can even use bar charts to show both positive and negative quantities.

Another thing you can do with bar charts is convert the bars into a line of symbols, the number of symbols used indicating the number of items (see Figure 14.9). The chief value of charts of this type, called pictograms, is their novelty. But from the standpoint of both accuracy and preparation time, pictograms leave a lot to be desired. Although they occasionally enhance a report, they tend to be less useful than other types of bar charts. As Chuck Wettergreen of Firestone points out, you should avoid using too many cute little symbols in a business message.

FIGURE 14.9
Pictogram

Technical sales	$$$$$$$$$$$$$$$$$$$$$$$$$$$$
Marketing management	$$$$$$$$$$$$$$$$$$$$$$
Wholesale sales	$$$$$$$$$$$$$$$$$$
Retail sales	$$$$$$$$$$$$

Figure 1 Starting Salaries for Sales Careers (in $ thousands)

Source: Adapted from David J. Rachman and Michael H. Mescon, Careers in Business, in Business Today, 5th ed. (New York: Random House, 1987), 574 - 575.

FIGURE 14.10
Pie Chart Combined with Bar Chart

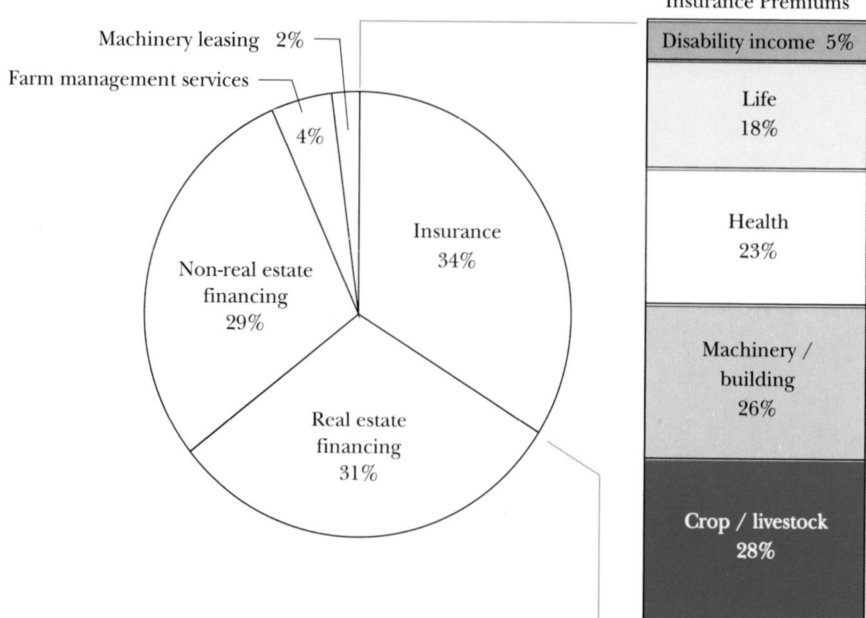

Figure 1 Insurance Accounts for Over a Third of Farmers' Expenditures on Services*
*** Average annual expenditure on services per farmer: $12,000**

Pie charts

Use pie charts to show the relative sizes of the parts of a whole.

Although they are somewhat less versatile than either line or bar charts, pie charts are nevertheless a valuable item in your inventory of visual aids. Nothing is better for showing the composition of a whole than a pie chart like the one in Figure 14.10, which also shows how a pie chart can be combined with another type of chart to expand its usefulness.

In composing pie charts, try to limit the number of slices in the pie to no more than seven. Otherwise, the chart looks cluttered and is difficult to label. If necessary, lump the smallest pieces together in a "miscellaneous" category. Ideally, the largest or most important slice of the pie, the segment you want to emphasize, is placed at the 12 o'clock position; the rest are arranged clockwise either in order of size or in some logical progression. You might want to shade the segment that is of the greatest interest to your readers or use color to distinguish the various pieces. In any case, be sure to label all the segments and to indicate their value in either percentages or units of measure so your readers will be able to judge the value of the wedges. The segments must add up to 100 percent.

Flow charts and organization charts

Use flow charts
- To show a series of steps from beginning to end
- To show relationships

Use organization charts to depict the interrelationships among the parts of an organization.

If you need to show physical or conceptual relationships rather than numerical ones, you might want to use a flow chart or organization chart.

Flow charts are indispensable in illustrating processes, procedures, and relationships. They can illustrate the entire sequence of activities from start to finish, as Figure 14.11 shows. The various elements in the process may be represented by pictorial symbols or geometric shapes, as in this example.

Organization charts, as the name implies, are used to illustrate the positions, units, or functions of an organization and the way they interrelate.

FIGURE 14.11
Flow Chart

Figure 1 Flow of Clients Through Health Center

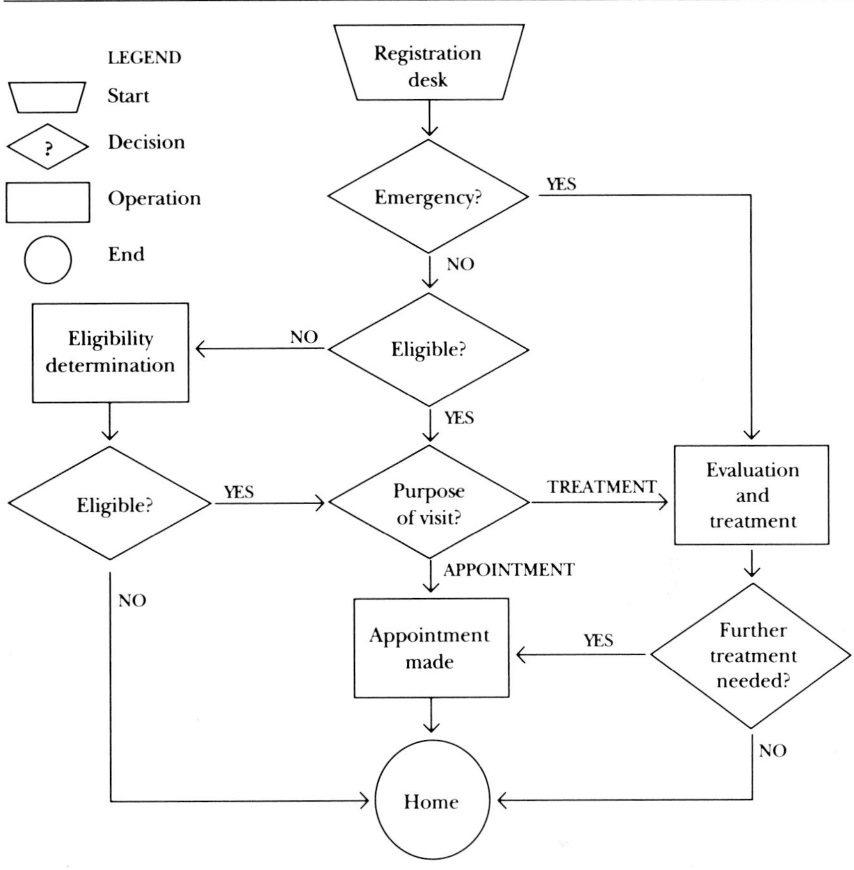

An organization's normal communication channels are almost impossible to describe without the benefit of a chart like the one in Figure 14.12.

Maps

Use maps
- To represent statistics by geographic area
- To show locational relationships

For certain applications, maps are ideal. One of the most common uses is to show concentrations of something by geographic area (see the Report Writer's Portfolio following page 432). In your own reports, you might use maps to show regional differences in such variables as your company's sales of a product. Or you might indicate proposed plant sites and their relationship to sources of supply or key markets.

Most office supply stores carry blank maps of this country, various regions of the country, and areas of the world. You can illustrate these maps to suit your needs, using dots, shading, labels, numbers, and symbols.

Drawings, diagrams, and photographs

Use drawings and diagrams to show
- How something looks
- How something is used

Business reports occasionally use drawings, diagrams, and photographs, although these tend to be less common than some of the other visual aids.

Drawings and diagrams are most often used in technical reports to show how something looks or operates. Figure 14.13, for example, is taken from a report describing furniture for use with computers. Although this diagram was professionally prepared, even a hand-drawn sketch can give

FIGURE 14.12
Organization Chart

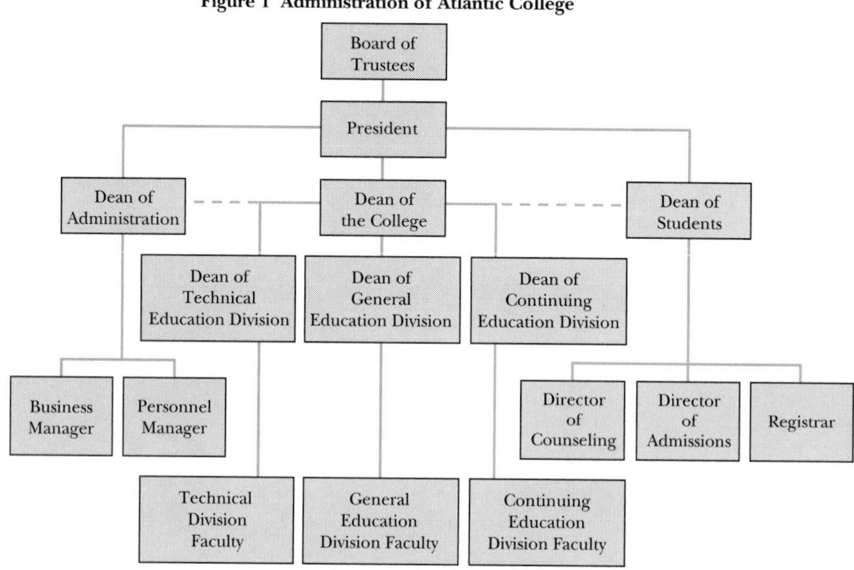

an audience a much clearer idea of how an item looks or can be used than words alone could. In many industries, such as engineering and architecture, computer-aided design systems are capable of producing detailed diagrams and drawings. In addition, a variety of widely available programs for use on microcomputers provide a file of symbols and pictures of various types that can be used (sparingly) to add a decorative touch to reports and presentations.

Use photographs
- For visual appeal
- To show exact appearance

Photographs have always been popular in certain types of business documents, such as catalogs and annual reports, where their visual appeal is used to capture the interest of readers. As the technology for reproducing photographs improves and becomes less expensive, even analytical business reports for internal use are beginning to have more photographs in them. Nothing can demonstrate the exact appearance of a new facility, a piece of property or equipment, or a new product the way a photograph can.

PRODUCING VISUAL AIDS

Computer graphics systems cut the time and cost involved in producing visual aids.

If you have any doubts about the importance of visual aids in business communication, this statistic should dispel them: American companies spend about $14 billion on visual presentations every year, creating over 1.2 billion slides and overhead transparencies.[3] And that's just the bill for the oral presentations! Billions more are undoubtedly spent on visual aids for written reports.

The price tag is high because, until recently, producing professional-looking visual aids was a labor-intensive, time-consuming activity. If you wanted to produce a series of slides, you had to sketch your ideas on graph paper, type the data on an accompanying sheet, then give the package to a graphic artist. After two or three days, you would get sketches back for approval; corrections might take another day or two. Then the visuals could be processed into slides. The price for all this? Roughly $1,500 for 15 slides. Today, however, companies like Firestone are discovering that

FIGURE 14.13
Diagram

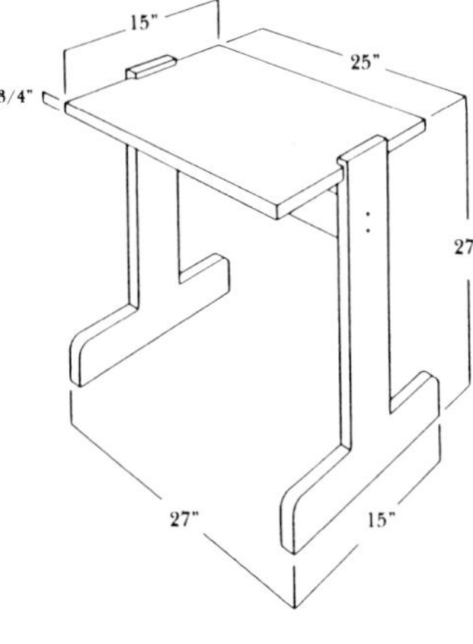

they can cut the costs and time involved in preparing visual aids with the help of computer graphics systems. Using such a system, you can prepare the same 15 slides yourself in about an hour for $150 to $225.[4]

Such systems are having a tremendous impact on how companies create and use visual aids. Instead of relying on graphic designers, business people are turning out their own professional-looking visual aids. The simplicity of the production process encourages people to present data in a graphic format. In fact, as Chuck Wettergreen notes, the technology is so seductive that some people go overboard and put everything in graphic form, thereby diminishing the effect they'd hoped to achieve.

USING A COMPUTER GRAPHICS SYSTEM

If you are lucky enough to work for a firm that, like Firestone, encourages employees to use microcomputers, one of the best things you can do to improve your communication skills is to master a computer graphics program. There are currently more than 150 different software packages on the market, and more are being introduced all the time.[5] These programs vary considerably in their capabilities, which means that you may need to learn several different programs to achieve the results you want.

Computer graphics systems vary widely in their capabilities and hardware requirements.

In general, there's a trade-off between inexpensive, versatile, easy-to-use programs that can produce "working" visual aids for everyday purposes and expensive, specialized programs that yield magazine-quality results. The workhorse programs can function with a microcomputer and a broad range of printers and plotters, but the presentation-quality programs require more expensive computer systems to live up to their potential.

As an individual employee, your choices in software and hardware are likely to be limited by your company's existing systems. Unless you work for a large corporation or a specialized firm that requires a lot of presentation-quality visual aids, you are more likely to encounter one of the workhorse systems. Although you may not be able to turn out charts worthy of *Fortune* magazine, you can create respectable charts and graphs. If you occasionally need to produce more professional-looking results, you can either delegate the final preparation to a specialized in-house department that handles all of the company's presentation-quality graphics or hire an outside service firm.

The workhorse graphics programs are becoming less intimidating all the time, but they do require some effort to master. Most come with established settings, called defaults, that reduce the number of decisions you have to make. Although these settings simplify the task of creating a chart or graph, they also limit your options in terms of layout and typography. With a little extra thought, however, you can override the default settings and gain more control over the finer points of graphic design.

A computer graphics system does more than draw charts; it enhances your analytical capabilities.

One of the great advantages of the workhorse systems is that they are both an analytical tool and a communication tool. As you enter numerical data on your computer, you can use the graphics program to automatically calculate trend lines and growth curves. You can print these out for use in reports or presentations or simply use them in your own analysis. You can also save the results, then enter additional data later. For example, if you track sales or profits by month, you can easily add the latest figures and whip out a new graph that shows the cumulative pattern.

The sophistication of visual aids should match the communication situation.

But before you get carried away with the technical possibilities, think about the kind of image you want to project. The style of your visual aids communicates a subtle message about your relationship with the audience. A simple, hand-drawn diagram is fine for a working meeting but inappropriate for a formal presentation or report. On the other hand, elaborate, full-color visuals may be viewed as extravagant for an informal memo but be entirely appropriate for a message to top management or influential outsiders. The image you want to project should determine your production technique.

FITTING VISUAL AIDS INTO THE TEXT

Once you have produced your visual aids, you face the problem of displaying them in an appropriate way. You have to fit them into the text in a manner that is convenient for the audience and practical from a production standpoint. (For information on how to handle visual aids in oral presentations, see Chapter 18.)

To tie visual aids to the text

- Introduce them in the text
- Place them near the points they illustrate
- Choose a meaningful title and caption for each one

To some extent, your approach to integrating text and visuals will depend on the type of report you're preparing. If you're working on a glossy public relations document, you'll handle the visual aids as though they were illustrations in a magazine, positioning them to attract interest and tell a story of their own. But in most business documents, where the visual aids clarify the text, you will need to tie them very closely to the discussion.

Introduce illustrations in the text

Every visual aid you use should be clearly referred to by number in the text of your report. Some report writers refer to all visual aids as exhibits and number them consecutively throughout the report; many others number tables and figures separately. (Everything that isn't a table is regarded as a figure.) In a very long report with numbered chapters, visual aids may have a double number consisting of the chapter number and an individual number within that chapter (as in this book), separated by a period or a hyphen. (Chapter 16 provides additional information on the mechanics of numbering and labeling visual aids.)

In-text references tell readers why the illustration is important.

A reference to a visual aid should precede the piece itself, so readers are not confronted with visual aids whose significance they can't yet understand. The reference should make readers understand why the table or chart is important. The following selection from a report on the market for motorcycles shows how the connection can be made:

> Figure 1 shows the financial history of the motorcycle division over the past five years, with sales broken into four categories. As the figure shows, total sales were steady over this period, but the mix of sales by category changed dramatically.
>
> The underlying reason for the remarkable growth in our sales of low-horsepower motorcycles is suggested by Table 4, which provides data on motorcycle sales in the United States by region and model.

Use references of this type to prepare your readers for all your visual aids.

In describing the data shown in your visual aids, be sure to emphasize the main point you are trying to make. Don't make the mistake of simply repeating the data to be shown. Paragraphs like the one that follows are guaranteed to put the reader to sleep:

Among women who replied to the survey, 14.6 percent earn less than $5 per hour; 26.4 percent earn $5-$7; 25.7 percent, $8-$12; 18.0 percent, $13-$24; 9.6 percent, $25-$49; and 2.9 percent, $50 and over.

The chart will provide these details; there is no need to repeat them in the text. Instead, use round numbers that sum up the message:

Over two-thirds of the women who replied earn less than $12 per hour.

Place visual aids near the points they illustrate

Put a visual aid as close as possible to its in-text reference to help readers understand the illustration's relevance.

Ideally, it is best to place each visual aid right beside or right after the paragraph it illustrates so readers can consult both the explanation and the visual aid at the same time. But unless your company has a specialized desktop publishing system, you'll have trouble creating layouts with artwork and text on the same page. With conventional office equipment, the most practical approach is to put visual aids on separate pages and mesh them with the text after the report has been typed.

But this solution raises the question of where you should put the pages with the visual aids. Some writers prefer to cluster them at the end of the report, either as a separate section or as an appendix. Others group them at the end of each chapter. Still others prefer to place them as close as possible to the paragraphs they refer to. Although a case can be made for each approach, the best one is generally to place the pages of visual aids right after the pages containing references to them. This arrangement encourages readers to look at the visual aids when you want them to, in the context you have prepared.

Choose titles and captions with a message

One of the best ways to tie your visual aids to the text is to choose titles and captions that reinforce the point you want to make. This precaution is especially necessary when the visual aids are widely separated from the text.

Titles and captions should

- Reinforce the point you want to make
- Be specific

The title of a visual aid, when combined with labels and legends on the piece itself, should be complete enough to tell the reader what the content is. For example, the title "Petroleum Tanks in the United States" is sufficient if, say, it's the title of a line chart labeled "Year" along the horizontal axis and "Number (in thousands)" along the vertical axis. However, if the visual aid were a map overlaid with dots of different sizes, the title would need to explain a bit more: "Concentrations of Petroleum Tanks in the United States in 1989." A legend might then explain how many petroleum tanks each size of dot represents.

When a visual aid is placed next to the text discussion that pertains to it, a clear label and a good title are usually enough; the text can explain the visual aid's significance and details. But when a visual aid is placed elsewhere or requires considerable explanation that would disrupt the flow of the text, a caption may be necessary. Captions, which are generally written as one or more complete sentences, should do more than repeat what's already clear from the title and labels. But it's better to be too specific than too general when you're identifying the content of an illustration. As a check, ask yourself whether you've covered the who, what, when, where, why, and how of the illustration.

If you are using informative headings in your report, you should usually carry this style over into the titles and captions. In other words, instead of simply identifying the topic of the illustration (descriptive title), call attention to the conclusion that ought to be drawn from the data (informative title). Here's the difference:

Descriptive Title: Relationship Between Petroleum Demand and Refinery Capacity in the United States

Informative Title: Shrinking Refinery Capacity Results from Stagnant Petroleum Demand

Regardless of whether your titles and captions are informative or descriptive, phrase them consistently throughout the report. By the same token, be consistent in your format. If the title of the first visual aid is typed entirely in capital letters, all the remaining titles should be typed that way as well. Although an employer may specify the placement of titles, as a general rule you should place all table titles at the top and all figure titles at the bottom. Use captions for all illustrations or for none, and make all captions roughly the same length.

CHECKING OVER THE VISUAL AIDS

Make sure each visual aid is necessary, convenient, accurate, and honest.

Before you give your visual aids a final stamp of approval, take a few extra minutes to review them. Ask yourself the following questions about each one: Is it necessary? Is it convenient? Is it accurate? Is it honest?

Is it necessary?

Avoid cluttering a report with too many visual aids.

As the old saying goes, "One picture is worth a thousand words." But that doesn't mean you should include one picture for every thousand words. A few well-placed visual aids clarify and dramatize your message, but an avalanche of illustrations may bury it. So avoid the temptation to overload your reports with unnecessary tables, graphs, and charts. Remember that your audience is busy. Don't give people information they don't need simply because you want to impress them or because you have fallen in love with the computer graphics system.

Is it convenient?

Make sure the audience can locate your visual aids and figure out what they mean.

In reviewing tables, particularly, be aware of convenience. The information should be laid out so the audience can grasp the important points easily. Be sure that columns are labeled properly and that units of measure are clearly identified. Ask yourself whether separating columns or rows with lines or extra spaces might make the table easier to follow.

Also, check the placement of your visual aids. Try to position them so your audience won't have to flip back and forth too much between them and the text, and be certain that the illustrations are clearly and correctly referred to in the text. If you have more than four visual aids, you should prepare a separate listing of them that can be placed with the table of contents at the front of the report. Some writers list tables separately from figures. The two lists should start on separate pages unless both lists will fit on the same page.

Is it accurate?

Proofread visual aids carefully for errors in data and consistency with the text.

Proofreading visual aids is a chore, but it has to be done, preferably several times. Before you release the final product, make sure that every number is correct, that every line is plotted accurately, that every scale is drawn to reflect reality, that every bit of information is consistent with the text.

If you rely on others to prepare the visual aids, you may be tempted to let them catch all the errors, but resist the temptation. Even the most conscientious staff members will miss a few mistakes, particularly because they may lack the information necessary to spot a data point that doesn't make sense.

When you're proofreading, be sure to check the source notes and the content notes too. Regardless of where reference notes for the text are placed, those for illustrations should appear right below the visual material (as Component Chapter E recommends). If you are the source, you may omit the source note, identify the source as "primary" or "internal data," or refer to the nature of the information (for example, "interviews with 50 soybean farmers").

Is it honest?

Make sure your graphs and charts don't create a false impression by

- Omitting key data points
- Ignoring an important outside influence on the data
- Shifting the scale of measurement

Accuracy and honesty are two different things. You can have all the numbers right and still give your audience a false impression by presenting those numbers in a distorted way. Graphs and charts, in particular, tend to oversimplify some numerical relationships. And deliberately leaving out important data points that don't fit your needs is a serious abuse.

Another possible source of distortion is the omission of an outside influence on the data being portrayed. For example, you might develop a bar or line chart that shows big improvements in your company's profits. Your audience might attribute this gain to lasting changes in the way the company does business, even though the source of the improvement might actually be a one-time change in accounting methods. If events not shown on the graph or chart are actually responsible for creating the results, let your audience know. A footnote is helpful, but the best solution is to revise the visual aid to create a more realistic picture of events.

The choice of scale on a graph or chart also introduces the possibility of distortion. You can make your sales appear to soar by compressing the horizontal scale or expanding the vertical scale, but you will mislead your audience in the process. They will either get the wrong impression or see through the deception. In either case, you're creating a problem, so be sure that the visual impression you create is an honest representation of the facts.

When you are the audience, interpreting data presented in a visual format, also be aware of the possibilities for distortion. Ask yourself whether any important data might have been omitted. Look closely at the scale. Don't let a pretty curve fool you. Bear in mind that visual images tend to oversimplify reality.

SUMMARY

Visual aids are illustrations in tabular, graphic, schematic, or pictorial form. They are used to reduce lengthy verbal descriptions and to emphasize key points. In presenting data graphically, observe conventions of continuity, contrast, and emphasis.

Tables are commonly used to present detailed, specific information; line, bar, and pie charts are used to clarify and dramatize trends and numerical relationships. Flow charts, organization charts, maps, drawings, and photographs, although somewhat less common, are useful for certain purposes.

The production of visual aids is becoming increasingly automated, as computers supplant graphic artists. But regardless of how it's produced, each visual aid should be clearly labeled and referred to in the text. And each should be able to pass the four-question test: Is it necessary? Is it convenient? Is it accurate? Is it honest?

COMMUNICATION CHALLENGES AT FIRESTONE

A company like Firestone Tire & Rubber can sell tires to three types of customers: consumers, automobile manufacturers, and retailers who sell the tires under another label. Of the three, auto manufacturers represent the most desirable customers, because their orders are extremely large and the costs of selling to them are relatively low. In recent years Firestone has focused on attracting more of this business, with considerable success.

At the upcoming annual shareholders' meeting, the general manager of the tire division plans to give a brief overview of efforts to capture a larger share of the auto manufacturer business. He has asked you to help him develop visual aids for his presentation, using this information supplied by Chuck Wettergreen:

- In 1980, 32 percent of Firestone's tires were sold to retailers for resale under their own private labels, 42 percent were sold to consumers, and 26 percent were sold to auto manufacturers.
- Today, only 7 percent of Firestone's tires are sold to retailers, 49 percent are sold to consumers, and 44 percent are sold to auto manufacturers.

The general manager of the tire division also hands you a copy of the 21st annual edition of *Modern Tire Dealer*'s "Facts/Directory." It estimates that last year the three U.S. auto manufacturers purchased tires from the major suppliers in the following proportions:

	AUTO MANUFACTURER		
TIRE MANUFACTURERS	FORD	GENERAL MOTORS	CHRYSLER
Firestone	39%	21%	1%
General	10	17	0
Goodyear	23	22	85
Michelin	21	4	14
Uni Good	6	34	0

Individual Challenge: Use these data to sketch a series of visual aids that will be appropriate for the shareholders' meeting. Your sketches will serve as the basis for presentation-quality slides, which will be produced on Firestone's computer graphics system.

Team Challenge: The general manager likes your ideas, but he has asked you to discuss them with members of Firestone's art department (represented by your classmates). Work together to improve your designs. Pay particular attention to continuity, contrast, and emphasis. Be sure to give some thought to your titles.

QUESTIONS FOR DISCUSSION

1. In what ways might visual aids help people overcome some of the barriers to communication discussed in Chapter 2?
2. What similarities do you see between visual aids and nonverbal communication?
3. What are some of the similarities and differences among tables, line charts, bar charts, and pie charts?
4. How does the information shown in flow charts, organization charts, and diagrams differ from the information shown in line, bar, and pie charts?
5. Would you expect to use the same visual aids for both a written report and an oral presentation covering the same material? Why or why not?
6. What are some of the advantages and disadvantages of preparing visual aids with a computer graphics system?
7. If you were preparing visual aids for an in-house meeting with peers and could choose any production method you preferred, which one would you use? What method would you choose to produce visual aids for an important presentation to an outside client?
8. What steps should you take to correctly describe and identify visual aids in a report? Why should you go to such lengths?
9. When would you use informative titles for visual aids in a written report? When would you use descriptive titles?
10. When you read a graph, how can you be sure that the visual impression you are receiving is an accurate reflection of reality?

DOCUMENTS FOR ANALYSIS

Document 14.A

Examine the pie charts in Figure 14.14, and point out any problems or errors you notice.

FIGURE 14.14
Pie Charts for Analysis (Document 14.A)

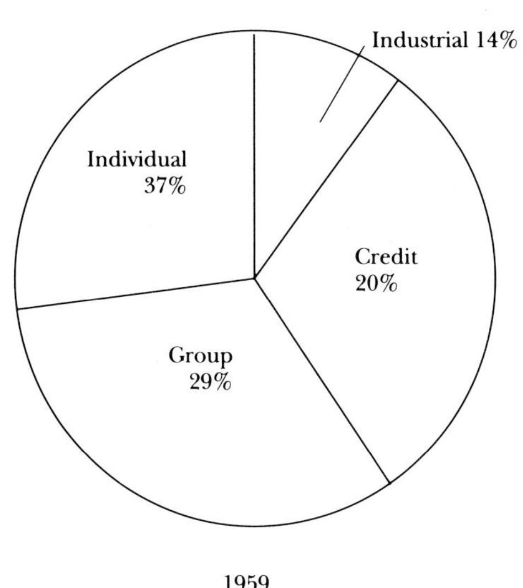

1959
Share of number of policies

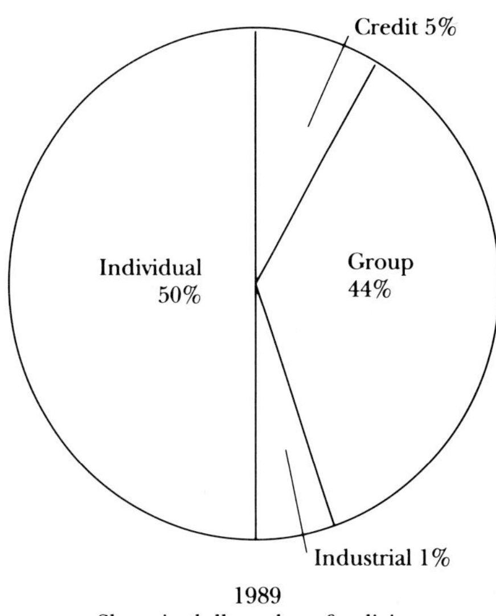

1989
Share in dollar value of policies

Figure 1 Life Insurance Policies Owned

Document 14.B

Examine the line chart in Figure 14.15, and point out any problems or errors you notice.

FIGURE 14.15
Line Chart for Analysis (Document 14.B)

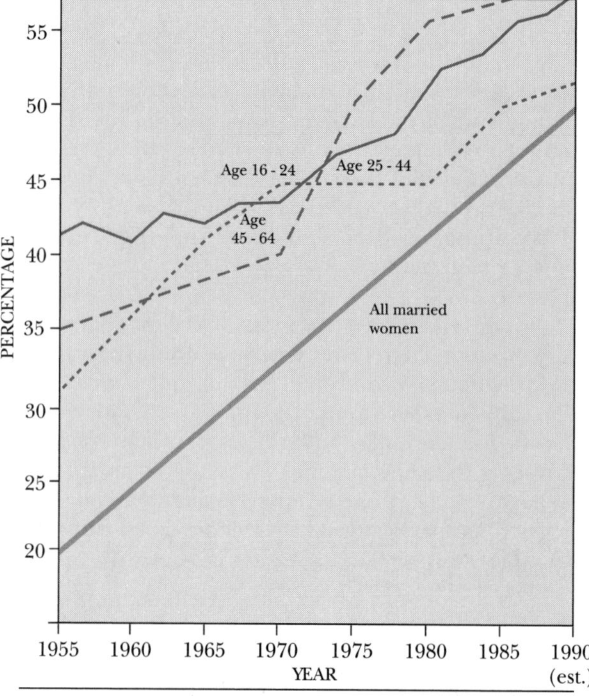

Table 1 The Dramatic Increase in the Number of Women in the Work Force, 1960 - 1990

EXERCISES

1. Prepare a bar graph that visually presents the following information about single-person households in 1989. Your visual should include combined totals for owners and renters ("total households").

AGE GROUP	OWNERS (in 000s)	RENTERS (in 000s)
18–24	143	1,208
25–29	454	1,796
30–34	596	1,326
35–44	816	1,545
45–54	824	986
55–64	1,697	1,348
65–74	2,513	1,655
75+	2,344	1,767

2. Present the following information in three separate visual aids: a table, a line chart, and a bar chart.

   Assets of international banks (in billions of dollars): 1980—47.6; 1981—55.0; 1982—59.8; 1983—46.5; 1984—34.1; 1985—42.2; 1986—47.6; 1987—45.0; 1988—44.9; 1989—49.3

3. Create a pie chart based on the following information, which shows where 1988 journalism school graduates went:

Media jobs	11,276
Newspapers/wire services	3,162
Broadcast/radio/TV	1,653
Public relations	2,407
Advertising	2,142
Magazines	286
Other media	1,626
Graduate study	1,346
Nonmedia jobs	5,324
Unemployed	2,454
Total graduates	20,400

4. You want to illustrate where the money comes from and where the money goes for your nonprofit organization, which puts on an annual animation festival. Your main expenses are rental of a hall for three nights, $1,250; advertising, $5,000; office supplies, $235; phone, $655; air fares for guest animators, $560; hotel expenses for guest animators, $380; miscellaneous administrative costs, $1,125. Your income is as follows: advance ticket sales, 320 at $6 each; at-door ticket sales, 640 at $7.50 each; corporate donations, $3,000; sale of festival posters, 83 at $3 each. Create matching pie charts for your income and expenses.

5. Develop an organization chart for a typical newspaper advertising department. The head of the department is the director of advertising. Under the director are the retail advertising manager, the classified advertising manager, and the general advertising manager. The classified ad manager supervises two departments: telephone sales and street sales. The retail ad manager supervises the sales staff, newspaper services, and the cooperative advertising coordinator. Under newspaper services fall copy, art, and production. The general ad manager supervises the newspaper's representatives in major advertising cities.
6. You are trying to raise capital to begin producing a new type of badminton racquet. Make a list of the various visual aids you want to include in your prospectus for the business.
7. For each of the following types of information, what form of visual aid would you choose?
   a. Data on annual sales for FretCo Guitar Corp. for the past 20 years
   b. Comparison of FretCo Guitar Corp. sales, product by product (electric guitars, bass guitars, amplifiers, acoustic guitars), for this year and last year
   c. Explanation of how a FretCo acoustic guitar is manufactured
   d. Explanation of how the FretCo Guitar Corp. markets its guitars
   e. Data on sales of FretCo products in each of 12 national sales territories
   f. Comparison of FretCo sales figures to sales figures for three other major guitar makers over the past ten years
8. What kind of visual aid would be most appropriate for illustrating each of the following? Write a brief paragraph explaining your decision in each case.
   a. The procedure for setting up a videocassette machine
   b. The average age of your city's residents in the last three censuses as compared to the corresponding average ages of residents in Toronto, New York, Chicago, Dallas, or Los Angeles (choose one)
   c. A comparison of the features, costs, and benefits of three employee compensation plans
   d. A breakdown of your monthly expenses
   e. Your annual income over the past five years
   f. The distribution of theme amusement parks throughout the United States
   g. A comparison of annual sales for all the stores in a nearby shopping center
   h. The schedule for completing a major term paper
   i. The structure of your school's hierarchy
   j. The total income of your family over each of the past five years and the income of every family member in each of those years
9. Last year's sales figures are in for the large department store where you are advertising manager (see Figure 14.16). Construct visual aids based on these figures that will help you plot your advertising budget for each department.

FIGURE 14.16
Store Sales in 1989, in Thousands

Month	Lingerie	Sporting Goods	Housewares
January	$ 39	$ 55	$ 83
February	37	50	81
March	37	51	78
April	25	55	77
May	26	60	79
June	30	65	85
July	30	65	79
August	27	60	77
September	27	51	77
October	27	53	78
November	31	60	82
December	40	65	85

10. In other textbooks or in *U.S. News & World Report*, *Fortune*, and other news magazines or business magazines, locate one example of each of the following types of visual aids: table, line chart, surface chart, bar chart, pie chart, flow chart, organization chart, map, diagram, photograph. Bring these samples to class and discuss the effectiveness of each. Is the information presented in a convenient format? Do you believe the effect to be honest? Is the visual aid clear, readable, and meaningful? Is it properly introduced and discussed in the text? As an alternative to class discussion, write an evaluation of the strong and weak points of each visual aid.

CHAPTER FIFTEEN

WRITING REPORTS AND PROPOSALS

After studying this chapter, you will be able to

- Decide on the proper format and length for your report
- Decide when to use direct versus indirect order
- Organize informational reports by using topical divisions of thought
- Organize analytical reports by using conclusions and recommendations or different types of logical arguments
- Establish an appropriate degree of formality in a report
- Establish a consistent time perspective
- Use headings, lists, transitions, openings, and summaries to guide readers through the report

William L. Beer

COMMUNICATION CLOSE-UP AT MAYTAG

A couple of years ago, The Maytag Company of Newton, Iowa, decided to build on its reputation for high-quality laundry and kitchen appliances by offering some new products. One concept that Maytag executives wanted to evaluate was "space-efficient" laundry equipment: a full-size washer and dryer set that could be stacked in a kitchen, bathroom, bedroom, or hall closet. The company's market researchers began by analyzing everything from demographic patterns to trends in the size and layout of new homes.

The results of this research were promising, so a prototype was designed. Panels of typical consumers were invited to give their opinions of the sample washer and dryer. William L. Beer, the company's manager of economic and survey research (essentially market research), attended all the sessions. "I listened to what people had to say about the appearance and features of the stacked laundry equipment," Bill recalls, "and also had them fill out a written evaluation."

With that basic data in hand, Bill set out to write a report summarizing the results of the research. His purpose was to give top managers the information they needed to decide whether to manufacture and market the new product. But he and his staff had developed their own opinion of

Behind the success of The Maytag Company's appliances are thousands of reports, some only conveying information and others also drawing conclusions and making recommendations.

what should be done. To build a case, Bill laid out the facts that contributed to the recommendation he would make: "I discussed in turn each of the research projects we'd conducted. I covered the high points of each particular project and the conclusions that we drew as a result."

That kind of detail is useful to product designers and others who want insights into consumer preferences. But busy decision makers don't necessarily want to wade through all the background material. They want concise, relevant, reliable information that will help them decide quickly what course to take. "That's why we included what we call an executive summary, which tied together all the research findings and listed several recommendations," Bill says. "Some of these recommendations dealt with features of the product itself; others dealt with ways to distribute and promote it. The final recommendation was our strong endorsement for getting stacked laundry equipment into the market as soon as possible." Maytag executives agreed and launched a new product that has been a gratifying success.

The reports that Bill and his staff write fall into two categories: analytical reports, like the one concerning stacked laundry equipment, and informational reports. "Our informational reports tend to have a lot of statistics and very little text," Bill says. "The most important thing in this type of report is to provide clear and logical headings so people know what's there. And our informational reports are usually organized from the general to the specific. For example, a sales report would start out with a summary of total sales for the United States. The second page might show sales for the same time period by our four sales divisions: eastern, central, northern, and western. We break down that information into smaller selling areas until we get to sales by county."

Analytical reports—such as strategic marketing analyses, forecasts of business conditions, and evaluations of advertising campaigns—are more text-oriented, and their organization is more complex. Bill and his staff usually follow a four-part plan: "First of all, we always provide a one-page explanation of how the research was conducted, which builds credibility for the rest of the report. The second thing is an executive summary, which highlights the significant research findings and provides just enough information to make readers want to go on. Next is a more detailed discussion, where we lay out findings, statistical information, analysis of statistics, and any conclusions that can be drawn from the statistics. The final section is the appendix, which contains written questionnaires, letters to respondents, source documents, and things like that. The appendix is very seldom read when the report first comes out, but it's useful when you go back to the report after a year or two and want to see how the information in the report was obtained."

The writing style used in these reports is rather formal, but Bill sees no need for "flowery, drawn-out statements and three-dollar words." He believes instead in conciseness: "Remember that the only purpose for ever writing a business report is to communicate in condensed form something that otherwise would take the reader a lot of time or effort to find out. I tell my people that it isn't the report I want on my desk, it's the results of the research. Explaining those results requires a report, but the report is only a means to an end."

PREPARING TO WRITE REPORTS AND PROPOSALS

Before you write your report, you may have to revise the outline you used to guide your research effort.

When the time comes to translate your own research into a finished report or oral presentation, you, too, face the challenge of finding the most effective way to communicate your message to an audience. Sometimes you can use the preliminary outline that guided your research as a final blueprint for your report. More often, however, you have to rework it to take into account both your audience's probable reactions and the things you learned during your study. The division of ideas that helped you do your research may be quite different from the division of ideas that will help your audience understand and accept your message, particularly if your message contains controversial material. In addition to the audience, you must consider your purpose and subject matter. All three elements—audience, purpose, and subject matter—should influence the format, length, and basic structure of your report or presentation.

DECIDING ON FORMAT AND LENGTH

One of the first issues you must decide is whether to create a written report or an oral presentation. Often, you will need to prepare both: a presentation to brief management on the results of your work and a written report to provide a lasting record. You can generally use the same basic outline for both, but reports and oral presentations obviously require different preparation methods. (Chapter 18 provides details on how to handle oral presentations; this chapter focuses on reports. However, the organizational principles discussed here pertain equally to both oral and written material.)

If you're writing a report, decisions about format and length may be made for you by the person who requests the document. This rigidity is often the case with monitor/control reports, justification reports, proposals, progress reports, and compliance reports. Generally speaking, the more routine the report, the less flexibility you have in deciding on format and length.

When you do have some leeway about these issues, your decisions should be based on your readers' needs. Your goal should be to tell them what they need to know in a format that is easy for them to use. In selecting a format for your report, you have four options:

You may present a report in one of four formats.

- *Preprinted form.* Basically for "fill in the blank" reports. Most are relatively short (five or fewer pages) and deal with routine information, often mainly numerical. Use this format when it is requested by the person authorizing the report.
- *Letter.* For reports of five or fewer pages that are directed to outsiders. These reports include all the normal parts of a letter, but they may also have headings, footnotes, tables, and figures.
- *Memo.* The most common format for short (fewer than ten pages), informal reports distributed within an organization. Memos have headings at the top: "Date," "To," "From," and "Subject." In addition, like longer reports, they often have internal headings and sometimes visual aids. Memos exceeding ten pages are sometimes referred to as memo reports to distinguish them from their shorter cousins. They, too, begin with the standard memo headings. The checklist at

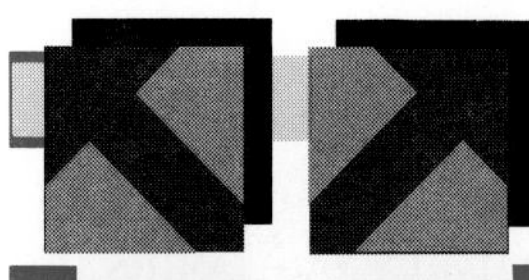
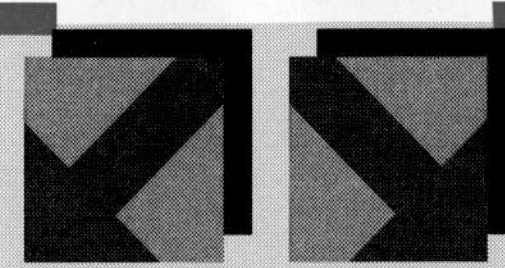

BUSINESS COMMUNICATION TODAY

How to Handle Crash Assignments

Most reports have deadlines, and those deadlines are frequently difficult to meet. If you are ever faced with the responsibility for a "crash" report, consult this list of time-management tips. They may help you write a better report and still make the deadline.

- *Isolate yourself.* Assemble all the materials and supplies you need to do the job in a quiet place where you can work undisturbed.
- *Don't procrastinate.* Get to work. You'll be done sooner. And don't be uneasy about the tasks ahead. Lack of confidence can slow you down. Instead, get started and give it your best.
- *Know your objectives.* Before you start to write, decide what you are writing about. What is the focus? To whom are you writing? What will your report be used for? Targeting it to the intended reader and actual use could save you hours of needless rewriting.
- *Give top priority to planning.* Report planning is just as important as report writing. Good preparation will speed your work.
- *Break the job into individual tasks.* Make a list of steps that are involved, estimate the time required for each, then use it as a checklist for the entire project. For example, planning and organizing the report might take two hours, analyzing data four hours, and writing the rough draft two hours.
- *Make choices.* "Is it more important today to do research or to outline the report?" The choice will help you define and set your goals.
- *Keep a time log.* It will tell you how you are spending your time and how you may be wasting it.
- *Reduce interruptions.* Unless a phone call takes priority over the task at hand, offer to call back later. Reduce visitor interruptions by limiting the "open-door policy" to certain hours.
- *Avoid clock watching and other diversions.* Refilling your coffee cup every few minutes can rob you of important work time.
- *Concentrate.* Keep your mind off personal problems or peripheral issues that could disrupt or halt the progress you are making.
- *Strive to meet the deadline.* Your ability to meet a deadline could have a critical effect on your chances for advancement.

Well-managed writing time pays off in clearer writing and in more time for the other priorities in your life. Ask yourself: "Do I understand the value of time and manage it well? Or am I willing to endure the frustration of long hours and unmet goals?"

1. Is it easier to handle a crash assignment alone or with a team? Explain your answer.

2. One way to make good use of your time when under a deadline is to take advantage of "wasted" periods, such as time spent standing in line, taking a shower, riding the bus, and so on. Choose a specific problem you need to solve, and for the next week use only your "wasted" time periods to ponder the problem. What do you learn from this exercise?

the end of this chapter provides guidelines for preparing memo reports and other short, informal reports.

- *Manuscript.* For reports, from a few pages to several hundred pages, that require a formal approach. As their length increases, reports in manuscript format require more elements before the text of the report (prefatory parts) and after the text (supplementary parts). Chapter 16 explains these elements and includes additional instructions and a checklist for preparing formal reports.

Component Chapter D, "Format and Layout of Business Documents," contains more specific guidelines for preparing these four kinds of reports.

Length depends on
- Subject
- Purpose
- Your relationship with the readers

The length of your report obviously depends on your subject and purpose but is also affected by your relationship with the readers. If they are relative strangers, if they are skeptical or hostile, if the material is nonroutine or controversial, you generally have to explain your points in greater detail. Thus you end up with a longer document. You can afford to be brief if you are on familiar terms with your readers, if they are likely to agree with you, and if the information is routine or uncomplicated. Generally speaking, short reports are more common in business than long ones, and you will probably write many more 5-page memos than 250-page formal reports.

ESTABLISHING A BASIC STRUCTURE

Choice of structure involves three decisions:
- What to say?
- Direct or indirect order?
- Topical or logical organization?

In addition to deciding on format and length, you have to decide on the basic structure of your report. This problem involves three issues:

- What information should you include, and what should you exclude? Should you cover all the material obtained during your research or eliminate some of the data?
- What psychological approach is best with your particular readers? Should you use direct order, leading off with the main idea (a summary of key findings, conclusions, recommendations)? Or should you use indirect order, which lays out the facts and gradually builds up to the main idea?
- What method of subdivision will make your material both clear and convincing? Should you use a topical organization based on order of importance, sequence, chronology, location, spatial relationships, or categories? Or should you organize your ideas around logical arguments?

Key points to cover

Your report should answer the audience's key questions.

In deciding on the content of your report, the first step is to put yourself in the audience's position. What major questions do you think your audience has about the subject? Your objective is to answer all those questions in the order that makes the most sense.

In most situations, your audience has one main question of greatest importance: "Why are we losing money?" "Is this a good investment?" "What will our sales and profits be over the next six months?" "What is the progress to date on the work assigned?" Whether it's one of these or another, you must define the main question as precisely as you can before you can begin to formulate your answer. Defining the main question may seem to require the skills of a mind reader, but nine times out of ten, the main question is simply the reason you have been asked to write the report or make the presentation.

Once you've defined the main question, you can sketch a general answer, based on the results of your research. Your answer, like the question, should be broad.

The next step is to determine what additional questions your audience is likely to ask based on your answer to the main question. A typical question-and-answer chain might go as follows:

Main question:	Why are we losing money?
General answer:	We're losing money because our production costs are higher than our prices.
Question 1:	Why are our production costs high?
Question 2:	Why are our prices low?

Your next step is to answer these questions, and your answers again raise additional questions. As the chain of questions and answers is forged, the points multiply and become increasingly specific, as Figure 15.1 illustrates. When you've identified and answered all your audience's probable questions, you have defined the content of your report or presentation. The process is akin to factoring the issues in order to conduct an investigation.

Pursue the chain of questions and answers from the general to the specific.

The question-and-answer chain clarifies the main idea of the report (your answer to the main question) and establishes the flow of ideas from the general to the specific. All effective reports and presentations are constructed in this way, with a mix of broad concepts and specific details. When the mix is right, the message works: Members of the audience grasp both the general meaning of the ideas and the practical implications of those ideas. They get the gist of the message and can relate the broad concepts to the everyday world of objects and actions. The general ideas sum up and give direction to the message, and the specific ideas clarify and illustrate their meaning.

Business communication tends to be concerned with the details: facts, figures, and hard data. Routine, recurring messages are especially heavy on details; analytical, problem-solving messages are heavier on generalizations. In either case, the trick is to draw conclusions and generalizations out of all the information and relate them to your audience's needs. For every piece of information that you are tempted to include, ask why the audience needs it and how it relates to the main question.

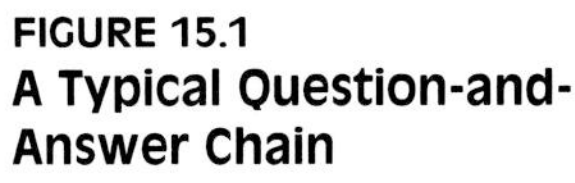

FIGURE 15.1
A Typical Question-and-Answer Chain

Q: Why are we losing money?
A: Production costs exceed prices.
Q: Why are production costs high?
A: Overhead is spread over low sales volume.
Q: Why are prices low?
A: Competitors establish the base that we must meet.
Q: Why is overhead high?
A: We have higher research and development expenses than our competitors.
Q: Why is volume low?
A: We distribute in only three states.
Q: How can competitors charge less?
A: They have lower costs and higher sales volume.
Q: Are consumers really concerned about price?
A: They appear to be, although other factors enter into the decision to buy.

Direct versus indirect order

The direct approach, which gives readers the main idea first, saves time and makes the report easier to understand.

As Chapter 4 explains, audience attitude is the basis for decisions about organization. When the audience is considered either receptive or open-minded, you should use the direct approach: Emphasize your key findings, conclusions, and recommendations. This approach, which is most common for business reports, enables readers to get the main idea of the report at the outset, which saves time and makes the rest of the report easier to follow. For those who have questions or want more information, later parts of the report provide complete findings and supporting details.

In addition to being more convenient for readers, the direct approach generally produces a more forceful report. You sound sure of yourself when you state your conclusions confidently at the outset instead of beating around the bush.

The indirect approach, which withholds the main idea until later in the report, helps overcome resistance.

However, sometimes confidence may be misconstrued as arrogance. If you are a junior member of a status-conscious organization or if your audience is skeptical or hostile, you may want to use indirect order. With this approach, you introduce the complete findings and supporting details before the conclusions and recommendations, which come last. The indirect approach gives you a chance to prove your points and gradually overcome your audience's reservations. By deferring the conclusions and recommendations, you imply that you have weighed the evidence objectively without prejudging the facts. You also imply that you are subordinating your judgment to that of the audience, whose members are capable of drawing their own conclusions when they have access to all the facts.

Although the indirect approach has its advantages, there is always the possibility that report readers will be in a hurry to get to "the answer" and will flip to the recommendations immediately, thus defeating your purpose. For this reason, length should enter into your decision on direct versus indirect order. Generally speaking, the longer the message, the less effective an indirect approach is likely to be. Furthermore, an indirect argument is harder to follow than a direct argument.

Because both the direct and indirect approaches have merit, business people often combine them. They reveal their conclusions and recommendations as they go along, rather then putting them either first or last. For example, Figure 15.2 contrasts the introductions from two reports with the same general outline. In the direct version, the writer makes a series of statements summarizing the conclusion reached in relation to each main topic on the outline. In the indirect version, the writer simply introduces the same topics (in the same order) without drawing any conclusions about them. The conclusions appear within the body of the report instead. So is the report that uses this second introduction direct or indirect? Real reports are often just as hard to classify.

Division of ideas

Regardless of whether you use the direct or indirect approach, you must still deal with the question of how your ideas will be subdivided and developed. For example, let's say you are writing a controversial report recommending that your company revise its policy on who reports to whom. You know that some of your readers will object to your ideas, so you decide to use indirect order. But how do you develop your argument?

FIGURE 15.2
Direct Approach Versus Indirect Approach in an Introduction

THE DIRECT APPROACH

Since the company's founding 25 years ago, we have provided regular repair service for all our electric appliances. This service has been an important selling point as well as a source of pride for our employees. However, we are paying a high price for our image. Last year, we lost $500,000 on our repair business.

Because of your concern over these losses, you have asked me to study the pros and cons of discontinuing our repair service. With the help of John Hudson and Susan Lefkowitz, I have studied the issue for the past two weeks and have come to the conclusion that we have been embracing an expensive, impractical tradition.

By withdrawing from the electric appliance repair business, we can substantially improve our financial performance without damaging our reputation with customers. This conclusion is based on three basic points that are covered in the following pages:

--It is highly unlikely that we will ever be able to make a profit in the repair business.
--Service is no longer an important selling point with customers.
--Closing down the service operation will create few internal problems.

THE INDIRECT APPROACH

Since the company's founding 25 years ago, we have provided repair service for all our electric appliances. This service has been an important selling point as well as a source of pride with our employees. However, the repair business itself has consistently lost money.

Because of your concern over these losses, you have asked me to study the pros and cons of discontinuing our repair business. With the help of John Hudson and Susan Lefkowitz, I have studied the issue for the past two weeks. The following pages present our findings for your review. Three basic questions are addressed:

--What is the extent of our losses, and what can we do to turn the business around?
--Would withdrawal hurt our sales of electric appliances?
--What would be the internal repercussions of closing down the repair business?

In the following sections, you'll see how people in a variety of situations have answered this question. The key is first to decide whether the purpose of the report is to provide chiefly information or analysis. From there, you can choose an organizational plan that suits your topic and goals.

ORGANIZING INFORMATIONAL REPORTS

The purpose of informational reports is to explain.

Informational reports have one basic purpose: to explain something in straightforward terms. Informational reports, which have hundreds of uses in business, include reports for monitoring and controlling operations, statements of policies and procedures, most compliance reports, most personal activity reports, some justification reports, some reports documenting client work, and some proposals.

Make clarity your main objective in informational reports.

In writing informational reports, you usually don't have to worry too much about reader reaction. Because readers will presumably respond unemotionally to your material, you can present it in the most direct fashion possible. What you do need to worry about with informational reports is reader comprehension. The information must be presented logically and accurately so readers will understand exactly what you mean and be able to use the information in a practical way.

In structuring an informational report, you can let the nature of whatever you're describing serve as the point of departure. For example, Bill Beer uses a geographic organization in his sales reports for Maytag, presenting results for the country as a whole, then for each of the four regions in turn. If you're describing a machine, each component can correspond to a part of your report. If you're describing an event, you can approach the discussion chronologically, and if you're explaining how to do something, you can describe the steps in the process.

Some informational reports, especially compliance reports and internal reports prepared on preprinted forms, are organized according to instructions supplied by the person requesting the information. In addition, many proposals conform to an outline specified in the request for proposal issued by the client: statement of the problem, background, scope of work, limitations, sources and methods, work schedule, qualifications of personnel, facilities, anticipated costs, expected results.

Informational reports take many forms, but the two examples that follow, a brief periodic report and a personal activity report on a conference, will give you an idea of the typical organization and tone.

A PERIODIC REPORT

Periodic reports are recurring monitor/control reports that keep managers informed about departments reporting to them.

A periodic report is a monitor/control report that describes what has happened in a department or division during a particular period. The purpose of these recurring documents, which are sometimes called status reports, is to provide a picture of how things are going so that managers will be up-to-date and can take corrective action if necessary.

Periodic reports are usually written in memo format and do not need much of an introduction; a subject line on the memo is adequate. They should follow the same general format and organization from period to period. Most are organized in this sequence:

Most periodic reports follow a set sequence.

- *Overview of routine responsibilities.* A brief description of activities related to each of the writer's normal responsibilities. In some cases, the overview focuses on statistical or financial results; in other cases, it is written in paragraph form.
- *Discussion of special projects.* A description of any new or special projects that have been undertaken during the reporting period.
- *Plans for the coming period.* A schedule of activities planned for the next reporting period.
- *Analysis of problems.* Although often included in the overview of routine or special activities, it is sometimes put in a separate section to call attention to areas that may require high-level intervention.

Periodic reports must expose any problems that exist.

The important thing to remember in writing periodic reports is to be honest about problems as well as accomplishments. In fact, the bad news is probably more important than the good news, because problems require action whereas good news often does not.

The periodic report in Figure 15.3 was prepared by Liz Rockwell, director of campus recruiting for the Minneapolis office of an accounting firm. Liz has this to say about her report: "Campus recruiting is a big deal for our firm, because we hire most of our staff right out of college. Between

FIGURE 15.3
Sample Periodic Report

MEMO

DATE: February 16, 1989
TO: Joyce Roberts, V.P., Personnel
FROM: Liz Rockwell, Director, Campus Recruiting
SUBJECT: Recruiting activities, February 1-15

ACTIVITIES COMPLETED

We've been working on three campuses February 1-15:

--University of Wisconsin. Jud Morgan and I had dinner with five good candidates identified by Professor Neiburgh. I have invited three of them to visit our offices and am awaiting their replies.

--University of Minnesota. We interviewed 54 undergraduate business/accounting majors during regular campus interviews on the 7th and 8th. Joe Damon and Linda Sawyer handled the candidates who had been invited to sign up in advance, and I handled the rest. We have reviewed the evaluations and are sending invitations to 10 students to come in for additional interviews at our office.

--Northwestern University. The resume book from Northwestern arrived on the 3rd, and we are now prescreening the graduating business majors. We expect to invite about 25 candidates to sign up for campus interviews, which will be held on March 3.

ACTIVITIES SCHEDULED

Recruiting activities scheduled for the next two weeks are indicated below:

Date	Activity	Responsibility
Feb. 18-19	University of Michigan, undergraduate business majors: 1st-round interviews	Rockwell, Lipp, Pritsky, Lloyd
Feb. 21	University of Chicago: 1st-round interviews	Taylor
Feb. 28	University of Iowa, undergraduate business majors: 1st-round interviews	Rockwell, Damon

PROBLEMS

Some of the staff are already complaining about the burden of interviewing so many candidates. In addition to screening resumes, contacting former professors, and helping with campus interviews, the staff will be talking with approximately 40 people here in our offices between now and April 14. Since each of the 40 will be seen by three staff members, we'll actually have to schedule 120 office interviews.

The scheduling problem is compounded by the fact that many of our people travel extensively. On any given day, only about 60 percent of them are in the office. Moreover, some interviewers are better than others, and I am reluctant to use those who lack confidence or ability in this area.

January and April, we visit eight or ten campuses and screen about 500 candidates in an effort to hire roughly 20 people. During the recruiting season, I prepare a memo twice a month to let my boss know where we stand. The rest of the year, I submit my report on a monthly basis."

A PERSONAL ACTIVITY REPORT

A personal activity report is a form of monitor/control report that calls for an individual's description of what occurred during a conference, convention, or trip, for example. It is intended to inform management of any important information or decisions that emerged.

Personal activity reports, often in the form of brief memos, describe the facts and decisions that emerge during conventions, trips, and business meetings.

Personal activity reports are ordinarily written in memo format. Because they are nonrecurring documents, they require more of an introduction than a periodic report does. They are often organized chronologically, but some are organized around topics that reflect the reader's interests.

Figure 15.4 gives an example of a personal activity report organized by topic. It is a conference report prepared by Chris Bowers, who is on the staff of a large housing-development company. Says Chris, "My boss sent me to the Manufactured Housing Convention to find out whether we might be able to use factory-built houses to reduce our development costs. Because I knew my boss was mainly interested in learning about different kinds of factory-built housing, I went to the seminars that covered the four main types. When I wrote my conference report, I devoted a section to each one."

ORGANIZING ANALYTICAL REPORTS

The purpose of an analytical report is to convince the reader that the conclusions and recommendations developed in the text are valid.

Analytical reports differ from informational reports in their purpose and thus in their organization. Informational reports are mainly intended to educate readers, but analytical reports are designed to persuade readers to accept certain conclusions or recommendations. In informational reports, the information alone is the focus of attention. In analytical reports, the information plays a supporting role. The facts are a means to an end rather than an end in themselves.

Analytical reports are generally written to respond to special circumstances. Most of the decision-oriented reports mentioned in Chapter 12 are analytical, such as justification reports, research reports, and troubleshooting reports. So are many proposals and final reports to clients.

Organize analytical reports around conclusions and recommendations (direct approach) or around logical arguments (indirect approach).

Regardless of which type of analytical report you are writing, you must organize your ideas so they will convince readers of the soundness of your thinking. Your choice of a specific approach should be based on your estimate of the readers' probable reaction: direct if you think they are likely to agree with you, indirect if you think they will resist your message. If you use the direct approach, you can base the structure of the report on your conclusions and recommendations, using them as the main points of your outline. If you employ an indirect approach, your organization should reflect the thinking process that will lead readers to your conclusions.

ORGANIZATION BASED ON CONCLUSIONS OR RECOMMENDATIONS

People from your own company who have asked you to study something are often the most receptive readers. They may know from past experience that you will do a thorough job, and they may trust your judgment. They are therefore likely to accept your conclusions. Thus you can usually come straight to the point and organize your report around conclusions or recommendations. The direct approach does have some limitations, however. If your readers have reservations about either you or your material, strong statements at the beginning may intensify their resistance. Focusing

FIGURE 15.4
Sample Personal Activity Report

MEMO

DATE: October 23, 1989
TO: Gary Boone
FROM: Chris Bowers
SUBJECT: Manufactured Housing Convention

My trip to the Manufactured Housing Convention, held October 16-20 in Miami, was extremely interesting. One clear point was made repeatedly by many speakers: Factory-built homes have the potential to transform the housing industry. By 1995, 37 percent of all new homes will be manufactured away from the development site, freeing the developer to concentrate on site acquisition, preparation, and marketing. The four main types of manufactured housing discussed at the convention are described below.

MOBILE HOMES

Design improvements and price advantages are both swelling demand for mobile homes. The new models are spacious and attractive--hard to distinguish from conventional site-built homes. In fact, most so-called "mobile" homes are never relocated once they are in place at their first site. With proper landscaping, they create an impression that is far better than the unattractive trailer camps of the 1940s. The attached brochures will give you an idea of how some of the new models look.

Sales of new mobile homes are growing at an annual rate of 6 percent and will reach 500,000 units per year by 1995. Currently, almost 50 percent of all new single-family homes priced at less than $80,000 are mobile homes. Buyers range from first-time homeowners to middle-income retirees.

MODULAR HOUSING

The main difference between modular and mobile homes is that modular homes must be trucked to their site, whereas mobile homes can be towed on their own chassis. Sales of new modular homes are increasing by 7 percent per year and should total 120,000 units by 1995.

PANELIZED HOUSING

Panelized housing is assembled at the development site from large factory-built components, such as walls, floors, and roofs. The developer has the option of using the components in various configurations. Shipments are increasing at an annual rate of 8 percent and will reach 175,000 units by 1995.

PRECUT HOUSING

People who want to build their own homes or act as their own general contractor can now buy precut but unassembled components packaged in kit form. This market has traditionally been dominated by mail-order firms featuring log cabins, geodesic domes, and A-frames, but a few manufacturers are currently trying to gear their packages to the development market. Sales are beginning to pick up. Shipments are growing by 6 percent annually and will reach 42,000 units by 1995.

on conclusions and recommendations may also make everything seem too simple. Your readers could jump on your report as being superficial: "But why didn't you consider this option?" or "Where did you get this number?" You're generally better off taking the direct approach in a report only when your readers trust you and are willing to accept your conclusions and recommendations.

Focusing on conclusions: A research report

Ellen Miller, who works on the planning staff of a forest-products company in Charlotte, North Carolina, was asked to investigate opportunities for getting into the mushroom-growing business. She has this to say about her analysis and report: "I've worked for my boss for five years, and our function in the company is to look for new business opportunities. An investment banker had sent us a prospectus on a little company that specializes in growing mushrooms, but we didn't want to acquire the company without taking a good, hard look at the mushroom industry as a whole. I spent about six weeks checking out the industry, and I had to conclude that growing mushrooms is a lot like eating hot-fudge sundaes: sounds good but has some serious drawbacks. I didn't feel that it was my place to say flat out that we shouldn't invest in the industry, but I did feel justified in warning my boss of the risks."

Ellen decided to organize her report into two main sections, as the outline in Figure 15.5 illustrates. Her basic conclusion was that growing mushrooms is a good business—but not for her company. The two main sections of the report develop this dual conclusion.

For the flavor of Ellen's report, look at Figure 15.6, which reproduces the beginning of the section describing the attractive features of the mushroom industry. Notice how Ellen uses one of her conclusions as the foundation. She tells her boss exactly what she thinks in clear, straightforward terms. She provides plenty of facts, but the facts are selected and arranged to prove her points.

When the reader is concerned with conclusions, use them as the main points.

You can use a similar organization whenever you're asked to analyze a problem or opportunity. If your reader is mainly interested in your conclusions, use them as the main points in your outline.

Focusing on recommendations: A justification report

When the reader is concerned about what action to take, use recommendations as the main points.

A similar but slightly different approach is useful when your readers want to know what they ought to do as opposed to what they ought to conclude. Ellen offered conclusions but stopped short of recommending specific steps that her company should take. Often, however, you will be asked to solve a problem as opposed to just studying it. If so, the things you want your readers to do become the main subdivisions of your report.

FIGURE 15.5
Outline of a Research Report Based on Conclusions

I. Introduction

II. Conclusion: Growing mushrooms is a good business--but not for us

III. Cultivating mushrooms is an attractive business opportunity
   A. Market is large and growing
   B. Growers are in a good position
   C. Leadership is possible

IV. Our company is poorly positioned to enter this business
   A. Stable earnings are unlikely
   B. Our management lacks sophistication to compensate for lack of experience
   C. Our strengths do not fit with requirements for success in mushroom-growing business

V. Summary

FIGURE 15.6
Excerpt Showing the Development of Conclusions in an Analytical Report

CULTIVATING MUSHROOMS IS AN
ATTRACTIVE BUSINESS OPPORTUNITY

Three characteristics of the mushroom-growing industry suggest that it offers attractive opportunities for growth:

1. The market demand for mushrooms is large and growing, with particularly rapid growth in the demand for fresh mushrooms.
2. The profit potential of growers appears to be high, particularly among growers who are able to build brand identification.
3. The opportunity to establish a dominant leadership position exists and has not yet been fully exploited.

Market Is Large and Growing

Industry data indicate that the market for mushrooms is large and that growth is likely to accelerate in the next five years.

--Retail mushroom sales (canned and fresh) are estimated to be $2.5 billion.
--In the past 15 years, growth in retail mushroom sales has been relatively constant at nearly 8 percent annually.
 --Per capita consumption of fresh mushrooms has increased to 10 percent annually in the last five years.
 --Expenditures on canned mushrooms as a percentage of personal consumption have remained constant.

An analytical report based on recommendations should follow a set sequence.

In organizing a report around recommendations, you must usually take five steps:

1. Establish the need for action in the introduction, generally by briefly describing the problem or opportunity.
2. Introduce the benefit that can be achieved, without providing any details.
3. List the steps (recommendations) required to achieve the benefit, using action verbs for emphasis.
4. Explain each step more fully, giving details on procedures, costs, and benefits.
5. Summarize the recommendations.

Raymond Verdugo, director of manufacturing engineering at a paper-products company in New Jersey, was asked by top management to suggest ways to increase the company's production of facial tissues without making a heavy investment. Says Raymond, "I must have looked at a dozen different ways we could increase our output. When I wrote up the results, I thought about discussing all the options I'd evaluated, but then it occurred to me that management wasn't really interested in the ideas that wouldn't work. So I just talked about the two things we could do to increase capacity." Raymond's memo appears in Figure 15.7. Notice how he uses recommendations to organize his discussion.

ORGANIZATION BASED ON LOGICAL ARGUMENTS

Focusing on conclusions or recommendations is the most forceful and efficient way to organize an analytical report. But it isn't the best solution

FIGURE 15.7
Sample Justification Report Focusing on Recommendations

MEMO

DATE: August 4, 1989
TO: Marshall Boswell, Plant Manager
FROM: Raymond Verdugo, Manufacturing Engineering
SUBJECT: Expansion of facial tissue production capacity

The steady increase in facial tissue sales is making it more difficult to keep our inventory levels where they should be for efficient distribution. Our back-order situation has become worse in recent months, and the marketing department is complaining about it. The new plant won't be ready until next March, so we can't expect any relief for at least ten months.

I've studied the product flow on our three facial tissue lines, and I believe we can increase capacity 22 percent by taking two short-term measures that do not require a significant investment:

1. Speed up cut-off machine on #1 line to eliminate bottleneck.
2. Eliminate the green, pine-scented tissue product.

SPEED UP #1 CUT-OFF MACHINE

The bottleneck on #1 line is the old Evans cut-off machine. This unit runs at a speed of only 200 packs per minute. The rest of the #1 line can handle 300 packs per minute, as can line #2.

I propose to speed up the Evans machine by installing a 20-horsepower motor to replace the old 15-horsepower motor, by thickening the transfer bolts, and by replacing two cams. Stress analysis shows that the machine can then safely be run at 300 packs per minute. This change will give us 50 percent more output on line #1 at a cost of roughly $6,500 and one day's lost production.

ELIMINATE GREEN, PINE-SCENTED TISSUE

Eliminating the green, pine-scented tissue is a sensitive subject. I'm aware of your running battle with marketing on this, but I'd like to urge you to try once again to get them to kill this product. When we run it on line #3, we can operate at only 120 packs per minute be-cause the tissue is weakened by the dye and pine perfume. The other colored tissues run on line #3 are capable of 200 packs per minute.

The green pine product constitutes only 4 percent of total tissue sales and, by marketing's own data, sells well only in Maine and northern Minnesota. I have to believe that those customers would buy one of our other colors if we pulled the green pine off the market. If you can swing this, I estimate that we can get another 9 percent out of line #3.

SUMMARY

I recommend the following steps:

1. Speed up #1 line cut-off machine; capital cost = $6,500; output increases from 200 to 300 packs/minute.
2. Eliminate green pine product on #3 line; cost = zero; output increases from 120 to 200 packs/minute.

for every situation. Often you can achieve better results by encouraging readers to weigh all the facts before you present your conclusions or recommendations.

There are four organizational plans for convincing skeptical readers that your conclusions and recommendations are well founded.

When you want your readers to concentrate on *why* your ideas make sense, your best bet is to let your logical arguments provide the structure for your report. The main points in your outline correspond to the main points in favor of your conclusions and recommendations. There are four basic organizational plans for arguing your case: the 2 + 2 = 4 approach, the chain reaction approach, the scientific method, and the yardstick approach. The best choice depends on the nature of the facts at your disposal. Essentially, you choose an organizational plan that matches the reasoning process you used to arrive at your conclusions.

The four approaches are not mutually exclusive. In analyzing a problem, you often pursue several lines of thought to arrive at a solution; you might want to lead readers along the same mental pathways in hopes they will follow you to the same conclusions. In a long report, particularly, you may find it convenient to use different organizational plans for different sections. Generally speaking, however, simplicity of organization is a virtue. You need a clear, comprehensible argument in order to convince skeptical readers to accept your conclusions or recommendations.

The 2 + 2 = 4 approach: A troubleshooting report

Use reasons as the main divisions in your outline to gradually build a case for your conclusions and recommendations.

Reports based on the accumulation of facts and figures are developed around a list of reasons that collectively add up to the main point you're trying to prove. Essentially, to persuade readers of your point of view, you demonstrate that 2 + 2 = 4. The main points in your outline are the main reasons behind your conclusions and recommendations. You support each of these reasons with the evidence you have collected during your analysis.

Gary Johansen, executive assistant to the president of a diversified company, was asked to prepare a memo analyzing the performance of the restaurant division. He was also asked to recommend what to do with it: continue the current course, sell off the chain, or remodel existing facilities and build new restaurants.

But Gary had a problem: "I knew that whatever I recommended would alienate somebody. My difficulties were compounded by the nature of the problem. I could have made a good case for any of the three options. But as an objective, neutral, and unbiased observer, I gradually came to a conclusion of my own: that we should sell some of the restaurants and use the proceeds to offset the cost of remodeling the remaining locations and adding new outlets. In writing my report, I decided that my strategy would be to build a case for this course of action by gradually presenting the various reasons that had emerged from my analysis of the options."

Gary's report is outlined in Figure 15.8. Notice the main idea: The company should strengthen the restaurant division by selling some facilities, upgrading others, and adding new sites. The main divisions of the outline are the reasons that support this recommendation.

When Gary translated the outline into a report, he changed the phrasing of the main points to reduce their immediate impact on readers. The table of contents showed five main sections, corresponding to the five roman numerals in the outline:

I. Introduction

II. Recent Performance of the Restaurant Division

III. Trends in the Restaurant Industry

IV. Analysis of Alternatives

V. Summary

Soften the force of controversial points

- By using descriptive (not informative) headings
- By writing a "neutral" introduction
- By placing recommendations at the end

By phrasing his thoughts as descriptive rather than informative headings, Gary gave his report a more objective flavor, which reassured his readers

FIGURE 15.8
Outline of a Troubleshooting Report Using the 2 + 2 = 4 Approach

Main idea: We should remodel selected restaurants and add some new locations, using funds generated by selling several existing sites.

I. Introduction
II. Reason: Although growth has slowed, the restaurant division shows underlying strength.
   A. Sales/profits have slipped, but division is still a major source of corporation's business.
   B. Slowdown is partially due to lower rate of restaurant start-ups.
   C. Older facilities have lost business, but newer locations have not.
   D. Patrons still like our formula.
III. Reason: The restaurant industry is entering a new phase, which can work to our advantage.
   A. Shakeout is likely; survivors will enjoy higher sales and profits.
   B. We are well positioned to survive the shakeout.
IV. Recommendation: Upgrade the chain by remodeling and adding restaurants in the Southeast; sell off older facilities to raise cash for reinvestment in better locations.
V. Summary

and prevented them from reacting negatively to ideas that had not yet been fully explained.

Figure 15.9 is a copy of Gary's report. Notice that the introduction does not reveal his position. Instead of summarizing his recommendations, he begins by discussing the report's purpose and scope, the background of the study, and his methods of research. In the body, he presents the facts in an objective tone, without revealing his own point of view. He saves his recommendations for the fourth section, where he finally adds up all the reasons (2 + 2 = 4).

The 2 + 2 = 4 approach works well when you have many reasons for your point of view but no single reason is overwhelming.

Organizing an analytical report around a list of reasons that collectively support your main conclusions or recommendations is a natural approach to take. Many problems are solved this way, and readers tend to accept the gradual accumulation of evidence, even though they may question one or two points. Because of its naturalness and versatility, the 2 + 2 = 4 approach is generally the most persuasive and efficient way to develop an analytical report for skeptical readers. In writing your own reports, this is the structure to try first. You will usually find that your arguments fall naturally into this pattern. However, not every problem or reporting situation can be handled with this organizational plan.

The chain reaction approach: A policy review

The chain reaction approach features a string of reasons that leads inevitably to your conclusions and recommendations.

In some reports, the reasons seem to proceed along a straight line from cause to effect, like a chain reaction: If *A* is true, then *B* is true; if *B* is true, then *C* must follow; and so on, until you have completed your argument. You begin a chain reaction report with an accepted fact or a definite goal, something readers will agree with. You proceed from there to unfold your argument step by step through a logical progression. Thus the order in which the reasons are given is crucial; the conclusions are simply the last link in the chain.

FIGURE 15.9
Sample Troubleshooting Report Using the 2 + 2 = 4 Approach

MEMO

DATE: March 27, 1989
TO: Alton Sanders, President
FROM: Gary Johansen, Executive Assistant to the President
SUBJECT: Possibilities for the Restaurant Division in the 1990s

INTRODUCTION

This report was authorized by President Alton Sanders on January 11, 1989. Its purpose is to analyze the performance of our restaurant division and to recommend a course of action. The analysis does not include institutional food-service operations.

The first Gateway restaurant was opened over 25 years ago in Falls Church, Virginia. Initially, the chain consisted of moderately priced cafeteria-style restaurants located in the suburbs of Washington, D.C. Encouraged by the success of these operations, Gateway management gradually expanded the chain into surrounding states, moving first into the Middle Atlantic and New England areas, then into the Southeast. As the chain grew, the cafeteria format was modified. Although some sites still feature a self-serve buffet, most of the restaurants now provide table service and a complete breakfast, lunch, and dinner menu.

Historically, the restaurant division has been one of Gateway's strongest operations, providing approximately 20 percent of the corporation's sales and 26 percent of its profits for much of the past decade. However, in the past two years the restaurant division's sales and profits have fallen below expectations. In an attempt to determine why, management has decided to take a closer look at the division's recent performance in light of trends in the restaurant industry as a whole. These issues are examined in the following sections. A final section analyzes the alternatives available to management and presents recommendations for the future.

In preparing this report, the study team analyzed internal data and reviewed published information pertaining to the restaurant industry. The team also analyzed demographic data furnished by the business development agencies of the 21 states in which Gateway restaurants are located. In addition, the team has interviewed over 50 restaurant owners and managers, politicians, civic leaders, and real estate professionals and has surveyed some 1,500 Gateway restaurant patrons.

RECENT PERFORMANCE OF THE RESTAURANT DIVISION

By historical standards, the restaurant division shows signs of slowing down. Instead of growing at the customary rate of 8 to 10 percent each year, the division's sales and profits have edged up by only 3 percent for the past two years (Figure 1).* Despite this leveling off, restaurant operations still account for approximately 25 percent of the corporation's business (Figure 2). Restaurant division sales in the most recent fiscal year totaled $44 million, and profits were $3.9 million.

A closer look at the division's financial results suggests that two internal factors are involved in the restaurant division's relatively slow growth:

*To conserve space, the figures are not included with this sample report.

Continued on next page

Terry Harmon is director of compensation for a company that manufactures a line of wallpapers and matching fabrics sold through independent interior decorating shops. Terry describes her report on sales force compensation policy this way: "My boss, the vice president of personnel, asked me to review the salaries and commissions that we pay our sales force, the people who call on the decorators who carry our lines. I concluded that we should make major changes in the compensation system, but I knew that my boss expected something quite different: a report that said

Figure continued from previous page

-2-

--In years past, the growth in sales and profits was fueled by the addition of new restaurants to the chain. However, in the past 2 years only three new restaurants have been opened. This record is less than half the average annual rate of openings throughout the 1970s and most of the 1980s (Figure 3).

--Performance has been uneven. Sales have declined in the Middle Atlantic and New England states, where facilities are aging, but sales have increased in the Southeast, where most of the newer restaurants are located (Figure 4).

These facts suggest that the leveling off in the restaurant division's growth is at least partially attributable to a lack of investment in the chain's facilities rather than to a fundamental weakness in the chain itself. In fact, a survey of Gateway patrons underscores the restaurants' continued popularity. Offering moderate prices in a pleasant, family-oriented environment still has broad appeal. (See Appendix A.)

TRENDS IN THE RESTAURANT INDUSTRY

Although Gateway's restaurant division appears to be fundamentally sound, the flattening of its growth curve reflects a slowdown in the restaurant industry as a whole. The rate of sales growth for full-service restaurants has fallen from 5 percent in the early 1980s to roughly 1.1 percent today (Figure 5).[1]

Many analysts contend that this slowing growth reflects a subtle shift in consumer behavior. In the 1970s and 1980s, as more women joined the work force, eating out became increasingly common, and restaurants sprang up to satisfy demand. In the past few years, however, the number of meals eaten in restaurants seems to have reached a plateau. Many people would rather pop a "gourmet" frozen dinner into the microwave and watch a movie on the VCR than pay restaurant prices.

Whatever the reasons, the leveling out of demand has left too many restaurants vying for too few patrons, a situation that spells trouble for many participants in the industry. Typically, when an industry has excess capacity, a shakeout period occurs; weaker companies fail and only the strong survive. Once the shakeout ends, the survivors generally enjoy a period of higher sales and profits.

If the restaurant industry follows the usual pattern, the small, independent restaurants will be most likely to fail. Larger chains can be expected to weather the shakeout because of their superior financial strength. Ultimately, the survivors will be the restaurants with the best locations and the most appealing combinations of food, price, atmosphere, and service.[2]

If a shakeout does occur, our restaurant division should be in a strong position, particularly in the Southeast. The division's facilities in this region are relatively new, and they are located in rapidly growing, affluent suburbs (Figure 6). Futhermore, Gateway patrons in the Southeast are particularly loyal, typically dining at a Gateway restaurant at least twice a month (Appendix A).

1. Steve Whitelaw, "Trends in the Restaurant Industry," speech delivered at the 1987 Western Restaurant Convention and Exposition, Los Angeles, California.
2. Conrad Hammond, "Recipes for Success in Restaurant Management," Restaurant News, December 1988, 24.

Continued on next page

our policy is fine but we need to add a little here and there to reflect changes in the cost of living. I figured that my report would have to be very convincing, so I decided to explain exactly how I had reached my conclusions."

The outline of Terry's report appears in Figure 15.10. The first major section focuses on issues related to sales force compensation in the company and in the industry. Nothing in this section is at all controversial. Terry's

Figure continued from previous page

-3-

ANALYSIS OF ALTERNATIVES

Management is considering three alternatives for the restaurant division:

--Continue to operate the existing restaurants, but minimize the capital reinvested in the business.
--Sell off the chain.
--Upgrade the chain by remodeling older facilities and adding new sites.

The first alternative is certainly viable. Although sales and profits have leveled off, the restaurant division is still a major source of earnings. One could argue that by maintaining the status quo, Gateway can generate approximately $4 million per year in cash to reinvest in other businesses with higher growth potential. On the other hand, without additional investment the restaurant division is likely to experience a further erosion as its aging facilities become less and less appealing to patrons.

The alternative of selling off the division is somewhat more appealing from a financial standpoint. Instead of gradually pulling cash out of the restaurant operation until the business deteriorates, Gateway could sell its holdings immediately while the business is still performing well. The restaurant operation has a market value of approximately $40 million, a sum that would go a long way toward funding management's diversification program. But selling the operation would mean the loss of about a quarter of our sales and profits. Unless management can immediately acquire a business of similar size, this loss would have a severe impact.

The third alternative is to expand and upgrade the restaurant operation in an effort to restore its historical growth pattern. According to division management, such a program would require an investment of approximately $22 million over the next three years for remodeling 20 of the older restaurants and adding 9 new sites (Figure 6). This expansion could result in a 10 percent annual growth in sales and a 12 percent annual growth in profits over the next five years (Figure 7).

The key stumbling block to this alternative is the required allocation of $22 million in investment capital. In the company's most recent strategic plan, management committed itself to a program of diversification into new, higher-growth businesses. The lion's share of the firm's investment funds is being channeled into new areas, leaving very little for shoring up existing operations.

One possible solution would be to sell off several of the restaurant division's existing sites, then use the money to refurbish other locations and add new restaurants to the chain. Discussions with real estate professionals suggest that a number of Gateway's older restaurants are located on land that has appreciated considerably in value. Many of these sites were purchased in the early 1970s, when land values were considerably lower than they are today. These same sites tend to be Gateway's oldest, least attractive restaurants, where sales have slipped most dramatically. As Figure 8 illustrates, by selling off 7 of the chain's 80 restaurants, Gateway could raise approximately $12.6 million, which is over half the amount required to fund the remodeling and expansion program. The remaining $9.4 million could be obtained by reinvesting the division's annual earnings for three years. Although selling the 7 sites would initially reduce the division's sales and earnings, over a five-year period the loss would be more than offset by gains from new and remodeled locations (Figure 9).

Continued on next page

readers were aware of these points and agreed with them, although they had not considered the implications for their own compensation system.

The second major section makes these implications clear. It is somewhat more controversial than the first section, but the logic is hard to resist. Terry is reasoning in a straight line, saying in so many words, "If this is true, then this must follow."

The final section, containing Terry's recommendations, is the most controversial part of the report. Once again, she builds on the chain of

Figure continued from previous page

-4-

SUMMARY

The restaurant division appears to be fundamentally sound. The fall-off in its sales and earnings growth is largely due to a reduction in the cash being reinvested in the business. Although the restaurant industry as a whole is maturing, strong chains like Gateway can expect to achieve continued growth in sales and profits as weaker operations fall by the wayside. By selling off some of its older, less appealing sites and using the cash to refurbish and expand the chain, the restaurant division can resume its historic growth pattern and continue to play a major role in the corporation.

logic. She makes specific recommendations that will satisfy the compensation requirements established in the previous section. Top management might argue with the specific dollar amounts, but they would have a hard time resisting Terry's basic concepts.

The success of the chain reaction approach depends on readers' acceptance of the first reason in the chain.

The chain reaction approach is very useful when you want to explain the rationale for conclusions and recommendations that are based on a series of related ideas. However, unless you can start with a set of facts that your readers will accept as being true, your whole argument will fall apart before it really gets under way. For this reason, you should use this structure for a report only when you have no other basis for convincing your readers of the validity of your conclusions.

The scientific method: A proposal

In organizing a report to reflect the scientific method, you discuss, one by one, hypothetical solutions to the problem.

When you are trying to discover whether an explanation is true, whether an option will solve your problem, or which one of several solutions will work best, you are likely to find the scientific method useful. Every day, hundreds of managers ask themselves, "What's wrong with this operation, and what should we do about it?" They approach the problem by coming up with one or several possible solutions (hypotheses), then doing experiments or gathering information to find the most effective one.

Reports based on the scientific method begin with a statement of the problem and a brief description of the hypothetical solution or a listing of possible solutions. In the body of the report, each alternative is discussed in turn, and evidence is offered that will either confirm the alternative or rule it out. Because many problems have multiple causes and complex solutions, several alternatives may be relevant. The final section of the report summarizes the findings and indicates which solution or solutions are valid. The report concludes with recommendations for solving the problem or eliminating the causes.

The scientific method, which is used in planning many studies, also provides a suitable outline for a proposal.

A variation of this pattern is often useful for the main section of a proposal. After defining the problem, you can suggest one or several solutions that you plan to investigate during the study. For each alternative, you explain why it may have a bearing on the problem and describe how you plan to investigate the issue. The next section of the proposal is a work plan showing the schedule for investigating each alternative. Additional sections describe your organization's past experience, facilities, personnel, and projected costs.

FIGURE 15.10
Outline of a Policy Review Using the Chain Reaction Approach

Main idea: The sales force compensation system requires fundamental changes.

I. Introduction

II. Starting point: We've got to have a good sales force to succeed in this business, but we have to control our compensation costs.
   A. Sales force relationships with decorators are key to success.
   B. Competition is increasing.
   C. Selling costs have major impact on profits.
   D. Sales force is growing.

III. Implications: Because of the nature of our selling environment, our compensation system has to do the following things:
   A. Reward activities that upgrade the sales force.
   B. Provide competitive cash compensation.
   C. Permit control over compensation costs and expense allowances.
   D. Offer specialized sales careers.
   E. Compensate sales management differently from sales personnel.

IV. Recommendations: To accomplish these things, we need to make major changes in our compensation system.
   A. Introduce salary grade and range system.
   B. Replace commissions with bonuses.
   C. Raise base salaries by 20 percent.
   D. Vary expense allowances by region.
   E. Introduce specialized career paths.
   F. Introduce standard compensation for regional managers.

An example of a proposal using the scientific method (see Figure 15.11) was prepared by John MacGregor, an account executive with an advertising agency. John's proposal was designed to win the advertising account for Cambridge, a soap introduced five years ago and promoted as a "family" soap: "Mom loves it because it's gentle; Dad loves its deodorant power; Suzie Teen-ager swears that it cures acne; and the little twins like the way it floats. By the end of the day, there's hardly any left for Grandma, who says it kills germs and costs less than other brands."

Despite the broad appeal, the public did not flock to the soap. The manufacturer, hoping to boost sales, asked John's agency to submit a proposal for developing a new advertising campaign. John explains: "We did some preliminary research, which revealed that the public buys soap for special qualities, not for versatility, so we decided to propose that the company market the product as a special-interest soap. The trouble was, everybody in the company had a different idea of which special quality to promote.

"But I knew what I wanted the client to do," John says. "I wanted them to promote Cambridge as the premium-priced soap for people who care about their bodies, people who drink Perrier, wear Reebok running shoes, jog three times a week, and drive a Mercedes-Benz. My theory was that if you can charge twice as much for your soap, you can afford to sell only half as many bars as your competitors."

Even though John had a strong case for his position, he couldn't boldly state his arguments without first acknowledging the merits of other ideas.

FIGURE 15.11
Outline of a Proposal Using the Scientific Method

Main idea: The client should market the soap as a premium-priced product for people who care about their bodies.

I. Statement of problem and purpose of proposal

II. Scope of work

III. Analysis of advertising concepts
- A. Alternative 1: Focus on purity of ingredients
  1. Basic idea--the "natural" motif
  2. Pros--approach is appealing to mothers, young adults
  3. Cons--competition from Ivory and Neutrogena would be hard to beat
- B. Alternative 2: Focus on deodorant protection
  1. Basic idea--the "macho-man" motif
  2. Pros--appeals to working-class men and teen-agers
  3. Cons--since women buy most of the soap, this concept has limited appeal; competition is heavy
- C. Alternative 3: Focus on complexion care
  1. Basic idea--moisture and/or cleansing power
  2. Pros--appeals to women and teen-agers
  3. Cons--strong competition from Noxzema, Dove, Phase III
- D. Alternative 4: Focus on scent, size, shape, color of soap
  1. Basic idea--physical qualities of soap
  2. Pros--Zest and Softsoap have succeeded with this approach
  3. Cons--hard to come up with the right feature (soap is soap)
- E. Alternative 5: Focus on high-priced, premium health image
  1. Basic idea--the "beautiful, healthy, rich" pitch
  2. Pros--market segment is growing rapidly; no single strong competitor; very high profit margins
  3. Cons--none apparent

IV. Methods and procedures for testing ad campaign
- A. Establish research objectives
- B. Conduct market survey
- C. Analyze competitors
- D. Develop preliminary ad campaign
- E. Conduct in-store tests

V. Work plan and schedule
- A. Schedule of tasks
- B. Project administration

VI. Qualifications
- A. Previous experience in consumer product advertising
- B. Resumes of key personnel

VII. Projected costs

When readers have their own ideas about how to solve a problem, you have to discuss those notions before you can sell your own solution.

"I decided to use a very balanced strategy in my proposal," he recalls. "I started with a complete review of the problem. Then I went through five competing advertising concepts, explained each one in detail, and examined whether each did or did not solve the problem. Ultimately, of course, I concluded that my approach was the best solution."

John's approach, analyzing each alternative, is very useful when you are trying to unify a divided audience. Your chances of bringing about a consensus are much better when you show the strengths and weaknesses of all the ideas. The main drawback to the scientific method is that many of the alternatives may turn out to be irrelevant or unproductive, but you have to discuss them all. And the more ideas you discuss, the more confused your readers may become and the more trouble they may have comparing pros and cons.

The yardstick approach: A research report

One way to reduce the confusion presented by having a lot of alternatives is to establish a yardstick for evaluating all of them. You begin by discussing the problem, as with the scientific method, but you then set up the conditions that must be met to solve the problem. These are the criteria against which you evaluate all possible solutions. The body of the report is devoted to an evaluation of those alternatives in relation to the criteria. The main points of the outline are either the criteria themselves or the alternatives.

In the yardstick approach, the report is organized around criteria; the solution is the alternative that best meets the criteria.

Yardstick reports are similar in some respects to those based on the scientific method, but in criteria-based reports each alternative is reviewed against the same standards. Another distinction is that criteria-based reports can be used to prove the need for action: The present situation can be measured against the criteria and shown to be wanting.

Some proposals are best organized by using the client's criteria as the main points.

The yardstick approach is useful for certain kinds of proposals, because the client who requests the proposal often provides a list of criteria that the solution must meet. Say, for example, that your company has been asked to bid on a contract to install a computer for a large corporation. The client has listed the requirements (criteria) for the system, and you have developed a preliminary design to meet them. In the body of your proposal, you could use the client's list of requirements as the main headings and, under each one, explain how your preliminary design meets the requirement.

The following example of a yardstick report was provided by Larry Hagen, director of new-business development for the medical products division of a large midwestern corporation. He explains: "My boss, the vice president of the division, asked me to prepare a plan for expanding our business into high-growth market segments. Our basic medical products were pretty ordinary: plastic tubing, stuff like that. It was obvious that we needed to get into higher-technology market segments, and I was delighted when my boss asked me to write a formal new-business plan."

Figure 15.12 shows the organization of Larry's report. The first section establishes six criteria for evaluating specific opportunities. The second section discusses trends in the health-care field that provide clues to new businesses; it identifies the surgical procedures, medical specialties, and hospital departments with the highest growth rates.

Analyzing these trends, Larry selected five market areas as being particularly attractive. He then prepared a profile showing how each of the five areas met the criteria established in the first major section. The final section was devoted to specific plans for pursuing the most attractive new businesses and for identifying other promising opportunities.

For the yardstick approach to work, readers must accept your criteria.

Using the yardstick approach is generally a useful way to show the soundness of an approach, by itself or in relation to alternatives. It's also useful when you're trying to persuade someone to take action in the first place. On the other hand, yardstick reports can backfire if readers disagree with your criteria. For this reason, the yardstick approach works best when you know in advance that your criteria will be acceptable or when you consciously want to stimulate discussion about them.

FIGURE 15.12
Outline of a Research Report Using the Yardstick Approach

Main Idea: We should diversify into high-technology medical products through internal development and acquisitions.

I. Introduction

II. Criteria for choosing new-business opportunities
- A. Market growth
- B. Profit potential
- C. Significant size
- D. Superior products
- E. Competitive advantages
- F. Good fit with current capabilities

III. Health-care trends
- A. Fastest-growing surgical and diagnostic procedures
- B. Fastest-growing hospital departments
- C. Fastest-growing medical specialties

IV. Specific new-business opportunities
- A. Respiratory therapy
  1. Market growth
  2. Profit potential
  3. Size
  4. Product qualities
  5. Possible competitive advantages
  6. Fit with current capabilities
- B. Hemodialysis [evaluated in terms of A-1 through A-6]
- C. Emergency care [evaluated in terms of A-1 through A-6]
- D. Cardiac care [evaluated in terms of A-1 through A-6]
- E. Burn care [evaluated in terms of A-1 through A-6]

V. Recommendations
- A. Begin action programs in selected areas
  1. Hemodialysis
  2. Cardiac care
- B. Analyze additional areas
- C. Establish sources of new business leads

Tables are useful in the yardstick approach
- To avoid repetition
- To make the options easier to compare

The yardstick approach has one other drawback: It can be a little boring. You will find yourself saying the same things over and over again: "Opportunity *A* has high growth potential; opportunity *B* has high growth potential; opportunity *C* has high growth potential." And so on. One way to minimize the repetition is to compare the options in tables and then highlight the more unusual or important aspects of each alternative in the body. Thus you get the best of both worlds. You compare all the alternatives against the same yardstick but call attention to the most significant differences among them.

MAKING REPORTS AND PROPOSALS READABLE

Choosing format, length, and a basic organizational plan for your report is an important set of decisions. But a number of other decisions also affect the way your report will be received and understood by readers.

CHOOSING THE PROPER DEGREE OF FORMALITY

Write informal reports in a personal style, using the pronouns *I* and *you.*

The issue of formality is closely related to considerations of format, length, and organization. If you know your readers reasonably well and if your report is likely to meet with their approval, you can generally adopt an informal tone. In other words, you can speak to readers in the first person, referring to yourself as *I* and to your readers as *you*. This informal, personal approach is often used in brief memo or letter reports, although there are many exceptions.

Being formal means putting your readers at a distance and establishing an objective, businesslike relationship.

Longer reports dealing with controversial or complex information are traditionally handled in a more formal vein, particularly if the audience is a group of outsiders. You achieve this formal tone by using the impersonal style, eliminating all references to *I* (including *we, us,* and *our*) and *you.* The style is borrowed from journalism, which stresses the reporter's objectivity. However, avoiding personal pronouns may lead to overuse of such phrases as "there is" and "it is," which are not only dull but also wordy.

But formality is more than a matter of personal pronouns; it is a question of your relationship with your audience. When you write in a formal style, you impose a certain distance between you and your readers. You remain businesslike, unemotional, and objective. You use no jokes, no similes or metaphors, and very few colorful adjectives or adverbs. You eliminate your own subjective opinions and perceptions and retain only the objective facts.

You are not being objective if you

- Omit crucial evidence
- Use exaggerated language

The formal style does not guarantee objectivity, however. In determining the fairness of a report, the selection of facts is far more important than the way they are phrased. If you omit crucial evidence, you are not being objective, even though you are using an impersonal style.

In addition, you can easily destroy objectivity by exaggerating and using overblown language: "The catastrophic collapse in sales, precipitated by cutthroat pricing on the part of predatory and unscrupulous rivals, has jeopardized the very survival of the once-soaring hot-air balloon division." This sentence has no personal references, but its objectivity is highly questionable.

Although the impersonal style has disadvantages, you should use it if your readers expect it.

Despite these limitations, the impersonal style is a well-entrenched tradition. Many readers are uncomfortable with informality in a report. They associate the personal tone with sloppy thinking, lack of objectivity, and excessive familiarity. You can often tell what tone is appropriate for your readers by looking at other reports of a similar type in your company. If all the other reports on file are impersonal, you should probably adopt the same tone yourself, unless you are confident that your readers prefer a more personal style. Most organizations, for whatever reasons, expect an unobtrusive, impersonal writing style for business reports.

ESTABLISHING A TIME PERSPECTIVE

Be consistent in the verb tense you use.

In addition to deciding on the formality of your report, you must also decide on the time frame. Will you write in the past or present tense? The person who wrote this paragraph never decided:

Twenty-five percent of those interviewed report that they are dissatisfied with their present brand. The wealthiest participants complained most frequently, but all income categories are interested in trying a new brand. Only 5 percent of the interviewees say they had no interest in alternative products.

By flipping from tense to tense in describing the same research results, the writer only confuses readers. Is the shift significant, they wonder? Or is the writer just being sloppy with the time perspective? Such confusion can be eliminated by using either the past or present tense consistently.

Follow a proper chronological sequence in your report.

You should also be careful to observe the chronological sequence of events in your report. If you're describing the history or development of something, start at the beginning and cover each event in the order of its occurrence. If you're explaining the steps in a process, take each step in proper sequence.

DEVELOPING STRUCTURAL CLUES

FIGURE 15.13
Differences in the Perspective of Writer and Reader

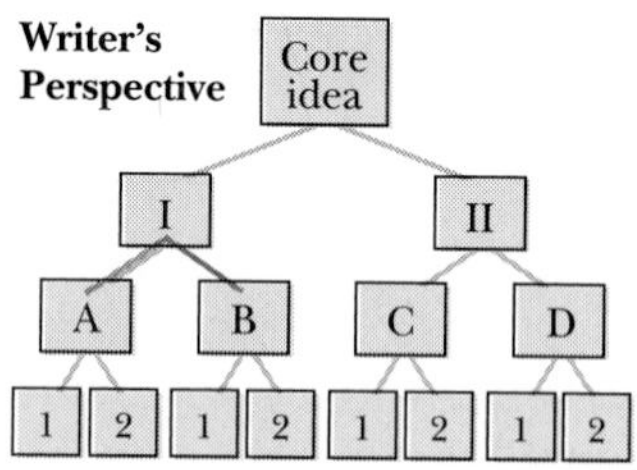

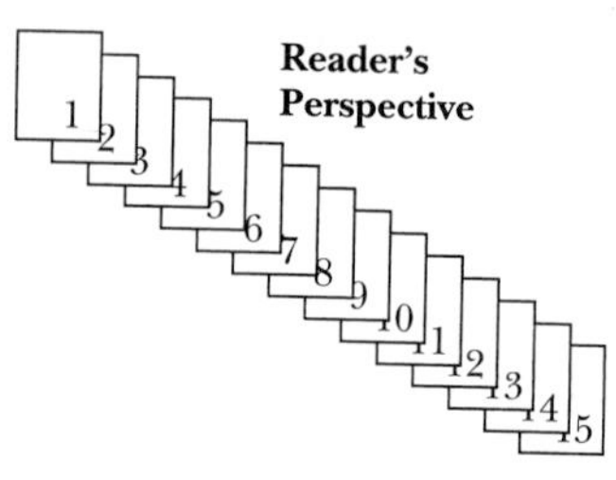

As you begin to write, remember that readers have no concept of how the various pieces of your report relate to one another. Because you have done the work and outlined the report, you have a sense of its wholeness and see how each page fits into the overall structure; but readers see the report one page at a time. (Figure 15.13 illustrates these differences in perspective.) Your job, as you begin to write, is to give readers a preview or road map of the report's structure so they too will see how the parts of your argument relate to one another.

In a short report, readers are in little danger of getting lost. But as the length of a report increases, so do readers' opportunities for becoming confused and losing track of the relationship among ideas. If you want readers to understand and accept your message, you must prevent this confusion. Four tools are particularly useful for giving readers a sense of the overall structure of your document and for keeping them on track as they read along: the opening, headings and lists, smooth transitions, and the ending.

The opening

A good opening must do at least three things:

- Introduce the subject of the report
- Indicate why the subject is important
- Give readers a preview of the main ideas and the order in which they will be covered

In the opening, tell readers what to expect, and orient them toward your organizational plan.

If you fail to provide readers with these clues to the structure of your report, they will read aimlessly and miss important points, much like drivers trying to find their way through a strange city without a map.

If your audience is skeptical, the opening should downplay the controversial aspects of your message while providing the necessary framework for understanding your report. Here's a good example of an indirect opening, taken from the introduction of a controversial memo on why a new line of luggage has failed to sell well. The writer's ultimate goal is to recommend a shift in marketing strategy.

SHARPEN YOUR SKILLS

Writing Headings That Spark Reader Interest

Headings help readers follow the main points presented in your report. But when carefully developed, they can do much more. They can capture the readers' attention and interest, inform them, and make them want to read the whole report.

Each heading offers you an opportunity to make an important point. For example, instead of "Introduction," your opening section might be called "An Insight into the Need." This title catches the eye and sparks interest. The title "Chart of Proposed Organization" gains impact when reworded "Organization for Results." So does "Cost Considerations" when retitled "A New Way to Cut Costs."

Headings fall into two categories. Descriptive (topical) headings, such as "Cost Considerations," identify a topic but do little more. However, they are fine for routine reports and in controversial reports, where they may defuse emotional reactions. Informative (talking) headings, such as "A New Way to Cut Costs," convey more information about the main theme or idea of the report. They are helpful because they guide readers to think in a certain way about the topic. For more effective reports, concentrate on developing informative headings rather than descriptive ones. However, be aware that informative headings are more difficult to create.

Try to avoid vague headings. In a chronological history of your company, for example, headings such as "The Dawning of a New Era" and "The Times They Are a-Changin' " may be cute, but readers will have no idea what time period you are referring to. Preferable would be headings along the lines of "The War Years: Gebco Outfits Our GIs" or "The 1970s See International Expansion."

Whatever types of headings you choose, try to keep them grammatically parallel. For example, this series of headings is parallel: "Cutting Costs," "Reducing Inventory," "Increasing Profits." This series of headings is not: "Cutting Costs," "Inventory Reduction," "How to Increase Profits."

1. Think about the headlines in a newspaper. What functions do they perform? How are they usually phrased? What can you learn from journalistic headlines that applies to report writing?

2. For practice in writing headings, collect some brochures, newsletters, or similar items and rewrite the headings to convey more information about the theme or main idea. Can you draw any conclusions about what works best?

In the two years since its introduction, the Venturer line has failed to achieve the sales volume that we expected. The disappointing performance of this product line is a drain on the company's total earnings. The purpose of this report is to review the luggage-buying habits of consumers in all markets where the Venturer line is sold so we can determine where to put our marketing emphasis.

This paragraph quickly introduces the subject of the document (disappointing sales), tells why the problem is important (drain on earnings), and indicates the main points to be addressed in the body of the report (review of markets where the Venturer line is sold), without revealing what the conclusions and recommendations will be.

Headings and lists

Use headings to give readers the gist of your report.

Headings are useful markers for clarifying the framework of a report. They visually indicate shifts from one idea to the next, and when subheadings and headings are both used, they help readers see the relationship between subordinate and main ideas. In addition, busy readers can quickly understand the gist of a document by simply scanning the headings.

Phrase all same-level headings within a section in parallel terms.

Headings within a given section that are of the same level of importance should be phrased in parallel form. In other words, if one heading begins with a verb, all same-level headings in that section should begin with verbs. If one is a noun phrase, all should be noun phrases. Putting comparable ideas in similar terms tells readers that the ideas are related. The only exception might be such descriptive headings as "Introduction" at the beginning of a report and "Conclusions" and "Recommendations" at the end.

Many companies specify a format for headings. If yours does, use that format. Otherwise, you can use the scheme shown in Figure 15.14.

Use lists to set off important ideas and show sequence.

Setting off important ideas in a list provides an additional structural clue. Lists can show the sequence of ideas or visually heighten their impact. Like headings, list items should be phrased in parallel form.

Transitions

Such phrases as "to continue the analysis," "on the other hand," and "an additional concept" are another type of structural clue. Transitions like these tie ideas together and keep readers moving along the right track.

Use transitions consisting of a single word, a few words, or a whole paragraph to provide additional structural clues.

Here is a list of some words and phrases frequently used to provide continuity between parts of sentences and paragraphs:

Additional detail	moreover, furthermore, in addition, besides, first, second, third, finally
Causal relationship	therefore, because, accordingly, thus, consequently, hence, as a result, so
Comparison	similarly, here again, likewise, in comparison, still
Contrast	yet, conversely, whereas, nevertheless, on the other hand, however, but, nonetheless
Condition	although, if
Illustration	for example, in particular, in this case, for instance
Time sequence	formerly, after, when, meanwhile, sometimes
Intensification	indeed, in fact, in any event
Summary	in brief, in short, to sum up
Repetition	that is, in other words, as has been stated

Although transitional words and phrases are useful, they are not sufficient in themselves to overcome poor organization. Your goal is first to put your ideas in a strong framework and then to use transitions to link them together even more strongly.

In longer reports, transitions that link major sections or chapters are often complete paragraphs that serve as mini-introductions to the next section or as summaries of the ideas presented in the section just ending. Here's an example:

Given the nature of this problem, the alternatives are limited. As the following section indicates, we can stop making the product, improve it, or continue with the current model. Each of these alternatives has advantages and disadvantages. [The following section discusses pros and cons of each of the three alternatives.]

FIGURE 15.14
Heading Formats for Reports

TITLE

The title is centered at the top of the page, underlined, and typed in capital letters. When the title runs to more than one line, the lines should usually be double-spaced and arranged as an inverted pyramid (longer line on the top).

FIRST-LEVEL HEADING

A first-level heading should indicate what the following section is about, perhaps by describing the subdivisions. All first-level headings should be grammatically parallel, with the possible exception of such headings as "Introduction," "Conclusions," and "Recommendations." Some text should appear between every two headings, regardless of their levels.

Second-Level Heading

Like first-level headings, second-level headings should indicate what the following material is about. All second-level headings within a section should be grammatically parallel. Never use only one second-level heading under a first-level heading. (The same is true for every other level of heading.)

Third-Level Heading

A third-level heading should be worded to reflect the content of the material that follows. All third-level headings beneath a second-level heading should be grammatically parallel.

Fourth-Level Heading. Like all the other levels of heading, fourth-level headings should reflect the subject that will be developed. All fourth-level headings within a subsection should be parallel.

Fifth-level headings are generally the lowest level of heading used. However, you can indicate further breakdowns in your ideas by using a list:

1. The first item in a list. You may indent the entire item in block format to set it off visually. Numbers are optional.
2. The second item in a list. All lists should have at least two items. An introductory phrase or sentence may be underlined for emphasis, as shown here.

The ending

Reemphasize your main ideas in the ending.

Research shows that the final section of a report leaves a strong and lasting impression, so use the ending to emphasize the main thrust of your message. In a report written in direct order, you may want to remind readers once again of your key points or your conclusions and recommendations. If your report is written in indirect order, you should end (except in short memos) with a summary of key points. In analytical reports you should end with conclusions and recommendations as well as key points.

In general, the ending ties up all the pieces and reminds readers how those pieces fit together. It provides a final opportunity to emphasize the wholeness of your message.

CHECKLIST FOR SHORT, INFORMAL REPORTS

A. Format

- ☐ 1. For brief external reports, use letter format, including a title or a subject line after the reader's address that clearly states the subject of the document.
- ☐ 2. For brief internal reports, use memo or manuscript format.
- ☐ 3. Present all short, informal reports properly.
  - ☐ a. Single-space the text.
  - ☐ b. Double-space between paragraphs.
  - ☐ c. Use headings where helpful, but try not to use more than three levels of headings.
  - ☐ d. Call attention to significant information by setting it off visually with lists or indention.
  - ☐ e. Include visual aids to emphasize and clarify the text.

B. Opening

- ☐ 1. For short, routine memos, use the subject line of the memo form and the first sentence or two of the text as the introduction.
- ☐ 2. For all other short reports, cover these topics in the introduction: purpose, scope, background, limitations (restrictions in conducting the study), sources of information and methods of research, and organization of the report.
- ☐ 3. If using direct order, place conclusions and recommendations in the opening.

C. Body (Findings and Supporting Details)

- ☐ 1. Use direct order for informational reports to receptive readers, developing ideas around subtopics (for example, chronologically, geographically, categorically).
- ☐ 2. Use direct order for analytical reports to receptive readers, developing points around conclusions or recommendations.
- ☐ 3. Use indirect order for analytical reports to skeptical or hostile readers, developing points around logical arguments.
- ☐ 4. Use an appropriate writing style.
  - ☐ a. Use an informal style (*I* and *you*) for letter and memo reports, unless company custom calls for the impersonal third person.
  - ☐ b. Use an impersonal style for more formal short reports in manuscript format.
- ☐ 5. Maintain a consistent time frame by writing in either the present or the past tense, using other tenses only to indicate prior or future events.
- ☐ 6. Give each paragraph a topic sentence.
- ☐ 7. Link paragraphs by using transitional words and phrases.
- ☐ 8. Strive for readability by using short sentences, concrete words, and terminology that is appropriate for your readers.
- ☐ 9. Be accurate, thorough, and impartial in presenting the material.
- ☐ 10. Avoid including irrelevant and unnecessary details.
- ☐ 11. Include documentation for all material quoted or paraphrased from secondary sources, using a consistent format.

D. Ending

- ☐ 1. In informational reports, summarize major findings at the end if you wish.
- ☐ 2. Summarize points in the same order in which they appear in the text.
- ☐ 3. In analytical reports using indirect order, list conclusions and recommendations at the end.
- ☐ 4. Be certain that conclusions and recommendations follow logically from facts presented in the text.
- ☐ 5. Consider using a list format for emphasis.
- ☐ 6. Avoid introducing new material in the summary, conclusions, or recommendations.

SUMMARY

Preparing the final draft of a report involves decisions on length, format, and organization. Short, informal reports often take the form of memos or letters; longer, more formal reports are presented in manuscript form.

When readers are receptive or open-minded, you may present your ideas in direct order, with the main point first. When readers are hostile or skeptical, use indirect order, with key findings, conclusions, and recommendations last. Informational reports are organized around subtopics. Analytical reports are organized around conclusions or recommendations or around a logical argument, such as the 2 + 2 = 4 approach, the chain reaction approach, the scientific method, or the yardstick approach.

The task of organizing a report is not complete until you decide on the proper degree of formality, establish a time perspective, and develop such structural clues as an opening, headings, lists, transitions, and an ending.

COMMUNICATION CHALLENGES AT MAYTAG

Consumer reaction to The Maytag Company's stacked washer-dryer combination has been uneven. Although sales have been disappointing in the eastern division, they have met projections in the northern, western, and central divisions. The product has performed particularly well in the Sunbelt, where many retirees have purchased the appliances for condominiums or small retirement houses.

Individual Challenge: One of Maytag's major shareholders, who happens to live in the eastern division, carried her proprietary interest in the new washer-dryer combination to the extent of trying to buy a set. The results shook her confidence in the company. In a long, rambling letter to Maytag's president, she made several complaints: Only two of the six dealers she contacted were even familiar with the product; the two that were had limited stock on hand and claimed that delivery would take more than a month; salesclerks hinted that she would be unhappy with the product and might prefer something "more traditional." She ended her letter with a deceptively simple question: "Why did you decide to go ahead with a product that no one appears to want and that seems to have a reputation for inferiority?"

Maytag's president has decided to respond with a personal letter explaining how well researched the decision to market the product was and how encouraging the results have been in most areas. He has asked Bill Beer to provide a brief report on the research process and the decision to proceed with the stacked washer-dryer combination. Bill delegates to you responsibility for preparing an outline that someone else can then flesh out. Keep in mind that the resulting report will be dropped, virtually intact, into the president's letter to the shareholder. Along with the outline, prepare a memo to Bill explaining your choice of organizational scheme.

Team Challenge: The product manager for the washer-dryer combination decided to attack poor sales in the eastern division by trying to increase sales to apartment developers in major eastern cities. He was highly enthusiastic about the concept, but he encountered some resistance in discussing the proposal with other Maytag executives. Several objected that the apartment market is too small; others raised the point that apartment owners are likely to demand price concessions. Now the product manager has invited a team of you to help him develop a report that will convince Maytag's top management to approve the effort to woo apartment developers. Begin by developing a question-and-answer chain. If you have unanswered questions, do some research. After deciding on the format, length, organization, and style of the report, design an outline and write the introduction.

QUESTIONS FOR DISCUSSION

1. What factors might influence your decision to use memo format rather than manuscript format for a short report?
2. Should a report always explain the writer's method of gathering evidence or solving a problem? Why or why not?
3. What are the advantages and disadvantages of the direct and the indirect approaches?
4. How can a writer achieve an indirect tone in a report?
5. What strategic considerations encourage use of the 2 + 2 = 4 approach?
6. What is the main danger in using the chain reaction approach?
7. What is the main drawback to using the scientific method?
8. What is the most vulnerable part of a report organized according to the yardstick approach?
9. Why do some companies require an impersonal tone in their reports? What are the advantages and disadvantages of such a tone?
10. How can a writer help readers understand the structure of a report?

EXERCISES

1. Locate an article of interest to you in a recent business publication, such as the *Wall Street Journal, Business Week, Fortune,* or *Forbes*. The article should contain at least 500 words and should preferably draw conclusions. If conclusions are not included, draw your own. Then, ignoring the article's actual organization, construct an outline of the material, using (a) direct order and (b) indirect order.
2. Make a list of five business situations or problems for which periodic reports would be written. Describe the purpose of each report, how often it would be submitted, what kinds of information would be included, and how it would be used in the decision-making process of a company.
3. Locate a business publication that has an article reporting in detail on a conference or convention. Write an outline for a personal report on the conference or convention as if you had attended yourself.
4. For each of the organizational approaches that follow, identify a business problem that could be reported using it. In each case, state the situation, the audience, and the main idea of the report.
   a. Organization based on conclusions
   b. Organization based on recommendations
   c. The 2 + 2 = 4 approach
   d. The chain reaction approach
   e. The scientific method
   f. The yardstick approach
5. Select a topic for an analytical report that you feel would best be organized by focusing on conclusions. Write out the main idea, and draft an informative outline with first- and second-level headings.
6. Select a topic for an analytical report that you feel would best be organized by focusing on recommendations. Write out the main idea, and draft an informative outline with first- and second-level headings.
7. Select a topic for an analytical report that you feel would best be organized by using the 2 + 2 = 4 approach. Write out the main idea, and draft an informative outline with first- and second-level headings.
8. Select a topic for an analytical report that you feel would best be organized by using the chain reaction approach. Write out the main idea, and draft an informative outline with first- and second-level headings.
9. Select a topic for an analytical report that you feel would best be organized by using the scientific method. Write out the main idea, and draft an informative outline with first- and second-level headings.
10. Select a topic for an analytical report that you feel would best be organized by using the yardstick approach. Write out the main idea, and draft an informative outline with first- and second-level headings.

CASES

INFORMAL INFORMATIONAL REPORTS

1. My progress to date: Periodic report on your academic career As you know, the bureaucratic process involved in getting a degree or certificate is nearly as challenging as any course you could take.

Your task: Prepare a periodic report detailing the steps you've taken toward completing your graduation or certification requirements. After examining the requirements listed in your college catalog, indicate a realistic schedule for completing those that remain. In addition to course requirements, include such steps as completing the residency requirement, filing necessary papers, and paying necessary fees. Use memo format for your report, and address it to anyone who is helping or encouraging you through school.

2. That's class: Personal report on class activities You may have experienced a peculiar or particularly interesting discussion in class sometime and had trouble telling friends why it was so notable. Here's your chance to practice.

Your task: Prepare a memo, addressed to a friend, about the discussion in one of your classes. Use made-up names to identify the instructor and students. Try to show how ideas took shape and what conclusions resulted from this discussion.

3. Gavel to gavel: Personal report of a meeting Meetings, conferences, and conventions abound in the academic world, and you have probably attended your share.

Your task: Prepare a report on a meeting, convention, or conference that you have recently attended. Use memo format, and direct the report to other students in your field who were not able to attend.

INFORMAL ANALYTICAL REPORTS

4. A new venture: Report organized around conclusions Read the classified ads in your local newspaper. Select a business for sale or a business opportunity.

Your task: Write a memo to yourself evaluating the item you read in the classifieds, assuming you had the money required for the venture. Call the person running the ad to get the information you need to complete this assignment.

5. My next career move: Report organized around recommendations If you've ever given yourself a good talking to, you'll be quite comfortable with this project.

Your task: Write a memo report directed to yourself and signed with a fictitious name. Indicate a possible job that your college education will qualify you for, mention the advantages of the position in terms of your long-range goals, and then outline the actions you must take to get the job.

6. A step toward simplification: Report using the 2 + 2 = 4 approach In modern life, policies and procedures abound. Whether at school or on the job, you have undoubtedly run across several.

Your task: Choose a policy or procedure that you are familiar with. Justify the adoption, modification, or elimination of it to an appropriate individual, using memo format.

7. Making it salable: Report using the chain reaction approach Your friend John is trying to sell his car, a 1967 red Mustang convertible. This car is John's favorite possession. He hates to sell it, but he is desperate for cash to complete his education. In his eyes, the car is perfect. But you know that it has a few little quirks. For example, the roof does not work properly; the left door does not open and close; the upholstery on the back seat is in poor condition. Because you care for your friend, you want him to get the best possible price for his car. You want to convince him to make a few basic repairs before he tries to sell it, but you know that he will resist your advice. He will claim that the car is beautiful just the way it is, that he can't afford to take the car in for repairs, and that he doesn't have enough time to make them himself.

Your task: Write a memo that will convince John to follow your advice. As a point of departure in establishing your chain of logic, begin with this point: The reason for selling the car is to get as much cash as possible by the time tuition is due (in about four weeks). In your memo, complete the chain of logic that will lead John to make the necessary repairs.

8. Planning my program: Report using the scientific method Assume that you will have time for only one course next term.

Your task: List the pros and cons of four or five courses that interest you, and use the scientific method to settle on the course that is best for you to take at this time. Write in memo format, addressing the memo to your academic adviser.

9. Section A, Section B: Report using the yardstick approach Choose a course that is taught by at least two different instructors at two different times, either one that you actually need to take or one that interests you. Which section should you enroll in?

Your task: Write a memo to your academic adviser that explains which section you plan to enroll in and why you chose it. Use three or four important criteria as a basis for analyzing the different sections or instructors.

10. "Would you carry it?" Sales proposal recommending a product to a retail outlet Select a product you are familiar with, and imagine that you are the manufacturer trying to get a local retail outlet to carry it.

Your task: Write a sales proposal in letter format to the owner (or manager) of the store, proposing that the item be stocked. Making up some reasonable figures, tell what the item costs, what it can be sold for, and what services your company provides (return of unsold items, free replacement of unsatisfactory items, necessary repairs, and the like).

11. Expanding operations: Justification report for business expansion Consider a job that you now hold or have held in the past. Imagine an expansion of the company's business, possibly addition of a new product line or new services (for example, adding brake repairs to a shop that currently only replaces mufflers).

Your task: Develop a budget for the enlarged operation, considering personnel, equipment, space, and possibly inventory. Next, write a report explaining your concept, describing the major budget items, and briefly predicting the future benefits that this expansion will bring. Write your report in memo format to the owner or manager of the business.

SHORT, INFORMAL REPORTS

12. Selling something special: Proposal to a business Pick a company or business that you know something about. Now think of a customized item or service that you believe the business needs. Examples might be a specially designed piece of equipment, a workshop for employees on improving their communication skills, a program for curtailing shoplifting, a catering service to a company's construction site, or a customized word-processing system, to name just a few possibilities.

Your task: Write a proposal directed to the owners or managers of this business. Persuade them that they need the product you're selling. Include a statement of the problem, purpose (benefits), scope (areas in which your product will help the business), methods and procedures, work plan and schedule, your qualifications, projected costs, and any other pertinent information. Use letter format.

13. Who's best? Report comparing job candidates Imagine that you're the interviewer for a company you have selected. You have just interviewed three people for the position of personnel management trainee.

Your task: Write a report in memo format to Mona Martin, director of personnel. In it, you must describe the three candidates (use three friends) and recommend them, in rank order, for the position. Consider at least the following areas for comparison: education, experience, and personal attributes.

14. Restaurant review: Report on a restaurant's food and operations Visit any restaurant, possibly your school cafeteria. The workers and fellow customers will assume that you are an ordinary customer, but you are really a spy for the owner.

Your task: After your visit, write a short memo to the owner, explaining (a) what you did and what you observed, (b) any violations of policy that you observed, and (c) your recommendations for improvement. The first part of your report (what you did and what you observed) will be the longest. Include a description of the premises, inside and out. Tell how long the various steps of ordering and receiving your meal took. Describe the service and food thoroughly. You are interested in both the good and bad aspects of the establishment's decor, service, and food. For the second section (violations of policy), you must use some common sense. If all the servers but one have their hair covered, you may assume that policy requires hair to be covered; a dirty window or restroom obviously violates policy. The last section (recommendations for improvement) involves professional judgment. What management actions will improve the restaurant?

15. Taste test: Report on the results of consumer research Here's your chance to check the advertising claims of soft-drink manufacturers. Blindfold four or five friends (one at a time), and ask them to taste several competing soft drinks.

Your task: After you have conducted the test, write a memo that summarizes your findings. Could your friends tell the difference between the soft drinks? If so, how did they describe the difference? Did they seem to prefer one of the brands? Did the order in which they tested the drinks seem to have any bearing on the results? You might also address the problem of whether soft drinks without sugar or caffeine taste as good to your friends as drinks containing these ingredients.

16. Mansfield Center or Cat Spring? Report comparing potential plant locations Current plant capabilities are inadequate for manufacturing Victory Valve's new line of gate valves, globe valves, check valves, ball valves, and butterfly valves. The company is seeking a new location removed from the strains of rapid urbanization and union pressures but still close to potential markets. Two locations have been proposed: Mansfield Center, Connecticut, and Cat Spring, Texas. Fellow members of the site-selection committee (you're in charge) submitted the following raw data about these two locations:

- *Mansfield Center, Connecticut.* An attractive town of about 5,000 near the Mansfield Hollow Reservoir, with rivers and forested recreation areas. Good schools, with moderately expensive housing available. Tax rates generally low and subject to negotiation; the town might forgive taxes during a three- to five-year start-up period. Adequate rail and road transportation available. Located within 50 miles of markets in Hartford, Providence, Springfield, Worcester, and New Haven. Energy costs ranging from average to high and rising. Experienced factory workers available. Steel must be brought in by rail, probably from Pennsylvania or the Chicago-Gary area. Moderate climate. The University of Connecticut, at nearby Storrs, might provide research facilities and assistance, as well as a supply of seasonal workers. In this heavily industrialized area, valves are in constant demand, but the presence of nearby competitors would force heavy price competition.

- *Cat Spring, Texas.* A tiny, dry town about 50 miles from the Gulf of Mexico; conveniently located on the Houston–Fort Worth rail line. Real estate prices low and taxes minuscule. Adequate labor available from the Houston and Dallas–Fort Worth areas, but housing would have to be built to accommodate the influx of workers. Local schools presently inadequate for any increase from workers' families but could presumably be expanded. Steel from Europe arrives at the port of Houston and could be delivered economically by rail to Cat Spring. The climate is hot and dry nine months of the year, making air conditioning of the plant necessary. Markets in Houston, Waco, Fort Worth, Dallas, and Austin are all about 200 miles away. The need for our type of valves appears to be growing as industrialization increases in southern Texas. Electricity and water expensive, although recent developments in solar power appear to be reducing the costs of air conditioning.

Your task: Write a memo in which you recommend one of the two locations and justify your recommendation. The report has been requested by Ron Wasserman, chief executive officer of Victory Valves, Inc.

17. In the driver's seat: Report on the best route for obtaining a new truck City Heights News Service, a partnership that supplies periodicals to various outlets in the area, has had the same used truck since it was founded three years ago. Business has expanded since then, and the old truck has become a little unreliable, so the owners of City Heights, Pam and Bill Oster, have decided to get a new set of wheels. They've given you the job of analyzing three options:

- Lease a truck for $320 per month for two years. At the end of that time, purchase the truck for $6,000. The lease payments are tax-deductible; thus 40 percent of the lease expense is covered through lower taxes.
- Lease the same truck for $700 a month for a two-year period, and then purchase it for a token payment of $1. Again, the lease payments are tax-deductible.
- Purchase a similar truck for $11,500.

Your task: Select an option and justify your choice in a brief memo.

18. On the books: Report on improving the campus bookstore Imagine that you are a consultant hired to improve the profits of your campus bookstore.

Your task: Visit the bookstore and look critically at its operations. Then draft a memo offering recommendations to the bookstore manager that would make the bookstore more profitable, perhaps suggesting products that the store should carry, hours that the store should remain open, or added services that the store should make available to students. Be sure to support your recommendations.

19. With an eye toward change: Report on converting a building to a new use The company you work for, Video Vendors, Inc., has just bought an abandoned fast-food restaurant with the intention of converting it to an outlet for renting and selling videotapes and video equipment. You are a planning specialist with Video Vendors, and it's your job to outline the architectural changes that will be necessary for successful remodeling.

Your task: Visit any fast-food restaurant in your area and draw a diagram that shows its current use of indoor and outdoor space. Next determine the architectural changes that will be necessary to convert the building into a video outlet, the major fixtures that must be removed, and the major items that must be purchased. Present your findings in a memo to Angelica Smythe, vice president of planning for Video Vendors, Inc. Include a diagram showing the proposed layout of the video outlet.

20. Prospects for growth: Report on a small firm Choose a small independent business in your area, and assume that the owners have hired you to help them approach a local bank for financial help with their expansion. The bank will require a complete financial statement and a brief narrative description of the business, covering such topics as the length of time it has been operating, its chief product lines and services, the size of its market area, its usual mix of customers, and the general prospects for growth in its neighborhood.

Your task: Draft the report that you will submit to the bank for your client. Several paragraphs of objective writing will be sufficient, and no financial figures are necessary, because they will appear in accompanying financial statements. Remember that your job is to describe the business, not to recommend that the bank lend money to it.

CHAPTER SIXTEEN

COMPLETING FORMAL REPORTS AND PROPOSALS

After studying this chapter, you will be able to

- Describe how organizations produce formal reports and proposals
- Prepare all the necessary parts of a formal report
- Assemble all the parts of a formal report in the proper order, using an appropriate format
- Prepare and assemble all the parts of a formal proposal
- Critique formal reports prepared by someone else

COMMUNICATION CLOSE-UP AT TUPPERWARE

Jane Trimble

Once upon a time at Tupperware Home Parties, the process of preparing formal reports and proposals was exasperating for everyone. Writers frequently made projections and commitments without double-checking the information. And the time the office staff required to prepare the final documents never seemed to match the time available. "But now we have modified the process and eliminated a lot of the problems," says Jane Trimble, director of public relations for the Orlando, Florida, company.

Each year, Jane prepares at least one "major, major" justification report for a public relations project, along with numerous smaller reports. One formal justification report Jane wrote suggested that Tupperware become a corporate sponsor at Sea World in central Florida, because "we both have the best seals anywhere" (Tupperware's seals are in the fit between its plastic containers and their lids). The report began with some background, explained the strategy and goals of the project, presented the recommendations in the middle, and ended with a calendar, cost estimates, and criteria for measuring success.

To ensure that reports and proposals like Jane's contain accurate, realistic information, Tupperware has instituted a process featuring built-

At Tupperware Home Parties, staffers concentrate on developing quality products, innovative marketing techniques—and carefully prepared formal reports.

in feedback. "For example," Jane explains, "when I write a plan for a public relations event, I might work with the financial planning department to get cost figures and revenue projections. I often check with the design group too, because they might have to design a brochure or audiovisual program to support the project. I have to make sure the calendar in my report reflects the time they need."

Publishing a formal document requires even more teamwork. After doing her research, Jane writes out her report by hand or on a typewriter. "I do my own editing for content and organization and style," Jane notes, "and then my secretary enters the report into a personal computer. I send the draft to my boss for comments. He makes sure that everything I say can be substantiated, that I am making a reasonable request, that the project will help the company fulfill its purpose and meet its yearly goals. Then I fine-tune the report; with a computer, it's easy to make changes. If we want multiple copies of the final document, the office services department reproduces it."

Early in the process, Jane figures out how much time she has: "Say that I need to have a public relations plan approved by a certain date. I can work back from that date to schedule all the different parts of the preparation process. If I know that I need to get a report out quickly, my secretary coordinates with office services well in advance to make sure they can make the copies I need as soon as the report is ready." Altogether, it takes about a week to get a formal report drafted, revised, produced, and delivered to the people who will make the decision. Only after all their questions have been answered and they have all signed on the cover sheet can Jane go ahead with the project.

Jane likes her reports and proposals to look clean, with plenty of white space. "I want them to have a lot of eye appeal," she says. "A page that isn't too cluttered makes a good first impression and gives readers a place to write their comments. I also try to use a lot of headings and bulleted lists within the text, so a busy person can just scan it and find the most important points immediately.

"I want my reports and proposals to look good because they reflect on me. More than that," she adds, "messy documents may not be read at all, even if the content is great. The people at Tupperware are busy, so I try to make it easy for them to understand my ideas."

THE REPORT PROCESS

Planning a report or proposal, conducting the necessary research, developing visual aids, organizing the ideas, and drafting the text are demanding and time-consuming tasks. But don't assume that the process of writing a report or proposal ends with them. When you are writing a formal document, one important task remains: producing a polished final version.

How the final version is actually produced depends on the nature of the organization. If you work for an organization that, like Tupperware, produces many reports and proposals, the preparation process is likely to involve the interaction of a number of people. You and other members of a study team may subdivide the writing job, an arrangement sometimes called collaborative writing. Working from a jointly developed outline, each of you may draft a section of the text, then delegate final preparation of the report or proposal to the company editor, the secretarial staff, and the art department. If this is the case, you won't be involved in the finer points of formatting, like setting up a title page or positioning page numbers properly. The support staff will handle these tasks, using the approved company format. Your role will be to review their work and be sure it reflects the proper professionalism. On the other hand, if you work for a small business with a limited staff, you may compose and type the entire report yourself, handling everything from the outline of the issues for analysis to the final version of the report.

In organizations that produce many reports and proposals, the preparation process involves teamwork.

The equipment available also has a bearing on the production process. If you draft the report on a personal computer, using a word-processing program and perhaps a computer graphics package, you can easily incorporate editorial changes and reviewer comments. In addition, you can let the computer handle such mechanical chores as setting margins, adding footnotes, numbering pages, and checking your spelling. Some software programs even edit your draft for readability. Without a computer, the preparation process may take longer. If you don't have access to a sophisticated electronic typewriter either, you may have to retype the entire document in order to make changes, and each page must be formatted separately.

Personal computers can automatically handle many of the mechanical aspects of report preparation.

Regardless of precisely how the final product is produced, you should allocate enough time for a thorough job. Be realistic in what you expect from the support staff. Secretaries can type only about 8 pages an hour; editors may spend 10 to 15 minutes on a single page; graphic artists may spend up to an hour or more preparing just one chart. And every person who reviews the draft of the report will take as much time as possible and will recommend changes that are time consuming to incorporate.

Be sure to schedule enough time to turn out a document that looks professional.

In terms of your own part in the process, remember that you don't have to start writing on page one. A person with a strong visual sense might begin by developing the visual aids. Someone who thinks in broad, general terms might start with the introduction. Someone else might prefer to write the main analytical sections first. If you are writing as part of a

FIGURE 16.1
Parts of a Formal Report

PREFATORY PARTS	TEXT OF THE REPORT	SUPPLEMENTARY PARTS
Cover	Introduction	Appendixes
Title fly	Body	Bibliography
Title page	Summary	Index
Letter of authorization	Conclusions	
Letter of acceptance	Recommendations	
Letter of transmittal	Notes	
Table of contents		
List of illustrations		
Synopsis or executive summary		

team, you will be forced to work on sections taken out of context and out of sequence. Although this practice may be disconcerting, it is often necessary in business. And it seems to work, provided that one person takes responsibility for assembling all the pieces, developing transitions, and editing the whole report to ensure consistency.

Ask for feedback, and learn from your mistakes.

When you've completed a major report and have sent it off to the readers, you will naturally expect a positive response, and quite often you'll get one. But in the real world, you won't always get the response you want. For instance, you may get half-hearted praise or no action on your conclusions and recommendations. Or worse, you may get some serious criticism. Try to learn from these experiences; don't consider them a personal insult. Constructive criticism will prepare you for the next time, so you'll have a better chance of succeeding.

Sometimes you won't get any response at all, which is frustrating. If you haven't heard from your readers within a week or two, you might want to ask politely whether the report arrived. In hopes of stimulating a response, you could also offer to answer their questions or provide additional information.

COMPONENTS OF A FORMAL REPORT

A formal report conveys the impression that the subject is important.

As Chapter 15 indicates, formal reports differ from informal ones in both format and tone. Manuscript format and an impersonal tone convey an impression of professionalism.

But a formal report can be either short (fewer than ten pages) or long (ten pages or more). It can be informational or analytical, direct or indirect. In many cases, a formal report is directed to readers outside the organization, but it may also be written for insiders. What sets it apart from other reports is its polish.

The three basic divisions of a formal report:

- Prefatory parts
- Text
- Supplementary parts

The longer the report and the more information in it, the greater the number of components it usually contains; complex information is easier to digest when presented in smaller pieces. Notice that the components listed in Figure 16.1 fall into three categories, depending on where they are found in a report: prefatory parts, text of the report, and supplementary parts. The parts included in a report depend on the type of report you are writing, the requirements of your audience, the organization you are working for, and the length of your report. For instance, the prefatory parts of a short report usually include only a title page, a letter of transmittal combined with a synopsis, and a table of contents; usually no supplementary parts are included. In very short reports the table of contents and letter of transmittal are omitted too. Long reports often include all the components listed in Figure 16.1. Later in this chapter, a sample formal report illustrates how the parts fit together.

PREFATORY PARTS

Prefatory parts may be written after the text has been completed.

Although the prefatory parts are placed before the text of the report, you may not want to write them until after you have written the text. Many of these parts—such as the table of contents, list of illustrations, and synopsis—are easier to prepare after the text is complete, because they directly reflect the contents. Other parts can be prepared at almost any time.

Cover

Many companies have standard covers for reports, made of heavy paper and imprinted with the company's name and logo. Report titles are either printed on these covers or attached with gummed labels. If a company does not have standard covers, you can usually find something suitable in a good stationery store. Look for a cover that is appropriate to the subject matter, attractive, and convenient and that can be labeled with the title of the report, the writer's name (optional), and the submission date (also optional).

Put a title on the cover that is informative but not too long.

Think carefully about the title before you put it on the cover. A business report is not a mystery story, so give your readers all the information they need: the who, what, when, where, why, and how of the subject. At the same time, try to be reasonably concise. You don't want to intimidate your audience with a title that is too long, awkward, or unwieldy. One approach is to use a subtitle: "Opportunities for Improving Market Share in the Athletic Shoe Department: Customer Attitudes Toward Marshall's Athletic Footwear, December 1989." You can reduce the length of your title by eliminating phrases like "A report of," "A study of," or "A survey of."

Title fly and title page

The title fly is a plain sheet of paper with only the title of the report on it. You don't really need one, but it adds a touch of formality to a report.

The title page usually includes four blocks of information.

The title page includes four blocks of information, as shown in the sample report later in this chapter: (1) the title of the report; (2) the name, title, and address of the person, group, or organization that authorized the report (which is usually the intended audience); (3) the name, title, and address of the person, group, or organization that prepared the report; and (4) the date on which the report was submitted. On some title pages, the second block of information is preceded by the words "Prepared for" or "Submitted to," and the third block of information is preceded by "Prepared by" or "Submitted by." In some cases, the title page serves as the cover of the report, especially if the report is relatively short and is intended solely for internal use.

Letter of authorization and letter of acceptance

If you were authorized in writing to prepare the report, you may want to include the letter or memo of authorization and the letter or memo of acceptance in your report. These documents are useful "for the record."

A letter of authorization usually follows the direct-request plan.

The authorization document normally follows the direct-request plan described in Chapter 6. It typically specifies the problem, scope, time and money limitations, special instructions, and due date.

Use the good-news plan for a letter of acceptance.

The reply is the letter or memo of acceptance, which acknowledges the assignment to conduct the study and to prepare the report. Following the good-news plan, the acceptance confirms time and money limitations and other pertinent details. This document is rarely included in a report.

Letter of transmittal

Use a less formal style for the letter of transmittal than for the report itself.

The letter (or memo) of transmittal conveys the report to the readers. (If you were writing a book, you might label it a preface instead.) The letter of transmittal says what you'd say if you were handing the report directly to the person who authorized it. Thus the writing style is less formal than that of the rest of the report. For example, the letter would use personal pronouns *(you, I, we)* and conversational language.

Generally, the transmittal letter appears right before the table of contents. But if your report is quite formal, with wide distribution, you may want to include the letter of transmittal only in selected copies of the report, in order to make certain comments to a specific audience. Say, for example, that you are recommending that two departments be merged, a change that will displace one of the department heads. In your report, you might not want to recommend either person for the remaining position, especially if both department heads will receive a copy of the report. Rather, you might want to discuss the issue privately in a letter of transmittal to top management.

Use the good-news plan for a letter of transmittal.

In terms of organization, the letter of transmittal should follow the routine and good-news plans described in Chapter 7. Begin with the main idea, officially conveying the report to the readers and summarizing its purpose. Typically, such a letter begins with a statement like "Here is the report you asked me to prepare on. . . ." The rest includes information about the scope of the report, the methods used to complete the study, and the limitations that became apparent. In the middle section of the letter you may also highlight important points or sections of the report, make comments on side issues, give suggestions for follow-up studies, and transmit any information that will help readers better understand and use the report. You may also wish to acknowledge help given by others. The concluding paragraph of the transmittal letter should be a note of thanks for having been given the report assignment, an expression of willingness to discuss the report, and an offer to assist with future projects.

The synopsis of short reports is often included in the letter of transmittal.

If the report does not have a synopsis, the letter of transmittal may summarize the major findings, conclusions, and recommendations. This material would follow the opening of the letter.

Table of contents

The table of contents outlines the text and lists prefatory and supplementary parts.

The table of contents indicates in outline form the coverage, sequence, and relative importance of the information in the report. In fact, the headings used in the text of the report are the basis for the table of contents. However, depending on the length and complexity of the report, the contents page may show only the top two or three levels of headings, sometimes only first-level headings. Excluding some levels of headings may frustrate readers who want to know where to find every subject you cover, but simplification of the table of contents also helps readers focus on the major points.

Be sure the headings in the table of contents match up perfectly with the headings in the text.

The table of contents should be prepared after the other parts of the report have been typed so that the beginning page numbers for each heading can be shown. The headings should be worded exactly as they are in the text of the report.

Also listed on the contents page are the prefatory parts (only those that follow the contents page) and the supplementary parts. If you have four or fewer visual aids, you may wish to list them in the table of contents too; but if you have more than four visual aids, you should list them separately in a list of illustrations.

List of illustrations

For simplicity's sake, some reports refer to all visual aids as illustrations or exhibits. In other reports, as in the sample report in this chapter, tables are labeled separately from all other types of visual aids, which are called figures. Regardless of the system used to label visual aids, the list of illustrations gives their titles and page numbers.

Put the list of illustrations on a separate page if it won't all fit on one page with the table of contents; start the list of figures and the list of tables on separate pages if they won't both fit on one page.

If there is enough space on a single page, type the list of illustrations directly beneath the table of contents. Otherwise, type it on a separate page following the contents page. When tables and figures are numbered separately, they should also be listed separately. Both lists can be typed on the same page if they fit; otherwise, start each list on a separate page.

Synopsis or executive summary

Provide an overview of the report in a synopsis or executive summary.

A synopsis is a brief overview (one page or less) of a report's most important points, designed to give readers a quick preview of the contents. It is particularly likely to be included in long informational reports dealing with technical, professional, or academic subjects. Because it is a concise representation of the whole report, it may be distributed separately to a wide audience; interested readers can then opt to order a copy of the entire report.

An informative synopsis summarizes the main ideas; a descriptive synopsis states what the report is about.

The phrasing of a synopsis can be either informative or descriptive, depending on whether the report is in direct or indirect order. With an informative synopsis, you present the main points of the report in the order in which they appear in the text. But a descriptive synopsis simply tells what the report is about, in only moderately greater detail than the table of contents; the actual findings of the report are omitted. Here are examples of statements from each type:

Informative Synopsis:	Sales of super-premium ice cream make up 11 percent of the total ice cream market.
Descriptive Synopsis:	This report contains information about super-premium ice cream and its share of the market.

The way you handle a synopsis should reflect the approach you use in the text. If you're using an indirect approach in your report, you are better

Use a descriptive synopsis for a skeptical or hostile audience, an informative synopsis for most other situations.

off with a descriptive synopsis. An informative synopsis, with its focus on conclusions and key points, may be too confrontational if you have a skeptical audience. You don't want to spoil the effect by providing a controversial beginning.

Put enough information in an executive summary so an executive can make a decision without reading the entire report.

Many business report writers prefer to include an executive summary instead of a synopsis. A synopsis is essentially a prose table of contents that outlines the main points of the report; an executive summary is a fully developed "mini" version of the report itself, intended for readers who lack the time or motivation to study the complete text. As a consequence, an executive summary is more comprehensive than a synopsis, generally about 10 percent as long as the document.

Unlike a synopsis, an executive summary may contain headings, well-developed transitions, and visual aids. It should be organized in the same way as the report, using a direct or indirect approach depending on the audience's receptivity. In analytical reports, enough evidence should be provided in the executive summary to make a convincing case for the conclusions and recommendations. After reading the summary, the executive should know the essentials and be in a position to make a decision. Later, when time permits, he or she may read certain parts of the report to obtain additional detail.

Many reports do not require either a synopsis or an executive summary. Generally speaking, length is the determining factor. Most reports of fewer than 10 pages either omit one or combine it with the letter of transmittal. But if your report is over 30 pages long, you should probably include either a synopsis or an executive summary as a convenience for readers. Which to provide depends on the traditions of your organization.

TEXT OF THE REPORT

If you have read Chapter 15, you should already know a good deal about how to write the text of a report. But apart from deciding on the fundamental issues of content and organization, you must also make decisions about the design and layout of the report. You can use a variety of techniques to present your material effectively. Many organizations have format guidelines that make your decisions easier, but the goal should always be to focus readers' attention on major points and on the flow of ideas.

Aids to understanding in the text of a report:

- Headings
- Visual aids
- Preview and summary statements

Headings are the most powerful format tool available to you. Each heading should give readers a clue to the material that follows. By skipping along from heading to heading, they should be able to pick up the structure or outline of your report. This skimming process is easier if the headings are phrased and typed in a consistent way. To highlight the headings, you can use typographical distinctions, such as all capital letters, initial capitals, underlining, italics, and boldface print. But be sure that you use these signals consistently, so that the hierarchy among the headings is visually apparent. You can also emphasize the headings by allowing extra white space between them and the text. In fact, in longer reports you should call attention to the major breaks in thought by beginning each main section or chapter on a separate page. In shorter reports the sections or chapters may run continuously, with only first-level headings separating the major divisions.

Visual aids are also useful tools for calling attention to key points and helping readers grasp the flow of ideas. By depicting important information visually, you capture the attention of readers who are leafing through the report. Eye-catching graphics dramatize the high points of the message, and informative captions explain their meaning.

It is also a good idea to preview key points at the beginning of each major section or chapter and to sum them up at the end. In other words, readers benefit when you

1. Tell them what you're going to tell them.
2. Tell them.
3. Tell them what you told them.

This strategy keeps readers positioned and reinforces the substance of your message.

Introduction

The introduction of a report serves a number of important functions:

- Puts the report in a broader context, tying it to a problem or an assignment
- Tells readers the report's purpose
- Lets readers know what to expect in terms of the report's contents and organization
- Establishes the tone of the report and the writer's relationship with the readers

The length of the introduction depends on the length of the report. If you're writing a relatively brief report, the introduction may be only a paragraph or two and may not be labeled with a heading of any kind. But the introduction to a major formal report may extend to several pages and should be identified as a separate section by the first-level heading "Introduction."

An introduction has a number of functions and covers a wide variety of topics.

Here's a list of topics that are generally covered in an introduction:

- *Authorization.* When, how, and by whom the report was authorized, who wrote it, and when it was submitted. This material is especially important when no letter of transmittal is included.
- *Problem/purpose.* The reason for the report's existence and what is to be accomplished as a result of the report being written.
- *Scope.* What is and what isn't going to be covered in the report. The scope indicates the report's size and complexity.
- *Background.* The historic conditions or factors that have led up to the report. This section should enable readers to understand how the problem developed and what has been done about it so far.
- *Sources and methods.* The secondary sources of information used and the surveys, experiments, and observations carried out. This section should tell readers what sources were used, how the sample was selected, how the questionnaire was constructed (a sample questionnaire and cover letter should be included in the appendix), what follow-up procedures were employed, and the like. It should provide

enough detail to give readers confidence in the work and to convince them that the sources and methods were satisfactory.

- *Definitions.* A brief introductory statement leading into a column of terms used in the report and their definitions. The terms may be unfamiliar but essential to understanding the report (such as "duosony") or familiar expressions used in a specific way (such as "business education" used only to mean the education of business teachers). Terms may be defined in other places as well: in the body, as the terms are used; in explanatory footnotes; or in a glossary, an alphabetical listing of terms placed at the end of the report.
- *Limitations.* Factors affecting the quality of the report, such as a budget too small to do all the work that should have been done, an inadequate amount of time to do all the research desired, unreliability or unavailability of data, or social or environmental conditions beyond your control. This is the place to mention doubts about any aspect of the report. Although candor may lead readers to question the results, it will also enable them to assess the results more accurately and will help maintain the integrity of the report. However, limitations are no excuse for conducting a poor study or writing a bad report.
- *Report organization.* The organization of the report (what topics are covered and in what order), along with a rationale for following this plan. This section is a road map that helps readers understand what is approaching at each turn of the report and why.

Some of these items may be combined in the introduction; some may not be included at all. Make your decision about what to include by figuring out what kind of information will help your readers understand and accept the report.

In preparing the introduction, give some thought to its relationship to the prefatory parts of the report. In longer reports, you may have a letter of transmittal, a synopsis or executive summary, and an introduction, all of which cover essentially the same ground. To avoid redundancy, you may need to juggle the various sections. If the letter of transmittal and synopsis are fairly detailed, for example, you might want the introduction to be relatively brief. However, remember that some people may barely glance at the prefatory parts; thus the introduction should be detailed enough to provide an adequate preview of the report. If you feel that you need to repeat information in the introduction that has already been covered in one of the prefatory parts, simply use different wording.

Body

The body of the report follows the introduction. It consists of the major sections or chapters, with various levels of headings, that present, analyze, and interpret the findings gathered as part of your investigation. These chapters contain the "proof," the detailed information necessary to support your conclusions and recommendations.

One of the decisions you have to make in writing the body of your report is how much detail to include. Your decision should depend on the nature of your information, the purpose of the report, and the preferences

Limit the body to those details necessary to prove your conclusions and recommendations.

of your readers. Some situations call for detailed coverage; others lend themselves to shorter treatment. However, in general, provide only enough detail in the body to support your conclusions and recommendations, and put additional detail in tables, charts, and appendixes.

You must also decide whether to put your conclusions in the body or in a separate section or both. Here again, circumstances dictate the best approach. If the conclusions seem to flow naturally from the evidence, you will almost inevitably cover them in the body. However, if you want to give the conclusions added emphasis, you may also include a separate section to summarize them. Having a separate section is particularly appropriate in longer reports; the reader may lose track of the conclusions if they are given only in the body.

Summary, conclusions, and recommendations

The final section of the text of a report tells readers "what you told them." In a short report, this final wrap-up may be only a paragraph or two. But a long report generally has separate sections labeled "Summary," "Conclusions," and "Recommendations." Here's how the three differ:

Summaries, conclusions, and recommendations serve different purposes.

- *Summary.* The key findings of your report, paraphrased from the body and stated or listed in the order in which they appear in the body.
- *Conclusions.* The writer's analysis of what the findings mean. These are the answers to the questions that led to the report.
- *Recommendations.* Opinions, based on reason and logic, about the course of action that should be taken.

If the report is organized in direct order, the summary, conclusions, and recommendations are presented before the body and are reviewed only briefly at the end. If the report is organized in indirect order, they are presented for the first time at the end and are covered there in detail.

Some report writers combine the conclusions and recommendations under one heading. Combined or separate, if you have several conclusions and recommendations, you may want to number and list them. An appropriate lead-in sentence to the list of conclusions is, "The findings of this study lead to the following conclusions." A statement that could be used for the list of recommendations is, "Based on the conclusions of this study, the following recommendations are made." No new findings should be presented in either the conclusions or the recommendations section.

In action-oriented reports, put all the recommendations in a separate section and spell out precisely what should happen next.

In reports that are intended to lead to action, the recommendations section is particularly important, because it spells out exactly what should happen next. It brings all the action items together in one place and gives the details on who should do what, when, where, and how. Readers may agree with everything you say in your report but still fail to take any action if you are vague about what should happen next. Readers have to understand what is expected of them and have some appreciation of the difficulties that are likely to arise. A timetable and specific assignments are therefore helpful, because concrete plans have a way of commanding action.

Notes

Give credit where credit is due.

In writing the text of the report, you will have to decide how to acknowledge your sources. You have a moral and legal obligation to give other people credit for their work. When you use someone else's research, it is unfair, and also illegal, to pass it off as your own. At the same time, acknowledging your sources enhances the credibility of your report. By citing references in the text, you demonstrate that you have thoroughly researched the topic.

Citing sources is desirable, but you want to do it in a way that doesn't make your report read like an academic treatise, dragging along from footnote to footnote. The source references should be handled as conveniently and inconspicuously as possible (see Component Chapter E, "Documentation of Report Sources," for some alternatives). One approach, especially for internal reports, is simply to mention a source in the text:

According to Dr. Lewis Morgan of Northwestern Hospital, hip replacement operations account for 7 percent of all surgery performed on women ages 65 and over.

If your report will be distributed to outsiders, however, you should include additional information on where you obtained the data.

SUPPLEMENTARY PARTS

The supplementary parts, which come after the text of the report, are the appendix(es), bibliography, and index. They are more common in long reports than in short ones.

Put in an appendix materials that are

- Bulky or lengthy
- Not directly relevant to the text

An appendix contains materials related to the report but not included in the text because they are too lengthy or bulky or because they lack direct relevance. Sample questionnaires and cover letters, sample forms, computer printouts, and statistical formulas are frequently put in appendixes; a glossary of terms may be put in an appendix or be made a separate supplementary part. The best place for visual aids to appear is in the text nearest the point of discussion, but if they are too large to fit on one page or are only indirectly relevant to the report, they too may be put in an appendix. Some organizations specify, however, that all visual aids be placed in an appendix.

Each different type of material deserves a separate appendix. Identify the appendixes by labeling them, for example, "Appendix A: Questionnaire," "Appendix B: Computer Printout of Raw Data," and the like. All appendixes should be mentioned in the text and listed in the table of contents.

List your secondary sources in the bibliography.

A bibliography is a list of sources consulted in preparing the report. The way a bibliography should be constructed is shown in the sample report at the end of this chapter and in Component Chapter E.

An index is an alphabetical listing of names, places, and subjects mentioned in the report and the pages on which they occur, as in the index for this book. An index is rarely included in unpublished reports.

SHARPEN YOUR SKILLS

Analyzing a Sample Formal Report: An In-Depth Critique

The report presented in the following pages was prepared by Andy O'Toole, an analyst in the cost accounting department of TriTech Industries, a medium-size company headquartered in San Francisco. TriTech's main product is optical character recognition equipment, which is used by the U.S. Postal Service for sorting mail. Andy's job is to help analyze the company's costs. He has this to say about the background of his report:

"For the past three or four years, TriTech has been on a roll. Our A-12 optical character reader was a real breakthrough, and the post office grabbed up as many as we could make. Our sales and profits kept climbing, and morale was fantastic. Everybody seemed to think that the good times would last forever. Unfortunately, everybody was wrong. When the Postal Service announced that they were 'postponing' all new equipment purchases because of cuts in their budget, we woke up to the fact that we are essentially a one-product company with one customer. At that point, management started scrambling around looking for ways to cut costs until we can diversify our business a bit.

"The vice president of administration, Jean Alexander, asked me to help identify cost-cutting opportunities in the travel and entertainment area. On the basis of her personal observations, she felt that TriTech was overly generous in its travel policies and that we might be able to save a significant amount by controlling these costs more carefully. My investigation confirmed her suspicion.

"I was reasonably confident that my report would be well received. I've worked with Ms. Alexander before and know what she likes: plenty of facts, clearly stated conclusions, and specific recommendations for what should be done next. I also knew that my report would be passed on to other TriTech executives, so I wanted to create a good impression. I wanted the report to be accurate and thorough, visually appealing, readable, and appropriate in tone."

In writing the analytical report that follows, Andy used an organization based on conclusions and recommendations, presented in direct order. The first two sections of the report correspond to Andy's two main conclusions: that TriTech's travel and entertainment costs are too high and that cuts are essential. The third section presents recommendations for achieving better control over travel and entertainment expenses. As you review the report, notice both the mechanical aspects and the way Andy presents his ideas.

Capitalize the title; use upper- and lower-case letters for all other lines.

REDUCING TRITECH'S TRAVEL AND ENTERTAINMENT COSTS

Follow the title with the name, title, and organization of the recipient.

Prepared for

Jean Alexander, Vice President of Administration
TriTech Industries

Balance the white space between the items on the page.

In centering the lines horizontally on the title page, allow an extra ½-inch margin on the left side if it's a left-bound report.

Prepared by

Andrew O'Toole, Director
Cost Accounting Services
TriTech Industries

For future reference, include the report's publication date.

May 15, 1989

The "how to" tone of this title is appropriate for an action-oriented report that emphasizes recommendations. A more neutral title, such as "An Analysis of TriTech's Travel and Entertainment Costs," would be more suitable for an informational report.

Use memo format for transmitting internal reports, letter format for transmitting external reports.

optional

MEMORANDUM

DATE: May 15, 1989

TO: Jean Alexander, Vice President of Administration

FROM: Andrew O'Toole, Director of Cost Accounting Services A.O'T.

SUBJECT: Reducing TriTech's Travel and Entertainment Costs

Here is the report you requested April 30 on TriTech's travel and entertainment costs.

Present the main conclusion or recommendation right away if you expect a positive response.

Your suspicion was right. We are spending far too much on business travel. Our unwritten policy has been "anything goes." We have no real control over T&E expenses. Although this offhanded approach may have been understandable when TriTech's profits were high, we can no longer afford the luxury of "going first class," particularly in light of recent changes in the tax laws.

The solutions to the problem are obvious: We need to put someone in charge of travel and entertainment; we need a clear statement of policy; we need an effective control system; and we need to retain a business-oriented travel service that can optimize our travel arrangements. Perhaps more important, we need to change our attitude. Instead of viewing business travel as a free vacation, we need to act as though we were paying the bills ourselves.

Use an informal, conversational style for the letter or memo of transmittal.

Getting people to economize is not going to be easy. In the course of researching this issue, I've found that our employees are deeply attached to their first-class travel privileges. I almost think they would prefer a cut in pay to a loss in travel status. We'll need a lot of top management involvement to sell people on the need for moderation. One thing is clear: People will be very bitter if we create a two-class system in which top executives get special privileges while the rest of the employees make the sacrifices.

Acknowledge any help that you have received.

I'm grateful to Mary Lehman and Connie McIllvain for their help in rounding up and sorting through five years' worth of expense reports. Their efforts were truly Herculean.

Close with thanks, an offer to discuss results, and an offer to assist with future projects, if appropriate.

Thanks for giving me the opportunity to work on this assignment. It's been a real education. If you have any questions about the report, please give me a call.

ghc

In this report, Andy decided to write a brief memo of transmittal and include a separate executive summary. Short reports (fewer than ten pages) often combine the synopsis or executive summary with the memo or letter of transmittal.

Word the headings exactly as they appear in the text.

Extend spaced periods (leaders) from the end of the heading to the page number. (For spaced periods, strike the space bar and the period alternately.) Align the periods under one another.

Type only the page numbers where sections begin; align the last digits of the page numbers.

Because figures and tables were numbered separately in the text, they are listed separately here. If all were labeled as exhibits, a single list would have been appropriate.

Number the contents pages with lower-case roman numerals centered 1 inch from the bottom.

CONTENTS

LIST OF ILLUSTRATIONS

iii

Andy included only first- and second-level headings in his table of contents, even though the report contains third-level headings. He prefers a shorter table of contents that focuses attention on the main divisions of thought. To save space, he also chose to list illustrations on the same page. Notice the informative titles, which are appropriate for a report to a receptive audience.

Begin by stating the purpose of the report.

Present the points in the executive summary in the same order as they appear in the report; use subheadings that summarize the content of the main sections of the report without repeating those that appear in the text.

Type the synopsis or executive summary in the same manner as the text of the report. Single-space if the report is single-spaced, and use the same format in both the executive summary and the text for margins, paragraph indentions, and headings.

EXECUTIVE SUMMARY

This report analyzes TriTech's travel and entertainment costs and presents recommendations for reducing those costs.

T&E Costs Are Too High

Travel and entertainment (T&E) is a large and growing expense category for TriTech Industries. The company currently spends about $10 million per year on business travel, and costs are increasing by 7 percent annually. Company employees make some 5,000 trips each year, at an average cost per trip of $2,000. Air fares are the biggest expense, followed by hotels, meals, and rental cars.

The nature of TriTech's business does require extensive travel, but the company's costs appear to be excessive. Every year, TriTech spends about twice as much on T&E for each professional employee as its main competitors do. Although the location of the company's facilities may partly explain this discrepancy, the main reason for TriTech's high costs is the firm's philosophy and management style. TriTech encourages employees to go first class and pays relatively little attention to travel costs.

Cuts Are Essential

Although TriTech has traditionally been casual about travel and entertainment expenses, management now recognizes the need to gain more control over this element of costs. The company is currently entering a period of declining profits, prompting management to look for every opportunity to reduce spending. At the same time, changes in the tax laws are making travel and entertainment expenses more important to the bottom line.

TriTech Can Save $4 Million per Year

Fortunately, TriTech has a number of excellent opportunities for reducing its travel and entertainment costs. Savings of up to $4 million per year should be achievable, judging by the experience of other companies. The first priority should be to hire a director of travel and entertainment to assume overall responsibility for T&E spending. This individual should establish a written travel and entertainment policy and create a budgeting and cost-control system. The director should also retain a nationwide travel agency to handle our reservations.

iv

Andy decided to include an executive summary because his report was aimed at a mixed audience. He knew that some readers would be interested in the details of his report and some would prefer to focus on the big picture. The executive summary was aimed at the latter group. Andy wanted to give these readers enough information to make a decision without burdening them with the task of reading the entire report.

The hard-hitting tone of this executive summary is appropriate for a receptive audience. A more neutral approach would be better for hostile or skeptical readers.

At the same time, TriTech should make employees aware of the need for moderation in travel and entertainment spending. People should be encouraged to forgo any unnecessary travel and to economize on airline tickets, hotels, meals, rental cars, and other expenses.

In addition to economizing on an individual basis, TriTech should look for ways to reduce costs by negotiating preferential rates with travel providers. Once retained, a travel agency should be able to accomplish this.

These changes, although necessary, are likely to hurt morale, at least in the short term. Management will need to make a determined effort to explain the rationale for reduced spending. By exercising moderation in their own travel arrangements, TriTech executives can set a good example and help make the changes more acceptable to other employees.

v

Number the pages of the executive summary with lower-case roman numerals centered about 1 inch from the bottom of the page.

This executive summary is written in an impersonal style, which adds to the formality of the report. Although the impersonal style is commonly used for a synopsis or executive summary, some writers prefer a more personal approach. Generally speaking, you should gear your choice of style to your relationship with the readers. Andy chose the formal approach because several members of his audience were considerably higher up in the organization. He did not want to sound too familiar. In addition, he wanted the executive summary and the text to be compatible, and his company prefers the impersonal style for formal reports.

Center the title of the report on the first page of the text, 1 inch (1½ inches if top-bound) from the top of the page.

Begin the introduction by establishing the need for action.

Single-space the report to create a formal, finished look; double-space if your readers prefer it or if your report is a preliminary document.

Mentioning sources and methods increases the credibility of a report and gives readers a complete picture of the study's background.

Use the arabic numeral 1 for the first page of the report; center the number about 1 inch from the bottom of the page.

REDUCING TRITECH'S TRAVEL AND ENTERTAINMENT COSTS

INTRODUCTION

TriTech Industries has traditionally encouraged a significant amount of business travel, in the belief that it is an effective way of conducting operations. To compensate employees for the stress and inconvenience of frequent trips, management has authorized generous travel and entertainment allowances. This philosophy has undoubtedly been good for morale, but the company has paid a price. Last year, TriTech spent $10 million on T&E, $5 million more than it spent on research and development.

This year, the cost of travel and entertainment will have a bigger impact on profits, owing to changes in tax laws. The timing of these changes is unfortunate, because the company anticipates that profits will be relatively weak for a variety of other reasons. In light of these profit pressures, Ms. Jean Alexander, Vice President of Administration, has asked the accounting department to take a closer look at the T&E budget.

Purpose, Scope, and Limitations

The purpose of this report is to analyze the travel and entertainment budget, evaluate the impact of recent changes in tax laws and government regulations, and suggest ways to tighten management's control over travel and entertainment expenses.

Although the report outlines a number of steps that could reduce TriTech's expenses, the precise financial impact of these measures is difficult to project. The estimates presented in the report provide a "best guess" view of what TriTech can expect to save. But until the company actually implements these steps, there is no way of knowing how much the travel and entertainment budget can be reduced.

Sources and Methods

In preparing this report, the accounting department analyzed internal expense reports for the past five years to determine how much TriTech spends on travel and entertainment. These figures were then compared with statistics on similar companies in the electronic equipment industry, obtained through industry association data, annual reports, and magazine articles. In addition, the accounting department studied publicly available information regarding the new tax laws and changes in government regulations. Magazine and newspaper articles were screened to determine how other companies are coping with the high cost of business travel.

1

In a brief introduction like this one, some writers would omit the subheadings within the introduction and rely on topic sentences and on transitional words and phrases to indicate that they are discussing such subjects as the purpose, scope, and limitations of the study. Andy decided to use headings because they help readers scan the document.

Using arabic numerals, number the second and succeeding pages of the text in the upper right-hand corner where the top and right-hand margins meet.

line 6 Report Organization

Derickson 2

1/2 in — line 3

This report reviews the size and composition of TriTech's travel and entertainment expenses, analyzes the impact of the new tax laws and changes in government regulations, and recommends steps for reducing the travel and entertainment budget.

THE HIGH COST OF TRAVEL AND ENTERTAINMENT

Although many companies view travel and entertainment (T&E) as an "incidental" cost of doing business, the dollars add up. Last year, U.S. industry paid an estimated $90 billion for travel and entertainment.[1] At TriTech Industries, the bill for air fares, hotels, rental cars, restaurants, and entertainment totaled $10 million. The company's travel and entertainment budget has increased by 12 percent per year for the past five years. By industry standards, TriTech's budget is on the high side, largely because management has a generous policy on travel benefits.

$10 Million per Year
Spent on Travel and Entertainment

TriTech Industries' annual budget for travel and entertainment is only 8 percent of sales. Because this is a relatively small expense category compared with such things as salaries and commissions, it is tempting to dismiss travel and entertainment costs as insignificant. However, T&E is TriTech's third-largest controllable expense, directly behind salaries and data processing.[2]

Last year, TriTech personnel made about 5,000 trips, at an average cost per trip of $2,000. The typical trip involved a round-trip flight of 3,000 miles, meals and hotel accommodations for three days, and a rental car. Roughly 80 percent of the trips were made by 20 percent of the staff. Top management and sales personnel were the most frequent travelers, averaging 18 trips per year.

Figure 1 illustrates how the travel and entertainment budget is spent. The largest categories are air fares and lodging, which together account for $7 out of every $10

Placement of visual aids titles should be consistent throughout a report. This sample report, however, shows all options for placement; above, below, or beside the visual aid.

Figure 1
Air Fares and Lodging Account for Over Two-thirds of TriTech's Travel and Entertainment Budget

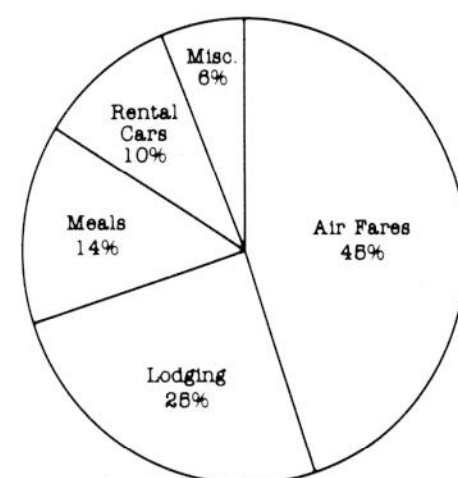

Notice how Andy opened the first main section of the body. He began with a topic sentence that introduced an important fact about the subject of the section. Then he oriented the reader to the three major points developed in the section. He put his data in perspective by comparing growth in travel and entertainment expenses to growth in sales. After all, if sales were also increasing by 12 percent a year, an increase of 12 percent in travel and entertainment expenses might be acceptable.

Introduce visual aids before they appear, and indicate what readers should notice about the data.

Number the visual aids consecutively, and refer to them in the text by their numbers. If your report is a book-length document, you may number the visual aids by chapter: Figure 4-2, for example, would be the second figure in the fourth chapter.

3

that employees spend on travel and entertainment. This spending pattern has been relatively steady for the past five years and is consistent with the distribution of expenses experienced by other companies.

Although the composition of the travel and entertainment budget has been constant, its size has not. As Figure 2 shows, expenditures for travel and entertainment have increased by about 12 percent per year for the past five years, roughly twice the rate of the company's growth in sales. This rate of growth makes travel and entertainment TriTech's fastest-growing expense item.

Figure 2
Travel and Entertainment Expenses Have Increased as a Percentage of Sales

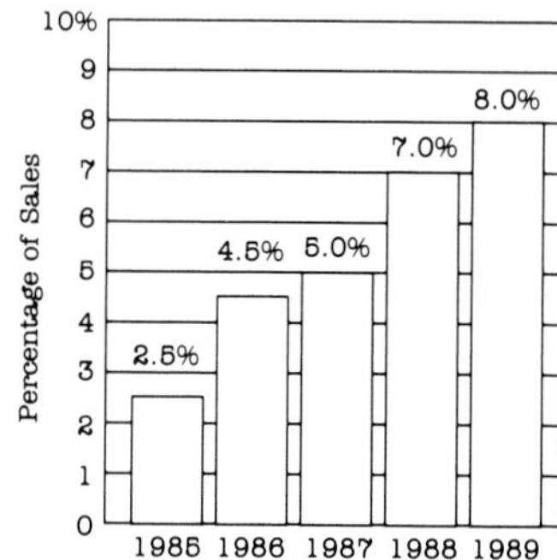

TriTech's Budget Exceeds Competitors'

There are many reasons why TriTech has a high travel and entertainment budget. TriTech's main customer is the U.S. Postal Service. The company's mode of selling requires frequent face-to-face contact with the customer, yet corporate headquarters is located on the West Coast, some 2,600 miles from Washington, D.C. Furthermore, TriTech's manufacturing operations are widely scattered; facilities are located in San Francisco, Detroit, Boston, and Dallas. To coordinate these operations, corporate management and division personnel must make frequent trips to and from company headquarters.

Although much of TriTech's travel budget is justified, the company spends considerably more on travel and entertainment than its competitors do, as Figure 3 indicates. Data supplied by the International Association of Electronics indicates that the typical company in our industry spends approximately $1,900 per month per professional employee on travel and entertainment.[3] TriTech's per capita travel costs for professional employees are running $4,000 per month.

Andy originally drew this bar chart as a line chart, showing both sales and T&E expenses in absolute dollars. However, the comparison was difficult to interpret because sales were so much greater than T&E expenses. The vertical axis stretched from 0 to $125 million. Switching to a bar chart, expressed in percentage terms, made the main idea much easier to grasp.

Place the visual aid as close as possible to the point it illustrates.

Give each visual aid a title that clearly indicates what it is about.

4

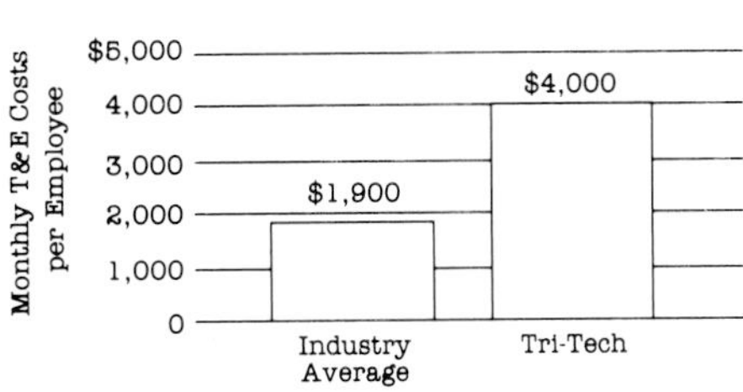

Figure 3
TriTech Spends Over Twice the Industry Average on Travel and Entertainment
Source: International Association of Electronics, 1988.

Spending Has Been Encouraged

Although a variety of factors may contribute to this differential, TriTech's relatively high travel and entertainment budget is at least partially attributable to the company's philosophy and management style. Because many employees do not enjoy business travel, management has tried to make the trips more pleasant by authorizing first-class air fare, luxury hotel accommodations, and full-size rental cars. The sales staff is encouraged to entertain clients at restaurants and to invite them to cultural and sporting events.

The cost of these privileges is easy to overlook, given the weakness of TriTech's system for keeping track of travel and entertainment expenses. The monthly financial records provided to management do not contain a separate category for travel and entertainment; the information is buried under Cost of Goods Sold and under Selling, General, and Administrative Expenses. Each department head is given authority to approve any expense report, regardless of how large it may be. Receipts are not required for expenditures of less than $100. Individuals are allowed to make their own travel arrangements. No one is charged with the responsibility for controlling the company's total spending on travel and entertainment.

GROWING IMPACT ON THE BOTTOM LINE

During the past three years, TriTech has enjoyed healthy profits; as a result, there has been relatively little pressure to push for tighter controls over all aspects of the business. However, the situation is changing. Management is projecting flat to declining profits for the next two years, a situation that has prompted the company to search for ways to cut costs. At the same time, changes in tax laws have increased the impact of travel and entertainment expenses on the company's financial results. The problem is compounded by a trend toward higher air fares, which represent TriTech's largest T&E expense category.

The chart on this page is very simple, but it creates an effective visual comparison. Andy included just enough data to make his point.

Informative headings focus readers' attention on the main points of the report. Thus they are most appropriate when the report is in direct order and is aimed at a receptive audience. Descriptive headings are more effective when a report is in indirect order and the readers are less receptive.

Pointing up the dollar impact of the changes in tax laws puts the data in perspective.

Lower Profits Underscore Need for Change

The next two years promise to be difficult for TriTech Industries. After several years of steady increases in spending, the U.S. Postal Service is tightening procurement policies for automated mail-handling equipment. Funding for TriTech's main product, the A-12 optical character reader, has been canceled. As a consequence, sales are expected to decline by 15 percent and profits to fall by 12 percent. Although TriTech is negotiating several promising research and development contracts with nongovernment clients, management does not foresee any major procurements for the next two to three years. Under the circumstances, every effort must be made to reduce costs.

New Tax Laws Increase
Travel and Entertainment Expenses

Even without the incentive of profit pressures, TriTech management would need to pay more attention to travel and entertainment costs in the coming years, because changes in the tax laws will increase the impact of these costs on our profits. Until recently, expenses for travel and entertainment were 100 percent deductible. Under the new tax laws, however, business meals and entertainment will be only 80 percent deductible. Furthermore, the IRS is cracking down on its interpretation of what qualifies as business entertainment. Companies were formerly allowed to deduct the cost of "goodwill" entertaining intended to build a long-term relationship with customers. Now companies must demonstrate that the expense was "necessary" to a particular business deal. In addition, companies are no longer allowed to deduct the cost of alcoholic beverages.[4] According to Gary Silverman, TriTech's outside tax consultant, these changes in tax laws and government regulations can be expected to increase the company's taxable income by approximately $600,000 per year. Given the maximum corporate tax rate of 38 percent, TriTech could pay an additional $228,000 in taxes each year.

Although air fares, hotel rooms, and rental cars will continue to be 100 percent deductible, changes in the tax laws will tend to push up the cost of some of these items. Less favorable treatment of hotel investments will tend to discourage construction of new hotels, which should gradually lead to an increase in room rates. At the same time, rental car companies can be expected to boost rates by 8 to 10 percent to compensate for revisions in depreciation schedules and the loss of the investment tax credit.[5]

Air Fares Are Rising

Over the next 8 to 12 months, rising air fares can also be expected to inflate TriTech's travel and entertainment costs. The recent round of mergers in the airline industry has reduced competition among carriers, thereby reducing the companies' incentive to cut ticket prices. In 15 of the nation's busiest airports, either half the business is already controlled by one airline or two share more than 70 percent.[6] The

Because air fares represent TriTech's biggest T&E expense, Andy included a subsection that deals with the possible impact of trends in the airline industry. Air fares are rising, so it is especially important to gain more control over employees' air travel arrangements.

Pointing out both the benefits and risks of taking action gives recommendations an objective flavor.

The indented list format calls attention to important points and adds visual interest. You can also use visual aids, headings, and direct quotations to break up large, solid blocks of print.

6

decline in competition is already leading to higher air fares. For example, the travel department of one major corporation based in St. Louis estimates that it will spend an average of 33 percent more for airline tickets this year than it did last year. The increases have been exceptionally high in St. Louis, but companies based in other cities are also facing fare increases that range from 2 percent to 15 percent.[7]

Given the fact that air fares account for 45 percent of TriTech's T&E budget, the trend toward higher ticket prices will have serious consequences on the company's expenses unless management takes action to control these costs.

METHODS FOR REDUCING
TRAVEL AND ENTERTAINMENT COSTS

By implementing a number of reforms, management can expect to reduce TriTech's travel and entertainment budget by as much as 40 percent. However, these measures are likely to be unpopular with employees. To gain acceptance for the changes, management will need to sell employees on the need for moderation in travel and entertainment allowances.

Three Ways to Trim Expenses

By researching what other companies are doing to curb travel and entertainment expenses, the accounting department has identified three promising opportunities that should enable TriTech to save about $4 million annually in travel-related costs.

Institute Tighter Spending Controls

A single individual should be appointed to spearhead the effort to gain control of the travel and entertainment budget. This individual should be familiar with the travel industry and should be well versed in both accounting and data processing. He or she should report to the vice president of administration and should be given the title of director of travel and entertainment. The director's first priorities should be to establish a written travel and entertainment policy and to implement a system for controlling travel and entertainment costs.

TriTech currently has no written policy on travel and entertainment, despite the fact that 73 percent of all firms have such policies.[8] Creating a policy would clarify management's position and serve as a vehicle for communicating the need for moderation. At a minimum, the policy should include the following provisions:

- All travel and entertainment should be strictly related to business and should be approved in advance.
- Instead of going first class, employees should make a reasonable effort to economize on air fares, hotels, rental cars, and meals.

Andy created a forceful tone by using action verbs in the third-level subheadings of this section. This approach is appropriate to the nature of the study and the attitude of the audience. However, in a status-conscious organization, the imperative verbs might sound a bit too presumptuous coming from a junior member of the staff.

When including recommendations in a report, specify the steps required to implement them.

The travel and entertainment policy should apply equally to employees at all levels in the organization. No special benefits should be allowed for top executives.

To implement the new policy, TriTech will need to create a system for controlling travel and entertainment expenses. Each department should prepare an annual T&E budget as part of its operating plan. These budgets should be presented in detail so management can evaluate how travel and entertainment dollars will be spent and recommend appropriate cuts.

To help management monitor performance relative to these budgets, the director of travel should prepare monthly financial statements showing actual travel and entertainment expenditures by department. The system for capturing this information should be computerized and should be capable of identifying individuals who consistently exceed approved spending levels. The recommended average spending level should range between $1,500 and $2,500 per month for each professional employee, depending on the individual's role in the company. Because they make frequent trips, sales and top management personnel can be expected to have relatively high travel expenses.

The director of travel should also be responsible for retaining a business-oriented travel service that will schedule all employee trips and look for the best travel deals, particularly in air fares. In addition to centralizing TriTech's reservation and ticketing activities, the agency will negotiate reduced group rates with hotels and rental car agencies. The agency selected should have offices nationwide so all TriTech facilities can channel their reservations through the same company. By consolidating its travel planning in this way, TriTech can increase its control over costs and achieve economies of scale.

Reduce Unnecessary Travel and Entertainment

One of the easiest ways to reduce expenses is to reduce the amount of traveling and entertaining that occurs. An analysis of last year's expenditures suggests that as much as 30 percent of TriTech's travel and entertainment is discretionary. For example, the professional staff spent $1.7 million attending seminars and conferences last year. Although some of these gatherings are undoubtedly beneficial, the company could save money by sending fewer representatives to each function and by eliminating some of the less valuable seminars.

By the same token, TriTech could economize on trips between headquarters and divisions by reducing the frequency of such visits and by sending fewer people on each trip. Although there is often no substitute for face-to-face meetings, management could try to resolve more internal issues through telephone contacts and written communication.

Andy decided to single-space his report to give it a "published" appearance. Double-spacing makes the text of a long report somewhat easier to read and provides more space for readers to write comments.

TriTech can also reduce spending by urging employees to economize. For example, instead of flying first class, employees can fly tourist class or take advantage of discount fares. Instead of taking clients to dinner, TriTech personnel can hold breakfast meetings, which tend to be less costly. Rather than ordering a $20 bottle of wine, employees can select a less expensive bottle or dispense with alcohol entirely. People can book rooms at moderately priced hotels and drive smaller rental cars. In general, employees should be urged to spend the company's money as though it were their own.

Obtain Lowest Rates from Travel Providers

Apart from urging individual employees to economize, TriTech can also save money by searching for the lowest available air fares, hotel rates, and rental car fees. Currently, few TriTech employees have the time or specialized knowledge to seek out travel bargains. When they need to travel, they make the most convenient and most comfortable arrangements. However, if TriTech contracts with a professional travel service, the company will have access to professionals who can be more efficient in obtaining the lowest rates from travel providers.

The use of an example adds credibility and makes the discussion more interesting.

Judging by the experience of other companies, TriTech may be able to trim as much as 30 to 40 percent from the travel budget by looking for bargains in air fares and negotiating group rates with hotels and rental car companies.[9] For example, by guaranteeing to provide selected hotels with a certain amount of business, Tandem Computer was able to achieve a 20 percent reduction in its hotel expenses. Now, instead of choosing between 40 or 50 hotels in a city like Chicago, Tandem employees stay at one of the 6 or 7 hotels where the company has negotiated a corporate rate.[10] TriTech should be able to achieve similar economies by analyzing its travel patterns, identifying frequently visited locations, and selecting a few hotels that are willing to reduce rates in exchange for guaranteed business. By the same token, the company should be able to save up to 40 percent on rental car charges by negotiating a corporate rate.

Pointing up the difficulties demonstrates that you have considered all the angles and builds readers' confidence in your judgment.

The possibilities for economizing are promising, but it's worth noting that making the best arrangements is a complicated undertaking, requiring many trade-offs. The airlines currently offer 4 million different air fares, and every week 120,000 of those fares change in some way.[11] In booking a particular reservation, the travel agent might have to choose between 20 or 25 options with varying prices and provisions. The best fare might not always be the lowest. For example, indirect flights are often less expensive than direct flights, but they take longer and may end up costing more in lost work time. By the same token, the cheapest tickets may have to be booked 30 days in advance, often an impossibility in business travel. Similarly, discount tickets may be nonrefundable, which is a real negative if the trip has to be canceled at the last minute. TriTech is currently not equipped to make these and other trade-offs. However, by employing a business-oriented travel service, the company will have access to computerized systems that can optimize its choices.

Notice how Andy made the transition from section to section. The first sentence under the heading on this page refers to the subject of the previous paragraph and signals a shift in thought.

The use of informative titles for illustrations is consistent with the way headings are handled and is appropriate for a report to a receptive audience. The use of complete sentences helps readers focus immediately on the point of the illustrations.

Even though estimated savings may be difficult to project, including dollar figures helps management envision the impact of your suggestions.

The Impact of Reforms

By implementing tighter controls, reducing unnecessary expenses, and negotiating more favorable rates, TriTech Industries should be able to reduce its travel and entertainment budget significantly. As Table 1 illustrates, the combined savings should be in the neighborhood of $4 million, although the precise figures are somewhat difficult to project. Reductions in air fares and hotel accommodations are the most important source of savings, accounting for about $2.3 million.

Table 1
TriTech Can Trim Travel and Entertainment Costs
by an Estimated $4 Million per Year

Source of Savings	Amount Saved
More efficient scheduling and selection of airline reservations	$1,400,000
Preferred rates on hotels	900,000
Fewer trips to conferences	700,000
Reduction in interdivisional travel	425,000
Reduced rates on rental cars	375,000
More economical choices by individuals	200,000
TOTAL SAVINGS	$4,000,000

Source: Accounting department estimates based on internal data and experience of other companies.

To achieve the economies outlined in the table, TriTech will incur expenses associated with hiring a director of travel and implementing a travel and entertainment cost-control system. These costs are projected at $60,000: $55,000 per year in salary and benefits for the new employee and a one-time expense of $5,000 associated with the cost-control system. The cost of retaining a full-service travel agency will be negligible, because agencies receive a commission from travel providers rather than a fee from clients.

The measures required to achieve these savings are likely to be unpopular with employees. TriTech personnel are accustomed to generous travel and entertainment allowances, and they are likely to resent having these privileges curtailed. To alleviate their disappointment, management should make a determined effort to explain why the changes are necessary. The director of corporate communication should be asked to develop a multifaceted campaign that will communicate the importance of curtailing travel and entertainment costs. In addition, management should set a positive example by adhering strictly to the new policies. To maintain morale, the limitations should apply equally to employees at all levels in the organization.

The table on this page puts Andy's recommendations in perspective. Notice how he called attention in the text to the most important sources of savings and also spelled out the costs required to achieve these results.

Use a descriptive heading for the last section of the text. In informational reports, this section is generally called "Summary"; in analytical reports it is called "Conclusions" or "Conclusions and Recommendations."

Emphasize the recommendations by presenting them in list format, if possible.

Do not introduce new facts in this section of the text.

10

CONCLUSIONS AND RECOMMENDATIONS

TriTech Industries is currently spending $10 million per year on travel and entertainment. Although much of this spending is justified, the company's costs appear to be high relative to competitors', mainly because TriTech has been generous with its travel benefits.

TriTech's liberal approach to travel and entertainment was understandable during years of high profitability; however, the company is facing the prospect of declining profits for the next several years. Management is therefore motivated to cut costs in all areas of the business. Reducing T&E spending is particularly important, because the impact of these costs on the bottom line will increase as a result of the new tax laws, changes in government regulations, and fare increases in the airline industry.

TriTech should be able to reduce travel and entertainment costs by about 40 percent by taking three important steps:

1. Institute tighter spending controls. Management should hire a Director of Travel and Entertainment who will assume overall responsibility for T&E activities. Within the next six months, this individual should develop a written travel policy, institute a T&E budgeting and cost-control system, and retain a professional, business-oriented travel agency that will optimize arrangements with travel providers.

2. Reduce unnecessary travel and entertainment. TriTech should encourage employees to economize on travel and entertainment spending. Management can accomplish this by authorizing fewer trips and by urging employees to be more conservative in their spending.

3. Obtain lowest rates from travel providers. TriTech should also focus on obtaining the best rates on airline tickets, hotel rooms, and rental cars. By channeling all arrangements through a professional travel agency, the company can optimize its choices and gain clout in negotiating preferred rates.

Because these measures may be unpopular with employees, management should make a concerted effort to explain the importance of reducing travel costs. The director of public relations should be given responsibility for developing a plan to communicate the need for employee cooperation.

Because Andy organized his report around conclusions and recommendations, readers have already been introduced to them. Thus he summarizes his conclusions in the first two paragraphs, presenting them in the same order in which they were presented in the text. A simple list is enough to remind readers of the three main recommendations. In a longer report, he might have divided the section into subsections, labeled "Conclusions" and "Recommendations," to distinguish between the two. If the report had been organized around logical arguments, this would be readers' first exposure to the conclusions and recommendations, and Andy would have needed to develop them more fully.

To simplify the typing process, most writers prefer to place all source notes together at the end of the text. (See Component Chapter E for details on handling documentation.)

11

NOTES

1. Susan Voyles, "Companies Clamp Down in Tight '87," USA Today, 23 February 1987, 1E.

2. Denis W. Day, "How to Fly the Low-Cost Friendly Skies of T&E," Management Accounting, June 1985, 33.

3. Analysis of Costs in the Electronics Industry (Washington, D.C.: International Association of Electronics, 1988), 23.

4. Kevin Maney, "Taxes: Business as Usual," USA Today, 23 February 1987, 1B.

5. Voyles, "Companies Clamp Down," 2E.

6. Scott Kilman, "An Unexpected Result of Airline Decontrol Is Return to Monopolies," Wall Street Journal, 20 July 1987, 1.

7. Kilman, "An Unexpected Result."

8. Voyles, "Companies Clamp Down," 2E.

9. Ray D. Dillon, Betty C. Horn, and Thomas S. Dudick, "Business Travel Expenditures: A Plan for Controlling Costs," Journal of Accountancy, October 1986, 146.

10. Voyles, "Companies Clamp Down," 2E.

11. Interview with Judith Dettinger, "Ways Businesses Can Save Billions on Travel Costs," U.S. News & World Report, 22 April 1985, 78.

List references alphabetically by the author's last name or, when the author is unknown, by the title of the reference. See Component Chapter E for additional details on preparing bibliographies.

BIBLIOGRAPHY

Analysis of Costs in the Electronics Industry. Washington, D.C.: International Association of Electronics, 1988.

Day, Denis W. "How to Fly the Low-Cost Friendly Skies of T&E." Management Accounting, June 1985, 33-36.

Dillon, Ray D., Betty C. Horn, and Thomas S. Dudick. "Business Travel Expenditures: A Plan for Controlling Costs." Journal of Accountancy, October 1986, 146-155.

Kilman, Scott. "An Unexpected Result of Airline Decontrol Is Return to Monopolies." Wall Street Journal, 20 July 1987, 1, 12.

Maney, Kevin. "Taxes: Business as Usual." USA Today, 23 February 1987, 1B.

Voyles, Susan. "Companies Clamp Down in Tight '87." USA Today, 23 February 1987, 1E-2E.

"Ways Business Can Save Billions on Travel Costs." U.S. News & World Report, 22 April 1985, 78-79.

Andy's bibliography is a reading list of sources cited in the notes. Some report writers use the bibliography to list additional sources.

COMPONENTS OF A FORMAL PROPOSAL

Bids to perform work under a contract and pleas for financial support from outsiders are nearly always formal. The goal, which is to impress the potential client or supporter with your professionalism, is best achieved through a structured and deliberate approach.

Formal proposals contain many of the same components as formal reports (see Figure 16.2). The difference lies mostly in the text, although a few of the prefatory parts are also different. With the exception of an occasional appendix, most proposals have few supplementary parts.

PREFATORY PARTS

Formal proposals contain most of the same prefatory parts as formal reports.

The cover, title fly, title page, table of contents, and list of illustrations are handled just as they are in a formal report. But other prefatory parts are quite different.

Use a copy of the request for proposal in place of the letter of authorization.

- *Copy of the RFP.* Instead of having a letter of authorization, a formal proposal may have a copy of the request for proposal (RFP) issued by the client to whom the proposal is being submitted. If the RFP includes detailed specifications, it may be too long to bind into the proposal; in that case, you may want to include only the introductory portion of the RFP. Or you can omit the RFP and simply refer to it in your letter of transmittal.

Use the good-news pattern for the letter of transmittal if the proposal is solicited; use the persuasive plan if the proposal is unsolicited.

- *Letter of transmittal.* The way you handle the letter of transmittal depends on whether the proposal is solicited or unsolicited. If the proposal is solicited, the transmittal letter should follow the pattern for good-news messages, highlighting those aspects of your proposal that may give you a competitive advantage. If the proposal is unsolicited, the transmittal letter takes on added importance; in fact, it may be all the client reads. The letter must persuade the reader that you have something worthwhile to offer, something that justifies the time required to read the entire proposal. The transmittal letter for an unsolicited proposal should therefore follow the pattern for persuasive messages (see Chapter 9).
- *Synopsis or executive summary.* Although you may include a synopsis or executive summary for your reader's convenience if your proposal is quite long, these components are somewhat less useful in a formal

FIGURE 16.2
Parts of a Formal Proposal

PREFATORY PARTS	TEXT OF THE PROPOSAL	SUPPLEMENTARY PARTS
Cover	Introduction	Appendixes
Title fly	Body	
Title page	Summary	
Letter of transmittal		
Table of contents		
List of illustrations		
Synopsis or executive summary		

Most proposals do not require a synopsis or executive summary.

proposal than they are in a formal report. If your proposal is unsolicited, your transmittal letter will already have whet the reader's appetite, making a synopsis or executive summary pointless. It may also be pointless if your proposal is solicited, because the reader is already committed to studying the text to find out how you propose to satisfy the terms of a contract. The introduction to a solicited proposal provides an adequate preview of the contents.

TEXT OF THE PROPOSAL

A proposal is both a selling tool and a contractual commitment.

The text of a proposal performs two essential functions: It persuades the client to award you a contract, and it spells out the terms of that contract. The trick is to sell the client on your ideas without making promises that will haunt you later.

Follow the instructions presented in the RFP.

If the proposal is unsolicited, you have some latitude in arranging the text. However, the organization of a solicited proposal is governed by the request for proposal. Most RFPs spell out precisely what you should cover, in what order, so that all bids will be similar in form. This uniformity enables the client to evaluate the competing proposals in a systematic way. In fact, in many organizations a team of evaluators splits up the proposals and looks at different sections. For example, an engineer might review the technical portions of all the proposals submitted, and an accountant might review the cost estimates.

Introduction

In the introduction, establish the need for action and summarize the key benefits of your proposal.

The introduction orients readers to the rest of the proposal. It should identify your organization and your purpose and outline the remainder of the text. If the proposal is solicited, the introduction should refer to the RFP; if not, it should mention any factors that led you to submit the bid. For example, you might refer to previous conversations you've had with the client or mention mutual acquaintances. Subheadings often include the following:

- *Background or statement of the problem.* A brief review of the client's situation, worded to establish the need for action.
- *Overview of approach.* Highlights your key selling points and their related benefits, showing how your proposal will solve the client's problem. The subhead for this section might also be "Preliminary Analysis" or some other heading that will identify this section as a summary of your solution to the problem.
- *Scope.* The limits of the study, what you will and will not do. This brief section may also be labeled "Limitations."
- *Report organization.* Orients the reader to the remainder of the proposal and calls attention to the major divisions of thought.

Body

The heart of the proposal is the body, which generally has the same purpose as the body of a report. In a proposal, however, the body must cover some specific types of information:

- *Proposed approach.* May also be titled "Technical Proposal," "Research Design," "Issues for Analysis," or "Work Statement." Regardless of the heading, this section is a description of what you have to offer: your concept, product, or service. For example, if you are proposing to develop a new airplane, you might describe your preliminary design, using drawings or calculations to demonstrate the soundness of your solution. To persuade the client that your proposal has merit, focus on the strengths of your product in relation to the client's needs. Point out any advantages that you have over your competitors. For example, you might describe how the unique wing design of your plane provides superior fuel economy, a particularly important feature specified in the client's request for proposal.

In the approach section, demonstrate the superiority of your ideas, products, or services.

- *Work plan.* Describes how you will accomplish the work that must be done (necessary unless you are proposing to provide a standard, off-the-shelf item). For each phase of the work plan, you describe the steps you will take, their timing, the methods or resources you will use, and the person or persons who will be responsible. Indicate any critical dates when portions of the work will be completed. If your proposal is accepted, the work plan will become contractually binding. Any slippage in the schedule you propose may jeopardize the contract or cost your organization a considerable amount of money. Therefore, be very careful in preparing this section of the proposal. Don't promise to deliver more than you can realistically achieve within a given period.

Use the work plan to describe the tasks to be completed under the terms of the contract.

- *Statement of qualifications.* Describes your organization's experience, personnel, and facilities in relation to the client's needs. If you work for a large organization that frequently submits proposals, you can usually borrow much of this section intact from previous proposals. Be sure, however, to tailor this "boilerplate" to suit the situation. The qualifications section can be an important selling point, and it deserves to be handled carefully.

In the qualifications section, demonstrate that you have the personnel, facilities, and experience to do a competent job.

- *Costs.* Typically has few words and many numbers but can make or break the proposal. If your price is out of line, the client will probably reject your bid. However, before you "buy in" with a low bid, remember that you will have to live with the price you quote in the proposal. It's rarely advantageous to win a contract if you're doomed to lose money on the job. Because it is often difficult to estimate costs on experimental projects, the client will be looking for evidence that your cost proposal is realistic. Break the costs down in detail so the client can see how you got your numbers: so much for labor, so much for materials, so much for overhead.

The more detailed your cost proposal is, the more credibility your estimates will have.

In a formal proposal, it pays to be as thorough and accurate as possible. Carefully selected detail enhances your credibility. So does successful completion of any task you promise to perform.

Summary

You may want to include a summary or conclusion section, because it is your last opportunity to convince the reader to accept your proposal. Summarize the merits of your approach, reemphasize why you and your firm are the ones to do it, and stress what the benefits will be. The section should be relatively brief, assertive, and confident.

CHECKLIST FOR FORMAL REPORTS AND PROPOSALS

A. Quality of the Research

- ☐ 1. Define the problem clearly.
- ☐ 2. State the purpose of the report or proposal.
- ☐ 3. Identify all relevant issues.
- ☐ 4. Accumulate evidence pertaining to each issue.
- ☐ 5. Check evidence for accuracy, currency, and reliability.
- ☐ 6. Justify your conclusions by the evidence.
  - ☐ a. Do not omit or distort evidence in order to support your point of view.
  - ☐ b. Identify and justify all assumptions.

B. Preparation of the Report or Proposal

- ☐ 1. Choose a format and length that are appropriate to your audience and the subject.
- ☐ 2. Prepare a sturdy, attractive cover.
  - ☐ a. Label the cover clearly with the title of the report or proposal.
  - ☐ b. Use a title that tells the audience exactly what the report or proposal is about.
- ☐ 3. Provide all necessary information on the title page.
  - ☐ a. Include the full title of the report or proposal.
  - ☐ b. Include the name, title, and affiliation of the recipient.
  - ☐ c. Give the name, title, and affiliation of the author.
  - ☐ d. Provide the date of submission.
  - ☐ e. Balance the information in blocks on the page.
- ☐ 4. Include a copy of the letter of authorization or request for proposal, if appropriate.
- ☐ 5. Prepare a letter or memo of transmittal.
  - ☐ a. Use a memo format for internal documents.
  - ☐ b. Use a letter format for external documents.
  - ☐ c. Include the transmittal letter in only some copies if it contains sensitive or personal information suitable for some but not all readers.
  - ☐ d. Place the transmittal letter right before the table of contents.
  - ☐ e. Use the good-news plan for reports and solicited proposals; use the persuasive plan for unsolicited proposals.
  - ☐ f. Word the letter to "convey" the report officially to the readers; refer to the authorization; and discuss the purpose, scope, background, sources and methods, and limitations.
  - ☐ g. Mention any special points that warrant readers' attention.
  - ☐ h. If you use direct order, summarize conclusions and/or recommendations (unless they are included in a synopsis).
  - ☐ i. Acknowledge all who were especially helpful in preparing the report or proposal.
  - ☐ j. Close with thanks, offer to be of further assistance, and suggest future projects, if appropriate.
- ☐ 6. Prepare the table of contents.
  - ☐ a. Include all first-level headings (and all second-level headings or perhaps all second- and third-level headings).
  - ☐ b. Give the page number of each heading.
  - ☐ c. Word all headings exactly as they appear in the text.
  - ☐ d. Include the synopsis (if there is one) and supplementary parts in the table of contents.
  - ☐ e. Number the table of contents and all prefatory pages with lower-case roman numerals centered at the bottom of the page.
- ☐ 7. Prepare a list of illustrations if you have more than four visual aids.
  - ☐ a. Put the list in the same format as the table of contents.
  - ☐ b. Identify visual aids either directly beneath the table of contents or on a separate page under the heading "List of Illustrations."
- ☐ 8. Develop a synopsis or executive summary if the document is long and formal.
  - ☐ a. Tailor the synopsis to the document's length and tone.
  - ☐ b. Condense the main points of the report or proposal, using either the informative approach or the descriptive approach, according to the guidelines in this chapter.
  - ☐ c. Present the points in the synopsis in the same order as they appear in the report or proposal.
- ☐ 9. Prepare the introduction to the text.

- ☐ a. Leave a 2-inch margin at the top of the page, and center the title of the report or proposal.
- ☐ b. In a long report or proposal (ten pages or more), type the first-level heading "Introduction" three lines below the title.
- ☐ c. In a short report or proposal (fewer than ten pages), begin typing three lines below the title of the report or proposal without the heading "Introduction."
- ☐ d. Discuss the authorization (unless it's covered in the letter of transmittal), purpose, scope, background, sources and methods, definitions, limitations, and text organization.

☐ 10. Prepare the body of the report or proposal.

- ☐ a. Carefully select the organizational plan (see Chapter 15).
- ☐ b. Use either a personal or an impersonal tone consistently.
- ☐ c. Use either a past or a present time perspective consistently.
- ☐ d. Follow a consistent format in typing headings of different levels, using a company format guide, a sample proposal or report, or the format in this textbook as a model (see Component Chapter D).
- ☐ e. Express comparable (same-level) headings in any given section in parallel grammatical form.
- ☐ f. Group ideas into logical categories.
- ☐ g. Tie sections together with transitional words, sentences, and paragraphs.
- ☐ h. Give ideas of equal importance roughly equal space.
- ☐ i. Avoid overly technical, pretentious, or vague language.
- ☐ j. Develop each paragraph around a topic sentence.
- ☐ k. Make sure all ideas in each paragraph are related.
- ☐ l. Double-space if longer than 10 pages.
- ☐ m. For reports and proposals bound on the left, number all pages with arabic numerals in the upper right-hand corner (except for the first page, where the number is centered 1 inch from the bottom); for top-bound documents, number all pages with arabic numerals centered 1 inch from the bottom.

☐ 11. Incorporate visual aids into the text.

- ☐ a. Number visual aids consecutively throughout the text, numbering tables and figures (other visual aids) separately if that style is preferred.
- ☐ b. Develop explicit titles for all visual aids except in-text tables.
- ☐ c. Refer to each visual aid in the text, and emphasize the significance of the data.
- ☐ d. Place visual aids as soon after their textual explanations as possible, or group them at the ends of chapters or at the end of the document.

☐ 12. Conclude the text of a report or proposal with a summary and, if appropriate, conclusions and recommendations.

- ☐ a. In a summary, recap the findings and explanations already presented.
- ☐ b. Place conclusions and recommendations in their order of logic or importance, preferably in list format.
- ☐ c. To induce action, explain in the recommendations section who should do what, when, where, and how.
- ☐ d. If appropriate, point up the benefits of action, to leave readers with the motivation to follow recommendations.

☐ 13. Document all material quoted or paraphrased from secondary sources, using a consistent format (see Component Chapter E).

☐ 14. Include appendixes at the end of the report or proposal to provide useful and detailed information that is of interest to some but not all readers.

- ☐ a. Give each appendix a title, such as "Questionnaire" or "Names and Addresses of Survey Participants."
- ☐ b. If there is more than one appendix, number or letter them consecutively in the order they're referred to in the text.
- ☐ c. Type appendixes in a format consistent with the text of the report or proposal.

☐ 15. Include a bibliography if it seems that readers would benefit or the document would gain credibility from it.

- ☐ a. Type the bibliography on a separate page headed "Bibliography" or "Sources."
- ☐ b. Alphabetize bibliography entries.
- ☐ c. Use a consistent format for the bibliography (see Component Chapter E).

SUMMARY

Preparing a formal report or proposal requires a team effort. Be sure to allow enough time for the various phases in the preparation process, from planning the report to reproducing the final copy.

In typing the final version, be sure to use the correct format, following company-approved guidelines. Long formal reports have a greater number of separate elements than do short ones. The text of the report (introduction, body, and final summary/conclusions/recommendations) is usually prepared first. Various prefatory and supplementary parts—such as the cover, title page, table of contents, appendixes, and bibliography—are added as needed, depending on the length and formality of the document.

Formal proposals are prepared in much the same way as formal reports, although they differ somewhat in prefatory parts, text elements, and supplementary parts.

COMMUNICATION CHALLENGES AT TUPPERWARE

Tupperware Home Parties is launching a new line of containers that can go from the refrigerator to the microwave oven to the table. The product has been designed for working mothers who are looking for convenient and economical ways to feed their families. Tupperware management has asked Jane Trimble to develop a public relations campaign to promote the new product among these consumers.

Jane has decided to hold a microwave cooking contest that will encourage people to use leftovers in a creative way with the help of Tupperware. Women from around the country will be encouraged to submit recipes for recycling leftovers. Five entrants, selected by a panel of judges, will be flown to New York to compete in a Tupperware cook-off contest. Filmed footage of the contest will be aired on TV talk shows, such as "Good Morning America."

Individual Challenge: Jane has asked you to develop a schedule for preparing a justification report that outlines the campaign. She expects the report to be about 20 pages long and to be illustrated with four or five visual aids. Make a list of the steps required in the preparation process, and estimate the amount of time required for each.

Team Challenge: Jane has cleared her preliminary ideas with all the necessary people within Tupperware. Now she is ready to begin working on the report itself. She has asked you and a few other members of the public relations department to help her brainstorm ideas and develop a detailed outline for the report. Be sure to identify all the prefatory and supplementary parts that will be included. Draft the memo of transmittal and an introduction.

QUESTIONS FOR DISCUSSION

1. How does the report writer's role differ from organization to organization?
2. What are the steps involved in the report preparation process, from initial planning through final editing and distribution? What percentage of the total preparation time do you suppose each step might take?
3. You know the old saying, "It isn't over 'til it's over." How does this comment relate to the report writing process?
4. How close to "perfection" should you strive to bring a formal report? Explain.
5. What are the distinguishing characteristics of a formal report?
6. What are the prefatory parts, text components, and supplementary parts of a formal report? What function does each subdivision serve?
7. How should you decide whether to use a synopsis or an executive summary?
8. What is the difference between conclusions and recommendations? What types of reports would have both?
9. How do the prefatory parts of a solicited proposal differ from the prefatory parts of an unsolicited proposal?
10. How does the text of a formal proposal differ from the text of a formal report?

CASES

SHORT FORMAL REPORTS

1. Who's eating what: Report using statistical data to analyze industry trends You are the assistant to Christie Thurber, the president of Restaurant Association of America, which recently commissioned a study of consumer eating habits. The association undertakes studies like these so it can relay results to member restaurants. The restaurants can then adapt to changing consumer needs.

To get the results shown in Tables 16.1, 16.2, and 16.3, telephone interviews were conducted with a nationwide sample of 1,035 people over 18. The interviewers prefaced their questions with this statement:

> In recent years some people say they have changed their diets by *increasing* their consumption of fruits, vegetables, and whole grains and by *decreasing* their consumption of refined sugar, animal fats, and salts.

TABLE 16.1 Percentages of Consumers Who Have Changed Eating Habits at Home

DEMOGRAPHIC CHARACTERISTIC	YES	NO	DON'T KNOW
GENDER			
Male	54%	46%	—%
Female	67	33	—
AGE			
18–24 years	48	52	—
25–34 years	61	38	1
35–49 years	64	36	—
50–64 years	60	40	—
65 years and older	65	35	—
MARITAL STATUS			
Married	62	38	—
Not married	57	43	—
EDUCATION			
College graduate	69	31	—
High school graduate	62	38	—
Not high school graduate	46	54	—
ANNUAL HOUSEHOLD INCOME			
$30,000 and over	67	33	—
$20,000–29,999	61	38	1
$15,000–19,999	60	40	—
Under $15,000	60	40	—
WOMEN'S EMPLOYMENT STATUS			
Employed full-time	69	31	—
Employed part-time	65	35	—
Not employed	66	34	—
REGION			
East	65	34	1
Midwest	59	41	—
South	52	48	—
West	66	34	—
FREQUENCY OF EATING OUT IN AVERAGE WEEK			
None	56	44	—
One	64	35	1
Two or three	62	38	—
Four or more	54	45	1
Average	60	40	—

TABLE 16.2 Percentages of Consumers Who Have Changed Eating Habits at Restaurants or Other Eating Places

DEMOGRAPHIC CHARACTERISTICS	YES	NO	DON'T KNOW
GENDER			
Male	35%	64%	1%
Female	44	54	2
AGE			
18–24 years	30	70	—
25–34 years	42	57	1
35–49 years	41	58	1
50–64 years	45	54	1
65 years and older	39	58	3
MARITAL STATUS			
Married	41	58	1
Not married	38	61	1
EDUCATION			
College graduate	47	52	1
High school graduate	41	58	1
Not high school graduate	27	70	3
ANNUAL HOUSEHOLD INCOME			
$30,000 and over	48	51	1
$20,000–29,999	39	60	1
$15,000–19,999	33	67	—
Under $15,000	42	55	3
WOMEN'S EMPLOYMENT STATUS			
Employed full-time	51	49	—
Employed part-time	42	58	—
Not employed	38	59	3
REGION			
East	41	56	3
Midwest	42	57	1
South	35	64	1
West	42	58	—
FREQUENCY OF EATING OUT IN AVERAGE WEEK			
None	31	65	4
One	40	59	1
Two or three	45	55	—
Four or more	40	60	—
Average	40	59	1

TABLE 16.3 Percentage of Consumers Who Have Made Various Types of Changes When Dining Out

DEMOGRAPHIC CHARACTERISTICS	LESS SALT	MORE SALT	LESS SUGAR	MORE VEGETABLES	MORE SALADS	FEWER FATS
AGE						
18–34 years	20%	16%	21%	24%	24%	12%
35–49 years	26	18	21	16	16	16
50 years and older	31	25	17	16	12	20
EDUCATION						
College graduate	18	28	20	23	15	15
Less than college graduate	28	17	19	17	19	16
ANNUAL HOUSEHOLD INCOME						
$30,000 and over	25	27	21	18	13	17
$15,000–29,999	22	17	22	20	21	18
Under $15,000	31	16	19	19	21	9
WOMEN'S EMPLOYMENT STATUS						
Employed	23	24	19	14	20	11
Not employed	31	16	14	20	21	18
REGION						
East	24	22	18	17	20	13
Midwest	30	19	21	15	21	23
South	17	22	18	25	13	13
West	30	17	20	18	14	14
FREQUENCY OF EATING OUT IN AVERAGE WEEK						
None	33	22	13	18	16	22
One	30	14	21	24	19	13
Two or three	22	18	23	14	16	18
Four or more	19	30	17	19	21	12
Average	25	20	20	18	18	16

Your task: Write a report to your boss that explains the results of the survey and its implications for restaurants. What trends in eating habits should they be concerned about? What changes should they make? Justify your conclusions and your recommendations by referring to the data in the tables.

2. Sailing past the sunsets: Report using statistical data to suggest a new advertising strategy As manager of Distant Dreams, a travel agency in Waco, Texas, you are highly interested in the information in Table 16.4. It appears that dollar income is shifting toward the 35–44 age group. Tables 16.5 and 16.6 are also broken down by age group.

Traditionally, your agency has concentrated its advertising on those nearing retirement, people who are closing out successful careers and now have the time and money to vacation abroad. But after examining the three sets of data, it occurs to you that a major shift in emphasis is desirable.

Your task: Write a report to Mary Henderson, who writes your advertisements, explaining why future ads should be directed to people besides those in their fifties and sixties who want to explore far reaches of the world. Justify your explanation by referring to the data you have examined.

TABLE 16.4 Percentage of Total U.S. Household Income Earned by Various Age Groups

AGE GROUP	YEAR 1975	1980	1985
25–34	23%	24%	26%
35–44	22	25	28
45–54	22	21	19
55–64	19	17	15
65 +	14	13	12

TABLE 16.5 Preferences in Travel Among Various Age Groups

TRAVEL INTERESTS	AGE GROUP 18–34	35–54	55 +
I am more interested in excitement and stimulation than rest and relaxation.	67%	42%	38%
I prefer to go where I haven't been before.	62	58	48
I like adventuresome travel.	62	45	32
I love foreign and exotic things.	41	25	21
Vacation is a time for self-indulgence, regardless of the cost.	31	16	14
I don't see the need for a travel agent.	67	63	52

TABLE 16.6 Basic Desire for Travel Among Various Age Groups

ATTITUDE TOWARD TRAVEL	AGE GROUP 18–34	35–54	55 +
Travel is one of the most rewarding and enjoyable things one can do.	71%	66%	56%
I love the idea of traveling and do so at every opportunity.	69	59	55
I often feel the need to get away from everything.	66	48	33

3. Picking the better path: Report assisting a client in a career choice You are employed by Open Options, a career counseling firm, and your main function is to help clients make career choices.

Today a client with the same name as yours (a truly curious coincidence!) came to your office and asked for help in deciding between two careers that you had yourself been interested in (an even greater coincidence!).

Your task: Do some research on the two careers and then prepare a short report that your client can study. Your report should compare at least five major areas, such as salary, working conditions, and education required. Interview the client to understand her or his personal preferences regarding each of the five areas. For example, what is the minimum salary the client will accept? By comparing the client's preferences with the research material you collect, such as salary data, you will have a basis for concluding which of the two careers is best. The report should end with a career recommendation.

4. Selling overseas: Report on the prospects for marketing a product in a foreign country Select (a) a product and (b) a country. The product might be a novelty item that you own (an inexpensive but accurate watch or clock, a desk organizer, or a coin bank, for example). The country should be one that you are not now familiar with. Imagine that you are with the international sales department of the company that manufactures and sells the novelty item and that you are proposing to make it available in the country you have selected.

The first step is to learn as much as possible about the country where you plan to market the product. Check almanacs and encyclopedias, paying particular attention to descriptions of the social life of the inhabitants and their economic conditions. If your library carries *Yearbook of International Trade Statistics, Monthly Bulletin of Statistics,* or *Trade Statistics* (all put out by the United Nations), you may want to consult them. And you should, of course, check the card catalog and recent periodical indexes for sources of additional information; look for (among other matters) cultural traditions that would encourage or discourage use of the product.

Your task: Write a short report that describes the product you plan to market abroad, briefly describes the country you have selected, indicates the types of people in this country who would find the product attractive, explains how the product would be transported into the country (or possibly manufactured there if materials and labor are available), recommends a location for a regional sales center, and suggests how the product should be sold. Your report is to be submitted to the chief operating officer of the company, whose name you can either make up or find in a corporate directory. The report should include your conclusions (how the product will do in this new environment) and your recommendations for marketing (steps the company should take immediately and those it should develop later).

5. Rating some textbooks: Report comparing textbook readability Gather the textbooks you are reading this term (if you have fewer than six, include some you used in previous terms to bring the total to at least six). Then do the following:

- Rank the books in order of the difficulty you are having in understanding them (the most difficult being number 1).
- Rank the books by how much you enjoy reading them (the least enjoyable being number 1).
- Rank the books by how well you are doing in the courses that they cover (the book for the course that you are doing worst in being number 1). If several books are used for the same course, assign them the same rank.

Next, determine the Fog Index for the prose in each book. (See Chapter 5 for an explanation.)

Your task: Write a short formal report, directed toward college professors, that (a) summarizes the relationship between the textbooks' scores on the Fog Index and your own evaluations of the textbooks; (b) displays your results graphically; (c) describes the methods you used and any special problems you encountered (did one contain poetry or contain works by many different authors?); (d) compares the Fog Index, which indicates the grade level for which a particular book is appropriate, to your grade level; and (e) evaluates and explains the use of the Fog Index as a measure of readability.

6. Is anyone out there listening? Report on radio advertising Martha McCreary is a vice president at Knowles-Mead, a small stock brokerage house in your city. In order to increase its clientele, the firm has decided to run a series of radio advertisements designed to catch the attention of potential investors.

Knowing of your interest in local radio, Martha asks your advice. Of the local stations, which one or two would be best for the low-key, factual advertisements that her firm has in mind? At what times during the day and the week might these spots be most effective?

Your task: Listen systematically to three or four radio stations in your area to determine (a) what types of products their advertisers generally are selling, (b) what their programming generally consists of, and (c) what type of listener they seem to appeal to. You should listen to each station at several different times during the day and at different times during the week. Chart your findings.

Then draft a formal report for Martha that contains the results of your research and your conclusions and recommendations. If the report is successful, Knowles-Mead should be able to choose the appropriate times and stations for a series of advertisements that would win new clients.

7. A park inspection: Report on the condition of public facilities As an employee of the city, you have been assigned to inspect some of its parks.

Your task: Visit a city park, and report back to your supervisor (Ben Willis, Commissioner of Parks) on the use and condition of the park that you have inspected. Your report should include at least the following information: the date and time of your inspection, a general description of the park and its facilities, an indication of who (if anyone) was on duty at the time of your inspection, an estimate of the number of people using the park at the time of your inspection, a breakdown by age and activity of these people, conclusions about the general use and condition of the park, recommendations for making the park more useful or attractive, and a statement of any problems more significant than ordinary day-to-day maintenance (such as inadequate parking or inadequate facilities).

Show in your report that you have inspected the park carefully. Check the bolts in the swings (for rust, wear, or inadequate lubrication), and make other observations necessary for a conscientious inspection. For your report, write factually. A serious inspector would write, "The swing area was littered with 12 empty soda cans," not "The swing area was filthy."

LONG FORMAL REPORTS REQUIRING NO ADDITIONAL RESEARCH

8. Getting to know you: Report analyzing bank customers The president of a local bank has been noticing that 35 percent of the bank's customers use the automated teller machines (ATMs) for most of their banking; the rest prefer the personal service of tellers inside the bank. This may be a useful distinction, but additional questions must be answered: Do the regular ATM users generally have a "financial life style" different from that of the nonusers? Which group would be more receptive to other changes in banking procedures? Which group is more price-sensitive (more likely to switch banks to get better rates on their accounts)? Are the economic aspirations of the two groups similar? Which group would be more likely to pay for additional banking services? The bank's president has accumulated the data in Tables 16.7 and 16.8 in an attempt to answer these questions.

Your task: Write a formal report that answers these questions through reference to the tables. Howard Sandler, the bank president who has commissioned your report, essentially wonders whether to reduce the

TABLE 16.7 Financial Life Style of Bank Customers

	ATM USERS		ATM NONUSERS	
	YES	NO	YES	NO
CONVENIENCE				
If I drive to a bank, I generally use the drive-in window rather than go in the lobby.	60%	40%	50%	50%
If a bank near me was open on Saturdays and my bank remained closed on Saturdays, I would consider switching my account to the bank open on Saturdays.	56	44	58	42
It would be very helpful to me if banks stayed open at night like department stores and supermarkets.	53	47	57	43
I would be very hesitant to use a bank in a department store or supermarket even if it was more convenient to do so.	29	71	44	56
The convenience of a bank's location is the most important factor in my selection of a bank.	70	30	31	69
TRANSACTION INNOVATIVENESS				
I would prefer to pay bills by telephone if I had the opportunity.	49	51	67	33
I would like to be able to make financial transactions from my own home-based teller terminal.	75	25	45	55
BARGAIN SHOPPING				
I would switch banks if I could earn 1 or 2 percent more interest on my checking account balance.	74	26	43	57
I would change banks if I had to keep $500 in my checking account to avoid a service charge.	77	23	56	64
ECONOMIC ASPIRATIONS				
In terms of wealth accumulation, my greatest achievements are ahead of me.	79	21	35	65
CREDIT UNION				
A credit union is an excellent place to have a savings account.	80	20	29	71
I would rather borrow money from a bank than a credit union, even if the interest rate was 2 or 3 percentage points higher.	16	84	71	29
Credit unions are really for working-class people—people who don't make a lot of money.	17	83	76	24
PERSONAL SERVICE				
It makes me feel better if the tellers at my bank know my name.	76	24	21	79
I think it is important to know personally the officers of the financial institution I deal with.	64	36	33	67
It doesn't matter to me whether tellers are friendly, as long as they are fast and efficient.	44	56	54	46

TABLE 16.8 **Bank Customers' Preferences for Financial Services**

	ATM USERS		ATM NONUSERS	
FINANCIAL SERVICES	YES	NO	YES	NO
Personal line of credit/overdraft protection	82%	18%	32%	68%
Transactions by phone	65	35	57	43
Bill paying	63	37	48	52
Investment advice	72	28	37	63
Estate planning/advice	65	35	43	57

bank's ATM services, continue them in their present form, or expand them into new locations. Another concern is the additional services that both types of customers might appreciate. Your report should profile both types of customers and then present your conclusions and recommendations.

9. The advertising director's decision: Report recommending a policy for certain types of advertising As the advertising director for *Living Well* magazine, you have been asked by the publisher, Phyllis Bradley, to consider the pros and cons of continuing to accept advertising for cigarettes and alcoholic beverages. Readers and staff members have questioned whether ads for these products are appropriate in a magazine devoted to physical fitness and healthful living.

Because your decision involves advertising revenue as well as reader and advertiser goodwill, you want to evaluate the alternatives carefully before making your recommendation. Your options include accepting all, none, or some part of the current advertisements for cigarettes and alcoholic beverages from five companies that have been doing business with your magazine for several years. You must also consider the likelihood of attracting other advertisers to take their place.

The financial aspects of the decision are an important consideration. In 1988, advertising income made up over 86 percent of *Living Well*'s $50.6 million in revenues, as shown in Figure 16.3. The combined 1988 revenue from the five accounts in question amounted to $1,262,880, or about 2.5 percent of total revenue. Although the loss of such a small portion of total revenue seems insignificant, you are concerned that you might jeopardize other advertising revenue as well, because the advertising agencies that represent these five accounts also represent some of the magazine's other advertisers. For example, the agencies currently holding the five accounts spent roughly $2.25 million on *Living Well* advertising in 1988, as Figure 16.3 shows.

FIGURE 16.3
***Living Well*'s Advertising and Circulation Revenue**

1988 REVENUE

Advertising revenue	$43.6 million
Circulation and other revenue	7.0 million
Total revenue	$50.6 million

Advertising as percentage of total revenue = $43.6/$50.6 = 86%

FIVE QUESTIONABLE ACCOUNTS—1988 REVENUE

Allied Tobacco Company	$ 354,980
Cardulla Winery	265,430
United Tobacco Products	259,200
Marston Liquor Distributors	238,070
Bausch Beer	145,200
Total of five accounts	$1,262,880

Revenue from five accounts as percentage of total revenue = $1,262,880/$50,600,000 = 2.5%

AGENCIES HOLDING QUESTIONABLE ACCOUNTS—1988 REVENUE

Applewood Incorporated (Marston, Bausch, and Cardulla)	$ 939,884
Larry F. Minn Agency (Allied Tobacco)	733,330
D. B. Powers and Company (United Tobacco)	575,000
Total from agencies	$2,248,214

Revenue from agencies as percentage of total revenue = $2,248,214/$50,600,000 = 4.4%

In making your decision, you must also consider whether readers might cancel their subscriptions because they disapprove of the ads. In just the past year, *Living Well* has received an increasing number of letters from readers who disapprove of cigarette and liquor ads. Over 300 readers have objected to ads for cigarettes; 112 have complained about ads for hard liquor, such as scotch, bourbon, gin, vodka, rum, and tequila; and 8 readers have objected to advertisements for wine and beer. A loss of these and other readers would not only decrease your income from selling magazines but would also affect your ability to attract advertisers, who are vitally interested in a magazine's

TABLE 16.9 Results of *Living Well's* Readership Survey

AGE GROUP	PERCENTAGE OF TOTAL	PERCENTAGE WHO OBJECT TO: CIGARETTE AND TOBACCO ADS	HARD-LIQUOR ADS	BEER AND WINE ADS
12–17	4%	Not surveyed	Not surveyed	Not surveyed
18–24	14	48%	36%	8%
25–34	21	51	42	6
35–44	23	58	47	9
45–54	11	52	41	8
55–64	16	47	38	6
65+	11	46	28	4

TABLE 16.10 Occupations of *Living Well's* Readers

OCCUPATION	PERCENTAGE OF TOTAL
Professional	12%
Key executive	8
Clerical	22
Trade	18
Service worker	12
Sales	11
Agricultural	9
Proprietor	8

TABLE 16.11 Total Family Income of *Living Well's* Readers

FAMILY INCOME	PERCENTAGE OF TOTAL
Under $8,000	1%
$8,000–15,999	2
$16,000–24,999	9
$25,000–29,999	23
$30,000–34,999	27
$35,000–$39,000	22
$40,000 and over	16

circulation figures. Tables 16.9, 16.10, and 16.11 show the results of a readership survey.

Looking at the disputed advertising in light of your magazine's editorial policy, you feel that the cigarette ads are most clearly out of harmony with your emphasis on physical fitness and healthy living. Although moderate use of alcoholic beverages has not clearly been identified as a health risk, the medical dangers of smoking are well established. At the same time, *Living Well* might not want to be perceived as advocating the use of hard liquor, because it can clearly lead to health problems if consumed in large quantities.

Your task: Write a full formal report to your publisher, Phyllis Bradley, that includes your data, conclusions, and recommendations. Do not omit significant data, even if they appear to contradict your final recommendations. Include justifications for your recommendations, possibly stated as assumptions about the future growth and development of the magazine if your recommendations are followed.

10. Equipping an office: Report analyzing buying decisions Your research firm has been commissioned to prepare a study examining the way small businesses decide what office products and services to buy. The national publication that has hired your firm would like evidence to support its contention that magazines are a good place to advertise office products to small businesses.

Your staff has conducted a telephone survey of 500 U.S. businesses ranging in size from 1 to 99 employees and representing a full range of businesses (manufacturing, retail, finance/insurance, real estate, service, and so on). Some of the more significant findings from the survey are presented in Tables 16.12 through 16.16 and in Figure 16.4.

Your task: After studying the findings, write a report summarizing the results and analyzing the implications for marketers of office products.

FIGURE 16.4
Employee Groups' Power to Purchase*

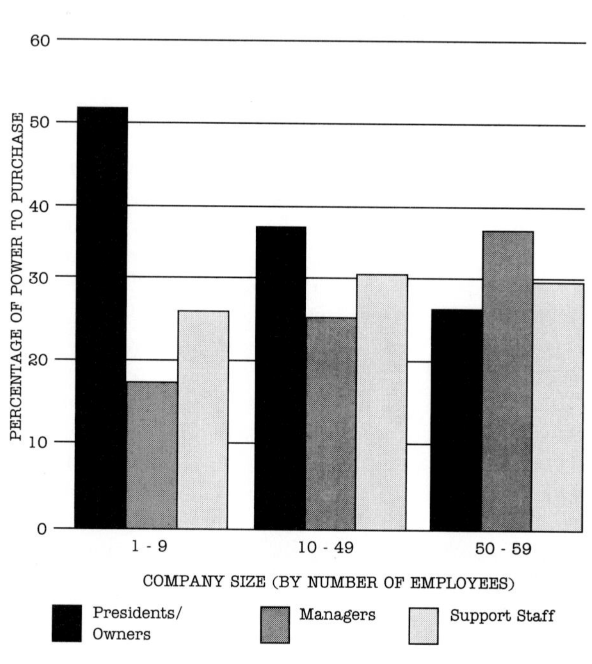

* Average for all product categories

TABLE 16.12 Percentage of Time That Employee Groups Determine the Need for Office Products and Services

OFFICE PRODUCT/ SERVICE	EMPLOYEE GROUP*		
	PRESIDENTS/ OWNERS	MANAGERS	SUPPORT STAFF
Telephone equipment	70%	22%	7%
Monthly telephone service	69	23	8
Personal computers	65	25	9
Computer software	59	26	13
Word processors	58	27	14
Copiers	57	30	11
Typewriters	56	26	16
Calculators	50	28	17
Pens/pencils	39	27	31
Stationery	39	27	31
Air couriers	31	17	9

* Numbers in table may not total 100 percent because of unspecified job title.

TABLE 16.13 Percentage of Expenditures That Employee Groups Influence

OFFICE PRODUCT/ SERVICE	EMPLOYEE GROUP*		
	PRESIDENTS/ OWNERS	MANAGERS	SUPPORT STAFF
Typewriters	26%	38%	37%
Word processors	28	60	12
Pens/pencils	29	36	34
Stationery	30	40	30
Computer software	36	50	14
Calculators	37	41	22
Copiers	38	29	33
Telephone equipment	40	33	28
Air couriers	45	34	21
Monthly telephone service	47	34	19
Personal computers	63	19	18

* Numbers in table may not total 100 percent because of unspecified job title.

TABLE 16.14 Sources of Product Information Used by Employee Groups

SOURCE OF INFORMATION	EMPLOYEE GROUP			
	PRESIDENTS/ OWNERS	MANAGERS	SUPPORT STAFF	TOTAL
Catalogs	74%	83%	81%	79%
Dealers	46	66	64	57
Friends/associates	52	58	55	54
Magazines	49	51	49	50
Newspapers	29	34	29	31
Television	12	14	8	12
Radio	10	16	9	12

TABLE 16.15 Factors That Influence Purchases by Employee Groups*

FACTOR INFLUENCING PURCHASE	EMPLOYEE GROUP		
	PRESIDENTS/ OWNERS	MANAGERS	SUPPORT STAFF
Service	4.36	4.56	4.58
Price	4.07	4.22	4.40
Manufacturer's reputation	4.33	4.27	4.30
Product features	2.93	3.18	3.04

* On a scale of 1 to 5, with 5 being most influential.

TABLE 16.16 Average Yearly Expenditure per Company on Office Products and Services

OFFICE PRODUCT/ SERVICE	SIZE OF COMPANY (BY NUMBER OF EMPLOYEES)			AVERAGE (1–99)
	1–9	10–49	50–99	
Monthly telephone service	$4,440	$ 9,839	$16,298	$5,714
Personal computers	1,555	3,195	7,576	2,000
Stationery	934	2,083	4,084	1,225
Telephone equipment	774	2,578	3,857	1,222
Computer software	242	623	2,322	374
Copiers	564	1,247	2,174	728
Air couriers	360	1,016	1,200	509
Typewriters	147	484	1,110	242
Pens/pencils	311	767	1,110	417
Word processors	226	502	730	288
Calculators	83	170	355	105
Total	$9,636	$22,504	$40,816	$12,824

LONG FORMAL REPORTS REQUIRING ADDITIONAL RESEARCH

11. Equipment purchase: Report on competitive product features Say that your office or home needs some new equipment. Choose one of the following, and figure out which brand and model would be the best buy.

a. typewriter
b. calculator
c. telephone answering machine
d. home security system
e. photocopier
f. microcomputer
g. word-processing software
h. dictation equipment

Your task: Write a long formal report comparing the features of available alternatives, and make your recommendation clear.

12. Is there any justice? Report critiquing legislation Plenty of people complain about their state legislators, but few are specific about their complaints. Here's your chance.

Your task: Write a long formal report about a law that you feel should not have been enacted or should be enacted. Be objective. Write the report using specific facts to support your feelings. Reach conclusions and offer your recommendation at the end of the report. As a final step, send a copy of the report to an appropriate state official or legislator.

13. Employment opportunities: Report comparing two employers As a student, the task of getting a job looms large. But you don't want just any job, so you're going to be doing some research.

Your task: Prepare a lengthy comparative study of two organizations that you might like to work for. Using annual reports, brochures, discussions with present or past employees, and all the other types of company information described in Chapter 10, analyze the suitability of these organizations to your own career goals and preferences for work environment. At the end of the report, recommend the best company to work for.

14. Group effort: Report on a large-scale topic The following topics may be too big for any one person, and yet they need to be investigated.

a. A demographic profile (age, gender, socioeconomic status, residence, employment, educational background, and the like) of the students at your college or university
b. The best part-time employment opportunities in your community
c. The best of two or three health clubs or gyms in your community
d. Actions that can be taken in your community or state to combat alcohol (or drug) abuse
e. Improvements that could be made in the food service at your college or university
f. Your college's or university's image in the community and ways to improve it
g. Your community's strengths and weaknesses in attracting new businesses

Your task: Because these topics require considerable research, your instructor may wish to form groups to work on each. If your group writes a report on the first topic, summarize your findings at the end of the report. For all the other topics, reach conclusions and make recommendations in the report.

15. Secondary sources: Report based on library research Perhaps one of the following questions has been keeping you awake at night:

a. What's the best way for someone with your financial status to invest $5,000?
b. What should be done about parking problems on campus?
c. Of three careers that appeal to you, which best suits you?
d. How do other consumers regard a product that you use frequently?
e. Which of three cities that you might like to live in seems most attractive?
f. What's the surest and easiest route to becoming a millionaire?

Your task: Answer one of these questions, using secondary sources for information. Be sure to document your sources in the correct form. Give conclusions and recommendations in your report.

16. Business problem: Report relating to business In the business or profession that you are in or are studying for, there are undoubtedly some issues that have not been resolved.

Your task: Choose one of these problems and write a long formal report on it, complete with your own conclusions and recommendations.

FORMAL PROPOSALS

17. Top dogs: Proposal to furnish puppies to Docktor Pet Centers You are the business manager for Sandy's Kennels of Alma, Kansas, one of the country's largest dog-breeding operations. Every year, you sell 7,500 puppies to pet shops around the country, at an average price of $130 per dog. The pet stores then sell the dogs for $225 to $300, depending on the breed.

Your business involves both breeding and reselling animals. In your own kennels, you raise 52 different kinds of dogs; in addition you buy dogs from other breeders at approximately $60 per dog and resell them to pet stores. Your dogs are all pedigreed animals with American Kennel Club papers. In addition, they come with all the required puppy vaccinations and are guaranteed to be healthy.

For several years, you have been trying to win a long-term contract to supply puppies to Docktor Pet Centers, the country's largest pet store chain. Finally you have been invited to submit a proposal to provide 2,000 dogs per year to Docktor's 220 retail outlets. The specifications stipulate that you will ship approximately 150 dogs per month from January through October and 250 dogs in November and in December. The puppies should be eight to ten weeks old at the time of shipment and should have all the necessary shots and AKC papers. Docktor is willing to accept a variety of breeds but has requested that each shipment contain a mix of large and small dogs and males and females. The chain is willing to pay from $115 to $130 per dog, depending on the breed.

Your task: Using your imagination to supply the details, write a proposal describing your plan to provide the dogs.[1]

18. Cruising out to sea: Proposal to host an American Medical Association convention The marketing department for Miami-based Carnival Cruise Lines, of which you are a member, is responsible for making sure that your firm's cruise ships are fully booked. The job has become increasingly challenging since several rival cruise ship lines have added new ships. The surge in capacity has prompted companies in the industry to scramble for passengers.

As part of your marketing program, you are trying to encourage large groups to book conventions on board your ships. You have recently purchased two new vessels, both capable of carrying 1,900 passengers, that are particularly suitable for such functions. The ships are essentially floating hotels with meeting rooms, restaurants, lounges, pools, and other recreational facilities. Staffed with a crew of 500, each vessel offers outstanding food, entertainment, and service. The ships can be scheduled for three-day or seven-day cruises. The price per passenger for shorter cruises ranges from $325 to $855, depending on accommodations and the group's choice of menu and activities. The average price per passenger for week-long cruises is $1,250. Both ships sail from Miami and cruise either the Caribbean or the Gulf of Mexico.

The Southeast Region branch of the American Medical Association is soliciting proposals for hosting a convention from February 8 through 11. An estimated 1,800 delegates and spouses are expected to attend the convention, which will feature lectures on medical topics as well as recreational activities. The AMA will be responsible for planning the medical portions of the program, but the hotel or convention center that gets the contract will be in charge of organizing recreational activities and planning food and beverage service. The AMA is prepared to pay $1,100 per person for food, lodging, and recreation for the four-day convention, a sum that Carnival management is willing to accept for such a large group.

Your task: Develop a proposal that describes how Carnival Cruise Lines can meet the AMA's needs. Emphasize the advantages of booking the convention on board a ship as opposed to holding it in a hotel or convention center. Use your imagination to flesh out the details of the proposal.[2]

19. A losing proposition: Proposal to run a weight-loss program for General Electric employees One of your duties as a marketing representative for Weight Watchers International is to encourage corporations to sponsor weight-loss programs for their employees. You are a firm believer in the value of such programs, because you have seen what they can do for a company's workers. For example, as a result of one or your recent five-week, company-sponsored programs, a group of 110 employees lost a total of 750 pounds. At the conclusion of the program, you had the satisfaction of knowing that you had left a healthier, happier staff. One woman who lost 20 pounds said, "You've changed my life!"

Weight Watchers' outstanding reputation in the diet industry helps make your job relatively easy. The program involves a combination of psychological support and nutritional counseling. Groups of dieters meet once a week to discuss their eating problems, check their progress, and learn good eating habits. A group leader, usually a successful Weight Watchers "graduate," runs the meeting and provides nutritional information and moral support. Participants are encouraged to use a variety of Weight Watchers products, which include cookbooks and frozen dinners.

The approach sounds simple, but it works. Since the organization was founded in 1963, 25 million people have joined Weight Watchers. Some 15,000 meetings are held each week, and over 700,000 dieters are currently enrolled in the program at a weekly cost of $6 or $7.

You recently met with the director of employee health and safety at General Electric headquarters in Fairfield, Connecticut. During your meeting, you proposed that Weight Watchers conduct a seven-week weight-loss program for GE employees. You suggested that the sessions be held during lunch hour and that as many employees as possible be encouraged to participate. You would subdivide the enrollees into groups of 25 to facilitate discussions. Each group would be headed by a professional Weight Watchers trainer. Participants would meet for an hour each day to share low-calorie lunches, prepared by the GE cafeteria using Weight Watchers recipes. During their meal, enrollees would get a pep talk from the group leader and share their own experiences.

After lunch, each group would take a brisk 15-minute walk before returning to work. In addition, employees would be encouraged to spend an hour each day working out in the GE gym before or after work. Weight Watchers trainers would be on hand at these times to run aerobics classes and advise participants on exercise programs.

The seven-week program would culminate with a ceremony honoring participants who had lost the most pounds and inches. The grand prize would be a one-week trip for two to Hawaii. General Electric would pay Weight Watchers a fee of $50 for each employee who enrolled in the program and would cover the costs of the award ceremony and the prizes.

Your task: Your contact at GE was very enthusiastic about your suggestions. He urged you to submit a formal, written proposal describing your program. Write the proposal.[3]

20. Tennis anyone? Proposal to convince the Chicago Unified School District to adopt a tennis program Back in the late 1970s, tennis was the "in" sport. Racquets were selling like hotcakes, and people were reserving court time three weeks in advance. But in recent years, enthusiasm for the sport has waned. The number of players has declined by 40 percent. According to industry analysts, one reason for the declining popularity of tennis is its elitist reputation. To a great extent, the industry has ignored the 71 percent of all players who use public courts and has focused instead on the affluent players who belong to private tennis clubs.

To broaden the appeal of the game, the United States Tennis Association (USTA) is now making a concerted effort to bring tennis to the average person. Part of this effort involves teaching young people to play the game. The USTA has allocated $1 million per year to run the Schools Program, which encourages local schools to provide tennis instruction for elementary and junior high school students. Some 2 million students at over 4,000 schools currently participate in the program.

You have been hired by the USTA as one of 17 regional coordinators for the Schools Program. Your job is to call on schools in Illinois, Wisconsin, Michigan, and Indiana to explain how the program works.

You recently met with the superintendent of schools for the Chicago Unified School District. You explained that the USTA could help participating schools convert their gymnasiums and basketball courts for use as temporary tennis courts. You also explained that the USTA works with equipment manufacturers to obtain free racquets and balls for students. In addition, you described how the district's physical education teachers would be trained by USTA officials to teach tennis to schoolchildren.

The superintendent was enthusiastic about your suggestions, particularly when you explained that the cost to the district would be minimal. He asked you to submit a formal written proposal that could be acted on by the school board.

Your task: Write the proposal, using your imagination to develop specific details.[4]

PART SIX

ORAL COMMUNICATION

CHAPTER SEVENTEEN

After studying this chapter, you will be able to

- Understand the importance of planning and editing your spoken comments
- Understand the role of listening in oral communication
- Identify the listening skills that suit different situations
- Identify the ingredients of a successful interview
- Understand group dynamics
- Identify the ingredients of effective meetings

LISTENING, INTERVIEWING, AND CONDUCTING MEETINGS

David Anderson

COMMUNICATION CLOSE-UP AT KELLY SERVICES

Kelly Services, Inc., of Troy, Michigan, is the ultimate service business. Its only product is people—namely, skilled workers who can provide temporary help to a large and diverse group of customers. David Anderson, Kelly's vice president of personnel, has found that oral communication is essential when you're dealing with 500,000 temporary workers as well as 3,000 full-time employees.

Dave spends most of his days talking to one person at a time. "I interview people for senior-level jobs, and I also interview people who have some sort of personnel-related problem. For example, one manager came to me complaining of excessive turnover. I used my interviewing skills to gather information; I asked probing questions to determine exactly what the problem was."

Asking questions is just one side of the story; listening to the answers is the other. "When someone's speaking with me, I don't try to draw conclusions or think of reasons why something that person's telling me

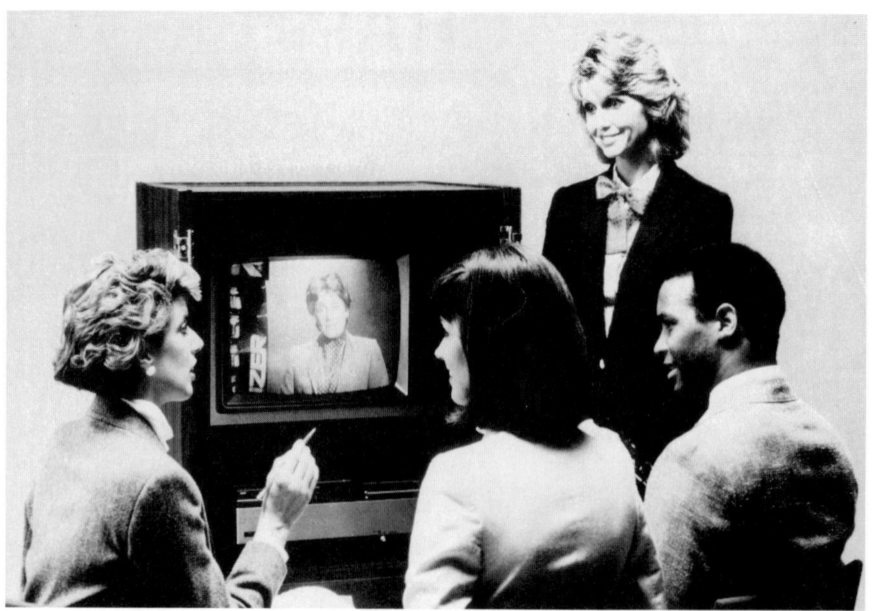

When your product is people, as at Kelly Services, one of the most valuable skills is the ability to get your ideas across to others while taking their responses into account.

will or will not work," Dave notes. "I don't try to think of my own answer; I just try to listen to what the other person is saying."

Occasionally Dave faces a more contentious situation. For example, a manager who believes that higher compensation will solve turnover problems may not be willing to accept Dave's arguments that lack of training or the manager's style may be to blame. "One way to handle a conflict like this," Dave says, "is to provide information so the other person can understand your point of view or the needs of the broader organization. You can say, 'Personally it doesn't matter to me, but if you look at it from a business viewpoint. . . .' That way the other person doesn't associate you with the problem. I don't need to say, 'I feel this way'; it's better to say, 'The facts of the situation show this and this and this.' "

Dave applies his oral communication skills in groups too. "There are three types of meetings," he says. "In information-giving meetings, I gather people together to explain a new program or some action. I always encourage questions, but it's basically a one-way flow of information. In information-sharing meetings, the flow of comments moves back and forth. I bring everybody in my department up-to-date and then get comments. Problem-solving meetings have even more interaction. The purpose is to reach a decision or coordinate the efforts of other people.

"A problem-solving meeting is the most difficult to conduct, but it's the most important. If you don't analyze the options correctly or assign tasks properly, you might jeopardize completion of the program. Furthermore, you have to follow up more carefully after the meeting ends."

Recently Dave organized a problem-solving meeting to work out a program of health-care benefits for temporary employees. The first step was to figure out who needed to be involved: "I didn't want to leave out someone who would play an integral part in implementing the program." Then he drew up an agenda that supplied as much background information as possible. "The agenda was designed so everyone would know why she or he was there. An agenda also helps me stick to the point and get a meeting concluded quickly." Dave sent out the agenda in advance and then contacted all the participants by phone: "I asked if they got the agenda, went over it briefly, and explained what I expected from them."

The meeting itself then went rather smoothly, with Dave asking each participant to express an opinion. After hearing from everybody, Dave asked each person to summarize her or his responsibilities and deadlines. "I wanted all the participants to understand clearly what took place and how their tasks dovetailed with others' jobs." Oral communication techniques like those Dave uses are a key to achieving that sort of understanding.

COMMUNICATING ORALLY

Dave Anderson's job may involve more oral communication than most, but his experience is by no means unusual. Speaking and listening are the communication skills we use most. Given a choice, most people would rather talk to each other than write to each other. Talking takes less time and doesn't involve composing, typing, editing, retyping, duplicating, and distributing the message.

Oral communication saves time and provides opportunities for feedback and social interaction.

More important, oral communication provides the opportunity for feedback. When people communicate orally, they are able to interact. They can ask questions and test their understanding of the message; they can share ideas and work together to solve problems.

In addition, they can convey and absorb nonverbal information that reveals far more than words alone. By communicating with facial expressions, eye contact, tone of voice, gestures, and postures, they can send subtle messages that add another dimension to the spoken words.

Oral communication has another advantage too: It makes people feel good. It satisfies one of our deepest needs, the need to be part of the human community. Talking things over helps people in organizations build morale and establish a group identity.

The spontaneous quality of oral communication limits your ability to edit your thoughts.

But oral communication also has its dangers. Under most circumstances, it occurs spontaneously. You have far less opportunity to revise your spoken words than your written words. You can't cross out what you just said and start all over. Your dumbest comments will remain etched in the other person's memory, regardless of how much you try to explain that you really meant something else entirely.

By the same token, you can't go back and reread what was just said. If you let your attention wander while someone else is speaking, you miss the point. You either have to muddle along without knowing what the other person said or admit you were daydreaming and ask the person to repeat the comment.

People often judge the substance of a remark by the speaker's style.

There's another problem too. Oral communication is very personal. People tend to confuse your message with you as an individual. They are likely to judge the content of what you say by your appearance and delivery style. Nobody will reject your sales letter because you are wearing white socks with a blue pin-stripe suit or because you say "um" a lot. But people might very well reject your oral presentation on those grounds.

When it comes to oral communication, your goal should be to take advantage of its positive characteristics while minimizing the dangers. To achieve that goal, you must become more adept at two key skills: speaking and listening.

SHARPEN YOUR SKILLS

Telephone Tactics

Even when using a telephone, you should keep the conversation courteous and efficient. Before you place a call, you may want to jot down a few notes outlining what needs to be discussed. In any case, have a pad handy for writing notes during the call. If it's going to be a complex discussion, be ready with copies of any pertinent background information. Don't expect the other person to wait while you scramble through your files. And follow these helpful tips:

- As soon as you say hello, identify yourself. Don't expect others to recall your voice.
- By placing your own calls, you let the other person know that you're particularly interested in reaching him or her.
- If you're placing a call to another time zone, make sure you will reach the other person during business hours. Avoid calling around 11 a.m. and 3 p.m., the two peak times for business calls.
- If the person you want to speak to is not available, be sure to leave not only your name, number, and purpose for calling but also a specific time when you can be reached. Or arrange to call the person back at a specific time. Don't just say, "Have her call me when she gets back."
- Treat switchboard operators and secretaries as human beings. If you are having difficulty getting through to someone, try to get the intervening people on your side without taking too much of their time. Ask questions that will be useful to you, such as "How do you pronounce the manager's name?" and "When is the best time to reach him?"
- Don't take up too much of the target person's time by talking too slowly, spending too much time in small talk, or complaining about how difficult it is to get in touch with him or her. Speak quickly and clearly, and get right to the point of the call. If the call is complex and will be time consuming, you may need to arrange to call back at a more convenient hour.
- Eliminate distractions. Don't call from a noisy pay phone or from an area where background machines and conversations will interfere with your concentration and your ability to hear and be heard. Similarly, don't tap a pencil or make other noises that might be picked up and amplified over the phone wires.
- Allow an adequate number of rings before hanging up. It's frustrating to others to rush to the phone only to have the caller hang up.
- When answering phone calls, immediately identify yourself. Always try to answer within two or three rings, and always greet callers in a courteous and friendly manner, even if you're having a bad day.
- Don't put callers on hold for long periods of time. If it's necessary to hunt for information or to take another call, offer to call back.
- It's bad manners to engage in a long phone conversation while you have a visitor in your office. If the call can't be handled quickly, say you'll call back later. Then remember to do so!
- Be cheerful and obliging when you answer your boss's phone. If your boss is not available, offer to take a message, with a brief explanation such as "She's not in her office right now. May I help?"
- It's important to take messages accurately. Check spellings of names, and repeat your notes to the caller to make sure the message is correct.

1. What are the advantages and disadvantages of using the telephone to deliver bad news? If you were being turned down for a job, for example, would you rather receive a letter or a phone call?

2. Think about the career you hope to pursue. What telephone skills will be particularly important in this profession? Make a list. Now examine your list to determine which of the skills you will need to improve. Develop a plan for improving those skills.

SPEAKING

Because speaking is such an ingrained activity, we tend to do it without much thought. But that casual approach can be a problem in business.

Suppose that a disgruntled client calls with a complaint. Work is piled a foot high on your desk, and your boss has just barked at you. The client's call is the last straw. He blames you, unjustly, for messing up an important shipment. Without thinking, you make a cutting reply, and the conversation goes downhill from there. Later, the client cancels his order and complains about your behavior to your boss, who is beginning to wonder whether you deserve that next promotion.

Learn to think before you speak.

To avoid problems like this, you must become more conscious of speaking as a tool for accomplishing your objectives. The first step is to break the habit of talking spontaneously without planning what you're going to say or how you're going to say it. You must learn to manage the impression you create by consciously tailoring your remarks and delivery style to suit the situation. That's not to say you should become manipulative or dishonest. But you should become aware of speaking, much as you are aware of writing.

With a little effort, you can learn to apply the same process you use in written communication to oral communication. Before you speak, think about your purpose, your main idea, and your audience. Organize your thoughts in a logical way; decide on a style that suits the occasion, then edit your remarks mentally. As you speak, watch the other person to see whether your message is making the desired impression. If not, revise it and try again.

Adjust your speaking style to suit the situation.

Bear in mind that different situations call for different speaking styles, just as different writing assignments call for different writing styles. Four distinct modes of speech are characterized by changes in vocabulary, voice quality, and sentence structure:

- *Expressive style.* Spontaneous, conversational, and uninhibited. We use it when we are expressing our feelings, joking, complaining, or socializing. For example: "No way I'm going to let that nerd represent us at the convention!"
- *Directive style.* Authoritative and judgmental. We use this style to give orders, exert leadership, pass judgment, or state our opinions. For example: "I want Mike Romig to represent us at the convention."
- *Problem-solving style.* Rational, objective, unbiased, and bland. This is the style most commonly used in business dealings. We use it when we are solving problems and conveying routine information. For example: "Stacy Lee might be able to represent us at the convention."
- *Meta style.* Used to discuss the communication process itself. Meta language enables us to talk about our interactions. For example: "We seem to be having a hard time agreeing on who will represent us at the convention."[1]

Be sure your nonverbal signals are consistent with your words.

As you think about which speaking style is appropriate, think too about the nonverbal message you want to convey. People derive less meaning from your words than they do from your facial expressions, vocal characteristics, and body language.

Apply the "you" attitude to oral communication.

Perhaps the most important thing you can do to project yourself more effectively is to remember the "you" attitude. It's even more important in oral communication than in written communication. The best way to earn other people's attention and goodwill is to focus on them.

LISTENING

The ability to listen is a vital skill in business.

If you're typical, you spend over half your communication time listening. But you'd be well advised to do more of it. Listening heads the list of essential managerial skills; it provides most managers with the bulk of the information they need to do their jobs. In addition, lack of listening ability at all levels is a major source of work-related problems.[2]

Most people need to improve their listening skills.

Most of us like to think of ourselves as being good listeners, but research suggests the opposite. The average person remembers only about half of what's said during a 10-minute conversation and forgets half of that within 48 hours.[3] Furthermore, when questioned about material they have just heard, people are likely to get the facts mixed up. In one study, people were exposed to two 30-second clips taken from TV programs and commercials. The subjects replied incorrectly to questions about these broadcasts about 30 percent of the time.[4]

It isn't surprising that many people are poor listeners. The average school curriculum ignores the subject. However, so important are listening skills to the conduct of business that a number of corporations now train employees in listening.

What happens when you listen

Listening involves five steps: sensing, interpreting, evaluating, remembering, and responding.

Listening is a process involving five related activities, which generally occur in this sequence:

1. *Sensing.* Physically hearing the message and taking note of it. Reception can be blocked by interfering noises, impaired hearing, or inattention; you must tune out distractions and focus on registering the message.
2. *Interpreting.* Decoding and absorbing what you hear. As you listen, you assign meaning to the words based on your own values, beliefs, ideas, expectations, roles, needs, and personal history. The speaker's frame of reference may be quite different, so you must try to determine what the speaker really means. Paying attention to nonverbal cues often increases the accuracy of your interpretation.
3. *Evaluating.* Forming an opinion about the message. Sorting through the speaker's remarks, separating fact from opinion, and evaluating the quality of the evidence requires a good deal of effort, particularly if the subject is complex or emotionally charged. It's also tempting to dismiss ideas offered by people who are unattractive or abrasive and to embrace ideas offered by charismatic speakers.
4. *Remembering.* Storing a message for future reference. To retain what you hear, you must take notes or make a mental outline of the speaker's key points. Good speakers facilitate remembering by clarifying their messages with previews, transitions, and summaries.
5. *Responding.* Acknowledging the message by reacting to the speaker in some fashion. If you are communicating one-on-one or in a small group, the initial response generally takes the form of verbal feedback. If you are one of many in an audience, your initial response may take the form of applause, laughter, or silence. Later on, you may act on what you have heard.[5]

As you can see, listening requires a mix of physical and mental activities, and it is subject to a mix of physical and mental barriers.

The four types of listening

To be a good listener, vary the way you listen to suit different situations.

Different situations call for different listening skills. For example, when you attend a briefing on the company's new medical insurance, you listen mainly for content. You want to know what the policy is. As the speaker describes the prescription drug plan, you begin to listen more critically, assessing the benefits of the new plan relative to your own needs. Later, as a friend talks to you about his problems, you listen empathically, trying to understand his feelings. If he blames you for his problems, you may use the technique of active listening to help resolve the conflict.

The four forms of listening:

- Content listening enables you to understand and retain the message.
- Critical listening enables you to evaluate the information.
- Empathic listening is used to draw out the other person.
- Active listening helps you understand the other person's point of view and resolve conflicts.

The four types of listening differ not only in purpose but also in the amount of feedback or interaction that occurs:

- *Content listening.* The goal is to understand and retain information imparted by a speaker. You may ask questions, but basically information flows from the speaker to you. Your job is to identify the key points of the message, so you concentrate and listen for clues to its structure: previews, transitions, summaries, enumerated points. In your mind, you create an outline of the speaker's remarks; afterward, you silently review what you've learned. You may take notes, but you do this sparingly so you can concentrate on the key points. It doesn't matter whether you agree or disagree, approve or disapprove—only that you understand.
- *Critical listening.* The goal is to evaluate the message at several levels: the logic of the argument, strength of the evidence, and validity of the conclusions; the implications of the message for you or your organization; the speaker's intentions and motives; the omission of any important or relevant points. But absorbing information and evaluating it at the same time is hard, so reserve judgment until the speaker has finished. Critical listening generally involves interaction as you try to uncover the speaker's point of view. You are bound to evaluate the speaker's credibility as well. Nonverbal signals are often your best clue.
- *Empathic listening.* The goal is to understand the speaker's feelings, needs, and wants in order to help solve a problem; the message is only a vehicle for gaining insight into the person's psyche. However, your purpose is not really to "solve" the problem. By listening, you help the individual vent the emotions that are preventing him or her from dealing dispassionately with the problem. You may be tempted to give advice, but don't. Try not to judge the rightness or wrongness of the individual's feelings. Just let the other person talk.
- *Active listening.* Psychiatrist Carl Rogers developed this technique to help people resolve their differences,[6] but it can be used in nearly any listening situation. Here's how it works: Before you can reply to another person's comment with a point of your own, you must restate the ideas and feelings behind the comment to the other person's satisfaction. You go back and forth this way, until each of you understands the other's position. The goal is to appreciate the other person's point of view, whether or not you agree.[7]

FIGURE 17.1
Ten Keys to Effective Listening

To Listen Effectively	The Bad Listener	The Good Listener
1. Find areas of interest	Tunes out dry subjects	Opportunizes; asks What s in it for me?
2. Judge content, not delivery	Tunes out if delivery is poor	Judges content; skips over delivery errors
3. Hold your fire	Tends to enter into argument	Doesn't judge until comprehension is complete; interrupts only to clarify
4. Listen for ideas	Listens for facts	Listens for central themes
5. Be flexible	Takes intensive notes using only one system	Takes fewer notes; uses 4 to 5 different systems, depending on speaker
6. Work at listening	Shows no energy output; fakes attention	Works hard; exhibits active body state
7. Resist distractions	Is distracted easily	Fights or avoids distractions; tolerates bad habits; knows how to concentrate
8. Exercise your mind	Resists difficult expository material; seeks light, recreational material	Uses heavier material as exercise for the mind
9. Keep your mind open	Reacts to emotional words	Interprets emotional words; does not get hung up on them
10. Capitalize on the fact that thought is faster than speech	Tends to daydream with slow speakers	Challenges, anticipates, mentally summarizes, weighs the evidence; listens between the lines to tone of voice

All four types of listening can be useful in work-related situations, so it pays to learn how to apply them.

How to be a better listener

Regardless of whether the situation calls for content, critical, empathic, or active listening, you can improve your listening ability by following the ten basic guidelines shown in Figure 17.1. In addition, you should put nonverbal skills to work as you listen:

- Maintain eye contact with the speaker.
- React responsively with head nods or spoken signals ("Yes," "Uh-huh," "Go on") to confirm continuing attention.
- Pay attention to body language for signs of stress, excitement, or anxiety.

Effective listening involves being receptive to both information and feelings.

Above all, try to accomplish two things as you listen: (1) the exchange of information that will lead to higher-quality decisions and (2) the open exchange of feelings that will build understanding and mutual respect. If you do, you'll be well on the way to becoming an effective interviewer and meeting leader, two roles that require especially good listening skills.

CONDUCTING INTERVIEWS ON THE JOB

Interview: any planned conversation with a specific purpose involving two people

Any time two people meet to discuss a particular matter, they are participating in an interview. Thus from the day you apply for your first job until the day you retire, you will be involved in a wide variety of business interviews. No communication activity is more dependent on oral communication skills.

In a typical interview, the action is controlled by the interviewer, the person who scheduled the session. This individual poses a series of questions, which are designed to elicit information from the interviewee. Thus the

When both the interviewer and the interviewee achieve their purpose, the interview is a success.

conversation bounces back and forth from interviewer to interviewee. Meanwhile, the interviewee also may seek to accomplish a purpose, perhaps to obtain or provide information, to solve a problem, to create goodwill, to persuade the other person to take action. If the participants establish rapport and stick to the subject at hand, both parties have a chance of achieving their objectives.

The interviewer establishes the style and structure of the session, depending on the purpose of the interview and the relationship between the parties, much as a writer varies the style and structure of a written message to suit the situation.

CATEGORIZING INTERVIEWS

Two types of interviews:

- Those dominated by the exchange of information
- Those involving the exchange of feelings

Not all interviews are alike. And all do not require the same set of skills. One major difference is that some interviews are dominated by the exchange of information, whereas others are geared more toward the exchange of feelings.

The following types of interviews are information-oriented:

- *Job interviews.* The job candidate wants to learn about the position and the organization; the employer wants to learn about the applicant's abilities and experience. Both hope to make a good impression and to establish rapport. Job interviews are usually fairly formal and structured. Content and critical listening skills are especially important.
- *Information interviews.* The interviewer seeks facts that bear on a decision or contribute to basic understanding. Information flows mainly in one direction: One person asks a list of questions that must be covered and listens to the answers supplied by the other person. Content and critical listening skills are dominant.
- *Persuasive interviews.* One person tells another about a new idea, product, or service and explains why the other should act on the recommendations. Persuasive interviews are often associated with, but are certainly not limited to, selling. The persuader discusses the other person's needs and shows how the product or concept is able to meet those needs. Thus persuasive interviews require skill in drawing out and listening to others as well as the ability to impart information.
- *Exit interviews.* The interviewer tries to understand why the interviewee is leaving the organization or transferring to another department or division. A departing employee can often provide insight into whether the business is being handled efficiently or whether things could be improved. The interviewer tends to ask all the questions while the interviewee provides answers. The departing employee should be encouraged to focus on events and processes rather than personal gripes.

These types of interviews focus on feelings:

- *Evaluation interviews.* A supervisor periodically gives an employee feedback on his or her performance. The supervisor and the employee discuss progress toward predetermined standards or goals and evaluate areas that require improvement. They may also discuss goals for the coming year, as well as the employee's longer-term aspirations and general concerns. Content, critical, and empathic listening skills may all be required.

- *Counseling interviews.* A supervisor talks with an employee about personal problems that are interfering with work performance. The interviewer should be concerned with the welfare of both the employee and the organization and should confine the discussion to business. (Only a trained psychologist should offer advice on such problems as substance abuse, marital tension, and financial trouble.) Critical and empathic listening skills are both important, because the employer needs to evaluate the facts of the situation and deal with the human emotions involved.
- *Conflict-resolution interviews.* Two competing people or groups of people (such as Smith versus Jones, day shift versus night shift, sales versus production) explore their problems and attitudes. The goal is to bring the two parties closer together, cause adjustments in perceptions and attitudes, and create a more productive climate. Empathic and active listening skills are useful in fostering these changes.
- *Disciplinary interviews.* A supervisor tries to correct the behavior of an employee who has ignored the organization's rules and regulations. The interviewer must not only get the employee to see the reason for the rules and agree to comply but must also review the facts and explore the person's attitude. Because of the emotional reaction that is likely, neutral observations are more effective than critical comments. Active and empathic listening skills are of prime importance.

Notice that all types of interviews deal to some extent in both emotion and fact; although some listening skills predominate in a particular interview, all may come into play. Furthermore, throughout your career you may find yourself in either the interviewer's or the interviewee's chair. Fully developing your interviewing skills is therefore a worthwhile pursuit.

PLANNING THE INTERVIEW

Plan an interview just as you plan other forms of communication.

Planning an interview is similar to planning any other form of communication. You begin by stating your purpose, analyzing the other person, and formulating your main idea. Then you decide on the length, style, and organization of the interview.

To accomplish their objectives, interviewees should develop a communication strategy.

Even as an interviewee, you have some control over the conversation. You need to anticipate the interviewer's questions, then plan your answers so that the points you want to make will be covered. You can also introduce questions and topics of your own. And by your comments and nonverbal cues, you can affect the relationship between you and the interviewer. Think about your respective roles. What does this person expect from you? Is it to your advantage to confirm those expectations? Will you be more likely to accomplish your objective by being friendly and open or by conveying an impression of professional detachment? Should you allow the interviewer to dominate the exchange, or should you try to take control?

The interviewer assumes the main responsibility for planning the interview.

If you are the interviewer, responsibility for planning the session falls on you. On the simplest level, you must schedule the interview and see that it is held in a comfortable and convenient location. These details may seem trivial, but they can make a big difference. Do you think you'd make the sale if you called on a client at 4:45 on the day before Thanksgiving? You also need to develop a set of interview questions and decide on their sequence. Having a plan will enable you to conduct the interview more efficiently, even if you find it advantageous to deviate from the plan during the interview.

Types of interview questions

The purpose of the interview and the nature of the participants determine the types of questions that should be asked. When you are planning the interview, bear in mind that you ask questions (1) to get information, (2) to motivate the interviewee to respond honestly and appropriately, and (3) to create a good working relationship with the other person.

Four basic types of interview questions:

- Open-end questions
- Direct open-end questions
- Closed-end questions
- Restatement questions

To obtain both factual information and underlying feelings, you will probably want to use various types of questions:

- *Open-end questions.* Questions like "What do you think your company wants most from its suppliers?" invite the interviewee to offer an opinion, not just a yes or no or a one-word answer. You can learn some interesting and unexpected things from open-end questions, but they diminish your control of the interview. The other person's idea of what's relevant may not coincide with yours, and you may waste some time getting the interview back on track. Use open-end questions to warm up the interviewee and to look for information when you have plenty of time to conduct the conversation.
- *Direct open-end questions.* This type of question suggests a response. For example, "What have you done about . . . ?" assumes that something has been done and calls for an explanation. With direct open-end questions, you have somewhat more control over the interview, yet you still give the other person some freedom in framing a response. This form is good to use when you want to get a specific conclusion or recommendation from someone.
- *Closed-end questions.* Closed-end questions require yes or no answers or call for short responses: "Did you make a reservation for the flight?" "Tell me your age group: 18–25, 26–35, 36–45, 46–55, 56 and over." Questions like these produce specific information, save time, require less effort from the interviewee, and eliminate bias and prejudice in answers. The disadvantage is that they limit the respondent's initiative and may prevent important information from being revealed. They are better for gathering information than for prompting an exchange of feelings.
- *Restatement questions.* Restatement, or mirror, questions invite the respondent to expand on an answer: "You said you dislike completing travel vouchers. Is that correct?" They also signal the interviewee that you are paying attention. Restatements provide opportunities to clarify points and correct misunderstandings. Use them to pursue a subject further or to encourage the other person to explain a statement. You can also use restatement questions to soothe upset customers or co-workers. By acknowledging the other person's complaint, you gain credibility.

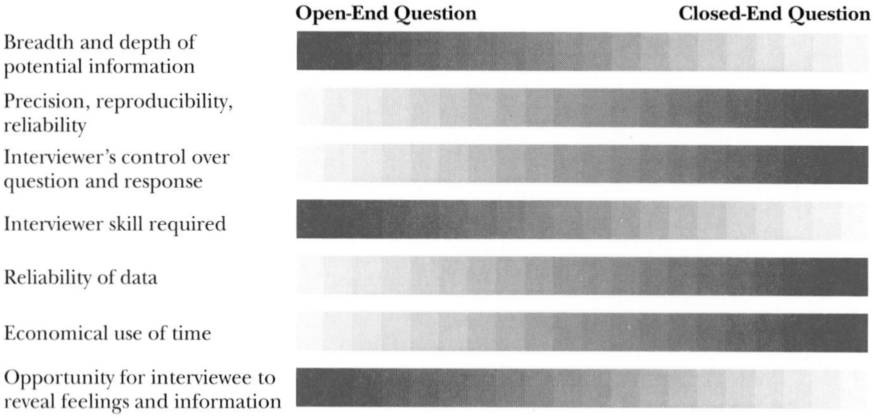

FIGURE 17.2
Choosing Questions with the Appropriate Degree of Openness

Open-End Question — Closed-End Question

Breadth and depth of potential information

Precision, reproducibility, reliability

Interviewer's control over question and response

Interviewer skill required

Reliability of data

Economical use of time

Opportunity for interviewee to reveal feelings and information

Figure 17.2 gives another view of the differences among questions. As the figure implies, most questions fall along a continuum of openness. To achieve any of the circumstances listed in the figure, frame a question toward the end of the spectrum that's inked more heavily.

The structure of the interview

Organize an interview much as you would organize a written message, with the interview's purpose and the audience's receptivity shaping the sequence of questions.

In some respects, the different types of questions are similar to the different types of paragraphs described in Chapter 5; they are tools for developing ideas. And, like paragraphs, they must be arranged in a sequence that will enable you to accomplish your purpose:

- *Informational purpose.* Topical organization, presented in direct order.
- *Analytical or problem-solving purpose.* Organization like that in a proposal (state the problem, review the background and objectives, suggest solutions, evaluate the pros and cons of each, identify the best option, and agree on implementation plans).
- *Persuasive purpose.* Organization based on the other person's receptivity (if receptive, focus on conclusions or recommendations that highlight the benefits of your ideas; if resistant, focus on a logical argument that gradually builds a convincing case for your position).

Don't try to cover more questions than you have time for.

From a practical standpoint, you need to be certain that your interview outline is about the right length for the time you've scheduled. People can speak at the rate of about 120 words (roughly one paragraph) per minute. Assuming that you are using a mix of different types of questions, you can probably handle about 30 questions in a half-hour (or about the same amount of information that you would cover in a seven- to ten-page document). However, you may want to allow more or less time for each question and response, depending on the subject matter and the complexity of the questions. Bear in mind that open-end questions take longer to answer than other types do.

Use the opening to set the tone and orient the interviewee.

Like a written message, an interview should have an opening, a body, and a close. The opening should be used to establish rapport and to orient the interviewee to the remainder of the session. You might begin by introducing yourself, asking a few polite questions, and then explaining the purpose and ground rules of the interview.

FIGURE 17.3
Choosing the Right Amount of Structure for an Interview

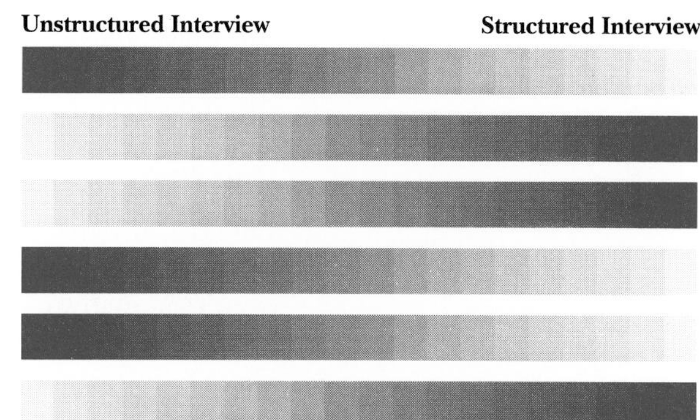

Informational interviews are generally more structured than interviews designed to explore feelings.

The questions in the body of the interview should reflect the nature of your relationship with the interviewee. For an informational session, such as a market research interview, you may want to prepare a detailed list of specific questions. This approach will enable you to control the interview and use your time efficiently. In addition, it will facilitate repeating the interview with other participants. On the other hand, if the interview is designed to explore problems or persuade the interviewee, you may prefer a less structured approach. You might simply prepare a checklist of general subjects, then let the interview evolve on the basis of the participant's responses. Figure 17.3 summarizes the advantages and disadvantages of both approaches.

Use a mix of question types to give the body of the interview rhythm.

In the body of the interview, use a mix of question types. One good technique is to use closed-end questions to pin down specific facts that emerge during an open-end response. For example, you might follow up by asking, "How many people did you contact to get this information?" or "Can we get this product in stock before May 15?"

Use the close to sum up the interview and leave the interviewee with a cordial feeling.

The close of the interview is a time for summarizing the outcome, previewing what comes next, and underscoring the rapport that has been established. To signal that the interview is coming to an end, you might lean back in your chair, smile, and use an open, palms-up gesture as you say, "Well, I guess that takes care of all my questions. Would you like to add anything?" If the interviewee has no comments, you might go on to say, "Thank you so much for your help. You've given me all the information I need to finish my report. I should have it completed within two weeks; I'll send you a copy." Then you might rise, shake hands, and approach the door. In parting, you could add a friendly comment to reaffirm your interest in the other person: "I hope you have a nice trip to Yellowstone. I was there when I was a kid, and I've never forgotten the experience."

When you've concluded the interview, take a few moments to write down your thoughts. If it was an information-gathering session, go over your notes. Fill in any blanks while the interview is fresh in your mind. In addition, you might write a short letter or memo that thanks the interviewee for cooperating, confirms understandings between you, and if appropriate, outlines next steps.

HANDLING DIFFICULT INTERVIEW SITUATIONS

Some interviews are easier to conduct than others. If you're simply trying to obtain information from a willing and interested party, chances are you will accomplish your purpose without too much trouble. But maintaining your composure and achieving your goals takes a great deal of skill when the stakes are high and emotions are aroused.

Handling negotiations

Life is full of transactions. Whether you're bargaining over the terms of your employment, the conditions of a lease, the price of a car, or the evening's dishwashing responsibilities, you want to get the best deal you can, preferably without alienating the other person. However, if you're like many people, you may have doubts about your negotiating skills. Perhaps you were taught as a child that it's impolite to haggle over money, or perhaps you lack experience in "doing deals."

Negotiators are made, not born.

But don't give up on yourself. You can learn to negotiate better if you follow a systematic approach:

- *Know what you want.* Before you enter negotiations, define your goals. If you know what you hope to obtain, you can explain your position more clearly to the other side. In addition, you are less likely to make concessions on the spur of the moment.
- *Do your homework.* Always approach the negotiations armed with information that supports your position. Let's say, for example, that you are trying to convince a potential employer to give you a more generous starting salary. If you know that comparable companies are paying that much for similar employees, you will have a strong basis for supporting your position.
- *Consider the other person's needs.* You can always get what you want more easily if the other person benefits too. Before your meeting, try to find out what might be acceptable to the other party. For example, if you're buying a new car, get the wholesale list price so you know the dealer's break-even cost.
- *Search for mutually satisfactory solutions.* Keep your eyes and ears open; ask questions that will help you understand the other person's wants. Look for compromises that result in joint gain.
- *Know your strengths and weaknesses.* In any negotiation, you are bound to have some advantages and disadvantages. Know what they are. Try to think of ways to minimize or offset your disadvantages. And be prepared to make the most of your strong points.
- *Resist the pressure to cave in.* Experienced negotiators know how to win concessions. Here are a few "tricks of the trade" to beware of: time pressure ("This sale ends tomorrow"); fear of loss ("Another customer wants the car, but . . ."); extreme proposals ("You must be crazy to ask for $10,000—$5,000 is my best offer").
- *Rehearse.* Negotiating is a lot like acting; the more you rehearse, the better your performance will be. Stand in front of a mirror and play out the scene. Practice what you will say; think of how you will respond to different proposals and tactics.[8]

The important thing to remember about negotiations is that usually both parties can get what they want if both are willing to compromise. In many cases, the negotiating process is chiefly an exchange of opinions and information that gradually leads to a mutually acceptable solution.

Overcoming resistance

It's not difficult to imagine why you might encounter resistance or hostility when you're offering criticism or trying to persuade people to change their minds. In these situations, you may well become frustrated. However, the best strategy is to remain calm and detached so you can avoid destructive confrontations and present your position in a rational manner. Here are some tips for defusing explosive situations:

When you encounter resistance or hostility, try to maintain your composure and address the other person's emotional needs.

- *Express understanding.* Most people are ashamed when they react emotionally, especially in business situations. They are insulted when you say, "You're reaction is emotional," and they respond by rejecting you and your viewpoint. The best way to handle an emotional reaction is to show sympathy, not necessarily agreement but understanding and acceptance. For example, you might say, "I can understand that this change might be difficult, and if I were in your position, I might be reluctant to do it myself." The point is to make the other person relax and talk about his or her anxiety so you have a chance to offer reassurance.
- *Make the person aware of the resistance.* When you encounter a noncommittal, silent reaction, you know that you aren't getting through to the other person. Although not actively resisting you, the person is tuning you out, possibly without even being aware of why. In such situations, continuing to present your own point of view is futile. Your best bet is to deal directly with the resistance, but not in an accusing way. You might say, "You seem cool to this idea. Have I made some faulty assumptions somewhere?" This sort of question will force the person to face up to her or his resistance and define it.
- *Evaluate objections fairly.* Don't just keep on repeating yourself. Focus instead on what the other person is saying. Deal with the feelings being expressed. Get the person to open up so you can understand the basis for his or her resistance. The person may raise some legitimate points. If your suggestions are going to create problems for people, you will have to discuss ways of minimizing those problems.[9]

When you're trying to convince someone of your viewpoint, hold your arguments until the other person is ready for them. Your success in getting your points across depends as much on the other person's frame of mind as it does on your arguments. You cannot assume that a strong argument will speak for itself. You must address the other person's emotional needs first.

Resolving conflict

Conflict is not necessarily bad, as long as it is handled in a constructive fashion.

Many business dealings involve conflict. People in organizations often compete for scarce resources or clash over differences in goals and values. These conflicts can be valuable, because they force important issues into the open and bring out creative ideas about solving problems. In fact, an organization that discourages constructive and open conflict may be asking for trouble. Eventually, hostility builds to the point that it has to be released in any way possible, even if it's damaging to individuals or the organization.

Although conflict itself can be healthy, some approaches to resolving conflict are destructive. If you believe that the only solution is for one

CHECKLIST FOR INTERVIEWS ON THE JOB

A. Preparation

- ☐ 1. Decide on the purpose and goals of the interview.
- ☐ 2. Set a structure and format based on your goals.
- ☐ 3. Determine the needs of your interviewee, and gather background information.
- ☐ 4. Formulate questions as clearly and concisely as possible, and plot their order.
- ☐ 5. Project the outcome of the interview, and develop a plan for accomplishing the goal.
- ☐ 6. Select a time and a site.
- ☐ 7. Inform the interviewee of the nature of the interview and the agenda to be covered.

B. Conduct

- ☐ 1. Be on time for the interview appointment.
- ☐ 2. Remind the interviewee of the purpose and format.
- ☐ 3. Clear the taking of notes or the use of a tape recorder with the interviewee.
- ☐ 4. Use ears and eyes to pick up verbal and nonverbal cues.
- ☐ 5. Follow the stated agenda, but be willing to explore relevant subtopics.
- ☐ 6. At the end of the interview, review the action items, goals, and tasks that each of you have agreed to.
- ☐ 7. Close the interview on an appreciative note, with thanks to the interviewee for her or his time, interest, and cooperation.

C. Follow-up

- ☐ 1. Write a thank-you memo or letter that provides the interviewee with a record of the meeting.
- ☐ 2. Provide the assistance that you agreed to during your meeting.
- ☐ 3. Monitor progress by keeping in touch through discussions with your interviewee.

Look for win-win solutions to conflict.

party to win and the other party to lose (win-lose strategy), the outcome of the conflict will surely make someone unhappy. On the other hand, if you approach the conflict with the idea that both parties can satisfy their goals, at least to some extent (win-win strategy), then there are no losers. Unfortunately, some conflicts degenerate to the point that both parties would rather lose than see the other party win (lose-lose strategy).

The win-win strategy suggests that parties to the conflict can better solve their problems if they work together than if they wage war. But for the win-win strategy to work, everybody must accept a few basic beliefs:

- It is possible to find a solution that both parties can accept.
- Cooperation is better for the organization than competition.
- The other party can be trusted.
- Higher status does not entitle one of the parties to impose a solution.

Managers have a special responsibility for resolving conflicts without making one party the loser and the other the winner. Here are seven measures a manager can take:

- Deal with minor conflict before it becomes major conflict.
- Get those most directly involved in the conflict to participate in solving it, and make sure they know that you expect them to communicate with each other.
- Get feelings out in the open before dealing with the main issues; try to understand each party's motivations, biases, and vested interests.

- Seek reasons for the problem before seeking solutions, but don't blame either party; make sure that reasons are based on fact, not on differing perceptions.
- Don't let anyone become locked into a position before considering other solutions.
- Don't let anyone avoid a fair solution by hiding behind the rules.
- Try to get the parties to fight together against an "outside force" instead of against each other.

By applying these techniques, a manager can turn potentially disastrous conflict into an opportunity for creative change.

CONDUCTING MEETINGS

Meetings are called to solve problems or share information.

Meetings, like interviews, are vital to the functioning of modern organizations. They provide a forum for making key decisions and a vehicle for coordinating the activities of people and departments. Theoretically, the interaction of the participants should lead to good decisions based on the combined intelligence of the group. Whether the meeting is held to solve a problem or to share information, the participants gain a sense of involvement and importance from their attendance. Because they share in the decision, they accept it and are committed to seeing it succeed.

Ineffective meetings are costly in many ways.

Unproductive meetings are frustrating, however. And they're expensive. The average cost of a manager's time, including overhead, is about $100 per hour. Multiply that by ten, and you get the bill for a one-hour meeting involving ten managers.[10] On top of all that, poor meetings may actually be counterproductive, because they may result in bad decisions. When people are pressured to conform, they abandon their sense of personal responsibility and agree to ill-founded plans.

UNDERSTANDING GROUP DYNAMICS

A meeting's success depends not only on what the goal is but also on how the group approaches the task.

A meeting is called for some purpose, and this purpose gives form to the meeting. In addition, however, the interactions and processes that take place in a meeting, the group dynamics, also affect the outcome. On one level, people are assembled to achieve a work-related task; but on another level, each individual has private motives that affect the group's interaction. The "hidden agendas" of the individual members may either contribute to or detract from the group's ability to perform its task.

Role playing

We all have many facets to our personalities; sometimes we are carefree and fun-loving, sometimes we are serious and hard working. We assume different roles to suit different occasions, playing the part that is expected of us in a particular context. The roles we assume are all consistent with our self-concept, but we vary the image we project depending on the demands of the situation and the cues we receive from other people.

Members of a group each play a role that affects the outcome of the group's activities.

The roles people play in meetings can be classified into three categories (see Figure 17.4). Self-oriented group members, who are motivated mainly

FIGURE 17.4
Roles People Play in Groups

Self-Oriented Roles	Group Maintenance Roles	Task-Facilitating Roles
Controlling: dominating others by exhibiting superiority or authority **Withdrawing:** retiring from the group either by becoming silent or by refusing to deal with a particular aspect of the group's work **Attention seeking:** calling attention to one's self and demanding recognition from others **Diverting:** focusing group discussion on topics of interest to the individual rather than those relevant to the task	**Encouraging:** drawing out other members by showing verbal and nonverbal support, praise, or agreement **Harmonizing:** reconciling differences among group members through mediation or by using humor to relieve tension **Compromising:** offering to yield on a point in the interest of reaching a mutually acceptable decision	**Initiating:** getting the group started on a line of inquiry **Information giving or seeking:** offering (or seeking) information relevant to questions facing the group **Coordinating:** showing relationships among ideas, clarifying issues, summarizing what the group has done **Procedure setting:** suggesting decision-making procedures that will move the group toward a goal

to fulfill personal needs, tend to be less productive than the other two types, who are far more likely to contribute to group goals. Those who assume group maintenance roles help members work well together. Those who focus on the task facilitate the problem-solving or decision-making process.

To a great extent, the role we assume in a group depends on our status relative to the other members. The people with the most status play dominant roles; those with less status play more passive parts. Status depends on many variables, such as personal attractiveness, competence in a particular field, past successes, education, age, social background, and organizational position. It also varies from group to group: We may have a good deal of status in one group (say, a college fraternity) and less status in another (say, a Fortune 500 company).

Group members' attempts to gain control interfere with the group's efforts to accomplish its mission.

In most groups, a certain amount of "power politics" occurs as people try to establish their relative status. One or two people typically emerge as the leaders, but often an undercurrent of tension remains as members vie for better positions in the pecking order. These little power struggles often get in the way of the real work. For example, one person might refuse to go along with a decision simply because it was suggested by a rival. Until roles and status have become relatively stable, the group may have trouble accomplishing its goals.

Group norms

A group that meets regularly develops unwritten rules governing the behavior of the members. To one degree or another, people are expected to conform to these norms. For example, there may be an unspoken agreement that it's okay to be 10 minutes late for meetings but not 15 minutes late. In the context of work, the most productive groups tend to develop norms that are conducive to business.

Some groups are more cohesive than others. When the group has a strong identity, the members all observe the norms religiously. They are upset by any deviation, and individuals feel a great deal of pressure to conform. This sense of group loyalty has both positive and negative implications. On the positive side, the members generally have a very

Because they feel pressured to conform, members of a group may agree to unwise decisions.

strong commitment to one another; they are highly motivated to see that the group succeeds. However, they are also susceptible to "groupthink." Because belonging to the group is very important to them, individual members are willing to set aside their personal opinions and go along with everyone else, even if everyone else is wrong.

Group decision making

Group decision making passes through four phases: orientation, conflict, emergence, reinforcement.

Groups usually reach their decisions in a predictable pattern. The process can be divided into four phases:

1. *Orientation phase.* Group members socialize, establish their roles, and agree on their reason for meeting.
2. *Conflict phase.* Group members begin to discuss their positions on the problem. If group members have been carefully selected to represent a variety of viewpoints and expertise, disagreements are a natural part of this phase. The point is to air all the options and all the pros and cons fully. At the end of this phase, group members begin to settle on a single solution to the problem.
3. *Emergence phase.* The group reaches a decision. Group members who advocated different solutions put aside their objections, either because they are convinced that the majority solution is better or because they recognize that arguing is futile.
4. *Reinforcement phase.* Group feeling is rebuilt, and the solution is summarized. Individual members are given their assignments for carrying out the group's decision, and arrangements are made for following up on these assignments.[11]

These four phases almost always occur, regardless of what type of decision is being considered. The members of the group naturally employ this process to reach agreement, even if they lack experience or training in group communication. However, just as a natural athlete can improve by practicing, the "natural" decision-making process can occur more easily if the leader of the group prepares carefully.

ARRANGING THE MEETING

By being aware of how small groups of people interact, meeting leaders can take steps to ensure that their meetings are productive. Careful planning of four elements—purpose, participants, agenda, and location—is the key. The trick is to bring the right people together in the right place for just enough time to accomplish your goals.

Determining the purpose

Before calling a meeting, ask yourself whether it is really needed.

Meetings may be classified as informational or decision making.

Meetings are expensive, so before you call one, satisfy yourself that a meeting is the best way to achieve your goal. Perhaps your purpose does not require the interaction of a group, or maybe you could communicate more effectively in a memo or through individual conversations.

Generally, the purpose of a meeting can be categorized as informational or decision making, although many meetings comprise both purposes. An informational meeting is called so the participants can share information and, possibly, coordinate actions. This type of meeting may involve individual briefings by each participant or a speech by the leader followed

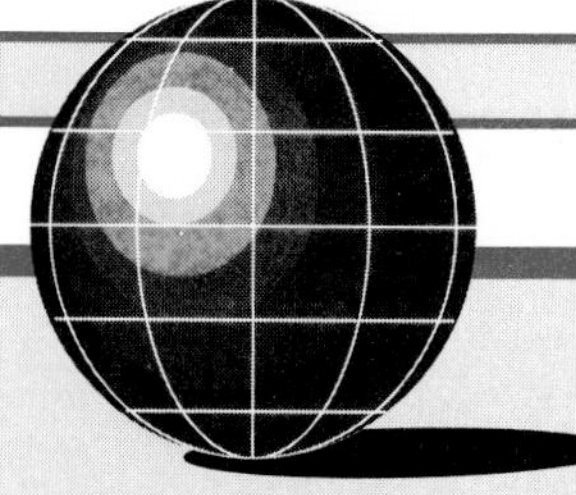

INTERNATIONAL OUTLOOK

Globetrotter's Guide to Mastering Meetings

Yes, meetings are meetings. But meetings that bring together people from diverse cultures present some special problems. Here are some important tips for those with international business dealings:

HOMEWORK

Learn everything you can about the homeland of meeting participants. Check into its history, its geography, its people and politics. Determine what subjects of discussion are welcome and those that should be avoided. The fact that you care enough to have learned something about their country will be very meaningful to the participants.

BUSINESS MEETINGS

You will need to know the rudiments of business meetings in the country you will be visiting. For example, in China teams of people will be brought in to see your presentation, over and over again. In Saudi Arabia, you'll usually deal with one person; you will be expected to drink three or four cups of coffee before the onset of the discussion; and your presentation will probably be interrupted by family members and associates striding in, as well as numerous phone calls. Be prepared to accept business practices in the country you're visiting.

RANK AND STATUS

Who is the decision maker, and how do you show the respect that is due? According people their proper rank and status is important in every country, and inadvertently failing to show your client that respect can endanger your negotiations. In China, the decision maker may never be made known to you; he or she will be one of the many who see your presentation. Be respectful to all, lest you unintentionally offend the one who is most powerful.

CORRECT FORMS OF ADDRESS

We all like to have our names written and pronounced correctly and to be addressed properly. Yet we frequently do not take the time to learn what is proper in other cultures. In China, for example, the one-syllable surname comes first, followed by the two-syllable first name. Thus Wang Chengwu is addressed as Mr. Wang and Chu Heshu is addressed as Madame Chu. In South America, a man's name might appear to be Jorge

by questions from the attendees. The information-giving and information-sharing meetings mentioned by Dave Anderson of Kelly Services fall into this category.

Decision-making meetings, like the one Dave Anderson conducted to develop a health-care program for temporary employees, are mainly concerned with persuasion, analysis, and problem solving. They often include a brainstorming session followed by a debate on the alternatives. These meetings tend to be somewhat less predictable than informational meetings. In planning a decision-making meeting, bear in mind that your purpose is to develop a course of action that the group can support. Therefore, each participant must be aware of the nature of the problem and the criteria for its solution.

Selecting the participants

In many organizations, being invited to this or that meeting is a mark of status, and as the one calling the meeting, you may be reluctant to leave someone out. But despite the pressure to include everyone even remotely concerned, try to invite only those whose presence is essential. The number of participants should reflect the purpose of the meeting. If the session is purely informational and one person will be doing most of the talking, you can include a relatively large group. However, if you are trying to

Rojas Neto. The word Neto is not a last name but rather means "the third," as in Jorge Rojas III.

ATTIRE

Dress codes vary from culture to culture, according to the formality of the occasion. Learn the rules governing dress, both for your own comfort and confidence and for the impression you wish to make.

NONVERBAL COMMUNICATION

Internationally, body language takes on many baffling nuances. For example, a Japanese nodding his head in an up and down manner is not saying yes or agreeing with you; he is saying no. In the Middle East, you should never pass anything to anyone using your left hand, because that hand is used for personal hygiene only. Although Americans are purported to be great back-slappers, hand-shakers, nodders, and pokers (actually, they are not), most of the world's people are more reserved. If you're not familiar with the local customs, avoid all physical contact or display.

BARGAINING/COMPROMISE

In some cultures, a deal is not a deal unless bargaining is involved. It is considered customary and necessary to win some concessions. Take this ploy into account when establishing price quotations.

ENTERTAINMENT

Business lunches and dinners are an important part of doing business. In North America and Europe, we frequently mix business discussion with pleasure. In many countries, however, no business will be transacted until several lunches and dinners have been held socially. Examples are Japan and Mexico.

PACE OF COMMUNICATIONS

The element of time in business negotiations varies with culture. The American attitude is generally "Let's get down to business." The general approach in Saudi Arabia is to avoid pressure or an overall sense of time limits. To Arabs, time is not a frame but a gratuitous gift from God. Hence, reaching agreements may take considerable patience.

1. Americans tend to be impatient in their international business dealings. What are the drawbacks to such impatience? How might an American businessperson deal with this trait?

2. Choose a country where you might want to conduct business. Try to pick one with a culture quite different from your own, such as Nigeria, Chile, or Japan. Research customs for that country, and report on adaptations you would need to make to conduct business successfully there.

solve a problem, develop a plan, or reach a decision, you should try to limit participation to between four and seven people.[12] The more people who attend, the more comments and confusion you're likely to get, and the longer the whole thing will take.

Limit the number of participants, but include all key people.

Although you don't want to invite too many people, be sure to include those who can make an important contribution and those who are key decision makers. Holding a meeting to decide an important matter is pointless if the people with the necessary information aren't there. For example, if your purpose is to develop the schedule for launching a new product, you'd better be sure you've invited someone from production as well as all the marketing people. Otherwise, you may end up with a great promotional campaign but nothing to sell.

Setting the agenda

Although the nature of a meeting may sometimes prevent you from developing a fixed agenda, you should at least prepare a list of matters to be discussed. Distribute the agenda to the participants several days before the meeting. The more participants know ahead of time about the purpose of the meeting, the better prepared they will be to respond to the issues at hand.

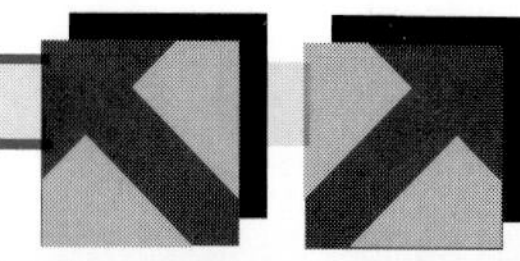

BUSINESS COMMUNICATION TODAY

Seven Deadly Blunders Made in Meetings

Many business meetings are "ineffective and boring." They are also "memorials to dead issues." That's the view of meeting expert Virginia Johnson, a market development supervisor for 3M (Minnesota Mining & Manufacturing Company), who travels the nation lecturing on how to conduct better business meetings.

"The biggest mistake is that meetings often have no specific goal." Preparation, says Virginia, is a must. The unprepared meeting leader is likely to be done in by the fact that listeners can think four times faster than the speaker can talk and are therefore likely to be distracted by the slightest delay or interruption.

One of Virginia's favorite solutions for improving meetings is simply this: "Tell people what time the meeting will end as well as when it will start." Meetings have a bad reputation, she says, because "they never seem to end."

Virginia also recommends avoiding what she terms the seven deadly blunders made in meetings:

- *Monopolizing.* "Your role as a meeting leader is to manage the participation of others, not to deliver a monologue."
- *Clowning.* "Allow humor, but don't be a clown. If you're good ol' comical Harry, you'll have trouble dealing with serious issues."
- *Losing control.* "Don't let participants take the meeting away from you by going off on tangents. Use the agenda to control events."
- *Scolding.* "If you embarrass a participant, all the others will fear being put in the same position and will become defensive."
- *Allowing interruptions.* "Don't allow outside distractions. Alert your staff to prevent phone messages and other interruptions."
- *Resenting questions.* "Acknowledge all questions, and if you don't know the answer to the question, assure the person that you or someone else will get it. Avoid answering a question with just a yes or no. That kind of answer can be very deflating."
- *Being unprepared.* "This is the deadliest sin and the most common. If you don't come prepared, the meeting will probably last too long, will have no logical flow, and will waste people's time."

Meetings should be "success experiences" for all involved, Virginia concludes. "Leaders should encourage people to participate and to feel that their participation has made a real difference."

1. Do you think meeting leaders should always use a participatory style, or are there some circumstances when this might not be advisable?

2. You are meeting with members of your project team to go over the draft of a report. Everyone agrees on the basic contents of the report, but one member keeps raising objections to points of style in the manuscript. At this rate you will be here for hours debating whether to use the word *criteria* or the word *parameter* on page 27. What should you do?

Prepare a detailed agenda well in advance of the meeting.

The agenda should include the names of the participants and the time, place, and order of business (see Component Chapter D). Some argue that the most important items should be scheduled first, but others favor an arrangement that provides warm-up time to accommodate latecomers. Regardless of the order of business, meetings should start on time and end on time.

Preparing the location

Give attention to the small details that help participants focus on the task at hand.

Decide where you'll hold the meeting, and reserve the location. (For work sessions, morning meetings are usually more productive than afternoon sessions.) Consider the seating arrangements. Are rows of chairs suitable, or do you need a conference table? Give some attention to such details as room temperature, lighting, ventilation, acoustics, and refreshments. These things may seem trivial, but they can make or break a meeting.

If you work for a large organization with teleconferencing capabilities, you may want to use this technology for your meeting. The most common form of electronic meeting is the conference call, using telephone equipment to allow several people at different locations to take part. Videoconferencing, another use of electronic technology, combines long-distance voice and video transmission. In companies where executives would otherwise have to spend countless hours and dollars traveling from one location to another, teleconferencing can be a real boon.

RUNNING A PRODUCTIVE MEETING

Whether the meeting is conducted electronically or conventionally, its success depends largely on how effective the leader is. If the leader is prepared and has selected the participants carefully, the meeting will generally be productive.

The meeting leader is the person most responsible for keeping the ball rolling. If you're the leader, avoid being so domineering that you close off suggestions, but don't be so passive that you lose control of the group. If the discussion lags, call on those who have not been heard from. Pace the presentation and discussion so you will have time to complete the agenda. As time begins to run out, interrupt the discussion and summarize what has been accomplished.

Another leadership task is either to arrange for someone to record the proceedings or to ask a participant to take notes during the meeting. (Component Chapter D includes an example of the format for minutes of meetings.)

The meeting leader's duties:

- Pacing the meeting
- Appointing a note taker
- Following the agenda
- Stimulating participation and discussion
- Summarizing the debate
- Reviewing recommendations
- Circulating the minutes

As the leader, you are also expected to follow the agenda; participants have prepared for the meeting on the basis of the announced agenda. However, don't be rigid. Allow enough time for discussion, and give people a chance to raise related issues. If you cut off discussion too quickly or limit the subject too narrowly, no real consensus can emerge.

As the meeting gets under way, you will discover that some participants are too quiet, others too talkative. To draw out the shy types, ask for their input on issues that particularly pertain to them. You might say something like "Helen, you've done a lot of work in this area. What do you think?" For the overly talkative, simply say that time is limited and others need to be heard from. The best meetings are those where everyone participates, so don't let one or two people dominate your meeting while others doodle on their notepads. As you move through your agenda, stop at the end of each item, summarize what you understand to be the feelings of the group, and state the important points made during the discussion.

At the conclusion of the meeting, tie up the loose ends. Either summarize the general conclusion of the group or list the suggestions. Wrapping things up ensures that all participants agree on the outcome and gives people a chance to clear up any misunderstandings. Before the meeting breaks up, briefly review who has agreed to do what by what date.

As soon as possible after the meeting has taken place, the leader should give all the participants a copy of the minutes or notes, showing recommended actions, schedules, and responsibilities. The minutes will remind everyone of what took place and provide a reference for future actions.

■ CHECKLIST FOR MEETINGS

A. Preparation

- ☐ 1. Determine the meeting's objectives.
- ☐ 2. Work out an agenda that will achieve your objectives.
- ☐ 3. Select participants.
- ☐ 4. Determine the location, and reserve a room.
- ☐ 5. Arrange for light refreshments, if appropriate.
- ☐ 6. Determine whether the lighting, ventilation, acoustics, and temperature of the room are adequate.
- ☐ 7. Determine seating needs: chairs only or table and chairs.

B. Conduct

- ☐ 1. Begin and end the meeting on time.
- ☐ 2. Control the meeting by following the agenda.
- ☐ 3. Encourage full participation, and either confront or ignore those who seem to be working at cross-purposes with the group.
- ☐ 4. Sum up decisions, actions, and recommendations as you move through the agenda, and restate main points at the end.

C. Follow-up

- ☐ 1. Distribute notes or minutes on a timely basis.
- ☐ 2. Take the follow-up action agreed to.

SUMMARY

Oral communication is of primary importance in business. The two key skills are speaking and listening, both of which are augmented by nonverbal communication. Speaking well requires a conscious effort to plan and edit your remarks in light of your audience's needs. Listening, too, requires conscious effort.

An interview is any planned, purposeful conversation involving two people. Informational interviews require mainly content and critical listening skills; emotion-sharing interviews may require empathic and active listening as well. Different types of interviews require different mixes of the four main types of questions: open-end, direct open-end, closed-end, and restatement. Planning an interview is much like planning a written message. The interview outline should be tailored to the subject, purpose, and audience and should include an opening, body, and close.

In business, a great deal of time is spent in meetings. Their effectiveness depends on careful planning and skillful leadership. The personal motives of the participants can affect the outcome of the meeting. The goal is to get all participants to share information or to contribute to a sound decision.

COMMUNICATION CHALLENGES AT KELLY SERVICES

As businesses began replacing their typewriters with word processors in the mid-1980s, Kelly Services ran into problems. Many of Kelly's temporary secretarial and clerical employees lacked experience with computers and word-processing software, and even those employees with some word-processing experience were generally familiar with only one or two software/hardware combinations. Yet Kelly's clients used a confusing array of incompatible programs and systems. Customers were demanding workers with specialized knowledge. Thus Kelly management faced an age-old problem: Its product (temporary workers with generalized typing skills) was becoming obsolete.

As vice president of personnel, David Anderson

landed in the middle of the debate on how to solve the problem. Should Kelly attempt to hire new workers who already had the required skills, or should it focus on retraining its existing corps of temporary employees?

Individual Challenge: Dave has decided to call a meeting of the four regional managers of Kelly's branch offices to discuss the problem. He has asked you to help him plan the meeting. Define the purpose of the meeting and prepare an agenda. Be sure to stipulate a starting and ending time. Use your imagination to supply any needed information.

Team Challenge: As a result of the meeting, Kelly Services has decided to develop its own intensive training program, which will teach its temporary employees the basics of the most popular word-processing programs. However, before creating the training program, Kelly management wants to interview a cross section of its clients to determine their word-processing needs. The branch managers will conduct the interviews, but a group of you in the personnel department have been given responsibility for developing an interview guide. Compose a series of questions that will enable the branch managers to gather enough information to create the training program. The interviews should take about 30 minutes. Try to use a mix of question types.

QUESTIONS FOR DISCUSSION

1. Do you feel that you are better at sending written, oral, or nonverbal messages? Why does this particular form of communication appeal to you? When receiving messages, are you better at reading, listening, or interpreting nonverbal cues?
2. Have you ever "stuck your foot in your mouth"? Describe the circumstances and explain the consequences.
3. What are your major problems as a listener?
4. How do interviews differ from general conversations?
5. What are the advantages and disadvantages of the different types of interview questions?
6. When was the last time you negotiated for something? Were you successful in achieving your aims? If you could repeat the experience, what would you do differently?
7. What is the value of conflict in an organization? How can the benefits of conflict be maximized?
8. How do information-sharing meetings differ from problem-solving or decision-making meetings?
9. How do individuals' goals affect a group's ability to achieve its goals?
10. Think of a meeting you have led (or one you have attended). Did the meeting achieve its objectives? What contributed to its success? What could have been done differently to make the meeting more successful?

EXERCISES

1. One aspect of oral communication that is often overlooked is the telephone, and yet the telephone is used extensively in business. Make a list of bad telephone habits that you have encountered, and recommend ways to overcome the undesirable effects of each.
2. On two consecutive nights, listen attentively to the evening news. During the first broadcast, take no notes but listen for key ideas. Then write down as much as you can remember of what you heard, in your own version of the speakers' words. Thus you would say "There's trouble in Central America," not "Then the commentator discussed troubles in Central America." Spell names phonetically (by the way they sound). During the next broadcast, take brief notes and then use them to write out your version of the news. Hand in your two drafts as written, together with a page or so explaining what you have learned about listening from this exercise.
3. What kinds of questions (open-end, direct open-end, closed-end, restatement) are most likely to be asked by the interviewers in these situations? Explain your answers.
   a. Someone conducting an opinion poll
   b. A management consultant evaluating a proposed personnel policy
   c. A job interviewer attempting to solicit additional information from a shy respondent
   d. A travel agent helping a vacationer plan her itinerary
   e. A travel agent firming up dates and times for a client

f. A teacher preparing an essay-type examination
g. A personnel counselor probing for more information in a sensitive area

4. Good interviewers and good interviewees plan in advance. In the following situations, think about the interview from the viewpoint of both participants. For each participant, what is the general purpose of the interview? What sequence of conversation might best accomplish this purpose? What type of information should be sought or presented?
   a. A high school debate coach has scheduled an appointment with the school principal in an attempt to obtain $250 to take her debate team to the state finals in Peoria, Illinois. The team is strong, and she feels that it has a good chance of winning some type of award. However, the school activities budget is limited.
   b. A counselor has scheduled an interview with a company employee who has a long, consistent record of excellent work. Recently, however, the employee has been coming to work late and often appears distracted on the job.
   c. As part of the job-evaluation process and in an attempt to have her civil service position upgraded, an employee has submitted a job description of her work. An evaluator from the civil service has scheduled an interview at the job location to discuss the candidate's requested upgrading.
5. Imagine that you have been asked to chair a discussion on a topic that is currently splitting your campus community: whether members of the security department should carry weapons. You know that, with both sides represented, the discussion will be animated. Arriving at any type of consensus is probably impossible; but you have been asked to gather information at the meeting and close it with a vote, which will serve as a recommendation to the campus president. As part of your planning, jot down eight to ten points to keep in mind as the meeting goes on. These may take the form of a proposed agenda, some suggestions to yourself for keeping the discussion on target, or ideas for bringing the meeting to a successful close.

CHAPTER EIGHTEEN

After studying this chapter, you will be able to

- Categorize speeches and presentations according to their purpose
- Analyze the audience for speeches and presentations
- Identify the steps required in planning a speech or presentation
- Develop an introduction, body, and final summary for a long, formal presentation
- Select, design, and use visual aids
- Deliver your speech or presentation effectively
- Handle questions from the audience

GIVING SPEECHES AND ORAL PRESENTATIONS

Martha Tapias

COMMUNICATION CLOSE-UP AT AT&T

Martha Tapias is a sales and marketing representative with AT&T Information Systems in Los Angeles, so she gives a lot of oral presentations. "I have to describe our major telecommunication systems to potential clients—movie studios, television and radio stations, publishing companies, amusement parks," Martha explains. "All our products are custom-designed to meet an individual customer's communication needs. I first determine what those needs are through on-site interviews and phone calls. I try to figure out how customers' businesses operate, how their information moves, and how some form of communication system could help them."

When she's collected the information she needs and has developed a proposal, Martha sets a date for a sales presentation to explain what AT&T can do for the client. "We meet in the setting that makes the client comfortable and invite the people the client wants. I try not to sit at the head of the table, because I want to get the audience involved. I want a dialogue. So I prefer that we sit at a round table.

"I describe our proposed system and explain how it will meet the client's needs. I keep throwing back what they've told me. I'll say, 'Are these still your needs, Mr. Jones?' Or I'll remind them of a problem: 'Didn't you tell me, Ms. Smith, that this roadblock exists?' I involve them at every possible point."

When AT&T Information Systems representatives make oral presentations to clients, visual aids like these often help clarify the important points.

Martha finds that flip charts and other visual aids are helpful devices for maintaining attention and clarifying points. "Mostly I use the charts to compare my client's current system to the system I'm proposing. But sometimes I also show financial information."

Because it's hard to keep everyone's attention during a presentation, Martha has learned an essential strategy: "You have to relate your proposal to each person's needs and wants. Talk sales to the salespeople. Talk production language to the production people. And if you've learned that someone is interested only in financial aspects, talk dollars and percentages."

When she encounters resistance or hostility, Martha says, "I listen to what that person is really saying and then try to rephrase it in less emotional terms. Once we both understand what the objection is, I can come back with my rationale.

"If you've never done it before, chances are that the idea of standing up in front of an audience and giving a speech is a bit intimidating," Martha notes. "But once you've had some practice, you'll probably find that you can speak to a group with confidence. In fact, you may even have fun. The important thing is to be prepared."

PREPARING TO SPEAK

Although they resemble interviews and meetings in some respects, speeches and presentations also have many of the characteristics of formal reports.

Speeches and oral presentations are much like interviews and meetings: In preparation, you must define your purpose, analyze the audience, and develop a plan for presenting your points. But speeches and presentations differ from interviews and meetings in several important respects. For one thing, speeches and presentations are usually delivered to larger groups, so the nature and amount of interaction between the audience and the speaker are different. Because speeches and presentations are somewhat public events, they generally do not deal with emotional issues or personal problems, as some interviews do. Finally, in terms of content and structure, speeches and presentations often have a good deal in common with formal reports; in fact, many of them are oral versions of written documents.

ANALYZING THE PURPOSE

During your career, you may be called on to give speeches and presentations for all sorts of reasons. If you're in the human resources department, for

FIGURE 18.1
How Purpose Affects Audience Interaction

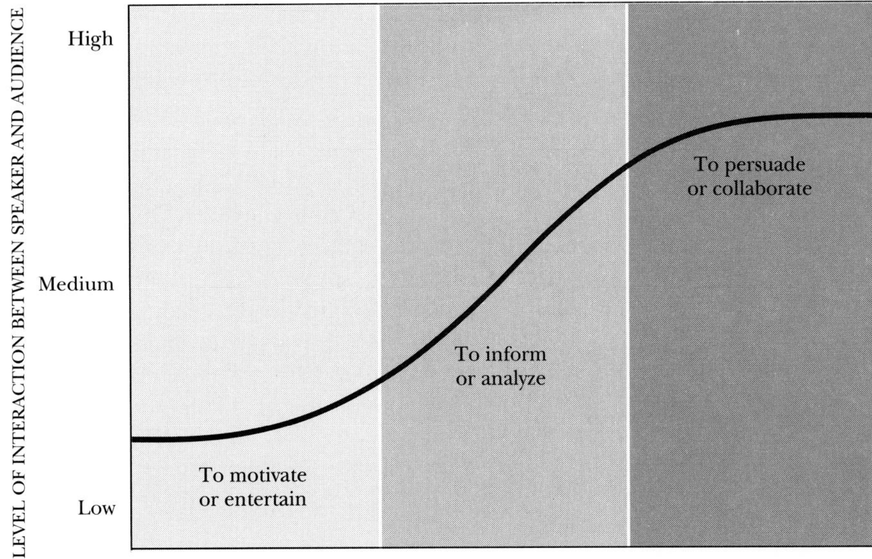

The amount of audience interaction varies from presentation to presentation, depending on the speaker's purpose.

example, you may give orientation briefings to new employees or explain company policies, procedures, and benefits at assemblies. If you become a department supervisor, you may conduct training programs. If you're a problem solver or consultant, you may give analytical presentations on the merits of various proposals. If you're involved in accounting or finance, you may have to brief management on the financial position of the company. As a scientist or engineer, you might explain technical matters to clients or make speeches at professional gatherings. If you're in sales or marketing, you'll explain your company's products and services to customers. And if you're the president, you may address securities analysts, the board of directors, the press, and the shareholders.

These speeches and presentations can be categorized according to their purpose, much as interviews and meetings are categorized. The purpose helps determine content and style. As Figure 18.1 illustrates, the purpose also affects the amount of audience participation that occurs.

- *To motivate or entertain.* When you are trying to motivate or entertain the audience, you generally do most of the talking. Let's say, for example, that you have been asked to say a few words in honor of a retiring employee. You would probably make a few affectionate or amusing comments about the individual and describe his or her contribution to the organization. In the process, you would make the employee happy and reinforce morale. During your speech, the audience would play an essentially passive role, listening to your remarks but providing little direct input in the form of comments or questions. You would control the content of the message.
- *To inform or analyze.* When your purpose is to provide information or analyze a situation, you and the audience generally interact somewhat. Basically, a group of people meet to hear the oral equivalent of a written report; then members of the audience offer comments or ask questions. Companies use these sorts of speeches and presenta-

tions like reports: to monitor and control operations, implement policies and procedures, comply with regulations, and explain the status of work for clients. They are very common in business.

- *To persuade or collaborate.* The most interaction occurs when, like Martha Tapias of AT&T Information Systems, you aim to persuade people to take a particular action or to collaborate with them in solving a problem or reaching a decision. You generally begin by providing facts and figures that increase the audience's understanding of the subject; you might also offer arguments in defense of certain conclusions or recommendations. But in addition, you invite the audience to participate by expressing their needs, suggesting solutions, and formulating conclusions and recommendations. Because persuasive and collaborative presentations involve so much audience interaction, you have relatively little control of the material. You must be flexible enough to adjust to new input and unexpected reactions; you cannot adhere to a prewritten script.

Often, a speech or presentation accomplishes several of these purposes simultaneously.

ANALYZING THE AUDIENCE

The nature of the audience affects your strategy for achieving your purpose.

Once you have your purpose firmly in mind, you should think about another basic element of your speech or presentation: the audience. Your choice of a strategy for accomplishing your purpose must take into account those who will be attending.

If you're involved in selecting the audience, you will certainly have information about their characteristics. Many times, however, you will be speaking to a group of people you know very little about. You have a much better chance of achieving your purpose if you investigate the audience's characteristics before you show up to speak. Ask your host or a contact person for help in analyzing the audience; supplement their estimates with some intelligent "guess-timates" of your own. Analyze which of the factors that characterize the audience are most important to your planning.

Gear the content, organization, and style of your message to the audience's size, background, and attitude.

First consider the size and composition of the audience. A relatively small group may sensibly be drawn into a decision-making process. But with more than 12 people, it's difficult to manage the give and take that are essential to building consensus, so your approach may lean more toward telling than toward asking. In addition, a homogeneous group (made up, for example, entirely of young engineers or entirely of East Coast sales representatives) benefits from a focused speech or presentation; a diverse group requires a more generalized approach.

You also need to put together some other relevant information about the audience. One very important factor is the likely reaction to your speech or presentation: In general, will they be hostile, receptive, or indifferent to your point of view? Do they care about the issues you will discuss? You should also learn as much as you can about their level of understanding: How much do they already know about your subject? Finally, you need to take a cold, hard look at their relationship with you: Do they already know you? Do they respect your judgment? The answers will help you decide on the best way to organize your material.

■ CHECKLIST FOR AUDIENCE ANALYSIS

A. Audience Size and Composition

- ☐ 1. Estimate how many people will attend.
- ☐ 2. Consider whether they have some political, religious, professional, or other affiliation in common.
- ☐ 3. Analyze the mix of men and women, age ranges, socioeconomic and ethnic groups, occupations, and geographic regions represented.

B. Probable Audience Reaction

- ☐ 1. Analyze why audience members are attending the speech or presentation.
- ☐ 2. Determine the audience's general attitude toward the topic.
  - ☐ a. Decide whether the audience is very interested, moderately interested, or unconcerned.
  - ☐ b. Review how the audience has reacted to similar issues in the past.
  - ☐ c. Determine which facets of the subject are most likely to appeal to the audience.
  - ☐ d. Decide whether portions of your message will create problems for any members of the audience.
- ☐ 3. Analyze the mood that people will be in when you speak to them: tired from listening to other presentations like yours or fresh because your presentation comes early in the agenda, interested in hearing a unique presentation, restless from sitting too long in one position and needing a minute to stretch.
- ☐ 4. Figure out which sort of backup information will most impress the audience: technical data, statistical comparisons, cost figures, historical information, generalizations, demonstrations, samples, and so on.
- ☐ 5. Predict audience response.
  - ☐ a. List ways that the audience will benefit from your message.
  - ☐ b. Formulate an idea of the most desirable audience reaction and the best possible result (what you want the audience to believe or do afterward).
  - ☐ c. Anticipate possible objections or questions.
  - ☐ d. Analyze the worst thing that might happen and how you might respond.

C. Level of Audience Understanding

- ☐ 1. Determine whether the audience already knows something about the subject.
  - ☐ a. Analyze whether everybody has about the same amount of knowledge.
  - ☐ b. Consider whether the audience is familiar with your vocabulary.
- ☐ 2. Estimate whether everybody is equally capable of understanding the message.
- ☐ 3. Decide what background information the audience will need to understand the subject.
- ☐ 4. Think about the mix of general concepts and specific details you will need to explain.
- ☐ 5. Consider whether the subject involves routine, recurring information or an unfamiliar topic.

D. Audience Relationship with the Speaker

- ☐ 1. Analyze how this audience usually reacts to speakers.
- ☐ 2. Determine whether the audience is likely to be friendly, open-minded, or hostile toward your purpose in making the speech or presentation.
- ☐ 3. Decide how the audience is likely to respond to you.
  - ☐ a. Analyze what the audience expects from you.
  - ☐ b. Think about your past interactions with the audience.
  - ☐ c. Consider your relative status.
  - ☐ d. Consider whether the audience has any biases that might work against you.
  - ☐ e. Take into account the audience's probable attitude toward the organization you represent.
- ☐ 4. Decide which aspects of your background are most likely to build credibility.

PLANNING YOUR SPEECH OR PRESENTATION

Developing a strategy for delivering an oral message is just as crucial as developing a strategy for a written message. If you can't put information in an easily digestible form, your audience will not only lose patience with you but may also fail to understand some important points. For maximum impact and achievement of your goals, therefore, you must define the main idea, construct an outline, estimate the appropriate length, and decide on the most effective style.

Developing a main idea

The main idea is a you-oriented statement that points up how the audience can benefit from your subject and purpose.

The first step is to define the main idea, or theme, that you want to get across in your speech or presentation. The main idea links your subject and purpose to the audience's frame of reference, much as an advertising slogan points out how a product benefits consumers. Your goal in developing a main idea is to make your subject as interesting to the audience as it is to you.

Try to state your main idea in one sentence that summarizes the chief argument you will use to convince the audience. Here are a few examples:

Demand for low-calorie, high-quality frozen foods will increase because of basic social and economic trends.

Reorganizing the data-processing department will lead to better service at a lower cost.

Placing an order with us makes sense because we offer fast delivery and quantity discounts.

We should build a new plant in Texas to reduce operating costs and to capitalize on growing demand in the Southwest.

The new health plan gives all employees more options for coverage.

Judy Semmerich has been a dedicated employee, and we are going to miss her when she retires.

After 18 months of sacrifice and uncertainty, we can all be proud of our company's successful efforts to compete effectively in a difficult environment.

Notice that each of these statements puts a particular slant on the subject, one that is positive and directly related to the audience's interests. This sort of "you" attitude helps keep the audience's attention and convinces people that your points are relevant. For example, a group of new employees will be much more responsive to your discussion of plant safety procedures if you focus on how the procedures can save their lives than if you point out how the rules conform to Occupational Safety and Health Administration guidelines. This emphasis on the needs and interests of the audience is one of Martha Tapias's main strategies in her job with AT&T Information Systems.

Developing an outline

With a well-crafted main idea to guide you, you can begin to outline the speech or presentation. The structure that you establish should be geared to the subject, the purpose, the audience, and the time allotted for your speech or presentation.

Structure a short speech or presentation like a letter or memo.

If you have 10 minutes or less to deliver your message, you should organize your thoughts much as you would a letter or brief memo, using the direct approach if the subject involves routine information or good news and using the indirect approach if the subject involves bad news or

FIGURE 18.2
Sample Outline for Brief Speech

WHO OWNS THE VAN GOGH?

Purpose: To convince executives that corporate art is a good investment

I. Introduction: On a cold night in March, collectors assembled at Christie's auction gallery in London to bid on Van Gogh's Sunflowers. Within 5 minutes, the price soared to $39.9 million. The buyer? A Japanese insurance company.

II. Corporations are becoming major consumers of art.

- A. Over 1,000 corporations now have art collections.
- B. Companies are motivated by three factors:
  1. Top executives' love of art
  2. Desire to provide public and employees with aesthetic value
  3. Potential for appreciation in the value of the work of art

III. Most corporate collections are conservative.

- A. Corporate collectors tend to avoid the controversial.
- B. The art is generally the work of 20th-century artists.
  1. Moderately priced, compared to Old Masters
  2. In plentiful supply

IV. Several corporate collections have soared in value.

- A. PepsiCo paid $150,000 for a sculpture by Alexander Calder, which is worth $1 million today. [slides]
- B. First Bank Systems, Inc.'s collection, acquired for $3 million, has doubled in value. [slides]
- C. Sterling Regal's collection of 180 works cost about $2 million and is now worth about $4.5 million. [slides]
- D. Domino's Pizza has invested $7.5 million in its collection, which is currently valued at $12 million. [slides]

V. Conclusion: Investing in art provides both aesthetic and monetary rewards. Corporations are the Medicis of the current art renaissance.

persuasion. Begin with an introduction that arouses the audience's interest and gives a preview of what's to come. In the body of the speech or presentation, explain the who, what, when, where, why, and how of your subject. In the final paragraph or two, review the points you have made. Close with a statement that will help the audience remember the subject of your speech. Figure 18.2 shows the outline of a brief persuasive speech delivered by an art dealer trying to interest a group of executives in investing in corporate art.

Organize longer speeches and presentations like formal reports.

Longer speeches and presentations should be organized like reports (see Chapter 15 for specific suggestions). If the purpose is to entertain, motivate, or inform, use a direct order imposed naturally by the subject. If the purpose is to analyze, persuade, or collaborate, organize around

FIGURE 18.3
Sample Outline for 30-Minute Presentation

NEW COMPETITORS ENTER THE FAST-FOOD RACE

Purpose: To make fast-food franchisees aware of the growing threat posed by convenience stores

I. Introduction: The battle for market share among fast-food franchises is heating up as convenience stores enter the business with hot menu items and in-store seating areas.

II. Convenience stores represent a growing threat.

  A. Convenience stores currently have fast-food sales of $3.7 billion, and sales are growing by 15% per year.

  B. The two C-stores with the heaviest commitment to fast food are Arco's AM/PM mini markets and 7-Eleven.

    1. Arco graduates from self-serve milkshakes to hot dogs and hamburgers.

    2. 7-Eleven moves beyond Slurpees.

      a. Experimenting with a fast-food restaurant prototype with self-serve condiment bar for hot dogs and hamburgers

      b. Conducting joint ventures with Church's Fried Chicken

  C. Many others have plans and test programs under way: [slide]

    1. Casey General Stores offers "Homemade Pizza to Go" through 230 stores

    2. Village Pantry not only makes pizza from scratch but delivers it as well

  D. The motivating force behind the move into fast food is a desire to boost gross profit margins.

    1. Margins on fast food are 47.4% compared to 35% for groceries and 7.3% for gas. [slide]

-1-

either conclusions and recommendations or a logical argument. Use direct order if the audience is receptive, indirect if you expect resistance. Figure 18.3 is the outline of a 30-minute analytical presentation, organized around conclusions and presented in direct order. The presentation was delivered to a group of fast-food franchisees by an expert on trends in the food service industry. His purpose: to convince the audience that convenience stores like 7-Eleven would soon represent a major source of competition for fast-food customers.

Regardless of the length of your speech or presentation, bear in mind that simplicity of organization is especially useful in oral communication.

-2-

2. As margins on groceries and gas slip, pressure to expand into fast food mounts.

3. Fast-food items now account for 13% of total convenience store sales, up from 1.5% in the early 1970s. [slide]

III. Convenience stores are adding in-store eating areas and interesting menu items to appeal to consumers.

A. Many offer in-store eating areas.

1. Small chains are more likely than large chains to offer seating. [slide]

2. More seating is on the way. [slide]

B. C-stores' menus are more than cold sandwiches wrapped in plastic. [slide]

C. A majority of C-store operators plan to add new menu items next year. [slide]

D. Close to 90% prepare the food on their premises. [slide]

IV. Savvy management and good advertising have helped the C-stores become strong competitors for the fast-food dollar.

A. C-stores are hiring talented executives from the food service industry to head their fast-food operations.

B. Big ad campaigns are changing the way consumers view convenience stores. [slide]

V. Conclusion: Ambitious convenience store chains are making the investment required to give the traditional fast-food industry a run for its money.

To accommodate the listeners' limitations, be as clear and direct as possible in organizing your ideas.

Once listeners lose the thread of your comments, they have a hard time tuning back in and following the remainder of your message. They don't have the luxury of reviewing a paragraph or flipping pages back and forth, as they can when reading. Thus you should look for the most obvious and natural way to organize your ideas, using a direct order of presentation whenever possible. Explain at the beginning how you have organized your material, and try to limit the number of main points to three or four—even when the speech or presentation is rather long. Be sure to include only the most useful, interesting, and relevant supporting evidence so you can keep the audience's attention. Remember, people cannot skim over

FIGURE 18.4
Sample Outline with Notes on Delivery

I. The company's sales growth has flattened in recent years because of weakening demand for cosmetics and our lack of new products.

A. Consumption of cosmetics has leveled off in the past 3 years. LINE CHART

1. Working women have more money but less time to spend it.

2. Recession has dampened demand and prompted a shift to cheaper brands. BAR CHART

B. Our market share has declined. LINE CHART

1. Consumers are going to new outlets. PIE CHARTS

2. Competitors have gained share by introducing cheaper lines for these outlets. TABLE

TRANSITION: Our loss of market share can be reversed.

II. We can regain our position in the cosmetics market if we introduce our own inexpensive line.

unnecessary information as they might when reading. In addition, you might reorient the audience at the end of each section by summarizing the point you have just made and explaining how it fits into your overall speech or presentation.

You may use an outline for a speech or presentation as the "script," but prepare some organizational alternatives if you plan to allow considerable audience interaction.

A carefully prepared outline may be more than just the starting point for composing a speech or presentation. If you plan to deliver your presentation from notes rather than from a written text, your outline will also be your final "script." For this reason the headings on the outline should be complete sentences or lengthy phrases rather than one- or two-word topic headings. Many speakers also include notes that indicate where visual aids will be used. You might also want to write out the transitional sentences you will use to connect main points. The excerpt from an outline shown in Figure 18.4 is a good example of all these techniques.

Keep in mind, however, that you may have to adjust your organization in response to input from the audience, especially if your purpose is to collaborate. You might want to think of several different organizational possibilities, based on "what if" assumptions about the audience's reactions. That way, if someone says something that undercuts your planned approach, you can switch to another line of argument.

Estimating length

Time for speeches and presentations is often strictly regulated. Several speakers may have to share a limited number of hours; the audience more than likely has plenty of other things to do too. You should learn to tailor your material to the available time so you can both fill the time allotted to you and keep within the limits.

The average speaker can deliver about one paragraph, or 125 to 150 words, in a minute.

Once you have developed an outline, you can estimate more accurately how long your speech or presentation will take. The average speaker talks at the rate of about 125 to 150 words a minute (or roughly 7,500 to 9,000 words an hour, which corresponds to 20 to 25 double-spaced, typed pages of text), and the average paragraph is about 125 to 150 words in length. Thus most of us speak at the rate of about one paragraph per minute.

Let's say that you want to make three basic points. In a 10-minute speech, you could take about 2 minutes to explain each of these points, using roughly two paragraphs for each point. If you devoted a minute each to the introduction and the conclusion, you would have 2 minutes left over to interact with the audience. If you had an hour, however, you could spend the first 5 minutes introducing the presentation, establishing rapport with the audience, providing background information, and giving an overview of your topic. In the next 30 to 40 minutes, you could explain each of the three points, spending about 10 to 13 minutes per point (the equivalent of 5 or 6 typewritten pages). Your conclusion might take another 3 to 5 minutes. The remaining 10 to 20 minutes would then be available for responding to questions and comments from the audience.

Be sure that your subject, purpose, and organization are compatible with the time available.

Which is better, the 10-minute speech or the hour-long presentation? The answer depends on the subject, on the audience's attitude and knowledge, on the relationship between the audience and the speaker. For a simple, easily accepted message, 10 minutes may be enough. But if your subject is complex or your audience is skeptical, you need more time. The important thing is to use good judgment. Don't try to squeeze a complex presentation into a period that is too brief, and don't draw out a simple talk any longer than necessary.

Deciding on the style

Another important element in your planning is the style most suitable to the occasion. Is this a formal speech or presentation in an impressive setting, with professionally developed visual aids? Or is it a casual, shirt-sleeves working session? The size of the audience, the subject, your purpose, your budget, and the time available for preparation all determine the style.

Use a casual style for small groups, a formal style for large groups and important events.

In general, if you are speaking to a relatively small group, you can often get away with a casual approach that encourages audience participation. A small conference room, with the audience seated around a table, may be appropriate. Use simple visual aids. Invite the audience to interject comments. Deliver your remarks in a conversational tone, using notes to jog your memory if necessary.

On the other hand, if you are addressing a large audience and the event is an important one, you should establish a more formal atmosphere. Hold the presentation in an auditorium or convention hall, and seat the audience in rows. Show slides or films to dramatize your message. Ask people to hold their questions until after you have completed your remarks. Use detailed notes or a complete script to guide your delivery. Formality is enhanced when you put physical and psychological distance between you and the audience.

DEVELOPING FORMAL SPEECHES AND PRESENTATIONS

Preparing a major speech or presentation is very much like writing a formal report, with one important difference: You must adjust your technique to the oral mode of communication. This is both an opportunity and a challenge.

The opportunity lies in the interaction that is possible between you and the audience. When you speak before a group, you can receive information as well as transmit it. As a consequence, you can adjust both the content

How formal speeches and presentations differ from formal reports:

- More interaction with the audience
- Use of nonverbal cues to express meaning
- Less control of content
- Greater need to help the audience stay on track

and the delivery of your message as you go along, editing your speech or presentation to make it clearer and more compelling. Instead of simply expressing your ideas, you can draw out the audience's ideas and use them in reaching a mutually acceptable conclusion. You can also capitalize on nonverbal signals to convey information to and from your audience.

But in order to get the benefits of oral communication, you have to make a few sacrifices. The biggest price you pay is loss of control. Dealing with an audience requires flexibility; the more you plan to interact, the more flexible you must be. Halfway through your presentation, an unexpected comment from someone in the audience may force you to shift to a new line of thought, which requires a good deal of skill. At the same time, you must also accommodate the limitations of listeners. To prevent the audience from losing interest or getting lost, you must use special techniques in developing the various elements of the presentation: the introduction, the body, the final summary, the question-and-answer period, and the visual aids.

THE INTRODUCTION

The introduction should capture attention, inspire confidence, and preview the contents.

You have a lot to accomplish during the first few minutes of your speech or presentation: You need to arouse the audience's interest in your topic, establish your credibility, and prepare the audience for what will follow. That's why the introduction often requires a disproportionate amount of your attention.

Arousing interest

Some subjects are naturally more interesting than others. If you happen to be discussing a matter of profound significance that will personally affect the members of your audience, chances are they will listen regardless of how you begin. All you really have to do is announce your topic (for example, "Today I'd like to announce the reorganization of the company").

Other subjects, however, call for more imagination. Say that you're explaining the pension program to a group of new clerical employees, none of whom will be full participants for another five years and most of whom will probably leave the company within two. In a case like this, how do you get people to listen to you?

Connect the topic to the listeners' needs and interests.

The best approach when you're dealing with an uninterested audience is to appeal to human nature. Encourage people to take the subject personally. Show them how they as individuals will be affected. For example, in speaking to clerical employees about the pension program, you might start off with an opening like this:

> If somebody offered to give you $200,000 in exchange for $5 per week, would you be interested? That's the amount you can expect to collect during your retirement years if you choose to contribute to the voluntary pension plan. During the next two weeks, you will have to decide whether you want to participate. Although for most of you retirement is many years away, this is an important financial decision. During the next 20 minutes, I hope to give you the information you need to make that decision intelligently.

Experienced speakers use several other tried-and-true techniques for connecting their subject to the audience's personal concerns. However, they always make sure that the introduction matches the tone of the speech or presentation. If the occasion is supposed to be fun, you may begin with something light; but if you're talking business to a group of executives, don't waste their time with cute openings. Avoid jokes and personal anecdotes when you're discussing a serious problem. If you're giving a routine oral report, don't be overly dramatic. Most of all, be natural. Nothing turns off the average audience faster than a trite, staged beginning.

Building credibility

One of the chief drawbacks of overblown openings is that they damage the speaker's credibility, and building credibility is probably even more important than arousing interest. Communication research clearly shows that acceptance of a message depends on the audience's confidence in the speaker.[1] Thus you must establish a good relationship with the audience—and quickly, because people will decide within a few minutes whether you are worth listening to.[2] You want the audience to like you as a person and to respect your opinion.

Establishing credibility is relatively easy if you're speaking to a familiar, open-minded audience. As long as you avoid sticking your foot in your mouth, you can coast on your reputation. The real difficulty arises when you must earn the confidence of strangers, especially those who are predisposed to be skeptical or antagonistic.

One way to handle the problem is to let someone else introduce you. This solution enables you to present your credentials without appearing boastful. Be certain, however, that the person doesn't exaggerate your qualifications. Some members of the audience are likely to bristle if you're billed as being the world's greatest authority on the subject.

Without boasting, explain why you are qualified to speak on the subject.

If you're introducing yourself, keep your comments simple. But don't be afraid to mention your accomplishments. Your listeners are curious about you. They want to know your qualifications, so tell them very briefly who you are and why you're there. Generally speaking, one or two aspects of your background are all you need to mention: your position in an organization, your profession, the name of your company. For example, you might say something like this:

> I'm Karen Whitney, a market research analyst with Information Resources Corporation. For the past five years, I've specialized in studying high-technology markets. Your director of engineering, John LaBarre, has asked me to brief you on recent trends in computer-aided design so you'll have a better idea of how to direct your research and development efforts.

Notice how this speaker establishes credibility by tying her credentials to the purpose of her presentation. She lets her listeners know immediately that she is qualified to tell them something they need to know. She connects her background to their concerns.

Previewing the presentation

Giving your audience a preview of what's ahead adds to your authority and, more important, helps people understand your message. A reader can get an idea of the structure of a report by looking at the table of

Let the audience know what lies ahead.

contents and scanning the headings. But in an oral presentation, the speaker must provide the framework. Otherwise, the audience may be unable to figure out how the main points of the message fit together.

Your introduction should summarize your basic message (the main idea), identify the supporting points, and indicate the order in which those points will be developed. Tell your listeners in so many words, "This is the subject, and these are the points I will cover." Once you have established the framework, you can move into the body of the presentation, confident that the audience will understand how the individual facts and figures relate to your main idea.

THE BODY

The body should transmit the three or four most important points you want to make.

The bulk of your speech or presentation should be devoted to a discussion of the three or four main points on your outline. You can use the same organizational patterns that you use in a letter, memo, or report, but strive for simplicity. You want the structure of your speech or presentation to be clear, and you don't want to lose the audience's attention.

Emphasizing structure

A written report uses typographical and layout clues—headings, paragraph indentions, white space between sections, lists—to show how ideas are related. For an oral presentation, however, you must rely more on words.

Help the audience follow your presentation

- By summarizing your remarks as you go along
- By emphasizing the transitions from one idea to the next

For the small links between sentences and paragraphs, one or two transitional words are enough: *therefore, because, in addition, in contrast, moreover, for example, consequently, nevertheless, finally*. But to link major sections of the speech or presentation, you need complete sentences or paragraphs, such as "Now that we've reviewed the problem, let's take a look at some solutions" or "We'll turn now to the three reasons for our loss of market share." Every time you shift topics, stress the connection between ideas. Summarize what's been said; preview what's to come.

The longer the speech or presentation, the more important the transitions become. When you present many facts and ideas, the audience has trouble absorbing them and seeing the relationship among them. Listeners need clear transitions to guide them to the most important points. Furthermore, they need transitions to pick up any ideas they may have missed. If you repeat key ideas in the transitions, you can compensate for lapses in the audience's attention. You might also want to call attention to the transitions by using gestures, changing your tone of voice, or introducing a visual aid.

Holding the audience's attention

You must make a special effort to keep an audience's attention, because listening is difficult.

Throughout a speech or presentation, you must continue trying to maintain the audience's interest. Here are a few helpful tips for creating memorable speeches:

- *Relate your subject to the audience's needs.* People are most interested in things that affect them personally. Present every point in light of the audience's needs and values.
- *Use clear, vivid language.* People become bored very quickly when they don't understand the speaker. If your presentation involves

SHARPEN YOUR SKILLS

Five Proven Ways to Get Attention and Keep It

In any speech or presentation, but especially a long, formal one, you need to use attention getters throughout your speech to maintain and revive the audience's interest. Here are five possibilities:

- *Use humor.* In business, the subject of most presentations is serious. But that doesn't mean you can't include a light comment now and then to perk up the audience. Just be sure the humor is relevant to the presentation.
- *Tell a story.* Most audiences will pay attention to a story, and you can generally find one that illustrates an important point. A speaker who was trying to explain his company's strategy of buying old, low-priced houses and fixing them up told this story: "One of the first properties we bought was in a very poor part of town, and we had serious reservations about buying it. We were especially worried about the motorcycle tracks on the wall, but we fixed that with a coat of paint. In fact, that house taught me the value of paint in general. Most of our properties don't look like much on the surface, but they are solid underneath. All they need is a few coats of paint, some basic carpentry, new landscaping, and *voila!* The ugly duckling emerges as a beautiful swan."
- *Pass around a sample.* Psychologists say that you can get people to remember your points by appealing to their senses. The best way to do that is to pass around a sample. If your company is in the textile business, let the audience handle some of your fabrics. If you sell chocolates, give everybody a taste.
- *Ask a question.* Asking questions will get the audience actively involved in your speech and, at the same time, give you information about them and their needs. A securities broker whose presentation was designed to arouse interest in tax-free municipal bonds used these questions at various points in her talk: "How many of you paid over $10,000 in taxes last year?" "What's the biggest risk you run when you invest in common stocks?" "How important is safety to your investment strategy?" "What kind of return do you want on your investments?" These questions made the audience think about what she was saying, and their answers helped her understand them.
- *State a startling statistic.* People love details, as the popularity of games like Trivial Pursuit demonstrates. If you can interject an interesting statistic, you can often wake up an audience. For example, in a presentation on opportunities in the computer field, you might say, "Experts estimate that 80 percent of the gross national product will depend on computers in one way or another by the turn of the century."

Regardless of which attention getters you use, remember to use them in moderation and with good taste. If you're giving a serious business presentation, you must keep the tone of your remarks on a businesslike level.

1. Which of your lecture classes do you enjoy the most? What techniques does the instructor use to keep students interested?

2. Suppose that you are giving a presentation on white-collar crime. Do a little creative thinking or research to come up with three attention getters you might use to enliven your talk.

abstract ideas, try to show how those abstractions connect with everyday life. Use familiar words, short sentences, and concrete examples.

- *Explain the relationship between your subject and familiar ideas.* By showing how your subject relates to ideas the audience already understands, you give people a way to categorize and remember your points.[3]

You can also maintain the audience's interest by introducing variety into your speech or presentation. One especially useful technique is to pause occasionally for questions or comments from the audience. Not only do you get a chance to determine whether the audience understands key points before launching into another section, but the audience also gets a chance to switch for a time from listening to participating. Visual aids are another source of both clarification and stimulation. Variety in your tone of voice and gestures helps too.

THE FINAL SUMMARY

The final summary should leave a strong and lasting impression.

When you have finished covering the main points, you may be tempted to wrap things up quickly. Avoid the temptation. The ending of a speech or presentation is almost as important as the beginning, because audience attention peaks at this point. Plan to devote about 10 percent of the total time to the ending.

Begin your conclusion by telling listeners that you are about to finish so they'll make one final effort to listen intently. Don't be afraid to sound obvious. Say something like "In conclusion" or "To sum it all up." You want people to know that this is the home stretch.

Restating the main points

Summarize the main idea and restate the main points.

Once you have everyone's attention, repeat your main idea. Be sure to emphasize what you want the audience to do or think. Then state the key motivating factor.

Reinforce your theme by repeating the three or four main supporting points. A few sentences are generally enough to refresh people's memories. For example, here's how one speaker ended a presentation on the company's executive compensation program:

> We can all be proud of the way our company has grown. But if we want to continue that growth, we will have to adjust our executive compensation program to reflect competitive practices. If we don't, our best people will look for opportunities elsewhere.
>
> In summary, our survey has shown that we need to do four things to improve executive compensation:
>
> * Increase the overall level of compensation
> * Install a cash bonus program
> * Offer a variety of stock-based incentives
> * Improve our health insurance and pension benefits
>
> By making these improvements, we can help our company cross the threshold of growth into the major leagues.

Notice how the speaker repeats his recommendations, then concludes with a memorable statement that motivates the audience to take action.

Outlining the next steps

Some speeches and presentations require the audience to reach a decision or agree to take specific action. In those cases, the final summary must provide a clear wrap-up.

If the audience has reached agreement on an issue handled in the speech or presentation, review the consensus in a sentence or two. If not, make the lack of consensus clear by saying something like "We seem to have some fundamental disagreement on this question." You can go on to suggest a method of resolving the differences.

Be certain that everyone agrees on the outcome and understands what should happen next.

If you expect any action to occur, you must explain who is responsible for doing what. One very effective technique is to list the action items, with an estimated completion date and the name of the person responsible. This list should be presented in a visual aid that can be seen by the entire audience. Each person on the list should be asked to agree to accomplish his or her assigned task by the target date. This public commitment to action is the best insurance that something will happen.

If the required action is likely to be difficult, make sure everyone understands the problems involved. You don't want people to leave the presentation thinking "This will be easy as pie," only to discover later that the job is a major undertaking. If that happens, they are likely to become discouraged and fail to complete their assignments. You want everyone to have a realistic attitude and be prepared to handle whatever arises. So use the final summary to point up pitfalls; alert people to potential difficulties.

Ending on a positive note

Your final remarks should be enthusiastic and memorable. Even if parts of your speech or presentation have been downbeat, you should try to close on a positive note. For example, you might point up the benefits of action or express confidence in listeners' ability to accomplish the work ahead. An alternative is to end with a question or with a statement that will leave your audience thinking.

Remember that your final words should round out the presentation. You want to leave the audience with a satisfied feeling, a feeling of completeness. The final summary is not the place to introduce new ideas or to alter the mood of the presentation. Although you want to close on a positive note, avoid a staged finale. Keep it natural.

THE QUESTION-AND-ANSWER PERIOD

In addition to having an introduction, a body, and a final summary, your speech or presentation should include an opportunity for questions and answers. Otherwise, you might just as well write a report. If you don't plan to interact with the audience, you waste the chief advantage of an oral format.

Encourage questions throughout if you are addressing a small group, but ask a large audience to defer questions until later.

Although you should generally interact with the audience, think carefully about the nature and timing of that interaction. Responding to questions and comments during the presentation interrupts the flow of your argument and reduces your control of the situation. If you are addressing a large group, particularly a hostile or unknown group, questions can be dangerous. Your best bet in this case is to ask people to hold their questions until after you have concluded your remarks. But if you are working with a small group and need to draw out ideas, you should encourage comments from the audience throughout the presentation.

Regardless of when you respond to questions, remember that they are one of the most important parts of your presentation. Questions give you a chance to obtain important information, to emphasize your main idea and supporting points, and to build enthusiasm for your point of view.

THE VISUAL AIDS

Visual aids help both the speaker and the audience remember the important points.

Most formal speeches and presentations incorporate visual aids. From a purely practical standpoint, they are a convenience for the speaker, who can use them as a tool for remembering the details of the message (no small feat in an hour-long presentation); novice speakers also like visual aids because they draw audience attention away from the speaker. More important, however, visual aids dramatically increase the audience's ability to absorb and remember information.

Although the visual aids used in speeches and presentations are similar in many respects to those used in documents (see Chapter 14), they also differ significantly. Thus their design and preparation merit special consideration.

Designing and presenting visual aids

Two kinds of visual aids:

- Text visuals help listeners follow the flow of ideas.
- Graphic visuals present and emphasize important facts.

Two types of visual aids are used to supplement speeches and presentations. Text visuals, which consist of words, help the audience follow the flow of ideas. As simplified outlines of your presentation, you can use them to summarize and preview the message and to notify the audience of major shifts in thought. On the other hand, graphic visual aids illustrate the main points. They help the audience grasp numerical data and other types of information that would be hard to follow if presented orally.

Simplicity is the key to effectiveness in designing both types of visual aids. Because people cannot read and listen at the same time, the visual aids must be simple enough so the audience can understand them within a moment or two.

Text visuals should consist of no more than six lines, with a maximum of six words per line. They should be typed in large, clear type, using upper- and lower-case letters, with extra white space between lines of type. Items in list format should be phrased in parallel grammatical form. The wording should be telegraphic ("Compensation Generous," for example) without being cryptic ("Compensation"); you are often better off to include both a noun and a verb in each phrase.

Many speeches and presentations begin with several text visuals. The first is usually the equivalent of a title page: It announces the subject and signals the audience that the presentation is under way. The second typically lists the three or four major points you will cover, providing a road map of what's to come. The remaining text visuals are used to emphasize the transitions between the main points on the outline. Like the headings in a written report, they signal that a new topic is about to be introduced.

Graphic visuals include line, pie, and bar charts, as well as flow charts, organization charts, diagrams, maps, drawings, and tables. Graphic visuals used in oral presentations should be simplified versions of those that appear in written documents. Eliminate anything that is not absolutely essential to the message. To help the audience focus immediately on the point of each graphic visual, use headings that state the message in one clear phrase: "Earnings have increased by 15 percent."

When you present visual aids, you want to give people a chance to read what's there, but you also want them to listen to your explanation. Here are a few tips for handling visual aids effectively:

Visual aids are counterproductive if the audience can't clearly see or understand them within a few moments.

- Be sure that all members of the audience can see the visual aids.
- Allow the audience time to read a visual aid before you begin your explanation.
- Limit each visual aid to one idea.
- Illustrate only the main points, not the entire presentation.
- Do not use any visual aids that conflict with your verbal message.
- Do not read the text of a visual aid word for word; paraphrase it instead.
- When you have finished discussing the point illustrated by the visual aid, remove it from the audience's view.[4]

Remember that you want the audience to listen to you, not to study the visual aids. The visual aids are there to supplement your words—not the other way around.

Selecting the right medium

Visual aids may be presented in a variety of media.

Visual aids for documents are usually limited to paper. But for speeches and presentations, you have a variety of media to choose from:

- *Handouts.* Even in a presentation, you may choose to distribute sheets of paper bearing an agenda, an outline of the program, an abstract, a written report, or such supplementary material as tables, charts, and graphs. Members of the audience can keep the handout to remind them of the subject and the main ideas of your presentation. In addition, they can refer to it while you're speaking. Handouts work especially well in informal situations where the audience takes an active role; they often make their own notes on the handouts. However, handouts can be distracting because people are inclined to read the material rather than listen to you, so many experienced speakers distribute handouts after completing the presentation.
- *Chalkboards and whiteboards.* When you're addressing a small group of people and want to draw out their ideas, use a board to list points as they are mentioned. Because visual aids using this medium are produced on the spot, boards provide flexibility. But they are too informal for some situations.
- *Flip charts.* Large sheets of paper attached at the top like a tablet can be propped on an easel; you flip the pages as you speak. Each chart illustrates or clarifies a point. You might have a few lines from your outline on one, a graph or diagram on another, and so on. By using felt-tip markers in different colors, you can highlight various ideas as you go along. Flip charts are most effective when you keep them simple. As a general rule, limit each sheet to three or four graphed lines or five or six points written in list format.
- *Overheads.* One of the most common visual aids in business is the overhead transparency, which can be projected on a screen in full daylight. Because you don't have to dim the lights, you don't lose eye contact with the audience. Transparencies are easy to make using a typed original on regular paper, a copying machine, and a page-size sheet of plastic. Opaque projections are similar to transparencies but do not require as much preparation. For example, you could use an

TABLE 18.1 Guidelines for Selecting Visuals

	OPTIMUM AUDIENCE SIZE	DEGREE OF FORMALITY	DESIGN COMPLEXITY	EQUIPMENT AND ROOM REQUIREMENTS	PRODUCTION TIME	COST
HANDOUTS	Fewer than 100	Informal	Simple	Typed text and photocopying machine	Typing or drawing time; photocopying time	Inexpensive
BOARDS AND FLIP CHARTS	Fewer than 20	Informal	Simple	Chalkboard or whiteboard or easel and chart, with writing implements	Drawing time only	Inexpensive
OVERHEADS	About 100	Formal or informal	Simple	Text, photocopying machine, plastic sheets, and projector and screen	Drawing or typing time; photocopying time	Inexpensive unless professionally designed or typeset
SLIDES	Several hundred	Formal	Anything that can be photographed	Slides, projector, and screen; dim lighting	Design and photographing time; at least 24 hours production time	Relatively expensive

opaque projector to show the audience a photograph or an excerpt from a report or manual.

- *Slides.* The content of slides may be text, graphics, or pictures. If you are trying to create a polished, professional atmosphere, you might find this approach worthwhile, particularly if you will be addressing a crowd and don't mind speaking in a darkened room. However, remember that you may need someone to operate the projector, and that person will need to coordinate the slides with your speech. Check in advance to be sure the equipment works, and practice beforehand with the operator.
- *Other visual aids.* In technical or scientific presentations, a sample of a product or material allows the audience to experience your subject directly. Models built to scale are convenient representations of an object. Audiotapes are often used to supplement a slide show or to present a precisely worded and timed message. Filmstrips and movies are effective for capturing the audience's attention with color and movement. Television and videotapes are good for showing demonstrations, interviews, and other events. However, audiotapes, filmstrips, movies, television, and videotapes require rather elaborate production and presentation equipment.

Table 18.1 summarizes some of the factors to consider in selecting a visual medium.

Use visual aids to highlight, not just substitute for, the spoken word.

With all visual aids, the crucial factor is how you use them. They should not just substitute for the spoken word but should also save time, create interest, add variety, make an impression, illustrate things that are difficult to explain in words alone. Let your visual aids highlight your presentation and call attention to points of interest.

MASTERING THE ART OF DELIVERY

Although some people memorize or read their speeches or presentations, using notes is generally the best way to handle delivery.

When you've planned all the parts of your presentation and have your visual aids in hand, you're ready to begin practicing your delivery. You have a variety of delivery methods to choose from, some easier to handle than others:

- *Memorizing.* Unless you're a trained actor, avoid memorizing an entire speech, particularly a long one. You're likely to forget your lines and botch the whole thing. Furthermore, a memorized speech often sounds very stiff and stilted. On the other hand, memorizing a quotation, an opening paragraph, or a few concluding remarks often strengthens your delivery.
- *Reading.* If you're delivering a technical or complex presentation, you may want to read it. Policy statements by highly placed government officials are generally read, because the wording is usually critical. If you choose to read your speech, practice enough so that you can still maintain eye contact with the audience. Triple-spaced copy, wide margins, and large type help too. You might even want to include "stage cues" for yourself, such as *pause, raise hands, lower voice.*
- *Speaking from notes.* Making a presentation with the help of an outline, note cards, or visual aids is probably the most effective and easiest delivery mode. It gives you something to refer to and still allows for eye contact and interaction with the audience. If your listeners look puzzled, for example, you can expand on a point or put it another way.
- *Impromptu speaking.* When you're asked to speak without any advance warning, your talk will be impromptu. For example, in a meeting you might be asked to give your opinion as the "resident expert" on something. In these situations, take a moment or two to think through what you're going to say. Then avoid the temptation to ramble.

Regardless of which delivery mode you use, be sure that you are thoroughly familiar with the subject. Your self-confidence will add a great deal to any speech or presentation.

PREPARING FOR SUCCESSFUL SPEAKING

Another good way to build self-confidence is to practice, especially if you have not had much experience in public speaking. You may deliver the speech or presentation to nobody but your image in a mirror, but try to visualize the room filled with listeners. Put your talk on tape to check the sound of your voice and your timing, phrasing, and emphasis. If possible, rehearse on videotape to see yourself as your audience will. Go over your visual aids and coordinate them with the talk.

Before you speak:
- Practice
- Prepare the location

If possible, check the location for your presentation in advance. Know beforehand what the seating arrangements will be, and make sure they are appropriate to your needs. For example, if you want the audience to sit at tables, be sure tables are available. Check the room for outlets that may be needed for your projector or microphone. Locate the light switches and dimmers. If you need a flip-chart easel or a chalkboard, be sure it is on hand. Check for chalk, an eraser, extension cords, and any other small but crucial items you might need.

DELIVERING THE SPEECH

Although common, the fear of speaking can be overcome.

When it's time to deliver the speech, you may feel a bit of stage fright. Most people do, even professional actors. You can overcome your fears, however, by taking a few tips from the professionals:

- Prepare more material than necessary. Extra knowledge, combined with a genuine interest in the topic, will boost your confidence.
- Think positively about your audience, yourself, and what you have to say. See yourself as polished and professional, and your audience will too.
- Be realistic about stage fright. After all, even experienced speakers admit that they feel butterflies before they address an audience. A little nervous excitement can actually provide the extra lift that will make your presentation sparkle.
- Use the few minutes while you are arranging your materials, before you actually begin speaking, to tell yourself you're on and you're ready.
- Before you begin speaking, take a few deep breaths.
- Have your first sentence memorized and on the tip of your tongue.
- If your throat is dry, drink some water.
- If you feel that you are losing your audience during the speech, don't panic. Try to pull them back by involving them in the action.
- Use your visual aids to maintain and revive audience interest.
- Keep going. Things usually get better, and your audience will silently be wishing you success.

Perhaps the best way to overcome stage fright is to concentrate on your message and your audience, not on yourself. When you're busy thinking about your subject and observing the audience's response, you tend to forget your fears.

Don't rush the opening.

However, as you deliver your presentation, do try to be aware of the nonverbal signals you are transmitting. To a great degree, your effectiveness will depend on how you look and sound. As you approach the speaker's podium, breathe deeply, stand up straight, and walk slowly. Face the audience. Adjust the microphone. Count to three slowly, then survey the room. When you find a friendly face, make eye contact and smile. Count to three again, then begin your presentation.[5] Even if you feel nervous inside, this slow, controlled beginning will help you establish rapport.

■ CHECKLIST FOR SPEECHES AND ORAL PRESENTATIONS

A. Development of the Speech or Presentation

- ☐ 1. Analyze the audience.
- ☐ 2. Begin with an attention getter.
- ☐ 3. Preview the main points.
- ☐ 4. Limit the discussion to no more than three or four points.
- ☐ 5. Explain who, what, when, where, why, and how.
- ☐ 6. In longer presentations, include previews and summaries of major points as you go along.
- ☐ 7. Close by reviewing your main points and making a memorable statement.

B. Visual Aids

- ☐ 1. Use visual aids to show how things look, work, or relate to one another.
- ☐ 2. Use visual aids to highlight important information and create interest.
- ☐ 3. Select appropriate visual aids.
  - ☐ a. Use flip charts, boards, or transparencies for small, informal groups.
  - ☐ b. Use slides or films for major occasions and large groups.
- ☐ 4. Limit each visual aid to three or four graphed lines or five or six points.
- ☐ 5. Use short phrases.
- ☐ 6. Use large, readable type.
- ☐ 7. Make sure equipment works.

C. Delivery

- ☐ 1. Establish eye contact.
- ☐ 2. Speak clearly and distinctly.
- ☐ 3. Do not go too fast.
- ☐ 4. Be sure everyone can hear.
- ☐ 5. Speak in your natural style.
- ☐ 6. Stand up straight.
- ☐ 7. Use gestures in a natural, appropriate way.
- ☐ 8. Encourage questions.
  - ☐ a. Allow questions during the presentation if the group is small.
  - ☐ b. Ask the audience to hold their questions until the end if the group is large or hostile.
- ☐ 9. Respond to questions without getting sidetracked.
- ☐ 10. Maintain control of your feelings in spite of criticism.

Once your speech is under way, be particularly careful to maintain eye contact with the audience. Pick out several people positioned around the room, and shift your gaze from one to another. Doing this will make you appear to be sincere, confident, and trustworthy, and it will also help you become attuned to the impression you are creating.

Use eye contact, posture, gestures, and voice to convey an aura of mastery and to keep your audience's attention.

Your posture is also important in projecting the right image. Stand tall, with your weight on both feet and your shoulders back. Avoid gripping the podium. Use your hands to emphasize your remarks with appropriate gestures. At the same time, vary your facial expressions to make the message more dynamic.

Think, too, about the sound of your voice. You should speak in a normal, conversational tone but with enough volume so everyone in the audience can hear you. Try to sound poised and confident, varying your pitch and speaking rate to add emphasis. Don't ramble or use meaningless filler words like "um," "you know," "okay," and "like." Speak clearly and crisply, articulating all the syllables and sounds. Try to sound enthusiastic.

HANDLING QUESTIONS

Many a speaker does very well at delivering the speech or presentation, only to falter during the question-and-answer period. The key to handling this segment effectively is preparation. Spend some time in advance thinking about the questions that might arise. Be ready with answers. In fact, some

SHARPEN YOUR SKILLS

Answering Questions from the Floor with Confidence and Courage

The question-and-answer period at the end of a speech or presentation gives you a chance to make sure the audience understood your facts and purpose. It also gives you insight into the audience's reaction to your topic. Most of all, it gives you a final opportunity to make points.

Here are some guidelines to help you deal with this important part of your presentation:

- *Be prepared.* If you have analyzed the audience for your presentation, you should already have some idea of which points and positions you may have to defend. Consider, too, the other presentations that the audience may hear on the same topic. Make a list of questions that might be asked by someone who lacks your knowledge and viewpoint. Then prepare possible answers, keeping in mind that circumstances may require some changes in the answers.
- *Admit ignorance.* If you don't know the answer to a question, don't pretend that you do. But do offer to find the answer and send the information to the questioner later.
- *Don't let the questioner become the speaker.* Some audience members will take advantage of the opportunity to mount the soapbox themselves. The rest of the audience may look to you to exert control in these situations. If the audience seems restless, break in, admit that you and the questioner have a difference of opinion, and then offer to get back to the questioner after you've had time to do some research. Then call on someone else. Or simply interrupt the questioner after a certain time and call on someone else. You might also respond with a very brief answer, thereby avoiding a lengthy debate with the questioner. Or you might break in, thank the person for her or his question, and then

experts recommend that you hold back some dramatic statistics as ammunition for the question-and-answer session.[6]

When someone poses a question, focus your attention on that individual. Pay attention to body language and facial expression to help determine what the person really means. Nod your head to acknowledge the question, then repeat it aloud to confirm your understanding and to ensure that the entire audience has heard it. If the question is vague or confusing, ask for clarification. Then give a simple, direct answer. Don't say more than you need to, because you want to have enough time to cover all the questions. If giving an adequate answer would take too long, simply say, "I'm sorry that we don't have time to get into that issue right now, but if you'll see me after the presentation, I'll be happy to discuss it with you." If you don't know the answer, say something like "I don't have those figures. I'll get them for you as quickly as possible."

Keep your answers short and sweet.

Don't allow one or two people to monopolize the question period. Try to give everyone a chance to participate; call on people from different parts of the room. If the same person keeps angling for attention, say

Don't let any member of the audience monopolize your attention.

remind the questioner that you were looking for specific questions. Don't indulge in put-downs, which may easily backfire and make the audience more sympathetic to the questioner.

- *Avoid overreacting to certain questions.* Some questioners will challenge your ideas, logic, or facts, perhaps with the goal of making you overreact in order to discredit your position. Needless to say, you must remain cool and collected. Defuse hostility and aggression by paraphrasing the question and asking the questioner to confirm that you've understood it correctly. Break long, complicated questions into parts that you can answer simply. Then answer honestly, accurately, and factually; avoid opinions. Address your answer to the entire audience instead of debating with the questioner. If necessary, remind the questioner that other audience members would like a chance to ask questions. You may refuse to continue if the questioner starts shouting, but be sure to provide a calm contrast to her or his outrageous behavior.
- *Prepare some questions in advance.* Just in case your audience is too timid or hostile to ask questions, plant some of your own. If a friend or the meeting organizer gets the ball rolling, other people in the audience will probably join in. You might also ask a question yourself: "Would you like to know more about . . . ?" If someone in the audience answers, act as if the question came from that person in the first place. When all else fails, say something like this: "I know from past experience that most questions are asked after the question period. So I'll be around afterward to talk." Members of large and diverse audiences are particularly likely to resist asking questions.

The question-and-answer period at the end of a speech or presentation is something more than a casual conversation, but don't be afraid of it. In some ways, it is more fun than the presentation itself.

1. In courses you have taken in the past year, to what extent have instructors invited questions? How has that technique affected your evaluation of the courses? Do some courses lend themselves more to questions than others do?

2. Suppose you were speaking to a student group about a controversial subject. What would you do if no one asked questions in the question period? If only one person asked questions, even though they were good ones? If someone began a long, emotional attack under the guise of asking a question?

something like, "Several other people have questions; I'll get back to you if time permits."

Respond unemotionally to tough questions.

Most of the people who ask questions will simply want clarification or additional information. Occasionally, however, you will encounter hostility. When that happens, keep cool. Look the person in the eye, answer the question as well as you can, and try not to show your feelings. Don't get into an argument. Simply state your response and move on to the next question. Avoid postures or gestures that might seem antagonistic. Don't put your hands on your hips or point your finger in a scolding fashion. Maintain a businesslike tone of voice and a pleasant expression.[7]

When the time allotted for your presentation is up, call a halt to the question-and-answer session, even if more people want to talk. Prepare the audience for the end by saying, "Our time is almost up. Let's have one more question." After you've made your reply, summarize the main idea of the presentation and thank people for their attention. Conclude the way you opened: by looking around the room and making eye contact. Then gather your notes and leave the podium, shoulders straight, head up.

SUMMARY

At some point in your career you are likely to be called on to give a speech or presentation. Brief speeches (5 to 15 minutes) are organized like letters and short memos. Formal presentations, lasting up to an hour or more, generally involve more complex subjects and require more interaction with the audience. They are organized like formal reports, with an introduction, a body, and a final summary.

Many long speeches and presentations make use of such visual aids as handouts, chalkboards, flip charts, overheads, and slides. These should be selected to suit your purpose and the size and needs of the audience.

Practice your presentation thoroughly in advance. As you address the audience, use nonverbal communication skills to enhance your effectiveness. Be sure to make eye contact and to speak so everyone can understand you. If you encounter difficult questions, remain unemotional. Respond as well as you can, then move on.

COMMUNICATION CHALLENGES AT AT&T

AT&T Information Systems has decided to create a training program for its new sales and marketing representatives. The trainees will take a course consisting of three hour-long segments: planning a persuasive sales presentation, developing and using visual aids, and delivering the presentation. Each of these segments will feature several speeches by experienced sales and marketing representatives, like Martha Tapias, interspersed with exercises in applying skills.

Individual Challenge: Present a 5-minute speech on some aspect of one of the three main topics to a group of trainees (your classmates). For example, you might give a speech on nonverbal techniques to use in delivering a sales presentation. In preparation for your speech, be sure to define your purpose, analyze the audience, state the main idea, outline the major supporting points, estimate length, and decide on a delivery style. Remember to think about the visual aids you will use. When you present the speech to your classmates, pay attention to both the verbal and nonverbal aspects of your communication style.

Team Challenge: A group of you have been asked to prepare one of the major segments of the training program, the one on developing and using visual aids. Prepare the script and supporting materials for a 50-minute presentation, then deliver it as a team to trainees (your classmates). Your presentation must not only cover techniques but also incorporate some application exercises. Of course, you need to show some examples of well-prepared visual aids.

QUESTIONS FOR DISCUSSION

1. How do speeches and presentations compare with interviews and meetings?
2. How does the purpose of a speech influence the amount of audience interaction that occurs?
3. Apart from length, what differentiates short speeches and presentations from long ones?
4. What factors determine the style of a speech or presentation?
5. How does the introduction to a formal speech or presentation differ from the introduction to a formal report?
6. Why is it important to emphasize transitions in a speech or presentation? What are some of the techniques you can use to emphasize the transitions?
7. What are the advantages and disadvantages of responding to questions from the audience throughout a speech or presentation?
8. What are the benefits and dangers of using various types of visual aids?
9. Which visual aids are most appropriate for small audiences? For large audiences?
10. What should you do when you encounter hostile questions?

EXERCISES

1. Prepare outlines or "scripts" for the following speaking situations:
   a. A 5-minute pep talk to 20 production workers straining to meet a deadline
   b. A 15-minute after-dinner speech on your community in the year 2000 to an audience of about 100 at the annual meeting of the local Chamber of Commerce
   c. A 10-minute informative presentation to a 15-member board of directors on the results of a search for a new executive director for a nonprofit organization
   d. A 20-minute analytical presentation to a 15-member board of directors on the relative merits of the three finalists for the position of executive director of a nonprofit organization
   e. A 30-minute sales presentation touting a new textbook to a five-member teachers' committee
   f. An hour-long presentation to a six-member group of top executives in which you and two colleagues present the results of marketing studies on trends in the fast-food market and facilitate an executive decision about which new opportunities to pursue
2. Give an oral presentation to the class (length specified by your instructor) based on the formal analytical report you prepared as an assignment for Chapter 16. You should mention the purpose of your report, your sources, and your conclusions and recommendations. If appropriate, use visual aids as well. Be sure to allow enough time for questions from your audience.
3. Choose a successful professional whom you know, and assume that this person will be speaking to a specific campus group (your choice too). Write a three-minute introduction that relates some of the speaker's accomplishments to the interests of the group. In other words, bring the speaker and the group together. Try to word your introduction as if you were actually speaking to the group.
4. Make a five-minute speech or presentation to your classmates on any business topic. When you finish, ask your audience to comment on your performance. If your instructor prefers, you might prepare evaluation forms for your audience to fill out anonymously.
5. Attend a speech or presentation, then write a page or two evaluating the speaker's delivery and effectiveness in handling problems associated with the audience or the speaking environment. For any area that the speaker handled poorly, suggest alternatives.

PART SEVEN

Special Topics in Business Communication

COMPONENT CHAPTER A

INTERCULTURAL BUSINESS COMMUNICATION

Managers of U.S. companies along the Mexican side of the Rio Grande have learned the hard way that the gap between the customs of U.S. and Mexican employees is as wide as the river separating the two countries. One company, for example, developed a carefully thought out three-tiered process for employees to present grievances. The manager of the plant assumed things were going well, because not a single grievance was lodged. Much to his embarrassment and surprise, however, the entire staff of Mexican employees walked off the job one day. What the manager had not known is that Mexicans consider it disrespectful to confront their bosses directly with grievances. In their culture, to complain is to challenge the role of authority.

In a similar incident, the manager of a computer component plant wanted to reduce the obvious differences in socioeconomic status between him and his Mexican managers. He dressed casually and called all the Mexican managers by their first names. He later found out that the Mexicans considered him uncultured and boorish. Mexican people place great importance on status and feel that one's appearance should reflect one's role: "The higher the importance of a job, the more formal the attire, the fancier the wristwatch, the shinier the shoes."[1]

At plants and factories all over the world, American managers are learning from such incidents that doing business with people from another country requires much more than memorizing a few important phrases in their language. To be successful, they have to know something about the other culture, especially those aspects that directly affect business communication: roles and status, business etiquette, decision-making customs, and verbal and nonverbal communication styles.

In your capacity as a business communicator, you too may have opportunities for dealing with people from other cultures. You may need to travel to another country to do business, or you may do business with foreigners who are traveling or living here. In this country, you may work for a foreign-owned firm or have dealings with other citizens who have distinctly different cultural backgrounds from your own. You will thus find an awareness of intercultural differences useful.

BASICS OF INTERCULTURAL BUSINESS COMMUNICATION

The first step in learning to communicate with people from other cultures is to become aware of what culture means. You may not realize it, but you belong to several cultures. The most obvious is the culture you share with all other people who live in this country. But you also belong to such other cultural groups as an ethnic group, a religious group, a fraternity or sorority, or perhaps a profession that has its own special "language" and customs.

UNDERSTANDING CULTURE

So what exactly is culture? More than 100 definitions have been offered; it's not an easy concept to pin down. However, it is useful to define *culture* as a shared system of symbols, beliefs, attitudes, values, expectations, and norms for behavior. Thus, all members of a culture have similar assumptions about how people should think, behave, and communicate, and they tend to act on those assumptions.

Cultural groups that exist within a major culture are more properly referred to as *subcultures*. Among groups that might be considered subcultures are Mexican Americans in East Los Angeles, Mormons in Salt Lake City, and longshoremen in Montreal. Subcultures without geographic boundaries can be found as well, such as wrestling fans, Russian immigrants, and Harvard MBAs.

Cultures and subcultures vary in several ways that affect intercultural communication:

- *Stability*. Conditions in the culture may be stable or may be changing slowly or rapidly.
- *Complexity*. Cultures vary in the accessibility of information. In some cultures, as in North America, information is contained in explicit codes, including words. In others, like Japan, a great deal of information is conveyed implicitly, through body language, physical context, and the like.
- *Composition*. Some cultures are made up of many diverse and disparate subcultures; others tend to be more homogeneous.
- *Acceptance*. Cultures vary in their attitudes toward outsiders. Some are openly hostile or maintain a detached aloofness. Others are friendly and cooperative toward strangers.

As you can see, cultures vary widely. It's no wonder that most of us need special training before we can become comfortable with a culture other than our own.

DEVELOPING INTERCULTURAL COMMUNICATION SKILLS

When faced with the need (or desire) to learn about another culture, you have two main approaches to choose from. One is to learn as much as possible—the language, cultural background and history, social rules, and so on—about the specific culture that you expect to deal with. The other is to develop general skills that will help you adapt in any culture.

The first approach, in-depth knowledge of a particular culture, certainly works. But there are a couple of drawbacks. One is that you will never be able to understand another culture completely. No matter how much you study German culture, for example, you will never be a German or share the experiences of having grown up in Germany. Even if you could understand the culture completely, natives might resent your assumption that you know everything there is to know about them.

The other drawback to immersing yourself in a specific culture is the trap of overgeneralization. When you overgeneralize, you look at people from the culture not as individuals with their own unique characteristics but as instances of "Germans" or "Japanese" or "black Americans." The trick is to learn useful general information but to be open to variations and individual differences.

The second approach to cultural learning, general development of intercultural skills, is especially useful if you will need to interact with people from a variety of cultures or subcultures. Among the skills you need to learn are

- *Taking responsibility for communication*. Don't assume that it is the other person's job to communicate with you.
- *Withholding judgment*. Learn to listen to the whole story and to accept differences in others.
- *Showing respect*. Learn the ways in which respect is communicated—through gestures, eye contact, and so on—in various cultures.
- *Empathizing*. Try to put yourself in the other person's shoes. Listen carefully to what the other person is trying to communicate, and imagine the person's feelings and point of view.
- *Tolerating ambiguity*. Learn to control your frustration when placed in an unfamiliar or confusing situation.
- *Looking beyond the superficial*. Don't be distracted by such things as dress, appearance, and environmental discomforts.
- *Being patient and persistent*. If you want to accomplish a task, don't give up easily.
- *Recognizing your own cultural biases*. Learn to identify when your assumptions are different from the other person's.

- *Being flexible.* Be prepared to change your habits, preferences, and attitudes.
- *Emphasizing common ground.* Look for similarities to work from.
- *Sending clear messages.* Make your verbal and nonverbal messages consistent.
- *Taking risks.* Try things that will help you gain a better understanding of the other person or culture.
- *Increasing your cultural sensitivity.* Learn about variations in customs and practices so that you will be more aware of potential areas for miscommunication or misunderstanding.
- *Dealing with the individual.* Avoid stereotyping and overgeneralization.

These are skills that will help you communicate with anybody, whether someone from your own culture or another.

DIFFICULTIES OF INTERCULTURAL BUSINESS COMMUNICATION

The more differences there are between the people who are communicating, the more difficult it is to communicate effectively. The major problems in intercultural business communication are language barriers, cultural differences, and ethnocentric reactions.

LANGUAGE BARRIERS

If you're doing business in London, you obviously won't have much of a language problem. You may encounter a few unusual terms or accents in the 29 countries in which English is an official language, but your problems will be relatively minor.

Let's say, for example, that you drive into a filling station in England and ask for gas. The attendant looks puzzled for a moment, then laughs and says, "You mean petrol." After filling your tank, the attendant asks, "Shall I look under the bonnet?" You're taken aback by this question, but then, as the attendant points toward the front of your car, you understand that the English *bonnet* translates into the North American *hood.*

Misunderstandings of this sort are not too serious. But suppose you're visiting New Zealand, not England. The people speak English, of course. But their pronunciation is quite different from ours. Becoming used to their pronunciation may take a little time.

Language barriers will also be relatively minor when you are dealing with people who use English as a second language (and some 650 million people fall into this category). Some of these millions are extremely fluent; others have only an elementary command of English. Although you may miss a few subtleties in dealing with those who are less fluent in English, you will still be able to communicate.

The pitfall to watch for is assuming that the other person understands everything you say, even slang, local idioms, and accents. One group of English-speaking Japanese who moved to the United States as employees of Toyota had to enroll in a special course to learn that "Jeat yet?" means "Did you eat yet?" and that "Cannahepya?" means "Can I help you?"

The real problem with language arises when you are dealing with people who speak virtually no English. In situations like this, you have very few options: You can learn their language, you can use an intermediary or translator, or you can teach them your language.

Becoming fluent in a new language (which you must do to conduct business in that language) is time-consuming. The U.S. State Department, for example, gives its Foreign Service officers a six-month language training program and expects them to continue their language education at their foreign posts. Even the Berlitz method, which is famous for the speed of its results, requires a month of intensive effort—13 hours a day, 5 days a week. It is estimated that minimum proficiency in another language requires at least 240 hours of study over 8 weeks; more complex languages, such as Arabic and Chinese, require more than 480 hours. Language courses can be quite expensive as well. Unless you are planning to spend several years abroad or to make frequent trips over an extended period, learning another language may not be worth the time and effort required.

A more practical approach may be to use an intermediary or translator. For example, if your company has a foreign subsidiary, you can delegate the communication job to local nationals who are bilingual. Or you can hire bilingual advertising consultants, distributors, lobbyists, lawyers, translators, and other professionals to help you.

The option of teaching other people to speak your language doesn't appear to be very practical at first glance; however, many multinational companies do in fact have language training programs for their foreign employees. Tenneco, for example, instituted an English-language training program for its Spanish-speaking employees in a New Jersey plant. The classes concentrated on practical English for use on the job. According to the company, these classes were a success: Accidents and grievances declined, and productivity improved.[2]

In general, the magnitude of the language barrier depends on whether you are writing or speaking. Written communication is generally easier to handle.

Barriers to written communication

One survey of 100 companies engaged in international business revealed that between 95 and 99 percent of their business letters to other countries are written in English. And 59 percent of the respondents reported that the foreign letters they receive are usually written in English, although they also receive letters written in Spanish and French. Other languages are rare in international business correspondence.[3]

Because many international business letters are written in English, North American firms do not always have to worry about translating their correspondence. However, even when both parties write in English, minor interpretation problems do exist because of different usage of technical terms. Usually, these problems do not pose a major barrier to communication, especially if correspondence between the two parties continues and each gradually learns the terminology of the other.

More significant problems arise in other forms of written communication that require translation. Advertisements, for example, are almost always translated into the language of the country in which the products are being sold. Documents such as warranties, repair and maintenance manuals, and product labels also require translation. In addition, some multinational companies must translate policy and procedure manuals and benefit plans for use in overseas offices. Reports from foreign subsidiaries to the home office may also be written in one language, then translated into another.

Sometimes the translations aren't very good. For example, the well-known slogan "Come alive with Pepsi" was translated literally for Asian markets as "Pepsi brings your ancestors back from the grave," with unfortunate results. Part of the message is almost inevitably lost during any translation process, sometimes with major consequences.

Barriers to oral communication

Oral communication usually presents more problems than written communication. If you have ever studied a foreign language, you know from personal experience that it's easier to write in a foreign language than to conduct a conversation.

Even if the other person is speaking English, you're likely to have a hard time understanding the pronunciation if the person is not proficient in English. For example, many foreigners notice no difference between the English sounds *v* and *w*; they say *wery* for *very*. At the same time, many people from North America cannot pronounce some of the sounds that are frequently used in other parts of the world.

In addition to pronouncing sounds differently, people use their voices in different ways, a fact that often leads to misunderstanding. The Russians, for example, speak in flat, level tones in their native tongue. When they speak English, they maintain this pattern, and we may assume that they are bored or rude. Middle Easterners tend to speak more loudly than Westerners and may therefore mistakenly be considered more emotional. On the other hand, the Japanese are soft-spoken, a characteristic that implies politeness or humility to Westerners.

Idiomatic expressions are another source of confusion. If you tell a foreigner that a certain product "doesn't cut the mustard," chances are that you will fail to communicate. The phrase does not make much sense to someone from another culture, who must interpret your words literally.

Even when the words make sense, their meanings may differ according to the situation. For example, suppose that you are dining with a German woman who speaks English quite well. You inquire, "More bread?" She says, "Thank you," so you pass the bread. She looks confused, then takes the breadbasket and sets it down without taking any. In German, *thank you* (*danke*) is used as a polite refusal. If the woman had wanted more bread, she would have used the word *please* (*bitte* in German).

When speaking in English to those for whom English is a second language, follow these simple guidelines:

- *Try to eliminate "noise."* Pronounce words clearly and stop at distinct punctuation points. Make one point at a time.
- *Look for feedback.* Be alert to glazed-over eyes or signs of confusion in your listener. Realize that nods and smiles do not necessarily mean understanding. Don't be afraid to ask, "Is that clear?" and to check the listener's comprehension through specific questions. Encourage the listener to ask questions.
- *Rephrase your sentence when necessary.* If someone doesn't seem to understand what you have said, choose simpler words; don't just repeat the sentence in a louder voice.
- *Don't talk down to the other person.* Americans tend to overenunciate and to "blame" the listener for lack of comprehension. It is preferable to use phrases such as "Am I going too fast?" rather than "Is this too difficult for you?"
- *Use objective, accurate language.* Americans tend to throw around adjectives such as "fantastic" and "fabulous," which foreigners consider unreal and overly dramatic. Calling something a "disaster" will give rise to images of war and death; calling someone an "idiot" or a "prince" may be taken literally.
- *Let other people finish what they have to say.* If you interrupt, you may miss something important. And you'll show a lack of respect.

CULTURAL DIFFERENCES

As you know, misunderstandings are especially likely to occur when the people who are communicating have different backgrounds. Party A encodes a message in one context, using assumptions common to people in his or her culture; Party B decodes the message using a different set of assumptions. The result is confusion and, often, hard feelings. For example, take the case of the computer sales representative who was calling on a client in China. Hoping to make a good impression, the salesperson brought along a gift to break the ice, an expensive grandfather clock. Unfortunately, the Chinese client was deeply offended, because clocks are a symbol of bad luck in China. Furthermore, expensive presents are a source of great embarrassment.[4]

Such problems arise because of our unconscious assumptions and nonverbal communication patterns. We ignore the fact that people from other cultures differ from us in many ways: in their religion and values, their ideas of status, their decision-making habits, their attitude toward time, their use of space, their body language, and their manners. We assume, wrongly, that other people are like us.

Religion and values

Although North America is a melting pot of people with different religions and values, the predominant influence in our culture is the Puritan ethic: If you work hard and achieve success, you will find favor in the eyes of God. We tend to assume that material comfort is a sign of superiority, that the rich are a little bit better than the poor, that people who work hard are better than those who don't. We believe that money solves many problems. We assume that people from other cultures share our view, that they dislike poverty and value hard work. But, in fact, many societies condemn materialism and prize a carefree life style.

As a culture, we are goal oriented. We want to get the work done in the most efficient manner, and we assume that everyone else does too. We think we are improving things if we can figure out a way for two people using modern methods to do the same work as four people using the "old way." But in countries like India and Pakistan, where unemployment is extremely high, creating jobs is more important than getting the work done efficiently. Executives in these countries would rather employ four workers than two.

Roles and status

Culture dictates the roles people play, including who communicates with whom, what they communicate, and in what way. In many countries, for example, women still do not play a very prominent role in business. As a result, female executives from American firms may find themselves sent off to eat in a separate room with the wives of Arab businessmen, while the men all eat dinner together.

Concepts of status also differ, and as a consequence, people establish their credibility in different ways. North Americans, for example, send "status signals" that reflect materialistic values. The big boss has the corner office on the top floor, deep carpets, an expensive desk, handsome accessories.

The most successful companies are located in the most prestigious buildings.

In other countries status is communicated in other ways. For example, the highest-ranking executives in France sit in the middle of an open area, surrounded by lower-level employees. In the Middle East fine possessions are reserved for the home, and business is conducted in cramped and modest quarters. An American executive who assumes that these office arrangements indicate a lack of status is making a big mistake.

Decision-making customs

In North America we try to reach decisions as quickly and efficiently as possible. The top people focus on reaching agreement on the main points and leave the details to be worked out later by others. But in Greece this approach would backfire. A Greek executive assumes that anyone who ignores the details is being evasive and untrustworthy. Spending time on each and every little point is considered a mark of good faith. Similarly, Latin Americans prefer to make their deals slowly, after a lengthy period of discussion. They resist an authoritarian "Here's the deal, take it or leave it" approach, preferring the more sociable method of an extended discussion.

Cultures also differ in terms of who makes the decisions. In our culture many organizations are dominated by a single figure who says yes or no to every deal. Likewise in Pakistan, where you can get a decision quickly if you reach the highest-ranking executive.[5] But in other cultures, notably China and Japan, decision making is a shared responsibility. No individual has the authority to commit the organization without first consulting others. In Japan, for example, the negotiating team arrives at a consensus through an elaborate, time-consuming process (agreement must be complete—there is no majority rule). If the process is not laborious enough, the Japanese feel uncomfortable.[6]

Concepts of time

Differing perceptions of time are another factor that can lead to misunderstandings. An executive from North America or Germany attaches one meaning to time; an executive from Latin America, Ethiopia, or Japan attaches another.

Let's say that a salesperson from Chicago calls on a client in Mexico City. After spending 30 minutes in the outer office, the person from Chicago feels angry and insulted, assuming, "This client must attach a very low priority to my visit to keep me waiting half an hour." In fact, the Mexican client does not mean to imply anything at all by this delay. To the Mexican a wait of 30 minutes is a matter of course.

Or let's say that a New Yorker is trying to negotiate a deal in Ethiopia. This is a very important deal, and the New Yorker assumes that the Ethiopians will give the matter top priority and reach a decision quickly. Not so. In Ethiopia important deals take a long, long, long time. After all, if a deal is important, it should be given much careful thought, shouldn't it?

The Japanese, knowing that North Americans are impatient, use time to their advantage when negotiating with us. One of them expressed it this way: "You Americans have one terrible weakness. If we make you wait long enough, you will agree to anything."[7]

Concepts of personal space

The classic story of a conversation between a North American and a Latin American is that the interaction may begin at one end of a hallway but end up at the other, with neither party aware that they have moved. During the interaction, the Latin American instinctively moves closer to the North American, who in turn instinctively steps back, resulting in an intercultural dance down the floor.

Like time, space means different things in different cultures. North Americans stand about five feet apart when conducting a business conversation. To an Arab or a Latin American, this distance is uncomfortable. In meetings with North Americans, they move a little closer. We assume they are pushy and react negatively, although we don't know exactly why.

Body language

Gestures help us clarify confusing messages, so differences in body language are a major source of misunderstanding. We may also make the mistake of assuming that a non-American who speaks English has mastered the body language of our culture as well. It therefore pays to learn some basic differences in the way people supplement their words with body movement.

Take the signal for no. We North Americans shake our heads back and forth; the Japanese move their right hands; Sicilians raise their chins.

Or take eye contact. North Americans read each other through the eyes. We may assume that a person who won't meet our gaze is evasive and dishonest. But in many parts of Latin America, keeping your eyes lowered is a sign of respect. It's also a sign of respect among many black Americans, which some schoolteachers have failed to learn. When they scold their black students, saying, "Look at me when I'm talking to you," they only create confusion for the children.

Sometimes people from different cultures misread an intentional signal, and sometimes they overlook the signal entirely or assume that a meaningless gesture is significant. For example, an Arab man indicates a romantic interest in a woman by running a hand backward across his hair; most Americans would dismiss this gesture as meaningless. On the other hand, an Egyptian might mistakenly assume that a Westerner sitting with the sole of his or her shoe showing is offering a grave insult.

Social behavior and manners

What is polite in one country may be considered rude in another. In Arab countries, for example, it is impolite to take gifts to a man's wife but acceptable to take gifts to his children. In Germany giving a woman a red rose is considered a romantic invitation, inappropriate if you are trying to establish a business relationship with her. In India you might be invited to visit someone's home "any time." Being reluctant to make an unexpected visit, you might wait to get a more definite invitation. But your failure to take the Indian literally is an insult, a sign that you do not care to develop the friendship.

Rules of etiquette may be formal or informal. Formal rules are the specifically taught "rights" and "wrongs" of how to behave in common situations, such as table manners at meals. Members of a culture can put into words the formal rule being violated. Informal social rules are much more difficult to identify and are usually learned by watching how people behave and then imitating that behavior. Informal rules govern how males and females are supposed to behave, how and when people may touch each other, when it is appropriate to use a person's first name, and so on. Violations of these rules cause a great deal of discomfort to the members of the culture, but they usually cannot verbalize what it is that bothers them.[8]

ETHNOCENTRIC REACTIONS

Although language and cultural differences are significant barriers to communication, these problems can be resolved if people maintain an open mind. Unfortunately, however, many of us have an ethnocentric reaction to people from other cultures—that is, we judge all other groups according to our own standards.[9]

When we react ethnocentrically, we ignore the distinctions between our own culture and the other person's culture. We assume that others will react the same way we do, that they will operate from the same assumptions, that they will use language and symbols in the "American" way. An ethnocentric reaction makes us lose sight of the possibility that our words and actions will be misunderstood, and it makes us more likely to misunderstand the behavior of foreigners.

Generally, ethnocentric people are prone to stereotyping and prejudice: They generalize about an entire group of people on the basis of sketchy evidence, then develop biased attitudes toward the group. As a consequence, they fail to see people as they really are. Instead of talking with Abdul Karhum, unique human being, they talk to an Arab. Although they never have met an Arab before, they may already believe that all Arabs are, say, hagglers. The personal qualities of Abdul Karhum become insignificant in the face of such preconceptions. Everything he says and does will be forced to fit the preconceived image.

Bear in mind that Americans are not the only people in the world who are prone to ethnocentrism. Often, both parties are guilty of stereotyping and prejudice. Neither is open-minded about the other. Little wonder, then, that misunderstandings arise. Fortunately, a healthy dose of tolerance can prevent a lot of problems.

TIPS FOR COMMUNICATING WITH PEOPLE FROM OTHER CULTURES

You may never completely overcome linguistic and cultural barriers or totally erase ethnocentric tendencies, but you can communicate effectively with people from other cultures if you work at it. Here are some tips for handling intercultural business communication more effectively.

LEARNING ABOUT A CULTURE

The best way to prepare yourself to do business with people from another culture is to study their culture in advance. If you plan to live in another country or to do business there repeatedly, learn the language. The same holds true if you must work closely with a subculture that has its own language, such as Vietnamese Americans. Even if you end up transacting business in English, you show respect by making the effort to learn the language. In addition, you will learn something about the culture and its customs in the process. If you do not have the time or opportunity to learn the language, at least learn a few words. Table A.1 (pp. 594–595) provides a list of useful phrases in several languages.

You should also read books and articles about the culture and talk to people who have dealt with its members, preferably people who have done business with them. Concentrate on learning something about their history, religion, politics, and customs, but don't ignore the practical details either. In that regard you should know something about another country's weather conditions, health-care facilities, money, transportation, communications, and customs regulations.

Find out as well about a country's subcultures, especially its "business subculture." Does the business world have its own rules and protocol? Who makes decisions? How are negotiations usually conducted? Is gift giving expected? What is the etiquette for exchanging business cards? What is the appropriate attire for attending a business meeting?

Seasoned business travelers suggest the following:

- In Spain, let a handshake last five to seven strokes; pulling away too soon may be interpreted as a sign of rejection. In France, however, the preferred handshake is a single stroke.
- Never give a gift of liquor in Arab countries.
- In England, never stick pens or other objects in your front suit pocket; doing so is considered gauche.
- In Pakistan, don't be surprised when business people excuse themselves in the midst of a meeting to conduct prayers. Moslems pray five times a day.
- Allow plenty of time to get to know the people you're dealing with in Africa. They're suspicious of people who are in a hurry. If you concentrate solely on the task at hand, Africans will distrust you and avoid doing business with you.
- In Arab countries, never turn down food or drink; it's an insult to refuse hospitality of any kind. But don't be too quick to accept, either. A ritual refusal ("I don't want to put you to any trouble" or "I don't want to be a bother") is expected before you finally accept.
- Stress the longevity of your company when dealing with the Germans, Dutch, and Swiss. If your company has been around for a while, the founding date should be printed on your business cards.

These are just a few examples of the variations in customs that make intercultural business so interesting.

HANDLING WRITTEN COMMUNICATION

Intercultural business writing falls into the same general categories as other forms of business writing. How you handle these categories depends on the subject and purpose of your message, the relationship between you and the reader, and the customs of the person to whom the message is addressed.

Letters

Letters are the most common form of intercultural business correspondence. They serve the same purposes and follow the same basic organizational plans (direct and indirect) as letters you would send within your own country. Figure A.1 (pp. 596–597) is an example of a business letter sent from an overseas branch of a U.S. company to someone in the host country.

Unless you are personally fluent in the language of the intended readers, you should ordinarily write your letters in English or have them translated by a professional translator. But if you and the reader speak different languages, be especially concerned with achieving clarity:

- Use short, precise words that say exactly what you mean.
- Rely on specific terms to explain your points.

TABLE A.1 **How to Say It: Some Basic English in Translation**

ENGLISH	FRENCH	GERMAN	SPANISH
Greetings	**Formules de politesse**	**Begrüssung**	**Saludos**
Good morning	Bonjour	Guten Morgen	Buenos días
Good evening	Bonsoir	Guten Abend	Buenas tardes
Good night	Bonne nuit	Gute Nacht	Buenas noches
Good-bye	Au revoir	Auf Wiedersehen	Adiós
How are you?	Comment allez-vous?	Wie geht es Ihnen?	¿Cómo está usted?
Very well	Très bien	Sehr gut	Muy bien
Thank you	Merci	Danke	Gracias
You are welcome	Il n'y a pas de quoi	Gern geschehen	De nada
General Conversation	**Conversation générale**	**Redewendungen**	**Conversación general**
Do you speak English?	Parlez-vous anglais?	Sprechen Sie Englisch?	¿ Habla usted inglés?
Your name?	Votre nom?	Ihr Name?	¿Cómo se llama usted?
I do not understand	Je ne comprends pas	Ich verstehe nicht	No entiendo
Yes/No	Oui/Non	Ja/Nein	Sí/No
Excuse me	Excusez-moi	Entschuldigen Sie	Dispénseme
Please	S'il vous plaît	Bitte	Por favor
Do you understand?	Comprenez-vous?	Verstehen Sie?	¿Me entiende?
Can you assist me?	Pouves-vous m'aider?	Können Sie mir helfen?	¿Puede ayudarme?
Money	**Argent**	**Geld**	**Dinero**
Bank	Banque	Bank	Banco
Change (money)	Change (devises)	Geldwechsel	Cambio (de dinero)
Check (note)	Chèque (traite)	Scheck (Bankscheck)	Cheque (giro)
Credit card	Carte de crédit	Kreditkarte	Tarjeta de crédito
Travelers check	Chèque de voyage	Reisescheck	Cheque de viajero
Communications	**Communications**	**Kommunikation**	**Comunicaciones**
Air Mail	Par avion	Luftpost	Vía aérea
Letter (registered)	Lettre (recommandée)	Einschreibebrief	Carta (certificada)
Post Office	Bureau de poste	Postamt	Oficina de Correos
Postage stamp	Timbre-poste	Briefmarke	Sello de correo
Telegram (cable)	Télégramme	Telegramm	Telegrama (cable)
Telephone	Téléphone	Telefon	Teléfono
Telex	Télex	Fernschreiber	Télex

Avoid abstractions altogether, or illustrate them with concrete examples.

- Stay away from slang, jargon, and buzz words. Such words rarely translate well. Nor do idioms and figurative expressions. Abbreviations, acronyms (such as NORAD and CAD/CAM), and North American product names may also lead to confusion.
- Construct sentences that are shorter and simpler than those you might use when writing to someone fluent in English.
- Use short paragraphs. Each paragraph should stick to one topic and be no more than eight to ten lines.
- Help readers follow your train of thought by using transitional devices. Precede related points with expressions like "in addition" and "first," "second," "third."
- Use numbers, visual aids, and preprinted forms to clarify your message. These devices are generally understood in most cultures.

Your word choice should also reflect the relationship between you and the reader. In general,

TABLE A.1 (continued)

ENGLISH	ITALIAN	CHINESE	JAPANESE
Greetings	**Saluti**	**Wen How**	**Aisatsu**
Good morning	Buon giorno	Tsao An	Ohayo gozaimasu
Good evening	Buona sera	Wu An	Konbanwa
Good night	Buona notte	Wan An	Oyasuminasai
Good-bye	Arrivederci	Tsai Tsien (Tsai Chien)	Sayonara
How are you?	Come sta?	Ni How Mà?	Ikaga desuka?
Very well	Benissimo	Heng How	Hijoni yoidesu
Thank you	Grazie	Shieh Shieh Ni	Arigato
You are welcome	Prego	Pu Ko Ch'i	Doitashimashite
General Conversation	**Conversazione**	**Pu Tung Hiu Hua**	**Ippan Kaiwa**
Do you speak English?	Lei parla inglese?	Ni Shoh In Wen Ma?	Anatawa eigo wo hanasemasuka?
Your name?	Il suo nome?	Ching Wen Kwei Sing?	Onamaewa?
I do not understand	Non capisco	O Pu Chu Tao	Wakarimasen
Yes/No	Si/No	Shu/Pu Shu	Hai/yie
Excuse me	Scusi	Tui Pu Chih	Sumimasen
Please	Per piacere	Ching	Dozo
Do you understand?	Capisce?	Ni Tung Ma?	Wakarimasuka?
Can you assist me?	Può aitarmi?	Ni Neng Pang O Meng Ma?	Tasukete kudasaimasuka?
Money	**Denaro**	**Chien**	**Okane**
Bank	Banca	Ying Heng	Ginko
Change (money)	Cambiare (denaro)	Hwan Chien	Ryogae (Okane)
Check (note)	Assegno (tratta)	Chu Piao	Kogitte
Credit card	Carta di credito	Shing Yung Chi'a	Kurejitto kaado
Travelers check	Travelers check	Nii Hsing Chu Piao	Torabera chekku
Communications	**Comunicazioni**	**Tung Hsun**	**Tsushin**
Air Mail	Posta aerea	Hang Kung Sing	Köökubin
Letter (registered)	Raccomandata	Kua How Sing	Tegami (kakitome)
Post Office	Ufficio postale	Yu Chü (U Chü)	Yubinkyoku
Postage stamp	Francobollo	Yu Pìao (U Piao)	Kitte
Telegram (cable)	Telegramma	Dìen Pao	Denpo (keiburu)
Telephone	Telefono	Dìen Hua	Denwa
Telex	Telex	Dìen Chuan Dien Pao	Terekkusu

be somewhat more formal than you would be in writing to people in your own culture. In many other cultures, people use a more elaborate, old-fashioned style, and you should gear your letters to their expectations. However, do not carry formality to extremes, or you will sound unnatural.

In terms of format, the two most common approaches for intercultural business letters are the block style (with blocked paragraphs) and the modified block style (with indented paragraphs). You may use either the American format for dates (with the month, date, and year, in that order) or the European style (with the date before the month and year). For the salutation, use *Dear (Title/Last Name)*. Close the letter with *Sincerely* or *Sincerely yours,* and sign it personally.

If you correspond frequently with people in foreign countries, your letterhead should include the name of your country and cable or Telex information. Send your letters by air mail, and ask that responses be sent that way as well. Check the postage too, because rates for sending mail to most other countries are not the same as rates for sending it within your own.

FIGURE A.1
International Business Letter, with Translation

ИБМ

IBM

ПОСТОЯННОЕ ПРЕДСТАВИТЕЛЬСТВО
ИБМ В МОСКВЕ

Гостиница «Националь»
Комната 265
Тел. 203-50-51, 203-83-84
Телекс: 7420 Монстар

IBM ACCREDITED OFFICE
MOSCOW

HOTEL "NATIONAL"
ROOM № 265
TEL : 203-50-51 - 203-83-84
TELEX : 7420 MONSTAR SU

Председателю
В/О "Внешторгиздат"
господину Моролеву Р.В.

17 декабря 19--

Уважаемый господин Моролев,

Постоянное Представительство фирмы ИБМ в СССР свидетельствует Вам свое уважение и подтверждает получение счета за работу,выполненную по заказу фирмы ИБМ по переводу и печатанию 50 экз. руководства для пищущей машинки "Селектрик" и 50 экз. словаря для пищущей машинки.

Поскольку в указанном счете показана только обшая стоимость всей работы отдельно по руководству и по словарю,мы бы просили Вас переделать счет с тем,чтобы в нем были отражены отдельные статьи затрат/т.е. стоимость перевода,изготовления оригинала,печатания/ как по руководству,так и по словарю.

Заранее благодар'м Вас за любезное содействие.

С уважением,

Р. Пинкертон
Постоянный представитель
ИБМ в СССР

In the letters you receive, you will notice that people in other countries use different techniques for their correspondence. If you are aware of some of these practices, you will be able to concentrate on the message without passing judgment on the writers. Their approaches are not "good" or "bad," just different.

The Japanese, for example, are slow to come to the point. Their letters typically begin with a remark about the season or weather. This is followed by an inquiry about your health or congratulations on your prosperity. A note of thanks for your patronage might come next. After these preliminaries, the main idea is introduced. If the letter contains bad news, the Japanese begin not with a buffer but with apologies for disappointing you.

Letters from Latin America look different too. Instead of using letterhead stationery, Latin American companies use a cover page with their printed seal in the center. Their letters appear to be longer than ours, because they use much wider margins.

Memos and reports

Memos and reports sent overseas fall into two general categories: those written to and from sub-

17 December 19—

Mr. R. V. Morolev
Chairman
c/o "Foreign Trade Publishers"

Dear Mr. Morolev,

The accredited IBM Office in the USSR sends its respects and verifies the receipt of the charges for the work fulfilled according to IBM's order for the translation and printing of 50 copies of the handbook for the "Selectric" typewriter and 50 copies of the typing dictionary.

Since the bill you sent shows only the aggregate cost of all the work for the handbook and the dictionary separately, we would like to ask that you redo the bill in such a way that the individual expenditures are delineated, that is, the cost of the translation, the preparation of the original, and the printing, first for the handbook, and secondly, for the dictionary.

We thank you beforehand for your kind cooperation in this matter.

With respect,

R. Pinkerton
Accredited Representative
IBM in the USSR

sidiaries, branches, or joint venture partners and those written to clients or other outsiders.

When the memo or report has an internal audience, the style may differ only slightly from that of a memo or report written for internal use in North America. Because sender and recipient have a working relationship and share a common frame of reference, many of the language and cultural barriers that lead to misunderstandings have already been overcome. However, if the reader's native language is not English, you should take extra care to ensure clarity: Use concrete and explicit words, simple and direct sentences, short paragraphs, headings, and many transitional devices.

If the memo or report is written for an external audience, the style of the document should be relatively formal and impersonal. If possible, the format should be like that of reports typically prepared or received by the audience. In the case of long, formal reports, it is also useful to discuss reporting requirements and expectations with the recipient beforehand and to submit a preliminary draft for comments before delivering the final report.

Other documents

Many international transactions involve shipping and receiving goods. A number of special-purpose documents are required to handle these transactions: price quotations, invoices, bills of lading, time drafts, letters of credit, correspondence with international freight forwarders, packing lists, shipping documents, and collection documents. Many of these documents are standard forms; you simply fill in the data as clearly and accurately as possible in the spaces provided. Samples are ordinarily available in a company's files if it frequently does business abroad. If not, you may obtain descriptions of the necessary documentation from the United States Department of Commerce, International Trade Administration, Washington, D.C. 20230. (For Canadian information, contact the Department of External Affairs, Trade Division, Ottawa, Ontario K1A 0G2.)

In preparing forms, pay particular attention to the method you use for stating weights and measures and money values. The preferred method is to use the other country's system of measurement and its currency values for documenting the transaction; however, if your company uses U.S. or Canadian weights, measures, and dollars, you should follow that policy. Check any conversion calculations carefully.

HANDLING ORAL COMMUNICATION

Oral communication with people from other cultures is more difficult to handle than written communication. But it can also be more rewarding, from both a business and a personal standpoint. Some transactions simply cannot be handled without face-to-face contact.

When engaging in oral communication, be alert to the possibilities for misunderstanding. Recognize that you may be sending signals that you are unaware of and that you may be misreading cues sent by the other person. To overcome language and cultural barriers, follow these suggestions:

- Keep an open mind. Don't stereotype the other person or react with preconceived ideas. Regard the person as an individual first, not as a representative of another culture.
- Be alert to the other person's customs. Expect him or her to have different values, beliefs, expectations, and mannerisms.
- Try to be aware of unintentional meanings that may be read into your message. Clarify your true intent by repetition and examples.
- Listen carefully and patiently. If you do not understand a comment, ask the person to repeat it.
- Be aware that the other person's body language may mislead you. Gestures and expressions mean different things in different cultures. Rely more on words than on nonverbal communication to interpret the message.
- Adapt your style to the other person's. If the other person appears to be direct and straightforward, follow suit. If not, adjust your behavior to match.
- At the end of a conversation, be sure that you and the other person both agree on what has been said and decided. Clarify what will happen next.
- If appropriate, follow up by writing a letter or memo summarizing the conversation and thanking the person for meeting with you.

In short, take advantage of the other person's presence to make sure that your message is getting across and that you understand his or her message too.

Speeches are both harder and simpler to deal with than personal conversations. On the one hand, speeches don't provide much of an opportunity for exchanging feedback; on the other, you may either use a translator or prepare your remarks in advance and have someone who is familiar with the culture check them over. If you use a translator, however, be sure to use someone who is familiar not only with both languages but also with the terminology of your field of business. Experts recommend that the translator be given a copy of the speech at least a day in advance. Furthermore, a written translation given to members of the audience to accompany the English speech can help reduce communication barriers. The extra effort will be appreciated and will help make sure that you get your point across.

QUESTIONS FOR DISCUSSION

1. What are the general goals of intercultural business communication? Why are they especially difficult to achieve?
2. What are some of the advantages and disadvantages of delegating your intercultural communication to intermediaries or translators?
3. Why is written communication less of a problem in intercultural interactions than oral communication is?
4. What are some of the communication barriers you might encounter in attempting to open a business in Tijuana, Mexico, a border city south of San Diego?
5. How would you characterize the "national personality" of people from your own country?
6. What are some of your own stereotypes and prejudices? For example, what are your beliefs and attitudes with respect to Germans? Japanese? Saudi Arabians? Cubans? Ethiopians? Mexicans? Tahitians?
7. How have episodes of terrorism affected your attitudes toward visiting other countries? Your perceptions of people from other countries?
8. What are some of the issues to consider in deciding whether to accept a job overseas?
9. Suppose you have decided to open a retail store that deals in imported handicrafts and you plan to visit several South American countries on a big initial buying trip. What cultural differences should you be prepared for?
10. Imagine that a multinational company has manufacturing operations in eight widely dispersed countries. The plants in these countries all have local managers who speak at least some English; however, the workers speak mainly their own native languages. What language should company headquarters use to communicate with these plants? Should it use a written or oral approach to communicating?

EXERCISES

1. Make a list of ten jobs you might enjoy that would involve intercultural communication. What would you have to do to qualify for these positions? What specific types of intercultural communication would each require? For information on intercultural job opportunities, check the reference room of a large college or city library. One useful source is *International Jobs: Where They Are and How to Get Them,* by Eric Kocher. Other places to check include your campus placement office, the foreign student office, the personnel office of multinational corporations, and the U.S. State Department or Canadian Department of External Affairs. You might also identify intercultural job opportunities through the classified section of such major newspapers as the *Wall Street Journal, Washington Post, Toronto Star, Los Angeles Times,* and *New York Times.*
2. Invite a student whose first language is not English to have lunch or dinner with you. Can you communicate with the person as easily as you can with someone born here? What specific communication problems do you encounter? Different vocabularies? Pronunciation differences? Different assumptions and beliefs? Different gestures and expressions?
3. Imagine that you have been assigned to host a group of Japanese students who are visiting your campus for the next two weeks. They have all studied English since they were ten years old and speak the language well. What things should you tell them that will help them fit into the culture on your campus and in your town? Make a list of behavioral rules they should know about.
4. Choose a specific foreign country, such as India, Brazil, China, Thailand, Malaysia, Nigeria. The less familiar you are with it, the better. Research the "business culture" of the country, and write a report summarizing what an American would need to know to conduct business successfully there (business etiquette, roles and status, decision-making customs, concepts of time, nonverbal communication styles, and so on).
5. Locate someone, preferably a businessperson, who has spent some time in another country, and interview him or her about the experience. What preparation did the person have before going to the country? In what ways was the preparation adequate? Inadequate? In hindsight, how might he or she have prepared differently? Ask for anecdotes about particular communication problems or mistakes.

COMPONENT CHAPTER B

BUSINESS COMMUNICATION TECHNOLOGY

In today's business world, much of the communication that takes place involves some sort of equipment. Even a simple letter requires typing. Oral communication is often conducted with the aid of such devices as telephones and microphones.

As impersonal and cold as the "nuts and bolts" of communication may seem, office hardware is currently a hot topic. You have undoubtedly been hearing a lot about word and information processing and the "electronic office." Before reading about the most advanced office equipment, however, you may want to learn about the functions of more typical office hardware.

A SURVEY OF OFFICE TECHNOLOGY

It is no easy task to describe in a limited space the wide variety of office machines that now exist, and anyone who sets out to make a comprehensive list would be stymied by the rapidly changing marketplace for office machines. This section, therefore, is divided according to the general functions that office machines fulfill: origination, production, reproduction, distribution/transmission, and storage. It includes a description of some of the most common equipment available for performing these tasks. With the help of this framework, you can categorize the equipment currently used in most organizations and still understand new developments.

ORIGINATION EQUIPMENT

The most versatile piece of origination equipment is the communicator's mind. But here we are concerned with the tools used to organize and record the ideas coming out of a mind. *Pens and pencils* applied to paper fall into this category. This simple technology may be used by someone writing in longhand; it may also be used by someone writing in shorthand as someone else dictates a message.

Personal dictation has a certain elegance, but it does require the coordination of two people's time. A *dictation machine*, which is like a tape recorder (see Figure B.1), is frequently more efficient. The transcriber uses a similar machine (but with headphones instead of a microphone) to play back the message and put it in written form, at his or her convenience.

Adding machines and calculators may also be considered origination equipment, because they can

FIGURE B.1
Dictation Equipment

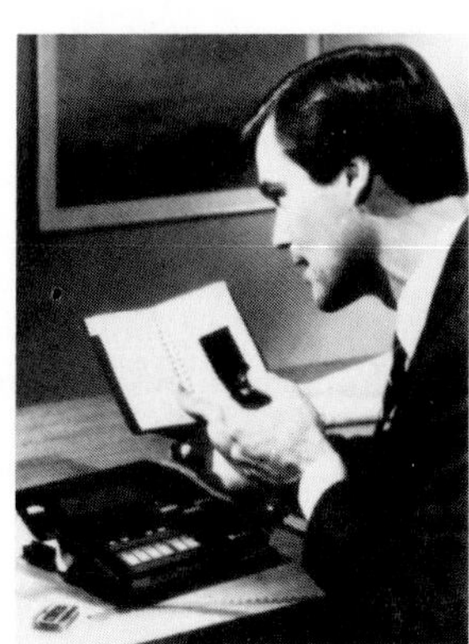

be used to generate the numbers for a letter, memo, or report. The microchip revolution has made electronic calculators very compact; one model can even be worn on the wrist like a watch.

Messages may also be originated on keyboard devices such as *typewriters, word/information processors,* and *microcomputers,* which are discussed more thoroughly in the next section. They are quick and easy to use for composing messages, as long as you know your way around a keyboard. Word/information processors and computers have an extra benefit: At the touch of a key (or keys) you can rearrange words, sentences, paragraphs, or pages.

PRODUCTION EQUIPMENT

Once the message has been composed, it must be put into polished form. That old standby, the *typewriter,* is the basic tool for transforming a draft into final copy. In the hands of a trained typist or secretary, a typewriter can produce a document that looks supremely professional.

A somewhat more sophisticated tool is the *electronic typewriter,* which has a memory unit that can show on a small screen what has been typed, before any characters are imprinted on the page. Typewriters with larger memories—usually augmented with separate magnetic disks, tape cassettes, or magnetic cards—can also store addresses or entire letters for replay when needed; or selected paragraphs or sentences can be put together for "customized" letters. The other main advantage of electronic typewriters is that they make it much easier for a typist to underline words, center titles, set up tables, and space characters so that all lines end at the same place on the right (called "justifying" lines on a page).

An electronic typewriter and a word/information-processing unit are very similar. The major difference is that a *word/information processor* usually has a large display screen, a separate printing device, and greater memory and computing power (see Figure B.2). A word/information processor may also be linked to other word/information processors. The advantage of such links is that one person can review what another has typed simply by looking at the display screen on his or her desk, thereby eliminating the need for producing a hard, or paper, copy. *Microcomputers* and *computer terminals* linked in a network, perhaps with minicomputers and mainframe computers, serve much the same function.

FIGURE B.2
Word-Processing Center

Organizations that produce a lot of documents for outside distribution—such as annual reports, brochures, and magazines—may also have *phototypesetting equipment* that produces a fully justified, precisely spaced page with all the indentions and headings automatically placed where they belong, just like a page of this book.

REPRODUCTION EQUIPMENT

Most business messages are copied in some way before they are sent to their intended receivers. If nothing else, it is often important to have a copy in the files for future reference. For many years, *carbon paper* was considered an indispensable aid for creating multiple copies. Now *carbonless copy sets,* made of several layers of coated paper, are also popular, especially for preprinted forms such as memos, order forms, and sales reports.

The most common type of reproduction equipment is the *photocopier,* which uses light and chemicals to produce, in essence, a photo of a document on paper (see Figure B.3). Some photocopiers can

FIGURE B.3
Photocopier

feed originals into the machine one page at a time, freeing the person who is making the copies to do something else; some can reduce or enlarge images. When hooked up to a computer, a photocopier may even be commanded to produce different kinds of copies by someone sitting at a keyboard in a distant room. Extra equipment is available that collates (sorts multiple copies of a multipage document into the proper order).

The *offset printing machine* has become popular for making a large number of copies. Photographs are made of the document, and the image is transferred to a metal or paper printing plate. The plate is then attached to a drum, which transfers the image to paper with ink as it rotates.

To reproduce a speech or presentation with all the intonation and gesture that might enhance its literal meaning, the business communicator can produce *audio and video tapes* and laser-read *video disks* that are compact and easy to use. Some organizations use audio cassettes for motivational messages to, say, the sales force. Others use video tapes or disks of executives to pass along company information. Equipment similar to that used by the music industry permits multiple copies to be made and sent to widely scattered branch offices.

The computer, the jack-of-all-trades of the modern office, can also be used to reproduce documents. Once a message has been perfected, the *computer printer* can be switched on to generate multiple copies of what look like hand-typed letters, in a fraction of the time a human typist would take.

DISTRIBUTION/TRANSMISSION EQUIPMENT

This category of office equipment is probably the most diverse and fastest growing. Given the dynamic status of this equipment, it is difficult to make a comprehensive list. The simplest way to categorize distribution and transmission equipment is to label it as either a physical delivery system or an electronic delivery system.

Physical delivery systems

A message can always be delivered from *hand to hand,* of course. In a large organization, or when many people are to receive a document, a company mail room may do the distributing (*interoffice mail*). In a sense, a *meeting* is also a physical distribution system, because the speaker delivers the message directly to the audience, without the help of any other devices.

The largest and best-known physical delivery system in the United States is the *U.S. Postal Service.* (In Canada, it's the *Canada Post Corporation.*) Each year, billions of messages are passed from one person to another by the friendly mail carrier in blue. Few of these messages get lost, and most arrive in a reasonable amount of time. The Postal Service does have rules and conventions that its users must follow, however, a few of which are detailed in Component Chapter D. For the most part, these guidelines were developed to allow the Postal Service to handle most business mail by machine.

Special mail-handling devices fall somewhere between the physical and electronic categories (see Figure B.4). However, they have been designed to aid in the physical delivery of mail, and so they're included here. *Mail conveyors* and *automated delivery carts* are machines for transporting mail from one spot to another. *Postage meters,* which are leased from the manufacturer and serviced by the Postal Service, weigh letters and imprint them with the appropriate amount of postage. *Mail sorters* help categorize mail mechanically by, say, ZIP code or department code. *Optical character readers* (OCRs) scan a piece of paper, change the information to an electronic code, and then store or sort the information in a computer. The Postal Service uses OCRs to sort mail by ZIP code.

Given the inevitable inefficiencies of an organization as large as the U.S. Postal Service, it is no wonder that such *private delivery services* as Federal Express and United Parcel Service (UPS) have sprung up. Some guarantee faster delivery (for a premium price, of course); some guarantee lower rates, especially for bulky or heavy packages. Another alternative for sensitive messages or for deliveries within a city is *messenger services,* which put someone in a car, on a motorcycle, or even on a bicycle to hand-deliver messages for a fee.

Electronic delivery systems

It is hard to imagine how the world economy could have developed to its present extent without the *telephone* being widely available to speed communication. Now even very small offices may have *multiple-line telephones*. Callers can be put on hold by pushing a button; pushing another button allows the phone to function as an intercom, so that people in the same building can talk to each other

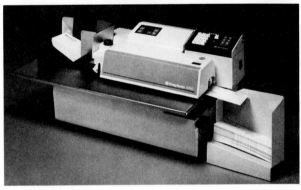

FIGURE B.4
Physical Distribution Equipment
(Upper left): Self-propelled Delivery Cart

(Upper Right): Horizontal Conveyor

(Lower Left): Postage Meter

without leaving their desks; calls can be transferred from one office to another; someone in one office can "cover" the phone for someone absent from another office.

On a large scale, these sorts of functions are handled by a *PBX (private branch exchange) system*, shown in Figure B.5. In many companies, a PBX operator screens and routes all calls. In others,

FIGURE B.5
Electronic Distribution Equipment

PBX System, AT&T

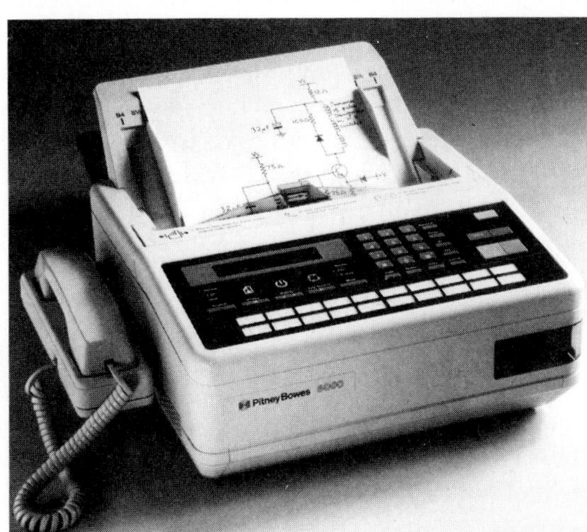

Pitney Bowes 8000 FAX (Facsimile) Machine

telephone operations are computerized, so that most calls (except those requesting general information) are handled automatically. *Centrex* and *PABX* (*private automatic branch exchange*) *systems* eliminate the need for a company operator, because callers can dial each phone directly.

The wires and satellites that make the phone system work can also be used to transmit purely electronic information (unlike the telephone, which transmits voice messages). *Teletypewriters* are used, like a regular keyboard, to produce letters and numbers that are coded electronically and sent over telephone lines for printout on teletypewriters in other locations. *Telegrams* are similar but are used more often by organizations that do not send a lot of electronic messages and therefore do not need an in-house teletypewriter. If the message is not urgent, the organization may choose instead to send a *mailgram*, which is transmitted from one telegraph office to another and then converted to a paper format that can be delivered with the regular mail. In general, teletype messages and telegrams are less expensive than phone calls, especially if the message must be transmitted a long way.

A modern development is called *electronic mail*. In brief, two or more computers are linked by telephone, and they send oral or written messages back and forth (see Figure B.5). *Data phones* are similar, but instead of linking the computer terminals of two users, they link a user with a data source. *FAX* (*facsimile*) *equipment*, one of the fastest-spreading distribution systems, uses a device like a photocopier to send copies of a document via telephone lines and radio waves. *Communicating word/information processors*, likewise, are linked by telephone lines to a computer memory; but instead of putting the message on a screen, the message is typed out on the printer. The major advantage of all these modern technologies is that messages can be encoded during the working day or at the sender's convenience, accumulated by the computer, sent when telephone rates are low or when transmission channels are less crowded, and decoded at a time convenient to the receiver.

Audiovisual equipment can distribute such messages as speeches and presentations. *Video players* and *film projectors* are necessary when a prerecorded message needs to be delivered. For simultaneous delivery of a speech or presentation to many people, a *public address system*, consisting of a microphone and speakers, or a *closed-circuit television system*, consisting of a video camera and television monitors, may be used.

Teleconferencing facilities use video equipment and telephones or computers to link meeting participants, with telephone lines and/or satellites, in two or more locations. Participants in a video conference must gather in a specially equipped room at a prearranged time. With computers, however, conferencing is conducted from regular terminals, and participants individually receive and transmit messages at their convenience. The disadvantage of computer conferencing is that the computer is less adept at conveying individual expressions of feeling than video and telephone equipment are.

STORAGE EQUIPMENT

Messages often need to be saved for later reference or for piecemeal distribution of copies over time. The most common and least complicated form of storage equipment is the *file cabinet*, although such devices as *card files*, *rotary files*, *disk files*, and *horizontal files* serve the same purpose: to categorize documents so they can readily be found (see Figure B.6). As you might guess, the computer revolution has left its imprint on this sort of equipment too. *Magnetic disks*, *tapes*, and *cards*, which store information for use on a computer or word/information processor, may be stored in special cabinets or folders according to some classification scheme. Some information may also be stored in the computer itself.

Magnetic and laser technology now make it possible to store *audio and video recordings* too. Important meetings and telephone conversations and significant events in the organization are likely prospects for storage. These recordings are sensitive to heat, dust, and magnetism, however, so they must be handled carefully.

In organizations with vast files of information, *micrographic equipment* is often used. Document pages are reproduced in miniature on film (microfilm) and then viewed with a special machine when someone needs to see the information (see Figure B.6). The main advantage of both microfilm and magnetic computer disks is that they take up much less space than paper would.

FIGURE B.6
Storage Equipment

Microfilm Reader/Printer

Motorized Rotary File

Floppy-Disk File

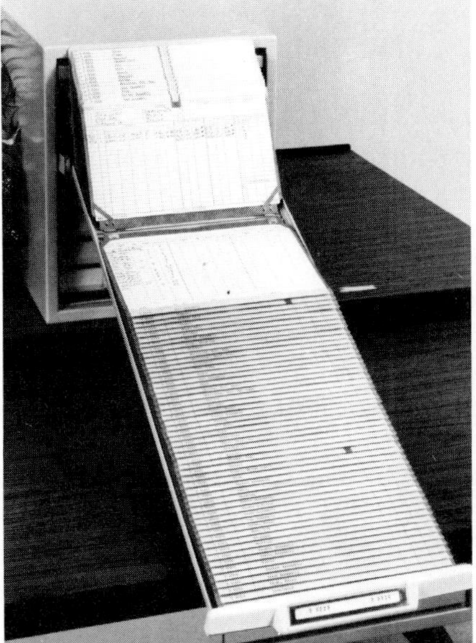
Visible Card File

Horizontal File

THE ELECTRONIC OFFICE

To the extent that an office (or even an entire company) is transmitting information electronically rather than by paper, it may be considered an electronic office. The advantages are many and central to better business: faster access to data, hence faster response to customers' needs, competitors' actions, and other developments in the business environment; greater accuracy in analysis; and elimination of many of the most routine and boring tasks, freeing a company's employees for more creative and interesting work.[1]

EQUIPPING THE ELECTRONIC OFFICE

In a sense, the development of office technology is coming full circle. Long ago, a mind and a hand putting pen to paper were all a businessperson needed to communicate with someone in another place or time. Then specialized machines were developed to handle specific parts of the communication process, such as producing a message and sending it. Now, however, the electronic office has fewer pieces of equipment, most related to the computer and telephone transmission lines, but they perform multiple functions.

Computer-based work stations

Companies of every size have emphatically joined the computer age by installing a computer on nearly every employee's desk. Each desk thus becomes a "work station." In some companies, a work station includes a terminal that is connected to a large *mainframe computer* or a somewhat smaller *minicomputer*; this setup allows a number of people to have access to the same data base. Other companies put a separate *microcomputer* at each work station, allowing employees to work independently. And some companies have both types of work stations or have hybrid systems that allow microcomputer users to tap into the greater computing power and larger data base of a mainframe computer or minicomputer.

The main uses for these work stations are word and data processing. In *word processing*, documents are drafted, polished, and produced on the computer. In *data processing*, raw numbers—sales, costs, inventories, and so on—are entered into the data base, manipulated, analyzed, and transformed into information that the organization can use to produce more efficiently and market more effectively.

Software is what makes a computer so versatile. For example, with the insertion of various diskettes, a single microcomputer can be used to draft and produce letters, calculate statistics from raw data, and keep mailing lists. A great selection of ready-to-use software is now available for microcomputers. Minicomputers and mainframe computers often use software that is specially designed to meet the organization's unique needs.

The most recent business function for computers is called *desktop publishing*. A combination of word processing and graphics, desktop publishing allows the production of polished newsletters, catalogs, and reports. Blocks of text, special headlines, and diagrams can be laid out together on-screen so that the user can see exactly what will come out on the printer (WYSIWYG—"wizzywig," or what you see is what you get). *Laser printers* produce pages that appear much more like professionally typeset material than like the "connect-the-dot" computer printouts of the past. Although a desktop publishing system cannot yet substitute for the artistic expertise of a professional designer or match the quality of professional typesetting equipment, it does give organizations a quick and relatively inexpensive alternative to printing.

Electronic networks

Computers are certainly versatile, but they have become even more versatile when linked together electronically. Within a building, computer terminals and microcomputers can be "hard-wired" (linked directly) to minicomputers and mainframe computers. *Local-area networks* (LANs) permit microcomputers to be linked together, along with such accessories as printers. With either arrangement, employees share access to computing power, data, and a wide variety of equipment, saving the company money and space. The computer links among employees also give them another channel for communicating.

Such links are no longer limited to employees within a single building either. Telecommunications gives anyone at the end of a telephone line the potential to communicate by computer with anyone else on the line. One popular use for this link is *electronic mail* (sometimes called an electronic bulletin board when confined to the organization): One user types or speaks a message into the computer, coded for access only by the intended receiver or receivers, and the message is stored in the computer at the other end until the receiver is ready to look at it or listen to it. A pilot study of electronic mail at a large office equipment corporation found that it reduced paper memos by 50 percent, interoffice mail by 94 percent, photocopying by 60 percent, and time on the phone by 80 percent.[2]

Small "laptop," or portable, computers take the concept one step further; they not only allow information processing almost anywhere but also let someone out in the field tap into a central data base back at headquarters. And if the organization's own data base isn't big enough, telecommunications allows any subscriber to consult the large data bases maintained by such information networks as CompuServe and The Source.

Computer messages have typically been written messages. But visual messages and spoken messages can now be transmitted through electronic networks too. *Voice mail* is similar to electronic mail, except that (1) it doesn't require each user to have a computer (only a Touch-Tone phone) and (2) it permits the sending, storage, and retrieval of spoken messages. *Teleconferencing* is a way of conducting a meeting when the participants are in scattered locations but all near a phone. *Video conferencing* uses phone lines too, but with cameras and special viewing equipment, it allows participants to be seen as well as heard.

The overall social and economic effect of these new communication links remains to be seen. Some speculate that *telecommuting*—working at home and keeping in touch with fellow employees, customers, and suppliers through computer and telephone networks—will become much more prevalent. One source estimates that 10,000 Americans working for 300 companies already telecommute every day and that 10 million workers may telecommute by the end of the century.[3]

WORKING IN THE ELECTRONIC OFFICE

Computers and electronic networks now serve employees at almost every level of the organization, from executive suite to production line. But to get an idea of how this new technology influences communication, imagine that you are the vice president of human resources for a moderately large company and that you are implementing a new benefit package.

In the process of deciding on the outlines of the package, you use the microcomputer at your work station to communicate by electronic mail with human resources managers at various branches of your company and to tap into data banks that have information about benefit packages offered by outside insurers and health plans. You use the numeric pad on your computer keyboard to calculate the costs to the company, storing the information that you want to refer to later, and even use some of the data to construct graphs and charts for a graphic analysis of various options.

Finally, you have most of the package outlined, but you need to confirm a few hunches with a couple of executives at widely separated locations. So you set up a video conference, with you and an assistant stationed in the video conferencing studio at headquarters and the other executives gathered at two or three other locations. With the video link, you can share on-the-spot calculations, as well as impressions of your colleagues' feelings about the proposal. One of your colleagues asks that you send a copy of one of the graphs that you developed on your computer, and you immediately transmit it by electronic mail.

Now it's time to put together the documents and supporting materials to tell all the company's employees about the program you've developed. Staff members, working on their own computers and tapping into previously written documents stored on disk, draft various pieces of the package and send them electronically to you for review. You make a few corrections (a keystroke here and there) and transfer some of the graphs you composed earlier into the document.

When the document is composed to your liking, you take the disk to your friend, the director of corporate communications. (Even an electronic office has room for person-to-person contact!) The communications staff does a final edit and uses its desktop publishing system to lay out professional-looking materials. After your final review, the material on the disk is transferred into the central computer, which distributes the information to all branch offices. In each branch, the electronic code is translated into paper copies, so employees can take them home. Simultaneously, the company's electronic bulletin board (on the computer again) advises everyone that you will be conducting a meeting about the new package.

On the day of the meeting, you and some of the top executives of the company gather in the video conferencing studio. Other employees gather in the studios at their own branch offices to see and hear what you have to say about the benefits they now have. Anyone who has a question has a chance to ask it, through a telephone speaker system.

All goes smoothly with the new program, but from time to time someone has a question about benefits or you come up with a refinement. The computer is a perfect medium both for answering individual questions (some of which you can answer with stock data you've already developed and stored on disk) and for providing updates.

What you have demonstrated in the process of preparing the new benefit package is that a computer-based work station and an electronic network give you considerable control over the information you need to do your job. Word and data processing, electronic mail, and video conferencing put you in touch with others more quickly than ever before, and your decisions are more likely to be based on the best data available.

QUESTIONS FOR DISCUSSION

1. Given the importance of keyboards in today's office, should everyone studying business be required to learn keyboarding? Why or why not?
2. What can a word/information-processing unit do that an electronic typewriter can't do?
3. In a small office, what sort of production equipment would be most versatile?
4. How does an optical character reader speed and simplify the distribution of messages?
5. What is electronic mail?
6. What are some qualities of a good system for information storage?
7. What is an electronic office, and how does it help the conduct of business? What are its disadvantages?
8. What are the main components of the electronic office, and how do they break down into the five categories of office equipment (origination, production, reproduction, distribution/transmission, storage)?
9. What makes a computer so versatile?
10. How does the electronic office affect business communication? What communication skills are most important in an electronic office? Be specific.

EXERCISES

1. Using whatever type of dictation equipment is available to you, dictate one of the sample letters in Component Chapter D; follow the steps in Chapter 4's "Checklist for Dictation." To gain an understanding of the transcriber's concerns, let the tape sit for a day or two, then try to transcribe the letter from your dictation.
2. Visit two or three different types of businesses in your area, such as an insurance company, a school, and a car dealership. Interview the office managers about each company's system for handling and storing records. Prepare a report comparing the systems and perhaps making recommendations for upgrading or improving them.
3. Visit the word-processing center at a large company or at your school. Develop a flow chart of how the word-processing system works, from origination to distribution and storage. Be sure to indicate the approximate time required at each step for different types of documents.
4. Consider any two types of office equipment designed to perform the same function, and compare their advantages and disadvantages. Take into account the purchase and operating costs of each, their ease of operation, their flexibility in handling varied assignments, their dependability, and other relevant matters. Remember to consider the time lost while staff members attend training programs to learn how to operate sophisticated equipment.
5. Imagine that you are a regional sales manager for Business Comfort, Inc., a California office furniture manufacturer that distributes its products throughout California and the West. Your territory is Idaho and Montana. Given the long distances between retail outlets and the difficulties of winter travel, you have convinced management to let you work out of your home in Horseshoe Bend, Idaho. Sales meetings with your five-member crew will be few, and if your equipment purchase plan is approved, most of the messages will be relayed from their microcomputers to yours and then to company headquarters. You like to have almost daily contact with your crew. Credit purchases are approved on a sale-by-sale basis, and the credit files are kept at headquarters. Prepare a list of equipment that you and your salespeople will need to work out of an electronic office in Horseshoe Bend, briefly justifying each item.

COMPONENT CHAPTER C

FUNDAMENTALS OF GRAMMAR AND USAGE

Grammar is nothing more than the way words are combined into sentences, and usage is the way words are used by a network of people—in this case, the community of businesspeople who use English. You will find it easier to get along in this community if you know the accepted standards of grammar and usage.

What follows is a review of the basics of grammar and usage, things you have probably learned but may have forgotten. Without a firm grasp of these basics, you may be misunderstood, damage your company's image, lose money for your company, and possibly even lose your job.

1.0 GRAMMAR

The sentences below look innocent, but consider the bombs they contain:

We sell tuxedos as well as rent.
(You might sell rent, but it's highly unlikely. Whatever you are selling, some people will ignore your message because of a blunder like this.)

Vice President Eldon Neale told his chief engineer that he would no longer be with Avix, Inc., as of June 30. (Is Eldon or the engineer leaving? No matter which side the facts are on, the sentence can be read the other way. You may have a hard time convincing either person that your simple mistake was not a move in a game of office politics.)

Now look at this sentence:

The year before we budgeted more for advertising sales were up.

Confused? Perhaps this is what you meant:

The year before, we budgeted more for advertising. Sales were up.

Or did you mean this?

The year before we budgeted more for advertising, sales were up.

The meanings of language fall into bundles called sentences. A listener or reader can take only so much meaning before filing a sentence away and getting ready for the next one. So writers have to know what a sentence is. They need to know where one ends and the next one begins.

But anyone who wants to know what a thing is has to find out what goes into it, what its ingredients are. Luckily, the basic ingredients of an English sentence are simple. They are called the parts of speech, and the content-bearing ones are nouns, pronouns, verbs, adjectives, and adverbs. They combine with a few functional parts of speech to convey meaning. Meaning is also transmitted by punctuation, mechanics, and vocabulary.

1.1 NOUNS

A noun names a person, place, or thing. Anything you can see or detect with one of your other senses has a noun to name it.

Some things you can't see or sense are also nouns—ions, for example, or space.

And so are things that exist as ideas, such as accuracy and height. (You can see that something is accurate or that a building is tall, but you can't see the idea of accuracy or the idea of height.) These names for ideas are known as abstract nouns.

But the simplest nouns are the names of things you can see or touch: car, building, cloud, brick.

1.1.1 Proper nouns and common nouns

So far, all the examples of nouns have been common nouns referring to general classes of things. The word *building,* for example, refers to a whole class of structures. Common nouns, like *building,* are not capitalized.

But if you want to talk about one particular building, you might refer to the Glazier Building. Notice that the name is capitalized, indicating that *Glazier Building* is a proper noun.

Here are three sets of common and proper nouns for comparison:

COMMON	PROPER
city	Kansas City
company	Blaisden Company
store	Books Galore

1.1.2 Plural nouns

Nouns can be either singular or plural. The usual way to make a plural noun is to add *s* to the singular form of the word:

SINGULAR	PLURAL
rock	rocks
picture	pictures
song	songs

But many nouns have other ways of forming the plural. For example, letters, numbers, and words used as words are sometimes made plural by adding an apostrophe and an *s*. As a rule, *'s* is used with abbreviations that have periods, lowercase letters that stand alone, and capital letters that might be confused with other words when made into plurals:

Spell out all *St.*'s and *Ave.*'s.

He divided the page with a row of *x*'s.

Sarah will register the *A*'s through *I*'s at the convention.

In other cases, however, the apostrophe may be left out:

They'll review their ABCs.

The stock market climbed through most of the 1980s.

Circle all *the*s in the paragraph.

Observe in these examples how letters and words used as words are italicized.

Other nouns, like those below, are so-called irregular nouns; they form the plural in some way other than simply adding *s*:

SINGULAR	PLURAL
tax	taxes
specialty	specialties
cargo	cargoes
shelf	shelves
child	children
woman	women
tooth	teeth
mouse	mice
parenthesis	parentheses
son-in-law	sons-in-law
editor-in-chief	editors-in-chief

Rather than memorize a lot of rules about forming plurals, use a dictionary. If the dictionary says nothing about the plural of a word, it is formed the usual way—by adding *s*. If the plural is formed in some irregular way, the dictionary will show the plural or have a note something like this: pl. *-es*.

1.1.3 Possessive nouns

A noun becomes possessive when it is used to show the ownership of something. Then you add *'s* to the word:

the man's car	the woman's apartment

But ownership does not need to be legal:

the secretary's desk	the company's assets

And ownership may be nothing more than an automatic association:

a day's work	a job's prestige

An exception to the rule about adding *'s* to make a noun possessive occurs when the word is singular but already has two *s* sounds at the end. In cases like the following, an apostrophe is all that is needed:

crisis' dimensions Mr. Moses' application

When the noun has only one *s* sound at the end, however, retain the *'s*:

Chris's book Carolyn Nuss's office

With hyphenated nouns (compound nouns) add *'s* to the last word:

HYPHENATED NOUN	POSSESSIVE NOUN
mother-in-law	mother-in-law's
mayor-elect	mayor-elect's

Forming the possessive of plural nouns may at first seem confusing, but it is really rather simple. Just begin by following the same rule as with singular nouns: add *'s*. But if the plural noun already ends in an *s* (as most do), drop the one you have added, leaving only the apostrophe:

the clients'~~s~~ complaints employees'~~s~~ benefits

1.2 PRONOUNS

A pronoun is a word that stands for a noun; it saves having to repeat the noun.

Drivers have some choice of weeks for vacation, but *they* must notify this office of *their* preference by March 1.

The pronouns *they* and *their* stand in for the noun *drivers*. The noun that a pronoun stands for is called the antecedent of the pronoun; *drivers* is the antecedent of *they* and *their*.

When the antecedent is plural, the pronoun that stands in for it has to be plural; *they* and *their* are plural pronouns because *drivers* is plural. Likewise, when the antecedent is singular, the pronoun has to be singular:

We thought the *contract* had been signed, but we soon learned *it* had not been.

1.2.1 Multiple antecedents

Sometimes a pronoun has a double (or even triple) antecedent:

Kathryn Boettcher and Luis Gutierrez went beyond their sales quotas for January.

Kathryn Boettcher, if taken alone, is a singular antecedent. So is *Luis Gutierrez*. But when both are the antecedent of a pronoun, they are plural and the pronoun has to be plural. Thus the pronoun is *their* instead of *her* or *his*.

1.2.2 Unclear antecedents

In some sentences, the pronoun's antecedent is not clear:

Sandy Wright sent Jane Brougham *her* production figures for the previous year. *She* thought they were too low.

Whom does the pronoun *her* refer to? Someone who knew Sandy and Jane and knew their business relationship might be able to figure out the antecedent for *her*. But even with such an advantage, a reader still might receive the wrong meaning. And it would be nearly impossible for any reader to know which name is the antecedent of *she*.

The best way to clarify an ambiguous pronoun is usually to rewrite the sentence, repeating nouns when needed for clarity:

Sandy Wright sent her production figures for the previous year to Jane Brougham. *Jane* thought they were too low.

But repeat the noun only when the antecedent is unclear.

1.2.3 Gender-neutral pronouns

The pronouns that stand for males are *he*, *his*, and *him*. The pronouns that stand for females are *she*, *hers*, and *her*. But you will often be faced with the dilemma of choosing a pronoun for a noun that refers to both females and males:

Each manager must make up (his, her, his or her, its, their?) own mind about stocking this item and about the quantity that (he, she, he or she, it, they?) can sell.

This sentence calls for a pronoun that is neither masculine nor feminine.

The issue of gender-neutral pronouns has arisen in response to efforts to treat females and males even-handedly. Here are some possible ways to deal with this issue:

Each manager must make up *his* . . .
(But not all managers are men.)

Each manager must make up *her* . . .
(Nor are all managers women.)

Each manager must make up *his or her* . . .
(This solution is acceptable but becomes awkward when repeated more than once or twice in a document.)

Each manager must make up *her* . . . Every manager will receive *his* . . . A manager may send *her* . . . (A manager's gender does not alternate like a windshield wiper!)

Each manager must make up *their* . . . (The pronoun can't be plural when the antecedent is singular.)

Each manager must make up *its* . . . (*It* never refers to people.)

The best solution is to make the noun plural or to revise the passage altogether:

Managers must make up *their* minds . . .

Each manager must decide whether . . .

But be careful not to change the original meaning.

1.2.4 Case of pronouns

The case of a pronoun tells whether it is acting or acted upon:

She sells an average of five packages each week.

In this sentence, *she* is doing the selling. Because *she* is acting, *she* is said to be in the nominative case.

But consider what happens when the pronoun is acted upon:

After six months, Ms. Browning promoted *her.*

In this sentence, the pronoun *her* is acted upon. The pronoun *her* is thus said to be in the objective case.

Contrast the nominative and objective pronouns in this list:

NOMINATIVE	OBJECTIVE
I	me
we	us
he	him
she	her
they	them
who	whom
whoever	whomever

Objective pronouns may be used as either the object of a verb (like *promoted*) or the object of a preposition (like *with*):

Rob worked with *them* until the order was filled.

In this example, *them* is the object of the preposition *with,* because Rob acted upon—worked with—them.

Here is a sample sentence with three pronouns, the first one nominative, the second the object of a verb, and the third the object of a preposition:

He paid *us* as soon as the check came from *them.*

He is nominative; *us* is objective because it is the object of the verb *paid; them* is objective because it is the object of the preposition *from.*

Every writer sometimes wonders whether to use *who* or *whom:*

(Who, Whom) will you hire?

Because this sentence is a question, it is difficult to see that *whom* is the object of the verb *hire.* You can figure out which pronoun to use if you rearrange the question and temporarily try *she* and *her* in place of *who* and *whom:* "Will you hire *she*?" or "Will you hire *her*?" *Her* and *whom* are both objective, so the correct choice is "*Whom* will you hire?"

Here's a different example:

(Who, Whom) logged so much travel time?

Turning the question into a statement, you get:

He logged so much travel time.

Therefore, the correct statement is:

Who logged so much travel time?

1.2.5 Possessive pronouns

Possessive pronouns are like possessive nouns in the way they work: They show ownership or automatic association.

her job	their preferences
his account	its equipment

But possessive pronouns are different from possessive nouns in the way they are written. That is, possessive pronouns never have an apostrophe.

POSSESSIVE NOUN	POSSESSIVE PRONOUN
the woman's estate	her estate
Roger Franklin's plans	his plans
the shareholders' feelings	their feelings
the vacuum cleaner's attachments	its attachments

Notice that *its* is the possessive of *it*. *Its*, like all possessive pronouns, does not have an apostrophe. Some people confuse *its* with *it's*, the contraction of *it is*. Contractions are discussed later, so remember this point.

1.3 VERBS

A verb describes an action:

They all *quit* in disgust.

Or it describes a state of being:

Working conditions *were* substandard.

The English language is full of action verbs. Here are a few you will often run across in the business world:

verify	perform	fulfill
hire	succeed	send
leave	improve	receive
accept	develop	pay

You could undoubtedly list many more.

The most common verb describing a state of being instead of an action is *to be* and all its forms:

I *am*, *was*, or *will be* you *are*, *were*, or *will be*

And so on.

But other verbs describe a state of being too:

It *seemed* a good plan at the time.

She *sounds* impressive at a meeting.

These verbs link what comes before them in the sentence with what comes after; no action is involved. (See Section 1.7.5 for a fuller discussion of linking verbs.)

1.3.1 Verb tenses

English has three simple verb tenses: present, past, and future.

PRESENT: Our branches in Hawaii *stock* different items.

PAST: When we *stocked* Purquil pens, we received a great many complaints.

FUTURE: Rotex Tire Stores *will stock* your line of tires when you begin a program of effective national advertising.

With most verbs (the regular ones), the past tense ends in *ed;* the future tense always has *will* or *shall* in front of it. But the present tense is a little more complex:

SINGULAR	PLURAL
I stock	we stock
you stock	you stock
he, she, it stocks	they stock

Notice that the basic form, *stock*, takes an additional *s* when *he*, *she*, or *it* precedes it.

In addition to the three simple tenses, there are three perfect tenses using forms of the helping verb *have*. The present perfect tense uses the past participle (regularly the past tense) of the main verb, *stocked*, and adds the present-tense *have* or *has* to the front of it:

(I, we, you, they) *have stocked*.

(He, she, it) *has stocked*.

The past perfect tense uses the past participle of the main verb, *stocked*, and adds the past-tense *had* to the front of it:

(I, you, he, she, it, we, they) *had stocked*.

The future perfect tense also uses the past participle of the main verb, *stocked*, but adds the future-tense *will have:*

(I, you, he, she, it, we, they) *will have stocked*.

Keep verbs in the same tense when the actions occur at the same time:

When the payroll checks *came* in, everyone *showed* up for work.

We *have found* that everyone *has pitched* in to help.

Of course, when the actions occur at different times, you may change tense accordingly:

A shipment *came* last Wednesday, so when another one *comes* in today, please return it.

The new employee *had been* ill-at-ease, but now she *has become* a full-fledged member of the team.

1.3.2 Irregular verbs

Many verbs do not follow in every detail the patterns already described. The most irregular of these verbs is *to be:*

	SINGULAR	PLURAL
PRESENT:	I *am*	we *are*
	you *are*	you *are*
	he, she, it *is*	they *are*
PAST:	I *was*	we *were*
	you *were*	you *were*
	he, she, it *was*	they *were*

The future tense of *to be* is formed the same way the future tense of a regular verb is formed.

The perfect tenses of *to be* are also formed as they would be for a regular verb, except that the past participle is a special form, *been,* instead of just the past tense:

PRESENT PERFECT:	you *have been*
PAST PERFECT:	you *had been*
FUTURE PERFECT:	you *will have been*

Here's a sampling of other irregular verbs:

PRESENT	PAST	PAST PARTICIPLE
begin	began	begun
shrink	shrank	shrunk
know	knew	known
rise	rose	risen
become	became	become
go	went	gone
do	did	done

Dictionaries list the various forms of other irregular verbs.

1.3.3 Transitive and intransitive verbs

Many people are confused by three particular sets of verbs:

lie/lay sit/set rise/raise

Using these verbs correctly is much easier when you learn the difference between transitive and intransitive verbs.

Transitive verbs convey their action to an object; they "transfer" their action to an object. Intransitive verbs do not. Here are some sample uses of transitive and intransitive verbs:

INTRANSITIVE	TRANSITIVE
We should include in our new offices a place to *lie* down for a nap.	The workers will be here on Monday to *lay* new carpeting.
Even the way an interviewee *sits* is important.	That crate is full of stemware, so *set* it down carefully.
Salaries at Compu-Link, Inc., *rise* swiftly.	They *raise* their level of production every year.

The workers *lay* carpeting, you *set* down the crate, they *raise* production—each action is transferred to something. But in the intransitive sentences, one *lies* down, an interviewee *sits,* and salaries *rise* without (at least grammatically) affecting anything else. Intransitive sentences are complete with only a subject and a verb; transitive sentences are not complete unless they also include an object, or something to transfer the action to.

Tenses are a confusing element of the *lie/lay* problem:

PRESENT	PAST	PAST PARTICIPLE
I *lie*	I *lay*	I have *lain*
I *lay* (something down)	I *laid* (something down)	I have *laid* (something down)

Notice that the past tense of *lie* and the present tense of *lay* look and sound alike, even though they are different verbs.

1.3.4 Voice of verbs

Verbs have two voices, active and passive:

PASSIVE:	A large amount *was paid* by the buyer.
ACTIVE:	The buyer *paid* a large amount.

Notice that the passive voice uses a form of the verb *to be.*

Notice also that the passive-voice sentence uses eight words, whereas the active-voice sentence uses six words to say the same thing. Thus the words *was* and *by* are unnecessary to convey the meaning of the sentence. In fact, extra words usually clog meaning. So always opt for the active voice when you have a choice.

At times, however, you have no choice:

Several items *have been taken*, but so far we don't know who took them.

The passive voice becomes necessary when the writer does not know (or doesn't want to say) who performed the action. But the active voice is bolder and more direct. It packs a punch.

1.3.5 Mood of verbs

You have three moods to choose from, depending on your intentions. Most of the time, you use the indicative mood to make a statement or ask a question:

The secretary *mailed* a letter to each supplier.

Did the secretary *mail* a letter to each supplier?

When you wish to command or request, use the imperative mood:

Please *mail* a letter to each supplier.

Sometimes, especially in business, a courteous request is stated like a question; in that case, however, no question mark is required.

Would you *mail* a letter to each supplier.

The subjunctive mood, most often used in formal writing or in presenting bad news, expresses a possibility or a recommendation. Usually it is signaled by a word such as *if* or *that*. Notice in these examples that the subjunctive mood uses special verb forms:

If the secretary *were to mail* a letter to each supplier, we might save some money.

I suggested that the secretary *mail* a letter to each supplier.

Although the subjunctive mood is not used very often anymore, it is still found in such expressions as *Come what may* and *If I were you*.

1.4 ADJECTIVES

An adjective modifies (tells something about) a noun or pronoun:

an *efficient* staff	a *heavy* price
brisk trade	*poor* you

Each of these phrases says more about the noun or pronoun than the noun or pronoun would say alone.

Adjectives should always tell us something we would not know without them. So avoid using adjectives when the noun alone, or a different noun, will give the meaning:

a *company* employee
(An employee ordinarily works for a company.)

a *crate-type* container
(*Crate* gives the entire meaning.)

At times, adjectives pile up in a series:

It was a *long, hot,* and *active* workday.

Such strings of adjectives are acceptable as long as they all convey a different part of the phrase's meaning.

Verbs in the *ing* form can be used as adjectives:

A *boring* job can sometimes turn into a *fascinating* career.

So can the past participle of verbs:

A freshly *painted* house is a *sold* house.

Adjectives modify nouns more often than they modify pronouns. But when adjectives do modify pronouns, the sentence usually has a linking verb:

They were *attentive.*	It looked *appropriate.*
He seems *interested.*	You are *skillful.*

Most adjectives can take three forms: simple, comparative, and superlative. The simple form modifies a single noun or pronoun. Use the comparative form when comparing two items. When comparing three or more items, use the superlative form.

SIMPLE	COMPARATIVE	SUPERLATIVE
hard	harder	hardest
safe	safer	safest
dry	drier	driest

Notice that the comparative form adds *er* to the simple form and the superlative form adds *est*. (The *y* at the end of a word changes to *i* before the *er* or *est* is added.)

But a small number of adjectives are irregular, including these:

SIMPLE	COMPARATIVE	SUPERLATIVE
good	better	best
bad	worse	worst
little	less	least

When the simple form of an adjective is two or more syllables, you must usually add *more* to form the comparative and *most* to form the superlative:

SIMPLE	COMPARATIVE	SUPERLATIVE
useful	more useful	most useful
exhausting	more exhausting	most exhausting
expensive	more expensive	most expensive

The only exception might be a two-syllable adjective that ends in *y*:

SIMPLE	COMPARATIVE	SUPERLATIVE
happy	happier	happiest
costly	costlier	costliest

If you choose this option, change the *y* to *i*, and tack *er* or *est* onto the end.

1.5 ADVERBS

An adverb modifies a verb, an adjective, or another adverb:

MODIFYING A VERB:	Our marketing department works *efficiently*.
MODIFYING AN ADJECTIVE:	She was not dependable, although she was *highly* intelligent.
MODIFYING ANOTHER ADVERB:	His territory was *too* broadly diversified, so he moved *extremely* cautiously.

Notice that most of the adverbs above are adjectives turned into adverbs by adding *ly*, which is how many adverbs are formed:

ADJECTIVE	ADVERB
efficient	efficiently
high	highly
extreme	extremely
special	specially
official	officially
separate	separately

But some adverbs are made by dropping or changing the final letter of the adjective, then adding *ly*:

ADJECTIVE	ADVERB
due	duly
busy	busily

Other adverbs do not end in *ly* at all. Here are a few examples of this type:

often	fast	too
soon	very	so

1.6 OTHER PARTS OF SPEECH

Nouns, pronouns, verbs, adjectives, and adverbs carry most of the meaning in a sentence. But four other parts of speech link them together in sentences: prepositions, conjunctions, articles, and interjections.

1.6.1 Prepositions

Prepositions are words like these:

of	to	for	with
at	by	from	about

They most often begin prepositional phrases, which function like adjectives and adverbs in telling more about a pronoun, noun, or verb:

of a type	*by* Friday
to the point	*with* characteristic flair

1.6.2 Conjunctions, articles, and interjections

Conjunctions are words that usually join parts of a sentence. Here are a few:

and	but	because
yet	although	if

The use of conjunctions is discussed in Sections 1.7.3 and 1.7.4.

Only three articles exist in English: *the, a,* and *an.* These words are used, like adjectives, to specify which item you are talking about.

Interjections are words that express no solid information, only emotion:

Wow!	Well, well!
Oh no!	Good!

Such purely emotional language has its place in private life and advertising copy, but it only weakens the effect of most business writing.

1.7 WHOLE SENTENCES

Sentences are constructed with the major building blocks, the parts of speech.

Money talks.

This two-word sentence consists of a noun (*money*) and a verb (*talks*). When used in this way, the noun works as the first requirement for a sentence, the subject, and the verb works as the second requirement, the predicate.

Now look at this sentence:

They merged.

The subject in this case is a pronoun (*they*), and the predicate is a verb (*merged*). This is a sentence, then, because it has a subject and a predicate.

Here is yet another kind of sentence:

The plans are ready.

This sentence has a more complicated subject, the noun *plans* and the article *the*; the complete predicate is a state-of-being verb (*are*) and an adjective (*ready*).

Without these two parts, the subject (who or what does something) and the predicate (the doing of it), no collection of words is a sentence.

1.7.1 Commands

In commands, the subject is only understood, not stated. It is always *you*:

(You) Move your desk to the better office.

(You) Please try to finish by six o'clock.

1.7.2 Longer sentences

More complicated sentences have more complicated subjects and predicates. But they still have a simple subject and a predicate verb. In the following examples, the simple subject is underlined once, the predicate verb twice:

Marex and Contron enjoy higher earnings each quarter.
(Marex [and] Contron did something; enjoy is what they did.)

My interview, coming minutes after my freeway accident, did not impress or move anyone.
(Interview is what did something. What did it do? It did [not] impress [or] move.)

In terms of usable space, a steel warehouse, with its extremely long span of roof unsupported by pillars, makes more sense.

(Warehouse is what makes.)

These three sentences demonstrate several things. First, notice that in all three sentences the simple subject and predicate verb are the "bare bones" of the sentence, the parts that carry the core idea of the sentence. When trying to find the simple subject and predicate verb, disregard all prepositional phrases, modifiers, conjunctions, and articles.

Second, notice in the third sentence that the verb is singular (*makes*) because the subject is singular (*warehouse*). Even though the plural noun *pillars* is closer to the verb, *warehouse* is the real subject. So *warehouse* determines whether the verb is singular or plural. Subject and predicate must agree.

Third, notice that the subject in the first sentence is compound (*Marex* [and] *Contron*). A compound subject, when connected by *and*, requires a plural verb (*enjoy*). Notice also in the second sentence that compound predicates (*did* [not] *impress* [or] *move*) are possible.

Fourth, notice that the second sentence incorporates a group of words—"coming minutes after my freeway accident"—containing a form of a verb (*coming*) and a noun (*accident*). Yet this group of words is not a complete sentence. It is a nonsentence for two reasons:

- *Accident* is not the subject of *coming*. Not all nouns are subjects.
- A verb that ends in *ing* can never be the predicate of a sentence (unless preceded by a form of *to be*, as in *was coming*). Not all verbs are predicates.

Because it does not have a subject and a predicate, the group of words "coming minutes after my freeway accident" (called a phrase) cannot be written as a sentence. That is, it cannot stand alone, beginning with a capital letter and ending with a period. Because a phrase cannot stand alone, it must always be part of a sentence.

Sometimes a sentence incorporates two or more groups of words that do contain a subject and a predicate; these word groups are called clauses.

My interview, because it came minutes after my freeway accident, did not impress or move anyone.

The independent clause is the portion of the sentence that could stand alone without revision:

My interview did not impress or move anyone.

But the other part of the sentence could stand alone only by removing because:

(because) It came minutes after my freeway accident.

This part of the sentence is known as a dependent clause; although it has a subject and a predicate, as an independent clause has, it is linked to the main part of the sentence by a word (*because*) showing its dependence.

To summarize, the two types of clauses—dependent and independent—both have a subject and a predicate. But dependent clauses do not bear the main meaning of the sentence and must therefore be linked to an independent clause. Nor can phrases stand alone; phrases lack a subject and predicate. Only independent clauses can be written as sentences without revision.

1.7.3 Sentence fragments

When an incomplete sentence (a phrase or dependent clause) is written as though it were a complete sentence, it is called a fragment. Consider the following sentence fragments:

Marilyn Sanders, having had pilferage problems in her store for the past year. Refuses to accept the results of our investigation.

This serious error can easily be corrected by putting the two fragments together:

Marilyn Sanders, having had pilferage problems in her store for the past year, refuses to accept the results of our investigation.

Not all fragments can be corrected so easily:

Employees a part of it. No authority or discipline.

Only the writer knows the intended meaning of these two phrases. Perhaps the employees are taking part in the pilferage. If so, the sentence should read:

Some employees are part of the pilferage problem.

On the other hand, it is possible that some employees are helping with the investigation. Then the sentence would read:

Some employees are taking part in our investigation.

But it is just as likely that the employees are not only taking part in the pilferage but are also being analyzed:

Those employees who are part of the pilferage problem will accept no authority or discipline.

In fact, even more meanings could be read into these fragments. Because fragments like these can mean so many things, they mean nothing. No well-written memo, letter, or report should ever demand that the reader be an imaginative genius.

One more type of fragment exists, the kind represented by a dependent clause. Notice what *because* does to what was once a unified sentence:

Our stock of sprinklers is depleted.

Because our stock of sprinklers is depleted . . .

Although it contains a subject and a predicate, the second version is a fragment because of *because*.

Words like *because* form a special group of words called subordinating conjunctions. Here is a partial list:

since	though	whenever
although	if	unless
while	even if	after

When a word of this type begins a clause, the clause is dependent and cannot stand alone as a sentence. But if a dependent clause is combined with an independent clause, it can convey a complete meaning. The independent clause may come before or after the dependent clause:

We are unable to fill your order, because our stock of sprinklers is depleted.

Because our stock of sprinklers is depleted, we are unable to fill your order.

Another remedy for a fragment that is a dependent clause is to remove the subordinating conjunction. That solution leaves a simple but complete sentence:

Our stock of sprinklers is depleted.

The actual details of a transaction will determine the best way to remedy a fragment problem.

There is one exception to the ban on fragments.

Some advertising copy contains sentence fragments, written knowingly to convey a certain rhythm. However, advertising is the only area of business in which fragments are acceptable.

1.7.4 Fused sentences and comma splices

Just as there can be too little in a group of words to make it a sentence, there can also be too much:

All our mail is run through a postage meter every afternoon someone picks it up.

There are two sentences here, not one. But the two have been blended so that it is hard to tell where one ends and the next begins. Is the mail run through a meter every afternoon? If so, the sentences should read:

All our mail is run through a postage meter every afternoon. Someone picks it up.

But perhaps the mail is run through a meter at some other time (morning, for example) and is picked up every afternoon:

All our mail is run through a postage meter. Every afternoon someone picks it up.

The order of words is the same in all three cases; sentence division makes all the difference. Either of the last two cases is grammatically correct. The choice depends on the facts of the situation.

Sometimes these so-called fused sentences have a more obvious point of separation:

Several large orders arrived within a few days of one another, too many came in for us to process by the end of the month.

Here the comma has been put between two independent clauses in an attempt to link them. When a lowly comma separates two complete sentences, the result is called a comma splice.

A comma splice can be remedied in one of three ways:

- Replace the comma with a period and capitalize the next word: ". . . one another. Too many. . . ."
- Replace the comma with a semicolon but do not capitalize the next word: ". . . one another; too many. . . ." This remedy works only when the two sentences have closely related meanings.
- Change one of the sentences so that it becomes a phrase or a dependent clause. This remedy often produces the best writing, but it takes more work.

The third alternative can be carried out in several ways. One is to begin the blended sentence with a subordinating conjunction:

Whenever several large orders arrived within a few days of one another, too many came in for us to process by the end of the month.

Another way is to remove part of the subject or the predicate verb from one of the independent clauses, thereby creating a phrase:

Several large orders arrived within a few days of one another, too many for us to process by the end of the month.

Finally, you can change one of the predicate verbs to its *ing* form:

Several large orders arrived within a few days of one another, too many coming in for us to process by the end of the month.

At other times, a simple coordinating conjunction (such as *or, and,* or *but*) can separate fused sentences:

You can fire them, *or* you can make better use of their abilities.

Margaret drew up the designs, *and* Matt carried them out.

We will have three strong months, *but* after that sales will taper off.

The use of coordinating conjunctions calls for caution: They should be used only to join simple sentences that express similar ideas.

Coordinating conjunctions should not be overused, because they say relatively little about the relationship between the two clauses they join: *and* is merely an addition sign; *but* is just a turn signal; *or* only points to an alternative. Subordinating conjunctions such as *because* and *whenever* tell the reader a lot more.

1.7.5 Sentences with linking verbs

Linking verbs were discussed briefly in the section on verbs (Section 1.3). Here you can see more fully the way they function in a sentence.

The following is a model of any sentence with a linking verb:

A (verb) B.

Although words like *seems* and *feels* can also be linking verbs, let's assume that the verb is a form of *to be:*

A *is* B.

In such a sentence, A and B are always nouns, pronouns, or adjectives. When one is a noun and the other's a pronoun, the sentence says that one is the same as the other:

She is president.

When one is an adjective, it modifies or describes the other:

She is forceful.

Remember that when one is an adjective, it modifies the other as any adjective modifies a noun or pronoun, except that a linking verb stands between the adjective and the word it modifies.

1.7.6 Misplaced modifiers

The position of a modifier in a sentence is important. Notice how the movement of *only* changes the meaning in the following sentences:

Only we are obliged to supply those items specified in your contract.

We are obliged *only* to supply those items specified in your contract.

We are obliged to supply *only* those items specified in your contract.

We are obliged to supply those items specified *only* in your contract.

In any particular set of circumstances, only one of these sentences would be accurate. The others very likely would cause problems. To prevent misunderstanding, modifiers like *only* must be placed as close as possible to the noun or verb they modify.

For similar reasons, whole phrases that are modifiers must be placed near the right noun or verb. Mistakes in placement create ludicrous meanings:

Antia Information Systems has bought new computer chairs for the programmers *with more comfortable seats.*

The anatomy of programmers is not normally a concern of business writing. Obviously the comfort of the chairs was the issue:

Antia Information Systems has bought new computer chairs *with more comfortable seats* for the programmers.

Here is another example:

I asked him to file all the letters in the cabinet *that had been answered.*

In this ridiculous sentence, the cabinet has been answered, even though no cabinet in history is known to have asked a question. *That had been answered* is too far from *letters* and too close to *cabinet.* Here's an improvement:

I asked him to file in the cabinet all the letters *that had been answered.*

Notice that in some cases, instead of moving the modifying phrase closer to the word it modifies, the best solution is to move the word closer to the modifying phrase.

2.0 PUNCTUATION

On the highway, signs tell you when to slow down or stop, where to turn, when to merge. In similar fashion, punctuation helps readers negotiate your prose. The proper use of punctuation keeps readers from losing track of your meaning.

2.1 PERIODS

Use a period (1) to end any sentence that is not a question, (2) with certain abbreviations, and (3) between dollars and cents in an amount of money.

2.2 QUESTION MARKS

Use a question mark after any direct question that requests an answer:

Are you planning to enclose a check, or shall we bill you?

Do not use a question mark with commands phrased as questions for the sake of politeness:

Will you send us a check today.

2.3 EXCLAMATION POINTS

Use exclamation points after highly emotional language. But because business writing almost never calls for emotional language, you should almost never use exclamation points.

2.4 SEMICOLONS

Semicolons have three main uses. The first is to separate two independent clauses when they are closely related:

The outline for the report is due within a week; the report itself is due at the end of the month.

A semicolon should also be used instead of a comma when the items in a series have commas within them:

Our previous meetings were on November 11, 1988; February 20, 1989; and April 28, 1989.

Finally, a semicolon should be used to separate independent clauses when the second one begins with a word such as *however, therefore,* or *nevertheless* or a phrase such as *for example* or *in that case:*

Our supplier has been out of part D712 for 10 weeks; however, we have found another source that can ship the part right away.

His test scores were quite low; on the other hand, he has a lot of relevant experience.

Section 4.4 tells more about using transitional words and phrases like these.

2.5 COLONS

Use a colon (1) after the salutation in a business letter and (2) at the end of a sentence or phrase introducing a list, quotation, or idea:

Our study included the three most critical problems: insufficient capital, incompetent management, and inappropriate location.

In some introductory sentences, *the following* or *that is* is implied by use of the colon.

A colon is optional when the list, quotation, or idea is a direct object or part of the introductory sentence:

We are able to supply
staples wood screws
nails toggle bolts

2.6 COMMAS

Commas have many different uses, the most common being to separate items in a series:

He took the job, learned it well, worked hard, and succeeded.

Put paper, pencils, and paper clips on the requisition list.

Be aware that company style often dictates omitting the final comma in a series. If you have a choice, however, use the final comma. It is often necessary to prevent misunderstanding.

The second place to use a comma is between clauses. A comma should separate independent clauses (unless one or both are very short):

She spoke to the sales staff, and he spoke to the production staff.

I was advised to proceed and I did.

A dependent clause at the beginning of a sentence is also separated from an independent clause by a comma:

Because of our lead in the market, we may be able to risk introducing a new product.

But a dependent clause at the end of a sentence is separated from the independent clause by a comma only when the dependent clause is unnecessary to the main meaning of the sentence:

We may be able to risk introducing a new product, because we have a lead in the market.

A third use for the comma is after an introductory phrase or word:

Starting with this amount of capital, we can survive in the red for one year.

Through more careful planning, we may be able to serve more people.

In short, the move to Tulsa was a good idea.

Yes, you may proceed as originally planned.

However, with short introductory prepositional phrases and some one-syllable words (such as *hence* and *thus*), the comma is often omitted:

Before January 1 we must complete the inventory.

Thus we may not need to hire anyone.

Fourth, commas are used to surround parenthetical phrases or words, which can be removed from the sentence without changing the meaning:

The new owners, the Kowacks, are pleased with their purchase.

Fifth, commas are used between adjectives modifying the same noun:

She left Monday for a long, difficult recruiting trip.

To test the appropriateness of such a comma, try reversing the order of the adjectives: "a difficult, long recruiting trip." If the order cannot be reversed, leave out the comma ("a good old friend" isn't the same as "an old good friend"). A comma is also not used when one of the adjectives is part of the noun. Compare these two phrases:

a distinguished, well-known figure

a distinguished public figure

The adjective-noun combination of *public* and *figure* has been used together so often that it has come to be considered a single thing: *public figure.* Thus no comma is required.

Sixth, commas should precede *Jr., Sr., Inc.,* and the like:

Cloverdell, Inc. Daniel Garcia, Jr.

In a sentence a comma should also follow the abbreviation:

Belle Brown, Ph.D., is the new tenant.

Seventh, commas are used both before and after the year when writing month, day, and year:

It will be sent by December 15, 1989, from our Cincinnati plant.

Some companies write dates in another form: 15 December 1989. No commas should be used in this case. Nor is a comma needed when only the month and year are present (December 1989).

Eighth, a comma may be used after an informal salutation in a letter to a personal friend. (In business letters, however, salutations are followed by colons.)

Ninth, a comma is used to separate a quotation from the rest of the sentence:

Your warranty reads, "These conditions remain in effect for one year from date of purchase."

However, the comma is left out when the quotation as a whole is built into the structure of the sentence:

He hurried off with an angry "Look where you're going."

Finally, a comma should be used whenever it is needed to avoid confusion or an unintended meaning. Compare the following:

Ever since they have planned new ventures more carefully.

Ever since, they have planned new ventures more carefully.

2.7 DASHES

Use a dash to surround a parenthetical comment when the comment is a sudden turn in thought:

Membership in the IBSA—it's expensive but worth it—may be obtained by applying to our New York office.

A dash can also be used to emphasize a parenthetical word or phrase:

Third-quarter profits—in excess of $2 million—are up sharply.

Finally, use dashes to set off a phrase that contains commas:

All our offices—Milwaukee, New Orleans, and Phoenix—have sent representatives.

Do not confuse a dash with a hyphen. A dash separates words, phrases, and clauses more strongly than a comma does; a hyphen ties two words so tightly that they almost become one word.

When typing a dash, type two hyphens with no spacing before, between, or after.

2.8 HYPHENS

Hyphens are used in three main ways. The first is to separate the parts of compound words beginning with such prefixes as *self, ex, quasi,* and *all:*

self-assured quasi-official
ex-wife all-important

But hyphens are usually left out and the words closed up when using such prefixes as *pro, anti, non, un, inter,* and *extra:*

prolabor nonunion
antifascist interdepartmental

An exception occurs when the prefix occurs before a proper noun or when the vowel at the end of the prefix is the same as the first letter of the root word:

pro-Republican anti-American
anti-inflammatory extra-atmospheric

If in doubt, consult your dictionary.

Hyphens are also used in some compound adjectives, which are adjectives made up of two or more words. Specifically, you should use hyphens in compound adjectives that come before the noun:

a first-rate company well-informed executives

But do not hyphenate when the adjective follows a linking verb:

This company is first rate.

Their executives are well informed.

You can shorten sentences that list similar hyphenated words by dropping the common part from all but the last word:

Check the costs of first-, second-, and third-class postage.

Finally, hyphens may be used to divide words at the end of a typed line. Such hyphenation is best avoided, but when you have to divide words at the end of a line, do so correctly (see Section 3.4). A dictionary will show how words are divided into syllables.

2.9 APOSTROPHES

Use an apostrophe in the possessive form of a noun (but not in a pronoun):

On *his* desk was a reply to *Bette Ainsley's* application for the *manager's* position.

Apostrophes are also used in place of the missing letter(s) of a contraction:

WHOLE WORD	CONTRACTION
we will	we'll
do not	don't
they are	they're

2.10 QUOTATION MARKS

Use quotation marks to surround words that are repeated exactly as they were said or written:

The collection letter ended by saying, "This is your third and final notice."

Notice two things: (1) When the quoted material is a complete sentence, the first word is capitalized; (2) the final comma or period goes inside the closing quotation marks.

Quotation marks are also used to set off the title of a newspaper story, magazine article, or book chapter:

You should read "Legal Aspects of the Collection Letter" in *Today's Credit.*

Notice that the book title is in italics. When typewritten, the title is underlined. The same treatment is proper for newspaper and magazine titles. (Component Chapter E explains documentation style in more detail.)

Quotation marks may also be used to indicate special treatment for words or phrases, such as terms that you are defining or terms that you are using in an unusual or ironic way:

In this report, "net sales" refers to after-tax sales dollars.

Our management "team" spends more time squabbling than working to solve company problems.

When using quotation marks, take care to put in both sets, the closing marks as well as the opening ones.

Although periods and commas go inside any quotation marks, colons or semicolons go outside them. A question mark goes inside the quotation marks only if the quotation is a question:

All that day we wondered, "Is he with us?"

If the quotation is not a question but the entire sentence is, the question mark goes outside:

What did she mean by "You will hear from me"?

2.11 PARENTHESES

Use parentheses to surround comments that are entirely incidental:

Our figures do not match yours, although (if my calculations are correct) they are closer than we thought.

Parentheses are also used in legal documents to surround figures in arabic numerals that follow the same amount in words:

Remittance will be One Thousand Two Hundred Dollars ($1,200).

Be careful to put punctuation (period, comma, and so on) outside the parentheses unless it is part of the statement in parentheses.

2.12 ELLIPSES

Use ellipsis points, or dots, to indicate that material has been left out of a direct quotation. But use them only in direct quotations and only at the point where material was left out. Notice how the first sentence is quoted in the second:

The Dow Jones Industrial Average, which skidded 38.17 points in the previous five sessions, gained 4.61 to end at 2213.84.

According to the Honolulu *Star Bulletin*, "The Dow Jones Industrial Average . . . gained 4.61" on June 10.

The number of dots in ellipses is not optional; always use three. Occasionally the points of ellipsis come at the end of a sentence, where they seem to grow a fourth dot. But don't be fooled: One of the dots is a period.

2.13 UNDERSCORES AND ITALICS

Usually a line typed underneath a word or phrase either provides emphasis or indicates the title of a book, magazine, or newspaper. If possible, use italics instead of an underscore.

3.0 MECHANICS

The most obvious and least tolerable mistakes that a business writer makes are probably those related to grammar and punctuation. However, a number of small details, known as writing mechanics, demonstrate the writer's polish and reflect on the company's professionalism.

3.1 CAPITALS

You should, of course, capitalize words that begin sentences:

Before hanging up, he said, "*We'll* meet here on Wednesday at 10 a.m."

A quotation that is a complete sentence should also begin with a capitalized word.

The names of particular persons, places, and things (proper nouns) are also capitalized:

We sent *Ms. Larson* an application form, informing her that not all *applicants* are interviewed.

Let's consider opening a branch in the *West,* perhaps at the *west* end of *Tucson, Arizona.*

As *office buildings* go, the *Kinney Building* is a pleasant setting for *TDG Office Equipment.*

Notice that Ms. Larson's name is capitalized because she is a particular applicant, whereas the general term *applicant* is left uncapitalized. Likewise, *West* is capitalized when it refers to a particular place but not when it means a direction. In the same way, *office* and *building* are not capitalized when they are general terms (common nouns) but are capitalized when they are part of the title of a particular office or building (proper nouns).

Titles within families, governments, or companies may also be capitalized:

My *Uncle David* offered me a job, but I wouldn't be comfortable working for one of my *uncles.*

We've never had a *president* quite like *President* Sweeney.

In addition, always capitalize the first word of the salutation and complimentary close of a letter:

Dear Mr. Andrews:

Yours very truly,

Finally, capitalize the first word after a colon when it begins a complete sentence:

Follow this rule: When in doubt, leave it out.

Otherwise, the first word after a colon should not be capitalized.

3.2 ABBREVIATIONS

Abbreviations are used heavily in tables, charts, lists, and forms. They are used sparingly in prose paragraphs, however.

Here are some abbreviations often used in business writing:

ABBREVIATION	FULL TERM
b/l	bill of lading
ca.	circa (about)
dol., dols.	dollar, dollars
etc.	et cetera (and so on)

FDIC	Federal Deposit Insurance Corporation
Inc.	Incorporated
L.f.	Ledger folio
Ltd.	Limited
mgr.	manager
NSF or N/S	not sufficient funds
P&L or P/L	profit and loss
reg.	regular
whsle.	wholesale

Notice that *etc.* contains a word meaning *and;* therefore, never write *and etc.*

3.3 NUMBERS

Numbers may correctly be handled many ways in business writing, so follow company style. In the absence of a set style, however, you should generally spell out all numbers from one to ten and use arabic numerals for the rest.

But there are some exceptions to this general rule. First, never begin a sentence with a numeral:

Twenty of us produced *641* units per week in the first *12* weeks of the year.

Second, use numerals for the numbers one through ten if they are in the same list as larger numbers:

Our weekly quota rose from *9* to *15* to *27*.

Third, use numerals for percentages, time of day (except with *o'clock*) and dates, and (in general) dollar amounts.

Our division is responsible for *7* percent of total sales.

The meeting is scheduled for *8:30* a.m. on August *2*.

Add *$3* for postage and handling.

Numbers with four digits should use a comma (*1,257*) unless the company specifies another style.

When writing dollar amounts, use a decimal point only if cents are included. In lists of two or more dollar amounts, use the decimal point either for all or for none:

He sent two checks, one for *$67.92* and one for *$90.00*.

3.4 WORD DIVISION

In general, you should avoid dividing words at the ends of lines. But when you must, follow these rules:

- Do not divide one-syllable words, such as *since, walked,* and *thought*; abbreviations (*mgr.*); contractions (*isn't*); or numbers expressed in numerals (*117,500*).
- Divide words between syllables, as specified in a dictionary or word-division manual.
- Make sure that at least three letters of the divided word are moved to the second line: *sin-cerely* instead of *sincere-ly*.
- Do not end a page or more than two consecutive lines with hyphens.
- Leave syllables consisting of a single vowel at the end of the first line (*impedi-ment* instead of *imped-iment*), except when the single vowel is part of a suffix like *able, ible, ical,* or *ity* (*respons-ible* instead of *responsi-ble*).
- Divide between double letters (*tomor-row*), except when the root word ends in double letters (*call-ing* instead of *cal-ling*).
- Divide hyphenated words after the hyphen: *anti-independence* instead of *anti-inde-pendence*.

4.0 VOCABULARY

Use of the right word in the right place is a crucial skill in business communication. However, many pitfalls await the unwary.

4.1 FREQUENTLY CONFUSED WORDS

Because the following sets of words sound similar, you must be careful not to use one when you mean to use the other:

WORD	MEANING
accede	to comply with
exceed	to go beyond
accept	to take
except	to exclude
access	admittance
excess	too much
advice	suggestion
advise	to suggest
affect	to influence
effect	the result
allot	to distribute
a lot	much or many
all ready	completely prepared
already	completed earlier
born	given birth to
borne	carried
capital	money, chief city
capitol	a government building
cite	to quote
sight	a view
site	a location
complement	complete amount, to go well with
compliment	to flatter
corespondent	party in a divorce suit
correspondent	letter writer
council	a panel of people
counsel	advice, a lawyer
defer	to put off until later
differ	to be different
device	a mechanism
devise	to plan
die	to stop living, a tool
dye	to color
discreet	careful
discrete	separate
envelop	to surround
envelope	a covering for a letter
forth	forward
fourth	number four
holey	full of holes
holy	sacred
wholly	completely
human	of people
humane	kindly
incidence	frequency
incidents	events

WORD	MEANING
instance	example
instants	moments
interstate	between states
intrastate	within a state
later	afterward
latter	the second of two
lead	a metal
led	guided
lean	to rest at an angle
lien	claim
levee	embankment
levy	tax
loath	reluctant
loathe	to hate
loose	free, not tight
lose	to mislay
material	substance
materiel	equipment
miner	mineworker
minor	under-age person
moral	virtuous, a lesson
morale	sense of well-being
ordinance	law
ordnance	weapons
overdo	to do in excess
overdue	past due
peace	lack of conflict
piece	a fragment
pedal	a foot lever
peddle	to sell
persecute	to torment
prosecute	to sue
personal	private
personnel	employees
precedence	priority
precedents	previous events
principal	sum of money, chief, main
principle	general rule
rap	to knock
wrap	to cover
residence	home
residents	inhabitants
right	correct
rite	ceremony
write	to form words on a surface

WORD	MEANING
role	a part to play
roll	to tumble, a list
root	part of a plant
rout	to defeat
route	a traveler's way
shear	to cut
sheer	thin, steep
stationary	immovable
stationery	paper
than	as compared to
then	at that time
their	belonging to them
there	in that place
they're	they are
to	a preposition
too	excessively, also
two	the number
waive	to set aside
wave	a swell of water, a gesture
weather	atmospheric conditions
whether	if

Notice in the above list that only enough of each word's meaning is given to help you distinguish among the words in each group. Several meanings are left out entirely. For more complete definitions, consult a dictionary.

4.2 FREQUENTLY MISUSED WORDS

The following words tend to be misused for reasons other than their sound. A number of reference books (including *The Random House College Dictionary*, Revised Edition, Follett's *Modern American Usage*, and Fowler's *Modern English Usage*) can help you with similar questions of usage.

a lot: When the writer means many, *a lot* is always two separate words, never one.

correspond with: Use this phrase when you are talking about exchanging letters, *correspond to* when you mean "similar to." Either *with* or *to* may be used to mean "relate to."

disinterested: This word means fair, unbiased, having no favorites, impartial. If you mean bored or not interested, use *uninterested*.

etc.: This is the abbreviated form of a Latin phrase, *et cetera*. It means "and so on" or "and so forth." The current tendency among business writers is to use English rather than Latin.

imply/infer: Both refer to hints. Their great difference lies in who is acting. The writer *implies;* the reader, in seeing between the lines, *infers*.

lay: This is a transitive verb. Never use it for the intransitive *lie*. (See Section 1.3.3.)

less: Use *less* for uncountable quantities (such as amounts of water, air, sugar, and oil). Use *fewer* for countable quantities (such as numbers of jars, saws, words, pages, and humans). The same distinction applies to *much* and *little* (uncountable) versus *many* and *few* (countable).

like: Use *like* only when the word that follows is just a noun or pronoun. Use *as* or *as if* when a phrase or clause follows:

She looks *like* him.

She did just *as* he had expected.

It seems *as if* she had plenty of time.

many/much: See *less*.

regardless: The *less* ending is the negative part. No word needs two negative parts, so it is illiterate to add *ir* at the beginning.

to me/personally: Use these phrases only when personal reactions, apart from company policy, are being stated (not often the case in business writing).

try: Always follow with *to*, never *and*.

verbal: People in the business community who are careful with language frown on those who use *verbal* to mean *spoken* or *oral*. Many others do say "verbal agreement." But strictly speaking, *verbal* means "of words" and therefore includes both spoken and written words. Be guided in this matter by company usage.

4.3 FREQUENTLY MISSPELLED WORDS

All of us, even the world's best spellers, sometimes have to check a dictionary for the spelling of some words. But people who have never memorized the spelling of commonly used words have to look up so many of them that they often become exasperated and give up on spelling words correctly.

You should not expect perfection, nor need you surrender. If you can memorize the spelling of just the words listed below, you will need the dictionary far less often and will write with more confidence.

absence
absorption
accessible
accommodate
accumulate
achieve
advantageous
affiliated
aggressive
alignment
aluminum
ambience
analyze
apparent
appropriate
argument
asphalt
assistant
asterisk
auditor

bankruptcy
believable
benefited
brilliant
bulletin

calendar
campaign
canceled
category
ceiling
changeable
clientele
collateral
committee
comparative
competitor
concede
congratulations
connoisseur
consensus
convenient
convertible
corroborate
criticism

definitely
description
desirable
dilemma
disappear
disappoint
disbursement
discrepancy
dissatisfied
dissipate

eligible
embarrassing
endorsement
exaggerate
exceed
exhaust
existence
extraordinary

fallacy
familiar
flexible
fluctuation
forty

gesture
grievous

haphazard
holiday

illegible
immigrant
incidentally
indelible
independent
indispensable
insistent
intermediary
irresistible

jewelry
judgment
judicial

labeling
legitimate
leisure
license
litigation

maintenance
mathematics
mediocre
minimum

necessary
negligence
negotiable
newsstand
noticeable

occurrence
omission

parallel
pastime
peaceable
permanent
perseverance
persistent
personnel
persuade
possesses
precede
predictable
preferred
privilege
procedure
proceed
pronunciation
psychology
pursue

questionnaire

receive
recommend
repetition
rescind
rhythmical
ridiculous

salable
secretary
seize
separate
sincerely
succeed
suddenness
superintendent
supersede
surprise

tangible
tariff
technique
tenant
truly

unanimous
until

vacillate
vacuum
vicious

4.4 TRANSITIONAL WORDS AND PHRASES

The following two sentences don't communicate as well as they might because they lack a transitional word or phrase:

Production delays are inevitable. Our current lag time in filling orders is one month.

A semicolon between the two sentences would signal a close relationship between their meanings, but it would not even hint at what that relationship is. Here are the sentences, now linked by means of a semicolon, with a space for a transitional word or phrase:

Production delays are inevitable; ___________, our current lag time in filling orders is one month.

Now read the sentence with *nevertheless* in the blank space. You are receiving one of many meanings that the writer may have had in mind. Now try *therefore, incidentally, in fact,* and *at any rate* in the blank. Each changes the meaning of the sentence.

Here are some transitional words (called conjunctive adverbs) that will help you write more clearly:

accordingly	furthermore	moreover
anyway	however	otherwise
besides	incidentally	still
consequently	likewise	therefore
finally	meanwhile	

The following transitional phrases are used in the same way:

as a result	in other words
at any rate	in the second place
for example	on the other hand
in fact	to the contrary

When one of these words or phrases joins two independent clauses, it should be preceded by a semicolon and followed by a comma, as shown here:

The consultant recommended a complete reorganization; moreover, she suggested that we drop several products.

QUESTIONS FOR DISCUSSION

1. Why is it important to have a working knowledge of grammar and usage?
2. What is the difference between a plural noun and a possessive noun, in both use and appearance?
3. How can pronouns be handled to avoid gender bias?
4. What is the difference between a transitive verb and an intransitive verb?
5. What is a sentence?
6. What is the difference between a phrase and a clause? Between a dependent clause and an independent clause?
7. How can a sentence fragment be fixed?
8. How can a fused sentence or comma splice be fixed?
9. What is the difference in the way semicolons and commas are used?
10. What are the three types of punctuation used to set off parenthetical comments, and when is each best used?

EXERCISES

1. Possessive nouns

Review Section 1.1.3. Then, beside each noun, write its possessive form.

a. women ____________________

b. secretaries ____________________

c. worker ____________________

d. Matthew Kitsos ____________________

e. editor-in-chief ____________________

f. children ____________________

g. Betsy Daniels ____________________

h. *Daily Times* ____________________

i. nobody ____________________

j. month ____________________

k. Jules ____________________

l. desks ____________________

m. office ____________________

n. today ____________________

o. the Rosses ____________________

2. Antecedents

Review Section 1.2.1. Then, for each sentence below, underline the correct pronoun and write its antecedent and its number (*S* for singular, *P* for plural) in the appropriate columns.

		ANTECEDENT	NUMBER
a. Joe, Frank, and Bob gave (their, his) opinions.	a.	____________________	____
b. Any company worth (its, their) salt has one.	b.	____________________	____
c. Los Angeles, as well as San Francisco, has (its, their) advantages.	c.	____________________	____
d. Because office decor is important to employees, (it, they) should be planned by professionals.	d.	____________________	____
e. Neither newcomers nor veterans knew (his, her, their) way around.	e.	____________________	____

f. Was it Marilyn or Lupe who sent (her, their) resume? f. ______ ___

g. Both candidates did well in (his, their) interviews. g. ______ ___

h. Each of the sales representatives went (his or her, their) own way. h. ______ ___

i. This ad campaign, despite excessive costs, has had (its, their) successes. i. ______ ___

j. Nancy is one of those people who know (her, their) business. j. ______ ___

3. Case of pronouns

Review Section 1.2.4. Then underline the correct pronoun in each sentence.

a. (We, Us) sales representatives are overworked.
b. (Who, Whom) do you trust to do a good job?
c. Just between you and (I, me), the pay is poor.
d. The programmer (who, whom) gets this job will have to work.
e. Give Terry and (I, me) that office.
f. The best positions went to Randolph and (she, her).
g. It's (he, him) who should get the raise.
h. I'll give the assignment to (whoever, whomever) isn't busy with another one.
i. He turned as large a profit as (I, me) did.
j. (Who, Whom) will you talk to?

4. Possessive pronouns

Review Section 1.2.5. Then underline the correct word choice in each sentence.

a. (Its, It's) imperative that we close escrow today.
b. In (its, it's) final clause, the contract states that we are accountable for defects.
c. BGT and Ramp Industries have changed the design of (there, their, they're) brakes recently.
d. It is (are, our) conviction that we can complete this job before the deadline.
e. Always be sure that (your, you're) employees understand what is expected of them.
f. Give each secretary a copy of (her or his, their) new schedule.
g. Do you know what (there, their, they're) planning for the sales meeting?
h. Take note of (your, you're) mistakes.
i. If (its, it's) warranty has not expired, we will not charge you for fixing it.
j. (Your, you're) mistaken if you think she will budge on that issue.

5. Verb tenses

Review Section 1.3.1. Then write the correct form of each verb in the space provided.

TO PROVIDE

a. present: I ______
b. past: you ______
c. future: we ______
d. present perfect: they ______
e. past perfect: she ______

TO ALLOW

f. present: he ______
g. past: it ______
h. future: you ______
i. present perfect: they ______
j. past perfect: I ______

TO SHRINK

k. present: they ______

l. past: she ______

m. future: it ______

n. present perfect: you ______

o. past perfect: we ______

TO BECOME

p. present: we ______

q. past: I ______

r. future: you ______

s. present perfect: he ______

t. past perfect: it ______

TO BE

u. present: you ______

v. past: she ______

w. future: we ______

x. present perfect: they ______

y. past perfect: I ______

6. Transitive and intransitive verbs

Review Section 1.3.3. Then underline the correct verb in each sentence.

a. After the walls are poured, there must be a way to (rise, raise) them into position.
b. (Sit, Set) up your display against that wall.
c. The contract has (laid, lain) forgotten in our safe for months.
d. I could see when I (lay, laid) it on Mary's desk that she was surprised.
e. It's important to know why production costs have (raised, risen).

7. Voice of verbs

Review Section 1.3.4. Then rewrite these sentences so that their verbs are in the active voice.

a. The delivery was made by Mercury Message Service.

______

b. Your report has been read by three of us.

______

c. A choice of color must be made by the buyer.

______

d. Complaints are handled by Jane Harper.

______

e. New ideas were picked up at the trade fair by our representatives.

______

______

8. Adjectives

Review Section 1.4. Then, for each simple adjective in parentheses, give the comparative or superlative (whichever is more appropriate) in the space provided.

a. Of the three, Paul's sales record is (good) ______.

b. Which check is the (large) ______ of the two?

c. Inspect our five branches before choosing the (promising) ______ one.

d. Send the (practical) ______ frame you have from the group.

e. Having lifted both, I can pick out the (heavy) ______ one.

9. Adverbs

Review Section 1.5. Then turn these adjectives into adverbs.

a. intense ______

b. poor ______

c. real ______

d. full ________

e. complete ________

f. good ________

g. whole ________

h. busy ________

i. secondary ________

j. due ________

10. Prepositions

Review Section 1.6.1. Then underline all the prepositions in these sentences.

a. Providing a few samples of cheese created better sales in many areas.
b. Lead into the letter without a break.
c. He brought with him the habit of using quick-freeze equipment.
d. If the right people are informed of your offer, word of mouth will take care of the rest.
e. The committee will meet behind closed doors for several reasons, none of which are secret.

11. Conjunctions, articles, and interjections

Review Section 1.6.2. Then, beside each word below, write *C*, *A*, or *I* to indicate whether the word is a conjunction, article, or interjection.

a. the ____
b. although ____
c. Oh no! ____
d. but ____
e. because ____
f. an ____
g. Good! ____
h. if ____
i. unless ____
j. and ____

12. Longer sentences

Review Section 1.7.2. Then underline the word that makes each sentence correct.

a. His presentation, coming after two of the most boring speeches I have ever heard, (was, were) refreshing.
b. When the full slate of officers (is, are) present, she doesn't write out their names.
c. (Although, However,) it was over by the time we got there.
d. The (secretary, secretaries) working in corporate headquarters the longest are going to be recognized.
e. All who are in the group (meet, meets) the selection criteria.

13. Sentence fragments

Review Section 1.7.3. Some of the following are sentence fragments; others are correct as they stand. Rewrite the sentence fragments to make them complete sentences; write *correct* in the space following sentences that are complete.

a. In just 14 days, with lots of promotion, the new outlet will open.

____

____

b. Nearly ten one-week sessions, beginning the first week in June, with no breaks.

____

____

c. Drop the economy model.

____

____

d. Who of all our employees?

____

____

e. Although Joan is well grounded in office procedure.

____

____

f. Charging our office with the task of counting supplies.

____

____

g. Having ordered a large quantity of wheat from the United States.

____

____

h. Nearly ten one-week sessions begin the first week in June, with no breaks.

____

____

i. Our coats, water-repellent, sleek, and undeniably tough.

____

____

j. Because the action would absorb the available supplies of short-term government securities.

____

____

14. Fused sentences and comma splices

Review Section 1.7.4. Some of the following are fused sentences; others are correct as they stand. Rewrite the fused sentences to make them correct; write *correct* in the space following correct sentences.

a. You like the idea of owning your own business, particularly because you have the capital to begin one.

____

____

b. Having met at a previous sales convention, we often had lunch with him you never know where you stand.

____

____

c. The big question is financing, will you have enough money?

____

____

d. If satisfaction is not forthcoming, we will be forced to cancel our order, find another supplier, and take legal action.

____

____

e. Over half of them are badly damaged, it looks like water damage.

____

____

15. Misplaced modifiers

Review Section 1.7.6. Then rewrite each of the following sentences so that modifiers are placed correctly.

a. Deliver the fastback to the customer with the leather upholstery.

____

____

b. An unauthorized caller can't get through this "smart" telephone, no matter how clever.

____

____

c. We interviewed several applicants with great speed.

____

____

d. The letters should be filed in the green cabinet from clients who have complaints.

____

____

e. I passed the new business center driving through Emerson City.

____

____

16. Punctuation A

Review Section 2.0. Then, in the space provided, write *C* if the sentence is punctuated correctly, *I* if punctuation is incorrect.

a. "Johnson and Kane, Inc., is gone, comments one Wall Street merger expert. ______

b. OPEC's uncertain outlook—its production has fallen drastically since

1978—makes attempts to defend the cartel's official price appear futile. ____

c. Over half of the combined debt loads of Argentina; Brazil; and Mexico fluctuates with the movement of the U.S. prime rate. ____

d. About 100 products bore the Can-Man trademark last May; there are nearly 300 today. ____

e. Stephen Raken says Oak Tree Realty now: "realizes that it can't keep up if it does it all in-house." ____

f. Seasoned, well-managed companies should explore this alternative. As they search for capital. ____

g. Several insurers (Gaston, Regis, DMA) maintain offices in Tennessee. ____

h. Is the private placement extinct? Yes. And no. ____

i. "Bricks and mortar," Johnson says, are history." ____

j. At Simtex, however, the union recently gave up a three-year-old profit-sharing plan—which has produced no bonuses—because the workers wanted an immediate wage increase; they had not had a raise in nearly two years. ____

17. Punctuation B

Review Section 2.0. Then correct the punctuation in the following sentences.

a. Will you please send us a check today so we can settle your account?

b. I find it hard to believe that we could miss such a promising opportunity!

c. His writing skills are excellent, however he still needs to polish his management style.

d. We'd like to address the issues of: efficiency, profitability, and market penetration.

e. During the highest level trials we will resume operations.

f. Mark is a bright competent young man.

g. The letter should be dated no later than April 14 1989 if it is to prove the point.

h. All along the production designers have insisted on using robots.

i. My boss the most senior executive in the company is well known for her concern for employees.

j. What is your career goal the interviewer asked.

18. Punctuation C

Review Section 2.0. Then insert correct punctuation in the following business letter:

Hardball Bearing Company
2206 Wheeler Boulevard
Newark New Jersey 07127

November 13 1989

Mr James R Capp Accounts Payable Manager
The Rollem Company
8321 Clearspring Way
Boston Massachusetts 02109

Dear Mr Capp

We are happy after five years of pleasant dealings with you to announce a change in our billing procedure one that will prove helpful to both of us

Until recently we have billed all of our customers on the first of each month beginning January 1990 we will mail billings in alphabetical order you will enjoy the following benefits of this change

> For the month of January the balance of your account with us will be in effect an interest-free loan
>
> Because most other suppliers continue to bill on the first our bill will not arrive during your peak accounting period
>
> Our company newsletter Bearing Up will continue to be enclosed with our billing

We know that an accountants life is never simple but we are doing our best to make it so

Yours very truly

Now count the number of items of punctuation you inserted and enter the total in this space: ____. Your instructor will tell you if you have missed some.

19. Capitals

Review Section 3.1. Then capitalize the appropriate words below by putting three short parallel lines under each letter that should be capitalized. (The first item in the first sentence is done for you.)

a. he was questioned about lifting the post-afghanistan embargo on grain sales to the u.s.s.r.

b. what did the senate foreign relations committee say about her as a human rights official?

c. at northern natural gas company, for one, president samuel f. segnar holds monthly luncheons with employees who have hit the five-year service mark.

d. margaret d. steele, head of faribault college's business department, recently conducted a semester-long program involving monthly lunches with professors.

e. "book me a flight to atlanta on airtrans airlines," he said, "so i can visit our southern wholesalers."

20. Word division

Review Section 3.4. Then correct the way the following words are divided by crossing through inappropriate hyphens and inserting slash marks where the words could more appropriately be divided.

a. cal-lable
b. a-gainst
c. self-anal-ysis
d. controll-ing
e. hasti-ly

21. Frequently confused words

Review Section 4.1. Then underline the correct word in each sentence.

a. To be successful, one must (accept, except) a certain amount of stress.

b. Our plans were (all ready, already) when the news came in.

c. The (incidence, incidents) of breakdowns has decreased.

d. No manager can afford to (loose, lose) his or her self-control.

e. Good lines of communication maintain company (moral, morale).

f. I've worked with both Tom and Rita, and I prefer the (later, latter).

g. Civilized people can (defer, differ) in their opinions without getting angry.

h. The (principal, principle) was sound, but the details were misleading.

i. In the future, sales representatives will be assigned (routes, routs) by the Chicago office.

j. See if this regulation can be (waived, waved).

k. I would (advice, advise) you to hedge your investments.

l. The color of that hat is a perfect (complement, compliment) to the colors in the dress.

m. Because employment matters are so sensitive, you will have to make some (discreet, discrete) inquiries if you want to find out about his previous performance.

n. I have received no greater compliment (than, then) the one she gave me yesterday.

o. That chair is (stationary, stationery), but the other one can be moved.

22. Frequently misused words

Review Section 4.2. Then underline the correct or preferable word in each sentence.

a. Each carton contained (fewer, less) packages than were indicated on the outside.

b. His letter (inferred, implied) that there was no charge for the damaged items.

c. We encountered no problems when we (laid, lay) the tiles.

d. We will have (a lot, allot) of openings in six months.

e. The usual mediator was formerly employed by one of the parties to the dispute, so a more (disinterested, uninterested) mediator was assigned to the case.

f. All seated passengers must be able to see the sign, just (as, like) they can on a 747.

g. Our popular poplin dress shirt is (as, like) our executive Essence shirt in many ways.

h. (Many, Much) of our sales effort would be enhanced by a computer.

i. Our Trade Division (corresponds to, corresponds with) their International Division; both have the same function.

j. Apparently I only (implied, inferred) that opinion from her report.

23. Frequently misspelled words

Review Section 4.3. Then underline the correct spelling of each word.

a. indispensible	indispensable	indespensable
b. permenent	perminent	permanent
c. consensus	concensus	consencus
d. benefitted	benifitted	benefited
e. changable	changeable	changible
f. noticeable	noticable	notisable
g. medeocre	mediocer	mediocre
h. catigory	category	cattegory
i. alignment	alinement	alinment
j. prefered	preferd	preferred

24. Transitional words and phrases

Review Section 4.4. Then, of the transitions listed below, choose the most appropriate for each sentence and write your choice in the space provided.

for example	meanwhile
on the contrary	still
in other words	furthermore
on the other hand	therefore
in the second place	in that case

a. Ms. Siegel worked for you in a similar capacity during the past two years; ________________ we are interested in getting your candid comments on her professional abilities.

b. We have experienced difficulties with your shipments of candy before; ________________ just last December, 5 of the 22 boxes you shipped arrived empty.

c. The enclosed information sheet contains names and telephone numbers of prospective clients; ________________________ it includes mailing addresses and ZIP codes.

d. Because you are a valued customer of Carrillo Images, we are rechecking the figures we used to prepare your invoice; ________________ we are discounting the new price.

e. Your acceptance of these conditions, signaled by your signing the enclosed check, will begin the process; ________________________ your signature on this check will release you to begin construction.

25. Grammar and usage

Edit the following memo so it conforms with all the rules presented in this chapter, as well as the principles of good writing presented in Chapter 5.

MEMO

DATE: June 22 1989
TO: All department heads
FROM: Alan Kitchener, vice president of human relations
SUBJECT: In-house training program

Several new training programs have been developed in response to the training needs assessment conducted in February, 1989. (27 highly-informative replies were recieved; I personally appreciated your comments). Our goal in developing these new programs was to give each employee the skills to do his job better, and to improve employee's moral.

These are the new programs, which will be available beginning July 1.

1. Making the Most of Microcomputers. Reviews microcomputer operations and provides hands-on experience in using the four main software packages owned by us: word processing, spreadsheet; data-base management and graphics.

2. Keeping Customers Happy. Covers methods for answering the telephone and correspondence--policies for handling complaints and requests for adjustment--as well as general marketing goals as they relate to customer service.

3. Writing Better for Business. Deals with the organization of messages, analyzing purpose and audience, and style and tone.

Each course will be offered once a month beginning at the first week and continuing for 4 sessions. Making the Most of Microcomputers on Tuesdays, Keeping Customers Happy on Wednesdays, and Writing Better for Business on Thursdays. They will be held in the second floor conference room from three to five p.m.

In general these courses have been designed for clerical and supervisory employees; although every-body on your staff who could benefit are welcome to attend. To register an employee must bring a signed authorization form, a packet are included with this memo, to the human relations office, Room 117, at least a week in advance of the start of the course.

Try and send all appropriate staff so our organiza-tion can better meet it's goals!

COMPONENT CHAPTER D

FORMAT AND LAYOUT OF BUSINESS DOCUMENTS

An effective letter, memo, or report does more than store words on paper. It must get to the right person, make an impression, and tell the recipient who wrote it and when it was written. The sender may also need to find out later how and by whom the document was processed.

Over the centuries, certain conventions for formatting and laying out business documents have developed. As with most matters of style, however, few hard-and-fast rules exist. Certain styles—namely, those described here—are more common than others. In addition, organizations often develop a variation of the standard style to suit their own needs. Each writer or organization should use a style that best conveys the types of messages it sends.

In most organizations, secretaries are expected to know how to put documents into the proper form and how to make them attractive to readers. But you should also be familiar with these conventions, if only to be sure you provide all the information that the secretary needs.

FIRST IMPRESSIONS

A letter or other written document is often the first or only contact that a person has with your organization. It is important, therefore, that documents look neat and professional and be easy to read. Several elements—the paper that you use, the letterhead, and the typing—tell readers a lot about you and your company's professionalism.

PAPER

Your own experience should tell you that a flimsy, see-through piece of paper gives a much less favorable impression than a richly textured piece. But you may not know that the quality of paper is measured in two ways.

The first method is by weight, specifically the weight of four reams (each a 500-sheet package) of letter-size paper. The quality most commonly used by business organizations is 20-pound paper, but 16- and 24-pound paper are also used.

The second measure of quality is the percentage of cotton in the paper. Cotton does not yellow over time the way wood pulp does, and it is simultaneously strong and soft. In general, paper with a 25-percent cotton content is an appropriate quality for letters and outside reports. For memos and other internal documents, lighter-weight paper and paper with a lower cotton content may be used.

The standard size of paper for business documents is 8½ by 11 inches. But legal documents are presented on paper that measures 8½ by 14 inches. And sometimes executives have heavier 7- by 10-inch paper on hand (with matching envelopes) for such personal messages as congratulations and recommendations.[1] Executives may also have a box of correspondence note cards imprinted with their initials and a box of plain folded notes for condolences or for acknowledging formal invitations.

Stationery may also vary in color. White, of course, is standard for business purposes, although sometimes neutral colors like gray and ivory are used. Memos are sometimes produced on pastel-colored paper so they can more easily be distinguished from outside letters; sometimes memos are typed on different colors of paper for routing to different departments. Although light-colored papers are distinctive and often appropriate, bright or dark colors are difficult to read and may convey too frivolous an impression.

CUSTOMIZATION

For letters to outsiders, businesses commonly use letterhead stationery printed with the company's name and address, usually at the top of the page but sometimes along the left side or even at the bottom of the page. Other information may be included in the letterhead as well: the company's telephone number, cable address, product lines, date of establishment, officers and directors, slogan, and symbol (logo). The idea is to give the recipient of the letter pertinent reference data and a better idea of what the company does. But the letterhead should be as simple as possible, because too much information gives the page a cluttered look, cuts into the space needed for the letter, and may become outdated before all the letterhead has been used.

Company letterhead should always be used for the first page of a letter. Successive pages should be typed on a plain sheet of paper that matches the letterhead in color and quality or on a specially printed second-page letterhead bearing only the company's name.

Many companies also design and print standardized forms for memos and for reports that are written frequently and that always require the same types of information (such as sales reports and expense reports). These forms may be printed in sets for use with carbon paper or in carbonless copy sets that produce multiple copies automatically with the original.

TYPING

Most business documents should be typed or printed out on a typewriter-quality computer printer. Typing is usually easier to read than handwriting and is smaller, so more words fit into less space. Some short, informal memos are handwritten, however, and it is appropriate to handwrite a note of condolence to a close business associate. The envelope should be handwritten or typed to match the document.

TABLE D.1 Guidelines for Establishing Line Lengths Using the "Picture Frame" Method

		LINE LENGTH		
LENGTH OF LETTER	NUMBER OF WORDS	INCHES	ELITE CHARACTERS	PICA CHARACTERS
Short	Under 100	4	50	40
Medium	100–200	5	60	50
Long	200–300	6	70	60
Two pages	Over 300	6	70	60

Even a letter on the best-quality paper with the best-designed letterhead may look unprofessional if it is poorly typed. All documents (but especially those that leave the company) should be centered on the page, with margins of at least an inch all around. This balance can be achieved in one of two ways: by establishing a standard line length or by establishing a "picture frame."

Most commonly, the standard line length is about 6 inches wide. Lines should usually not be justified, or aligned exactly with both margins, because a justified letter is hard to read and looks too much like a form letter. Variations in line length look more personal and interesting. If the typewriter or word processor has larger, pica type, each line will have 60 characters; if smaller, elite type is used, each line will have 72 characters. Sometimes a guide sheet, with the margins and the center point marked in dark ink, is used as a backing when typing a page. The number of lines between elements of the document (such as the date line and inside address in a letter) can be adjusted to ensure that the document fills the page vertically or, if it's a longer document, extends to at least three lines of body on the last page.

Fitting type into a picture frame with even margins all around requires more skill. First the length of the document is estimated; then the number of characters for each line is determined. Table D.1 gives the most commonly used guidelines for estimating line length; however, tables, set-off quotations, and exceptionally long or short opening and closing elements all affect the size of the margins.

Another important aspect of a professional-looking document is the proper spacing after punctuation. For example, you should always leave two spaces at the ends of sentences and after colons; single spaces are used after commas and semicolons. Each letter in a person's initials is followed by a period and a single space. Abbreviations for organizations, such as U.S.A., may or may not have periods, but they should never have internal spaces. Dashes should be typed as two hyphens with no space between or on either side of the dash. Other details of this sort are provided in most secretarial handbooks.

Most business documents should be cleanly typed. Electric/electronic typewriters, word processors, and some computer printers produce a clearer, more regular impression than manual typewriters do. In addition, a carbon or plastic ribbon produces a darker, more uniform image than a cloth ribbon. Finally, messy corrections are dreadfully obvious; a letter, outside report, or memo to a higher-up that requires a lot of corrections should simply be retyped. This sort of mess can be avoided by using a self-correcting typewriter or a word processor that can produce correction-free documents at the push of a button.

LETTERS

For a very long time, written messages from one person to another have begun with some type of phrase in greeting and have ended with some sort of polite expression and the writer's signature. In fact, books printed in the sixteenth century prescribed letter formats for writers to follow. Styles have changed some since then, but all business letters still have certain elements in common. Several of these parts appear in every letter; others appear only when desirable or appropriate. In addition, these parts are usually arranged in one of three basic letter formats.

STANDARD LETTER PARTS

All business letters typically include seven elements, in the following order:

1. Heading
2. Date
3. Inside address
4. Salutation
5. Body
6. Complimentary close
7. Signature block

The letter in Figure D.1 shows the placement of these standard letter parts. Because it's a personal business letter, it includes a typed heading instead of a printed letterhead.

Heading

Letterhead, the usual heading, shows the organization's name, full address, and (almost always) telephone number. Executive letterhead bears the name of an individual within the organization as well. If letterhead stationery is not available, the heading consists of a return address (but not a name) starting 13 lines from the top of the page, which leaves 2 inches between the return address and the top of the page.

Date

If you are using letterhead paper, the date on which the letter is typed should be placed at least one blank line beneath the lowest part of the letterhead. Without letterhead, the date is typed immediately below the return address.

In typing the date, the full name of the month (no abbreviations) is followed by the day (in numerals), a comma, and then the year: July 14, 1989. This is the standard method of writing the date. In some industries and in government, however, the date is typed with the day (in numerals) first, followed by the month (unabbreviated), followed by the year—with no comma: 14 July 1989. In this country, the date is rarely typed all in numerals. Also, it is old-fashioned to put *rd* or *th* after the numeral representing the day at the top of a letter.

Inside address

The inside address, which identifies the recipient of the letter, is typed one or more lines below the date, depending on how long the letter is.

The addressee's name is preceded by a courtesy title, such as *Dr.*, *Mr.*, or *Ms.* The accepted courtesy title for women in business is *Ms.*, although a woman who is known to prefer the title *Miss* or

FIGURE D.1
Standard Letter Parts

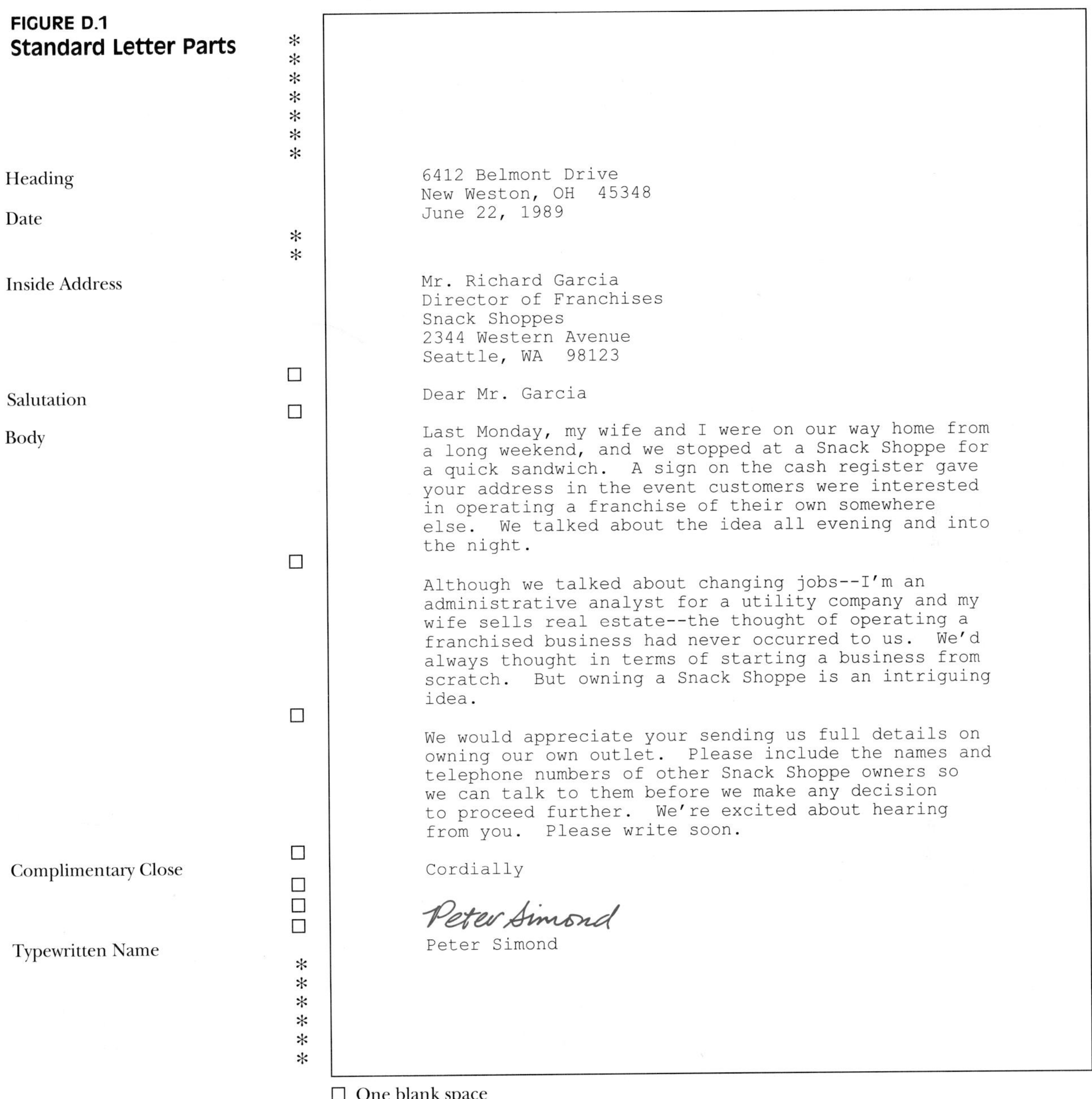

☐ One blank space
* Variable spacing, depending on length of the letter, except for the top margin, which should be two inches

Mrs. should be accommodated. Any other titles, such as *Professor* or *General*, should not be abbreviated. Table D.2 shows the proper forms of address for various dignitaries.

The person's organizational title, such as *Director*, may also be included on this first line (if it is short) or on the line below; the name of a department may follow. If the name of a specific person is unavailable, the letter may be addressed to the department or to a specific position within the department.

This example shows all the information that may be included in the inside address and its proper order:

TABLE D.2 Forms of Address for Dignitaries

PERSONAGE	NAME IN ADDRESS	SALUTATION
President of the United States	The President	Dear Mr. or Madam President
Cabinet member	The Honorable [first and last name]	Dear Mr. or Madam Secretary
Attorney General	The Honorable [first and last name]	Dear Mr. or Madam Attorney General
U.S. Senator	The Honorable [first and last name]	Dear Senator [last name]
U.S. Representative	The Honorable [first and last name]	Dear Mr. or Ms. [last name]
Governor	The Honorable [first and last name]	Dear Governor [last name]
State senator or representative	The Honorable [first and last name]	Dear Mr. or Ms. [last name]
Mayor	The Honorable [first and last name]	Dear Mayor [last name] or Dear Mr. or Madam Mayor
Judge	The Honorable [first and last name]	Dear Judge [last name]
Lawyer	Mr. or Ms. [first and last name]	Dear Mr. or Ms. [last name]
University president	Dr. [first and last name], President	Dear Dr. [last name]
Dean	Dr. [first and last name], Dean of [school or college]	Dear Dr. [last name]
Professor	Professor [first and last name]	Dear Professor [last name]
Rabbi	Rabbi [first and last name]	Dear Rabbi [last name]
Protestant clergy	The Reverend [first and last name]	Dear Dr., Mr., or Ms. [last name]
Roman Catholic priest	The Reverend Father [first and last name]	Reverend Father or Dear Father [last name]
Roman Catholic nun	Sister [name]	Dear Sister

Ms. Linda Coolidge, Director
Corporate Planning Department
Midwest Airlines
Kowalski Building, Suite 21-A
7279 Bristol Avenue
Toledo, OH 43617

Canadian addresses are similar, except that the name of the province is usually spelled out or abbreviated and two spaces separate the province name from the Postal Code:

Dr. H. C. Armstrong
Research and Development
Commonwealth Mining Consortium
The Chelton Building, Suite 301
585 Second Street SW
Calgary, Alberta T2P 2P5

Salutation

The salutation of a letter should use the person's name if at all possible. Your relationship with the addressee affects the formality of the salutation. If, in conversation, you would say "Mary," your letter's salutation should be *Dear Mary*, followed by a colon. Letters to people you do not know well enough to address personally should use the courtesy title and last name, followed by a colon. Presuming to write *Dear Lewis* instead of *Dear Professor Chang* demonstrates a disrespectful familiarity that a stranger will probably resent.

Don't overlook an especially important point with personalized salutations: Whether they are informal or formal, make sure names are spelled right. A misspelled name is glaring evidence of carelessness, and it belies the personal interest you are trying to express.

Choosing a salutation for a letter addressed to a group or to an unknown person is one of the least-settled issues related to salutations. Several choices are available:

- *Ladies and Gentlemen*—unless it is known that the group is made up entirely of women or men or unless your organization dictates the use of *Gentlemen* for mixed groups

- *Dear Sir or Madam*—again, unless the gender of the recipient is known or company policy requires the use of *Sir*
- *Dear Colleague*—or *Dear Policyholder, Dear Customer,* or some other appropriate title
- *To Whom It May Concern*

Dear Sir (or *Dear Madam*) and *To Whom It May Concern* are quite stiff and formal; use them only when you wish to establish a polite barrier.

In an attempt to avoid the awkwardness of a salutation, some letter writers use a salutopening on the salutation line. A salutopening omits *Dear* but includes the first few words of the opening paragraph along with the recipient's name. After this line, the sentence continues a double space below as part of the body of the letter, as in these examples:

Thank you, Mr. Brown,	Salutopening
for your prompt payment of your bill.	Body
Congratulations, Ms. Lake!	Salutopening
Your promotion is well deserved.	Body

Body

The body of the letter is the message. Almost all letters are typed single-spaced, with double spacing (one blank line) before and after the salutation or salutopening, between paragraphs, and before the complimentary close.

The body may include indented lists, entire paragraphs indented for emphasis, and even subheadings. If so, all similar elements should be treated in the same way. A department or company often selects a format to be used for all letters.

Complimentary close

The complimentary close is typed on the second line below the body of the letter. A number of alternatives for wording are available, but currently the trend seems to be toward using one-word closes, such as *Sincerely* and *Cordially*. In any case, the complimentary close should reflect the relationship between the writer and the recipient of the letter.

Be wary of closes that are too cute, such as *Yours for bigger profits;* if the recipient doesn't know you well, your sense of humor may be misunderstood.

Signature block

After leaving three blank lines for a written signature below the complimentary close, the sender's name is typed (unless it appears in the letterhead). The person's title may appear on the same line as the name or on the line below:

Cordially,

Raymond Dunnigan
Director of Personnel

Use of letterhead indicates that the writer is representing the company. But if the letter is typed on plain paper or runs to a second page, the writer may want to emphasize that she or he is speaking legally for the company. The accepted way to do that is to type the company's name in capital letters a double space below the complimentary close and the sender's name four lines below that, with the title following:

Sincerely,

WENTWORTH INDUSTRIES

(Mrs.) Helen B. Taylor
President

If the writer's name could be taken for either a man's or a woman's, a courtesy title indicating gender should be included in the typewritten name, with parentheses or without. Women who prefer to be addressed as *Mrs.* or *Miss* should also include a courtesy title.

ADDITIONAL LETTER PARTS

Letters vary greatly in subject matter and thus in the identifying information they need and the format they adopt. The following elements may be used in any combination, depending on the requirements of the particular letter, but generally in this order:

1. Addressee notation
2. Attention line
3. Subject line

FIGURE D.2
Additional Letter Parts

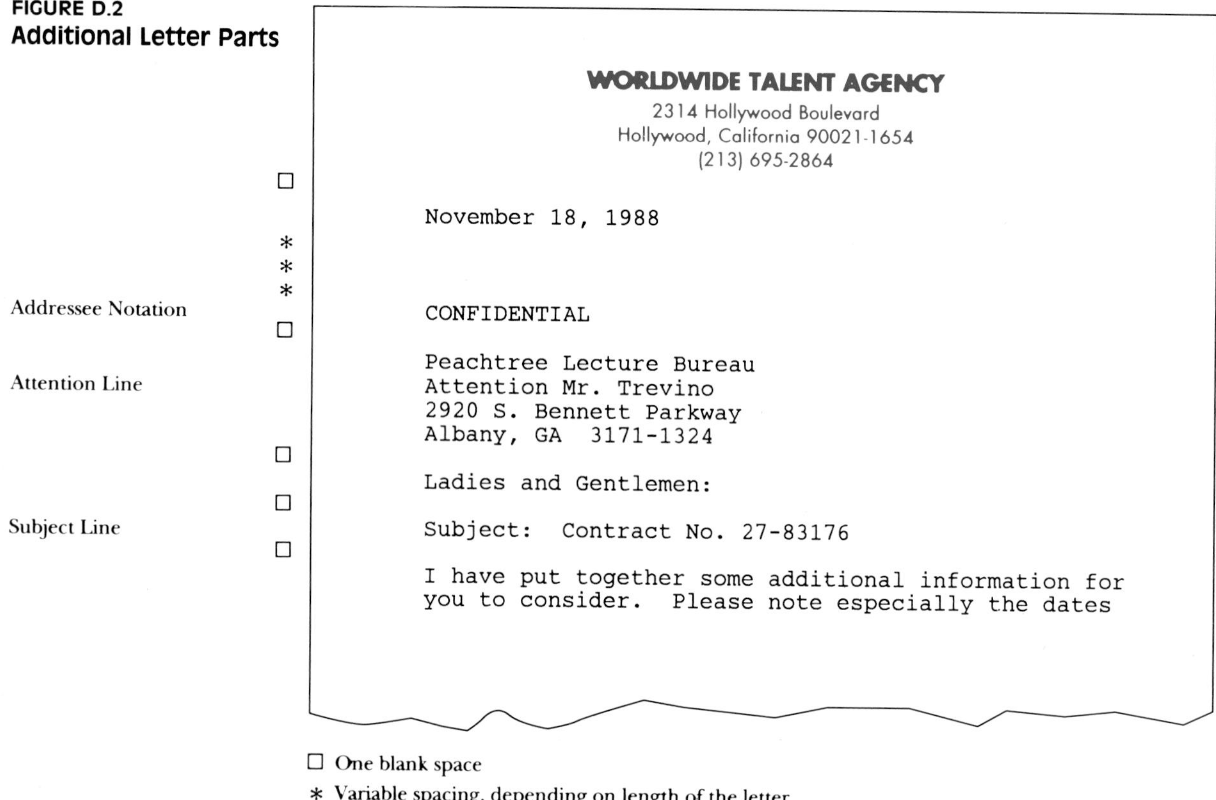

4. Second-page heading
5. Company name
6. Reference initials
7. Enclosure notation
8. Copy notation
9. Mailing notation
10. Postscript

The letter in Figure D.2 shows how these additional parts should be arranged.

Addressee notation

Letters that have a restricted readership or that must be handled in a special way should include such addressee notations as *Personal, Confidential,* or *Please Forward.* This sort of notation appears two lines above the inside address in capital letters.

Attention line

Although today an attention line is not commonly used, you may find it useful if you only know the last name of the person to whom you are writing. An attention line can also be used to direct a letter to a position title or department. An attention line may take any of the following forms or variants of them: *Attention: Dr. McHenry, Attention: Director of Marketing,* or *Attention: Marketing Department.* You may place the company name on the first line and use an attention line as the second line of the inside address.

Some companies prefer an alternative approach in which the attention line is placed a double space below the inside address. It may be typed against the left margin (the most common procedure), indented as the paragraphs in the body of the letter are, or centered. The word *Attention* or the whole line may also be underlined.

With either approach, the address on the envelope should always match the style of the inside address shown in Figure D.2, in order to conform to postal specifications.

Subject line

The subject line is a device to let the recipient know at a glance what the letter is about; it also helps indicate where to file the letter for future reference. It is usually typed below the salutation—against the left margin, indented as the paragraphs in the body of the letter are, or centered on the line.

FIGURE D.2
Additional Letter Parts (continued)

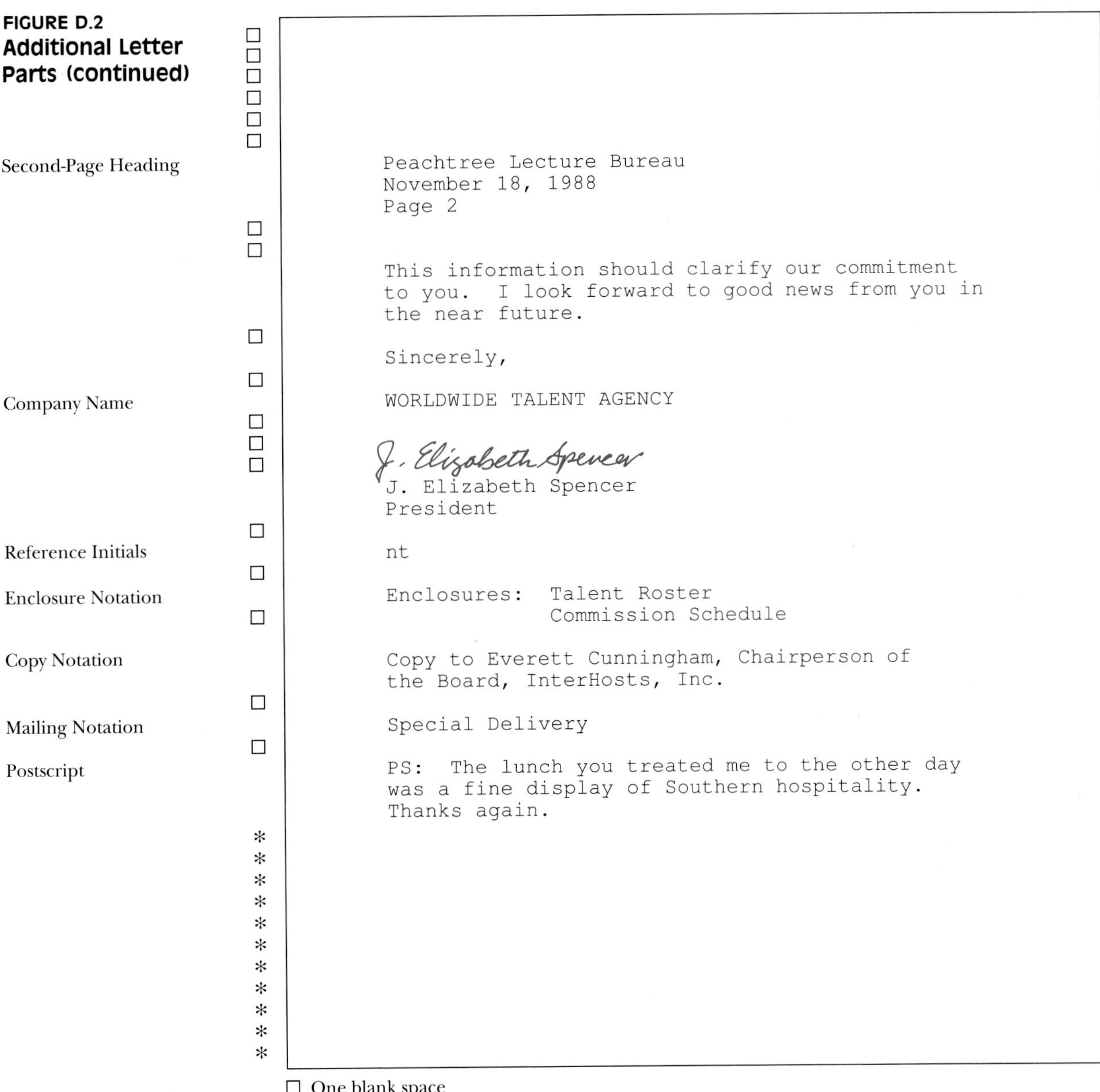

Second-Page Heading

Peachtree Lecture Bureau
November 18, 1988
Page 2

This information should clarify our commitment to you. I look forward to good news from you in the near future.

Sincerely,

Company Name

WORLDWIDE TALENT AGENCY

J. Elizabeth Spencer
J. Elizabeth Spencer
President

Reference Initials

nt

Enclosure Notation

Enclosures: Talent Roster
Commission Schedule

Copy Notation

Copy to Everett Cunningham, Chairperson of the Board, InterHosts, Inc.

Mailing Notation

Special Delivery

Postscript

PS: The lunch you treated me to the other day was a fine display of Southern hospitality. Thanks again.

□ One blank space
* Variable spacing, depending on length of the letter

Sometimes the subject line is typed above the salutation or at the very top of the page.

Like the attention line, the subject line may take a wide variety of forms, including the following:

Subject: RainMaster Sprinklers

About your February 2, 1989, order

FALL 1989 SALES MEETING

Reference Order No. 27920

Sometimes the subject line (or the last line of a long subject "line") is underscored. And some writers omit the word *Subject* and put the other information all in capitals to distinguish it from the other parts of the letter.

Second-page heading

If the letter is long and an additional page is required, a second-page heading must be used. Some companies have second-page letterhead, with the company name and address on one line and in smaller type than the regular letterhead. In any case, the second page must bear the name of the person (preferably) and/or organization receiving the letter, the page number, and the date of the letter; a reference number may also be included. All of the following are acceptable:

Ms. Melissa Baker
May 10, 1989
Page 2

Ms. Melissa Baker, May 10, 1989, Page 2

Ms. Melissa Baker -2- May 10, 1989

Triple-space (leave two blank lines) between the second-page heading and the body.

Company name

The company's name, if included in the signature block, is typed all in capital letters a double space below the complimentary close. The company's name is usually included in the signature block only when the writer is serving as the company's official spokesperson or when letterhead has not been used.

Reference initials

It is very common in business for one person to dictate or write a letter and another person to type it. Reference initials show who helped prepare the letter.

Reference initials always appear at the left margin and are typed a double space below the last line of the signature block. When the writer's name has been typed in the signature block, only the typist's initials are necessary. But if only the department name appears in the signature block, both sets of initials should appear, usually in one of the following forms:

RSR/sm

RSR:sm

RSR:SM

The first set of initials is the writer's; the second is the typist's.

Sometimes the writer and the signer of a letter are two different people. In that case, at least the file copy of a letter should bear both their initials as well as those of the typist: JFS/RSR/sm (signer, writer, typist).

Enclosure notation

Enclosure notations also appear at the bottom of a letter, one or two lines below the reference initials. Some common forms:

Enclosure

Enclosures (2)

Enclosures: Resume
Photograph

Attachment

Copy notation

Copy notations may follow reference initials or enclosure notations. They indicate who is receiving carbon copies or photocopies (*cc* or *pc* or just *c*) of the letter, preferably in order of rank or in alphabetical order. Among the forms used:

c: David Wentworth

pc: Martha Littlefield

Copy to Hans Vogel

Addresses may be included, along with notations about any enclosures being sent with the copies.

Sometimes it is desirable to keep the sending of copies a secret from the person who receives the original copy of the letter. In that case, the notation *bc*, *bcc*, or *bpc* (for blind copy, blind carbon copy, or blind photocopy) appears with the name—but only on the copy, not on the original—where the copy notation would normally appear.

Mailing notation

A mailing notation, such as *Special Delivery* or *Registered Mail*, may be placed after reference initials, enclosure notations, and copy notations at the bottom of the letter; or it may be placed at the top of the letter, either above the inside address on the left-hand side or just below the date on the right-hand side. For greater visibility, mailing notations may be typed in capital letters.

Postscript

Letters may also bear postscripts, which are afterthoughts to the letter, messages that require emphasis, or personal notes. The postscript is usually the last thing on any letter and may be preceded by *P.S.*, *PS.*, *PS:*, or nothing at all. A second afterthought would be designated *P.P.S.*, meaning post postscript.

FIGURE D.3
Block Letter Format

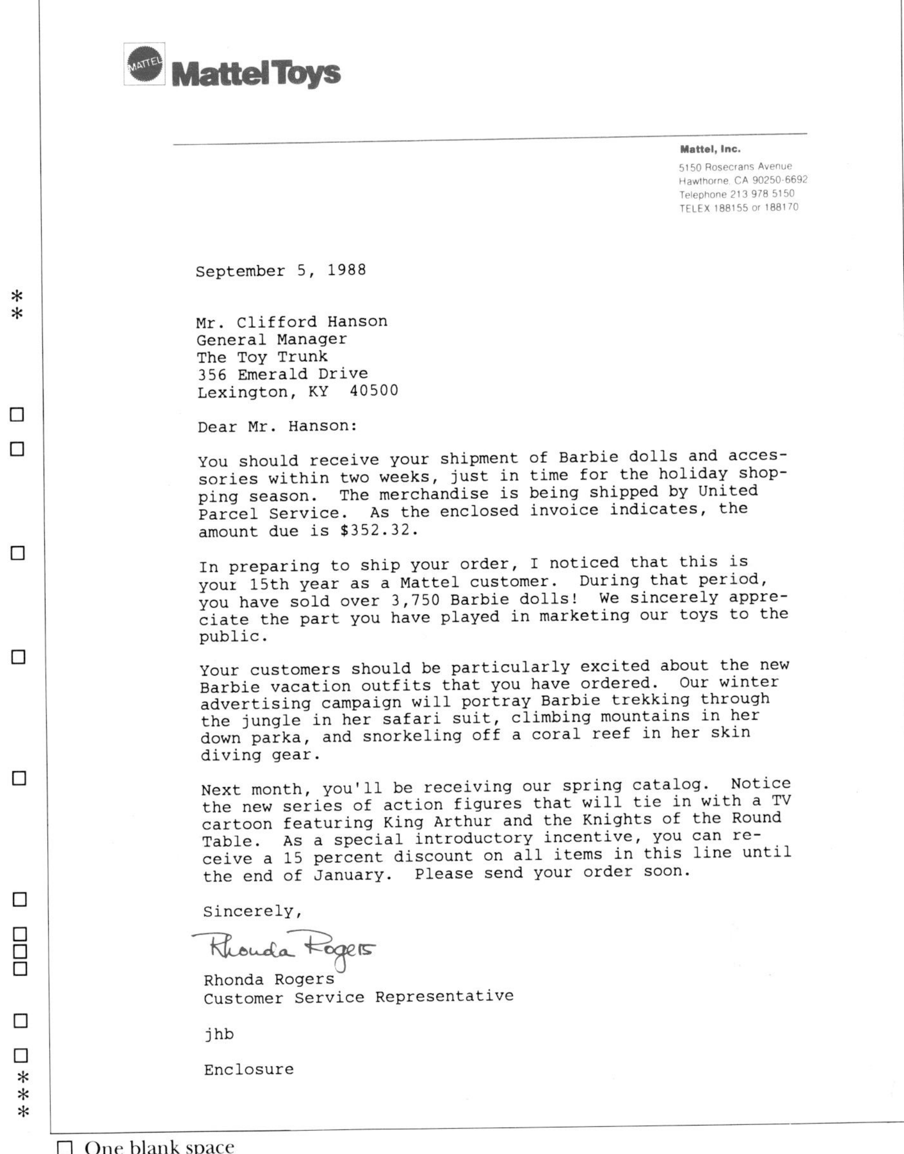

Mattel Toys

Mattel, Inc.
5150 Rosecrans Avenue
Hawthorne CA 90250-6692
Telephone 213 978 5150
TELEX 188155 or 188170

September 5, 1988

Mr. Clifford Hanson
General Manager
The Toy Trunk
356 Emerald Drive
Lexington, KY 40500

Dear Mr. Hanson:

You should receive your shipment of Barbie dolls and accessories within two weeks, just in time for the holiday shopping season. The merchandise is being shipped by United Parcel Service. As the enclosed invoice indicates, the amount due is $352.32.

In preparing to ship your order, I noticed that this is your 15th year as a Mattel customer. During that period, you have sold over 3,750 Barbie dolls! We sincerely appreciate the part you have played in marketing our toys to the public.

Your customers should be particularly excited about the new Barbie vacation outfits that you have ordered. Our winter advertising campaign will portray Barbie trekking through the jungle in her safari suit, climbing mountains in her down parka, and snorkeling off a coral reef in her skin diving gear.

Next month, you'll be receiving our spring catalog. Notice the new series of action figures that will tie in with a TV cartoon featuring King Arthur and the Knights of the Round Table. As a special introductory incentive, you can receive a 15 percent discount on all items in this line until the end of January. Please send your order soon.

Sincerely,

Rhonda Rogers

Rhonda Rogers
Customer Service Representative

jhb

Enclosure

☐ One blank space
* Variable spacing, depending on the length of the letter

Postscripts are usually avoided, because they indicate poor planning. However, they are commonly used in sales letters, not as an afterthought but as a punch line to remind the reader of a benefit in taking advantage of the offer.

LETTER FORMATS

Although the basic letter parts have remained the same for centuries, ways of arranging them do change. Sometimes a company adopts a certain format as its policy; sometimes the individual letter writer or secretary is allowed to choose the format most appropriate for a given letter or to settle on a personal preference.

Today, three major letter formats are commonly used:

- Block format
- Modified block format
- Simplified format

The major differences among these formats are the way that paragraphs are indented, the placement of letter parts, and some of the punctuation. However, the elements are always separated by at least one blank line, and the typewritten name is

FIGURE D.4
Modified Block Letter Format

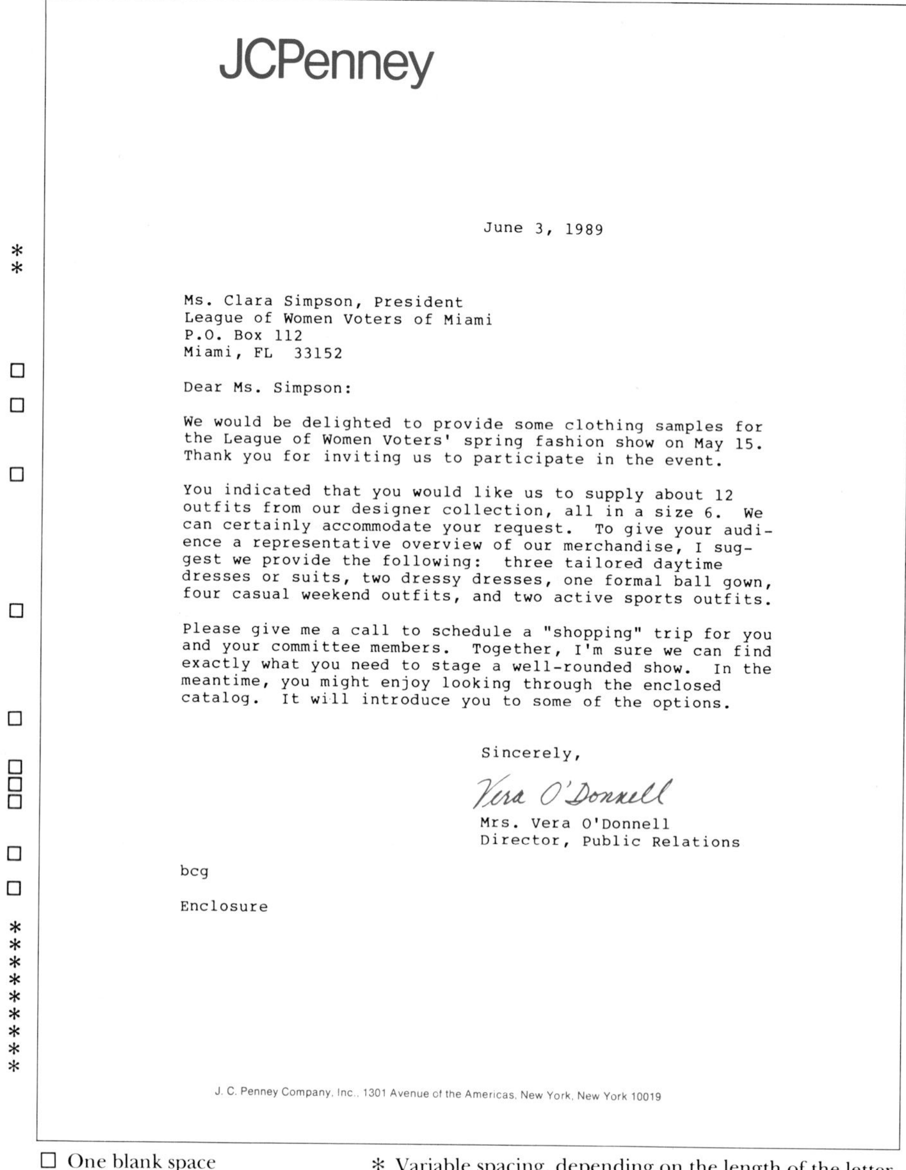

JCPenney

June 3, 1989

Ms. Clara Simpson, President
League of Women Voters of Miami
P.O. Box 112
Miami, FL 33152

Dear Ms. Simpson:

We would be delighted to provide some clothing samples for the League of Women Voters' spring fashion show on May 15. Thank you for inviting us to participate in the event.

You indicated that you would like us to supply about 12 outfits from our designer collection, all in a size 6. We can certainly accommodate your request. To give your audience a representative overview of our merchandise, I suggest we provide the following: three tailored daytime dresses or suits, two dressy dresses, one formal ball gown, four casual weekend outfits, and two active sports outfits.

Please give me a call to schedule a "shopping" trip for you and your committee members. Together, I'm sure we can find exactly what you need to stage a well-rounded show. In the meantime, you might enjoy looking through the enclosed catalog. It will introduce you to some of the options.

Sincerely,

Vera O'Donnell

Mrs. Vera O'Donnell
Director, Public Relations

bcg

Enclosure

J. C. Penney Company, Inc., 1301 Avenue of the Americas, New York, New York 10019

□ One blank space * Variable spacing, depending on the length of the letter

always separated from the line above by at least three blank lines to allow space for a signature. If paragraphs are indented, the indention is normally five spaces.

In addition to these three letter formats, letters may also be classified according to the style of punctuation they use. *Standard*, or *mixed, punctuation* uses a colon after the salutation (a comma if the letter is social or personal) and a comma after the complimentary close. *Open punctuation* uses no colon or comma after the salutation or the complimentary close. Either style of punctuation may be used with block or modified block letter formats. But because the simplified letter format has no salutation or complimentary close, the style of punctuation is irrelevant.

Block format

As you can see in Figure D.3 (p. 647), each part of a letter typed in block format begins at the left margin. The main advantage of this format is that letters can be typed quickly and efficiently.

Modified block format

This format is similar to the block format. However, as Figure D.4 shows, the date, complimentary close,

FIGURE D.5
Simplified Letter Format

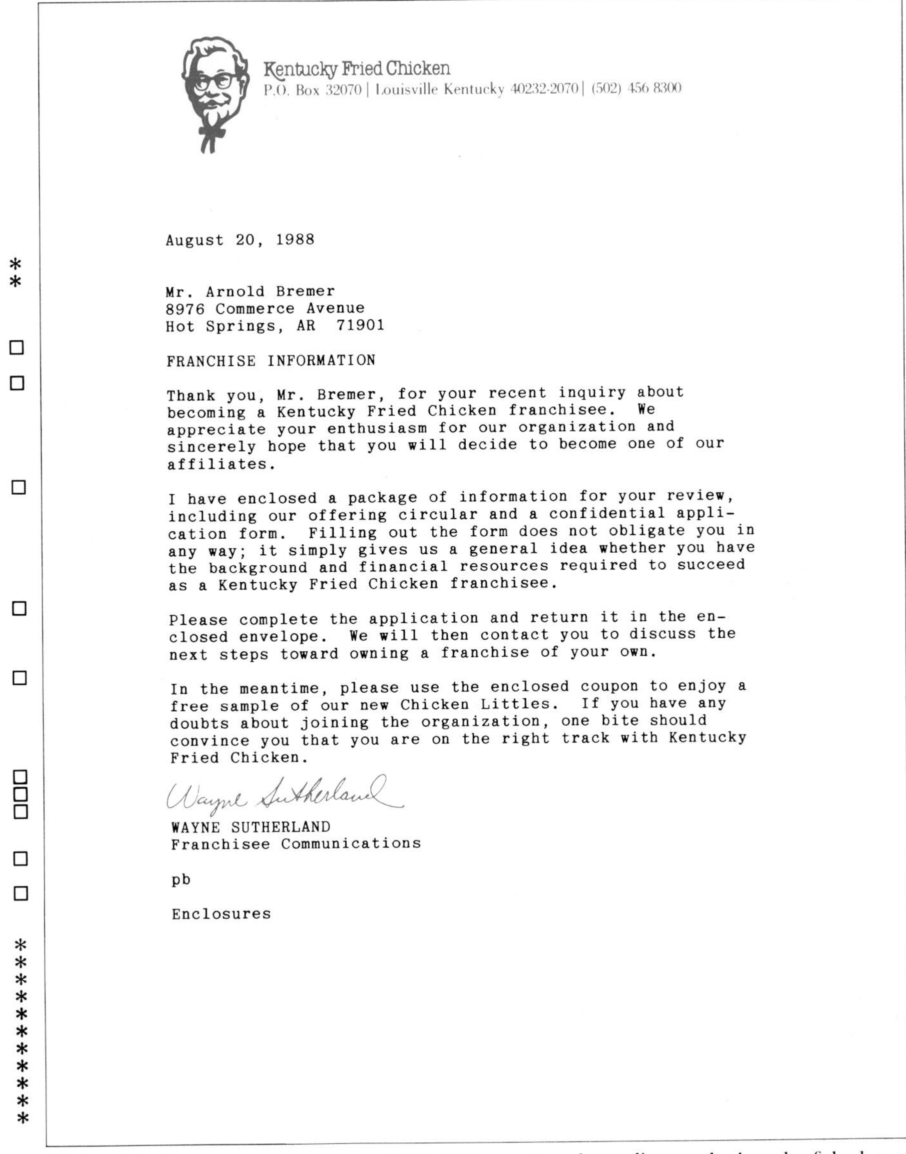

and signature block start near the center of the page. Although the letter in Figure D.4 does not show indented paragraphs, the modified block format does permit indention as an option. This format mixes speed of typing with traditional placement of some letter parts. It also looks more balanced on the page than the block format does.

Kentucky Fried Chicken
P.O. Box 32070 | Louisville Kentucky 40232-2070 | (502) 456 8300
August 20, 1988
Mr. Arnold Bremer
8976 Commerce Avenue
Hot Springs, AR 71901
FRANCHISE INFORMATION
Thank you, Mr. Bremer, for your recent inquiry about becoming a Kentucky Fried Chicken franchisee. We appreciate your enthusiasm for our organization and sincerely hope that you will decide to become one of our affiliates.
I have enclosed a package of information for your review, including our offering circular and a confidential application form. Filling out the form does not obligate you in any way; it simply gives us a general idea whether you have the background and financial resources required to succeed as a Kentucky Fried Chicken franchisee.
Please complete the application and return it in the enclosed envelope. We will then contact you to discuss the next steps toward owning a franchise of your own.
In the meantime, please use the enclosed coupon to enjoy a free sample of our new Chicken Littles. If you have any doubts about joining the organization, one bite should convince you that you are on the right track with Kentucky Fried Chicken.
Wayne Sutherland
WAYNE SUTHERLAND
Franchisee Communications
pb
Enclosures
□ One blank space
* Variable spacing, depending on the length of the letter

Simplified format

Instead of a salutation, this variation of the block format sometimes works the recipient's name into the first line or two of the body and often includes a subject line in capital letters (see Figure D.5). It also omits the complimentary close; the writer signs between the body of the letter and the typewritten name. The simplified format is convenient when you don't know the reader's name, because no salutation is required. On the other hand, some people object to this format because it seems mechanical and impersonal (a drawback that may be overcome with a warm writing style, however). Notice in Figure D.5 that the elimination of certain letter parts changes some of the spacing between lines.

ENVELOPES

The quality of the envelope is just as important to first impressions as the quality of the stationery. In fact, letterhead and envelopes should be of the same paper stock, have the same color ink, and be imprinted with the same address and logo.

Most envelopes used in business are No. 10 envelopes (9½ inches long), which are sized to contain an 8½- by 11-inch piece of paper folded in thirds. Some occasions call for a smaller, No. 6¾ envelope or for envelopes proportioned to fit special stationery. Figure D.6 shows the two most common sizes used in business.

ADDRESSING THE ENVELOPE

No matter what size an envelope is, the address should always be typed in block form—that is, with all lines aligned on the left—and the lines should be single-spaced.

The inside address on the letter and the address on the envelope should be in the same style and present the same information. The order to follow is from the smallest division to the largest:

1. Name and title of recipient
2. Name of department or subgroup
3. Name of organization
4. Name of building
5. Street address and suite number, or post office box number
6. City, state or province, and ZIP code or Postal Code
7. Name of country (if the letter is being sent abroad)

Because the post office uses optical scanners to sort mail, envelopes for quantity mailings, in particular, should be addressed in the prescribed format. Notice in Figure D.6 that everything is typed in capital letters, that no punctuation is included, and that all mailing instructions of interest to the

FIGURE D.6
Prescribed Envelope Format

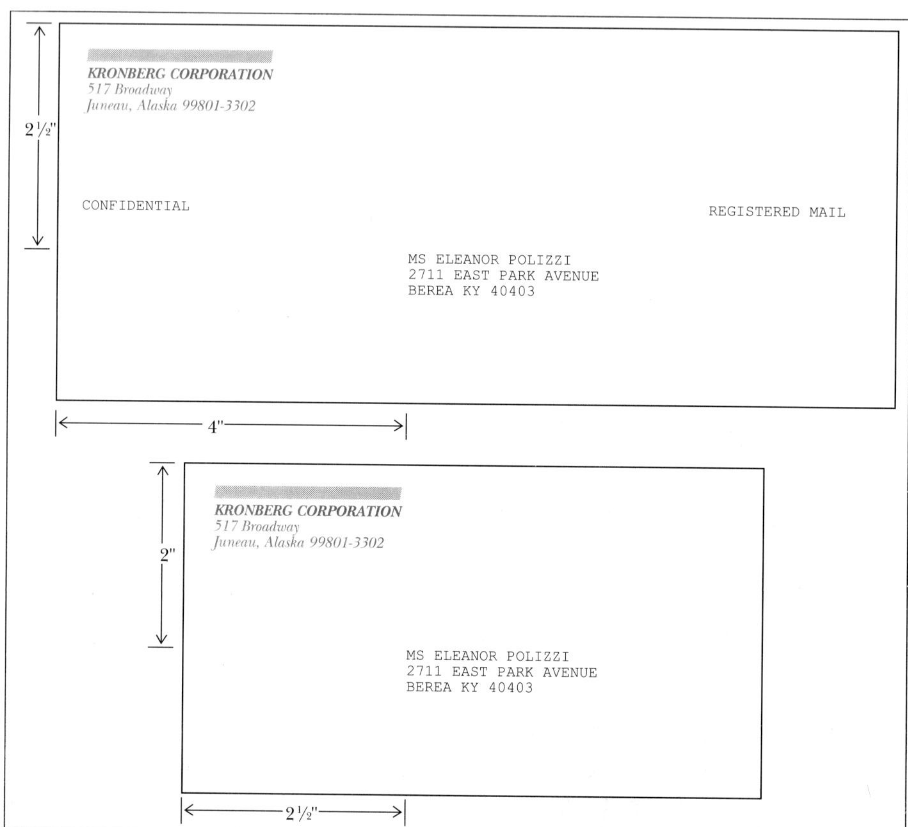

TABLE D.3 Two-Letter Mailing Abbreviations for the United States and Canada

STATE/TERRITORY/PROVINCE	ABBREVIATION	STATE/TERRITORY/PROVINCE	ABBREVIATION	STATE/TERRITORY/PROVINCE	ABBREVIATION
UNITED STATES					
Alabama	AL	Michigan	MI	Utah	UT
Alaska	AK	Minnesota	MN	Vermont	VT
Arizona	AZ	Mississippi	MS	Virginia	VA
Arkansas	AR	Missouri	MO	Virgin Islands	VI
American Samoa	AS	Montana	MT	Washington	WA
California	CA	Nebraska	NE	West Virginia	WV
Canal Zones	CZ	Nevada	NV	Wisconsin	WI
Colorado	CO	New Hampshire	NH	Wyoming	WY
Connecticut	CT	New Jersey	NJ		
Delaware	DE	New Mexico	NM		
District of Columbia	DC	New York	NY		
Florida	FL	North Carolina	NC	CANADA	
Georgia	GA	North Dakota	ND	Alberta	AB
Guam	GU	Northern Mariana Islands	CM	British Columbia	BC
Hawaii	HI	Ohio	OH	Labrador	LB
Idaho	ID	Oklahoma	OK	Manitoba	MB
Illinois	IL	Oregon	OR	New Brunswick	NB
Indiana	IN	Pennsylvania	PA	Newfoundland	NF
Iowa	IA	Puerto Rico	PR	Northwest Territories	NT
Kansas	KS	Rhode Island	RI	Nova Scotia	NS
Kentucky	KY	South Carolina	SC	Ontario	ON
Louisiana	LA	South Dakota	SD	Prince Edward Island	PE
Maine	ME	Tennessee	TN	Quebec	PQ
Maryland	MD	Trust Territories	TT	Saskatchewan	SK
Massachusetts	MA	Texas	TX	Yukon Territory	YT

post office are placed above the address area. (Canada Post requires a similar format, except that only the city is typed all in capitals and the Postal Code is placed on the line below the name of the city.) The post office scanners read addresses from the bottom up, so if a letter is to be sent to a post office box rather than a street address, the street address should appear on the line above the box number.

The U.S. Postal Service and the Canada Post Corporation have published lists of two-letter mailing abbreviations for states, provinces, and territories (see Table D.3), to be used without periods or commas. But some executives prefer that state and province names be typed out in full and that a comma be used to separate the city and state or province names. Thus the use of a comma between the name of the city and the two-letter abbreviation is an unresolved issue. Most commonly, the comma is included; sometimes, however, the comma is eliminated to conform with the post office standards.

Quantity mailings should follow post office requirements. But for letters that are not mailed in quantity, a reasonable compromise is to use traditional punctuation and upper- and lower-case letters for names and street addresses but two-letter state or province abbreviations, as shown here:

Mr. Kevin Kennedy
2107 E. Packer Drive
Amarillo, TX 79108

For all out-of-office correspondence you should use ZIP codes and Postal Codes, which have been assigned in an attempt to speed the delivery of mail. The U.S. Postal Service has divided the United States and its territories into ten zones, each represented by a digit from 0 to 9; this digit comes first in the ZIP code. The second and third digits represent smaller geographic areas within a state,

FIGURE D.7
Letter Folds for Standard-Size Letterhead

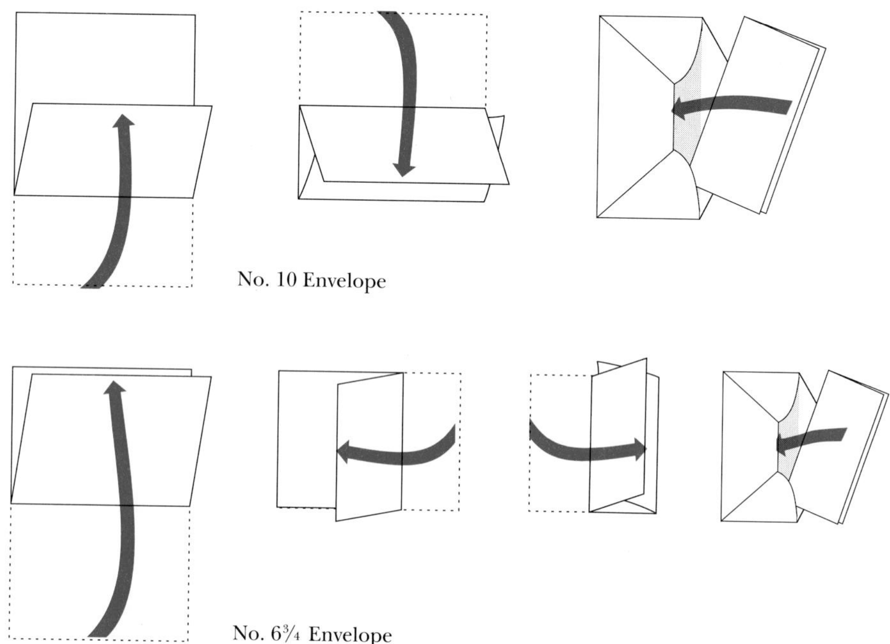

and the last two digits identify a "local delivery area." Canadian Postal Codes are alphanumeric, with a three-digit "area code" and a three-digit "local code" separated by a single space (for example, K2P 5A5). ZIP codes and Postal Codes should be separated from state and province names by two spaces. As an alternative, a Canadian Postal Code may be put on the bottom line of the address all by itself.

The U.S. Postal Service has introduced ZIP+4 codes, which add a hyphen and four more numbers to the standard ZIP codes. The first two of the new numbers may identify an area as small as a single large building, and the last two digits may identify one floor in a large building or even a specific department of an organization. The ZIP+4 codes are therefore especially useful for business correspondence. The Canada Post Corporation achieves the same result with special postal codes assigned to buildings and organizations that receive a large volume of mail.

FOLDING TO FIT

Trivial as it may seem, the way a letter is folded also contributes to the recipient's overall impression of your organization's professionalism. A standard-size piece of paper sent in a No. 10 envelope should be folded in thirds, with the bottom folded up first and then the top folded down over it (see Figure D.7); the open end should be at the top of the envelope and facing out. Smaller stationery should fit neatly into the appropriate envelope simply by folding it in half or in thirds. But when a standard-size letterhead must be sent in a No. 6¾ envelope, it should first be folded in half from top to bottom and then in thirds from side to side.

MEMOS

Interoffice memos are not distributed outside the organization and thus may not need to be typed on the best-quality paper according to all the format rules of letter writing. But they nevertheless convey important information. Clarity, careful arrangement, and neatness are therefore important. As with letters, the guidelines that have developed for formatting memos help recipients understand at a glance what they have received and from whom.

Many organizations have memo forms printed, with labeled spaces for the date, the recipient's name (or sometimes a checklist of all departments in an organization or persons in a department), the sender's name, and the subject (see Figure D.8).

FIGURE D.8
Preprinted Memo Form

MEMO

DATE: ____________________

TO: ____________________ FROM: ____________________

DEPT: ____________________ TELEPHONE: ____________________

SUBJECT: ____________________ *For your* ☐ APPROVAL ☐ INFORMATION ☐ COMMENT

Message, Comment, or Reply

If such forms do not exist, memos are typed on plain paper or sometimes on letterhead.

Memos typed on plain paper or on letterhead should always have a title like *Memo* or *Interoffice Correspondence* (all in capitals) centered at the top of the page or aligned with the left margin. The words *Date, To, From,* and *Subject*—followed by the appropriate information—should also appear at the top with a blank line between, as shown here:

MEMO

DATE:

TO:

FROM:

SUBJECT:

Sometimes the heading is organized like this:

MEMO

TO: DATE:

FROM: SUBJECT:

These four pieces of information may be arranged in almost any order, as long as they are present. Sometimes the date is typed without the heading *Date*; the subject may also be presented without the heading, but in that case it is typed in capital letters so it stands out clearly. A file or reference number, introduced by the word *File,* may also be included at the top.

If the memo is to be sent to a long list of people, the notation *See distribution list* or *See below* goes into the *To* position at the top, and the names are placed at the end of the memo. Alphabetical arrangement of such a list is usually the most diplomatic course, although high-ranking officials may deserve more prominent placement. Sometimes memos are addressed to groups of people—for example, *All Sales Representatives, Production Group, Assistant Vice Presidents.*

Courtesy titles need not be used anywhere on a memo; in fact, first initials and last names, first names, or even initials alone are sometimes sufficient. As a general rule, however, you should use a courtesy title if you would use one in face-to-face encounters with the person.

The subject line of a memo helps busy colleagues find out quickly what the memo is about. Although the subject "line" may overflow onto a second line, it is most helpful when it is short but still informative.

The body of the memo starts on the second or third line below the heading. Like the body of a letter, it is usually single-spaced. Paragraphs are separated by blank lines but may or may not be indented. Lists, important passages, and subheadings may all be handled as they are in letters. If the memo is very short, it may be double-spaced.

If the memo carries over to a second page, the second page is headed just as the second page of a letter is.

Unlike a letter, a memo does not require a complimentary close or a signature, because the writer's name is already prominent at the top. However, the memo writer may initial the memo—beside the name typed at the top or at the bottom of the memo—or even sign his or her name at the bottom, particularly if the memo deals with money or confidential matters.

All other elements—reference initials, enclosure notations, and copy notations—are treated as they would be in a letter.

Memos may be delivered by hand, by the post office (when the recipient doesn't work at the same location as the memo writer), or through interoffice mail. Interoffice mail may require the use of special reusable envelopes that have spaces for noting the recipient's name and department or room number; the name of the previous recipient is simply crossed out. If a regular envelope is used, the words *Interoffice Mail* should be typed where the stamp normally goes so it isn't accidentally stamped and mailed with the rest of the office correspondence.

Many times, informal, routine, or brief reports for distribution within a company are presented in memo form (see Chapter 12). Such report parts as a table of contents and appendixes are not included, but the body of the memo report is written just as carefully as a formal report.

TIME-SAVING MESSAGES

In the business world, time is money. So if there's a way to speed up the communication process, the organization stands to gain. Telephones and electronic mail systems are very quick indeed, as are mailgrams, telegrams, facsimile, and the like. In addition, organizations have developed these special formats that reduce the amount of time spent writing and typing short messages:

- *Memo-letters.* Printed with a heading somewhat like a memo's, although they provide a space for an inside address so the message may be sent outside the company (see Figure D.9). Folded properly, the address shows through a window in the envelope, thereby eliminating the need to address the envelope separately. Memo-letters often include a space for a reply message as well, so that the recipient will not have to type a whole new letter in response; carbonless copy sets allow sender and recipient to keep on file a copy of the entire correspondence.
- *Short-note reply technique.* Used in many organizations, even without a special form. The recipient of a memo (or sometimes a letter) simply handwrites a response on the original document, makes a copy for the files, and sends the annotated original back to the person who wrote it.
- *Letterhead postcards.* Another time-saving device, ideal for short, impersonal messages. Organizations that often deal by mail with individuals (such as mail-order companies and government agencies) frequently have postcards and sometimes letters preprinted with a list of responses; the "writer" merely checks the appropriate response(s) and slips the postcard into the mail.

The important thing to realize about these and all message formats is that they have developed over time to meet the need for clear communication and to speed responses to the needs of customers, suppliers, and associates.

REPORTS

The way a report is laid out and typed may enhance its effectiveness. Therefore, pay careful attention to the margins, headings, spacing, indention, and page numbers of a report.

MARGINS

Each prefatory part and supplementary part of a report and the first page of its text should have a two-inch top margin. All remaining pages of the report should start one inch from the top of the page. For very long reports, you may wish to start each major section or chapter on a new page; the first-level headings for each new section should then be typed two inches from the top of the page.

The side and bottom margins for all pages of a report should be at least an inch wide. If you are going to bind your report, at the left or at the top, add half an inch to the margin on the bound edge (see Figure D.10 on page 656). Because of the space taken by the binding on left-bound reports, the center point of the typed page is a quarter inch

FIGURE D.9
Memo-Letter

MEMO

TO: Green Ridge Gifts
786 Century Road
Nashua, NH 03060
USA

FROM: Whiteside Import/Export, Ltd.
601 Ronson Drive
Toronto, Ontario M9W 5Z3
CANADA

SUBJECT: Order for Royal Dorchester china completer sets

DATE: October 11, 1989

MESSAGE:

The six Wellington pattern completer sets that you ordered by telephone October 9 are on their way and should reach your shop by October 18.

The three Mayfield pattern completer sets are coming from the factory, however, and will not arrive here until October 26 or 27. That means you will get them around November 2 or 3.

Do you still want the Mayfield sets? Or would you like us to bill you for the Wellington sets only, so you can place the Mayfield order at a later date? Please add your reply below, retain the yellow copy for your records, and send us the white and pink copies.

SIGNED: Barbara Hutchins

REPLY: PLEASE SEND THE MAYFIELD SETS AS SOON AS POSSIBLE. YOU MAY BILL FOR BOTH MAYFIELD AND WELLINGTON SETS

DATE: OCT. 15, 1989

SIGNED: William L. Smith

to the right of the center of the paper. Be sure that centered headings are centered over the typed portion, not centered on the paper.

Other guidelines for typing a report can be found in the sample report near the end of Chapter 16.

HEADINGS

Headings of various levels provide visual clues to a report's organization. Figure 15.14, on p. 477, illustrates one good system for showing these levels, but many variations exist. No matter which system you use, be sure to be consistent.

SPACING AND INDENTIONS

The spacing and indention of most elements of a report are relatively easy. If your report is double-spaced (and long or technical reports probably should be, for reading ease), all paragraphs should be indented five spaces. In single-spaced reports,

FIGURE D.10
Margins for Formal Reports

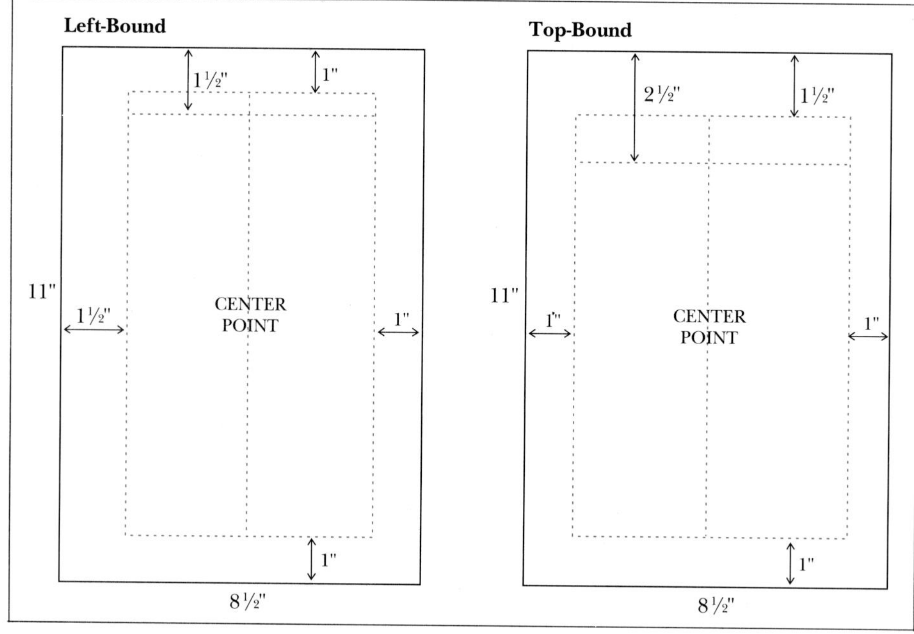

the paragraphs are usually blocked (no paragraph indentions); one blank line is left between paragraphs.

Properly spacing the material on the title page is more complicated, however. For reports that will be bound on the left, start a quarter inch to the right of center. From that point, backspace once for each two letters in the line, so that the line will appear centered once the report is bound.

To correctly place lines of type on the title page, first count the number of lines in each block of copy, including blank lines. Subtract the total from 66 (the total number of lines on an 11-inch page) to get the number of unused lines. To allocate these unused lines equally among the spaces between the blocks of copy, divide the number of unused lines by the number of blank areas (always one more than the number of blocks of copy). The result is the number of blank lines to devote to each section. The title page of the sample report in Chapter 16, which appears on page 497, shows how this procedure produces a balanced-looking page.

PAGE NUMBERS

Remember that every page in the report is counted but that not all pages have numbers shown on them. For instance, the first page of the report, normally the title page, is not numbered. But all other pages in the prefatory section are numbered with a lower-case roman numeral, beginning with ii and continuing with iii, iv, v, and so on. The unadorned (no dashes, no period) page number is centered one inch from the bottom of the page.

The first page of the text of the report carries the unadorned arabic numeral 1, centered one inch from the bottom of the page. In left-bound reports the following pages, including the supplementary parts, are numbered consecutively with unadorned arabic numerals (2, 3, and so on), placed one inch from the top edge of the page at the right-hand margin. For top-bound reports, these page numbers are typed one inch from the bottom of the page and at the center.

MEETING DOCUMENTS

Meetings are an important forum for business communication. But the success of any meeting depends on the preparation of the participants and on the follow-up measures they take to implement decisions or to seek information after the meeting. Meeting documents—agendas and minutes—aid this process by putting the meeting plan and results into permanent, written form.

FIGURE D.11
Agenda Format

AGENDA

PLANNING COMMITTEE MEETING
TUESDAY, AUGUST 21, 1989
10:00 A.M.
EXECUTIVE CONFERENCE ROOM

I. Call to Order

II. Roll Call

III. Approval of Agenda

IV. Approval of Minutes from Previous Meeting

V. Chairperson's Report

VI. Subcommittee Reports

A. New Markets

B. New Products

C. Finance

VII. Unfinished Business

VIII. New Business

A. Carson & Canfield Data

B. Reassignments

IX. Announcements

X. Adjournment

Small, informal meetings may not require a written agenda, but any meeting involving a relatively large number of people or covering a lot of ground will run more smoothly if an agenda is distributed in advance. The advantage of having a written agenda is that it helps participants prepare by telling them what will be discussed and helps keep them on track once the meeting begins.

The typical agenda format (shown in Figure D.11) may seem stiff and formal, but it helps structure a meeting so as little time as possible is wasted. At the same time, it provides opportunities for discussion, if that's what is called for.

The presentation, a special form of meeting that allows for relatively little group interaction, may also require an agenda or a detailed outline. Special visual aids, such as flip charts, help attendees grasp the message, and copies of the charts are often provided for future reference.

After a meeting, the secretary who attended prepares a set of minutes for distribution to all attendees and to any other interested parties. The minutes are prepared in much the same format as a memo or letter, except for the heading, which takes this form:

MINUTES

PLANNING COMMITTEE MEETING
MONDAY, AUGUST 21, 1989

Present: **[All invited attendees are listed here, generally by rank, in alphabetical order, or in some combination.]**
Absent:

The body of the minutes, which follows the heading, should note the times at which the meeting started and ended, all major decisions reached at the meeting, all assignments of tasks to meeting participants, and all subjects that were deferred to a later meeting. In addition, the minutes should objectively summarize important discussions, noting the names of those who contributed major points. Outlines, subheadings, and lists help organize the minutes, as in letters, memos, and reports. Additional documentation, such as tables or charts submitted by meeting participants, should be noted in the minutes and attached.

At the end of the minutes, the words *Submitted by* should be added, followed by a couple of blank lines for a signature and then the preparer's typed name and title (if appropriate). If the minutes have been prepared by one person and typed by another, the typist's initials should be added, as in the reference initials on a letter or memo.

An informal meeting may not require minutes. Attendees simply pencil their own notes onto their copies of the agenda. Follow-up is then their responsibility, although the meeting leader may need to remind them through a memo, phone call, or face-to-face talk.

QUESTIONS FOR DISCUSSION

1. What type of information does the ideal letterhead convey?
2. What are the pros and cons of justifying typed documents along the right-hand margin?
3. If you were writing a form letter to customers telling them about a product recall, what would you use as a salutation? Explain your answer.
4. What are the qualities of a good subject line in a letter or memo?
5. Which letter format do you prefer? Why?
6. In what order are the elements of an address arranged? Why is it important that they be arranged that way?
7. Besides saving time, what other advantages accrue from using time-saving message formats?
8. What is the purpose of using different levels of headings in a report?
9. When is a report double-spaced? When is it single-spaced?
10. Why is it important to distribute an agenda in advance of a meeting?

EXERCISES

1. What salutation or salutopening would you use in the following situations? Explain your answers.
   a. A letter to your local historical society requesting information on membership
   b. A letter to Samuel Harrington, Ph.D., asking him to speak about careers in anthropology during your college's annual careers week
   c. A form letter that will go to all persons who purchased cars at your dealership in the past two years, informing them about discounts on car repair and maintenance services
   d. A letter to Lee Massey, trustee of the estate of Byron Randall, regarding interest accrued on an account with your bank
   e. A congratulatory letter to Louise Hernandez of Valley High School for being awarded a scholarship by your trade association
2. Over the next week or so, collect a dozen business letters sent to you or someone you know. Classify each letter by format (block, modified block, simplified). Then scrutinize each letter for deviations from the formats recommended in this chapter.
3. Create a letter in block format that includes an addressee notation, an attention line, a subject line, reference initials, enclosure notations, and a postscript. Recast your letter into modified block format and then simplified letter format.
4. Prepare an agenda for a meeting of a group that you belong to. If you do not belong to a group, attend an open meeting of a group on campus, such as the student council, and prepare an agenda based on the meeting itself.
5. Attend a meeting of a group or organization and take notes throughout. Afterward, prepare formal minutes of the meeting.

COMPONENT CHAPTER E

DOCUMENTATION OF REPORT SOURCES

Documenting a report through source notes and bibliography is too important a task to undertake haphazardly. When you provide information about your sources, the facts and opinions that you present gain credibility. By documenting your work, you also give readers the means for checking your findings and pursuing the subject further. Finally, documentation is the accepted way to give credit to the people whose works you have drawn on.

The specific style you use to document your report may vary from the style recommended here. Not only do experts disagree on the "correct" form, but you may also find that your company or organization has adopted a form somewhat different from any suggested by the experts. Don't let this discrepancy confuse you. If your employer specifies a form, use it; the standardized form is easier for colleagues to understand. If the choice of form is left to you, however, adopt a style like one of those described here. Just be consistent within any given report, using the same order, punctuation, and so on from one source note or bibliography entry to the next.

SECONDARY SOURCES

Chapter 13 describes the difference between primary data and secondary data and tells how to gather both kinds. Most of this component chapter describes how the results of secondary research are reported in source notes and bibliographies. (Studies and surveys that you conduct as the basis for a report, however, are usually documented through descriptions of your methods and findings within the text of the report.) But before reviewing documentation formats, you must know how to get enough information. Most business research depends on secondary sources, which are traditionally stored in libraries.

A LIBRARY'S RESOURCES

"Just go to the library and look it up." That isn't as straightforward a proposition as it may sound. The *American Library Directory* lists more than 30,000 public, college, university, and special libraries in the United States and 3,000 in Canada. In addition, many companies have their own libraries. Today, the first hurdle in getting information is to figure out which library to visit or to phone with your query. Most libraries, however, harbor the same types of information sources.

Basic references

Once you've decided which library to use, you should head for the reference section. A librarian with specialized knowledge of general sources of information can direct you to the appropriate dictionaries, encyclopedias, almanacs, atlases, biographical reference books, handbooks, manuals, directories of companies and associations, and perhaps even a collection of corporations' annual reports.

FIGURE E.1 Major Reference Works

- *Biography Index:* Indexes biographical data from more than 2,400 periodicals as well as from English-language books.
- *Books in Print:* Lists more than 425,000 books in 62,000 subject categories currently available from over 6,000 U.S. publishers. Also indexes books by author and by title.
- *Business Periodicals Index:* Lists articles from about 280 business-related periodicals; companion is *Canadian Business Index.*
- *Current Biography:* Features biographical data about individuals who have achieved fame during the period covered.
- *Directory of Directories:* Indexes several thousand business, industrial, and professional directories.
- *Dun & Bradstreet, Inc., Million Dollar Directory:* Lists more than 120,000 U.S. companies by net worth. Includes names of officers and directors, goods and services, approximate sales, and number of employees.
- *Encyclopedia of Associations:* Indexes thousands of associations by broad subject category, by specific subject, by name of association, and by geographic location.
- *Moody's Manuals:* In a series of publications for specific industries—such as banks and financial institutions, public utilities, and international companies—list financial data of the sort found in corporate annual reports.
- *Reader's Guide to Periodical Literature:* Indexes articles in some 190 popular periodicals by subject and author.
- *Standard & Poor's Register of Corporations:* Indexes more than 37,000 U.S., Canadian, and major international corporations. Lists officers, products, sales volume, and number of employees.
- *Standard Periodical Directory:* Describes more than 66,000 U.S. and Canadian periodicals.
- *Statistical Abstract of the United States:* Presents U.S. economic, social, political, and industrial statistics.
- *Survey of Current Business:* Features national business statistics on construction, real estate, employment and earnings, finance, foreign trade, transportation, communication, and other key topics.
- *Thomas Register of American Manufacturers:* Presents information on thousands of U.S. manufacturers, indexed by company name and product.
- *U.S. Government Publications: Monthly Catalog:* Lists titles of more than 1,000 new U.S. government publications in each issue.
- *Who's Who in America:* Summarizes the achievements of living U.S. citizens who have gained prominence in their fields; *Canadian Who's Who* and *Who's Who in Business and Finance* are similar.
- *World Almanac and Book of Facts:* Presents statistical information about many events, people, and places. Index contains both general subject headings and specific names. Similar information is available in the *Canadian Yearbook* and the *Corpus Almanac of Canada.*
- Other indexes of articles in newspapers, magazines, and journals:

  Accountants' Index
  Applied Science and Technology Index
  Art Index
  Biological and Agricultural Index
  Computer Literature Index
  Education Index
  Engineering Index
  General Science Index
  Humanities Index
  Index Medicus
  Index to Legal Periodicals
  The New York Times Index
  Predicasts (U.S. and international editions)
  Public Affairs Information Bulletin
  Social Sciences Index
  The Wall Street Journal Index

In the absence of a knowledgeable reference librarian, consult *Reference Books: A Brief Guide* or *Business Information Sources.* Or refer to Figure E.1, which lists the major reference books used by business researchers.

Books and articles

Both books and articles provide in-depth coverage of specific topics. Although articles are more timely than books, books have a broader focus. A combination of the two often provides the best background for your report.

So many books and articles are published every year that a library must be very selective in choosing those to put on its shelves. For specialized information, therefore, a public library is not very useful. You will have better luck finding books and articles on technical subjects at college libraries (assuming the college offers courses in those subjects) and in company libraries.

All libraries provide bibliographies of the books and back issues of publications they stock. The traditional card catalog contains vast numbers of index cards organized by subject, title, and author;

a code on each card directs you to the shelf where the book or publication is located. Some libraries have converted their card catalogs to microfilm or microfiche, however, which takes up far less space. Inserted in a special viewing device, microfilm and microfiche tell you where to find what you want. Other libraries have now computerized information about their holdings.

Abstracts

One way to find out a lot relatively quickly is to consult abstracts. Instead of just supplying a categorized list of article titles, as indexes do, abstracts summarize each article's contents as well. Many fields are served by abstracts that regularly review articles in the most useful periodicals. Here are the names of a few abstracts that may prove useful:

ABS Guide to Recent Publications in the Social and Behavioral Sciences

Book Review Digest

Business Publications Index and Abstracts

Computer Abstracts

Dissertation Abstracts International

Educational Research Information Center (ERIC)

Personnel Management Abstracts

Psychological Abstracts

Sociological Abstracts

Government documents

When you want to know the exact provisions of a law, the background of a court decision, or population and business patterns, you can consult the government documents section of a library. The ins and outs of this sort of research are rather complicated, but a librarian can direct you to the information you need. Just know what government body you're interested in (for example, U.S. Congress, Ninth Court of Appeals, or Department of Labor) and some sort of identification for the specific information you need (such as the Safe Drinking Water Act of 1974, *Price* v. *Shell Oil Co.*, or 1980 Census). If you have a date and the name of a publication containing the document, so much the better.

COMPUTERIZED DATA BANKS

One resource available in some companies is a computerized data base (referred to as a management information system) containing company-generated statistics on sales and expenses, product specifications, inventory status, market research data, and perhaps reports and correspondence as well. Employees can often tap into that information directly through the computers or terminals on their desks, or they may be able to ask the data-processing department to get them a printout of the information they need.

Your access to information expands greatly when you also subscribe to one of the commercial data bases, such as Management Contents, National Newspaper Index, and Trade and Industry Index. (More and more libraries are also data base subscribers.) Their extensive files are continuously updated, thoroughly indexed, and readily accessible over standard telephone lines. See Appendix I, "Business Communicator's Resource Directory," for the names and addresses of more data bases and data base vendors.

NOTE CARDS

Many people check books containing information they need out of the library. Or they make photocopies or printouts of articles and other documents, so they can study them more carefully in their own offices. (Good researchers carefully note all necessary bibliographic information so they don't have to go back to the library or supply incomplete information in their documentation.) Photocopying is legal as long as you are not doing it to avoid buying the publication or to resell it.

Sometimes, however, you just need to note a point or two from a document; you don't need to have the whole document. In such cases, you will find note cards useful. You should make a separate note card for each fact, quotation, or general concept you want to record. Summarize in your own words unless you think specific data or quotations may be useful.

Bear in mind that the reason for using note cards is to help you remember and retrieve useful information for your report. As a practical matter, then, you should write the author's name, the book's or article's title, and other necessary bibliographic information at the top of each card. (As an alternative when you're collecting several pieces of information from each source, you might prepare a bibliography card for each, number the cards, and then use these numbers to cross reference your note cards.) It is also helpful to note at the top of the card the general subject of the material, in a simple phrase or with identifying numbers from your preliminary outline, so you can sort your notes more easily when it comes time to write your report. Figure E.2 shows a sample note card.

II-B-2a

William Hoffer, "Businesswomen: Equal but Different," Nation's Business August 1987, 46-47.

Liz Claiborne, Inc., launched by Elisabeth Claiborne Ortenberg, Arthur Ortenberg, & Leonard Boxer w/ $250,000 initial funding (p.47)

FIGURE E.2
Sample Note Card

COPYRIGHT AND FAIR USE

There is an important reason for carefully documenting the sources you consult during secondary research: Although ideas belong to no one person, the way they are expressed provides the livelihood for many scholars, consultants, and writers. To protect their interests, most countries have established copyright laws. Transgress those laws, and you or your company could be sued, not to mention embarrassed.

In addition to printed materials like books and magazines, copyright law covers audiovisual materials, many forms of artistic expression, computer programs, maps, mailing lists, even answering machine messages. However, copyright law does not protect

- Titles, names, short phrases, and slogans
- Familiar symbols or designs
- Listings of ingredients or contents
- Ideas, procedures, methods, systems, processes, concepts, principles, discoveries, or devices (although it does cover their description, explanation, or illustration)

A work is considered copyrighted as soon as it is put into fixed form, even if it has not been registered.[1]

How do you avoid plagiarism (presenting someone else's work as your own)? Here are a couple of guidelines:

- Whenever you quote another person's work, whether published or unpublished, tell where you found the statement. This rule applies to books, articles, tables, charts, diagrams, song lyrics, scripted dialogue, letters, speeches, anything that you take verbatim (word for word) from someone else. Even if you paraphrase (change the wording somewhat), you should give credit to the person who has found an effective way to express an idea.
- You do not, however, have to cite the source of general knowledge or specialized knowledge generally known among your readers. For example, everyone knows that Franklin Roosevelt was elected to the presidency of the United States four times. You can say so on your own authority, even if you have read an article in which the author said the same thing.

The way to provide credit through source notes is detailed in the rest of this component chapter.

Merely crediting the source is not always enough, however. The fair use doctrine says that you can use other people's work only as long as you do not unfairly prevent them from benefiting as a result. For example, if you reproduce someone else's copyrighted questionnaire in a report you are writing (and identify the source thoroughly), you are preventing the author from selling a copy of that questionnaire to your readers.

It is generally best to avoid relying to such a great extent on someone else's work. But when it can't be avoided, you must write to the copyright holder (usually the author or publisher) for permission to reprint. You will usually be asked to pay a fee.

Fair use is decided in the courts on a case-by-case basis. Thus you will not find any hard-and-fast rules about when you must get permission and when permission is unnecessary. In general, however, you should probably get permission to use

- More than 250 words quoted from a book
- Any reproduction of a piece of artwork (including fully reproduced charts and tables) or excerpt from commercially produced audiovisual material
- Any dialogue from a play or line from a poem or song
- Any portion of consumable materials, such as workbooks
- Multiple copies of copyrighted works that you intend to distribute widely or repeatedly, especially for noneducational purposes

You do not need permission to use materials published before 1907, news articles more than three months old, or materials originally published by the government. Nor do you need permission if you intend to use copies as the basis for "criticism, comment, news reporting, teaching (including multiple copies for one-time classroom use), scholarship, or research."[2]

In deciding whether you may use someone else's work without permission, remember that the courts (if they get involved) will consider the length of your quotation in relation to the total length of the work from which it is taken, the type of work you are taking it from, your purpose, and the effect your action has on the original author's efforts to distribute the work. If you think you may be infringing on the author's rights, write for permission and provide a credit line. In any case, be sure to acknowledge the original author's work with a source note.

SOURCE NOTES

Traditionally, source notes are presented as footnotes at the bottom of report pages. But endnotes, typed at the end of each chapter or at the end of the report (just before the bibliography), have also become quite common. Each practice has pluses and minuses. Footnotes, for instance, are harder to type within the margins of the page, but they are handier for the reader. Endnotes, on the other hand, are much easier to type, but the reader may become annoyed at having to flip to the end of the report.

The solution to the dilemma may lie, in part, in distinguishing between two types of notes. *Source notes* are used to document quotations (word-for-word selections from another work), paraphrased passages (someone else's ideas stated in your own words), and visual aids. Any information taken from another source requires a source note.

The *content note* is the second type. From time to time, you may want to supplement your main text with asides about a particular issue or event. Or you may want to provide a cross reference to another section of your report or direct the reader to a related source, explaining the connection between one thing and the other. Any note that contains more than a simple reference to another work is a content note.

Content notes are often presented at the bottom of the page they refer to, for the reader's convenience; source notes are less distracting when placed at the end. Sometimes a report presents source notes as endnotes and content notes as footnotes. As a less confusing alternative, you might consider which type of note is most common in your report, then choose whether to present them all as endnotes or all as footnotes. Regardless of the method you choose for references to text information, however, remember that both content notes and source notes pertaining to visual aids are placed on the same page as the visual aid.

MECHANICS

Notes of all varieties are single-spaced and separated from one another by a double space. In footnotes to text information, the identifying number is indented five spaces, placed on the line, and followed by a period. Two spaces are left after the period, then the entry begins (see the section containing examples). Endnotes, however, are typed beginning at the left margin. Notes referring to visual aids are handled differently too: A source note, preceded by the underlined word *Source* and a colon, is placed at the bottom of the visual aid; content notes, if any, are listed below the source note. Figure 14.1, on page 431, shows the placement of these notes on visual aids.

When using footnotes, you must plan carefully to leave enough space for the footnote at the bottom of the page and still maintain the standard margin. A line about 1½ inches long (15 spaces in pica type, 20 in elite), made with the underscore key on a typewriter, separates the footnote(s) from the text.

Reference marks

Content notes and source notes pertaining to text are signaled with superscripts, which are arabic numerals placed just above the line of type. Usually superscripts come at the end of the sentence containing the referenced statement; but occasionally, to avoid confusion, a superscript is placed right after the referenced statement:

Rising interest rates put a damper on third-quarter profits in all industries,[1] and profits did not pick up again until the Federal Reserve loosened the money supply.[2]

Notice that the first superscript in the example comes after the comma. Superscripts follow all punctuation marks except the dash, which is placed after the superscript.

Reference marks are numbered consecutively throughout the report. (In very long reports, they may be numbered consecutively throughout each chapter instead.) If a note is added or deleted, all the reference marks that follow must be changed to maintain an unbroken sequence. If you change the reference marks, be sure to renumber the notes as well.

In visual aids, content notes are marked with asterisks and other symbols (or italicized small letters if the visual aids contain many numbers).

Quotations

Quotations from secondary sources must always be followed by a reference mark. However, quotations may appear in one of two forms, depending on their length. A brief quotation (three lines or less) can be typed right into the main body of the text. Quotation marks at the beginning and end of the quotation separate the other person's words from your own.

Longer quotations must be set off as extracts. An extract begins on a new line, and both right and left margins are indented five to seven spaces. No quotation marks are needed. Although the main text may be single- or double-spaced, an extract is always single-spaced.

Often you will want to leave out some part of a quotation. Ellipsis points (or dots) are the three period-like punctuation marks that show something is missing:

> Brant has demonstrated . . . a wanton disregard for the realities of the marketplace. His days at the helm are numbered. . . . Already several lower-level executives are jockeying for position.[3]

In this example, you can see how ellipsis points are handled between sentences: A period is followed by the three dots. Notice, too, that ellipsis points are typed with spaces between them.

FORM

Many schemes have been proposed for organizing the information in source notes. But all break the information into two main parts: (1) information about the author and the work and (2) publication information. The first part includes the author's name, the title of the work, and such other identifying information as the edition and volume number. The second part includes the place of publication, the publisher, and the date of publication, followed by relevant page numbers. A few details about these elements are described in the sections that follow.

Author's name

If the author of the work is only one person, her or his name is spelled out and followed by a comma. Two authors are listed similarly, with *and* separating their names. For three authors, you should separate the names with commas and insert *and* before the last author's name. But four or more authors may be handled more concisely. After the first author's name, you simply insert *et al.* or *and others,* with no preceding comma.

Title of the work

Titles are usually typed upper- and lower-case, which means that the first and last words start with a capital letter, as do all nouns, pronouns, verbs, adverbs, and adjectives. However, prepositions, conjunctions, and articles start with a small, lower-case letter; exceptions are prepositions that are an inseparable part of an expression (as in "Looking Up New Words") and, often, prepositions and conjunctions with more than four letters.

Works often have a two-part title; a colon should be used to separate the two parts:

<u>Managerial Communications: A Strategic Approach</u>

Leave two spaces after the colon, and capitalize the letter that comes right after the colon.

Titles of books, periodicals (journals and magazines published at regular intervals), and other major works are usually printed in italics, which means that when using a typewriter you should underline them. Sometimes, however, they are typed all in capitals, with no underlining, to make the typing task easier and to make the title stand out more. Titles of articles, pamphlets, chapters in books, and the like are placed in quotation marks.

Publication information

Source notes referring to periodicals do not usually include the publisher's name and place of business (see sample source notes 7, 12, and 13), but source notes for books, pamphlets, and other hard-to-find works do. Such publication information is set off in parentheses.

In a reference to a book, the first item following the opening parenthesis is the city where the publisher is located. If the city is large and well known and if there are no other well-known cities by the same name, its name can appear alone. But if necessary for proper identification, the state, province, or country should also be indicated. Abbreviations (the standard kind, not the two-letter postal abbreviations) are used for states and provinces, but the names of countries are spelled out. A colon follows the name of the place.

The publisher's name comes after the colon, often in a shortened form. For example, Random House, Inc., can easily be identified when shortened to Random House. If you begin with shortened publishers' names, be sure to carry through with the same short forms throughout your source notes and bibliography. But use a publisher's full name if it is not well known or might be confused with some other organization.

The publication date you should use is the most recent year on the copyright notice. Ignore the dates of printing. After the date, close the parentheses.

A source note often refers to a specific page number. If so, the closing parenthesis is followed by a comma, which in turn is followed by the page number(s).

Repeated source notes

You may need to cite the same reference more than once in the course of your report. When you do, you can save time and effort by using a full citation for the first source note and a shortened form for later references to the same work. If your report has a comprehensive alphabetical bibliography, you may opt to use the short form for all your source notes, not just first citations.

The information in repeated source notes can be handled in two ways. One is a formal, traditional style; the other is informal. The formal style uses Latin abbreviations to indicate certain information; the informal style uses shortened versions of that information instead.

Here are some repeated source notes using the formal style:

4. Thomas W. Horn, Business Valuation Manual (Lancaster, Penn.: Charter Oak Press, 1985), 59-60.

5. Ibid., 130. **[refers to page 130 in the Horn book]**

6. Robert Levering, Milton Moskowitz, and Michael Katz, The 100 Best Companies to Work For in America (New York: New American Library, 1985), 9.

7. Steven Fink, "Planning for a Crisis," Nation's Business, April 1986, 49.

8. Levering, Moskowitz, and Katz, op. cit., 28. **[refers to a new page in the book cited in note 6]**

9. Fink, loc. cit. **[refers to page 49 of Fink]**

Ibid. means "in the same place"—that is, the same reference mentioned in the immediately preceding entry but perhaps a different page (indicated by giving the page number). *Op. cit.* means "in the work cited"; because it is used when at least one other reference has come between it and the original citation, you must include the last name of the author. You must also use a new page number; otherwise, you would use *loc. cit.* ("in the place cited") and omit the page number.

The informal style, which is commonly used today, avoids Latin abbreviations by adopting a shortened form for the title of a reference that is repeated. In this style, the previous list of source notes would appear as follows:

4. Thomas W. Horn, Business Valuation Manual (Lancaster, Penn.: Charter Oak Press, 1985), 59-60.

5. Horn, Valuation Manual, 130.

6. Robert Levering, Milton Moskowitz, and Michael Katz, The 100 Best Companies to Work For in America (New York: New American Library, 1985), 9.

7. Steven Fink, "Planning for a Crisis," Nation's Business, April 1986, 49.

8. Levering, Moskowitz, and Katz, 100 Best Companies, 28.

9. Fink, "Planning for a Crisis," 49.

Notice that only the author's last name, a short form of the title, and the page number are used in this style of repeated source note.

EXAMPLES

With these few general guidelines in mind, take a closer look at how the form of a source note depends on the type of reference being cited. You'll find some additional examples in the sample report in Chapter 16.

Books

In their simplest form, references to books look like source notes 4 and 6 in the preceding set of examples. Sometimes, however, you will want to note the edition of a book:

10. William Strunk, Jr., and E. B. White, The Elements of Style, 3d ed. (New York: Macmillan, 1979), 27.

When you need to cite a volume number, place *vol. 3* (or the correct number) after the title or edition number and before the publication data.

On other occasions, you'll need to use the name of an editor instead of an author:

11. Warren K. Agee, Phillip H. Ault, and Edwin Emery, eds., Perspectives on Mass Communications (New York: Harper & Row, 1982).

Periodicals

The typical periodical reference looks like source note 7 in the previous examples. The article author's name (if there is one) is handled as a book author's is, but the title of the article appears in quotation marks. Like the title of a book, the title of the magazine or journal appears either in italics (underlined) or in all capital letters.

The rest of the periodical note can be tricky, however. For popular and business magazines, you need include only the date and page number(s) after the title. (Notice that the date is inverted, unlike dates used in text.)

12. "Now Introducing Son of Greenmail," Time, 8 June 1987, 62.

But for scientific or academic journals, you should include the volume number and treat the page number as shown here:

13. John A. Quelch and Kristina Cannon-Bonventre, "Better Marketing at the Point of Purchase," Harvard Business Review 61 (November/December 1983): 165. [volume 61, page 165]

As a rule of thumb, you should use the more scholarly style of source note 13 if your report is weighted heavily toward serious research in professional journals; if popular and trade magazines dominate your references, you may stick with the simpler style that leaves out the volume number. Your guiding principle in choosing a style should be to provide the information that your readers need to find your source easily.

Newspapers

When a newspaper article does not have an author, the citation begins with the name of the article. The name of the newspaper is treated like the title of a book or periodical. Many of the best-known newspapers—for example the *New York Times, Wall Street Journal*, and *Christian Science Monitor*—cannot be mistaken for other newspapers, but many smaller newspapers are not so easily identified. If the name of the city (plus the state or province for obscure or small cities) does not appear in the title of these newspapers, you should put the place name in brackets after the title. Finally, a newspaper reference should specify the date of publication in the same way a magazine does, and it should end with a section name and/or number (if appropriate) and a page number:

14. "In the U.S. Today, 'Common Courtesy' Is Contradictory Phrase," Wall Street Journal, 12 March 1987, sec. 1, p. 1.

Public documents

Government documents and court cases are often useful in business reports, but source notes referring to them are hard to construct. As you struggle with a complex set of "authors" and publication data, remember that the goal is to provide just enough information to identify the work and to distinguish it from others.

Here are some examples of source notes for government and legal documents:

15. U.S. Department of Commerce, Task Force on Corporate Social Performance, Corporate Social Reporting in the United States and Western Europe (Washington, D.C.: Government Printing Office, July 1979), 3. **[identifies the group issuing the document as specifically as possible]**

16. U.S. Congress, House Committee on Labor, An Investigation Relating to Health Conditions of Workers Employed in the Construction and Maintenance of Public Utilities, 74th Cong., 2d sess., 16-29 January 1936.

17. Simpson v. Union Oil Co. of California, 377 U.S. 13 (U.S. Sup. Ct. 1964). **[provides the name of the case, the volume and page numbers of the law report, the name of the court that decided the case (the U.S. Supreme Court here), and the date of the decision]**

For more information on documenting specialized sources like these, consult the librarian in the documents section or one of the style books cited at the end of this component chapter.

Unpublished material

Theses, dissertations, and company reports—which are usually prepared for a limited audience of insiders—are handled similarly. The title, like an article title, is in quotation marks, and "publication" data that will help the reader find the work is put in parentheses:

18. John Peter Randolph, "Development and Implementation of Public Access Through Cable Television" (Master's thesis, San Diego State University, 1975), 73-74.

19. Frances Asakawa, "Recommendations for Replacing the Sales Fleet Based on a Comparison of Three Midsize Automobiles" (Report to Daniel Standish, Director of Sales, Midwest Marketing, Inc., 17 November 1988), 17.

This format can be used for any written source that doesn't fall into one of the other categories, such as a sales brochure or a presentation handout. Identify the author, title, and place and date of publication as completely as you can, so your readers have a way to refer to the source.

Letters, speeches, interviews, and other types of unprinted references should also be identified as completely as possible to give readers some means of checking the source. Begin with the name, title, and affiliation of the "author"; then describe the nature of the communication, the date and possibly the place, and if appropriate, the location of the files containing the document:

20. Nancy Sjoberg, President, Del Mar Associates, welcoming address at CRM Reunion, San Diego, California, 15 August 1987.

21. Victor Schoenberg, letter to Barbara Parsons, 10 February 1988.

22. Dorothy Gabbei, interview with the writer, Emporia, Kansas, 14 July 1988.

You may want to weave references to these sorts of sources into the text of your report. If you have many of them, however, you may just as well put them into notes so they won't be distracting to readers.

Electronic media

Television and radio programs, films, computer programs, and the like should also be documented. It may be more difficult for a reader to refer to these media (especially television and radio programs), but you should at least acknowledge ideas and facts borrowed from someone else.

Many times, you can weave references to electronic media into the text of your report. When you prefer to use source notes, however, your citations should look something like this:

23. Mike Wallace, "60 Minutes," CBS-TV, 26 July 1987.

24. Group Productivity (Del Mar, Calif.: CRM/McGraw-Hill Films, 1985), videotape, 22 min.

25. OverVUE Release 2.1 (Huntington Beach, Calif.: ProVUE Development Corporation, 1986), software for Macintosh computer.

The exact information you provide depends on your subject and audience and on the context of the reference. For example, in citing a film, it may be appropriate to note the scriptwriter or director. When it comes to electronic media, which are rather new sources of information for business researchers, you must use good judgment in constructing source notes.

BIBLIOGRAPHIES

The reason for including a bibliography in a report is to give your readers a complete list of the sources you consulted. In addition, a bibliography serves as a reading list for readers who want to pursue the subject of your report further. The bibliography should therefore present, in alphabetical order, every source that appears in the notes and perhaps additional references that you didn't specifically refer to in the body of your report.

If all your sources are listed in endnotes, you may find that a bibliography is unnecessary. However, the longer and more formal the report, the greater the need for a separate bibliography.

Because a bibliography may serve as a reading list, you may want to annotate each entry—that is, to comment on the subject matter and viewpoint of the source, as well as its usefulness to your readers:

> Baldrige, Letitia. Complete Guide to Executive Manners. New York: Rawson Associates, 1985. Thorough review of etiquette as it relates to the business world. Two parts: Human Relations at Work and Business Protocol; 499 pages.

Annotations may be written in either complete or incomplete sentences.

MECHANICS

Depending on the length of your report and the complexity and number of your sources, you may either put the entire bibliography at the end of the report (after the endnotes) or put relevant sections at the end of each chapter.

Another way to make a long bibliography more manageable is to subdivide it into categories (a classified bibliography), either by type of reference (such as books, articles, and unpublished material) or by subject matter (such as government regulation, market forces, and so on).

In typing the bibliography, each entry should start at the left margin, with the author's last name first. In general, the content of the entries and the order of the elements are the same as in source notes. Like source notes, bibliographic entries are single-spaced, with a double space between them. However, some of the punctuation is different, and bibliographic entries are indented after the first line (hanging indent). The sample report in Chapter 16 includes a complete bibliography.

EXAMPLES

To point up the differences between source notes and bibliographic entries, the following examples use the same works as sample source notes 10 through 19. The major content difference is that bibliographic entries do not include page numbers (unless they are articles or chapters in books), because the reader is being referred to the work as a whole.

To be sure you have all the information you need when it comes time to construct a bibliography, use this same format during your research. Many writers use a separate index card for each work consulted, which makes alphabetizing the entries relatively painless.

Books

Notice that only the first author's name is typed in reverse order and that parentheses are not used around the publication data:

> Agee, Warren K., Phillip H. Ault, and Edwin Emery, eds. Perspectives on Mass Communications. New York: Harper & Row, 1982.

> Strunk, William, Jr., and E. B. White. The Elements of Style. 3d ed. New York: Macmillan, 1979.

For more than one work by the same author, use six hyphens in place of the author's name. But repeat the name if one of the books is by a single author and another is by that author with others.

Periodicals

Use the same information that appears in the source note, but use inclusive page numbers (page numbers for the whole article):

"Now Introducing Son of Greenmail." Time, 8 June 1987, 62-63.

Quelch, John A., and Kristina Cannon-Bonventre. "Better Marketing at the Point of Purchase." Harvard Business Review 61 (November/December 1983): 162-169.

Notice the differences in punctuation between bibliographic style and source note style.

Newspapers

Again, the major difference is in the punctuation:

"In the U.S. Today, 'Common Courtesy' Is Contradictory Phrase." Wall Street Journal, 12 March 1987, sec. 1, p. 1.

Because no author is listed, this entry would be alphabetized by the first word of the article title (*In*) instead of by author's name.

Public documents

Here, in alphabetical order, are bibliographic entries for sample source notes 15, 16, and 17:

Simpson v. Union Oil Co. of California. 377 U.S. 13 (U.S. Sup. Ct. 1964).

U.S. Congress. House. Committee on Labor. An Investigation Relating to Health Conditions of Workers Employed in the Construction and Maintenance of Public Utilities. 74th Cong., 2d sess., 16-29 January 1936.

U.S. Department of Commerce. Task Force on Corporate Social Performance. Corporate Social Reporting in the United States and Western Europe. Washington, D.C.: Government Printing Office, July 1979.

Legal cases are often not listed in bibliographies, just mentioned in the text or cited in source notes.

Unpublished material

Letters, casual interviews, and telephone conversations are rarely included in bibliographies. But theses, dissertations, company reports, and formal interviews may be if the source is accessible to readers. Here are two examples, in alphabetical order:

Asakawa, Frances. "Recommendations for Replacing the Sales Fleet Based on a Comparison of Three Midsize Automobiles." Report to Daniel Standish, Director of Sales, Midwest Marketing, Inc., 17 November 1988.

Randolph, John Peter. "Development and Implementation of Public Access Through Cable Television." Master's thesis, San Diego State University, 1975.

Electronic media

Here, in alphabetical order, are bibliographic entries for sample source notes 23 through 25:

Group Productivity. Del Mar, Calif.: CRM/McGraw-Hill Films, 1985. Videotape, 22 min.

OverVUE Release 2.1. Huntington Beach, Calif.: ProVUE Development Corporation, 1986. Software for Macintosh computer.

Wallace, Mike. "60 Minutes." CBS-TV, 26 July 1987.

The information provided in these entries is sufficient to give readers a clear idea of the works you consulted, but more information may be needed if they are to easily consult the works themselves.

REFERENCE CITATIONS

Another method of documenting report sources has become popular in recent years. In an attempt to eliminate the need for separate source notes and bibliography, references are listed at the ends of chapters or at the end of the report, in much the same format as a regular bibliography. However, superscripts and source notes are eliminated.

Three popular ways of handling so-called reference citations are explained here. All three were designed to streamline the report and to eliminate some of the tedium of preparing both source notes and bibliography.

AUTHOR-DATE SYSTEM

One simple system uses regular bibliographic style for the list of references. However, if the reference list has many instances of multiple works by one author or if the report writer wants to highlight the currency of the research, the date of publication may be moved to the spot just after the author's name. This is the style recommended by the American Psychological Association.

In the text, reference to a given work is documented mainly with the author's last name and the date of publication (with a page number added when necessary):

. . . a basic understanding of the problem (Randolph 1975, 67).

An alternative is to weave the name of the author into the sentence:

According to Randolph (1975), no solution is likely to come . . .

When no author is named, use a short form of the title of the work. If the "author" is an organization, then shorten the name of the organization. In either case, make sure a reader can easily find the entry in the bibliography:

. . . with an emphasis on environmental matters (U.S. Department of Commerce 1979).

If this entry were identified as "Department of Commerce," a reader would be searching the *D*'s instead of the *U*'s for the correct reference.

In listing more than one work by the same author, rely on the year of publication to distinguish between them. A lower-case letter (*a*, *b*, and so on) after the year differentiates two works by the same author published in the same year.

KEY-NUMBER SYSTEM

The second approach numbers each bibliography entry in sequence, with an arabic numeral followed by a period. Sometimes the "bibliography" is arranged in order of the appearance of each source in the text instead of in alphabetical order.

In the text, references are documented with numbers. The first is the number assigned to the source, the second is the page number:

. . . a basic understanding of the problem (12:7).

This reference cites page 7 of item 12 in the reference list.

MLA SIMPLIFIED STYLE

Like the author-date system, the documentation system recommended by the Modern Language Association lets you weave references into the text. However, instead of using the author's name with the date of publication, MLA simplified style uses the author's name and a page reference:

. . . giving retailers some additional options (Quelch and Cannon-Bonventre 166).

Often parenthetical references can be reduced to just the page number or eliminated entirely (when you refer to the work as a whole instead of specific pages):

In her chapter on international business manners, Baldrige emphasizes Japanese customs (171-76).

Strunk and White offer a few simple guidelines that cover most writing problems.

The reference list at the end of the report (usually labeled "Works Cited" or, when uncited works are included, "Works Consulted") is arranged alphabetically in a format much like the bibliography format recommended in this component chapter. The main difference is that publication information—especially the names of months, the names of easily recognized periodicals, and portions of publishers' names—is often abbreviated:

United States Dept. of Commerce. Task Force on Corporate Social Performance. <u>Corporate Social Reporting in the United States and Western Europe.</u> Washington: GPO, 1979.

In addition, punctuation is minimized in newspaper and periodical citations:

"In the U.S. Today, 'Common Courtesy' Is Contradictory Phrase." <u>Wall Street Journal</u> 12 Mar. 1987, sec. 1: 1.

"Now Introducing Son of Greenmail." <u>Time</u> 8 June 1987: 62-63.

The goal, as in other methods of using reference citations, is to simplify the traditional documentation style.

FURTHER INFORMATION ON DOCUMENTATION

As mentioned earlier, a wide variety of style books provide information on constructing source notes and bibliographies. These are a few of the guides most commonly used:

Achtert, Walter S., and Joseph Gibaldi. *The MLA Style Manual.* New York: Modern Language Association, 1985.
Basis for the note and bibliography style used in much academic writing and recommended in many college textbooks on writing term papers; provides lots of examples in the humanities.

American Psychological Association. *Publication Manual of the American Psychological Association.* 3d ed. Washington, D.C.: American Psychological Association, 1983.
Details the author-date system, which is preferred in the social sciences and often in the natural sciences as well.

Campbell, William Giles, Stephen Vaughan Ballou, and Carole Slade. *Form and Style: Theses, Reports, Term Papers.* 6th ed. Boston: Houghton Mifflin, 1982.
Compares documentation styles recommended by the Modern Language Association and by the *Chicago Manual of Style.*

The Chicago Manual of Style. 13th ed. Chicago: University of Chicago Press, 1982.
Known as the *Chicago Manual* and widely used in the publishing industry; detailed treatment of documentation in Chapters 15, 16, and 17.

Shields, Nancy E., and Mary E. Uhle. *Where Credit Is Due: A Guide to Proper Citing of Sources—Print and Nonprint.* Metuchen, N.J.: Scarecrow Press, 1985.
Invaluable for its exhaustive treatment of troublesome sources, such as pamphlets, reports, oral messages, and electronic media.

Turabian, Kate L. *A Manual for Writers of Term Papers, Theses, and Dissertations.* 4th ed. Chicago: University of Chicago Press, 1973.
Based on the *Chicago Manual,* but smaller and limited to matters of concern to report writers; many examples of documenting nonstandard references.

U.S. Government Printing Office Style Manual. Rev. ed. Washington, D.C.: Government Printing Office, 1973.
Known as the *GPO Manual;* particularly useful for styling references to government documents.

QUESTIONS FOR DISCUSSION

1. **Why is it so important to document report sources?**
2. **What are the advantages of each of the major sources of information in libraries (basic reference works, books, articles, abstracts, and government documents)?**
3. **How can you avoid plagiarism and violation of the fair use doctrine?**
4. **When would you use endnotes, and when would you use footnotes? What are the advantages and disadvantages of each?**
5. **On visual aids, how should source notes and content notes be handled?**
6. **What are the differences between the formal and the informal style of repeated source notes?**
7. **How can you decide which information to include when citing an unusual source?**
8. **In what ways can a long bibliography be made more manageable?**
9. **What are the main ways that source notes and bibliography entries differ?**
10. **What is the purpose of using reference citations, and what is the general principle behind them?**

EXERCISES

1. **Using your library's card catalog, select three to five books that you think would be particularly useful in preparing a report on a topic of your choice. Using various guides to periodicals, locate**

three to five articles that seem like pertinent resources. Locate these sources and prepare a bibliography card for each. Prepare note cards containing information that will be of use to you in your report.

2. Write a preliminary draft of a report on the topic you chose in exercise 1, basing it on the data you recorded. Provide footnotes throughout to support the data you present.
3. Create a bibliography for the report you drafted in exercise 2.
4. For each of the following items, indicate whether you would need to write to obtain permission to use the material in your company's annual report, which will be distributed to 5,000 shareholders, employees, and customers. If permission is needed, to whom should you write?
   a. A Gahan Wilson cartoon ("I didn't know the harpoon was loaded") from the May 15, 1985, issue of the *New Yorker*
   b. A 500-word excerpt from Herman Melville's *Moby Dick*
   c. A 500-word excerpt from Ernest Hemingway's *The Old Man and the Sea*
   d. Two lines from Randy Newman's song "Sail Away"
   e. A 150-word excerpt from a syndicated newspaper article, "The Old Man at Sea World" by Art Buchwald, published June 22, 1986
   f. A pie chart from the brochure "Modern Uses for Whale Meat," published by the U.S. Food and Drug Administration
5. Revise the following bibliography to reflect the proper format and style:

   Copetas, A. Craig, "The selling of the entrepreneur," Inc., March 1986. Pp. 32-36.

   TV Basics 1986 (New York, Television Bureau of Advertising), 1986.

   Alsop, Ronald, and Stevens, Pat. 'Advertisers Go Beyond Soaps to Reach Daytime Audience,' The Wall Street Journal, 19 Sept. 1985, p. 33-34.

   Gay, V., "Pressure on TV Networks Grows." Advertising Age, April 14, 1986, 1.

   Mandese, Joe. "Is Home Video The Real Fourth Network?" Adweek, (March 18, 1986), P. 4.

   Stevenson, R. W.; and Self, V. "Bartering for TV Ad Time." The New York Times. August 1985, p. 19.

   Barr, D. S. Advertising on cable: A practical guide for users, Englewood Cliffs, N.J., Prentice-Hall, 1985.

   Bovee, Courtland L., and William F. Arens, 1989. Contemporary Advertising. 1989. 3rd Edition. Homewood, IL: Richard D. Irwin, Inc.

   Miller, M. "SPAM's Media Plan: It Might Surprise You." Marketing and Media Decisions 32 (October 1985), 69-72.

   Steinberg, Janice, Trends in Radio Advertising, 1960-1985. University of New Mexico master's thesis, 1989.

APPENDIX I

Business Communicator's Resource Directory

Sometimes you must call on outside resources for specialized help. In fact, you expand your ability to do a job when you know where to go for information that you lack. The resources listed here have been selected especially for business communicators who have not yet compiled their own list of favorite writing books, handbooks and manuals, periodicals, newsletters, computer data bases, computer software, professional associations, and career information.

BOOKS ON WRITING AND LANGUAGE

The following books are the best on writing and language and should be in almost everyone's library:

The Careful Writer, Theodore M. Bernstein, Atheneum Publishers, 115 Fifth Avenue, New York, NY 10003

The Elements of Style, William Strunk, Jr., and E. B. White, Macmillan Publishing Company, 866 Third Avenue, New York, NY 10022

How to Write, Speak and Think More Effectively, Rudolf Flesch, New American Library, 1633 Broadway, New York, NY 10019

On Writing Well, William Zinsser, Harper & Row, 10 East 53d Street, New York, NY 10022

The Technique of Clear Writing, Robert Gunning, McGraw-Hill Publishing Company, 1221 Avenue of the Americas, New York, NY 10020

Writing That Works, Kenneth Roman and Joel Raphaelson, Harper & Row, 10 East 53d Street, New York, NY 10022

HANDBOOKS AND MANUALS

The following books provide guidelines on English usage and grammar, as well as document styles and other technical details of business communication. For a list of additional handbooks and manuals, consult the subject guide to *Books in Print.*

American Usage and Style: The Consensus, Roy H. Cooperud, Van Nostrand Reinhold Company, 135 West 50th Street, New York, NY 10020

A to Z Business Office Handbook, Robert E. Swindle and Elizabeth Swindle, Prentice-Hall, Englewood Cliffs, NJ 07632

Gregg Reference Manual, William Sabin, Gregg Division, McGraw-Hill Book Company, 1221 Avenue of the Americas, New York, NY 10020

Harper Dictionary of Contemporary Usage, William Morris and Mary Morris, Harper & Row, 10 East 53d Street, New York, NY 10022

HOW: A Handbook for Office Workers, James L. Clark and Lyn R. Clark, Kent Publishing Company, 220 Park Plaza, Boston, MA 02116

Reference Manual for Office Personnel, Clifford R. House and Kathie Sigler, South-Western Publishing Company, 5101 Madison Avenue, Cincinnati, OH 45227

Wiley Office Handbook: Reference Guide, Word Finder, Word Processing Guide, Rita Kutie and Virginia Huffman, John Wiley and Sons, Inc., 605 Third Avenue, New York, NY 10158

PERIODICALS

The following scholarly journals, professional and trade publications, and newsletters are those most useful to business communicators. Write for subscription information, or look for them in any well-stocked library.

SCHOLARLY JOURNALS AND PROFESSIONAL/TRADE PUBLICATIONS

For an exhaustive list of periodicals in the United States and Canada, consult the *Standard Periodical Directory* or *Ulrich's International Periodicals Directory*.

Administrative Management, 1123 Broadway, New York, NY 10010

Communication World, International Association of Business Communicators, 870 Market Street, Suite 940, San Francisco, CA 94102

Direct Marketing, 224 Seventh Street, Garden City, NY 11530

Journal of Business Communication, Association for Business Communication, 100 English Building, 608 South Wright Street, Urbana, IL 61801

Journal of Technical Writing and Communication, 120 Marine Street, Box D, Farmingdale, NY 11753

Journal of the International Listening Association, c/o Richard L. Quianthy, Broward Community College, 1000 Coconut Creek Boulevard, Pompano Beach, FL 33066

Management Solutions, American Management Association, 135 West 50th Street, New York, NY 10020

Modern Office Technology, 1100 Superior Avenue, Cleveland, OH 44114

Office Administration and Automation: The Operations Magazine for Administrative and Systems Executives, 51 Madison Avenue, New York, NY 10010

The Professional Communicator, Women in Communication, P.O. Box 9561, Austin, TX 78766

Today's Office, 645 Stewart Avenue, Garden City, NY 11530

Words, Association of Information Systems Professionals, 1015 North York Road, Willow Grove, PA 19090

Writer's Digest, 9933 Alliance Road, Cincinnati, OH 45242

NEWSLETTERS

For an exhaustive list of newsletters, consult the *National Directory of Newsletters and Reporting Services*.

The Business Writer, 407 South Dearborn, Chicago, IL 60605

Communication Briefings, 806 Westminster Boulevard, Blackwood, NJ 08012

Communications Concepts, Box 1608, Springfield, VA 22151-0608

Decker Communications Report, 2718 Dryden Drive, Madison, WI 53704

COMPUTER DATA BASES

A great variety of information is now available via computer. For comprehensive listings of data bases, vendors, and related subjects, consult *Encyclopedia of Information Systems and Services* or *COIN: Computerized Information in Canada*.

DATA BASE VENDORS

The most popular data base vendors are listed here. Each has many data bases to choose from. Although there tends to be a great deal of overlap, different vendors frequently offer different data bases. Simplicity of access, support services, and fees also vary from one vendor to another.

BRS, BRS Information Technologies, 1200 Route 7, Latham, NY 12110

BRS After Dark (night-time, lower-rate version of BRS), 1200 Route 7, Latham, NY 12110

Dialcom, 1109 Spring Street, Suite 410, Silver Spring, MD 20910

Dialog, Dialog Information Services, 3460 Hillview Avenue, Palo Alto, CA 94304

HRIN, Human Resource Information Network, 9585 Valparaiso Court, College Park North, Indianapolis, IN 46268

Knowledge Index (night-time, lower-rate version of Dialog), Dialog Information Services, 3460 Hillview Avenue, Palo Alto, CA 94304

Mead Data Central, 9393 Springboro Pike, P.O. Box 933, Dayton, OH 45401

SDC Orbit, SDC Information Services, 2525 Colorado Avenue, Santa Monica, CA 90406

VU/TEXT, VU/TEXT Information Services, 1211 Chestnut Street, Philadelphia, PA 19107

DATA BASES

The following data bases are some of the most popular. Some can be accessed directly, and others must be accessed through a data base vendor. Each data base supplier can provide access details.

ABI/Inform, Data Courier, Inc., 620 South Fifth Street, Louisville, KY 40202

Books in Print, R. R. Bowker Company, 245 West 17th Street, New York, NY 10011

Business Dateline, ABI/Inform, 620 South Fifth Street, Louisville, KY 40202

Dissertation Abstracts Online, Dissertation Publishing, University Microfilms International, 300 North Zeeb Road, Ann Arbor, MI 48106

ERIC, National Institute of Education, 4833 Rugby Avenue, Suite 303, Bethesda, MD 20014

Legal Resource Index, Information Access Company, Inc., 11 Davis Drive, Belmont, CA 94002

Magazine Index, Information Access Company, Inc., 11 Davis Drive, Belmont, CA 94002

Management Contents, Information Access Company, Inc., 11 Davis Drive, Belmont, CA 94002

MENU—The International Software Database, The International Software Database Corporation, 1520 South College Avenue, Fort Collins, CO 80524

Microcomputer Index, Database Services, Inc., 885 North San Antonio Road, Suite H, Los Altos, CA 94022

MLA Bibliography, Modern Language Association, 62 Fifth Avenue, New York, NY 10011

National Newspaper Index, Information Access Company, Inc., 11 Davis Drive, Belmont, CA 94002

Trade and Industry Index, Information Access Company, Inc., 11 Davis Drive, Belmont, CA 94002

COMPUTER SOFTWARE

To compose on a computer, you need word-processing software and, possibly, a style checker. For a comprehensive list of directories of software, hardware, and related subjects, consult *The Directory of Directories*. For an extensive list of Canadian software, consult the *Canadian Directory of Software*.

WORD-PROCESSING SOFTWARE

These are currently the five best-selling programs:

Microsoft Word, Microsoft Corporation, 10700 Northup Way, Bellevue, WA 98004

MultiMate, Ashton-Tate, 10150 West Jefferson Boulevard, Culver City, CA 90230

PFS: Professional Write, Software Publishing Corporation, 1901 Landings Drive, Mountain View, CA 94043

Word Star, MicroPro International Corporation, 33 San Pablo Avenue, San Rafael, CA 94903

WordPerfect, Satellite Software International, 266 West Center Street, Orem, UT 84057

STYLE CHECKERS

These are the most popular programs for feedback on spelling, grammar, and punctuation:

Grammatik II, Reference Software, 330 Townsend Street, Suite 135, San Francisco, CA 94107

Improved Writing Style, Right On Programs, Distributed by Menu, 1520 South College Avenue, Fort Collins, CO 80524

Punctuation + Style, Oasis Systems, 7907 Ostrow Street, San Diego, CA 92111

Rightwriter, Decisionware, Inc., Distributed by Menu, 1520 South College Avenue, Fort Collins, CO 80524

Word Plus, Oasis Systems, 7907 Ostrow Street, San Diego, CA 92111

PROFESSIONAL ASSOCIATIONS

Associations offer many benefits, among them the opportunity to meet others with professional interests like your own and publications focusing on issues of importance to those in your field. For details on more than 1,000 associations, consult *The Encyclopedia of Associations.*

American Society for Training and Development, 1630 Duke Street, Alexandria, VA 22313

Association for Business Communication, 100 English Building, University of Illinois, 608 Wright Street, Urbana, IL 61801

Council of Communication Management, P.O. Box 3970, Grand Central Post Office, New York, NY 10163

International Association of Business Communicators, 870 Market Street, Suite 940, San Francisco, CA 94102

International Listening Association, c/o Richard L. Quianthy, Broward Community College, 1000 Coconut Creek Boulevard, Pompano Beach, FL 33066

International Communication Association, P.O. Box 9589, Austin, TX 78766

International Training in Communication, 2519 Woodland Drive, Anaheim, CA 92801

Society for Technical Communication, 815 15th Street NW, Suite 506, Washington, DC 20005

Speech Communication Association, 5105 Blacklick Road, Suite E, Annandale, VA 22003

Toastmaster's International, 2200 North Grand Avenue, Santa Ana, CA 92771

Women in Communication, P.O. Box 9561, Austin, TX 78766

World Communication Association, c/o Dr. Ronald L. Applbaum, Pan American University, Edinburg, TX 78539

CAREER INFORMATION

Whether you are just getting started in a career or plotting future career moves, you may find the following resources useful. In addition, consult *Career Employment Opportunity Directory, Dictionary of Occupational Titles, Encyclopedia of Careers and Vocational Guidance, Encyclopedia of Managerial Job Descriptions,* and *Occupational Outlook Handbook.* Many other periodicals and books are available at libraries and bookstores.

PERIODICALS

For regular updates on jobs, job hunting, and careers, look at the following:

Business Week's Guide to Careers, 1221 Avenue of the Americas, New York, NY 10020

Career Opportunity News, Garrett Park Press, Garrett Park, MD 20896

Journal of Career Planning and Employment, College Placement Council, 62 Highland Avenue, Bethlehem, PA 18017

Occupational Outlook Quarterly, Superintendent of Documents, U.S. Government Printing Office, Washington, DC 20402

BOOKS

The books listed here are currently the five best-selling books on the subject of careers and job hunting.

Beyond the Resume, Herman Holtz, McGraw-Hill Book Company, 1221 Avenue of the Americas, New York, NY 10020

The Inside Track: A Successful Job Search Method, William Lareau, New Century Publishers, 220 Old New Brunswick Road, Piscataway, NJ 08854

Jobs! What They Are . . . Where They Are . . . , Robert O. Snelling, Simon and Schuster, 1230 Avenue of the Americas, New York, NY 10020

What Color Is Your Parachute, Richard N. Bolles, Ten Speed Press, P.O. Box 7123, Berkeley, CA 94707

Winning Moves: Career Strategies for the Eighties, Thomas Chorba and Alex York, Anchor Books, 245 Park Avenue, New York, NY 10017

APPENDIX II

CORRECTION SYMBOLS

Instructors often use these short, easy-to-remember correction symbols and abbreviations when evaluating students' writing. You can use them too, to understand your instructor's suggestions and to revise and proofread your own letters, memos, and reports. Refer to Component Chapter C for additional information on grammar and usage.

CONTENT AND STYLE

Acc	Accuracy. Check to be sure information is correct.
ACE	Avoid copying examples.
ACP	Avoid copying problems.
Adp	Adapt. Tailor message to reader.
Assign	Assignment. Review instructions for assignment.
AV	Active verb. Substitute active for passive.
Awk	Awkward phrasing. Rewrite.
BC	Be consistent.
BMS	Be more sincere.
Chop	Choppy sentences. Use longer sentences and more transitional phrases.
Con	Condense. Use fewer words.
CT	Conversational tone. Avoid using overly formal language.
Depers	Depersonalize. Avoid attributing credit or blame to any individual or group.
Dev	Develop. Provide greater detail.
Dir	Direct. Use direct approach; get to the point.
Emph	Emphasize. Develop this point more fully.
EW	Explanation weak. Check logic; provide more proof.
Fl	Flattery. Avoid flattery that is insincere.
FS	Figure of speech. Find a more accurate expression.
GNF	Good news first. Use direct order.
GRF	Give reasons first. Use indirect order.
GW	Goodwill. Put more emphasis on expressions of goodwill.
H/E	Honesty/ethics. Revise statement to reflect good business practices.
Imp	Imply. Avoid being direct.
Inc	Incomplete. Develop further.
Jar	Jargon. Use less specialized language.
Log	Logic. Check development of argument.
Neg	Negative. Use more positive approach or expression.
Obv	Obvious. Do not state point in such detail.
OC	Overconfident. Adopt more humble language.
Org	Organization. Strengthen outline.
OS	Off the subject. Close with point on main subject.
Par	Parallel. Use same structure.
Plan	Follow proper organizational plan. (Refer to Chapter 4.)
Pom	Pompous. Rephrase in down-to-earth terms.
PV	Point of view. Make statement from reader's perspective rather than your own.
RB	Reader benefit. Explain what reader stands to gain.
Red	Redundant. Reduce number of times this point is made.
Ref	Reference. Cite source of information.
Rep	Repetitive. Provide different expression.
RS	Resale. Reassure reader that he or she has made a good choice.
SA	Service attitude. Put more emphasis on helping reader.

Sin	Sincerity. Avoid sounding glib or uncaring.
SL	Stereotyped language. Focus on individual's characteristics instead of on false generalizations.
Spec	Specific. Provide more specific statement.
SPM	Sales promotion material. Tell reader about related goods or services.
Stet	Let stand in original form.
Sub	Subordinate. Make this point less important.
SX	Sexist. Avoid language that contributes to gender stereotypes.
Tone	Tone needs improvement.
Trans	Transition. Show connection between points.
UAE	Use action ending. Close by stating what reader should do next.
UAS	Use appropriate salutation.
UAV	Use active voice.
Unc	Unclear. Rewrite to clarify meaning.
UPV	Use passive voice.
USS	Use shorter sentences.
V	Variety. Use different expression or sentence pattern.
W	Wordy. Eliminate unnecessary words.
WC	Word choice. Find a more appropriate word.
YA	"You" attitude. Rewrite to emphasize reader's needs.

GRAMMAR, USAGE, AND MECHANICS

Ab	Abbreviation. Avoid abbreviations in most cases; use correct abbreviation.
Adj	Adjective. Use adjective instead.
Adv	Adverb. Use adverb instead.
Agr	Agreement. Make subject and verb or noun and pronoun agree.
Ap	Appearance. Improve appearance.
Apos	Apostrophe. Check use of apostrophe.
Art	Article. Use correct article.
BC	Be consistent.
Cap	Capitalize.
Case	Use cases correctly.
CoAdj	Coordinate adjective. Insert comma between coordinate adjectives; delete comma between adjective and compound noun.
CS	Comma splice. Use period or semicolon to separate clauses.
DM	Dangling modifier. Rewrite so modifier clearly relates to subject of sentence.
Exp	Expletive. Avoid expletive beginnings, such as *it is*, *there are*, and *there is*.
F	Format. Improve layout of document.
Frag	Fragment. Rewrite as complete sentence.
Gram	Grammar. Correct grammatical error.
HCA	Hyphenate compound adjective.
lc	Lower case. Do not use capital letter.
M	Margins. Improve frame around document.
MM	Misplaced modifier. Place modifier close to word it modifies.
NRC	Nonrestrictive clause. Separate from rest of sentence with commas.
P	Punctuation. Use correct punctuation.
Par	Parallel. Use same structure.
PH	Place higher. Move document up on page.
PL	Place lower. Move document down on page.
Prep	Preposition. Use correct preposition.
RC	Restrictive clause. Remove commas that separate clause from rest of sentence.
RO	Run-on sentence. Separate two sentences with comma or semicolon.
SC	Series comma. Add comma before *and*.
SI	Split infinitive. Do not separate *to* from rest of verb.
Sp	Spelling error. Consult dictionary.
Stet	Let stand in original form.
S-V	Subject-verb pair. Do not separate with comma.
Syl	Syllabification. Divide word between syllables.
WD	Word division. Check dictionary for proper end-of-line hyphenation.
WW	Wrong word. Replace with another word.

PROOFREADING MARKS

SYMBOL	MEANING	SYMBOL USED IN CONTEXT	CORRECTED COPY
=	Align horizontally	meaningful result	meaningful result
||	Align vertically	1. Power cable 2. Keyboard	1. Power cable 2. Keyboard
(uc)	Capitalize	(uc) Do not immerse.	DO NOT IMMERSE.
≡	Capitalize	Pepsico, Inc.	PepsiCo, Inc.
⁀	Close up	self- confidence	self-confidence
ℯ	Delete	harrassment and abuse	harassment
(STET)	Restore to original	all of the (STET)	all of the
^	Insert	tirquoise shirts (u; and white)	turquoise and white shirts
^,	Insert comma	a, b and c	a, b, and c
⊙	Insert period	Harrigan et al ⊙	Harrigan et al.
/	Lower-case	TULSA, South of here	Tulsa, south of here
⊏	Move left	Attention: Security	Attention: Security
⊐	Move right	February 2, 1989	February 2, 1989
⊔	Move down	Sincerely,	Sincerely,
⊓	Move up	THIRD-QUARTER SALES	THIRD-QUARTER SALES
⊐ ⊏	Center	Awards Banquet	Awards Banquet
⌐	Start new line	Marla Fenton, Manager, Distri- bution	Marla Fenton Manager, Distribution
⊋	Run lines together	Manager, Distribution	Manager, Distribution
¶	Start paragraph	¶ The solution is easy to deter- mine but difficult to imple- ment in a competitive environ- ment like the one we now face.	The solution is easy to determine but difficult to implement in a competitive environment like the one we now face.
#	Leave space	realestate testcase	real estate test case
◯	Spell out	(COD)	cash on delivery
(SP)	Spell out	(SP) Assn. of Biochem. Engrs.	Association of Biochemical Engineers
∿	Transpose	airy, light, casaul tone	light, airy, casual tone

REFERENCES

CHAPTER 1

1. Michael Skapinker, "Xerox Searches for Life Beyond Boxes," *International Management,* June 1986, 24–30; David T. Kearns, "Xerox's Productivity Plan Is Worth Copying," *Planning Review,* May 1985, 14–16, 31. Note: For follow-up on the vignette, see Norman Deets and Richard Morano, "Xerox's Strategy for Changing Management Styles," *Management Review,* March 1986, 31–35.
2. J. Michael Sproule, *Communication Today* (Glenview, Ill.: Scott, Foresman, 1981), 327.
3. Walter D. St. John, "You Are What You Communicate," *Personnel Journal,* October 1985, 40.
4. Thomas J. Peters, "In Search of Communication Excellence," *Communication World,* February 1984, 12–15; Thomas J. Peters and Robert H. Waterman, Jr., *In Search of Excellence* (New York: Warner Books, 1984), 220.
5. "Employees Rate Company Information," *Small Business Report,* December 1986, 15.
6. Michael Brody, "Listen to Your Whistle Blower," *Fortune,* 24 November 1986, 77.
7. Sproule, *Communication Today,* 329.
8. Donald B. Simmons, "The Nature of the Organizational Grapevine," *Supervisory Management,* November 1985, 40.
9. Simmons, "Organizational Grapevine," 40.
10. Phillip V. Lewis, *Organizational Communication* (New York: Wiley, 1987), 50–53.
11. M. E. Shaw, "Some Effects of Problem Complexity upon Problem Solution Efficiency in Different Communication Nets," *Journal of Experimental Psychology* 48 (1954): 211–217.
12. David E. Sanger, "Challenger's Failure and NASA's Flaws," *New York Times,* 2 March 1986, sec. 4.
13. "Hands Off Managers Need a Firm Grasp: Four Basic Methods of Management," *San Diego Union,* 10 March 1987, C-1.
14. Douglas McGregor, *The Human Side of Enterprise* (New York: McGraw-Hill, 1960), 33–34, 47–48.
15. William G. Ouchi, *Theory Z: How American Business Can Meet the Japanese Challenge* (Reading, Mass.: Addison-Wesley, 1981), 17.
16. James C. Shaffer, "Seven Emerging Trends in Organizational Communication," *IABC Communication World,* February 1986, 18.
17. Courtland L. Bovée and William F. Arens, *Contemporary Advertising,* 2d ed. (Homewood, Ill.: Irwin, 1986), 47.
18. Sproule, *Communication Today,* 204–205.
19. Dianna Booher, "Don't Put It in Writing," *Training and Development Journal,* October 1986, 46.
20. Lynn Asinof, "Copious Copies," *Wall Street Journal,* 28 August 1986, 1.
21. John S. Fielden, Jean D. Fielden, and Ronald E. Dulek, *The Business Writing Style Book* (Englewood Cliffs, N.J.: Prentice-Hall, 1984), 7.
22. Lloyd Shearer, "Intelligence Report," *Parade,* 1 January 1983, 9.
23. "1987 Business Letter Cost Tops $9.00," *Dartnell Target Survey,* Dartnell Institute of Business Research, 1987, 1.
24. Shearer, "Intelligence Report," 9.
25. Dan Cook, "Why Gerber Is Standing Its Ground," *Business Week,* 17 March 1986, 50–51.
26. "Survey: 47% of Firms Have Crisis Communication Plans," *Marketing News,* 26 April 1985, 15.
27. Edwin McDowell, "In a Crisis, 'Tell It All and Tell It Fast,' " *New York Times,* 28 December 1986, sec. 3.
28. William J. Seiler, E. Scott Baudhuin, and L. David Schuelke, *Communication in Business and Professional Organizations* (Reading, Mass.: Addison-Wesley, 1982), 7.

CHAPTER 2

1. David Givens, "You Animal! How to Win Friends and Influence Homo Sapiens," *The Toastmaster,* August 1986, 9.
2. Mark L. Hickson III and Don W. Stacks, *Nonverbal Communication: Studies and Applications* (Dubuque, Iowa: Wm. C. Brown, 1985), 4.
3. Dale G. Leathers, "The Impact of Multichannel Message Inconsistency on Verbal and Nonverbal Decoding Behaviors," *Communication Monographs,* 46: 88–100.
4. Dale G. Leathers, *Successful Nonverbal Communication: Principles and Applications* (New York: Macmillan, 1986), 13.
5. Nido Qubein, *Communicate Like a Pro* (New York: Berkley Books, 1986), 97.
6. Leathers, *Successful Nonverbal Communication,* 19.
7. Leathers, *Successful Nonverbal Communication,* 102.
8. Jill Neimark, "Reach Out And . . .," *Savvy,* February 1985, 42.
9. Stuart Berg Flexner, "From 'Gadzooks' to 'Nice,' the Language Keeps Changing," *U.S. News & World Report,* 18 February 1985, 59.
10. Phillip Morgan and H. Kent Baker, "Building a Professional Image: Improving Listening Behavior," *Supervisory Management,* November 1985, 35, 36.
11. Irwin Ross, "Corporations Take Aim at Illiteracy," *Fortune,* 29 September 1986, 49.
12. Janet Maker and Minnette Lenier, *College Reading* (Belmont, Calif.: Wadsworth, 1982), 1.

CHAPTER 3

1. Mary Munter, *Guide to Managerial Communication* (Englewood Cliffs, N.J.: Prentice-Hall, 1982), 9.
2. William P. Dommermuth, *Promotion: Analysis, Creativity, and Strategy* (Boston: Kent Publishing, 1982), 282.
3. Morgan W. McCall, Jr., and Robert L. Hannon, *Studies of Managerial Work: Results and Methods,* Technical Report no. 9 (Greensboro, N.C.: Center for Creative Leadership, 1978), 6–10.
4. Thomas J. Peters and Robert H. Waterman, Jr., *In Search of Excellence: Lessons from America's Best-Run Companies* (New York: Harper & Row, 1982), 150–151.
5. Ernest Thompson, "Some Effects of Message Structure on Listener's Comprehension," *Speech Monographs* 34 (March 1967): 51–57.

CHAPTER 4

1. Carol S. Mull, "Orchestrate Your Ideas," *The Toastmaster,* February 1987, 19.
2. Bruce B. MacMillan, "How to Write to Top Management," *Business Marketing,* March 1985, 138.
3. MacMillan, "How to Write to Top Management," 138.
4. Based on the Pyramid Model developed by Barbara Minto of McKinsey & Company, management consultants.
5. Roger P. Wilcox, *Communication at Work: Writing and Speaking* (Boston: Houghton Mifflin, 1977), 30.
6. John S. Fielden, Jean D. Fielden, and Ronald E. Dulek, *The Business Writing Style Book* (Englewood Cliffs, N.J.: Prentice-Hall, 1984), 7.

CHAPTER 5

1. Robert Half International, "Message Lost in Some Memos," *USA Today,* 25 March 1987, 1A.
2. Alinda Drury, "Evaluating Readability," *IEEE Transactions on Professional Communication,* vol. PC 28 (December 1985), 11.
3. Portions of this section are adapted from Courtland L. Bovée, *Techniques of Writing Business Letters, Memos, and Reports* (Sherman Oaks, Calif.: Banner Books International, 1978), 13–90.
4. Edward Tenner, "Cognitive Input Device in the Form of a Randomly Accessible Instantaneous-Read-Out Batch-Processed Pigment-Saturated Laminous-Cellulose Hard-Copy Output Matrix," *Discover,* May 1986, 61.
5. Judy E. Pickens, "Terms of Equality: A Guide to Bias-Free Language," *Personnel Journal,* August 1985, 24.
6. Robert W. Kent, ed., *Money Talks* (New York: Pocket Books, 1985), 283.
7. Drury, "Evaluating Readability," 12.

Exercise notes

1. Milton Moskowitz, Michael Katz, and Robert Levering, eds., *Everybody's Business: An Almanac* (San Francisco: Harper & Row, 1980), 131.
2. Randolph H. Hudson, Gertrude M. McGuire, and Bernard J. Selzler, *Business Writing: Concepts and Applications* (Los Angeles: Roxbury, 1983), 27.

CHAPTER 6

Case notes

1. Adapted from Wendy Lowe, "Sales Are Roaring at Jungle Stores," *USA Today,* 22 May 1986, 1B; Henry Weil, "Keeping Up with the (Indiana) Joneses," *Savvy,* February 1986, 43–46; *Banana Republic Travel & Safari Clothing Co. Catalog,* no. 30, Holiday 1986, 51.
2. Adapted from Steven Greenhouse, "The Big Bucks in Knees and Elbows," *New York Times,* 1 February 1987, sec. 3.
3. Adapted from Albert Scardino, "Marketing Real Estate with Art: Luring Tourists as Well as Tenants," *New York Times,* 1 February 1987, sec. 3.
4. Adapted from Pat Guy, "Merrill Lynch Is Back to Running Bull in Ads," *USA Today,* 12 August 1986, 1B.
5. "Fuller Brushes Up Its Image, Product Line," *USA Today,* 2 September 1986, 2B.

CHAPTER 7

1. Susan Stobaugh, "Watch Your Language," *Inc.,* May 1985, 156.

Case notes

1. Adapted from Barbara Basler, "A Sleuth's Newest Venture," *New York Times,* 26 October 1986, sec. 3.
2. Adapted from Susan Spillman, "What Has 31 Flavors and a New Image?" *USA Today,* 20 August 1986, 1B.
3. Adapted from *L. L. Bean Catalog, Christmas 1986,* 20–21.
4. Adapted from George Russell, "Where the Customer Is Still King," *Time,* 2 February 1987, 56.
5. Adapted from Fern Schumer Chapman, "Executive Guilt: Who's Taking Care of the Children?" *Fortune,* 16 February 1987, 30–37.
6. Adapted from William Dunn, "Sabbaticals Aim to Cool Job Burnout," *USA Today,* 25 July 1986, 1, 2B.
7. Adapted from Mike Tharp, "Nike Recoups Laurels in the Sportswear Market," *Wall Street Journal,* 19 March 1986, 6.

CHAPTER 8

Case notes

1. Adapted from "Ford Recalls 1,230 Taurus, Sable Cars That May Be Unsafe," *Wall Street Journal,* 31 October 1986, 16.
2. Adapted from Lillian Vernon catalog, vol. 612.
3. Adapted from Trish Hall, "Wendy's Is Seen Dropping Pepsi for Coca-Cola," *Wall Street Journal,* 15 October 1986, 12; "Wendy's Sues PepsiCo over Soft Drinks; Is Countersued," *San Diego Union,* 14 November 1986, C-1; Robert L. Barney, "An Open Letter from Robert L. Barney, Chairman of the Board, Wendy's International," *Wall Street Journal,* 16 October 1986, 29.
4. Adapted from Scott McMurray, "United Airlines Is Dismissing 1,016 Workers," *Wall Street Journal,* 2 February 1987, 4; "Air Fare War Costs United 1,016 Jobs," *San Diego Union,* 31 January 1987, E-1.
5. Adapted from Eileen White, "Northrup's Failure to Sell F-20 Casts Pall on Bid for Contractors to Bear More Risks," *Wall Street Journal,* 3 November 1986, 2; Robert S. Greenberger and Roy J. Harris, Jr., "Northrup, Lockheed to Build Prototypes of Jet; General Dynamics Gets F-16 Job," *Wall Street Journal,* 3 November 1986, 2.
6. Adapted from Lisa Belkin, "Redesigning Liz Claiborne's Empire," *New York Times,* 4 May 1986, sec. 3.

CHAPTER 9

1. Abraham H. Maslow, *Motivation and Personality* (New York: Harper & Row, 1954), 12, 19.
2. Jeanette W. Gilsdorf, "Executives' and Academics' Perceptions on the Need for Instruction in Written Persuasion," *Journal of Business Communication* 23 (Fall 1986): 67.
3. Direct Mail Advertising Association, New York, 1987.
4. William North Jayme, quoted in Albert Haas, Jr., "How to Sell Almost Anything by Direct Mail," *Across the Board,* November 1986, 50.

Case notes

1. Adapted from Patrick Wallace, "Golf Course Builders Play on Popular Sport to Sell Costly Housing," *Wall Street Journal,* 29 October 1986.
2. Adapted from Janice Castro, "Battling Drugs on the Job," *Time,* 27 January 1986, 43; Janice Castro, "Battling the Enemy Within," *Time,* 17 March 1986, 52–61.
3. Adapted from Karl Schoenberger, "In Skies over Tokyo, Kodak and Fuji Fight Battle of the Blimps," *Wall Street Journal,* 30 December 1986, 1.
4. Adapted from Lisa Belkin, "Pushing Fashion in the Fast Lane," *New York Times,* 9 November 1986, sec. 3.
5. Adapted from Selwyn Feinstein, " 'Short-Time' Pay Fails to Catch On as a Way to Hold Down Layoffs," *Wall Street Journal,* 3 February 1987, 35.
6. Adapted from Clifford Krauss, "Is Hartz Mountain Breeding Parakeets on Idyllic St. Lucia?" *Wall Street Journal,* 24 March 1986, 1.
7. Adapted from Ronald Alsop, "Grand Openings Aren't Just Ribbon Cutting Affairs Any Longer," *Wall Street Journal,* 30 October 1986, 35.
8. Adapted from Steve Weiner, "Sears' Move to Cover Uncollectible Debt May Signal Trouble for U.S. Economy," *Wall Street Journal,* 22 October 1986, 4.

CHAPTER 10

1. Sewell Whitney, "On-Line Resumes Put Job Candidates in Line," *Advertising Age,* 7 March 1985, 48.
2. Joseph E. McKendrick, "Managers Talk About Careers," *Management World,* September/October 1986, 18–19.
3. Robert J. Gerberg, *Robert Gerberg's Job Changing System,* summarized by Macmillan Book Clubs, Inc., in the "Macmillan Executive Summary Program," April 1987, 4.
4. Adapted from Burdette E. Bostwick, *How to Find the Job You've Always Wanted* (New York: Wiley, 1982), 69–70.

CHAPTER 11

1. Sylvia Porter, "Your Money: How to Prepare for Job Interviews," *San Francisco Chronicle,* 3 November 1981, 54.
2. Harry Bacas, "How Companies Avoid Mistakes in Hiring," *Nation's Business,* June 1985, 34, 36.
3. Robert Gifford, Cheuk Fan Ng, and Margaret Wilkinson, "Nonverbal Cues in the Employment Interview: Links Between Applicant Qualities and Interviewer Judgments," *Journal of Applied Psychology* 70, no. 4 (1985): 729.
4. Dale G. Leathers, *Successful Nonverbal Communication* (New York: Macmillan, 1986), 225.
5. Shirley J. Shepherd, "How to Get That Job in 60 Minutes or Less," *Working Woman,* March 1986, 119.
6. Shepherd, "How to Get That Job," 118.
7. Marilyn Moats Kennedy, "Are You Getting Paid What You're Worth?" *New Woman,* November 1984, 110.

CHAPTER 12

1. Roger P. Wilcox, *Communication at Work: Writing and Speaking* (Boston: Houghton Mifflin, 1977), 49–51.

CHAPTER 13

1. Rudolf Flesch, "How to Say It with Statistics," *Marketing Communications,* 8 December 1950, 23–24.
2. Flesch, "How to Say It with Statistics," 23–24.

CHAPTER 14

1. Alexander Petofi, "The Graphic Revolution in Computers," *The Futurist,* June 1985, 30.
2. Maureen Jones, "Getting Good Graphs," *PC Magazine,* 23 July 1985, 217.
3. Christopher O'Malley, "Graphics," *Personal Computing,* October 1986, 105.
4. Abigail Reifsnyder and Roxane Farmanfarmaian, "Saying It with Pictures," *Working Woman,* April 1986, 98, 102.
5. O'Malley, "Graphics," 110.

CHAPTER 16

Case notes

1. Adapted from Nicholas E. Lefferts, "What's New in the Pet Business," *New York Times*, 28 July 1985, sec. 3.
2. Adapted from Justine Kaplan, "What's New in Cruises," *New York Times*, 3 August 1986, sec. 3.
3. Adapted from N. R. Kleinfield, "The Ever-Fatter Business of Thinness," *New York Times*, 7 September 1986, sec. 3.
4. Adapted from David Tuller, "What's New in the Tennis Business," *New York Times*, 7 June 1987, sec. 3.

CHAPTER 17

1. J. Michael Sproule, *Communication Today* (Glenview, Ill.: Scott, Foresman, 1981), 167–170.
2. James J. Floyd, *Listening: A Practical Approach* (Glenview, Ill.: Scott, Foresman, 1985), 5–6.
3. Phillip Morgan and H. Kent Baker, "Building a Professional Image: Improving Listening Behavior," *Supervisory Management*, November 1985, 35–36.
4. Andrew D. Wolvin and Carolyn Gwynn Coakley, *Listening* (Dubuque, Iowa: Wm. C. Brown, 1985), 6.
5. Lyman K. Steil, Larry L. Barker, and Kittie W. Watson, *Effective Listening: Key to Your Success* (Reading, Mass.: Addison-Wesley, 1983), 21–22.
6. Sproule, *Communication Today*, 69.
7. Sproule, *Communication Today*, 55–70.
8. Janis Graham, "Sharpen Your Negotiating Skills," *Sylvia Porter's Personal Finance*, December 1985, 54–58.
9. Jesse S. Nirenberg, *Getting Through to People* (Englewood Cliffs, N.J.: Prentice-Hall, 1973), 134–142.
10. Andrew S. Grove, "How (and Why) to Run a Meeting," *Fortune*, 11 July 1983, 132.
11. B. Aubrey Fisher, *Small Group Decision Making: Communication and the Group Process*, 2d ed. (New York: McGraw-Hill, 1980), 145–149.
12. "Successful Meetings: Management's Ongoing Challenge," *Small Business Report*, January 1987, 77.

CHAPTER 18

1. H. C. Kelman and C. I. Hovland, " 'Reinstatement' of the Communicator in Delayed Measurement of Opinion Change," *Journal of Abnormal and Social Psychology* 48 (1953): 327–335.
2. Walter Kiechel III, "How to Give a Speech," *Fortune*, 8 June 1987, 180.
3. *Communication and Leadership Program* (Santa Ana, Calif.: Toastmasters International, 1980), 44 and 45.
4. *How to Prepare and Use Effective Visual Aids*, Info-Line series, Elizabeth Lean, managing ed. (Washington, D.C.: American Society for Training and Development, October 1984), 2.
5. Judy Linscott, "Getting On and Off the Podium," *Savvy*, October 1985, 44.
6. Sandra Moyer, "Braving No Woman's Land," *The Toastmaster*, August 1986, 13.
7. Robert L. Montgomery, "Listening on Your Feet," *The Toastmaster*, July 1987, 14–15.

Component Chapter A

1. Mariah E. de Forest, "Offshore Across the Border," *Manufacturing Systems*, February 1987, 37.
2. Vern Terpstra, *The Cultural Environment of International Business* (Cincinnati: South-Western, 1979), 19.
3. Retha H. Kilpatrick, "International Business Communication Practices," *Journal of Business Communication*, 21 (Fall 1984): 36.
4. Kathleen K. Reardon, "It's the Thought That Counts," *Harvard Business Review*, September/October 1984, 141.
5. "Pakistan: A Congenial Business Climate," *Nation's Business*, July 1986, 50.
6. Herschel Peak, "Conquering Cross-Cultural Challenges," *Business Marketing*, October 1985, 139.
7. Edward T. Hall, "The Silent Language of Overseas Business," in *Dimensions of Communication*, ed. Lee Richardson (New York: Appleton-Century-Crofts, 1969), 442.
8. Sharon Ruhly, *Intercultural Communication*, 2d ed., MODCOM (Modules in Speech Communication) (Chicago: Science Research Associates, 1982), 14.
9. Ruhly, *Intercultural Communication*, 28.

Component Chapter B

1. David J. Rachman and Michael H. Mescon, "Computers and Information Technology," *Business Today*, 5th ed. (New York: Random House, 1987), 381.
2. International Data Corporation, "Office Systems for the Eighties: Automation and the Bottom Line," White Paper to Management, *Fortune*, 3 October 1983, 142.
3. "Telecommuting," *Openline: For the Pacific Bell Customer*, August 1986, 1–2.

Component Chapter D

1. Patricia A. Dreyfus, "Paper That's Letter Perfect," *Money*, May 1985, 184.

Component Chapter E

1. Dorothy Geisler, "How to Avoid Copyright Lawsuits," *IABC Communication World*, June 1984, 34–37.
2. Robert W. Goddard, "The Crime of Copying," *Management World*, July/August 1986, 20–22.

ACKNOWLEDGMENTS

TEXT, FIGURES, AND TABLES

6–7 "Eight Ways Communication Skills Can Help Advance Your Career": Adapted from Henry H. Beam, "Good Writing: An Underrated Executive Skill," *Human Resource Management,* Spring 1981, 2–7. **9** (Figure 1.1): Adapted from David J. Rachman and Michael H. Mescon, *Business Today* (Copyright © 1987, Random House, Inc.), 127. **10** (Table 1.1): "Lack of Communication," *The Wall Street Journal,* 2 July 1985, 29. Reprinted by permission of *The Wall Street Journal,* © Dow Jones & Company, Inc. 1985. All Rights Reserved. **13** (Figure 1.3): Adapted from "Who Told You That?" *The Wall Street Journal,* 23 May 1985, 33. Reprinted by permission of *The Wall Street Journal,* © Dow Jones & Company, Inc. 1985. All Rights Reserved. **13** (Figure 1.4): Adapted from David J. Rachman and Michael H. Mescon, *Business Today* (New York: © Random House, Inc.) 1987, 127. **15** (Figure 1.5): From *Organizational Communication,* Phillip V. Lewis. Copyright © 1987, 5. Reprinted by permission of John Wiley & Sons, Inc. **15** (Table 1.3): Adapted from *Organizational Communication,* Phillip V. Lewis. Copyright © 1987, 53. Reprinted by permission of John Wiley & Sons, Inc. And from *The Administrator's Job: Issues and Dilemmas* by R. K. Ready. © McGraw-Hill, Inc. As adapted by Allan D. Frank in *Communicating on the Job,* Scott, Foresman & Company, 1982, 27. **24–25** "Check Your Communication Skills": Adapted from *Listening: The Forgotten Skill,* Madelyn Burley-Allen. Copyright © 1982, 12–15. Reprinted by permission of John Wiley & Sons, Inc. **33** "How Does Your Nonverbal Credibility Measure Up?": Adapted from Dale G. Leathers, *Successful Nonverbal Communication: Principles and Applications,* 161–163. Reprinted with permission of Macmillan Publishing Company from *Successful Nonverbal Communication: Principles and Applications* by Dale G. Leathers. Copyright © 1986 by Dale G. Leathers. **37** (Figure 2.1): Adapted from Phillip Morgan and H. Kent Baker, "Building a Professional Image: Improving Listening Behavior." Reprinted, by permission of the publisher, from *Supervisory Management,* November 1985, 34. © 1985 American Management Association, New York. All rights reserved. **44–45** "Communication Barriers to Watch For and Avoid": Adapted from C. Glenn Pearce, Ross Figgins, and Steve F. Golen, *Principles of Business Communication: Theory, Application, and Technology,* 520–538. Copyright 1984, John Wiley & Sons, Inc. **45** (Figure 2.3): From *Communicating on the Job,* Allen D. Frank. Copyright © 1982 by Scott, Foresman and Company, 20. Reprinted by permission. **68–69** "Ten Tips for Communicating Successfully with a Global Audience": Adapted from Lennie Copeland and Lewis Griggs, *Going International: How to Make Friends and Deal Effectively in the Global Marketplace,* 2d ed., 102–116. Copyright © 1985, Random House, Inc. **81, 82** (Figures 3.2, 3.4): Courtesy of General Mills, Inc. **104–105** "How Personal Computers Aid the Composition Process": Adapted from Ronald J. Donavan, "Writing Made Easier with Personal Computers," *Writer's Digest,* September 1982, 33–34; Michael O. Boccia, "How to Write Better Using Your Computer," *Systems/3X World,* May 1986, 40, 42, 46; Peter Bates, "How to Turn Your Writing into Communication," *Personal Computing,* October 1984, 84–85, 87–88, 91, 93; Steve Ditlea, "How Wordsmiths Write Smarter," *Personal Computing,* March 1986, 58, 61, 63, 65. **108–109** "Tailor Your Writing Style to Get the Results You Want": Adapted from the book *The Business Writing Style Book* by John S. Fielden, Jean D. Fielden, Ronald E. Dulek, © 1984, 32–36. Used by permission of the publisher, Prentice-Hall, Inc., Englewood Cliffs, N.J. **124–125** Adapted from "Fifteen Secrets of Successful Business Writers": *Feel Free to Write: A Guide for Business and Professional People,* John Keena. Copyright © 1982, 41–43. Reprinted by permission of John Wiley & Sons, Inc.; adapted from *Writing That Works,* by Walter E. Olie, Charles T. Brusaw, and Gerald J. Alfred, 31–34. Copyright 1980 by St. Martin's Press, Inc. and used with permission. **126** (Figure 5.2): Adapted from Robert Gunning, *The Technique of Clear Writing* (New York: McGraw-Hill, 1973), 38–39. Used by permission of the copyright owner, Gunning-Mueller Institute, Inc., Santa Barbara, California. Fog Index is a service mark of Gunning-Mueller. **127** "How to Proofread Effectively": Adapted from Philip C. Kolin, *Successful Writing at Work,* 2d ed., 102. Used with permission of D. C. Heath and Company; Dennis Hensley, "A Way with Words: Proofreading Can Save Cash and Careers," *Dalla Magazine,* May 1986, 57–58. Reprinted with permission. **137** "Plain-English Laws": Adapted from Randolph H. Hudson, Gertrude M. McGuire, and Bernard J. Selzler, *Business Writing: Concepts and Applications* (Los Angeles: Roxbury, 1983), 79–82; Alan Siegel, "The Plain English Revolution," *Across the Board,* February 1981, 22. **160–161** "Pitfalls of Writing International Business Letters": Adapted from Lennie Copeland and Lewis Griggs, *Going International: How to Make Friends and Deal Effectively in the Global Marketplace,* 2d ed., 24–27. Copyright © 1985, Random House, Inc. **172–173** "Writing Claim Letters That Get Results": Adapted from David Klein, "How to Write a Complaint Letter," *Fifty Plus,* June 1979, 30; and adapted from *How to Write a Wrong: Complain Effectively and Get Results* (Washington, D.C.: American Association of Retired Persons and Federal Trade Commission, 1983). Reprinted by permission of AARP. **198** "Turn Complaining Customers into Company Boosters": Adapted from "So You Think You Have Unhappy Customers?" *The Reporter,* San Diego Better Business Bureau, August 1982, 1; Lloyd W. Moseley, *Customer Service: The Road to Greater Profits* (New York: Chain Store Age Books, 1972), 147, 153. **204–205** "Hazards of Writing Recommendation Letters": Adapted from Arthur G. Sharp, "See You in Court," *Supervision,* April 1986, 3–5. Reprinted by permission of © by The National Research Bureau, Inc., 424 North Third Street, Burlington, Iowa 52601-9989; adapted from Arthur G. Sharp, "The Revenge of the Fired," *Newsweek,* 16 February 1987, 46–47. Copyright 1987. Newsweek, Inc. All rights reserved. Reprinted by permission. **210** (Figure 7.3): Courtesy of Time, Inc. **213** (Figure 7.4): Courtesy of Trans World Airlines, Inc. **246–247** "How to Criticize yet Maintain Goodwill": Adapted from *How To Have Confidence and Power In Dealing With People* by Les Giblin © 1956, 132–133. Used by permission of the publisher, Prentice-Hall, Inc. Englewood Cliffs, N.J. **263** (Figure 9.1): Adapted from Abraham H. Maslow, "A Theory of Human Motivation," *Psychological Research,* July 1943, 370–396. Reprinted with permission of Springer-Verlag, Inc. **275** (Figure 9.3): Adapted from Lillian Eichler Watson, *The Standard Book of Letter Writing and Correct Social Forms* (Waterford, Conn.: Bureau of Business Practice, 1958), 269–270. **307** (Figure 10.1): Adapted from Joseph E. McKendrick, "Managers Talk About Careers," *Management World,* September/October 1986, 18–19. Reprinted from *Management World,* September/October 1986, with permission from AMS, Trevose, PA 19047. Copyright (1986) AMS; Michael Scott-Blair, "What's a Diploma Worth?" *San Diego Union,* 30 June 1985, B-1. Reprinted with permission from *The San Diego Union.* **309** (Figure 10.2): Adapted from *Guerrilla Tactics in the Job Market* by Tom Jackson, 197. Copyright © 1978 by Tom Jackson. Reprinted by permission of Bantam Books. All rights reserved. **313** (Figure 10.3): Adapted from Burdette E. Bostwick, *How to Find the Job You've Always Wanted* (New York: Wiley, 1982), 53–54. **315** (Table 10.1): Adapted from *The Perfect Resume* by Tom Jackson, 69–70. Copyright © 1981 by Tom Jackson. Used by permission of Doubleday, a division of Bantam, Doubleday, Dell Publishing Group, Inc. **323** "Ten Skills That Can Help You Succeed in Any Career": From *The Complete Job-Search Handbook: All the Skills You Need To Get Any Job and Have A Good Time Doing It* by Howard Figler, 233–235. Copyright © 1979 by Howard Figler. Adapted by permission of Henry Holt and Company, Inc. **325** "Eight Ways to Sidestep Hidden Job-Hunting Hazards": Adapted from Chapter 17, "Avoid the Hidden Hazards of Job Hunting," in *How to Get A Better Job Quicker,* Richard A. Payne, 3d ed., 1987 (New York; Taplinger Publishing Co., Inc.), 213–233. Used by permission. **339** (Figure 11.1): From Joseph E. McKendrick, "Managers Talk About Careers," *Management World,* September/October 1986, 19. Reprinted from *Management World,* September/October 1986, with permission from AMS, Trevose, PA 19047. Copyright (1986) AMS. **344** (Figure 11.3): Adapted from *The Northwestern Endicott Report* (Evanston, Ill.: Northwestern University Placement Center). **345** (Figure 11.4): Adapted from H. Lee Rust, *Job Search: The Complete Manual for Jobseekers* (New York: American Management Association, 1979), 56. **346–347** "15 Interview Questions": Adapted from "Career Strategies," *Black Enterprise,* February 1986, 122. **348** (Figure 11.5): Adapted from *The Northwestern Endicott Report* (Evanston, Ill.: Northwestern University Placement Center). **352–353** "Turning Tough Interview Situations to Your Advantage": Adapted from Chapter 9, "Tough Interview Situations," in *How to Get A Better Job Quicker,* Richard A. Payne, 3d ed., 1987 (New York: Taplinger Publishing Co., Inc.) 133–144. Used by permission. **410–411** "Plugging into Electronic Data Bases": Adapted from Andrew P. Garvin and Hubert Bermont, *How to Win with Information or Lose Without It* (Glenelg, Md.: Bermont Books, 1980), 67–84. **416** (Figure 13.5): From David J. Rachman and Michael H. Mescon, *Business Today,* 5th ed. 587. Copyright © 1987, Random House, Inc. **418** "Seven Errors in Logic That Can Undermine Your Reports": From Mary Munter, *Guide to Managerial Communication* 2d ed., © 1982, 31. Adapted by permission of Prentice-Hall, Inc., Englewood Cliffs, New Jersey. **427** (Table 14.1): Adapted from *Elements of Graphics* by Robert Lefferts; 18–35. Copyright © 1981 by Robert Lefferts. Reprinted by permission of Harper & Row, Publishers, Inc. **432** (Figure 14.2): From *Rand McNally Places Rated Almanac* by Richard Boyer ad David Savageau, 194. Copyright © 1985 by Prentice Hall Press. Used by permission of the publisher. **Color Insert** "Creating Colorful Visual Aids with Computers": Adapted from David M. Kroenke and Kathleen A. Dolan, *Business Computer Systems: An Introduction* (Santa Cruz, Calif.: Mitchell Publishing, 1987), 1, 3, 5–7, 8, 14; Hideaki Chijiiwa, *Color Harmony: A Guide to Creative Color Combinations* (Rockport, Mass.: Rockport Publishers, 1987), 138–141. **Color Insert** (Figure A): Courtesy of IBM. **Color Insert** (Figure B): Data from *National Restaurant News,* 3 August 1987, 7. **Color Insert** (Figure C): Data from *Psychology Today,* May 1980, p. 72. By permission of the American Psychological Association. **Color Insert** (Figure D): Courtesy of Paladin Press, Boulder, Colorado, from *Life After Doomsday,* Dr. Bruce Clayton, 1980. **433** (Figure 14.4): Data from U.S. Department of Commerce. **433** (Figure 14.5): Cynthia Kramer, "Production Statistics Raise Intriguing Questions," *Industrial Outlook,* 12 April 1988, 24. **433** (Figure 14.6): Adapted from Gene Zelazny, *Say It with Charts* 112, Richard D. Irwin, Inc., © 1985. **435** (Figure 14.9): Adapted from David J. Rachman and Michael H. Mescon, "Careers in Business," in *Business Today,* 5th ed. (New York: Random House, 1987), 574–575. **437** (Figure 14.11): Adapted from *How to Prepare Charts and Graphs for Effective Reports* by Robert Lefferts, 126. Copyright © 1981 by Robert Lefferts. Reprinted by permission of Harper & Row, Publishers, Inc. **438** (Figure 14.12): Adapted from John M. Lannon, *Technical Writing,* 3d ed. (Boston: Little, Brown, 1985), 269. **474** (Figure 15.13): Adapted from James W. Souther and Myron I. White, *Technical Report Writing,* 41. Copyright © 1977 by John Wiley & Sons, Inc. **519–520** (Tables 16.1,16.2, 16.3): Adapted from "Changes in Consumer Eating Habits," survey conducted for the National Restaurant Association, September 1983. **520** (Tables 16.4, 16.5, 16.6): Adapted from Thomas D. Dupont, "Consumer Travel: The New Breed of Travel Consumers," *Madison Avenue,* July 1983, 32, 34. **522–523** (Tables 16.7, 16.8): Adapted from Thomas Stanley and George P. Moschis, "The ATM-Prone Consumer: A Profile and Implications," *Journal of Retail Banking,* Spring 1983, 46–51. **524–525** (Tables 16.12, 16.13, 16.14, 16.15, 16.16, Figure 16.4): Adapted from "Purchase Influence Study for Small Business Office Products," prepared by Wharton Center for Applied Research for *People Weekly,* 1987. **538** (Figure 17.1): Adapted from material prepared by Dr. Lyman K. Steil, President, Communication Development, Inc., St. Paul, Minnesota, for the Sperry Corporation. Reprinted with permission of Dr. Steil and the Unisys Corporation. **542** (Figure 17.2): Adapted from Charles J. Stewart and William B. Cash, Jr., *Interviewing Principles and Practices,* 4th ed., 86. Copyright © 1985 by Wm. C. Brown Publishers, Dubuque, Iowa. All Rights Reserved. Reprinted by permission. **543** (Figure 17.3): Adapted from Charles J. Stewart and William B. Cash, Jr., *Interviewing Principles and Practices,* 4th ed., 71. Copyright © 1985 by Wm. C. Brown Publishers, Dubuque, Iowa. All Rights Reserved. Reprinted by permission. **548** (Figure 17.4): Adapted from *Communication Today* by J. Michael Sproule, 292. Copyright © 1981 by Scott, Foresman and Company. Reprinted by permission. **550–551** "Globetrotter's Guide to Mastering Meetings": Adapted from Sondra Snowden, "How to Gain the Global Edge," *IBAC Communication World,* August 1986, 29, 30. Reprinted with permission of International Association of Business Communicators. **552** "Seven Deadly Blunders Made in Meetings": Adapted from Beth Ann Krier, "How to Avoid Boring Meetings," *Los Angeles Times,* 8 August 1982, Part 8, 1–2. **563** (Figure 18.2): Adapted from Faye Rice and Adam Bartos, "The Big Payoff in Corporate Art," *Fortune,* 25 May 1987, 106–112. **564–565** (Figure 18.3): Adapted from Toni Lydecker and Lisa Bertagnoli, "Convenience Stores: The New Fast-Food Merchants," *Restaurants and Institutions,* 5 August 1987, 34–47, 50–51. Reprinted with permission of *Restaurants and Institutions,* a Cahners publication. **576** (Table 18.1): Adapted from Marya W. Holcombe and Judith K. Stein, *Presentations for Decision Makers,* Lifetime Learning Publications, Van Nostrand Reinhold, 1983. **580–581** "Answering Questions from the Floor with Confidence and Courage": Adapted from Ronald L. Applbaum and Karl W. E. Anatol, *Effective Oral Communication: For Business and the Professions* (Chicago: Science Research Associates, 1982), 240–244. **594–595** (Table A.1): U.S. Department of Commerce, International Trade Administration, *A Basic Guide to Exporting* (Washington, D.C.: Government Printing Office, 1981), 71. **596–597** (Figure A.1): Reprinted by permission of Dr. Thomas E. Berry, University of Maryland. **639** (Table D. 1): Adapted table, p. 6, from *The Secretary's Handbook,* Third Edition, by Doris H. Whalen, copyright © 1987 by Harcourt Brace Jovanovich, Inc., reprinted by permission of the publisher. **642** (Table D.2): Adapted from *The Amy Vanderbilt Complete Book of Etiquette* revised and expanded by Letitia Baldridge; 568–581, 594–603. Copyright © 1978 by Curtis B. Kellar and Lincoln G. Clark, Executors of the Estate of Amy Vanderbilt Kellar and Doubleday, a division of Bantam, Doubleday, Dell Publishing Group, Inc. Copyright © 1952, 1954, 1955, 1956, 1958, 1963, 1967, 1972, by Curtis B. Kellar and Lincoln G. Clark, Executors of the Estate of Amy Vanderbilt Kellar. Used by permission of the publisher. **647** (Figure D.3): Courtesy of Mattel Toys, Inc. **648** (Figure D.4): Courtesy of J.C. Penny Co., Inc. **649** (Figure D.5): Courtesy of Kentucky Fried Chicken Corp.

PHOTO CREDITS

xii (top) John Feingersh/Stock, Boston **xii (bottom)** Wayne Cable/Cable Studios **xiii** Tom Hollyman/Photo Researchers **xiv** George Haling/Photo Researchers **xv** Jeff Smith **xvi (top)** Great Valley Commercial Photography **xvi (bottom)** Jules Allen/Vision Foto/Wheeler Pictures **xvii** Paul R. Solomon/Wheeler Pictures **xviii** Gabe Palmer/The Stock Market **xix** Marc Jefferies/The Stock Market

3, 4 Xerox Corporation **30** Camera 1 **31** Sepp Seitz/Woodfin Camp & Associates **61** Courtesy of Irma Cameron **62** General Mills, Incorporated **87** Courtesy of David Petree **88** Courtesy of Mercy Hospital **121** Courtesy of Marcus Smith **122** Bear Creek Corporation **159, 160** Toucan-Du **189** Pepsico Foundation **190** Jessica Katz/SUNY, Purchase **225** Southland Corporation **226** Tom Kelly **260** Newsweek photo by Bernard Gotfryd **261** Courtesy of Newsweek **301** Price Waterhouse **302** Gary Gladstone **335** Apple Computers **336** Three Lions **367, 368** Calvin Klein, Limited **398, 399** Lowry Associates **424** Firestone Tire and Rubber Company **425** Tom Kelly **448, 449** Maytag Company **484, 485** Tupperware Home Parties **531, 532** Kelly Services, Incorporated **557, 558** AT&T Information Systems **603** (top left), Bell and Howell (top right), Novak Company **603** (center and bottom right) Pitney Bowes Facsimile Systems **603** (bottom left), AT&T Information Systems

ORGANIZATION INDEX

SUBJECT/PERSON INDEX